John Henry Newman: The Challenge to Evangelical Religion

JOHN HENRY NEWMAN

The Challenge to Evangelical Religion

FRANK M. TURNER

Yale University Press

New Haven & London

Designed by James J. Johnson and set in Monotype Ehrhardt Roman type by Keystone Typesetting,
Inc. Printed in the United States of America by R. R. Donnelley & Sons.

Library of Congress Cataloging-in-Publication Data

Turner, Frank M. (Frank Miller), 1944–
 John Henry Newman : the challenge to evangelical religion / Frank M.
Turner.
    p.   cm.
Includes bibliographical references and index.
   ISBN0-300-09251-2 (cloth : alk. paper)

 1. Newman, John Henry, 1801–1890.   I. Title.
   BX4705.N5 T87 2002
   282'.092—dc21   2002001086

A catalogue record for this book is available from the British Library.

10 9 8 7 6 5 4 3 2 1

Contents

Acknowledgments   ix

Introduction   1

CHAPTER 1. The Evangelical Impulse   24

CHAPTER 2. Men in Motion: John Keble, Richard Hurrell Froude,
              Edward Bouverie Pusey   65

CHAPTER 3. John Henry Newman and the Call to Obedience   110

CHAPTER 4. What the Early Tracts Said   162

CHAPTER 5. The Hampden Case   207

CHAPTER 6. The Assault on the Protestant   255

CHAPTER 7. The Pursuit of the Catholic   293

CHAPTER 8. Proving Cannon   353

CHAPTER 9. In Schism with All Christendom   404

CHAPTER 10. Monks, Miracles, and Popery   474

CHAPTER 11. Endgame   527

CHAPTER 12. Paths Taken and Not   587

Abbreviations   643

Notes   645

Index   725

Acknowledgments

Scholarship happily involves education in friendship. Five remarkably generous colleagues read virtually all of the manuscript for this book and contributed detailed comments and criticisms. Professor Robert Sullivan of the University of Notre Dame afforded me the insights of his vast knowledge of both modern British and European religious history, as well as of Christian theology. Professor Robert K. Webb of the University of Maryland, Baltimore County, pressed me toward improved clarity of expression and argument. Dr. Braxton McKee not only read the manuscript-in-process but also for several years over luncheons cheerfully tolerated my speculations about Newman's psychological development and on more than one occasion restrained overly eager enthusiasms on my part. Professor Linda Peterson of the Yale University English Department allowed me to benefit from her deep knowledge of Newman's *Apologia Pro Vita Sua* and of more general Victorian studies. Professor Nicholas Wolterstorff of the Yale University Divinity School aided my understanding of Newman's grasp of British philosophy. Professors Richard Davis, Jeffrey Cox, Jacob Ellens, Mark Noll, and Harry Stout read individual chapters. Dr. Mark Curthoys furnished me with innumerable details of the nineteenth-century administration of the University of Oxford. Professor Donald Smith, Dr. Richard Lofthouse, Dr. Darrin McMahon, and Ms. Elisa Milkes aided my checking of manuscript sources. Professor Jeffrey Von Arx, S.J., of Fordham University, Professor Francis Oakley of Williams College, and Professor Bernard Lightman of York University provided insights and encouragement at more than one crucial moment. I also wish to thank the two anonymous Yale University Press reviewers, who so thoughtfully and thoroughly examined the manuscript. The errors, of course, remain my own.

As this book was being researched and written, the Birmingham Oratory edition of the *Letters and Diaries of John Henry Newman*, initiated by C. S. Dessain and continued by Ian Ker and Thomas Gornall, has been moving toward completion under the editorship of Gerard Tracey, with all but the last two volumes of Newman's years in the Church of England having appeared. Mr. Tracey made available to me the typescripts for those last two volumes and put at my disposal the full manuscript resources at the Oratory. I have also used the John Henry Newman Papers Microfilm, copies of which reside at Yale University, Fordham University, and the University of Notre Dame. My references to these materials reflect those consulted for individual documents. Virtually all of Newman's own letters are cited either to the published volumes or to the original manuscripts, with a very few to the typescript. In manuscript and typescript citations I have attempted to indicate the location of the original copy, though all such information will be available when the last two volumes of the letters and diaries are published. I have referenced in all instances unpublished correspondence received by Newman as it is reproduced in the microfilms. The originals are to be found at the Birmingham Oratory.

Many scholars have explored the Tractarian Movement and the life of John Henry Newman. I wish to mention, in addition to the editors of the letters and diaries, six without whose work no scholar of Victorian religion could begin to approach Newman. They are Professor Marvin O'Connell, Dr. Peter Nockles, Professor Owen Chadwick, Professor A. Dwight Culler, and Newman's two most recent biographers, Sheridan Gilley and Ian Ker. However much we may differ in our assessments of Newman, we have shared the experience of being drawn to his personality, his life, and his times.

I am grateful to the various depositories of manuscript materials for permission to publish the extracts that I have quoted. I acknowledge the gracious permission of Her Majesty Queen Elizabeth II for quotations from the Melbourne Papers in the Royal Archives at Windsor. I wish to extend particular thanks to the Provost and Fathers of the Birmingham Oratory, the Warden and Fellows of Keble College, the Principal and Chapter of Pusey House, the Librarian and Archivist of Oriel College, the Keeper of Manuscripts of Southampton University, the Manuscript Division of the British Library, the Lambeth Palace Library, the Bodleian Library, and the Keeper of the Archives of Oxford University. I also acknowledge with much appreciation the permission of the various owners of the reproduction rights of the materials that illustrate the book. These include the Provost and Fellows of Oriel College, the Warden and Fellows of Keble College, the National Portrait Gallery, Oscott College, Birmingham, The International Centre of Newman Friends, and Ms. Johanna Woodmansterne.

This book could not have been completed without the generous help of the staffs of the Yale University Library System, most particularly those working in the Seeley G. Mudd Library, the Yale Divinity School Library, the microtext room of Sterling Memorial Library, and the Beinecke Rare Book Library. In Great Britain a whole series of librarians of Pusey House and of Oriel College provided enormous assistance, as did librarians of Ushaw College, the National Library of Scotland, the British Library, the Bodleian Library, the University of Southampton, and the Colindale Newspaper Division of the British Library

This research originated under the auspices of a Guggenheim Foundation Fellowship. During 1994 I benefited from a semester in residence at the Woodrow Wilson Center in Washington, D.C. Leaves of absence accorded by Yale University made the research and writing possible. I wish to extend warm thanks to my friend Benno C. Schmidt, who as President of Yale University made it possible for me, after a time in academic administration, to continue a life of active scholarship.

I have been privileged to deliver portions of this study as lectures at numerous universities. These include the Erasmus Institute and history department of the University of Notre Dame; the University of Maryland, Baltimore County, where I delivered the R. K. Webb Lecture in 2001; Ball State University, which invited me to present the Dorothy J. and Richard W. Burkhardt Lecture in 1996, as well as the California Institute of Technology, St. Louis University, the Catholic University of America, and York University. The Yale University Divinity School honored me in 1998 with appointment as Roland Bainton Lecturer. It was an invitation now many years ago from the Ontario Victorian Studies Association to deliver a keynote address that provided the occasion for writing a lecture from which this book eventually emerged.

Over the years of research and writing my sisters-in-law and their husbands Elizabeth and Ralph Brown and Marianne and Snowden Rowe provided measures of support for which full thanks cannot be given, as did my cousin Tacy French and her husband, Lafayette, along with her daughter Tacy and son-in-law Mark Ranney. My sister Sarah Morgan, her husband, John, and my niece Kelly were similarly supportive as was my mother, Betty M. Turner. Donald Kagan, Steven Ozment, Ramsay Macmullen, Paul Bushkovitch, Maija Jansson, Anne Fabbri, Ed and Joan Woodsum,

Bernard and Norma Lytton, Myles and Nancy Alderman, Cheever and Sara Tyler, and David and Julie Pease provided the warmth of friendship and unfailing good cheer. My agent Glen Hartley was supportive throughout the placement of the manuscript. At Yale University Press, Larisa Heimert has proved both a demanding and helpful editor. Daniel Heaton extended enormous aid in the transformation of the manuscript into a book.

This book is dedicated to the memory of Nancy Batson Nisbet Rash, to whom I was married from 1984 to 1995 and who would be pleased that the project has at last come to fruition. That it was finished is very much the result of the unfailing encouragement and patience with the burdens of the scholarly life that I have received from Ellen Louise Tillotson, whom I married in 1999.

Introduction

The protagonist of this volume is *not* John Henry *Cardinal* Newman, whom many people regard as the father of the Second Vatican Council, whose name adorns Roman Catholic student societies on numerous North American college and university campuses as well as scores of websites, and the cause of whose sainthood has been pressed for some time. Nor do these pages address John Henry Newman of the Birmingham Oratory, author of *The Idea of a University,* the most influential work on the liberal education in the English language; *A Grammar of Assent,* an enduring exploration of religious belief; and *The Dream of Gerontius,* a poetic meditation on death, a copy of which was found on General Charles George Gordon's body after his defeat at Khartoum in 1885 and which Edward Elgar at the turn of the last century provided with a still performed musical setting. This book is not even about the writer of the *Apologia Pro Vita Sua,* that most effective of all Victorian autobiographies. Nor is it about the person whom at the second centenary of his birth in 2001 Pope John Paul II described as belonging "to every time and place and people."[1]

The subject of this book is John Henry Newman, fellow of Oriel College, Vicar of St. Mary the Virgin Church in Oxford, and between 1833 and 1845 chief leader of the Tractarian Movement in the Church of England. This earlier cleric who late in life and in the Roman Catholic Church became Cardinal Newman is a historical figure belonging very much to a particular time, a particular place, and a narrowly self-selected circle of sympathizers. Commencing in 1833 with the publication of the controversial *Tracts for the Times,* Newman of Oriel had drawn about himself a coterie of friends and acolytes determined, in Matthew Arnold's words, "to renew what was for us the most national and natural institution in the world, the Church of England."[2] In the pursuit of that renewal the Oriel Newman and other Tractarians sought nothing less than to carry out in England a Second Reformation, first by resisting the political influence of evangelical Dissent on the established church, then by purging the establishment of Protestant innovations, especially recent evangelical ones, and finally by recovering ancient Catholic faith and practice. Like so many other religious and political revolutionaries, Newman and his fellow Tractarians embraced a rhetoric of tradition for the ends of radical change. The effort to revolutionize the national church through tactics of intransigence, ecclesiastical disruption, clerical pretension, and devotional experiment redolent of Roman Catholicism resulted by 1840 in what one commentator termed "the civil war now so furiously raging in the Anglican Church."[3]

This radical high-church agitation fomented by the Newman of Oriel College and St. Mary the Virgin Church has from its own day to the present often been called the Oxford Movement, after the university within which it arose and to which in one way or another all of its other major leaders— including, in addition to Newman, John Keble, Richard Hurrell Froude, and Edward Bouverie Pusey—as well as many secondary figures were associated. But Oxford as a university expressing itself through its various decision-making authorities stood deeply divided over the movement whose leaders appropriated its name when first designating the origins of the authors of the tracts. Furthermore, to continue today using the term Oxford Movement risks confusing nineteenth-century events and personalities with the very different twentieth-century moral rearmament crusade of Frank Buchman also designated by many commentators as the Oxford Movement. But most important, the first and primary hallmark of what was sometimes also termed the Religious Movement of 1833 was the publication of the tendentious *Tracts for the Times* proclaiming a new radical agenda for the clergy of the Church of England and assailing contemporary evangelical Protestant religion. Oxford was the setting for their actions, but the substance of the movement comprised the *Tracts for the Times;* Newman's sermons, as well as his *Lectures on the Prophetical Office of the Church* and *Lectures on Justification;* the articles in the *British Critic;* Froude's posthumously published *Remains;* and devotional innovations, including the revival of monasticism within the Church of England. Because this book concerns itself with the ideas and ecclesiastical agenda of the authors of the tracts and other publications, in these pages their challenge to evangelical religion and their revolt against complaisant establishment ecclesiastical life will consistently be termed the Tractarian Movement and its progenitors the Tractarians.

Within a few years of its beginnings the Tractarian Movement not only displayed itself as an innovative anti-Protestant religious experiment but also embraced a number of adherents troublesomely attracted to the Roman Catholic Church. As a result, by 1841 Newman's problem had become how to hold his restless followers in the English Church. To that end he published the infamous *Tract 90*, proposing through highly contorted arguments the possibility of clergy subscribing to the 39 Articles of the Church of England in a fashion compatible with a set of indeterminate beliefs dubbed Catholic, about which not even the Tractarians themselves agreed. With *Tract 90* quickly condemned by university authorities and not long thereafter criticized by numerous bishops, Newman organized a monastic retreat in the village of Littlemore, just outside Oxford, where he and the men attracted to him and to his self-styled Catholic religion engaged in a conventual life of prayer, confession, study, fasting, and liturgical innovation. Most religious and nonreligious observers at the time regarded all this behavior as "Romanizing," and many believed Newman and company to be secret Roman Catholics boring into the life of the English Church. By late summer 1843 in response to broad criticism from bishops and the conversion of one of his followers to Roman Catholicism, Newman resigned St. Mary's and devoted himself entirely to the Littlemore community, while remaining a fellow of Oriel College. In October 1845, along with a number of his close followers, Newman himself entered the Roman Catholic Church. Shortly before that event one of his young, radical confidants and fellow converts told him, "The English Church without you w[oul]d be, as they say, like the Play of Hamlet without the character of Hamlet."[4] But in point of fact and contrary to later Newman hagiography, most people in the Church of England by the autumn of 1845 were genuinely delighted to see this difficult priest, so beclouded by distrust, resentment, and calumnies, at long last depart.

After that departure, Newman virtually disappeared from the English public scene. Following study in Rome, he established in 1848 a small Oratory of St. Philip Neri in Birmingham, a provincial city far from the religious ferment of Oxford. Eventually that Oratory established a second house in London, which acrimoniously split from the Birmingham establishment in 1856. In 1851, Newman answered the call of Pope Pius IX and Cardinal Paul Cullen to organize a Roman Catholic university in Dublin. There he composed the lectures that became *The Idea of a University*, initially published in 1852 under a different title to modest notice. During those same years Newman unsuccessfully stood trial on the accusation of libel against Giovanni Achilli, a former Italian Roman Catholic priest turned anti-Catholic lecturer, and was assessed a fine and received public judicial rebuke. For a short time toward the end of the decade Newman cooperated with liberal English Catholics on *The Rambler,* of which he became briefly editor. His article in that journal "On Consulting the Faithful in Matters of Doctrine" prompted an English Roman Catholic bishop to report Newman to Rome on charges of heresy. Although those charges were after some years resolved in Newman's favor, Roman Catholic authorities and laymen, often of ultramontane sympathy, thereafter distrusted him on ecclesiastical matters. They also wondered why he was so hesitant to draw converts into the Roman Catholic communion. At this point in his life Newman had become personally and religiously an isolated figure whose present life and past career interested few people and whose inner spirit was very close to having been broken by two churches. In 1863 he confided to his journal, "O how forlorn & dreary has been my course since I have been a Catholic! Here has been the contrast—as Protestant, I felt my religion dreary, but not my life—but, as a Catholic, my life dreary, not my religion."[5]

And so might the story of John Henry Newman of the Birmingham Oratory have ended. Even as early as 1857 he had written his closest friend, "To the rising generation itself, to the sons of those who knew or read me 15 or 20 years ago, I am a character of history—they know nothing of me; they have heard my name, and nothing more—they have no associations with it."[6] But in 1864 a chance occurrence allowed Newman to resurrect and publicly defend that nearly forgotten "character of history," his earlier self in the English Church. Near the beginning of that year the Rev. Charles Kingsley, a well-known Church of England clergyman, novelist, and historian of both broad church and fervent anti-Catholic instincts, published an anonymous book review in the course of which he accused Newman and by implication other Roman Catholic priests of untruthfulness. The charge against Newman personally and Roman Catholic priests generally would not have surprised mid-Victorian readers, dwelling as they did in an atmosphere of public opinion deeply polluted with anti-Catholicism. Moreover, many people who had encountered Newman during his years in the English Church still deeply doubted his honesty. Roman Catholics had for sometime doubted his orthodoxy.

Under those circumstances, Newman, like an ecclesiastical Achilles long removed from battle, reemerged into the public arena once again to do battle, this time not to defend either the Church of England or the Roman Catholic Church, but to redeem his own personal reputation as an honest Englishman. Onto a much changed religious and intellectual landscape, where liberal Protestant theologians, ultramontane Roman Catholics, and proponents of scientific naturalism now commanded central attention, Newman hurled his *Apologia Pro Vita Sua*, first as a series of pamphlets and then as a separate book. Immediately and against all predictable odds, it proved to be the most effective religious polemic of the age.

A powerfully infuriated Newman challenged Kingsley and without quarter rhetorically vanquished him. Newman had long contended that English literature was fundamentally Protestant in character. By composing a commanding work for that literature, he ironically secured for himself an enduring base of sympathetic support in the English Protestant world during the very decade when he faced enormous difficulties among Roman Catholics. Newman thus transformed himself into the figure who became the much admired late Victorian sage and man of letters whose personal narrative of a difficult personal spiritual journey resonated with the religious restiveness of the last third of the century and beyond.

In 1864 John Henry Newman of the Oratory seized the occasion of relating the history of the religious opinions of John Henry Newman of Oriel College to set the rules and conditions for his own subsequent self-presentation and historical interpretation and judgment. At the outset of the *Apologia*, Newman appealed to the fairness of Englishmen rather than to that of any particular religious community to judge his defense of his public reputation. The writer who had long ago carried out one polemic after another callously stereotyping his opponents now demanded that his readers look at something other than the straw man he charged Kingsley with having created. But quite carefully and deliberately Newman did *not* ask to be judged according to a dispassionate investigation of the events and documents of the 1830s and 1840s. His tactic worked: the details of his life, thought, and publications in the Church of England afterward received at best limited independent investigation. Those earlier decades of his life certainly received virtually no examination in 1879, when as a result of political considerations among English Roman Catholics, Pope Leo XIII made Newman at the age of seventy-eight a cardinal. Surviving another eleven years, Newman outlived and outwrote all of his former opponents and quite literally had the last word. The prose and presence of the elderly, magisterial Newman of the *Apologia*, an almost ghostly survivor from a different era living quietly as a monk in Birmingham, determined the ground of engagement with the young, angry, fiercely polemical Oxford Newman so that at the end of his life he could be praised as "the great Anglican, the great Catholic, the great Englishman."[7] Rarely in any culture has a public reputation undergone so remarkable a self-generated transformation. Not even Lytton Strachey would dare to turn the contempt of Bloomsbury against this particular eminent Victorian.

Most important, save for a few late Victorian writers whose credibility was undermined by their overt anti-Catholicism, no one challenged the *Apologia* that had made Kingsley look so small and foolish. Consequently, the *Apologia* stands as the dazzling autobiographical creation of Newman's determination to forge into a linear narrative structure the history of his shifting religious opinions from his youth to the day of his reception into the Roman Catholic Church. The volume tells the story in his own way so that it will at last make sense to those who knew him in the Church of England, to the Roman Catholics with whom he had lived and worked for nineteen years, and perhaps most significant to himself. The powerful, seductive autobiographical narrative of the *Apologia* portrays Newman's Roman Catholic faith and personality as emerging from a Protestant chrysalis through a difficult process of self-discernment, spiritual development, and combat with opponents of dogmatic religion—the liberals. In its pages the ecclesiastical tumult of the Reform Act years, the interdenominational religious struggles of the 1830s and 1840s, and the simultaneous venomous internal debates over the future of the Church of England stand transformed into events within the universal battles between Protestantism and Roman Catholicism, faith and doubt, religion and secular liberalism, as well as roadmarks on Newman's own journey of religious discovery.

Furthermore, the Newman of the *Apologia* afterward reorganized, reworked, and refurbished his earlier publications to establish himself as one of the chief authors and preeminent stylists of the high Victorian age. Those republished books from his years in the English Church, accompanied by his own Roman Catholic commentary on his previous Protestant opinions, the sermons he had delivered in the English Church as well as certain of his Roman Catholic writings, most prominent *The Idea of a University,* commanded an extensive following among Protestants in both Britain and America. Indeed, one reason he confessed for making no substantial changes or additional comments in his autobiography was that "at present my Apologia sells very fairly."[8] Continuing sales of the *Apologia* in turn spurred those of his other books, providing much welcome income for his work at the Birmingham Oratory. Consequently, by the close of his life and beyond, Newman's fierce polemics of another era had become domesticated essays encased in the multivolume sets of his collected works published by Longmans, one of those great-library monuments of the worthies of Victorian intellectual life. As a further result, the Tractarian Movement of the 1830s and 1840s, as constituting the most extensive, vigorous theological and intellectual assault of the century on evangelical Protestantism, became lost to memory or became transformed, and thus tamed, into a struggle for a universal Catholic truth in the face of an opposing liberal religion. Furthermore, the documents of Tractarianism, which revealed its powerful antievangelical thrust, sat generally undisturbed and unread on the shelves of country rectories and university libraries, while Newman's own books continued to be printed and reprinted and widely read.

In this manner Newman's *Apologia* became the most significant and enduring account of the Tractarian Movement. All later Victorian histories and many in the twentieth century relied upon it often in the most uncritical fashion. Resort to the *Apologia* as the fundamental document of the Tractarian Movement and of Newman's early life presupposed a necessarily Roman Catholic outcome. The author of the *Apologia* knew how the story ended; the protagonist actually leading the life recounted in the narrative of the *Apologia* did not. With the exception of a handful of professional historians, too many commentators, especially those writing from religiously engaged stances, have from the late Victorian period to the present relied on Newman's compelling history of his religious opinions instead of exploring the harsh polemics of the generally unread *Tracts for the Times* and the vast pamphlet literature and newspaper commentary they evoked. Nor did later commentators generally examine, except to confirm, Newman's derogatory judgments on the lives and thought of Tractarian opponents. Because Kingsley had been unfair, it became assumed that everyone else who had criticized Newman and fellow Tractarians had been similarly unfair. It has only rarely been recognized that Newman in the pages of the *Apologia* created not a few straw men of his own. For that reason the voices, often highly critical voices, of the non-Tractarians of the Tractarian era will figure prominently in this study.

That the Newman of the *Apologia* had selectively reshaped many of the realities of the Tractarian Movement and his behavior therein was apparent even to Victorian observers who were not hostile because of antipathy to Roman Catholicism. In 1865, reacting to his reading of the *Apologia*, F. J. A. Hort, the distinguished Cambridge biblical scholar, wrote, "How strangely distant from 1864 the whole book sounded! . . . No critique that I have

seen has at all grasped either Newman's own significance, or what it is
that separates those years from the present generation by so impassible a
chasm." At the time of Newman's death in 1890, Hort observed, "I hardly
know whether to rejoice more or be anxious more at the general tone of
comment in England on his character and career. A large proportion of it is
sadly unreal, founded on the vaguest impressions, and showing no knowledge of the Church history of our own time." What Hort recognized, unlike
many others of the late Victorian generation, was that the Newman of more
than a half-century earlier "seemed to revel in religious warfare, and as a
combatant . . . was bitter and scornful beyond measure." Having "found the
temptation to use his remarkable controversial powers unscrupulously too
strong for him," it was "sadly uncommon" to discover that earlier Newman
"showing gentleness, or forbearance, or even common fairness." Hort, although he believed that after the publication of the *Apologia* Newman had
personally become more peaceful and more reconciled to "things English"
than he had been previously, nonetheless insisted that it was "misleading to
keep out of sight the strife and violence of nearly all his active life." Hort
held "a large share of reverence" for Newman and rejoiced "at what not long
ago would have seemed an impossible overleaping of the barriers of English
prejudice" manifest in the plaudits arising across the religious spectrum
accorded Newman at his passing. Yet Hort knew the history of Tractarianism had been different from the picture embodied in the *Apologia* and later
works drawing upon it. He understood that whatever " 'saintliness' " may
have characterized Newman's "old age," it had not marked "his early and
middle life."[9]

Hort's private judgment was very much on target. Newman's *Apologia*
sowed as much historical confusion as clarity. Not unsurprisingly, Newman's autobiography emphasized first his hostility and then his attraction to
Roman Catholicism while he was in the English Church. For most readers
in 1864 and after, that was the issue requiring explanation for two reasons.
First, there was the obvious one of Newman's having reversed his religious
stance, a situation that became even more interesting once he was made a
cardinal. Second, there was the necessity of Newman's demonstrating that
the process of change had been one of honest religious development and
not of concealment of religious conviction while a priest in the English
Church. In 1864 he also needed to prove to Roman Catholics that he was
firmly and permanently a part of their communion and an orthodox adherent to a dogmatic faith. Consequently, the story of Newman the oppo-

nent of Roman Catholicism giving way to Newman the convert to Roman Catholicism—with both all the while championing dogmatic religion—dominated the narrative.

But what the structure and purpose of Newman's narrative of 1864 by its very nature concealed was his antipathy as the Newman of Oriel and St. Mary's to evangelical Protestantism, a dislike bordering on hatred that had been the single most energizing force in his thought and theology during the 1830s and early 1840s. In point of fact, as will emerge in more detail later, Newman's anti-Roman polemics had been relatively rare, eccentric, and markedly different from more widely diffused popular early Victorian anti-Catholicism. In neither extent nor intensity did his criticisms of Roman Catholicism ever remotely approach his carefully articulated assault on evangelical religion, or what he and other Tractarians usually termed "ultra-Protestantism" or "popular Protestantism." Indeed, when received into the Roman Church, Newman was the most outspoken and probing critic of evangelical religion on the English scene, the person whom in 1856 the Unitarian theologian James Martineau recalled as having "assailed the Evangelical party with every weapon of antipathy which could be drawn from the armory of imagination or logic, Scripture or history."[10]

In the *Apologia* and later, however, Newman assiduously recast that Tractarian assault on evangelical religion into a struggle against liberals and liberalism whose victim he claimed to have been. Newman transformed the liberalism of the 1830s into something to be deplored in 1864 by both Roman Catholic and Protestant audiences. In the key passage he declared,

> The most oppressive thought, in the whole process of my change of opinion, was the clear anticipation, verified by the event, that it would issue in the triumph of Liberalism. Against the Anti-dogmatic principle I had thrown my whole mind; yet now I was doing more than any one else could do, to promote it. I was one of those who had kept it at bay in Oxford for so many years; and thus my very retirement was its triumph. The men who had driven me from Oxford were distinctly the Liberals; it was they who had opened the attack upon *Tract 90*, and it was they would gain a second benefit, if I went on to abandon the Anglican Church. But that was not all. As I have already said, there are but two alternatives, the way to Rome, and the way to Atheism: Anglicanism is the halfway house on the one side, and Liberalism is the halfway house on the other.[11]

For English Protestants inside and outside the established church after the publication of *Essays and Reviews* (1860) and for English Roman Catholics after the promulgation of the *Syllabus of Errors* (1864), the word *liberalism* carried an immediate connection with hostility to biblical and ecclesiastical orthodoxy. To both communions Newman could thus appear as a longtime champion of dogmatic religious truth against its current enemies. Ever an enemy of liberals and liberalism, he deserved to be rehabilitated after a defeat at their hands a generation earlier. Most particularly Roman Catholic authorities should trust him to defend dogmatic religion against its detractors. Furthermore, emphasizing the Tractarian opposition to the interference with ecclesiastical affairs by the political liberals of the 1830s appealed to those in the Church of England who deplored various decisions by ecclesiastical and secular courts inimical to Anglo-Catholicism and favorable to either evangelicals or liberal theologians. The same emphasis gained the sympathy of English Roman Catholics long subject to denunciations from national political figures. Thus from 1864 onward opposition to something called *liberalism* decades earlier served Newman well in all the quarters that concerned him most and especially in the Roman Catholic Church, where in 1879, on the occasion of receiving his cardinal's hat in Rome, he declared that his entire life had been a struggle against liberalism.

Newman himself, however, provided a hint of the evidentiary problem involved in this transformed rhetoric. In his note on "Liberalism," one of the appendices added to the *Apologia* in 1865, he observed differences in the meaning of the term at different moments. At one point he wrote, "Now by Liberalism I mean false liberty of thought, or the exercise of thought upon matters, in which, from the constitution of the human mind, thought cannot be brought to any successful issue, and therefore is out of place." Of course, the problem not explored lay in determining what constituted just such matters. He enumerated eighteen principles he associated with Liberalism during the Tractarian era but commented, "I need hardly say that the above Note is mainly historical. How far the Liberal party of 1830–40 really held the above eighteen Theses, which I attributed to them, and how far and in what sense I should oppose those Theses now, could scarcely be explained without a separate Dissertation."[12] Characteristically, he neither supplied that "separate Dissertation" nor identified the persons associated with "the Liberal party of 1830–40." As will be seen in later chapters, as often as not Newman associated the antidogmatic principle and false liberty of thought with Protestant private judgment and more particularly with an evangelical reading of the Bible which, of course, most contemporaries regarded as highly dogmatic, though not in Newman's sense of the word. In almost no serious instance did he associate liberalism during the Tractarian era with secular rationalism or secular critical thought which was the chief connotation of liberalism in Victorian intellectual life during the second half of the century.

The personal religious development of Newman of Oriel, rather than constituting either combat with a critical liberalism or a spiritual pilgrimage concluding in Roman Catholicism, as portrayed in the *Apologia,* more nearly resembled the typical pattern of Victorian loss of Protestant religious faith. The most fundamental religious experience of Newman's life was his adolescent conversion to evangelical religion. His reception into the Roman Catholic Church almost thirty years later represented the final step in what had been a long process of separation from that adolescent faith. That the conclusion of the process, which commenced in his mid-twenties, was Roman Catholicism does not make it any less a loss of evangelical faith than if, like others of his and later generations, he had ended in Unitarianism, like his brother Francis, or in agnosticism. No less than those who lost evangelical faith for more liberal modes of Protestantism or complete unbelief, Newman in his pursuit of the Catholic demanded new latitude for religious faith, practice, and devotion within the English Church. If his brother had not more than a decade earlier already used the title to describe his own religious journey, John Henry Newman might just as easily and correctly have entitled the history of his own religious opinions *Phases of Faith.*

In some respects, Newman's skepticism was more profound than that of more typical Victorian unbelievers, extending from the adequacy of the Bible to doubt about his or any one else's capacity to discern a church that could teach true doctrine. Newman feared at least from the late 1830s that he might not with certainty be able to locate that true church. His ecclesiastical skepticism had equally serious consequences for his religious life and thought as did the biblical skepticism entertained by himself and more religiously radical or secular contemporaries. Although he and other Tractarians championed the authority of religious tradition, Newman of Oriel actually wrote about the subject in a manner that removed any clear signposts or certain authority indicating which elements in Christian tradition were true or false. By the time of his conversion, he claimed that the choices that lay before him were total skepticism or faith in the Roman Catholic Church. Newman's skepticism at that point in his life must be taken as seriously as his conversion.

Ecclesiology, or concern over the identity, character, and constitution of the Christian Church in England, stood at the fountainhead of the Tractarian enterprise. Tractarianism and Newman's leadership, if not his own early personal faith, arose from the high-church wing of the Church of England, a fact that traditional high churchmen later sought to diminish in order to distance themselves from the radicalism and Romeward movement of Newman and a younger Tractarian generation. Late Victorian Anglo-Catholics similarly sought to obscure this key connection because they saw the early-nineteenth-century high-church party as overly concerned with accommodation to establishment and hence insufficiently spiritual.

The term *high church* originated in the fierce English political and ecclesiastical polemics of the seventeenth and early eighteenth centuries.[13] Many clergy whose opinions fell under the epithet would have preferred, and often later adopted, the term *orthodox* to describe their position. The latter word, of course, consciously imputed a lack of orthodoxy to opponents. Over the years high churchmen had particularly emphasized their firm adherence to trinitarianism in an effort to cast doubt on the faith of their opponents in both the English Church and the ranks of Protestant Dissent.

Early-nineteenth-century high churchmen, about whom so much more is now known because of the exceptional scholarship of Peter Nockles, generally understood the Church of England to be a branch of the universal catholic church because, through the descent of its bishops, it possessed apostolical succession. In turn, such high churchmen denied religious legitimacy to reformed Protestant groups, at least in England, who lacked bishops. At the same time, they vigorously criticized the Roman Catholic Church as a profoundly corrupt institution filled with false, superstitious practices, which they denoted as "Romish." High churchmen so vehemently faulted Rome both from genuine conviction and from the necessity of refuting longstanding accusations of harboring their own papist sympathies. These high churchmen saw themselves as heirs of Archbishop Laud's liturgical tradition and emphasized grace as communicated through the sacraments of baptism and the eucharist. They often espoused a deep, even mystical spirituality, stressed holy living, condemned the contemporary evangelical emphasis on conversion that resulted from preaching, and generally distrusted emotional religion. For their rule of faith, these high churchmen affirmed the authority of the Bible, but generally as interpreted through tradition, embodied primarily in the Prayer Book and the creeds. They held patristic writings in high regard, but might or might not have any significant familiarity with the Church Fathers.

Traditional high churchmen, in contrast to some Tractarians, were at all times deeply committed to the fact and wisdom of establishment, the outlook most associated with them in the public mind. This was the point at which their politics and ecclesiology met. All ecclesiastical irregularity, especially any interaction with Dissenters, however informal, was to be eschewed. Willingness to seek accommodation with Dissenters was the mark of latitudinarians, whom high churchmen often called liberals if not worse, but who except for their ecumenical sympathy were generally theologically orthodox in other matters. Though often accused of only aggrandizing the privileges of establishment, high churchmen genuinely regarded the English Church as sacralizing the English state, though that view had much diminished by the early nineteenth century. Those who regarded establishment as fulfilling an almost civic function were known as "high and dry" churchmen.

For all their claims to upholding principle, traditional high churchmen had no inclination toward political or ecclesiastical martyrdom. In this they again differed sharply from the generally younger, more radical Tractarians. Traditional high churchmen were unwilling to pursue the path of the late-seventeenth-century Nonjurors, the group of about five hundred clergy, including several bishops, who after the Revolution of 1688 had departed the Church of England and formed their own short-lived church rather than take an oath to William and Mary. In contrast to the Nonjurors, high churchmen managed to rationalize their continuing in the established church even as over the years one problem after another flowed from that relationship. In the course of the nineteenth century, the Tractarians revolutionized high churchmanship, largely through a process of creative destruction, to the point that by the third quarter of the century the high church outlooks of 1800 had largely vanished from the English Church, a situation also important for the reception and particular later influence of Newman's *Apologia*.

During the 1830s, in their opposition to evangelical Protestantism and its impact on political life, the Tractarians had conflated and confused to their own ends two important long-standing high-church quarrels with other English Christians. The first was the familiar conflict, dating from the Restoration, between the Church of England and Protestant Dissenters. During the Restoration and the early eighteenth century, establishment polemicists had decried Dissent as leading politically to turmoil and theologically to antitrinitarian heterodoxy. Here there existed a feedback mechanism in which accusations of lack of Trinitarian orthodoxy served to demonstrate concomitant political inadequacy or vice versa.

The second previously existing religious dispute engaged by the Tractarians was that between evangelicals and high churchmen *within* the Church of

England, a dispute most recently manifesting itself in the quarrels of the 1820s over baptismal regeneration. Because evangelicals within the Church of England were willing to cooperate, however modestly, with evangelical Protestant Dissenters, and because they shared the same attachment to distinctly evangelical doctrines, high churchmen had portrayed them as potentially or actually disloyal to the establishment and as theologically uncertain. In point of fact, by the 1830s most evangelicals in the Church of England, and especially their leaders, whatever their ecumenical sympathies, strongly supported establishment. Nonetheless, they found themselves the targets of the kind of accusations on other occasions usually directed toward Dissenters. Both the earlier high-church and later Tractarian conflicts with the evangelicals were quarrels over the internal definition of the English Church as it pursued new strategies of competition in the increasingly voluntaristic religious marketplace. Over time, but only over time, the Tractarians extended this quarrel and made a second conflation by identifying virtually all forms of historic Protestantism with what they regarded as the most offensive elements of evangelical Protestantism. This second development will be explored more fully later.

The Tractarians, as other high churchmen before them, not infrequently accused usually unnamed opponents both inside and outside the church of a tendency toward Socinianism. The term, derived from the name of the radical sixteenth-century Protestant Lelio Sozzini, had originally indicated a heterodox view of the Trinity that understood Jesus to be less than fully coequal with the Father, but throughout the eighteenth century it had acquired the status of a party epithet in England. High churchmen and on occasion evangelicals would use *Socinian* as a term of opprobrium against political and theological opponents. Most particularly advocates of a minimally dogmatic Christianity based on reason and toleration—what was known at the time as Rational Dissent—or spokesmen for a latitudinarian ecclesiology, as well as the relatively small body of actual English Unitarians, often found themselves accused of Socinianism in actuality or tendency. Persons of any theological position who emphasized the supremacy of Scripture might also find themselves so berated, because English Unitarians argued against the doctrine of the Trinity on the basis of reading the Bible. High churchmen usually insisted that Socinians and contemporary Unitarians were not Christians.

Late-eighteenth-century political turmoil had brought new life and confusion to this rhetoric.[14] Unitarians, distinguished for vociferous advocacy of radical reform and early sympathy toward the French Revolution, then assumed leadership roles among politically active Dissenters at almost exactly the same time as all Dissenting denominations except the Unitarians embraced evangelical religion. Consequently, with Unitarians frequently voicing radical political demands that benefited evangelical Dissenters, the entire body of English Dissent, no matter how evangelical, became subject to the public accusation of Socinianism. The continued prominence of Unitarians in the leadership of political Dissent and the early-nineteenth-century cooperation between rationalistic Unitarians and evangelical Dissenters in the British and Foreign Bible Society gave surface plausibility to these accusations. Yet despite partisan polemics, as R. K Webb has concluded after careful examination of the realities of English religious life, "Unitarianism was not the inevitable accompaniment to or result of Rational Dissent."[15] By the 1830s the term *Socinian,* as some who raised the charge readily admitted, no longer carried substantial theological meaning but served only to conjure up fears and prejudice against the persons so designated.

But to return to the beginning, Tractarianism originated in the reaction of English high-church clergy to the ecclesiastical constitutional changes enacted by Parliament between 1828 and 1833 and the vibrant spiritual and institutional renewal that transformed early-nineteenth-century transatlantic Christianity. Because of its role in the initiation of the movement, the former has generally received more attention, but the climate of Christian renewal in both the evangelical Protestant and the Irish Roman Catholic communions was what actually made the political issues of such importance to English high churchmen.[16]

Throughout Europe, as well as in the Americas, the political upheavals of the late eighteenth and early nineteenth centuries required often painful and disruptive renegotiations of church-state relations.[17] On the Continent the Roman Catholic Church and eventually the papacy itself had to respond to the destructive ecclesiastical policies first of enlightened monarchs in eastern Europe and then of the French Revolution and the more general violent anticlericalism and destruction of ecclesiastical structures, political privilege, and property holding that spread in its wake. In Great Britain the much more peaceful but still tumultuous renegotiation of the relation of the various religious groups to the state was part and parcel of the larger movement of political reform. Whether or not one agrees with recent analysis of eighteenth- and early-nineteenth-century England as a confessional state, there is no question that the Church of England was one of the national institutions most deeply touched by reform.[18] Early in the nineteenth century both Protestant Dissenters and Roman Catholics still endured a broad

structure of discriminatory legislation dating from the seventeenth century
that seriously inhibited Dissenters and effectively excluded Roman Catholics from holding political office. Both groups also faced a host of other civil
disabilities. Dissenters, in contrast to the more quiescent English Roman
Catholic minority, had from the late eighteenth century become increasingly
associated with political radicalism as they combined their demands for civil
equality with the broad political reform agenda. By the 1820s Irish Roman
Catholics had similarly attained new political consciousness and undertaken
disruptive organizational behavior.

Beginning in 1828, the politics of constitutional reform and religious
pluralism directly converged to initiate the entire reform era. In that year,
with little public debate and no public turmoil, Parliament repealed the
Corporation Act of 1661 and the Test Act of 1673, formally opening participation in political office to Protestant Dissenters.[19] The former legislation had been intended to exclude Dissenters from participating in municipal corporations, and the latter had imposed discriminatory religious oaths
upon officeholders. Because this repeal legislation affected neither the franchise nor electoral districts, contemporaries did not see it as holding portent
for other immediate action or as significantly affecting political structures.
Moreover, Dissenters through various legislative loopholes, such as their
taking communion once annually in the Church of England, had actually
participated in politics though under duress. The 1828 legislation removed
visible, humiliating barriers. Furthermore, despite their ongoing grievances
regarding other disabilities, no one could doubt that the Dissenters were
loyal to the Protestant constitution.

But events in Ireland—not for the first or last time—then unexpectedly
and radically transformed the entire political scene. Early in 1829 the Roman Catholic Irish nationalist Daniel O'Connell was elected to Parliament
from County Clare.[20] The Test Act of 1678 effectively prohibited Roman
Catholics from being seated in the Westminster Parliament, but not from
being elected to it. Fearful of possible civil war in Ireland if O'Connell did
not enter Parliament, the Duke of Wellington reversed long-standing Tory
policy and sponsored Catholic emancipation. The emancipation measure
permitted the seating of Roman Catholics while simultaneously restricting
the electoral franchise in Ireland to relatively wealthy property owners.

Robert Peel, the Tory leader of the Commons, though previously one of
the most outspoken opponents of Catholic emancipation, carried the measure through the house with a combination of votes from eager Whigs and
from reluctant but loyal Tory supporters of the ministry. It is difficult for

the present generation to realize the impact of Catholic emancipation on the English political imagination of its day, but it was staggering. A nation that had defined much of its self-identity through Protestantism saw the Protestant political monopoly on officeholding vanish. Evangelical Protestants saw the loathed and fearsome Roman Catholic monster invading their national government. As Asa Briggs long ago importantly observed, "It was in 1829 not in 1831 or 1832 that a provincial newspaper, specially edged for the occasion in black, exclaimed—'Died, full of good works, deeply lamented by every HONEST BRITON, MR. CONSTITUTION. His decease took place on the 13th of April in the year of our Lord 1829, at the House of the *Incurables*."[21] The religious-political monopoly of the Church of England, however imperfect, had been one of the chief ideological linchpins of pre–Reform Act politics. Its sudden disappearance within a matter of months proved politically and religiously disorienting.

Fast upon these events George IV died in late June 1830, and a new parliamentary election was required. Internal resentment and rancor growing out of Catholic emancipation divided the Tory majority in the House of Commons, many of whom suddenly believed parliamentary reform necessary on the grounds that only the corruption of the present system could have allowed emancipation to pass. Shortly after the new House of Commons gathered, Wellington's ministry fell. The Whigs came into office, opening the way for the passage of the Great Reform Act in 1832 and all the reform legislation that followed. An outburst of popular anticlericalism in the months leading up to that act included attacks on bishops of the Church of England, the burning of the bishop's palace in Bristol, and political unrest in both cities and the countryside. Thereafter on both the national and local scene Protestant Dissenters and Roman Catholics could exercise new influence and seek to alleviate long-standing grievances. This new political situation compounded the challenges facing the established church clergy, who, as a result of the removal of officeholding proscriptions against both Dissenters and Roman Catholics, found themselves required to compete religiously for the loyalty of members without the advantage of assuring them a privileged position in political life.

In 1829 a chance political circumstance galvanized Oxford University, making it the center for immediate, organized ultraconservative clerical opposition to the Tory ministry's policy of Catholic emancipation and to subsequent modifications in the relation of the English Church and English state.[22] Robert Peel sat as Member of Parliament for the university, in large part because of his long opposition to Catholic emancipation. Early in

February 1829, as he submitted the emancipation legislation to the Commons, Peel informed the Oxford Vice Chancellor of his policy reversal, resigned his seat, and prepared to stand for reelection. This set the stage for a bitter electoral contest in the Oxford Convocation, the university electoral and legislative body composed of resident and nonresident M.A.s, the latter returning to the city to vote. On February 28 Peel lost the by-election to Sir Robert Inglis, an anti-Catholic Tory of evangelical outlook, strongly supportive of church establishment.

The Peel reelection contest permanently changed Oxford ecclesiastical political life. Oxford authorities, including most of the heads of colleges, who for years had cooperated with the Tory government and were prepared to do so again even in the emancipation crisis, unexpectedly ran headlong into newly organized anti-Peel forces. These included the future Tractarians Newman, Keble, and Froude, who had united around the banner of university independence from ministerial subservience more than around rejection of Catholic emancipation itself. Peel's university opponents no longer believed that any government, even a Tory one, could be trusted to protect the interests of the English Church or the privileges of Oxford as an outpost of clerical, political, and religious orthodoxy. Nor were they willing ever again to see themselves taken for granted by London political managers who expected deference from Oxford. Throughout the next decade and beyond, those who had opposed Peel believed that Oxford, expressing itself through Convocation, must act as the conscience of the church to protect orthodoxy and ecclesiastical independence against opportunistic university and ecclesiastical political trimmers, who might be willing to accommodate the forces of reform, including, in the most limited manner, Dissenters. These university ultraconservatives disliked Oxford Peelite conservatives as much or possibly even more than they did the Whigs, and that dislike was mutual.

After reform of Parliament in 1832, many Oxford-connected high-church clergy were convinced that the Whig ministry, supported by Irish Roman Catholics and Protestant Dissenters, would radically reform the Church of England, thus endangering its property and further diminishing their own clerical standing. During 1833 the debate over and eventual passage of the Irish Temporalities Act, which reorganized bishoprics and rationalized the uses of income in the Church of Ireland, sparked the opposition of Newman, Keble, and Froude, who in protest against the government and the inaction of more traditional high churchmen undertook the publication of *Tracts for the Times*. Over the next several years the authors of these brief, sharply outspoken, self-consciously alarmist pamphlets warned fellow clergy of the danger posed to their social and religious status by possible radical parliamentary intrusions into the property, faith, and liturgy of the Church of England. The Tractarian Movement in this respect originated in what on the surface appeared to be a straightforward high-church political response to a dispute over state influence on the administration of the church and its property. This was the situation upon which Newman focused in the *Apologia* when he marked as the beginning of the movement John Keble's sermon on national apostasy of July 14, 1833, decrying the Irish Temporalities Act.

But a key element in this situation has often been overlooked. The most serious critics and opponents of the Church of England in the reformed Parliament, as elsewhere in the political nation, were not any secular-minded Benthamite philosophic radicals or other freethinkers, but rather other Christians, most of whom were of an evangelical persuasion. The overwhelming number of people who in 1833 might be termed liberals and who demanded reform of the English Church were devout, politically active Christians. The Church of England since 1688 had defended itself as the intellectually sensible, politically stable, theologically orthodox alternative to the enthusiasm of Puritans, the superstition of Roman Catholics, and the antitrinitarianism of Unitarians. Now spokesmen for and from all those religious groups sat in the reformed Parliament legislating for the established church and found allies among bishops of the establishment who from either conviction or prudence believed accommodation necessary. Moreover, as reform moved forward, Unitarians and evangelical Dissenters would occupy parliamentary commissions, reformed municipal corporations, poor-law commissions, even vestries, and similar bodies influencing areas of vital interest to the Church of England.

It was this political participation by nonestablishment Christian religious groups and the sympathy they might elicit from latitudinarians and evangelicals in the established church itself that Keble decried as national apostasy, rather than the rise of a secular or anti-Christian politics. To resist parliamentary reform of the church was indeed to resist liberals, but those liberals were more often than not evangelical Dissenters and people within the established church willing to extend latitudinarian sympathy or cooperation to Dissent. Because their real opponents were evangelical Dissenters, the Tractarians, like high churchmen before them, presented the enemy as endangering true religion in the land and—because of the new political structures—true religion in the established church.

The Tractarian leaders had for some years before 1833 criticized evangelical religion inside and outside the church; now they could draw upon that criticism to underscore their political stance against any ecclesiastical policies actually or apparently accommodating to the grievances of Dissenters. Although they could hope for cooperation with establishment evangelicals on the basis of a common defense of ecclesiastical establishment, the more general Tractarian hostility to evangelical Protestant theology short-circuited that cooperation except on rare, short-lived occasions.

The Tractarians feared that if the Church of England made significant compromises in light of the new political structures and constituencies influencing it, the church would find itself increasingly pressured to become a more nearly evangelical Protestant religious body. To the extent that that situation occurred, they believed that the church's clergy would become more vulnerable to the opinions and tastes of their congregations and thus lose their already diminished privileged status. Moreover, the Tractarians were equally convinced that the Church of England would lose its competitive religious position if it did become merely one more evangelical Protestant church not very much different from the Dissenting denominations. They consequently believed that the English Church and its clergy, whom they generally identified as constituting the church itself, could survive in the newly competitive religious and political climate only by defining themselves in direct opposition to evangelical religion, externally among Dissenters and internally against establishment evangelicals. In the face of what they portrayed as a dire, almost apocalyptic, situation arising from the advancing political and cultural influence of evangelical Protestantism, the Tractarians contemplated an imagined, radical refounding of the English Church as a Catholic religious body, embracing novel theological and devotional practices while retaining little or no dependence on the English state.

Within a year of the launching of *Tracts for the Times* in 1833, most of the accusations the Tractarians had first directed against evangelical political Dissent found targets among evangelicals inside the Church of England itself. When by 1836 the danger from external religious and political enemies had declined, that smoldering internal struggle between Tractarians and establishment evangelicals intensified. Thereafter, the Tractarians functioned very much as Catholic Dissenters inside the Church of England. But to the anger and consternation of both religious and secular observers, they refused to behave as earlier English Dissenters, who from the early Congregationalists through the Methodists had always eventually separated from the established church. By contrast, the Tractarians remained determined to function inside the Church of England while sharply dissenting from the prevalent understanding of subscription to the 39 Articles and adopting novel elements of faith and practice. In reality, the most tendentious quality of the Tractarians was not their much decried attraction to Rome, for which they became famous or infamous, and which Newman reasserted in the *Apologia*, but rather their determination to remain outside the Roman Catholic Church as long as they could. The Tractarians by 1840 essentially constituted a quasi-schismatic or sectarian movement within the Church of England. That they used the rhetoric and tropes of Catholicism to advance their ends did not make them any less sectarian; indeed, it was just such self-referential language that established their sectarian stance and identity. The entrance of Newman into the Roman Catholic Church itself was the result of the collapse of a whole series of social and ecclesiastical relationships that had permitted him to remain in the English Church despite his sectarian tendencies. Indeed, Newman delayed his decision to be received into the Roman Catholic Church for as long as possible, and in the end found that decision largely forced upon him, another fact concealed by the narrative of the *Apologia*.

No contemporary commentator better clarified the dual character of Tractarianism—its initial rejection of political intrusion and its permanent challenge to evangelicalism—than did Newman himself in his too-little-consulted lectures of 1850 on *Certain Difficulties Felt by Anglicans in Catholic Teaching*. He composed and delivered these in the wake of the evangelical victory in the Gorham judgment from the judicial committee of the Privy Council that formally recognized the legitimacy in the Church of England of evangelical views on the long-vexed question of baptismal regeneration. The decision, which occasioned many more conversions to Roman Catholicism than the end of the Tractarian Movement itself, demonstrated both the political influences on the English Church and the manner in which those influences could protect and advance evangelical doctrine in that institution. Under these circumstances Newman addressed people still sympathetic to what he then called "the Religious Movement of 1833." These were people whom he wished to draw to the Roman Catholic Church by reminding them that the forces of evangelical religion that they had opposed almost twenty years earlier were alive, well, and at that moment triumphant in the Church of England. He used the occasion to explain why the Tractarian Movement had failed and why that failure illustrated the inherent political and theological inadequacy of the English Church. In these lectures Newman forcefully delineated the relation of the two generally conflated elements of the

Tractarian Movement—opposition to the erastian influence of the English
state and opposition to evangelical religion. First, he claimed that the primary target of the tract writers had been the erastianism that, as demonstrated in the Gorham judgment, made the English Church in its faith and
practices a creature of the state and victim of political forces. According to
Newman in 1850, the Tractarians had taught that erastianism constituted
"the one heresy which practically cut at the root of all revealed truth" and
that "the man who held it would soon fraternise with Unitarians, mistake
the bustle of life for religious obedience, and pronounce his butler as able to
give communion as his priest." Erastianism thereby "destroyed the supernatural altogether, by making most emphatically Christ's kingdom a kingdom of the world." By contrast, the Tractarians had taught that "the whole
system of revealed truth was . . . to be carried out upon the anti-Erastian or
Apostolical basis."[23]

Newman then immediately identified evangelical Protestantism as the
power injecting the actual theological poison into erastian political structures. The movement of 1833, he argued, had ultimately failed to transform
the English Church into an apostolical body because the Tractarians had
failed to grasp that Protestantism, most especially in its evangelical guise, so
infused the political framework of the English Church as to render the latter
incapable of realizing Catholic principles. In relation to that national religion, Anglo-Catholic teaching appeared as something "most uncongenial
and heterogeneous, floating upon it, a foreign substance, like oil upon the
water." Consequently, the Tractarian Movement had unwittingly "from its
very beginning engaged in propagating an unreality," with the English
nation having been "provoked, not persuaded, by Catholic preaching in the
Establishment."[24] He declared that in fact the Church of England in its
evangelical Protestant political bondage had been as likely a vehicle for
making the English nation Catholic as Islamic authorities were for bringing
the Gospel to Turkey.

More particularly, he continued, during the past fifty years evangelicals,
supported by "the spirit of the age" and in turn "congenial with the age," had
shaped and energized that national Protestantism, fostering an increasingly
Protestant interpretation of the formularies of the English Church, by which
he meant the 39 Articles. "Did the nation grow into Catholicity," Newman
explained, those formularies might easily have been "made to assume a
Catholic demeanour; but as it has matured into its Protestantism, they must
take, day by day, a more Evangelical and liberal aspect." Thus conforming
itself through its erastianism to the surrounding evangelical Protestant cul-

ture, the Church of England had necessarily concealed its inner Catholic aspirations. Countering all these forces, the Tractarians had steadfastly attempted to realize Catholic principles within the English Church. To that end, Newman recalled, the Tractarians had appealed to antiquity, considering it irrelevant whether antiquity told for or against Rome because, he announced, "their great and deadly foe, their scorn, and their laughing-stock, was that imbecile, inconsistent thing called Protestantism."[25]

In this last phrase, more clearly than in any other moment of his post-conversion writings, Newman identified the religious force against which for a decade and a half he and his fellow Tractarians had battled in the Church of England. In 1850 Newman the religious controversialist spoke and wrote with characteristic aggressiveness and uncharacteristic clarity. Evangelical Protestantism and not political or secular liberalism in and of itself had been the Tractarian enemy. It was this assault against evangelical Protestantism lying at the heart of the Tractarian Movement that fourteen years later Newman omitted and concealed in the *Apologia*, where he wrote as a controversialist seeking to reshape and rescue his personal public reputation. There evangelical Dissenters, churchmen willing to accommodate modestly their grievances, moderate Protestants, and establishment evangelicals were all reduced to *liberals* whose goals and values embodied *liberalism*, terms that meant one thing from 1830 to 1845 and another in 1864. Newman's *Certain Difficulties Felt by Anglicans* of 1850, with its overt attack on evangelical Protestantism, had not succeeded in gaining him any significant hearing or public support. He did not make that mistake again in the *Apologia*, with its indictment of a diffuse liberalism onto which his readers whether Protestant or Roman Catholic might project their own particular religious and political antipathies. The purpose of this book, however, is to explore the Tractarians and the career of John Henry Newman of Oriel in their challenge to evangelical Protestant religion. In that respect, the choice has been to take Newman at his word in 1850 rather than in 1864.

CHAPTER I

The Evangelical Impulse

EVANGELICAL PROTESTANT religion was the most dynamic force within North Atlantic Christianity from the middle of the eighteenth century through at least the middle of the nineteenth. In many of the cultures originally touched by that evangelical faith its influence lingered, often reasserting itself well into the twentieth century and beyond. David Hempton has perceptively commented, "Religious cultures are not static, nor are they isolated from their social setting, rather they are made and remade by the people who live them, and therefore hardly ever conform to the fixed boundaries commentators have designed for them."[1] Such was certainly true of the evangelical impulse which was simultaneously always in a state of being and in a state of becoming. Evangelicalism in its various transmutations in different locations over the decades manifested a considerable degree of continuity and consistency. Yet like the broader contemporary Christianity of which it was a part, evangelicalism also proved to be an evolving entity, with its adherents choosing different theological, social, and political emphases at particular moments and pursuing different tactics in different locales. Recognizing both the consistent and the dynamic elements of evangelical religion is thus essential for its historical analysis and for that of the Tractarians who challenged it.

The Tractarians initially encountered a broad heritage of mainstream evangelical faith and practice dating from the middle of the previous century and institutionalized among the several Methodist connections, the Dissenting denominations, most of which were then expanding, and evangelically minded clergy and laymen active and influential within the Church of England, as well as within a wide variety of religious, missionary, and reform societies and a vast literature of sermons, tracts, journals, devotional manuals, and biblical commentaries. By the late 1820s, however, the Tractarians confronted more recently emerged evangelical groups, often with roots in Scotland, who embraced a more literalist approach to the Bible, novel modes of interpreting prophecy, virulent anti-Catholicism, and charismatic ministries. These new evangelicals had been quick to distinguish themselves from such older evangelicals as Charles Simeon of Cambridge, who saw the novel tendencies as displaying "an *ultra-Evangelical* taste."[2] Tractarian writers often collapsed these new strains of evangelicalism—which were influencing politically active Dissenters as they achieved unprecedented political influence—and the more moderate establishment evangelicals into a single entity that they denounced as "ultra-Protestantism."

THE RISE OF EVANGELICAL PROTESTANTISM

The point of origin of the evangelical impulse appears to lie among early-eighteenth-century continental pietists who saw Protestantism under siege as Roman Catholicism began to exert a new sway in their midst.[3] About the same time revivals occurred in the Connecticut River valley of New England, and the news of those occurrences, spreading among a network of other American congregations and as later recalled and recounted by local pastors and historians, fostered the belief that a general awakening had taken place. English Protestants, especially among the Dissenters, had connections with both the Moravians and the Americans, as did, somewhat later, Wesley and Whitfield. Thereafter, evangelical religion established a presence in Britain, commencing in 1739 with the rise of Methodism, then extending itself further into the world of the Dissenting denominations and the Scottish Church, as well as into important pockets of influence in the Church of England. British evangelical religion, which burst upon the public scene in the heat of field revivals, had by the close of the eighteenth century achieved relatively stable theological and organizational contours as well as social respectability, notably in the Clapham Sect, whose number included William Wilberforce, Henry Venn, Hannah More, James Fitzjames Stephen, and Henry Thornton. Furthermore, between Wesley's death in 1791 and the passage of the Reform Bill in 1832 evangelical religion enjoyed a period of steady, if frequently fractious, expansion and consolidation, especially outside the established church.

Evangelicals sought to realize what they termed vital or serious or true

Christianity over "nominal Christianity." The former presupposed a strong
personal religious experience of faith in the atonement of Jesus Christ and
the determination to conduct one's life in the light of that experience and
the reading of Scripture. Although some early Methodist leaders, most
particularly the Wesleys, came from high-church backgrounds with an emphasis on personal holiness, proponents of evangelical religion among both
clergy and laity generally stressed the preaching of the Gospel in its fullness, meaning primarily the message of repentance and justification by
faith in Christ's atonement, only after which followed good works. Theirs
was also a faith grounded in Scripture and in a conviction of the capacity of
all Christians to read and study Scripture. In all these respects the evangelical faith was a religion of the heart. One of its most famous and influential devotional manuals, written by Hannah More, was entitled *Practical Piety; or, The Influence of the Religion of the Heart on the Conduct of
Life* (1811).

Evangelical Christianity, however, extended itself well beyond the confines of believers' personal piety or their personal church or chapel. Evangelicals often sought Christian fellowship and possible religious cooperation
across denominational lines with believers of similar outlooks and values. In
addition to the institutional churches, evangelicals looked to the family,
Sunday schools, private prayer meetings, and a host of voluntary societies
characterized by pan-Protestant memberships to further the work of vital
Christianity in the world. Life among evangelical Christians was rarely
simple, and division and conflict could arise at almost any moment. For
much of the eighteenth century and well into the nineteenth, evangelical
Christians usually agreed to disagree or to carry out their disputes with
civility, but the possibility of incivility, harsh theological polemics, organizational strife, and schism always lurked within the evangelical fold. In particular, evangelicals in the Church of England disapproved of the harsh
political attacks on that institution and the vigorous demands for its disestablishment originating from evangelical Dissenters.

These diverse but more or less well defined elements of religious doctrine, piety, and organization, which resided within but extended beyond
the Church of England, the Church of Scotland, and the various Dissenting
and Methodist chapels, embodied what both Alan Gilbert and Mark Smith
have termed an "evangelical consensus" in early Victorian Britain. Scholars
attempting to outline that broad evangelical consensus, however, have often
unwittingly tended to conceal the protean character of evangelical faith,

the potential for which perhaps lay inherent in its revivalist origins but was no less grounded in its open-ended approach to Scripture and ecclesiology. For example, the four characteristics that D. W. Bebbington has associated with evangelical religion—conversionism, activism, biblicism, and crucicentrism—received different emphasis at different times, and, as he himself points out, received quite different interpretations over the years. Consequently, evangelical religion could display shifting faces depending on which element or elements prevailed at a given moment. Elizabeth Jay has distinguished between "the essential" and "the non-essential" evangelical doctrines.[4] The essential included original sin, conversion, justification by faith, and the authority of the Bible, while the nonessential embraced eternal punishment, millenarianism, special providence, and assurance. In fact, however, during certain decades the doctrines that Jay considered nonessential proved absolutely essential to various evangelically minded Christians whose commitment to those doctrines led them into conflict with other evangelicals.

Both David Newsome and Sheridan Gilley have described the evangelical departures of the 1820s and 1830s—into stricter biblical literalism, premillenialism, charismatic ministries, prophesyings, and denominational secessions—which so stirred the Tractarians, as a "crisis" in the evangelical movement.[5] This presumed crisis, which coincided with the deaths of the Clapham leaders and the vast changes in English political-religious structures, actually more nearly represented still one more stage in an ongoing, self-generated transformation of evangelical beliefs and institutions that dated from the origins of the movement. From the 1730s onward evangelical religion had repeatedly reshaped itself; the emergence of the politically well-connected, self-publicizing Clapham Sect was only one of the most influential of those transformations. What has appeared as the "crisis" of the late 1820s actually represents the intrusion upon the more respectable upper-class London, Oxford, and Cambridge religious circles of radical religious ideas and practices that had previously manifested themselves with much complexity among evangelical religionists in Scotland, Wales, and Ireland, as well as among English Methodists and Dissenters. Rather than being seen as new, eccentric, or extreme, these non-Clapham forces need to be understood as representing elements of evangelical religious life already present by the late eighteenth century in various provincial locales and among metropolitan working-class congregations but now beginning to appear among respectable London religious groups.

THE EVANGELICAL MESSAGE
AND EXPERIENCE

Commencing in the 1720s, English Dissenting ministers, as well as Jonathan Edwards in New England, had begun to write about the necessity of preaching a direct, simple message of faith in Christ for salvation while simultaneously exploring new methods of preaching that would touch the heart or the affections, producing a new heart and a sense of being washed over by the love of God and being inculcated with the love of the Holy Spirit. These spokesmen for an affectionate religion had defined the chief function of the minister as that of preaching particular doctrines in a fashion designed to lead the congregation to achieve particular subjective religious experiences. As Isaac Watts once urged his fellow Dissenting ministers, "Contrive all lively, forcible, and penetrating forms of speech, to make your words powerful and impressive on the hearts of your hearers, when light is first let into the mind. Practice all the awful and solemn ways of address to the conscience, all the soft and tender influences on the heart. Try all methods to rouse and awaken the cold, the stupid, the sleepy race of sinners; learn all the language of holy jealousy and terror, to affright the presumptuous; all the compassionate and encouraging manners of speaking, to comfort, encourage, and direct the awakened, the penitent, the willing, and the humble; all the winning and engaging modes of discourse and expostulation, to constrain the hearts of every character to attend."[6] Thus from its earliest days evangelicalism, though a profoundly laicized religion, validated the status of those ministers who preached a religion of the heart by transforming them into the vessel whereby God spoke to convict the sinner of sin and to bring the sinner to repentance. Such preaching of salvation through faith in Christ became the chief vehicle for evangelical revival from that time onward in Dissenting, Methodist, Church of England, and Church of Scotland settings.

This message began to assume a somewhat different emphasis in the late eighteenth and early nineteenth centuries, with stricter meditation directed toward the actual blood sacrifice of Christ on Calvary and the atonement achieved thereby. By that time concepts of the atonement actually covered a reasonably wide spectrum. Some evangelicals pointed to Christ's having restored divine law to a proper balance, others stressed Christ's example of self-sacrificing love, but most emphasized Christ's loving substitution of himself for sinners. That is to say, evangelicals taught that God was reconciled to sinners (made "at one" with them) when the guilt and penalty that sinners had brought upon themselves for their violation of divine law was placed on Christ at the cross. The atonement, according to this view, was thus *penal* and *substitutionary:* Christ took the penalty that should have come to sinners, and he suffered and died in their place. Across the spectrum of evangelical opinion there was an emphasis on the perfection of Christ, as living a sinless life that did not deserve punishment and as dying a sinless death so that others might live. The resurrection of Christ provided the divine seal on the transaction, showing that the same Christ who had suffered for sinners had also triumphed over sin, death, and the devil. J. C. Philpot, an Oxford evangelical who eventually left the Church of England, captured this teaching in a single sentence when he asked, regarding non-evangelical clergy, "What description can they give of the entrance of the law into their conscience, bringing with it guilt, condemnation, and death, and of a deliverance by the inward revelation of Christ and the application of the 'blood of sprinkling'?"[7]

In the context of preaching the Word, the doctrine of the atonement functioned as both truth and instrument because evangelicals believed that the preaching of the atonement in and of itself constituted the chief vehicle for achieving conversions. Thus the substitutionist atonement became the centerpiece of doctrine, devotion, and persuasion. According to evangelical preaching, faith in Christ's atonement for one's sin preceded good works— that is to say, sanctification followed upon justification by faith. Whether preached in fields, churches, chapels, barns, or cottages, the atonement for personal sins by Christ's sacrificial death constituted the vital center of the vital faith of evangelical Christianity from the late eighteenth century onward. Although in preaching the atonement it was possible to emphasize the depravity of humankind, its sinfulness, and utter unworthiness, most moderate evangelicals, while not rejecting such a view, tended to emphasize the love of God in Christ and the power of Christ's sacrifice. As Boyd Hilton has commented, "Enthusiasm for the Cross, rather than mere repression of one's own depravity, was the secret of moderate evangelical religion."[8] The evangelical faith promised assurance of salvation to believers, and as time passed and allegiance to Calvinism waned, evangelicals became increasingly expansive in their understanding of the circle of those embraced by the power of the atonement. The Tractarians repeatedly identified both the evangelical doctrine of the atonement and the manner in which it figured so predominantly in contemporary evangelical preaching as the chief fault of what they often called "the modern system" of religion which they so decried. They were especially troubled by the evangelical belief that good

works followed and need not precede justification by faith in Christ's atoning work.

For evangelicals, subjective, personal religious experience confirmed
one's assurance or provided the grounds for inferring that one had actually placed faith in the atonement of Jesus and had received deliverance.
Although many evangelical writers indicated from their own spiritual histories that the reading of Scripture and prayer could foster such experience,
the more general tendency among evangelical Christians was to emphasize
preaching, and most particularly the preaching of the atonement itself, as
the vehicle for persuasion and conversion. Yet such preaching, and the
resulting conversions, posed certain difficulties for thoughtful evangelical
Christians. All of them agreed that at some point in one's life it was necessary for a person to place faith in Jesus Christ as atoning savior and that from
that moment forward a life of practical piety must follow. They firmly
rejected high-church theories of baptismal regeneration largely because
they could see that numerous baptized people often led flagrantly sinful,
irreligious lives.

Beyond this agreement, complex, differing strains of thought informed
evangelical teaching about conversion. There did exist a view of conversion
associated with revivals in Wales, Scotland, and America and more generally
with early-nineteenth-century Methodism that regarded conversion as an
intense, virtually instantaneous experience.[9] This understanding of conversion was also often combined with the belief that a converted person could
possess full assurance about salvation, an outlook extending well beyond the
Methodist circles to which it is usually tied. Certain other evangelicals,
usually known as hyper-Calvinists by their foes and consistent Calvinists by
themselves, taught that persons who by faith accepted the free gift of grace
were henceforth accounted as righteous before God and that such righteousness was merely reflected in but never achieved through personal piety
or holy living. Critical observers, including both the Tractarians and conservative evangelical Christians themselves, thought the concepts of instantaneous conversion, personal assurance, and final perseverance could lead to
an easy or cheap faith, antinomianism, or worse.

But within the wider tradition of evangelical religion itself many people
had often distrusted instantaneous, emotional conversion experience. Wesley, for example, had taught the ideal of Christian perfection whereby those
converted sought to pursue a life of holiness. Moreover, evangelical devotional literature was full of firm injunctions to holy living. Evangelical
congregations and other institutions, such as Sunday schools, famously

fostered powerful modes of personal and social discipline. Even those evangelicals who did believe in some form of instantaneous conversion frequently stressed the expectation that religious rearing or religious experience within a Christian home, a Sunday school, or either a Church of England or a Dissenting congregation would predate the conversion. Evangelicals had themselves often received religious instruction from their mothers or other Christian women, and most particularly they were acquainted with the moral expectations of Christian living. For many people it appears that acute awareness of personal failure to meet those expectations—often in relation to the onset of sexuality—and a consequent fear of damnation or eternal punishment played a large role in triggering the conversion experience itself.

Other late-eighteenth-century evangelicals, most particularly within the Church of England but also including some of the more staid Dissenters, who did not wish to be conflated with Methodists, were often as fearful of bursts of religious passion being mistaken for true faith and conversion as they were of outbursts of sexual passion being confused for true love. Such evangelicals as Charles Simeon and the Clapham Sect, who shared the experience of Christian childhoods and the sense of personal spiritual inadequacy, understood conversion as arising from Christian growth manifested in the sanctity of life after one had placed personal faith in Christ. Wilberforce, following Jonathan Edwards, believed that the Bible taught "that it is the religion of the affections which God particularly requires"—including "love, zeal, gratitude, joy, hope, trust"—as "our bounden duty, and commended to us as our acceptable worship." At the same time, he vigorously stated the advisability of guarding

> against a mistaken supposition, that the force of the religious affections is to be mainly estimated by the degree of mere animal fervor, by ardors, and transports, and raptures, of which, from constitutional temperament, a person may be easily susceptible; or into which daily experience must convince us that people of strong conceptions and of warm passions may work themselves without much difficulty, where their hearts are by no means truly or deeply interested. These high degrees of the passions bad men may experience, good men may want. They may be affected; they may be genuine; but, whether genuine or affected, they form not the true standard by which the real nature or strength of the religious affections is to be determined.

Further distinguishing between emotional conversion and the full Christian life, Wilberforce explained that "true Christians," who "cordially and unreservedly" devoted themselves to God, thereafter became "the sworn enemies of sin," allowing "it in no shape," admitting "it to no composition," and declaring against it "universal, irreconcilable" war.[10] Thomas Scott, Charles Simeon, Hannah More, and numerous other evangelicals voiced similar warnings about the necessity of a disciplined character for the Christian life following genuine repentance.

Such conservative admonitions within the Church of England as well as in certain Dissenting groups came, however, after more than fifty years of very emotional, often ex tempore preaching during which numerous evangelical ministers had pursued homiletic strategies of affectionate religion to induce among their listeners either conversion or a longing for conversion. The admonitions indicated the profound tension that moderate and conservative evangelicals understood to exist between legitimate religious emotion and undisciplined enthusiasm. Church of England evangelicals were especially concerned with preserving church order and discipline and clear recognition of a regularly ordained clergy. Yet for every voice emphasizing an evangelical experience of quiet piety and moderate preaching, there were scores of preachers across the land who delivered the message of an emotional religious experience as indicating faith in an atoning Savior or the presence of the Holy Spirit in the believer's life. Consequently, evangelicalism both inside and outside the Church of England was almost always equated, especially by its critics, with a religion of emotional conversion or incitement of intense religious feeling. No other aspect of evangelical religion received as careful and probing an exploration on the part of the Tractarians.

The emphasis on conversion also made evangelicalism a religion of motion, change, and self-transformation. For many evangelicals the conviction of having placed personal faith in the atoning Christ, whether manifested in a conversion experience or more quietly through a growing sense of faith, might be followed by a lifetime effort of personal self-discipline and pious living. But for other evangelicals with more restless minds and spirits, the emphasis upon subjective experience and the search for inner assurance led to long periods, even lifetimes, of restless religious searching, probing, experiment, and occasionally despair. Indeed, one of the remarkable elements of British religious life from approximately 1820 onward is the number of persons—among them John Henry Newman, Francis Newman, Edward Irving, John Nelson Darby, Marian Evans, Francis Power Cobbe, William Gladstone, and J. A. Froude—who recounted experiences of relatively rapid ongoing religious transformation lasting often a decade or longer.[11] For these figures and others the evangelical conversion was the first of many, and their spiritual lives, like the prototype in Bunyan's *Pilgrim's Progress*, constituted a lifelong journey.

Beyond the realm of preaching and personal conversion, evangelical religion, like other examples of previous Christian revival, found its chief social foundation in the home. Evangelicals looked to the home rather than to the services of the church or the chapel as the fundamental arena for Christian education, inculcation of self-discipline, family devotion, prayer, and Bible reading.[12] The home prepared children to experience faith in Christ and nurtured a life of Christian sanctification thereafter. Although during the early years of Methodism, Wesley recommended celibacy, and evangelical leaders, such as Charles Simeon and Hannah More, remained unmarried, evangelicals more generally firmly believed that the best setting for a life of sanctity was a traditional family circle in which a man and a woman loved each other, married, dwelled together, produced children, and reared those children in the faith. Evangelicals also assumed that sexual relations would be heterosexual, and, like other Protestants, that their clergy would be married. These outlooks constituted one of the major foundation stones for Victorian domesticity.

The family, including the wider household of servants, thus served as one of the chief institutions for the expansion and intergenerational replication of the evangelical faith. Henry Venn found himself "at a loss for words strong enough" to convey to parents their duty "to provide, as far as lies in them, for *the spiritual and everlasting welfare* of their offspring." He further observed, "The command of God . . . to educate their children in the service, and for the honor of their Maker and Redeemer, is universally acknowledged by pious parents." The task belonged to both parents, but in the household setting, though the father often led family worship, there is no question about the frequently prominent role of the mother as religious and spiritual teacher and guide. Parents who failed to nurture the faith of their children, Venn contended, cast "an invincible obstacle, humanly speaking, to the success of the preacher of the Gospel."[13] Henry Thornton declared, "It is through the institution of families that children are brought up in an orderly manner; and that the knowledge of God and his laws is handed down from generation to generation."[14] To that end he and other evangelicals composed a large literature of manuals for family worship, instruction, and nurture. Furthermore, to rectify the situation among poor families that failed in their duty, evangelical philanthropists organized the Sunday school movement in the hope of training children both for their own sakes and for their potential influence on their parents.[15] Evangelicals by no means exercised a monopoly on viewing the family as an instrument of religious education and nurture, but that outlook became particularly associated with them.

EVANGELICALS AND THE BIBLE

In solid Protestant fashion, the chief manual for the evangelical faith whether in the home or in the pulpit was the Bible itself. Evangelical Christians saw their faith as based either strictly on the authority of the Bible alone or on the authority of the Bible along with a body of faithful teachers and tradition whose authority was never as great as the Bible's. As we shall see, they generally thought that the study of nature confirmed biblical truths. Evangelicals quoted Scripture to prove their points of doctrine, appealed to Scripture as the basis of their moral teaching, and read the Scripture as the center of their devotional lives. Evangelicals like the young John Henry Newman might construct elaborate tables of biblical references to various theological questions and then draw upon their own expositions.[16] Evangelicals tended to orient their entire religious lives around biblical narratives and personalities. They saw their faith very much as the faith that St. Paul had delivered to the saints of the New Testament churches. It is hardly an exaggeration to say that they regarded St. Paul as one of their own contemporaries, even as one of their personal friends and companions in the faith.

Because the term *evangelicalism* in the late twentieth century often became conflated with the term *fundamentalism*, it is important to understand more precisely what eighteenth- and early-nineteenth-century evangelicals believed about the Bible.[17] Most important, the Bible provided them with the information necessary to receive salvation through faith in the atoning Christ. Evangelicals who believed that Scripture contained all things necessary to salvation differed considerably in their thinking about the nature of biblical inspiration, but very few until the third decade of the nineteenth century defined the biblical message through verbal or plenary inspiration in the modern sense. Fearful of both antinomianism and false teaching, evangelicals read the Bible within the context of a system of faith established by a vast evangelical literature of biblical commentaries, devotional guides, sermons, and sermon outlines and in the social context not only of individual reading but also of Bible reading groups and instruction by their local ministers or lay leaders. Such reading and exposition were generally non-literal, devotionally oriented, and theologically sophisticated. The Bible as read through the lenses of these commentaries and devotional manuals provided evangelical Christians with a providentialist framework for understanding world history and divine redemption. For a small but influential portion of the evangelical community, the reading of the Bible and most particularly of prophecy furnished a framework of millennialist expectation. Late-eighteenth- and early-nineteenth-century evangelicals did not, however, like their successors, search the Scriptures for scientific knowledge of nature.

Perhaps the most famous eighteenth- and early-nineteenth-century evangelical commentator on Scripture was Thomas Scott, whom Newman described as the writer "to whom (humanly speaking) I almost owe my soul." Scott, originally a Unitarian, had become a minister of the Church of England and between 1788 and 1792 published and later republished with revisions a multivolume Bible with commentary. The notes and exposition derived from his own study of Scripture as well as from earlier commentaries, including those of such distinguished Nonconformist scholars of Scripture as Philip Doddridge. *Scott's Bible,* as it was then called, constituted a lengthy evangelical exposition of the chief theological doctrines of atonement, repentance, faith, the dispensation of grace replacing that of the law, and the necessity of obedience. But Scott, who repeatedly distinguished between real and apparent Christians, also concluded the commentary on each chapter of Scripture with a set of "Practical Observations" that related the passage to the everyday life of the Christian dwelling in a world filled with temptations. So understood, Scott asserted, "The Bible, received in true faith, becomes the foundation of our hope, the standard of our judgment, the source of our comfort, the lantern of our feet, and the light of our paths: and implicit faith always produces unreserved obedience."[18]

What the Bible thus understood communicated was God's revelation of Jesus Christ and other distinct religious truths that were not to be confused with the truths of history or science or nature. Scott, in the spirit of earlier eighteenth-century evangelical commentators, declared that "the DIVINE INSPIRATION, and not merely the *authenticity* or *genuineness*, of each part of the sacred writings" constituted the significance of the Bible's teaching. By divine inspiration Scott meant "such a complete and immediate communication, by the Holy Spirit to the minds of the sacred writers, of those things which could not have been otherwise known; and such an effectual superintendency as to those particulars concerning which they might otherwise obtain information, as sufficed absolutely to preserve them from every degree of error, in all things which could in the least affect any of the doctrines

1. Thomas Scott (1747–1821) was the evangelical writer best known for his autobiography *The Force of Truth* and his multivolume edition of the Bible with footnotes and commentary. Newman described him as the person "to whom (humanly
speaking) I almost owe my soul" (*Apologia,* p. 18). (Reproduced from frontispiece,
John Scott, [ed.], *Memoir of the Rev. Thomas Scott, Rector of Aston Sandford, Bucks;
Including a Narrative Drawn Up by Himself, and Copious Extracts of His Letters*
[New York: Protestant Episcopal Society for the Promotion of Evangelical Knowledge, 1856].)

or precepts contained in their writings, or mislead any person who considered them as a divine and infallible standard of truth and duty." According
to Scott, the reasons for believing the Bible to be "the infallible word of
God" included the testimony of "vast numbers of wise and good men,
through many generations and in distant countries," the agreement of the
biblical writers among themselves, the miracles by which the divine writers
confirmed their mission to contemporaries, the fulfillment of the prophecies
contained in Scripture, the "simplicity, majesty, and authority" with which
God speaks in Scripture, the tendency toward good behavior on the part of
those who believe and obey the Bible as divine revelation, the depth of
meaning included in the Scriptures, and the promise which God fulfills to

those who read the Bible in the light of faith.[19] The fact that Jesus quoted Hebrew Scripture and treated it as fully authoritative further demonstrated that the entire Bible, and not simply the words of Jesus and the rest of the New Testament, were inspired. Finally, Jesus' promise to the apostles of the presence of the Spirit of Truth assured the inspiration of their own writings.

Scott posited the divine inspiration of the Bible so that the Scriptures could be considered the sole source of knowledge of saving revelation and thus serve as the sole rule of faith. According to Scott, God had created human beings to be religious, but only the Bible could have led them to a personal conviction of sin and the understanding of the human need for salvation. Scott asserted that no record existed of human beings un-acquainted with the Bible having actually achieved the alleged insights of natural religion that were supposed to originate either in innate human faculties or from observation of physical nature. He thus unhesitatingly declared that "*without revelation, there never was any true religion on earth since the fall of Adam.*" He further explained, "Indeed were men fully ac-quainted with all the glorious perfections of God; with his holy law; with the nature and malignity of sin; with their own real character and situation as sinners; and with the rule and consequence of the future judgment: and were they left at the same time utterly destitute of the encouragements and assistances which the Gospel proposes, and which form the grand pecu-liarity of the Bible; their knowledge, so far from rendering them religious, would probably, by leaving them without hope, annihilate all appearances of religion." Scott furthermore considered holy Scripture, with its message of human salvation through Christ, "as a *complete* revelation: so that nothing need be known, believed, or practised, as essential to religion, except what may be plainly proved from them." On that basis he denounced "*Tradition*" as "so uncertain a way of conveying the knowledge, either of truths or facts, that no dependence whatever can be placed on it" and suggested that it was "highly improbable, that without written revelation, any one thing revealed to the prophets and apostles would have been transmitted to us uncor-rupted." Scott went so far as to opine the probability that God had commu-nicated the art of writing to Moses "in order to perpetuate, with certainty, those facts, truth, and laws, which he was first employed to deliver to Israel," and he also gave thanks "to God for this most important advantage; and also for the invention of printing, by which copies of the scriptures are rendered so cheap and plentiful."[20] In this regard, there existed in Scott's mind, as in those of Protestants before him, no doubt that the expansion of print culture in terms of both technology and distribution had worked providentially for the evangelization of the world.

For Scott, the testimony of God in Scripture must be received and believed even when it seems unreasonable. But the unreasonableness that Scott envisioned related to the possible rejection of certain portions of Scripture on theological grounds rather than because of discrepancies between the Bible and critical reason, history, or science. He explained, "If we believe the scriptures to have been written by inspiration from God, and have any suitable apprehensions of his omniscience, veracity, and perfections; we must be convinced, that it is the height of arrogance for us, short-sighted erring creatures of yesterday, to speak of any doctrine contained in them, as false or doubtful, because it is not coincident with our reasonings and conceptions. . . . And seeing it is evident that the Lord hath in the scriptures required the belief of certain doctrines, as absolutely necessary to salvation, to insinuate that these doctrines are either false, doubtful, or of no value, must involve in it the grossest and most affronting blasphemy imaginable." In this passage Scott was addressing himself to eighteenth-century rationalist skeptics, optimistic moral philosophers like Shaftesbury and Hutcheson, and contemporary Unitarians who in his view chose what they approved in Scripture according to humanly preconceived views of a rational God or a rational faith. Denouncing the overestimation of the rational powers of human beings used in this manner, he at one point wrote, "They who are most proud of their reasoning powers, often form the grossest conceptions of spiritual things: they speak of God, as if he were altogether such an one as themselves, and of heaven with carnal ideas and imaginations; so that they are commonly fighting with shadows, when they start objections to the doctrines of the Gospel. If they understood the plain meaning of the scriptures, or had any proper ideas of the divine power, they must be convinced of the futility of their own arguments; which seldom need any other answer, than a fair statement of the truths which they oppose." This emphasis on the plain meaning of Scripture became a constant trope among most mainline biblical commentators and evangelical writers. For example, in 1819 Thomas Chalmers, the foremost Scottish evangelical of his day, explained that not "till, humbled by the mortifying experience that many a simple cottager who reads his Bible and loves his Saviour has got before him," not until the philosophic Christian put himself "on a level with the most illiterate of them all, and prays that light and truth may beam on his darkened understanding from the sanctuary of God," would such a Christian truly understand the Bible.[21]

THE RADICAL RECASTING OF
EVANGELICALISM

Eighteenth-century evangelicals—and many nonevangelical Christians, for that matter—had believed that Jesus would return, but their general post-millennialism had led them to see it as a far-off event. During the years of the French Revolution and Napoleonic Wars there occurred a significant resurgence of eschatological speculation among some British Christians. By the mid-twenties a new school of premillennialist prophetic interpretation, which eventually led directly to modern religious fundamentalism in the English-speaking world, arose in Scotland. These believers proclaimed a climactic end of the age involving the restoration of the Jews to Palestine, a judgment upon contemporary Christianity, and the imminent return of Christ.[22] This premillennialist reading of prophecy, which soon extended to evangelical circles in England and Ireland, became substantially institutionalized through a series of prophecy conferences hosted during the late 1820s by the evangelical banker and former member of Parliament Henry Drummond at his estate at Albury in Scotland and attended by clergy from both the Church of England and the Church of Scotland. Beyond the Albury conferences, premillennialists and others concerned with prophecy, such as the Society for Investigating Prophecy (1826), quickly established their own press, including *The Morning Watch* (1829–1833), the Dublin *Christian Herald* (1830–1835), and the *Investigator* (1831–1836).

The advent of premillennialist thought and institutions, as well as sharply divisive debates within the British and Foreign Bible Society over inclusion of the Apocrypha in bibles shipped to the Continent, led some evangelicals toward biblical literalism and increasingly narrow interpretations of biblical inspiration. Many more traditional evangelicals sharply demurred from these new outlooks. Premillennialists, who often despaired of human efforts to revive religion or to prepare the world progressively for the eventual coming of Christ, exuded the utmost confidence in the power of the human mind to delineate the exact, literal meaning of the most abstruse prophecy of the Bible. For those who believed that they could tease out the intricate meaning of prophecy or who could find scientific knowledge in the exact letter of Scripture, the Bible became a text not to be followed in a pietistic manner but to be expounded by human reason, investigation, and ingenuity—the very tendency against which Thomas Scott had warned. In such heady confidence the quiet faith that earlier evangelicals had placed in the capacity of the human mind to delineate biblical truths necessary for salvation suddenly ran wild in one area of extravagant speculation after another.

Within this new climate of premillennialism and biblical literalism there emerged a group of young evangelical Scots who on January 1, 1828, began to publish the *Record*, a new religious newspaper that produced a large and enduring impact on the Victorian religious world.[23] The most influential of its proponents was Alexander Haldane, a Scottish evangelical who had attended the conferences at Albury and who had been active in the fierce struggles of the Apocrypha controversy. In virtually every edition the biweekly *Record* took the evangelically more radical stance in contrast to the staid *Christian Observer* associated with the Clapham Sect. The columns of the *Record*, like those of the even more radical prophetic journals, implicitly, and sometimes explicitly, hurled against the earlier generation of British evangelicals the accusations of cold, nominal Christianity that the latter in their prime had directed against both the Church of England and older Dissenting congregations. Although the *Record* represented only a narrow spectrum of evangelical religion, it achieved influence far beyond evangelical circles by virtue of its circulation of approximately four thousand and its being until 1843 the only newspaper published for members of the Church of England. Though many evangelicals disagreed with the *Record*, Newman and other Tractarians often saw it as the major voice of their evangelical enemy.

The appearance of the *Record* and the new emphasis on prophecy fostered a rabid anti-Catholicism that characterized a large segment of evangelical religion for much of the rest of the century.[24] Antipopery was, of course, nothing new to British political and religious culture or evangelical religion, but from the mid-1820s onward anti-Catholicism became one of the defining features of much advanced establishment evangelicalism, with the British Society for Promoting the Religious Principles of the Reformation being founded in 1827. By contrast, Dissenters, though theologically critical of Roman Catholicism, sometimes extended sympathy to Roman Catholics as fellow religionists suffering from establishment intolerance. The debates over Catholic emancipation intensified anti-Catholicism although evangelicals themselves divided sharply over the issue. Both the increase in Irish immigration and the actual revival of Roman Catholicism in Britain fed the phenomenon of antipathy to the Roman Church, as did the religious and political aggressiveness of Irish Catholics. From the middle of the 1830s Peel's Conservative Party played the anti-Catholic card. Its firm Protestant stance attracted support throughout the nation, including the endorsement of numerous evangelicals who might or might not trust Peel himself. Anti-Catholicism as both a political and cultural phenomenon, as well as the numerous religious issues surrounding Irish Catholicism that shook English politics for more than two decades, also kept the English Reformation at the fore as a symbol of Protestant and evangelical Protestant self-identity.

Anti-Catholicism also fostered that integration of evangelical religion with British self-identity that Newman so decried in 1850. Evangelicals proudly found their roots in the experiences of the English, Scottish, and continental reformations, with their doctrines of justification by faith alone, *sola scriptura*, and the priesthood of all believers. Evangelical religion appropriated to itself the religious and cultural heritage encompassed by the experience of the Reformation, the Protestant calendar, Foxe's *Book of Martyrs*, Bunyan's *Pilgrim's Progress*, and the reading of the Authorized Version of the Bible. In the wake of Catholic emancipation, evangelical religion, with its capacity to extend sympathy across English Protestant denominational boundaries as well as to coreligionists in Scotland and Ireland, provided a receptacle for national Protestant loyalties that no longer existed in the political sphere. Evangelicalism might be distasteful, priggish, and possibly antinomian or enthusiastic, but it could not be regarded as either un-English or un-British, which was one of the many accusations directed against Tractarian affinities for Roman Catholicism.[25]

THE INVISIBLE CHURCH

Evangelical ecclesiology aided this identity with the Protestant nation that was no longer congruent with the state. Evangelical Christians, both lay and clerical, often had very powerful loyalties to their individual denominations, which could lead them into conflict with other evangelical groups, but they had nonetheless long declined to identify the true church with any single formal contemporary religious organization. As with Luther and Calvin, theirs was the invisible church of believers. For evangelicals in the United States, Canada, Scotland, England, Ireland, Wales, or German-speaking Europe this concept of the invisible church allowed self-identification with a vast host of the faithful through the ages who had experienced the evangelical faith and championed its doctrines. Explicating the idea of the invisible church in the first introduction to his widely read and influential *History of the Church of Christ* (1794), Joseph Milner wrote, "It is certain that, from our Saviour's time to the present, there have ever been persons whose dispositions and lives have been formed by the rules of the New Testament; men who have been REAL, not merely NOMINAL Christians: who believed the doctrines of the Gospel, loved them because of their divine excellency, and suffered gladly the LOSS OF ALL THINGS, THAT THEY MIGHT WIN CHRIST, AND BE FOUND IN HIM. It is the history of these men which I propose to write. It is of no consequence with respect to my plan, nor of much importance, I believe, in its own nature, to what EXTERNAL Church they belonged." Thus for evangelicals there always existed a religious appearance, which they often disparaged and sought to escape, and a genuine religious reality, which they championed and sought more fully to realize. According to the polemical caricature of one late Victorian critic of evangelicalism, Milner's view, which embodied that of virtually all evangelicals, established "not *one* Church, holy, catholic and apostolic, but two Churches, one visible and one invisible, one (apparently) delusive and one real."[26] It was, however, exactly that twofold vision that allowed considerable latitude for evangelical pan-Protestant cooperation.

Identification with the invisible church permitted evangelical Christians to transcend the inherent parochialism of their prayer meetings, devotional groups, barn congregations, and isolated chapels by filling their minds and spirits with the image of a Christian community that included not only themselves but like-minded people elsewhere in Britain, on the Continent, on the American frontier, and in the struggling missionary congregations in the most remote parts of the globe. It was the community of those who since the coming of the Holy Spirit to the apostles at Pentecost had experienced faith in the atonement of Jesus Christ and who in modern times could trace their spiritual lineage to the Reformation. Their spiritual lives thus stood joined across the centuries to those of the ancient Christians visited by St. Paul, who had taught them the same gospel truths that now, thanks to the achievements of the Reformers, were proclaimed, believed, and inwardly experienced in modern evangelical settings. Theirs was a faith existing through the centuries which must again and again be revived after periods of declension and corruption in the realm of visible Christian institutions. This view stood in sharp contrast to the doctrine of the Roman Catholic Church and to the outlook of both traditional high churchmen in the English Church and later Anglo-Catholics, who insisted on the authority of a visible church and its priesthood.

Faith in the reality over time and space of the invisible church meant that eighteenth- and nineteenth-century evangelical Christians in a very real sense constituted what in a different context Benedict Anderson has termed *an imagined community*. Evangelical Christianity—the imagined community of real, vital Christians at work in the world—depended, as Anderson contends was the case with early nationalism, upon a print culture and upon both clerical and lay evangelical intellectuals who, like nineteenth-century nationalistic scholars, constructed both a history of the invisible church and an agenda for its current and future activity. Whereas Anderson points to a "philological-lexicographic revolution" that created the modern reality of the possession of unique languages and history among various ethnic groups, the transatlantic evangelical revival witnessed a no less vast outpouring of evangelical publications that forged for evangelical Christians a common social and theological self-identity.[27] The bookshelves of evangelicals stood lined with the sermons, tracts, volumes of family prayers, church histories, ecclesiastical biographies, biblical commentaries, annual society reports, monthly journals, newspapers, and later the reports of missionary activity around the globe that constituted a self-referential world of the mind and spirit of the invisible church.

This division of the church into a visible organization of questionable spiritual validity and an invisible one of true faith meant that evangelical Christians were more likely than other Christians within the very real constraints of denominational rivalry and competition to undertake ecumenical relations across contemporary religious boundaries.[28] Evangelicals within and without the Church of England retained the strong denominational ties characteristic of the day, but evangelicals were modestly willing, at least in principle, to cooperate with one another. The cooperation might involve something so simple as an establishment evangelical attending an evening chapel service to hear a particularly gifted Methodist or Dissenting preacher. Or cooperation might take the form of evangelicals from the various denominations cooperating in one of the many pan-Protestant evangelical societies, the boards of which often included members of more than one religious denomination. The May meetings at Exeter Hall normally included figures across the denominational spectrum.

Enormous complexity marked evangelical cooperation as it waxed and waned over the decades. Evangelicals within the Church of England considered the Anglican establishment as a historical accident of a providential nature rather than a divinely ordained ecclesiastical structure. Nonetheless, from the French Revolution onward they generally strongly supported the parish system and disapproved of Dissent while still modestly cooperating as individuals with evangelical Dissenters. The leaders of the Church Missionary Society firmly and consistently defended the Anglican establishment and its processes for ordaining clergy. During the 1820s and 1830s even such radical evangelicals as the Recordites strongly supported establishment and often harshly criticized Dissenters. That criticism grew as Dissenters, following the passage of the Reform Act, launched their highly politicized crusade to remove all religious disabilities. Evangelicals could also vehemently differ among themselves about issues of Sunday school instruction, cash flows for missions, and even anti-Catholic activity. But the extent and tenor of these disputes differed from one locale to another and shifted with changing national and ecclesiastical politics. Despite these very real difficulties and frequent mutual hostilities, evangelicals, whether in the area of social reform or the distribution of bibles, were more likely to seek some mode of formal or informal religious cooperation than any other groups of the day. In all these ways, evangelicalism blurred and stretched religious denominational boundaries by fostering what the high-church historian Johnson Grant denounced as "philandering associations betwixt the Establishment and Dissent."[29]

To high churchmen such as Grant, evangelicals with their criticisms of the gospel inadequacy of the visible, established Church appeared as a kind of fifth column who failed to recognize the sin of schism on the part of Dissenters. Modest evangelical cooperation with Dissent or the Church of Scotland, the use of Dissenting hymns in English Church services, and the raising of money for ecumenical societies only gave these fears more substance. Grant for his part deplored the "unbecoming concessions" whereby evangelicals "compliment the Dissenters," "invest them with the titles of Reverend," and "acknowledge their sacerdotal character." He saw in "such misplaced liberality" a tendency "to degrade the dignity and to destroy the pre-eminence of the Church" while elevating "the sectarists to a consequence they never ought to possess," abolishing "all the boundaries and differences between the one and the other," and thus paving "the way for the triumph of irregularity, and the overthrow of the Apostolic Church." Even while working within the established church, evangelicals purchased parishes to be assigned to clergy of their own persuasion and constructed proprietary chapels in the midst of other parishes, carrying out, in Grant's mind, "a design to establish every where an *imperium in imperio*, a parish within a parish, and to deprive the parochial incumbents of all voice in those congregations—these new subdivisions of their flocks—for the doctrines taught in which they were responsible; nay, to open a secret leak in the vessel; to divide the house against itself."[30] In the eyes and prose of such hostile commentators, evangelicals within the Church of England, despite their usually strong support of the parish system and discouragement of itinerant ministries, appeared as potential seceders who might suddenly constitute themselves into a new Methodist movement. Yet after the great Methodist secession, such fears were not realized, though a few individual evangelical clergy left the church for Dissent. Instead, ironically, the major Victorian secessions from the English Church were by high churchmen entering the Roman Catholic Church and contributing to its midcentury renewal.

Evangelical clerical irregularity was an expanding reality outside the Church of England in the early nineteenth century. Methodism had entered the ranks of Dissent and become within itself and by its example a vast force throwing off new religious groups and new religious experiments. As Michael R. Watts has argued, it was evangelical Dissenters emulating Methodism and appropriating its evangelical devices who expanded during these years.[31] The most important Methodist device appropriated by Dissenters was the itinerant ministry. So extensive had such ministries become that in 1811 Lord Sidmouth attempted unsuccessfully to curtail them. Not only did that effort fail, but the next year Parliament repealed the Conventicle and Five Mile Acts of the Restoration Clarendon Code, thus creating a vast zone of domestic free trade in religion. In 1813 Parliament revised the East India Company Charter to permit missionary activity on the south Asian subcontinent.

Numerous causes explain this expansion of clerical itinerancy. First, Methodism had long demonstrated its efficacy. Second, among Dissenters the moderating of the Calvinist doctrine of election and the concomitant embracing of a more universalistic vision of redemption encouraged the expansion of ministry in all areas of evangelistic endeavor. As the Baptist Midland Association of 1817 declared, "How encouraging is the thought to ministers, to missionaries, to the teachers of youth, to village preachers, to the visitors of the sick, that God will gather together the number of his elect! And perhaps the words we are speaking in a barn, or a sunday school, or the cottage of affliction, at a dying bed, may be the word which the Holy Spirit will bless to the conversion of a soul, who will shine for ever among the angels of glory. God will fulfil his designs: let us be workers together with God."[32] Finally, home missions undertaken by itinerant clergy answered criticisms that the foreign mission effort that had commenced in the 1790s neglected the unconverted in England.

American revivalism also energized certain portions of British evangelical Dissent and contributed to clerical irregularity.[33] Reports of the

American revivals appearing in the British religious press, travelers' accounts, and contemporary histories provided information on the phenomenon. A British edition of Charles Grandison Finney's enormously important *Lectures on Revivals* (1835) appeared in 1837 and was soon translated into Welsh. These publications led to the adoption of such American revival techniques as weeks of special meetings, prayer meetings, Bible study, the praying for particular persons, the call to the altar rail, and emotional preaching. Certain American evangelists also actually came to Britain to preach and in a very real sense rivaled many of the local itinerants. Early in the century the American Methodist Lorenzo Dow had conducted such enthusiastic British revivals that the Wesleyan Conference refused him permission for further meetings. He then found a welcome among the Primitive Methodists. Between 1841 and 1847 James Caughey, an Irish-born American Methodist revivalist, preached extensively across the British Isles, achieving considerable numbers of conversions. Though much less vulgar than Dow, Caughey still used many of the techniques perfected in the American revivals. During these decades, lesser-known American clergy preached and conducted revivals in Britain. Although British revivals, with the possible exception of those in Wales, proved less extensive than the contemporaneous American revivals, they nonetheless added new ferment to British religious life.

EVANGELICAL SECEDERS

Itinerancy and revivals had helped to produce a new variety of clergyman who became a familiar figure on the social religious landscape—the seceder who founded either a new independent congregation or a new denomination. Long part of the inner dynamic of Methodism, these figures now appeared within the Church of Scotland, the Church of England, and the major Dissenting denominations. Discontented in his denominational situation, such a clergyman would usually clash with church or chapel authorities and then leave or be asked to leave or be relieved of his license to preach. Thereafter he might join the ministry of another denomination. Or he might establish his own church or house of worship, if he could carry a congregation off with him or secure the financial resources to support his ministry in a new worship space.

The most formidable evangelical secession to occur in Victorian Britain was the Great Disruption in the Church of Scotland, which took place in 1843 under the leadership of Thomas Chalmers and resulted in the forma-

tion of the Free Church of Scotland. Before that momentous and insufficiently explored event, two less expansive examples of clerical secession
and subsequent congregation building, well known to the Tractarians, took
place among religious communities in London and Oxford. The first involved the charismatic Edward Irving (1792–1834), originally a minister of
the Church of Scotland, whose religious career manifested most of the
elements of the advanced evangelicalism of the 1820s.[34] Beginning in 1819
he served for two years as the assistant in Glasgow to Chalmers, then the
most dynamic figure in contemporary Scottish evangelicalism and the Scottish Church in general. In 1822, however, Irving moved to London to
assume duties as the minister of the Caledonian Chapel in Hatton Garden,
an obscure chapel where for a time his preaching attracted vast crowds from
fashionable London society. Irving visited Scotland from time to time,
participating in the Albury prophecy conferences, at which he pressed a
premillennialist view of the imminent return of Christ. He also criticized
the Roman Catholic Church and later Protestant churches for rejecting
charismatic ministries and prophesying in their congregations. In 1827
Irving transferred his ministry to the large National Scotch Church in
Regent Square, where he pressed all the most extreme ideas of contemporary evangelicalism, including not only premillennialism but also a very
expansive understanding of Christ's atonement. In contrast to more moderate evangelicals, Irving long displayed a fundamental pessimism bordering
on despair about the capacity of the contemporary institutional church
either to convert the world or to make it the scene of righteousness. This
same dark pessimism appeared among the Tractarians during the early
1840s.

During the second half of the 1820s areas of Scotland became the scene
of persons speaking in tongues, prophesying, and carrying out miraculous
healing.[35] The General Assembly of the Church of Scotland, dominated by
strong but conventional evangelicals, eventually condemned the clerical
leadership associated with these events. In 1830, however, Irving and other
London clergy concluded that the occurrences in Scotland were genuinely
the work of the Holy Spirit. The next year John Bate Cardale, a London
lawyer who had attended the Albury conferences, joined Irving's Regent
Square church, where shortly thereafter prophecies and speaking in tongues
began to attract large gatherings. In April 1832 the Presbytery removed
Irving from the ministry of his church, and the next year the Presbytery of
the Church of Scotland deposed him from its ministry. Irving then joined
with Cardale and others who were in the process of founding what became

the Catholic Apostolic Church, which successfully developed its own highly sacramental liturgy, devotional literature, and distinct ecclesiology, as well as institutional structures that allowed it to survive for about a century as a distinct, if minor, denomination on the British religious scene. Irving ministered within the newly organizing church but in a role subordinate to Cardale. Irving died of consumption on December 8, 1834, as "an outcast among the millenarian party, his very name transformed into a term of reproach among evangelicals and decent citizens."[36] Not until the collapse of the career of John Henry Newman in the Church of England and his subsequent reception into the Roman Catholic Church did the public reputation of another major British religious figure undergo such rapid change and public condemnation. In both cases the protagonist found himself repudiated by onetime allies prepared to protect the structure of their respective churches from what they regarded as untoward innovation: firm but ecclesiastically moderate Scottish evangelicals in the case of Irving, high churchmen in the case of Newman. In both cases the religious group receiving the outcast immediately refused to permit him to assume a position of significant leadership.

Whereas the Irvingite phenomenon and the Catholic Apostolic Church originated in the interaction of evangelical Anglicans with evangelical Scottish Presbyterians, the Plymouth Brethren movement originated in Ireland among largely premillennialist evangelical establishment clergy. During the 1820s in Dublin a small number of clergy and laymen in the Church of Ireland became disillusioned with both the established church and what they regarded as the narrowness of Dissent. They were concerned with Christian unity, the return of Christ, pious living, and the outpouring of the Holy Spirit. Finding none of these issues satisfactorily addressed in the Irish Protestant religious world in the years just before and after Catholic emancipation, they began to meet in private homes for the breaking of bread and the sharing of their faith experience. John Nelson Darby, the son of well-to-do parents and a godson of Lord Nelson, emerged as the key figure among these discontented Christians.[37] Educated at Trinity College and then trained for the law, Darby in the early 1820s pursued Holy Orders, becoming a priest in 1826. During the debates over Catholic emancipation, Darby abandoned briefly held high-church views, composed tracts championing the concept of the invisible church, and then in 1828 or 1829 resigned his curacy to become an itinerant clergyman. He had already begun to develop his particular premillennial views of prophecy, involving the concept of the Rapture. His ideas had enormous influence later in the century throughout the world of prophecy study, especially in the United States, where his ideas constituted the framework for the *Schofield Reference Bible,* a key text to modern American fundamentalism.

In 1828 in the midst of all this inner change and turmoil Darby became acquainted with Francis W. Newman, a younger brother of John Henry Newman and recent graduate from Oxford. The younger Newman was a tutor in the home of Sergeant Pennefather, Darby's brother-in-law, who later became the chief justice of Ireland.[38] Francis Newman became the link between the nascent radical evangelical community in Ireland and sympathetic figures in Oxford. Not long after meeting Darby and falling deeply under the spell of his message, Newman returned to Oxford and renewed his acquaintance with B. W. Newton, an outspoken Calvinist evangelical whom he had tutored in Exeter College and whom he later introduced to Darby. Newton and Darby became significant figures in the early days of the Plymouth Brethren, though the two later went separate ways. In 1830 Newman himself set off on a missionary venture to Persia, not returning until the summer of 1833.

Meanwhile, in 1831 Darby became involved in the furor surrounding the Rev. Henry B. Bulteel, who became one of the renowned seceders from the Church of England. Bulteel was a fellow of Exeter College and in 1826 a curate at St. Ebbe's Church in Oxford, where he preached so extreme an evangelical message that authorities forbade students to attend the church. In a university sermon of February 6, 1831, Bulteel disassociated justification by faith from any injunction to holy living by equating complete justification with the gift of righteousness. Bulteel announced to the congregation in St. Mary's that God "doth but reckon that such and such sinners shall become righteous, and, lo! they become righteous instantly, God bestowing upon them faith to lay hold on the robe of Christ's everlasting righteousness, and clothe themselves with these garments of salvation." He further contended that this righteousness was freely given by God and in no manner the result of humankind's exercising its alleged free will. He contended that many clergy in the Church of England clearly misrepresented the teaching of the 39 Articles as understood by the Reformers in regard to these questions and thus failed to preach Christ. As a result of political influence on church appointments, the Articles, "which were set up as barriers to keep out all but spiritual men from the ministry," had been "easily explained away, and made to mean any thing but what they do mean." Men of worldly pleasure and sin thus entered the Church of England ministry, and consequently "those who, professing themselves to be set apart from the peculiar service of God and his Christ, are to be generally found in the front rank of Baal's worshippers in his temples." Bulteel also sharply complained that various college and university authorities denied proper recommendations to graduates of strong Calvinist persuasion while giving good recommendations to "men notorious for nothing so much in their day as profaneness, debauchery, and all kind of riotous living."[39] Finally, he denied that the Church of England actually preached the doctrines and practices of its Reformers and argued that the English Church, no less than the Church of Rome, required reformation. Edward Burton, the Regius Professor of Divinity, denounced Bulteel's Calvinistic interpretation of the Articles, contending instead for the presence of Lutheran influences. Darby countered with a defense of Bulteel's interpretation of the Articles and thus associated himself with the young curate's theological and ecclesiastical radicalism.

During the summer of 1831 Bulteel conducted an open-air ministry in the West Country. William Tiptaft, a friend of Bulteel who also later left the Church of England, indicated the tenor of that West Country tour in a letter to his brother: "We shall preach in churches, chapels, barns, rooms, or in the open air. We shall, if the Lord strengthens us for the work, give great offence. But it is a glorious work to preach the everlasting gospel. It is the very purpose for which I was ordained. Christ will not turn us out of His Church for following His steps in preaching the gospel in every city and village. I should not be surprised if the Bishop withdraw Bulteel's license, as he is only a curate." Indeed, shortly after this irregular, itinerant mission, Bishop Richard Bagot of Oxford revoked Bulteel's license to preach. Responding to the revocation, Bulteel denounced the worldliness of the Church of England, its "arbitrary Prelates," the bishop's misreading of the Canons, and his failure to explain the basis for his hostile action. Bulteel, like Wesley before him, claimed that his ordination was grounded in his college fellowship rather than in his license and that he could thus preach where he wished without episcopal authorization. He attacked "governors of the Establishment" as "more anxious to hug their own treasures and corruptions, than to retain true ministers of the Gospel in her pale." Relieving Bishop Bagot of personal responsibility, Bulteel blamed instead "a *system*, which compels a man, however gentle he may be, to become a persecutor of the Gospel of our Lord Jesus Christ." In both a public letter and a pamphlet, he further accused Bagot of being "an officer of the Church of Antichrist" and not "a true pastor of the flock of our great Shepherd."[40] For a time the ejected Bulteel preached to large open-air crowds in and around Oxford. Later he purchased land and established St. Ebbe's Chapel, then often known as Bulteel's Chapel, which later became the Commercial Road Baptist Chapel. Under the influence of Irving he gave up his Calvinism, but he later rejected Irvingism and returned to Calvinist opinions. Bulteel's ministry remained a fact of Oxford religious life throughout all the years of the Tractarian Movement. When he departed Oxford in perhaps 1846, he appears to have joined the Plymouth Brethren.

Bulteel's experience deeply disillusioned Darby, Newton, and others who later gathered in Plymouth and founded the Plymouth Brethren in hope of pursuing the strictest observance of Christianity as taught in the Bible. The small movement initially took the form of Monday evening meetings in an abandoned chapel rented for the occasion. A number of evangelical Church of England clergy attended the early gatherings, but most soon abandoned them when the Lord's Supper began to be conducted by laymen and when Sunday morning services commenced. By 1832 prophecy conferences at Powerscourt House in Ireland convinced Darby that both the established church and the regularly organized churches of Dissent, as well as the Roman Catholic Church, represented the Babylon of prophecy against which the true church must stand. On those grounds he advocated withdrawal from the established church.[41] By 1834 he urged the free preaching of the Gospel by laymen as well as clergy and launched the *Christian Witness*. Within the next several years the Brethren established a number of substantial congregations in both England and Ireland.

The stance of these seceders and radical itinerants relative to older and more established evangelicals actually quite closely resembled that of some earlier Methodists and evangelicals to the eighteenth-century established church. Wherever either generation looked, they saw the faith in decline. The letter written by J. C. Philpot in 1835 explaining to the Provost of Worcester College his decision to leave the Church of England illustrates the point. Philpot was an evangelical disheartened with what he regarded as the worldliness of the established church, but he was no less impatient with fellow evangelical clergy who dwelled in quite comfortable complaisance in that institution. Of the latter he wrote,

> What are these, however, as a body, now generally doing but making common cause with the worldly clergy, whom in their hearts they consider to be neither Christians nor ministers, to uphold an unholy system? They are for the most part compounding their sermons out of Simeon's dry and marrowless "Skeletons," looking out for preferment, buying and selling livings, training up their unregenerate sons for the ministry, and "putting them into the priest's office that they may eat a piece of bread." . . . Under their

ministry the spiritual children of God will not sit; for knowing little or
nothing of the work of regeneration, and the trials, temptations, or consolations of the people of Christ, they cannot approve themselves to the
consciences of the spiritual, either as called by grace or as sent to preach
the gospel.[42]

The return of such seceders to a strict sense of doctrine, their emphasis on a
spiritual religion of the heart, their often literalist reading of Scripture, and
their founding of new religious congregations, organizations, and publications fulfilled a long-existing pattern of renewal and self-transformation
within evangelical religion. That new generation saw in their own evangelical predecessors and contemporaries little more than another generation of
hypocritical and complaisant Pharisees and Sadducees.

EVANGELICALISM AND THE PUBLIC SPHERE

Throughout the 1820s and 1830s the forces of evangelical religion were on
the march, moving well beyond what had seemed for a time to be rather set
channels established in the wake of its original eighteenth-century explosion. Yet those channels had never really been particularly sturdy, and firm
discipline, despite efforts of many of its leading proponents, had never really
encumbered the evangelical religious impulse. Revivals had continued to
take place. Methodism had continued to divide. Scottish evangelical religion
in particular had proved a source of ongoing ferment and disputatiousness
that spread beyond its borders. Evangelical ministers of strong conviction
and feisty personality left various established religious folds to found their
own congregations. Significant quarrels among the major evangelical societies during the 1820s and 1830s cast doubt upon their capacity to sustain
pan-Protestant cooperation. At the same time the activities of those societies
continued to expand in both the religious and philanthropic spheres. Evangelical Dissent assumed an increasingly politicized face as those congregations became increasingly angry over remaining disabilities. Dissenters' political affiliation was almost invariably Whig.

In all these respects the advocates of the invisible church made themselves highly visible throughout the British Isles and among all strata of
society, as well as across a global mission field. By tactics and doctrines
alike—whether in Methodist field preaching or the expanding missionary
enterprise or the vast crusades against slavery and for moral reform or
during the May meetings at Exeter Hall or within the secessionist congregations and denominations—the champions of evangelical faith and action

forged a religion of what Jürgen Habermas long ago termed *the public sphere*. Through this fertile concept Habermas sought to explain how an emerging, complex European middle class learned to regulate civil society in an autonomous fashion outside the confines of the absolutist state and aristocratic institutions. Habermas portrayed the institutions and structures of bourgeois life and social discourse as creating a sphere for the public discussion of matters relating to politics and the economy that became characteristic of nineteenth-century liberal, commercial society. Historians have raised significant questions about the general applicability of Habermas's concept to the British situation as a whole, but it does serve to illumine the contours of late-eighteenth- and early-nineteenth-century British religious life.

Evangelicals, to whom the forces of Roman Catholic revival in Ireland bore affinities, carried a popular and significantly laicized religion front and center in the public life of the English-speaking world. Paralleling Habermas's secular vision of the public sphere as emerging from the exploration and extension of private life during the eighteenth century, evangelical religion drew deeply upon private religious experience to challenge the spiritual and ecclesiastical adequacy of religious establishments in both England and Scotland, as well as of traditional Dissent. Evangelicals thrust aside the authority of the efforts of governments and religious establishments since the Restoration to contain the expansive, enthusiastic, and self-determining sides of Protestantism. In chapels, barns, cottages, fields, and a host of religious societies, evangelicals provided a multitude of locations where both the poor and the middle classes encountered the preaching of irregular clergy and learned to discuss theological, biblical, ecclesiastical, moral, and social questions outside the spaces and authority of the established churches and traditional Dissenting denominations. Evangelical religion helped to determine the character of civil society and shaped much of the public sphere as its faithful participated in reform activities, philanthropic societies, Sunday schools, and an extensive world of religious publication and religious voting constituencies. Evangelical values and practices also instilled individual and collective social discipline. Commentators as different as Marx, Tocqueville, and Mill agreed on the power of evangelical religion as a shaping force in contemporary civil society.

By associating the emergence of the public sphere with the critical use of reason and the embracing of non-Christian enlightenment ideas, Habermas, as well as the host of scholars who both embraced and criticized his thought, almost totally ignored this vast role of evangelical as well as other forms of religion in eighteenth- and nineteenth-century civil society. Instead, they devoted attention to Masonic lodges, coffeehouses, salons, and secular print culture. That approach reflected the association of enlightenment in the middle of the twentieth century almost exclusively with a secular or non-Christian approach to the world. It was part of a larger phenomenon of simply excluding religion from the consideration of modern European history and social experience, a practice less followed in more recent historiography.[43]

Today, however, it is easier to recognize a number of qualities shared by enlightenment writers and evangelicals. Evangelical religion, like the secular activities analyzed by Habermas, was rooted in the private sphere of the heart, the family setting, and small congregations where evangelical Christians learned to apply their individual critical reasons to religious questions.[44] Evangelical religion taught people to feel, but evangelical religious discourse over Scripture, doctrine, personal morality, and the enterprise of moral reform taught evangelical Christians to think and to make critical judgments. No less than Kant in *What Is Enlightenment?* (1784), devout evangelicals urged Christians to dare to use their own reason and inner resources to challenge established ecclesiastical authorities, including those who emerged within evangelical structures themselves. To a remarkable degree, evangelical laity decided what would constitute the character of their religiosity rather than receiving it from any ecclesiastical authority.

In this respect evangelical Christianity paralleled the secular activities explored by Habermas. In his view, emerging from the new eighteenth-century attention to the private self and cultivation of civility, politeness, and family intimacy were sets of social skills and a capacity to reason that were carried into public life and public discussion. Whereas previously culture had been the possession of the monarchy and the aristocracy, and as such enjoyed an exclusive aura about itself, in the world of the emerging middle class the products of culture became widely and publicly accessible. As a result of this process, culture itself became a commodity. Habermas portrayed this transformation as nothing less than a kind of desecration of established culture: "The private people for whom the cultural product became available as a commodity profaned it inasmuch as they had to determine its meaning on their own (by way of rational communication with one another), verbalize it, and thus state explicitly what precisely in its implicitness for so long could assert its authority." In this fashion the public itself became "a critical authority" with the ultimate intention of forging "the self-enlightenment of individuals" who might provide for "the regulation of civil society" on the basis of the values, skills, and critical reason that had originally developed in private life.[45]

Evangelical religion, rooted consciously and sometimes unconsciously in the Protestant ideal of the priesthood of all believers, often acknowledged only modest boundaries between clergy and laity, with the latter in large measure determining what they regarded as germane to their religious and spiritual lives. In that fashion, the expanding host of evangelicals profaned established religion in the same sense that Habermas's expanding citizenry profaned secular culture. Evangelical clergy saw themselves as teachers or ambassadors making religious truths accessible to the laity so that the laity might make judgments upon them and incorporate them into their own lives. From Wesley onward evangelicals designed a simple message easily accessible and subject to examination and debate on the part of all who believed. They were determined to furnish the laity with religious language and theological concepts that might be discussed in an open, public manner, not reserved to a secluded sacred space or closed priesthood. As Wesley declared, "I design plain truth for plain people. Therefore of set purpose I abstain from all nice and philosophical speculations, from all perplexed and intricate reasonings, and as far as possible from even the show of learning, unless in sometimes citing the original Scripture. I labour to avoid all words which are not easy to be understood, all which are not used in common life; and in particular those kinds of technical terms that so frequently occur in bodies of divinity, those modes of speaking which men of reading are intimately acquainted with, but which to common people are an unknown tongue." Later evangelicals, particularly moderate ones, stood as heirs of Wesley in their dislike of theological system. By eschewing system, they rejected most sharp boundaries of religious and theological understanding and embraced a largely antidogmatic stance toward Christian truth. As Charles Simeon wrote in one of his prefaces, "The Author is no friend to systematizers in Theology. He has endeavored to derive from the Scriptures alone *his* views of religion. . . . He is disposed to think that the Scripture system, be it what it may, is of a broader and more comprehensive character than some very exact and dogmatical [Calvinist and Arminian] theologians are inclined to allow."[46] Early Victorian evangelicals did not ultimately escape such divisions and conflict or systematization of their theology, particularly their reading of prophecy, but the earlier generation ending with Simeon had largely postponed conflict while at the same time communicating the critical and rhetorical skills which many in the next generation employed to quarrel among themselves. The evangelicals thus democratized religion and in democratizing it made religion something about which Christians through the exercise of their private judgments could reason, debate, and choose. And such democratization continued to mark the later development of the evangelical impulse despite the efforts of figures such as the early Victorian Methodist leader Jabez Bunting to exert greater centralized clerical control.

EVANGELICALISM AND THE COMMERCIAL SPIRIT

As a religion of the public sphere and as a religion manifesting itself in and through the institutions of civil society, evangelicalism also in the most profound sense was a religion shaping itself by and through British commercial culture.[47] What Coleridge termed "the spirit of commerce" deeply informed what evangelicals regarded as the work of the Holy Spirit. Commercial wealth, competition, values, tactics, and rhetoric became intertwined with virtually every facet of evangelical religion. Evangelicalism provided one of the modes, if by no means the only one, of personal and social discipline undergirding middle-class commercial life; in turn, commercial practices and institutions provided devices whereby evangelicals publicized their faith and put it into action. If Britain was a nation of shopkeepers, that may also be one reason, though assuredly only one, why it also became a nation of evangelicals—evangelicals who by doctrine and practice transformed the religious landscape into a free market for competing religious commodities offered to self-consciously critical and discriminating religious consumers. As in the late eighteenth and early nineteenth centuries people all over the British Isles experienced more and more opportunities to exercise choice in consumption in various areas of their lives, it is not surprising that this idea of the free exercise of choice extended into their religious lives. The expanding free trade in religion inevitably worked against the interests and claims of the Church of England. Methodist circuit riders, itinerant Dissenting ministers, and seceders from established churches and denominations resembled the English smugglers on the high seas, who for decades pressed against every fault line of the Spanish trading monopoly in the Americas. Evangelicals supplied varieties of spiritual and religious goods that the Anglican monopoly failed to supply, just as the smugglers supplied commodities that the Spanish monopoly withheld from its subjects.

Evangelicals, whether laymen from the business world such as Henry Thornton or entrepreneurial clergy such as Charles Simeon, believed money and commerce to be tools for the spread of the Gospel faith. As Simeon wrote in regard to his purchase of livings for the Simeon Trust, which assured the placement of evangelically minded clergy, "The securing of a faithful minis-try in influential places would justify any outlay of money that could be expended on it; and if I were able to effect it by any funds of my own, they would be most gladly supplied for the attainment of so great an end. If our blessed Lord came down from heaven and died upon the cross, for the salvation of immortal souls—sure I am, that nothing which we can do for the promotion of His glory and of man's salvation can be justly deemed super-fluous or inexpedient. . . . I purchase *spheres*, wherein the prosperity of the Established Church, and the kingdom of our blessed Lord, may be advanced; and not for a season only, but, if it please God, in perpetuity also."[48] Money and commercialized religion allowed evangelicals to work the system of parish appointments within the established church and to create in their various societies a vast extramural and often pan-Protestant infrastructure controlled jointly by the laity and the clergy.

Evangelical leaders could invest capital to assure the presence of evan-gelical preaching, doctrines, and literature in the religious market, but the real test for the adequacy of their religious products resided with the deci-sions of religious consumers themselves. As an overwhelmingly laicized mode of religious life, evangelicalism very much oriented itself toward con-sumer satisfaction on the part of its congregations, an accommodation the Tractarians would denounce from the publication of their very first tract. Evangelical clergy, and most particularly the Methodist Conference, might attempt to assert firmer clerical control, but at the end of the day the pursuit of lay satisfaction drove much of the inner structure of evangelical worship, congregational life, and reform society activity. What held evangelical con-gregations was the message preached by the evangelical minister rather than his administration of the sacraments or possession of clerical, social, or religious authority. If the congregation or particular members of the con-gregation were dissatisfied by the content and delivery of his sermons, they would move to another minister. Furthermore, the availability of this world of open, expanding religious choice could prove tempting to dissatisfied members of the Church of England, especially after Catholic emancipation removed one of the political advantages of membership in the establishment.

What Boyd Hilton has termed "an 'economy of redemption' " per-meated the evangelical theology preached in this newly opened arena of free trade in religion. From the mid-seventeenth century onward, in the English-speaking world Protestants of Calvinist and Arminian convictions had debated the character of the atonement using metaphors of judicial-commercial transaction, with God as judge as well as financier. As Calvinist critics attacked late-eighteenth-century Methodist views of the atonement and justification, participants on both sides of the dispute debated the question using commercial terms and rhetoric. Thomas Scott appropriated commercial metaphors when exploring justification by faith through a comparison with the function of a banknote: "The intrinsic value of the paper is not one farthing, but it refers the creditor to a company who are engaged, and competent to pay the demand, and therefore it is accounted to the debtor as so much paid in specie. Thus faith refers God the Father to Christ, who is able and willing to answer for every believer, and therefore 'it is imputed to us for righteousness:' so that if a man should die, immediately after the first exercise of true faith, (as the thief on the cross did), and before he had time to perform one further act of obedience, he would certainly enter heaven as a justified person; though all who are spared, will as certainly show their faith by their works." Chalmers, in his *Lectures on the Epistle of Paul the Apostle to the Romans*, provided one of the most extensive discussions of the atonement through commercial terms. There Chalmers explained that Christ

> undertook to be surety for all who should believe; and having finished his undertaking, the matter was closed, and the creditor now ceased from putting in any further claim. . . . In the covenanting of ordinary trade, a deficiency from our engagements brings us into debt; but should an able cautioner liquidate the whole, we, in him, may be said to have sustained the prosecution, and borne the damage, and are now clear of the weight of conscious debt—because in him we have made full and satisfactory payment. . . . It is detracting from the richness and the efficacy of Heaven's boon, for us to cherish the haunting imagination of a debt, that the revealed Surety has done away—or, changing the terms, to cherish the haunting imagination of a guilt, for which the High Priest whom god Himself has set forth, has made a sacrifice wherewith God Himself has declared that He is well pleased.[49]

Such contractual language, though not the exclusive rhetoric of evangelical theology, continued to appear in various evangelical publications throughout the Victorian era and provided one of the chief targets for critics from other theological viewpoints, particularly Unitarians.

Reflecting on the evangelicalism of his youth, Gladstone observed that such a faith "did not ally itself with literature, art and general cultivation; but it harmonized very well with the money-getting pursuits." Gladstone did not exaggerate. Evangelical moral treatises echoed contemporary Scottish political economists, warmly embracing commercial society, and championed as fundamentally Christian the personal honesty required for the fair and proper functioning of commerce. Henry Venn in *The Complete Duty of Man* related Christian virtues directly to contractual arrangements in business conduct. When explaining the role of sincerity in personal relations, he stated,

> As a Christian, then, you will esteem it your duty constantly to speak the truth, according to the information you have received, in all affairs and occurrences of life. . . . When you have bound yourself by a promise to do any good office, or confer any benefit the right of the thing promised hath, in the court of conscience and before the God of truth, passed over from you to the person receiving the promise; wherefore you have, without his leave, no more power to recall or reverse it, than if you had given him a legal bond. Consequently you will esteem yourself obliged to stand to the performance of your word, though it may be much to your prejudice. And this in every instance where you have made a promise, unless some conditions were specified which have not been fulfilled, or something has afterwards come to light which annuls its obligation.

Sincerity thus constituted "the cement of society and the only foundation of mutual confidence." Venn went so far as to assert, "It is impossible, therefore, to be a Christian and at the same time live under the dominion of a false and deceitful tongue." Personal sincerity also encompassed the virtue of justice, which included paying bills, especially to tradesmen who "are daily tortured with the dilemma of bankruptcy, if they recover not their debts; or of ruin through the cruel resentment of their opulent creditors, if they do." The Christian businessman would not allow himself to be corrupted by the love of money, nor would he deal with false goods. Assigning long-standing Christian morality direct applicability to the commercial world, Venn advised, "You know that God, who indispensably requires you to be honest, leaves no foundation for the worldly and infidel excuses constantly urged to palliate cheating, viz. the necessity of being dishonest in order to prosper; for he pledges his own most sacred word for your provision, if you will deal uprightly." Similar advice appeared in other evangelical works, such as Thomas Gisborne's *Enquiry into the Duty of Men in the Higher and Middle Classes of Society*, as well as Wilberforce's *Practical View* and Scott's *Essays*.[50]

The emphasis on sincerity, justice, honesty, and fairness in trade and contracts undergirded evangelical competition in the religious marketplace, where evangelicals claimed to replace a deficient religious product—*nominal Christianity*—with the real thing—*vital Christianity*. They defined real religion as spiritual religion and theirs as the best path to such a faith. As

Francis Power Cobbe, one of the sharpest mid-Victorian critics of evangelicalism, commented, "It is not to be calculated how vast a force Evangelical Christianity has derived in our country from the position it early assumed, and long claimed undisputed, of being the only form of a really *spiritual* religion."[51] Evangelicals thus constantly presented themselves as furnishing the pure, unadulterated Gospel product as opposed to other inadequate or inferior products. Portraying much of the Church of England and nonevangelical Dissent as self-satisfied and overly formal and Roman Catholicism as inherently corrupt, evangelicals claimed that their own religion, realized through preaching, private and family devotion, and social reformation, would provide theological truth, personal salvation, and broad spirituality unavailable elsewhere.

Evangelical Christians did not only discuss the market, they also organized an array of voluntary societies that operated as businesses selling religious products, the most important of which involved inexpensive publications. Evangelicalism was the product of print culture, which allowed sermons and tracts to be published, advertised, and distributed in vast quantities. Through such organizations as the Religious Tract Society (1799), evangelicals printed and successfully marketed literally millions of copies of tracts. Indeed, it is one of the supreme ironies of English religious history that a radical high-church movement rather than the evangelical movement came to be called the Tractarian Movement and its activists the Tractites. But the most important of these evangelical publishing enterprises was the British and Foreign Bible Society (1804). Its founders became convinced, with apparent justification, that there existed a vast need and demand for the Scripture throughout the ranks of British society, especially among the poor. They were also desirous to see that the Scriptures circulated throughout the world in adequate translations on the Continent and where needed by missionaries.

The Bible Society epitomized the pan-Protestant evangelical commercial enterprise. Its central committee, composed entirely of laymen drawn from the commercial and professional classes, included fifteen Anglicans, fifteen Dissenters, and six foreign representatives. The Bible Society was an extremely Protestant organization firmly rooted in the belief that the sheer availability of the Bible would make it possible for people to find their own faith through reading its pages. On the basis of that conviction, the Society distributed the Authorized Version of the Bible "*without note or comment*," a practice that evangelicals could embrace either because of their conviction about the power of the sacred word or because of the presence of numerous biblical commentaries. Consequently, as Luke Howard, an early Quaker supporter, observed, it was "a society for furnishing the means of religion, but not a religious society."[52] By its production and distribution through paid subscriptions of hundreds of thousands of copies of the Christian Scripture, the Bible Society, as well as other societies dedicated to the distribution of the Scriptures, made possible the very existence of a Bible Christianity.

In addition to the Bible, the other book of divine revelation—nature— also linked many evangelical Christians to British commercial society. Although certain evangelical writers, such as Scott, devoted much less attention to nature and natural theology than to the Bible, other evangelicals had frequently appealed to natural theology and shared many of its presuppositions. As early as 1763 John Wesley had published *A Survey of the Wisdom of God in the Creation; or a Compendium of Natural Philosophy*. As John Brooke has commented, Wesley's readers would have concluded "that a science of nature, not bedeviled by arrogant theorizing, could offer rational support for Christian piety—revealing . . . a marvelous organization and adaptation within the created order."[53] There were evangelical literalists who were suspicious of both science and natural theology and others who disliked the utilitarian bent of much natural theology, but the wider vision of the firm compatibility of knowledge of the Bible and nature dominated. The most notable evangelical natural theologian was Chalmers, who contributed one of the Bridgewater Treatises, *On the Power, Wisdom, and Goodness of God* (1833). Years before writing that book he had held Glasgow evangelical circles spellbound with lectures on astronomy and natural theology. There were also numerous early Victorian Church of England evangelical studies of natural theology, including those by J. B. Sumner, Bishop of Chester and later Archbishop of Canterbury. As Hilton has urged, only an analysis of evangelicalism which overemphasizes the biblical extremists can ignore the powerful confidence that moderate evangelicals placed in the knowledge of God revealed in the natural order, though to be sure, they never conflated that knowledge with the revelation of saving gospel knowledge in Scripture.

An empirical Baconian spirit informed the exploration of each book, as did the assumption that God intended his creatures to take an active role in discovering his truth, whether in the natural order or in the Bible. The faith in the revelation of the two books and the role of reason in discerning that truth allowed many evangelicals to see their own faith as rational, grounded in empirical fact, and resistant to superstition.[54] Such was true of both traditional evangelicals and the new, adventuresome explorers of prophecy.

Thus evangelicals saw both the Bible and nature as arenas for the reverent exercise of human reason in pursuit of knowledge that God had revealed to humankind. This outlook, which pervaded evangelical circles on both sides of the Atlantic, provided the foundation for confidence that knowledge of science and the Bible, when properly examined and understood, would prove compatible and mutually self-supporting.

Natural theology, like biblical faith, also furnished a platform for pan-Protestant cooperation in the midst of harsh, unrelenting denominational quarrels. Arnold Thackray and J. D. Morrell have explored the manner in which natural theology allowed natural philosophers drawn from various competing religious denominations to cooperate in the fledgling British Association for the Advancement of Science.[55] Such cooperation among men of science of diverse religious backgrounds resembled the functioning of the Bible Society. Furthermore, many of the scientists who took leadership roles were either moderately evangelical or sympathetic to moderate evangelical Christianity. In this context, such evangelicals served the important function of constituting a buffer for science against the more extreme literalists.

From the time of John Ray and the early-eighteenth-century Boyle Lecturers through the Bridgewater Treatises, natural theologians had repeatedly devised arguments to demonstrate that God had designed the earth for commercial and capitalistic exploitation that was realized most appropriately in the society and economy of northwestern Europe. Natural theology, which since the early eighteenth century had justified commercial life tempered by benevolence, thus provided grounding for evangelical convictions that money and commerce could properly expand the knowledge of the Gospel and Christian activity. Whether with conscious intent or not, evangelical philanthropic and reform societies sought to instill manners and self-discipline that would allow the poor to function in commercial and industrial society that natural theology portrayed as providentially ordained. The antislavery movement combined the highest of humanitarian aspirations with a vision of the economic exploitation of the earth based on free labor and the substitution of goods produced by free labor for those produced by slave labor. The various missionary societies tended to believe that the global expansion of English commerce based on capitalistic enterprise had been providentially devised to allow the spread of the Gospel. As one historian has contended, "The Victorian churches, which had been compelled to adjust their domestic strategies in order to come to terms with the advent of free trade in religion, marketed their gospel to the world as the commodity of surpassing value, confident that providence would honour a faithful performance of their duty with a substantial return on their investment."[56] Evangelical Christians saw the Pax Britannica, based on an empire of free trade, as analogous to the Pax Romana, which had in their view providentially allowed for the spread of early Christianity.

All of these factors contributed to an enormous sense of confidence and satisfaction on the part of early Victorian British evangelical Christians as they looked out upon the world. They might have differing political loyalties in regard to specific issues of the reform era; they might differ in their degrees of optimism and pessimism about immediate social problems; they might sharply disagree on interpretation of the millennium and the desirability of ecclesiastical establishments. Nonetheless, they believed they stood as heirs of three quarters of a century of faithful evangelical advance in numbers and activity about which they could rejoice and seek to further. During those decades they saw increasing numbers of congregations across the spectrum of British religious life embracing evangelical theological doctrines, religious tactics, and reform causes. They had seen the slave trade abolished and slavery made illegal in the colonies. They saw Sunday schools dotting the landscape. They were witnessing an unprecedented distribution of Bibles and expansion of missionary effort at home and abroad. Each day as they read the Bible, they found confirmation that God had redeemed them through the atonement of Jesus Christ. As they further studied Scripture, the prophecies assured them that at the end of time Jesus would return and all things would be made aright. Whether of a premillennialist or postmillennialist outlook, they essentially shared that broad assurance. And as they cast their eyes upon nature, they saw the power, wisdom, and benevolence of God realizing itself in the creation and confirming the correctness of their social and economic life. To be sure, there was much work to be done: souls to be saved, sin to be discouraged, Roman Catholicism to be checked, and social and moral evils to be eradicated. Yet evangelical Protestant Christians generally stepped into the world with confidence that the Bible, nature, and history as revealed through prophesy promised that the Lord God reigned in a very special way in their personal lives, in the fortunes of their nation, and the larger contours of their epoch. The world of man and nature, however fallen, still belonged to God and displayed divine presence, purpose, and providence, even if imperfectly realized.

At the same time, there were other Christians in early Victorian Britain who systematically dissented from those evangelicals in regard to the expansive nature of Christ's atonement, the character of the church, the adequacy of the Bible, the role of the clergy and the laity, the purpose of preaching, the function of the sacraments, the desirability of ecumenical relations, and the commercialization of religion. A small group of such Christians had come to know each other in Oxford. During the second quarter of the nineteenth century these high churchmen would challenge evangelicalism on each and every one of its most cherished convictions. Their dislike of and even contempt for evangelical religion had various sources in their social situation, personal sensibilities, and theological presuppositions. But at some level of their being, about which the historian may speculate but perhaps cannot really intrude upon, they were unable in the fashion of so many contemporary evangelicals to affirm the world and the possibility of its fundamental rightness under the providence of God even if in a fallen state.

Late in his life John Henry Newman, the primary leader of this group, for his part reported that when he looked out of himself "into the world of men" he saw a sight that filled him "with unspeakable distress." He mused that if he looked into a mirror and did not see his face, he should have "the sort of feeling" which actually came upon him when he looked "into this living busy world" and saw "no reflexion of its Creator." Admitting that he could not deny "the real force of the arguments in proof of a God, drawn from the general facts of human society and the course of history," he nonetheless confessed that those arguments "do not warm me or enlighten me; they do not take away the winter of my desolation or make the buds unfold and the leaves grow within me, and my moral being rejoice." For Newman "the sight of the world" was "nothing else than the prophet's scroll, full of 'lamentations and mourning, and woe.'"[57] However stark the evangelical vision might be on occasion, it was never this stark because the evangelical saw the world as redeemed by God and much of it bound ultimately for union with God at the end of time. It will be well to keep in mind this vast difference in temperament of spirit as we explore the Tractarian challenge to the manifestations of the evangelical impulse.

CHAPTER 2

Men in Motion

John Keble, Richard Hurrell Froude, Edward Bouverie Pusey

IN THE HAGIOGRAPHY of the Tractarian Movement, John Keble, Richard Hurrell Froude, Edward Bouverie Pusey, and John Henry Newman often appear as figures of innate Catholic sensibility, who stepped magisterially into the ecclesiastical struggles of the Reform Act era to defend ancient Catholic truths of faith and practice. In point of fact, in the years before 1833, they actually *became* the Tractarians as they decided that only through a major challenge to evangelical religion both inside and outside the Church of England could that institution and its clergy survive in the rapidly shifting religious climate. Throughout the 1820s the future Tractarian leaders had been young men in motion acquiring, through different paths, the values and outlooks that would more fully manifest themselves during the next two decades. That motion would not cease when the Tractarian Movement commenced; indeed, motion was part of its essence.

ORIEL COLLEGE

Although the Tractarians addressed themselves to the state of a national church and employed the rhetoric of a universal Catholicism, their most fundamental point of reference was that relatively small spot of land in Oxford encompassed by the walls of Oriel College. There each was elected a fellow, and there each entered young adulthood among a group of quite remarkable contemporaries. None of the other places the Tractarians would spend most of their lives ever so thoroughly captured their imaginations or furnished them with friends or companions of so powerful spirit and intellect. Throughout their lives it was against the minds, spirits, and achievements of other current and past Oriel fellows that they would usually first measure themselves. It was in the Oriel Common Room with its eighteen fellows and provost, as well as visiting former fellows, that they learned to think, to criticize, to fight, and to pursue ambition. In that same cramped, all-male environment they also learned to forgive only rarely a slight and never to forget it. They could fulfill their not inconsiderable personal ambitions only by leaving Oriel, but having left it, they remained permanently shaped by the experience.

During the 1820s the life of the Oriel fellowship provided the backdrop against which the future Tractarian leaders, despite different social and religious backgrounds, forged bonds of friendship and eventual theological affinity. Under the leadership of Edward Copleston, who was its provost from 1814 to 1828, Oriel had taken the lead in the reenergizing of Oxford academic life following its eighteenth-century doldrums. During those years the university had instituted a new tutorial and examination system designed to demand more of teachers and to infuse recognition of merit among students. To be sure, Oxford and its colleges remained clerical and privileged, but they had nonetheless recognized that they must provide real instruction for those who desired it. Oriel had gone at least one step further by devising its own set of examinations for entrance into its fellowship. That device meant that Oriel was prepared to make its own judgments on the qualities of future fellows rather than depending on the outcome of previous examinations taken by prospective fellows. It gave young men a second chance to prove themselves. That structure was particularly to benefit Newman and Froude. As a result of the Oriel fellowship selection process and the intellectual climate fostered thereby, over the course of time its fellows filled numerous positions of leadership in both the church and the university. A person could retain the fellowship and its income for life, but had to resign it upon marriage. As fellows married or for other reasons resigned their fellowships as their careers advanced, new personalities appeared on the Oriel scene, with the remaining fellows displaying a keen interest in their election.

The Oriel fellowship which the Tractarians, as young men, entered was the most accomplished of any early-nineteenth-century Oxford college. It was also the home of the so-called "Noetics," a loose-knit group of Oriel fellows known for their intellectual prowess and supposed intellectual, political, and ecclesiastical liberalism.[1] More rhetoric than reality surrounded the collective life of these Noetics, whose number included Edward Copleston, John Davison, Richard Whately, Edward Hawkins, R. D. Hampden, Baden

Powell, Blanco White, and Samuel Hinds. They were never in residence all at the same time, nor did they work and cooperate exclusively with each other. What marked their public careers was a quiet determination to eschew ecclesiastical partisanship, to advance Catholic emancipation, and to accommodate modestly the interests of the church and university to the grievances of Dissenters. During the 1820s and 1830s, despite their reputations for liberalism, certain Noetics received patronage under Tory, Whig, and Conservative ministries.

Though most noted for their public activities, the Noetics displayed lives of deep, sincere, and consistent religious devotion. Indeed, regular chapel attendance after dinner by all fellows distinguished the Oriel of their day from many other Oxford colleges. Colin Matthew correctly emphasized that in the writing of the Noetics "nothing is more striking . . . than the fervour of their faith"; he also observed that nothing could be "more misleading than to present them as incipient secularists, as is shown by their eagerness to refute both utilitarianism and Unitarianism."[2] Theologically, the Noetics stood for moderation in most things. In contrast to the Calvinists against whom they polemicized, they believed that Jesus had died for all and that all who received him would be saved. They looked to the Bible as the foundation of Christian truth, but saw the Bible as proving what the church taught. They firmly supported good ecclesiastical order and were suspicious of ecclesiastical irregularity among evangelical groups. At the same time they sharply differed from many high churchmen and eloquently denounced any effort to equate the English Church with its clergy or to present clergy as something resembling a sacerdotal order. In regard to the issue of Christian tradition, they believed that all Christian revelation had ceased with the death of the apostles. The Noetics were profoundly critical of Roman Catholicism, which they regarded as a manifestly corrupt form of Christianity. In other words, the Noetics—to the extent they had any collective presence at all—were strong traditional, learned Protestants and moderate churchmen who believed in ecclesiastical discipline and eschewed any antinomian tendencies or ecclesiastical irregularity with contemporary Protestantism. All of these points require highlighting, because a very different, almost unfailingly hostile and even antireligious, picture of these men appeared in Tractarian writings, both public and private.

The later Tractarian hostility to many Oriel fellows with whom they had once been friendly arose in part from different reactions to the national political-ecclesiastical struggles of the late 1820s and in part to three events that had occurred in Oriel College itself. Each of these occurred before the publication of the *Tracts for the Times* in 1833, but very much remained on the minds of all the protagonists. These events need to be mentioned, however briefly, at this point so as to clarify them when they appear in later contexts.

First, in late 1827 Copleston was appointed Bishop of Llandaff, thus providing the occasion early the next year for the election of a new Oriel provost. Some college friends urged John Keble, who had left Oxford five years earlier but still retained his fellowship, to stand for the provostship against Edward Hawkins, who was then Vicar of St. Mary's Church, a position that lay in the gift of Oriel. Keble, who doubted that he could command a majority of the votes, let alone unanimity, and who may not have wanted the responsibility, declined. Keble's decision not to stand for the leadership of Oriel became in the minds of many Tractarians a path not taken. Both Newman and Pusey supported Hawkins's election, the former on the grounds that restoration of undergraduate discipline in the college required Hawkins's firm hand.[3]

The second event was the Oxford parliamentary election of 1829, in which the university electors refused to reelect Robert Peel, whom they believed had betrayed them by his recent about-face on Catholic emancipation. Although Newman had favored Catholic emancipation, he joined with Keble and Froude, as well as many others in the university, to protest Peel's reelection. The candidate they supported was Sir Robert Inglis, an evangelical Tory, firmly committed to the ecclesiastical establishment. Blanco White, a former Spanish Roman Catholic priest who enjoyed privileges in the Oriel Common Room and proved a shrewd if troubled observer of the Oxford scene, regarded the event as the key moment in the transformation of Newman's personality and the emergence of a fervent, uncompromising clerical party within the university identifying the true church with themselves.[4] There was, however, an important Oriel dimension to the election. Hawkins, acting on his own initiative and without consultation, had promised Oriel votes to the Peel cause. Much to his consternation, he faced an open rebellion in his own common room, where he encountered fervent opponents of Peel. Thus the common room that had not long before unanimously elected Hawkins as provost now stood sharply divided and no longer fully supportive of his leadership.

The third occasion for Oriel disruption touching the lives of the future Tractarians was the dispute over the college program of instruction. The weeks of the Oxford election had coincided with the introduction of a plan, originating with Newman, to revise tutorial instruction in Oriel. Newman and his fellow tutors, who included Froude, Henry Wilberforce, and Joseph Dornford, attempted to organize a clericized instructional system whereby certain better students would benefit from private tuition and a close personal and pastoral relationship with a tutor.[5] They had commenced this effort just before the Peel election without securing Hawkins's permission. All four tutors had opposed Peel and thus contributed to their provost's political humiliation. Hawkins, who became aware of the new tutorial structures only in early 1830, sharply disapproved. After weeks of difficult, fruitless negotiation by correspondence, Hawkins decided in late May 1830 to send no further students to Newman, Froude, or Wilberforce. Hawkins replaced Newman with R. D. Hampden, a former Oriel fellow who later loomed large in Newman's life and in the events of the Tractarian era. Thereafter, Newman and Hawkins, who had once been quite friendly, retained a correct but hardly cordial relationship.

Each of these Oriel episodes remained very much alive in the minds of the future Tractarian leaders as throughout the 1830s and 1840s they attempted to reshape both their church and their university. We must now turn our attention to those men and their own personal development. Newman was to become the most prominent and famous of this group, but his own personality and outlook can be understood only by first looking at the other major Tractarian figures. Moreover, at certain points in the history of Tractarianism the actions and thoughts of Keble, Froude, and Pusey very much came to the fore determining both the wider public response and Newman's own state of mind.

JOHN KEBLE

Newman always dated the commencement of the Tractarian Movement from July 14, 1833, and John Keble's delivery of his Oxford Assize Sermon on national apostasy.[6] The issue at hand was a bill then working its way through the Whig-controlled Parliament relating to the Church of Ireland, the established Protestant church in that overwhelmingly Roman Catholic country. Keble delivered his sermon seized with fury at the Irish Temporalities Bill, which abolished ten Irish bishoprics as part of a larger scheme to reform Irish Church finance by substituting the income from those sees for income previously drawn from charges against the general Irish population. The bill clearly embodied the contemporary reform spirit. The surfeit of bishoprics in the Church of Ireland permitted the alleviation of the obvious evil of requiring Irish Roman Catholics to pay for a church of a different faith and simultaneously increased ecclesiastical administrative efficiency. The measure enjoyed wide support, including that of a number of bishops, among them Edward Copleston, Bishop of Llandaff, and Richard Whately, Archbishop of Dublin, both former Oriel fellows. To the Tory Keble, however, the bill simply constituted Whig buckling to radical Irish Roman Catholics and English Dissenters, who were wreaking further havoc on the established church and now threatening its property.

Keble's strategy was that of a firm high churchman. He did not defend ecclesiastical establishment as such, but rather portrayed the immediate legislative events as an assault on God's one true church in the realm. Throughout his sermon Keble eschewed the terms *establishment*, Church of England, and English Church. Rather adopting standard high-church rhetoric, he spoke of the "apostolical Church" in the English realms, the distinct authority and legitimacy of which resided in the apostolical descent of its bishops, now assaulted by Parliament, rather than in their political connection or legal privileges. That "apostolical Church," as distinct from Dissenting and Roman Catholic congregations, embodied the true church within the kingdom and had been "established among us for the salvation of our souls."[7] Nonetheless, as opposed to the evangelical "invisible Church" of true believers across the ages and several denominations, Keble's "apostolical Church" in England was visible and did for all intents and purposes stand coterminous with the national establishment. That relationship in the mind of Keble and others constituted its enormous advantage and at the same time its enormous burden.

Drawing his text from 1 Samuel 12:23, Keble translated his political denunciation into a more general jeremiad against national apostasy engulfing the English realms. Recent English constitutional and ecclesiastical changes sponsored by "impatient patrons of innovation" recalled to his mind the ancient Hebrews' demand for government by a king, a demand that in their day had manifested "a fresh development of the same restless, godless spirit which had led them so often into idolatry." Among the "omens and tokens of an apostate mind in a nation" Keble included ecumenical understanding and mutual religious forbearance, which he equated with a "growing indifference, in which men indulge themselves, to other men's religious sentiments" while acting "under the guise of charity and toleration" accompanied by self-congratulation "on the supposed decay of what they call an exclusive system." All such outlooks, which might have been found among either evangelical Dissenters or establishment latitudinarians, manifested "the fashionable liberality of this generation." A nation that began by persecuting the successors of the apostles, Keble contended, would under the guise of pursuing "toleration" or "state security" or "sympathy with popular feeling" in all likelihood end by persecuting the true church itself. Furthermore, the disrespect of the Whig ministry toward the successors of the apostles—that is, the Irish Bishops—constituted "an unquestionable symptom of enmity to him who gave them their commission at first, and has pledged himself to be with them forever."[8]

Keble followed his rousingly harsh critique of the Whig ministry with a remarkably timid and self-consciously apolitical solution in line with traditional high-church thought on the matter. Should "the apostolical Church be forsaken, degraded, nay trampled on and despoiled by the state and the people of England," Keble suggested that both clergy and laity offer prayers of intercession for all in political authority and then, "when the Church landmarks are being broken down," voice steady remonstrance. Individual Christians should thus support "the cause of the apostolical church in these realms" grounded in the sure knowledge that eventually, perhaps even after death, they would stand on the winning side, having achieved "complete, universal, and eternal" victory against "the triumph of disorder and irreligion."[9] Keble thus enjoined the apostolical church within the English realms to do little more than hunker down in anticipation of passively resisting the events and policies of a forthcoming period of testing and persecution.

A week later in the advertisement to the published version of the sermon, Keble adopted a significantly different rhetoric and analysis, declaring that the by-now-completed Irish legislation indicated "that the apostolical Church in this realm is henceforth only to stand, in the eye of the state, as *one sect among many,* depending, for any pre-eminence she may still appear to retain, merely upon the accident of her having a strong party in the country." That emergence of the established church as "*one sect among many*" in the religious marketplace had, of course, not actually occurred because of the "profane intrusion" and "tyranny" of the Irish Temporalities Bill, but rather because of the recent political advance, first, of evangelical religion in England through the accommodation of Dissent from the Toleration Act of 1812 through the repeal of political disabilities against Protestant Dissenters in 1828, and, second, of Roman Catholicism in Ireland as accommodated by the passage of Catholic emancipation in 1829. Keble's comments left unclear whether churchmen should continue to defend retention of the privileges of establishment or in some other fashion maximize the position of the English Church as one of several competing religious groups operating in a free market of religion. Despite many public and private comments, the Tractarians never really permanently clarified that point for themselves. Keble's immediate advice—that churchmen decide first how most effectively henceforth to answer the charge of the Bishop of Rome that the Church of England is "a mere parliamentarian church" and second how in the future to maintain the purity and integrity of the sacred order of the priesthood—embodied that ambiguity.[10]

The John Keble whose jeremiad of July 14, 1833, so stirred his friend Newman had not always been a person of narrow, angry, and extreme opinion. There had been another, younger John Keble of keener intellect, more moderate temper, and famously sweet disposition. Keble once told Isaac Williams that his years with Newman and Pusey in the Tractarian Movement constituted "a sort of parenthesis" in his life when he had departed from the outlook of his rearing and for a time had actually believed that religious truths as he understood them might be popular and undespised.[11] But before his entry into the parenthesis of the movement, Keble had not secured for himself a settled personal or professional life or more than modest position in the church.

Born in 1792, reared and educated in a clerical home, Keble was the oldest of the Tractarians. In 1807 he entered Corpus Christi, where under the recently revised examination statute of 1800 he achieved a Double First for his outstanding examinations in both classics and mathematics, only the second Oxford student to do so, the first having been Robert Peel. Keble became a fellow in 1811 and later was a tutor in Oriel College, where younger acquaintances seem naturally to have confided in him as he easily assumed the role of mentor. While serving there and later as his father's curate, the devout Keble on more than one occasion actively discouraged overly introspective or ascetic tendencies that would later become a hallmark of many Tractarian sympathizers.[12]

In one important case Keble exercised such moderating influence over Thomas Arnold, who in 1819 found himself unable to assent to the damnatory clauses of the Athanasian Creed or to clarify for himself certain aspects of the doctrine of the Trinity. His particular problem was the not unfamiliar one of reconciling elements of those doctrines to the letter of Scripture itself, a process made all the more difficult by English Unitarians who denied the doctrine of the Trinity on the basis of Scripture. As a result of his inner questioning, Arnold became undecided as to whether he should move forward toward ordination as a deacon. Arnold confided his difficulties to Keble, his senior by only three years. The latter, without any apparent sense of breaking a personal or spiritual confidence, reported to J. T. Coleridge, a mutual friend, that if Arnold "were not so good a fellow I think he would be a sceptic." Keble quite wisely mused to Coleridge that Arnold in all probability simply required "a domestic circle, constant employment *in company*, & perhaps pastoral cares" as a cure for "this defect of his intellectual life" and as a means "to drown effectually the scruples & doubtings by which in spite of himself he is every now & then so harassed and brought so low, that he needs all his strong sense & Xtian Resolution to bear up against them." He saw Arnold's perplexity as reflecting "a mere morbid state of mind, a severe probation," which he believed "superior intellects not seldom go thro" and which were "cured without much talking or arguing about it, by mere force of holy living."[13] Keble thus advised Arnold to pursue a good diet, practical piety, family, and parish life as the source of genuine cure for significant religious questioning. Keble's counsel struck a receptive chord in Arnold, who reported to Coleridge that he had "practically followed" Keble's advice, laying "the Controversy aside" and "endeavouring to bring myself to a better Temper by avoiding such pursuits as tend to feed my Pride and Vanity." For his part, the young Keble appears to have been relatively unperturbed by Arnold's possible lack of orthodox views on significant theological questions and generously understood how to direct him toward a practical resolution of inner uncertainties. Deeply appreciative of Keble's aid, counsel, and patience, Arnold told Coleridge in the spring of 1820, "I know by my own experiences how excellent a friend & Comforter he [Keble] is in any Sorrow whether outward or arising from within one's self."[14]

The Keble of 1819, willing to tolerate and aid the resolution of a friend's doubt over the Trinity and the Athanasian Creed, had by a decade later transformed himself into a political and religious reactionary prepared to break friendships, even that with Arnold, over ecclesiastical politics. It is not altogether certain what so changed Keble, though his family and social environments played major roles. In 1822 he left Oxford to take up country parish work, serving except for a brief interval until 1835 as his father's unmarried curate while remaining a fellow of Oriel and drawing the annual income associated with that position. These are the years when most young early-nineteenth-century adults, as well as those of other eras, normally successfully differentiated their lives from those of their parents and immediate family, acquired new mentors and friends, married, and also often modified their religious views.[15] During his Oxford years Keble had clearly been developing into his own person, but he abandoned that emerging independence and chose to reenter his father's parish world. There he read

extensively on ecclesiastical matters and became acquainted with the writings of the Nonjurors. Keble's high estimation of the supernatural role of
ordained English clergy developed from this reading and his father's mentoring. That outlook served in their own eyes to distinguish father and son
from both Dissenting and evangelical ministers with whom they competed
and likewise to counter the carping criticism of the established church from
political liberals and radicals.

    Although Keble had at least two opportunities to move to other parishes,
his sense of duty to his father and sisters led him to refuse the offers and to
restrict his life. From 1824 to late 1827 he unsuccessfully courted a woman
about half his age. Biographers suggest that the death in 1826 of his younger
sister Mary Anne, to whom he was devoted, changed his character or at least
aged him. The next year, during which he declined to stand for the Oriel
provostship, Keble published *The Christian Year*, the most famous and enduring work of English devotional poetry of the century.[16] That volume
accorded him a considerable reputation within the church and in the university, where in 1831 Convocation elected him poetry professor, a position he
could hold for ten years. Still, he did not have a parish of his own or an
independent position in the church.

    During the same period Keble developed the theological outlook he was
to carry for life. Both before and during the 1820s Keble's sermons emphasized repentance, good works, and the facing of eventual divine judgment.
He told one congregation in 1818, "This . . . is Christian repentance,
namely, to cease to do evil, and learn to do well for Christ's sake, and by the
assistance of His Holy Spirit blessing the ordinances of Christian religion.
Nothing short of this can with any safety be trusted to as likely at all to avail
us in the hour of death, or the day of judgment." The theme of judgment
runs throughout the sermons of this decade. Moreover, though he would
become a poet of considerable sensibility, he consistently warned against
equating a true religious life with religious feelings or emotions. In 1823 he
counseled against depending upon "overpowering feelings" as evidence of
the work of God in one's life and reminded his listeners, "Men are better
pleased, in general, to imagine that the love of God must excite a sort of
tumult in their minds, so that their heart shall feel as if it were full, and not
know which way to turn itself from excess of emotion, than that the same
love should make them ashamed of their sins, and set them soberly upon
redeeming the time, and doing all their duty more carefully and humbly for
the time to come." Keble urged that "sound Scriptural hope" depended
"not on inward fancies and feelings" but was "always joined with *good*

2. John Keble (1792–1866), here portrayed at the age of forty-one, became famous in Church of England circles during the late 1820s as the author of *The Christian Year*, a volume of devotional poetry. He was professor of poetry at Oxford from 1831 to 1841. Newman considered his sermon on national apostasy, preached on July 14, 1833, as marking the beginning of the Tractarian Movement. Keble was the person to whom Newman most often turned for advice. (Reproduced with the permission of the Warden and Fellows of Keble College.)

works." In a sermon of the next year he criticized those "who insist upon their strong feelings, and the delight they find in prayer, as a surer and more necessary sign of their being in a good way, than the sober and quiet keeping of the Commandments." In 1827 he declared, "If any one thing is plainer than another out of the Holy Scriptures, it is this, that no one must expect to be saved by Christ hereafter, who has not sincerely endeavoured to be like Him in this present world." Keble consistently tied such Christian obedience to respect for social superiors associating in 1826 criticism of one's superiors with "the hateful tempers" of "presumption, self-will, and cowardice." Unsurprisingly, in late 1830 he denounced the disobedience of agricultural riots in his neighborhood that had led to violence and property destruction.[17]

Although a strong upholder of the social order, Keble was not altogether convinced of the desirability of ecclesiastical establishments. As early as 1820 he had objected to "making religion too much a matter of politics," by which he meant the equation of the Church of England with establishment.[18] His subsequent reading in the Caroline divines, the royalist historians of the seventeenth century, the Nonjurors, and William Law, as well as contemporary literature on the relationship of church and state, did not dissuade him from that view. Keble appears to have contemplated as early as 1827 the free competition of the English Church with its rivals through a separation of the Church of England from the English state, but he remained understandably apprehensive over the manner in which such separation might be accomplished. At the time of Catholic emancipation and afterward, Keble was deeply troubled that persons outside the Church of England would be able to legislate for it and might eventually separate it from the state on their own terms.

Throughout all his comments on the issue of establishment, which were never systematic or consistent, he entertained a lively, even vitriolic hatred of the Whigs, having long lived in a Whig stronghold, where with his father he had been hooted on the way to the parliamentary election. Writing to Coleridge in 1831, Keble facilely associated liberal political and evangelical religious outlooks as he bemoaned the "Liberal-reforming-Jacobino-Socino-puritanical crew." Early in 1833, in the wake of the Reform Act, he told the same correspondent, "I look upon them [church and state] as virtually dissolved, and as soon as they are avowedly the better," adding that as far as he could discern, such dissolution might be "better for true Religion than going on in Union with a Whig State."[19]

The presence of evangelicals in the English Church also caused Keble to ponder the desirability of some kind of disruption. His dislike for evangelicals was personal as well as theological, for the owner of his father's benefice was an evangelical between whom and the Kebles there existed little sympathy. In 1832 John Keble complained about the presence of a young evangelical vicar at Fairfield who went "about making converts to the 'peculiar views'" and who had "so bewitched divers of the neighborhood" that there was hardly any whom he "would trust to baptize a child or bury a corpse" in his own absence. Keble further commented, "I am now more & more inclined to think, that the sooner we come to an open separation from these people, the better both for ourselves & our flocks." Such a separation, he thought, might well arise from "the progress of Revolution," which he associated with the Reform Act turmoil.[20] Thus John Keble was willing to contemplate very considerable disruption in the English Church for the sake of ridding it of the influence of establishment evangelicals or of a Whig government dependent upon evangelical Dissenters.

Keble's increasingly conservative political opinions transformed his relationship with Thomas Arnold, who during the years of Keble's country parish obscurity had become an historian of note, Headmaster of Rugby, a husband, and a father, one of whose children, Matthew, was Keble's godson. Arnold had also moved steadily away from strong Tory sentiments toward ecclesiastically liberal ones which Keble deplored but which did not prevent him from admiring the manner in which Arnold had begun his Rugby career. Once appointed headmaster, Arnold was ordained to the priesthood of the Church of England. Over the next few years he became an increasingly outspoken critic of the establishment and certainly did not regard the Church of England as the only Christian church in the realm. At that point Keble firmly and permanently broke with his former student because of differences in ecclesiology as he had not broken over Arnold's questioning of the Trinity more than a decade earlier. Keble wrote to Coleridge, "With all my respect for Arnold he really shows himself so wilful and presumptuous in his way of dealing with holy things, a most erroneous and dangerous way, I think and a palpably sophistical way, that I cannot any longer look on him as a fellow-worker in the same cause. He seems to me now like a well-meaning heretic." The heresy referred to Arnold's ecclesiastical politics, not to his theology. Keble's opinion was only confirmed in 1833, when Arnold published an exceedingly controversial and politically ill-advised pamphlet on church reform, suggesting among other things that the various Christian denominations share time in the buildings of the Church of England. If Keble could later describe even modest cooperation between Baptist and

Church of England missionaries as "super-ultra-liberal," his contempt for
Arnold's scheme was even deeper. By late 1836, after Arnold had vigorously
opposed the Tractarian enterprise, Keble denounced him to Coleridge for
"treason towards the Holy Catholic Church" and for having "taken part, a
prominent part, with the prevailing forms of Antichristianism." Keble even
deplored Coleridge's visit to Arnold's home that year as "something like
disloyal communication with our Master's Enemies."[21]

The rupture in friendship, trust, and esteem had been mutual. By October 1833, reacting to Keble's sermon on national apostasy and the clericalism of the early tracts, Arnold sadly told Coleridge that his former mentor
now illustrated

> a melancholy Instance of how a good Man may so degrade and destroy his
> Understanding that Fanaticism at last reacts upon his heart and impairs his
> Clarity. I cannot tell you how I have been pained by all that I have seen of
> Keble's lately;—he seems to be on the edge of any Atrocity, like Dominic or
> the Puritans of old,—from being so completely overpowered by Fanaticism:
> a Fanaticism as furious as Irvine's [Irving's], and actually less reasonable;
> for Irvine at least appealed to outward & visible signs, while Keble & his
> Party, like the Quakers in their worst Extravagances, set up their own mor-
> bid Feelings as the Criterion of Truth & Holiness, and call those who dis-
> pute them aliens from the Church of God and Rebels against their Saviour.

Arnold feared that under Keble's influence the English clergy might "begin
to exhibit an aggravation of the worst Superstitions of the Roman Catholics,
only stripped of that Consistency which stamps even the errors of the
Roman System with something of a character of Greatness."[22] Though
writing from personal hurt, anger, and disappointment, Arnold had predicted correctly the direction and tenor of Keble's religious zeal. In addition
to having perceived the single-mindedness in Keble's opinions, Arnold had
intuitively grasped the affinities and parallels that Tractarian actions and
outlooks bore to both contemporary disruptive evangelical experimentation
and historic subjective, radical Protestantism.

In the autumn of 1835, upon the death of his father, Keble at the age
of forty-three surprised and chagrined his Tractarian friends, who championed clerical celibacy, by resigning his fellowship to marry. The same year
William Heathcote, a landlord who refused to accept Dissenters as tenants,
had also presented him to the parish of Hursley. Keble had thus secured for
himself a place of excellent income and social position where he personally
would encounter little need to compete in the evolving religious marketplace. Indeed, Keble sought to exercise a considerable clerical presence in

his parish. Like some other Tractarians, though by no means all, he favored the revival of confession as a device whereby the English clergy might reassert authority within the life of their parishes. In 1843 he complained to Coleridge of "not knowing what men are really doing" in his parish and discovering "a fearful state of things" when he did find out. He said his "one great grievance" was "the neglect of Confession," without the revival of which "we shall not have the due severity in our religion" that was required for it not to fail.[23]

By this point in his career confirming his earlier outlook, Keble regarded evangelical religion as the chief enemy of such religious severity and consequent proper respect for priests of the Church of England. In 1844 he again complained to Coleridge of "working in the dark, and in the dark it will be, until the rule of systematic Confession is revived in our Church." In the same context he criticized evangelicalism, which he described as "the tradition which goes by the name of Justification by Faith, and which in reality means, that one who has sinned, and is sorry for it, is as if he had not sinned, blights and benumbs one in every limb, in trying to make people aware of their real state." This situation led Keble to "deprecate the word and the idea of Protestantism," which in his own mind he could not separate from the concept and reality of " 'Every man his own absolver,' " which he thought amounted to declaring "Peace where there is no Peace, and mere shadows of Repentance."[24] For Keble, absolution from sin could truly emanate only from episcopally ordained priests, who through an intimate knowledge of their parishioners' lives, gained at least in part through the confessional, would foster social and spiritual discipline in their flocks.

This vision of moral asceticism and clerical authority, both of which challenged evangelical religion, far more than antierastianism constituted the fundamental theological thrust of the Tractarian message. It was the realization of such austerity that the Tractarians over time found difficult to achieve within the traditional devotional and ecclesiastical boundaries of the English Church. But the person responsible for bringing a fervent desire for ascetic religion to the fore in the emerging Tractarian consciousness was not Keble but rather Richard Hurrell Froude.

RICHARD HURRELL FROUDE

Richard Hurrell Froude, the shortest-lived of the Tractarian leaders, played two distinct roles in the movement. Froude epitomized the person without responsibility who can and does say whatever pleases him, encountering few, if any, consequences. In that role he pressed a small circle of friends toward a radical anti-Protestant and antiestablishment position. After his death in early 1836, Froude became a far more widely known and even more tendentious presence in English religious life through the publication in 1838 and 1839 of his manuscripts and otherwise previously little-noticed articles, edited by Keble and Newman. The four volumes of *Remains of the Late Reverend Richard Hurrell Froude,* though inflaming anti-Tractarian sentiment in the press, soon became an inspiration and rallying point for a second generation of younger Tractarians drawn to Froude's radical Catholic ideas and novel devotional ideals.

Froude was an unlikely figure to have generated such enthusiasm. He was born in 1803, studied at Eton, and then entered Oriel College in 1821. His friendship with Keble, who reminded him of his mother, commenced during a reading party in 1823, shortly after Keble had left Oxford. The friendship grew slowly. Keble was always hesitant about Froude's love of paradox, beneath which Keble nonetheless discerned real concern for morality and personal spirituality. After completing undistinguished undergraduate examinations, Froude began serious study, most particularly relating to seventeenth-century English history, hoping to gain an Oriel fellowship. In 1826 he attended the theology lectures of Charles Lloyd, Regius Professor of Divinity and later Bishop of Oxford, and the same year succeeded in winning his fellowship. At the time Keble wrote Coleridge, "I am glad that H F has succeeded in something at last," further observing that he had encountered "this good luck" just "when his conceit was working off and he wanted a little encouragement to industry."[25] For reasons of either health or laziness, Froude's industry never developed very fully or fruitfully. He continued to relish the display of his considerable gifts for irony and impudence. Throughout his adult life he adopted condescending language toward both Dissenters and evangelicals and employed similarly deprecating language toward persons of color whom he later met on Barbados.

In 1826, having taken up the Oriel fellowship, he spent several weeks reading the personal journal of his mother, who had died five years earlier. Froude began to fill his own journal with passages of self-criticism and self-excoriation.[26] During this inner turmoil, which extended into 1827, he repeatedly attempted to pursue a regimen of fasting and appears, as is true of many twentieth-century persons with eating disorders, to have become fixated on his unsuccessful efforts to confine his consumption of food. Overall, the journal for this period presents a young adult possessing little sense of vocation or sustained conviction about anything who makes resolution after resolution to change behavior, all of which ultimately come to very little, and then suffers self-inflicted pangs of conscience. During this period of depression, not unlike that recounted in John Stuart Mill's *Autobiography*, Froude, like Arnold before him, turned to Keble for advice and mentoring. Keble, who until taking up his duties as Froude's editor a decade later remained unaware of the depths of his young friend's despair, advised him to be cheerful and to constrain his penchant for self-abasement.

The reasons for that self-abasement remain mysterious but appear to have had a sexual component, as suggested by a sermon, written several years later. There Froude presented childhood innocence as the highest human moral condition, cited portions of the Bible that either "connect the idea of sin with that of filthiness" or equate it with "a kind of bodily pollution" requiring "external purification," and pointed to the necessity "not only to avoid sinful actions, but to hate and erase from our minds all relish for sinful pleasures." Froude also urged that Christ's words about coming to him as little children be understood "in the full sense which they literally convey, that we are not to find out partial explanations of them, but to believe that we really must aim at becoming again as little children" who have not disobeyed parents nor tasted the pleasures of disobedience. Those who would truly seek God's acceptance, Froude declared, "will have to regard as filth what they now set their affections on, and to vomit from their minds every pleasant recollection connected with sin." Many people would find this difficult and would ultimately return to God "not as a little child, but as a diseased and deformed man." Yet those who approached God feeling "grieved" and "intolerably burdened at the recollection of all their bad thoughts and deeds" that had opposed God's will, and who observed in themselves "with disgust and anguish the traces of those bad pleasures" which they had indulged, might still hope to be admitted to God's presence, though they could not rank with the great saints, apostles, or martyrs.[27] Froude's emphasis on literally returning to childhood with its then-presumed innocence and his repeated discussion of sin as related to filth suggest considerable sexual anxiety on Froude's part, the nature of which cannot be determined. His use of the verb "to vomit" to express the removal of pleasant recollections from the mind also recalls his identification of sinfulness with food and eating. Froude's anxiety and frustration over his incapacity to alleviate sin appears to have fostered a determination on his part not only to lead a celibate life but also to find relief for his burden of sin through physical privation first attempted through fasting.

In this sermon and others of the early 1830s, only some of which were delivered, Froude espoused a severe moral rigor that firmly rejected the supposition that "religion is a matter of feeling, to be attained to, and judged of, in quite a different way from other tempers and habits." He ridiculed evangelicals who affected "an unnatural voice and manner, when talking on religious subjects" and who thus seemed "more like men acting a part than like persons whose conduct arose out of their feelings." In contrast to such public evangelical preaching and witnessing, Froude declared, "We must lead lives of voluntarily endured privation, if we would ever give Jesus Christ that place in our affections which He has promised to supply for those who seek Him earnestly." Overwhelmed with the impossibility of erasing the lingering effects of bad habits, he thought that they might themselves "be healed by care and discipline, and their worst consequences prevented by timely remedies," but, he nonetheless insisted, "the scars will remain to the last." Just as an amputated arm though healed at the shoulder would not return, Froude claimed, "so also purity of heart will not come again, though we strive ever so successfully to repress the encroachments of sin." The deformity of earlier bad habits remained a part of a person's nature, which he could no more rid himself of than the Ethiopian could "change his skin, or the leopard his spots." For those reasons Froude directly spurned the evangelical conviction that repentance could occur through "a sudden feeling" induced by preaching, conversation, or personal suffering. Indeed, in another sermon he went so far as to say, "Let us be *sure* that our spirit is martyred, before we feel so very comfortable at our not resembling those who suffered in the body."[28]

Although Froude emphasized the necessity of personal mortification during the same period that he espoused radical views on possible new relationships of the English Church with the state, the former exhortation in the long run proved far more influential and disruptive than the latter, especially among Tractarian followers early in the next decade. It is significant that those second generation Tractarians attracted to Froude's asceticism, made public in the *Remains* in 1838, were themselves then about the same age as Froude had been during his crisis. Several of these young men later moved toward their own ascetic pursuits involving serious fasting in Newman's self-styled monastery at Littlemore.

Within Oriel by late 1828 Froude and Newman had become very close friends, and Froude also encouraged a deepening of friendship between Newman and Keble, already acquainted but not closely so. The Oxford election of 1829 permanently established political bonds among the three as with others they resisted the efforts of Provost Edward Hawkins to reelect

Robert Peel. Those bonds became further cemented in 1830 when Hawkins relieved Froude, Newman, and Wilberforce of their tutorial duties.[29]

Health concerns dominated Froude's spirit more than disappointment over the failed tutorial reform. He suffered from tuberculosis and its consequent fatigue and enforced physical inactivity. His extravagant prose and conversation may have compensated for the absence of an active life. Illness may also account for his interest in celibacy. The tuberculosis steadily weakened Froude, prevented his seriously seeking a parish, and provided the reason for a Mediterranean trip in late 1832 and early 1833 on which Newman accompanied the Froude family. The conversations of that journey, as well as the immediate experience of Italian Roman Catholicism, proved a momentous turning point in Newman's own thought and religious development and accounted for the receptive frame of mind in which he heard Keble's assize sermon a few days after his return.

Froude was studying English ecclesiastical history during the very months and years of the momentous constitutional transformation of the English Church. Watching those events as he delved more deeply into the ecclesiastical past had moved him to the contemplation and advocacy of a radical restructuring of the English Church in the life of the nation and the society. Froude appears to have been more willing than others in the Tractarian circle to imagine a genuinely formal severance of the Church of England from the state, even if the separation involved significant loss of ecclesiastical property. For example, as early as 1830 he informed his father, Archdeacon Robert Froude, "I am quite making up my mind to lose every thing and to be thrown on my own resources before long, and I do not consider the prospect a gloomy one. I cannot but believe that the Church will surprise people a little when its latent spirit has been roused; and when the reasons for caution have been removed by disconnecting it with the State. And though I am not blind to the evils which must accompany such a convulsion, so that I would not for the world have a hand in bringing it about, I own it is not with unmixed apprehension that I anticipate its approach."[30] It was perhaps easy for Froude and other future Tractarians, including Keble near that time, to speak and write bravely, even if in private, about giving up privileges when they did not yet have parishes of their own or family responsibilities and still retained their Oriel fellowship incomes. Nonetheless, there did exist in their minds the distinct idea of a sufficiently radical transformation of the relationship of the English Church and state as to constitute in effect the refounding of the former.

Froude himself wished a plague on all contemporary parties in the

Church of England. Consistently critical of the evangelicals, all of whom he regarded as ultra-Protestants and puritans in disguise, Froude also disliked the caution and timidity of the traditional high-church party, whom he dubbed the "Z's." For some time Froude had adopted the term *Apostolical* to describe an advanced high-church position, distinct from that of the Z's, that would distinguish the Church of England from other denominations in the land on the basis of its unique possession of apostolic succession and a monopoly of grace through its sacraments. In October 1832 he wrote, "If it was not for a personal hatred of the Whigs, I should care comparatively little for the Reform Bill. For the Church can never right itself without a blow-up." In June 1833, shortly after his return from the Mediterranean voyage, while walking in the Trinity College gardens, he told Isaac Williams, "Isaac, we must make a row in the world. Why should we not? Only consider what the Peculiars, *i.e.* the Evangelicals have done with a few half truths to work upon! And with our principles, if we set resolutely to work, we can do the same. . . . Church principles, forced on people's notice, must work for good. However, we must try; and Newman and I are determined to set to work as soon as he returns, and you must join with us."[31] This comment again indicates the frame of mind with which Newman encountered Keble's sermon a few days later. He and Froude had decided they must forge a Catholic position in the established church as distinct as that long enjoyed by evangelicals.

Froude's rhetoric in June 1833, like that of Keble's sermon the next month, outpaced his immediate action, which consisted of dispatching a few poems by Williams, Keble, and himself to the *British Magazine*, edited by high churchman Hugh James Rose of Cambridge. The three also contacted William Palmer of Worcester College, an Irish born high-church expert on liturgy, about their concern for the church. Two weeks after Keble's sermon, Froude joined Palmer at a small clerical gathering held between July 25 and July 29 at Rose's Hadleigh rectory to devise a strategy for high-church resistance to Whig policy. Despite the fame this Hadleigh conference attained in high-church historiography, it accomplished nothing except to persuade Froude of the worthlessness of any traditional high-church protest. He left Hadleigh convinced that significant differences of purpose existed between high churchmen and those whom he and Newman had over the years come to describe as Apostolical. That was an important if negative fallout, because it confirmed his and Newman's view that they must pursue their own strategy. Publication of *Tracts for the Times* was the result of that decision. At the same time, despite the Tractarian view of the indecisiveness of the older high churchmen, it is worth noting that one of the participants preaching on the Sunday that fell in the middle of the Hadleigh gathering had declared, "All the signs and tokens of evil which marked the days when good King Charles was put to death, are gathering around, and showing themselves again. . . . The ministers of religion are openly reviled and abused. . . . The property which the piety of former days gave to support the clergy . . . is the object of men's covetousness. . . . Too soon, I fear, many of us may be called upon to put in practice those lessons which the Scriptures teach, of how to suffer persecution."[32] Such profound apprehensions expressed and energized by such extreme rhetoric filled all those who launched the Tractarian enterprise, including the high churchmen whom Froude regarded as overly timid.

In late 1833, after the tracts had commenced, Froude, in hope of regaining his health, departed England for Barbados. There he remained until May 1835, continuing with Newman through correspondence their radical Mediterranean conversations. While in the Caribbean, Froude more fully developed a private criticism of the English Reformers that had been emerging in his mind for at least two years. While reading in 1832 about the Reformation, Froude had found Cardinal Pole to be the person from that era whom he liked best. He had also decided that the Council of Trent marked the point at which the Roman Catholic Church had become corrupt through its codification of informal practices not previously possessing formal ecclesiastical approval. In late 1833 Froude indicated that secretly he was uncertain that justification by faith was part of doctrine necessary to salvation and that he would also willingly give up the 39 Articles and keep the creeds. Significantly, references to Scripture or the authority of Scripture rarely appear to have informed Froude's views on any of these matters.[33]

Throughout other letters and manuscripts of 1834 and 1835 Froude continued his diatribes against the English Reformers, as well as against the Protestant doctrine of the eucharist and Protestant interpretation of Scripture. That interpretation, along with the Protestant emphasis on preaching over the sacraments in worship, he described as manifestations of "rationalism."[34] His introduction of that term into Tractarian discourse—to disparage both historic Protestant theology and contemporary evangelical practices—and his personal example of asceticism were Froude's most distinctive contributions to Tractarian thought. In the hands of others these contributions were to have momentous consequences for the relationship of the Tractarians with other parties in the English Church.

But Froude with somewhat less expansiveness pointed his immediate friends and the later readers of his *Remains* in still more radical theological directions. Writing from Barbados in early 1834, he told a correspondent, "You will be shocked at my avowal, that I am every day becoming a less and less loyal son of the Reformation." It by then appeared to him "that in all matters that seem to us indifferent or even doubtful, we should conform our practices to those of the Church which has preserved its traditionary practices unbroken." Then in words that forecast the developmental theological framework that Newman was to pursue to logical conclusions a decade later, Froude urged, "We cannot know about any seemingly indifferent practice of the Church of Rome that it is not a development of the apostolic *ethos;* and it is to no purpose to say that we can find no proof of it in the writings of the six first centuries; they must find a *dis*proof if they would do anything." Froude here planted a seed for the use of the concept of development to incorporate somehow into English Church life what he regarded as "indifferent" devotional practices that both evangelicals and more moderate English Protestants regarded as Romish corruptions. In early April 1834 Froude explained how he overcame possible scruples about the 39 Articles: "In the preface to the Articles it is said that we are to understand them in their grammatical sense; which I interpret into a permission to think nothing of the opinion of their framers." Froude thus cast himself adrift from any lingering loyalty to the English Reformers, asserting his capacity to determine in his own antinomian manner the meaning of the Articles. In early March 1835 he further suggested that the Articles might be interpreted in a fashion compatible with Roman Catholicism.[35] It was exactly Newman's attempt in *Tract 90* of February 1841 to interpret the 39 Articles without regard to the intention of their framers and as patient in some degree of compatibility with Roman Catholicism that became the rock against which the entire Tractarian enterprise shattered.

Froude did not, however, advocate outright union with Rome, and neither did the other original Tractarians. Although Froude had written respectfully of the Church of Rome, while in Italy in 1833 he had deplored the laughter of priests in the confessional, the absence of discipline in monasteries, and the carnival experiences in Roman Catholic society. On arriving in Rome, he and Newman had initially thought that achieving terms of communion between the English and Roman Churches lay within the power of the Pope or that some reconciliation could be made on a basis of the relationship between the two churches before the Council of Trent. But Monsignor Nicholas Wiseman, whom they visited, much to their chagrin informed them that "the doctrine of the infallibility of the Church made the acts of each successive Council obligatory for ever, that what had been once decided could never be meddled with again; in fact, that they were committed finally and irrevocably, and could not advance one step to meet us, even though the Church of England should again become what it was in Laud's time, or indeed what it may have been up to the atrocious Council, for M.[onsignor Wiseman] admitted that many things, e.g., the doctrine of the mass, which were fixed then, had been indeterminate before." Froude left the interview wishing "for the total overthrow of their system," having concluded that the only model for a church now to be entertained was " 'the ancient Church of England,' and as an explanation of what one means, 'Charles the First and the Nonjurors.' "[36]

Once settled in Barbados, Froude reaffirmed his admiration for the Nonjurors. In February 1834, less than a year after the Wiseman conversations, he wrote, "I begin to think that the Nonjurors were the last of English divines, and that those since are twaddlers." His reading about those clergy who had rejected the 1688 settlement and separated from the church "reconciled" Froude "to the present state of things in England and prospects of the Church" in the current political tumult. In light of this new perspective, contemporary ecclesiastical disarray and confusion amounted to "only the fermentation of filth which has long been in existence and could not be got rid of otherwise." On April 8, 1834, Froude reported "becoming a more and more determined admirer of the Nonjurors."[37] It was on that basis that he also declared his independence from the intentions of the framers of the 39 Articles.

Angry with the contemporary Church of England, admiring of the Nonjurors, and finding any acceptable path to union with Rome closed, Froude freely speculated upon a Christianity in England originating in the English Church liberated from the trammels of establishment. Froude, like the other Tractarians, believed such a church must have the capacity to enforce holy living and personal righteousness in the lives of its members. A national church, such as currently existed, could not enforce righteousness because by definition it must allow anyone who wished to enter its membership. By similar reasoning, a church that could enforce discipline necessarily could not be national. Froude's remarks in this regard are very revealing, as in 1834 he wrote, "The true cause of the decay of Church Discipline is not that nations have become Christian, but that the clergy have wished to make them appear Christian, either before they were so or after they have ceased to be so. And if at the present day it is difficult to enforce Church Discipline in England, it is not because we have a national Church, but because the

clergy are too anxious to keep up the show of one." Froude directly condemned English clergy who wanted to preserve the privileges and advantages of establishment at the cost of a true Christian religion requiring
personal righteousness and holiness. Froude insisted on a visible church
that embodied the true faith and exercised discipline over members which
evangelical Dissenters believed existed only within an arena of voluntary
religion and which evangelicals within the Church of England believed
possible only through the concept of the invisible church and various modes
of nonecclesiastical or nonclerical spiritual discipline. Froude for his part
declared, "The body of the English nation either are sincere Christians or
they are not: if they are, they will submit to Discipline as readily as the
primitive Christians did. If not, let us tell the truth and shame the devil: let
us give up a *national* Church and have a *real* one."[38] Looking in a fashion not
all that far removed from evangelical thought for a real Christianity that
would displace an inadequate national church, Froude envisioned a refounding of the Church of England rooted in Catholic principles and sustained by popular support not unlike that received by Dissenting congregations and evangelical voluntary societies. He stood willing for the Church of
England—or those in it who wished to enforce and accede to righteous
discipline—to constitute what amounted to an independent denomination
or what Keble in his assize sermon had disparagingly termed "one sect
among many."

Paradoxically, Froude embraced a more or less Lockean concept of religious bodies as voluntary societies functioning without state support and
possessing the right to enforce discipline over those members willing to
submit themselves to such discipline. In a letter of February 25, 1835,
describing the Tractarians as "Catholics without the Popery, and Church-
of-England men without the Protestantism," he outlined a thought experiment that he had been conducting about the possibility of endowing a new
church foundation. He stated quite bluntly, "The present Church system is
an incubus upon the country. It spreads its arms in all directions, claiming
the whole surface of the earth for its own, and refusing a place to any
subsidiary system to spring upon. Would that the waters would throw up
some Acheloides, where some new Bishop might erect a see beyond the
blighting influence of our upas tree." Froude denounced the collection of
tithes by the civil authority on the basis of constituting "a legal debt and
religious offering at the same time" as amounting to a religious desecration.
Resisting, however, the conclusion that voluntary religion must necessarily
end in something resembling Methodism, he contended, "I think talking

broadly against the Voluntary System, because it fails under one particular form, is as unfair, as it is inexpedient to make the clergy think an Establishment necessary."[39] All of these remarks suggest the organizing of a Church Catholic as some kind of voluntary association distinct from a legally established national church.

Structurally, Froude's vision was not all that far from the evangelical seceders founding the Plymouth Brethren or those radical evangelicals organizing the new Catholic Apostolic Church or the early Methodists. Froude's thought experiment proposing a newly organized voluntary church emerging from an establishment would actually with much turmoil be carried out in Scotland following the Great Disruption of 1843. At some level, as indicated by his letter of February 1835, Froude understood that his thought experiment in many respects potentially resembled a Methodist departure. Such a departure or disruption was the logical conclusion that the Tractarians repeatedly confronted and then resisted. As a result, they could never quite locate their church except where clergy of their outlook ministered and officiated. Moreover, they were never able to establish either an infrastructure for such a new church or a message that would sustain congregations, as had Methodists in the previous century, radical English and Scottish seceders in their own day, and late Victorian Anglo-Catholics in the next generation.

Froude returned to England in late 1835 only to die a few weeks later, never having pursued a parish ministry and only briefly having borne responsibilities as an Oriel tutor. During Froude's last months Keble's marriage had led to a cooling of affection between the two friends. Keble failed to write to Froude in his final illness. No such distance ever came between Froude and Newman, for whom the departed friend stood as a brilliant, prematurely extinguished flame about which in both life and remembrance Newman fluttered and circled like a moth, then destroyed himself by allowing the fire to engulf him. Froude functioned theologically in John Henry Newman's life as the radically eccentric evangelical John Nelson Darby did in Francis Newman's. Froude and Darby appealed to the separatist and seeker strains lodged deeply in the religious personalities of both brothers. Darby was the strange, physically and socially uncouth clergyman who persuaded Francis of the deficiencies of the Church of England and drew him into the Plymouth Brethren, from which Francis departed eventually to Unitarianism. Froude similarly beguiled John Henry Newman with the shortcomings of the contemporary English Church and pointed him and others toward an indeterminate vision of a Church Catholic.

Froude more than any other single person pressed Newman toward embracing tradition, ascetic devotion, celibacy, monasticism, use of the Breviary, a high view of the eucharist, the authority of an apostolic priesthood, dislike of the Reformation, contempt for the existing Church of England and its authorities, an elastic interpretation of the Articles, and doctrinal development. Yet Froude did *not* push John Newman toward Rome, just as Darby did not push Francis toward Unitarianism. Rather Froude ignited in John Newman directly, and in others who knew him only through his posthumous *Remains*, a zeal for personal devotion and holiness that could not realize itself in the contemporary Church of England. In Froude questions of devotion had always loomed larger than those of ecclesiastical politics, and such would be the same pattern in John Newman's life.

In that respect, although contemporaries saw the Tractarians as drifting toward Rome, it would be more nearly correct to say that within the confines of the English Church, they attempted to explore, to realize, and to expand upon Froude's ecclesiastical and devotional ideas. His ideal of a "real" versus a "national" church particularly resonated with a generation formed not by the constitutional struggles of the church but by the religious and theological stirrings of the tracts in an ever-competitive religious marketplace. But there existed one crucial difference between Froude and his posthumous admirers. Froude had envisioned a Church Catholic emerging from the Church of England filled with new devotional zeal and sustained by popular support. To reach that goal, he had, however, been willing at least in theory to entertain real economic sacrifices of ecclesiastical property and livings. Those who pursued his vision after his death encountered enormous conflict and hostility not only because of the Froudean ideals they pursued but also because of their unwillingness to make the sacrifices he assumed would be necessary for a real Catholic Christianity to establish itself in England. The late Tractarians demanded that they be permitted to pursue Froudean ideals within the existing structure. Froude himself would hardly have been surprised at the disastrous result.

EDWARD BOUVERIE PUSEY

All scholars of the Tractarian Movement confess that the relationship of Edward Bouverie Pusey, Regius Professor of Hebrew, to the movement was complicated, but they display little agreement on the source of that complexity. Pusey came to the movement late in 1833, having had nothing to do with the instigation of the tracts and bearing only marginal sympathy with the immediate issues of church and state. In addition to his professorial standing with its canonry in Christ Church, Pusey brought to the Tractarian enterprise an aristocratic connection that could normally achieve access to the Bishop of Oxford or London ecclesiastical and political circles. Theologically, Pusey's arrival immediately associated the tracts with religious asceticism in the form of fasting, the subjects of his first tract, and with highly controversial opinions on baptismal regeneration and the problem of sin after baptism, the subjects of his single most important tract and issues that deeply divided religious parties inside the English Church. His views on baptism and his allegedly inadequate appreciation for the doctrine of justification by faith alone provoked from the evangelical press the hostile epithets Puseyite and Puseyism, the terms with which *Tractarian* and *Tractarianism* became virtually interchangeable in the religious and secular press throughout the rest of the century.[40]

Although through the Oriel fellowship he had enjoyed a long-standing acquaintance with Keble, Froude, and Newman, continuing after he moved to Christ Church as Regius Professor, Pusey was never entirely intimate with their most deeply held opinions nor always familiar with their actions. He also often trod his own independent path. The wealthiest of the Tractarian leaders by virtue of family money and professorial income, Pusey could afford to be holy, to be willful, and to outlast as well as to outspend his opponents. Pusey embodied enormous personal arrogance cloaked under a carefully crafted life of asceticism and devotional holiness. He refused, unless given no legal escape, to acknowledge in more than a cursory fashion the authority of bishops or of other ecclesiastical and university institutions, resting his faith and actions instead upon the authority of the Church Catholic as he personally understood and interpreted that authority.

As far as the vexing issue of ecclesiastical establishment was concerned, Pusey combined theological inflexibility with a certain tactical flexibility, even opportunism. As early as the debates of the 1830s over the Irish Church, Pusey preferred having "the maintenance of the national Churches left to the Xtian feeling of the public" than to embrace other modes of finance that would support all churches irrespective of their theology. To further among the religious public at large his understanding of the faith, he looked to new institutional structures, including clerical training schools associated with cathedrals, sisterhoods pursuing charitable and devotional ends, and churches constructed and financed for the employment of sympathetic clergy. By 1868, stating in a forthright fashion thoughts held over three decades earlier in a more tentative and unformed fashion by his

Tractarian colleagues, Pusey told H. P. Liddon, his later biographer, "I have long foreseen that some form of Denominationalism must sooner or later replace Establishments. Denominationalism sacrifices money, not principle or faith. . . . Denominationalism, rude as it is, has something earnest about it."[41] In that regard, he somewhat resembled evangelicals in the Church of England, who with no intention of departing, instead forged institutions that allowed their faith to flourish in and around that church. Pusey's fundamental quarrel with evangelicals involved not a rejection of their tactics but rather a conviction of the incapacity of evangelical theology to foster genuine holiness and true repentance, issues that haunted his own life and family.

Born in 1800 into a prosperous family of minor aristocracy, Pusey was the second son of a stern, overbearing father then in his mid-fifties. The father was politically favorable to Tories and religiously hostile to evangelicals, to whom he ascribed insufficient emphasis on good works and holy living. In 1827, conveying to his fiancée views held by his father—which resembled Keble's critique of the impact of evangelical religion on parish life—Pusey reported, "My father from hearing and seeing the abuses of preaching faith (as it has been often preached) *without* works, connects no other idea with the 'being justified by faith only' than by faith *exclusive* of works—not only as not entitling us to salvation, but as being in no way necessary to it."[42] Pusey's father and mother practiced a faith very much involving works. Both engaged in extensive charity, and his mother, also not a source of personal affection, appears to have undertaken various acts of self-denial. Pusey as an adult would revert to his parents' behavior, carrying it to what even friends and admirers regarded as extremes.

Like Froude, Pusey attended Eton and later received further instruction from the Rev. Edward Maltby, who as Bishop of Durham became a severe critic of the Tractarians. Passion as much as intellect, however, drove the young Pusey, who at age eighteen fell in love with Maria Barker. Both of their fathers forbade any courtship, and for almost a decade, until 1827, the couple remained apart. In the meantime Pusey, often in a state of depression, threw himself into intense undergraduate study in Christ Church. In 1823 he became a fellow of Oriel and soon a friend of Newman, who more than sixty years later recalled Pusey "as being the first good man I had come very near who was not an Evangelical." During these years Pusey favored the Whigs and advocated repeal of disabilities against both Dissenters and Roman Catholics. Symptomatic of his political liberalism and his sympathy toward Trinitarian Dissenters, Pusey denounced the Test and Corporations

Acts as "a disgrace and detriment to religion," keeping "alive the bitterness of party spirit among Christians agreeing in the same essentials of faith in England."[43] Like Froude and Newman, he studied with Charles Lloyd, who encouraged him to become familiar with German theology. Pusey made two trips to study in Germany, the first in 1825 and the second in 1826 and 1827.

The German connection led the young Pusey into a major theological controversy with Hugh James Rose, the conservative Cambridge high churchman who would have numerous difficult relationships with the Tractarians. In 1825 Rose had delivered a series of not overly informed lectures on *The State of the Protestant Religion in Germany* in which he blamed critical, rationalist tendencies in German theology on the absence of episcopal structures based on apostolical succession.[44] At the urging of German colleagues hoping for clarification of the situation, Pusey in 1828 replied to Rose in *An Historical Enquiry into the Probable Causes of the Rationalist Character Lately Predominant in the Theology of Germany*. There Pusey contended that the rationalist character of German theology had arisen not from the absence of episcopal structures and articles of faith but rather from the religious behavior of two groups of German Lutherans.

First, Pusey pointed to a rigid Lutheran orthodoxy whereby successors to the Reformers had "strangely reversed" the "pre-eminence of scriptural above human systems" with the result that interpretation of Scripture "instead of being the mistress and guide, became the handmaid, of doctrinal Theology." Those later German Lutherans, unlike the Reformers, had forced the language of the Bible "into the fetters of a narrowing and monotonous conception of system." In particular, Pusey criticized their interpretive assumption "that the whole of Scripture was immediately dictated by the Holy Spirit," a principle that led to their second assumption "that all must be of equal value." Lutheran interpreters had then conflated the Law and the Gospel, regarded as distinct by Luther, and consequently "held that all the distinguishing doctrines of Christianity were even to the Jews as much revealed in the Old Testament as in the New," with knowledge of those doctrines considered "as necessary to their salvation as to ours." Such interpreters had thus reduced the "living Word" of Scripture to "a dead repository of barren technicalities" and could admit "no error, however minute" existing in Scripture, even in "historical passages, in which no religious truth was contained." That "palpable perversion of the doctrine of Inspiration," susceptible to so many critical, historical challenges, had prepared the way "for the indiscriminate rejection of the doctrine itself." Without the substitution of "the influential faith of the heart" for "the barren contentious scholasticism, by which the understanding alone was occupied, or rather was distracted," this framework of biblical interpretation devoid of concern for Christian practice and ecclesiastical history necessarily "contained within itself the seeds of its own dissolution." In place of a return to the good sense of Luther there had occurred endless debates that provoked "the inconsiderate rejection" of the whole structure of interpretation. The consequent failure "to return from the light of their self-kindled fire, to the sun of pure Christianity" had allowed "the storm of unbelief" to burst over German Protestants.[45] What Pusey did not note was that biblical interpretation among British evangelicals had in the past decade taken a turn similar to that which he associated with an earlier Lutheran scholasticism.

Pusey located a second source for rationalism within German Lutheranism in the rise of Pietism, which had challenged that cold scholasticism. The trajectory of German Pietists, commencing with the teaching of Jacob Spener (1635–1705), appeared closely to parallel the activity of British evangelicals moving from the restraint of the Clapham Sect to the excesses of the next generation. Spener attracted congregations through his emphasis on Christian morality, the Bible, and personal religious experience. He organized groups independent of formal worship services to discuss Scripture and the Christian life, revived catechism and confirmation, taught that clergy were simply teachers guided by the Holy Spirit, and encouraged people to express their faith in their own words. He also reached beyond the confines of his own Lutheran communion. Furthermore, one of Spener's disciples formed a business that printed millions of Bibles, and "as among the first Reformers" the reading of Scripture became "the root of theological study."[46] The University of Halle became the center of Pietism, and from its classes emerged thousands of clergy imbued with Pietist sentiments. Many of these practices, of course, resembled those of later English Methodists, as well as other British evangelical groups who had familiarity with the continental developments.

Pusey, however, pointed to "the liabilities to degeneracy" within this remarkably admirable Pietist system. He noted sympathetically, "All religious forms, and especially those expressive of religious feeling, have a tendency to lose the spirit by which they were originally animated." Like the Lutheran formalists whom Spener had resisted, his later followers fell into a narrow, technical formalism that attached "a mere vague and general meaning" to terms that "had originally conveyed definite Christian ideas." Within the Pietist devotional groups there arose a tendency to hypocrisy "engendered by the too great stress laid upon private edifying and Christian conversation" and the gradual, unconscious replacement of "practical, living Christianity" with "external duty" pursued "mechanically." Over time, despite the genuinely devout persons associated with it, German Pietism eventually appeared to the external world "as a speculative system, oppressive to the intellectual without communicating energy to the moral powers, as the garb of hypocrisy, or the dream of a bewildered imagination."[47] Thus by its untoward self-confidence, oppressive morality, and susceptibility to accusations of fanaticism, Pietism invited criticism on both theological and ecclesiastical grounds.

According to Pusey both decayed Lutheran scholasticism and decayed Pietism had become highly vulnerable to the attacks of well-meaning reformers imbued with eighteenth-century rational morality. These reformers attempted to extract from the formalized manifestations of German Lutheranism a mode of Christian faith and morality compatible with the critical spirit of the eighteenth century itself. The consequent decline of German faith into rationalism had been steady. Pusey summarized his analysis by presenting the orthodox as having converted Christianity into "speculation," after which the Pietists "superficialized" it, and finally the reconcilers treated it "as uncertain and vague." By the end of the eighteenth century German Christianity had been thus rendered so insubstantial that it could be united with earnest systems of rational morality "by which it was opposed, but to which it had been gradually approaching."[48]

In contrast to Rose, Pusey thought episcopacy could have done little or nothing to deflect the forces that had worked their way through the past two centuries of German Protestantism. Throughout the *Enquiry* Pusey understood religious truth and the desire for personal sanctity as distinct from both formal statements of theology and formal ecclesiastical arrangements. Pusey even went so far as directly to question the efficacy of formal articles of faith to protect gospel truth, and indicated that the real question behind "any relaxation of the binding force" of articles was whether it would "produce not merely deviation from their doctrines within Christianity, but the abandonment of the principles and the authority of Christianity itself." He suggested that too great advocacy of articles of religion might actually indicate abandonment of the "fundamental" Protestant principle of "the independence and the inherent power of the word of God."[49] Complicated articles of faith could furthermore themselves furnish occasion for rationalistic dispute that might or might not pertain to the core of the Christian faith. Historical evidence, of course, supported Pusey's cautionary remarks, which also inadvertently forecast much of the debate that was to poison the life of the Church of England during the next several decades.

Pusey's writing of the first edition of the *Enquiry* coincided with the resumption of his long-delayed courtship of Maria Barker, possible only because of her father's death and his own father's grudging permission. Early in the relationship, Maria Barker, whom Pusey had really only seen from afar, indicated her own very considerable skeptical puzzlement about internal contradictions of Scripture and the consequent disagreement and confusions among Christians.[50] She also discussed her dislike of the evangelical ministry of Francis Close, a clergyman then active in Cheltenham who later became Dean of Carlisle. Pusey, though not yet ordained, thus found himself having to reconcile the woman whom he so loved to the faith to which he intended to devote his life. Having just escaped parental constraints to the fulfillment of his romantic and sexual longings, he suddenly found the authority of the Bible and evangelical religious admonitions posing new difficulties. In his letters to Maria at this time, Pusey recapitulated themes that he explored in the *Enquiry*, with the causes he assigned to the emergence of rationalism in Germany appearing very close to those underlying Maria's skeptical indifference to contemporary Christianity.

Pusey's correspondence criticized several of the most favored views of evangelicals and questioned overly formalized or restrictive articles of faith. In contrast to Close's narrow understanding of those who might receive salvation, Pusey displayed warm generosity to virtually all sincerely religious people. For example, prefiguring his attack on the Lutheran scholastics, he explained to Maria that in his view modern Jews, like the heathen, would "be tried by the degree of the spirituality to which under their dispensation they could attain, not by their acknowledging or non-acknowledging of Christianity." He extended similar ecumenical charity toward Roman Catholics, whose political emancipation both he and Maria favored, writing that despite numerous superstitions and errors into which Roman Catholic faith and practice had fallen, he had no doubt "that there have been hundreds of thousands of sincere men among the Roman Catholics, and that every sincere man has been led into that degree of truth which was necessary for salvation." Pusey's liberality embraced not only a tolerant understanding of other faiths but also an undogmatic attitude toward Christianity as a whole, which Maria clearly thought proper. Drawing upon the biblical criticism he had encountered in Germany, Pusey willingly agreed with Maria about the presence of historical discrepancies in the Bible, which did not, however, affect the "*essentials*" of the faith. Pusey also told her that he did not believe that divine revelation was complete, declaring, "Revelation was, and must be, *progressive*."[51] During his courtship with his future wife, Pusey thus argued that irrevocably fixed beliefs or doctrines need not constrain the Christian faith. For the moment sincerity of mind and spirit appeared to provide the touchstone for Pusey's judgment of religious behavior.

Pusey also sharply faulted evangelical criticism of contemporary popular recreations, such as Close preached and Maria hated, just as in the *Enquiry* he was similarly to criticize the narrow, joyless moralism of German Pietists. In each instance Pusey distinguished between the necessity of holy living following sincere repentance on one hand and undue or formalistic physical and spiritual asceticism on the other. Maria was particularly sensitive to the issue of asceticism because Close had encouraged one of her friends toward restriction in diet, self-deprecation, and long periods of isolated prayer on bended knees. In contrast to such excessive evangelical piety, which was not altogether unlike that which Froude was near the same time secretly pursuing and recording in his journals, Pusey outlined to Maria a rather expansive concept of Christian repentance, according to which he termed "mischievous," "delusive," "unduly elating to some," and "distractingly depressing to others," the practice of "employing the feelings as a criterion of religion." Contending "that a *deep* repentance is perfectly distinct from a *painful* or distressing one," he commended the practice as "defined by our Church with a beautiful moderation, 'a repentance whereby we forsake sin.'" He indicated that he understood both those who "have *predominately* the hatefulness of sin before their eyes" and those who "contemplate principally the mercies of God in His pardon of it" though equally straining "to avoid sin, cannot equally dwell upon it, or be equally pained by it." A few months later he deplored to Maria the "far-fetched asceticism" of the Port Royal Jansenists. Pusey was determined that repentance must result in new kinds of actions, not merely strong subjective feelings of grief, but nonetheless moderate, restrained actions that might equally well entail rejoicing at divine mercy as well as pain over sin remembered. Furthermore, as he told Maria on May 16, 1828, "The past must be to every Christian a source of sorrow; yet one knows that on repentance the past is forgiven us, that our sins are blotted out in the blood of Christ, that in the sight of God they are pardoned, as though they had never been." In the same letter, he assured her, "Christianity is not intended to go contrary to, to annihilate our natural feelings but to sanctify them."[52] It is uncertain whether Pusey actually believed what he wrote to his prospective bride or whether he was shaping his views to a receptive reading on her part. The issue is not minor because in the years following their marriage both he and she moved toward rigorous modes of physical self-denial in their own lives and those of their children.

Whether Pusey would have failed to marry Maria Barker had she continued in her skepticism is not known. It is clear, however, that Pusey attributed much of Maria's skepticism and indifference toward Christianity to her experience of ascetic evangelicalism and to a lesser extent conflict among Christians over achieving scriptural precision regarding articles of faith. The young Pusey had encountered rationalism in the mind and spirit of his beloved and ascribed its sources to overly formalized theology and extreme evangelicalism. These issues arising from his courtship then profoundly influenced the composition of his *Enquiry*, where he adopted the interpretive framework of a pure German Protestantism declining into rationalism as a result of reactions against narrow systematic interpretations of Scripture, constricting articles of faith, and formalized pietistic morality. The story of Germany was the story of Maria Barker. Just as at the time Pusey saw a promising future for Christianity in Germany through new scholarship, he saw himself as restoring faith to his prospective wife on the basis of that same understanding of Christianity.

The scholarship and religious latitudinarianism by which Pusey had accommodated his wife's religious skepticism soon landed him in the middle of considerable controversy. The first edition of the *Enquiry* appeared about a month before their wedding on June 12, 1828. Anticipating difficulties, Pusey had told Maria that he expected "to be thought 1 / 3 mystic, 1 / 3 sceptic, and 1 / 3 (which will be thought the worst interpretation of all,) a Methodist, though I am none of the 3."[53] His prediction proving all too correct, Pusey encountered stinging attacks from Rose and other high churchmen who questioned his views of inspiration and ecclesiastical discipline and who because of his remarks on the historical books of Scripture suspected personal sympathy for rationalism on his part.

This whirlwind of criticism quickly ceased to be academic when on September 25, 1828, Alexander Nicholl, the young Regius Professor of Hebrew, died. Charles Lloyd, by then both Bishop of Oxford and Regius Professor of Divinity, as well as the person to whom Pusey had dedicated the *Enquiry*, very much wanted Pusey appointed to the now vacant Hebrew chair, which carried with it a canon's stall in Christ Church worth more than £1,000 annually. Pusey's recent reputation for heterodox latitudinarianism suddenly posed a stumbling block to his professional advancement and the achievement of considerable permanent income.

On Saturday, October 4, 1828, Lloyd, in whose Christ Church apartment Pusey and his bride had been living, explained the difficulties to the young scholar. On the following Monday, Pusey replied with a letter which, while defending his position regarding biblical inspiration, stated that he did not "abate the slightest tittle of the authority of any syllable in the Scriptures" but derived that authority somewhat differently from those who regarded inspiration "as dictation." He suggested that the inerrancy of the historical books stood upon a somewhat different foundation than that of the Gospels and that prophecy as a portion of Scripture stood by itself. He defended his sympathetic treatment of Spener, whom Pusey's high-church critics must have seen as the prototype of a Methodist, on the grounds that the latter had consistently prevented and opposed disunion in the Lutheran Church. Asserting that he felt himself "more and more removed from what is called the Low Church," Pusey further added that he did not know "any subject of controversy between the high & the low Church, in which I do not agree with the former," though he did not expect to preach on any of these.[54] A presumably similarly trimming letter eventually worked its way through normal ecclesiastical channels to the Archbishop of Canterbury.

Following these private epistolary exchanges in which Pusey not uncomfortably set himself in opposition to much recent evangelical emphasis on biblical inerrancy as well as evangelical ecclesiastical outlooks, he received appointment as Regius Professor of Hebrew in early November and was ordained November 25. Lloyd himself, whom Pusey described as a "guardian friend," died six months later at the end of May 1829, having the previous month vigorously championed the passage of Catholic emancipation, which Pusey had also favored.[55] The death of Bishop Lloyd corresponded almost exactly with the appearance of Rose's long-delayed public attack entitled *Letter to the Lord Bishop of London in Reply to Mr. Pusey's Work on the Causes of Rationalism in Germany*.

As a direct response to Rose's appeal to the Bishop of London, Pusey submitted the draft of the second edition of the *Enquiry* to Bishop Blomfield, who in January 1830 replied with two long critical letters. Pusey's ascription of earnestness and love of God to German rationalists "who mutilate & pervert the Word of God & strip Christianity of its characteristic attributes" had, Blomfield insisted, been "more than charity requires" and displayed "a manifest tendency to strengthen the opinion that their errors are not such as to affect the essence of religion." He also bluntly told Pusey, "The *tone* of many of your inconsiderate observations is too latitudinarian, & savours too strongly of the channel through which the current of your reading has recently of necessity flowed." But Blomfield reserved the main thrust of his criticism for Pusey's assertion that articles of faith are useful but not necessary. Regarding that issue, Blomfield declared, "If Articles of Faith are not *necessary*, it will be hard to show that they are *lawful*. And if a Church may subsist without them, then its teachers may be Socinians, or Anabaptists, or Antinomians, or any thing whatever, as long as they profess to believe that the Bible is the Word of God. If this evil can only be avoided by the use of Articles, then Articles are not only expedient, but necessary." According to Blomfield, "the real use of Articles" for clergy was "not so much to teach them what they are to believe, as to show them what they are to believe, if they wish to act as *teachers* of religion." He thought that "uniformity of *doctrine*, even with some possible errors on points not funda-mental," to be "better, for the religious interests of the people at large, than an arbitrary and licentious exposition of Scripture truth." In this respect, Blomfield considered "it therefore to be a fundamental principle of church polity, that Articles of belief are 'absolutely necessary.'" He further ob-served that "in good truth the real object of Articles, such as ours, is not to systematize Scripture, but to prevent the teaching of any thing contrary to Scripture." In a second letter, Blomfield simply told Pusey that the latter's confused views on articles of faith were "incompatible with any sound view of church polity."[56]

Blomfield's comments clearly pertained to his apprehension about evan-gelical clergy, who by expostulating on the Bible outside the confines of the Articles had long constituted a serious threat to the internal ecclesiastical order in the English Church. The next year Henry Bulteel and fellow radical Oxford evangelical clergy provoked turmoil in the diocese by their radical Calvinism and brought down upon themselves the wrath of Bishop Bagot. Paradoxically, however, during the following fifteen years it would actually be radical high-church clergy emerging from the Tractarian Movement itself who would most vex episcopal authority and disturb the peace of the English Church through their determination to press for Catholic lati-tude in the interpretation of the Articles. In 1845 Bishop Blomfield again emerged as the defender of the 39 Articles by prosecuting the Tractarian Frederick Oakeley in the Court of Arches, thus occasioning the last great crisis of the Tractarian era.

Throughout the second edition of the *Enquiry* Pusey assumed a defensive tone. He portrayed himself as poorly used by Rose, who had unfairly rendered him "an object of suspicion to many, whose general views I share, and whose characters I admire." Deeply offended by Rose's public charges and Blomfield's private comments, Pusey complained, "It is indeed a painful task to have to clear away imputations, foreign to every sentiment which I cherish; it is yet more painful that, ushered into the world as these charges have been, I can scarcely entertain a hope ever wholly to efface them: like the separate counts against a criminal, each would appear to the by-standers to throw a degree of probability upon the remainder; no one could, it would be thought, contract so much suspicion without some share of guilt."[57] Pusey thus stood as the first major Victorian English churchman to have to defend himself in such a fashion. For the next three quarters of a century and beyond similar protests echoed through the corridors of English religious life from Pusey to R. D. Hampden, persecuted in 1836 upon his appointment as Regius Professor of Divinity, to Newman, castigated for the publication of *Tract 90*, to the authors persecuted for their contributions to *Essays and Reviews*, again to Newman, as a Roman Catholic attacked by Kingsley, to the *Lux Mundi* group associated with the late Victorian high church, and finally, after the turn of the century, to the authors of *Foundations*. Curiously, and perhaps not accidentally, often the victim of one event became a persecutor in a later exchange.

Despite his protests, Pusey's second edition did accommodate itself to the public and private attacks. He directly reversed himself, strongly stating the necessity of articles of faith and even adopting part of the wording from Blomfield's letter. In the revised *Enquiry* Pusey declared,

> I may repeat, in order to obviate misconception, that I also consider articles, *absolutely necessary*, . . . to the *well-being* of a Church; that I regard a mere subscription to Holy Scripture absolutely nugatory; that, although articles should be limited, as far as is practicable, to essentials, the subscription must then not be left vague and indeterminate, but (in order to prevent, as much as possible, dishonest evasion) must be absolute and definite. It is evident that every Church has a right to require of its ministers, as long as they profess to be ministers of that Church, to teach the doctrines which she holds; and that thereby no undue restraint, no hard yoke is placed upon them, whenever the articles are good, and exceed not in their definitions the just bounds. There could even be no question, (if it were necessary to choose,) that uniformity of doctrine in essentials, even with some *possible* errors in points not fundamental (although these, of course, should be

corrected as soon as discovered) is better for the religious interests of
the people at large, than an arbitrary and licentious exposition of Scripture truth.

Yet while so emphasizing the necessity and expedience of articles of faith,
Pusey still insisted, no doubt with his wife in mind, that the purview of such
articles could, as he believed to have been the case in seventeenth-century
Germany, be extended too far and do "unintentional injury to the cause of
religion."[58] Pusey thus once again firmly resisted equating complete truth in
religion with articles of faith while acquiescing in their use to provide a
discipline to clerical discretion. He also left undefined which ecclesiastical
authorities were to enforce and interpret the articles of faith. From his
experience with the friendly Bishop Lloyd and the critical Bishop Blomfield
he had rapidly learned that bishops could differ and persons such as himself
be caught in the middle. Unlike Newman, from 1830 onward Pusey did not
trust bishops or give much countenance to their authority.

Pusey also systematically answered other charges from Rose in regard to
his views of episcopacy, the character of Scripture, inspiration, and what he
regarded as a newly dawning era of theology. But Pusey actually did not
retreat appreciably from his previous firm approval of Luther's views on the
authority of Scripture. As in the first edition, Pusey accounted for changes
in German theology as arising primarily from internal religious conflicts
rather than from forces outside religious life. He reasserted the advantage of
simple gospel truth over complicated, scholastic statements of doctrine. He
repeated that the overly formalized character which German theology assumed in the generations after Luther had made it susceptible to rationalism and that a decayed pietism brought religious spirituality into contempt.
He again defended both the religious sincerity and honesty of those scholars
whose thought may have inadvertently fostered later rationalism.

One reason for Pusey's refusal to back down more substantially may
have been that to abandon his latitudinarianism might have upset the religious accommodation he had recently achieved with his new wife. One
passage in particular from the second edition of the *Enquiry* would appear to
repeat the thrust of arguments he had made to her during the correspondence of their courtship. When discussing why Lutheranism had lost its
religious hold over certain Germans, Pusey argued, "Indisposition to the
Lutheran system as a whole was created by the wearisomeness of its controversies, its unpractical character, the manifest untenableness of parts, the
offensiveness of others, which persons were yet unable to separate from the

sounder portions. Hostility or indifference to religion was engendered by the different exhibitions of it in a degraded form, as a lifeless and spurious orthodoxy, a formal Pietism, or a wild fanaticism, which had been confounded in the public mind with genuine Pietism, or all earnest endeavours after holiness."[59] This criticism of undue Lutheran orthodoxy and formalistic pietism paralleled Pusey's critique of evangelicalism whereby he had sought to draw Maria from skepticism to faith. In that regard both editions of the *Enquiry* displayed a vigor, pugnacity, and clarity of prose never again achieved in the hundreds of pages that were to flow from Pusey's pen. Those two volumes had been composed not only with the enthusiasm of youth but with the passion of young love finally consummated against formidable odds. They were the volumes wherein Pusey had bonded his soul with Maria Barker's.

The years immediately following Pusey's marriage, his appointment to the Hebrew Chair, and the controversy over the *Enquiry* were the only period of his life associated with scholarly activity, as he completed the catalogue of Arabic manuscripts in the Bodleian Library begun by his predecessor. Thereafter a deeply depressive strain came to the fore in Pusey's mind, leading to an overweening concern about personal moral austerity, religious asceticism, and experiments in devotional holiness. Such depression and melancholy had marked his adolescence and young adulthood, perhaps because of the absence of parental affection and his long separation from Maria Barker. This situation had moderated briefly during the couple's courtship, but severe personal difficulties and sadnesses (heralded by the death of Maria's father just before the formal courtship and of Pusey's own just before their wedding) marked the entire decade of the Puseys' marriage.[60] Four children were born in rapid succession to the couple, but they brought little happiness. In November 1832, the Puseys lost the third of their four children, a daughter, in infancy. Before that loss Pusey had experienced a prolonged, severe illness during late 1830 and early 1831. By the middle of the decade Maria had contracted the tuberculosis that was to lead to her own premature death in 1839, after which Pusey acceded to a virtual vocation of mourning.

Their intense stresses, familial losses, and profound experiences of the unfairness of things transformed the Puseys personally and religiously, as was the case in some other Victorian homes visited by disease and early childhood death.[61] In the case of the Puseys, a profound sense of guilt overcame both of them, as if they felt that their pursuit of mutual happiness, religious accommodation, marriage, sexuality, and family, as well as Edward's professional ambitions, in some fashion stood divinely condemned as revealed through paternal deaths, unfair public controversy, a child's passing, mutual frailty, and chronic illness.

Pusey attempted to work through the meaning of these experiences in terms of his own spiritual life. On November 4, 1835, he recalled to Mrs. Pusey his letter of 1827 about repentance in which he had rejected "the acuteness or bitterness of the grief" as "the proof that our sorrow was a godly sorrow" emphasizing instead "that we must look to our lives, not to our emotions." He reasserted "the real *test* of repentance" as "change of life, to cease to do evil and learn to do well—not matter of feeling." He lamented that people found Newman's statement of this matter "attractive" but his own "repulsive." Pusey saw Newman as having been contemplative, tranquil, self-denying, and humble, whereas in his own study of evidences and German theology and in his general pursuit of activity he had been busy, self-indulgent, and self-exultant. Pusey asked his wife to pray for him "that this and everything else of sin may be forgiven me." Two days later, he explained to Mrs. Pusey that part of the problem with weak repentance, which he clearly associated with both evangelical assurance and his own former views, was a forgetfulness of the sin itself. He then told his wife that the loss of their infant daughter Catherine on November 8, 1832, should be understood not as a trial but rather as God's personal chastisement and "as a merciful correction, although still as a correction." He furthermore confided to his wife that he could not with happiness recall the years of love for her before their marriage because he had failed to wait patiently on God's will. Pusey wrote that he could not "without doing harm to myself" even refer to those years "without the solemn memory of past sinfulness." The same month as this letter, he commenced Friday fasting and forbade his wife to use a Bible incorporating evangelical commentary, which he saw as embodying "much of the Rationalism of the day" because of its attempts to explain "difficulties" rather than receiving them "in their plain sense."[62] Mrs. Pusey appears to have eagerly joined in her husband's regimen.

From at least this time onward, the Puseys, in pursuit of repentance and avoidance of further sin, organized their household according to an extreme ascetic discipline, which during their courtship both husband and wife had regarded as fanatical. Least harmful, Pusey made substantial donations for the building of a church in London, which required a significant paring down of household expenses and Maria's disposal of jewelry. Both Puseys became fixated on fasting and imposed the same rigorous self-discipline upon their small children. In 1839, when Mrs. Pusey was seriously ill, Pusey became so concerned about her excessive fasting that, invoking his own priestly authority in an attempt to mitigate it, he admonished her, "Take care of yourself, dearest, about fasting: I, as your priest, am the person to give you a dispensation: it is a blessing, when you can; but one for which you do not seem to be in a state now; at least not for 2 days together, certainly."[63] Only a year earlier a physician had questioned their manner of child rearing and had urged more food, air, and exercise to overcome the sickly appearances of their children. Mrs. Pusey had resisted the advice.

Beyond and more troubling than the fasting, the Puseys submitted their children to severe corporal punishment, the applications of which are carefully recorded in their correspondence. From at least 1834, and probably earlier, Pusey whipped his children, as did Mrs. Pusey. She also with his approval confined them to their rooms for considerable periods and tied them to the bedpost. On one occasion when her daughter Mary encountered difficulty with her spelling lessons, Mrs. Pusey wrote her husband, "Mary has been whipped four times today, and tied to the bed post all day, and seems as proud as the wicked spirit could wish. . . . I told her calmly, but decidedly I must punish her more each day, till it was done, and that I should go on for weeks, months or years: she scarcely uttered a murmur at the punishment before me, and seems too proud to do so, but after I leave her, I hear her cry, and she told Hannah she did very much dislike being up stairs." Responding to his wife over his own brother's disapproval of such harsh practices, Pusey wrote, "Our system, if it is worth anything, must be contrary to the world's system, and so must cost us something."[64] Even by what often appear the austere practices of Victorian child rearing, the Pusey household was extreme and even abusive.

The charity, fasting, and efforts to curb the will of his children appear related to Pusey's personal concern with sin after baptism and his conviction that Christians must undertake with God's aid to combat such sin and achieve holiness in their lives. Pusey, like many others who believed in baptismal regeneration, understood baptism to remove sin, but believed that baptized persons then endured a subsequent life during which post-baptismal sin might overwhelm baptismal grace. In his mind the solutions to this problem were the active pursuit of holiness, which involved the suppression of sinful tendencies through self-denial, and the practice of penance. Pusey thought that under proper circumstances even fallen, baptized persons were capable with God's help of achieving genuine holiness. He criticized those evangelicals who stressed instant conversion and assurance of salvation for ignoring such pursuit of holiness. He explained to a correspondent early in 1835 that many evangelicals viewed "it as derogatory to Christ's Atonement, if we are represented as any other than weak, miserable, sinning creatures, who are to go on sinning and polluted unto our lives' end." The result of that outlook, according to Pusey, was "a miserably low standard of human attainment, or rather a want of faith as to what God can and has and does work in man, if he gives himself up to Him."[65] Because of his conviction of the power human beings achieved through their union with God, Pusey's outlook partook in part of the impulse to Christian perfectionism associated with Methodism.

Pusey also thought that the eucharist could remove the presence of sin subsequent to baptism. After having ministered to a friend's dying child in the spring of 1835, Pusey reported that "since she received the Blessed Sacrament perhaps during all this illness, she had been kept free from sin even here, and was already a holy angel, before she parted from among us." That autumn he published the first edition of his long three-part tract on *Scriptural Views of Holy Baptism,* championing baptismal regeneration and extensively criticizing both evangelical theology and the more general heritage of continental Protestantism. His personal crisis over repentance in regard to his courtship and loss of his youngest child followed weeks later. Then in February 1836, Pusey preached a highly controversial sermon emphasizing, perhaps with his own recent experience in mind, the difficulty of becoming a Christian and the danger of falling from baptismal grace. T. L. Claughton believed that Pusey's "extreme" views on these matters had arisen in reaction to "the awful calmness with which the Evangelicals hold out assurance of Salvation to any man, who suddenly struck with a sense of sin, would comfort himself with Heavenly Hopes."[66]

Pusey's near obsession with baptism and postbaptismal sin provoked still another crisis within his own household. In the original edition of *Scriptural Views of Holy Baptism* Pusey had spoken of the continental reformed churches as churches. But in notes to his wife's copy of that edition and in the later printed revised edition, he referred to those churches simply as "bodies" and their liturgies as "services." These modifications indicated that Pusey no longer regarded the reformed tradition as part of the true church. With this shift in her husband's opinions, Mrs. Pusey became quite apprehensive over the validity of her own baptism, which had been administered by a Dissenting minister. Apparently fearful of not having experienced regeneration through that baptism, she sought to have the sacrament performed again. Bishop Bagot gave permission for her to receive a conditional baptism, which Newman administered on April 14, 1838.[67] The very same apprehensions must also have driven her toward the extreme fasting that marked her last months.

During the late 1830s and 1840s Pusey's asceticism moved in several different directions. He began to believe that there existed in the Prayer Book a vague authority for private confession that might to some extent relieve persons of what he had transformed into an almost unbearable burden of sin. In 1838 he instituted his own practice of hearing confessions, especially those of young men who were dealing with adolescent sexuality.[68] In 1843 he urged the Headmaster of Eton to encourage students to confess to clergy on the faculty. Pusey also became actively interested in sisterhoods at least as early as 1841, when he visited Roman Catholic convents in Ireland. He later claimed to support founding such institutions in part as a result of his daughter Lucy's expression of a wish to live an unwed life in service to God. Her death in 1844 during early adolescence appeared to Pusey as another expression of divine punishment realized within his own family. Within these sisterhoods Pusey either cultivated or permitted extravagant fasting and other forms of physical self-denial criticized by physicians and other onlookers. These latter practices represented an extension into the sisterhoods of the ascetic regimen he had imposed on his family, including his most recently deceased daughter. Pusey also heard confessions of the women in the new sisterhoods, a practice that encountered resistance from other clergy, including John Keble.

By the middle of the 1840s Pusey persuaded Keble to act as his personal confessor and to approve rigorous forms of spiritual and physical discipline that Pusey would appear to have already contrived for himself. In 1844, a few months after his daughter Lucy's death, while preparing to adopt Keble formally as his confessor, he told his friend, "I am scarred all over and seamed with sin, so that I am a monster to myself; I loathe myself; I can feel of myself only like one covered with leprosy from head to foot; guarded as I have been, there is no one with whom I do not compare myself, and find myself worse than they; and yet, thus wounded and full of sores, I am so shocked at myself, that I dare not lay my wounds bare to any one: . . . and so I go on, having no such comfort as in good Bp. Andrewes' words, to confess myself 'an unclean worm, a dead dog, a putrid corpse,' and pray Him to heal my leprosy as He did on earth, and to raise me from the dead."[69] Here Pusey embraced the mode of self-denigration and confession of incapacity for holiness that almost a decade early he had criticized in certain evangelicals. Pusey no doubt drew the rhetoric of this letter from the language of the Fathers and other more recent devotional literature. Possibly having wrestled unsuccessfully with his own sexuality after his wife's death, Pusey applied to himself the same language of personal uncleanness that he used when writing of the sexual temptations confronting young men in the public schools and universities. Seeking to assuage a burden of personal sin, Pusey, as well as other men of his acquaintance such as Gladstone and some of Newman's younger followers of the early 1840s, sought modes of repentance that they could not discover within the standard devotional life and practices of the Church of England. There seems little doubt that in most of these cases the pressing sense of sin related to sexuality, but there is usually little or no evidence of the exact reason their sexuality or sexual practices rendered them so full of guilt. It may simply have been an overwhelming inner fear of the power of sexuality and the inner fantasies it nurtured to challenge and overwhelm the remarkable discipline they so thoroughly imposed upon and expected of themselves.

Pusey's contemporaries regarded his devotional enterprise private and public as tending toward Roman Catholicism, in part because he edited or translated continental Roman Catholic works in the 1840s and later. In reality, Pusey functioned quite simply as a Protestant deeply convicted of his sinfulness who used spiritual exercises of the Roman Catholic Church in the manner in which a Protestant thought or more properly imagined they would be used. He functioned as his own priest, picking and choosing on the basis of his own private judgment Roman Catholic devotional conventions unconnected to actual Roman Catholic practice or guidance. Early in 1836 Pusey, having already commenced his household experiment in asceticism, inquired of Newman whether the early monastic brotherhoods had been founded on the principle of penance. Newman, just then publishing articles about early Christian monasticism, discounted the role of penance in those orders, stating "that *gloom* as connected with Monastic rule came in with the Gothic ethos (original in Greek)," and then claiming that St. Anthony and St. Athanasius had been "bright and cheerful" in regard to monasticism, Newman also insisted that "early asceticism had more of a striving after perfection in it, than a penance." Pusey could not accommodate himself to Newman's vision of cheerful monastic life, just as he could not accept the evangelical invitation to forgiveness through emotional conversion. In pursuit of penitential asceticism and self-denial Pusey from 1839 onward transformed his quarters in Christ Church into a personal monastic cell of the Church Catholic whose truth and spiritual exercises he alone understood and mandated. With remarkable perception, Newman, commenting as a Roman Catholic, understood the uniqueness of Pusey's situation, and told a correspondent, "Dear Dr. Pusey does not witness his virtues for his Church, he witnesses for himself, he witnesses for his own opinions."[70] Pusey's was the witness of an ascetic Protestant.

It is difficult to overestimate the significance of these distinct but loosely intertwining strands of personal asceticism among the major Tractarian leaders and later among the second generation of their followers who joined Newman at Littlemore. Asceticism, not antierastianism, lay at the core of Tractarianism. More than any other single factor, the desire for the pursuit of obedience through novel, ascetic devotional practices led Newman and others first to reject evangelical theology as manifested among both Dissenters and fellow members of the Church of England, then to press for a broader reading of the 39 Articles, and finally to undertake a monastic experiment within the English Church.

CHAPTER 3

John Henry Newman and the Call to Obedience

W HATEVER THE CONTRIBUTIONS of Keble, Froude, and Pusey, the disruptions and transformations the Tractarians unleashed in the Church of England would not have occurred without John Henry Newman. He alone possessed the psychic energy and the polemical gifts required to make Froude's envisioned "row" in the English Church. Whereas Keble, Froude, and Pusey were men in motion, Newman for the thirty years between 1815 and 1845 personified the impetus to religious self-transformation that over the course of the Victorian decades recast both the British and transatlantic religious landscapes. During those years Newman's religious life and thought underwent one indeterminate metamorphosis after another, with no certain teleological direction necessarily leading him into the Roman Catholic communion. The apparent teleology of those many transitions appears only retrospectively in his *Apologia Pro Vita Sua* (1864) and the many subsequent interpretations drawing upon that work. In reality, contingency after contingency determined the emergence of Newman's religious character and thought.

THE EXPERIENCE OF PATERNAL FAILURE

The main outlines of Newman's early years are relatively familiar but not properly understood for their impact on his later development. John Henry Newman was born in February 1801, the eldest child in a middle-class commercial family of comfortable means, his father John being a partner in various banking establishments.[1] By 1809 there were six children—three boys and three girls. Charles was born in 1802, Harriett in 1803, Francis in

1805, Jemima in 1808, and Mary in 1809. Throughout John Newman's life he measured much of his own religious thought against that of his younger siblings, and his interaction with them often generated new directions or reactions in his own development. The Newmans attended the established church regularly and appear to have held moderate religious opinions. To the extent that religion had impact on the children, it came from outside rather than within the family circle. Their parents sent John, Charles, and Francis to Ealing School, one of whose masters was the father of Thomas Henry Huxley, the chief voice of late Victorian scientific naturalism.

Serious and prolonged economic problems commenced for the Newman family when the bank of Ramsbottom, Newman & Ramsbottom failed in early March 1816, about the time that many other banks also went under. Brought home briefly from school in mid-March to be told of the bank's collapse, John Henry Newman then returned to Ealing, where he remained to the end of the term and then during the summer. Although the bank collapse did not result in a formal bankruptcy and all creditors were paid, the Newman family's standard of living nonetheless began a steadily downward spiral. Having failed at banking, John Newman moved his family from Richmond to Alton in Hampshire, where he became a brewer. Away from home throughout the family's relocation, Newman suddenly found his family removed to a dismal new setting without his having been able to spend any significant time at their longtime residence before the move. Thus at the age of fifteen and a half, Newman experienced his home as literally vanishing, and no doubt also entered a period of grief and confusion over that loss and separation. The Newman family would never know another place of settled residence. During the same weeks Newman, again while at school, experienced a severe illness. Nothing specific is known about his malady, but it appears to have deeply frightened him.[2]

Children and especially adolescents can react in a variety of ways to the difficulties encountered by their parents. In Newman's case during the summer of 1816 subsequent to the collapse of his father's bank, he underwent his first conversion through the influence of the Rev. Walter Mayers, a Calvinist evangelical classics master at Ealing School.[3] In turning to Mayers, the young Newman sought a strong, new mentor to substitute for his faltering father. Such transitions are not uncommon among adolescents, but John Newman's business difficulties, as well as his son's serious illness, certainly moved the process along. From that time until his death in 1828, Mayers appears to have exerted more influence on Newman and his brother Francis than any other single figure except possibly their mother. Both brothers

consulted him for advice about their faith and their careers. Francis later
served as an assistant in Mayers's parish, where in 1824 John preached his
first sermon. For his part the senior John Newman was deeply suspicious
and sometimes directly critical of his oldest son's evangelical religiosity. The
younger man's persistence in such piety served to separate him from his
father's values and influence. The same may have been true for Francis
as well.

Through Mayers's instruction and extensive reading of Calvinists William Romaine and Thomas Scott, Newman in the summer and autumn of
1816 came to believe himself embraced by a heavenly father whose promises
were certain and who could provide an eternal home. The most important
element of that Calvinist creed was "the doctrine of final perseverance,"
which had assured Newman of his election "to eternal glory."[4] In light of the
frequent evangelical fiduciary analysis of the atonement in terms of commercial debts and payments, Newman's first conversion may also have assured him of eternal solvency as well as of salvation. His concern at the time
to assure friends that John Newman's bank had preserved good faith with
its customers may also have reflected a desire to assure himself that both
earthly and heavenly fathers kept their commitments.

For some time, even after entering Trinity College, in December 1816,
Newman remained under Mayers's religious tutelage, possibly because in
contrast to Cambridge there were relatively few evangelicals in Oxford, and
they were generally of low social standing, a point that Samuel Wilberforce
made to his father in 1823. Seeking to clarify his beliefs, Newman read
widely in evangelical theology and found himself particularly drawn to the
then sharply debated question of baptismal regeneration, which he and
Mayers considered in detail. Mayers insisted that in addition to receiving
the sacrament of baptism, a person must undergo personal conversion,
which Mayers understood as an experience leading to holiness of life "consisting in an entire change of views, of temper, and conduct," as "produced
by the Spirit of God." Mayers thought such conversions "very rarely *sudden*
or *instantaneous* but generally *slow* and *gradual*" and caused by "fortuitous"
events often associated with "sickness or adversity," later understood "to
have been directed by God."[5] The seeds for such a change leading to holiness might be sown in baptism, but Mayers, like most evangelicals of the
day, believed that the conversion even of baptized persons required the
instrument of the Holy Spirit and thereafter the practice of repentance.

In the *Apologia* Newman recounted reaching a second decision shortly
after his conversion in 1816, a decision that has received too little attention.

As he wrote in 1864, "I am obliged to mention, though I do it with great reluctance, another deep imagination, which at this time, the autumn of 1816, took possession of me,—there can be no mistake about the fact; viz. that it would be the will of God that I should lead a single life." Almost nothing is known about why he chose this path, though Mayers appears not to have been involved. Virtually nothing is known of Newman's relationships with either men or women during his childhood. Francis Newman recalled that his brother rarely played games and never swam, presumably in the nude, with other boys.[6] His mother and sisters provided his only close and ongoing contact with women during his youth and early adulthood. Consequently one can only speculate why a fifteen-year-old boy might decide against marriage. Newman may have blamed his awakening sexuality for his family's recent misfortunes. Although no evidence presents itself, he may have encountered confusion over his own sexual orientation. He may have feared that sexual thoughts, fantasies, longings, or activity might indicate the absence of the requisite marks of personal holiness. Many of the evangelical works that Newman read or may have read contained injunctions to family responsibility and commercial honesty immediately following discussions of conversion and holiness. Newman might have doubted his capacity to sustain a family in the manner that evangelical religion urged, something that his comment of 1864 that the decision "strengthened my feeling of separation from the visible world" may suggest. Whatever the occasion for his decision to pursue a celibate life, which in 1816 had no relationship to vocation, Newman's determination to remain unmarried, to avoid intimacy with women, and later to live among other unmarried men would constitute the single most consistent element in his personal life.

While Newman was attending Oxford, his family encountered further downward social mobility and dislocation. Unsuccessful as a brewer, John Newman in late 1819 moved his family to London and became a tavern-keeper. The next year, after exhausting himself by overstudy, his son fared poorly on his Oxford examinations and regarded himself as having disappointed both his family and Mayers. In late 1821 family disaster followed, when Newman's father fell into formal bankruptcy and was listed in the *Gazette*.[7] In January 1822, while Newman remained in Oxford, his family's goods were auctioned on the street in front of their rented residence. Thereafter for some time the family moved from one spot to another in London.

The bankruptcy and auction of family goods were moments that seem never to have left John Henry Newman's memory and spirit. They were events about which fifty years later he still believed he "was obliged to shuffle" with people outside his family. He felt a personal responsibility for one part of the collective family disappointment and sadness. During October 1821 his father in anticipation of the bankruptcy had urged him to take his own property to Oxford. Newman did not do so. In particular, he left all of the music for his violin, an instrument on which he had become accomplished, giving much pleasure to his family. His mother especially had hoped the music might be saved or at least purchased during the auction, but their bid was too low. At a distance of a half-century Newman still recalled to his sister Jemima "how sad My Mother was at dinner, and how my Father said he would try to get it all from the purchaser." That effort also failed. Newman believed the cause of the disappointment "*was* my negligence." In 1871 a friend, not knowing this story, happened across a volume of the music bearing the young Newman's name and gave it to him, thus occasioning his letter to Jemima, and the remark, "The poor book is like a voice from the grave."[8] All his years Newman was haunted by his father's failure, about which he wished no one to know, and those moments of his own failure commencing with his undergraduate examinations.

THE YOUNG ORIEL FELLOW

In the midst of the family turmoil Newman's father advised him to decide upon a career. Within two weeks of his father's formal bankruptcy, Newman decided to stand for an Oriel fellowship, and less than two months later he also decided to enter Holy Orders to strengthen his qualifications for the fellowship. His undergraduate examination failure haunted him, but the Oriel system of administering its own examinations as part of its election process gave him a second chance. Even his success in those examinations did not give him confidence. In July 1822 he expressed thanks in his diary for having been able to take them at the particular time he did rather than with a later possibly stronger group of competitors, when he might "have failed the second time." All of his life Newman would avoid direct competition with persons who might be as or more effective than himself. Thankful for his election to Oriel, he exclaimed, "And now I have a home, and every comfort about me." Newman must have felt that a college that had stood for centuries would not disappear in his absence as had first his childhood home in Richmond and later his family's goods on the streets of London. In good evangelical fashion he regarded that Oriel fellowship, which was his so long as he did not marry, as "God's gift."[9]

That gift included not only lodging and physical comforts but also access to the possibility of university social mobility. As a result, less than five years after his father's formal bankruptcy the young man had achieved a secure income, a position of trust in his college as junior treasurer, another position of responsibility as Richard Whately's vice principal at St. Alban Hall, an Oriel tutorship, and friends from among excellent families in the church, the aristocracy, and London commerce. His social advance could even allow his sisters to imagine marrying into the Wilberforce family. In his ascent, Newman had demonstrated the financial acumen and social skills that had eluded his father.

Even when Newman entered the Oriel fellowship, Walter Mayers's influence dominated his life. Mayers's counsel, as Newman later recalled, had allowed him "to go through the dangerous season of my Undergraduate residence" without "wounding" his conscience or experiencing "any gross or scandalous sin." He had also become zealously and introspectively—his father thought morbidly—evangelical, displaying considerable moral fastidiousness and priggishness. Although warned by his father against showing "ultraism in anything," Newman, like Froude after him, attempted a regimen of fasting and strict observance of the Sabbath even when receiving social invitations within Oriel. During these early Oriel years, his journal also records extensive personal Bible study and much interest in prophecy. For some time he also privately judged Oriel colleagues by Calvinist standards—for example, privately wondering whether despite his apparent goodness Pusey really stood among the elect and observing Hawkins as moving toward fuller spirituality. In his journal Newman repeatedly castigated himself for personal and spiritual shortcomings and asked how he as a sinner could receive the various blessings that had come upon him. Quite curiously, without any further explanation, he recorded in his birthday meditation of February 21, 1826, "What I want is a humble, simple, upright, sincere, straightforward mind. I am full of art and deceit, double dealing, display."[10] The hyperbolic rhetoric was that of pious evangelical self-examination, but the words also hinted at mature, even incisive, self-knowledge.

The ability and willingness of Oriel College to welcome and nurture such an odd young man as John Henry Newman has received too little appreciation. What differentiated the Oriel fellows, including those regarded as Noetics, from all but a few other Oxford Colleges and what made Oriel a safe haven for the young Newman was a genuine sympathy for evangelicals, ignored by historians but clearly recognized by Newman himself. In his autobiographical memoir he recalled that religiously the Oriel fellowship stood as "neither high Church nor low Church" but as "a new school" marked by "its spirit of moderation and comprehension." Their enemies, according to Newman, were "the old unspiritual high-and-dry, then in possession of the high places of Oxford" and the residents of lesser colleges who "felt both envy at their reputation and took offence at the strictness of their lives." Newman then significantly stated, "Their friends . . . as far as they had exactly friends, were of the Evangelical party." As one of that party Newman had himself felt "drawn in heart" to those Oriel associates "in proportion as he came to be intimate with them."[11] Such Oriel friendliness to evangelicals may account for William Wilberforce's having sent his sons there.

Consequently, although Oriel was most certainly not an evangelical college, it was a college in which a narrow Calvinist evangelical such as Newman could feel an affinity with the other fellows who were religiously serious. For his first six years in the Oriel fellowship he would have rubbed shoulders with Provost Edward Copleston, who once, after denouncing the Calvinist doctrines of election and final perseverance, had continued his discourse by reminding his audience of clergy, "It may be your glorious destiny . . . that you may *increase* that number [who are saved]—that you may provide guests for that heavenly feast, who would never have heard of it but for your preaching—never have sought after it, but for your persuasion—never have found their way to it, but for your guidance. Happy indeed shall he be who turns one sinner to righteousness—who adds one sheep to the fold into which his Lord's flock will then be gathered: and when the chief Shepherd shall appear, from his hands will he doubtless receive a crown of glory that fadeth not away." Though not an evangelical, Copleston's sentiments were certainly compatible with Newman's own image of himself in the mid-1820s as "Christ's soldier" and as one having "a commission to preach the gospel."[12] He had held to that evangelical vocational self-conception even after having attended during 1823 and 1824 Divinity Professor Charles Lloyd's generally high-church lectures.

In the summer of 1824, shortly before his father's death and after consulting with Mayers, Newman, having been ordained a deacon, became curate of St. Clement's Church in Oxford. He distinguished himself in three ways in this position. First, he was an accomplished fund raiser, an efficient organizer of a more effective Sunday school program, and a generally strong figure in revivifying his parish. As a result of these efforts, undertaken to halt leakage to Dissenting congregations, he recorded, "I find I am called a Methodist." Second, while attempting to strengthen St. Clement's,

3. Edward Copleston (1776–1849) was Provost of Oriel College when Newman became a fellow in 1821. He became Bishop of Llandaff in 1827, thus giving occasion for the election of Edward Hawkins as Oriel provost, which in turn opened the pulpit of the Church of St. Mary the Virgin for Newman's appointment. Copleston remained involved in Oxford life and was a moderate critic of the Tractarians. (Portrait by Thomas Phillips reproduced with the permission of the Provost and Fellows of Oriel College.)

Newman refrained from hostility toward Dissenters. As early as August 1823 he had told his brother Charles that he "did not confine salvation to one sect—that in any communion whoever sought truth sincerely would not fail of heaven." Moreover, once working in St. Clement's, Newman found so much "irreligion in the place" that he avoided conflict with the competing

Dissenting minister though he still thought "a good Churchman . . . better than a good dissenter." This behavior very much reflected the outlook of Richard Whately's Bampton Lectures of 1822 on *The Use and Abuse of Party-Feeling in Matters of Religion,* which had contended that it was necessary "to oppose Dissenters *as such,* without being wanting in charity towards them as men, and as Christians;—to be steady in maintaining the sinfulness of schism, yet without censuring as unpardonable those who fall into it." Third, Newman proved himself a stern preacher, emphasizing damnation more than his congregation appreciated and insisting on the necessity of real changes in moral life beyond what they felt they could achieve. The message proved too difficult for most. But for a time he persevered, explaining to his mother that, while striving to preach the Christian doctrine of increasing peace and joy in Christ, he remained determined "at the same time to warn people that it is quite idle to pretend to faith and holiness, unless they show forth their inward principles by a pure, disinterested, upright line of conduct."[13]

The letters and diary of Newman's first months in St. Clement's display both his energy for the tasks of his vocation and his consternation at the vast array of religious opinions, denominational loyalties, moral misbehavior, confusing family situations, and human suffering he confronted in parish ministry. During August 1824 Edward Hawkins, Oriel fellow and Vicar of the Church of St. Mary the Virgin, came to Newman's aid. This relationship flourished just as Mayers, who by then had a parish in Oxfordshire, married.[14] As the Calvinist Mayers entered upon matrimony, Newman, moved toward Hawkins's mentoring influence, began to entertain serious criticism of Calvinism, and opened himself to more moderate evangelical influence. Such was not an infrequent pattern of changing friendships for Newman, who virtually always had difficulty with close clerical friends or acquaintances when they married and often regarded them as having abandoned him.

Hawkins, responding to Newman's frustration over his inability to discern who in his congregation did and did not stand among the elect, commended to his reading *Apostolical Preaching* by John Bird Sumner, a moderate evangelical whose natural theology Newman had previously studied earlier under Bishop Lloyd's tutelage. While stressing preaching over liturgy and urging the individual clergyman to remember "his situation as the messenger of Christ," whose "business" was that of "converting sinners from the error of their way," Sumner's volume also attacked Calvinist theology as incompatible with the preaching of St. Paul. According to Sumner,

4. Richard Whately (1787–1863), an Oriel fellow at the time of Newman's election, became Principal of St. Alban Hall, where he appointed Newman vice principal. A prolific writer on ecclesiastical, philosophical, and economic topics, in 1831 he was appointed Archbishop of Dublin. From that position he continued to influence university matters and ecclesiastical patronage. He was a strong supporter of R. D. Hampden and one of the most incisive of Tractarian critics. (Portrait from the Circle of Thomas Phillips reproduced with the permission of the Provost and Fellows of Oriel College.)

Calvinist doctrines prevented congregations from understanding or fulfilling their baptismal covenant and grasping the love of God. Sumner conceived baptism administered by the Church as a medium for regeneration, which, however, had to be realized through the active faith of the baptized person in Christ's sacrifice. To exercise such faith, a person must "individually embrace the doctrine of the Gospel" and "must look for salvation through Christ's death with as much personal gratitude as if Christ had suffered for him alone." If adults failed to embrace the Gospel, then the covenant of baptism "is made void."[15]

By eschewing "indiscriminate severity" against those "who do not answer the preacher's idea of entire *regeneracy*," the minister, according to Sumner, could sustain those who had quietly grown into their baptismal vows, awaken others to new awareness of them, and draw back to those vows members of the congregation who had long fallen away from them. Sumner presented St. Paul as having understood "that there would always be many in the visible church, to whom the grace of the Gospel would be offered in vain" and that any congregation would include many "who have not ratified their baptismal vows, or given the requisite diligence to 'make their calling and election sure.' " He reminded the clergy that "the worst of those whom a minister addresses, may become subjects of grace, and finally recover; the best may swerve from the faith." While emphasizing the importance of sanctification following upon justification, Sumner denounced any efforts to substitute "justification by works," that "error most flattering to the human heart," for "justification by faith alone" as "the foundation of the Christian scheme."[16]

Hawkins also sought to discourage Newman from too strong a commitment to the nondenominational Bible Society, which he had joined in 1824, with its emphasis on individuals reading Scripture without commentary or instruction from other Christians. To that end, Hawkins gave Newman his own sermon on *Unauthoritative Tradition*, which Newman had apparently heard him deliver in 1818. The issue that Hawkins had addressed was why "many of the Christian doctrines" were "so *indirectly taught* in the Scriptures?" He found "an aid and guide" to those doctrines existing "in *tradition*, the traditions conveyed from age to age by the Church in general." Recognizing that Protestants would resist the idea of tradition guiding the reading of the Bible, Hawkins asked, "Why may it not have been the general design of Heaven that by early oral, or traditional, instruction the way should be prepared for the reception of the mysteries of faith; that the Church should carry down the *system*, but the Scriptures should furnish all the *proofs* of the Christian doctrines; that tradition should supply the Christian with the *arrangement*, but the Bible with all the *sustenance* of divine truth?" Hawkins quickly rejected any notion that his idea resembled tradition as taught by the Roman Catholic Church because he assigned "*no independent authority* for the traditions conveyed to us by the Church."[17] Rather he argued that this independent tradition must always agree with the Bible and receive its authority through that agreement. Doctrines could be proved from the Bible, but only after they had first been received from other Christians who had served as teachers.

Hawkins thought the Reformers themselves had acknowledged this process through their provision for catechetical instruction. St. Paul's mention of instructions that he had delivered orally to the early churches, as well as the provision for "a perpetual *succession of ministers* and teachers," further indicated the perceived necessity of teaching in addition to the reading of Scripture. Yet Hawkins asserted that such clergy were "by no means the sole depositories, or sole vehicles of unauthoritative tradition, although upon the whole they have been efficient guardians of it." Rather he declared, "Every Christian, who received the doctrines of his faith, becomes by the very nature of the case the keeper of tradition, so far as he knows the Christian doctrines." Hawkins's view of who should communicate the tradition that should inform the reading of the Bible very closely resembled evangelical manuals of instruction as he stated, "Private religious instruction . . . becomes involved in the circle of almost every Christian's duties at some period of life or other. Masters of families or of schools, and parents in a more especial manner, are bound to contribute their services to the common cause; women may here perceive their appropriate and important province; it would be difficult to overrate their usefulness when discreetly employed in this career."[18] In this regard Hawkins, like the other Oriel Noetics, consistently rejected a clerical definition of the church. At the same time he opposed the Bible Society policy of distributing bibles without commentary. His position, however, was quite compatible with that of evangelicals who, like Thomas Scott, incorporated commentary alongside the word of Scripture and other evangelicals who strongly supported the corporate authority of the church against the antinomianism always present in the evangelical impulse.

Sumner's *Apostolical Preaching* and Hawkins's sermon, as well as his own parish experience, began to draw Newman away from Calvinism and toward more moderate evangelical religion. Nonetheless, he remained an active member of both the Bible Society and the Church Missionary Society. In

March 1825, Richard Whately, who had already commissioned articles from Newman for the *Encylopaedia Metropolitana*, appointed him Vice Principal of St. Alban Hall. His work with Whately associated Newman with one of the most acute and independent minds in the university and with a person who himself entertained doubts about the wisdom of ecclesiastical establishment. About a year later Newman became tutor of Oriel and resigned both the vice principalship and his work at St. Clement's. He now commanded a significant income, with his fellowship paying approximately £250 each year and the tutorship worth approximately £300 annually.[19]

CONFLICTS IN FAMILY, UNIVERSITY, AND COLLEGE

Parallel to forging a career within Oriel and moderating his theological opinions, Newman remained deeply involved with his family, an involvement that no less than his university experiences reshaped his theological and ecclesiastical outlooks. The troubles of his family had stirred much anger in Newman, who later castigated himself for displaying too little sympathy toward his father. In his capacity as eldest son and brother, Newman effectively assumed a very nearly paternal role and became substitute head of household. He provided firm emotional support for his mother, spiritual and educational mentoring for his brothers and sisters, and money for virtually everyone in the family. On October 27, 1821, his father had commended him for having "by example as well as by precept and instruction so greatly contributed to the Moral Beauty as well as to the cultivation and enlargement" of the minds of his brothers and sisters. In late February 1822, just after John's twenty-first birthday and the auction of the family goods, Mrs. Newman praised him for having been "a second father" to whom his siblings were "much indebted for the improvement and cultivation of their minds."[20] Newman had also become the driving force in securing the family's economic well-being, a role that he would continue to fill until his mother's death and the marriages of his two sisters in 1836.

Throughout the early 1820s Newman's journal entries indicate a virtual obsession with finding and borrowing enough money to ensure that Francis could continue at Oxford. Again and again he prayed about his financial problems and repeatedly saw those prayers answered, as if by magic, when small amounts of money arrived unexpectedly in the mail. For example, his journal of February 9, 1824, recorded, "O gracious Father, how could I for an instant mistrust Thee? On entering my room, I see a letter, containing

£35!" His financial and instructional attention to Francis, which often generated friction between the two, paid off handsomely. In contrast to John's weak undergraduate performance, Francis in 1826 emerged from his examinations with a Double First and soon qualified for a Balliol fellowship, a triumph that caused John to see his brother as the avenger of his own collapse. Early the next year John confided to his journal, "Frank is off my hands, but the rest are now heavier."[21] His aunt ran a small school, which floundered and incurred debts that he and Francis paid. He was also repeatedly concerned with housing arrangements for his mother and sisters, which were rarely very satisfactory.

Newman also became in point of fact chaplain to his own family. In that context he first directly confronted radical secularism and radical evangelicalism, the two contemporary cultural forces that he eventually considered most dangerous to the Christian faith. Those encounters deeply influenced the history of his religious opinions but remained largely unmentioned in the *Apologia*.

Commencing in 1823, Newman engaged in a long religious debate with his brother Charles, who had become involved with politically and religiously radical working-class London Owenites, followers of the socialist pioneer Robert Owen. During the summer of that year Charles told John that the "antecedent improbability of eternal punishment" was "so great that it is absurd to believe it," and that he thought people "not in earnest, when they call themselves the vilest of sinners." Charles had also asked, "Why not read the Bible, and employ reason at once?" rather than seeking grace for the process. Two years later Charles challenged the authority of Christianity and the validity of the Bible, telling his brother, "I think Mr Owen for practical motives to action . . . beats St Paul hollow." Newman, assigning such opinions to his brother's lack of emotional balance and good judgment, as well as to his tendency "to be self-willed," told Charles, "A dislike of the *contents* of Scripture is at the bottom of unbelief." Throughout this correspondence, the most extensive of this decade, Newman argued that to believe in Christianity was to believe in a revelation, the contents of which were "not to be brought into evidence for or against revelation, *because* man is not in a state to judge of them; not, that is, from the fault of the *contents*, but from the weakness of *man*." In response to a paper by Charles on the authenticity of the Gospels, Newman urged "that the New Testament is not *Christianity*, but the *record* of Christianity."[22] Consequently, biblical errors or discrepancies did not invalidate the faith itself, which existed apart from Scripture.

Newman engaged in an even more dogged quarrel with Francis. Whereas Charles Newman had fallen in with Owenites, Francis Newman embraced the new extreme evangelicalism of the decade, with its novel readings of biblical prophecy and millennial speculation. Just after taking his degree, Francis had been elected a fellow of Balliol College and shortly thereafter left for Ireland, where he became a private family tutor. Through connections he developed in Ireland during 1827, Francis became deeply involved with John Nelson Darby and the fledgling Plymouth Brethren, and later with other radical, evangelical seceders from the Church of England. Once in Ireland, Francis engaged John in long debate over the scriptural authority for infant baptism, which Francis rejected on the ground of Scripture and John affirmed on the ground of tradition. In Francis's rejection of church tradition on the basis of personal reading of Scripture, John saw a demand analogous to that which Charles had voiced from an Owenite point, "Why not read the Bible, and employ reason at once?"[23]

As far as John was concerned, both brothers had resorted to their subjective private judgments. Francis, along with the Darbyites, saw himself using his reason to reclaim from Scripture a primitive version of Christianity predating the Fathers. Francis's thinking embodied the very mode of nontraditional reading of Scripture that Hawkins had decried in his sermon and that he associated with the Bible Society. Curiously, in John's critical remarks and admonitions to his two brothers, he as the eldest among them and the person assigned by his parents as a second father to them was actually reverting to the kind of advice their father had given him against falling prey to extreme, dogmatic, or "ultra" opinions.

Faced with aggressive if divergent modes of skepticism on the part of Charles and Francis, who thus challenged his dominance as eldest sibling, Newman acted swiftly to assert religious dominance over the rest of his family. In early 1827 he composed a long essay of sixty-six quarto pages for his sisters, refuting Francis's rejection of infant baptism. This private paper marked a considerable advance in Newman's criticism of evangelical religion, now embodied by Francis in the family setting. Just as Newman had accounted for Charles's unbelief on the grounds of emotional instability, he blamed Francis's "excessive opinions" on his health and changes in seasonal weather.[24]

The quarrel with Francis unfolded while Newman encountered the single most devastating personal event of his early adulthood. As already noted, his sisters were the only women with whom he had a close, intimate relationship. On October 30, 1825, he wrote in his journal, "O how I love them. So much I love them, that I cannot help thinking. Thou wilt either take them hence, or take me from them, because I am too set on them. It is a shocking thought." He also told his sisters directly in letters of his love for them. Then just over two years later, in early January 1828, without warning his youngest sister Mary died after an illness of less than a day. Alluding to the many difficulties his family had confronted, Newman described Mary's death to Hawkins as "of many troubles . . . the most acute Providence has visited us with." Relating her deathbed in evangelical fashion to Hawkins, he observed that although Mary had indicated "that she could not fully satisfy her mind as to the *certainty* of her salvation, and was in some fear," nonetheless "her entire hope was in Christ."[25] Newman's own growing conviction of the communication of regenerative grace, if not necessarily justification, through baptism may well have arisen as a response to Mary's uncertainty of her own salvation as she lay dying. Both Mary and her deathbed remained on his mind throughout 1828, when he preached sermons more nearly embracing baptismal regeneration than he had previously done. Newman, who was nine years old when Mary was born, would have had clear recollections of her as an infant and no doubt of her baptism and may well have wished to assure himself of her salvation through baptism.

Whereas the death of his father had passed with virtually no comments in his letters, Newman for many months visited and revisited his sister's passing and recalled it for the rest of his life. Expressing to Jemima anxiety that he might forget what Mary had said, he declared that she would "flourish from the tomb" and that in the meantime he would "try to talk to her in imagination and in hope of the future, by setting down all I can think about her." Riding to Cuddesdon in May, he thought, "Dear Mary seems embodied in every tree and hid behind every hill. What a veil and curtain this world of sense is! beautiful but still a veil." The next day he wrote a poem, which he sent to Jemima, about Mary's death, in which he meditated on the bed where she had died and the same bed which he claims to have visited in grief as Mary lay in her casket. He also slept in his dead sister's bed on one of his visits home. In June he told Harriett, "Not an half hour passes, but dear Mary is before my eyes." In late August 1828 the sight of a letter from Mary could still lead to his discomposure. In November he found Mary's voice seeming to chant from everything in nature as he rode about the countryside. He also reported to Harriett, "Her form is almost nightly before me, when I have put out the light and lain down. Is not this a blessing? All I lament is, that I do not think she ever knew how much I loved her." In February 1829, a year after Mary's death, he still found himself "dreaming most vividly of her."[26] When recording these feelings, Newman was a man of twenty-eight and not an adolescent.

Other significant events touched Newman's life during 1828. On February 27, Walter Mayers had also suddenly died. Newman preached his memorial sermon in April. In March, with Hawkins formally elected Provost of Oriel, Newman replaced him as Vicar of the Church of St. Mary the Virgin, the name of which may have evoked each day memories of his beloved deceased virgin sister. Appointment to St. Mary's also meant that Newman had become answerable to a bishop. Then in June, Pusey married, and by October he was installed in Christ Church as Regius Professor of Hebrew. For some time the two friends saw little of each other, an eventuality that Newman blamed on the new Mrs. Pusey. In December, Hawkins, who had recently been his closest Oriel friend, also married. Part of Newman's participation during the following year in conflicts within Oriel over the election of Robert Peel and the tutorial system, both of which challenged Hawkins's authority, may have had roots in Newman's anger and disappointment over his friend's marriage.

During the spring of 1828, Newman appears to have recognized that changes in Oriel relationships and his own placement at St. Mary's would considerably modify his circle of acquaintances. On April 29 an intercollegiate dining group first gathered at his instigation. A few days later he told Jemima, "In accordance with my steady wish to bring together members of different Colleges I have founded a dinner Club of men about my own standing. . . . We meet once a fortnight—one fundamental rule is to have very plain dinners." Excluding his youthful organization of a secret order of boys at Ealing School with himself as the "Grand Master," his dining club, about which very little is known and which ceased to meet in late 1833, represented the first of Newman's efforts to gather around himself in some organized manner a group of celibate males, part of whose camaraderie was based on simplicity in meals. In 1829, the year after founding that club and while he still grieved for his lost sister, Newman firmly decided upon a celibate life. One can only wonder how the family sadnesses of 1828, as well as those that had come earlier, had pressed him in that direction. In a letter of November 23 he had written, "Home has the memory of too many trying events to inspire a merely earthly pleasure."[27] For more than ten years home and family had brought embarrassment, humiliation, personal sacrifice, and grief to Newman. It may be no wonder that he would avoid domesticity.

As the months of 1828 passed, Newman's friendship with Froude, whose brother also died during the spring, began to intensify. Froude, unlike the recently deceased Mayers or the recently married Pusey and Hawkins, championed celibacy. During the same months Newman's admiration grew for Keble's sacramental poetry, which had been much loved by Mary. This development allowed Froude to encourage a renewal of contact and friendship between Newman and the unmarried Keble. Froude was also interested in Roman Catholicism, about which he and Newman sought instruction from Blanco White, the former Spanish priest, who as previously noted had privileges in the Oriel Common Room. In early July, Newman commenced his study of the Church Fathers, but later that month he still praised the appointment of the evangelical John Bird Sumner to the see of Chester. As late as September 1828 Froude continued to call Newman "a heretic" because of his ongoing evangelicalism.[28] But Froude continued to introduce him to his radical Catholic views of the English Church as an apostolic foundation, and in time the terms *Apostolic* and *Apostolical* began occasionally to appear in Newman's correspondence.

Newman's public behavior quickly reflected his new friendships and social acquaintances. Early in 1829, almost exactly one year after Mary's death, Newman sharply disrupted his previously carefully cultivated Oriel relationships by joining the university protest against the reelection of Robert Peel. Newman, somewhat confusedly, had supported the policy of Catholic emancipation but nonetheless opposed Peel's reelection because of the latter's personal political about-face on the issue and the consequent effort by his Oxford supporters to accommodate the university to the switch in Tory policy. The opinions that Newman followed with unprecedented zeal were those of Froude and Keble in opposition to those of Hawkins and Pusey, both of whom were now married. The Peel election demonstrated that the M.A.s in the university could forge an effective alliance in Convocation with the country parsons to oppose the senior members of the university, who often boasted London political connections, as was also the case at this time with both Hawkins and Pusey. That alliance continued to function during the next decade, quite often to Tractarian advantage. Furthermore, Keble's subsequent election by Convocation to the poetry professorship appeared to demonstrate that, within the university, resisting Peel's reelection provided genuine political benefits.

Beyond resistance to those politically well connected in the university, the battle over Peel's reelection for the first time elicited from Newman an extremely harsh ecclesiastical-political rhetoric directed against liberals, Dissenters, and advanced evangelicals. To his sisters he portrayed Peel's reversal of policy as part of a larger attack on the church led by "Utilitarians and Schismatics" that required the "Guardians and Guides of Christ's Church" to demonstrate its independence from the state. To his mother, he contended that the church confronted the spirit of "latitudinarianism, indifferentism, republicanism, and schism, a spirit which tends to overthrow doctrine, as if the fruit of bigotry, and discipline as if the instrument of priestcraft." Representatives of that spirit included "useful knowledge people" associated with utilitarian institutions, "schismatics, in and out of the Church," Baptists, "the high circles in London," and "political indifferentists," as well as the uneducated masses who read radical authors. He bemoaned the absence of "mental endowments" as well as "activity, shrewdness, dexterity, eloquence, practical powers" in the church party and its dependence "on prejudice and bigotry."[29] Throughout these family letters Newman indicated that the tie between the English Church and the English state might at some time be severed for the good of the church. It should be noted that Newman's description of the opponents of the church closely paralleled the challenges that he, an ordained establishment priest, had confronted within the confines of his own family, first from the radical politics of Charles and then from the advanced evangelicalism of Francis. Almost all the terms of opprobrium he hurled at Peel's supporter could have been directed at one or the other of his brothers.

In mid-March, Newman told the St. Mary's congregation, who would have been fully sensitive to the election campaign, "that those who attempt to please all parties, please fewest; and that the best way to gain the world's good opinion . . . is to show that you prefer the praise of God." He also enjoined them and no doubt himself, "Make up your mind to be occasionally misunderstood, and undeservedly condemned."[30] In many respects, that last injunction became for many years Newman's own self-serving and self-interpretive motto, as he would again and again portray himself as undeservedly condemned after having been misunderstood.

The weeks of the Oxford election coincided with the introduction of Newman's plan to revise tutorial instruction in Oriel, which Hawkins abruptly ended about a year later. His formal departure from the Tutorship in 1832, when he had completed the instruction of students previously assigned to him, caused Newman to forfeit approximately half of his annual income. Though he later interpreted his dismissal as providentially allowing him to pursue the activities associated with the tracts, it is by no means clear that such were his thoughts at the time.

Newman's effort to reorganize the Oriel tutorial structures directly followed from the convictions about the plight of the English Church that he

5. Edward Hawkins (1789–1882) preceded Newman as Vicar of the Church of St. Mary the Virgin. He was elected Provost of Oriel College in 1828. As provost, Hawkins in 1830 ended Newman's tutorial reform in Oriel and later proved to be the most effective university opponent of the Tractarians. (Portrait by Sir Francis Grant, reproduced with the permission of the Provost and Fellows of Oriel College.)

voiced to his family at the time of Peel's election struggle. The reorganization would have allowed him and his colleagues through private, pastoral instruction to equip a subsection of Oriel undergraduates for the upcoming struggles of the church. About two weeks after Peel's defeat Newman had forecast to his sister the need for such a group, complaining, as if describing his own brothers, of the "republican times" and "the *forwardness of young persons*" who had no respect for their superiors. Newman then declared, "See what a bigot I am getting—I am more than ever imprest too with the importance of staying in Oxford many years . . . nay feel more strongly than ever the necessity of there being men in the Church, like the R Catholic friars, free from all obstacles to their devoting themselves to its defence." Newman thus envisioned a celibate order of defenders of the Church of England against its secular and religious detractors. His reformed tutorial system would have allowed Oriel instruction to produce such a brotherhood, which, unlike his own brothers, would have been dedicated to orthodoxy and obedience rather than to infidelity and schism. Newman appears to have justified to his mother and sisters his own decision for celibacy in those terms. By December 1829 Mrs. Newman, apparently reconciled to her son's forgoing of marriage, told him, "If we could move advantageously, I should vote for a nice little cottage with a garden *near you,* as you seem to intend to be a sort of 'Monk' for some time." By the summer of 1830 his sister Harriett also spoke of him as a "monk."[31]

Simultaneously with the Oriel struggle, Newman entered his first public dispute with radical evangelicals. Throughout the late 1820s, despite the growing influence of Froude and his own patristic studies, Newman remained, broadly speaking, within an evangelical frame of mind, preaching evangelical sermons, studying prophecy from an evangelical standpoint, and retaining membership in evangelical societies. He continued his activity in the Oxford Auxiliary of the Church Missionary Society, which elected him secretary in March 1829 the month of the Peel election. The auxiliary membership included a number of the more extreme Oxford evangelicals, most importantly his brother Francis and Henry Bulteel, both of whom would soon separate from the Church of England.

Newman's experience with these people, as well as his new alliances arising from the Peel election, led him to become vocal in his criticism of both extreme Church of England evangelicals, who had little loyalty to the church establishment as such, and mainstream Dissenters. In November 1829, in a sermon on "Submission to Church Authority" directed toward those radical evangelicals in the English Church, he deplored the contemporary disregard of "religious unity and peace" and the popularity of "novel doctrines and new measures." He produced a litany of reasons why contemporary religious people ignored the authority of the church and championed heresy and schism. Those drawn to such novelties argued that "Christianity is an universal gift" not limited to one party or embodied in one set of forms, or that the best way to achieve unity was to relax strictness and to allow all sects to join together, or that all groups should surrender their adherence to particular forms of worship, ministry, or ecclesiastical organization. Those resisting church authority also argued that faith is a matter of the heart that required not only correct creed but also inner vitality. Yet Newman answered uncompromisingly, "Now let it be carefully noted, that if order is to be preserved at all, it must be at the expense of what seems to be of more consequence, *viz.*, the so-called communion of the heart between Christians." This injunction struck at a core belief of moderate Dissenting and establishment evangelicals as well as of the radicals. To seek in such communion of the heart, as were some local extreme evangelicals, "a less formal, more spiritual religion" outside the church, Newman urged, was to break a commandment. He finally declared, "We must transmit as we have received. We did not make the Church, we may not unmake it. As we believe it to be a Divine Ordinance, so we must ever protest against separation from it as a sin. There is not a dissenter living, but, inasmuch as so far as he dissents, is in a sin." Such Dissent flowed from pride, restlessness, impatience, and self-will and led to such actions as "wilful separation," "turbulent conduct," the "forming of religious meetings" independent of the church, and the exercise of private judgment.[32]

Toward the close of 1829, as indicated by this sermon, Newman found his discontent with the radical Oxford evangelicals and his brother Francis growing. He then attempted to persuade the Oxford Church Missionary Society Auxiliary to refuse to accept the collections received when its extreme members preached. Though failing in this instance, he published on February 1, 1830, *Suggestions in Behalf of the Church Missionary Society*, which directly criticized evangelical irregularities of that society. These included laying "out anew the Church's territory, dividing it into districts of its own appointing," remodeling "our ecclesiastical system, the functions of which are brought under the supreme direction of a committee of management in London," sending out its own representatives, including both clergy and laymen, to preside over assemblies and make collections, giving a "prominence to preaching over other religious ordinances," and making "the people not the Bishops, the basis and moving principle of her constitution."[33] Newman proposed to alleviate these typically evangelical practices by flooding the local auxiliaries of the Church Missionary Society with clergy whose votes could conform its practices to the governing ecclesiastical structures of the church. The Oxford radical evangelicals quickly derailed Newman's quixotic move when in March 1830, on a motion of Bulteel supported privately if not publicly by Francis Newman, the local Oxford Church Missionary Society auxiliary deposed John Henry Newman as secretary. Benjamin P. Symons, the Subwarden and later Warden of Wadham College and a major future detractor of the Tractarians, chaired the meeting. Not insignificantly, however, Newman continued to attend meetings of the society through at least early 1831 and possibly later.

The exact significance of Newman's privately circulated pamphlet of 1830 may never be fully known. His correspondence indicates that he and his friends were genuinely concerned over the evangelical ecclesiastical irregularities. In light of the controversy recently roused among high churchmen by Pusey's controversial book about Germany, Newman may have felt it politic to champion episcopal authority and ecclesiastical regularity. He may also, however, have hoped through this challenge to extreme evangelicalism and ecclesiastical irregularity to mend fences with Hawkins, who strongly objected to the absence of adequate ecclesiastical supervision within the Church Missionary Society.[34] If such was his plan, it clearly failed. In the spring of 1830 Hawkins concluded his drive against the revised tutorial structures with the effectual dismissal of the offending tutors in June.

Despite all the difficulties over the Oriel tutorial program, Newman continued until October 1831 to handle the college financial accounts. Furthermore, Whately in September 1831 upon his appointment to Dublin offered Newman reappointment as Vice Principal of St. Alban Hall, perhaps as an act of friendship to compensate Newman for the loss of tutorial income. Newman refused, hoping to receive from Whately a different but never proffered position in Dublin, and even fantasizing about appointment as Principal of St. Alban Hall. Newman planned to decline these avenues for advancement, but he was declining offers never made. Except for his duties at St. Mary's, Newman was to hold no other university occupation or significant college responsibility.[35]

Toward the end of the tutorial struggle in Oriel and shortly after his ouster as secretary of the Church Missionary Society, Newman experienced an explosive religious conflict with his two brothers. Within a day or so of each other in May 1830, both Charles and Francis reentered Newman's by then highly vexed life. Charles wished to recommence the theological debate that he and John had abandoned in 1825. That demanding invitation, about which John complained to his sisters, resulted in one of the longest letters he ever wrote. He repeated to his Owenite brother his views of faith, revelation, and evidence, once again distinguishing between the contents of revelation, which involved doctrines, and the contents of the Bible, which did not.[36]

During the same week that he had received Charles's letter, John learned of Francis's intention to undertake an ecclesiastically unauthorized missionary journey to Persia with other Darbyites. Francis was also to resign his Balliol fellowship on the grounds that he could no longer in good conscience subscribe to the 39 Articles. John was furious that Francis, whose resignation caused still another loss to the collective family finances, had neither consulted him nor told him his reasons. John did think, however, that "from F's great dissatisfaction with every thing as it is," it might "be a relief to his mind to be free from the irritation which I believe the sight of every thing around him occasions." He also speculated that in some manner the church should be able to employ usefully abroad such persons as Francis who were mischievous at home. Once again Mrs. Newman looked to her eldest son to sort out the family problems by mentoring his younger brother, urging him to put Francis "on his guard, that, from a false idea of being under the guidance of the Spirit, he may be following his own enthusiastic inclinations." In late August, observing the earnestness of Charles in the cause of Owen and of Francis in the cause of preaching the Gospel in Persia, she characterized each as "similarly self-willed" believing "that they *alone* see things rightly." Failing to dissuade Francis, Newman admitted to his mother in late August, "Frank's departure has had its sufficient share in knocking me up."[37] In this manner Newman both shared with his mother a common sadness and frustration over the behavior of his brothers and reasserted his position of the most loyal and obedient of her sons. He was again the only son who had some financial security, even if of a much reduced nature.

Whereas Mrs. Newman saw a self-willed son, Newman could have regarded Francis's departure and resignation of his Balliol fellowship as nothing less than the self-destruction of the brilliant brother-creation intended to compensate for his own examination collapse. Radical evangelical religion had in effect consumed all the personal expense and psychic energy that John had devoted to his brother's education and his achieving a secure social and economic position. Newman's only direct action in the summer of 1830 was his resignation in early June from the Bible Society. About two months later Newman wrote Simeon Lloyd Pope that the Bible Society contributed toward liberalism or "a thinking established notions worth nothing," the very attitude he had ascribed to Francis. Newman stressed that "authority of some kind of [or] other" residing in the Church established by the apostles must enforce moral truth, but that liberals "in every possible manner [were] trying to break it up." He then added, "I think the B. S. (unconsciously) is a means of aiding their object." Newman further asserted that the inclusion of both churchmen and Dissenters in the administrative structure of the Bible Society "MAKES CHURCHMEN LIBERALS" by leading them to "undervalue the guilt of schism" and to "feel a wish to conciliate Dissenters at the expence of truth." In this fashion the Bible Society was "preparing the downfall of the Church."[38] Newman had, of course, witnessed that very downfall in his own family. Significantly, he directed far more vitriol against the evangelicals of the Bible Society than he ever expressed to Charles about the Owenites. Here, as throughout his life, he was always more angry at Christians with whom he differed than with those who set themselves outside the Christian fold. Heresy, so to speak, was for Newman worse than apostasy.

Having been defeated by radical evangelical schismatics in both the Oxford Church Missionary Society and his family, Newman took the offensive from the pulpit of St. Mary's. Energized by anger, disappointment, and frustration, he lifted the private battles located in his family to a universal plane of criticism, where he associated the evangelical impulse with contemporary material optimism, political reform, and overmuch trust in reason and science. In the process, he enunciated a vision of Christian faith and experience as constituting a religion of obedience to conscience. He also set forth perhaps the most penetrating psychological critique ever written in the English language of the modern evangelical impulse.

The driving psychic force behind that critique had originated in Newman's family setting, where in the radical evangelicalism of Francis he first directly witnessed an articulate religious life shorn of what he considered real concern for obedience. In 1830 Newman castigated Francis for standing among those "in the so-called religious world" who "account themselves Christians because they use Scripture phrases" or consider themselves "to believe in Christ with the heart and to be changed in their moral nature because they assent fully to certain doctrines . . . that we can do nothing of ourselves, have no merit, or are saved by faith;—or (again) imagine they have habits or a character when they have only feelings." Francis and others like him applied "high Christian doctrines as medicine" thus offering "truths, which require a faith (to understand and receive them) grounded on deep self-knowledge and a long course of self-discipline."[39] Of course, what stirred Newman's anger at Francis was not only his brother's religious experimentation but the manner in which that new religious commitment encouraged him to flout John's authority. There was a direct parallel between Francis's refusal to submit to the church and his simultaneous rejection of deference to his eldest sibling.

DENOUNCING THE RELIGION OF THE DAY FROM ST. MARY'S PULPIT

Newman, along with other future Tractarians and more traditional high churchmen, loathed evangelical preaching. He was quite sharp on the matter during his Roman Catholic years, when he privately denounced the Protestant introduction of "a popular theology, with all the formality, coldness, and incomprehensibleness, which is incident to theology," resulting in the issuing "from the Preacher's mouth the difficult words vicariousness, gratuitousness, innate corruption, private judgment, Bible Christianity, and all the rest of these themes." In 1870 he recalled his dislike of "what, when I was young, R. Wilberforce and H. Froude used to call '180 degree sermons,' that is, sermons which were resolved to bring in the whole circuit of theology in the space of twenty minutes." They considered it "the great fault of Evangelicals—that they would not let religious topics come in naturally, but accused a man of not being sound in religion if he dared to speak of sanctification without justification, regeneration, etc., etc." Still later in life in a mutually civil exchange Newman told a late Victorian evangelical that while a young man, "I thought the Evangelical Preaching of the Atonement was irreverent, oratorical, and vulgar." He explained that he had "considered the Atonement as an Object for *devotion,* not for conversion, not denying of course that it was adapted in itself to convert *religious minds,* but that it was not the instrument, in the case of *irreligious,* as the Evangelicals used it. It was a profanity thus to use it." The result of such preaching was what seemed to Newman "a superstition, viz the fancied obligation of introducing the whole gospel into every Sermon" whereby "all Sermons are repetitions of each other."[40] These comments stand among Newman's clearest, most straightforward, and least self-serving of personal explications of his thinking during his years in the English Church.

In contrast to both moderate and radical evangelicals, the young Newman preached the impossibility of genuine faithfulness in and to the Gospel without obedience. In that respect, he transformed Mayers's comments on conversion necessarily occurring over time into a process of joint pursuit of faith and obedience. He told his congregation on February 21, 1830, approximately three weeks after circulating his pamphlet criticizing the irregularities of the Church Missionary Society, that the states of mind embodying faith and obedience "are altogether one and the same" and that it was a matter of indifference "whether we say a man seeks God in faith, or say he seeks Him by obedience" because faith and obedience were "not divided one from the other in fact." Assuming that faith and obedience "are but one thing viewed differently," Newman regarded "whole masses of men . . . at this day, who are commonly considered religious" to be in "a most serious error" by putting obedience into a second place after faith "as if it were rather a necessary consequence of faith than requiring a direct attention to its own sake." As a consequence, "they believe in a coming judgment as regards the wicked, but they do not believe that all men, that they themselves personally, will undergo it." Newman argued that people could miss the fundamental scriptural injunction to both obedience and faith by "perplexing themselves with their human systems, and measuring and arranging its inspired declarations by an artificial rule." Such "strained interpretations" avoided the plainest teaching of Scripture.[41]

During the spring of 1830 Newman more fully explored the issue of obedience. In "The Influence of Natural and Revealed Religion Respectively" of April 13, restating arguments he previously had addressed to his brother Charles and was to repeat to him a few weeks later, Newman portrayed conscience as "the essential principle and sanction of Religion in the mind." The functioning of conscience implied "a relation between the soul and a something exterior, and that, moreover, superior to itself" that embodies "an excellence which it does not possess" and constitutes "a tribunal over which it has no power." This external authority stood at the center of "the system of relations existing between us and a Supreme Power, claiming our habitual obedience." For all of its moral depth and inner demands, as attested by "the actual state of religious belief of pious men in the heathen world," this "Natural Religion" lacked "an object on which the affections could be placed, and the energies concentrated," an object that only revelation could supply. Over and against this "Dispensation of Paganism," the purpose of revealed religion was "to relate some course of action, some conduct, a life (to speak in human terms) of the One Supreme God." In this context Newman redefined the full preaching of Christ—a notion associated with evangelicals as the preaching of the atonement—to mean that "in the Christian scheme we find *all* the Divine Attributes (not mercy only, though mercy pre-eminently) brought out and urged upon us, which were but latent in the visible course of things." The life of Christ had brought together and concentrated "the chief good and the laws of our being, which wander idle and forlorn over the surface of the moral world, and often appear to diverge from each other."[42] Christianity thus sustained and completed the moral law that the natural religion of conscience had first, but deficiently, impressed upon humankind.

In "Obedience to God the Way to Faith in Christ," preached on October 31, 1830, Newman urged that the Gospel is "but the completion and perfection of that religion which natural conscience teaches." Consequently, it was a mistake to believe "that strict obedience is not necessary under the Gospel, and that something else will be taken, for Christ's sake, in the stead of it." Some Christians erroneously assumed "that Christ came to gain for us easier terms of admittance into heaven than we had before." Instead, the way to Christ lay through obedience. In this respect Newman explained, "The Gospel leaves us just where it found us, as regards the necessity of our obedience to God; that Christ has not obeyed instead of us, but that obedience is quite as imperative as if Christ had never come; nay, is pressed upon us with additional sanctions; the difference being, not that He relaxes the strict rule of keeping His commandments, but that He give us spiritual aids, which we have not except through Him, to enable us to keep them."[43] The Christian must come to God through keeping his commandments. Those who have lived openly in sin must come to a repentance that must occur over time as they learn to walk in obedience.

Pursuing a moral rigor that appeared in Froude's sermons of the same years, Newman sharply rejected equating the life of obedience with any "sudden change of heart" or sudden emotional conversion associated with so much evangelical preaching. He denounced "the false doctrines now so common" that encouraged the irreligious to "look forward for a possible day when God will change their hearts by His own mere power, in spite of themselves, and who thus get rid of the troublesome thought that now they are in a state of fearful peril." Still others living "by a dreadful deceit of Satan" believed themselves personally unable to follow divine commandments, thinking that they "must wait for the successive motions of God's grace to excite them to action." This approach to Christianity, involving much talk of religion but little obedience to God's will, led people to embrace "a self-indulgent life" within which "they veil their self-indulgence from themselves by a notion of their superior religious knowledge, and by their faculty of speaking fluently in Scripture language." With an eye to radical evangelical practices in his own day, Newman observed, "Men fancy that certain strange effects on their minds—strong emotion, restlessness, and an unmanly excitement and extravagance of thought and feeling—are tokens of that inscrutable Spirit, who is given us, not to make us something *other than* men, but to make us, what without His gracious aid we never shall be, upright, self-mastering men, humble and obedient children of our Lord and Saviour." Newman returned to the theme of the deceit and falseness of a religion of feeling in "Religious Emotion" of March 27, 1831, where he decried the mistaking of "mere transient emotion, or mere good thoughts, for obedience" as a "deceit" and "a counterfeit earnestness" often misleading men "from the plain path of obedience." Transient religious feelings might or might not accompany obedience, whereas good actions were "the fruits of faith" that assure us "that we are Christ's." He warned his congregation that they would take more comfort on their deathbeds reflecting "on one deed of self-denying mercy, purity, or humility" than by recollecting "the shedding of many tears, and the recurrence of frequent transports, and much spiritual exultation."[44]

In "The Religious Use of Excited Feelings" of July 3, 1831, Newman denied that religious emotion, feeling and sensibility could lead people to change their ways or to do their duty to God. He deplored the contemporary emphasis on "impassioned thoughts, high aspirations, sublime imaginings" which had "no strength in them" and could "no more make a man obey consistently" than they could "move mountains." True repentance must be the result not of feelings and passion but "of a settled conviction" of guilt and "a deliberate resolution" to leave sin and serve God. Newman asserted, "Conscience, and Reason in subjection to Conscience, *these* are those powerful instruments (under grace) which change a man." He admitted that "earnest, ardent feelings" might remove the "*grievousness*" associated with "the *beginnings* of obedience," but people reveling in emotion alone confused the temporary feelings intended by God "to encourage them to set about their reformation" with "the substance and real excellence of religion." Moreover, such religious feelings could easily become an end in themselves as people too easily learned to "indulge themselves in these warm feelings for their own sake, resting in them as if they were then engaged in a religious exercise, and boasting of them as if they were an evidence of their own exalted spiritual state; not *using them* (the one only thing they ought to do), using them as an incitement to *deeds* of love, mercy, truth, meekness, holiness."[45] This conflation of ends and means served to avoid the necessity of habitual obedience.

Perhaps with his experience of Francis in mind, Newman saw the evangelical religion of feeling as containing within itself the seeds of future skepticism and as fostering the pursuit of infinite religious innovation. As religious excitement diminished, those who had confused it with genuine religion might believe they were "losing their faith, and falling into sin again." Thereafter they might eschew religious obedience "as a mere un-enlightened morality" and "seek for potent stimulants to sustain their minds in that state of excitement which they have been taught to consider the essence of a religious life, and which they cannot produce by the means which before excited them." In pursuit of new, ongoing religious stimulation they would "have recourse to new doctrines, or follow strange teachers, in order that they may dream on in this their artificial devotion" and thus evade the conviction of sin that might lead them to obedience and hence to a true understanding of the Christian faith.[46]

Never did Newman more forcefully summarize this outlook than a little more than a year later, on November 4, 1832, when he declared to his congregation: "Praise to the obedient, punishment on the transgressor, is the revealed rule of God's government from the beginning to the consummation of all things. The fall of Adam did not abolish, nor do the provisions of Gospel-mercy supersede it."[47] Here and elsewhere in his sermons of this period, Newman's voice from St. Mary's pulpit resembled that of an eldest child insisting upon order among disobedient younger siblings in hope of restoring to himself the primary and once exclusive love of parents disrupted by the advent of those new children. He was recalling the necessity of obedience over and against what he may have regarded as too lenient parental treatment of young siblings, and most particularly his family's (and especially his mother's) continuing love and concern for Charles and Francis. Beyond presenting an alternative to evangelical religion, his sermons expressed a profound personal wish that within his family his own obedience might receive praise and the willfulness of his brothers be condemned.

Reflecting on his preaching of the early 1830s, Newman portrayed himself to one friend as "up in arms against the Shelleyism of the day, which resolves religion into feeling, and makes it possible for bad men to have holy thoughts." He saw subjective religious emotion and religious egoism, which he here associated with both the emotion and political radicalism of the poet Shelley, as "not worth a straw" and being even "pernicious, if it does not lead to *practice*." The chief benefit of good thoughts was their capacity to be "taken as a means to exact *obedience*." In 1835, writing to Samuel Wilberforce, Newman admitted emphasizing sanctification over justification in his sermons because he had been convinced *"that we required the Law* not the Gospel in this age—we want rousing—we want the claims of duty and the details of obedience set before us strongly." He told Wilberforce, "In truth men *do* think that a saving state is one, where the mind merely looks to Christ—a virtual antinomianism." Later that year Newman confessed to Wilberforce that his most recent volume of sermons "on the whole induces fear, and depression" because what was required of Christians is "a continual Ash-wednesday."[48]

What so profoundly offended Newman about evangelicalism within both the larger British religious landscape and his own family was what he regarded as its easy repentance and its inherently optimistic view of human nature. In a sermon of April 1832, Newman presented human beings in both barbarous and non-Christian civilized societies as having rejected such a view of the human situation because their own consciences had recognized the presence of evil in their lives. Overwhelmed with guilt about their disobedience to conscience, they had embraced all manner of public and private devices, including elaborate rituals and self-torment, to assuage that guilt, and those practices had constituted "man's truest and best religion, *before* the Gospel shines on him." Although later Christians had regarded such behavior as superstition, Newman thought it might still retain value as he strikingly announced, "They who are not superstitious without the Gospel, will not be religious with it: and I would that even in us, who have the Gospel, there were more of superstition than there is; for much is it to be feared that our security about ourselves arises from defect in self-knowledge rather than in fullness of faith, and that we appropriate to ourselves promises which we cannot read."[49] However distasteful or painful, superstitious practices in pursuit of obedience bore witness to the natural conscience persuading human beings of their disobedience to God. Without such persuasion, even persons benefiting from the Christian dispensation, which perfected the insights of natural religion, could not become genuinely religious.

Newman contrasted his stark religion of conscience with what he regarded as the more optimistic religious views of his own day, all of which he subsumed under the single term Socinianism, which remained otherwise undefined. Among those outlooks he included the beliefs that divine government is benevolent, that evil is remedial and sin venial, that "repentance is a sufficient atonement" for sin, that the moral sense is an instinct of benevolence, and that "doctrinal opinions do not influence our character or prospects, nor deserve our serious attention." Newman associated these beliefs with the "false cheerfulness, and the ill-founded hope, and the blind charitableness" of what he termed "the man of the world." His specific targets were the natural theologians, identified in later notes with William Paley, who in seeing creation working toward universal good and happiness had fostered "an unreal and unpractical view of human nature."[50]

In "The Religion of the Day," preached on August 26, 1832, Newman explored affinities between that widespread natural theology and evangelical religion. He defined the "religion of the world" as a protean tendency that from age to age stressed one element of the Gospel over all others and "in reality attends to no part at all." In his own time Newman saw this "religion of the world" as having taken "the brighter side of the Gospel" while forgetting "all darker, deeper views of man's condition and prospects" and eschewing religious austerity. He pointed to certain unnamed contemporary religious persons speculating on the millennium as having "more or less identified their vision of Christ's kingdom with the elegance and refinement of mere human civilization" and as having "hailed every evidence of improved decency, every wholesome civil regulation, every beneficent and enlightened act of state policy, as signs of their coming Lord." Such persons looked to natural theology and human enlightenment rather than to Scripture and conscience to understand God's will. Furthermore, not caring about the means for achieving reformist ends, they cooperated with men "who openly profess unchristian principles."[51]

Criticizing this rational, optimistic evangelical religion, Newman declared that he did "not shrink from uttering" his "firm conviction, that it would be a gain to this country, were it vastly more supersticious, more bigoted, more gloomy, more fierce in its religion, than at present it shows itself to be." He equated the religion of the present age with "the sleep of Jonah" in the whale, which under the appearance of peace concealed the great danger around him. Rejecting the evangelical theology that produced a similar false assurance and confidence, Newman told his congregation, "I do not wish you to be able to point to any particular time when you renounced the world (as it is called), and were converted; this is a deceit. Fear and love must go together; always fear, always love, to your dying day." Miserable as were the superstitions of the dark ages and the tortures of the heathen of the East, Newman thought it better "to torture the body all one's days, and to make this life a hell upon earth, than to remain in a brief tranquility here, till the pit at length open under us, and awakens us to an eternal fruitless consciousness and remorse." Christians might properly comfort themselves with knowledge of Christ's desire for their salvation, his death for them, and their baptism. "But," Newman firmly added, "at the same time, you never can be sure of salvation, while you are here; and therefore you must always fear while you hope."[52] Thus a sermon that commenced with criticism of natural theology closed with a rejection of the optimistic assurance of salvation that in one way or another so much evangelical religion had promised for almost a century.

Both evangelicalism and natural theology embodied what Newman in late 1831 termed "the usurpations of Reason" that had commenced with the Reformation and that informed a more general Baconianism.[53] Evangelicals in general, and more particularly recent radical evangelicals, believed that through the empirical study of Scripture the human mind could probe and solve divine mysteries. The natural theologians believed that they could achieve the same end through the empirical study of nature. Consequently, both diminished the authority of the church as a traditional teacher of religious truth. For Newman, the evangelical gospel of easy repentance and assurance paralleled natural theologians' rationalizing the evil in the world that required repentance. In this regard both evangelicals in the Bible Society and natural theologians in the British Association embodied "the religion of the day" as they espoused the values and embraced the vehicles of commercial society in pursuit of religious agendas that self-consciously manifested themselves in the public sphere, as opposed to the private sphere of conscience.

Newman directly criticized the great evangelical reform societies as providing the means to such false religious assurance by substituting commercial transactions for genuine obedience. As he told Pope in 1834, "There is a great tendency in mankind to get rid of habitual duties, and substitute occasional practices. The Bible etc Societies encourage this—the giving a guinea being a substitute for personal holiness." Newman saw the cheap currency of commercialized evangelical religion driving out of circulation the sound currency of personal holiness through obedience. Similarly, Newman directly connected the same evangelical impulse with that broad, diffuse religious heresy that he denoted as Socinianism. In February 1835 he told James Stephen of his conviction that the spirit of evangelicalism "tends to liberalism and Socinianism." Newman further condemned the "corrupt" school of evangelicalism as "a system of doctrine which eats out the heart of godliness, where truer and holier instincts do not exclude it from producing its legitimate results." Not long thereafter Newman denounced the evangelicals to Samuel Wilberforce: "Rightly or wrongly, *I think they tend as a body to Socinianism.*"[54]

ANCIENT ARIANS AND MODERN EVANGELICALS

Newman expanded his public crusade against evangelical religion begun in St. Mary's pulpit by writing *The Arians of the Fourth Century*, commissioned in 1831 and published in late 1833. Throughout this volume, as in his contemporaneous sermons, Newman presupposed a natural primitive revelation promulgated before the rise of the Christian Church with its "*authoritative documents* of truth, and *appointed channels* of communication" with God. Extending the concept appearing in his sermon of 1830, he identified a "*Dispensation of Paganism*" that denoted a "vague and unconnected family of religious truths, originally from God, but sojourning without the sanction of miracle, or a definite home, as pilgrims up and down the world, discernible and separable from the corrupt legends with which they are mixed, by the spiritual mind alone." Christ and the apostles had proclaimed a new dispensation that supplemented and completed the pagan dispensation. According to Newman, however, the early Church had long hesitated before enunciating a formal public creed because the Fathers had realized that "when confessions do not exist, the mysteries of divine truth, instead of being exposed to the gaze of the profane and uninstructed, are kept hidden in the bosom of the Church, far more faithfully than is otherwise possible; and reserved by a private teaching, through the channel of her ministers, as rewards in due measure and season, for those who are prepared to profit by them; for those, i.e. who are diligently passing through the successive stages of faith and obedience." In consequence, the primitive church had wisely refrained from instructing believers in the Lord's Prayer, the creed, and the full doctrines of the Trinity, incarnation, and atonement, as well as withholding access to the eucharist until shortly before baptism. Before encountering those spiritual riches, believers in antiquity had received instruction in the doctrines of repentance, pardon, the necessity of good works, baptismal regeneration, and the immortality of the soul. Through this "*disciplina arcani*" the ancient church had thus established moral discipline and self-restraint on the part of believers before providing instruction in the most sacred doctrines.[55]

With modern evangelical practices clearly in mind, Newman suggested that these practices of the early church had avoided "much of that mischievous fanaticism" which "at present abounds from the vanity of men, who think that they can explain the sublime doctrines and exuberant promises of the Gospel, before they have yet learned to know themselves and to discern the holiness of God, under the preparatory discipline of the Law and of Natural Religion." Echoing his letter of 1830 to his brother Francis, Newman criticized the "very many sincere Christians of the present day, who consider that the evangelical doctrines are the appointed instruments of conversion, and, as such, exclusively attended with the Divine blessing" and who "appeal, not to Scripture, but to the stirring *effects* of this (so-called) Gospel preaching, and to the inefficiency . . . of mere exhortations respecting the benevolence and mercy of God, the necessity of repentance, the rights of conscience, and the obligation of obedience." But Newman also emphasized the inadequacy of Scripture in and of itself to convey the message of revealed religion and pointed to "the obscurity of the inspired documents," the unsystematic nature of both Scripture itself and the doctrinal truths embedded therein, "the incommunicable nature of God," and the "mysteriousness of the doctrine" of the Trinity.[56]

Newman then portrayed the emergence of Arianism itself, the foremost heresy of antiquity, as closely paralleling the rise of modern evangelical religion from the time of Wesley onward. Newman cited Tertullian's criticism of heretics who allowed believers and catechumens to meet and pray together, who discussed religious doctrine in the presence of nonbelievers, who regarded catechumens as full of faith before they were properly instructed, and who permitted women to teach and argue about the faith, and even to baptize. Methodist and other evangelical groups had embraced one or more of all these practices. Then claiming that "the heretical spirit is ever one and the same in its various forms," Newman described specific actions of Arius, who, again resembling modern evangelical Christians, threw "out his questions as a subject for debate; and at once formed crowds of controversialists, from those classes who were the least qualified or deserving to take part in the discussion," as well as "composing and setting to music, songs on the subject of his doctrine for the use of the rudest classes of society, with a view of familiarizing them to it." Furthermore, Arius himself, like Wesley and later moderate evangelicals, had been "distinguished by a certain reserve and loftiness in his personal deportment," only to be succeeded by "less refined successors." Against this assault, the ancient church, as might have been said of the modern English Church of the eighteenth century, had difficulty defending itself because of "the very sacredness and refinement of its discipline."[57]

In their effort to erect "a witness for the truth" that might stand "against the lying spirit which was abroad in the Church," the Nicene Fathers could not simply appeal to Scripture because its words "were the very subject in controversy." In line with his criticism of the Bible Society, Newman decried as endangering true faith the search for nominal unity under the banner of "assent to the text of Scripture." Such mistaken, if well intentioned, efforts to conceal fundamental differences allowed enemies of the church to weaken it by persuading "us to fraternize with those who, differ-

ing from us in essentials, yet happen, in the excursive range of opinion
somewhere to intersect that path of faith, which centres in supreme and
zealous devotion to the service of God." Clergy should stand against innovation and define precisely the grounds of Christian communion whether
the words of such definition were or were not contained in Scripture. Possibly echoing the second edition of Pusey's *Enquiry* or even Blomfield's letter
to Pusey, Newman urged that only a formal creed defining the faith could
"give security to the Church, as far as may be, that the subscriber take the
peculiar view of it which alone is the true one." Later Newman admitted
some difficulty in permanently devising such a creed when he observed in
regard to antiquity, "There will, of course, be differences of opinion, in
deciding how much of the ecclesiastical doctrine . . . was derived from direct
Apostolical Tradition, and how much was the result of intuitive spiritual
perception in scripturally-informed and deeply religious minds."[58] The
latter clause opened the possibility of considerable indeterminacy in creed
and practice, a possibility that Newman was to explore fulsomely over the
course of the next decade.

Throughout *The Arians of the Fourth Century* Newman's targeted enemy
was an ancient religious party that time and again he equated with the
modern evangelicals. Toward the close of the volume he pointed to "the
present perils" of the English Church as bearing "a marked resemblance to
those of the fourth century." On both occasions there existed "the prospect,
and partly the presence in the Church, of an Heretical Power enthralling it,
exerting a varied influence and a usurped claim in the appointment of her
functionaries, and interfering with the management of her internal affairs."
He took comfort that "should the hand of Satan press us sore, our Athanasius and Basil will be given us in their destined season, to break the bonds of
the Oppressor, and let the captives go free."[59] Significantly, Newman used
the term Heretical Power precisely to denote his modern religious enemy as
one internal to the English Church and not as an external political or secular opposition. His remarks furthermore retain a certain ambiguity as to
whether the liberation of the captives will free them to dwell inside or
outside of the church.

In late October 1832, Hugh James Rose and Archdeacon W. R. Lyall, the
high churchmen who had commissioned Newman's study, rejected, or as
Newman later wrote "plucked," the manuscript though with somewhat differing degrees of disapproval.[60] Lyall thought Newman's views overly favorable to a Roman Catholic outlook, objected to the concepts of the *disciplina
arcani* and the dispensation of paganism, and rejected the contention that

the ante-Nicene fathers had not spoken openly of the atonement and Christ's divinity. Though concerned with a possible drift toward Romanism, Rose and Lyall were even more concerned about a drift into doctrinal indeterminacy on Newman's part, which Rose had earlier sensed in the first edition of Pusey's *Enquiry*. High churchmen had long opposed evangelicalism, but had done so largely on the basis of its ecclesiastical irregularities and ecumenical sympathies. What Lyall and Rose confronted in Newman was a profound critique of evangelical religion tied to an alternative understanding of Christianity that opened the path to a theological indeterminacy every bit as disturbing to them as evangelicalism itself. They did eventually aid the publication of Newman's book, but not as part of a series bearing their imprimatur. Newman now stood rebuffed by Oriel Noetics, Oxford evangelicals, and influential high churchmen as well as by his two brothers.

MEDITERRANEAN MOMENTS AND AN APOSTOLIC BROTHERHOOD ENVISIONED

About a month and a half after Rose and Lyall rejected his manuscript, Newman set sail with the Froude family on a seven-month Mediterranean journey. The weeks of travel to Gibraltar, Malta, Corfu, Sicily, and Rome allowed Newman and Froude to speculate broadly about the Church of England and contemporary Christianity in general. On their arrival in Italy, Newman and Froude encountered a Roman Catholic Church that in the wake of the wars of the French Revolution and Napoleon had experienced almost forty years of pillage, turmoil, and uncertain restoration. On February 28, writing to his mother from Naples, Newman interpreted the plight of that church as an indication that Satan had been "let out of prison to range the whole earth again." In the midst of his description of the Italian Church injured by clerical "infidelity and profligacy," as well as much poverty resulting from confiscation, he mentioned the Whig Irish Temporalities bill, which he equated with such confiscation and robbery. Then envisioning the entire Western world as "tending toward some dreadful crisis," Newman voiced the hope "that England is after all to be the 'Land of Saints' in this dark hour, and her Church the salt of the earth." Yet he found the English churches in Italy deeply troubled, with one congregation having just experienced a formal secession of members who had chosen their own "*preacher*."[61] Even in Italy he could not escape the specter and reality of radical evangelicalism.

While residing in Rome, Newman's epistolary meditations on the domestic English religious scene reached near paranoid dimensions. Expressing anxiety over what people in England thought of the "cursed Irish spoliation bill," he told Henry Wilberforce that it was "useful" to dwell on the problems of the Roman Catholic Church in Italy "because it is so likely to be the case with ourselves at home." He pondered that he "should feel a great deal at being ejected from St Mary's, and seeing another person appointed to it," and trusted that "our Clergy may quit" their livings "like men—if some of the Bishops would but give the signal." Newman could thus imagine bishops, perhaps similar to the seventeenth-century Nonjurors, leading clergy to leave their benefices and then presumably establishing some alternative ecclesiastical foundation. Continued concern over the Irish legislation led him to tell George Ryder, "For myself, I am perhaps not sorry, in a bad matter, to see things proceed so quickly to a crisis—since it is very annoying and disheartening to linger on in an ague, and to feel every one around you neither hot nor cold. The time is coming when every one must choose his side. On the other hand, I am much afraid we shall not know our own principles, if we are not allowed a little time to get them up." Later in March, having heard that Keble was roused against the Irish Temporalities Bill, he predicted that "he will prove a second St Ambrose."[62] In other letters from Rome, Newman expressed hope that the clergy in Ireland would act with more heroism than Italian priests whom he criticized for passivity, formality, lack of respect for their ecclesiastical duties, and loss of respect by their congregations.

During these same weeks, confused, contradictory thoughts about the Roman Catholic Church virtually overwhelmed Newman. In criticism resembling that previously leveled against evangelicalism, he faulted the fasting practices of the Greek Church and the Latin Masses of the Roman Church as providing "a substitute apparently for moral obedience, and an opiate to the conscience." He further decried "the Saint worship [of the Roman Church], which is demoralizing in the same sense that Polytheism was," but explained that such worship "is not the Church's *act*, (tho' it in fact sanctions it) but the people's corruption of what is good—the honor due to Saints—whereas the doctrines of the Mass and Purgatory are not perversions but inventions." In March, despite these strong reservations, Newman speculated to Pusey about a possible future reunion of the English and Roman Churches, but immediately qualified his thoughts, claiming that the Roman Church would have to reform itself. He declared that "no means short of some terrible convulsion" could achieve such reform and then concluded, "Nothing short of great suffering, as by fire, can melt us together in England one with another." Later, after his and Froude's unsatisfactory conversation with Wiseman on April 6, he told his friend Christie, "A union with Rome, while it is what it is, is impossible; it is a dream. As to the individual members of the cruel church, who can but love and feel for them?" Finally, to his sister he announced, "Oh that Rome were not Rome; but I seem to see as clear as day that a union with her is *impossible*. She is the cruel Church—asking of us impossibilities, excommunicating us for disobedience, and now watching and exulting over our approaching overthrow."[63] The contemporary Roman Catholic Church clearly was not an alternative for Newman in the spring of 1833.

At exactly the same time, however, there arose in Newman's mind strong ambivalence about Protestantism and the English Reformation fostered by conversations with Froude. Newman wrote to Henry Jenkyns, "I do not like to talk of the lamentable mixture of truth with error which Romanism exhibits—the corruption of the highest and noblest views and principles, far higher than we Protestants have, with malignant poisons." He told his sisters, "I *do not* like Cr[anmer]'s character—his death must ever make him an object of reverence—but his conduct! his marriage! his taking part against Catherine! I cannot bear it." He suggested that the devout Roman seminarians "may be as near truth (at the least) as that Mr B. [Burgess] whom I like less and less every day." Burgess was a Church of England clergyman ministering in Rome whom Newman had previously described as "one of the most perfect watering place preachers I ever heard, most painfully so . . . and a true specimen of the experimentally abortive style" of preaching marked by "mischievous semi-evangelical" doctrine.[64] Consequently, when in mid-April the Froudes headed northward, Newman, who retraced his steps toward southern Italy and Sicily, left Rome profoundly skeptical about the character and adequacy of both Roman Catholicism and Protestantism.

Throughout the weeks in Rome, Newman had begun to imagine himself or other clergy like him experiencing some kind of persecution resulting in loss of standing and property that would justify their undertaking a new religious departure. This anxiety served to justify in Newman's mind his return to the warmth and beauty of southern Italy and Sicily. He told Walter John Trower, an Oriel friend, that he would never have another holiday because evil days lay before the English Church and difficulty for its clergy. He further declared that because the legislation of recent years had disconnected both Tories and Whigs from the Church, it was no longer "the duty of a Churchman to be a Politician." Drawn to neither party, he wrote, "I shall be neuter, with a tendency, which may grow, towards agitating for a more effectual Church discipline, for the independence of Bishops of the Crown which has now become but a Creature of an Infidel Parliament, and for the restoration of the practice of excommunication."[65] Newman's use of the term *neuter*, rather than *neither* or *neutral*, was perhaps not insignificant. The word *neuter* did have contemporary usage denoting neutrality in political or military conflict, but Newman also fully understood that he, unlike the married Cranmer for whom he had expressed contempt to his sister, would undertake his agitation for what he would later term a Second Reformation as a celibate, monastic clergyman.

Newman had first established that role as a celibate clergyman within the Oriel fellowship, and he carried with him on the Mediterranean voyage considerable concern over the spring Oriel fellowship elections during which he would be absent. One of the candidates was Frederic Rogers, the last of his Oriel tutees and a student who, like his brother Francis, had achieved a Double First in 1832.[66] Concern over Rogers's election, as well as his other by now long-standing angers over Oriel, came to the fore in Newman's mind in a dream that occurred during the night of April 16, while he was in Naples waiting for a ship to Sicily. The dream so powerfully affected him that he felt the need to recount it in extensive detail the next day in a letter to his mother.

With travel expenses, family finances, and no doubt his recently sacrificed tutorial income on his mind, Newman assured his mother that the delay in Naples incurred no significant additional cost, though his hotel did command a higher price for meals than the one he and the Froudes had chosen a few weeks earlier. His indulging in good dining and new foods stood at odds with his more general concern about simplicity in meals and his later practices of fasting. At such an expensive dinner the previous evening, he had found himself tempted by a piece of cheese and "had in consequence a nightmare dream when I went to bed." The nightmare commenced with the sense of "a sort of weight and a horror" falling upon him as he found himself in the Oriel College Tower, where the fellows were attending the annual audit of the college accounts, an occasion familiar from his time as college treasurer and as a recipient of a generous portion of college income through his fellowship, vicarship, and former tutorship. Henry Jenkyns, one of the fellows, and Provost Hawkins had been quarreling. Hawkins left the room, and Jenkyns "to expedite matters had skipped on in the accounts and entered some items without the P.'s superintendence." As the dream continued, Newman shook hands with Dornford, his former associate in the tutorial program, and then with G. A. Denison and W. J. Copleston, two of the new tutors now receiving income that had once been his. Copleston then introduced him to two new fellows who were "two of the most clumsy awkward looking chaps I ever set eyes on" and who had "awkward unintelligible names." Newman "with great grief of heart, but a most unembarrassed smiling manner" shook hands with them and chatted with the other fellows "while longing to get away and with a sickness within me." Once he did get away, he could "find no means of relief" as he searched in vain for his friends Froude and J. F. C. Christie. Thus frustrated, Newman found himself wishing "to retire to the shrubberies, which were those of Ham," his residence near Richmond from 1804 to 1807, which in boyhood dreams he had equated with heaven. Newman felt that this retreat to Ham would allow him to recover from the previous scene. Instead he again found himself in Oriel rooms, where he encountered continual interruptions from a father and son "intending to stand for some Sicilian (which I thought meant Merton) scholarship," then "a brace of Gentlemen Commoners with hideous faces" even though he was no longer a tutor, and, finally his "companion down here from Rome," who "made his appearance with a lady under his arm," whom Newman knew well but in the dream did not recognize. He told his mother, "This was part of the dream—but only part—and all, I say, so vivid—who shall say a bit of cheese has not the poetical faculty? I hope simply poetical, and not the historical." Convincing himself that Rogers and not those two ugly fellows had been elected to Oriel, Newman reported having "grown calm out of spite" and becoming "now so confident R [Frederic Rogers] has succeeded, that I do not think about it."[67]

The dream of April 16 and the extensive letter of the following day to his mother wove together numerous strands of Newman's anxieties and angers regarding his family, Oriel, and the English Church. In the letter he associated a defensive account of his indulging in a very good meal with a dream about the Oriel audit, which determined each fellow's annual income and the payment to be allotted to the college tutors—payment he would no longer receive. In the dream Henry Jenkyns, who had supported Hawkins during the tutorial dispute and had again supported the provost's authority the previous summer over issues raised regarding Newman's assuming the Oriel deanship, quarrels with Hawkins, perhaps suggesting Newman's wish to find Jenkyns defending him or at least see Hawkins lose his allies.[68] The provost's departure and the moving on with accounts may indicate Newman's wish that his quarrel with Hawkins be settled by Hawkins's vanishing from the scene and someone changing the books and perhaps restoring his forfeited income. Newman must also have had similar wishes about his father and his father's finances and reputation. Within the dream Newman shakes hands with fellows who had assumed the tutorial responsibilities from which he had been ousted. They in turn introduce him to two new singularly awkward fellows who resemble new siblings to the Oriel family. Their entrance upon the scene causes Newman grief of heart, but he hypocritically welcomes them; then, feeling sick, he rapidly seeks to escape. In his own family the infidelity of Charles and the radical evangelicalism of Francis had similarly sickened, embarrassed, and appalled him, facts that made him wish them ugly in his mother's sight. Both brothers had also cost him money. Newman seeks refuge where as a child he had found peace, safety, and security, his father's garden at Ham, a place recalled from his years of three to six, when his siblings were still too weak to challenge him significantly and when it might have appeared to him that they would never really be able to do so. It was also a home enjoyed by the Newman family before their father's financial difficulties commenced.

Failing in that effort to escape to Ham, Newman finds himself again in Oriel but now interrupted by a father and son seeking a scholarship outside Oriel, then by hideous students approaching him even though he is no longer a tutor, and finally by his hired traveling servant, accompanied by an unidentifiable woman. Both the awkwardness of the two new fellows and the ugliness of the two prospective students may well suggest Newman's anger at the married Hawkins (perhaps the servant and unidentifiable woman) and his spiteful wish that with the rejection of his tutorial plan and his loss of personal income, Oriel might experience decline into awkward fellows, ugly undergraduates, families seeking scholarships in other colleges, and a married provost transformed into a servant.

Thereafter, having been genuinely frightened by the plethora of foreboding elements in the dream and the feelings of angry spitefulness so released, Newman states that he hopes its vividness relates to poetry rather than to history. He hoped, of course, that Rogers and not two ugly men had been chosen by Oriel. But on another level, he may have hoped the dream poetical so that he could distance himself from the feelings that the dream indicated of enormous anger and spite about Oriel, feelings which to no small extent paralleled those toward his family. In hoping that Rogers had succeeded, Newman was hoping that he might be able to embrace a brother Oriel fellow who would treat him differently than other Oriel fellows and his own brothers had done. The advent of Rogers, then a grateful former student, or persons like Rogers would have allowed Newman to break out of the personally frustrating and disappointed sibling or siblinglike relationships he had experienced first in his family and later in Oriel. Indeed, in pushing Rogers for the fellowship, Newman was selecting his own brother fellow as he had not been able to select the brothers in his own family.

Issues of family, Oriel, and brotherhood also appear in a second letter of April 17, 1833. Writing to H. A. Woodgate, another Oriel fellow, Newman again expressed apprehension about the recent Oriel election and spitefulness toward Hawkins. Commenting that Hawkins was about to become a father, Newman hoped that he would have twins followed by ten more children to distract him from Oriel business. In the dream, of course, Hawkins had abandoned college business. Turning to current ecclesiastical politics, Newman declared that supporters of the church should avoid half measures and urged that bishops should have the power of excommunication and should not be appointed by the Crown, which under current circumstances could not function independently. Then returning to the idea, first mentioned in March 1829, about the need for something resembling Roman Catholic friars in the Church of England, Newman asked Woodgate, "Why will you not be in the humour to devote yourself to the Apostolical cause? I do not wish you to come back to College, but to join the brotherhood of those who wish a return to the primitive state of the Church, when it was not a mere instrument of civil government, which it approaches to be now." Imagining this brotherhood as an ecclesiastically irregular organization, Newman explained, "I almost think the time has come to form clubs and societies under title of Apostolical—that we may have some approximation towards a system of discipline. They should be somewhat on the plan of the Temperance Societies, with the professed object of strengthening the Church, and the promise to disband whenever the Church has recovered its power of governing itself."[69] Newman thus associated his apostolical brotherhood with an evangelical-like organization, suggesting that henceforth disciplined, reforming priests of apostolical outlook and sentiment could not resort to traditional modes of high-church organization and protest.

This desire for some kind of brotherhood in which members would defer to his judgment and leadership had become one of the most important forces in Newman's life. By 1833 his hope for a settled home among Oriel brothers had floundered as various fellows had married, quarreled over politics and religion, and then abandoned him over the tutorial project and other college matters. He still hoped to recoup his losses in Oriel through the election of new fellows such as Rogers, but by the spring of 1833 he also had come to speculate upon a new brotherhood founded on Apostolic principles.

On April 19, having posted the letters to his mother and Woodgate the previous day, Newman departed Naples for Sicily, where he soon fell near fatally ill with fever. Both at the time and through a series of later recountings, Newman understood the fearful experience of this illness and his recovery as a providential sign that he must redirect the course of his life. He did so upon his delayed return to England in early July.

THE TRACTS AND ANCIENT MONASTICISM

Newman's arrival in Oxford on July 9 coincided with the last days of debate over the Irish Temporalities Bill, during which Keble on July 14 preached his sermon on national apostasy. This sermon was the first that Newman, still weak and temporarily hairless from his Sicilian fever, heard after coming home. His Italian meditations upon continental anticlericalism, his tendency to interpret contemporary events in categories of apocalyptic prophecy, his brooding over Oriel and his family, his looking for new direction in his life after the end of his tutorial career, and his conviction that he had been spared death for a providential purpose allowed Keble's antierastian message to strike him with particular force.

As has long been noted, virtually no one else at the time attached much importance to Keble's sermon.[70] Such dismissive views seek to credit traditional high churchmen with having previously nurtured an Anglican ethos upon which the Tractarians drew and then besmirched by their later radical actions. That Keble's sermon was neither much noticed nor overly original is, however, actually beside the point, for there is no doubt that the sermon did at a particularly crucial moment galvanize Newman's determination to align himself with Froude's rejection of traditional high church reticence and timidity and for them together to craft their own distinctive response to the difficulties confronting the English Church.

The immediate impact of Keble's sermon on Newman received further energy when Froude returned from Rose's Hadleigh conference convinced of the tactical ineptitude of more traditional high churchmen. Newman agreed but argued that for the moment he, Froude, and others of Apostolical outlook must cooperate with Rose, who did not favor disestablishment but hoped for some kind of synod that might govern the church more or less independent of state interference. By early August 1833 Newman, Keble, and Froude, with Palmer as a hesitating ally, had decided to launch a secret association of clergy (which always existed more in their own minds than in any kind of concrete reality) to press theological issues in preparation for the next session of Parliament. Then on August 8 Keble momentously suggested to Newman that they might "perhaps in tracts and pamphlets" pursue their goals. Explaining the precise ecclesiology that informed their then projected activities, Newman told Charles Golightly, "Our main doctrine is the Apostolical Succession and the exclusive privilege of Bishops and Priests to consecrate the Bread and Wine."[71] The Oxford group intended to oppose formal separation of church and state while at the same time remaining willing to contemplate such a situation. Furthermore, they hoped to make the Church of England more popular, to organize similar societies in other regions, to circulate books and tracts, to prevent heretical appointments to bishoprics, and to prevent Socinian alterations to the Prayer Book, both of the latter two points being a direct slap at evangelicals. The first of the subsequent *Tracts for the Times*, to be more fully explored in chapter 4, appeared that September.

But simultaneously with the appearance of *Tracts for the Times* in the autumn of 1833 Newman also undertook other publications that opened the way for his championing not only a new ecclesiastical politics but also controversial new departures in the devotional and institutional life of the English Church. These departures, like the tracts themselves, were gauged directly to challenge the attractions of evangelical religion as well as to address some of his own most profound inner concerns. All of Newman's writings of late 1833 and early 1834 must be considered in order to grasp the full ambition of his devotional and theological aspirations for the English Church. The tracts constituted only part of the story.

As early as August 5, 1833, before the publication of the first tract, Newman wrote Thomas Mozley about "poking into the Fathers with a hope of rummaging forth passages of history which may prepare the *imaginations* of men for a changed state of things, and also be precedents for our conduct in difficult circumstances."[72] Those circumstances were the anticipated persecution of the English Church and confiscation of its property that Newman had pondered in his Italian correspondence. This patristic study resulted in the first of what eventually became twenty "Letters on the Church of the Fathers," which between 1833 and 1837 Newman published anonymously in the *British Magazine*. In this series, as in the *Arians of the Fourth Century*, which he was carrying through the press during these same months in late 1833, antiquity provided materials to rethink modern religious issues, in this instance religious authority disentangled from establishment and an ascetic religion of obedience sharply contrasting with the evangelical religion of feeling.

In the earliest of these articles, which appeared in October 1833, Newman recounted the history of St. Ambrose in Milan to demonstrate "by *what instruments* the authority of religion is to be supported, when the protection and recommendation of the government are withdrawn." Both St. Ambrose in Milan and St. Basil in Caesarea had through "their popularity with the laity and the vigour of their discipline" successfully resisted Arian clergy, whom Newman's *Arians of the Fourth Century* equated with evangelicals, as well as an Arian sovereign, a situation not all that different from that Newman saw prevailing under the reformed Parliament. Those two ancient saints had demonstrated that direct resistance to powerful governments achieved more politically than accommodation and compliance. At the same time their lives proved that bishops promoting discipline and apostolicity must necessarily expect to be regarded as turbulent disturbers of the peace.[73]

Newman, however, reserved his warmest praise not for St. Basil's politics but for his founding of monasteries as havens for the Catholic faith during politically tempestuous times and for his and St. Gregory's emphasis on celibacy. Newman championed monasticism throughout "The Church of the Fathers," describing it as "a system which, with all its dangers . . . has undoubtedly some especial place in the providential conduct of our dispensation." He presented monasteries as institutions preserving a kind of saving remnant outside the formal structures of the ancient church and aiding "the maintenance of the truth, at times and places in which the Church had let it slip from her." For Newman, no strong counterarguments or theological presumption should inhibit efforts within the English Church to establish some such subsidiary devotional foundations. The absence of scriptural authority worked against monasticism no more than against other practices that the church embraced. Moreover, even if monasticism were a corruption, it was a corruption from primitive Christianity and had at various times served the faith well. Furthermore, Newman declared, "If people lift up their hands and eyes and cry out this is Popery, I beg to ask them in which of the Articles monasticism is condemned? and, since I do not force them to agree with me, I claim that liberty of 'private judgment' in indifferentials which I accord to them."[74] Within Protestant countries, Newman contended, the desire to achieve such serious religious devotion drove persons into Dissent and separatism from the established churches. He also suggested that the Nonjurors would have been wise to have founded such institutions to preserve their outlook.

Despite misgivings about his boldness in pursuing the theme, Newman explored monasticism more fully in his life of St. Antony, the solitary hermit considered the founder of the system. Antony's life demonstrated how the Church of England could channel religious feelings that seemed to have no place in its own system and that led persons into Dissent. Although it was not necessary for Christians to quit their temporal callings and consequent prosperity, Newman contended that "such an abandonment is often allowable, and sometimes praiseworthy," as demonstrated by Christ's injunction to the rich young ruler. Directly attacking the emphasis on commerce, family, and social obligations in evangelical social morality, Newman condemned "ultra-protestantism" for forbidding "all the higher and more noble impulses of the mind" and forcing men to remain in worldly pursuits. By contrast, he explained, "The mind of true catholic Christianity is expansive enough to admit high and low, rich and poor, one with another."[75]

Justifying this embrace of monastic values and settings, Newman claimed that the genius of the early gospel system, which had prevented schism, lay in its permitting broad scope to devotional practices "correcting them the while, purifying them, and reining them in, before they get excessive." What he termed "true catholicism" did not enforce "a strict and rigid creed, extending to the very minutest details of thought, so that a man can never have an opinion of his own" but rather, with a "short and simple" creed, provided "cautious and gentle" decisions that distinguished "between things necessary and things pious to believe, between wilfulness and ignorance," while still asserting "the supremacy of faith, the guilt of unbelief, and the duty of deference to the church." In that manner reason was "brought round against and subdued to the obedience of Christ, at the very time when it seems to be launching forth without chart upon the ocean of speculation." Reason so disciplined opposed "the intolerance of what are called '*sensible* protestants,' as much as that of papists." Such reason also stood "shocked at the tyranny of those who will not let a man do anything out of the way without stamping him with the name of fanatic."[76] In a culturally Protestant fashion, but under the banner of true Catholicism, Newman demanded the liberty to pursue in a relatively isolated celibate setting such devotional practices as he and St. Antony long before him had seen fit for their own lives and for the lives of some others.

Through the life of St. Antony, Newman attempted "to shew how enthusiasm is sobered and refined by being submitted to the discipline of the church, instead of being allowed to run wild externally to it." He reminded readers that monasticism emphasized not only solitude but also austerity and prayers that were certainly Christian. In the present day, Newman speculated, Antony would have become some kind of sectarian because the Church of England provided too little elasticity to accommodate one "panting after some higher rule of life than that which the ordinary forms of society admit of." He challenged his readers to compare Antony's monasticism "with the sort of Christianity into which the unhappy enthusiast of the present day is precipitated by the influences of sectarianism, and he will see how much was gained in purity, as well as unity, to Christianity, by that Monastic system which, with us, is supplied by methodism and dissent." Whatever Newman's reservations about monasticism as a form of popular religion, he preferred its emphasis on self-denial over that modern religion of the day which, as argued in his sermons, made religious faith comfortable.[77]

Newman offered other important comments on monasticism in the second portion of "Home Thoughts Abroad," composed in mid-1835 but not published in the *British Magazine* until March 1836. These remarks appeared in a three-person dialogue contemplating, among other things, the possible future of a reformed English Church no longer dependent upon the English state. In that context, despairing of any serious engagement with the Roman Catholic Church, the speakers discussed a refounding of a true English church on the basis of a purified Protestantism. One participant proposed adopting Catholic practices drawn from the Middle Ages to counter those of Dissent. He provided a list of practices to which, because of the absence of modern clarity about a legitimate priesthood, evangelical Dissenters, as well as some establishment evangelicals, had resorted, thus displacing richer medieval Catholic practices. He explained,

"Texts for every day in the year" are the substitute for the orderly calendar of scripture lessons; prayer meetings stand for the daily service; farewell speeches to missionaries take the place of public ordinations; public meetings for religious oratory, the place of the ceremonies and processions of the middle ages; charitable societies are instead of the strict and enthusiastic Religious Institutions. Men know not of the legitimate priesthood, and therefore are condemned to hang upon the judgment of individual and self-authorized preachers; they defraud their children of the initiatory sacrament, and therefore are forced to invent a rite of dedication instead of it; they put up with legends of private Christians, distinguished for an ambiguous or imperfect piety, narrow-minded in faith, and tawdry and discoloured in their holiness, in the place of the men of God, the meek martyrs, the saintly pastors, the wise and winning teachers of the catholic church.[78]

Practices supposedly recovered from the ancient and medieval church tied to a reassertion of the authority of the priesthood in a reformed English Church might in their own turn displace those shallow substitutes that had arisen during the evangelical revival.

Newman's revived Catholic devotion constituted a nineteenth-century religious experiment intended to counter the eighteenth-century evangelical religious experiment and all that had flowed therefrom. Monasticism lay at the heart of this novel devotional departure. Urging revived medieval practices as "imperatively called for to stop the progress of dissent," the proponent of such change in the dialogue declared, "I conceive you necessarily must have dissent or monachism in a Christian country; so make your choice." There existed in England at present, he asserted, a demand for "some stricter religion than that of the generality of men," but the Church of England did "not provide innocent outlets for the sober relief of feeling and excitement," and consequently people move into Dissent. Echoing Froude's views, the speaker claimed that the living example of self-denying clergy might foster conversions among the urban poor, "just as argument may be accounted the medium of conversion in the case of the educated, or parental authority in the case of the young." Another participant suddenly interjected that this suggestion resembled Roman Catholic monasticism. Without disagreeing, the advocate of monasticism declared that the present generation had not "yet learned the distinction between Popery and Catholicism." He then added, "But, be of good heart, it will learn many things in time."[79]

Although from almost the beginning evangelical commentators, and then later disillusioned high churchmen, regarded the Tractarians as potentially Roman Catholic, the Tractarians at the time and later always denied those accusations, and properly so. The experiment that Newman, Keble, Froude, and Pusey envisioned was not a movement toward Rome, which they thought impossible, but rather the introduction into the Church of England of a whole host of novel devotional practices, including monasticism, that would in their eyes counter evangelicalism and Dissent and provide outlets for their own personal ascetic religious enthusiasm. Such asceticism served to sustain a religion of the private sphere that was the mirror image of the evangelical religion of the public sphere with its powerful engagement with the world. In each case Tractarian asceticism stood rooted in the personal psychological needs of its proponents. Froude and Newman appear to have consistently pursued lives of austere devotion from a very young age. Pusey came to it through the sadnesses of his marriage. Keble fostered such devotion but most certainly after his marriage stood somewhat removed from its pursuit while modestly encouraging others in it.

One contemporary Oriel observer, Blanco White, had understood very early that the issue for Newman and other Tractarians was not sympathy for Roman Catholicism as such but rather a vision of the Christian faith embracing frequent sacraments, intense personal devotion, ascetic exercises, and possibly monasticism. White had become closely acquainted with the future Tractarians while a member of the Oriel Common Room in the late 1820s and early 1830s. White, who eventually became a Unitarian, personified the quintessential early-nineteenth-century religious seeker for whom Christianity represented "neither an *occupation,* nor a *science*" but rather a spiritual and ethical enterprise. With his Tractarian acquaintances in mind, White during 1834 noted in his journal, "It is curious . . . that if we admit the principle that Christian piety consists in devotional *practices,* there is no sound reason to object to Monachism." White further stated,

> Allow the piety which Keble and Newman wish to introduce;—lay it down that having service at church three times a-week is desirable for the promotion of Christian piety, and then exert your ingenuity to discover why we should wish for so much and no more. Of course, cathedral service every day must be still more desirable. Still more desirable would it be to have Monasteries, where Christians should pass their lives in singing psalms, in meditation, in pious reading—to which if they added preaching, and visiting the poor and sick, and fasting, and some other means which their desire of keeping the body under control would easily suggest—we should have Monasteries among Protestants, exactly upon the plan of the Popish Orders.—I conceive, however, that this prospect would not deter my friends.

Despite his own profound anti-Catholicism, White understood that Newman and others did not propose a return to Roman Catholicism itself but rather the establishment within the Church of England of new devotional life with more formal religious observances, possibly including monasticism. For his part White did not see "anything positively wrong in all this" except that in his view as a spiritual religious seeker despairing of the formality of religion, "it is *not Christianity.*" In contrast to "the Oxford High Church Pietists" among his Oriel acquaintances, White believed that the entire life of a Christian, not merely discrete devotional moments, must become "an uninterrupted exercise of piety."[80]

While grasping the monastic imperative in the Tractarian enterprise,

White did not perceive the manner in which that imperative, at least in Newman's thought, tied itself to an apocalyptic vision. Toward the close of the final dialogue of "Home Thoughts Abroad," one of the participants, believing it impossible to achieve an immediate reformation of the English Church, contemplated instead something like a *gathered Church Catholic*, torn from the present privileged establishment, consisting of men working outside the parish system without "the endearments and anxieties of a family," functioning as a saving remnant during the last days, and employing "the ancient system" of religious practice as "the providentially designed instrument" to keep "alive the lamp of truth in the sepulchre of this world till a brighter era." During the "day of trial," these Catholic clergy "driven from the established system of the church, from livings and professorships, fellowships and stalls" would "muster amid dishonour, poverty, and destitution, for higher purposes." Thus "severed from possessions and connexions of this world," they would educate those whom the church had neglected, especially in the great cities, where they would "attempt to be evangelists in a population almost heathen." They would also "educate a certain number, for the purpose of transmitting to posterity our principles and our manner of life."[81] This speaker essentially recapitulated in the contemporary setting functions for a reformed English Church that in "Letters on the Church of the Fathers" Newman had ascribed to ancient monasticism.

From 1833 to his entry into the Roman Catholic Church in 1845, Newman anticipated at least in his imagination an apocalyptic moment when the forces of evangelical religion aligned with the power of the state would persecute such persons as himself. He virtually invited upon himself a vocation of rejection and cultural martyrdom and regarded his faith and outlook as vindicated and authenticated by that experience. These thoughts, appearing in his sermons as early as 1829, embodied a call for martyrdom and ejection not wholly unlike that experienced by the Puritan clergy in the 1660s, the late-seventeenth-century Nonjurors, the eighteenth-century Methodists, and contemporary radical evangelical seceders. Newman actually, though in all likelihood unknowingly, depicted the exact situation of ouster and rejection previously imagined by certain late-eighteenth-century establishment evangelical clergy, who thought that in time proponents of the true Gospel faith might be ejected from the Church of England through confiscation that would require the nurturing of that faith in separate congregations. Newman for his part at least as early as the spring of 1833 had envisioned some mode of clerical secession, quite possibly monastic in character with himself as its prophetic leader, a fact underlined by his comparing himself to Elijah as early as 1836.[82] No less was it a vision of secession simply because he conceived it occurring under the name of Catholicism. Furthermore, at some level in his mind he may have felt that if he could carry out such a role, he might again achieve the deference, or at least the respect, of his brothers, who had followed their own Owenite and Darbyite prophets.

CHAPTER 4

What the Early Tracts Said

PARADOXICALLY the *Tracts for the Times* themselves have remained among the least read and least cited documents of the Tractarian Movement. In 1841 they received credit for having initiated an "increased reverence and regard manifested . . . for the Liturgy, Creeds, Sacraments, Episcopal polity, and Apostolical succession of the Church," a "greater apprehension of the fearful sin of schism," and a "more diligent attention given to the study of Ecclesiastical History, and of Christian Antiquity," but within a generation of their appearance the tracts remained quietly ignored by many people originally associated with them and then by later commentators and scholars. Newman for his part virtually excluded any significant account of the content of the tracts from the *Apologia*, where *Tract 90* alone stood forth as igniting a reaction that propelled him from the English to the Roman Church. Mid- and late-Victorian high churchmen, who regarded the tracts as having commenced well but having ended disastrously, wished to separate themselves from the whole questionable enterprise. Toward the close of the century, in his sympathetic history of the movement, R. W. Church noted the "surprise, dismay, ridicule, and indignation" roused by the "strong and peremptory language" of the tracts and "their absence of qualifications and explanations."[1] Although Church did quote *Tract 1* in its entirety, he failed to probe the others. Neither admirers nor detractors in the twentieth century systematically examined the tracts.

THE HISTORICAL SILENCE SURROUNDING
TRACTS FOR THE TIMES

The tacit silence regarding *Tracts for the Times* served the purposes of both later generations and those Tractarians who lived long into the century. The tracts had initially provided a powerful political and ecclesiastical counterpunch to the forces of religious pluralism and Dissent. By the third year of publication, however, Newman, Keble, and Pusey, under the guise of further deepening the understanding of antiquity, began to clarify their other agenda of advancing a religion of obedience and ascetic devotion. Then, paradoxically, the very religious pluralism that they had previously so vehemently repudiated in regard to Dissent became a necessity for themselves as it did later in the century for both the Roman Catholic Newman and Anglo-Catholics. Furthermore, in the second half of the century the battle to save the Bible from theological critics united Anglo-Catholics, high churchmen, and evangelicals in the English Church, none of whom wanted to recall the divisive conflict spawned by the earlier Tractarian attacks on evangelical championing of a scriptural faith. Moreover, in point of fact the later Tractarianism that Newman associated with the term *Via Media* had, as he himself admitted, failed as a religious experiment, with some of its adherents converting to Roman Catholicism and others to religious skepticism. Consequently, for committed Roman Catholics, Anglo-Catholics, high churchmen, evangelicals, and the few surviving former Tractarians of the late Victorian world, it was wise to let the confusions of 1833 to 1845 lapse into distant memories.

The alarmist rhetoric and near-apocalyptic vision that characterized the first three years of the tracts quickly posed a problem even to their authors once it became clear to everyone that the reformed government under either party had no intention of significantly undermining the Church of England or confiscating its property. But if in 1836 the polemical language of the early tracts, criticized even at their onset as making "too rapid an advance upon events, which may or may not be coming on," stood discredited by the absence of any ecclesiastical disaster, then the fuller Tractarian agenda of constructing a Church Catholic within the Church of England might have been undermined as well. Consequently, as early as the autumn of 1836, Newman sought to transform the tracts into statements prophetic of Catholic truth, lest readers recognize them for the overstated political documents they were. In the advertisement for the third volume of the tracts, dated November 1, 1836, by which time seventy-seven had been published, Newman defensively recast his image of the ecclesiastical climate of three years earlier in which "the prospects of Catholic Truth were especially gloomy, from the circumstance that irreligious principles and false doctrines, which had hitherto been avowed only in the closet or on paper, had just been admitted into public measures on a large scale, with a probability of that admission becoming a precedent for future." The authors of the tracts had then "spontaneously used the language of alarm and complaint" to rouse the members of the Church "to comprehend her alarming position" and to help them recognize "the gradual growth, allowance, and establishment of unsound principles in the management of her internal concerns." They had written the tracts "as a man might give notice of a fire or inundation," with only so much doctrine and argument necessary to justify their publication and to answer "more obvious objections to the views therein advocated." That "peculiarity in their composition" had "occasioned them to be censured as intemperate and violent."[2]

Intemperance of spirit and violence of language had been part of the strategy of Newman, Froude, and Keble from the beginning. They were personally and institutionally angry men in the summer of 1833, more angry and more committed to radical departures than other high churchmen, as demonstrated by Froude's contempt for the ideas discussed at Rose's Hadleigh Conference. Furthermore, Newman, Froude, Keble, and Pusey, who would join them in a few months, had embraced not only an ecclesiastical politics of protest but also an ascetic religion of obedience. Consequently, both their anger and their religious vision distinguished them from other high churchmen. The publication of the tracts had originated in just that distinction, and the original chasm separating the Tractarians from their high-church contemporaries never closed but actually widened over time. One consequence was the distance that high churchmen eventually sought to set between themselves and the tracts as well as the Tractarian leaders.

THE PUBLICATION OF
TRACTS FOR THE TIMES

The first tract appeared in September 1833. There was no immediate certainty that it would initiate a substantial series or that the high-church protest would become primarily associated with the radical Oxford Apostolicals. Ten additional tracts appeared between September and early November 1833. At that point, however, William Palmer of Worcester College wanted the series halted. For a time Newman obliged, as Palmer continued to press for a clerical association organized across diocesan boundaries, possibly without episcopal approval, for the purpose of affording "Churchmen an opportunity of exchanging their sentiments, and co-operating together on a larger scale." Simultaneously, Palmer and others, at Newman's suggestion, organized a successful clerical petition to the Archbishop of Canterbury that eventually attracted several thousand signatures across the spectrum of the English Church in a pledge to carry "into effect any measures that may tend to revive the discipline of ancient times, to strengthen the connexion between the bishops, clergy, and people, and to promote the purity, the efficiency, and the unity of the Church."[3] A second petition to the Archbishop of Canterbury from more than two hundred thousand lay heads of households similarly championed the ecclesiastical status quo.

After the brief hiatus, however, much to Palmer's chagrin, Newman resumed the publication of the tracts, refusing to trim their extreme clericalism, ecclesiology, sacramentalism, and opposition to evangelical religion. He also insisted that they stand distinct from the faltering organization of a clerical association. From the first tract in September 1833 through the last in February 1841, Newman as both author and editor assumed full responsibility for the series and regarded himself accountable essentially to no one but himself and perhaps John Keble. He rejected any oversight committee, which Palmer advocated. Despite their rhetoric of episcopal obedience, the Tractarians actually distrusted the bishops, repeatedly challenged them, and whenever possible ignored them. After years of career frustration and blocks to his ideas and actions, Newman had found an arena of personally untrammeled action, where he described himself to Samuel Rickards as standing "connected with no Association, answerable to no one except God and His Church, committing no one, bearing the blame, doing the work."[4]

Although Newman was not alone in the cause, he was the prime mover of what J. W. Bowden termed "the imperium in imperio, the knot of Tract writers."[5] No fewer than eighteen authors contributed to *Tracts for the Times,* though Newman with thirty contributions led the list. Keble had eight; Pusey, seven; and Bowden, five; Thomas Keble and Benjamin Harrison each wrote four. Froude, A. P. Perceval, and Isaac Williams wrote three apiece. Other authors included Alfred Menzies, C. P. Eden, R. F. Wilson, Anthony Buller, Henry Manning, George Prevost, and Charles Marriott. A number of the tracts reprinted passages from approved Church of England divines of the past, including Bishops Beveridge, Cosin, Wilson, Bull, and Andrewes, as well as Archbishop Ussher. Bishop Wilson was by far the most frequently reprinted author. A few of the tracts were anthologies of briefer extracts from other favored Anglican authors on particular subjects. One tract consisted primarily of translated portions of the Roman Breviary.[6]

The tract authors paid their own publication costs and reaped whatever financial reward might accrue. In some cases it was not insignificant. Except for Pusey's contributions, which at his insistence carried his initials, they appeared as anonymous publications by members of Oxford University, a self-conscious publishing tactic intended to generate interest and speculation. In so announcing themselves as published by "Members of the University," the tracts appropriated the cultural and religious aura of that university.[7] By moving the high-church protest from widely dispersed country parishes to Oxford, the Tractarians also fostered a situation that transformed internal university conflicts into debates over the character and direction of the Church of England. Because Oxford, unlike Cambridge, did not permit students to matriculate without subscribing to the 39 Articles, Oxford graduates and college fellows regarded their university as the peculiar seat of national religious orthodoxy. As we have seen, commitment to this viewpoint had become a particular point of honor among Oxford men in the aftermath of the recent ecclesiastical and reform legislation. As in the Peel reelection contest of 1829, gatherings of Convocation permitted Oxford graduates, who were overwhelmingly clerics, to return to vote on university matters and thus presumably to provide an indication of the collective mind of the clergy. Although ultimately such votes in Convocation would crush the Tractarians, in their early years the votes worked to their advantage.

In addition to the ninety tracts the Tractarians also published twenty-five *Records of the Church*. Appearing between 1834 and 1838, these pamphlets presented translations or paraphrases of the Church Fathers accompanied by polemical introductions. Initially the goal of the *Records of the Church* was "to familiarize the imagination of the reader to an *Apostolical state* of the Church" and thus "to prepare the public mind for a restoration of the old Apostolic System" when the contemporary establishment collapsed through what the Tractarians expected to be state persecution.[8] Over time, however, the *Records of the Church* came to provide a small anthology of patristic writings which would otherwise not have been widely available. Later the Tractarians also undertook the much more extensive projects of the Library of the Fathers and the Library of Anglo-Catholic Theology.

Physically the *Tracts for the Times* underwent various transformations. The first several appeared only with titles and a price on the front cover and sometimes a date. Often the date took the form of the feast day on which the tract had been completed for publication. Headings indicated certain tracts as intended *ad Clerum;* others, *ad Populum* or *ad Scholas.* The early tracts were very brief, usually no more than four pages, and printed on inexpensive paper. Only in late 1835, with Pusey's *Tract 67* on baptism, did they become substantially longer. Thereafter, except for the reprints of earlier Anglican divines, the tracts quite often constituted brief monographs or expanded articles. Each of the tracts was published initially in batches of 1,000 and was then reprinted, with total circulation for most of them standing between 4,500 and 7,000 copies. More than 14,500 copies of *Tract 90* were printed. Differing unauthorized versions of many of the tracts appeared in both England and the United States.

In 1834 the previously published individual tracts began to appear as collections in bound volumes, three of which included important introductory advertisements. The distinct volumes produced a collective effect, which Newman had forecast as early as November 22, 1833, when he told the critical Rickards in regard to the then emerging series, "The truth is, there is an extreme difficulty in hitting the exact thing that will do. It is only attained by a series of experiments. Nor is it fair to look at each Tract by itself; each is part of a whole intended to effect one or two great ends. Hence the different *tone* of them (which you notice) and which . . . does not arise from difference in the writers—the same writer aiming (whether or not from error of judgement) at the same ends in a different way."[9] Publication in bound volumes gave the tracts a permanent published life, encouraged their purchase as a set, and gave a clear physical presence to a new school of English theology. Only after the appearance of the bound volumes did the tracts receive extensive periodical reviews. For that reason significant journalistic commentary often appeared months or even years after the initial publication of an individual tract.

The first sixty-six tracts, which appeared between the autumn of 1833 and the close of 1835, constituted the fundamental statement of early Tractarian ecclesiastical principles. The content of the last twenty-four tracts, from late 1835 through 1841, differs in considerable measure because of the end of the perceived constitutional crisis, the events surrounding the Hampden affair of 1836, the concentration of later authorship into a very few hands, and the undertaking of a more nearly systematic attack on evangelical theology inside the Church of England in addition to that among Dissenters. At the same time there are important continuities. From 1836 onward the tracts much more fully and directly explored the Catholic devotional experiment toward which Newman and Pusey had already pointed in pre-1836 publications. Readers of Newman's *Arians of the Fourth Century*, "Letters on the Church of the Fathers," and his early volumes of sermons, as well as of Pusey's tract on fasting, saw those works as previewing the later tracts. Nonetheless, despite admitted and real continuities, the close of 1835 does provide a convenient endpoint for analyzing what the early tracts said.

But answering the question "What did the early tracts actually say?" is neither simple nor easy because the authors of the tracts—most particularly, but not only, Newman and Pusey—kept revising what they published. Both major and minor revisions appeared in tracts that carried indications of being second and third editions or proclaimed themselves New Editions. But substantive revisions also appeared without any mention in later editions of some tracts. Tractarian opponents repeatedly pointed to these silent revisions, and their unacknowledged presence was one of the main reasons that the Tractarians rapidly encountered accusations of dishonesty. They had quite simply said one thing and then another or advocated one position and then another without any admission of change. The evangelical *Christian Observer* could consequently decry a "sort of slipperiness" permeating the tracts.[10]

APOSTOLICAL SUCCESSION

Late in the century R. H. Hutton, one of the friendliest commentators on the movement, observed, "Now Tractarianism was clerical to the core—more clerical, I conceive, in some real sense than the Roman Catholic Church herself."[11] Although such was also the view of most contemporary opponents of the Tractarians, historians have not fully appreciated this clericalism or the reasons for its presence. The Tractarians in the tracts, in contrast to Keble in his sermon on national apostasy, defined the particular religious and political crisis of the day as a clerical one and proposed a clerical response. Rather than concentrating on the collective or institutional life of the Church of England, the initial tracts instead contemplated the possible downfall of the English clergy with subsequent loss of income, social standing, and congregational respect. They portrayed Church of England clergy as suddenly naked to their religious enemies and required to compete at distinctly new disadvantage with Dissenting ministers for the attention of their congregations.

The Church of England clergy of the second quarter of the nineteenth century had more at stake than their predecessors.[12] Only from the late eighteenth century onward had a significant number of English clergy been reasonably well educated and sufficiently secure economically to mix at ease with the local gentry. Their incomes had risen substantially with the prosperity of English agriculture occasioned by the Napoleonic Wars. As the clergy had entered local political and social power structures, they also had become the objects of attack by critics of those structures. The turmoil surrounding passage of the Reform Act, which numerous bishops had opposed in the House of Lords, had exposed those bishops and local Church of England incumbents, including Archdeacon Froude and the Kebles, to popular abuse, criticism, and even physical danger. The individual Church of England clergyman, often leading an isolated parish existence, consequently faced the questions of how to assure continuing local respect and how to define his personal vocation when he served an ecclesiastical establishment that no longer even in theory defined the nation.

Many Church of England clergy, having lost much of their civic status, entertained considerable apprehension about the adequacy of the English Church as a distinctly religious and spiritual body. The Methodist schism, no matter how often or deeply anathematized, stood as a constant, lively reminder of the religious failures of the previous century. During the decade of the twenties new modes of evangelical religion had emerged across the country. Church of England clergy each week witnessed the progressive strengthening of Dissent and often observed dual religious attendance on the part of many of their parishioners. Through Irish immigration Roman Catholicism was spreading within the cities where the Church of England had difficulty competing successfully. The power of the early *Tracts for the Times* resided in their capacity to tap into these numerous clerical apprehensions of both social and religious inadequacy.

In *Tract 1*, dated September 9, 1833, Newman issued a clarion call for the reasserting of social authority on the part of Church of England clergy and directly addressed the innermost fears of those clergy lacking former protections for their individual status. He demanded of his fellow clergy, "Should the Government and Country so far forget their GOD as to cast off the Church, to deprive it of its temporal honours and substance, *on what* will you rest the claim of respect and attention which you make upon your flocks? Hitherto you have been upheld by your birth, your education, your wealth, your connexions; should these secular advantages cease, on what must CHRIST's Ministers depend? Is not this a serious practical question? We know how miserable is the state of religious bodies not supported by the State . . . and the question recurs, on *what* are we to rest our authority, when the State deserts us?"[13] By thus presupposing a disastrous hypothetical situation, which his clerical readers did not actually confront but feared, Newman consciously appealed to their deeply shared apprehensions and insecurities.

Newman understood whereof he wrote. Only a few months earlier he had personally witnessed the results of the despoliation of the Italian Church. But there was a deeper source for his image of clerical collapse. That was the experience of his own family. In his vision of clerical deprivation and confiscation Newman projected onto the collective body of the English clergy the situation that he and his family had undergone during John Newman's bankruptcy of 1821. English law that had once protected the Newman family had then occasioned its economic and social downfall. English law in the past five years had similarly left the clergy of the Church of England adrift. Those clergy, though still upheld by establishment, nonetheless found themselves required to function in an increasingly voluntary church, stood newly dependent on the goodwill of their congregations, and needed to justify their own function and status. In late 1833 they also were convinced that they faced the likelihood of additional state intrusion into their lives and property. Newman asked what, if anything, those clergy could offer their congregations to avoid the loss of personal property and social deference that he had seen his father experience from his first financial collapse in 1816 until the end of his life.[14]

Newman waved before his clerical readers the image of social decline into the insecure world of congregational dominance that would every day require them to demonstrate their worth. Evoking the enormous condescension in which the English clergy held their Dissenting counterparts, he declared, "Look at the Dissenters on all sides of you, and you will see at once that their Ministers, depending simply upon the people, become the *creatures* of the people." He then asked, "Are you content that this should be your case? Alas! can a greater evil befall Christians, than for their teachers to be guided by them instead of guiding?" The clergy must not, as Newman insisted in *Tract 2*, "be accounted the mere creation of the State as schoolmasters and teachers may be, or soldiers, or magistrates, or other public officers."[15] The clergy reading the tract could easily have grasped that those whose social status had been created by the state could be destroyed by the state.

Having imagined a situation of disestablishment, economic deprivation, and social decline, Newman urged his fellow clergy in the Church of England to reconstruct their social and professional standing on "the real ground on which our authority is built,—OUR APOSTOLICAL DESCENT." The clergy should keep this descent before their minds "as an honorable badge, far higher than that secular respectability, or cultivation, or polish, or learning, or rank which gives you a hearing with the many." He enjoined them, "Speak out now, before you are forced, both as glorying in your privilege, and to ensure your rightful honor from your people." He virtually commanded the clergy, "Exalt our Holy Fathers, the Bishops, as the Representatives of the Apostles, and the Angels of the Churches" so as to magnify their own local office within their parishes "as being ordained by them to take part in their Ministry."[16] In later publications and in his *Apologia* Newman would emphasize the dogmatic character of true religion, but in the early *Tracts for the Times* true religion stood defined in terms of clergy of apostolical descent.

The Tractarians were determined that the clergy of the Church of England should be regarded as *priests* possessing by virtue of their episcopal ordination distinctly supernatural sacramental powers and consequent rights to social respect. In defiance of the evangelical emphasis on an invisible church of believers through the centuries, the Tractarians defined the church "on earth as an existing Society, Apostolic as founded by the Apostles, Catholic because it spreads its branches in every place; i.e. the Church Visible with its Bishops, Priests, and Deacons." The apostles themselves remained with the visible church through succeeding generations in the presence of the bishops and episcopally ordained clergy. Those clergy stood appointed by God, Newman explained, as "a company of men as the especial medium of His instruction and spiritual gifts" and the proper response from the laity to them was "the duty of gratitude." In *Tract 15* adding the duty of lay obedience to that of gratitude, Newman asserted, "The Christian Church is a body consisting of Clergy and Laity; this is generally agreed upon, and may here be assumed. Now, what we say is, that these two classes are distinguished from each other, and united to each other, by the commandment of God Himself; that the Clergy have a commission from GOD ALMIGHTY through regular succession from the Apostles, to preach the Gospel, administer the Sacraments, and guide the Church; and, again, that in consequence the people are bound to hear them with attention, receive the Sacrament from their hands, and pay them all dutiful obedience." In *Tract 16* Benjamin Harrison portrayed God's "duly appointed Ministers sent before Him to prepare us for His coming" as divine gifts along with the commandment of love and the inspired word.[17]

Keble similarly pressed hard on the matter of apostolical succession and episcopal ordination. In *Tract 52* he pointed to the calling of Matthias as the successor-disciple to Judas to argue that Christ had obviously meant for the apostles to replace each other and had given them the power to do so. Indeed, according to Keble, Jesus had personally abstained from appointing a successor to Judas in order to illustrate that this appointive power passed to the apostles. Persons so appointed and ordained, Keble contended, "our LORD will consider . . . as commissioned and ordained by Himself." Furthermore, Keble argued that members of the early church had regarded themselves as connected to Christ through the apostles. For fifteen hundred years Christian believers understood themselves as actually partaking of valid sacraments only when the latter were celebrated by an apostolically ordained priest. Keble concluded that the scriptural example of the ordination of Matthias, the practices of the early church, and the teaching of universal church "all agree to show that Communion with GOD Incarnate, such communion as He offers in His holy Supper, cannot be depended on without an Apostolical Ministry."[18]

Within Keble's thought, bishops functioned as "a divinely-appointed guard, meant to secure the integrity of Apostolical doctrine." To question or criticize or demean that episcopal ministry carried with it grave consequences. Throughout the history of the church, whenever the doctrine of apostolical succession supporting bishops and their powers of ordination had been surrendered, confusion had arisen in the faith. Keble then demanded of Dissenting clergy and their congregations, who had for so long complained of the dominance of the Church of England and its bishops, *"What will be the feelings of a Christian, particularly of a Christian pastor, should he find hereafter that in slighting or discouraging Apostolical claims and views (be the temptation what it may), he has really been helping the evil spirit to unsettle men's faith in* THE INCARNATION OF THE SON OF GOD?"[19] According to Keble, those who attacked episcopal church government in point of fact put the core of the Christian faith itself in danger and, knowingly or not, cooperated with the forces of evil. The great question for the Christian faith in England was whether the English bishops would remain to define and protect doctrine and to identify and anathematize heresy. Such appeals to the apostolical authority of Church of England clergy had not originated with the Tractarians, but they revived and transformed the concept into an aggressive weapon against evangelical Dissent, as had American episcopalian leaders more than a decade earlier. Unlike the Americans, however, the Tractarians actually retained the advantages of establishment, all the while forecasting its destructive demise to give credence to their views.

Contemporaries attached considerable significance to the Tractarian assertion of apostolical succession, as is witnessed in the immediate and on-going criticism it aroused in the evangelical wing of the English Church even though the ostensible Tractarian target had been Dissenting clergy. In that respect, some establishment evangelicals saw themselves as the object of Tractarian scorn from the beginning of the enterprise. In its first notice of the tracts, as part of its religious overview of 1833, the *Christian Observer* portrayed the Church of England as at the moment endangered on the one side by extreme Dissenters allied with "infidels, radicals, and Socinians to raze her foundations." On the other side, however, stood "a Society formed at Oxford, the members of which, professing themselves to be the most orthodox upholders of the Church, have begun to scatter throughout the land publications which, for bigotry, Popery, and intolerance surpass the writings even of Laud and Sacheverall." Early the next year a correspondent in the same journal deplored Tractarian emphasis on apostolical succession for provoking "a new and most prolific source of discord" by placing Episco-palians "in a warfare against all churches, and all followers of Christ, of whatever name, who do not agree with us in matters of discipline as well as in doctrine" rather than uniting "more closely upon spiritual principles all who love our Lord Jesus Christ in sincerity." Later in 1834 the *Christian Observer* criticized the tracts for contending "for the power of the keys to the fullest range of the Roman Catholic priesthood," thus rendering those pub-lications "not more undisguisedly Popish" than "the decrees of the Council of Trent, centuries ago."[20]

In an editorial of December 5, 1833, the *Record* regretted "melancholy and wicked Popish delusions" in the tracts, such as the language suggesting eucharistic sacrifice and the transformation at the priest's hand of the bread and wine into the body and blood of Christ. But the paper actually focused stronger criticism on the Tractarian assertions of apostolic succession. The *Record* first regarded those claims as absurd because Protestants must con-sider many persons through whom that succession had necessarily passed "to be rejected and lost." Second, the doctrine of apostolical succession ignored the ongoing work of the Holy Spirit in the present day, directly calling men to ministry through one of "the infinitely more noble, the in-comparably more precious communications, under whose life-giving power the spiritually dead hear the voice of the Son of God and live."[21] Later that month the *Record* contended that apostolical succession built a stronger case for Rome than for the Church of England, that the succession had not pre-served the Roman church from enormous corruption, and that the Scottish Church, foreign churches, and Dissenters with no claim to apostolical suc-cession had known, loved, and preached the Gospel in its fullness.

The deeply anti-Catholic *Record* by the middle of the decade denounced the Tractarians as Roman Catholic sympathizers, if not possibly "a body of Jesuits" sent "into this country" by the Pope and then assuming "the garb of clergymen of the Church of England." Tractarian adherence to apostolical succession constituted a major factor in those accusations. According to the *Record* in late 1836 the Oxford writers' founding the safety of the Church of England on the basis of "a long succession of men, who though visibly and carnally ordained, were never called or ordained by Christ, but who, as perverters of his Gospel and abusers of his Sacraments, he declares to be *accursed,* is a fond and vain thing, discountenanced by the Articles of our Church, repudiated by the most distinguished Reformers, and strikingly repugnant to the Word of God." Moreover, because the Tractarians must regard as true the succession that had passed through the corruptions of medieval popery, they would dismiss the necessity of the Reformation restoring the church to truth. In August 1837 the *Record* described the Tractarians as "this new sect" that had established the church as "the object of worship," but not "the Church mystical, composed of the living members of the body of Christ throughout the world," but rather "the outward visible Church" of which the largest section was "apostate Rome" accompanied by the English Church and "any other Episcopal bodies which glory in the true apostolic succession." Later that year the *Record* berated the Tractarians for, on the basis of apostolical succession, embracing Roman Catholic priests as genuine ministers of Christ while rejecting those of "the Protestant Churches which did not pay that attention to the Apostolic Succession which marked our Church, in effecting their separation from Antichrist." In contrast to apostolical succession, the external marks required of true Christian ministers, as indicated by Scripture and recognizable by their congregations, included their teaching of "certain fundamental doctrines, clearly revealed in Scripture," their possession of "a certain spirit revealed in Scripture of separation from the world, of devotedness to God, of joy in invisible and heavenly things," and their understanding the profound differences between the morals of Christianity and those of the world. The *Record* further denounced "the Puseyite notion" of apostolical succession as "*Antichristian*" and as an idea that "ought, accordingly, to be cast out of the Church of Christ."[22]

SACRAMENTAL CLERICALISM

A sacramental definition of the clerical calling was essential to Tractarian social and ecclesiastical aims to furnish the Church of England a unique product in the religious marketplace and unique claim to congregational loyalty. The Tractarian argument was quite simple. The sacraments were necessary for salvation; episcopally ordained clergy held the sacraments; only by receiving the sacraments from such clergy could a person be assured of salvation. Therefore, those clergy deserved respect, honor, gratitude, and obedience.[23] Whereas evangelical clergy attracted and held their congregations by providing through preaching a weekly subjective religious experience, episcopally ordained Tractarian clergy expected to attract and hold congregations by providing grace through the frequent administration of what they claimed to be the only valid sacraments in the parish. Whereas evangelicals gave the dominant role to the religious consumer who might move from preacher to preacher, the Tractarians sought to claim a monopoly on the channels of grace unaffected by fluctuating consumer taste.

Evangelical establishment ministers as well as high churchmen could make a case for the protection of clerical interests from uncertain, shifting congregational influence. For example, in 1834 the Rev. Hugh McNeile, a strongly proestablishment, evangelical minister in the Church of Ireland who disliked Dissent, urged the necessity of clerical independence from congregational pressures, explaining, "To obtain a voluntary support the man [ministering to a Dissenting congregation] must dilute his teaching to meet the prejudices of fallen man; he must only assail the natural character as far as conscience will bear it, setting forth, what they know already, that they are indeed what they ought not to be, so as to do it gently, so as not to alarm and disturb too much; and thus measuring his statements of doctrine, so that he may not bring forward what may make them recoil from him; seeking to be palatable, instead of seeking to be true; he must consider the prejudices of his people in preparing his discourses, instead of considering the contents of the word of God."[24] According to McNeile and others like him, the security of religious establishment allowed an evangelical minister the freedom to carry out his responsibility to preach the Gospel in a manner that might offend members of his congregation.

In light of Newman's concern for a religion of obedience, Pusey's for penance, and Keble's for clerical parish oversight, it might have been expected that they would urge an argument similar to McNeile's, but they did not. The danger to Church of England clergy as portrayed in the tracts was not that loss of establishment would harm them in their distinctly religious ministry or prevent their preaching a faith of obedience but rather that loss of establishment would rob them of the respect of their congregations and hence their social standing. Like McNeile, they emphasized issues of conscience and conduct, but they did so in order to retain their social authority, not their capacity to preach a difficult message of obedience. McNeile no doubt also wanted to protect his own economic and social interests, but his argument for doing so sharply differed from the Tractarians' emphasis on controlling access to the sacraments as a means of exercising local clerical social authority.

To secure their position as possessors through episcopally valid ordination of the only valid channels of grace, the Tractarians, like Newman in his sermons, necessarily had to challenge the evangelical faith in grace mediated through feeling and subjective religious experience induced by preaching. Consequently, the tracts both implicitly and explicitly contrasted the religion of valid sacraments with the religion of sincere feelings associated with Methodism and virtually all other evangelically oriented religious groups, including those in the Church of England. The initial Tractarian targets were politically active Dissenters, but the manner in which the tract writers shaped their attack almost immediately brought establishment evangelicals within their compass. Moreover, it should be remembered that Newman's *Arians of the Fourth Century*, with its implicit attack on all forms of evangelical religion, appeared in November 1833 and his first volume of *Parochial Sermons*, with their polemic against a religion based on feeling, in March 1834.[25] The criticisms in both applied to Dissenters and establishment evangelicals alike.

The Tractarians directly questioned whether sincerity as such had any distinct religious validity whatsoever. As early as *Tract 2* Newman, in contrast to his remarks of 1823 to his brother Charles, sharply criticized the definition of the church as consisting of "a number of sincere Christians scattered through the world" instead of constituting a visible church known through its bishops and clergy. In *Tract 11* he berated those who contended that "a *right state of the affections* is the test of vital religion in the heart." In *Tract 29* Bowden berated Dissenters who taught that the real question in religion was "the state of our heart." In *Tract 52* Keble argued that the Church Fathers had not judged the correctness of a Christian communion "by those tests which we now hear most insisted on; not by convictions, and emotions, and highly-wrought feelings." In *Tract 60* Keble broadly condemned virtually all evangelical vital religion as wrongly teaching "that in the matter of acceptance with GOD, sentiment, feeling, assurance, attachment, towards JESUS CHRIST, is all in all: that definite notions of His Person, Nature, and Office, may very well be dispensed with, provided only the heart feel warm towards Him, and inclined to rely upon Him entirely for salvation: that the high mysteries of the orthodox Catholic Faith, the Trin-

ity, the Incarnation, and Communion with our Lord through His Sacraments, are either unnecessary to be distinctly believed, or that such belief
will come of itself, if only the above-mentioned feeling of dependence on
CHRIST be sincere." Keble noted that "various classes of religionists, who
think themselves, and are in many respects, diametrically opposed to each
other" shared this religious outlook which as far as he was concerned merely
embodied "human presumption."[26]

In opposition to a religion of feeling, Keble linked, as Newman had in
Tract 1, exclusive access to grace necessary for salvation with a particular
kind of clergy. Seriously and fervently pressing the argument that there
might be no path to salvation in England outside the English Church,
he asked,

> Why then should any man here in Britain, fear or hesitate boldly to assert
> the authority of the Bishops and Pastors of the Church, on grounds strictly
> evangelical and spiritual; as bringing men nearest to CHRIST our SAVIOUR,
> and conforming them most exactly to His mind, indicated both by His own
> conduct and by the words of His SPIRIT in the Apostolic writings? Why
> should we talk so much of an *Establishment*, and so little of an APOSTOLICAL
> SUCCESSION? Why should we not seriously endeavour to impress our people
> with this plain truth;—that by separating themselves from our communion,
> they separate themselves not only from a decent, orderly, useful society, but
> from THE ONLY CHURCH IN THIS REALM WHICH HAS A RIGHT TO BE QUITE SURE
> THAT SHE HAS THE LORD'S BODY TO GIVE TO HIS PEOPLE?

It is certain that Keble's concern in this matter related as much to the social
status of the clergy as the salvation of the laity because he concluded "that
among other results of the primitive doctrine of the Apostolical Succession,
thoroughly considered and followed up, it would make the relation of Pastor
and Parishioner far more engaging, as well as more awful, than it is usually
considered at present." So long as the laity saw a pastor on a human mission
for an establishment, that minister could hardly evoke "a *religious* veneration" because "there is nothing, properly, *sacred* about him." But once
viewed in the full character of his apostolic ordination, "every thing about
him becomes changed, every thing stands in a new light."[27]

In particular Keble and Newman related the high standing of the clergy
to the spiritual benefits conveyed through the eucharist. Keble bemoaned
the tendency of the clergy to rest "our claim on the general duties of
submission to authority, of decency and order, of respecting precedents long
established; instead of appealing to that warrant, which marks us, *exclusively*, for GOD'S AMBASSADORS." Congregations could be certain that they

were "Partakers of the Body and Blood of CHRIST" only if clergy ordained by bishops descended from the Apostles administered the eucharist. In a letter in the autumn of 1833 Keble referred to this concept of the clergy as analogous to "the Aronical priesthood."[28]

Newman for his part connected this argument to his characteristically apocalyptic reading of what might soon happen to the clergy. In the first edition of *Tract 10*, in a passage directed toward the laity, he wrote,

> Yes! the day may come, even in this generation, when the Representatives of CHRIST are spoiled in their sacred possessions, and degraded from their civil dignities. . . . Then you will look at us, not as gentlemen, as now; not as your superiors in worldly station. . . . Then you will honor us, with a purer honor than you do now, namely, as *those who are intrusted with the keys of heaven and hell, as the heralds of mercy, as the denouncers of woe to wicked men, as intrusted with the awful and mysterious gift of making the bread and wine* CHRIST'S *body and blood, as far greater than the most powerful and the wealthiest of men in our unseen strength and our heavenly riches.*[29]

Newman quickly revised the first edition of this tract when his extreme sacerdotal claims encountered stiff resistance from otherwise sympathetic clergy, who regarded the powers being ascribed to Church of England clergy as resembling those they associated with Roman Catholic priests. Some Tractarian critics pointed to this process of revision as exemplifying the Tractarians' original Romanizing intentions and their subsequent concealment of those goals. These accusations ignored Newman's having asserted such full clerical powers not in the cause of Romanizing but in the cause of establishing a theological basis for securing the local social standing of Church of England clergy deprived of other means of protecting their status. Newman's social goal was not hidden in his rhetoric but stood completely out in the open.

Newman encountered considerable complaint even from friendly correspondents, not only about his language regarding the eucharist but also about his extreme political rhetoric. For example, Samuel Rickards expressed the puzzlement with which many clergy must have first received the tracts, telling Newman in November 1833 that "in the whole circuit of a very large neighbourhood which I have been searching into with no little care and labour, I have not been able to find a single person, lay- or clergyman, x, y, or z, who believes the Church or its Liturgy or any thing belonging to it is in any serious danger. The tracts they either utterly abhor or else they consider them the work of men whose brains are cracked by their own melancholy and fanciful temper working on very partial and cloudy views of their subject: and I myself am looked upon as a mere alarmist." Rejecting such words of well-intentioned caution, as well as harsher comments, Newman pressed forward, eschewing both compromise and public apologies for his original statements and his later revisions. He reported to Rose, who only months earlier had refused to include *The Arians of the Fourth Century* in his series, "I am in all sorts of scrapes with my Tracts—abused in every quarter (amid some cheering criticisms) and I doubt not with considerable reason. No one person can hit off the exact truth, much less exact propriety . . . so I must be forced to suffer criticism, in order to tend towards effecting certain ends—and take blows and wounds as in a battle;—only, alas!, they are not generally considered so honorable as scars." Again employing the military metaphor in another letter, he urged issuing the tracts singly rather than as a magazine because "we do not want regular troops, but sharpshooters."[30]

During the summer of 1834 Froude, another of the sharpshooters, also clearly outlined the implications of apostolical succession and a sacramental priesthood for clerical social standing. In Barbados, attempting to recover from his consumption, he speculated upon undertaking "another reform," which "every clergyman can make for himself without difficulty." He advised "that every one should receive the communion as often as he has opportunity; and that if he has such opportunity every day of the week, it is his duty to take advantage of it every day of the week." Admitting that daily communion was difficult, he saw no problem with instituting monthly communion, which would hardly be regarded as a change and which would most certainly assure the attendance of communicants. Froude directly related celebration of communion to the religious and social status of the clergy, commenting, "The administration of the Communion is one of the very few religious duties now performed by the clergy for which Ordination has ever been considered necessary. Preaching and reading the scriptures is what a layman can do as well as a clergyman. And it is no wonder the people should forget the difference between ordained and unordained persons, when those who are ordained do nothing for them, but what they could have done just as well without Ordination."[31] Froude offered the spiritual experience of a frequent eucharist celebrated exclusively by an episcopally ordained priest as a religious counterattraction for the spiritual stirrings of preaching. A sacramental ministry by priests of the apostolic succession would thus forestall the spiritual, social, and political claims of any other clergy—or, in his mind, pretended clergy—who defined themselves through a preaching vocation.

In pursuing these assertions of a Church of England monopoly on the channels of grace in the more nearly voluntaristic English religious world, the Tractarians fulfilled a prediction that Adam Smith had made a half-century earlier in *The Wealth of Nations* (1776). Smith had observed that clergy under a well-endowed establishment often became learned gentlemen and gradually lost "the qualities, both good and bad, which gave them authority and influence with the inferior ranks of people," thus leaving them essentially defenseless "when attacked by a set of popular and bold, though perhaps stupid and ignorant enthusiasts." In his own day he saw Dissent and Methodism flourishing because the established clergy had neglected "the arts of popularity, all the arts of gaining proselytes." In the past, establishment clergy in such trouble could call upon the civil government "to persecute, destroy, or drive out their adversaries, as disturbers of the public peace." Smith then recalled Hume's forecast in his *History of England* of the behavior to be expected from establishment clergy left to their own devices for securing their social standing and maintaining perceived utility: "Each ghostly practitioner, in order to render himself more precious and sacred in the eyes of his retainers, will inspire them with the most violent abhorrence of all other sects, and continually endeavour, by some novelty, to excite the languid devotion of his audience. No regard will be paid to truth, morals, or decency in the doctrines inculcated. Every tenet will be adopted that best suits the disorderly affections of the human frame. Customers will be drawn to each conventicle by new industry and address in practising on the passions and credulity of the populace."[32] Newman, Froude, and Keble, recognizing that the Whig ministry and the reformed Parliament were not about to persecute Dissenters, adopted modes of behavior very closely resembling those that Hume had darkly predicted of clergy suddenly finding themselves lacking the support of the civil magistrate. The Tractarians attempted to make themselves "more precious and sacred" in the eyes of their congregations by asserting through apostolical succession possession of a monopoly on the supernatural authority required for salvation. The Tractarians later associated themselves with novel devotional practices which religious as well as nonreligious contemporaries thought manifested "the disorderly affections of the human frame" and appealed to the "passions and credulity of the populace."

THE DENIGRATION OF DISSENT AND ALTERNATIVE ECCLESIOLOGIES

With the old political critique that Dissent leads to revolution ringing hollow in the mid-thirties, the Tractarians pounded instead the religious or spiritual inadequacy of Dissent in a fashion that generally presented a mirror image of the Tractarian claims *for* the Church of England. They denigrated both the ordination of Dissenting clergy and the religious authority of the congregations who called them and whom they served. In *Tract 7* Newman accused Presbyterian clergy, by whom he meant those of the continental and Scottish Reformed tradition, of spiritual usurpation, asserting, "It is not merely *because* Episcopacy is a *better or more scriptural form* than Presbyterianism, (true as this may be in itself,) that the Episcopalians are right, and Presbyterians are wrong; but because the Presbyterian Ministers have assumed a power, which was never intrusted to them. They have presumed to exercise the power of ordination, and to perpetuate a succession of ministers, without having received a commission to do so. This is the plain fact that condemns them; and is a standing condemnation, from which they cannot escape, except by artifices of argument, which will serve equally to protect the self-authorized teacher of religion." According to Newman, a permanent standing authority must vest clergy with spiritual powers which by the very nature of things could not derive from congregations, "which can scarcely be considered to be vested with any powers such as to require the visible authority which a Succession supplies." In *Tract 15* William Palmer and Newman declared that the succession of clergy among Dissenters "does nothing for *them;* for, their succession, not professing to come from GOD, has no power to restrain any fanatic from setting up to preach of his own will, and a people with itching ears choosing for themselves a teacher."[33] Here Palmer and Newman ascribed to all Protestant clergy outside the Church of England the characteristics of the recently emerging itinerant ministers and knowingly ignored the rigidly organized clerical structures of both Methodism and the Scottish Kirk.

The Tractarians emphatically denied sacramental powers to Dissenting clergy who, of course, had never claimed them in the first place. In *Tract 35* A. P. Perceval explained, "A person not commissioned from the bishop, may use the words of Baptism, and sprinkle or bathe with the water *on earth*, but there is no promise from CHRIST, that such a man shall admit souls to the *Kingdom of Heaven*. A person not commissioned may break bread, and pour out wine, and pretend to give the LORD'S Supper, but it can afford no comfort to any to receive it at his hands, because there is no warrant from CHRIST to lead communicants to suppose that while he does so here *on earth*, they will be partakers in the SAVIOUR'S *heavenly* Body and Blood." Directly and personally attacking Dissenting clergy, Perceval further declared, "And as for the person himself, who takes upon himself without warrant to minister in holy things, he is all the while treading in the footsteps of Korah,

Dathan, and Abiram, whose awful punishment you read of in the book of Numbers." Perceval informed his readers that apostolic commission and it alone "can give you any security that the ministration of the Word and Sacraments shall be effectual to the saving of your souls." As if there were still any doubt about his intentions, he then bluntly asserted, "*The Dissenting teachers have it not.*"[34]

In *Tract 36* Perceval explicated a schema of English religious groups according to the manner in which they taught complete or incomplete religious truth. He opened quite forthrightly, stating, "The English Church, which is a true branch or portion of the 'One Holy, Catholic, and Apostolic Church' of CHRIST, receives and teaches the entire Truth of God according to the Scriptures: the Truth, the whole Truth, and nothing but the Truth." Adherents to the other religious sects (and it should be noted that the term *sect* itself was pejorative) he divided into three groups: those who "*reject the Truth,*" those "*who receive and teach a part but not the whole of the truth,* erring in respect of one or more fundamental doctrines," and those "who teach more than the truth."[35] The first group included Socinians, Jews, deists, and atheists; the second encompassed Presbyterians, Independents, Methodists, Baptists, and Quakers, who had either improper ordination or inadequate appreciation of one or more of the sacraments; the third group included Roman Catholics, Swedenborgians, Southcottians, and Irvingites.

At different times in the past the Church of England had encountered persecution from those religiously inadequate groups: from unbelievers in the fourth through the sixth centuries, from Roman Catholics in the sixteenth, and from Protestant Dissenters in the seventeenth. Seeing the English Church currently confronting unprecedented danger, Perceval contended, "At the present time, these three Classes of opponents have united their forces; and unbeliever, Papist, and Protestant Dissenter, obeying Satan's bidding, are endeavouring to do that together, which they have failed to do singly, namely, to overthrow and destroy our branch of the Catholic and Apostolic Church."[36] The reference to Satan was not casual, but appeared with some frequency in the tracts as a means of transforming the contemporary political conflict into a larger transhistorical struggle between the forces of darkness and light.

The Dissenters, according to the Tractarians, behaved with willful and sinful intransigence toward the Church of England. In *Tracts 29* and *30* Bowden, one of the few lay writers of the tracts and a close friend of Newman from undergraduate days, presented a dialogue between an established church clergyman and a parishioner named John Evans, who with his family more or less regularly attended the local chapel to experience vital Christianity. The narrator commented, "It will be seen from what follows, that . . . John Evans did not understand that he was disobeying the GOD, whom he was trying to serve, and putting a slight upon that SAVIOUR, whose disciple he not only professed himself, but in good earnest desired to be." As the dialogue proceeds, Evans equates his chapel attendance with the exercise of Christian liberty and claims that he responds better to the Dissenting worship service. The parson replies, "You would have been right, if GOD had not chosen a Minister for you. In that case perhaps you might have used our Christian Liberty, as you call it, and joined any congregation you pleased. But His having given a clear command alters the case, and makes that which would otherwise have been a matter of indifference, an act of disobedience and sin." The Church of England, the parson claims, unlike any of the Dissenting sects "is sprung from that very Church which CHRIST set up at Jerusalem when He came upon earth." When Evans, in good evangelical fashion, indicates that he understands the word *church* to include "all sincere Christians," the parson reprimands him, urging that by *church* Christ signified "a body of men, bound by the same laws, acting together, speaking the same thing, attending the same worship, reverencing the same Pastors and Teachers, and receiving at their hands the Sacraments which CHRIST has ordained." Lest there be any further doubt, the parson firmly states, "He meant a Church such as the Church of England." In the second portion of the dialogue, Evans asks the parson to name the sin of those "who separate themselves from that [true] Church altogether, and join one or other of the many sects which reject her authority." That sin, the parson replies, is called *schism* and constitutes a person exercising "a disregard of Church authority, and a notion that so long as his doctrine is pure, he may join what sect he pleases, or even set up one for himself." Returning to his earlier comments, the parson notes that some people confuse the sin of schism with the exercise of " 'Christian Liberty.' "[37]

In *Tract 47* Newman described Dissent as residing "not 'in CHRIST' " and then located it on the spectrum of human religious life as standing "between us and heathenism." That location meant that Dissent, especially "long established dissent," was "attended with a portion of blessing . . . which does not attach to those who *cause* divisions, found sects, or wantonly wander from the Church to the Meeting House." Long established Dissent Newman regarded as sharing in a "Divine favor, which is utterly withheld from heresy."[38] The perpetuation of such established orthodox sects as well as of Roman Catholicism appeared to indicate possession on their part of some portion of divine truth. Consequently in this tract, as in "Home Thoughts Abroad," Newman drew a distinction between older orthodox Dissenting sects in England and new heresies, which he associated with evangelical religion since the rise of Methodism.

In *Tract 51*, R. F. Wilson expanded upon this analysis, announcing "that Dissent is a sin," while simultaneously refusing to condemn all Dissenters as sinners. Certain persons, whom he termed "*conscientious* Dissenters," might have separated from the Church of England because of some sense of an alleged obstacle to personal salvation. Even these Dissenters, however, displayed "a very erroneous" conscience, which understood nothing of the New Testament teachings on the sin of schism, the authority of the church, and the duty of obedience. Wilson did not hesitate to portray even the clearly conscientious Dissenter as "*heretical*." He explained that Scripture taught the necessity of a unified, visible church, as well as obedience to spiritual superiors, provided injunctions against giving offense to one's brother, and associated schism with heresy, bad passions, bad actions, and vicious dispositions. Both the Old and New Testaments upheld the awfulness of the fate of the rebellious, dissenting Korah. To dissent was to oppose Christ's own petition for the unity of the Church and to act "as if Christianity required of us no surrender whatever of the private judgment" and acceptance of dutiful obedience to legitimate authority. Consequently, unless persons were driven by true conscientious dissent, which itself might be the result of "false conviction of their deceitful hearts," it seemed better to remain a member of the established church following the example of their forefathers, their country, and holy martyrs and to rest their faith "on the authority of those who are, by virtue of their office, successors of the Apostles." According to Wilson, those "careless or weak-minded persons" who dissented on issues involving little substantial difference with the Church of England fully embodied "the sinfulness of Dissent" as taught in the Scripture.[39] For those people Wilson could conjure up neither sympathy nor charity.

According to the tracts, Dissenters, whether for good or bad reasons, willfully excluded themselves from the Catholic truth of the apostles and all the spiritual benefits that flowed therefrom. In *Tract 61* Buller announced, "Submission to Church authority is the test whether or not we prefer unity, and the edification of CHRIST's body, to private fancies." Dissenters who separated over points of ritual displayed "a rebellious spirit" embodying a parochial particularism that contrasted with the Catholic or universal qualities of the Church of England. Buller explained,

The spirit of Schism, in addition to its other inherent characters of sin, implies the desire of establishing minor points as Catholic or essential points, or the spirit of *exclusiveness.*

The desire of novelty is *restlessness;* the maintenance of *our own* novelty is *selfishness.*

Zeal is the effort to maintain *all* the Truth; *party spirit* is a perverse maintenance of this or that tenet, even though true, yet to the suppression and exclusion of every thing else.[40]

In this manner Buller and other Tractarians denied the significance of any points of disagreement that Dissenters believed important and by implication any new modes of religious activity that evangelicals within or without the Church of England might have sought to bring to the fore as issues of conscience or of fundamental religious importance.

The final area of the Tractarian denigration of Dissent regarded religious inadequacy arising from ecclesiastical polity. The Tractarians, like Rose in his book on Germany, charged that the absence of bishops left the preservation of apostolical truth insufficiently protected and created a situation that over the course of time led to the denial of the incarnation and a drift into some mode of Socinian theology. In *Tract 54* Keble, presenting the single most strenuous Tractarian indictment of nonepiscopalian polity leading to doctrinal error, argued that "the evil spirits" from the earliest ages of Christianity had labored to corrupt the faith in regard to the incarnation and human communion with God through Christ. To protect that essential core of revelation, God had appointed "persons in His Church to watch the treasure of Divine Truth, to try and assay, by comparison with it, whatever doctrines from time to time became current, and to give notice, with all authority, wherever they found GOD's mark wanting." Clergy who worked under the commission of those bishops could "expect more abiding results from their labours, than any, however zealous, who may venture to take this honour to themselves." The early apostles and St. Paul acknowledged the rights of the bishops, as their successors, "to mark out such heretics as might arise from time to time, and put the faithful on their guard against them." In that manner, "the Apostolical succession of pastors has continued, as a divinely-appointed guard, meant to secure the integrity of Apostolical doctrine." That "chain of rightly-ordained Bishops" had assured to present-day members of the church the inheritance of the true doctrine of the incarnation.[41]

In *Tract 57* Keble used this argument to question the widespread notion "that the *temper* of faith in the heart is every thing, and the *substance* of the faith in the creed comparatively nothing." That notion permeating

Christendom from the time of the Reformation had fostered churches that "have been so bold as to dispense with primitive discipline and government." Virtually all such churches had succumbed to doctrinal turmoil and fallen away from the apostolical truth of the incarnation. In passing Keble reminded readers that the "first spring" of Arius's heresy had been "a rebellious and envious feeling towards his Bishop."[42]

In the same tract Keble briefly surveyed the status of the doctrine of the incarnation across the contemporary transatlantic world. In Germany, he discerned the presence since the eighteenth century of "Rationalist" views, which pretended "to give account, on principles of mere human reason, of Christianity and every thing connected with it." Drawing upon Pusey's book on Germany, he noted the source of those ideas had been English deists whose thought had produced little impact in England because of the presence of bishops but which flourished in the nonepiscopalian German religious world. In Geneva, Keble saw a church generally drifting toward "profaneness" and teaching "the very lowest standard of doctrine consistent with nominal Christianity." Furthermore, despite Calvin's persecution of them, Socinians had always felt kinship with Calvinism. Keble portrayed the Church in Holland as having embraced a "Liberal or Latitudinarian" divinity that tended to explain away all mystery. In England itself the Presbyterian Churches had "subsided, one after another, into a cold and proud Socinianism." The Scottish Church stood as an exception to those tendencies usually found in presbyterian communions, but Keble ascribed that situation to its close geographical proximity to the English Church without explaining why the even closer proximity of English Presbyterians had not produced a similar result. Although among English independent congregationalist churches Keble could find no falling away from reverence for the incarnation, the absence of bishops had allowed them to disparage the sacraments, to disregard antiquity, and "to make Faith a matter of *feeling* rather than a strict relative duty towards the persons of the HOLY TRINITY." That situation, he thought, was "not very gradually preparing the way for lamentable results among them also." Finally, in America, where unrestrained congregationalism predominated, Keble discovered "the only country which witnesses the rapid and unmitigated growth of Unitarian principles of *doctrine*."[43]

From this survey of transatlantic Protestant churches, Keble concluded that "when once men have learned to think slightly of the testimony borne by the ancients to the primitive discipline, they will naturally lose some part of their respect for the testimony borne by the same ancients to the primitive interpretation of Scripture." Absence of reverence for bishops and their discipline would eventually produce absence of reverence for the apostles themselves. Finally, clergy lacking proper episcopal ordination necessarily could not benefit from "the gracious assistance of the HOLY GHOST" in guiding their minds to scriptural truth, and consequently the "evil spirit and the tempting sophistry of the world" would have a greater influence over those so improperly ordained. The present advances "in intellectual light and liberty" and "the appetite for knowledge of good and evil" required the Church to embrace "all the supernatural means and aids which our Lord has provided."[44] Those who scorned such aids bore an especially heavy responsibility. Thus Keble saw heterodoxy of the most serious kind flowing directly from any ecclesiastical organization that departed the contours of episcopacy founded on apostolical succession.

Keble's standing charge, repeated by other Tractarians, was that ecclesiastical irregularity and latitudinarian sympathy on the part of English churchmen for Christians outside the established church would lead inevitably to Socinianism. Although they directed that charge equally against latitudinarians, evangelicals were their chief concern. Given the Tractarians' tactic of protecting clerical status through the argument for apostolical succession and a monopoly of grace through the sacraments, it was virtually inevitable that they would eventually direct their fire against establishment evangelicals, who favored a preaching ministry, stressed private judgment on the part of laity, and occasionally cooperated with Dissenters. Establishment evangelicals nurtured a climate of religious thought and practice that softened the boundaries between church and chapel. As Keble wrote Newman early in 1834 regarding his own parish, "The Dissenters here are making frightful progress: owing *almost* entirely to our friends the Augustinians."[45] By the latter term, he denoted evangelical English churchmen. Although the presuppositions of *Tracts for the Times* were from the beginning potentially hostile to establishment evangelicals, and though during 1834 some tracts criticized their outlooks, only with the publication in late 1835 of Pusey's tract on baptism did the series formally turn from attacking Dissenters to criticizing Church of England evangelicals, thus provoking years of internal disruption.

PUSEY AND BAPTISM

Although Tractarianism is closely and properly associated with a high view of the eucharist, to which in point of fact some eighteenth-century evangelicals had first devoted new importance, the center of sacramental controversy from the 1820s to the 1850s throughout the English Church was baptism.[46] With the appearance in the late summer and autumn of 1835 of Pusey's *Tracts 67, 68,* and *69* on *Scriptural Views of Holy Baptism,* the Tractarian Movement became drawn into that previous long-standing dispute and shifted its focus of attention away from evangelical Dissent to evangelicalism within the English Church. Indeed, it was Pusey's particular and largely idiosyncratic teaching on baptism that led the editor of the evangelical *Record* to ascribe the term Puseyite to the entire Tractarian cause to signal its fundamentally antievangelical orientation.[47] The subsequent, ongoing baptismal controversy finally led to the Gorham Judgment of 1850, which by formally admitting Calvinist views of baptism as permissible within the Church of England occasioned the most significant number of mid-Victorian conversions from the English to the Roman Church. None of those converts ever wrote so compelling an account as Newman's of his conversion of 1845, so the later, more widespread influx never achieved the same kind of standing in historical and religious memory. Moreover, the reason for the conversions following the Gorham Judgment was public and theologically clear, while almost everything about Newman's last years in the Church of England had been private and murky to bystanders, hence the fascination with his subsequent account.

Pusey's three tracts on *Scriptural Views of Holy Baptism,* printed with continuous pagination and soon thereafter published in a single long volume, was the first of the tracts to boast extensive footnotes. For that reason it has sometimes been regarded as turning the series away from its early alarmist polemics and toward scholarship. Such was not the case. Though eschewing the rhetoric of alarm, Pusey's tract may nonetheless have been the single most polemical of the early tracts. Pusey's understanding of baptismal regeneration raised all the theological problems relating to the issue of sin after baptism and justified his advocacy of ascetic penance and his deep interest in the subject of purgatory. His discussion not only opposed the views on baptism held by Dissenters and establishment evangelicals but also directly attacked the continental Reformation and its influence in England. Pusey worked his way to the theology of this tract in the very months that he was writing to his wife about the difficulties associated with true repentance and when he was turning his own family life into a stronghold of rigid ascetic practices.

Pusey's discussion of baptism both supported sacramental clericalism and attacked evangelical religion. Pusey contended that baptism regenerated in a very literal sense and that the physical water itself, as administered by a properly ordained priest, was the channel of grace. The sacrament of baptism removed sin and regenerated its recipient, but thereafter left the person with no recourse for the removal of sin committed in later life. Consequently, for Pusey, if the sacrament of baptism was necessary for salvation and provided the actual, even physical, channel of divine saving grace, then the priests who administered that baptism were themselves necessary instruments of salvation and would also be the instruments for devising vehicles to deal with postbaptismal sin.[48] Any view, of course, that contended for a symbolic rather than regenerative interpretation of baptism lowered the unique powers and authority of the clergy.

Evangelicals and others in the Church of England understood baptism as a more or less symbolic initiation into the Christian communion or as planting seeds of regeneration that must later be awakened. Repentance later in life, usually indicated or accompanied by some form of religious feeling or sincerity associated with a subjective conversion experience, would assure forgiveness of sin. Pusey, however, specifically rejected such significance attached to religious feeling, stating that "to judge of doctrines by their supposed influence upon men's hearts, would imply that we know much more of our own nature, and what is necessary or conducive to its restoration, than we do." As a correlative to this position, he also contended that the efficacy of a preaching ministry had been overemphasized.[49]

Directly challenging evangelicals on their own biblical turf, Pusey undertook a long, complicated argument to demonstrate that Scripture itself taught his version of baptismal regeneration. Deploring "fanatic spirits, who depreciate the majesty of Baptism, and speak wickedly thereof," Pusey denounced those who equated baptism with an initiatory rite similar to Jewish circumcision as having pursued "the very error of rationalists" by supposing "that GOD'S HOLY SPIRIT, when he took the words used in Jewish Theology [sealed by circumcision], and employed them to express Christian Truth [sealed by baptism], conveyed nothing more by them, than they would have meant in the mouth of any ordinary Jew."[50] Such symbolic interpretations of baptism sought to explain a religious mystery that must more properly simply be accepted.

For Pusey this evangelical, rationalist misinterpretation of Scripture evaded the burden of postbaptismal sin through the idea and practice of easy postbaptismal repentance. Contrasting the views of the Fathers with those of evangelical writers, Pusey explained, "It is indeed a hard and toilsome path which these Fathers point out, unsuited to our degraded notions of

Christianity, as an easy religion, wherein sin and repentance are continually to alternate, pardon and Heaven are again and again offered to all who can but persuade themselves that they are sorry for their sins, or who, from circumstances, from time of life, or any other outward cause, have abandoned the grossest of them." Pusey declared, "We must bear the scars of the sins, which we have contracted: we must be judged according to our deeds." Strongly condemning any concept of "easy remission" of postbaptismal sin, he further urged that "wilful sin, after Baptism, is no such light matter as the easiness of our present theology would make it" and "that repentance is not a work of a short time, or a transient sorrow, but of a whole life."[51]

By the end of 1835, Newman formally embraced Pusey's tract as an essential contribution to the Tractarian critique of evangelicalism inside as well as outside the English Church. In the advertisement to the second volume of the tracts, Newman blamed "certain celebrated Protestant teachers, Puritan or Latitudinarian," for having led people to embrace "the doctrine, that GOD conveys grace only through the instrumentality of the mental energies, that is, through faith, prayer, active spiritual contemplation, or (what is commonly called) communion with GOD" rather than presenting the church and her sacraments as "the ordained and direct visible means of conveying to the soul what is in itself supernatural and unseen." Indeed Newman identified "the essence of Sectarian Doctrine" as considering faith rather than the sacraments "the proper instrument of justification and other gospel gifts." Such, Newman urged, was the "cardinal deficiency" of what he termed "the religion of the day" marked by "extensive popularity and great speciousness." Pusey's tract on baptism constituted a fundamental "delineation, and serious examination" of that defective modern system.[52]

Theologically, no single Tractarian publication so profoundly troubled and angered the evangelical press and other evangelical commentators as Pusey's discussion of baptism. In 1836 the *Record* urged that baptism is a sign and not the instrument of regeneration and that the spiritual fruits of one's life, not the fact of baptism constitute the true evidence of the state of one's soul. From that standpoint it denounced Pusey's view of the sacrament as requiring "great ignorance of Scripture united to much genuine Popish feeling and superstition" and as dishonoring Christ himself and his regenerating power in the lives of those who believed in him. A year later, portraying Pusey's teaching as compromising the doctrine of justification by faith, the *Record* asserted that the doctrine of baptismal regeneration lay "at the root" of all the Tractarians' "serious and destructive errors." What Pusey offered was grace through baptism followed by a life of sin from which only repentance and labor could bring one again into a regenerate state. He consequently misunderstood "the grand object of the Gospel," which was "to bring sinners home to the Saviour," an object achieved "when, *convinced* of their lost and sinful condition, they come to Christ 'by faith,' 'with their whole heart,' acting under the assurance of that Gospel truth 'that he is able to save them to the uttermost that come unto God by Him.'" By January 1838 the *Record* decried the Puseyites as nothing less than "perverters of the Gospel, and the most formidable enemies in the present day of our beloved Church," who through their emphasis on baptismal regeneration dishonored God, heaped contempt on the new birth of the spirit, and led "men into a fatal deceit and security as to their state before God" by ignoring the fruits of a lively faith that transformed lives. The Tractarians thus demonstrated that they "do not themselves perceive, or at best perceive thorough a glass darkly, the Gospel of the grace of God."[53]

The *Christian Observer,* in a similar vein, asserted that Pusey rested his concept of baptism on "the authority of the darkest ages of Popery, when men had debased Christianity from a spiritual system, a 'reasonable service,' to a system of forms, and ceremonial rites, and *opera operetta* influences." The journal found Pusey's specific interpretation of baptismal regeneration "crushed by it own weight," if one contemplated that, according to his view, all the patriarchs and prophets of the Old Testament were "not regenerate persons" or "sons of God," whereas Voltaire could claim such status because "he had been baptized by a Popish priest." It was "the very bathos of theology, an absurdity not worthy to be gravely replied to" that Pusey could consider those in whom the spirit of God had dwelled, but who were unbaptized, as "still 'unregenerate,' and therefore, in Scripture language, 'children of the devil.'" Pusey's teaching constituted "absurdity," "irrational fanaticism," and "intellectual driveling" proclaimed under the name of faith. Teaching that God conveyed saving grace through the instrumentality of baptism, rather than through faith, did more harm than the open preaching of Socinianism. In conclusion, the *Christian Observer* declared, "The Church of England teaches, after Holy Scripture, that we are 'justified by faith'; Professor Pusey teaches that the Sacraments are the appointed instruments of justification. The learned Professor ought to lecture at Maynooth, or the Vatican, and not in the chair of Oxford, when he puts forth this Popish doctrine." After noting that Pusey "may construe some of *the offices* of the Church after his manner," in a question that would long haunt the Tractarians the *Christian Observer* inquired, "But what does he do with the Articles and Homilies?"[54] It would, of course, be upon the rock of their

Catholic interpretation of the 39 Articles that the Tractarian ship would eventually founder.

This hostile reading of Pusey's tract on baptism provoked Newman to write an important series of letters in 1837 to the *Christian Observer* from which eventually emerged his volume of lectures on justification. The letters themselves constituted only a few printed pages, but the editor, as Newman complained almost a half-century later, "effectually smothered" him by surrounding his remarks with scores of pages of finely printed editorial footnotes that constitute a major evangelical critique of early Tractarianism and particularly its understanding of baptism. The editor and other evangelicals believed that God through enormous love and generosity for humankind had provided grace for the salvation of those persons who placed their faith in Christ as savior. They understood Pusey's, and by implication Newman's, concept of baptismal regeneration as a frightening doctrine that in contradiction to Scripture left human beings with only uncertain mercy for sins committed after baptism. The *Christian Observer* considered Pusey's doctrine of baptism as consequently embracing "a thrilling of terror, and not of holy joy," and as designed to "restore the tyranny of the Romish Priesthood over the consciences of men" and to set forth "the most bigoted, the most intolerant, the most superstitious opinions" of Christian ministers in the minds of the laity. The *Christian Observer* finally condemned Pusey's tract as "Protestantism rejected and Popery spoiled," with the result affording "the post-baptismal penitent neither the sacrament of penance, nor the Scriptural appropriation of the blood of Christ."[55]

The *Christian Observer,* throughout its commentary on Newman's letters defending Pusey, related their teaching regarding baptism to the wider Tractarian effort to champion a clerical sacramentalism exclusively available in the Church of England. In this regard the journal pointed to a larger picture of what it regarded as unfair and in some cases dishonest tactics whereby the Tractarians depicted anyone whose sacramental views differed from theirs as "fellow-workers with 'the Rationalists of Germany,' and with Deists and Socinians." The journal declared, "The whole spirit of the Oxford tracts, under all their veil of calmness, is . . . unjust and full of subtlety." As one part of that subtlety, the *Christian Observer* deeply deplored the Tractarian "air of being a suffering party—moral martyrs for truth," when they had actually emerged "as public assailants" who in "three volumes of closely-printed tracts and treatises" had taught "that the 'majority of the members' of the Church of England have cast aside her doctrines, and differ only in degree, but not in principle, from 'Rationalists' and

'Socinians.'" The journal further decried the Tractarian contention "that there was not, from the days of Adam to the advent of Christ, a child of God in the whole world; and that there is not in this hour a single individual in covenant with God—not one baptized person, not one regenerated person, not one communicant—among all the Protestant churches, Lutheran or Reformed, except in the Church of England and its daughter churches." While the Tractarians regarded it "a crime and 'personal' insult" to be asked how they reconciled "these Popish tracts with the doctrines of the Church of England," they saw "nothing 'unkind,' or unbrotherly, in telling the world that the great body of the clergy and professed members of the Church are traitors to her cause." In the eyes of the editor, and no doubt other establishment evangelicals, the Tractarians had not learned "anything new respecting the unity of Christ's church," but had succeeded in acquiring "the bigotry of expelling from it upon earth those whom Christ will not expel in heaven."[56]

THE TRACTS AND ROMAN CATHOLICISM

In light of the contemporary accusations of Tractarian sympathy for Roman Catholicism, what may surprise the later reader of *Tracts for the Times* is the relative paucity of direct comment on the subject. What they did say was, however, at once simple and complicated. Echoing his letters of the previous spring from Italy, Newman declared in *Tract 20* of December 1833, "AN UNION IS IMPOSSIBLE" because the Roman communion had "established a lie in the place of GOD's truth" and thus stood "infected with heterodoxy" from which those in the English Church must flee as from "a pestilence." He resoundingly concluded this brief diatribe with the Cato-like remark, "Popery must be destroyed; it cannot be reformed."[57] There, except for a brief subsequent comment in the advertisement to the first bound volume of the tracts in late 1834 indicating that both Dissent and Roman Catholicism supplied perceived deficiencies of the English Church, the issue lay more or less dormant for two years.

In late 1835 Newman and Keble discussed the options of concluding the tracts or launching a new anti–Roman Catholic series, which they thought might gain new supporters for the Tractarian cause. Newman told J. W. Bowden on September 11, 1835, that he and others had determined to begin during the next year a new series of tracts against popery, to which he saw numerous advantages attached. As he explained to Bowden, "Two years since the cry was against the Dissenters—this helped us—now Popery is the popular alarm—and we shall be able to convey the very same doctrines and in all parts of them under this economy. Besides we shall be anticipating the S.P.C.K. and co., and in a great measure the peculiar and ultra-protestant parties— who have not yet met the demand. Further we shall be showing we are not Papists." In October he told Bowden that a series of "Tracts against Popery," in addition to distinguishing the Tractarians from Papists and allowing them to benefit from popular anti-Catholicism, would also provide the opportunity for "a very effectual though unsuspicious way of dealing a backhanded blow at ultra-protestantism."[58] Thus, even in a projected attack on the Roman Catholics, Newman's chief opponent remained the evangelicals.

Such a series attacking Roman Catholicism did not actually come to pass. Neither Newman nor Keble really wanted it. More important, the dispute over the appointment of R. D. Hampden to the Regius Professorship of Divinity in February 1836 allowed them to reassert their already successful anti-Dissent strategy in their drive against a latitudinarian churchman patronized by the Whigs. In January 1836, just before the explosion of the Hampden matter, Newman did publish *Tract 71*, entitled "On the Controversy with the Romanists," and possibly intended as the first of an anti–Roman Catholic series. He opened the tract with the astonished observation, "The controversy with the Romanists has overtaken us 'like a summer's cloud.' We find ourselves in various parts of the country preparing for it, yet, when we look back, we cannot trace the steps by which we arrived at our present position. We do not recollect what our feelings were this time last year on the subject,—what was the state of our apprehensions and anticipations." He noted that for many decades members of the Church of England had found it unnecessary to explain why they were not Roman Catholics. Because of government protection and religious exclusiveness, the clergy had neglected "to inform themselves on subjects on which they were not called to dispute." Furthermore, they and others had assumed that Roman doctrines were untenable and could not prevail "in an educated country." That situation had now changed, Newman insisted, as "we hear of the encroachments of Romanism around us."[59]

Neither publicly nor privately did Newman indicate the specific nature of those encroachments. Bishop Nicholas Wiseman had delivered London lectures the previous year. Irish Catholics sat in Parliament, and O'Connell continued to rouse nationalistic disturbances. More Irish immigrants entered England each year. But these do not seem to have been issues particularly on Newman's mind. In all likelihood, through *Tract 71* Newman hoped to set the stage for a new series of tracts attacking Roman Catholicism by resorting to his by now well-practiced exaggeration of contemporary dangers to the Church of England. Just as almost three years earlier he had used alarm as a rhetorical weapon against political enemies allied with Dissent, he now intended to use alarm as a rhetorical weapon against Roman Catholics. In neither case was the actual situation commensurate to the tone of the rhetoric.

Only three subsequent tracts directly addressed themselves to Roman Catholicism, and in no case critically. *Tract 72* of January 1836 reprinted passages from Archbishop Ussher on prayers for the dead. In June 1836 in *Tract 75* Newman published translated portions of the Roman Breviary for use in personal devotion. In the introduction to those selections, however, he announced, "Till Rome moves towards us, it is quite impossible that we should move towards Rome."[60] In *Tract 79* of March 1837, Newman contributed an extensive and largely historically rather than theologically critical discussion of the Roman Catholic doctrine of purgatory.

Consequently, only *Tract 71* contained a substantive discussion of Roman Catholicism. There Newman contended, as in the advertisement of 1834, that the same forces leading people to Dissent led them also to Rome: the novelty of its worship and the attraction of its modes of devotion. In explaining why members of the Church of England should not join Rome, Newman pointed to apostolic injunctions against disorder and schism and similar urgings for people to remain in the religious communion into which they had been born. Departure from the religious communion of one's birth might properly occur either because that communion stood "involved in some damnable heresy" or because it was "not in possession of the sacraments."[61] Neither, he contended, was the situation of members or clergy of the Church of England who might find themselves tempted to Rome.

In thus seeking to sustain the English Church and to undermine the Roman, Newman granted far more to the Roman case than would most Church of England writers. Newman wrote how gratified he felt that it was unnecessary to debate with Roman Catholics such high doctrines as the incarnation, the Trinity, and the eucharist because the conduct of such debates in and of itself seemed to result in "a rationalistic line of thought" and "profane and rationalistic thoughts in the minds of the many." Instead of questioning specific statements of Roman doctrine, such as the decrees of the Council of Trent, Newman insisted that only the practical errors of Rome required critical examination. Accordingly he stated, "We have indirectly opposed the major premise of our opponents' argument, when we should have denied the fact expressed in the minor."[62] Consequently,

Newman criticized Roman teaching neither for being false nor for being incompatible with Scripture but rather for its incongruence with apostolical teaching. According to Newman in *Tract 71*, the Roman Church was guilty of seven major practical errors. These included the denial of the cup to the laity, the requirement of the priest's intention for the validity of the sacraments, the necessity of confession, the doctrine of purgatory, the invocation of saints, the worship of images, and the unwarranted anathemas of the Roman Church. All of these corrupt practices, he urged, lay near the center of contemporary Roman Catholic worship, devotion, and teaching, with antiquity providing warrant for none of them.

In the same tract Newman admitted that the Church of England itself was imperfect and in certain respects "*incomplete,*" not, he urged, an unexpected situation considering that it stood "at the distance of 1500 to 1800 years from the pure fountains of tradition" and had suffered political bondage. The sudden and violent change of the Reformation had harmed the Church, as had the Reformers' tendency to depart further than had been necessary from previous Catholic practices. The 39 Articles, Newman explained, "are scarcely more than protests against specific existing errors of the 16th century, and neither are nor profess to be a system of doctrine." But even taking all such shortcomings into account, the errors of the English Church were at worst those of omission, while those of Rome were of commission. Whatever the defects of the Church of England, they did "not interfere with the perfect development of the Christian temper in the hearts of individuals, which is the charge fairly adducible against Romanism."[63]

Throughout *Tract 71* Newman did not attack the Roman Catholic Church. Rather he compared the deficiencies of the Roman communion and those of the English, finally concluding the English was the less deficient Christian body. This evaluation of Rome and unenthusiastic endorsement of the Church of England represented only one facet of a larger meditation on Newman's part about the essential incompleteness of all contemporary English Christian churches. Recognition of Newman's sense of the spiritual and devotional incompleteness of that religious world is essential to understanding his thought and behavior in regard to Roman Catholicism and for an appreciation of his sense of religious isolation and that of his later followers.

In the advertisement to the first bound volume of the tracts, dated November 1, 1834, or about one year after the series had begun, Newman voiced regret over "a lamentable increase of sectarianism" in English religious life resulting from the neglect of the church to instruct its members about apostolical ministry and the sacraments as "the sources of Divine Grace." Pondering deeper sources of sectarianism, he observed that longings for religious experiences left unsupplied by the English Church touched human beings both individually and collectively. He then portrayed "Methodism and Popery" as functioning "in different ways" as "the refuge of those whom the Church stints of the gifts of grace" and filling the role of "the foster-mothers of abandoned children." Newman pointed to such "deficiencies" in the Church of England as "the neglect of the daily service, the desecration of festivals, the Eucharist scantily administered, insubordination permitted in all ranks of the Church, orders and offices imperfectly developed," as well as "the want of Societies for particular religious objects." The existence of those "deficiencies" eventually had led "the feverish mind, desirous of a vent to its feelings, and a stricter rule of life, to the smaller religious Communities, to prayer and bible meetings, and ill-advised institutions and societies, on the one hand,—on the other, to the solemn and captivating services by which Popery gains its proselytes."[64] Newman understood one of the fundamental goals of the Tractarian enterprise to be devising possibilities for devotional life and community within the English Church that would compensate for those perceived deficiencies or incompletenesses. But his remarks on the deficiencies of the English Church stand in parallel to others regarding the deficiencies of the Roman Catholic Church. The goal of Newman's Catholic ambitions was at least for a long time to remedy both, a point that most of his English contemporaries either ignored or missed.

Contemporaries simply saw in Newman and other Tractarians secret papists or open Roman sympathizers. *Tract 10*, with Newman's remarks on the powers of the priest changing the elements into the body and blood of Christ during the eucharist, had especially elicited such responses, as did more general Tractarian clericalism, emphasis on baptismal regeneration, and the later monastic experiment at Littlemore. In 1845 and again in 1850 the conversions to Rome of persons associated with the Tractarians seemed to confirm those early suspicions. Yet only two tract writers, Newman and Manning, actually converted. Manning hardly counts as a Tractarian, having contributed only one part of one tract and having always had a difficult relationship with Newman. Moreover, for his part Newman consistently rejected the Romanizing accusations and portrayed himself as pressing English religious life not toward Rome but toward a body of religious observances found in neglected rubrics and in antiquity. As we shall see, even when he turned to the concept of development to legitimize an even broader array of devotional practices, it is by no means clear that he wished to do so in order to justify conversion to Roman Catholicism.

Newman's insistence that he was seeking in his own and collective English religious life something different from Roman Catholicism must be taken seriously. Commenting privately on his strategy in late 1833, Newman wrote, "I expect to be called a Papist when my opinions are know[n]—but (please God) I shall lead persons on a little way, while they fancy they [are] only taking the mean, and denounce me as the extreme." He repeatedly claimed that the devotional practices he propagated constituted elements of a larger Catholic, as opposed to Roman Catholic, heritage, which at the time of the Reformation settlement had been "lost through inadvertence" and were now to be recovered by the Tractarians through "an act of re-appropriation."[65] This outlook appears to be a consistent element in his personal and theological thinking throughout his days in the Church of England. Like many radicals before and after, Newman portrayed himself as a restorer of a lost past. That stance is essential to understanding his relationship and that of other Tractarians to the Roman Catholic Church of which they were not a part until they became part of it through conversion.

THE TRACTS AND THE REFORMATION

The Tractarian path to the unfettered reappropriation of the faith and practices of antiquity stood blocked by the historical realities of the English Reformation, including both the events and personalities of that era and the legal and religious documents they had generated. Tractarian criticism of the Reformation and the Tractarian interpretation of Reformation era documents, the 39 Articles being the most important, stirred more broad public resistance and criticism than their pronouncements on any other single subject. Unlike Tractarian comments on apostolical succession, the sacraments, and ecclesiastical polity, their interpretation of the Reformation elicited opposition throughout the *entire* Church of England, including once-sympathetic high churchmen. Although the Reformation debate largely originated in 1838 with the publication of Froude's *Remains* and then climaxed in 1841 with the publication of Newman's *Tract 90* and subsequent key articles in the *British Critic,* the Tractarian assault on the Reformation had actually commenced much earlier.

For the Tractarians, as for other high churchmen, the Church of England constituted a branch of the Holy Catholic Church with doctrines rooted in antiquity about which very few practicing clergy had even modest knowledge. That ancient lineage was a fact more often asserted than demonstrated, though William Palmer wrote a key treatise showing the parallels between the English and the ancient liturgies.[66] For these churchmen corruptions had entered the life of the medieval and early modern English Church at some more or less unspecified point. English bishops had addressed these corruptions during the Reformation, but a foreign party of radical continental Reformers and their English adherents had almost immediately thereafter entered the scene, introducing extreme Protestant measures and new confusion. Thereafter, certain seventeenth-century English divines had attempted to restore pure Catholic teaching to the Church. The Tractarians, again like other high churchmen, contended that the Roman Church by its adherence to the papacy and its popish doctrines stood in schism with the English Church and now constituted a corrupt branch of the Holy Catholic Church. There was general agreement that the decrees of the Council of Trent had marked a point of no return from popery, but the situation before that council remained unclear.

On the basis of this outlook, the Tractarians, again not unlike other high churchmen, refused to regard the English Reformation as a founding of the English Church. The English Reformation proper simply constituted one important, highly tumultuous moment in the much longer history of the Catholic Church in England. The unruliness of the event raised doubts about the adequacy of its accomplishments. Indeed, to the early Tractarians even the necessity of the Reformation was by no means certain. In *Tract 57* Keble, in regard to the abolition of episcopacy in the continental and Scottish reformed churches, declined to dispute "the necessity of what was done at the Reformation" but added the parenthetical note, "(although it would be wrong to allow such necessity, without proof quite overwhelming)." In *Tract 71* Newman suggested that the turmoil and violence of the Reformation provided "antecedent ground for anticipating wants and imperfections in the English Church." Drawing a highly charged parallel between the turbulence of the Reformation and that of the French Revolution, he observed, "It is now universally admitted as an axiom in ecclesiastical and political matters that sudden and violent changes must be injurious; and though our own revolution of opinion and practice was happily slower and more carefully considered than those of our neighbours, yet it was too much influenced by secular interests, sudden external events, and the will of individuals, to carry with it any vouchers for the perfection and entireness of the religious system thence emerging."[67] During the sixteenth-century upheaval, some parts of Catholic truth had been rescued while other parts had been sacrificed. The English Reformation and its doctrinal arrangements thus could not constitute the defining religious benchmark for the Church of England of Newman's own day.

The villains in the Reformation from the Tractarian standpoint were the continental Reformers whom they always attempted to distance from their English counterparts. William Palmer, who made the first significant mention of the Reformation in *Tract 15*, argued that the English bishops, who could without taint of Roman corruption trace themselves back to the apostles, had possessed spiritual credentials that had not required aid from the Continent. While narrowly approving the actions of the continental Reformers, Palmer commented, "At the same time it is impossible not to lament, that they did not take the first opportunity to place themselves under orthodox Bishops of the Apostolical Succession. Nothing, as far as we can judge, was more likely to have preserved them from that great decline of religion, which has taken place on the Continent." Although initially Palmer indicated that Luther "had taught true doctrine," he later modified his judgment to Luther's having "in the main" upheld true doctrine.[68] As far as the Roman Church was concerned, Palmer indicated that its clear apostasy dated with certainty only from the Council of Trent.

In *Tract 45* Newman undertook a still more direct criticism of the continental Reformation. There he contended that the evil tendencies inherent in early Protestantism, as well as the better-known corruptions of popery, deserved the attention of modern English audiences. By rejecting the authority of the Church and substituting Scripture as "the sole document both for ascertaining and proving our faith," the Geneva Reformers, Newman asserted, had established a "system of self-will," the same fault he had long ago associated with his brother Francis. This continental resort to Scripture meant that matters of faith could be demonstrated only through controversy and dispute that often resulted in rigid black-and-white interpretations and which later in *Tract 71* Newman was to claim led to rationalism and Socinianism. As a result of this process of scriptural disputation, he contended, "It followed, that in course of time, all the delicate shades of truth and falsehood, the unobtrusive indications of GOD's will, the low tones of the 'still small voice,' in which Scripture abounds, were rudely rejected; the crumbs from the rich man's table, which Faith eagerly looks about for, were despised by the proud-hearted intellectualist, who, (as if it were a favour in him to accept the Gospel,) would be content with nothing short of certainty, and ridiculed as superstitious and illogical whatever did not ap-

prove itself to his own cold, hard, and unimpassioned temper." Such argumentative understanding of religious truth had most fully realized itself in
"the spirit of ultra-Protestantism, *i.e.,* that spirit, to which the principles of
Protestantism *tend,* and which they have in a great measure *realized." Ultra-
Protestantism* was a term that Newman appears to have invented and consistently applied to contemporary evangelical religion among Dissenters and
in the establishment. Newman then asked, "This being considered, can we
any longer wonder at the awful fact, that the descendants of Calvin, the first
Presbyterians, are at the present day in the number of those who have denied
the Lord who bought them?"[69] The assertion that historic mainline continental Protestantism, especially as it taught the doctrine of *sola scriptura,*
held within itself inherent tendencies first toward ultra-Protestantism and
then toward an almost necessary Socinianism provided an ongoing theme
for the tracts and other Tractarian publications. It was to provide the core
idea for the assault in 1836 on the appointment of Hampden to the divinity
professorship.

In his 1835 tract on baptism Pusey had gathered together these themes to
produce the single most extensive Tractarian assault on the continental
Reformation. He accused all those who in any substantial sense doubted or
denied the regenerative power of baptism as being guilty of degrading the
sacraments and associated that degradation with the interpretation of Scripture in the continental Reformation. Although both Luther and Zwingli, in
different and sharply opposing ways, had attempted to explain the nature of
the sacraments rather than accepting their mystery, Pusey traced the chief
Protestant errors to the Swiss Reformer's particular approach to Scripture. According to Pusey, Zwingli's theology manifested "an arrogant self-
confidence, which thinks lightly of any belief opposed to his own, although it
were that of the universal Church; and he became the author of tenets which
immediately well nigh effaced the Sacraments of his Lord. His rationalistic
tone sowed the seeds of a dreadful harvest, which his country is now reap-
ing." Zwingli's "decidedly rationalist" frame of mind, unable to open itself
to the mysteries of the faith as presented in Scripture, had carried him to
symbolic interpretations of the sacraments. His emphasis on human reason
and his attempt to make faith rationally understandable "appeased at once
both conscience, and those common cravings of intellect, which a more
vigorous faith restrains." Zwingli and Calvin after him had thus excluded
"all that is hyperphysical, in other words, all that is supernatural" from the
sacraments.[70] This rejection of the supernatural and the tendency to rationalism had drawn the Swiss Reformers very close to Socinianism, a brand

of theology that had taken its rise from the example of later Calvinistic reading of Scripture in Geneva.

In the second printing of *Scriptural Views of Holy Baptism*, appearing in 1836, Pusey directly related the alleged rationalism stemming from the Swiss reformers to the deficiencies of modern evangelical religion. He there declared, "The preaching of the Cross is now no stumbling-block to the mind of man; it offers no difficulties to the rationalism of the day; nay, it is subjected to illustration, and the system of Redemption is made cognizable by us, and we understand it, and extol the wisdom of the scheme! The Holy Eucharist it has rationalized, and in that degree, as a Sacrament destroyed: the efficacy of Infant-Baptism it cannot rationalize, and therefore denies it." In this second edition Pusey further associated such rationalism with American evangelicalism and with "popular" preaching that "claimed to itself the exclusive title to warmth and sincerity and undefiledness." Such preaching in effect denied the efficacy of the sacraments and led men "to ascribe our whole spiritual life simply to the action of faith, not of GOD's gifts in the Sacraments, whereof faith is the mere channel only."[71] The line of descent from Switzerland to the arena of transatlantic evangelical revival was thus clearly drawn.

Pusey, like the other Tractarians, outlined a mixed picture of the course of religious and spiritual events during the Reformation, an era about which he found much to regret and much that would cause later decline of the Catholic faith. He observed, "At least we ought never to forget, that in the great commotion of the Reformation, there were brought to the surface not only treasures which had long lain hid, but froth and scum also: would one might say, froth and scum only! Every thing, which before had lain concealed under the thick veil of outward conformity, was laid bare: the Gospel was again eminently a savor of life and a savor of death,—to those who embraced it with an honest and true heart, life; others profited by the security given only to manifest the unbelief or heresy which lurked within. To others, death and life were mingled in the cup." Not content to portray the Reformation in terms of an almost gothic narrative of demons rising from previously unopened doors, Pusey redefined the meaning of Protestantism itself. He declared, "'Protestantism' then, as now, was often as negative as its very name; Protestant was often another name only for 'infidel.' The deadly, stupefying heresy (if it may even be called such) of Socinus was, we must recollect, one product of the Reformation." The Council of Trent had directed its decrees against such Protestant excesses and errors as had manifested themselves among the continental foreign party who had undermined much but by no means all Catholic truth during the English Reformation. In the context of these charges, Pusey reminded his readers that the continental Reformers had always regarded the Church of England "as a distinct and peculiar Church" and urged contemporary English churchmen "not to identify ourselves with them."[72]

The early tracts would have led readers to draw several general conclusions about Reformation. First, the theology of the continental Reformers held within itself the seeds of later heresies, such as Socinianism, and intellectual outlooks, such as rationalism, that denied the true Catholic faith or contributed to its degradation. Second, these continental theologies and their advocates had tainted the events and results of the English Reformation itself. Those foreigners had infected English religion with the tendencies toward puritanism that had led to seventeenth-century political revolution and eighteenth-century Socinianism. Third, most early-nineteenth-century English evangelical religion, whether inside or outside the Church of England, descended from that earlier puritanism and partook potentially or actually of those Zwinglian and Calvinist errors.

From these conclusions the Tractarians argued that nineteenth-century evangelicals had driven doctrines and practices within the Church of England far beyond the intentions, institutions, and Articles of the Reformers themselves and that this damage to Catholic truth must be repaired. During mid-1834 in *Tracts 38* and *41* on the *Via Media* (one of the rare appearances of this term in Tractarian literature), Newman, in contrast to Pusey's later tract on baptism, had rather ironically embraced a quasi-prescriptive portrait of the Reformation for the purpose of criticizing modern evangelicals, including those in the English Church. In the dialogue of *Tract 38*, Clericus, after recalling "our Martyrs at the Reformation," contends that modern English Christians must recognize how far over the course of years puritan activity had driven the Church of England beyond the original principles of its Reformers. Clericus claims that members of the present-day English Church "differ from the principles of the Church of Rome more than our forefathers differed." Neglect of rubrics in the Prayer Book provided the most important evidence for these departures, as did the denunciation as "Popish" of practices established or left intact by the Reformers themselves. The practices and doctrines of the true English Church as taught in the Prayer Book and the rubrics constituted a *via media* between those extreme Protestants descended from "the foreign party, who afterwards went by the name of Puritans," and the Romanists. Even the original continental Protestants, such as Calvin, would regard present-day English Protestants, such as the Wesleyans, as far more Protestant than themselves. Clericus, urging that the modern English Church had "deviated from the opinions of our Reformers, and become more opposed than they were to the system they protested against," observes, "Men seem to think that we are plainly indisputably proved to be Popish, if we are proved to differ from the generality of Churchmen now-a-days." He then asks, "But what if it turn out that they are silently floating down the stream, and we are upon the shore?"[73]

Pressing his argument further, Clericus denies that the 39 Articles contain all of the true Christian faith because the founding of the Church long predated the Reformation era. He explains to his interlocutor, Laius, "I receive the Church as a messenger from CHRIST, rich in treasures old and new, rich with the accumulated wealth of ages." For their part, the Articles constitute only one portion, though a true portion, of that accumulation of treasure, whereas, in one of the rare criticisms of the Roman Church in this tract, Clericus notes that the teachings of Trent are false. When Laius quickly observes that Clericus had subscribed to the Articles, the latter replies with opinions which, as they worked their way through the English Church, were to wreak havoc for many decades to come, "There is a popular confusion on this subject. Our Articles are not a *body of divinity*, but in great measure only protest against certain errors of a certain period of the Church. Now I will preach the whole counsel of God whether set down in the Articles or not. I am bound to the Articles by subscription; but I am bound, more solemnly even than by subscription, by my baptism and by ordination, to believe and maintain the *whole* Gospel of CHRIST. The grace given at those seasons comes from the Apostles, not from Luther or Calvin, Bucer or Cartwright." According to Clericus, the Articles had opposed sixteenth-century superstition whereas the problem of the contemporary age was unbelief. Because of the changed circumstances, Clericus indicates in words again pregnant with future developments that he would "lay especially stress upon doctrines only indirectly contained" in the Articles and "say less about those which are therein put forth most prominently." Because now the danger is that of "unbelief" rather than "superstition," protests must be lodged against the errors of the current day.[74]

The debate fostered by the Tractarians over the next decade involved exactly which of those doctrines only indirectly encompassed by the Articles—part of what Newman here termed "the whole gospel of Christ"—would be tolerated in the Church of England. Fervent evangelical clergymen might also have declared their intention to preach the "whole gospel of Christ" beyond the content of the Articles, but they would have looked to Scripture for their understanding of the full Gospel. Such evangelical preaching of a full Gospel, based on private readings and interpretation of Scripture, had infused English-speaking Christianity with one new sect after another arising during the past century. By contrast Newman's full gospel looked less to Scripture than, first, to his private interpretation of the teaching and practices of the apostles, then later to the medieval Church, and finally to what he would soon term Prophetical Tradition. Although Newman's full Catholic gospel did not achieve the same organizational boundaries as the full evangelical gospel, it nonetheless stirred more than its share of controversy and division within the Church of England and gave rise to what contemporaries regarded as nothing less than a sect within the church.

In *Tract 41* Newman further clarified his thinking as he again asserted that over time intrusions of advanced Protestant thought and worship within the English Church had undermined the achievement of the English Reformers. Perhaps still with the example of his brother Francis in mind, he decried all the manifestations of "the religion of so-called freedom and independence, as hating superstition, suspicious of forms, jealous of priestcraft, advocating heart-worship; characteristics, which admit of a good or a bad interpretation, but which, understood as they are instanced in the majority of persons who are zealous for what is called Protestant doctrine, are (I maintain) very inconsistent with the Liturgy of our Church." Those embracing such outlooks displayed "that arrogant Protestant spirit," so fully manifest in Francis, that ascribed formalism and superstition to all those who hold to the old Catholic faith. It was now necessary for persons of the Catholic faith within the Church of England to assert their position and exercise their own system of faith and practice. In his concluding speech, Clericus exclaims, "I cry out betimes, whatever comes of it, that corruptions are pouring in, which, sooner or later, will need a SECOND REFORMATION."[75] Whereas the seventeenth-century Puritans had sought to purify the Church of England of residual Roman Catholic elements, Newman proposed that his Catholics purify the same institution of novel Protestant practices and reclaim devotional elements from centuries before the Reformation, including fasting, penance, celibacy, and monasticism.

In their pursuit of this Second Reformation within the English Church, demanded less than a year after they had commenced their movement as an assault on Dissent, the Tractarians hoped to achieve a radical restructuring of both the ecclesiology and the devotional life of the Church of England and to exalt the role of its clergy in contemporary English society. Theirs was a radical clericalism championed under the banner of Catholicism but carried out within a Protestant religious body. Though calling themselves Catholics, the Tractarians behaved very much as traditional Protestants, attacking the structural and spiritual inadequacy of the contemporary church. Simultaneously, they functioned as Catholic prophets pressing their own religious experiment from one extreme to the next on the basis of their claim to a unique discernment of the pure faith and practice of Christian antiquity. Their location within an essentially Protestant institution was essential to both prongs of this drive because, despite their demands to the contrary, only the absence of strong central ecclesiastical authorities within the English Church allowed their protest and their devotional experiment to go forward.

The nomination of R. D. Hampden by the Whig ministry to the Oxford Regius Professorship of Divinity in 1836 provided the Tractarians with an unexpected opportunity to demonstrate their determination to purify the contemporary English Church. Their opposition to this nomination confirmed them as a stubborn, revolutionary presence on the English religious landscape prepared to provoke one conflict after another and to take no prisoners. It was also the single instance in their history when they constructed a temporary alliance with other parties in the English Church.

CHAPTER 5

The Hampden Case

IN FEBRUARY 1836, Lord Melbourne appointed Renn Dickson Hampden as Regius Professor of Divinity at Oxford. The Tractarians, along with others in the university, unsuccessfully opposed the nomination, then vehemently assaulted Hampden's theology and religious character, and finally secured by vote of Convocation a minor but symbolically important limitation on his new professorial duties. The affair erupted after several years of private academic rivalry and two years of public political controversy between Hampden and various Tractarians. The attack on Hampden marked the peak of Tractarian influence in the university and ironically legitimated similar later hostile actions being taken against the Tractarians themselves.

THE OXFORD DEBATE ABOUT SUBSCRIPTION REFORM

During 1834 and early 1835 the reformed Parliament, under pressure from Dissenters, debated possible abolition or modification of the Oxford regulation that required students to subscribe to the 39 Articles at the time of matriculation. Initially the entire university opposed any accommodation on the grounds of the self-governing authority of the individual colleges and the sacrifice of the exclusively Church of England character of Oxford. Newman contributed lengthy letters to the *British Magazine* and to the *Standard* newspaper opposing reform. Other university spokesmen issued numerous pamphlets on the subject. In the spring of 1834 Vaughan Thomas of Corpus Christi College organized a petition from Oxford graduates to the Duke of Wellington, the Chancellor of the university, opposing change in subscription. On May 2, 1834, all of the Heads of Houses and a large number of tutors signed a declaration that denounced subscription reform as subverting "the System of Religious Instruction and Discipline, so long and so beneficially exercised by us," and endangering "the security" of both the university and the church "by dissolving the union" between them.[1] Among those signers was R. D. Hampden, Principal of St. Mary Hall and professor of moral philosophy.

During the summer of 1834, when parliamentary repeal seemed possible, Wellington urged the university authorities themselves to undertake modification of subscription.[2] Parliamentary abolition of subscription failed, and by November a Tory ministry was back in office. During the brief Peel ministry that governed from the close of 1834 through the spring of 1835, the Oxford Heads of Houses continued to debate an arrangement whereby a declaration of willingness to receive instruction in the Articles would replace subscription. This declaration, if adopted under a Conservative ministry, would avoid the appearance of Oxford intransigence, protect the university from further, more intrusive parliamentary interference, and accommodate some real, internal Oxford concerns about the propriety of requiring boys in their mid-teenage years to subscribe to the Articles before having been educated about their meaning.

The Heads of Houses stood sharply divided over the subscription issue, but until the late summer of 1834 none had publicly called for actual repeal of subscription. Then in August, while the Whigs still held office, Hampden published *Observations on Religious Dissent*, a pamphlet that carried his name on the title page. Three months later he published a revised edition, though the differences between the two elicited no appreciable attention. In this pamphlet Hampden advocated admission of Dissenters to Oxford on grounds different from those of any other commentators. At the outset he challenged what he termed "the common prejudice, which identifies systems of doctrine—or theological propositions methodically deduced and stated—with Christianity itself—with the simple religion of Jesus Christ, as received into the heart and influencing conduct." On the basis of that distinction he traced the origins of religious Dissent to the "confusion of theological and moral truth with Religion." Once religious opinions embodied in creedal statements came to be regarded "as identical with the objects of faith," the zeal aroused by Dissent over genuine objects of faith became "transferred to the guiltless differences of fallible judgments" exercised "on the admitted facts of Scripture." Distinguishing original Christianity from later theological speculation, Hampden stated "that no conclusions of human reasoning, however correctly deduced, however logically sound, are properly religious truths—are such as strictly and necessarily belong to human salvation through Christ." He further explained "that *conclusions* from Scripture are not to be placed on a level with truths which Scripture itself simply declares."[3] Consequently, he argued, the various grounds of exclusiveness among Christian denominations were not based on matters essential to the Christian faith.

For further elaboration of this argument and of the precise meanings he ascribed to his terms, Hampden referred his readers to his Bampton Lectures of 1832. There he had argued with considerable skill and subtlety that Scripture reveals great facts about God's relationship to humankind, but that over time there had occurred an inevitable distortion in human understanding of the original divinely revealed facts. Christian theologians, employing human reason, had established logical statements of doctrine, which they confused with or substituted for scriptural facts. Hampden particularly linked this confusion to scholastic philosophy supporting the theology and structures of the Roman Catholic Church. On the basis of this analysis, Hampden had stated, in direct contradiction of Newman's soon to be published argument in *The Arians of the Fourth Century*, "The only ancient, only catholic, truth is the Scriptural fact." Hampden also believed that, despite their best efforts, the Protestant Reformers had continued to substitute logic for revelation. Summarizing his thesis, Hampden went so far as to assert, "Strictly to speak, in the Scripture itself there are no *doctrines*." Despite the distinction he drew between articles of religion, including those of the Church of England, and the facts of Scripture, Hampden nevertheless firmly defended, like Bishop Blomfield to Pusey, the practical necessity of such formularies to accommodate "the Social Profession of Christianity," to preserve the presumed agreement about "Scripture-facts" within a Christian community, "to guard it from a latitudinarianism which would virtually annul it; and to prevent its dissolution by innovators, either within or without the religious society."[4] As of the summer of 1834 Hampden's lectures and their arguments illustrated primarily from medieval intellectual history stood almost universally ignored.

By the point in *Observations on Religious Dissent* at which Hampden directed the reader to his Bampton Lectures, he had associated himself with a thoroughly undogmatic concept of Christianity rooted in Scripture and emphasizing a religion of the heart, love of Christ, sincerity of faith, and practical piety reminiscent of moderate evangelicalism, though he made no reference to the necessity of a conversion experience. His argument against subscription thereafter carried him to what all of his readers regarded as a much more extreme position. In his enthusiasm to extend Christian charity and theological benefit of doubt, Hampden declared that despite the misguided theology and dogmatism of Unitarians, they must nonetheless be called Christians, explaining, "For when I look at the reception by the Unitarians, both of the Old and New Testament, I cannot, for my part, strongly as I dislike their theology, deny to those, who acknowledge this basis of divine facts, the name of Christians. Who indeed is justified in denying the title to any one who professes to love Christ in sincerity?" Hampden further expressed his willingness to set the Unitarian "on the same footing precisely of earnest religious zeal and love for the Lord Jesus Christ, on which I should place any other Christian." What he deplored among Unitarians was their "theological dogmatism," which rather than "religious belief" he suggested accounted for their Dissent. While regarding the Church of England as "preeminently a church of Christ beyond all others," Hampden refused to identify its formularies with those of the primitive church or to deny another person the right "to regard his own communion in the same light." In evangelical fashion Hampden stated that the true unity of the church was not one of formal, visible creedal agreement but rather was "an invisible one . . . the communion of saints; the union of Christians with the Holy Spirit himself."[5]

For all the expansiveness of Hampden's argument, there were distinct limits to his projected reform. He advocated the admission of Dissenters to Oxford, but only under the condition that they receive instruction exclusively informed by the faith and theological views of the Church of England. He rejected the admission of Dissenters as Dissenters intending to maintain their own sects in the university. Hampden seems quite sincerely to have believed that this position would accommodate the basic demands of Dissenters while still shielding the authority and orthodoxy of the English Church within the university. He believed that in practice subscription neither assured the authority of the church over the mind of the subscribing student nor secured orthodoxy within the university. Indeed, rather than serving as "parts of religious *education*," religious tests constituted "merely boundaries of exclusion."[6] Concluding that the university and not Parliament must change subscription, Hampden defended his signing the declaration of May 2, 1834, as a protest against possible parliamentary legislation rather than as an indication of his approval of the practice itself.

Within Oxford and among many clerical graduates, subscription carried immense symbolic meaning. Much that the church and its clergy had lost socially and politically on the national level during the era of reform seemed capable of retention within the privileged Oxford enclave. Like the Peel reelection campaign of 1829, the subscription debate rallied the most conservative elements in the university to attack with impunity Whigs, Dissenters, and anyone else perceived as sympathetic to reform, including those who thought accommodation a protection to Oxford's best interests. Philip Nicholas Shuttleworth, the president of New College sympathetic to the Whigs, warned Lord Holland on October 2, 1834, that any further drive toward subscription reform would allow opponents "to get up a holy war, and to make conscience a plea for creating political confusion." He further observed, "No one not resident in the University can form a notion of the degree of false and violent reasoning which our prominent men indulge in at this moment; and though one cannot but despise the folly which is thus hourly uttered, yet on the ground of common policy it certainly would seem advisable not to provoke it."[7] It was just exactly that hostility which the ambitious Hampden aroused in his pursuit of Whig patronage.

There is no question that Hampden intended both his original pamphlet and the subsequent *Postscript to Observations on Religious Dissent* of 1835 to spark the interest of the Whig ministers. Although the specific theological basis for his pamphlet originated in his Bampton Lectures, Hampden's more general notion of voluntary religious association echoed John Locke's *Letter on Toleration* and reflected widely known Whig views on religion. Furthermore, the radicalism of his pamphlet distinguished Hampden from other politically better connected but trimming Oxford Whigs such as Shuttleworth. At the same time Hampden's private correspondence with the radical Lord Radnor confirmed his genuine convictions that the university should undertake subscription reform for itself, that Dissenters would benefit from university education, that not all Dissenters' grievances could be met, and that "the ascendancy of Church-of-England principles [be] maintained, as those which I believe to be the best guardians of pure Christianity."[8] Hampden's pamphlet and private political correspondence paid off. About a year after the publication of *Observations on Religious Dissent*, Lord Melbourne was sounding out Archbishop Whately, with whom he consulted on Oxford ecclesiastical patronage, about Hampden's possible promotion to a small bishopric.

Hampden's quite public ambition had in recent months clashed with the more private ambition of Newman. In early 1834, having launched the tracts and published *The Arians of the Fourth Century*, Newman had also been seeking a position providing new influence to replace that which he

had lost after his defeat over the Oriel tutorial reform. In January 1834 he
had presented himself as a candidate for the professorship of moral philosophy. The office provided no significant income, but Newman saw it as a
"situation which combines respectability with lightness of responsibility
and labour" and believed that "the name is a good thing." Had Newman
obtained the appointment, Tractarians would have held three Oxford professorships as well as the pulpit of the Church of St. Mary the Virgin. Until
a day or so before the election Newman was the only candidate. So certain
was he of the appointment that he wished his presumed new office inserted
on the title page of his forthcoming volume of sermons. But just before the
election Hampden also chose to stand and with little or no effort succeeded.
As Newman wrote to Keble, "I am floored as to the Professorship by the
great Hampden."[9] This was the second occasion when Hampden had intruded upon Newman's life and ambition. After Hawkins had removed
Newman and his friends from Oriel teaching responsibilities, Hampden had
replaced Newman as tutor. This long-standing rivalry was a key reason that
Hawkins considered the Tractarian battle within the university fundamentally the extension onto a larger terrain of a college quarrel.

After the defeat over the moral philosophy professorship, Newman lost
no chance to oppose or attack "the great Hampden." The latter's *Observations on Religious Dissent* presented the first opportunity. On August 20,
1834, without having actually read the pamphlet, Newman told Rose that
Hampden "calls all articles impositions of human authority, and advocates
their removal as a test on matriculations—and assures his reader that all this
is in no wise inconsistent with his being partner to the Declaration of May
last." Newman feared Hampden's statements would allow "the enemy to be
able to suggest that half the signatures meant nothing more than his," but
he thought it prudent to remain quiet until that claim had actually been
made.[10] Perhaps to Newman's personal disappointment, Hampden's pamphlet seems initially to have stirred very little public notice or debate.

But in mid-November 1834 the Heads of Houses, who in their collective
capacity because of their weekly meetings were known as the Hebdomadal
Board, began to debate the substitution of a declaration of willingness to
receive instruction in the Articles in place of subscription. Hampden then
published the second edition of *Observations on Religious Dissent* and sent a
copy to Newman, who appears only then to have read it. Although admitting privately that the proposed accommodation would only bring Oxford
to the state of Cambridge, Newman continued to present a public case for
the great danger posed to the Christian faith at Oxford. On November 28 he

6. Renn Dickson Hampden (1793–1868) was an Oriel fellow whom Provost Hawkins brought back to the college to replace Newman as tutor after the collapse of the Oriel tutorial reform effort. In 1834 Hampden advocated the admission of Dissenters to Oxford. Upon his nomination as Regius Professor of Divinity in 1836, the Tractarians organized a successful effort to censure him in Convocation. Hampden remained Regius Professor of Divinity until his appointment as Bishop of Hereford in 1847. (Reproduced from frontispiece, Henrietta Hampden, *Some Memorials of Renn Dickson Hampden, Bishop of Hereford* [London: Longmans, Green, 1871].)

informed Hampden of his "very sincere and deep regret" over the publication of the pamphlet containing principles "tending as they do in my opinion altogether to make shipwreck of Christian faith." He warned Hampden that his "interrupting that peace and mutual good understanding" so long prevailing in Oxford would "be succeeded by dissensions the more intractable because justified in the minds of those who resist innovation by a feeling of imperative duty."[11] Of course, it was just such disruption that Newman hoped to loose throughout Oxford.

There was an important difference between the letter that Newman sent to Hampden and the draft he had actually considered sending. In the draft Newman charged that Hampden's principles legitimately led to "formal Socinianism," but in the version sent he replaced that accusation with the vague phrase about making "a shipwreck of Christian faith." Fostering a tendency toward Socinianism was exactly the charge that in other correspondence Newman had already directed toward Evangelicals who, like Hampden, emphasized a scriptural Christianity, an invisible church, and various modes of ecumenical cooperation. Hampden, who had no idea that Newman had considered accusing him of Socinianism, replied that he did "not intend to enter into any *personal* controversy on the subject," but stood prepared "to hear any arguments that may be alleged against my positions."[12] Hampden seems naively to have expected a debate over the issues and the politics of subscription. What he very rapidly encountered without any warning was a substantial debate over the character of his own personal religious faith.

Throughout the opening months of 1835 Newman remained determined to resist subscription reform, to foment party divisions within the university, and to designate all reformers as "the Hampden party" even though, as he well knew, Hampden had no personal following whatsoever and Hawkins led the effort to substitute a declaration for subscription.[13] On March 23, the day on which by a single vote the Heads decided to propose to Convocation the substitution of a declaration for subscription, Newman urged Henry Wilberforce to write a pamphlet with the projected title, "Socinianism in Oxford," a topic made opportune by Blanco White's recent apostasy to Unitarianism. This was the first of several occasions on which Newman turned to a younger friend or follower to compose a hostile pamphlet or article on his behalf. Wilberforce was particularly vulnerable to the request because his recent marriage had badly strained his friendship with Newman. Wilberforce wanted to repair the relationship and to demonstrate that marriage had not interfered with his apostolical principles.

Instigating internecine strife among Oriel men, Newman explained to Wilberforce that the proposed pamphlet should respond to Hawkins's *Letter to the Earl of Radnor*, which had denied any connection between Socinianism and the removal of subscription. Wilberforce should indicate that in regard to certain university reformers he believed "their motives pure etc and that some of them at least . . . do not mean to approximate to Socinianism." He should then note that Hampden's was the only pamphlet to justify subscription reform on religious grounds and then link Hawkins's pamphlet to Hampden's school of thought. Wilberforce should quote Thomas Arnold, Richard Whately, and Blanco White and connect the current proposals for change in subscription with those of 1772, which had actually been associated with anti-Trinitarian sentiment in the Church of England. By the end of the pamphlet, Newman counseled, the reader should be asking himself, "Who can doubt, with these facts before him, that the movement at Oxford is but the *advanced guard* of a black host, and that it desires to achieve the first of a series of changes?" Quickly agreeing to compose the pamphlet, Wilberforce declared, "There is no doubt all this tends towards Socinianism and infidelity."[14]

In May 1835 Wilberforce published *The Foundation of the Faith Assailed in Oxford: A Letter to His Grace the Archbishop of Canterbury*. There he presented the function of the university as "training up her members, from the first, in pure and uncalculating loyalty to the Church," which they should learn to regard "as the sacred ark wherein the truth has been preserved to us." University teachers should instruct students "not as sceptical disputants, who would investigate for themselves a new road to the shrine of truth; but as humble and teachable disciples, labouring to ascertain what has been the Church's faith and practice, assured that the path by which fathers, and confessors, and martyrs attained the high prize, will more certainly conduct them to it, than any which their own acuteness and the modern development of intellect can enable them to discover." The Christian faith, according to this view, was a matter for dogmatic teaching by an authoritative church upheld by university instruction. Challenging this concept of the church and university education, according to Wilberforce, stood a party associated with the publications of Arnold, White, and Hampden. This group encouraged within Oxford "a series of liberal changes" that embodied tendencies "to make knowledge, rather than moral discipline, the object of our studies, and to cultivate rather the habit of bold and irreverent inquiry, often conducted in the most flippant tone and spirit" in place of "that humility and self-distrust which characterizes the true philosopher."

Persons so educated would adhere to the Church of England over other religious alternatives only by personal preference and would regard Christian verities as "a mere matter of opinion, unconnected with moral and religious character."[15]

The impetus to modify subscription, originating with the Dissenters, had now become, according to Wilberforce, genuinely dangerous because of the presence in the university of persons prepared, along with Hampden, to open its doors to Unitarians. While specifically refraining from accusing "Dr. Hampden or his supporters of any unequivocal assertion of doctrines directly Socinian," Wilberforce nonetheless asserted that Hampden's views went beyond those of Socinus and Crellius and urged that Hampden "certainly paves the way for others to formal Socinianism, however he may himself escape it." Then Wilberforce, after citing numerous quotations from Hampden, Arnold, and White, stridently concluded "that in the University there exists a party on which I think I should hardly lay an unjust censure were I to apply to them the awful name of SOCINIAN."[16] Those accusations ensured for the upcoming meeting of Convocation the attendance of nonresidents, inflamed against the proposal to substitute a declaration for subscription. The pamphlet also assured turmoil within Oriel because all the alleged Socinian protagonists were associated with Oriel College and were friends of Provost Hawkins, who had removed both Newman and Wilberforce from their tutorships.

Wilberforce's anonymous pamphlet, transforming the subscription controversy (and the Oriel strife) into one of orthodoxy versus heterodoxy, cut Hampden to the quick. Of all the persons cited and censured, he alone was still resident at Oxford. As head of a house, he was the only person named who had been part of the Hebdomadal Board's decision to modify subscription. Perhaps most important, in his *Parochial Sermons* (1828) he had made a powerful presentation of the scriptural basis for the doctrine of the Trinity and had emphasized the necessity of Christian belief in that doctrine.[17] Furthermore, as a head and a professor, he did not expect to find himself the object of such a calumnious accusation. Having never resorted to anonymity in his own writings, Hampden demanded that the publisher of *The Foundation of the Faith Assailed* immediately disclose to him the name of the author.

On May 20, 1835, the day of the Convocation, in a note to Hampden dated from Oriel College, where he was staying, Wilberforce acknowledged his authorship, explaining that he had published the pamphlet anonymously because he had not written all of it. Hampden replied, deploring "the insinuations against his sincerity of belief contained in that Pamphlet with indignation, as utterly false and unjustified by any thing that he has written."[18] He demanded that Wilberforce make public his authorship and reveal the name of his assistant. Two days later Hampden similarly demanded the identity of the accomplice in a letter to Newman, who had introduced the offensive pamphlet into the Oriel Common Room.

While this dispute raged, Hampden simultaneously engaged Pusey in a separate controversy. In *Subscription to the Thirty-Nine Articles: Questions Respectfully Addressed to Members of Convocation,* Pusey had anonymously suggested that Hampden's charity toward Unitarians laid the groundwork for an attack on the great doctrines of Christianity. Describing Pusey's tactics as "very impertinent & unfair," Hampden particularly denounced his use of "the cover of an anonymous signature." Pusey defended himself as having wished not to address the university from a position of professorial authority. The plain fact of the matter, Hampden replied, was that only on the authority of his "own vain pretensions" had Pusey "propagated in an unmanly way an unwarranted scandal against me." He challenged Pusey, "Produce your *reasons;* valid ones, if you can, against the principles which I have established." Pusey then submitted his pamphlet and Hampden's correspondence to Hawkins for an opinion. The latter disapproved of the pamphlet and pronounced an apology to be in order. On May 27, commenting on the draft of a possible apology, Hawkins adjudged Pusey's extracts from Hampden to be unfair and observed that even if they had been fair, "it does not follow that you had a right to give them *on such an occasion;* viz, taking occasion from a question about Subscription to make Hampden's opinions the object of an oblique attack." He also chastised Pusey for omitting any reference to passages in which Hampden "professes his attachment to the Church of England & his conviction of the use & necessity of Articles." As if to anticipate events of the next few months, Hawkins added, "Mere detached passages can scarcely ever" express "opinions faithfully." Pusey replied that he owed Hampden no apology and that the attack on his theology was appropriate because it directly related to his proposal to change subscription. Pusey added, "I certainly think Dr. H's language calculated to foster Unitarianism (at least one form of it) & to make it less distrusted." Pusey apparently did not send the drafted apology, which Hawkins on May 27 had criticized for not being "anything like a full & fair" one.[19]

On May 21, 1835, Hampden informed Lord Radnor of Convocation's rejection on the previous day of the proposal to substitute a declaration for subscription. Reflecting on the general political and religious situation at Oxford, he indicated that his hope "that the University should make a change in the matter of the Tests by its *own act*" now seemed unlikely to be fulfilled and that the university "must therefore be eventually indebted for the benefit . . . to other hands." He reported the presence of "a very active party" who were "bent on resisting any alteration of our practice with the most determined enthusiasm" and who would raise "a clamour" against those persons "who express an opinion in favor of it." He noted that he had himself "been made the object of the most unjustifiable attacks" for the part he had taken and primarily because he had "put forward the *religious* grounds . . . on which . . . a change ought to be made in regard to the Tests."[20] Other trials awaited Hampden in the upcoming weeks.

On June 11 Newman published *Pamphlets in Defence of the Oxford Usage of Subscription to the XXXIX Articles at Matriculation*, a collection designed to reaffirm the Tractarian image of a university sharply divided between theological parties embodying truth and falsehood. However, the volume actually published on June 11 was *not* the collection as originally conceived or even as initially printed. Newman had edited the initial version, which was printed but not published, to demonstrate that subscription protected Oxford from Socinianism and Arianism. That original collection contained several pamphlets all from Tractarian hands, including Wilberforce's and Pusey's, that directly implied that Hampden fostered Socinianism. The second version, which was published, omitted Wilberforce's pamphlet as well as others, and generally refrained from imposing the Socinian and anti-Hampden interpretation on the subscription controversy.

In the original version, following an anonymous introduction probably written by John Keble, there had appeared an anonymous postscript concerning the insinuations appearing in Wilberforce's pamphlet. The author of the postscript stated that all the authors represented in the collection understood the author of *The Foundation of the Faith Assailed* "in no respect to refer to the personal faith of Dr. Hampden, or to be desirous of passing any judgment upon him in matters which lie solely between every man's soul and his Maker, but to speak of certain of his *opinions*, and of him so far forth as he is the *advocate* of those opinions." The author of the postscript then asserted as "a plain matter of fact" that "the sense in which Dr. Hampden interprets the doctrine of the Atonement or Reconciliation is Socinian, or that in which Socinus and his school received it." There followed a few rather obscure and heavily edited passages on the atonement from Hampden's Bampton Lectures, after which appeared a further series of unexplicated quotations from Socinus and Crellius. The postscript concluded, "It is plain then that in a main article of religion, in which our Church takes one side and the Socinians the other, Dr. H. sides with the Socinians, and on this account the writer of the pamphlet in question appears to call his school Socinian."[21] The purpose of the postscript was to suggest that all of the authors included in the collection agreed with Wilberforce's accusations.

On June 23, having learned about the contents of the original pamphlet collection and the postscript, which had already been printed but not yet circulated for sale, Hampden went on the offensive. He vehemently protested to Newman, describing him as a person acting "with dissimulation, and falsehood and dark malignity" and as one who "worked the machine, but hid yourself behind it." He declared that Newman had no ground of assault except for "a fanatical persecuting spirit." More to the point, Hampden stated that William Sewell, one of the authors included in the collection, had permitted use of his own pamphlet only if the others refrained from personal attacks. Yet the editors had aimed the entire project against Hampden: four of the pamphlets directly attacked him and several others had little to do with the subscription question. In contrast to Newman's coterie, Hampden claimed to have "neither willed, nor thought, nor done, any thing to hurt the feelings of a single person, by what I have written, or by any part that I have taken in the late question" and to have neither "provoked resentment" nor to have shown "resentment in any other way than becomes a man, and, I trust, a Christian."[22] Hampden was correct, if also overwrought. At no time in his public urging of subscription reform had he made personal attacks or attacks on other groups. Nor had he cast any aspersions on the honesty, sincerity, or orthodoxy of his opponents.

On June 24 Newman replied that he saw no reason to remove the anonymity of editorship of the collection because Hampden had encountered no difficulty in discovering his identity. Newman asserted that his letter of November 28, part of which he quoted, had made clear his disapproval of *Observations on Religious Dissent* and that thus his later actions could not be construed as concealed. He stated that Sewell had been given proofs of the objectionable postscript, whose authorship he refused to reveal.

At this point Sewell, a high-church opponent of subscription reform but not yet a Tractarian sympathizer, intervened. He admitted having not carefully read the proofs of the preface and indicated that he did not want his pamphlet included with one that made so direct a personal attack as did Wilberforce's. Newman very much wanted Sewell's pamphlet included, to indicate disapproval of subscription reform by a person regarded as unaligned in the university. Consequently, after consulting Keble and Pusey, Newman rapidly recast the collection, removing Wilberforce's *Foundation of the Faith Assailed* as well as another anti-Hampden pamphlet, thus rendering inclusion of the postscript unnecessary. Consequently, what had commenced as a pamphlet collection assaulting Hampden in order to portray the subscription controversy as a conflict over religious truth ended as a rather nondescript collection, more or less objecting to parliamentary interference with Oxford and voicing the usual protests against the danger of Dissent. Newman thought that Hampden, whom he described as in a state "like a red hot iron," would still be angered that Sewell had remained as part of the enterprise. But Hurrell Froude believed that Hampden would "certainly reckon" the removal of Wilberforce's pamphlet "a triumph."[23]

By late June 1835 Hampden probably believed that he had turned back his detractors. The subscription pamphlet incident was the third occasion on which he had bettered Newman. Hampden continued his teaching and administrative duties, published his lectures on moral philosophy—which, like everything else he had ever written, remained publicly ignored—and directed little or no further attention toward the Tractarians. By the end of the year he knew that his publication of *Observations on Religious Dissent* had brought him to the attention of Lord Melbourne and that a bishopric might await him.

Yet Hampden remained very much on the minds of the Tractarians and other high churchmen. On New Year's Day, 1836, writing to Newman, Rose criticized Hampden's recent volume on moral philosophy as "an aggravation of the offence of his former book" and condemned the "mischievous" and "Anti-Christian" character of the author's sharp distinction between the spheres of religious and moral truth. Arguing for the necessity of public rebuke, Rose regretted the continuation of "the same injurious policy" of silence that had followed the publication of other offensive books. Although the obscurity and vagueness of Hampden's works assured their current neglect, Rose feared that they might in later years acquire authority by default. The next day Newman, writing to Pusey, termed the policy of silence a "deplorable evil—a breach, it seems to me, of Vincentius's great rule, that error, as a witness for posterity, should be protested against, on its first appearing." But on January 3 Newman explained to Rose the difficulty of instigating any university action against Hampden on the grounds of Oxford having enjoyed "the blessing of a profound peace." As a consequence, Newman observed, "We are morbidly tender—afraid to stand up for the Truth—willing rather to offend against it than to offend man."[24] Newman saw no hope for leadership from either Edward Burton, the Regius Professor of Divinity, or Geoffrey Faussett, Lady Margaret Professor of

Divinity, whose amicability and caution made them unwilling to challenge any particular person or group on theological or ecclesiastical grounds. But that climate of "profound peace" dissolved more rapidly than Newman or anyone else might have expected when on January 19, 1836, Edward Burton unexpectedly died, leaving the divinity professorship vacant.

THE HAMPDEN CONTROVERSY OF 1836

Among the Tractarians there existed a fundamental tension between ambition for place in the university and the church and a wish for the martyrdom of failure. If the forces of erastian corruption informed by evangelical Dissent frustrated their ambitions, they found opportunity to display spiritual strength in the face of that worldly corruption, to confirm their own public and private sense of moral and spiritual superiority, and to indict those who had rejected their faithful prophetic remnant. Consequently the unexpected vacancy in the divinity professorship aroused in them both anxiety and hope.

In line with a self-image of one facing imminent persecution, Newman at first feared that the Whig ministry's decision on Burton's successor might open an era of persecution "if Hampden or other such 'forerunner of Antichrist', (for it does not now do to mince matters) be placed in the Divinity Chair." But that apocalyptic stance also served to mask an overweening ambition on the part of the Tractarians and a desire for vindication. Such hope for vindication quickly replaced Newman's original anxiety as he imagined even Hampden's nomination rallying new support to the Tractarian cause and fostering a realignment of university religious parties because "numbers would approximate to us and open themselves to our views, from fear of him, who at present are suspicious of us."[25]

For a brief moment, the Tractarians also actually fantasized themselves capturing the divinity professorship, with its annual income of almost £2,000, when on January 29 they learned that a list of potential candidates submitted to Lord Melbourne by the Archbishop of Canterbury had included the names of Keble, Pusey, and Newman. Pusey and Newman thought their own nomination unlikely but believed Keble's possible. Newman urged Keble to accept the position should it be offered. Pusey told William Gladstone that Keble's nomination "would be too great a blessing, for us to dare in these days to hope for—tho we may pray for it."[26]

On Monday, February 8, however, harsh political reality manifested itself as word arrived in Oxford that Lord Melbourne had appointed Hampden.

Hampden accepted the professorship the same day but requested permission to retain the principalship of St. Mary Hall, which, he claimed, brought him no significant pecuniary reward.[27] Retention, of course, maintained his Whig presence on the powerful Hebdomadal Board and also prevented the much-speculated-upon advancement of Vaughan Thomas, a major opponent of subscription reform. Hampden was nothing if not political.

On the evening of February 8 Pusey, with hopes dashed of capturing the divinity professorship for the Tractarian cause, invited to dinner a group whom J. B. Mozley termed "the leaders of orthodoxy in the University."[28] These guests, who included Newman, decided to circulate a public petition protesting the nomination and to issue a pamphlet attacking Hampden's theology. Although other Oxford religious parties were to join this effort, Newman and Pusey from beginning to end manipulated the drive that continued their long-standing conflict with Hampden. Reverting to Newman's original strategy, they sought to polarize the Oxford religious parties to achieve their own dominance. They intended to use that influence to assert the independent authority of Oxford, in place of that of the erastian institutions of the church, to define religious orthodoxy, to condemn religious error, and hence to determine in some measure ecclesiastical appointments.

The Tractarians quickly forged a broad alliance against Hampden's nomination because within the university itself there was no reward for supporting and no political cost for opposing Hampden, whom even supporters regarded as obscure in his expression and opportunistic in his ambition. The vehicle for protest was a caucus of Hampden opponents, who first met on February 10 in the Corpus Christi Common Room and thus designated themselves the Corpus Christi Common Room Committee. In addition to the names of Newman and Pusey, the major statements emanating from this committee bore the names of Vaughan Thomas, who had whipped Convocation to defeat the subscription reform efforts, William Sewell, who though disapproving subscription reform had previously dissented from attacking Hampden's theology, Edward Greswell, a high churchman from Corpus Christi College, and John Hill, a conservative evangelical from St. Edmund Hall.

Hampden always claimed that opposition to his nomination arose from the subscription controversy. He was correct, but in 1836 and after it was to Tractarian advantage to emphasize the breadth of opposition to draw as many participants as possible into sharing the guilt of the affair. Some years afterward, disillusioned allies, such as William Palmer, stressed the broad character of the opposition to Hampden so as not to appear to have been stalking horses for a Tractarian leadership, later deeply associated with Romanizing practices.[29] Nonetheless, Newman and Pusey spearheaded the attack with virtually all of the accusatory documents bearing the impress of their prose and echoing Wilberforce's *Foundation of the Faith Assailed.*

The evangelical link to the anti-Hampden alliance requires comment because, as Palmer noted in 1842, Hampden's theological emphasis on Scripture was not far removed from theirs. But as Peter Nockles has noted, Hampden did not, like the evangelicals, "appear to deduce dogma from self-evident scriptural truth, and above all, rejected scripture-consequences." Thomas Arnold privately suggested that evangelicals had honestly associated any accommodation on subscription with the petitions of 1772, which had arisen from anti-Trinitarians in the church. In 1836, however, the issue for Oxford evangelicals, such as Hill, as well as the evangelical press appeared to be protection of establishment against radical Dissent leagued to the Whig ministry. The *Record* supported the campaign against Hampden because it regarded admission of Dissenters to Oxford as offering the fundamental principles of the church in "sacrifice to the idol of an unprincipled *Liberalism*." According to the paper, Hampden's nomination had emerged from "the present O'Connell-ridden—Papist-ridden Cabinet" exercising what amounted "in simple verity, the powers of the temporal head of the Church."[30] The *Record* appears to have thought aid to Dissenters presaged later aid to Roman Catholics. The *Christian Observer* was critical for similar reasons during the spring of 1836. Additional evangelical skepticism toward Hampden appears to have reflected strife within the Bible Society, where earlier in the decade certain Church of England evangelicals had unsuccessfully attempted to impose a test to exclude Unitarians in the same manner that Oxford excluded them. For these reasons evangelicals opposed Hampden in early 1836, but by late in that year and thereafter most, despite occasional reservations, stood shoulder to shoulder with him in opposition to Tractarianism and all its works.

Because Regius professorships lie in the gift of the crown, there existed no regular legal channels to challenge an objectionable appointment. Keble suggested "a sort of respectful memorial" to the bishops in hope that they would "remove candidates for Orders out of" the king's "reach." Pusey advocated a petition asking the monarch to permit the Archbishop of Canterbury a veto over divinity appointments in the university. On February 10, however, the meeting of the Corpus Christi Common Room bypassed any appeal to episcopal authority and decided to petition the king directly. The extraordinary anti-Hampden petition, which by February 11 had received seventy-six signatures, declared that from the statements that Hampden had "put forth in his published works, we should apprehend the most disastrous consequences to the soundness of the faith of those whom he would have to educate for the sacred ministry of the Church, and so to the Church itself." The petition also contended that the Regius Professor of Divinity must "possess the full confidence" of the other instructors in the university, a "confidence which we unhappily cannot repose in Dr. Hampden." Looking back on these accusations from the standpoint of 1842, the Roman Catholic *Tablet* commented, "Up to this point the University had patiently endured the Bampton heresies; but the Whig patronage it could not stomach."[31]

On February 10 Hampden informed Melbourne that those who had attacked him on subscription reform were now circulating a memorial against his appointment and were also "putting together passages from my published works as proofs of what they consider unsound theology." Assuring Melbourne of his loyalty to the Church of England and directing attention to his volume of parochial sermons, Hampden concluded, "I fear not to stand the most strict examination as to every thing that I have written, if it can be only fairly weighed."[32] The next day he directly encountered the efforts to oppose him and fairness proved to be in short supply.

On February 11 a bitterly and narrowly divided meeting of the Heads of Houses, with Hampden present and voting in his own behalf, refused to forward the petition to either the king or the Archbishop of Canterbury. The proctor, E. G. Bayly, reported to Lord Holland that after portions of Hampden's Bampton Lecturers were read aloud, it was generally admitted that some passages required interpretation, "but neither from these, nor from other passages of his writings could anything like heresy or heterodoxy be substantiated." Bayly further stated, "The Board could bring no charge ag[ain]st him—in fact, by general confession no body *doubted* of his orthodoxy."[33] Furthermore, at this and at subsequent meetings a majority of Heads consistently refused to forward Hampden's work to a board of six doctors, the prescribed university setting for adjudicating accusations of heresy or heterodoxy, because as Regius Professor of Divinity, Hampden would have been a member of the board, and he had already demonstrated that he would not withdraw from proceedings involving himself.

After the February 11 meeting, nine of the Heads drew up their own petition informing the Archbishop of Canterbury, "Dr. Hampden is known to have expressed himself in printed publications, in such a manner as to produce on the minds of many an impression, that he maintains doctrines and principles fundamentally opposed to the integrity of the Christian

Faith."[34] Neither the university petition nor that of the nine Heads—nor any other subsequent attack on Hampden—listed any specific theological errors, and all rested their case on his having conveyed "an impression" of heterodoxy. The absence of specificity indicates the political nature of the opposition to Hampden and the determination of the various Oxford religious parties for different reasons to deny a Whig ministry exercise of patronage in the university.

On February 13 the pamphlet that Newman had composed at the instigation of Pusey's dinner guests appeared. *Elucidations of Dr. Hampden's Theological Statements* was the single most effective instrument devised against Hampden's nomination and reputation. Newman intended this pamphlet, which against Pusey's advice from his previous encounter with Hampden appeared anonymously, to appeal beyond the Heads of Houses to the larger university community and the wider church. The *Elucidations*, unlike any of Hampden's own writings, received wide circulation and provided the only information most observers received about Hampden during the weeks of controversy. Rivingtons sold it in London. Rose arranged to have it stitched into the March edition of the *British Magazine*. Batches were also posted to sympathetic clergy for wider circulation. A. T. Gilbert of Brasenose sent a copy to Melbourne. Edward Cardwell, Principal of St. Alban Hall and private university secretary to Wellington, told the Chancellor that the pamphlet fairly represented the issues in dispute.[35]

The *Elucidations* launched the attack Newman had wanted to deliver against his rival the previous year but had delegated to Wilberforce. Determined to leave Hampden's reputation in tatters, Newman boldly opened the *Elucidations*, perhaps the most abusive of all his polemics, with a bill of heterodox particulars. He declared that Dr. Hampden considered

that the only belief necessary for a Christian, as such, is belief that the Scripture is the word of God; that no statement whatever, even though correctly deduced from the text of Scripture, is part of the revelation; that no right conclusions about theological truth can be drawn from Scripture; that Scripture itself is a mere record of historical facts; that it contains no dogmatic statements, such as those about the Trinity, Incarnation, Atonement, Justification, &c.; that theological statements, though natural and unavoidable, are in all cases but human opinions; that even the juxtaposition of the actual sentences of Scripture, is a human deduction; that an individual is not abstractly the worse for being a Unitarian; that it does not follow that another is worse because I should be worse for being so; that, though a deduction be correct, logical, and true, yet a denial of it must not be pronounced to be more than an error of judgment; that infinite theories

may be formed about the text of Scripture, but that they ought not to be
made of public importance to Christian communities, badges of fellowship,
reasons for separation, and the like; that the Articles of the Nicene and Athanasian Creeds are merely human opinions, scholastic, allowing of change,
unwarrantable when imposed, and, in fact, the product of a mistaken philosophy; and that the Apostles' Creed is defensible only when considered as
a record of historical facts.[36]

Every one of these statements could be challenged as at best unfair and
at worst maliciously distorted presentations of Hampden's thought and
technical theological terminology. After this opening blast, Newman cited
numerous quotations from *Observations on Religious Dissent* and from the
Bampton Lectures. Many of them were taken out of context; none of them
was self-explanatory. Virtually all of Hampden's theology depended upon
the precise definitions that he had given to words such as *facts.* Newman
provided none of those definitions, nor did he even hint at their presence in
Hampden's works.

Throughout the *Elucidations,* as in the previous Tractarian attacks on
Hampden, Newman combined guilt by association and assertions that
Hampden's thought necessarily led to Socinianism, the strategy that a year
earlier had defeated subscription reform in Convocation. Newman assumed
that it would similarly turn back Hampden's professorial nomination or at
least demolish his credibility in that position. In the *Elucidations* Newman
contended, "Language such as he [Hampden] has used, is frequent in the
mouths of Socinians and others. These religionists urge, after his manner,
that all doctrine is matter of opinion, varying according to the character of
individual minds. We wait for him then to complete his view, and to draw the
line between himself and them, lest Churchmen perchance who listen to
him, turn Socinians before he is aware of their danger. He says, that it is a
matter of opinion, whether a man believe in the Divinity of Christ or not.
Now, supposing hearers of his were to take up with Socinianism, would he be
earnest in reclaiming them or not?"[37] Hampden had never said, nor even
hinted, that belief in the divinity of Christ was a matter of opinion. Consequently, Newman could not provide an illustrative quotation; instead he
quoted Blanco White, claiming that White and Hampden commenced their
thinking from the same point. In further accusatory comments on Hampden's statements about the Trinity, the incarnation, the atonement, the
sacraments, original sin, and morals, Newman rehearsed the same argument:
Hampden himself may not hold heterodox opinions, but persons of a Socinian outlook may find support or comfort in what he has said.

Though admitting that Hampden himself believed "in the doctrines of the Trinity and Incarnation . . . and considers them influential on conduct," Newman nonetheless argued that Hampden did not regard them as revealed and felt that he had no right to impose them on others. It was consequently necessary that "a Christian University should have some safeguard against Socinians sheltering themselves behind, and using the authority of, Dr. H., which in the present state of his published teaching they might do, were they inclined."[38] Newman thus uncompromisingly portrayed Hampden as a thoroughgoing latitudinarian, possessing no certain principles, no clear adherence to the major doctrines of the faith, no firm allegiance to the Church of England, and no distinct convictions separating himself from Unitarians.

Newman saw the eruption of "another row" with Hampden as resulting in both personal satisfaction and the extension of Tractarian influence in the university. On February 17 Newman admitted to Bowden that the absence of prior objections to the Bamptons and the noncontroversial appointment to the moral philosophy professorship would probably prevent the successful blocking of Hampden's nomination. Still angry over losing that professorship, Newman mused, "Now I am malicious enough to feel some amusement at this—for Gaisford and the Vice Chancellor were afraid of me as being ultra, and thought Hampden a safer man." Yet, should Hampden withdraw from his new professorship, that victory would mean that Hampden's successor "will be virtually curbed in any liberalistic propensities by our present proceedings and their success." If Hampden's nomination did go through, then the moral philosophy professorship and the principalship of St. Mary Hall would open. Keble might be drawn to the principalship, thus putting a Tractarian on the Hebdomadal Board. The entire anti-Hampden fray could only renew political animosities fruitful to Tractarian ends. Newman predicted: "Again the Ministry will be at open war with the Church—the Archbishop will be roused, and a large number of waverers in this place will be thrown into our hands." Finally, the confirmation of Hampden's appointment would allow "a formal investigation into his opinions before the Vice Chancellor—and nothing would do us more good in these times than the precedent of a judicial investigation and sentence."[39] How little did Newman suspect that in just a few years similar machinations and academic judicial devices would be turned upon himself, Pusey, and their sympathizers.

Because Newman's diatribe against Hampden reached a level of vendetta beyond that displayed in any other of his previous or later publications, it invites a fuller examination. Factors other than theological disagreement and frustrated ambition fueled Newman's anger. His private description of Hampden as "worse than a Socinian" and "the most lucre loving, earthly minded, unlovely person one ever set eyes on," betrayed a deep-seated visceral hatred of the man.[40] To be sure, almost every step of Hampden's success marked for Newman a moment of failed ambition and professional displacement, first in Oriel over the tutorial program and then in the university over both the moral philosophy and divinity professorships. In early 1836, as Hampden achieved new eminence and vast income, Newman remained the odd man out, possessing a college fellowship and a pulpit but no students, no professorship, an income significantly reduced from a few years earlier, but accompanied by no diminishment of his financial responsibility for his sisters and mother. Beyond giving vent to private vindictiveness, the public assault on Hampden for a brief time allowed Newman to attain the university preeminence to which he so aspired. The Provost of Oriel, the electors of the moral philosophy chair, and the prime minister might have rejected him, but now he would command a university-wide agitation to discredit his rival and to defend orthodoxy and the church against those in the university who, as at the time of the Peel reelection campaign, had curried the favor of London politicians.

There also existed an important link between John Newman's relentless drive against Hampden and his ongoing conflict with his brother Francis. During 1834 and late 1835, while subscription reform sparked Oxford controversy, John had again clashed with Francis over the authority of Scripture versus that of the church, the very issue of Hampden's offending pamphlet.[41] Francis had flatly rejected his brother's call to obedience as contrary to the Pauline theology of the Bible. Christianity based on a direct personal approach to Scripture versus that based on the church as a body teaching through its creeds also lay at the heart of Newman's disagreement with Hampden. Furthermore, Francis in the family, as Hampden in the university, prevented John from establishing the position of sustained, acknowledged leadership he so sought. The public and private objects of anger reinforced each other.

On November 17, 1835, Newman complained to Froude of Francis's having decided to preach the Gospel by undertaking a preaching ministry outside the Church of England and reported that he had broken socially with his brother, as he must do as a churchman. Fearing his brother's "verging towards liberalism," Newman observed, "That wretched Protestant principle about Scripture, when taken in by an independent and clear mind, is almost certain to lead to errors I do not like to name."[42] Both

Newman and Froude saw private judgment of Scripture as accounting for Blanco White's apostasy to Unitarianism, about which Froude was at the time composing an article.

Shortly after writing Froude, Newman shared his angry dismay directly with Francis. Declaring his brother to exemplify the popular notion that "latitudinarianism *is* a secret Socinianizing," John explained that he had not realized how deeply Francis had imbibed "that wretched, nay (I may say) cursed Protestant principle, (not a low principle in which our Church has any share, but the low arrogant cruel ultra-Protestant principle)" of private interpretation of Scripture. He then demanded of Francis, as he might have of Hampden,

> On what ground of reason or Scripture do you say that every one may gain the true doctrines of the gospel for himself from the Bible? where is illumination promised an *individual* for this purpose? where is it any where hinted that the aid of teachers is to be superseded? where that the universal testimony of the Church is not a principle of belief as sure and satisfactory as the word of Scripture? . . . Till you give it up, till you see that the unanimous witness of the whole Church (as being a witness to an historical *fact*, viz that the Apostles so taught), where attainable, is as much the voice of God (I do not say as sacredly and immediately so, but as really) as Scripture itself, there is no hope for a clearheaded man like you. You will unravel the web of selfsufficient inquiry.

As far as Newman was concerned, his brother's faith in the adequacy of independent, private interpretation of Scripture represented "a snare of the devil."[43] Francis epitomized the religious impulses of Protestantism gone awry and embodied the pursuit of scriptural religion unencumbered by the restraints or aided by the guidance of the church with its creeds and articles. In that manner, he exemplified for Newman the fate of the Christian religion should Hampden's latitudinarian critique of the theological inadequacy of articles of religion prevail.

Moreover, just as John Henry Newman could not defeat Hampden in the university, neither could he oust the latitudinarian Francis from the circle of family affection. In his letter of November 23, he told Francis that he objected to meeting him "in a familiar way" or sitting "at table" with him. Only a few days later John received a letter from their mother indicating her intention shortly to relieve him of some of the burden of the financial support he had been providing her and his sisters. She then also told him of her plan to invite Francis and his Unitarian bride for a family visit after their forthcoming marriage at Christmas. Mrs. Newman said, "It may lead to good, and would be very pleasing to your Sisters and myself."[44] Newman's mother and sisters simply would not, like John, eject the religiously errant and soon-to-be-married Francis from the family, no matter how schismatic his faith. Indeed, from Newman's standpoint they may have seemed to love him even more. Newman may have been even angrier with Francis because of the marriage itself, representing still one last step in Francis's moving away from his older brother's influence.

Also possibly accounting for the stridency of his behavior against Hampden, two of Newman's key friendships encountered serious difficulty in late 1835 and early 1836. In October 1835 John Keble had unexpectedly married and resigned his Oriel fellowship. Newman wrote critically of the event, which removed from the celibate state the Tractarian leader whom he had once compared with Ambrose.[45] His "Church of the Fathers" articles championing monasticism were in course of publication at the time, and Newman may have felt his opinions, well known to Keble, to have been spurned by his elder friend. Second, during these crucial weeks Froude entered his final illness, which took his life on February 28. Anticipating Froude's death, Newman had written Jemima, "I shall be truly widowed, yet I hope to bear it lightly."[46] Newman's harsh attack on Hampden allowed him to demonstrate one last time his solidarity with Froude and perhaps to vent his anger that one such as Froude was about to die, leaving him bereft of his closest friendship, while Hampden achieved position, influence, and income.

Finally, early in 1836 Newman may ironically have felt the necessity of shoring up his reputation among his own allies as a defender of creeds, tradition, and church authority. As we shall see, during the previous year he had been engaged in a newspaper controversy with a French abbé over the rule of faith in the English Church. Newman had strongly rooted the rule of faith for the Church of England in Scripture, only to encounter sharp criticism from Benjamin Harrison, the author of an extremely hostile anti-Hampden subscription pamphlet.[47] Harrison thought Newman's argument essentially ultra-Protestant and compromising of the entire Tractarian position. Newman displayed little patience with the younger man but may well have felt that the renewed attack on Hampden—whose position on Scripture, if carried to extremes, certainly did point to what the Tractarians regarded as an ultra-Protestant position—allowed him to reestablish his credentials with his own party.

As the pamphlet war raged in Oxford, William IV became aware of the turmoil, though neither of the petitions protesting Hampden's appointment reached his desk. The concerned monarch made inquiries of Melbourne, who reported having consulted with the Archbishop of Canterbury, the Archbishop of Dublin, and Bishop Copleston, among others, before making the nomination. As Newman had privately forecast, Melbourne noted that certain of the Heads now criticizing Hampden had approved his appointment as head of St. Mary Hall and as professor of moral philosophy. Throughout the controversy Hampden's having achieved the latter appointment without protest was the single most telling argument in favor of his orthodoxy. After Melbourne visited the king in Brighton and forcefully stated his case, William accepted the nomination, which became official on February 18. On February 19 the Oxford protesters learned that the Archbishop of Canterbury had not presented their petition to the king and that the appointment stood approved.[48]

Although Melbourne had a reputation for caring little about the theology of his ecclesiastical appointees, his correspondence demonstrates that Hampden's orthodoxy, as well as that of other potential appointees, did indeed concern him. Melbourne rightly distrusted the patronage advice of Archbishop Howley, who had opposed the current reform of the church and would happily embarrass the Whig ministry on any occasion. Furthermore, Howley did not raise theological concerns when advising about the divinity professorship. Consequently, Melbourne had consulted Copleston and Whately over the appointment, apparently after receiving a list of names from the archbishop. In the wake of the furor over his decision for Hampden, he did so again. After delving into the Bamptons, Copleston, who was not a Whig, though obviously a strong Oriel man, pronounced Hampden's lectures orthodox. Whately defended Hampden at length, pointing to the existence of unused university procedures against preachers thought to be heretical. He also suggested that if the anonymous tracts published by Hampden's opponents had been preached as sermons, he might himself, if still in the university, have brought formal action against them.[49]

On February 21, in a second letter, Whately revisited the Hampden matter. He stated that both Hampden and Arnold encountered "the *imputation* of heresy" because their independence of mind led them "to express even generally-received notions in such terms as seem to themselves most appropriate, without tying themselves down to hackneyed phrases." Many of their critics could not distinguish between matters of opinion and "what are, & what are not, portions of the *Creed of their Church*." Unable to make these distinctions, such people were likely to pronounce "a man heterodox who does not agree with them in *every* point." Whately observed, "Many trump up a charge of heresy, disloyalty, or what not, (& often bring themselves in time, sincerely to believe it) from some aversion to the man on other grounds, whether of personal jealousy, or dislike to some *other* position of his (real or supposed) conduct or tenets." Hampden's own difficulty arose directly from his favoring "the relaxation of subscription to the Articles at matriculation." As a consequence, he confronted "a charge of heresy," which if his opponents "had been sincere & honest," they would have raised at the time of the delivery and publication of the Bampton Lectures. Applauding Melbourne for upholding the appointment, Whately concluded that Hampden was "chiefly unpopular at *Oxford*, from *academical* causes" and added, "I do not think he w[oul]d have been so much opposed as A[rnold] in appointment to the Bench."[50]

There were others at Oxford, not associated with Oriel or with the Whigs, who also declined to attack Hampden. One was Thomas Legh Claughton, later Bishop of St. Alban's. On February 23, 1836, explaining to Roundell Palmer, then a strong Tractarian and critic of Hampden, his refusal to sign the protest against the nominee, Claughton quite simply reported, "I saw a number of persons rushing with furious haste to condemn a man, of whose opinions I was satisfied, many of them knew nothing—and setting myself to examine one or two points, as the time allowed, I found in *them* nothing to justify the common report."[51] Though he lamented the appointment, he found the accusations unfounded. Claughton seems to have been one of the few persons in Oxford who in early 1836 actually read Hampden's writings and compared what he found to the accusations.

The measured letters of Whately and Claughton stand in marked contrast with the one that Pusey composed to Lord Melbourne on February 22 urging the withdrawal of Hampden's nomination. Why Pusey waited until after the appointment had become official is unclear, though he most likely had heard from his brother of Melbourne's displeasure with events at Oxford. Some people believed that Pusey challenged Hampden in order to deflect public censure against a recent antievangelical sermon of his own on the difficulties attendant on achieving forgiveness of sin after baptism.[52]

Pusey condescendingly suggested that he could give the prime minister information about Hampden's appointment that he might not otherwise receive. Asserting the importance of cooperation among the Regius Professor of Divinity, the Lady Margaret Professor of Divinity, and the Regius Professor of Hebrew, Pusey claimed that in no German university would the crown appoint to a divinity post someone in whom the rest of the faculty lacked confidence. The Germans understood that differing professorial opinions undermined each other and could lead students to "float about, without any opinions at all" or to embrace one set of opinions in extravagant opposition to others. Pusey asserted, "It is confidently thought by sober & well-judging men in this place, that those trained in Dr. Hampden's school, would end in a state of universal scepticism (altho' no one accuses him of being as yet a sceptic)." Pusey also predicted that Hampden "would probably be prohibited from preaching" and that his lectures would be ill attended "except by a few lovers of novelty." Pusey then rebuked Melbourne for having ignored the names forwarded by the Archbishop of Canterbury, "the Spiritual head of our Church," and for having consulted Whately and Copleston, "neither of whom indeed possess the confidence of persons in this place." While denying that political opinions determined university opposition to Hampden and other appointments, Pusey added, "But we do feel deeply concerned whether their religious character give us ground to think that he will benefit or corrupt the Church of God; and to prevent any such corruption, (should the occasion unhappily be offered) I feel assured that any sacrifice will be made, which may, by God's blessing, help to avoid it."[53]

On February 24 Melbourne replied at considerable length, reminding Pusey that his information, like all reports collected from rumor, was "partly true & partly false." He chastised Pusey for petitioning the king, then advised, "If you want a thing done, take my advice, and hereafter, go to the man who has to do it." He rejected Pusey's plea for unanimity among divinity professors, noting, "Your principle would make the opinions of the present Professors the standard & measure of every future appointment" and also necessitate examining the tenets of the present occupants of theological chairs. Melbourne reminded Pusey that he himself stood connected with certain anonymous tracts "which are represented to me to be of a novel character & inconsistent with the . . . doctrines of the Church of England."[54] Melbourne also expressed his regret over the destructive tactics that Pusey had predicted would be launched against Hampden and urged those governing the university to seek the furtherance of religion and the spirit of Christianity.

In his reply, Pusey stressed to Melbourne that the differences he had discussed lay not between Hampden and the two other divinity professors but between Hampden and the entire university, with men of all shades of religious opinion opposing him. Only a common fear of the peril to the church posed by Hampden's being "the chief teacher of theology in this place" could have achieved such unity. Pusey regretted that any one had "taken alarm" at the tracts but assumed that the few who had done so lacked knowledge of Christian antiquity or the more ancient theology of the Church of

England. Pusey, only a few years away from having had his own orthodoxy questioned, assured Melbourne that the tracts, as edited by Keble and Newman, did not contain "a single expression" that was "not altogether consonant with the purest ages of the Christian Church, as well as the brightest & best period of our own." In their concern for the regulation of the church, veneration for antiquity, and high valuation of the sacraments, he declared, "They are not innovative."[55]

Returning to the matter at hand, Pusey stated that Hampden's works had gone astray only since the time of the Bampton Lectures, when "he appears to have been bewildered by a modern French philosophy," an accusation that never received any explanation. Hampden's previous faith had thus far preserved him from the conclusions stemming from the logic of his own views, but might not safeguard others. Trying to make Melbourne appreciate the intensity of the Oxford opposition, Pusey wrote, "We are truly persuaded that Dr. Hampden's appointment would have a direct tendency to corrupt our Church, to bring in a vague & uncertain way of teaching Scripture truth, to lower & profane men's notions of the Holy Sacraments, to produce Socinianism and scepticism." That being the case, Pusey predicted that the opponents of the appointment would probably seek "to condemn publicly the errors of Dr. Hampden's works" and urge the archbishop and bishops to accept only the Lady Margaret Professor's certificates for ordination, thus reducing Hampden's "office to merely a sinecure."[56] Pusey thought it proper to report that these proceedings were afoot rather than leave unnoticed the prime minister's injunction for the university to seek peace.

THE QUESTION OF RATIONALISM

Pusey's letters, the most outspoken ever written by a Tractarian to a person in authority, left the terms of engagement clearly drawn. Hampden's opponents would appeal to Convocation in an effort to destroy his theological credibility and with it the efficacy of Whig patronage in Oxford. The vehicle of the Corpus Committee was to be a statute passed by Convocation to prohibit Hampden from participating in choosing select preachers for the university and from serving on the panel of six doctors called to inquire into the orthodoxy of teaching or preaching in the university. To bring the motion for this statute before Convocation, the Corpus Committee required a majority recommendation from the Hebdomadal Board.

To achieve that end, during late February and early March the Corpus Committee issued both signed and anonymous broadsides describing Hampden as "one, in the soundness of whose doctrinal opinions the university can place no confidence" and decrying both "the evil principles and doctrines" and "the evil tendency of his past publications." On March 5, shortly after Hampden had publicly defended himself in *The Times*, the committee declared, "No explanation or even recantation of his opinions at this moment can sufficiently restore . . . confidence."[57] This strategy eliminated Hampden's possible escape from censure through a restatement or reconsideration of his views, as Pusey some years earlier had accomplished in private letters and a revised edition of his book on German theology. Following Newman's example, the committee issued its own set of unexplicated Hampden quotations without any indication of context.

Initially Hampden continued to be accused of a Socinian tendency of thought, but on March 10 his detractors shifted the accusation. The Report and Declaration of the Corpus Common Room Committee on that date insisted that what lay at stake in the controversy concerned neither an individual, nor a book, nor "even an ordinary system of false doctrine" but rather "a *Principle;* which (after corrupting all *soundness of Christianity* in other countries) has at length appeared among us, and, for the first time, been invested with Authority within the University of Oxford." The Corpus Committee then announced, "This principle is the *Philosophy of Rationalism,* or the assumption that uncontrolled human reason, in its present degraded form, is the primary Interpreter of God's Word, without any regard to those rules and principles of Interpretation, which have guided the judgments of Christ's Holy Catholic Church in all ages of its history, and under every variety of its warfare." This hitherto unmentioned principle accounted for both the errors of Hampden's past writings and the theological danger posed by his future teaching. Although refraining from imputing to Hampden "personally those unchristian doctrines," the Corpus Committee asserted that Hampden resembled J. S. Semler, a late eighteenth-century German biblical scholar of personal piety, whose thought had allegedly produced rationalistic consequences. The declaration denounced Hampden's "assertions of principles which necessarily tend to subvert not only the authority of the Church, but the whole fabric and reality of Christian truth." Then, like the previous pronouncements from the Corpus Common Room, the declaration stated that no "explanations of insulated passages or particular words" could be permitted to excuse the manner whereby "the Articles of our Church are described as mere human speculations, the relics of a false and exploded philosophy, and full at once of error and mischief."

The declaration further protested "against principles, which impugn and injure the Word of GOD as a revealed Rule of Faith and Practice, in its sense and use, its power and perfection, and which destroy the authority of the Church as a Witness and a Keeper of Holy Writ." Finally, the Corpus Common Room Committee resolved to oppose "the spread of that false philosophy" to which Hampden's principles could be traced, "a philosophy, which in other countries has poisoned the very fountains of Religious Truth, which for a long time reduced Protestantism, in its original seat, almost to an empty name, and changed the Religion of the Cross into the Theology of Deism."[58] Hampden stood accused of all of these intellectual faults despite the fact, alluded to neither by himself nor by anyone else in 1836, that he had extensively denounced any extravagant use of reason and rationality throughout his Bampton Lectures.

Not only did the Corpus Committee Report and Declaration cite no specific instances of violation of the Articles, rejection of the creed, or questioning of Scripture on Hampden's part, but it also left the new charge of *rationalism* to explain itself. Pusey certainly knew, from his experience with Rose and Blomfield between 1829 and 1831, that a reputation for supporting *rationalism*, meaning the questioning of the authority and practical expedience of religious articles, could arouse episcopal criticism and distrust. The committee must have resorted to the term in hope of thus dissuading bishops from accepting certificates of attendance at Hampden's lectures if presented by would-be ordinands. In particular, Pusey may have hoped the accusation would bring Bishop Blomfield to support the anti-Hampden forces even though Hampden had very carefully underscored the social necessity and expediency of articles of religion.

But in 1836 the meaning of *rationalism* within Tractarian and high-church circles was quite complicated. A few years earlier, during their debate on rationalism in Germany, both Rose and Pusey had acknowledged the difficulty of precise definition. Commentators on their dispute in the *Edinburgh Review* alluded to "the system called Rationalism in Germany," by which they meant a critical use of reason, a naturalistic interpretation of natural phenomena, an empirical account of human experience, a critical examination of biblical history, and a rejection of "whatever is supernatural in the Judaical and Christian revelations." During the Hampden controversy of 1836, however, rather than relating to a naturalistic analysis of the Bible, nature, or history, the term *rationalism* denoted a critical approach to clerical and ecclesiastical authority. In the earliest comment on the Corpus Committee use of the term, E. G. Bayly, one of the proctors who was to veto the initial censure of Hampden, reported to Lord Holland that the Committee Report and Declaration "contained no specific charge of heresy or heterodoxy against Dr. Hampden's writing, but only a general one of rationalism (a term which remains yet to be explained by that party) or it may mean too low a view of church authority and discipline."[59]

Private and public Tractarian comments confirmed Bayly's judgment. Froude in his "Essay on Rationalism, as Shown in the Interpretation of Scripture," composed in 1834 on Barbados but not published until 1839, associated the term with an evangelical concept of ministry. After citing passages of a century earlier from the evangelical Adam Clarke and the notoriously low-church Bishop Benjamin Hoadly to illustrate rationalism in theology, Froude commented, "A lower modification of Rationalism, in one or other of its shapes, is exhibited to us in the disposition now so prevalent, to set up Sermons as means of grace, to the disparagement of Sacraments." He later described as "essentially rationalist" any view which "assumes that the experimental good of Sermons is commensurable with the promised blessings of the Eucharist." In 1835 Froude privately denounced as "rationalistic" Bishop Cosin's tract denying transubstantiation.[60]

John Keble also equated rationalism with the broad principles of Protestantism and more particularly evangelicalism. On April 2, 1835, criticizing the proposal to accommodate Dissenters at Oxford by substituting a declaration for subscription, Keble told Robert Wilberforce, "I shall be much pained if you do not view the matter in the same light as we do, viz. as a contest between Faith & Rationalism." Keble did not use the term *rationalism*, as one might suspect, to equate all Dissenters with rational Unitarianism. He directly included evangelical Dissenters in the circle of his rationalism. Over a year later Keble expressed fears to his friend J. T. Coleridge that in the absence of a real church party, Parliament might mandate changes in the liturgy especially regarding baptismal regeneration. Such liturgical modifications, he observed, "would alike meet the purpose of the Hampdenian & Simeonite Rationalists."[61] The term Simeonite, here linked to Hampden and rationalism, referred to Charles Simeon of Cambridge, who like other prominent evangelicals looked to the Bible alone to defend the doctrines of the atonement and justification by faith and to criticize baptismal regeneration. What Keble privately denounced as rationalism was essentially the historic Protestant emphasis on supremacy of Scripture and priesthood of all believers championed by contemporary evangelicals of all persuasions.

Later in 1836, as discussed in chapter 4, Pusey made such denunciations publicly in the second printing of *Scriptural Views of Holy Baptism*. There he directly related the alleged rationalism emerging from the Swiss Reformers to the deficiencies of modern American evangelical religious practices and to the "popular" evangelical mode of preaching.[62] By drawing a line of rationalistic descent from the Swiss reformers to modern evangelicals, Pusey associated his critique of rationalism with a critique of the entire tradition of reformed Protestantism.

Pusey further clarified the connection he drew between rationalism and evangelicalism in a letter of 1838 to his German friend and theologian Augustus Tholuck. Assuming that Tholuck would "think our strong measures" against Hampden amounted to persecution, he defended them by explaining, "In our present state it was enough to show that Dr. H's system, as a system, went counter to that of the Articles, to show the leprous spot, and warn people to flee the infection." The condemnation of Hampden had strengthened emphasis on church authority as no mere teaching of it could have done. Had such a tactic been used in Germany at the time of the publication of the Wolfenbuttel fragments, Pusey contended, "Rationalism . . . might never have gained a head among you." As a result of this preemptive attack, Pusey reported that in England "people whom one would least have expected are coming to Catholic views, and leaving the narrowness of the so-called Evangelic party."[63]

As early as a sermon of 1831, Newman had announced, "The usurpations of the Reason may be dated from the Reformation." In overturning the authority of the church, the Reformation had undermined the very institution upon whose testimony the authority of Scripture itself had previously rested. Newman illustrated and criticized a key example of what he regarded as the inappropriate Protestant exercise of Reason in a private memo of 1834 regarding evangelical criticism of the doctrine of baptismal regeneration. There he described the evangelical argument that "*the lives of baptized Christians show that they are not regenerate*" as "an argument of *sight* or *reason*, an argument of *unbelief*" that manifested "the essence of rationalism." He further lamented "the popular comparison of baptism to circumcision," thus equating the former with "an outward rite of admission to the Church," as "arising from the rationalizing spirit."[64] In both instances, Newman regarded the questioning by Protestants of the authority as well as of the substantive content of ecclesiastical teaching to constitute a departure into rationalism

During the months before Hampden's nomination, while so deeply distraught about his brother's evangelical religious activity, Newman undertook his most extensive discussion of rationalism—an essay, published in the spring of 1836 as *Tract 73*, entitled "On the Introduction of Rationalistic Principles into Religion." Newman had commenced this tract in September 1835 and later claimed that its contents had no relation to the Hampden controversy. The tract, an extended commentary on the writings of the Scottish lay evangelical Thomas Erskine and the New England Congregationalist Jacob Abbott, assailed the two targets that Newman most intimately associated with rationalism—the exercise of private judgment and subjectivity in religious matters. In this context Newman declared, "To Rationalize is to ask for *reasons* out of place; to ask improperly how we are to *account* for certain things, to be unwilling to believe them unless they can be accounted for, i.e. referred to something else as a cause, to some existing system as harmonizing with them or taking them up into itself." Such rationalizing was characterized by "its love of systematizing, and its basing its system upon personal experience, on the evidence of sense." Both outlooks stood opposed "to what is commonly understood by the word Faith, or belief in Testimony."[65] Newman here as elsewhere conflated philosophic empiricism dependent on the senses with the evangelical religion dependent on subjective feeling. Both rejected the testimony of authority that could not be tested by sense experience on the one hand or by subjective religious experience on the other.

As he explored rationalism as the exercise of private judgment, Newman surprisingly drew his examples not from modern critical philosophy but from Scripture itself. Among the biblical practitioners of rationalism, he included the rich Samaritan lord who asked how Elisha's prophecy would be fulfilled; Naaman, who resisted bathing in the Jordan; Nicodemus, who objected to the doctrine of regeneration; and St. Thomas, who questioned Christ's resurrection. Each biblical account illustrated the "desire of judging for oneself" or of judging on the basis of one's own personal experience in matters of religion.[66]

When he turned to modern examples of rationalism rather than pointing to critical or skeptical philosophy, Newman discerned rationalism in the practices of everyday life whereby, "our private judgment is made everything to us,—is contemplated, recognized, and referred to as the arbiter of all questions, and as independent of every thing external to us." Rationalism thus transformed the human mind and its power of comprehension into the arbiter of religious truth and led people to seek to understand before believing. Rationalism thus by its very nature excluded other possible paths to

knowledge of religious truth. As Newman explained, "The notion of half
views and partial knowledge, of guesses, surmises, hopes and fears, of truths
faintly apprehended and not understood, of isolated facts in a great scheme
of Providence, in a word, of Mystery, is discarded."[67] These constituted the
very kinds of truth that in lectures of the spring of 1836, as in his French
controversy of the previous year, Newman associated with what he termed
"Prophetical Tradition."

According to Newman in *Tract 73*, practitioners of rationalism erroneously associated religious truth with subjective experience or subjective
reality. But Newman, as always, provided very special meanings for his
terms, meanings that had little to do with contemporary philosophic concepts of subjective or objective. In language that Pusey was to echo in his
letter to Tholuck, Newman explained, "By objective Truth is meant the
Religious System considered as existing in itself, external to this or that
particular mind: by Subjective, is meant that which each mind receives in
particular, and considers to be such. To believe in Objective truth is to
throw ourselves forward upon that which we have but partially mastered or
made Subjective; to embrace, maintain, and use general propositions which
are greater than our own capacity, as if we were contemplating what is real
and independent of human judgment." For Newman, there existed within
tradition a body of religious truth the content of which was to be accepted
on faith without substantial criticism or explanation, a set of beliefs which,
he readily acknowledged, "seems to the Rationalist superstitious and un-
meaning." The Rationalist consequently confined "faith to the province of
Subjective Truth, or to the reception of doctrine, as, and so far as it is met
and apprehended by the mind, which will be different in different persons,
in the shape of orthodoxy in one, heterodoxy in another."[68] The issue under
debate was not whether or not this traditionary knowledge existed but
rather whether it was to be accepted unquestioningly or only after some
kind of explanation or explication.

In *Tract 73* Newman directly contrasted the objective Catholic faith to
the subjectivity of what he termed "the popular theology of the day," which
taught the atonement as "the chief doctrine of the Gospel" and emphasized
not "its relation to the attributes of GOD and the unseen world, but . . . its experienced effects on our minds, in the change it effects where it is believed."
Further relating rationalism to evangelical religion, Newman urged, "There
is a widely spread, though various admitted School of doctrines among us,
within and without the Church, which intends and professes peculiar piety,
as directing its attention to the *heart itself,* not to any thing external to us,

whether creed, actions, or ritual. I do not hesitate to assert that this doctrine is based upon error, that it is really a specious form of trusting man rather than God, that it is in its nature Rationalistic, and that it tends to Socinianism."[69] According to Newman, such preaching produced within the listener a good feeling or state of mind but one that involved virtually no connection between the atonement and God's forgiveness of sin. This approach to Christianity resulted in neglect of the creeds and hence, as he had repeatedly argued elsewhere, a tendency to Socinianism, which as usual he left without definition.

For the purposes of the Hampden controversy, what is important to note is that Newman understood the quarrel with rationalism as occurring not between religious writers and secular skeptics but rather among religiously committed persons who despite disagreements about religious knowledge all presupposed its existence, importance, and accessibility. In that regard, the Hampden controversy was very much a quarrel among priests and, contrary to Tractarian rhetoric, not a dispute between believers and nonbelievers. For both Hampden and Newman there existed a mode of religious knowledge or revelation available for the salvation of human beings, a revelation that should remain uncontaminated by critical human reason. For Hampden it was Scripture; for Newman, tradition. In *Tract 73* Newman contended that the doctrines of the Catholic faith, including the Trinity, the incarnation, the atonement, the church, and the sacraments as channels of grace, constituted "a Mystery; that is, each stands in a certain degree isolated from the rest, unsystematic, connected with the rest by unknown intermediate truths, and bearing upon subjects unknown."[70] These doctrines demanded reverence, not theological systemization. Newman's hostility to theological system and skepticism about the capacity of systems to inculcate full religious truth in a very real sense echoed the formal argument of Hampden's Bampton Lectures, which indicted similar skepticism about the capacity of creeds, devised by human reason, to embody the full truth of the divine facts contained in Scripture.

In September 1837 Newman made his last significant remarks about the Hampden dispute in a letter to Lord Lifford. After posing his objections to evangelical emphasis on subjective emotion as proof of justification and after citing *Tract 73* for his argument regarding the Socinianizing tendency of evangelical Dissent, Newman stated, "As to the affair of Dr. Hampden, I do believe that this great good will result from it,—that it will alarm pious and serious men . . . who have hitherto held what is called the Evangelical System, without seeing the tendency of their opinions. That system has become Rationalistic in Germany, Socinian in Geneva—Socinian among English Presbyterians and Arian among Irish—Latitudinarian in Holland—it tends to Socinianism among our own Evangelical party. Let us profit by the examples of Watts and Doddridge, and of Dr. Hampden himself who though neither Socinian nor Evangelical, speaks like both at once, and is received by both."[71] The goal of the censure of Hampden was thus to serve notice on Church of England clergy sympathetic to evangelicalism within or without their church that they would face stiff Tractarian opposition and potential condemnation.

Among Tractarian sympathizers *rationalism* and its cognates remained for some time terms of opprobrium hurled at evangelicals. In late 1837 Arthur Perceval, then still friendly to Tractarians, in a letter to the *British Magazine* attacked an unnamed writer who, in the evangelical *Record*, had described the doctrine of baptismal regeneration as " 'an awful, unscriptural, and soul-destroying delusion.' " In response to that accusation Perceval declared, "Here rank, unblushing *rationalism* shews itself." He then denounced the *Record* itself as "a presbyterian, rationalistic, and semi-Socinian paper" and deplored the manner in which through its influence "the lurking hyaenas of rationalism" had crept into the Church of England. The *Record* replied on December 18, "Rationalistic! This new sect are very fond of the term. When their superstitious notions are attacked, immediately there is an accusation raised against the assailants of Rationalism." What the Tractarians thus condemned as rationalistic, the *Record* regarded as "an appeal to *common sense,*" with the charge of rationalism itself appearing in such cases "very foolish and very unscriptural."[72]

Early Victorians openly recognized the self-consciously confusing and destructive dynamic into which all of this public religious hostility could decline as polemicists claimed exclusive truth for their own positions and substituted name-calling for actual recognition of other points of view. W. F. Hook, the high-church rector of Leeds who long sympathized with the Tractarians, captured the character of these exchanges when in 1838 he confessed in the *British Magazine,* "When I speak of that class of persons represented by the 'Patriot,' the 'Record,' &c., as Socinianizing Christians, I deal with them as they deal with churchmen. They contend that church principles lead to popery, and therefore, trusting on the infallibility of their logic, they call us papists. Now we think that it is only their ignorance of logic which prevents their perceiving how *their* principles, if properly carried out, lead on to Socinianism. It is therefore on the same principle that we call them Socinians as they call us papists."[73] This statement clarifies much about the Victorian religious world where advocates of differing religious, theological, and ecclesiastical opinion and ambitions sought to prosper through a premeditated confusion of tongues.

In the spring of 1842, during an unsuccessful effort by the Heads of Houses to have Convocation rescind the 1836 Hampden censure, evangelicals in a reversal of their previous position supported Hampden, whom they now regarded as a Protestant champion. Thomas Mozley, Newman's hand-picked successor as editor of the *British Critic,* on that occasion declared that Hampden's newfound supporters now confessed "that their so-called evangelical system is compatible with a wish that there should be no theological opinion at all, and that two at least of the Creeds, viz. the Nicene and Athanasian, should be dispensed with as bonds of Christian union, or marks of discrimination between Christian and Christian." Mozley boasted that for ten years the Tractarians had warned that evangelicals, by instructing "the Christian to look *into* rather than *out* of himself, and to realize his own spiritual progress rather than the objects of faith," had "eaten away the substance of doctrinal Christianity, and left to the believer nothing but a so called spiritual, but really moral and rational scheme." He further claimed that the Tractarians had long presented reasons "for fearing that the 'Evangelical' school do not hold, in any *proper,* that is, real sense, the Divinity of the Son of God, the Incarnation, or the Atonement, or other Catholic doctrines; or at least that they do not act and speak as if they did."[74] Thus evangelical theology and Hampden's alleged rationalism finally formally blended into each other in the self-referential realm of Tractarian polemic.

Drawing upon these various discussions, one must conclude that for Tractarians *rationalism* indicated little more than a firm adherence to Protestantism in general and evangelicalism in particular and to theology that based Christianity on Scripture, justification by faith, and the priesthood of all believers rather than on the Articles, tradition, sacramental grace, and a sacerdotal priesthood.[75] Certainly such was the case with Hampden, whose alleged rationalism essentially consisted in his believing and having written that the fundamental truth of Christianity lay in Scripture and not in church tradition or creeds. Hampden possessed an exceedingly exalted view of Scripture and a profound distrust of human institutions, including creeds or articles, to contain or maintain the ultimate truth that God had revealed in the Bible. This distrust of human reason set him far apart from persons traditionally associated with Socinianism or Rational Dissent, as did his unswerving conviction that Christianity involves issues of human salvation and not merely ethical teaching. Hampden, however, had opened himself to accusations of Socinian tendencies through his friendship with Blanco White and his opportunistic tolerance toward Unitarians attending Oxford, as well as through careless wording and overstatement in his Bampton Lectures. It is worth noting, however, that neither earlier in Hampden's career nor later were there any indications that his teaching ever led any one to leave the Church of England for Unitarianism or for any other version of Dissent or for Roman Catholicism. Hampden's alleged rationalism seems to have been the only variety in the century that led no one into skepticism or away from the English Church.

HAMPDEN CONDEMNED

In late March 1836 Hawkins wrote Whately, "The violent party in Oxford will never rest until they are fairly beaten & exposed; but not until *after* H's condemnation. For Gentlemen who are pledged to Declarations, etc. will carry their point first & perhaps read his writing afterwards."[76] It took more than a decade after the fulminations of the Corpus Christi Common Room Committee for the results of reading what Hampden had actually written to take effect. It also required that profound distrust of Tractarian behavior and truthfulness settle over much of the English Church, distrust confirmed by the conversions of 1845. Hampden's reputation eventually benefited from those developments.

In 1847 Lord John Russell nominated Hampden to the see of Hereford. Archbishop Howley, initially approving the appointment, reported to the prime minister, "During the ten years that have passed since Dr. Hampden was appointed Regius Professor of Divinity at Oxford, I have no reason to believe that he has taught from the Chair any doctrine at variance with the Articles of our Church: and in justice to him I must say I have discovered nothing objectionable [in] the few publications of his which I have seen, and which are ably written."[77] When a new and again destructive but ultimately unsuccessful anti-Hampden high-church agitation erupted upon the nomination's being made public, Howley retreated from this position, but he had spoken the truth at the beginning.

Samuel Wilberforce, Bishop of Oxford in 1847, also found himself having to reconsider his previous thinking on Hampden. He at first strongly opposed the nomination but eventually reversed that position as a result of conversations with Hawkins, his long-ago Oriel tutor. Wilberforce admitted that in 1836 he had not read the Bampton Lectures. Having now under pressure from Hawkins finally done so, he found them orthodox if "disagreeable" and "obscure" in content and had also become "convinced that Newman's extracts, &c., were *most* unfair—so unfair as scarcely to let one hope they were not consciously unfair."[78] Wilberforce still insisted that *Observations on Religious Dissent* had deserved condemnation, but because the pamphlet was no longer in circulation, it was irrelevant to Hampden's current nomination. The reversal was embarrassing for Wilberforce, but unlike Howley he stood by it.

Hampden's nomination to Hereford allowed others in the church to become familiar with the events of 1836. During the 1847 agitation Julius Hare, the scholarly, Cambridge educated, theologically liberal Archdeacon of Lewes was asked to oppose the appointment. He was previously unacquainted with Hampden. Upon receiving a reprint of the 1836 Corpus Committee extracts, he read the 1832 Bampton Lectures and reported himself "quite amazed to find the utter groundlessness of the charges" lodged against Hampden. While subsequently writing a pamphlet to persuade clergy "to withdraw from this shameful persecution," Hare told William Whewell, Master of Trinity College, Cambridge, of having encountered throughout the published attacks "not mere misunderstandings, but gross & malignant misrepresentations" arising from the "faculty of lying" as "cultivated by this new Oxford religionism" whose proponents "really seem to have an incapacity of speaking the truth."[79]

A stunning private, personal apology came to Hampden almost a decade after he arrived at Hereford. In 1856 Gladstone, while, as a member of the London King's College Council, resisting the effort to condemn F. D. Maurice, recognized the similarities to the 1836 Hampden case. On the previous occasion as a Tractarian confidant, having received personal letters from Pusey as well as the public Corpus Committee materials, he had expected to vote against Hampden, though he had actually not attended the relevant meeting of Convocation. In 1856, suddenly finding himself conscience stricken by that memory, Gladstone wrote an apparently much surprised Bishop Hampden to apologize for "the injustice of which I had unconsciously been guilty in 1836" by acquiescing "in a condemnation couched in general terms which did not really declare the point of imputed guilt, and against which perfect innocence could have no defence."[80]

Still another decade later, during the *Essays and Reviews* controversy, W. F. Hook refused to condemn the authors, telling Bishop Wilberforce, then leading that agitation, "After the sin I committed in taking part against Hampden, without having first examined his works, prompted by zeal than by a spirit of justice, I vowed a vow that I would never take part in similar proceedings until I had thoroughly investigated the subject. We at that time placed ourselves under the leading of a man whose subsequent conduct has shown that he loved darkness better than light."[81] Hampden, however, for his part ever the champion of the sole authority of Scripture, did join the persecution of the authors of *Essays and Reviews.*

Roundell Palmer, another strong Tractarian supporter in the 1830s and, like Gladstone, always a high churchman, confessed many years later in his autobiography that those few of his Oxford friends who had abstained from the censure in 1836 had been correct. He observed, "The truth is, that most readers gave Hampden credit for meaning more than he said; and his previous publication of a pamphlet in favour of the admission of Dissenters to the university may perhaps have affected their judgment. The *Bampton Lectures* appeared to be directed against all definite or dogmatic theology. But they were capable of a construction, which would reduce their logic to a protest against the abuse of human logic on theological subjects; against a confusion of the form with the substance of revelation; and against disregard of the history and structure of the books of Scripture."[82] Palmer also noted that as a bishop Hampden had shown no signs of heterodoxy and was neither worse nor better than his fellow members of the bench.

Despite these much later apologies, recognitions of wrongs done, and other second thoughts, Hampden in 1836 had to defend himself more or less alone. Following his own political instincts, personal faith, and the advice of Oriel friends, he wrapped himself in the cloak of historic Protestantism, a stance from which he never wavered for the rest of his life. Ignoring the political roots of the assault on his appointment that generally united his university critics, Hampden raised the controversy between himself and the Tractarians to a dispute between Protestant truth and Roman Catholic falsehood. The progress of Tractarianism over the next decade toward Romanizing devotion and eventual conversions to the Roman Catholic communion served after the fact to confirm the interpretation he had set upon his own situation.

Hampden's defense in 1836, undertaken in the midst of what Hawkins termed "this discipline of persecution," not surprisingly proved inadequate to halt the Convocation censure. The prime minister and the monarch stood behind the appointment, as did much of the secular press in London, Oxford, and elsewhere. Hampden received modest support from within the university. He and his supporters, the most important of whom was Hawkins, first attempted to prevent the closely divided Hebdomadal Board from recommending any condemnation to a decision of Convocation. On March

4, with Hampden himself casting the deciding vote, the board postponed action until after his inaugural lecture. On March 11, however, the day after the Corpus Committee Declaration and Report, the Heads, with two of Hampden's supporters absent, sent Convocation a statute to prohibit him as Regius Professor from participating in the choosing of select preachers and serving on the panel of six doctors called to render judgments over allegedly heretical sermons. Edward Cardwell, an implacable enemy of Hampden's, explained to Wellington, "It is admitted that there was no great danger to be apprehended from the exercise of these powers [traditionally exercised by the Regius Professor]; but they promised a good opportunity for enabling Convocation, if they thought fit, to put on record a declaration of their want of confidence."[83]

When Convocation met on March 22, the proctors vetoed the statute and thus prevented a vote. Four days later, the young Tractarian supporter W. J. Copeland commented, "When Heads of Houses or Doctors take it into their heads to act the part of corks to a ginger beer bottle which seems to be pretty nearly their position now, it is true we may all froth out or evaporate and vanish in the explosion, but they may be blown no one knows whither. We really ought to be ready to sacrifice the University entirely in a cause of so deep interest to the Church."[84] Supported by such opinion, the Corpus Committee determined to carry the fight to a second meeting of Convocation when there would be new proctors. At the May gathering of Convocation the condemnatory statute passed and remained in effect until Hampden's elevation to the bench of bishops.

Throughout the political maneuvering Hampden made a series of public statements, the first of which was a letter of February 27 to Archbishop Howley published in *The Times*. Responding to the various hostile petitions and Newman's *Elucidations*, Hampden emphasized his belief in and support for "the doctrines and established formularies of the Church of England." He claimed his Bampton Lectures to have been "simply a history of the technical terms of theology" and to have displayed not "the slightest tendency, in my view and intention, to impugn the vital truths of Christianity." He had intended *Observations on Religious Dissent* only "to induce a charitable construction" on the views of groups differing from the Church of England. Declaring "a belief in the great revealed truths of the Trinity and the Incarnation" to have been "my stay through life," Hampden disclaimed "the imputation of inculcating any doctrines at variance with these foundations of Christian hope." Acknowledging failure always to have stated his views "with the precision and clearness" that he might have wished, he nonetheless insisted that he had attempted to declare the truth and "to maintain the Articles of the Church."[85] He referred the archbishop to his volume of parochial sermons, which had never been criticized, and requested a hearing with the archbishop.

Neither on this nor on subsequent occasions did Archbishop Howley make any substantial reply or request any further theological explanation. He was not about to transform what he knew to be a politically advantageous dispute over patronage into a more questionable contest over theology. For several months Howley maintained political pressure on Melbourne's ministry by emphasizing the vague impression of heterodoxy that he understood Hampden's writings to have conveyed to others.

In his inaugural lecture of March 17, Hampden resolutely asserted his faith in the doctrines of the Trinity, baptismal regeneration, justification by faith, and consubstantiation. But emphasizing his central duty as the preaching of Christ, he declared, "The great foundation . . . that I would lay for all my teaching is no other than that on which all our Scriptural instruction is built, Jesus Christ himself." He asserted his intention to point "to the Scriptures themselves as the sole supreme Authority of all revealed truth" and spoke of the "subordinate capacity" of the church. Hampden, following advice from Bishop Copleston, apologized for any lack of clarity in his previous writings, but he refused to retract anything. In remarks about the 39 Articles congruent with his Bampton Lectures and *Observations on Religious Dissent,* Hampden indicated his recognition of their "essential use for maintaining the Christian religion in its integrity, in holding together the faithful in fast communion, in keeping the unity of the Spirit in bonds of peace," but he nonetheless set them "at a vast distance from the sole authentic records of the Divine Will, the Scriptures themselves." He further described the value of the Articles as "relative to the Scriptures and derived from the Scriptures."[86] The church itself deserved reverence, he urged, because care of the Scriptures had been placed in its hands.

Then, following Whately's advice, in words that curiously anticipated those of Newman's *Apologia* a quarter-century later, Hampden acknowledged that he faced his audience "under a cloud of prejudice and clamour" and "insinuations of heterodoxy, of latitudinarianism, of scepticism." The charges leveled against him, he observed, bore "so vague a nature that each person adapts to them the chimera of his own fears or fancies, and there is no knowing to what point to address a refutation." Hampden then mused, "When once suspicions have been scattered among the public, it is no light task to undo the delusion. The sophistry may be exposed, but the impression on the mind of many remains; all have not the power to revert to their former simplicity: their feelings have been alienated, and they hear only to disapprove and condemn." He demanded henceforth to contend with persons who would argue from reason and not merely "by censure, and intimidation, and the array of hostile numbers." At the same time he categorically refused to yield "to misrepresentation, and clamour, and violence."[87] Of all the replies to religious persecution that marked Oxford life from the time of Pusey's publication of his book on Germany through the condemnation of W. G. Ward in 1845, Hampden's was the most forthright and trimmed the least, but it produced at best only modest impact.

One observer from afar, Sidney Smith, wholly misjudging the ferocity of the situation at Oxford, wrote privately, "A sad affair, this inaugural lecture of Hampden; instead of being like the worldly Hampden, martial and truculent, it is elegiac, precatory and hypocritical. I would have fetched blood at every sentence." Other observers less cynical than Smith and more intimately acquainted with the Oxford scene took a very different view. Filled with anger, bewilderment, and sadness as he watched the vicious spat among men with whom he had once shared the Oriel Common Room, Blanco White wrote Lord Holland about ten days before the inaugural lecture of being "incessantly haunted by the Oxford persecution of Hampden" and unable to conceive "a more impudent display of bigotry and thorough priestly spirit." White recalled that before he left Oxford, it had been "an established doctrine" among the Tractarian set "that no Dissenter should be allowed to live within the English dominions, but that an Englishman should of necessity, be a member of the Church of England." In "the Protestant Popery" that he saw "growing up at Oxford," White detected a spirit of persecution worse than that of the Inquisition, observing, "There is a consistency in the one which may excuse that dangerous error; but the practical contradiction implied in Protestant persecution shows a perverseness of heart which is to me perfectly odious."[88] White grasped perhaps more clearly than any other contemporary observer that the Oxford conflict arose not between orthodoxy and heterodoxy or between Protestantism and Roman Catholicism but rather between persons of differing religious temperaments and clerical persuasions within the English Church as a Protestant body.

What united Hampden's sympathizers was their cooperation with the government of the day, their opposition to Tractarian disruptiveness and clericalism, and their general sense of fairness. But his supporters were no party, and he was no leader. In 1836 Hampden's one outspoken public defender associated with Oxford was Thomas Arnold, who shared his views on the supremacy of Scripture and the centrality of Christology, as well as his suspicion of clericalism and willingness to extend broad toleration to Dissent. Once the controversy erupted, Arnold encouraged Hampden to "stand up firmly to redeem Oxford if it be yet possible from the utter degradation to which the Fanatics and the factions together are endeavouring to reduce it." He described the *Elucidations,* which he thought Pusey had composed, as "the last seal of the perfect Triumph of the lowest Fanaticism over a noble Nature."[89]

Seeking to prevent "Folly and Malice and Dishonesty" from having "everything their own way," Arnold published in the April *Edinburgh Review* an article which editor McNavy Napier infamously entitled "The Oxford Malignants and Dr. Hampden." There denouncing the political character of the controversy, Arnold recounted all the university honors received by Hampden, observed the considerable lapse of time between the publication of the Bampton Lectures and the persecution, and criticized his detractors' failure to use regular ecclesiastical and university channels to examine his teaching. Arnold also contrasted the falsehoods of the contemporary pamphlets attacking Hampden with the orthodoxy of his printed sermons and the simple piety of the inaugural lecture. After comparing the Tractarians with the judaizers in early Christian congregations and with the seventeenth-century Nonjurors, Arnold deplored the attack on Hampden for manifesting "the character, not of error, but of *moral wickedness.*" With a vast roll of rhetorical thunder, Arnold denounced the Oxford proceedings as displaying "nothing of Christian zeal, but much of the mingled fraud, and baseness, and cruelty, of fanatical persecution" in the breaking "through the charities and decencies of life, to run down a good and pious individual," in the appeal "not to any legal and competent tribunal, but to the votes of an assembly where party spirit is notoriously virulent," in the garbling of the writings of the "intended victim," the ignoring of context, and the "keeping out of sight the writer's general object, as to produce an impression unfair and false," and the laboring "to ruin" Hampden's character.[90]

Arnold's essay, for all the unpleasant truth it contained, proved too strident to achieve any good for Hampden. Because of the strong Whig orientation of the *Edinburgh Review* and its well-known antipathy toward the high-church party and Oxford generally, Hampden may indeed simply have suffered further political guilt through association. Even some among Arnold's admirers found the article too vitriolic. In April 1836 the young A. P. Stanley, for example, defensively apologizing for the tone of Arnold's

7. Thomas Arnold (1795–1842) was a fellow of Oriel and, during their early lives, a close friend of John Keble. Later, while Headmaster of Rugby School, he wrote actively on ecclesiastical matters, urging church reform and advocating accommodation with Dissenters. An outspoken critic of the Tractarians, he defended R. D. Hampden in the columns of the *Edinburgh Review*. In late 1841 he was appointed Regius Professor of Modern History at Oxford. (Portrait by a follower of Thomas Phillips, reproduced with the permission of the Provost and Fellows of Oriel College.)

essay, claimed that no one who had not compared the condemnatory pamphlets with Hampden's writings could "duly appreciate the appearance that must have presented itself to Arnold's mind of shameless and wilful fabrication." But Stanley also revealed why he as well as others in the university found it impossible fully to approve Arnold's blanket condemnation, observing, "If they (the extracts) had been made by anyone else than Newman and Pusey, I should not have hesitated to attribute them to wilful dishonesty; as it is, I must call it culpable carelessness, blindness, and recklessness, in matters of the most vital importance to the Church and nation, and to the peace of a good man. . . . It is certainly a deep disgrace upon Oxford, but it shows what can be done by men of commanding influence and undaunted energy like Newman and Pusey."[91] Seeing only the pious external appearances of Newman and Pusey, Stanley could not comprehend the inner private ambitions and angers of the Tractarian leaders. He could hardly have imagined the tutorial in techniques of character assassination that in 1834 Newman had provided Henry Wilberforce before the latter undertook writing *The Foundation of the Faith Assailed at Oxford*. Nor did Stanley fully appreciate the calumnious tactics to which since the Peel reelection of 1829 Tractarians and other Oxford high churchmen had unhesitatingly resorted to advance their version of ecclesiastical truth and clerical pretension.

On April 26, 1836, preparatory to the May 5 meeting of Convocation, when new proctors would permit Hampden's censure, the Corpus Committee issued its last major statement, asserting that the university was enjoined by its statutes "to prevent any principles, detrimental to the Christian Faith, from circulating uncondemned, under the sanction of its name." Hampden's publications were "conscientiously believed to abound" in such principles. Past forbearance could not continue because "Dr. Hampden is no longer a private individual." Because "the avowedly dangerous tendency" of Hampden's writings and his consequent "unfitness" to direct clerical education and not his personal faith were the issue, "No profession of personal belief could alter the tendency of those works; or restore a just confidence in the writer as an authoritative teacher of Theology." Furthermore, Hampden's inaugural lecture had "left the original charges wholly untouched," had "even increased the noxiousness of the previous errors, by the assumption that they are not inconsistent with the integrity of Christian doctrine," and had rendered "the soundness and safety" of his religious teaching "still more dubious." Returning to the Bampton Lectures, the Corpus Committee accused Hampden of seeking to prove that the phraseology of the Articles "was framed, not on the statements of the Bible, but on a false and mischievous philosophy, foreign and injurious to the Gospel!" Such reasoning could lead a reader "to believe, either that the assertions of our Church on the most solemn truths of Christianity, have no corresponding realities—are words, and nothing more; or that the notions which we are taught to embody in them are unscriptural and false."[92] Convocation must therefore formally condemn such teaching so as to present the feeling of the university and to give some warning to students. Curiously, the previous accusations of Socinianism and rationalism did not appear in this last public accusation from the Corpus Committee.

On May 5, 1837, Convocation, by a vote of 474 to 94, out of more than 2,000 possible votes, passed the statute circumscribing Hampden's professorial duties. Though deprived of certain prerogative responsibilities, Hampden remained the Regius Professor of Divinity. Furthermore, thriving in his new professorial position, he attracted significant numbers of students, much to the consternation of Pusey, who reported to C. A. Olgilvie on June 9 that Hampden's lectures were "carrying on the Inaugural Lecture, & so taking in people, & if matters are allowed to go on, we must have a young rationalizing party springing up in this place."[93] In the same letter Pusey suggested that students attended the lectures because they believed that bishops would continue to require certificates of attendance from the professor of divinity rather than the Lady Margaret Professor, a comment that suggests that the Convocation condemnation had failed to render Hampden's position a mere sinecure. For his part, Hampden lost no opportunity over the years to play off his own strongly self-espoused allegiance to historic Protestantism against the innovative Catholicism of the Tractarians.[94]

The Tractarians had been able to mount a united attack on Hampden's appointment in 1836 because people of differing religious opinions in the university still rallied to antierastianism. In particular, evangelicals at that moment distrusted the Melbourne ministry for its alliance with Irish Roman Catholics and radical Dissenters. As time passed, evangelicals, including the editors of the *Record* and the *Christian Observer*, became less fearful of the government than they were of a betrayal of the Protestant faith within the English Church itself. The publication of Pusey's tract on baptism of late 1835 and the anti-Roman tracts of 1836 fed the fires of those evangelical fears, as did the more general Tractarian assault on the Protestant and pursuit of the Catholic.

At the same time, through their drives against subscription and Hampden, the Tractarians had forged the weapons of their own eventual destruction. First, they had created a set of able, implacable personal and theological enemies. Second, they had established rules of religious encounter that threw decency, fairness, and truthfulness to the winds. Finally, they had succeeded in transforming Oxford University institutions into engines of theological and ecclesiastical discipline that were otherwise lacking in the Church of England. Within five years the hostility, unfairness, and university discipline first unleashed on Hampden would be turned against the Tractarians themselves. Meanwhile, they carried out a program of publication and devotional experiment that reconfigured the sensibilities of English religious and cultural life.

CHAPTER 6

The Assault on the Protestant

FROM 1833 and through 1835 the *Tracts for the Times* had heaped fulsome opprobrium on the religious and ecclesiastical inadequacy of Dissent, repeatedly portraying it as tending toward the ill-defined but much dreaded Socinianism of eighteenth-century Rational Dissent. Except, however, among Unitarians, the theology of early Victorian Dissent was profoundly evangelical. Consequently, the Tractarian critique of Dissent necessarily comprised a more general assault against evangelical religion, which, especially after Pusey's tract on baptism of late 1835, embraced that of evangelicals inside the Church of England. Moreover, the Tractarians' drive against evangelicalism *inside* as well as *outside* the establishment broadened into a frontal assault against historic Protestantism itself, as they gradually equated the religion of evangelicals with the religion of all Protestants.

Anti-Protestantism was as essential to the character and outcome of Tractarianism as was its more widely recognized sympathy for Roman Catholicism. The latter remained longer in historical consciousness because of the midcentury conversions to Rome and then because of the rise of Anglo-Catholicism in the English Church. At least one nonreligiously engaged contemporary observer, however, recognized anti-Protestantism as the chief Tractarian novelty. In late 1839 John Stuart Mill, describing the Tractarians to a French friend, first carefully outlined their relatively familiar high-church clericalism. Then, however, characterizing "the principal peculiarity of this school" as their "hostility to what they call ultra-Protestantism," Mill reported, "They dislike the word Protestant altogether, as a word which denotes only negation and disunion." Mill further noted that the new

Oxford School "urge all the arguments of the 19th century against the 18th. . . . All these they urge against Protestantism of the common English kind." Becoming more specific, Mill wrote, "They reprobate the 'right of private judgment' & consider *learning* rather than original thinking the proper attribut[ion] of a divine. They discourage the Methodistical view of religion which makes devotional feeling a state of strong *excitement*, & inculcate rather a spirit of humility & self-mortification. . . . It is one of the forms, & the best form hitherto, of the *reaction* of Anglicanism against Methodism, incredulity, & rationalism. . . . Their doctrine, which is spreading fast among the younger clergy, is giving great offence to the evangelical part of the Church . . . which had previously been increasing very much in numbers & influence."[1] In his appreciation of the Tractarian reduction of such Protestantism to "disunion and negation," Mill recognized that Tractarian anti-Protestantism pertained to the life of the larger culture and not merely to the life of the English Church. It was, of course, religious and cultural criticism directly derived from Tractarianism that later deeply informed Matthew Arnold's equation of Dissenting Protestant politics and religion with anarchy.

In the long run Tractarian criticism of all things Protestant proved more inviting, energetic, convincing, and coherent than their championing of Catholic faith and practice. For a minority of people in the late-Victorian and early-twentieth-century English-speaking world, Roman Catholicism and Anglo-Catholicism would provide substitutes for evangelical and historic Protestantism. But by the turn of the century, the broad assault on Protestant faith and culture associated with scientific naturalism, historical criticism of the Bible, aestheticism, literary modernism, the social sciences, and secular ethics largely carried the day among the educated classes. The Tractarians had prepared the way for these developments. Not only had they convinced many of their fellow English clergy that Protestant self-identity was socially and religiously inadequate, but they also fostered a climate in which other intellectuals, perhaps most often those connected with universities, found Protestant cultural self-identity lacking. The Tractarians did not defeat Protestant faith in the English-speaking world, but among certain important groups they certainly did, in Newman's previously quoted words of 1850, reduce it to "that imbecile, inconsistent thing called Protestantism."[2] In doing so, they provided a previously absent intellectual respectability to criticizing the Protestant faith, and thus, along with other very different secular-minded intellectuals, contributed to the late-century religious and cultural vacuum in the English-speaking world which secular forces would fill long after the Tractarians had left the scene.

In a very real sense the Tractarians behaved like Catholic puritans. Purging the Church of England of recently accumulated residues of radical evangelical Protestantism was a key goal of their projected Second Reformation, just as removing residual elements of Roman Catholicism had been a major objective for the seventeenth-century Puritans' ongoing reformation. But as the Tractarians pressed their case against evangelical faith and practice, they repeatedly found themselves very quickly criticizing the historical doctrines of the Protestant Reformation itself, which the evangelicals had carried to new extremes. For this reason, the Tractarians, commencing with hatred of particular contemporary evangelical religious practices, almost unwittingly stumbled into a stance of hostility toward the larger Protestant tradition. Indeed, between 1836 and 1839 Newman's chief publications loosed thunderbolts against the historic Protestant doctrines of the priesthood of all believers, justification by faith alone, and the supremacy of the Scriptures.

PRIVATE JUDGMENT DECRIED

During the spring of 1836 Newman delivered in the Adam de Brome Chapel of the Church of St. Mary the Virgin a series of discourses, which he published in early 1837 under the elaborate title *Lectures on the Prophetical Office of the Church, Viewed Relatively to Romanism and Popular Protestantism*. Within high-church and Tractarian circles the book soon became known as *Against Romanism*, a designation that, as Newman had hoped, served to deflect accusations of Tractarian sympathy for Roman Catholicism. More than twenty-five years later in the *Apologia* Newman portrayed himself as having attempted in this book, as well as in other works of the period, to construct an ecclesiastical *via media* that during the 1840s failed any longer to hold his convictions. Then in 1877, forty years after their original appearance, he republished the lectures of 1836 with an important new introduction in the two-volume collection of his Tractarian writings that he entitled *The Via Media*. Those volumes, largely because of his extensive commentary from a Roman Catholic standpoint on his writings while in the English Church, imposed the appearance of far more system to his thought of the 1830s than it possessed at the time. This process of transformation continued during the twentieth century with a critical scholarly edition of *Lectures on the Prophetical Office of the Church* appearing under the title *The Via Media of the Anglican Church,* with the editor discussing the Preface of 1877 more extensively than the lectures themselves.[3] The changing titles and formats reflect the shifting atmospheres in which Newman's lectures were delivered, published, read, interpreted, and reinterpreted, as well as the manner in which the original polemic against popular Protestantism, which Mill had recorded, was allowed quietly to disappear.

It is neither easy nor simple to recapture Newman's frame of mind when he composed and published the *Lectures on the Prophetical Office of the Church.* He had commenced their composition shortly after Froude's death in February 1836, continued writing them during the Hampden affair, and delivered the first just one day before his mother's unexpected death on May 17. His sister Jemima had married John Mozley, a printer, shortly before their mother's passing. Harriett married Thomas Mozley, John Mozley's brother, not long thereafter. John Newman was now without any immediate family circle, but was simultaneously relieved of family financial responsibilities except for helping his aunt. He did, however, experience pangs of guilt about this situation, because he had been hard-pressed for money until his mother's death and his sisters' marriages and for a year had been going into debt. Certainly those financial anxieties had informed his anger at Hampden's success in achieving major government patronage. Newman for some time had prayed that God would solve his problems of family obligation, mounting debt, and insufficient income. When Mrs. Newman so suddenly died, it seemed to him "just as if I had been praying for the death of her, which I had always looked forward to as living for many years."[4]

Newman's inner ambivalence about his own prayer life and uncertainty about what it was wise to ask from God may also have touched upon his lectures of 1836. Despite powerfully critical remarks against Romanism in these lectures, which Newman thought would prove he was not a Papist, his fundamental target remained evangelical religion and its proponents. Even in the midst of the Hampden contest, when being aided by Oxford evangelicals, Newman had complained to Miss Giberne, "The truth is this—the Ultra Protestants have had every thing their own way for about a Century, and now when things are coming to a crisis, God's good Providence is lifting about a Standard against them."[5] As the chief bearer of that standard, Newman in these lectures led an assault on the exercise of private judgment in religion that quickly expanded from a criticism of evangelicalism into a general questioning of the larger tradition of historical Protestantism. He did so just as his mother's death had sparked the most serious inner doubts and possibly inner fears about the wisdom of his own private judgment.

Like the comment to Miss Giberne, Newman's remarks in his letters about the *Lectures on the Prophetical Office of the Church* were extremely aggressive. In early January 1837, Newman told his sister Jemima that his forthcoming statements about evangelicals were "so strong that everything I have as yet said is milk and water to it," resembling the "difference between drifting snow and a hard snow ball." He thought that they would have an effect "like hitting the Peculiars, etc. a most uncommon blow in the face." Late the next month he wrote Manning that the publication of his new volume was "an anxious thing," explaining, "I am aware that I deserve no mercy from your Protestants—and if they read me, shall find none. . . . The amusing thing is that the unfortunate Peculiars are attacked on so many sides at once that they are quite out of breath with having to run about to defend their walls—Tradition, Baptism, Apostolical Succession, Faith and works, etc etc. No sooner do they recover their breath after one blow, but they receive another in their stomach." A few weeks later after he reported brisk sales of the book, he declared to Jemima that if misrepresented by the *Record*, he would "take it out in an attack on popular Protestantism" that demonstrated how far the contemporary Church of England had departed from the Reformation. Nonetheless, he did admit that according to his own lights the true ethos of the English Church in many points more nearly resembled popery than Protestantism. "So one must expect," he concluded, "a revival of the slander or misapprehension in some shape or other—and we shall never be free of it, of course."[6]

Lectures on the Prophetical Office of the Church marked a key moment in Newman's thinking as well as in his family life. By 1836 he was no longer forecasting an apocalyptic political cataclysm, wrought by unbelievers and Dissenters, that would require clergy in the Church of England to set out on an independent course of action. The Hampden case had served notice to the Whig government about the cost of latitudinarian appointments designed to assuage Dissenting grievances. The attack on Hampden, like the publication of the tracts themselves, had struck a broad responsive chord in both the university and larger church. Newman now became emboldened to forge a distinctive theological position and vocation for Catholics within the establishment. That goal meant that the Tractarians would necessarily redeploy their energy to an antievangelical struggle inside the Church of England, where the evangelical impulse provided the strongest hindrance to the Catholic cause. There had been direct hints in certain of the early tracts that the determination to carry out a Second Reformation would require conflict with establishment evangelicals. Most of the private Tractarian exchanges in regard to the efficacy of sacramental grace directly opposed the most basic theological assumptions of Church of England evangelicals. Pusey's tract on baptism had signaled the end of possible mutual accommodation, and Newman's lectures made the point even more directly. Henceforth there would be no question that Tractarians saw their enemy within the English Church.

To conceptualize this redefined struggle, Newman proposed an ecclesiastical vision based on the concept of a *via media* lying between what he and the late Froude regarded as the confusions of popular Protestantism and the corruptions of Roman Catholicism. Newman actually used the term *via media* quite infrequently in the 1830s. As the term appeared in both the *Apologia* and in the title of his subsequent collection of Tractarian writings, it suggested to later generations a tenor of moderation that had never characterized the Tractarian cause in its own day. Newman's *via media* sought nothing less than to reform the Church of England through the repudiation of the Protestant theological presuppositions that permeated both the church and its surrounding culture.

Newman's *via media* between popular Protestantism and Romanism assumed the necessity of at least transforming, if not overturning, the erastian structure of the Church of England. Newman argued that the English Church, by which he meant the Catholic body in that church, could no longer depend on "mere political religion; which, like a broken reed, has pierced through the hand that leaned upon it."[7] This rejection of "political religion" meant for Newman the rejection of evangelical Protestantism, which in his view dominated the politics of erastianism, thus smothering the Catholic presence in the Church of England. From Newman's standpoint, since the Reformation era itself, the religion of the English Church had been historically Protestant because politically it had become the creature of a state dominated by a Protestant culture. Renunciation or radical reform of the political link to the English state would allow the inherent Catholic character of the English Church to flourish because that church would no longer stand hostage through political pressure to that surrounding Protestant culture. Newman and other Tractarians had commenced with a hatred of evangelical Protestantism, but the more they probed the sources of that recent Protestantism, the more they saw it as the logical and historical outcome of earlier Protestantism. As a result, the Tractarians soon held in contempt all things Protestant. Consequently, as Newman elaborated his analysis, the rejection of political religion actually required the rejection of the deepest cultural forces that had forged the English self-identity of members of the Church of England as both participants in that communion and members of the nation. The progenitor of this hostility to Protestantism was, of course, Froude.

Although claiming equal hostility to Roman corruptions, the Tractarians felt much less need to criticize Roman Catholicism because the latter enjoyed so little cultural authority in either the English past or the present. Throughout *Lectures on the Prophetical Office of the Church* Newman assumed hostility to Rome on the part of his readers. He then portrayed first popular and later historic Protestantism as an inadequate and even contemptible opponent of Rome, indeed an opponent incapable of refuting Rome's arguments and theological positions. Once denied its capacity to resist Roman Catholicism, the religion of Protestants stood naked to a paradoxical Tractarian assault. If Protestant principles could not repulse the claims of Rome, those principles, according to Newman, should give way to Catholic ones that could stand against Rome. Thus Newman appealed to the anxieties of Protestants inculcated by antipopery to sustain his claims for the advance of Tractarian Catholicism. Newman recognized that the seventeenth-century English divines, whose Catholic theology he championed, would "offend the prejudices of the age at first hearing," as had the original teaching of the apostles.[8] But only that Caroline theology, as interpreted by the Tractarians, could prevent an eventual drift toward Rome in response to ever-widening manifestations of indeterminate, and what he regarded as virtually nihilistic, Protestantism.

Newman's general argument in *Lectures on the Prophetical Office of the Church* portrayed contemporary popular Protestantism as necessarily leading from orthodox trinitarian faith and toward rationalistic Socinianism. In the wake of the vast transatlantic explosion of evangelical Protestantism, Newman urged, the Church of England had assumed a special "mission, hitherto unfulfilled, of representing a theology, Catholic but not Roman." While in Italy in 1833, Newman had come to see the English Church as a kind of saving remnant, protecting the faith from the forces that had led to turmoil and confiscation in Roman Catholic lands. He now expanded that providential role to one of protecting a true saving faith from destructive forces at work elsewhere within contemporary Protestantism. According to Newman's analysis, "Before Germany had become rationalistic, and Geneva Socinian, Romanism might be considered as the most dangerous corruption of the gospel. . . . But at this day, when the connexion of Protestantism with infidelity is so evident, what claim has the former upon our sympathy? and to what theology can the serious Protestant, dissatisfied with his system, betake himself but to Romanism, unless we display our characteristic principles, and show him that he may be Catholic and Apostolic, yet not Roman?"[9] With broad strokes Newman thus portrayed contemporary popular Protestantism as a religious system associated with forces inevitably fostering unbelief and what he regarded as the religious indifference of latitudinarianism. It is important to understand that in this passage what he denoted as "rationalistic" and "Socinian," and elsewhere as in some fashion latitudinarian, was evangelical religion.

Popular Protestantism, Newman argued, constituted "that generalized idea of *religion,* now in repute, which merges all differences of faith and principle between Protestants as minor matters, as if the larger denominations among us agreed with us in essentials, and differed only in the accidents of form, ritual, government, or usage." Such doctrinally diffuse ecumenical activity, seen in the cooperation of Dissenting and Church of England clergy within evangelical societies, displayed the English proclivity to "exult in what we think our indefeasible right and glorious privilege to choose and settle our religion for ourselves" and to stigmatize "as a bondage to be bid take for granted what the wise, good, and many have gone over and determined long before, or to submit to what almighty God has revealed." Newman further criticized the English tendency to account "that belief alone to be manly which commenced in doubt, that inquiry alone philosophical which assumed no first principles, that religion alone rational which we have created for ourselves." Whereas in the sciences men did not dispute, but deferred to the knowledge of Newton or Cuvier, in religious matters they turned to private judgment, sought open questions, and asserted "the prerogative of being heretics or infidels."[10] This concept of religion and its associated behavior, which Newman had seen in the lives of his brothers Charles and Francis and among the radical Oxford evangelical clergy, resulted necessarily in unsettled opinions among both those seeking personal religious truth and those living around them.

In the *Lectures on the Prophetical Office of the Church* Newman largely equated popular Protestantism with the long-standing Protestant exercise of private judgment in the reading of Scripture. The idea that ordinary human beings might actually draw clear religious truth from their personal reading of the Bible constituted "an unreal doctrine" because God had never intended it "to teach doctrine to many." This exercise of private judgment among both Protestants and Romanists had given rise to a vast number of theological errors and heresies, including Unitarianism, Arianism, irrespective predestination, purgatory, and papal supremacy. Beyond doctrinal error and heresy, exercise of private judgment in the absence of adequate ecclesiastical authority also resulted in schism. Although Protestants might appeal to the Bible as the foundation of faith, "no two," he reminded his readers, "agree as to the *interpreter* of the Bible, but each person makes himself the interpreter, so that what seemed at first sight a means of peace, turns out to be a chief occasion or cause of discord." He had, of course, experienced just exactly such schismatic discord within his own family a decade earlier in his debates with Charles and Francis. Moreover, Newman urged, no one in point of fact really accepted the Bible on the basis of a discursively reasoned decision. Rather, in an argument that echoed Hume on political consent, Newman declared, "The great multitude of Protestants believe in Scripture precisely on the ground which the Romanists trust in behalf of their erroneous system, viz. because they have been taught it." The clear result of the exercise of private judgment must be confusion because, "Scripture is not so clear . . . as to hinder ordinary persons, who read it for themselves, from being Sabellians, or Independents, or Wesleyans."[11]

In place of private judgment, Newman appealed to Catholic tradition to interpret the Bible. "Scripture, when illuminated by the 'Catholic Religion,'" he declared, "or the Catholic Religion when fortified by Scripture, may either of them be called the Gospel committed to the Church, dispensed to the individual." His understanding of Catholic tradition, he insisted, differed in both character and content from that taught by Rome. Unlike Protestants, Newman explained, the Romanists "openly avow that they regulate their faith by something else besides Scripture, by the existing Traditions of the Church" that embrace "the whole system of faith and ordinances which they have received from the generation before them, and that generation again from the generation before itself." Newman compared this view of Roman Catholic tradition to English common law: "When Romanists say they adhere to Tradition, they mean that they believe and act as Christians have always believed and acted; they go by the custom, as judges and juries do." Newman, however, rejected such Roman tradition for ignoring the authority of antiquity as the decisive authority in matters of both Scripture and tradition. Although Rome appealed to tradition, its doctrines were actually "innovations" running "counter to the doctrine of Antiquity" and resting "upon what is historically an upstart Tradition."

Newman further declared that Rome cared "very little for the Fathers, whether as primitive or as concordant," and taught "the existing Church to be infallible, and if ancient belief is at variance with it, which of course they do not allow, but if it is, then Antiquity must be mistaken; that is all."[12] This neglect of antiquity indicated a lack of Catholic reverence that had permitted the beliefs of the Roman Church to continue to increase. By contrast, the English Church, according to Newman, reverently claimed antiquity itself as the chief authority upon which the faith stood and stood fixed.

Despite many pages of discussion, Newman left both unclear and indeterminate how modern Christians were to interpret the guidance afforded by antiquity. Newman, like traditional high churchmen, saw the Church Catholic, in contrast to the evangelical invisible church, as divided into branches having concrete, identifiable historical existence and as possessing the gift, purpose, and duty of teaching the truth. In her teaching the Church Catholic was "ever divinely guided" by a discernment of the truth "secured by a heavenly as well as a human rule."[13] Newman, however, significantly departed from the traditional high-church viewpoint. While claiming the Church of England to constitute the local branch of the Church Catholic, he simultaneously asserted that the English Church itself, because it had for three centuries been pervaded by the spirit of Protestantism, had not yet fully realized or enunciated Catholic theology. Protestantism had thus captured and misguided the Church Catholic in England as the Antichrist had captured and misguided the Church of Rome. Newman and those whom he influenced, consequently, contemplated serious theological and devotional reformation as necessary for both the contemporary English and the contemporary Roman churches.

Self-conscious Protestants in the Church of England of both evangelical and nonevangelical outlook, Newman understood, would consider his outline of the Catholic faith inadequate because he did not assert the necessity of faith in the Bible. Christians, he noted, had taught their faith long before establishing the canon of Scripture. The Nicene Creed itself embodied the essential elements of the Catholic faith without asserting the necessity of belief in Scripture. On these grounds, Newman contended, "Scripture is the foundation of the Creed; but belief in Scripture is not the foundation of belief in the Creed." The mass of Christians did not and never had derived their faith from the Bible but rather from tradition as taught by the Church Catholic. Newman even went so far as to "venture to deny that belief in the Scriptures, is, abstractly, necessary to Church communion and salvation." He furthermore termed the designation Bible Christian as being in fact "very unchristian," because holding definite doctrines on the basis of the Bible alone was impossible.[14] Paradoxically, for very different reasons neither Newman nor his nemesis Hamden believed that Scripture in and of itself conveyed doctrine.

For Newman, Protestants within or without the Church of England might preach the Bible and the leading doctrines of the Reformation, but they did not teach the Catholic faith expounded in antiquity, the witness whereof alone constituted the vocation and identity of the Church Catholic. In England, only Catholics inside the Church of England and Roman Catholics could actually claim to bear witness to that Catholic Faith. Those English Catholics and Roman Catholics were essentially at one in teaching "the doctrines of Three Persons in One indivisible Divine Nature; of the union of two Natures, Divine and Human, in the One Person of Christ; of the imputation of Adam's sin in his descendants; of the death of Christ to reconcile God the Father to us sinners; the application of His merits through external rites; the singular efficacy and mysteriousness of Sacraments; the Apostolical ministry; the duty of unity; the necessity of good works; these and other doctrines are maintained, and maintained as the chief doctrines of the Gospel, both by us and them." Such unity did not, and presumably could not, exist between the Catholics in the Church of England and Protestants with their ever-expanding theological novelties. Nevertheless, despite points of important agreement between the English Catholics and Roman Catholics, there were other points of fundamental divergence, including the Roman doctrines of purgatory, the supremacy of the Pope, and the infallibility of the Church, as well as Rome's "denying the cup to the laity, her idolatrous worship of the Blessed Virgin, her Image-worship, her recklessness in anathematizing, and her schismatical and overbearing spirit."[15] Those corrupt doctrines and practices, which Newman fiercely criticized here as in *Tract 71* of the previous year, should prevent Catholics within the English Church from leaving that fold for Rome.

Newman's *Lectures on the Prophetical Office of the Church* presented a highly controversial, indeed profoundly tendentious, interpretation of authority in religion and theology as a middle way, an Aristotelian mean. He established a unique and distinctly minority position within the English Church as the fundamental middle course between radical evangelicalism and Roman Catholicism. So long as he could state his position in isolation, it could hold that benign appearance. Critics, however, would not let that be the case. For example, in 1839 Christopher Nevile, a Lincolnshire rector, bluntly declared, "There can be no *via media* between the right of Private

Judgment and Church Infallibility." He portrayed Newman and his fellow Tractarians as "a small number of prejudiced individuals, in a prejudiced Church, setting themselves up as infallible guides to their fellow creatures" in abstruse matters of doctrine. This "small knot of individuals," he continued, made "the monstrous assumption" that they "are and must be right, because antiquity is an infallible test of truth, and they can decide infallibly what *is* antiquity, and what she says." Those same people then found themselves "justified in considering these fellow-creatures and fellow-wanderers as sinners and schismatics in the exact proportion in which they may differ in opinions with their self-proffered instructors."[16] That judgment exactly described the position that the Tractarians effectively assumed toward other groups within the English Church, though how much they actually admitted this situation even to themselves is unclear.

QUESTIONING JUSTIFICATION BY FAITH ALONE

In March 1838, with the publication of *Lectures on Justification*, Newman carried the Tractarian offensive to the heart of Protestant theology, what Charles M'Ilvaine, evangelical Bishop of Ohio, called "the master-principle of the Reformation." This volume, undoubtedly the greatest of Newman's theological works composed while he remained in the English Church, had originated in the two letters of January 1837 defending Pusey's tract on baptism, published in the *Christian Observer*. At the conclusion of this correspondence, which had provoked the extensive footnote commentary by the editor, Newman promised to take up the question of justification. Rather than doing so in another letter, he delivered a series of lectures that resulted the next year in his book on the subject.[17]

In *Lectures on Justification*, which the *Record* later described as "obviously directed against that body in the Church which is known by the name of Evangelical," Newman both extended his critique of religion rooted in feeling and sought to secure a firm theological foundation for the practical morality, personal piety, and religion of obedience that he had advocated in his parochial sermons. On September 12, 1837, responding to Lord Lifford's criticism that he had paid insufficient attention to the best examples of evangelical religion, such as Milner, Scott, and Simeon, Newman had argued that the evangelical system of doctrine must be judged by the character of its long-run development and not by the virtues of individuals who had forwarded it. Newman boasted of not having "spoken against *individuals* at least as individuals" but rather against "a system which works its way independently of individuals," while using them and then discarding them "till in the course of generations it arrives at its full dimensions." It was thus against "the so called Evangelical School" and "against their system," understood in terms of its long-term development, that Newman claimed to have written.[18] Considering the life of that school as viewed over several generations, Newman discerned a clear movement away from objects and works of faith toward "a direct contemplation of our feelings as *the* means, *the* evidence of justification."[19]

Newman understood his assault on the evangelical, and more broadly Protestant, doctrine of justification by faith as involving more than correction of erroneous doctrine. In his mind the evangelical understanding of subjective feeling as both the means and the evidence of divine justification constituted nothing less than an effort to destroy genuine religion. He most fully explained that position in *Tract 83*, "Advent Sermons on Antichrist," published in June 1838. There he decried a vast contemporary "effort to do without religion," which involved "an attempt to supersede religion altogether, as far as it is external or objective, as far as it is displayed in ordinances, or can be expressed by written words,—to confine it to our inward feelings, and thus, considering how transient, how variable, how evanescent our feelings are, an attempt in fact, to destroy religion." This effort "to destroy religion," manifesting itself in evangelical teaching and practice, arose "from the Evil One and savour of death," indicated a turn to apostasy, and foreshadowed the possible appearance of the Antichrist.[20] The core of Newman's discussion of justification, appearing earlier that year, had criticized exactly this evangelical subjectivity.

Directly targeting evangelical theology, Newman, in the advertisement to the first edition of *Lectures on Justification,* announced his intention of putting to rest a prejudice that existed "in many serious minds against certain essential Christian truths, such as Baptismal Regeneration and the Apostolical Ministry," on the grounds "that they fostered notions of human merit, were prejudicial to the inward life of religion, and incompatible with the doctrine of justifying faith, nay, with express statements on the subject in our Formularies."[21] Engaging this prejudice, Newman claimed that, when properly understood, the doctrine of justification was perfectly compatible with both baptismal regeneration and recognition of the necessity of sacraments administered by an episcopally ordained clergy. The sacraments administered by such clergy, who also as representatives of the Church Catholic interpreted the Scripture, embodied an objective religion

that avoided religious delusions based on subjective feeling. Along with
Pusey three years earlier, Newman thus addressed the long-standing baptismal controversy in a manner designed to divide the Church of England into
uncompromising camps and to uphold Tractarian clericalism. Furthermore, as in *Lectures on the Prophetical Office of the Church,* Newman quickly
adopted the language of "we" and "our Church" when advocating a radical
doctrine of baptismal regeneration actually held by only a very circum-
scribed Tractarian circle.

Newman opened the lectures with a characteristic explication of two
radically opposed extremes—"justification by faith" and "justification by
obedience"—to be mediated by his own argument. Although it was possible
to hold one or the other or both simultaneously according to circumstance,
Newman wished to avoid making either the exclusive or leading idea of a
religious system, as, he contended, Protestants did with faith and Roman
Catholics with obedience. He explained, "Justification by faith only, thus
treated, is an erroneous, justification by obedience is a defective view of
Christian doctrine," with the former standing "beside" and the latter "short
of the truth." Assigning prominence to obedience alone introduced the
issue of "the proper merit of good works," while emphasizing faith alone
suggested "the notion that good works are prejudicial to our salvation."
Newman then announced that he would treat "what is commonly called
Protestantism" as fundamentally erroneous in theology and unproductive
of good works.[22] It is significant that in this passage he employed the more
inclusive term *Protestantism* rather than either *ultra-Protestantism* or *popular
Protestantism,* each of which he often used to described both moderate and
radical evangelicalism. Moreover, Newman directly associated the Protestant view of justification by faith alone with Martin Luther, thus directing
his critique to the fountainhead of the Reformation itself rather than to
contemporary evangelical doctrine. Nevertheless, what Newman termed
Lutheran more nearly related to evangelicalism than to historic or contemporary Lutheranism in any deeply examined sense.

According to Newman, what separated the Lutherans from the Church
of England was a set of differences in regard to faith *or* baptism as the
instrument of justification. He explained, "These two views indeed need not
be, and have not always been, opposed to one another. Baptism may be
considered the instrument on God's part, Faith on ours; Faith may receive
what Baptism conveys. But if the word *instrument* be taken to mean in the
strictest sense the *immediate* means by which the gift passes from the giver to
the receiver, there can be but one instrument; and either Baptism will be

considered to convey it (whether conditionally or not is a further question), or Faith to seize, or, as it is expressed, to apprehend it,—either Faith will become a subordinate means, condition, or qualification, or Baptism a mere sign, pledge, or ratification of a gift otherwise received." For Newman, the fundamental problem with the Lutheran doctrine was that of explaining exactly what constituted *faith*. Protestants who emphasized justification by faith alone, he contended, could not really explain what they meant by faith and defined it "not by its *nature*, but by its *office;* not by what *it is*, but by what it *does*." To regard faith as "trust *in Christ*" differentiated it from "historical faith, or intellectual knowledge" and thus dissolved any precise meaning.[23]

Criticizing popular preaching, Newman argued that when "the gospel mercy is proclaimed openly and universally to all who will accept it," there appeared to be "no special state of mind" as "necessary for appropriating it." Nor did a person need to inquire whether he was fit to appropriate this mercy because "his warrant for making it his, is the freeness of the proclamation." Discerning nothing permanent or particularly holy in such practices, Newman declared that the Protestant upheld a mode of faith that "as little admits of a definition as putting out the hand or receiving alms" and as possessing "as little of a permanent form or shape as running, or kneeling." This Protestant faith constituted "a momentary act or motion rather than a moral virtue or grace." Such faith represented "the reaching forward of the heart towards Christ, determining and resting in the thought of Him as its limit, and thus deriving its character, and, as it may be called, its form from Him."[24] If further challenged, Newman claimed, the Protestant would confess the essential impossibility of expressing the exact character of faith or of the state of mind manifesting it.

Newman associated this inability with Luther's view "that the Moral Law was not binding on the conscience of the Christian" because Christ had fulfilled that law and through the substitution of his righteousness for ours freed us from it. The doctrine of justification by faith alone thus removed belief that our actions, rather than the righteousness of Christ, in any way contribute to our justification. Protestants, Newman argued, proclaimed this concept of justification by faith alone even though for many centuries Christians had believed that other rites and ordinances provided the path to salvation. Protestants, citing Scripture passages speaking of free gifts of grace, had long regarded such gifts "dispensed without any intermediate channel between God and the soul; on the ground that they would not be *freely* given, if given *through* any of God's servants or ministers, Angel or

Apostle, Prophet or Priest."[25] Protestants thus inherently and necessarily confused the nature of righteousness. They called men righteous who were not, rather than understanding that God makes them righteous first by imputing the righteousness of Christ to forgive their past sins and then imparting that righteousness for their future lives. Protestants in this fashion ignored the issue of obedience and abolished any substantial necessity for the clergy in regard to the instrumentality of salvation.

Newman equated this rejection of clergy and the sacraments to setting up "calves at Dan and Bethel" in place of "the true Temple and the Apostolic Ministry." The rejection of "Baptism as a token of God's election" and the "recourse to certain supposed experiences" of the heart constituted "the idolatry of a refined age, in which the superstitions of barbarous times displease, from their grossness." In one of the most virulently denunciatory passages in all his prose, Newman declared, "Away then with this modern, this private, this arbitrary, this tyrannical system, which promising liberty conspires against it; which abolishes Sacraments to introduce barren and dead ordinances; and for the real participation of Christ, and justification through his Spirit, would, at the very marriage feast, feed us on shells and husks, who hunger and thirst after righteousness." The doctrine of justification by faith alone, according to Newman, had emerged only at the time of the Reformation, opposing fifteen hundred years of previous Christian preaching of the duty of obedience, and that novel doctrine should hold no real claim on modern Christians. This "new gospel" attempted "to take from our hearts the power, the fulness, the mysterious presence of Christ's most holy death and resurrection, and to soothe us for our loss with the name of having it."[26]

Newman flatly rejected as "a mere phantom to frighten the mind from strict obedience" contemporary Protestant claims that other understandings of justification except their own novel one constituted adherence to *legalism* that in some disguised fashion rendered justification contingent upon obeying the Old Testament law. Evangelicals or others who accused the Church Catholic of idolatry were themselves the real legalizers of the day. Explaining this paradox, which he associated with the entire historical development of Protestantism, Newman observed "that a system of doctrine has risen up during the last three centuries, in which faith or spiritual-mindedness is contemplated and rested on as the end of religion instead of Christ. I do not mean to say that Christ is not mentioned as the Author of all good, but that stress is laid rather on the believing than on the Object of belief, on the comfort and persuasiveness of the doctrine rather than on the doctrine itself. And in this way religion is made to consist in contemplating ourselves, instead of Christ; not simply in looking to Christ, but in *seeing* that we look to Christ, not in His Divinity and Atonement, but in our conversion and faith in them." This modern Protestant legalism set "the state of a believer as a *more prominent* subject of the Gospel than the nature, attributes, and work of Him who has given it" and further insisted on that subjective state "as a special point for the consideration of those who have as yet lived without seriousness." Through the preaching of conversion rather than Christ, "faith and (what is called) spiritual-mindedness are dwelt on as *ends* and obstruct the view of Christ, just as the Law was perverted by the Jews."[27]

In *Lectures on Justification* Newman associated all the shortcomings of historic Protestant and contemporary evangelical approaches to that doctrine with Luther, whom he had not studied deeply, just as Pusey had blamed Zwingli and Calvin for an inadequate appreciation and understanding of baptism in particular and the sacraments in general. In a devastatingly broad polemic against the German Reformation, Newman wrote that Luther had met "the great corruptions," countenanced by the "highest authorities" in the Church, not "with divine weapons" but rather with "one of his own" when he adopted "a doctrine original, specious, fascinating, persuasive, powerful against Rome, and wonderfully adapted, as if prophetically, to the times which were to follow." Having "found Christians in bondage to their works and observances," Luther had "released them by his doctrine of faith" and then "left them in bondage to their feelings."[28]

Furthermore, according to Newman, "For outward signs of grace," Luther had "substituted inward; for reverence towards the Church contemplation of self." It was this shift which later in 1838, in his "Advent Sermons on Anti-Christ," Newman equated with the destruction of religion itself. For Newman, historic Protestantism ultimately led to a subjective psychological nihilism that reduced religious experience to a Humean realm of mind receiving impressions lacking any real connections or sense of causality. Newman equated Protestantism, whether contemporary or historic, to an idolatry of feeling that substituted subjective mental states for religious obedience and that could easily lead to antinomianism and self-contemplation. In a feisty footnote, Newman demanded, "When are we to escape from the city of Shadows, in which Luther would bewilder the citizens of the Holy Jerusalem?"[29]

In contrast to his relentlessly harsh assault against the Protestant doctrine of justification, Newman described the Roman Catholic version of that doctrine as "not unsound or dangerous in itself, but defective,—truth, but not the whole truth" and "not a perversion, but what Saints and Martyrs have in substance held in every age." While explicating the Roman outlook, he interjected almost no criticisms and allowed the Roman doctrine to blend with his own. Indeed, he judged the Roman Catholic understanding of justification as spiritual renewal to be "*in the main,* the true doctrine," even though its isolation from other doctrines rendered the Roman teaching defective. Newman explained that the Roman Church taught that "Justification . . . viewed relatively to the past is forgiveness of sin, for nothing more it can be; but considered as to the present and future it is more, it is renewal wrought in us by the Spirit of Him, who withal by His death and passion washes away its still adhering imperfections, as well as blots out what is past." Understood in this fashion, faith justified "first, as continually plead-ing that Passion before God," and then "secondly, as being the first recipient of the Spirit, the root, and therefore the earnest and anticipation of perfect obedience."[30] A new and holy life, achieved in the believer by the presence of the Holy Ghost, glorified God and justified the believer in His sight. In that manner, the obedience of the believer led to justification.

Newman urged that the Roman doctrine of justification was thoroughly biblical and not, like Protestant justification by faith alone, taught only in a few isolated passages of Scripture. Responding to those who would dis-tinguish between justification and renewal, Newman stated that "the pres-ent broad separation of justification and sanctification, as if they were two gifts, is technical and unscriptural." Turning to the Pauline epistles, the biblical stronghold of Protestant theology, he emphasized those passages that discussed the internal work of the Holy Ghost achieving righteousness by transforming the law of God into the will of the believer, infusing the Christian with love, and thus allowing the Christian to perform good works and acts of love in obedience to the law. Directly challenging evangelical theology and biblical exegesis, Newman declared that, according to St. Paul, "the regenerate please God, not merely by the imputation of Christ's obe-dience, but by their own obedience: by their obedience therefore are they justified. . . . Christ then does not keep the power of justification solely in His own hands, but by His Spirit dispenses it to us in due measure, through the medium of our own doings. He has imparted to us the capacity of pleasing Him; and to please Him is that in part, which justification is in fulness, and tends towards justification as its limit." In contemporary tech-nical theological language the issue was "whether justification means in Scripture *counting* us righteous, or *making* us righteous," or whether human righteousness was the imputed righteousness of Christ's atonement or the imparted righteousness of the presence of the Holy Spirit.[31] Newman contended that the 39 Articles supported his fusing of justification and sanctification because they spoke of justification in terms of accounted righteousness and the presence of the grace of Christ and of the inspiration of the Holy Spirit.

To understand God as making possible our future obedience after declaring our past sins forgiven, Newman thought, in no manner detracted from human dependence on God. Justification constituted "an act external to us, continued on into an act within us" and "a divine Voice issuing in a divine work, acceptance on the one part leading to acceptableness on the other, imputation to participation." The work of justification sees the Word of God entering people, transforming and renewing them, and making them capable as free agents of good actions that are pleasing to God. This view of justification involved a profoundly intimate indwelling of Christ in the very being of the Christian. As Newman explained, "Christ then is our Righteousness by dwelling in us by the Spirit; He justifies us by entering into us; He continues to justify us by remaining in us. *This* is really and truly our justification, not faith, not holiness, not (much less) a mere imputation; but through God's mercy, the very Presence of Christ."[32] But how was this justifying presence brought into the life and being of the Christian?

For Newman, the certain answer was by the sacraments and, most important, by the sacrament of baptism, through which justification takes us "out of original sin, and leads us all through life towards the purity of Angels." Emphasizing the necessity of baptism and the application of the sign of the cross, Newman again contrasted his sacramentalism with evangelical justification by faith alone, induced through emotional preaching of the atonement. He declared, "Men sit, and gaze, and speak of the great Atonement, and think this is appropriating it; not more truly than kneeling to the material cross itself is appropriating it. Men say that faith is an apprehending, and applying; faith cannot really apply it; man cannot make the Savior of the world his own. The Cross must be brought home to us, not in word, but in power, and this is the work of the Spirit. This is justification; but when imparted to the soul, it draws blood, it heals, it purifies, it glorifies." This understanding of justification, taught by the Church Catholic, Newman argued, takes the mind off self and "buries self in the absorbing vision of a present, an indwelling God."[33]

Newman repeatedly attacked the ordinary Protestant understanding of justifying faith as simple trust in the sacrifice of Christ. Criticizing that position, Newman wrote, "Faith in the abstract is a mere creation of the mind. The devils believe, and Christians believe; we may compare the two together, and observe that the outline of the faith in each is the same; they both realize the unseen and future on God's word." Furthermore, lively justifying faith must give birth to other virtues, a process which faith understood merely as trust could not foster. The Protestant "idea of faith," Newman declared, "is a mere theory, neither true in philosophy nor in fact; and hence it follows that their whole theology is shadowy and unreal." There was no question that people did trust in Christ's mercy for their salvation and received comfort as a result. Both bad and good people could experience that subjective feeling of trust, but as Newman commented, "What is so unreal, is to say that it is necessarily a holy feeling, that it can be felt by none but the earnest, that a mere trust, without any thing else, without obedience, love, self-denial, consistent conduct, conscientiousness, that this mere trust in Christ's mercy, existing in a mind which has as yet no other religious feeling, will necessarily renew the soul and lead to good works." A religion based on this "mere baseless and extravagant theory" must necessarily display a character of "vagueness and equivocation" without practical consequences. If faith was to be a reality and not simply a matter of words, it must manifest itself in love, fear, obedience, and newness of mind. Returning to his long-standing distinction between natural and revealed religion, Newman observed, "Faith, which in the natural man has manifested itself in the fearful energy of superstition and fanaticism, is in the Gospel grafted on the love of God, and made to mold the heart of man into His image."[34]

While relentlessly rejecting any Protestant understanding of justification that made the personal faith of the Christian the primary instrument, Newman did need to explore more fully the relationship of faith and the sacraments because Article 11 declared that "we are justified by Faith only." Newman sought this reconciliation by instrumentalizing both faith and baptism, explaining, "Justification . . . needs a perpetual instrument, such as faith can, and Baptism cannot be. Each, then, has it own office in the work; Baptism at the time, and faith ever after. Faith secures to the soul continually those gifts which Baptism primarily conveys. The Sacraments are the immediate, faith is the secondary, subordinate, or representative instrument of justification. Or we may say, varying our mode of expression, that the Sacraments are its instrumental, and Faith its sustaining cause." Newman continued, "Faith, then, being the appointed representative of Baptism, derives its authority and virtue from that which it represents. . . . Faith does not precede justification; but justification precedes faith, and makes it justifying." Newman contended that Protestant doctrine mistakenly regarded faith as "the sole instrument, not after Baptism, but before; whereas Baptism is the primary instrument, and creates faith to be what it is and otherwise is not, giving it power and rank, and constituting it as its own successor." The Books of Homilies commended by the 39 Articles, according to Newman, assumed a Christian congregation already baptized, hence their emphasis on faith rather than on baptism. Consequently, "when the Homily speaks of faith as an instrument, it means a sustaining instrument; what the primary instrument is, being quite a separate question."[35] Baptism itself transformed faith into an instrument of justification, and, of course, Newman believed that valid baptism depended upon administration by an episcopally ordained clergyman.

Lectures on Justification stands as Newman's most powerful, eloquent, and moving theological work. Its arguments often carried to further extremes, especially regarding the efficacy of baptismal regeneration, deeply informed all later Tractarian theological polemics against evangelical religion and historical Protestantism.[36] Newman's volume, with its emphasis upon the inadequacy of any religion based on subjective feeling alone to produce true repentance and righteous living, constituted a major foundation for Tractarian asceticism. It also provided one of the deepest nineteenth-century theological probings of religious subjectivity, an accomplishment often ignored because of its more immediate contribution to inter- and intradenominational controversy.

THE INADEQUACY OF THE BIBLE

Having previously disposed of fallacies he discerned in private judgment and justification by faith alone, Newman in *Tract 85*, "Lectures on the Scripture Proof of the Doctrines of the Church" of late September 1838, turned his critical anti-Protestant prowess against *sola scriptura*. Late in the century, both Leslie Stephen and T. H. Huxley pointed to this tract, with its harsh and extensive attack on the religious and historical authority of the Bible, as providing arguments against Christianity as powerfully effective as those written by any unbeliever.[37] This polemic illustrates all too clearly how in quarrels among themselves Christians have provided weapons to their most serious opponents.

Tract 85 originated in Newman's growing impatience with evangelical criticism of the authority that the Tractarians ascribed to the church of antiquity in formulating their ecclesiastical and sacramental doctrines. For example, in 1836 the *Record* had described as "a lamentable delusion" the Tractarian conviction that the church during its first three or four centuries had "possessed a unity of judgment, a simplicity and expansion of scriptural knowledge, and a sobriety in the interpretation of Scripture." Both the *Record* and the *Christian Observer,* as well as other evangelical voices, pointed to the confusions and corruptions of the ancient church suggestive of later Roman Catholic practices as a ground for dismissing its supposed authority. Furthermore, evangelicals consistently contended that there existed no basis in Scripture for Christians to defer to the judgments of the patristic age. Asserting that "the primitive church is no authority to us," the *Record* demanded that patristic authority, as used by the Oxford writers, be cast "away from us, as the dust in the balance."[38]

On another occasion, the *Record* had commented, "If we cannot agree in interpreting the Bible, we are much less likely to agree in interpreting the voluminous writings of the Fathers, who very often contradict, without scruple, both themselves and one another." Newman in *Tract 85* seized upon and reversed that argument to demonstrate that the evangelical rejection of antiquity would necessarily undermine the authority that they and all other Protestants ascribed to the Bible itself. Adopting what he admitted to be "a kill-or-cure remedy," Newman argued that if those who appealed to "the want of *adequate* Scripture evidence for the Church doctrine" were to be consistent, "they ought, on their own principles, to doubt or disown much which happily they do not doubt or disown." They could not "consistently object against a person who believes more than they do, unless they cease to believe so much as they do believe." Newman then pressed his evangelical opponents to confess that if they criticized the doctrines the Tractarians drew from antiquity, they must necessarily undermine their own position. Recognizing that his scorched-earth policy against Protestantism might possibly trouble the faith of some Christians, Newman bluntly stated, "Those who are to stumble must stumble, rather than the heirs of grace should not hear."[39]

Newman defended Church or Catholic doctrines—he used the terms interchangeably in the tract—by claiming that to attack such doctrines with consistency, one must simultaneously undermine Scripture itself. He proposed that "the Canon of Scripture" rested on the foundation of Catholic doctrine; "those who dispute the latter should, if they were consistent, . . . dispute the former," and "in both cases we believe, mainly, because the Church of the fourth and fifth centuries unanimously believed." The testimony of the Church of that era had established the canon and provided the theological foundation for later clarification of doctrines. If one believed the Church of the fourth and fifth centuries corrupt in its understanding of doctrines and rites, it must also have been corrupt in its formulation of the canon. It was consequently necessary to defend Catholic doctrines that were "the first object of attack"; otherwise, "we should at this very time be defending our belief in the Canon."[40]

Tractarian opponents claimed that Scripture said relatively little about Apostolical succession, baptismal regeneration, priestly absolution, and other rites. Paucity of biblical evidence for a particular doctrine, Newman urged, did not necessarily constitute an argument against it, because many doctrines for which much evidence existed, such as the divinity of Christ, encountered difficulty of certain explication by the complexity of the evidence. Furthermore, he contended, "If silence in Scripture, or apparent contrariety, is an argument against the Church System, it is an argument against system at all." Indeed, the argument against the Church system could be turned against numerous core doctrines held at one time or another by virtually all Christians. For example, Scripture did not furnish warrant for infant baptism, for keeping the first day of the week instead of the seventh, for going to church, for having established religions, for permitting the civil magistrate to take lives, or for prohibiting polygamy. Nor, for that matter, did the Bible declare its own inspiration: different passages contradicted each other, such as those in the epistles of St. Paul and St. James on justification and works. Moreover, Newman darkly reminded his readers, "If the words Altar, Absolution, or Succession, are not in Scripture (supposing it), neither is the word Trinity."[41]

The fundamental issues, according to Newman, were the manner in which Scripture contained divine truth and how it was to be gleaned therefrom. He argued, "Either there is *no* definite religious information given us in Christianity at all, or it *is* given in Scripture in *an indirect* and covert way, or it *is* given, but *not* in Scripture." People he designated as latitudinarians embraced the first view, Roman Catholics the latter. According to these unnamed and undefined latitudinarians, who in this tract functioned as rationalists and liberals did in others, "every man's view of revealed religion is acceptable to God, if he acts up to it; that no one view is in itself better than another, or at least that we cannot tell which is the better." Newman denounced this attitude as "that mere dream of religion, which pretends that modes of thinking and social conduct are all one and all the same in the eyes of God, supposing each of us to be sincere in his own." But Newman could not "conceive a serious man, who realized what he was speaking about, a consistent Latitudinarian." Assuming that God had revealed something to humankind, there would have been no point in leaving that message indefinite. To say that the message of Scripture was uncertain was simple enough "for educated persons, at their ease, with few cares, or in the joyous time of youth," but it would not serve human beings encountering a "consciousness of sin" or sorrows of life. To treat Scripture as uncertain or open to infinite interpretation would ultimately send people to Rome, which provided very clear, definite interpretations that satisfied what Newman regarded as an inherent human desire for dogmatic certainty in religious matters. In one of his most important statements on the character of religion, Newman asserted,

> The truth, which men are told they cannot find in Scripture, they will seek *out* of Scripture. They will never believe, they will never be content with, a religion without doctrines. The common sense of mankind decides against it. Religion cannot but be dogmatic, it ever has been. All religions have had doctrines; all have professed to carry with them benefits which could be enjoyed only on condition of believing the word of a supernatural informant, that is, of embracing some doctrines or other. It is a mere idle sophistical theory, to suppose it can be otherwise. *Destroy* religion, make men give it up, if you can; but while it exists, it will profess an insight into the next world, it will profess *important* information about the next world, it will have points of faith, it will have dogmatism, it will have anathemas.

Human nature demanded creeds, the Scripture sanctioned them, and the Church Catholic provided them. Only "the non-descript system of religion now in fashion," by which he meant evangelicalism, prescribed belief only in those matters directly and distinctly taught by Scripture.[42] The Church Catholic over the centuries had interpreted the Scriptures and the faith to those who demanded dogma. Newman's readers could choose between the Church Catholic or the Roman Catholic Church, but they could not expect to meet normal human religious expectations without dogma.

The Church Catholic, according to Newman, had always recognized a system of religion existing outside the Bible: "The Apostles refer to a large existing fact, their system; history informs us of a system, as far as we can tell, contemporaneous, and claiming to be theirs;—what other claimant is there?" If that system taught things in addition to Scripture, there was no excuse for not admitting those additions. If it taught things "but *indirectly taught* in Scripture," then it must be admitted "as an interpreter or comment upon Scripture." But however one might decide the apostolic system related to Scripture, "there it stands, that consistent harmonious system of

THE ASSAULT ON THE PROTESTANT

faith and worship, as in the beginning; and, if history is allowed any weight in the discussion, it is an effectual refutation of Latitudinarianism." No matter what may have been added to the apostolic system, no matter how it may have become corrupted, no matter what misinterpretations of it may have taken place—"from the first a system exists." Its authority could not be refused on the grounds of Scripture because its absence from the Bible would not disprove its truth, and its possible contrariety to the Bible "might after all be caused simply by our own incompetency to judge of Scripture."[43]

From this standpoint Newman asserted that the "irregular and un-methodical" structure of Scripture itself indicated that its message must be "indirectly and covertly recorded there, under the surface." This assertion of the unsystematic character of Scripture, an argument dating at least from Erasmus and other early critics of the Reformation, was essential to New-man's anti-Protestant polemic. The more confusion, incoherence, contra-diction, and lack of system that Newman could discover, the stronger was his position for the necessity of both the indirect reading of Scripture and the use of interpretations from antiquity. The unsystematic, incomplete character of Scripture suggested to Newman the necessity for its interpreta-tion or commentary from Catholic antiquity, the rejection of which led necessarily to virtual skepticism regarding the meaning of biblical language. Of Scripture he wrote, "We want a comment,—they are evidently but a text *for* comment,—and as they stand may be turned this way or that way, according to the accidental tone of mind in the reader." In that regard, "The indirectness of the Scripture proof of the Catholic system is not an objection to its cogency, except as it is an objection to the Scripture proof of every other system." As Protestant sects confronted the complexities posed by the unsystematic character of the Bible, "They must leave off their exceptions against our proofs of our doctrines as insufficient not being stronger in their own proofs themselves."[44] The kinds of questions that Protestants posed to the Tractarian understanding of Catholic doctrines could just as easily be posed to their claims about the sufficiency of the Bible for all knowledge necessary to salvation, the inspiration of the New Testament, the doctrines of justification by faith alone and of election, the right to leave the Church over disagreements with the clergy, and self-ordination. Protestants could not consistently admit some doctrines and rule out others.

Pressing the necessity of a dogmatic system or authority external to Scripture, Newman urged that without such a system no antecedent rea-son existed to believe the Bible itself to be inspired. The Bible was not a single book but a collection of separate compositions written in "as free and unconstrained a manner, and (apparently) with as little consciousness of a supernatural dictation or restraint, on the part of His earthly instruments, as if He had no share in the work." Then, in a passage that stunningly foreshadowed Benjamin Jowett's contribution to *Essays and Reviews* a generation later, Newman observed of the Bible, "Whatever else is true about it, this is true,—that we may speak of the history or mode of its composition, as truly as of that of other books; we may speak of its writers having an object in view, being influenced by circumstances, being anxious, taking pains, purposely omitting or introducing things, leaving things incomplete, or supplying what others had so left. Though the Bible be inspired, it has all such characteristics as might attach to a book uninspired,—the characteristics of dialect and style, the distinct effects of times and places, youth and age, of moral and intellectual character." After recognizing these factors, a person's most natural reading of the Bible would not assume it to contain all necessary revelation. Indeed, Newman declared, "It is . . . far from being a self-evident truth that Scripture must contain all the revealed counsel of GOD; rather the probability lies the other way at first sight." The history and character of the composition of the Bible worked "against its being a complete depository of the Divine Will, unless the early Church says it is." Even the early church had not claimed for Scripture total adequacy in regard to morals, church government, rites, or discipline. To the extent that doctrines and other teachings were present in Scripture, they resided there "by a sort of accident," and thus it was not strange that they must be discerned indirectly. But, Newman reminded the reader, "GOD affects His greatest ends by apparent accidents."[45]

Expanding upon the unsystematic character of Scripture, Newman highlighted the inconsistencies in both the Old and the New Testaments. These included the two creation narratives in Genesis, the distinctions between God's image and Adam's image, the failure to identify the serpent in the Garden with the devil, the two accounts of Abraham denying his wife, discrepancies between Deuteronomy and Exodus in the history of Moses and in the account of the commandments, and numerous other historical inconsistencies and conflicting dual narratives throughout the Old Testament. Within the New Testament, Newman noted the presence of only a single narrative of the raising of Lazarus, the different texts of the Sermon on the Mount in Matthew and Luke, accounts disagreeing about who bore the cross on the way to Calvary, discrepancies between Matthew and Acts over the death of Judas, and distinct accounts of the resurrection and ascension. Insisting that one portion of Scripture must supplement another, Newman urged, "As distinct portions of Scripture itself are apparently inconsistent with one another, yet are not really so, therefore it does not follow that Scripture and Catholic doctrine are at variance with each other, even if they too seem to be so."[46]

Newman did not rest his argument at this point, however, but asserted that the logical outcome of any Protestant attempt to deny the scriptural validity of Catholic doctrine must result in "an invalidating of Scripture itself." Doubts posed to the Catholic system applied to the Bible as well. The accusations launched against antiquity for the unsystematic, incomplete, contradictory, and sometimes erroneous character of its information were, as Newman had just demonstrated, equally applicable to the Bible. He concluded, "I do not see then, if men will indulge that eclectic spirit which chooses part and rejects part of the primitive Church system, what is to keep them from choosing part, and rejecting part of the Canon of Scripture." There were books of the Bible, such as Esther, Ecclesiastes, and the Song of Songs, that "any candid person would grant are presented to us under circumstances less promising than those which attend upon the Church doctrines."[47] Their function in the Bible was not immediately clear, for they contained no prophecy and received no reference in the New Testament. Similar objections to lack of clear purpose might be lodged against the epistles of St. James and St. Jude, the second book of St. Peter, the second and third books of St. John, and Revelation.

Many people objecting to the Church system, Newman admitted, did so because it seemed to be a mysterious, superstitious product of priestcraft. Yet except for "the strength of habit, good feeling, and our Lord's controlling grace" there was nothing to prevent similar objections against Scripture. Only the habitual reading of the Bible in a spirit of reverence prevented readers from regarding much of its contents "as fanciful and extravagant." If Protestants could believe the narrative of the serpent speaking to Eve and accounts of demoniacs healed and devils being sent into swine, then why should they not trust the Church system? Newman further asked, "If Balaam's ass instructed Balaam, what is there fairly to startle us in the Church's doctrine, that the Water of Baptism cleanses from sin, that eating the consecrated Bread is eating His Body, or that oil may be blessed for spiritual purposes, as is still done in our Church in the case of a coronation?" Consequently, those who would critically examine the church, the creed, or Scripture must understand that their thought was headed toward the destruction of "Church, Creed, Bible altogether,—which obliterates the very Name of CHRIST from the world." In this regard, Newman wrote, "Sectaries commonly give up the Church's doctrines, and go by the Church's Bible; but if the doctrines cannot be proved true, neither can the Bible; they stand or fall together."[48] Those who now stood prepared to give up the Church Catholic would soon find themselves compelled to give up the Scripture, and, of course, with the Scripture, the faith as they knew it.

Throughout *Tract 85* Newman indulged in a mischievous and inherently self-destructive analysis of Holy Scripture. Yet Newman portrayed the defense of Catholic or Church doctrines and principles as the first line of defense in what he anticipated to be a full-scale assault on the Christian faith through the undermining of the Bible. Determined to convince Protestants that even they had a real stake in the preservation of the authority of antiquity, he argued that if antiquity were surrendered, then the Bible must itself also soon lose the authority that Protestants so fervently attached to it. The same kind of destructive arguments now leveled by Protestants against antiquity, Newman urged, would soon be employed

> not to prove that Christianity was not true, or that CHRIST was not the SON of GOD, or the Bible not inspired, or not on *the whole* genuine and authentic, but that every part of it was not *equally* divine; that portions, books, particularly of the Old Testament, were not so; that we must use our own judgment. Nay, as time went on, perhaps it would be said that the Old Testament altogether was not inspired, only the New,—nay, perhaps only parts of the New, not certain books which were for a time doubted in some ancient Churches, or not the Gospels according to St. Mark and St. Luke, and the Acts, because not the writing of Apostles, or not St. Paul's reasonings, only his conclusions. Next, it would be said, that no reliance can safely be placed on single texts; and so men would proceed, giving up first one thing, then another, till it would become a question what they gained of any kind, what they considered they gained from Christianity as a definite revelation or a direct benefit.

As people thus retreated from faith in the unique character of biblical revelation, they would eventually consider Christianity itself merely an event in history altering human thought and improving human society, but not "as independent, substantive, and one, specially divine in its origin, and directly acting upon us." Viewing the age as moving steadily in this direction, Newman predicted, "The view henceforth is to be, that Christianity does not exist in documents, any more than in institutions; in other words, the Bible will be given up as well as the Church."[49] Newman here presciently outlined one key strain of future religious development among the educated classes of both Europe and America in the next century and correctly saw that impulse as arising from Protestant theology. Newman deeply believed that if the authority of the Church Catholic were not secured, there would be no institution prepared to defend the authority of the Bible itself.

Like Newman in *Tract 85*, Pusey in his *Letter to the Bishop of Oxford* of 1839 also criticized those who professed to draw their faith from Scripture alone. In the same spirit in which three years earlier he had attacked Hampden, Pusey declared, "All true Theology must of necessity be Scriptural; but that which terms itself a 'Scriptural Theology,' has always been a steppingstone to Socinianism or Rationalism."[50] According to Pusey, both the Roman Catholic and the ultra-Protestant appealed to their own interpretations of Scripture against that of antiquity. Both claimed infallibility, the Roman Catholic through the Spirit promised to the Church, the ultra-Protestant through the Spirit promised to individuals. Both referred without system or consistency to individual Church Fathers when useful and cast them aside at other times. Both believed that the Holy Spirit had reserved to later times what was withheld from earlier ones.

Throughout his pamphlet Pusey drew parallels between ultra-Protestants and Roman Catholics, asserting that they stood "united in an unnatural league against our Church." These elements of commonality were not "accidental" but stood rooted in the agreed necessity "to support modern corruptions of doctrine, unknown to Christian Antiquity." Adherents to Rome and to evangelical religion consequently refused to trust antiquity, "knowing beforehand that they will be condemned by her." Evangelicals refused to consult the testimony of antiquity because rather than finding that it supported Rome, they had "to escape hearing the testimony which she would give against the Anti-sacramental system of Geneva." Whereas the Roman Catholic appealed to antiquity and the ultra-Protestant to Scripture, "the genuine English system, being founded on Holy Scripture as interpreted by Christian Antiquity, possesses a deep reverence for Scripture as the source of the Faith, and for Antiquity, as its witness and expositor."[51] What both Pusey and Newman left for other occasions was any effort to delineate how Catholics and other Christians of their day were actually to understand Scripture as interpreted by Christian antiquity. They remained satisfied with having thrown into doubt the Protestant faith in *sola scriptura*.

ISAAC WILLIAMS AND RESERVE IN COMMUNICATING RELIGIOUS KNOWLEDGE

The Tractarians criticized the practice as well as the doctrines of evangelical Protestant religion. The most important example of this criticism was Isaac Williams's 1837 assault on evangelical preaching in *Tract 80*, "On Reserve in Communicating Religious Knowledge." Except for Newman's *Tract 90* and Pusey's tract on baptism, no Tractarian publication encountered more widespread condemnation. The term *reserve*, which Newman suggested for the published title of the tract, became a source of much criticism and confusion.

The well to do, Welsh-born Williams enjoyed warm relationships with the Tractarians leaders. As a fellow of Trinity College in the late 1820s, he had become a friend of Newman, whom he served as curate both at St. Mary's and Littlemore. He was also close to John Keble and his brother Thomas, serving much later in life as the latter's curate. Yet Williams had attached himself with much more enthusiasm to the Tractarian assault on the Protestant than to their pursuit of the Catholic, from which he consistently demurred. Williams concentrated his ire against ultra-Protestants' frequent, open preaching of the atonement over all other Christian doctrines. In this criticism he stood at one with Newman, who in 1835 had told James Stephen that he shrank from "the rudeness, irreverence, and almost profaneness . . . of making a most sacred doctrine a subject of vehement declamation, or instrument of exciting the feelings, or topic for vague, general, reiterated statements in technical language." Newman further denounced to Stephen "the lightness and hardness with which a certain school speaks of the adorable works and sufferings of our Saviour."[52] Here as in his sermons Newman decried ministers who portrayed God as offering free grace through faith in Christ before demanding obedience to the law.

Writing in the same spirit throughout *Tract 80*, Williams bemoaned that contemporary phenomenon, so fervently advanced by evangelicals, which he described as "the *knowledge* of GOD, hastening to cover the earth, as the waters cover the sea," and complained about the concomitant "impatience at any book being held back from any person, as too high or sacred for them." He specifically regretted the "indiscriminate distribution of Bibles and other religious publications" as incapable of leading to lives of holiness and true religious devotion, as he claimed that "any form of religion that does not support devotional habits must be essentially wrong." He further criticized the "inclination to put aside the Old Testament for the more exclusive use of the Gospel itself, which is contained in it." Williams thus denounced evangelical religion as a vast explosion of feverish public activity that avoided coming to grips with those portions of the Christian message that indicated "the necessity of mortification and obedience on the part of man."[53]

In his autobiography, Williams denoted the Low Church Party and "their hollow mode of proceeding" as having been the target of *Tract 80*. He boasted that among evangelicals the tract had been "understood as it was meant" and had done "its intended work," for which he had been "well content to bear with the outcry and opposition."[54] What provoked that evangelical outcry was not merely Williams's criticism of evangelical methods, but rather his propounding the ironic proposition that the ready availability of religious knowledge in the contemporary world should be directly curtailed through the exercise of reserve in Christian teaching.

According to Williams, God did not immediately reveal full knowledge of himself to all men, but only as they proved themselves obedient. In conjunction with God's desire to communicate knowledge of Himself there also appeared "a tendency to conceal, and throw a veil over" that knowledge "as if it were injurious to us unless we were of a certain disposition to receive it." Williams noted, for example, the absence among the heathen of important knowledge about God's relationship to humankind, the paucity of comment about eternal life in the books of Moses, and the Psalmists' conviction that religious truth lay hidden from them. Furthermore, for thirty years Christ himself had lived inconspicuously before declaring his ministry and had then indicted his own reserve in communicating divine knowledge by his apparent "intention of veiling the truth in the Parables." Throughout his ministry, Christ had also practiced reserve or concealment in regard to his divinity, addressing people according to their wants and their ability to deal with his message. The Gospels themselves indicated that Christ had conferred benefits "in a sort of measured proportion, according to the faith of the recipient or person engaged," and they also taught that the evidence of such faith was "a certain state of the heart" acquired by such means as "prayer and fasting" rather than by "a mere effort of the feelings or imagination." Situation after situation in the Gospel narratives demonstrated Jesus' "habit of concealing, in a remarkable manner, His divine power and majesty, excepting so far as persons might be found capable of receiving it."[55] Even the risen Christ did not immediately make himself known on the road to Emmaus. Williams further speculated that Jesus may have concealed his divinity to prevent people from rejecting it and thus becoming guilty of sin against the Holy Ghost.

According to Williams, God had only indirectly revealed other great mysteries of the faith such as the Trinity, Christ's presence in the eucharist, and the conveyance of grace through baptism. Contending like other Tractarians that true faith came through obedience, not through reason or religious feeling, Williams wrote, "All these topics contain great sacred truths of the very highest possible importance that we should know; but if we attempt to arrive at any knowledge of them by speculation, or any other mode but that of practical obedience, that knowledge is withheld, and we are punished for the attempt: in the same manner that it was of the highest importance that they should know our Lord; but unless they were sincerely and humbly seeking Him, He was hid from them." The danger of sin after baptism and other issues relating to salvation particularly demanded the exercise of reserve and of obedience preceding knowledge. Williams explained, "What I would say is, that fully to know that we are saved by faith in CHRIST only, and not by any works of our own, and that we can do nothing, excepting by the grace of GOD, is a great secret,—the knowledge of which can only be obtained by obedience,—as the crown and end of great holiness of life."[56] From his own reading of Scripture and of human nature, Williams concluded clergy should not preach all doctrines to all persons at the same time but rather communicate knowledge of Gospel truth only as a person grew in obedience, personal holiness, and accompanying humility.

As W. F. Hook once pointed out, whatever sense reserve may or may not have made in the context of the early church, its advocacy made no sense in a nation where all of the principal elements of the Gospel had been openly preached for centuries. The argument for reserve functioned primarily as a platform from which to attack evangelical religion. Personal holiness and obedience, presumably inculcated through reserve, indicated for Williams the real presence of the Holy Spirit, which was "not to be found in religious enthusiasm," where "the feelings are strongly moved by religion, but the heart is not adequately purified nor humbled." Those attracted to enthusiasm were persons of irregular lives, who had long ignored religion but then suddenly confronted it. In responding to enthusiastic preaching, such people encountered not the God of Scripture "as of infinite holiness, but a fiction of the imagination, as each man feigns the idea of God according to his own heart." Enthusiastic religion produced neither a "genuine effect of humbling the natural man" nor "a self-denying and consistent performance of religious duties in secret" but rather "a tendency to feel after sensible signs."[57]

Williams regarded "the prevailing notion that it is necessary to bring forward the Atonement *explicitly* and *prominently* on all occasions" as the most distressing element of this undisciplined, emotional, public outpouring of religious knowledge. Indiscriminate preaching of that doctrine, more than any other practice, indicated the harm sustained in English religious life by the failure of the Church of England to teach the correct doctrine of baptismal regeneration, with its deeper understanding of the atonement.

Williams urged, "The apparent paradox which we witness, of Christianity having become publicly acceptable to the world, contrary to our Lord's express declarations, can only be accounted for by its having been put forward without its distinguishing characteristic, the humiliation of the natural man: the doctrine of the Cross having been in some manner hidden: or those truths connected with it, which are most agreeable to mankind being brought forward alone." The ultimate end of concealing the necessity of obedience and personal humiliation, Williams contended, stood manifest in the evangelical system, working toward its logical conclusion of allowing individuals to apply "familiar and irreverent expressions" to Christ, a practice that constituted "a disguised shape of Socinianism." Offending evangelicals even further, Williams compared the open preaching of the atonement to the Roman Catholic veneration of Mary and condemned both practices as illustrating how "the natural heart lowers the object of its worship to its own frailty, so as to approach that object in Prayer without Holiness of life," a development that he saw as constituting "in fact the object of every false or perverted religion."[58] Here Williams clearly was attacking recent advanced evangelical preaching and appears either to have ignored or to have been unaware of the centrality of holiness of life in Wesley's own teaching, as well as in that of numerous evangelicals in the English Church.

Three years later, in *Tract 86*, "Indications of a Superintending Providence in the Preservation of the Prayer Book and in the Changes Which It Has Undergone," Williams attempted to deflect criticism of his position arising from critics in the Church of England. In that tract he specifically identified erroneous enthusiastic religion with Wesleyanism, which "in conveying a call to repentance," he urged, "so treats the penitent, that persons are placed thereby, not in the position of servants, but are called to strong spiritual joys and assurances, and assume at once the character as it were, of sons and the privilege of adoption." The result was a pursuit of spiritual righteousness through "internal emotions and sensibly felt assurances" in place of obedience.[59] Williams's effort to target Wesleyanism alone did not quiet the flood of criticism provoked by his more general denunciation of evangelical preaching. Furthermore, even nonevangelicals had considerable difficulty with the proposition that the preaching of the Gospel and more particularly the atonement should in some manner be curtailed.

The same year as *Tract 86*, however, Williams returned to his original subject in a second tract advocating reserve in communicating religious knowledge that further advanced his polemic against a religion of feeling.

In *Tract 87* he described the evangelical system, which he accused of always bringing the atonement to the fore while disparaging the sacraments, church authority, fasting, works of holiness, universal judgment, and scriptural injunctions to obedience, as "throughout *peculiar,* in distinction from what is Catholic," and he flatly denied its scriptural basis. He denounced evangelicals for disallowing "an unreserved appeal to the written Word" by maintaining that "only, when the HOLY SPIRIT was given, did Holy Scripture set forth the Atonement with that fulness which they require." Williams bitterly concluded, "In fact, this system is nothing else but a method of human device, which is able to quote a part of Scripture for its purpose."[60]

What Williams termed "this new scheme of religion" had led congregations to believe "that the efficacy of a preacher consists in human eloquence and activity, and not in the power of his Divine commission, which is, in fact, to set up something else, which may be sensibly felt, for the Divine gifts of the SPIRIT." In fact, for Williams evangelical religion amounted to "substituting a system of man's own creation for that which GOD has given." The evangelical stress on externalities resembled Roman corruptions, avoided genuine repentance and pursuit of holiness, and "instead of the process of painful secret self-discipline and gradual restoration, or the open and salutary penance of the Ancient Church," afforded "an instant and ready mode for assuming at once all the privileges and authority of advanced piety." Williams urged, "As we keep the commandments we shall embrace the Atonement, and so far only, whether we speak of it or not." In direct opposition to radical evangelical doctrine and Calvinism, Williams declared, "He . . . who most of all induces men to practise good works, under the awful sense of their condition as baptized Christians, brings them most of all to the Cross of CHRIST; and he who, by his teaching, leads men to think that such works are of minor importance, and speaks slightingly of them, i.e., works of charity, of humiliation, and prayer, teaches men false and dangerous doctrine, flattering to human indolence, but opposed to Scripture, opposed to the Church, opposed to the first principles of our moral nature." To disparage good works and piety, which Williams saw preachers of popular Protestantism as doing, was to separate men from Christ himself. By ignoring baptismal regeneration, evangelicals disparaged the necessity of practicing good works as baptized Christians. Williams further contended that evangelicalism had "about it something which falls in with, and encourages, nay, assumes its own character and complexion from, the spirit of disobedience and lawlessness, which is to prevail in the last days." The ancient Catholic system anchored itself in the invisible world, whereas "this modern system, partaking of the character of our own age of expediency, and mostly founded on feeling, is moved by every wind" and "partakes of the weakness of human things, and cannot stand when the floods arise."[61] Again, as in the past, Williams ignored the vast outpouring of evangelical publications urging the Christian toward the experience of personal sanctification following the experience of personal justification through placing faith in Christ.

Both Williams's tracts on reserve constituted loud eruptions of controlled rage against the democratization of religion within the public sphere. The Tractarian attack on preaching came from clergy who appear often to have written sermons to be read rather than to be heard. When the Tractarians could find no other charges to hurl at evangelical preaching, they accused it of eventually or logically producing liberalism, rationalism, latitudinarianism, Socinianism, and blasphemy against the Holy Spirit. Williams's demands for reverence and reserve were equivalent to a schoolboy during a playground scuffle demanding that his combatants hold still until he can strike them. To evangelicals and others, it appeared that Williams simply wanted to withhold the Gospel message and retain its power in the hands of a few priests.

PROTESTANTISM AS A NEGATIVE FORCE

The result of these Tractarian criticisms of evangelical doctrine and practice was the reduction of Protestantism in their pages to a negative, vacuous, disruptive force in the English Church. In his *Letter to the Bishop of Oxford*, Pusey claimed that ultra-Protestants charged Tractarians with being guilty of "disaffection" from the English Church as well as "unfaithfulness to her teaching, a desire to bring in new doctrines, and to conform our Church more to the Church of Rome, to bring back either entire or 'modified Popery.' " In response, Pusey claimed that the Tractarians, unlike the ultra-Protestants, had no desire to change the liturgy or, like members of evangelical societies, to escape the ecclesiastical authorities under whom they lived. Pusey asserted "that the '*via media*,' along which we, with our Church, would fain tread, though distinct from the bye ways of Ultra-Protestantism, is a broad and tangible line, not verging towards, or losing itself in Romanism." Rather, the Tractarian *via media* constituted "the 'old path' of the Primitive Church, after whose model our own was reformed, and which amid the entanglement of the modern deviations of Rome, our reformers wished, I believe, to trace out."[62] Both ultra-Protestantism and Roman Catholicism represented declines and departures from that ancient faith.

Evangelical charges of popery leveled against the Tractarians were, according to Pusey, necessarily vague because the ultra-Protestant defined as popish all that "which in solemnity of observance is greater than his own, or a doctrine, or rite of Antiquity which he holds not." Furthermore, to find anything commendable in the Breviary or "to doubt whether the Pope is *the* Antichrist, even while asserting that there is much anti-Christian in the system of Rome" had come to be regarded as a manifestation of popery. Pusey complained that for many people even the expression of dislike for the word Protestant implied a popish leaning when, in fact, the term indicated an affinity for Lutheranism rather than a rejection of Rome. Indeed, he asserted, "Protestant" was simply a negative epithet "ill-fitted to characterize the faith of any portion of the Christian Church."[63]

The same year as Pusey's *Letter to the Bishop of Oxford*, Frederick Oakeley expanded upon the negative character of the concept of Protestantism. Oakeley, a fellow of Balliol two years younger than Newman and a member of his short-lived dining society, became closely associated with the Tractarians only late in the decade, along with a considerably younger, more engaged coterie of Oxford men, whose most famous member was W. G. Ward. As we shall see, Oakeley was to play a key role in events of 1845 that culminated in the disintegration of Tractarianism. His comments of 1839, published as the preface to a volume of his sermons, illustrate the conclusions that a zealous, new adherent to Tractarianism might draw from the assault on the Protestant undertaken by Newman and to a lesser extent by Pusey and Williams.

Oakeley engaged essentially in a word game that manipulated the meaning of *Protestantism* with little or no reference to contemporary or historical religious realities. He defined and redefined Protestantism until eventually it lacked either substantive meaning or religious integrity. Oakeley described the popular religion of the day as "the modified form which the characteristic principle of mere undiscriminating Protestantism has assumed under the control of Church formularies." That same principle had "under less favourable circumstance" developed into rationalism, Socinianism, Calvinism, and puritanism. Oakeley asserted that the term Protestant simply indicated "one who is not a Roman Catholic" and thus functioned as "a merely negative term; expressing of what religion a man is not, but leaving it doubtful of what religion his is, or whether of any religion at all." Protestantism, so far as it "expresses an opposition to what is erroneous in Romanism," must be considered "as a term expressive of what is good," but because it denoted opposition to all Roman Catholicism, it "cannot express what is altogether right, unless Roman Catholicism be altogether wrong." Consequently, "Protestantism . . . expresses what is good, if it be opposed to Popery, and what is bad, if it be opposed to Catholicism." Indeed, "to call a man a Protestant, *and no more*," was to deny that he belonged to the Roman Church "which holds truth mixed with error, but not to affirm of him (necessarily) that he is more than a Socinian, or an infidel." A "*mere* Protestant" denoted a man standing as "a critic of mysteries, and a framer of his own creed." Oakeley associated the Protestant frame of mind with that of the ancient sophists of Plato's day and the Pharisees and Sadducees of the time of Christ. Protestants, like those ancient groups, exalted in the self, and, like modern utilitarians, displayed a "morbid and faithless craving after *visible results.*"[64]

Oakeley thought the term "anti-Catholic" might "advantageously" be substituted "for those of Protestant and ultra-Protestant." The anti-Catholic principle, like the Calvinist assurance of election, led to "the tendency of some popular views of religion to favour self-indulgence and unscrupulousness" against the looseness and self-complacency of which fasting might produce a salutary effect. For all of these reasons, Oakeley concluded, "Catholicism, *as distinguished from Popery*, is an essentially divine, Protestantism, *as contrasted with it*, an essentially human and worldly, principle."[65]

Oakeley's broad, sweeping, indiscriminate critique of Protestantism without any specific references to particular Protestants or particular Protestant writings flowed naturally from the Tractarians' polemics that had explored a pathology of diseased Protestant corruptions which they intended to remove from the Church of England and English religious life in general. In doing so, the Tractarians had projected a Protestant phantom largely of their own imagining and self-serving construction. If, as Pusey charged, evangelicals failed to define popery, the Tractarians similarly failed to define ultra-Protestantism. They examined evangelical Protestantism only from the exterior, and at a discrete distance, repeatedly devising caricatures of evangelical doctrine and practice, which they proceeded to demolish.

It was essential to the entire Tractarian enterprise to project a dark realm of evangelical Protestant ecclesiastical disorder, theological confusion, and spiritual laxity that bore only a modest relationship to reality. From the beginning, Newman had believed that only when the imaginations of clergy saw ruin around them would they be moved to new departures for the Church of England. His first effort in that direction had been the apocalyptic tenor of the early tracts enjoining clergy to speculate on how they would retain their social status if state confiscation of church property occurred. His second effort was the denigration of Dissent, then of evangelicalism, and finally of Protestantism in general as affording an inadequate foundation for clerical status and authority. Consequently, in the late 1830s, as clergy of the Church of England found themselves no longer fearful of disestablishment, the Tractarians sought to make them anxious over their traditionally recognized status as ministers of a Protestant faith. Even as inhabitants of a reasonably secure establishment, they must, according to the Tractarians, necessarily turn to new faith and practice if they were to be successful in the religious marketplace. The assault on the Protestant thus displaced the initial assault on erastianism as the device to induce anxiety to a point where clergy might contemplate the necessity of novel Catholic theological and devotional departures.

By the second half of the 1830s Newman, Pusey, and Keble really sought only the possibility of such novel departures for individual clergy or a small Tractarian party within the English Church rather than the actual transformation of the whole institution. Equating Catholic Christianity and its fate in England with themselves, they embraced a Catholic, or universalistic, rhetoric to serve their own narrow sectarian purposes. They carried out their program of creative destruction of the Protestant ethos of the Church of England so they might freely pursue their own novel pursuit of Catholic devotion and practice. In the process, they attracted to themselves a small coterie of zealous followers, such as Oakeley, who rushed even more rapidly through the breaches in the wall of traditional Protestant faith and practice of the English Church, causing the earlier Tractarians to have to run to keep up. At the same time, the Tractarian leaders had so undermined conviction in the adequacy of Protestantism that if any of their young followers lost faith in the Catholic experiment itself, their choice might well lie between Roman Catholicism and skepticism. In that respect, the Tractarian assault on the Protestant had unwittingly prepared some minds and spirits for both ecclesiastical doubt and theological unbelief, an outcome widely recognized at the time.

CHAPTER 7

The Pursuit of the Catholic

I N LATE October 1833, when Oxford Apostolicals considered organizing a clerical society, Newman's old friend J. W. Bowden advised, "In choosing a name for your Society, let the word 'Catholic' appear. Our great error has been that we have forgotten ourselves, or at least forgotten to teach others, that we, Churchmen, are the Catholics of England; and, unless we can wrest the monopoly of the term from the Papists, we do nothing. We *must* disabuse our fellow churchmen of the idea that we belong to a Church, comparatively new, which, some 300 years ago, *supplanted* the old Catholic Church of these realms. Let us then bear, by all means, our Catholic title on our front." Bowden immediately admitted that "an inconvenience" surrounded the word " 'Catholic' alone," which "might mislead some people," but suggested that combining " 'Catholic and Apostolic' together" would avoid confusion with Roman Catholicism.[1] The Tractarians, however, never overcame the ambiguities that even Bowden saw attached to the concept of the Catholic. Each of their efforts only further confused matters for themselves and presented new opportunities for criticism to their religious and secular opponents. It is indicative of the imprecisely defined boundaries of early-Victorian religion that Bowden could suggest as a designation for the radical Oxford high-church departure the very name appropriated less than two decades later by the mid-Victorian Catholic Apostolic Church descended from the charismatic Scottish evangelical Edward Irving's London congregation.

The focus for the Tractarian assault on the Protestant had been a well-defined body of historic Christian doctrine and contemporary evangelical practice. Such was not the case with their pursuit of the Catholic, which, even among its warmest sympathizers, was marked from its inception by an absence of clarity. Constructing Catholicism was a process of exploration, selective appropriation, and rediscovery of ideas and devotion that the Tractarians claimed had lain long hidden in English religious life. Like religious buccaneers pirating devotional and doctrinal treasures wherever their religious fancy led them, the Tractarians roamed through the faith and practice of the pre-Reformation church and the writings of favored English Church divines, as well as through Roman Catholic devotional literature, such as the Breviary, to forge their own concept of a Catholic tradition. They published tracts, pamphlets, and books incorporating selections from all of these sources. With difficulty they also published multivolume libraries of the Fathers and of Anglo-Catholic Theology.[2] In some cases, in order to make texts fit their own Catholic ecclesiastical and theological ends, they gave individual anthologized works titles different from those assigned by the original authors. In other cases, they could assert only the presence of a tradition that had remained mysteriously and, they asserted, providentially concealed for long periods of time.

Contemporaries across the religious spectrum repeatedly judged Tractarian ecclesiology, theology, and devotion as distinctly un–English and antithetical to dominant cultural values, the very same values with which evangelical religion in its multitudinous manifestations had so successfully and intimately intermeshed itself. Consequently, the Tractarian pursuit of the Catholic led as much to *cultural* as to *religious* apostasy, though it did lead to the latter.[3] Roman Catholicism in the popular and even learned English imagination resided across a boundary that partitioned true and false religion, private judgment and priestcraft, freedom and tyranny, rationality and superstition, marriage and celibacy, England and Ireland, Britain and most of the Continent. The *cultural*, as distinct from the *religious*, apostasy of the Tractarians lay in their violating those boundaries and spurning English Protestantism while accommodating elements of what contemporaries regarded as foreign superstition and heterodox social practices, including clerical celibacy and monasticism. Newman understood just exactly what was at stake in displacing the Protestant for the championing of the Catholic, noting in 1837 as an unassailable fact of contemporary life that "viewed *politically*, Protestantism is at this day the rallying point of all that is lofty and high-minded in the nation."[4]

TOWARD PROPHETICAL TRADITION

Because of its exploration of the "disciplina arcani," based, as he later told Froude, "on the hypothesis of Apostolical Traditions co-ordinate with

Scripture," Newman's *Arians of the Fourth Century* may stand as the first major Tractarian effort to reclaim for the nineteenth century pre-Reformation faith and practice. But the work that most pointedly laid the foundation for the reclamation of the Catholic centuries was "Home Thoughts Abroad," the series of articles that Newman wrote in 1833 and 1835 and published in Rose's *British Magazine* between 1834 and 1836.[5] The first two installments of "Home Thoughts Abroad," written in 1833 as the first tracts appeared and echoing his letters of the previous winter and spring, included meditations on the city of Rome, the Roman Church in prophecy, and the character of the Roman Church compared with that of the English Church.

In these articles, Newman presented the shortcomings of the Roman Catholic Church as twofold. First, Rome did not lead its members toward the rigorous righteousness that for many years he had preached from the pulpit of St. Mary's. The Roman Church actually discouraged ordinary Christians from pursuing obedience by "virtually" substituting "an external ritual for moral obedience; penance for penitence, confession for sorrow, profession for faith, the lips for the heart." The hope of the unrepentant sinner for salvation through the mediation of the saints constituted an easier path to forgiveness than judgment by the Son of God. The priest's celebrating mass for the people and for the dead, "so holding out a hope that, though a man live and die in sin, yet he may be saved," compounded these shortcomings. The doctrine of purgatory suggested to unrepentant and disobedient persons that "by their own brief suffering, they may cleanse themselves for heaven." All these practices manifested Rome's "*degradation of the human mind*" in the sense of "obliterating the command, the desirableness and the effort of aiming at high moral excellence, at the perfection of truth, holiness, justice, and love." In this fashion, Newman declared, the Roman Church "destroys *personal* religion, and so makes the world what it would be if the gospel had not been given."[6]

Second, Newman charged that the Roman Church had corrupted legitimate ancient Catholic religious and devotional practices that he hoped to see reintroduced into the Church of England. To substantiate this conclusion, Newman presented a novel interpretation of the Roman Catholic Church in prophecy. According to Newman, St. Paul and St. Peter had established the Catholic Church in Rome, which had later succeeded in making itself "undeniably the most exalted church in the whole world" and a political authority that through its "high-mindedness, majesty, and the calm consciousness of power" exceeded the excellence of Rome itself. Newman believed that one of the Four Monsters of the prophet Daniel's vision had inhabited the ancient Roman polity and eventually had "seized upon Christianity as the new instrument of its impieties." Once so captured by the Antichrist, the Roman Church stood as an object of pity, "spell-bound, as if by an evil spirit," and "in thralldom." As a consequence, the "corrupt papal system," through "its cruelty in its unsparing sacrifice of the happiness and virtue of individuals to a phantom of public expediency, in its forced celibacy within, and its persecutions without, its craft in its falsehoods, its deceitful deeds, its lying wonders, and its grasping ambition in the very structure of its polity, in its assumption of universal dominion," manifested iniquities not unlike those of ancient republican Rome. Newman presented Jesus' parable of the tares enmeshing irreconcilable elements of good and evil as "a prophetical reference to the case of Rome" that permitted him to draw a distinction between the Church of Rome infused with the monstrous spirit of Antichrist and the Antichrist itself. That distinction, which separated Newman from evangelical anti-Catholic interpreters of prophecy, permitted him to identify valuable, truly Catholic elements residually present in Roman Catholicism distinct from its corruptions. In effect, the Antichrist inhabited and corrupted the Roman Catholic Church and thus accounted for its popery without being identical with its true essence. By thus disowning the equation of Rome with Antichrist and regarding Rome as a true, though profoundly corrupted church, Newman believed that he had secured the legitimacy of the apostolical succession that passed through it and had thereby devised "a solution of the great difficulty which perplexes Protestants—how to avoid popery without giving up the church."[7]

By its having corrupted ancient Catholic religious practices, including free-will offerings of the heart, private self-sacrifice of riches and goods, and celibacy, the Roman Church, possessed by the Antichrist, had infected all such pure, original modes of Catholic devotion with sin or absurdity to the detriment of later Protestantism. Newman declared, "In these, and many other instances, Rome has robbed us of high principles, which she has retained herself, though in a corrupt state. When we left her, she suffered us not to go in the beauty of holiness; we left our garment and fled. Too much of what is angelic in devotion, and stately in teaching, and vigorous in discipline, and high-minded in practice, is lost to us." Whatever the corruption present within Roman devotional practices, they nonetheless retained and manifested "the *reverential* principle, which is indissolubly connected with real religion, and which the church of Rome inherits from old catholic times."[8] What Newman did not explain in these passages was the principle whereby he would sort and separate the mixed wheat and tares of legitimate Catholic and corrupt popish practices in the pre-Reformation Christian heritage.

His earliest substantial exploration of that issue occurred between late 1834 and early 1836 in a newspaper controversy with the French Abbé Jean-Nicolas Jager. This debate had originated in an exchange of public letters in the French press between Benjamin Harrison and Jager over the respective roles of tradition and Scripture, but Harrison soon turned the dispute over to Newman. Throughout his letters to Jager, which his sisters translated into French for him, Newman firmly asserted the supremacy of Scripture while simultaneously disassociating himself from an evangelical or ultra-Protestant emphasis on the Bible. For example, he wrote, "The main principle which we of the Anglican Church maintain, is this: that Scripture is the ultimate basis of proof, the place of final appeal, in respect to all fundamental doctrine." In another passage, he urged, "We consider Scripture to be the court of ultimate appeal, which has the right of definitely settling all questions of faith." Newman repeatedly asserted that all the fundamentals defining the limits of communion within the Anglican Church lay rooted in Scripture, and he presented tradition as subordinate and not coordinate with Scripture.[9] Furthermore, he presented the Gospel as constituting a deposit of divine truth given to the church and existing prior to it. The church had been empowered to develop into Articles the creed originating in apostolic tradition, but not to establish new fundamentals.

In addition to this definition of apostolic tradition, which, as we have seen, Harrison regarded as excessively Protestant and potentially rationalistic, Newman articulated the concept of a prophetical tradition that was "equally primitive, and equally claims our zealous maintenance." Prophetical Tradition, Newman explained to Jager, originated with unnamed prophets, who, different from the Apostles and their episcopal successors, "are the interpreters of the divine law," and who "unfold and define its mysteries, . . . illuminate its documents, . . . harmonize its contents, . . . apply its promises."[10] The various portions of the consequent Prophetical Tradition bore different degrees of authority, with the earliest having the greatest. Moreover, by its very nature Prophetical Tradition, unlike the apostolical, was subject to corruption because it had not been carefully handed down from bishop to bishop but had come into existence and received its maintenance through a much more diffuse process.

While discussing Prophetical Tradition, which he claimed deserved "the greatest veneration," Newman stated that the decrees of the Council of Trent deserved similar veneration although he did "not receive them as the body of doctrines." Those decrees stood as "ruins of primitive antiquity, worthy of respect, although they are . . . often altered, and they introduce

great corruptions into the practice of Christians who receive them." Newman regarded "the capital fault of that council" to consist not "precisely in
the exposition of Christian doctrines (although in many points they are in
opposition to antiquity), but in the right it arrogates to itself to impose its
belief as being part of the fundamental dogmas of Christianity, and as a
necessary condition of being received into the Church."[11] These statements
clearly reflect Newman's continued disillusionment originating in his and
Froude's conversation with Wiseman in 1833 and suggest that the difficult
issue for Newman was much less the content of Tridentine doctrines than
the authority claimed by the post-Tridentine church.

Froude himself had not been altogether pleased with Newman's thinking in the Jager exchange, about which Newman had corresponded with
him. Recognizing the infinitely expandable character of Prophetical Tradition, Froude commented to Newman,

> But if you allow tradition an interpretative authority I cannot see what is
> gained. . . . Also you lug in the Apostles' Creed and talk about expansions—
> What is to be the end of expansions? will not the Romanists say that their
> whole system is an expansion of 'the H. C. C. [Holy Catholic Church] and
> the Communion of Saints'? Also what are the Nicene and Athanasian
> Creeds but expansions? Also to which class of tradition do you refer the
> Athanasian Creed? for I suppose you will admit that it carries in its form the
> assertion of fundamentality. In short—Why treat a subject of great perplex-
> ity and deep and general interest on a narrow and insufficient ground which
> may avail in one or two controversies with the Romanists (supposing i.e.
> that you can prove what you think you can from the fathers) but which in
> no way serves to meet the general question, or to guide our own practice?[12]

Had the issue been, as Froude suggested, controversy with the Roman
Church, the exploration of Prophetical Tradition might not have been
worth the trouble, but the Roman controversy was not the fundamental
issue for Newman. It was instead his personal life and faith. He could fulfill
his own deepest spiritual longings only through a life of novel devotion
potentially validated through Prophetical Tradition that did not require the
authority and discipline of Roman Catholic ecclesiastical structures.

The peculiar, indeterminate expansiveness of Newman's theology, pushing into a largely untracked terrain of devotion and belief far beyond the
boundaries of Scripture and the formularies of the Church of England, was
no secret to his Oxford contemporaries. As early as January 1835 the young
F. W. Faber, later an important Roman Catholic convert but then an evangelically minded undergraduate, wrote of his having become more than ever

convinced of the "falsehood" of "Newmanism," which he characterized as "deeply tinctured by that mystical allegorizing spirit of Origen and the school of Alexandria." Regarding "with deep sorrow the spread of this amiable devotional mysticism in Oxford," Faber forecast that "a very serious blow may be given to the Church by bodies of young men going out to be parish priests, believing that there are inner doctrines, which *it is as well* not to reveal to the vulgar—mysteries—I am using Newman's own words, which are his peculiar treasure—'*thoughts which it is scarcely right to enlarge upon in a mixed congregation.*'" As a result of having himself been for a time "an unprejudiced acolyth [*sic*] of Newman's, an attentive reader of his works, a diligent attender at his church," Faber found "the impressive simplicities of the Bible irksome" and "all its quiet consolations" knocked from under him as his soul craved for "vague, bodiless Platonic reveries." Such Faber speculated might result in Newman's followers becoming "a sort of Christian Essenes." Closely observing Newman's pattern of thought, Faber had "seen indistinct visions become distinct embodiments" and "the conclusion of one proposition become the premise of a next," resulting in a theology that appeared to him at that point in his life "more like the blind march of error than the steady uniformity of truth."[13] Faber's own thinking was to change in the coming years, but his comments of 1835 capture the personal and intellectual qualities of Newman's religious teaching that both drew men into his sphere and eventually disturbed many early Tractarian sympathizers, as well as Oxford University authorities.

The articulation of the concept of Prophetical Tradition opened a vast arena of pre-Reformation faith and practice wherein Newman could exercise his private judgment in regard to what did and did not constitute the Catholic faith. Sheridan Gilley has described "the Prophetical Tradition" as loosing Newman "from his moorings" and pushing "him out into an unknown sea."[14] It would be closer to the mark to say that Newman seized upon Prophetical Tradition as a barque upon which to launch himself and those who would join him on a spiritual voyage to an undetermined port.

THE 1836 EXCHANGE WITH ROSE

Seeking to probe Prophetical Tradition, Newman in late 1835 approached Pusey on the question of prayers for the dead. Admonishing caution, Pusey insisted that there was no need to broach an issue which "perhaps more than any other" subject "would bring down the outcry, not only of the Ultra-Protestants, but of most Anti-Catholics" and which in the wrong hands might lead to much abuse in practice. Rejecting this warning, Newman moved ahead with *Tract 72*, published the next year, which incorporated much of Bishop Ussher's discussion of prayers for the dead. On the basis of Ussher's assurance that such prayers in the ancient church had nothing to do with the later Roman teaching of purgatory, Newman claimed that "the tenet of Purgatory . . . is but the gradual creation of centuries, and has no claim on our consideration," while prayers for the dead were clearly of apostolic origin. In what was by then normal Tractarian practice, Newman blamed the omission of such prayers on the English Reformers' fear, fired by their continental advisers, that both ordinary and educated people would assume prayers for the dead supported the doctrine of purgatory. By contrast, modern discussion of these prayers, Newman argued, would allow a member of the English Church "securely to expatiate in the rich pastures of Catholicism, without the reasonable dread, that he, as an individual, may fall into that great snare which has bewildered the whole Latin Church, the snare of Popery."[15] Pusey, having reconsidered his initial doubts, supported prayers for the dead in "An Earnest Remonstrance to the Author of 'The Pope's Letter,'" published independently in late April 1836 and later as *Tract 77*.

These publications led a perplexed Hugh James Rose to seek clarification of the future aims of the Tractarians, with whom from the publication of Pusey's book on Germany through the Hadleigh conference of July 1833 his relations had been troubled. Although Newman had recognized Rose's usefulness as a link to traditional high churchmen and London ecclesiastical circles and had cooperated with him in attacking Hampden, he was never willing to defer to him. In early 1836 Rose reacted quite negatively to passages in Pusey's tract on baptism, the first tract "Against Romanism," and the discussions of prayers for the dead, as well as to the Tractarian issuance of the partial translation of the Roman Breviary. Two distinct but interrelated issues worried him. The first was the Tractarian insistence on using antiquity as a benchmark for determining doctrine and practice. Rose knew such a resort to antiquity opened a theological morass not least because Unitarians such as Joseph Priestley, in his history of Christian corruptions, had effectively appealed to it. The second matter troubling Rose was the Tractarians' growing hostility to both the contemporary Church of England and the sixteenth-century Reformation. During the next decade controversy surrounding these two issues of the authority of antiquity and the relationship of the modern English Church to the Reformation overturned cooperation between high churchmen and Tractarians, eventually leading the former to seek the destruction of the latter, while their common evangelical opponents watched with delight.

In early April, Rose initiated a long correspondence with Newman that encapsulated almost all the elements of the later dispute and pointed to the fundamental radicalism of the Tractarian project. Rose's point of departure was criticism of Newman's final installment of "Home Thoughts Abroad," published that month in the *British Magazine*. After raising the possibility of disestablishment or confiscation of church property, Newman had speculated on new Catholic departures in devotional practice that might attract voluntary worshipers to a dispossessed English Church. On April 10 Newman assured Rose that he had intended only "to encourage Churchmen to look boldly at the possibility of the Church's being made to dwell in the affections of the people at large," a possibility that would "look like a dream" until real evil occurred against the church. He claimed to have raised the prospect of Catholic additions to the Prayer Book only "to frighten the Evangelicals" into halting their own efforts to alter the baptismal liturgy. At the same time, however, Newman indicated his personal readiness to entertain new ideas regarding religious " 'Excitements' " that might be permitted in the English Church. At present, he commented, "The Roman Church stops the safety valve of the Excitement of Reason—we that of the Excitement of Feeling. In consequence Romanists turn Infidels, and Anglicans Westleyans [*sic*]."[16] Newman's remarks about novel religious excitements clearly indicated the direction that Tractarian devotion was to move over the next decade.

Dissatisfied with Newman's response, Rose complained to Pusey that after having reawakened many young men to Catholic principles, the tracts in their new departures would alienate those allies and that "very many from fear, very many from conviction, will break away." Furthermore, the recent tracts played into the hands of hostile evangelicals. Consequently, "The enemy will have the best possible hand to use *against* you, and *for* himself and his own ends." Pusey turned Rose's letter over to Newman, who on May 1 insisted that the Tractarians must not only attack evangelicalism but also actively pursue Catholic truth, the benefits of which the English Church had not yet fully afforded itself. Newman stated his fundamental conviction "that the Anglican system of doctrine is in matter of fact not *complete*—that there are hiatuses which never have been filled up—so that, though one agrees with it most entirely as far as it goes, yet one wishes something more." Both Catholics in the Church of England and Roman Catholics knew of devotional practices dating from antiquity that the English Church omitted in its worship. Refusing to smother aspirations for the revival of such devotions, Newman asked, "When Romanists taunt us with not praying for the dead in Christ, what are we to say? to evade the question? or boldly say, *you* are not perfect, nor are we—or rather you have corrupted, we have only omitted—we do not hinder Christians praying in private for the dead—you damn them if they do not believe in purgatory."[17] The times were particularly ripe in Newman's opinion to explore devotional options that would both meet the Catholic aspirations of members of the English Church and repulse Roman Catholic incursions onto the contemporary religious scene.

For Rose, who had served as an examining chaplain to potential ordinands, the prospect of allowing clergy to explore antiquity held as little attraction as permitting Ranters to explicate Scripture. On May 9, once again hoping to temper his Oxford colleagues, he told Newman, "*All* that is in Antiquity is not good; and much that was good for Antiquity would not be good for us." Modern clerical readers loosed into antiquity "without the *tether*, without strict and authoritative guidance in short," were "just as likely to get harm as good: to deduce very false and partial conclusions from very insufficient premises; and to set up as object for *imitation* what may catch the fancy and strike the imagination, but what is utterly unfit for our present condition." Without "good guides and experienced drivers" providing "full, clear, and explicit directions" about how to derive good from antiquity and "to avoid the sort of quackery of *affecting* Antiquity," clergy might well regard ancient practices valuable quite simply because they were found in antiquity. Rose foresaw that "quick and ingenious men, once set on the track of thinking that we are in a very imperfect state, and that we have deserted Antiquity," would "pour a thousand follies and falsehoods out upon us, and indispose very many to all such fair consideration as I speak of." Clergy should be taught the truths residing in antiquity as having been always held and "not as a thing, which they are to go and look for, and find out, and prove by themselves." Rose firmly declared that corrective additions to Church of England doctrine, even involving nonessentials, could not safely be proposed to most clergy, who, lacking "the means of knowing or discovering how *much* or how *little*" improvement might be required, would become "merely converted into *ignorant* Reformers."[18] Rose clearly feared the consequences of ignorant clergy loosed into the pastures of antiquity as much as Newman feared individual Christians being allowed to roam at will the pastures of Scripture.

Newman steadfastly refused to retreat, claiming on May 11 that with the new absence of government support for the Church of England, "Our only chance of safety now lies in boldness." Portraying "the Revolution Protestantism" [of 1688] as "too cold, too tame, too Socinian-like to reach the affections of the people," he insisted that the English Church must be invested with "its treasures" and its communion made "a privilege as well as a duty" lest schism follow after schism just "as the Westleyans [*sic*] arose when the nonjurors were disowned." Newman then added quite ominously sentiments he would more fully expatiate upon in his circle of young acquaintances, "Now *supposing* a man thinks that, greatly as the Romanists have sinned, we have sinned too, supposing he has suspicions that perchance judgments are upon the Anglican Church in consequence, he cannot allow himself to proclaim the existing system of things perfect."[19] Under those circumstances, antiquity provided the basis for both perfecting the theological imperfections of the English Church and nurturing new internal practices that would prevent future schism. Both goals required recognition that the contemporary Church of England, like the Church of Rome, required genuinely substantial reformation and reconstruction. Just as the advanced evangelicals of the 1820s had pointed to the inadequacies of their more moderate immediate forebears, Newman pointed to the theological and ecclesiastical trimming of traditional high churchmen whose opposition to evangelicalism and erastianism had proved so inadequate. Similarly, he stood prepared to undertake a novel exploration of the antiquity championed by high churchmen in the same manner that the advanced evangelicals had undertaken new readings of the Bible more radical than those of their evangelical predecessors.

In an addendum to Newman's letter, Pusey stated that the Oxford writers had advised the use not of a single ancient Father but of many and had urged that only truths found in all of the Fathers should have authority. Pusey did not, of course, say that the tracts provided no substantial instructions for reading the Fathers or determining the collective patristic mind. Nor did he admit that neither sets of the Fathers nor scholarly commentaries were readily available to the isolated and frequently impoverished parish clergy. Nonetheless, embracing the indiscriminate searching of the Fathers, Pusey glibly reminded Rose, "This is what I meant by saying that we must spread our sails, not knowing whither we should be carried."[20]

Resisting even modest Catholic innovation, Rose declared on May 13, "Make men understand what *we* mean by 'the *Holy Catholic Church*' and 'the *Communion of Saints*,' and what can be done by any power to win the heart, will be done." Reverting to his previous letter, Rose asserted that "the search for *Catholic* antiquity must . . . be made for nine-tenths of the Ministry at least, and the results GIVEN them." Such was the case with the Roman Catholic priesthood in virtually every country. In a direct slap at Pusey's postscript, Rose firmly declared that in venturing into antiquity, "*We* are not like our own Reformers, *looking* for Truth and not knowing what will break upon us. We know exactly what the Truth is. We are going on no voyage of discovery. We know exactly the extent of shore. There is a creek here, and a bay there,—*all laid down in the charts;* but not often entered or re-surveyed. We know all this beforehand, and therefore can lay down our plans and not, (as I think), feel any uncertainty where we are going, or feel it necessary or advisable to spread our sails and take our chance of finding a New Atlantis."[21] Many early customs and beliefs from apostolic times did not constitute the great truths of the Gospel witnessed by antiquity. Furthermore, defending a practice present in Scripture was very different from defending one discovered in antiquity but unnoticed in Scripture. For example, Rose would not uphold the traditional practice of exorcism before baptism in order to defend the doctrine of baptismal regeneration.

On May 23 Newman fulsomely opened himself to Rose about his views of the English Church. While first indicating his love for the ecclesiastical vision of Andrewes, Laud, Hammond, Ken, and Butler "(so far as they agree together, and are lights shining in a dark place)," Newman stated his contrasting powerful dislike for *the idea* of the English Church that took the form of the law church organized first by Henry VIII and later reorganized by William III. Uncertain that the English Church could ever meaningfully transform itself beyond that status, Newman claimed, "The 'Church of England' has never been one reality, except *as* an Establishment," and that "viewed *internally*," it had been "the battle field of two opposite principles; Socinianism and Catholicism—Socinianism fighting for the most part by Puritanism its unconscious ally."[22]

Even assuming that there had occurred "a deliverance at the Reformation," Newman could not be "more than thankful for it" and could not "rejoice and exult," seeing that it had been "coupled with the introduction of doctrinal licentiousness, in my opinion as bad and more like a 'brothel.'" In regard to the 39 Articles, Newman thought it fortunate that "none of them are positively Calvinistic" and that "what is wanting in one is supplied in another." But he added, "How can I love them for their own sake, or their framers!" Regretting the loss of Catholic devotion during the Reformation, Newman defiantly asked Rose, "Why may I not in my own heart deplore the hard heartedness and coarsemindedness of those, whoever they were, who gave up (practically) to the Church of Rome what we *might have kept*—so much that was high, elevating, majestic, affecting, captivating—so depriving us of our birthright that the Latins now claim it as if theirs solely." He further confessed, on the basis of his "Home Thoughts Abroad" analysis of the Roman Church, "My heart *is* with Rome, *but not* as Rome, but as, and so far as, she is the faithful retainer of what we have practically thrown aside." By raising "impassable barriers" to certain illegitimate devotions, such as the worship of the Virgin, it might be possible to reclaim others that were genuinely Catholic against which the Articles said nothing. According to Newman, the additions that he and unspecified others would reclaim for the English Church were "in the main *restorations*, recoveries of the faith of the 17th century." But they also contemplated other restorations that might well appear as novelties including "the rise of Monastic bodies." Along with monasticism, he boldly demanded, "Why not claim the Breviary as ours, *showing historically* that the addresses to the Virgin are in matter of fact modern interpolations?" For the immediate present, however, Newman stated his aim as that of "getting up a feeling towards Antiquity among the members of the Church, leaving it to work in time *on* the Church itself as Providence shall order."[23]

This letter outlined the course of devotional innovation and theological apologetic Newman would pursue for the rest of his years in the English Church. He later regretted his openness with Rose and sought to withhold the correspondence from possible publication in a projected but never completed biography of the high churchman.[24] Rose had understood that the Tractarian appeal to antiquity, in the absence of any acknowledged center of ecclesiastical authority for determining doctrine and practice, contained within itself no less potential for Catholic antinomianism and schism than the evangelical impulse held for Protestant disruption. As the Catholic ethos spread in the English Church so did all of the disquieting forces that Rose so feared and that Newman had confessed to actively fostering.

THREE TRACTARIAN APPROACHES TO CATHOLIC TRADITION

Tractarian theology was never fully unified or systematic. It was a body of religious thought involving complementary writings each of which in different ways pressed against the generally acknowledged restraints of contemporary Protestant interpretations of the formularies of the English Church. More often than not, the point of Tractarian theology was to open new possibilities of devotion and faith rather than to delineate with any precision just what those possibilities were. Such was especially the situation with the discussions of tradition on the part of Keble, Newman, and Pusey.

John Keble's sermon on *Primitive Tradition Recognized in Holy Scripture* delivered on September 27, 1836, in Winchester Cathedral outlined broad contours for the Tractarian exploration of Catholic tradition that high churchmen such as Rose could do nothing to discourage. Keble's text was from St. Paul's second epistle to Timothy (1:14): "That good thing which was committed unto thee keep by the Holy Ghost which dwelleth in us." According to Keble, St. Paul here referred to a deposit of certain unwritten truths committed to Timothy, which included "the treasure of apostolical doctrines and church rules: the rules and doctrines which made up the charter of CHRIST's kingdom." In the present day, people so connected the word *tradition* with the errors of Rome, Keble observed, that few were willing to consider that the deposit assigned to Timothy actually comprised "matter, independent of, and distinct from, the truths which are directly Scriptural." Yet according to Keble, the New Testament itself, as well as patristic writings, provided evidence for the existence and use of such extra-scriptural traditionary knowledge. Keble further declared, first, that "to think lightly" of this unwritten, primitive tradition "must be the same *kind* of sin" as to think lightly of the written word of God itself and, second, that God's "*unwritten* word, if it can be any how authenticated, must necessarily demand the same reverence from us . . . *because it is His word*." This ill-defined, primitive, extrascriptural deposit of Christian truth, he argued, had provided a touchstone for evaluating the texts of the Scripture canon as well as for its interpretation, the discipline, formularies, and rites of the early church. Consequently, Keble argued that because "the Scriptures themselves, as it were, do homage to the tradition of the Apostles; the despisers . . . of that tradition take part, inadvertently or profanely, with the despisers of the Scripture itself."[25]

Tradition, according to Keble, despite the presence therein of undiscerned truths, functioned as a bulwark against theological novelty and the incursion of rationalism. Tradition assumed "that in the substance of the faith there is no such thing as improvement, discovery, evolution of new truths; none of those processes, which are the pride of human reason and knowledge, find any place here." But Keble then claimed as self-evident propositions that in any particular age or nation *the restoration* of lost apostolical truth "must for the time look new" and that those who restored it must contend "with the prejudice which constantly waits on the disturbers of things established." What was properly to be deplored in theology was "not novelty . . . relative to us, but novelty relative to the primitive and original standard," no matter by what "plausible air of originality, ingenuity, completeness, it may seem to recommend itself." Consequently only an appeal to primitive tradition existing more than fifteen hundred years earlier could serve to determine the definition of what was or was not actually new in the Church Catholic. Disguising the radical character of his claim for the pursuit of lost or undiscovered traditionary religious knowledge, Keble wrote, "New truths, in the proper sense of the word, we neither can or wish to arrive at. But the monuments of antiquity may disclose to our devout perusal much that will be to this age new, because it has been mislaid or forgotten; and we may attain to a light and clearness, which we now dream not of, in our comprehension of the faith and discipline of CHRIST." Keble's injunction thus embodied the very nightmare vision of clergy loosed into the pastures of antiquity against which Rose had warned Pusey less than six months earlier. In late 1836 Newman praised Keble's sermon as the boldest statement yet of Apostolical principles while Hawkins tartly described the same sermon to Whately as "puerile."[26]

Whereas Keble's sermon openly proclaimed the mutual value of Scripture and tradition, Newman's *Lectures on the Prophetical Office of the Church*, delivered in 1836 and published in 1837, mapped the contours of the vast arena for theological speculation and devotional appropriation lying within misunderstood or discarded traditionary thought and practice. Newman contrasted the rich, amorphous, open-ended Prophetical Tradition, first broached in his exchange with Jager and now reexplored in almost exactly the same language, with what he termed Episcopal Tradition, consisting of "a collection of definite articles set apart from the first, passing from hand to hand, rehearsed and confessed at Baptism, committed and received from Bishop to Bishop, forced upon the attention of each Christian, and demanding and securing due explanation of its meaning."[27] Rooted in Scripture and visibly transmitted through history, Episcopal Tradition embraced fundamental religious truth necessary for communion and salvation.

According to Newman, however, in addition to apostles and bishops who ruled and preached, God had raised prophets in his church who unfolded and defined mysteries of the church and illuminated its documents, harmonizing their contents and applying their promises. Prophetical Tradition consequently extended beyond the words of Scripture and the sentences of the creed to embrace the deposit to Timothy about which Keble had preached. Within Newman's argument, the teaching of these prophets con-

stituted "a vast system, not to be comprised in a few sentences, not to be
embodied in one code or treatise, but consisting of a certain body of Truth,
permeating the Church like an atmosphere, irregular in its shape from its
very profusion and exuberance; at times separable only in idea from Episcopal Tradition, yet at times melting away into legend and fable; partly written,
partly unwritten, partly the interpretation, partly the supplement of Scripture, partly preserved in intellectual expressions, partly latent in the spirit
and temper of Christians; poured to and fro in closets and upon the house-
tops, in liturgies, in controversial works, in obscure fragments, in sermons."
In his controversy with Jager, Newman had distinguished between *faith*,
embracing "what is fundamental" to salvation and church communion, and
religion, embracing "Prophetical Tradition." Newman told Froude that Prophetical Tradition constituted "the privilege of the Christian when admitted
[to Church communion], not a condition of his admission." He further informed Froude that whereas, "The Bible . . . has a sanction independent of
the Church, the (Prophetical) Tradition has none."[28]

By 1837, while again admitting that Prophetical Tradition was more
readily subject to corruption than Episcopal Tradition and that it was highly
differentiated among the different portions of the church, Newman reaffirmed that it was "equally Apostolical, and equally claims our zealous maintenance," and should receive no criticism. Responding to the question of how
much church doctrine drawn from Prophetical Tradition was also included
in the creed, Newman replied, "There is no precise limit; nor is it necessary
there should be." Nonetheless he asserted that church members "must either
believe or silently acquiesce in *the whole*" of Prophetical Tradition.[29]

Evangelicals quickly attacked Newman's position. The *Christian Observer* declared bluntly, "There is no absurdity, no impiety, that may not be
paralleled in the writings of some of those who are called, most unjustly, 'the
Fathers.'" The much-vaunted patristic instruction was nothing but "the
notion of poor frail fallible men like ourselves." The *Christian Observer*
naturally linked tradition to popery and the Roman Catholic Church, but
more interestingly it emphasized, as had the *Record* a year earlier, the uncertainty and confusions in Newman's own understanding about exactly
what was and was not included in the "wonder-working weapon of tradition." The appeal to tradition would eventually require some authority to
designate which traditions are true, and the *Christian Observer* suggested
that the Tractarians and their high-church friends were themselves "virtually" claiming "infallibility for what they consider the catholic church—

which, by the way, is a very small section of Christendom, if we deduct the Romanists."[30]

In a curious manner, Pusey actually confirmed the assessments of the *Christian Observer* by devising a concept of a *disciplina arcani* in the English Church that paralleled Newman's Prophetical Tradition in the wider Church Catholic. In 1837 Pusey attached a preface to *Tract 81*, "Testimony of Writers of the Later English Church to the Doctrine of the Eucharistic Sacrifice," a group of selections on the subject chosen by Benjamin Harrison. The purpose of the anthology, the contents of which Pusey termed *catenae*, a term normally used to describe extracts from ancient patristic writers, was "to exhibit the practical working of the system, and peculiar temper and principles of our Church upon the minds of the more faithful of her sons." Without indicating how they were chosen, Pusey argued that in some cases these particularly faithful sons had conveyed their doctrines "definitely and tangibly," while in others "a general tone, which runs throughout," constituting the ethos or "spirit of the Church," had transmitted doctrines, "retained by oral tradition" and ultimately preserved "by her uniform spirit of deference to the early Church, whose hallowed lamp she carries on, and whose handmaid she is." Pusey explained that the English Church did not dogmatically teach some Catholic truths, such as the spiritual benefits conveyed through absolution, confirmation, and ordination, but rather "presupposed" them "as already known through the successive teaching of her Ministers." Among points of doctrine thus originally committed to Church of England clergy but withdrawn from common use and dogmatic teaching or indicated only slightly because they had been or might be "misapplied or profaned" was that of "a Sacrifice in the Blessed Eucharist." Drawing a parallel between the secret doctrines Newman had found preserved in the early church and the practice of protecting reserved doctrines in the English Church, Pusey stated, "This might, by a sort of analogy, as far as relates to the *object*, be called the 'disciplina arcani' of the Anglican Church; only, it was so far a hazardous experiment, in that no provision was made (as in the ancient Church) for authoritatively inculcating upon those fit to receive it, the doctrine thus withheld from the unworthy or uninstructed. It was left to tradition, but that tradition was not guarded. One must, also, herein not speak of the wisdom or foresight of individuals, but of the good Providence of God, controlling and guiding the genius of the Church."[31] In this tortuously diffuse fashion Pusey located within the English Church an extrascriptural, latent, or secret tradition of

Catholic doctrines protected by divine Providence rather than by any group of individuals.

According to Pusey, the presence of some persons in the contemporary Church of England embracing the mystery of the eucharistic sacrifice indicated that a full Catholic doctrine had once inhabited that church because "a mere Protestant body could not have given rise even to the lowest statements" of such mystery. Pusey blamed Cranmer personally for the "half-suppression of true doctrine" in the Prayer Book, because in revising the Second Prayer Book of Edward VI he had "yielded to foreign advisers" and excised "the explicit statements of the Catholic doctrine" rather than leaving the correction of possible abuses to "ALMIGHTY GOD, who gave that doctrine." Yet Pusey happily reported that the Articles, liturgy, and catechism of the Reformation era had nonetheless been "preserved free from the errors into which the foreign Reformers fell, and expressed the truth fully on all points necessary to salvation," including a sufficiently primitive understanding of the eucharist. With Cranmer's respect for the Fathers preventing accommodation to the worst errors of ultra-Protestantism, the revisions of Edward's Second Prayer Book involved "no change of doctrine as to the Christian Sacrifice . . . but only a suppression, and timidity in their statement."[32] Pusey's unexpected authority for this assertion was the preamble to the Act of Parliament confirming the revised prayer book. The authority of the state was no problem for Pusey when it supported his own argument.

In the process of Prayer Book revision, according to Pusey's analysis, "The doctrine of the Commemorative Sacrifice was committed rather to the faithfulness of individual Ministers, than to the explicit teaching of the Church." Such ministers during much of the seventeenth century, but most especially during the Restoration, had taught the doctrine of eucharistic sacrifice until "the violent convulsion of 1688, and the subsequent ingratitude of the State, casting out some of our best bishops" caused the doctrine to become located primarily among the Nonjurors and the Scotch Church. Thereafter, Pusey admitted, in England the eucharistic sacrifice had never enjoyed so many adherents as baptismal regeneration. Yet, he speculated, it had been "held probably by far more than we deem, but still out of sight as it were, in the secret sanctuary of men's heart [sic], and is not handed down in any very distinct and authoritative way." The doctrine had thus become "a stranger and wayfarer in the Church, which was once its home."[33] Later in the century, Pusey was wont to say that in the 1830s the Tractarians were simply learning. In reality they were simply making things up as they went along.

NEWMAN'S ANTI-ROMANISM

Emphasizing the corruption of the Roman Catholic Church was an essential and necessary counterpoint to the Tractarian effort to reclaim Catholic antiquity. Rome had either hopelessly corrupted and transformed ancient practices or retained them in a decayed fashion. Newman, more than the other Tractarians, pursued this anti-Roman polemic. His goals were, first, to permit the embrace of Catholic sentiment distinguished from Roman Catholicism itself and, second, to prevent those people in whom Tractarianism had raised Catholic devotional aspirations from converting to Rome. But enormous confusion marked this entire effort, which required both acknowledgement of truth in the Roman Catholic Church and broad condemnation of the institution. Hence Tractarian anti-Romanism differed markedly from more general Victorian anti-Catholicism.

These difficulties can be seen quite clearly in Newman's consideration of purgatory. During 1836 he began to compose a tract on that subject. Pusey reacted quite negatively to an early draft. He thought that Newman not only contradicted his position in the first tract "On Romanism" but also in effect now argued "that Purgatory is no such dreadful invention after all; and that the sacrifice of Masses not 'dangerous fables nor blasphemous deceits,'" as Article 31 declared. Pusey exclaimed, "Conceive how a Protestant wd write!" At the heart of Pusey's concern was the tone of Newman's anti-Romanism, which differed from that to which people were accustomed, and which "hardly seems to come heartily . . . but comes laggardly." Pusey considered Newman "reluctant to say that the Romanists are in the wrong, although at the end truth" compelled him "to do so!" Pusey returned the manuscript having marked passages he thought "would most startle people" and added notes "which might soften the effect," while also telling Newman that within his explanation of purgatory, "something stronger against the practice is the more needed."[34] Pusey correctly, if naively, caught the narrow gauge of Newman's critique of Roman Catholic devotional life, much of which as he had told Rose he wished to reclaim for the English Church.

Essentially in *Tract 79,* "Against Romanism III—On Purgatory," of March 1837, Newman asked what Rome might do to remove corruption from an otherwise true doctrine. While describing both the doctrine and devotion associated with purgatory as "untenable," he stated that the practical corruptions connected to the doctrine, as taught in Roman Catholic countries, afforded "a strange contrast to the simple wording and apparent innocence of the decree by which it is made an article of faith." Although

Newman had noted those negative practical effects, presumably at Pusey's urging, he based his rejection of purgatory on the absence of catholic consent among the Fathers. For Newman, the important question in regard to Roman error was that of weighing "accurately how much the Romanists have committed themselves in their formal determinations of doctrine, and how far, by God's merciful providence, they had been restrained and overruled; and again how far they must retract, in order to make amends to Catholic truth and unity."[35] Thus despite critical comments, Newman gave purgatory historical standing in antiquity, a vague position of honor, though not consensus, among some of the Fathers, and thus presumably a substantive presence within the expansive confines of Prophetical Tradition, though he did not explicitly make that claim.

Newman justified his evenhanded approach to the highly controversial subject on the grounds that "we are in no danger of becoming Romanists, and may bear to be dispassionate, and (I may say) philosophical in our treatment of their errors." But the *Christian Observer*, as Pusey might have forecast, declared that Newman's calm anti-Roman rhetoric conveyed "a very inadequate view of the magnitude of the offences of the Papal anti-Christ, and especially of the peril in which it has placed the souls of men, by its false doctrines as well as by its corrupt practices." Deploring *Tract 79* for its hesitant refutation of transubstantiation, its silence on the authority of Scripture, and the absence of any critique of the Roman doctrine of justification by human merit, the journal accused the tract of pursuing a Jesuit strategy of showing "how fallacious are the strongest arguments ordinarily used by Protestants in answer to such objections." The *Christian Observer* feared that the battle of the Reformation must be refought within the English Church because the tracts embodied "the very spirit of Popery against which the Reformers protested, and from which, through the mercy of God, this nation has for nearly three centuries been delivered."[36]

Newman returned to his curious critique of Rome, which so irked evangelicals, in *The Prophetical Office of the Church*, in which he complained that the Roman Church through neglect of antiquity lacked reverence for Catholic truth. After providing various quotations indicating Romanist departures from antiquity, Newman asserted, "They will be found to care very little for the Fathers, whether as primitive or as concordant; they believe the existing Church to be infallible, and if ancient belief is at variance with it, which of course they do not allow, but if it is, then Antiquity must be mistaken; that is all." Furthermore, the authority of the Roman Church had become confused with the authority of the Pope: "And thus their boasted reliance on the Fathers comes, at length, to this,—to identify Catholicity with the decrees of Councils, and to admit those Councils only which the Pope has confirmed."[37] The Romanists thus claimed the authority only of their contemporary institution, while the English Church appealed to the authority of antiquity. The beliefs of Rome consequently continued to increase; those of the Anglican communion were fixed.

Tractarian anti-Catholicism projected an enemy to be reformed rather than repudiated. The relation of Rome to true Catholicism was not "the absence of right principle" or the presence of errors but rather "perversions, distortions, or excesses" of truth that implied "misdirection and abuse." Denouncing the Roman Church more in grief than in anger, Newman wrote,

> We must deal with her as we would towards a friend who is visited by derangement; in great affliction, with all affectionate tender thoughts, with tearful regret and a broken heart, but still with a steady eye and a firm hand. For in truth she is a Church beside herself, abounding in noble gifts and rightful titles, but unable to use them religiously; crafty, obstinate, wilful, malicious, cruel, unnatural, as madmen are. Or rather, she may be said to resemble a demoniac; possessed with principles, thoughts, and tendencies, not her own, in outward form and in outward powers what God made her, but ruled within by an inexorable spirit, who is sovereign in his management over her, and most subtle and most successful in the use of her gifts. Thus she is her real self only in name, and, till God vouchsafe to restore her, we must treat her as if she were that evil one which governs her.[38]

Through this language of regret and sadness over one lost to disease, madness, or demonic possession, Newman distanced himself from the contemporary Roman Catholic Church while embracing a hidden, undistorted ancient Catholic essence somehow residing under the external excrescence of popish corruption. At moments over the next several years Newman and his closest associates entertained the fantasy that through their own pursuit of the Catholic they might liberate true Catholicism within the confines of the Roman Church while restoring it in the Church of England.

FROUDE'S *REMAINS* AND THE ALIENATION OF HIGH CHURCHMEN

The year 1838 marked a major turning point in the history of the Tractarian Movement. First, early that year Newman became the editor of the *British Critic*, which had a circulation of approximately 1,200, thus establishing a distinctive Tractarian platform in the world of early-Victorian periodicals. Newman would attract to the journal a new group of Catholic writers more radical than the authors of the tracts. Even more important, he and Keble oversaw publication of the *Remains of the Late Reverend Richard Hurrell Froude*, an event recognized throughout the Church of England as a transforming moment in the whole Tractarian enterprise. At the time Newman expected the assimilation of Froude's *Remains*, along with the other growing "mass of Catholic Literature," to expand the boundaries of the Church of England, "marking out the broad limits of Anglicanism, and the differences of opinion which are allowable in it." But he recognized that the process would be anything but easy, telling Henry Wilberforce, "Bold hearts will stand the gust, but the reeds are bending, and the shallow [trees] may be uprooted."[39]

Froude's posthumous volumes publicly exposed the Tractarians' hostility not only toward evangelical Dissent and evangelicals in the English Church but also toward the larger historic Protestantism that characterized the reformed Church of England. Froude's pages also presented more fully than ever before the private rigorist devotional life that the Tractarians sought to foster. In 1850, stating a position somewhat different from that of the *Apologia*, where he located the founding of the movement in Keble's antierastian sermon on national apostasy, Newman wrote, "You cannot . . . do any thing in the way of an account of the Oxford movement without going to Froude's Remains."[40] Newman was exactly correct in 1850, admitting then what he largely sought to conceal in 1864. The *Remains* exposed a deep religious discontent with the English Church that had little or nothing to do with the religious politics of the Reform Act era. Tractarianism with the appearance of Froude's *Remains* stood revealed as an effort to disrupt the internal life of the English Church by equating the presence of both historic and evangelical Protestantism therein with heresy while demanding recognition and toleration of a Catholicism designed to fill perceived hiatuses in the faith and practice in that institution. The Catholic anti-Protestant cat was out of the bag, and everyone recognized the fact.

Initially Keble and Newman had undertaken the editing of Froude's manuscripts as an act of friendship to their recently departed comrade and his father. Over the months, however, their purpose shifted as they transformed Froude, whose manuscripts Newman once described as "certainly" portraying "a saint," into a spiritual model for modern Catholics.[41] Originally Archdeacon Froude had furnished the editors with only his son's sermons and essays. Then in August 1837 he sent them the private journals,

including the account of his son's intense fasting, which Newman immediately seized upon as a providential accumulation "for something especial,"
probably meaning as providing a modern non–Roman Catholic example of
monastic asceticism and devotion.[42]

But there was a very significant problem dampening this enthusiasm. Neither Froude's diary nor his personal meditations mentioned Jesus
Christ. To account for this omission, Keble suggested that in reaction to the
surrounding climate of evangelical religion, Froude's "great dread of insincerity would naturally make him almost morbidly cautious of using expressions and making allusions which he saw in every quarter so lightly and
insincerely employed." For his part, Newman proposed to rationalize the
omission on the grounds, first, that Froude's intimate friends were aware of
his faith in Christ and, second, "that a mind alive to its own real position,
often shrinks to utter what it most dwells upon, and is too full of awe and
fear to do more than silently hope what it earnestly wishes."[43] Seeking
to avoid insincerity, Froude had wisely used the prayers provided by the
Church rather than his own words to voice his feelings and reverence toward
God. Thus for both Keble and Newman the youthful Froude already embodied the virtues of Tractarian reserve.

On the other hand, revealing Froude's most private thoughts flouted the
principle of reserve. Despite receiving friendly admonitions to withhold
those journal passages, Keble and Newman claimed that Froude's memory
"would be sadly tarnished" if he were approached "in any spirit but that of
unshrinking openness like his own." Once set on this course, they compared
the tone of Froude's journals with that "of the Catholic Fathers, and (if it
may be urged without irreverence) of the Sacred Writers themselves." Neither the Fathers nor the biblical writers had kept anything back "merely
because it would prove startling"; rather, "openness, not disguise, is their
manner." The practice of those writers, the editors urged, "should not be
forgotten in a compilation professing simply to recommend their principles," which included in Froude's diary morbidly self-denying asceticism.[44]

Defending Froude's life and devotion, Newman and Keble defined the
Church Catholic in a fashion that paralleled the evangelical invisible church.
They suggested that Froude, discontented with the English Church and
repelled by the Roman, had regarded himself as "a minister not of any
human *establishment,* but of the one Holy Church Catholic, which, among
other places, is allowed by her Divine Master to manifest herself locally
in England." Pious members of that English Church Catholic had provided
it with endowments which the state, however, later secured "by various

conditions calculated to bring the Church into bondage." Froude had believed that Catholic clergy in that encumbered institution must consequently keep themselves "from the snare and guilt" of state enactments and
"observe only such a literal acquiescence as is all that the law requires in any
case, all that any external oppressor has a right to ask." Those clergy whose
"*loyalty*" was "already engaged to the Church Catholic" could not "enter
into the drift and intentions of her oppressors without betraying her." Catholic clergy could submit to existing statutes, but they could not "defend or
concur in the present suspension in every form of the Church's synodal
powers, and of her power of Excommunication," nor could "they sympathize in the provision which hinders their celebrating five out of the seven
daily Services which are their patrimony equally with Romanists."[45] These
statements may or may not have described Froude's own views, but they did
fit those of Tractarians for whom by 1838 neither the Roman nor the English Church properly embodied Catholic principles. At the same time that
group of aspiring Catholics, like evangelicals before them, intended to realize their disruptive principles while maintaining positions and incomes
within the Church of England and its associated institutions.

The preface to the first two volumes of the *Remains* also used Froude to
distinguish Catholicism from Roman Catholicism by portraying him as one
"looking and longing for some fuller development of Catholic principles
than he could easily find, but who was soon obliged to confess, with un-
dissembled mortification and disappointment, that such development was
not to be looked for in Rome." Admitting that some passages in the *Remains*
might indicate a tendency toward Romanism, the editors countered by
noting the inherent vagueness of the charge. Popery, they argued in one of
their key statements on the subject, must mean "either a predilection for the
actual system of the Church of Rome . . . or an overweening value for
outward religion, for Sacraments, Church polity, public worship,—such a
respect for these, as renders a man comparatively inattentive (so it is sur-
mised) to the inward and spiritual part of religion."[46] This important definition confined popery as such to external institutions and practices, resisted
the inclusion of private ascetic devotion within its compass, and avoided all
historic differences surrounding such doctrines as justification. Froude had
not been guilty of popish errors, as the editors defined them. What he had
sought, as would the later Tractarians with increasing ardor, was a religion
of internal self-discipline and external self-denial, producing a sense of
obedience contrasting with both more lenient Roman Catholic penitential
practice and evangelical subjectivity.

Newman once privately described Froude's as "a character fitted above all others to kindle enthusiasm." However unlikely that assessment seemed to most contemporaries, as well as to later readers, it proved to be correct for a second generation of Oxford men drawn by Froude's example to the late Tractarian cause and participation in the *British Critic*. Those newly committed sympathizers, the most important of whom proved to be W. G. Ward and Frederick Oakeley, found in Froude what his editors described as an example of "one endeavouring to feel, and to be, as much as possible alone with his God;—secretly training himself, as in His presence, in that discipline which shuns the light of this world."[47] The zeal of this second Tractarian generation for Catholic devotion and ascetic self-denial, their hatred of evangelicalism, and their contempt for traditional high churchmanship commenced where Froude's had ended. Froude's private radical Catholicism would become their public cause.

Where both younger and older Tractarians discerned Catholic piety in Froude's *Remains*, both evangelicals and high churchmen smelled superstition. What most awakened their hostility were Froude's unremittingly nasty comments about the English Reformation, such as, "The Reformation was a limb badly set—it must be broken again in order to be righted." The *Record* thought the result of the teachings of the Oxford writers becoming "generally prevalent and their principles adopted" would not be Roman Catholic conversions but rather the reentry into the English Church of "the superstitions and corruptions which were swept away at the Reformation" and their eventual increase "till the Church becomes as corrupt as before." In contrast to Keble and Newman, the *Record* defined "the essence of Popery" not as conformity to Roman Catholicism but rather as "modifying Christianity to suit the corruption of human nature," and in that respect, it contended, there was much in the *Remains* that might be considered popish and that might foster corruption. The distinction here drawn between "popish" and "Roman Catholic" is a significant one. Whereas the Tractarians argued that Roman Catholicism in its modern sense began with the Tridentine decrees, the *Record* consistently emphasized that the decrees of the Council of Trent had legitimized and revived previous errors in Roman faith and practice. It was the reintroduction of those errors swept away by the Reformers that constituted for the *Record*, as well as for many others of much more moderate Protestantism in the Church of England, the reintroduction of popery, raising the profound question of "whether the glorious Reformation was, on the whole, a good or an evil."[48]

High churchmen no less than evangelicals were skeptical of Froude's

Remains and the expanding novelty of Tractarian devotion. As early as January 1838, Hugh James Rose saw the Froude volumes as embodying "a disposition to find fault with our Church for not satisfying the wants and demands,—not of the human heart,—but of the imagination of enthusiastic, and ascetic, and morbidminded men," a task that "no Church does or can do by any honest means."[49] Rose thus succinctly stated the high-church objection to Tractarian Catholicism that would grow steadily from 1838 through the events of 1845.

High churchmen on the scene in Oxford were even more distraught by the new turn of events. On May 20 Godfrey Faussett, Lady Margaret Professor of Divinity, in an Oxford sermon that directly paralleled the late divinity professor Edward Burton's attack on Bulteel's radically Calvinist sermon in 1831, denounced the new direction of Tractarianism exemplified in Froude's *Remains*. In *The Revival of Popery*, after recalling the hopes for a reassertion of Church Principles initially raised by the tracts, Faussett complained of "Popish error and superstition" having more recently "undeniably insinuated itself" through the Tractarians' overrating the importance of apostolical tradition and the authoritative teaching of the church, exaggerating unscriptural statements about baptism and the eucharist, and deprecating the principles of Protestantism and the conduct of the Reformers. These writers now denied "the grosser corruptions of Popery" and the Roman Church while displaying "in the most favorable light whatever remnant of good she still retains," and thus banished "from the mind of the unwary Protestant every idea of the extreme guilt and anger of a reunion with an Idolatrous and Antichristian Apostasy." Faussett further deplored "the gloomy views of sin after Baptism" associated with Pusey, as well as "those rigid mortifications, and self-abasements, and painful penances, which call us back at once to the darkest period of Roman superstition" present in Froude's writings. Faussett criticized "the naked and unqualified and therefore ambiguous expression *real presence*" in relation to the eucharist as dangerous and objectionable, coming from those who had once written about the power of priests turning the elements into the body and blood of Christ. While resisting the temptation to call the Tractarians papists, Faussett could equally not "pronounce them safe and consistent members of the Church of England" or deny "the obvious tendency of their views to Popery itself."[50]

Faussett, like the *Record*, denied the crucial Tractarian distinction between Rome before Trent and Rome after Trent, as well as Newman's distinction between the Roman Church and the Antichrist. Faussett discerned idolatry and superstition in the Roman Church from at least the fourth century with monasticism, clerical celibacy, pretended miracles, purgatory, transubstantiation, and the worship of the Virgin Mary flowing from "the whole train of superstitions and abuses" associated with that church. Although Trent may have rendered these corruptions immutable, they had existed for centuries before the Reformation. Faussett cautioned against allowing "impatient zeal, and the premature and vain expectation of realizing Catholic views in the midst of the surrounding desolation" to lead to an incautious entanglement "in those mysteries of iniquity, from which God's mercy has once granted us so signal a deliverance." In conclusion he declared, "If we desire to be hereafter *Catholic*, not merely in theory and in prospect, but in happy experience, let us be assured that we must be strictly *Protestant* now."[51]

Replying in his *Letter to Dr. Faussett*, Newman proclaimed nothing less than a right of Catholic private judgment when exploring the devotional boundaries of Prophetical Tradition. By condemning Froude's *Remains*, Newman claimed, Faussett had attempted to establish articles of religion for the nineteenth century narrower than those established in the sixteenth century. Newman again distinguished between doctrines necessary to salvation and church communion and the shifting, floating opinions involving the actual practice of religion. Affecting a Protestant stance to defend Catholic liberty in the English Church, he demanded, "Why must this right of private judgment be infringed? Why must those who exercise that right be spoken of in terms only applicable to heretical works, and which might with just as much and just as little propriety be retorted upon the quarter they came from?" After further engaging the details of Faussett's arguments, Newman concluded that the real way to oppose Roman Catholicism was "not by cries of alarm, and rumours of plots, and dispute, and denunciation" but rather by "living up to the creeds, the services, the ordinances, the usages of our own Church without fear of consequence, without fear of being called Papists."[52]

In July 1838, while reviewing in the *British Critic* a novel whose heroine left the Church of England for the Church of Rome, Newman urged English laity to demand the devotional riches already present in the Prayer Book. The realization of as rich a devotional life as anyone might desire required only "the will to bring into existence what the Prayer Book contains—a will, which, if it exists in the individual himself, will enable him either at once or with a short delay to make all these exist, at least for his own comfort." Regarding devotion and ceremonies Newman pointed to unresolved religious questions that constituted "the true field for the religious exercise of private judgment" provided by Providence to allow "some play" to the human intellect. He further contended, "We might have been told peremptorily not to let our minds expatiate at all beyond what is positively revealed; but we are not so told; and the consequence of forbidding what God has not forbidden, will be like stopping a safety-valve." If the mind were precluded from examining "secondary questions of religion," Newman argued, it would soon be tempted "to employ itself on subjects, where thought *is* precluded, the sacred and fundamental articles of faith."[53] Private judgment exercised in the sphere of devotion would prophylactically inhibit its exercise in the sphere of doctrine.

In August 1838, less than two months after Faussett's sermon and Newman's reply, Bishop Richard Bagot of Oxford delivered his triennial charge. While praising the restoration of neglected truths, stricter adherence to rubrics, and observation of fasts and festivals, Bagot warned the Tractarians against both fostering "fresh schism" and reverting "to practices, which heretofore have ended in superstition."[54] Feeling deeply hurt and personally unappreciated, Newman immediately considered both withdrawing the tracts and halting their further publication out of deference to his bishop. However, when Bagot, through private channels, indicated that such had not been his intention, Tractarian publication went forward on all fronts.

Yet Bagot's charge did seem to require some response. At moments of perceived crisis, when they needed to address authority, Pusey was usually their author of choice. Hawkins had noted as early as 1836 that for the Tractarians "the Church" sometimes stood for "the Regius Professor of Hebrew closeted by himself." So it was early in 1839, when Pusey published his prolix *Letter to the Bishop of Oxford,* summarizing his relatively simple strategy in the title to an appendix of extracts from Tractarian writings *"Showing That to Oppose Ultra-Protestantism Is Not to Favour Popery."*[55] Pusey conflated all criticism of the Tractarians, including that of firm high churchmen, with mindless, theologically ignorant evangelical carping. He attributed the accusations of popery to the continuing influence of Zwinglian-Calvinist theology, which, he claimed, caused people to regard as Popish any doctrine, no matter how distant from Roman, that enhanced the status of the sacraments for which he then provided standard Tractarian interpretations.

Pusey further insisted that the Tractarians wished "to set forth no new doctrines" but only to "revive what circumstances connected with the sin of 1688" had "thrown into a partial oblivion" and to "appeal to the formularies of our Church as interpreted by our standard Divines, and agreeing with the best and purest ages," the designation of which lay in Pusey's own private

judgment. He also admitted that such publications as the Tractarians undertook were "but a rude way of disseminating truth" and that they thus
remained "unadapted to particular cases." That situation almost necessarily
bred some undisciplined use of Catholic devotion whereby Satan perverted
those practices to the benefit of Rome. Pusey justified that unfortunate
situation by observing that "so it often happens, as in the case of human
medicines, that persons will misapply them, those who need them will
neglect them, others use them wrongly, or employ them, while continuing
in habits of life, which neutralize them, or make them pernicious."[56]

Pusey's letter made clear to both the Bishop of Oxford and other high
churchmen that the Tractarians did not intend to retreat from a path of
action about which their leaders and younger supporters had been remarkably open. For example, early in 1838 Frederic Rogers, the last of Newman's
tutorial students and an Oriel fellow, contributed to the *British Critic* a
review of Froude's *Remains* that may in part have provoked both Faussett's
sermon and Bagot's critical remarks. After observing that both the Prayer
Book collects and the Homilies hinted at the constant presence of the Holy
Spirit in the hearts of Christians, Rogers pointed to sources of religious
truth, such as the Apocrypha, beyond the boundaries formally approved by
the English Church. He then asked, "Why . . . do we shrink from allowing in
so many words, that as in the Jewish, so more fully in the Christian Church,
there is, and has been always, a system of inspiration going on, of which we
cannot presume to define the extent? . . . Must we . . . speak as if for 1700
years the voice of God had been silent amongst us?" Then addressing
prayers for the dead in Christ, Rogers asserted, "It is hard, indeed, to be
forbidden the exercise of our most purifying feelings because others have
perverted them." According to Rogers, the rubrics of the Prayer Book
already recognized excommunication, absolution, the episcopal power of
ordination, and "the mystical virtue of the Sacraments" that "have lain, like
seeds, in our Ritual unexpanded and undwelt on, till we have too generally
forgotten that they are living truths." Those words should "be the habitual
energies of the Church" and had "yet their destinies to fulfil."[57] Pusey's
Letter to the Bishop of Oxford had served notice that such Catholic aspirations were not to be denied by either episcopal or professorial authority.

THE TRACTARIAN APPEAL TO MYSTERY

The Tractarians' championing of the devotional possibilities inherent in
Prophetical Tradition required the rejection of both Protestant and Enlightenment outlooks that during the eighteenth century had converged into a

mutual attack on the alleged superstition of Roman Catholicism. What evangelicals and high churchmen no less than the secular utilitarians of the 1830s regarded as popish or Romanish superstitions in both Catholic and Roman Catholic religious life the Tractarians redefined and defended as *mysterious* and as thereby possessing unique spiritual value. Because Tractarian writers asserted the necessity of religious mystery, they rejected both evangelicalism and rational Christianity, intuitively recognizing the paradoxical affinity between the evangelical impulse and religious thought influenced by the Enlightenment. The evangelical impulse involved the exercise of private judgment in reading the Bible, and Enlightenment-influenced thought through natural theology similarly looked to private judgment to discern religious truth from the book of nature. For the Tractarians, the claims to discern religious knowledge empirically from the Bible and nature represented mutually self-reinforcing examples of private judgment setting itself against and eluding the independent theological authority of the Church Catholic.

In the 1830s the fledgling British Association for the Advancement of Science, operating under a self-proclaimed ideological umbrella of natural theology, pursued the same kind of ecumenical cooperation previously pioneered by the great evangelical societies. Agreement about nature as a nondenominational path to divine knowledge provided the foundation for the one as agreement about the Bible as a common guide to divine truth grounded the other. Grasping this parallel, the Tractarians criticized the British Association from its inception for drawing together in peaceful, public, productive cooperation persons from diverse religious denominations. The Tractarians displayed a remarkable understanding of how science as a multifaceted social phenomenon fostering an ecumenical religious climate might within the culture at large displace what they regarded as the distinctive concerns of Christian religion. As Bowden declared in 1839, the man of science was "tempted . . . to put scientific fellowship, in his thought, into the place of the communion of the Church—to substitute, that is, an earth-built temple of unity and concern for that shrine of true harmony and peace, which the great Lord of nature and of grace has chosen to put His name there." By emphasizing social unity facilitated by science, the British Association, led by ecumenically minded clergy, had linked itself to "the chain of rationalism—the latitudinarianism—the anti-church, and therefore anti-Christian, theology of our time."[58] These were, of course, exactly the same charges that Newman several years earlier had lodged against the Bible Society. Furthermore, the culture of science championed by the British

Association combined the values of natural theology with those of useful knowledge. Evangelicals, who numbered among the members and leaders of the association, had long fostered the same combination, often understanding the progress of material civilization to aid the advance of the Gospel. Material civilization and Christianity were undergirding each other. The Tractarians set themselves foursquare against utility, the spirit of improvement, material civilization, and the culture, though not necessarily the truth claims, of science so that they might establish cultural and religious space for the mysterious, the mystical, and the superstitious in contemporary religious life.

In 1838, reviewing a volume on the Middle Ages, J. B. Mozley indicated that he "could never understand on what authority the present age sets up the advancement of science as the great, the only standard in short, of civilization." Certainly the medieval era should be regarded as civilized, though lacking modern science and countenancing much superstition. While giving way to superstition in some practices, the medieval Church had been "no friend to superstition" but rather had served as "a receptacle for genius, talents, and application of mind" functioning "in the situation which the middle classes occupy now, as representing what we call the intelligence of the day."[59] Despite the corruptions of transubstantiation, image worship, and invocation of saints, the medieval Church had still preserved the true creed.

In modern times, however, with science and reason so predominate, the church, according to Mozley, must assume a new role of calling people to mystery. More generally he proposed, "The Church should be always enlightened indeed, and always mysterious; but it is of special moment that she should be enlightened in a superstitious age, mysterious in a scientific." In an age of light the church should not embrace the "dark, for that is an ill-omened, forbidding word," but rather stand forth "deep, impenetrable, occult in her views and character." Urging "a retreat from our too much light" into a light "of the dim and awful kind," Mozley declared that the church should constitute an independent shelter amid "the powerful and noxious glare which settles upon her from without" and establish herself as "an interior empire of peace, an unseen world under the full light of reason and science." Only "a somewhat deeper system [of theology] than has prevailed for some time past, for the last century especially," Mozley contended, would allow the church thus to hold out against the scientific influence of the age. Unless religion distinguished itself from science, men of science would regard religion as merely a less satisfactory and by implication inadequate form of scientific knowledge. Mystery, he concluded, exactly suited the wants of the present age, "if it only knew what its wants were."[60]

Earlier in 1838 William Sewell had criticized the entire enterprise of natural theology as pursued by Paley, Sumner, Chalmers, and the Bridge-water authors as at best managing "to illustrate the existence of vague and undefined power above us" while drawing men's minds away from the real basis of belief. Natural theology actually undermined Christianity through a fundamentally incorrect approach to the faith, leading us to "believe Christianity, not because the Church has told us, in recognition of her authority and in obedience to her commands as our lawful superior, but because its doctrines are conformable to our individual reason." For Sewell, teaching systems of religious evidences encouraged a situation in the Church little different from that in which the crew of a man of war devised their own individual reasons for obeying their officers. He concluded, "In a Christian, credulity is far wiser and far better than scepticism."[61] Of course, what Sewell here termed scepticism many people would have regarded as the everyday use of reason.

Early the next year, Thomas Mozley, Newman's brother-in-law, actually questioned the propriety of even studying Christian evidences as "a branch of divinity at all." Although since Locke the evidences had provided "a fashionable pretence and framework of theology," Christians should believe without requiring evidences because "the great *prima facie* evidence for the truth of Scripture is the visible Church." Though designed to refute criticism of the faith, evidences necessarily drew both their authors and readers into those same destructive arguments. Evidences, moreover, naturalized religion by making "Christianity a matter of sight, testimony, and of moral and ordinary, as opposed to spiritual and extraordinary, agencies." But most important, so far as Mozley was concerned, evidences did not in fact inhibit unbelief. Authors of Christian evidences incorrectly assigned an intellectual origin to unbelief, whereas in reality it arose "always as a certain *tone* of mind: a state of the feeling, a gradual effect of habit, a mode of viewing things, a spirit;—not as a conviction or a question of the reason." Spreading itself by appeals "not to the intellect, but to the feelings," infidelity poisoned "the weak and unoccupied mind with irreverence, with fear or love of ridicule, with hope of licence, with pride, or some such spiritual delusion." Emphasizing those affective springs of infidelity, Mozley declared, "In other words, unbelief of the reason is subsequent to unbelief of the heart." He also denounced authors of evidences, as Newman had evangelicals, for fostering "the idea that Christian faith is distinct from Christian obedience." Because neither the authority of church nor the creeds provided matter for empirical demonstration, such authority lay outside the purview of evidences. To make matters worse, the English emphasis on the evidences rather than on church authority could allow Rome to claim that the English Church in effect admitted that it possessed "no authoritative voice," could not "put forth the Bible" in its own name, and was "*therefore* . . . driven to make the Bible stand by itself, by a cumbrous apparatus of Evidences."[62]

Among theologically sophisticated Protestants, the Tractarian assault on reason, natural theology, and the evidences provoked far more concern than did their alleged popery. These critics saw the rejection of an evidentiary basis for the Christian faith and the appeal to tradition without a verifying institution as necessarily resulting in religious skepticism. The most penetrating of these Protestant critics of the indeterminacy of Tractarian theology and its appeal to mystery was Baden Powell, whose *Tradition Unveiled* appeared in early 1839. Born in 1796, Powell had studied at Oriel, received appointment in 1827 as Savilian Professor of Geometry at Oxford, and later contributed to *Essays and Reviews*. His was an important intellectual presence in the university, though one that the Tractarians never publicly acknowledged.

For Powell the central difficulty with Tractarian theology was its failure to distinguish between divine revelation and human additions and the religious skepticism that he believed necessarily resulted. For example, in 1838 Newman had written, "It appears to us very plain that the primitive Church held the existence of a fundamental faith, and very hard to determine what that faith was," and then added, "and how can we detect additions unless we know what it is which is added to?" Newman used this appeal to uncertainty to defend the validity of elements of Prophetical Tradition against evangelical accusations of their lack of biblical foundation. Powell, who was no evangelical, believed there could be no authority for tradition distinct from that of Scripture. In *Tradition Unveiled* he argued, quite probably in direct response to Newman's statement, "If the disclosure of Christian truth began by inspiration, nothing afterwards can add to it but an authority equivalent to inspiration." The "Universal consent" to which the Tractarians appealed as authority for tradition was "but *human* opinion still; which can therefore only bind those who agree in it." The Tractarian concept of tradition accorded all ages of the church equally high authority, with "the latest and darkest ages of superstition and corruption" being "inseparably united in one chain of evidence with the earliest and purest times." According to this outlook, both the apostles and their present-day successors "*are placed on the same footing; both must be equally inspired and divine; or . . . both equally uninspired and human.*" In a subsequent pamphlet, Powell stated that "the system of Catholic consent" confounded "together *all* distinctive evidence of Divine revelation" and thereby subverted "the very notion, as usually understood, of any such revelation having been given."[63]

Moreover, according to Powell, those who would uphold such tradition must either support the veracity of miracles in all ages or reject it in all ages. This strategy essentially landed them in the same position as those who rejected the occurrence of miracles, with the result "that all distinctive evidence is virtually lost, confounded, or rejected." That situation, he contended, accounted for the general Tractarian desire to avoid consideration of the evidences by alleging its "*irreverence.*" For the Tractarians, the argument "*that we cannot be sure it is* NOT *so*" represented "a substantial ground of faith" and served as "an indication of that reverential frame of mind which peculiarly harmonizes with the humility of a true disciple of the church." That submissive frame of mind, Powell argued, displayed both "the very essence of superstition" and "a singular accordance with rationalism or scepticism." What Christian apologists had long regarded as "the ordinary views of the evidences of revelation" had in Tractarian publications come to be included "among the errors of 'popular Protestantism.' "[64]

Powell pilloried Mozley's demand for mystery in the present age as "the mere impotent bravado of bigotry in its dotage," and as the response of those who, if questioned about their faith, chose "to recur to mystery, and repose in the incomprehensibility of the doctrine." That embrace of mystery was the natural result of a party "arrogating to itself the exclusive title of 'the Church,' proclaiming aloud *the dissociation of religion and reason, of Christianity and its evidences.*" People outside the Church and even some within might well conclude "that Christianity cannot really stand inquiry" and then finding "ordinary events made into miracles" might soon regard "miracles as ordinary events." Thus for Powell, the Tractarian assumption of mystery as meeting the needs of the day could provide a "more convenient and decent cloak to cover total unbelief and confirmed irreligion." Indeed, he contended, "Faith, being reduced to an act of obedience, loses all connexion with real conviction; all test of distinct evidence being abandoned, and all appeal to reason discarded, the only substitute is a mere vague feeling, or sentiment, common to all religions, true or false." For Christianity to stand secure over the centuries, it had been necessary "to preserve a well-marked boundary of the depository of the Christian Word in authentic written records." By discarding rational consideration of evidence and championing mystery, the Tractarians put "truth and fable on the same level," neutralized the difference between revelation and tradition, and thus cast into *entire ambiguity the landmarks of the Christian truth.*[65]

In August 1839 Blanco White, now living with Unitarians, also pondered the skepticism latent in Tractarian antipathy toward Christian evidences. In a long journal entry, White recalled that "the strange school of Divinity" at Oxford had originated in "the dissatisfaction of its founders, in regard to the external evidences of what, according to my judgment, is improperly called Christianity." Unable to perceive "the moral attractions of the *Spirit of the Gospel*" independent of "the Church machinery of direct revelation, proved by miracles," and "aware that the common grounds of their faith were sinking under the pressure of enlightened reasoning and correct information," they had "fallen back upon the Church for support." Because they refused to "acknowledge Rome as the *determining* mark of that Church which they seek," the Tractarians' concept of the Church Catholic was "absolutely a *non-descript*," not being able to "be found by any mark whatever" and in point of fact constituting "only THEMSELVES."[66] White, like Powell, understood that despite their powerful critique of religious subjectivity, the Tractarians were themselves deeply subjective, in a more or less typically Protestant fashion, because their Church Catholic actually possessed no recognized basis of authority outside their own assertions grounded in subjective feelings.

White further believed that Tractarian appeals to the supernatural actually arose from inner anxiety over unbelief rather than from faith. In October 1839 he wrote to the American Unitarian William Ellery Channing that for many centuries people had believed real devotional feeling could not exist "unless it be supported by the *Imagination*" and that nothing heavenly could manifest itself "but what assumes the shape of a visible wonder." This state of mind had nurtured "the dangerous mistake of supposing the essence of Christianity to be inseparable from the firm belief in *historical* miracles, in *revealed* books, in unintelligible dogmas, called mysteries." White told Channing, "The Oxford *Puseyites* originate in the fulness of this persuasion, combined with a most wilful determination of maintaining a supernatural mysticism." The natural piety of their minds roused in them fear of being "inevitably led on to *unbelief;* and being too clever to be satisfied with the *historical* proofs of miraculous Christianity, they flung themselves on the bosom of a phantom, they call Church." According to White, the Tractarians planned "to stop all inquiry, and to believe because *they like it.*"

Assigning "full credit for good intentions" to their leaders, whom he described as "still young, and as such possessed of an all-powerful *Will*," he nevertheless concluded that their effort "must prove ineffectual every way; except in leading some rather weak persons to Romanism."[67]

Newman could, and no doubt would, have dismissed White's private observations as those of a rational Unitarian. Nor did he ever directly respond to Powell. But in April 1839, after the appearance of Powell's pamphlet, Newman defended the pursuit of the Catholic by exploring its affinity with contemporary romantic literature. His essay on the "State of Religious Parties" in the English Church resembled Carlyle's earlier meditation in *Sartor Resartus* (1833–1834) on the necessity of new church-clothes and religious symbols. Catholic principles, Newman explained, appealed to young men who like the age itself had experienced "the spiritual awakening of spiritual wants," a situation accounting for much that critics derided as "enthusiastic, extravagant, or excessive" in "the present revolution of religious sentiment." According to Newman, accidental factors peculiar to a particular time and place "influence the mind in embracing certain doctrines" and "permanently fix the expression and development of them afterwards." Indeed, as if again explicating Prophetical Tradition in a possibly indirect response to Powell, he saw "a great characteristic in fact of the true system" as its ability "to be thus free and spontaneous, to vary its aspect, to modify, enlarge and accommodate itself to times and places without loss of principle." Over time, Newman argued, "according as change was wanted," different schools of theology were intended to emerge in the Christian world to provide "fulness and expression" to the truth with "the inward basis and substance of truth in doctrine and discipline of course continuing the same all along."[68]

Having thus stated that each era needed to achieve its own peculiar realization and articulation of constant Catholic principles, Newman asked, "How, then, are satisfied in our age those wants and feelings of human nature, which is always the same, formerly supplied by symbols, now that the symbolical language and ritual are almost perished?" Poetry, he thought, might now substitute for "the deep contemplative spirit of the early Church." By drawing men "away from the material to the invisible world," poetry had become "our mysticism" and in that respect fulfilled a religious vocation. Contemporary Catholic doctrines were "the just expression" of the wider cultural change manifest in the poetry of Sir Walter Scott and Samuel Taylor Coleridge, as well as of Keble. Riding the crest of the spirit of modern poetry, it seemed possible that a Catholic religious system might arise "superior to the age, yet harmonizing with and carrying out its higher points, which will attract to itself those who are willing to make a venture and face difficulties, for the sake of something higher in prospect."[69] Thus, just as empiricism and science had informed much theology of the Church of England since 1688, epitomized in its best contemporary form in Powell's pamphlet, Newman saw the mysticism of romantic poetry—a mysticism at odds with evangelical Christianity, natural theology, and rational evidences—informing the Catholic movement.

Newman fiercely dismissed the staying power of either latitudinarian or evangelical Protestantism for this process of necessary historical adaptation. In his view, both liberals and puritans in the English Church lacked "any permanent inheritance" upon which they might draw for such a task. Devoting less than a paragraph to the liberals whom he was to so criticize in the *Apologia* a quarter-century later, Newman in 1839 expansively condemned contemporary puritanism as a "motley Protestantism" marked by "intrinsic hollowness and imbecility." Whereas the wider European "current of opinion" now pointed to "dogmatism, to mysticism, or to asceticism" on the one hand and to "pantheism" or "democracy" on the other, it most assuredly did not, he asserted, point "to the schools of the Reformation." Whether appearing in "Lutheranism, or Presbyterianism, or Jewellism, or Burnetism, or Paleyism, or Jacob-Abbotism," the cultural and religious power of Protestantism appeared exhausted. Consequently, Newman triumphantly proclaimed, "The spirit of Luther is dead; but Hildebrand and Loyola are still alive." Only Catholicism or Roman Catholicism could address the spiritual needs of the age, with those abandoning or spurning the former finding themselves eventually left with the latter. Newman warned, "Though the current of the age cannot be stopped, it may be directed; and it is better that it should find its way into the Anglican port, than that it should be propelled into Popery, or drifted upon unbelief."[70]

In his determination to advance the cause of religion as mystery indeterminately revealed, Newman went beyond the direct association of Catholicism with the spirit of romantic poetry. During the winter and spring of 1839 he delivered a series of sermons that recast the meanings of reason, faith, and superstition in a fashion similar to the redefinition of philosophic terms that had occurred in the romantic literary theory of the early century. In *The Arians of the Fourth Century* Newman had pondered "how much of the ecclesiastical doctrine ... was derived from direct Apostolical Tradition, and how much was the result of intuitive spiritual perception in scripturally-informed and deeply religious minds."[71] In his 1839 sermons, Newman attempted to provide a theological basis for trusting such "intuitive spiritual perception."

Countering people who, like the unnamed Powell, regarded faith as "a moral quality, dependent upon Reason," Newman variously defined faith as "the reasoning of a religious mind, or of what Scripture calls a right or renewed heart, which acts upon presumptions rather than evidence," "the reasoning of a divinely enlightened" mind, "an exercise of presumptive reasoning," and "a moving forward in the twilight, yet not without clue or direction." Faith so defined stood to reason in Newman's thought as the passions did in Hume's, with faith activating the mind before the functioning of reason. Newman further insisted, however, that a particular internal moral disposition must inform the mind even before the exercise of faith. To this end, he distinguished between faith and "right faith," a distinction reminiscent of Coleridge's between the fancy and the imagination, with the former drawing upon empirical observation and the latter being informed by transcendental knowledge. Clarifying his own bimodal concept of faith, Newman explained, "Right Faith is the faith of a right mind. Faith is an intellectual act; right Faith is an intellectual act, done in a certain moral disposition. Faith is an act of Reason, viz. a reasoning upon presumptions; right Faith is a reasoning upon holy, devout, and enlightened presumptions. Faith ventures and hazards; right Faith ventures and hazards deliberately, seriously, soberly, piously, and humbly, counting the cost and delighting in the sacrifice." Conscience established the foundation of religious actions, which in turn reason scrutinized. Consequently, Newman contended in another sermon that "Reason may be the judge, without being the origin, of Faith; and . . . Faith may be justified by Reason, without making use of it." He regarded "previous notices, prepossessions, and (in a good sense of the word) prejudices" rather than "direct and definite proof" as the chief influences on one's faith. Human beings acted upon and by faith because they could not by the nature of things reason their way to each and every action. Probabilities within the mind provided the basis of faith, with "moral temperament" determining how one weighed those probabilities.[72]

Whereas in the early 1830s Newman had emphasized the necessity of obedience to indicate the shortcomings of the evangelical religion of feeling, at the close of the decade he pointed to obedience and moral temperament to locate the shortcomings of the rational Christianity of natural theology that was often allied with evangelicalism. He understood that in the absence of a prior temperament of religious faith on the part of the scientific investigator, the empirical study of physical nature did not necessarily lead one to ponder first causes or a divine origin. The system of natural physical causes was "so much more tangible and satisfying than that of final" causes that without the presence in an inquirer's mind of "a pre-existent and independent interest . . . leading him to dwell on the phenomena which betoken an Intelligent Creator," his observations would certainly terminate "in the hypothesis of a settled order of nature and self-sustained laws." In this respect, Newman considered it "a great question whether Atheism is not as philosophically consistent with the phenomena of the physical world, taken by themselves, as the doctrine of a creative and governing Power." Consequently, only "the inward need and desire, the inward experience of that Power, existing in the mind before and independent of their examination of His material world," provided a real "practical safeguard against Atheism" on the part of men of science.[73]

Early in 1841, in a series of letters in *The Times* signed "Catholicus," Newman explored these same ideas. Better known as "The Tamworth Reading Room," these frequently anthologized satiric essays ridiculing a speech by Sir Robert Peel, attempted to demonstrate that genuine religious faith could arise only from Catholic truth and not from natural theology. This attack on natural theology paralleled that of *Tract 85* against Bible-based Christianity, which Newman, in a rejection of the Baconian vision of two books of divine revelation, saw functioning together in an unholy alliance. To the readers of *The Times* Newman declared, "The truth is, that the system of Nature is just as much connected with religion, where minds are not religious, as a watch or a steam-carriage. The material world, indeed, is infinitely more wonderful than any human contrivance; but wonder is not religion, or we should be worshipping our railroads. What the physical creation presents to us in itself is a piece of machinery, and when men speak of a Divine Intelligence as its author, this God of theirs is not the Living and True, unless the spring is the god of a watch, or steam the creator of the engine."[74] The subjective wonder associated with natural religion was in Newman's opinion as ephemeral and untrustworthy for a religious foundation as the feelings evoked by evangelical preaching. In both cases empirical experience failed to result in faith, in certain religious knowledge, or most important in obedience.

Thus, without the impact of any novel scientific theory, Newman short-circuited the entire debate over natural theology that was to erupt throughout the British scientific community from the mid-1840s through the 1870s, generally centering on questions associated with evolution. Like the later proponents of scientific naturalism, Newman rejected the broad religious

synthesis based on the Bible in combination with natural theology that so
deeply informed much pre-Darwinian British science. Long before the evolution controversy Newman had argued, "A mutilated and defective evidence suffices for persuasion where the heart is alive; but dead evidences,
however perfect, can but create a dead faith."[75] A preparation of the inner
self, not the presentation of evidences, must precede faith. Disposition must
necessarily lead reason. In Newman's rejection of any empirical base for
faith, whether in Scripture or nature, lay the origin of the skepticism that
Powell had forecast and that some Tractarians would soon encounter.

In the sermon series of 1839, however, Newman had criticized reason
and natural theology not only to defend Catholic principles but also to
transform the meaning of superstition itself in reply to the charges of popery lodged against Froude's *Remains*. In May 1839, in "Love the Safeguard
of Faith Against Superstition," one of the sermons in which he also distinguished faith and right faith, Newman openly admitted that his concept of
faith could "be made an excuse for all manner of prejudice and bigotry" and
might lead "directly to credulity and superstition." Most people held religious faith for reasons internal to themselves and required some safeguard
to prevent their faith "from running (as it were) to seed, and becoming
superstition or fanaticism." People conceiving religion as based on Scripture, natural evidences, or rationality might appeal to reason as a bulwark
against superstition. But Newman, denying, in contrast to Powell, that "any
intellectual act is necessary for right Faith besides itself," directly rejected
the proposition that "Reason is the safeguard of Faith." Instead, he contended that "a right state of heart" informed by love, obedience, holiness,
and dutifulness provided "the partition-wall which separates faith from
Superstition." Such love guided faith "in a clear and high path, neither
enervated by excitement, nor depressed by bondage, nor distorted by extravagance," and thus provided the moral disposition constraining faith to
its proper, high path. Rejecting the standard of reason and returning to his
views of 1830 on natural religion, Newman stated, "Superstition is a faith
which falls below that standard of religion which God has given, whatever it
is." Superstition so defined was not religion lacking reason but rather religion wanting an inward disposition of obedience. Faith "perfected, not by
intellectual cultivation, but by obedience" degenerated into superstition not
when it ignored reason but rather when it emancipated itself "from this
spirit of wisdom and understanding, of counsel and ghostly strength, of
knowledge and true godliness, and holy fear."[76]

Through these sermons Newman hoped to insulate Tractarian theology against the assaults of learned Protestants and to secure for it the power of mystery. He had established a realm of largely self-referential definitions that would resonate in the minds of a generation already imbued with romantic poetry and romantic aesthetics. These sermons also served another purpose. In "State of Religious Parties" he had argued, "Anglo-Catholicism is a road leading off the beaten highway of Popery; it branches off at last, though for some time it seems one with it."[77] By linking that Catholicism to contemporary romantic impulses, he hoped to provide it with a foundation distinct from historic Roman Catholicism. Achieving that theological and cultural goal was a necessity for his maintaining around himself the young Catholics of the English Church for whom he had set forth the self-referential body of new definitions of reason, faith, and superstition.

CATHOLICISM AS COMPANIONSHIP AND COTERIE

Newman had long thought that while the evangelicals built churches and purchased livings, the Tractarians would raise up a generation of new clergy who, even if the English Church were "separated from the State" and experienced "certain parties torn from it," would themselves "be brought into a clearer and more complete Christianity," with the church in the process being made "purer."[78] The Tractarian leaders took various steps to foster the emergence of such clergy. In late 1835 Pusey organized the Theological Society, which met Friday evenings at his lodgings to read and discuss papers, some of which, such as Williams's on reserve, later appeared as tracts. Early the next year students began to live in Pusey's residence, an arrangement during the summer of 1838 modified with Newman's aid into a separate house of study rented in St. Aldate's. Commencing in February 1837 Newman entertained men at weekly soirees in his Oriel rooms. He also raised money for a fund to finance continuing residence in Oxford for men not elected to college fellowships. These as well as other informal gatherings, pastoral conversations, and after 1838 private confessions provided the institutional settings for the rise of "Newmania" in Oxford, whereby men generally younger than Newman came to look to him for personal counsel, theological guidance, and ecclesiastical leadership.

Several of these men, as Rose had predicted, quickly outpaced Newman's own Catholicism and often proved to be impulsive, erratic, and lacking in judgment. When their aspirations for advanced Catholic devotion did not receive easy accommodation in the English Church, they became quite uncertain about the religious adequacy of that institution. Thereafter, a major part of Newman's vocation was to overcome their doubts and to devise measures to hold them in the Church of England. To that end, Newman willingly and necessarily subjected himself to the prodding of these advanced Catholics while resisting other moderating voices. By 1839 he was expressing himself far more expansively among these new companions, depicted by William Dodsworth as "*half* learned men, with *half* a catholic spirit," than he was with Keble, Pusey, or other older friends. Newman himself only too well understood the problem. As he complained to Woodgate in late 1839, the Tractarians were "educating persons for Rome somewhat the way that Evangelicalism does for Dissent," and while it was "comparatively easy to get up a Catholic movement, it was "not easy to see what barriers are to be found to its onward progress."[79]

In the process of erecting barriers, Newman transformed his own pursuit of the Catholic into persuading these figures that they might fulfill advanced Catholic devotional ambitions within an English Church setting. As long as he succeeded in that effort, he could enjoy their companionship and a position of acknowledged leadership that elsewhere eluded him. Newman's coterie—recognized as such by Tractarians and non-Tractarians alike—included at one time or another Robert Williams, Charles Marriott, William Lockhart, Robert J. Spranger, W. J. Copeland, Thomas Mozley, R. W. Church, J. R. Scott, J. R. Bloxam, Ambrose St. John, J. B. Morris, Frederic Rogers, Frederick Oakeley, F. W. Faber, J. D. Dalgairns, W. G. Ward, Mark Pattison, Richard Stanton, and J. A. Froude. Many of them became associated with Tractarianism well after the erastian dangers associated with the Reform Bill had subsided. What linked them to the original Tractarians was their rejection of evangelical religion and their desire for a Catholic devotional life. These men had flocked to the various Tractarian gatherings, and many later spent time at Littlemore. Several wrote for the *British Critic,* with Mozley in 1841 replacing Newman as editor, while several during 1844 and 1845 also contributed to the *Lives of the English Saints* series. Newman exercised spiritual authority over these men, cultivating a sense of dependence on himself. They in turn trusted him to find a way for them to remain Catholics in the Church of England. Conversion of any of them to Rome represented not the logical outcome of the Tractarian pursuit of the Catholic, but its fundamental failure.

The first serious challenge to the possibility of their remaining faithfully Catholic in the English Church arose in late 1839. In mid-September Robert Williams, at the time the most restless of the group, directed Newman's attention to a *Dublin Review* essay in which Bishop Wiseman compared the Church of England to the fifth-century Donatist heresy and hurled St. Augustine's condemnation of Donatism against all parties in the English Church, including the Tractarians. Wiseman unsparingly declared that even "the new Oxford school" would not easily persuade observers "that their Anglican Church forms no part of the great *Protestant* defection." Wiseman further denounced "the arrogant pretensions of the Anglican High Churchmen" who "charge others with the mote of schism from a national church, seeing not the beam of schism from the universal Church, which fearfully presses on their own cause."[80]

Newman, who had himself long drawn analogies between ancient and modern Christianity, read Wiseman's essay with a particularly receptive mind. Throughout the summer he had been studying ancient heresies for the first time since 1835, paying particular attention to the Monophysites. This group of ancient Christians living in Egypt had powerfully opposed the Arians of Syria. The Monophysites held a particularly exalted view of the nature of Christ, ultimately leading them to deny his full humanity and hence to fall into heresy. Paradoxically, opposition to one great ancient heresy had spawned another. In the *Apologia* Newman elaborated, as he had originally in 1850 in *Certain Difficulties Felt by Anglicans*, on the historical analogy between the ancient Monophysites and ancient Catholics and modern Tractarians and modern Roman Catholics. Writing in 1864, Newman recalled that reading Wiseman's article after his own study of ancient heresies, he had confronted a startling conclusion: "My stronghold was Antiquity; now here, in the middle of the fifth century, I found, as it seemed to me, Christendom of the sixteenth and the nineteenth centuries reflected. I saw my face in that mirror, and I was a Monophysite. The Church of the *Via Media* was in the position of the Oriental communion, Rome was, where she now is; and the Protestants were the Eutychians."[81] The issue at hand for Newman was the analogy of the two situations, not the substantial content of the theologies. That is to say, Newman dated his concern about the validity of the Church of England, and more particularly of the position of Catholics in that institution, as a church, to an argument based on issues of unity and schism. Curiously, at no point did Newman recall that Wiseman had largely recapitulated an idea that Newman himself had ventured in "Home Thoughts Abroad."

As Stephen Thomas has so cogently argued, however, the difficulty for the historian in accepting Newman's account rendered in 1864 is the absence of clear supporting evidence from 1839. There is considerable evidence that

Wiseman's article, which Newman told Bowden "is the only good thing which has been written against us" and "is worth your while" reading, did have real impact on him. Newman had previously described the article to Frederic Rogers as "the first real hit from Romanism which has happened to me" and stated that the Tractarian vessel had "sprung a leak." He also told Jemima that Wiseman's piece "is the only formidable thing I have seen on the Roman side—but I cannot deny it is good and strong, and calculated to do harm, considerable harm." What is not certain is whether in 1839 Newman connected Wiseman's article with the Monophysite parallel. There is a published recollection by Henry Wilberforce in 1869 of Newman's having related the recognition of the analogy to him in the fall of 1839, but the recollection came thirty years later and then as a result of Newman having first privately reminded Wilberforce of the incident in 1844, his mentioning it publicly in 1849 in the dedication of his first volume of Roman Catholic sermons, then having the next year expanded on it in *Certain Difficulties Felt by Anglicans,* and finally returning to it in the *Apologia.* On November 17, 1839, however, when Newman wrote his sister, "Our Church is not at one with itself—there is no denying it. We have an heretical spirit in us," he was directly referring to the evangelicals.[82] There and elsewhere in the correspondence of those months, he unhesitatingly equated the Tractarian Apostolicals with the party of truth in the Church of England.

Newman's several efforts to highlight the influence of Wiseman's *Dublin Review* essay long after the fact served four important functions. First, as Thomas has argued, Newman's initial public mention of the essay in *Certain Difficulties Felt by Anglicans* served to discredit his entire constructive theological activity in the English Church and thus to undermine any remaining faith in that theology that might still have been present in 1850 among former Tractarians, whom he hoped at that date to draw to the Roman Catholic communion. Second, in both the mid-1840s and later this strategy, pursued privately through Wilberforce, allowed Newman to point to an event changing his religious convictions before the polemical onslaught occasioned in 1841 by *Tract 90.* That is to say, he had come to Rome, if ever so slowly, as one genuinely convinced of the inadequacy of the Catholicity of the English Church rather than as one repudiated by that institution. Third, in the Roman Catholic politics of his conversion, pointing to the Monophysite parallel allowed Newman in 1849 to give Wiseman credit for instigating a conversion occurring over a period of considerable gestation.[83] Finally, pointing to Wiseman's essay served as the starting point for Newman's later, personally constructed conversion narrative that imposed a structure of spiritual search on what in actuality had been a series of contingent events infused with enormous personal confusion, anger, despondency, and mixture of other motives.

Newman's actual behavior in late 1839 suggests that he was much more concerned with disruptive activities among young Tractarians than with Wiseman's polemic, whatever its power. Robert Williams was seriously contemplating joining the Roman Church, a move that Newman directly, sharply, and successfully discouraged in what he confessed to be "a very cold style." Morris had preached for Newman at St. Mary's on two controversial occasions, once on fasting and then on "the Roman doctrine of the Mass," telling those present for the latter sermon, including the Heads of Houses, "that every one was an unbeliever, carnal, and so forth, who did not hold it." Then Newman received a report that Bloxam, while attending mass at Lord Shrewsbury's Roman Catholic Chapel, had prostrated himself at the raising of the host. Newman reported the second incident to Bishop Bagot, who may already have heard about Morris from other university sources. Bagot left it to Newman's own discretion to decide whether Bloxam had "acted in a manner unbecoming a Minister of our Protestant Church." His bishop took the opportunity of a second letter, however, to entreat Newman "to exert your own high and influential name among a numerous body of the Clergy, and young men destined for orders who look up to you,—to discourage by every means in your power indiscretions similar to Mr. Bloxam's or any little extravagances, the results of youth—harmless perhaps in themselves, but which I am sure, when they occur, and are known, tend to retard the progress of sound and high Church principles which you would inculcate."[84] Newman actually needed no such episcopal encouragement; he had been concerned about this problem for weeks.

In late August 1839 Henry Manning had brought to Newman the case of a woman considering conversion to the Roman Catholic Church. Quite perplexed and even uncertain about the right action, Newman looked beyond the individual situation. Complaining to Manning "that our Church has not the provisions and methods by which Catholic feelings are to be detained, secured, sobered, and trained heavenwards," he bluntly exclaimed, "Our blanket is too small for our bed." The Tractarians, he continued, had raised "longings and tastes which we are not allowed to supply" and the fulfillment of which "impatient minds" would seek in Rome "till our Bishops and others give scope to the development of Catholicism externally and visibly." In the spirit of Pusey's *Letter to the Bishop of Oxford*, Newman urged that when secessions to Rome did occur—"for which we must not be unprepared"—Catholics in the Church of England should set the blame squarely on "the Protestant section of our Church," demand conciliation, and require the institution to become "more suitable to the needs of the heart, more equal to the external pressures." Those Catholics must demand of Protestants, "Give us more services—more vestments and decorations in worship—give us monasteries—give us the 'signs of an Apostle—' the pledges that the Spouse of Christ is among us. Till then, you will have continual defections to Rome." Newman concluded, "I think nothing but *patience* and *dutifulness* can keep us in the Church of England—and remaining in it is a test whether we have these graces."[85] He had here outlined the twofold strategy he would pursue for the next several years: demanding latitude for Catholics in the English Church and blaming evangelicals for any consequences flowing from failure to provide that Catholic latitude.

Later that autumn John Keble, in the preface to the second two-volume installment of Froude's *Remains,* substantially expanded the compass of such Catholic latitude by presenting an unprecedented radical case for the authority of antiquity. Keble asserted that in Froude's prose readers witnessed a mind "thoroughly uncompromising in its Catholicity," which considered antiquity prescriptively binding Christians "alike to all doctrines, interpretations, and usages, for which it can be truly alleged." Froude's respect for antiquity, according to Keble, embraced as worthy of "dutiful veneration" and emulation not only ancient doctrines and practices but also "the cast of thought and tone of character of the Primitive Church, its way of judging, behaving, expressing itself, on practical matters, great and small as they occur." Then, speaking for himself, Keble pronounced as "a sacred and awful truth" that Catholics must unquestioningly accept "the propriety of any sentiment, allowed to be general in Christian Antiquity, how remote soever from present views and usages." So led by those remote precedents, the mind of the modern Catholic, Keble urged, "must be awake to the possibility of special providences, miraculous interferences, supernatural warnings, and tokens of the divine purpose, and also to indications of other unseen agency, both good and bad, relating to himself and others: subjects of this sort, if a man be consistent, must fill up a larger portion of his thoughts and affections, and influence his conduct far more materially, than the customs and opinions of this age would readily permit." Refusing to flinch from the widespread accusations of superstition, fanaticism, and extreme asceticism launched against the earlier volumes of the *Remains,* Keble here espoused religious practices, including belief in all manner of modern supernatural occurrences and miracles realized by "the Presence of a

wonder-working God," that churchmen across the spectrum of the English
Church believed the Reformation had wisely and blessedly extinguished
from English soil. Keble then momentously declared it wrong for anyone
committed to antiquity to adhere to a church, even a national one, whose
faith and practice proved "contradictory to the known consent of Antiquity." Froude, according to Keble, had believed, "(and so far all lovers of
Antiquity among us appear to agree with him)," that Protestantism, "as
distinct from true Catholicism, here in the Anglican Church," *did so contradict* ancient consent.[86]

Froude's hostility to the Reformation, Keble argued, was not gratuitous.
As demonstrated by evangelical appeals to the Reformers to sustain rationalistic principles and by those of high churchmen to defend erastian
authority, the continuing influence of the Reformation era "lies straight not
only *in* but *across* the way of an English Churchman inculcating adherence
to Antiquity." Taking Froude as his authority, Keble pointed to the immense difficulty, if not impossibility, of finding common ground between
antiquity and the Reformation. On a whole host of subjects including "Fasting, Celibacy, religious Vows, voluntary Retirement and Contemplation, the
memory of the Saints, Rites and Ceremonies recommended by Antiquity,
and involving any sort of self-denial," as well as on the question "of giving
men divine knowledge, and introducing holy associations, not indiscrimi-
nately, but as men are able to bear it," Keble found "the tone of the fourth
century" markedly different from that of the sixteenth. Then, declaring it
"absolutely impossible for the same mind to sympathize with both," he
directly commanded his readers, "You must choose between the two lines:
they are not only diverging, but contrary."[87]

Keble's starkly uncompromising distinction between Catholic antiquity
and the erastian Protestant Reformation, and not Wiseman's article about
modern English Church parallels with ancient heresies, baldly, perhaps
fatally, posed the dilemma that would fatally disrupt Tractarianism. Over
the coming months for certain members of Newman's personal circle the
question would become the more pointed one of how Catholics seeking
ordination could subscribe to the 39 Articles without by that act countenancing what a few years earlier Newman himself had privately described
as "a vile Protestantism" accidentally embedded in the Articles? Could
one subscribe without in the process actually condemning things Catholic?
The new generation of Tractarian adherents, drawn to the movement by
Froude's *Remains*, by their private desire for lives of rigorist, ascetic Catholic devotion, and by personal loyalty to Newman, wished to be clergy of the

Church Catholic primarily and of the Church of England secondarily. Keble
had assured such persons that despite the Reformation there still existed
inside the English Church "the ancient Church waiting to receive them, and
the Prayer-book, and the Anglican divines of the 17th century, ready to
cover their retreat towards it."[88] Newman, however, understood that advanced Catholics could not be so easily satisfied.

HOLDING CATHOLICS IN
THE CHURCH OF ENGLAND

Between late 1839 and early 1841, to hold Catholics in the Church of
England, Newman answered Wiseman's article, explored the experience
of pious religious communities living apart from churches, and published
Tract 90 to provide a basis for Catholic clerical subscription to the 39 Articles. The response to Wiseman took the least energy and does not appear
to have been the center of Newman's real attention. The consideration
of alternative religious communities and the composition of *Tract 90* addressed the very real problem that Keble's preface had posed to the advanced Catholic coterie.

Newman's immediate response to Wiseman's article was his own *British
Critic* essay on the "Catholicity of the Church," which he later portrayed as
having stated a case that for the time being satisfied him about the situation
of the English Church within Christendom. When Newman published this
article in January 1840, however, he actually presented arguments less in
support of the English Church than in defense of religious movements
noted for Christian sanctity while living separated from any historic Christian communion. The clear implication was that English Catholics might
need to dwell apart from either the Church of England or the Roman
Catholic Church. For that reason he expected the essay to "excite much pain
in the quarters" of high churchmen.[89]

After posing the mutual criticisms of the English and Roman Churches,
Newman denied the Roman claim that the Church of England stood in
schism. He based his contention largely on the Anglican argument that
regarded "each diocese," headed by an apostolically ordained bishop, as "a
perfect independent Church, sufficient for itself." According to that theory,
to which Newman was also to revert privately over the next several years,
"Considered as bishops, each is the ultimate centre of unity and independent channel of grace; they are all equal; and schism consists in separating

from them, or setting up against them in their particular place." On those grounds, the English Reformation had not constituted schism, even though the English and Roman Churches did stand in a state of disunity. But the character of their situation required substantial analysis beyond that of Wiseman's casting the Church of England in the role of "the profligate Arians or the fanatical Donatists." Newman suggested that whatever the power of Augustine's attack on the Donatists, it could not be supposed to have been "intended as a theological verity equally sacred as an article in the Creed." Newman also dispensed with the charge that the Church of England had infrequently applied the term Catholic to itself by claiming that the term had been "cherished by us in a sort of *disciplina arcani,* not claimed, but not abandoned."[90]

For Newman the most important point was the vitality and energy present in the Church of England. Throughout three centuries of conflict and turmoil, "as far as its formularies are concerned," he claimed, the English Church had "grown towards a more perfect Catholicism than that with which it started at the time of its estrangement." The theology of the English Catholic divines had fortunately expanded "after their death in the minds of their readers into more and more exact Catholicism as years rolled on." Moreover, there now existed in the English Church "a heavenly principle after all, which is struggling towards development and gives presage of truth and holiness to come." Whatever notes of a church the English Church might lack, she still held "the note of possession, the note of freedom from party titles; the note of life, a tough life and a vigorous," as well as "ancient descent, unbroken continuance, agreement in doctrine with the ancient Church."[91]

The Catholic vitality and drive toward holiness in the English Church contrasted with what Newman regarded as the very real shortcomings of the contemporary Roman communion. That church, he advised, must strive to achieve genuine sanctity until it could finally display "more straightforwardness, truth, and openness, more of severe obedience to God's least commandments, more scrupulousness about means, less of a political, scheming, grasping spirit, less of intrigue, less that looks hollow and superficial, less accommodation to the tastes of the vulgar, less subserviency to the vices of the rich, less humoring of men's morbid and wayward imaginations, less indulgence of their low and carnal superstitions, less intimacy with the revolutionary spirit of the day." Rome would never gain the real attraction of Englishmen who "like manliness, openness, consistency, truth" until she "learns these virtues, and uses them."[92] In this critique Newman clearly had in mind not only popular religious practices of continental Roman Catholicism but also the political upheavals associated with Irish Roman Catholics.

More important for Newman's own future course of action than these arguments on the merits of the English and Roman Churches, he provided several sketches of ecclesiastics from the period of the Arian controversy who displayed "notes" of "churchmanship" which "outweighed" separation from Rome and Alexandria and which thereby proved "that saints may be matured in a state which Romanists of this day would fain call schism."[93] These examples included the semi-Arians as well as Meletius, Bishop of Antioch, and Lucifer, Bishop of Cagliari in Sardinia, all of whom had been marked by sanctity of life and stood recognized as Christian by orthodox fathers.

This citation of ancient Christians residing outside recognized ecclesiastical boundaries represented the first of several efforts on Newman's part during 1840 and thereafter to find models in Christian history or Scripture for his own behavior and situation, which, because of the hostility evangelicals held for Catholic Apostolicals in the English Church, he understood involved the potential for secession or separation. Perhaps not insignificantly, he much later recalled that shortly after writing the "Catholicity of the Church," he had attempted to explain his position to Pusey while they stood across from the Oxford chapel built by the radical evangelical seceder Henry Bulteel.[94]

As in the past, the model that most appealed to Newman for a possible contemporary Christian community dwelling separate from the dominant church and fulfilling providential purposes in a time of crisis was monasticism. In March 1840 he for the second time publicly explored monasteries in an anonymous book-length version of *The Church of the Fathers*, which he reported to be "so dreadfully monastic, that I have some tremours what will happen to me." In this volume, which in 1857 he admitted to have been an attack on evangelicalism, he first thoroughly denigrated the spiritual adequacy of contemporary Protestant devotional life to justify the reclamation of the monastic imperative of Catholic antiquity as a refuge from modern heresy. Thrusting aside previous public caution, Newman directly urged the revival of monasteries in the Church of England, claiming that monasticism constituted "a system which, with all its dangers, . . . has undoubtedly some especial place in the providential conduct of our dispensation." He recalled that monasteries in the past had preserved "the truth, at times and places in which the Church had let it slip from her." For example, during the age of

Augustine, "when the increasing spread of religion made the Church more secular," monasteries had provided refuges for Christian piety. Rejecting "the cruel spirit of ultra-Protestantism" that opposed monasteries and convents on the grounds of historic corruptions associated with them, Newman asserted that at least such corruption flowed from shortcomings inherent in primitive Christian faith and practice, whereas contemporary English Protestant religious corruptions, such as preaching justification by faith alone, displayed no such primitive origins. Indeed, early Christian history provided no examples "of that peculiarity, or *peculiarism*, in religion (if I may give it a significant appellation,) which is now so much in favor." So far as the Fathers were concerned, Newman stated, "It is pretty well acknowledged that there is nothing ultra-Protestant in them." Then echoing Keble's preface of 1839, Newman concluded, "Clearly, then, whether or not monasticism is right, *we* at least are wrong, as differing in mind and spirit from the first ages of Christianity."[95]

On March 7, 1840, about the time *The Church of the Fathers* would have appeared in bookstores and less than a month after he turned thirty-nine, Newman settled in Littlemore to observe a very ascetic Lent while on various occasions Spranger, Copeland, Church, Cornish, and Ward carried out his duties at St. Mary's. The Littlemore village and church were closely associated with Newman's family. He had paid his mother and sisters for their work in the parish before hiring a proper curate. On July 21, 1835, his mother had laid the first stone at the dedication of the new church, and she had then died unexpectedly less than a year later. On June 20, 1839, Newman placed a monument by Richard Westmacott to her in the Littlemore church. That summer he discussed with Jemima Mozley the needs of the church for a pulpit cloth, curtains for the organ, and a covering for a litany stool. The next spring she furnished her brother with an altar cloth that received high approbation from the parish. At this moment in his life Newman also seems to have wanted the company of children and spent much time in the spring of 1840 teaching the local Littlemore children to sing and catechizing them.[96] His private memoranda, letters, and activities of the time very much suggest that he actually sought to create at Littlemore his own celibate version of a family.

Ten days after settling in Littlemore, Newman composed a personal memorandum on why he might choose to live there. Along with the idea of Littlemore as "a home," chief among his reasons was his hope "for a *Monastic* house" that would be "a *model* for others" and that "might *train up* men for great towns" where other such houses might be founded. He imagined that the Littlemore monastic house would allow him to remain at St. Mary's and Oriel and even possibly permit him to be "considered as the head of a hall offspringing from and in a way dependent upon Oriel as in old times St Mary's Hall." These musings recapitulated the themes that had run through his mind since the 1820s, when he had first found a home in Oriel among unmarried men, then pursued an energetic urban ministry at St. Clement's, and finally sought to establish himself as the leader of a celibate apostolic brotherhood. In August 1839 Newman had told Henry Wilberforce, that "for some time" his imagination had "roved after being a sort of brother of charity in London," though he feared "it is more imagination than heart," a thought he repeated not long thereafter to Frederic Rogers. Newman saw both male and female monastic communities not only as satisfying his own yearnings, but as providing a vehicle for retaining Catholics in the Church of England. He told Thomas Mozley in December 1839 that "the women would be going [to Rome], unless nunneries are soon held out to them *in* our Church."[97]

Because monasteries were illegal under English ecclesiastical law, Newman understood that in launching what twenty years later in *On Liberty* John Stuart Mill would term an experiment in living, he must proceed cautiously at Littlemore. The same day Newman penned the aforementioned memorandum, he confided to Wood his hope of establishing "some day a real Monastery here, and coming up myself to it, though I do not wish it talked about." If "a *complete* type" could be set up, he told Wood, the model might spread, whereas approximations would "slip back into nothing." He thought that £1,500 might cover the building costs and requested the name of an architect. He shared these thoughts with other close friends such as Bloxam, whom he asked on March 29, "What should you say, if I am thinking of wheedling Mr Laffer out of some land to build a Monastery on? *This is a secret.*" By May 20, with the help of Charles Marriott, Newman had purchased nine acres, and he soon commenced carefully but enthusiastically to share news of his monastic enterprise. To his sister Jemima he wrote, "We have bought nine or ten acres of ground at Littlemore . . . and, so be it, in time shall erect a Monastic House upon it—but I do not wish this mentioned. This may lead *ultimately* to my resigning my fellowship—but these are visions as yet." With Woodgate he let his imagination playfully soar, portraying his Littlemore "coenobitium," like the ancient monasteries of *The Church of the Fathers*, as providing refuge from anticlericalism so that "when parsons are turned out of their livings, and rail roads have superseded turnpikes, and you and yours are mounted on horses with one or two poneys for (the) luggage, I will give you bread and beer at the House of the Blessed Mary of Littlemore." One can only wonder whether Newman associated the Blessed Mary of Littlemore with his own beloved and now long dead sister Mary, thus adding still another family association to the place. To Miss Giberne later in the summer he fancied the building at Littlemore of "a magnificent Abbey . . . which is to rival Glastonbury or Osney."[98] Each of these letters indicates an early-middle-age imagination run riot, escaping present constraints, and seeking a new life that would fulfill long-standing, perennially frustrated yearnings for a position of mentoring leadership in a circle of loyal male friends who would not abandon him for women, marriage, and family.

If ancient monasticism provided the model for a celibate community over which Newman hoped to preside, early Methodism paradoxically provided a model for its relationship to the ecclesiastical establishment. Indeed, one may wonder whether if in reality during the autumn of 1839 Newman had not looked into the mirror and seen a Methodist rather than a Monophysite. In "Catholicity of the English Church," Newman stated that Methodism, not "heretical in the outset," had served "to rouse and stimulate us, when we were asleep." In *The Church of the Fathers*, he equated Methodism's drawing unto itself "many a sincere and zealous Christian, whose heart needed what he found not in the Established Church" with the function of early monasteries.[99] He elaborated more fully on the parallel during the spring of 1840, when reviewing the *Memoir of the Countess Huntingdon*, the noblewoman who had sponsored a separatist group of Methodists.

In this *British Critic* essay, replete with ambivalent statements of both fulsome condemnation and hesitant commendation, Newman recognized certain attractive elements in Methodism while nonetheless holding the movement at a firm distance. After initially declaring Methodist history "the history of a heresy," Newman immediately added, "But never surely was a heresy mixed up with what was good and true, with high feeling and honest exertion,—never a heresy which admitted of more specious colouring or more plausible excuse—never a heresy in which agent must be more carefully discriminated from agent, persons from their tenets, their intentions from their conduct, their words from their meaning, what they held of truth from what they held of error, their beginnings from their endings." Even if subsequent Methodist behavior required disapproval, Newman argued that the Methodists' early achievements commanded sympathy, insisting, "If the choice lay between them and the reformers of the 16th century (which we thankfully acknowledge it does not,) a serious inquirer would have greater reason for saying, 'Sit anima mea cum Westleio,' than 'cum Luthero,' or 'cum Calvino,' and 'cum multis aliis,' as the grammar has it, 'quos nunc perscribere longum est.'"[100]

Wesley and Whitfield, benefiting from grace conveyed to them through the baptism and ordination of the English Church, Newman argued, had preached "repentance to those who needed repentance" when the Church Catholic, as enmeshed in the eighteenth-century church establishment, stood "under eclipse or at least behind a thick fog in those our northern parts," unable to guide its children. In that era of faint Catholic religiosity, Wesley and Whitfield could have occupied a place in the "economy" of the Church Catholic "as truly as St. Francis, or St. Philip Neri," had there existed "minds able and free to solve the problem." Moreover, "faulty" as Methodism may have been, it was nonetheless still "a living acting thing, which spoke and did, and made progress, amid the scattered, unconnected and inconsistent notions of religion which were feebly opposed to it." Yet the English Church, wanting "precision and consistency" in its own conduct, had not been able to take "one clear consistent *view* of Methodism" or to "take it as a whole." It did not require any deep analysis to recognize "abundant evidence" of "the imbecile policy of the Establishment of the day in dealing with this living and vigorous offspring, of which to its horror and perplexity it had been delivered."[101]

Methodist history demonstrated that if ecclesiastical authorities failed to provide forms and disciplines of worship and devotion that human beings naturally sought, people would find them elsewhere. To underscore that point, Newman warned that if those authorities "will not act, others will act for them." As if drawing a role model for himself from the previous century, Newman explained that Lady Huntingdon had so acted in her own day when "the rulers of the Church did not understand her mission, and Lady Huntingdon became acting bishop instead of them." Newman quoted and commended Whitfield's description of Lady Huntingdon's "acting the part of a mother in Israel more and more" and assuming the guise of "*a good archbishop, with his chaplains around him*" as she welcomed evangelical clergymen into her home. Whitfield had further portrayed that home as "a Bethel" and "a college," where he and others had "the sacrament every morning, heavenly conversation all day, and preach[ed] at night." So described, Lady Huntingdon's household largely anticipated the ecclesiastically irregular, monastic house that Newman envisioned establishing at Littlemore during the spring and summer of 1840. His effort, like those of Wesley, Whitfield, and Lady Huntingdon, demonstrated "that what the Church will not do well, others will do ill instead."[102]

Methodists embodied a vibrant religious movement that "had a message to deliver, a position to defend, and that one and the same to all" while their opponents in the Church "had none." Turning to the Tractarians, Newman observed that the by now long-standing failure of the English Church to articulate a clear, decisive dogmatic response to "persons of what have been called evangelical sentiments" accounted for the "style of certain publications" of the past seven years "accused . . . of intemperance and harshness," whose authors wished only to have "a whole positive consistent external system" to be "recognized as a creed, and to have the attention due to one."[103] Though posing Tractarianism as a long-delayed response to Methodism and evangelical religion in general, Newman inevitably cast both Methodism and Tractarianism as similar movements providentially pointing a dormant, uncomprehending church establishment to its proper role in the divine economy. Newman's fascination with and ambivalence toward Methodism continued to his last days in the Church of England, when he incorporated a considerable discussion of Wesley into *An Essay on the Development of Christian Doctrine* (1845).

Newman's hope for a monastery at Littlemore and his writing about early Methodism coincided with an extensive correspondence with his brother Francis, their first direct communication since 1837. In early April 1840 John renewed their by now long-troubled relationship after learning that Francis was no longer preaching in Dissenting settings. Replying cautiously to John's initiative and feeling it necessary to explore his own ecclesiology, Francis observed, "*You* call it sectarianism, to promote any church but that of the Establishment: I do not mean to offend, when I say that *I* am conscientiously convinced that every Baptist or Independent meeting in the land is (to speak temperately) *as true* a church as yours, and yours as much a sect as those. . . . It is true that I see much sectarianism in dissenters, but I see a worse sectarianism in the Establishment. The former are narrow from want of information or misapplied principle; the latter, when they are so, are from false principle. My heart and understanding alike long for something larger far than either."[104] Without knowing it, Francis Newman had very nearly articulated John's own private view of the English Church and had in the last line directly expressed his brother's longing in regard to the Church Catholic.

John immediately responded, "I dare say you would be surprised to find how much more I agree with you in detail than you at present think," then agreed that sectarianism could exist without outward separation, and affirmed that the establishment "is internally in a sectarian state." He added, "All this I would confess and yet, if I had to explain definitely what I meant,

8. Francis William Newman (1805–1897), John Henry Newman's youngest brother, became a radical evangelical in the late 1820s and later moved toward Unitarianism, a passage traced in his book of 1850, *Phases of Faith*. Throughout their lives the two brothers quarreled and disagreed over religious and theological matters. Much of John Newman's thought and action may be traced to these disputes. In 1845 Francis Newman advised John to start his own denomination. (Reproduced with the permission of the National Portrait Gallery.)

and was probed to the bottom, doubtless you would think me more like the Roman Catholics than perhaps you do at present."[105]

On April 29 Francis indicated that John's difference from Roman Catholics on minor subordinate matters did not prevent his holding all the main principles that made Francis "feel so much aversion for the Roman church as a religious system." Francis then explained that not until he had been able to "embrace with Christian charity all Roman Catholics, priests and people," had he found a way to admit his brother to the same charity. He had discovered that he must either demand agreement to a creed in order to designate a person Christian or, casting off that requirement, "to judge of men by their sincerity, their reverential spirit, and practical benevolence and purity." Francis stated "that far deeper in the heart than all which is theologically prominent, there lies an inner element of the moral and spiritual, which is infinitely precious in God's sight, and if we are wise, may suffice to make us love each other when it [is] duly cherished and kindly estimated."[106] This last sentiment encapsulated the ecclesiastically plastic spiritual impulse that informed practically all nineteenth-century liberal Protestant seekers.

Quickly claiming Francis's expansively latitudinarian sentiment for his own, John indicated that Catholics in the Church of England required the exact comprehensive religious sympathy that Francis had outlined. He further stated, "If there is at present a party, (if it must be so called) of great *capacity*, of greater *actual* latitude than any other, ours is that one." No less important, John indicated his willingness "to abide" by Francis's "test of religious truth the moral peculiarities of a Christian," though he thought that test left perhaps as many grounds for disagreement as did differing estimates of creeds and indicated his "great distress and even horror" at the "notion of fraternizing with Unitarians."[107] Thus despite all manner of qualification and hesitancy John Newman had placed himself into a mental framework of religious Dissent and potential separation, largely abandoning his earlier ecclesiology and emphasis on dogmatic creeds. Only through a theory of latitudinarianism could he carry out his projects of establishing a monastery, Catholicizing the English Church, and maintaining the loyalty of his coterie.

Where John Newman's thought was heading appeared in a long letter of July 26, 1840, to W. C. A. Maclaurin, a clergyman in the Church of Ireland then contemplating going over to Rome. Newman urged Maclaurin not to act from private judgment, arguing, that the English Church "must become much less like a church than it is, must have less signs of life and truth," before one could think of such a change. At present, Newman announced, "A great experiment is going on, whether Anglocatholicism has a root, a foundation, a consistency, as well as Roman Catholicism, or whether (in the language of the day) it be 'a sham.'" Those within Oxford who had "embraced Apostolical doctrines" had "taken them up in a deeply religious,

practical, earnest and (what is sometimes called) spiritual way" and included "some of the most highly gifted, holy and heavenly persons in the
Church." Newman then asked, "Now is it likely that God would leave these
men in error? can such a body be abandoned to a lie? are they not seeking
God in the way of His commandments? will they not find?" Enjoining his
correspondent to observe "the steps of this body of earnest inquirers and see
whither God is leading them," Newman directly admonished Maclaurin,
"*They are the Church to you*—If Rome be true, they are her Messengers
guiding you to her. If England be true, they again are hers."[108] Newman thus
transformed his coterie into a saving Catholic remnant making their way,
like so many previous seekers in the history of the Christian faith, as a
gathered church.

The process of seeking entailed both ecclesiastical and spiritual ambiguities, which Newman could at his age personally tolerate but which proved
an enormous burden to his younger followers, who demanded the kind of
sharp delineation of thought characteristic of their time in life. On October 22, 1840, again corresponding with Francis, John described latitudinarianism as "an unnatural state" within which "the mind cannot long rest"
because if a revelation really exists, human reason should be able to determine its meaning. Skepticism in religious matters opened the way "for the
revival of a strong ecclesiastical authority" to make determinations, as had
been the situation when Christianity first arose and "the popular religions
had lost their hold on the mind." No doubt with the skepticism of his
own followers about the validity of the English Church in mind, he suggested that, despite deep aversion to Roman Catholicism, the English people "would embrace even Romanism rather than acquiesce in absolute uncertainty." While personally entertaining "no fears . . . for the ultimate
fortunes of Catholicism," he did "grieve and sigh over those who are destined to fall by the way in the wilderness."[109]

Newman's personal confusion and concern over the possibility of losing
men to Roman Catholicism reappeared four days later when he sounded out
Keble about resigning St. Mary's, an issue he was to debate in his own mind
for the next three years. Newman complained that his Oxford city parishioners failed to attend either the saints' days or daily services, the weekly
communion, or his lectures in Adam de Brome's Chapel, whereas despite
disapproval and discouragement on the part of authorities, university people did. Among the latter his preaching tended to lead his hearers "to the
Primitive Church if you will, but not to the Church of England." As a
consequence, his preaching was disposing his listeners toward Rome, where

there existed greater scope for many of the doctrines he advocated. In that regard he confessed, "I am troubled by doubts, whether, as it is, I have not in what I have published spoken too strongly against Rome." He added his concern "that this very circumstance that I have committed myself against Rome, has the effect of setting to sleep men's suspicions about me, which is painful now that I begin to have suspicions about myself."[110]

With a single letter from Keble having resolved his self-doubt, Newman declared that it remained to be seen how great "an infusion of Catholic Truth" the Church of England could receive without damage. Meanwhile, "Rationalism," he stated, remained "the great evil of the day," and his pulpit at St. Mary's constituted "a place of protest against *it*." In that respect, he was "more certain that the Protestant ethos which I oppose leads to infidelity than that which I recommend leads to Rome." Newman thought that the Tractarians had not "yet made fair trial how much the English Church will bear." That trial, he stated, resembled "a hazardous experiment, like proving Cannon," but they must not "take it for granted the metal will burst in the operation."[111]

A few days after recommitting himself to St. Mary's, the Catholic experiment, and the challenge to evangelical religion, Newman attempted to refute Francis's altogether correct accusation of his acting according to private judgment. Defending himself, John compared his situation to that of an inferior officer separated from his commander in the midst of battle but nonetheless having to act according to his understanding of the commander's intentions. Under similar circumstances, he claimed, there existed "no inconsistency in upholding the authority of the Church, and yet, when she did not speak or could not be heard, going by private judgment." While seeking "to set up no philosophy, or clearly arranged system," and "very ready to allow difficulties," John wished only to ask himself "in this mysterious world, what is *most likely* to be God's will, and how can I best please Him?" Private moral choices were inevitable, but he contended, "This should not properly be called 'private judgment', which is commonly taken to be a conscious act of the reason, not the spontaneous piety of the heart."[112] The phrase "the spontaneous piety of the heart" differed little from the historic rhetoric of Protestant antinomianism, whatever Newman's Catholic guise, and pointed to the growing subjectivity that was to inform his thinking and action for the next five years.

Admitting to having been accused of making "a church half visible, half invisible," John stated that he did not mind allowing, despite "whatever ridicule attaches to it, that it *is* like a building seen through a mist." That mist was the haze of the historical experience of the emergence of Christian doctrine. Through external and internal causes, the doctrines of "Apostolic Christianity" that stood clearly delineated only by the fourth century had, according to Newman, undergone development entailing "the more accurate statement and the varied application of ideas from the action of the reason upon them according to new circumstances." Although vast areas of dispute existed over specifically what had occurred to doctrine between the apostolic age and the present, Newman broadly asserted, "No one seems to deny that from the first the mass of Christianity tended straight to what is afterwards known as Catholicism, and was such, as far as it went." He then told Francis, "Here then we have one religion in all ages; I profess it. I sacrifice my private judgment to it whenever it speaks; I use my private judgment only in accidental details, where it does not speak, or to determine what it speaks."[113]

Of course, all that John Newman here so boldly proclaimed about his personal use of private judgment to discern the historic Catholic faith could just as easily have been stated by any evangelical Protestant determining the meaning of the Bible or by a more antinomian Protestant determining the insight of private revelations. Moreover, both he and they could have been charged with rationalism, according to the Tractarian sense of the term, in arriving at their respective discernments. It was in this state of mind that Newman had been composing and just over three months later published his momentous *Tract 90*.

CHAPTER 8

Proving Cannon

IN 1833 the Tractarians had commenced their enterprise by denouncing Dissent and within a matter of months had extended their critique to establishment evangelicals. By early 1841 the advanced Catholics among them were demanding their own right to dissent within the Church of England by subscribing to the 39 Articles in a manner that did not repudiate the expansive Catholic faith and devotion they now pursued. On February 27, 1841, Newman undertook to satisfy their concerns and thus to preserve his own Catholic constituency by publishing *Tract 90*, innocuously entitled *Remarks on Certain Passages in the Thirty-Nine Articles*. His contentious justification of Catholic discretion in clerical subscription immediately provoked reproofs from Oxford authorities and the bench of bishops that permanently changed the Victorian Church of England.

THE TRACTARIANS AND THE 39 ARTICLES

From the beginning, Tractarian Catholics had seen themselves as drawing from antiquity knowledge and practices that would complement the timebound contents of the 39 Articles and also supplement Scripture itself. Froude and Newman had corresponded over the character of the Articles, which they, like others in the church, regarded as inherently more Protestant than the Prayer Book and as having been subject to strongly Protestant interpretations since the late seventeenth century. In *Tract 38*, "Via Media," of 1834, Newman had refused to allow the 39 Articles to circumscribe his personal understanding of the ancient Catholic faith, just as evangelicals would have refused to permit them to circumscribe their reading of the

Bible. Two years later Newman told Arthur Perceval that the framing of the
Articles in the sixteenth century had been "a great mistake" because thereby
"the Church of a particular age" had set "forth its own *opinion* of the truth,
instead of simply bearing witness to a *fact,* the fact of its having received
certain doctrines by tradition." In *Lectures on the Prophetical Office of the
Church* of 1837, Newman argued that those formularies were not received
"from individuals, however celebrated, but as recommended to us by our
Church itself." He further contended that the English Church intended the
Articles to be received "as portions of Catholic teaching, as expressing
and representing that Ancient Religion, which of old time found voice
and attained consistency in Athanasius, Basil, Augustine, Chrysostom, and
other primitive Doctors." The divines who had drawn up the Articles had
not dreamed of them "in any degree superseding or interfering with the
Ancient Catholic teaching, or of their burdening us with the novelties of any
modern school." Furthermore, according to Newman, following up an earlier suggestion of Froude's, there existed nothing "in their 'literal and grammatical sense,' of which the King's Declaration speaks, inconsistent with
this Ancient Teaching, whatever obscurities may hang over their origin
historically, a subject, which that Declaration renders unimportant." While
defending his right to appeal to a tradition not mentioned in the Articles,
Newman, for the benefit of evangelicals, pointed to their similar silence
regarding the inspiration of Scripture, observing, "There are, as all parties
must confess, great truths not in the Articles."[1]

   In 1837 Pusey also pressed the case for Catholic devotional latitude in
the use of the Prayer Book on the part of clergy who had subscribed to the
Articles. Recognizing the hostility of evangelicals, as well as of more moderate Protestants, to any concept of eucharistic sacrifice, he cautioned clergy
who might wish to revive the doctrine to regard the issues surrounding it as
"not subjects for discussion, for speculation, for display of recently acquired
knowledge" but rather as "high, mysterious, awful Christian *privileges.*" He
advised those who wished to initiate observance to place the elements of
bread and wine on the altar and then say silently the oblation of the old
service for which he supplied the words from the Second Prayer Book of
Edward VI. Because this language was that of the ancient church, it was
"not dependent for its interpretation on the views of its revisers," who may
or may not have clearly understood what they delivered. Because, according
to Pusey, the Reformers, who had conveyed those ancient prayers, regarded
themselves as "refiners of corruptions" rather than "forgers of a new religion," those who had come after them did not actually "depend upon them"

but derived "their doctrine mainly from Catholic Antiquity, the common stay of both." Consequently, those ancient devotions "must be obviously understood in the sense of those ages, *i.e.* of the Old Catholic Fathers, to whom also they themselves appeal."[2]

In 1839, directly addressing the authority of the Articles in his *Letter to the Bishop of Oxford*, Pusey stated, "We are not bound to have no opinion *beside* them, provided we hold none *against* them." He claimed that the Articles were "not the only, often not the fullest, statements of the doctrines or tenets of our Church" and that they needed "often to be interpreted or to be filled up out of her other documents." It was necessary, Pusey argued, for the English Church to adopt this expansionary vision to persuade "imaginative and ardent minds" among its children "that all which they would seek for in Rome, they may find in the Church wherein they were baptized, if they will but study her character and avail themselves of their privileges." The same year, in his preface to the second installment of Froude's *Remains*, Keble contended that Catholic clergy and laity in the English Church enjoyed "the right and duty of taking her formularies as we find them, and interpreting them, as, God be thanked, they may be always interpreted in all essentials, conformably to the doctrine and ritual of the Church Universal." Such, Keble claimed, had been Froude's own conclusion in his growing adherence to "the pure theory of the ancient Church."[3]

The evangelical press had frequently commented on the absence of easy congruence of Tractarian theology and ecclesiology with the Articles. Discussing Newman's views of justification, the *Christian Observer* declared in 1837, "You know full well, Mr. Newman, that the Thirty-nine Articles do not contain your creed." Two years later, the *Record* claimed that in Pusey's *Letter to the Bishop of Oxford* the Articles were "evaded, added to, and even contradicted" by the author's "interpreting literally some expressions in the Liturgy" and by his "taking the expressions of charity and hope as the definitions of a doctrine." The paper further accused Pusey of selectively addressing the documents defining the faith of the English Church and then, like early Christian heretics with Scripture, stretching even those selected portions "beyond their proper bearing." The publication of the second portion of Froude's *Remains* led the *Record* to charge the Tractarians with lacking "the common decency to maintain a veil on their disbelief of those great and fundamental truths of the Reformation, which, according to their plain and grammatical meaning, they have subscribed."[4]

In his Bampton Lectures of 1840 Oriel Provost Edward Hawkins, certainly no evangelical, issued the Tractarians a more important warning

about the relationship of their teaching to the Articles. While firmly urging
the necessity for "*the teaching of the Church of Christ as an Introduction to the
truths of the Gospel,*" Hawkins steadily demurred from Tractarian assertions
of clerical authority, as well as from what he termed "the superstitious, the
almost idolatrous, reverence with which our Creeds" had come to be regarded. Of more immediate significance, however, Hawkins directly repudiated the Tractarian appeal to Catholicity for determining faith and practice
in the English Church. Despite having long confessed the necessity of an
unauthorized tradition in conveying Christian truth from generation to
generation, Hawkins stated, "Nothing can be more remote from my meaning than to assert, with some modern writers, that 'Catholicity is the only
test of truth.' It is not to many articles of faith that the test applies at
all; and we are blessed with a superior and a supreme authority in the sacred Scriptures." In words that echoed Rose's 1836 letters to Newman,
Hawkins advised "discretion and discrimination" in the exploration of antiquity which constituted "neither our only guide, nor always a safe guide."
He further added in response to numerous Tractarian assertions to the
contrary, "The treasures of Christian Antiquity invite and demand, instead
of superseding, the most discriminating exercise of our Reason."[5]

The subject of clerical subscription to the 39 Articles had framed the
context of Hawkins's observations. Like Blomfield a decade before, he affirmed the necessity of any Christian society settling their "*terms of Church
Communion.*" In the midst of religious controversy that process, according
to Hawkins, involved the church "pronouncing her judgment upon some of
the more important subjects of debate" and demanding "a concurrence in
that judgment on the part of her *Pastors and Teachers.*" In the case of the
Church of England, setting those terms of communion meant requiring the
assent of members to the Apostles' Creed and the Church Catechism and
"of the Ministers of the Word to her larger 'Articles of Religion.' "[6] In the
coming months and years enforcing that clearly articulated position, Hawkins would assume the leading university role in condemning and otherwise
frustrating any and all Tractarian efforts to foster Catholic clerical subscription to the Articles.

Yet in the months immediately after their delivery and publication,
Newman appears to have paid no attention to what Hawkins had said in his
Bampton Lectures, though he was aware of the provost's hostility to the
Tractarians. Determined to assure his followers of the possibility of consci-
entious Catholic subscription, Newman cast caution to the winds and made
an irreparable political miscalculation about the Oxford scene.

Although in the *Apologia* and in his correspondence, Newman often appears as a person moving almost ploddingly on the basis of considered thought, in fact emotion frequently drove his actions. When wishing to act aggressively or beyond the bounds of prudent judgment, he pictured himself as an instrument of divine Providence, thus avoiding personal responsibility and making the immediate landscape conform to his own wishes. He so portrayed himself and a willfully fantasized image of the situation in Oxford on December 22, 1840, when he wrote Miss Giberne, "Oxford or the English Church may be carried forward in a certain line, which may subserve Providential Purposes and tend to perfection without being perfect. With this explanation I think it allowable to speak, as I often do, of the great Chess player, who uses us most wonderfully as his pawns." Through Providence, he explained, the situation of the two Oxford divinity professors gave the Tractarians at that moment considerable room for maneuver. He saw Hampden's influence diminished by his censure, thus leaving only Faussett, "a fat old watchman to waddle after us as best he could." In combining against Hampden, the evangelicals and traditional high churchmen had worked for the Tractarians "just as tools might." Newman added, "And now they don't know what on earth to do, and are all lackadaisying."[7] This reduction of the Tractarians' Oxford opponents to the two unpopular professors of divinity and his self-deceiving appeal to Providence removed from Newman's own mind serious obstacles to the reckless strategy of championing an implausible, tendentious reading of the Articles to retain troubled young Catholics within the English Church.

The alternative to rapid aggressive action on behalf of Catholic subscription was for Newman to witness his emerging vision of a monastic community with himself at its head collapsing, through conversions to Rome, before it had really begun. Newman published *Tract 90* to protect the possibility of that monastic experiment. Thereafter, he stood prepared to endure all manner of ecclesiastical abuse as long as he could in one way or another convince himself and others that the tract with its defense of Catholic subscription had not been authoritatively condemned, that Catholics were thus allowed to thrive in the English Church, and that his monastic community could be realized. The desire to retain recruits for his monastery was the emotional driving force leading to his political miscalculation.

Newman also had to undertake his painfully contorted interpretation of the Articles because by January 1841 neither he nor Pusey was convinced that English divinity would support the Tractarian cause. To counter the recently founded Parker Society's volumes of Reformation theology, some

Tractarians had launched a Library of Anglo-Catholic Theology. On January 8, 1841, Pusey told Newman that he doubted "whether any of us are sufficiently acquainted with our divines to be able to fix definitively upon the list of what it wd be advisable to publish." He thought it possible to find "Catholic & unCatholic works from the same writer," and urged that to the editors be reserved "the right of explaining ambiguous phrases in a Catholic sense." In the end there might, Pusey feared, really be rather few books in the Anglo-Catholic Library, a project for which he "never had any great affection." On January 12 Newman stated his general agreement.[8] Clearly neither he nor Pusey was certain that an adequate theology of the Church Catholic resided within the volumes of English divinity. Newman then moved quickly to complete his own project, almost a year in the making, of explaining "ambiguous phrases in a Catholic sense," but this time in the 39 Articles themselves. If the Articles could be proved patient of a Catholic interpretation, discerning or not discerning Catholicism in English divinity would no longer be a substantial issue.

TRACT 90

In *Tract 90* Newman defended the ongoing presence within the Church of England of pre-Reformation Catholic faith and practice that Catholic-minded clergy did not through their subscription to the Reformation-era Articles repudiate. To achieve that end, he commenced *Tract 90* by posing a problem that most contemporaries were unaware existed or that in no manner disturbed them. "It is often urged," he wrote, "and sometimes felt and granted, that there are in the Articles propositions or terms inconsistent with the Catholic faith." If such were the case, then "persons who profess to be disciples of the early Church" might be regarded as "silently" concurring with a relaxation of subscription.[9] For Newman whatever difficulties Catholics might experience in the Church of England, articles of faith inconsistent with Catholicity were not one of them.

Before *Tract 90,* Newman's larger argument had been that Catholics must make the best of the absence of Christian unity for which both the English and Roman Churches were at fault. In *Tract 90,* however, while claiming that at some point through "a supernatural influence" the English Church would achieve that more desirable Catholic unity, Newman urged that Catholics within its walls must for the moment tolerate significant shortcomings, being assured of its essential, though clearly imperfect, Catholicity. Here primarily the sharp imperfections of the English Church or what Pusey regarded as exhibiting "her only on the depressing side" came to the fore, with Newman's arguments suggesting how Catholics might make the best of them. Equating Catholics with the true church, Newman declared, "Till her members are stirred up to this religious course, let the Church sit still; let her be content to be in bondage; let her work in chains; let her submit to her imperfections as a punishment; let her go on teaching with the stammering lips of ambiguous formularies, and inconsistent precedents, and principles but partially developed." Under these circumstances Catholics must console themselves "that, while our Prayer Book is acknowledged on all hands to be of Catholic origin, our Articles also, the offspring of an uncatholic age, are through GOD's good providence, to say the least, not uncatholic, and may be subscribed by those who aim at being catholic in heart and doctrine."[10]

Newman's subsequent argumentative strategies included interpreting the Articles through his own recent theology, drawing distinctions between popular Roman Catholic devotion and Tridentine doctrine, reading from the silences of the Articles, self-serving logic-chopping and word-splitting, appeals to phrases without context in the Homilies, and rejecting the intentions of their authors as a basis for understanding the Articles. Through these tactics he championed the existence of a Catholic truth lying behind the Articles, obfuscated by the conditions of their composition and concealed throughout most later interpretation. By the conclusion of the process of arguing for the presence of this obscured Catholicism, as James Anthony Froude later stated, Newman "had broken the back of the Articles."[11]

Newman first needed to disencumber the Articles from the Protestant gloss according to which they had long been read. Articles 6 and 20, declaring the Scriptures to contain "all things necessary to salvation," as well as Articles 11, 12, and 13, expounding justification by faith, constituted the most obvious bulwarks for that Protestant reading. On the authority of his own publications, Newman argued that the creed rather than the Scriptures established the rule of faith for the English Church. He urged that the silence of the Articles on the subject of individual private judgment as comprising "the ultimate standard of interpretation," allowed tradition as well as Scripture to be considered the rule of faith. Drawing upon his *Lectures on Justification*, he posited an intermediate state between justifying grace and utter destitution of grace, a condition "of which the Article says nothing, but which must not be forgotten, as being an actually existing one."[12]

In other instances, Newman simply defined terms according to his own inclination. Of all such word-splitting and logic-chopping, none proved more notorious than his remarks on Article 21, which states that general councils can err and that things they ordained have "neither strength nor authority, unless it may be declared that they be taken out of holy Scripture." Newman agreed that general councils called by princes were, as the article stated, subject to error. But then, again appealing to an argument from a silence in the article, he wrote:

> General councils then may err, *unless* in any case it is promised, as a matter of express supernatural privilege, that they shall *not* err; a case which lies beyond the scope of this Article, or at any rate beside its determination.
>
> Such a promise, however, *does* exist, in cases when general councils are not only gathered together according to "the commandment and will of princes," but *in the Name of* CHRIST, according to our Lord's promise. . . . While councils are a thing of earth, their infallibility of course is not guaranteed; when they are a thing of heaven, their deliberations are overruled, and their decrees authoritative. In such cases they are *Catholic* councils. . . . Some general councils are Catholic, and others are not. Nay, as even Romanists grant, the same councils may be partly Catholic, partly not.
>
> If Catholicity be thus a *quality*, found at times in general councils, rather than the *differentia* belonging to a certain class of them, it is still less surprising that the Article should be silent about it.[13]

Without ever attempting to indicate exactly what constituted the recognizable marks of a Catholic council, Newman asserted that certain ecumenical councils, in spite of the wording of the article, by virtue of being Catholic might not err. He also omitted all reference to the portion of the article stating that "things ordained" by councils "as necessary to salvation have neither strength nor authority, unless it may be declared that they be taken out of holy Scripture."

In the most hotly contested portion of the tract, Newman explored Article 22, which condemns "the Romish doctrine concerning purgatory, pardons, worshipping and adoration, as well of images as of relics, and also invocation of saints" as having no grounding in Scripture and being repugnant to the Word of God. Directly addressing the anxieties of his followers that such passages condemned Catholic truth, Newman drew his crucial distinction between Romish doctrines on these matters and primitive doctrine. The article, he asserted, condemned the former but not the latter. Enunciating what became for many the key argument of the entire tract, he wrote, "And further, by the 'Romish doctrine,' is not meant the Tridentine doctrine, because this Article was drawn up before the decree of the Council of Trent. What is opposed is the *received doctrine* of the day, and unhappily of this day too, or the doctrine of the *Roman schools;* a conclusion which is still more clear, by considering that there are portions in the Tridentine doctrine on these subjects, which the Article, far from condemning, by anticipation approves, as far as they go." Newman thus strictly limited Roman Catholic teaching proper to the decrees of the Council of Trent. The Articles, he claimed, by chronology could not have condemned and were consequently not necessarily at odds with that official teaching of the Roman Catholic Church. Through this argument Newman sought, first, to remove from the Roman Church the onus of officially teaching those elements of popular Roman Catholicism most offensive to Protestants and, then, to extend the scope of primitive Catholic devotional practice possible in the Church of England. He also hoped to open the way for a far distant Christian unity on the basis of mutually reformed English and Roman Churches as embodied in Bowden's hopeful assessment of "an Anti-Tridentine feeling there meeting the Anti-Protestant feeling here."[14]

Continuing this mode of reasoning, which most contemporaries regarded as disingenuous, Newman stated that Article 31, condemning "the sacrifice of masses," referred to a Romish practice and not to the mass itself as defined by the creed of the Roman Church. He explained, "Here the sacrifice of the *Mass* is not spoken of, in which the special question of doctrine would be introduced; but 'the sacrifice of *Masses*,' certain observances for the most part private and solitary, which the writers of the Articles saw before their eyes, and knew to have been in force in time past, and which involved certain opinions and a certain teaching." The article, he urged, condemned the blasphemy of regarding the mass as a repeated sacrifice and the practices of using the celebration of the mass for gain. Newman concluded, "On the whole, then, it is conceived that the Article before us neither speaks against the Mass in itself, nor against its being an offering for the quick and the dead for the remission of sin; but against its being viewed, on the one hand, as independent of or distinct from the Sacrifice on the Cross, which is blasphemy, and on the other, its being directed to the emolument of those to whom it pertains to celebrate it, which is imposture in addition."[15] Newman's reading of the Articles thus permitted the liturgy of the Church of England to embrace the mass in a manner that virtually no one outside Tractarian circles believed it could be or had been embraced.

Newman's discussion of Article 35, which commends the second book as well as the first book of Homilies as containing "a godly and wholesome doctrine," illustrated his tactic of selective quotation. During the early nineteenth century evangelicals had drawn upon the language of the Homilies to attack the Roman Catholic Church and to portray it as Antichrist. Newman produced sixty-seven quotations to indicate that the Homilies contain "a number of propositions and statements of more or less importance which are too much forgotten at this day, and are decidedly opposed to the views of certain schools of religion, which at the present moment are so eager in claiming the Homilies to themselves." As in other Tractarian works, many of these quotations, some of which were merely isolated words, appeared without reference to any context whatsoever. Newman cited these quotations to argue for the presence of Catholic elements in the Homilies, including support for "the authority of the Fathers, of the six first councils, and of the judgments of the Church generally, the holiness of the Primitive Church, the inspiration of the Apocrypha, the sacramental character of Marriage and other ordinances, the Real Presence in the Eucharist, the Church's power of excommunicating kings, the profitableness of fasting, the propitiatory virtue of good works, the Eucharistic commemoration, and justification by inherent righteousness."[16] Although Newman contended that subscription to the Article did not necessarily involve subscription to all the doctrines and teachings of the Homilies, consistent readers, he urged, could not embrace language of the Homilies portraying the Bishop of Rome as Antichrist and still exclude other language expounding Catholic truths. For his own part, Newman suggested the passages equating Rome with the Antichrist should be interpreted prophetically.

Newman's last formal topic was the passage in Article 37 declaring, "The Bishop of Rome hath no jurisdiction in this realm of England." The "hath" in this article, Newman claimed, should be interpreted as " 'ought to have' " no authority to make it conform to the Oath of Supremacy. But then further discussing the nature of papal authority, he explained, "Anglicans maintain that the supremacy of the Pope is not directly from revelation, but an event in Providence. . . . What revelation gives, revelation takes away; what Providence gives, Providence takes away. . . . The Papacy began in the exertions and passions of man; and what man can make man can destroy. Its jurisdiction, while it lasted was 'ordained of GOD'; when it ceased to be, it ceased to claim our obedience; and it ceased to be at the Reformation."[17] On the one hand, this argument released Catholics in the English Church from any necessity of obedience to the Pope, but on the other hand it did not condemn the papacy. More important, Newman's argument presented earlier papal power as an instrument, however temporary and expedient, of

Providence and thus implicitly suggested that the papacy could again become a providential instrument.

Preemptively responding to the inevitable evangelical charge that assigning the Articles "any other than a Protestant drift" constituted "an evasion" of their well-known meaning, Newman closed with a general gloss on their interpretation. In a passage derivative of Froude and holding even wider implications than what had gone before, he stated, "It is a *duty* which we owe both to the Catholic Church and to our own, to take our reformed confessions in the most Catholic sense they will admit; we have no duties towards their framers." He thus disconnected the meaning to be ascribed to the Articles from their authors, from the Reformation context of their composition, and from the institutional authority of the Church of England. But then for his own purposes quickly ignoring this injunction, Newman contended that the framers had themselves constructed the Articles "in such a way as best to comprehend those who did not go so far in Protestantism as themselves." Present day "Anglo-Catholics," he explained, were "but the successors and representatives of those moderate reformers," with "their case" having been "directly anticipated in the wording of the Articles." Consequently, he announced, Anglo-Catholics were "not perverting" the Articles but rather "using them, for an express purpose for which among others their authors framed them." That Anglo-Catholic interpretation of the Articles "was intended to be admissible; though not that which their authors took themselves." In a ringing conclusion Newman declared, "The Protestant Confession was drawn up with the purpose of including Catholics; and Catholics now will not be excluded. What was an economy in the reformers, is a protection to us. What would have been a perplexity to us then, is a perplexity to Protestants now. We could not then have found fault with their words; they cannot now repudiate our meaning." Despite the stentorian urgency of this paragraph, described by one observer as "truly Newmanic," the previous distinctions asserted between primitive and Romish practice and between popular and official Roman Catholic teaching left utterly indeterminate the faith that Newman ascribed to Catholics in either the sixteenth or the nineteenth century.[18]

Throughout *Tract 90* Newman exposed himself and those associates who subsequently wrapped themselves in its mantle to religious and secular attacks, doubts, and criticisms that could not be satisfactorily answered. Even family members and close Tractarian associates found themselves troubled. His sister Harriet reminded Jemima, "*We* know J.H.N. is sincere, though with that feeling a sense of the *tickling* nature of his expressions is not incompatible, whether he allows it or not." Bowden complained, "One thing, (candidly) I do *not* like in the tract is its vagueness—it does not clearly tell us what you *do* mean—what you really wish to say, and *what not.*" Pusey anticipated "a lasting impression of our Jesuitism" flowing from the tract. Even one of the most sympathetic twentieth-century observers of the Tractarian Movement would sadly note, "Tract 90 is and remains a very melancholy document. It shows how a really great man can become little in a false and ambiguous position. It is hard not to affirm a certain double-dealing when one compares Newman's later presentation of the matter with the contents of the disputed document."[19] Never did any other major figure of Victorian religious and intellectual life suffer a so profoundly self-inflicted wound.

Why did Newman start down the not altogether inevitable path to this publishing nightmare? Newman told Thomas Mozley that he had written *Tract 90* "to keep our young friends etc from stumbling on the Articles and going to Rome," and later reported to Perceval that the tract had been "necessary to keep people either from Rome or schism or an uncomfortable conscience." Yet by insisting shortly after its publication that *Tract 90* had been "addressed to one set of persons" but "used and commented on by another," Newman convinced contemporaries that Catholic subscription might be secret, even esoteric, and that Catholics, once ordained according to their own private understanding of the Articles, might constitute a self-concealed Romanizing presence within the English clerical body.[20] *Tract 90* and Newman's own interpretation of it thus served to confirm the most serious accusations that evangelicals had hurled against the Tractarians.

Tract 90 represented a continuation of Newman's previous tactic of taking as much ground as possible for the Catholic cause. In the spring of 1840 he had written to a correspondent, "The newest Tract or Volume has always been *the* indiscreet one, and our last point but one has been that at which we ought to have stopped."[21] Those earlier aggressive tracts or articles or books had then provided the new base point for debate or negotiation within the church. Newman appears to have thought that such might also be the case with *Tract 90,* by which he would make the giant leap over the obstacle posed by the Articles to a recognized Catholic clerical presence in the English Church and through which even with some later retreat he would accommodate the perceived aspirations of his followers and open the way for further Catholic innovations. Such was certainly the strategy Newman followed in the weeks after the publication of the tract.

THE HEBDOMADAL BOARD AND
THE BISHOP OF OXFORD

To some university members *Tract 90* presented a perverse mode of subscription that required formal denunciation, a fate all previous Tractarian publications, no matter how controversial, had escaped. Moreover, because it addressed the issue of *clerical* subscription and the ordination vows or contract between clergy and their bishops, the tract implicitly challenged ecclesiastical discipline. Bishops could not easily have ignored it even if they had wished to do so, and Tractarian opponents had no intention of allowing them to avoid the issue. Consequently, by provoking both an internal university censure and unprecedented, hostile episcopal responses, *Tract 90* marked the single most crucial turning point in both the Tractarian Movement and Newman's career in the Church of England.

On March 8, 1841, four Oxford tutors addressed a letter to *The Times* claiming that *Tract 90* displayed "a highly dangerous tendency from its suggesting that certain very important errors of the Church of Rome are not condemned by the Articles of the Church of England." By so underestimating the differences between the two churches, the tract worked "to the prejudice of the pure truth of the Gospel" and tended "to shake the confidence of the less learned members of the Church of England in the spiritual character of her formularies and teaching." Although advocating freedom in the interpretation of the Articles, the tutors portrayed *Tract 90* as embracing "new and startling views as to the extent to which that liberty may be carried" and as removing the security "that the most plainly erroneous doctrines and practices of the Church of Rome might not be inculcated in the lecture-rooms of the University and from the pulpits of our Churches."[22] Criticizing the anonymity of the tract, the four tutors requested that its author come forward publicly.

Although Archibald Tait was the primary author of the letter, the person most responsible for instigating it was Charles P. Golightly, a firm Protestant who had once served as Newman's curate at Littlemore.[23] After they parted ways, Golightly continued to live in Oxford, as a busybody, carrying gossip and generally making himself a thorn in the side of the Tractarians. By 1841 he had become Tait's own curate at Baldon near Oxford. Intellectually and otherwise a person of neither substance nor standing, Golightly directed his largely underemployed energy to publicizing Tractarian activities in hopes of provoking, if possible, official responses from university and church authorities. In this role of self-appointed ecclesiastical agent provocateur, Golightly persuaded a group of Oxford evangelical and more moderate Protestant acquaintances to undertake a high-profile attack on *Tract 90*. The letter to *The Times* turned the appearance of *Tract 90* into a nationally publicized event that reflected badly on the competence of the Oxford authorities to maintain orthodoxy within the university that regarded itself as the seat of orthodoxy.

The Oxford Heads of Houses hastily moved to defend their reputation. By March 10 Edward Cardwell informed the Duke of Wellington that Vice Chancellor Philip Wynter considered *Tract 90* "so jesuitical & mischievous" that he had laid it before the Hebdomadal Board. Cardwell, indicating a clear understanding of the arguments of the tract, told Wellington that its thrust was to make the Articles "consistent with the real system of the Church of Rome, & exclusive only of its local & grosser corruptions." By March 12 Newman already feared himself "clean dished." The same day, with the prospect of Hebdomadal action looming, Pusey attempted to explain to Wynter the intent of *Tract 90* as alleviating the qualms of persons who would be alienated from the church if through the Articles "she have condemned what is Catholic."[24]

The next day, rebuffing that entreaty, Wynter replied that after initially according the tracts his "entire approval," he had found himself eventually unable to defend "many a deviation" from their "leading principle," particularly as coupled with an "apparent recklessness" in risking "the unsettling of the minds of young men for the purpose of clearing or correcting their views of some truth by no means indispensable to a saving knowledge of God and of Christ." Wynter further stated, "The mooting of such points has seemed to me to be something more, than a humble declaration of the Truth as it is in Jesus: and though not intended so, seemed to carry with it the constant hazard of tempting God." These issues, however, now stood as "the shadow of a shade" compared to "the inculcation of a principle which being applied to all the Doctrines of the Church suggests such a laxity and indefiniteness of interpretation as would speedily render men indifferent to religion itself." Wynter pointedly reminded Pusey that just such indefiniteness of interpretation had occasioned Hampden's censure in 1836. But the wide circulation of the tracts "among a Class of persons more pliant" meant that *Tract 90* posed a greater danger than Hampden's "abstruse & obscure" work. Newman's tract left the impression on Wynter's mind that its object was "nothing more nor less" than "to reconcile men to Romish Doctrines instead of drawing over Romanists to the Anglican branch of the Catholic

Church."[25] For those reasons the authorities must act to disconnect the university from *Tract 90*.

Moving according to their own convictions and under enormous pressure from national and local newspapers and parliamentary comments, the Hebdomadal Board refused to permit further debate or to await, as Newman requested of Hawkins on March 14, "a *short* explanation" from the author of the tract. On March 15 the Heads adopted and early the next day promulgated a formal condemnation. Their statement described the "modes of interpretation" advanced by *Tract 90* "as evading rather than explaining the sense of the 39 Articles," as "reconciling subscription to them with the adoption of errors, which they were designed to counteract," and as defeating "the object" and being "inconsistent with the due observance" of the university statutes.[26]

By this single formal public declaration the Heads hoped to delimit the damage they perceived as having been done to the university by *Tract 90*. Privately urged toward moderation for the peace of the church by the Archbishop of Canterbury, they did not press the matter to a calling of Convocation, which almost certainly would have condemned Newman and the tract. As Wynter wrote to the Duke of Wellington, the resolution against the tract that "could render subscription to the Articles themselves mere mockery" constituted "an Act of the Board & not the university." Even John Keble felt "on the whole relieved by the turn the Heads have given to their document," which condemned neither the tracts as a series nor any specific doctrines. He told Newman, "I do not see how the Heads could do anything more innocuous, if they did anything at all."[27]

Keble was correct in this judgment. The Heads had wanted to condemn *Tract 90* without at the same time allowing the document to become the occasion for what high churchman Joshua Watson termed "*a great triumph of the Low Church party.*" The Hebdomadal Board and the Archbishop of Canterbury intended to avoid succumbing to popular evangelical demands, such as that of the *Record,* for a condemnation by Convocation. More liberally minded Oxford figures had their own reasons for not wanting matters pressed any further. A. P. Stanley cautioned Tait, "Do not draw these Articles too tight, or they will strangle more parties than one."[28] But as the weeks passed no one could dampen ongoing extreme actions by the Tractarians themselves, which in turn generated further hostile response.

Newman at this time found himself fighting a four-front campaign against the four tutors, the Hebdomadal Board, the Bishop of Oxford, and friendly private critics including Pusey. Each antagonist presented a different problem, leading to strategies somewhat at cross-purposes. Newman's defense *A Letter Addressed to the Rev. R. W. Jelf D.D., Canon of Christ Church in Explanation of the Ninetieth Tract*, completed on March 13, went to press late on March 16, the day that he publicly acknowledged authorship and the Hebdomadal Board promulgated its condemnation. He learned of the board's action just as his pamphlet went to print. This timing is important because it meant that Newman had addressed his initial defense of *Tract 90* to the furor unleashed by the strongly Protestant Letter of the Four Tutors rather than to the statement of the heads.

In the *Letter to Dr. Jelf,* during the composition of which Newman consulted Pusey, W. G. Ward, and possibly Keble, who was then in Oxford, he contended that the four tutors, and other readers presumed to be anti-Catholic evangelicals had misconstrued his meaning. This had been the standard Tractarian response to evangelical criticism, particularly when such criticism involved accusations of sympathy for Roman Catholicism. Defending his original position in *Tract 90*, Newman restated that the Articles condemned "the authoritative teaching of the Church of Rome" in regard to purgatory, pardons, worship and adoration of images and relics, the invocation of saints, and the mass, but he repeated his assertion that the Articles by virtue of their date did not condemn the decrees of the Council of Trent. Drawing a further, new distinction between the decrees of Trent and "the authoritative teaching of the present Church," Newman contended that the 39 Articles did speak condemnation "not of certain accidental practices, but of a *body* and *substance* of divinity, and that traditionary, an existing ruling spirit and view in the Church; which, whereas it is a corruption and perversion of the truth, is also a very active and energetic principle, and, whatever holier manifestations there may be in the same Church, manifests itself in ambition, insincerity, craft, cruelty, and all such other grave evils as are connected with these." Although the decrees of Trent did not themselves embrace such corruptions, they must yet "ever tend to foster and produce them, as if principles and elements of them—that is, while these decrees remain unexplained in any truer and more Catholic way." All that he had maintained in *Tract 90*, he now claimed, was the possibility "that Rome is *capable* of a reformation; its corrupt system indeed cannot be reformed; it can only be destroyed; and that destruction is *its* reformation." Thus the problem for Newman became not the teachings or doctrines of Trent but their explication within the Roman Church, which like the Articles of the English Church, Newman suggested, required a more fully

Catholic interpretation. In each case such Catholic explication would apparently involve a destructive reformation. One reason for his optimism about potential changes in Rome would appear to have been his private sense that "an Anti-papal feeling *is* rising among the English RC's."[29]

The destructive reform that Newman envisioned for the English Church, however, necessarily involved a repudiation of evangelical religion, which in his *Letter to Dr. Jelf* he portrayed as embodying popular Protestant corruption parallel to popish corruption in the Roman Church. Alluding to evangelicalism, he pointed to the presence in the English Church of "a traditionary system" extending "beyond and beside the letter of its formularies" and "ruled by a spirit far inferior to its own nature." That system, he explained, "not only inculcates what I cannot receive, but would exclude any difference of belief from itself." He then stated, "To this exclusive modern system, I desire to oppose myself; and it is as doing this, doubtless, that I am incurring the censure of the Four Gentlemen who have come before the public."[30] By portraying the four tutors as avenging evangelicals determined to drive Catholics from the Church of England, Newman hoped to shore up support among high churchmen by one more time attacking their common evangelical opponents.

Advocating the possibility of differing interpretations did not, Newman argued, leave the Articles "without their *one legitimate sense* in preference to all other senses." Admitting, however, that his sense differed from that most widespread at the moment, he asserted that "whereas it is usual at this day to make the particular *belief of their writers* their true interpretation, I would make the *belief of the Catholic Church* such." The latter interpretation would allow liberty within the Church of England to those wishing to adhere to primitive beliefs and practices that neither were specifically condemned by the Articles nor were Roman corruptions. Returning to the argument of his 1839 article on religious parties, Newman observed that the "great progress in the religious mind of our Church to something deeper and truer than satisfied the last century" had led Catholics to their yearning for the primitive church. As the age moved toward realizing those feelings and aspirations, "the one religious communion among us" standing "practically in possession of this something" was the Church of Rome, which "amid all the errors and evils of her practical system, has given free scope to the feelings of awe, mystery, tenderness, reverence, devotedness, and other feelings which may be especially called Catholic." To persons remaining with difficulty in the English Church while moved by such feelings, which included the desire for life in a monastic setting, Newman had addressed *Tract 90*. Urging that "we must consent either to give up the men, or to admit their principles," he concluded, "I have no wish or thought to do more than to claim an admission for these persons to the right of subscription."[31]

On March 17, the day after publication of both the Hebdomadal Board censure and the *Letter to Dr. Jelf*, Bishop Bagot became involved. He told Pusey of his hope that Newman, without saying what he did not believe, could find it "in his power to declare certain of the most obnoxious opinions to be opposed to the *spirit* of the Articles, if not to the *letter*, for it is their non-opposition to the *letter* only that the tract asserts." To Newman himself, Bagot wrote with uncharacteristic bluntness that he felt it his duty "to express my regret" over the publication of *Tract 90* and "to state plainly tho generally my honest conviction of its containing much which I am sure is directly the reverse of what the writer would wish or expect from it, but which would in my opinion tend both to disunite and endanger the Church." He then expressed his "anxious wish that,—for the peace of the Church:—discussions upon the Articles should not be continued in the publication of the 'Tracts for the Times.' "[32] Bagot and others at the time, such as Jelf, genuinely feared that *Tract 90* would generate schism, while Oakeley, ever the radical Catholic, welcomed an open engagement between the opposing parties in the church.

Subsequent to this correspondence, there followed twelve days of vexed negotiations between Bagot and Newman, with Newman cutting a hard bargain. On March 18 Newman informed the bishop that there would "be no more discussions upon the Articles" in the tracts. Bagot accepted this step but indicated that something else might be necessary, such as a letter to himself. On apparently the same day, writing Pusey, Bagot distinguished his concerns from those of the four tutors over heresy and those of the Hebdomadal Board over instruction, stating that his "responsibility as a Bishop" involved "control over those who are to *give* instruction, not merely (as in the case of the University) over those who are to receive it." On March 20, employing self-deprecating, obsequious language, gauged to conciliate, Newman assured Bagot that he had been "altogether unsuspicious" that *Tract 90* would "make any disturbance," but that he thought "matters would not have gone better for the Church" had he not written. He pleaded the difficulty of his situation when so many people asked him to give opinions on ecclesiastical matters. "Keeping silence looks like artifice," he wrote. Under those circumstances he had felt "the Tract necessary," though he stood prepared to say "in print anything which I can honestly say to remove false impressions created by the Tract."[33]

While in the midst of these negotiations, Newman undertook a relatively brief postscript to the *Letter to Dr. Jelf,* composed as a response to the Hebdomadal censure, Bagot's concerns, and private criticisms he had received from friends. The critics addressed in this addendum, written by March 19 and made public by March 20, were thus not the evangelicals targeted in the main body of the pamphlet but rather high churchmen offended by the tract. This hastily written and ultimately ill-conceived postscript stated that the purpose of *Tract 90* had been "quieting the consciences of persons who considered (falsely as I think) that the Articles prevent them from holding views found in the Primitive Church." Then, in the previously quoted statement that long haunted him, Newman wrote, "The Tract was addressed to one set of persons, and has been used and commented on by another." Claiming to have assumed his readers' familiarity with his previous criticisms of Rome, Newman admitted to "a vagueness and deficiency" in the tract's depiction of the differences between the Articles and the actual Roman system. His explication of the Articles through the Homilies had also allowed the Articles to be given "in some cases an inadequate representation."[34] He withdrew the phrase " 'ambiguous Formularies,' " though he thought it not inappropriate because both Calvinists and Arminians signed the article on predestination. He had not meant to suggest that high churchmen had difficulty subscribing to the Articles while holding Catholic opinions. He hoped to leave as open questions the character of the Reformation and the practices of invocation of saints, veneration of relics and the like. Whatever one concluded about them, however, those practices were not Catholic in the same sense as the incarnation or the episcopal principle. Finally, Newman denied that his injunction to interpret the Articles in a Catholic sense would lead to lax subscription.

In a similar vein of accommodating his bishop and high churchmen without surrendering his fundamental principles, Newman had quickly published a second edition of *Tract 90,* sent off to the printer on March 17, introducing several revisions proposed by Pusey, Keble, and Hook.[35] The most important of these stated that the Articles did in fact condemn the present-day Roman Catholic belief in purgatory and veneration of relics. Second, Newman removed the offensive phrase about the Church of England speaking with "stammering lips." These modest revisions, like the *Letter to Dr. Jelf* and its postscript, essentially replicated the established Tractarian practice of revising strongly worded publications that received harsh criticism without actually retracting the thrust of their argument. The revision of *Tract 90,* which for the first time in the history of the series actually indicated the revisions, eventually circulated in many thousands of copies, bringing Newman a significant amount of income.

The postscript to the *Letter to Dr. Jelf*, however, provoked an immediate unforeseen response from an unexpected quarter. On March 19 Archbishop Howley wrote to Bagot, generally approving his actions but observing that many moderate people thought the *Letter to Dr. Jelf* unsatisfactory. On March 22, having examined Bagot's correspondence with Newman and Pusey, Howley expressed doubt whether the "objectionable" passages in *Tract 90* "would admit of an explanation satisfactory in all respects" and thought it more advisable to let things rest than for Newman "to come forward with explanations inconsistent with the apparent sense of the propositions which have given offence, or expressing the same sense, with little variation, in different words." Then, apparently while in the course of writing this letter, Howley received Newman's postscript. It so angered the archbishop and so convinced him of Newman's intractability that he immediately changed his instructions, telling Bagot, "I have this instant seen Mr. Newman's Postscript to his second edition, and as he can go no further in explanation he should, in my opinion, explain no more; but it seems most desirable that the publication of the Tracts should be discontinued for ever." The same day Howley consulted Bishop Blomfield, who on his behalf informed Dr. Jelf and thus the university of the prelate's desire for the end of the tracts. Also on March 22, Blomfield wrote William Palmer expressing his displeasure with Palmer's early support for *Tract 90*.[36] The tracts were to conclude, and the Tractarians were to be isolated from older more traditional high-church allies.

Upon receipt of the archbishop's instructions, Bagot reopened negotiations through Pusey. Newman was willing to end the tracts as a series but not to withdraw *Tract 90* from circulation at his bishop's bidding. To so accede would in his opinion indicate the bishop's concurrence with the Hebdomadal Board and effectively constitute episcopal condemnation of Catholic subscription to the Articles. Consequently, on March 24 Newman stated that he could not agree to the suppression of *Tract 90* "without surrendering *interests* with which I am providentially charged at this moment, and which I have no right to surrender." Believing that the London authorities were using him against himself, Newman told Pusey, "When they thought me obstinate, they spoke only of not writing more in the Tracts about the Articles. When they find me obedient, they add the stopping of the Tracts and the suppression of No. 90."[37] Newman did not realize that his own aggressive, uncompromising postscript had convinced the archbishop that he was anything but obedient.

By this time Newman was receiving other advice to hold firm on *Tract 90*, with Hook even suggesting that he demand an appearance before the bishop's court. With such encouragement Newman raised the stakes, telling Pusey, "I have almost come to the resolution, if the Bishop publicly intimates that I must suppress it, or speaks strongly in his charge against it, to suppress it indeed, but to resign my living also." On March 26 Keble urged that any suppression of *Tract 90* must be done publicly on grounds of obedience to the bishop and "not at all giving up the view" enunciated in the tract. That being the ground of suppression, Keble explained, the bishop would in effect permit "his clergy to hold the view, as consistent with the literal and grammatical sense; which is a great point gained."[38] The same day, after extensive negotiation with Pusey, who had informed him of Newman's threat to resign, Bagot relented on the issue of suppression and informed Howley, who approved his decision.

Bagot insisted, however, upon a public letter from Newman acknowledging the bishop's objections to *Tract 90* and announcing the cessation of the tracts at his request. Thinking Bagot had made an excellent arrangement, the archbishop agreed that *Tract 90* could appear at the end of the last volume of tracts under the assumption that it would be followed by the *Letter to Dr. Jelf* and by a selection of Newman's anti-Roman writings. *Tract 90* never circulated in that manner, but its second edition appeared as the concluding tract to volume 5 of *Tracts for the Times*, a set that Archbishop Whately realized would constitute a library of Tractarian divinity.[39]

Newman's *Letter to the Bishop of Oxford* of March 30, 1841, composed the previous day, surrendered virtually no Catholic ground. In this pamphlet, which really constituted *Tract 91*, Newman acknowledged that his bishop found *Tract 90* objectionable and harmful to the peace of the church and had advised the discontinuation of the tracts, a step to which Newman announced his acquiescence. Having kept the letter of his agreement, Newman then directly rebuffed any accusation that the tract writers had pursued "wanton inconsiderateness towards the feelings of others" in mooting questions about Christian antiquity, exploring the principle of reserve, raising the reverence for baptism and the eucharist, or asserting the devotional value of the Breviary. In the course of the pamphlet, Newman provided extensive exposition and defense of each of these Tractarian positions so that in accepting the pamphlet the bishop could in Newman's view be regarded as offering no objection to them if not actually sanctioning them. Newman also stated that his intention in *Tract 90* had been explicating the broad principle of the Catholicity of the Articles rather than tempting men to see how close they might approach Rome. By emphasizing his own intention, Newman carefully avoided considering how advanced Catholic readers might themselves intend to interpret his arguments. Asserting his belief that the church over which his bishop presided constituted "the Catholic Church in this country" and denying a desire for union with Rome, he declared, implicitly attacking evangelicals, "Our business is with our-selves—to make ourselves more holy, more self-denying, more primitive, more worthy our high calling." He then added, "Let the Church of Rome do the same, and it will come nearer to us, and will cease to be what we one and all mean, when we speak of Rome." If the Roman Catholics were visited with divine grace, they would also acknowledge the Church of England "as the Catholic Church in this country, and would give up whatever offended and grieved us in their doctrine and worship, and would unite themselves to us."[40]

More than satisfied and no doubt relieved at the turn of events, Bagot hoped that Newman's pamphlet would end the matter, as did the Bishop of London. Newman, despite feeling bruised by the university authorities, took considerable satisfaction in the outcome of the negotiations, boasting to his sister on March 31 of being "quite satisfied with the bargain I have got," and telling Thomas Mozley the same day, "If you knew what was threatened, you will see that I have reason to be satisfied." He subsequently wrote Keble that he was "sanguine" about his letter to the bishop, into which he had "managed to wedge in a good many bits of Catholicism, which *now* come out with the Bishop's sanction." He added, "How odd it is that one should be able to act from the heart, yet from the head too—yet I think I have been honest—at least I hope so." In a second letter of April 1, Newman discouraged further controversy, telling Keble, "I am not at all sure but our game, if I may use the word, is to let the matter drop at present. We have got the *principle* of our interpretation admitted in that it has not been condemned—Do not let us provoke opposition—Numbers will be taking advantage silently and quietly of the admission for their own benefit. It will soon be *assumed* as a matter of course." To Woodgate, he wrote, "It is a *great* gain to have it recognized that one fair interpretation of our Articles is 'according to the Catholic sense.' "[41]

A large measure of Newman's confidence stemmed from his belief that during Pusey's negotiations with Bagot assurance had been given that except for a very few evangelicals on the bench, the bishops would not condemn *Tract 90*. That conviction led Newman to undertake no further defense of *Tract 90* and accounted in large measure for his later sense of betrayal as over the next several years one bishop after another criticized the tract. In early April 1841, however, Newman believed and encouraged others to believe that what could be asserted without condemnation stood in effect approved and that the absence of episcopal condemnation constituted Catholic victory. He firmly believed in his own mind that by avoiding any formal episcopal censure, he had achieved recognition of his version of a Catholic interpretation of the Articles, which benefited his followers. On June 18 he instructed Thomas Mozley, then assuming the editorship of the *British Critic*, "*Drop* the subject of Number 90, but *use* it."[42]

THE TRACTARIAN RESPONSE TO *TRACT 90*

Tract 90 powerfully confirmed the evangelical conviction of the fundamental incompatibility of Tractarian theology with the 39 Articles.[43] Paradoxically this vast outpouring of predictable evangelical hostility did the Tractarians much less harm than their own publications, which sowed confused discord among themselves and disillusioned anger among their previous high-church allies and which negated the possibility of that general episcopal silence about which Newman had felt himself assured.

Sharp fissures quickly appeared among the early Tractarians about the wisdom and meaning of *Tract 90*. Pusey himself voiced the first doubt. On the same day that the four tutors issued their public letter, Pusey wrote Newman a highly critical private letter, a document not reprinted in the nineteenth century and to which Newman denied Pusey's biographer Liddon access. In words recalling his warning of almost four years earlier regarding the tract on purgatory, Pusey stated that "the whole object" of *Tract 90* "as well as particular parts will be startling to people who have not felt the need of such views of the articles, or met with those to whom they will be a comfort." He predicted that people would be "annoyed too at having their broad, i.e. vague notions of what is Romish taken away from them" and that such annoyance would prove "a considerable trial for the time, tho good in the end." Pusey concluded, "We must bide our time with patience until the storm be over, & pray it damage not the truth. I should hardly have thought people in general ripe for it; tho some may need it, & they ought to be regarded; I hope this will not put you out of heart; I have an implicit confidence in all you do."[44]

Undoubtedly miffed at not having seen a draft of *Tract 90*, Pusey keenly sensed Newman's unpropitious timing, for Parliament was then debating a grant to the Irish Roman Catholic seminary at Maynooth. Refusing to retreat in the face of Pusey's criticism, Newman asserted, "I do think that an alternative is coming on when a Bishop must consent to allow what really does seem to me quite a legitimate interpretation, or to witness quasi-secessions, if not real ones, from the Church"[45] Newman responded only modestly to other questions and revisionary suggestions from longtime sympathizers.

Pusey's private differences with Newman became known immediately in Tractarian circles and marked the first of a number of disagreements between them during the year. The general fractiousness of the post–*Tract 90* atmosphere brought a conclusion to the Friday meetings of the Theological Society at Pusey's lodgings. Nonetheless, Pusey strongly supported Newman within the university and during the Bagot negotiation. Furthermore, although, as already noted, Pusey in mid-April complained to J. R. Hope about "a lasting impression of Jesuitism" produced by *Tract 90*, he at the same time confessed that it had struck a blow against "the pseudo-traditionary and vague ultra-Protestant interpretation of the Articles" from which "it will not recover." He also reluctantly concluded, "People will abuse *Tract 90*, and adopt its main principles."[46] What lay in dispute, however, even among the Tractarians was the real character of those "main principles."

Even though on April 1 Newman had advised Keble on the benefits of a period of Tractarian silence, such was not to be.[47] Indeed, the publication of *Tract 90* and the deal with Bagot emboldened both Keble and certain second-generation Tractarians. Keble, unlike Pusey, had seen a draft of *Tract 90* and no doubt agreed with the details as well as the general argument. Early in April, in *The Case of Catholic Subscription to the Thirty-Nine Articles Considered: With Especial Reference to the Duties and Difficulties of English Catholics in the Present Crisis,* Keble stated that for "persons imbued with Catholic principles" from "sacred Antiquity" who stood "in some point staggered by the tone and wording of the Articles," Newman's tract could serve "as a kind of manual to assist in what was believed to be the true, legitimate, catholic exposition of the Articles." Keble assured Catholics within Oxford that the Hebdomadal Board's declaration represented "no *authoritative* censure" of *Tract 90* on the part of the university, whereas a similar action by Convocation would have amounted to the establishment of "a new test." A future ratification of the censure by Convocation, he warned, would consequently constitute "no slight stumbling block in the way of academical tutors" who might "think it their duty so to interpret ambiguous phrases in the Articles, as to bring them most nearly into conformity with the primitive Church, and to throw no unnecessary censure on other Churches." Such persons "ordained to serve at God's Altar" and seeing college tuition as "a branch of the Pastoral Care" might have no alternative than either to "teach Catholicism, or not teach at all."[48] No doubt if Hawkins read this pamphlet, he would have found himself confirmed in the wisdom of his decision to halt Newman's tutorial initiative of a decade earlier.

Keble did not, however, limit his opinions to university authority. Whereas Newman had repudiated the intentions of the sixteenth-century composers in ascertaining the meaning of the Articles, Keble directly rejected the dispositive authority of sitting bishops. According to his argument, Catholic subscription to the Articles did not require acquiescence in "the particular interpretation which the Bishops and other authorities for the time being might happen to put upon the several ambiguous passages, as most probable in their own private opinion." Instead, the real rule of subscription must be "the known judgment of the primitive, and as yet undivided, Church." Exclusion of Catholic subscription would drive toward Rome those at present in the English Church "whose Catholic feelings are stronger than their principles are clear and consistent."[49] Keble predicted that such Catholics would be unable to give their energy to the English Church and would probably eventually fall into schism if the church itself moved further toward Protestantism, a term which by now Keble like other Tractarians used interchangeably with evangelicalism.

The two most radical defenses and explications of *Tract 90* came from Ward and Oakeley, who tied their fervent embrace of *Tract 90* as much to a rejection of Protestantism as any advocacy of Catholicism. Regarding neither the English nor the Roman Church as an adequate Christian institution, Oakeley and Ward summoned both communions to judgment in a whirlwind of prophetic Catholic criticism. Yet what most disturbed their readers was their unprecedented diatribe against Protestantism and the English Reformation through which they interpreted *Tract 90*.

Ward, a graduate of Arnold's Rugby and a fellow of Balliol, where he was a mathematics lecturer, quickly established himself in the spring of 1841 as the radical Catholic bulldog who for the next four years was to wreak havoc over the Oxford religious landscape. His initial appearance in this role occurred during April and May through the publication of *A Few Words in*

Support of No. 90 and *A Few More Words in Support of No. 90,* in which he interpreted the tract in the most Roman sense possible. At the same time, like Froude before him, he powerfully condemned the English Reformers and vehemently criticized imperfections of the contemporary Church of England. In his first pamphlet, without hint of subtlety or compromise, Ward announced his conviction that *Tract 90* "*did* imply . . . the Articles do not condemn the decrees of the Council of Trent, and that in point of fact there is no *necessity* for any Roman Catholic either then or at the present day to hold on these points opinions which the Articles condemn." In both pamphlets he distinguished between actual teachings of the Roman Catholic Church as a true branch of the Church Catholic and corruptions that had appeared in Rome over the centuries. He claimed that *Tract 90* taught that the Articles were "directed against *the authoritative teaching* so lamentably prevalent throughout the Roman Church, not the *authoritative statements* of that Church herself."[50] From the era of the Reformation to the present, he urged, the conflation of the two had sowed much confusion.

Ward's subsequent interpretation of the intentions of the Reformers astonished readers and created a general perception of Tractarian contempt for the authority of the Articles. According to Ward, the framers of the Articles had attempted "to present an imposing external appearance of Protestantism, while nothing is really decided which might prevent those who deferred more really than they did to primitive authority from subscribing." Within the Homilies he pointed to the presence of "*truth* of *doctrine* in declaring certain opinions condemnable, *error* in *fact* in considering them held by the more religious Roman Catholics." Ward regarded much in *Tract 90* that had "struck some persons as disingenuousness" to be "referable to this cause." Catholic Christians in the English Church must tolerate those who regarded it as Protestant, but at the same time must demand mutual toleration: "In a word then, we raise no question about others who interpret our formularies by the spirit of Cranmer and Jewel, why are they found fault with who interpret them by St. Gregory and St. Augustin?"[51]

Ward restated his original themes even more forcefully in *A Few More Words.* Condemning the residual Protestantism lurking in the Articles and criticizing even Newman's accommodation, Ward charged that the English Church "fails in one of her very principal duties, that of witnessing plainly and directly to Catholic truth; that she *seems* to include whom she ought to repel, to teach what she is bound to anathematize; and that it is difficult to estimate the amount of responsibility she year by year incurs on account of those . . . who remain buried in the darkness of Protestant error, because she fails in her duty of holding clearly forth to them the light of Gospel truth." Harsh though these words might be, Ward thought them necessary in order "to waken the minds of their brethren to a sense of her present degradation" that had followed upon "the schism of the sixteenth century." The pain that Protestants experienced from criticism of the Reformers and the Articles stood matched by the pain Catholics experienced from ongoing criticism of "those whom *we* revere as eminent saints, the Popes and others of the middle ages." Ward then vigorously defended the paradox "that the Articles in themselves breathe a Protestant spirit, and yet were intended to admit persons of Anti-Protestant feeling."[52] He called upon Catholics who feared they could not subscribe to read the Articles more carefully finding the protections there afforded them against Protestant doctrines.

At one point in *A Few More Words* Ward declaimed "that either plain words must be put forth" about the Articles or those persons agreeing with Froude and his editors and still subscribing to the Articles "must be accused, without the power of self-defense, of dishonesty and unfair dealing." People reading *Tract 90* without sufficient knowledge of earlier Tractarian works had considered it "a wanton exercise of ingenuity, instead of . . . a most important step towards claiming for all members of the Church of England a full right to that *substratum* of Catholic doctrine on which Catholic feeling and practice may be reared up." Newman's omission of explicit criticism of the Roman Church in the tract was explicable because he presumed his readers knew already his opinion on this subject. Furthermore, such repetition of anti-Roman polemic offended many Catholics, ill became a church itself so full of failings, and caused people to forget "our own practical corruptions" and "the true character and claims of the Roman Church, as being a true Church." Concluding *A Few More Words*, Ward called upon Catholics to work patiently within the English Church despite its failings and to throw themselves "in a loving spirit upon the thoughts of unworldliness, purity, self-denial, from what ever quarter they are presented" so as "to build up our own Church into a form truly *Catholic*."[53]

In the *Apologia* Newman was to describe Ward, with whom he had many conflicts in their Roman Catholic years, and other radical Catholics of the early 1840s as "younger men, and of a cast of mind in no small degree uncongenial to my own," who represented "a new school of thought . . . sweeping the original party of the Movement aside, and . . . taking its place." According to that later retrospective, "These men cut into the original Movement at an angle, fell across its lines of thought, and then set about

turning that line in its own direction." Newman also complained of their
needing "to be kept in order," a burden he undertook because of their "great
zeal" for him. But in reality during 1841 and for some time thereafter
Newman treated the brilliantly brash Ward as an intimate theological confidant and repeatedly urged the inclusion of his articles in the *British Critic*.
Newman afterward stated first privately and then many years later publicly
that his own intentions had not embraced efforts to make the Articles
compatible with Rome, but throughout 1841 there is no evidence that he
sought to dissuade or silence Ward, but rather repeatedly defended him to
detractors. Indeed, Newman told Thomas Mozley, as the new editor of the
British Critic, in late August 1841, "Ward is *full* of ideas of writing—and it
would be a great point to *expand* him. He is most desirous to be moderate."[54]

By early July, Ward, whose pamphlets resulted in the forced resignation
of his Balliol College lectureship, enjoyed company in his advanced interpretation of Newman's position when Oakeley published *The Subject of
Tract XC. Examined, in Connection with the History of the Thirty-Nine Articles, and the Statements of Certain English Divines*. Seeking to refute the
contention that Newman had presented an interpretation of the Articles
"unprecedented in the Church of England," Oakeley asserted that the English Church had long been "remarkably unwilling to protest, *as a Church*,
against the doctrines of Rome." That situation had prevailed even during
the Reformation, when "history gives *no countenance whatever* to the opinion that, the Articles were drawn up *with the view of excluding Catholics*."
Oakeley claimed "that with the English Reformers, Protestantism was, as I
may say, an *after-thought*" because their initial concern had been politics,
not religious corruption. Not taking up Protestantism "as a comprehensive
system," as had Luther and Calvin, but rather "in details and by degrees,"
the English Reformers had not tried "to create a new Protestant community;
but sought rather to remodel the existing, and long-established, English
Church." Then, jumping to the nineteenth century, Oakeley demanded
modern toleration for Catholics against an evangelical system "manifestly
breaking to pieces."[55]

The same month that his *Tract 90* pamphlet appeared, Oakeley also
contributed the most infamous article ever to appear in the *British Critic*.
His essay on Bishop Jewel, which Newman regarded as able though ill
timed, constituted a declaration of open hostilities upon Protestantism in
the contemporary Church of England that far outdistanced the most offensive passages in Froude's *Remains*. Oakeley baldly announced that the English Church had for so long regarded separation from Rome "as *inevitable*,

that we have almost ceased to esteem it an evil, if we have not gone the still further length of hailing it as a boon, and glorying in it as a privilege." Yet that division did constitute "an evil" and "a most grievous penalty upon sin *somewhere;* upon the corruption which provoked, or the sacrilege which assailed, or both together." Oakeley advised, "Let us never plume ourselves upon our isolation, and call it independence." Indeed, the English Church owed gratitude to the Church of Rome, which Oakeley described as "our 'elder sister' in the Faith" and "our Mother; to whom, by the grace of God, we owe it that we are what we are."[56]

Turning to the issue of subscription, Oakeley affirmed that "a true Catholic" might, "conscientiously, subscribe" to the Articles. He also contended, however, that "without some more stringent test of Catholicity than we are likely to obtain," the English Church would remain "(in the great body of her members,) the *apparent* representative of a very different principle." What Oakeley termed the " 'uncertain sound' " of the Articles that failed explicitly to contradict "some of the less obvious, but no less essential, characteristics of the Protestant error" might prevent most English clergy from being "secured against more or less of sympathy with those relaxed views of religion, which are quite certain to be rife in an intellectual age and a commercial country." Fortunately, despite the shortcomings of the Articles, Catholic principles had always proved strong enough to protect the faithful against the pitfall of Protestantism, which Oakeley described as "so characteristically the religion of corrupt human nature." Should, however, the Church of England "be considered as in any degree pledged to the private opinions, or individual acts, of her so-called Reformers," the current return to Catholic principles would be seriously impeded.[57]

Although according to Oakeley Froude's *Remains* had provided a safety rope to those feeling the need to chose between the ancient and the modern church, the pressing question of the day remained how a person who believed "that the Protestant tone of doctrine and thought is essentially Antichristian" could remain in a communion that consciously disavowed "the judgment of Rome, not merely in this or that particular, but in its general view of Christian Truth." Oakeley proclaimed that such a person could do so only through "the *unprotestantizing* (to use an offensive, but forcible, word) of the national Church." Catholics could not stand in place but must move forward to restore and to state clearly truths "which as yet have been but intimated, and others developed which are now but in germ." During that process of restoration and clarification, Catholics "must recede more and more from the principles, if any such there be, of the English Reformation."

If Reformation principles proved Catholic, then they would be accepted, but, Oakeley warned, "If they be not Catholic, then, no matter whom we alienate, or to whom we give cause of triumph, *they must be abandoned.*"[58]

Although Oakeley's rhetoric made his article one of the most notorious of all Tractarian declarations, Newman himself in the same number of the *British Critic* issued a similar, if more muted, warning to ecclesiastical authorities. Lamenting that English Christians ignored the absence of unity among the branches of the Holy Catholic Church, Newman stated that the distinctions separating the English and Roman Churches were not those existing between true and false religions or true and false prophets. Rather, he explained, the separation of the Churches of England and Rome more nearly resembled those among New Testament Christian groups adhering to either St. Peter or St. Paul or to other early Christian teachers, with each pertaining to the Catholic Church and gaining nothing from their separations. It was the duty of Catholics remaining within the English Church "to recognize" in their church "not an establishment, not a party, not a mere Protestant denomination, but the Holy Church Catholic which the traditions of men have partially obscured,—to rid it of these traditions, to try to soften bitterness and animosity of feeling, and to repress party spirit and promote peace as much as in us lies." They must prosecute their "search after the promised Teacher" while admitting the presence of "certain imperfections" in their own church and "certain corruptions" in Rome. What he termed the "incidental Protestantism" of the English Church (not far removed from Oakeley's Protestantism as an "afterthought") was no reason for quitting it. But Newman quickly warned, "If the profession of ancient truth were to be persecuted in our Church, and its teaching forbidden,— then doubtless, for a season, Catholic minds among us would be unable to see their way." Hinting at the path they might then follow, Newman recalled, as he had a year and a half earlier, Meletius, Bishop of Antioch who received the favor, support, and canonization of St. Chrysostom and St. Basil and "who in St. Augustine's own day lived and died out of the communion of Rome and Alexandria."[59] Newman clearly already contemplated such a role for himself.

TRACTARIANS DIVIDED AGAINST THEMSELVES

By mid-summer Pusey for his part stood to Newman more or less as Rose had in 1836, a voice indicating affection for an imperfect English Church and seeking to moderate its more extreme Catholic critics. In early May he had published *The Articles Treated on in Tract 90 Reconsidered and Their Interpretation Vindicated in a Letter to the Rev. R. W. Jelf*, a pamphlet that Newman in light of Pusey's essential lack of sympathy for his tract had wished he would not publish. Whereas in J. B. Mozley's words Ward's pamphlet was "a kind of strong interpretation" of *Tract 90*, Pusey's was "a mollifying one." In his typically diffuse, ungainly pamphlet Pusey accused the Hebdomadal Board of condemning " 'modes of interpretation,' which they inferred to be contained" in *Tract 90* "but which never had any real existence." Then agreeing that the English Reformers had been Catholic in outlook and that the Articles did not actually condemn anything Catholic, Pusey, departing from Newman, declared the issue best considered without reference to the Council of Trent. Further dissenting from Newman's position, Pusey asserted that priests in the Church of England, having received their commissions through her bishops, possessed "ample scope for teaching, in what she holds and delivers out of or agreeable to Holy Scripture" and thus had "no commission to teach opinions, which she practically excludes." Pusey specifically advised against prayers for departed saints and explanation of "*any* purgatorial process." After various other excursions into justification and baptismal regeneration, he eventually returned to *Tract 90* again asserting that Newman's interpretation of the Articles as "in conformity and subordination to the teaching of the Church Catholic, is not only *an* admissible, but *the* most legitimate, interpretation of them." But the basis to which Pusey pointed for their Catholicity was not their congruence with primitive doctrine but their approval by the Convocation of 1662, convened at a moment "when the deference owed to Catholic Antiquity, which the Reformers felt, was most fully developed and understood."[60] Pusey's pamphlet at once failed to move the Tractarian enterprise back from the brink of sympathy for the Roman Catholic communion and demonstrated just how far he stood from Newman's own position and that of Newman's more advanced defenders.

Not surprisingly, Pusey deeply disapproved Ward's pamphlets of the late spring, which had appeared before his own, and so indicated to Oakeley. In late June, Oakeley informed Pusey that Ward "does not go 'at all further' than most of the persons with whom he lives at Oxford," meaning those "who are intimate with N." Oakeley stated that Ward "certainly wd *not* pledge himself not to join Rome under *any* circumstances," and thought the same true of Newman. Their departure might occur if the English Church lost the notes of a true church such as might occur through "her committal to Heresy by some authoritative decision." A week later Oakeley defended Ward's criticism of the Reformers on the ground that he had gone no further than Froude, quoting Keble's 1839 preface to make his point. Reminding Pusey of the shortcomings of the evangelicals, he contended that their "anti-catholicism is a system tending to the idolatry, not of an external object (such as the B.V.) but of inward feelings, experiences, & the like." He thought "the subjective system" of evangelicalism "far more subversive of the first principles of religious Truth, than an error, however grievous in *objective* Religion."[61]

During July, Pusey visited Ireland for the purpose among other things of inspecting convents, an excursion that plunged him directly into the midst of that traditionary Roman Catholicism which Newman had wished to distinguish from authoritative teaching. Pusey reacted with hostility to the "miserable slavery to politics & sad degeneration" of Irish Roman Catholics and lamented their priests' maintaining Marian devotion as "the characteristic of Romanism." He regretted that "the more Catholic truth is distinctly recognized among us, the more obstinately do" Irish Roman Catholic priests "hold to what is distinctive," and then speculated that they did so "not for its own sake, but as a means of keeping the poor people and as enlisting human affections."[62] This experience led Pusey to read with renewed Protestant sensibilities the July *British Critic*, which included Oakeley's and Newman's articles.

On July 20, 1841, Pusey expressed to Newman his grief over Oakeley's and Ward's thinking "it necessary to act as 'public prosecutors' against the Reformers." No longer leaving the Reformation an open question even among the Tractarians, their publications had committed the *British Critic* itself "to a view of a certain section." Criticizing the "indefiniteness" of Oakeley's injunction to go forward, Pusey asked, "Why may not such as I, if we can, think the English Reformers meant to be Catholic?" Oakeley's disruptive behavior would play into the hands of Rome because, Pusey wrote, "It must be a great additional temptation to secede from our Church when even the one section of it, which such people would be inclined to trust, is at variance within itself." Although the new aggressiveness of the *British Critic* disturbed Newman on political grounds, he told Pusey it provided "safety valves" for restless Catholics. Furthermore, on July 30 Newman finally confessed to Pusey that in his heart he disliked "the Reformers as much as any one" but did not "see the need of saying so except so far as the purpose of self-justification goes and the duty of honesty."[63] He also wished that the subject of the Reformation could be dropped.

This confession came after Ward on July 23 had written a garrulous letter to Pusey in response to the latter's criticism of June, communicated to him through Oakeley. Ward stated that "entire confidence in Newman" served as the "great bond of union" among young Catholics such as himself and that in his own case Newman's views would remain authoritative. He reported having read one of his controversial *Tract 90* pamphlets of the late spring to Newman, who had indicated "that he did not know a single sentiment expressed in it in which he did not altogether concur," a conclusion from which Newman did not demur upon later reading the letter himself. Ward also reported to Pusey other disturbing information about Newman's private opinions. For example, after reporting that Newman thought neither the Puritans nor the Cavaliers had a moral edge during the seventeenth century, Ward stated,

> Indeed Newman says that from the time of the Reformation our most respected divines (including Archbishop Laud) have shewn an eagerness for preferment most painful to read of & most difficult to account for. And as to doctrine, when we say that our Articles do not actually *condemn* Catholic truth, we are *compelled* in Newman's judgment (for I have heard him say so frequently) to have recourse to the supposition of their being framed with more or less dishonesty; & if they are to be taken as *teaching[,]* they teach on many points nothing else than heresy. Consider also the state of the prayer book[.] I have heard Newman say that it is to say the least *doubtful* whether there can be said to be a valid sacrament administered unless the Priest adds mentally what our Eucharistic service omits.

Ward further indicated that Newman actually believed the Reformers to be disingenuous. Throughout the letter, Ward emphasized the close relationship that he and others had developed with Newman, in effect, ignoring Pusey. Reminding Pusey of people's "tendency to consider you almost his authorized interpreter," Ward claimed to have published his own two pamphlets to prevent Pusey's then forthcoming one from blinding people to Newman's actual anti-Reformation sentiments.[64]

Ward's letter also portrayed the dark, almost despairingly hopeless situation that he and presumably other radical Tractarians saw prevailing in contemporary Christendom, a vision that does much to explain their actions during the next several years. He told Pusey of his long-standing conviction "that all branches of the Church since the schism of the sixteenth century have been so lamentably corrupt that without faith in the promises of permanence, we cd hardly believe the Church still to exist upon earth [,] and the fact of such general corruption is in itself so awful & subduing that it is sad work to cast stones at each other." Ward thought the Church of England "corrupt in every sense in which we can use the word, except so far as corruption implies the *perversion* of truth." That church might "in some respects" actually "appear to be *without* the truth than to have perverted it," a situation of imperfection "even worse than corruptions." The Roman Church had always "held up for the veneration of the faithful the highest standards of holiness," whereas the English Church had sneered "at such as 'Popish' & fanatical." He thought that "the more a person feels this deficiency in the practical apprehension of unseen things," the more he desired the image of a visible church such as that of Rome and the spiritual discipline available in its prods, teachings, and confessional practices. Ward particularly deplored the absence of spiritual rigor among English evangelicals, such as the Bishop of Chester, who failed to relate justification to judgment and thus sanctioned "the Protestant heresy on that subject, a heresy which *consistently* carried out will subvert all morality & contradict the plainest dictates of conscience." He concluded his judgment by telling Pusey, "If then the Roman authoritative teaching be on the whole (with some exceptions) *idolatrous,* is not ours (with some exceptions) *schismatical & heretical?*"[65] Over the next several years Ward's utopian striving for a life of rigorous holiness, satisfactory devotion, and Catholic doctrine, each conceived in direct opposition to evangelical religion, would lead him to one theological extreme after another, an effort in which the entire Tractarian cause became implicated and ultimately repudiated.

Having become aware of Ward's letter, Newman explained to Pusey in early August that Ward "knows more what I think than you do, because he has asked me more questions, but I am as sure that he has often not taken in my exact meaning; and often mistaken a conjecture or an opinion for a formal assertion." Newman also reported that he had "given up the notion of a monastic body at present, lest talk should be made."[66] Rather than turning Littlemore into a monastery, he would simply make spare rooms available to those who wished to go there to study. That momentary decision, it should be noted, did not retreat from the idea of some kind of community of celibate Catholic men. Why he hesitated at this point is unclear, but he may have been troubled by the enormous controversy and bad publicity surrounding Pusey's visit to the Irish convents.

On August 9 Pusey wrote of his ignorance of Newman's opinions of the Reformers because the preface to the second part of Froude's *Remains* had not fallen his way. Pusey, thus astonishingly oblivious to the anti-Reformation tone of the second set of Froude's *Remains*, had concluded from *Tract 90* that Newman thought the Reformers "took the Articles in a less Catholic sense than we do; but I had no thought that you held them to be 'disingenuous.'" Pusey himself considered their appeals to antiquity sincere though entangled with Zwinglian notions from foreign Reformers. He asserted to Newman, "Our reformation has had amid whatever reverses, a steady tendency to develope itself into Catholicism, and to throw out the impure elements which came into our Church; the foreign reformation has developed the contrary way into rationalism and Pantheism; and therefore, I think, we have a right to infer that there was a difference in their original ethos; our's intrinsically Catholic, though with something unCatholic cleaving to the agents in it, their's intrinsically unCatholic, though with some semblance of Catholicism." Pusey added that he thought Oakeley's and Ward's obsession with the single subject of the Reformers displayed "a diseased state of mind."[67]

Assigning the authorship of the preface to the second part of Froude's *Remains* to Keble, Newman wrote Pusey with some exasperation, "I fear I must express a persuasion that it requires no deep reading to dislike the Reformation." He claimed that Oakeley and Ward were not eager to run down the Reformers as an end in itself, but from the "feeling that our Church cannot be right till they are exposed, till their leaven is cast out, and till the Church repents of them." Indicating his agreement, Newman considered such an event simply a matter of time, claiming, "Truth *will* work."[68]

For several months, the coterie around Newman had decided that the truth required some nudging. In April, apparently unbeknownst to anyone else, Ward and Dalgairns published an anonymous letter in the French Roman Catholic newspaper *L'Univers* stating that the author of *Tract 90* looked "upon the Thirty-Nine Articles as a burden which God in His anger has placed upon us for the sins of our ancestors." Ward and Dalgairns expressed regret over "the sins committed by our ancestors in separating from the Catholic world" and indicated "a burning desire to be reunited with our brethren." They also voiced an "unfeigned affection" for "the Apostolic see, which we acknowledge to be the head of Christendom." At the same time they bemoaned "the sins not only of England but of Rome," defended the apostolic succession in the English Church, and mentioned practical abuses that must be removed from the Roman Church before any reunion.[69] By July 28, 1841, Ward in the company of Oakeley visited the Catholic College at Oscott, which Bloxam had visited previously. Ward also became acquainted with the Roman Catholic A. L. Phillipps and visited the Cistercian Monastery of Mount St. Bernard's. Yet throughout these months

Ward and others sympathetic to reunion were not prepared to countenance conversions to Rome or any other action suggesting that the Church of England was less than a full, even if imperfect, branch of the Holy Catholic Church.

At the same time Ward, presumably as a result of his interpretation of private conversations, apparently thought Newman under certain conditions prepared to go over to Rome. Ward openly discussed with Phillipps how the modern Roman Catholic Church might accommodate patristically minded members of the Church of England. What Ward desired was the possibility of Newman's converting and then being able to say, " 'I protested against Rome on account of certain doctrines she practically professes; behold, in going over, I have a public protection against being expected to profess such doctrines.' "[70] Such was the profoundly self-referential fashion in which English Catholics had decided that the entire religious world of the West orbited around themselves and their chief leader.

Ward further explained that members of the Roman Catholic Church in England should assume "that wherever are found strictness and purity of life, anxious conscientiousness, etc., there are her friends," and that persons possessing those qualities "really belong to her, and should be looked on as secret fellow-workers with her." Ward disapproved Roman Catholics who appeared "to take up a sectarian position" and to be more devoted to promoting "the temporal welfare of the Roman Church than of promoting God's glory as He would have it." It was much more important for Roman Catholics to "sympathise with and pray for those who through the English Church are preaching the true doctrine of the Cross, obedience and self-denial, to the overthrow of Lutheran heresy" than to "show anxiety for the immediate union of some few individuals." Ward thought it important for Phillipps to know the obstacles placed in the way of reunion "by whatever may even seem to mark your communion as leavened with a Protestant, or sectarian, or worldly character." Fully revealing the complexity and confusion of religious nomenclature, Ward reproved Roman Catholics for a moral laxity that he also discerned in evangelicalism, "In a word, in return for your charging me with Protestantism, I charge you with implicit and unconscious Lutheranism: no sympathy is felt for the inculcation of habits of self-denial and scrupulous obedience till they are developed into veneration of saints and love of ceremonial."[71] Ward and presumably others genuinely saw themselves as a Catholic remnant in the English Church seeking cooperation with an analogous Catholic remnant in the Roman Church.

Together, they might establish a pure Catholic religious communion embracing antiquity, discipline, and self-denial.

At this point Newman and his advanced followers regarded themselves as the representatives of a pure, ascetic Catholicism that might correct the imperfections and corruptions of both historic churches. But Newman's ecclesiology, as well as his desire to retain a group drawn to his own leadership, inhibited action. On March 2 he had told Bloxam that people other than the bishops "have no right to take the initiative [toward reconciliation with Rome], except when the essential truth of the Gospel is in jeopardy." Having later described Rome to Bowden as "hollow, insincere, political, ambitious, & unscrupulous," and as lacking "the Note of Sanctity," Newman in May refused even to meet with Dr. Charles Russell of Maynooth College, telling the Irish cleric for whom he later developed the warmest respect, "We have too great a horror of the principle of private judgment, to trust it in so immense a matter as that of changing from one communion to another. We may be cast out of our communion, or it may decree heresy to be truth—you shall say whether such contingencies are likely; but I do not see other conceivable causes of our leaving the Church in which we were baptised." Newman had posed similar arguments to other Roman Catholic correspondents during the spring, pointing out the problems which the Irish Roman Catholic Church in particular presented to Catholics in the English Church. Moreover, reasserting his understanding of each diocese as constituting "an integral Church," he took his stand on the bargain he had completed through the publication of his *Letter to the Bishop of Oxford,* which he saw as having "had the effect of bringing the preponderating *authority* of the Church on our side."[72] Such was his position into the autumn of 1841, a stance that continued to hold his coterie and potential inhabitants for Littlemore at his side. At the same time the various Tractarian commentaries on *Tract 90,* both public and private, had served to isolate Newman and his closest friends more than ever and to confirm all of the most hostile suspicions about their intentions.

THE SPECTER OF HERESY

By early 1841 Newman had come to see the Church of England and more specifically the Catholics therein as dwelling in a climate of ever-growing evangelical Protestant heresy. On March 2 he recalled the climate surrounding the launching of the tracts themselves, telling Bloxam that "their authors" had published them as the result of having "felt that heresy was stealing all around their Church, if it had not already entered it." Once the explosion occurred over *Tract 90*, the image of Catholics dwelling in a church where evangelical heresy was rapidly intruding itself into the highest levels of authority again seized Newman's mind. Thereafter he saw heretical progress in even so minor an event as the Archbishop of Canterbury's acknowledging receipt of an anti-Tractarian petition from evangelical Cheltenham clergy. This image of the English Church overwhelmed by internal evangelical heresy replaced the earlier Tractarian concept of an institution endangered by the anticlericalism of evangelical Dissent and radical politicians. This redefinition of the danger confronting the church was another example of Newman's responding to the concerns of the second Tractarian generation for whom, unlike the first, politics held little interest. Beginning in 1841, forging a role for Catholics in both a church and wider culture besieged by heretics became a fundamental factor in Newman's framing of his personal vocation and that of his followers as forming a saving remnant. By the close of the year, genuinely reflecting the anxieties of his coterie, Newman observed to Keble, "It is not love of Rome that unsettles people, but *fear of heresy at home*."[73] Newman himself had done much to fan those fears because the specter of heresy both liberated him from deference to ecclesiastical authority and justified his Littlemore monastic experiment.

For Newman himself, the episcopal charges of the summer of 1841 provided the first evidence of the rising heretical tide. As Bishop Bagot had immediately recognized, unlike previous Tractarian publications, *Tract 90*, by addressing the question of clerical subscription, impinged directly on episcopal authority and ecclesiastical discipline. Forestalling anything resembling formal episcopal censure had been Newman's primary goal during his intricate negotiation with Bagot. Both Keble and Pusey in their pamphlets supporting *Tract 90* had attempted to deflect the impact of possible future episcopal censure. Ironically, the diffuse character of episcopal authority in the English Church, previously so lamented by the Tractarians, rendered a collective episcopal response difficult if not impossible. That situation did not, however, preclude individual bishops from voicing their opinions.[74]

John Bird Sumner, the evangelical Bishop of Chester, loosed the first blast from the episcopal bench. It had not been unexpected. The future Archbishop of Canterbury, whose book on apostolical preaching had proved important for Newman's own theological formation, combined his attack on *Tract 90* in his diocesan charge of May and June 1841 with an extensive critique of Williams's tract on reserve. Satan, according to Sumner, had ever sought to assail the simple Gospel truth that we are justified by faith in Jesus Christ. Danger to the preaching of that truth now arose from persons who claimed "that the doctrine of the Gospel, the propitiation made for sin, is a doctrine too dangerous to be openly disclosed, too mysterious to be generally exhibited" and who would thus "deprive the sinner at once of his motive to repent and his comfort in repenting." That same theological system obscured the truth of justification by conflating "what has been done for us, and what is to be wrought in us," thus "practically" inducing man "to look to himself and not to his Redeemer, for acceptance with God."[75]

Sumner then denounced "learned men" who by elaborately arguing "that outward rites and services are the only means of holiness on which we can depend" attempted to set the Church in the place of Christ. The Christian Church consisted of a congregation of faithful men with a ministry ordained to serve it, not to define it. The true minister of God was not a person possessing exclusive apostolical rights but rather one "animated with no other feeling than zeal for God's glory, and compassion for his fellowmen," going "forth with the Bible in his hand to meet the contradiction of the infidel and the sneers of the lover of this world." In England, "this land of light," the clergy could not maintain "the fatal claims which the Romish priests assume, and which nothing except the darkness in which they shroud their people could enable them to preserve." Sumner proclaimed the power of the Gospel when "diligently inculcated in the spirit" of the Articles to "enlist many hearts on their side, and on the side of those who preach them."[76]

Turning to *Tract 90* in an appendix to his charge, Sumner specifically rejected the notion that the 39 Articles might be interpreted according to the teaching of the Church Catholic. In his diocese, he emphasized, clergy subscribed to them "as articles, not of the Universal Church of Christ, but of the United Church of England and Ireland, of which the subscriber is a member." Consequently, those Articles did not "admit of interpretation borrowed from any remote or undefined authority, professing to be that of a church calling itself, or imagined to be, the Church Catholic."[77] In his exploration of reserve, justification, the church, and Catholic subscription, as well as in his extensive citing of offensive Tractarian quotations, Sumner established the format and much of the tone for other hostile charges, such as that issued later in the year by his brother, Charles Richard Sumner, Bishop of Winchester, in whose diocese Keble resided.

In late July and August 1841 Charles Thomas Longley, the evangelical

Bishop of Ripon and also later Archbishop of Canterbury, praised Tractarian efforts to revive a higher view of the sacraments and to foster personal
piety and self-denial. He wished, however, that the Tractarians had not
deprecated the Reformation or spoken "tenderly of practices to which our
standard Divines have usually affixed strong terms of reprobation," such as
invocation of the saints and the worship of images. By accusing the English
Church of providing "no free scope to the higher devotional feelings," the
Tractarians had brought some in its midst to the "verge of schism." Longley
also criticized the idea of reserve in preaching the atonement and deplored
Pusey's view of sin after baptism as contradicting both the liturgy and
the Homilies. While supporting a broad approach to the Articles, Longley
nonetheless espoused the existence of "limits beyond which this forbearance
cannot be carried." He understood Catholic interpretation of the Articles to
endanger "the integrity of subscription" itself. Directly rejecting Newman's
argument to the contrary, Longley declared, "There can be but one true and
legitimate meaning to an Article, and that must be the meaning intended by
the framer." For his own part, he would not take "advantage of any ambiguity in the wording" or affix his own notion of Catholic sense to an article
unless he "had found it impossible to ascertain what was the special sense
originally designed by the authors." Recognizing "the respect in which our
Reformers held Catholic antiquity," Longley opined "that *they* were more
likely to have correctly embodied that sense in it, than *I* as an individual
should be, to discover that sense for myself."[78] Longley here, as had Francis
Newman in 1840, ridiculed the implicit practice of private judgment on the
part of Tractarians when it suited their own purposes. As far as the bishops
were concerned, private judgment leading to Romanism was no more welcome than private judgment leading to Protestant Dissent.

In his August charge, Edward Maltby, Bishop of Durham, once Pusey's
tutor and more recently another of Newman's targets in the February "Catholicus" Letters, deplored the "misplaced zeal" embodied in the tracts
and culminating in "an elaborate attempt" to "explain away the real meaning of our Articles, and [to] infuse into them a more kindly spirit of accommodation to the opinions and practices of the Church of Rome." Maltby
declared that instead of emphasizing the Fathers and tradition, the Tractarians would have been better advised "to recollect . . . that before the Fathers
wrote, or any matter of opinion or of fact could be conveyed through those
who succeeded them, there existed the infallible Word of God, dictated by
his Holy Spirit, and preserved, for our study and edification, by the special care of His good Providence." Study of the best critical expounders of

the Scriptures would lead to a clearer knowledge of "the truth as it is in Jesus" than could be gleaned from "the fallacies or sophistries of Tradition." Maltby also criticized the tracts for upholding "antiquated Forms and Ceremonies" so as "to threaten a revival of the follies of by-gone superstition," and thus bringing into contempt both the Reformation and the name Protestant.[79]

That evangelical bishops or the recently maligned Maltby deplored *Tract 90* and much of the rest of the Tractarian enterprise was not surprising. But the tract had no less filled "with astonishment and concern" the nearly blind James Monk, conservative high-church Bishop of Gloucester and Bristol. Whereas, he wrote, it was well known that the Articles had been directed against Rome and had led to martyrdom among the Reformers, *Tract 90* through "much ingenuity" and "much sophistry" attempted to prove that upon full examination of the Articles and the Decrees of Trent the differences between the Church of England and of Rome would vanish. Furthermore, the tract writers had pursued "a constant and industrious endeavour to compliment the Papal Church, to extenuate its faults, and to apologize for its enormities." Monk questioned whether the Church of England still remained a "Scriptural Church, the glory of the Reformation, at once Catholic and Protestant, which appeals to the Apostles and Evangelists as to its fathers and its founders?" Or whether that Church stood in danger of being "seized and taken from us by a party of our own forces, and given up to the allegiance of an antichristian power?"[80]

While praising Tractarian concern for piety and church discipline, as well as for study of the Anglican Divines and the Church Fathers, Monk nonetheless regretted the Tractarians' having discouraged the availability of the Bible. Although according to Monk the Church appealed to the practices of antiquity, it did so only when those practices found confirmation in Scripture. Citing the clarity of Article 6, regarding the supremacy and full adequacy of Scripture, Monk insisted, "What is found in the inspired Scriptures has come to us with the warranty of Heaven: what is handed down through other sources of primitive belief rests, after all, upon the authority of man, exposed to the errors, distortions, and corruptions arising from the ignorance, superstition, or presumption of our nature, from which the early ages of Christianity were not exempt."[81] Consequently, those who would use tradition as an equal coordinate with Scripture must necessarily appeal to some human authority invested with divine infallibility, the very error upon which the Roman Church rested.

What most amazed and angered Monk, however, was the Tractarian advocacy of reserve in the preaching of the atonement. On that issue he declared, "That Christ died to save sinners; that our nature had become corrupt and depraved through sin; and that by the Sacrifice of our Blessed Lord upon the cross once offered, Atonement and satisfaction were made, and the wrath of God averted,—are among the first truths which we communicate to the youthful Christian; they are likewise inculcated in the reception of the Blessed Eucharist, as well as in the various parts of the Formularies of our Church. Upon what principle, then, can they be held back in our Christian teaching?" Despite the possibility of distortion in the preaching of the atonement, Monk could imagine no reason to cease proclaiming Christ crucified as "the sole ground upon which we teach our hearers to rest their hopes of forgiveness and reconciliation to God." Although clergy of genuine piety and concern for evangelical truth in his diocese might acknowledge Tractarian teachings, their real duty remained "to preserve to the Church that Scriptural purity in which it has been handed down to us by our Reformers."[82] That purity for Monk obviously included the open preaching of the atonement.

The statements of these bishops, large extracts of which Newman copied, left no doubt in his mind that his bargain with Richard Bagot did not obtain in other dioceses of the Church of England.[83] Whether issued by strongly evangelical bishops, such as the Sumner brothers, or by high churchmen, such as Monk, possibly seeking to insulate themselves from local evangelical assault, the episcopal charges of 1841 addressed themselves directly to clerical subscription as interpreted in *Tract 90* and to other major historic Protestant doctrines that had been questioned or criticized in the tracts. Neither the letter nor the spirit of these charges, which despite later claims to the contrary, were quite well informed about Tractarian theology, demonstrated sympathy for tender Catholic consciences.

Throughout the autumn of 1841 Newman, implicitly recognizing the theological power of these charges, complained to correspondents about the heterodoxy rather than the authority of the bishops. Late in October he wrote to Keble, "Our Church seems fast protestantising itself, and this I think it right to say everywhere; (not using the word protestant) but not lightly. Have you seen the Bishop of Chester's Charge? He seems to me, as far as in him lies, to have cut off Chester by it from the Catholic Church. In such cases I only see the alternative of obeying or of calling the Bishop heretic." About the same time, Newman told Mozley, "The truth is, we must if we can indite [*sic*] such charges as the Bishop of Chester's of heresy, or we shall [be] cast out of the Church," and somewhat later he expressed to Henry Wilberforce the hope that Bishop Sumner "will be arraigned before the proper Tribunal for heresy."[84] Newman thus chose to engage in name-calling and accusations of heresy rather than substantive argument. Through this projection of heresy upon the English episcopacy, along with that of corruption upon the Roman Church, Newman nurtured among his own Catholic followers the sense that they and they alone represented the Christian faith in England. It had been exactly that view that during the same month, as the letters quoted above, Ward had conveyed to Ambrose Phillipps when he urged the cooperation of Catholics in the English and Roman Churches.

In the late summer of 1841 another event occurred unmentioned publicly by Newman and unnoticed by historians of the Tractarian Movement. During the last week of the Whig ministry, Lord Melbourne appointed to the recently vacant Regius Professorship of Modern History Thomas Arnold, author of "The Oxford Malignants" in defense of Hampden. The prime minister had long wished to do something for Arnold, as had Archbishop Whately and Edward Hawkins. The history professorship, in contrast to a politically impossible theological appointment, provided the vehicle for bringing to Oxford a man known throughout the university, church, and nation for his plain-speaking and truthfulness, just as the Tractarians generally and Newman in particular encountered the most severe doubts about their own truthfulness. Arnold would have been a strong voice opposing both the theology and the morality of the Tractarians, whom from the inception of their enterprise he had criticized.[85] Arnold, whose volume of recent sermons Ward attacked in the October *British Critic,* died of heart disease less than a year after receiving the appointment, but no one could have predicted that eventuality when he was appointed. His anticipated ongoing presence as a part of Oxford life may have been another reason for Newman's more general discouragement during late 1841 and for his eventual decision to move to Littlemore early in the next year. With Arnold in Oxford, Newman for the first time would have faced the presence of a strong, charismatic voice competing with his own within the university and opposing all for which he stood.

In the wake of the summer charges against *Tract 90* and Arnold's appointment came the affair of the Jerusalem bishopric, which demonstrated still more pervasive evangelical influence within the English episcopacy, including the Archbishop of Canterbury. The Jerusalem bishopric was a proposal originating with Baron Bunsen, the Prussian ambassador, and his evangelical monarch Frederick IV for the appointment, alternately by

England and Prussia, of a bishop to minister to German Protestants and Church of England communicants residing in Jerusalem.[86] Lord Ashley, the most prominent English evangelical layman, strongly supported the plan as furthering international pan-Protestant causes and possibly aiding the conversion of the Jews preparatory to the second coming of Christ. High churchmen including Hook, Perceval, and Palmer also approved the idea as strengthening episcopacy and also undoubtedly as signaling distance between themselves and their former Tractarian allies.

From its inception, the Jerusalem bishopric provoked a negative reaction in Newman, recognized by almost all his friends as disproportional, extreme, and vehement. In his mind the specter of evangelical heresy attacking Catholicism linked the episcopal charges and the Jerusalem project. In early October, shortly after Archbishop Howley had consecrated the new Bishop of Jerusalem, Newman announced to his sisters, "The Archbishop is doing all he can to unchurch us." In a draft letter of the same month, left unpublished but intended for *The Times*, he wrote, "Surely it is an evil great enough to find Bishops heretics, without going on to make heretics Bishops." Newman further complained to his sister Jemima that by cooperating with the Prussians in appointing a bishop for Jerusalem, the Church of England was "forming a special league which she has never done before with the foreign Protestants."[87] In that cooperation Newman believed he was witnessing a contemporary intrusion by continental Protestants against Catholicism in the English Church, aided and abetted by its own bishops, that paralleled the cooperation of the English Reformers with their foreign Protestant advisers during the 1540s.

After much consultation among Tractarian colleagues, Newman on November 13 sent the Bishop of Oxford and the Archbishop of Canterbury a personal protest, dated November 11, against the Jerusalem project. Although Pusey thought the document should be published, Keble advised caution, and the protest remained only privately circulated until reprinted in the *Apologia*. In exaggerated, angry prose Newman stated that because the claim of the English Church "on the allegiance of Catholic believers" lay in its being a branch of the Church Catholic, he must protest "the recognition of heresy, indirect as well as direct" involved in the formation of a bishopric with Lutheranism and Calvinism, which he pronounced "heresies, repugnant to Scripture, springing up three centuries since, and anathematized by East as well as West."[88] Both bishops appear to have ignored the protest, whereby in the eyes of those close to him Newman had challenged the highest authorities in the English Church and suffered no resulting chastisement.

On November 24, acknowledging the harshness of his protest, Newman explained to J. R. Hope, a politically well-connected London lawyer and Tractarian supporter, that having long assured others that the English Church was a branch of the Church Catholic, he now stood "deeply pained" by the Jerusalem bishopric, which "tends to cut from under me the very ground on which I have been writing and talking, and to prove all I hold a mere theory and illusion, a paper theology that facts contradict." With ecclesiastical authorities ignoring and possibly preparing to disown Catholic doctrines, he feared that "the true living Catholic spirit" that had once inhabited the English Church now no longer did so. Through the protest he was asserting the right to warn church leaders "that there are those who think that our Church is on the brink of measures which will obscure the Notes of her Apostolic authority."[89]

What Newman did not say, of course, was that virtually the only people likely to see those notes so obscured were his closest associates, whose possible loss of confidence in the English Church would not only confuse their religious lives but also cause his own personal world to fall apart. On December 8 Newman wrote to Hope regarding the success of the Jerusalem bishopric project, "On me it falls very hard—here am I labouring with all my might to keep men from Rome, and, as if I had not enough trouble, a new element of separation is introduced."[90] Those Catholics enthusiastic for cooperation with persons of similar outlook in the Roman Church but knowing it impossible to pursue it other than through clandestine meetings and correspondence, such as that of Ward and Dalgairns, now had to watch bishops of their own church aid a joint venture between domestic and foreign evangelicals.

It was the potential evaporation of his personal coterie persuaded of the hopelessness of the situation for Catholics in the English Church that accounts for Newman's otherwise puzzling, explosive anger over the Jerusalem bishopric. But the vehemence of Newman's protest and the aggressiveness of his correspondence with Hope served another purpose beyond the expression of principles of Tractarian ecclesiology. In late 1841, by raising his rhetoric to new extravagances and provoking similar rhetoric privately in Hope and then publicly in Pusey, Newman intended to induce fears among ecclesiastical authorities not of conversions to Rome but of a secession more along the lines carried out by Wesley or the Nonjurors, an

eventuality about which Hook had already warned Blomfield.[91] Newman
had learned from his negotiations with Bagot during the previous March
the power of hints of secessions and of his own resignation from St. Mary's
for securing his goal of Catholic latitude in the English church. His interaction with Bagot had clearly emboldened him and his followers to believe
that they could sustain and even expand their position in the English
Church. To the extent that Newman's strategy won accommodations, all
was to the good; if it failed, then he was confirmed as the leader of a Catholic
remnant opposing heresy.

In 1850, in a marginal comment on a letter from early 1842, Newman
described his prose of that earlier date as illustrating an " 'ad terrorem'
argument of my being disgusted, so that any thing might happen, which was
true in prospect." That such a strategy was at work in his November 24
letter to Hope is suggested by a November 25 letter to Keble in which
Newman reported that he knew of no people at Oxford about to move to
Rome. He then further explained to Keble, "There is doubtless *great* danger
in prospect—but the persons in danger are far too serious men to act suddenly or without waiting for what they consider God's direction—and I
should think *very few indeed* realize to themselves yet the prospect of a
change, or nay *would* change, *if* our rulers showed us *any* sympathy, or their
brethren kept from saying and believing that they *would* change. In that case
the dangerous seed might lie dormant, like a disease, for *many* years. It is a
very bad thing to accustom them to the notion that people *think* they will
change."[92] These comments to Keble presumably reflect the relatively stable
situation that Newman believed he had achieved through his agreement
with Bagot and that he hoped to preserve by further aggressive actions
toward ecclesiastical authorities. He hoped to discourage change among his
followers while raising among his opponents the fear of its occurring.

Further energizing the anti-Tractarian climate of late 1841 was the contest over the Oxford poetry professorship, in which the forces of evangelicalism again triumphed. Keble's term in the professorship expired that year.
During the autumn some Tractarians decided to attempt to replace him with
Isaac Williams, who was soon opposed by James Garbett, a staunch evangelical with an election committee chaired by Lord Ashley. Pusey published an
ill-advised public letter that further polarized the situation, leading the
Record to declare that Williams's election would constitute "a great victory of
Tractarian error over scriptural truth." Never favoring the contest, Newman
feared that it might result in a meeting of an evangelical-dominated Convocation that would, as he told his sister, proceed "to measures which are to

have the effect of 'driving us clean out of the University.' " In the joint evangelical crusades over the Jerusalem bishopric and the poetry professorship, Newman saw "a movement of the Church as a whole in all its ranks to disown Catholic truth, in its Bishops, Societies, popular organs, and the like," and a plan "for organizing a large Protestant league throughout the world" that required putting "the Church of England on a more Protestant footing than it has hitherto acknowledged."[93] Consequently, no good could come from the disputed election of the Oxford poetry professor.

Eventually Gladstone, working with numerous Tractarian high-church sympathizers in London and with the Bishop of Oxford, defused the situation by persuading Williams to withdraw before any formal vote was taken. The outcome of the contest had never been in doubt, with the Roman Catholic *Tablet* describing the Tractarians as having been "defeated without striking a blow." Furthermore, the Tractarians, and most particularly Pusey and Keble, lost the sympathy of the long-suffering Bishop of Oxford, who declared that there could be no peace in the church if Pusey and others could not "restrain those younger men, who, professing to be your followers, run into extremes, but who, in fact cease to follow any persons who do not go to the same extent they themselves judge to be right."[94]

As 1841 passed into 1842, Bagot's role in the poetry contest was only one of several signals both public and private to traditional high churchmen that after the various condemnations of *Tract 90* they should severely distance themselves from the Tractarians, a development that further led Newman to see the entire English Church succumbing to evangelical heresy. The older high-church group consisting of the Joshua Watsons and the Edward Churtons had, like Bagot, lost all patience. Churton wrote Pusey on December 9, 1841, castigating him for his failure, along with that of Keble and Newman, to keep control of their party: "Instead of controlling the ebullitions of the young wrong-heads, you have suffered yourselves to be inoculated with their frenzies. Instead of saying to them, what, I do not use the proscribed term of *common* sense, but what *good* sense would have suggested . . . you have let them get ahead of you, and drag you after them." Churton further criticized Pusey for having visited the Irish convents and lamented Newman's protest, which he thought beside the point. Pusey firmly and directly resisted all of Churton's advice and, despite previous misgivings, decided one more time to defend the Tractarian cause before the authorities of the English Church. Pusey, whatever his inner hesitations, Newman told Henry Wilberforce, could not "bear to be left behind."[95]

By early January 1842 Pusey had begun to compose his *Letter to the*

Archbishop of Canterbury, even though during the previous autumn Howley
had advised a period of Tractarian silence. Pusey may have felt that after
having encouraged Newman's protest, he needed to do something himself
to retain the respect of advanced Catholics. But once he had begun work on
the pamphlet, another factor may well have impinged on his thinking and
that of other Tractarians. On January 22 Sir Robert Peel, as his first appointment to the episcopal bench, named A. T. Gilbert, leader of the university
campaign against Williams in the poetry professorship contest. The *Christian Observer* termed the appointment "a manifesto of Sir R. Peel against
Tractarianism," and the *Morning Chronicle* described it as "a severe blow" to
the Puseyites, demonstrating "that while Sir Robert Peel is in power Puseyism will not be the road to preferment in the church."[96] The appointment
represented a personal affront to Pusey and persuaded other Tractarians
that the forces of heresy were taking charge of the English Church.

A few days after Gilbert's appointment, Newman, who loathed Peel's
politics, shared for the first time with Robert Wilberforce his conviction of
the parallel between ancient and modern heresies and the doubts it raised in
his mind about the Catholicity of the English Church. Newman told Wilberforce that the analogy "seems something *prophetic*—it scares me." Recent events—unspecified, but surely including Gilbert's appointment—now
caused Newman to lack "an implicit faith in the validity of the *external*
Notes of our Church" and hence to rely on its internal notes. Observing, as
in the past, the relevance of the example of St. Meletius, he reported entertaining "a growing dread lest in speaking against the Church of Rome I may
be speaking against the Holy Ghost." In a postscript, Newman pondered
whether the degraded state of Rome might not be raised by his own joining
her or by her union with the English Church, by which he meant with
Catholics in that church. At the same time, in a new departure Newman
wondered whether one might not join the Roman Church before it had been
reformed "from her present degradation." These last remarks indicate the
impact of Ward's privately stated position of being willing under certain
conditions to join an unreformed Rome. Indeed, on the day of his letter to
Wilberforce, Newman castigated Mozley for extending insufficient editorial
sympathy toward Ward and defended the latter's intentions and views while
separating himself from Oakeley, whom for unspecified reasons he was
"suspicious of."[97]

Hope was apparently no less angered by Gilbert's appointment. On
January 31 he advised Pusey in composing his pamphlet not to fear being
"misunderstood as despising the Bishops." Influenced by his correspon-

dence with Newman and by Keble's pamphlet of a few months earlier, Hope encouraged Pusey to "give a distinct view of the authority both of individual and collective Bishops of *our* (not the Universal) Church, showing that (as I conceive) they may be listened to for *discipline's sake*, but must be judged, *as regards authority over Conscience* by the Church Catholic. And that the very same principle which leads to submission to them in the one case, implies (if need be) rejection in the other."[98] Hope thus advocated the fundamentally Protestant principle of private judgment, on the basis of which, despite repeated denials, the Tractarians now actively pursued their course of appealing to the authority of an invisible Church Catholic not altogether unlike that of the evangelical invisible church. In this vein Pusey's *Letter to the Archbishop of Canterbury* was to champion the presence and actions of a gathered Church Catholic within the Church of England.

With enormously condescending belligerence, reminiscent of his letter to Melbourne during the Hampden affair, Pusey castigated before the bar of the Church Catholic those bishops who in recent months had criticized the Tractarians. After faulting the bishops for failing to realize the weight their charges now carried as a result of the spread of Tractarian ecclesiology, Pusey criticized the evangelical theology that made several of those documents "at first sight, seem to involve a denial" or "a contradiction" of Catholic truth. In criticizing the preservation of Catholic truth and primitive devotions now sought by Catholics in the English Church, the bishops had unwittingly aggravated the disease by "applying stimulants, when they would if they knew it, use lenitives."[99]

Throughout his letter Pusey insisted upon the bishops' ignorance of Tractarian theology, claiming that they had read only "detached passages" or "insulated Tracts" without inquiring whether a portion of one corrected another. The bishops had consequently condemned what they feared that the tracts said rather than what they really contained. In short, Pusey declared, "These Bishops mean to condemn what they think us to be." Pusey particularly argued that the bishops had confused Williams's intention of correcting "irreverence in handling religious truth" with the withholding of the doctrine of the atonement. Had the bishops "fully considered *both*" Williams's tracts "instead of singling out one topic for condemnation," they might "have recommended their general teaching, as a corrective of so much under which we are now suffering."[100]

According to Pusey, the bishops' charges assumed a Genevan viewpoint, reflecting those foreign influences that three centuries earlier had corrupted the Catholicism of the native English Reformation and thus prepared the way for both the seventeenth-century Puritans and the eighteenth-century evangelicals. Pusey admitted to finding, "as far as it was true, the value and power of the popular system in its warnings against the world, its urgent calls to conversion, its pointing to our Blessed Lord as the Author and Finisher of our faith." But he also condemned that evangelical system as "in part defective, in part erroneous" in its shrinking "from inculcating 'Judgment to come,' 'according to our works,' the value of good works, of regular devotion, of self-discipline, of alms-deeds, and mercifulness," and its insufficient emphasis on the sacraments and on "the mysteriousness of our life in Christ, our responsibilities, or the nature of repentance." These deficiencies arose from evangelicals' having "condensed the whole Gospel into the two fundamental truths of nature and of grace, that by nature we are corrupt, by grace we are saved."[101]

The subsequent appropriation within the English Church of this " 'Nonconformist' system" incapable of spanning "the largeness of Catholic truth" could lead, Pusey determined, as in the charge of the Bishop of Chester, "even to unconscious heresy." That bishop, along with the bishops of Winchester and of Gloucester and Bristol, in teaching "that the individual must by his personal faith cleave unto his Lord," had "overlooked that no human faith nor longings can make a man a member of his Incarnate Saviour, that they only can be united with Him, whom He receives into His mystical Body, and that this His act is the Sacrament of Baptism." Proper recognition of the role of baptismal regeneration clarified the authority of the "collective wisdom of the Church" as the chief interpreter of Scripture in place of the alleged "sufficiency of self," fostered by evangelical theology and constituting for Pusey "one of the signs of the last Apostasy."[102]

Although the Tractarians stood accused of novelty, in fact, Pusey contended, the actual religious novelty of the day lay in "the contrary naked system," which neglected Catholic truth residing in the seventeenth-century divines, the Homilies, the Reformers, and the long span of Catholic tradition before them. In restoring an appreciation for the sacraments, piety, holiness, and church order, the tract writers had done far more good for the church than had the evangelical party. The drawing of the tracts to "a disgraced close" had not established peace in the English Church, as witnessed by the charges of the bishops and the contested election over the poetry professorship. Indeed, those charges had provided occasion for additional clerical attacks using "language little fitted for the sanctuary of God, where our Lord is 'in the midst' of us." Those who hated church principles "for their strictness, or for subjecting the individual will," and who "mix up ribaldry and profaneness" with the condemnation of what they hate, could now conduct "their unholy warfare under the banner of our Bishops." So long as the Church of England remained "the very battle-field of evil spirits," some people would leave for Rome as the cost of the struggle to restore the full Catholicity of the English Church, which could not be achieved on the foundation provided by the "miserable sin" and Zwinglian language of the Reformation.[103] Thus, with Pusey's *Letter to the Archbishop of Canterbury*, the religious movement that had commenced by exalting the authority of bishops and their possession of exclusive channels of grace resorted to publicly chastising them while simultaneously admitting that the pursuit of Catholic truth would lead some people to Rome. Consistent with both the tone and content of the earliest tracts was Pusey's denunciation of evangelical religion now presented as much as an internal as external danger to the Church of England and as a danger present at the highest levels of that institution.

CHAPTER 9

In Schism with All Christendom

LTHOUGH FROM 1833 onward evangelical and nonevangelical
commentators hurled epithets of *popish, papist,* and *Romish* at the
Tractarians, other no less hostile observers refused to embrace that
tempting Protestant–Roman Catholic binary opposition in their analysis of
the movement unleashed by *Tracts for the Times.* They saw a different category of religious behavior at work, that of schism. For example, during the
Tract 90 controversy of March 1841, the *Morning Herald* declared,

> However paradoxical it may at first appear, schism is the very essence and
> element of Puseyism. . . . Ask the papist what *he* thinks of Puseyism. He will
> tell you it is but another variation of Protestantism . . . that it is a protest
> against Protestantism—a schism within a schism—a schismatic attempt to
> maim the true church—a base, cowardly, counterfeit Catholicism. Ask the
> Protestant what *he* thinks of Puseyism. He will tell you it is a schismatical
> project to divide the followers of the reformation—that it apes Popery,
> without acknowledging the Pope—that it professes Protestantism without
> adherence to its doctrines—that it seeks to *unchurch all the Calvinistic and
> Lutheran Churches*—that it is in a state of schism with all Protestants, and is
> in a state of schism both with the Greek and Roman Churches.

The *Morning Herald* concluded its diatribe by relegating the situation of the
Tractarians to that of "a state of schism with the whole Christian world."[1]

The same day the *Morning Chronicle,* also pointing to Tractarian isolation, described Newman as "one who could make up his mind to live the
life of an anchoret." That spring Whately wrote privately of "the Tractite
Schism." The *Christian Observer* in 1842 described the Tractarians as "the
sect of the Ninety Articles." The same year the *Standard* denounced "the

Tractarian *schism*" and during the next wrote of "the *dissenting sect*" who had borrowed their name from Pusey. By 1844 Baden Powell, in the *British and Foreign Review*, criticized Tractarianism as "this Protestant Catholicism," "the pseudo-Catholics among ourselves," "reformed Catholicism," and "English Protestants who disclaim that title, and style themselves Anglo-Catholics." The Roman Catholic *Dublin Review*, which was particularly attuned to the peculiar position of the Tractarians, decried them as manifesting "the presumption of modern schism, that pretends alliance with ancient Catholicity."[2]

To join these early Victorian commentators in recognizing the Tractarians' schismatic character permits the historian to perceive their similarity to the Irvingites, such Oxford seceders as Bulteel, the Plymouth Brethren, the splintering Methodist connections, and the Scottish Free Church, with which those observers compared them.[3] Considered in this broader contemporary religious context, the Tractarians appear as an unsuccessful, short-lived, self-imploding schism constructed around Catholic devotion and sacramentalism, personal asceticism, monastic life, and Newman's uncertain personality.

ELIJAH IN THE WILDERNESS

On December 1, 1841, exploring his increasingly difficult position in the Church of England, Newman admitted to Samuel Rickards that he had been for two years in "a state of great uneasiness," owing to the consciousness that his opinions "went far beyond what had been customary in the English Church." Fearing that he himself might, while remaining in Oxford, become a "sort of schismatist or demagogue supporting a party against the religious authorities of the place," he told Rickards that he had "many schemes floating" in his mind about how to extricate himself from the status of "a teacher setting himself up against authority," a condition he thought "most odious." After supposing that "(if it may be said reverently) our Saviour bore this Cross as others," Newman stated that the Hebdomadal Board censure, the Bishop of Chester's charge, and the Jerusalem bishopric had "in great measure taken away that delicacy towards authorities which hitherto has been so painfully harassing to me." Because he now regarded the Board as "not defending the English Church, but virtually and practically . . . joining with this heretical spirit and supporting *it*," he thought the issue no longer one of "a quasi-Romanism against Anglicanism, but of Catholicism against heresy."[4]

This letter set the terms of Newman's future engagement with the English Church. The true faith of Catholicism must stand against an ever-rising tide of evangelical heresy. This characterization of the current struggle was not a casual reference. Newman, throughout the day on which he wrote Rickards, had been laboring on his edition of Athanasius's writings, a task that would continue for several years. In *The Arians of the Fourth Century* Newman had drawn direct parallels between the ancient Arians and modern Protestant evangelicals. That parallel now more directly than ever seemed to manifest itself in and give shape to his own experience. But Newman remained unsure what models drawn from Christian history and biblical narrative would best furnish a model for his own action. Already in 1840 he had considered St. Meletius from the early church, as well as the Nonjurors and various eighteenth-century Methodists. He also continued to contemplate St. Athanasius, the greatest ancient foe of heresy. But during late 1841 and for sometime thereafter, it was the prophet Elijah that most appealed to Newman's by then highly combative imagination.

None of Newman's models for behavior in the face of heresy provided an example of a person leaving one religious affiliation for another; that is to say, none provided a model pointing to conversion to Roman Catholicism. Newman fully recognized numerous alternatives lying between full commitment to either Canterbury or Rome that would not require him to exchange the one for the other, but he was not eager to follow any of them precipitously. In late 1841 some people thought Newman might retrace the path of the Nonjurors, but he specifically rejected that alternative, in part because on some occasions he actually believed that, as demonstrated by his agreement with Bagot, "every year adds to the strength of true principles in the Church."[5]

Although beginning not later than 1839, Newman behaved as a potential seceder, there is virtually no evidence that he intended to leave the Church of England or genuinely wished to enter the Roman Catholic Church, even in 1845. Considerable evidence points to the contrary on both scores. Newman told Dodsworth in early 1842, "It is a strange thing to me, that no one can speak of *facts as they are* [in the English Church], but he is supposed *at once* to be leaping into the Church of Rome."[6] Indeed Newman personally made every possible effort *not* to convert. He also counseled others such as Oakeley and Thomas Mozley against passing to Rome, deplored those who like R. W. Sibthorp and William Lockhart did so precipitously, and repeatedly discouraged or disowned efforts such as Bloxam's to work toward union or serious cooperation with the Roman Catholic Church. Neither Newman nor most of the other major Tractarian leaders wanted to move into the social wasteland of early-Victorian English Roman Catholicism with all its Irish associations at the cost of their present or future clerical livings, college fellowships, professorships, or other possible emoluments, as well as their social standing and positions of influence.

The problem of retaining Catholics in the English Church was largely one of Newman's own making. As he entered middle age, Newman had extended himself to a circle of vulnerable, enthusiastic young men of some-times uncertain and unstable late-adolescent personality. He responded to their loneliness and isolation as a solution to his own. The situation puzzled and disturbed not only high churchmen and his bishop but also his family. On November 30, 1841, Harriett, after surveying those comrades for whom John had provided "perfectly unsound, childish and pettish" arguments in *Tract 90,* complained to Jemima, "These certain friends are impetuous undisciplined spirits, impatient and restless—and why is the whole thinking world to be sacrificed for a few such?" Ironically, only a day later, J. D. Dalgairns, one of those "certain friends," more or less agreed, when he praised Newman's "wonderful love for all men" and particularly his ten-dency "to love persons the better the wilder and younger they are" and asserted that he "alone for a moment can hold things together."[7] Newman very much chose his own circle of anxious followers, with his energies and theirs mutually feeding off each other.

Newman's vehicle for nurturing the affection of his curious, often emo-tionally vulnerable, coterie had been the pursuit of the Catholic, which he had personally assured them could find a home in the English Church. By the close of 1841 events in both the church and university had cast increas-ing doubt on that assurance. Newman had to devise new tactics to hold his group in the church and thereby near himself. Attempting once more to redefine the role of Catholics in the world of contemporary religious life, he prepared a series of four sermons delivered in late November and early December 1841. Whereas *Tract 90* had explained why Catholics could in good conscience remain in the Church of England, Newman's four sermons at the end of 1841 attempted to demonstrate why they must remain despite all of that institution's now obvious shortcomings and recent open engage-ment with foreign heretics through the Jerusalem bishopric.

In these sermons, somewhat revised for publication in late 1843, New-man paradoxically grounded his personal understanding of the Catholic faith and Church Catholic in an internal subjectivity that resonated with the evan-gelical faith of his youth and late adolescence, though avoiding the typical evangelical appeal to the authority of Scripture. Outlining the foundations of what effectively constituted a Catholic antinomianism, he explained,

> If religion be a personal matter, its reasons also should be personal. Wherever it is present, in the world or in the heart, it produces an effect, and that effect is its evidence. When we view it as set up in the world, it has its external proofs, when as set up in our hearts, it has its internal. . . . Nay, with some little limitation and explanation it might be said, that the very fact of a religion taking root within us, is a proof, so far, that it is true. If it were not true, it would not take root. Religious men have, in their own religiousness, an evidence of the truth of their religion. That religion is true which has power, and so far as it has power; nothing but what is Divine can renew the heart. . . . And in this sense the presence of religion in us is its own evidence.

In thus commending a Catholic sense of assurance experienced from "inward effects," Newman carried to its logical conclusion the subjective redefinition of truth, first explored in his university sermons of the late 1830s.[8] He here asserted a religion of the inner self, lacking fixed authorities, save a subjective sense of its own power. Religious truth resided within the self rather than in Scripture, nature, or even the much-vaunted Tractarian tradition. Newman thus defined religion so as to unleash the exercise not only of private judgment but also of private will.

Like the leader of almost any gathered Christian congregation, Newman appealed to the intensity of Catholics' personal, subjective religious feelings and aspirations as denoting the presence of Christ, and thus also as manifesting the presence of the true church within the Church of England, despite the failure of the English Church to realize fully a Catholic devotional and liturgical life. Urging the recognition of the truth present in the English Church as demonstrated through this subjective experience of Christ's presence, Newman declared, "How great a blessing is it, my brethren, at all times, but especially in an age like this, that the tokens of Christ are not only without us, but more properly within us!" On the authority of that internal sense, Newman told Catholics, "We will cling to the Church in which we are, not for its own sake, but because we humbly trust that Christ is in it; and while He is in it, we will abide in it. He shall leave before we do." Newman contended that "at a time like this, when the public notes of the Church shine so faintly and feebly among us," Christians must look to "those truer and more precious tokens" that functioned inwardly to indicate God's presence. Echoing his remarks of 1840 about the age of Wesley and Whitfield, Newman announced, "The Church of God is under eclipse among us." In such an era, "What really and practically attaches any one to the Church, is not any outward display of magnificence or greatness, but the experience of her benefits upon himself."[9] Catholics could presumably continue to experience those spiritual benefits within the Tractarian devotional circles of the English Church. Newman left unsaid that in addition to those spiritual benefits still available in a few select places in the Church of England, that institution also afforded external benefits of livings, fellowships, and other avenues for income, employment, and advancement.

For Catholics doubtful about the adequacy of the Church of England, Newman erected a high, near impassable, barrier against leaving it, which in fact for his close friends meant leaving the confines of his personal ministry and religious influence. He recognized only two reasons for departing the religious communion into which one had been born: first, "some clear indisputable command of God to leave it," or, second, "some plain experience that God does not acknowledge it."[10] These conditions loomed even more starkly when he published these sermons in late 1843 after having resigned St. Mary's. On both occasions Newman was attempting to hold Catholics in the English Church and thus under his personal dominance by denying them the right to leave and by portraying an unreformed Roman Church as providing no solution to their difficulties. If Newman's coterie were to be Catholics, they would be so in his sphere of influence where the true church resided.

Yet Newman realized that he could not retain Catholics or secure his own ministry simply by carrying on business as usual. Consequently, though he had long asserted the ecclesiastical authority of episcopally ordained priests, by the close of 1841 he had himself begun to undertake a prophetic ministry, often associated with radical Protestantism. But it was a complexly constricted prophetic ministry that on the one hand rejected existing church authority and on the other resisted the impulse to radical reconstruction. In a sermon of December 12, 1841, entitled "Elijah the Prophet of the Latter Days," Newman articulated a vision of a modestly reformist religious community dwelling apart from institutions of official religion. He observed that Elijah "was not in communion with the Church of Moses in his lifetime, did not worship at the Temple," a fact that might comfort both Dissenting religious bodies and those English Catholics "who, though not without the Apostolical line and the possession of the Sacraments, are separated from the great body of the Church." Teaching and preaching when Israel had allowed the religion of Moses to fall into great corruption, "Elijah and Elisha, and their brethren, acquiesce in the disorders which surround them; and rather strive to make the best of things as they are, than to bring back a rule of religion which had passed away." Suggesting the limitations he set for his own actions, Newman explained that God, having for the moment dispensed with his laws, had not appointed Elijah to restore them. Rather, God had raised up Elijah "for a certain definite work, and for that alone, neither more nor less." Elijah had been God's instrument for executing "the Divine sentence upon Baal's priests" and for anointing "Jehu for the same work," but he "did no more; to this his mission was limited."[11] Elijah had attempted not to restore the Temple, but to reform the Israelites as he found them.

Newman confessed that he found all of this strange but had to admit that, for whatever reason, "Elijah and Elisha kept the people shut up under that system . . . in which they found them, and sought rather to teach them their duty, than to restore to them their privileges." They and other prophets had rested content with the partial mission of preaching the Ten Commandments rather than enforcing ecclesiastical duties. Yet those prophets had been divine instruments in preserving a remnant and thus proving that there was indeed a prophet in Israel. The contemporary lesson provided by those prophets was "to be patient, to pray, and to wait."[12]

Throughout his sermons of the next two years, Newman cast himself into the role of a prophet of the last days pronouncing judgments on the Church of England as its authorities pronounced judgment against him. Appealing to contemporary apocalyptic sensibilities, he repeatedly resorted to such phrases as "these latter times," "these latter days, which are days of the Gospel, though they be degenerate," "in this fallen time," and "this disordered dreary time, when the heaven above us is so dark, and its stars so hidden." Yet Newman did not move beyond the limits of action he had established in his initial sermon on Elijah. Such a restricted mission, Newman had then admitted, might well surprise modern Christians who thought nothing done until it was fully completed. Nonetheless, he explained, God worked according to his own, not human, understanding as he raised up prophets and gifted them "with miraculous power, to do a half work; not to heal the division of the kingdoms, but to destroy idolatry; not to restore outward unity, but to repress inward unbelief; not to retrace the steps of the wanderers, but to keep them from wandering still further." This mode of identification with Elijah and the last days served both to validate and to constrict Newman's own mission to the nurturing of a separatist monastic enclave at Littlemore. On December 13, the day after preaching the first sermon on Elijah, Newman told S. F. Wood, "I am content to be with Moses in the desert—or with Elijah excommunicated from the Temple."[13] As a prophet dwelling in the last days, Newman would attempt to preserve a saving Catholic remnant living apart from any corrupt contemporary ecclesiastical institutions, whether English or Roman. The embrace of Elijah and his delimited mission may very well suggest a fantasy on Newman's part of concluding his own ministry by relinquishing further responsibility for change, escaping present attacks and personal confusion, avoiding unpalatable choices, and, like the ancient prophet, eventually finding his life divinely validated by being miraculously carried away from the conflict, turmoil, and anger that filled him from within and confronted him from without. Or in his self-identification with Elijah, Newman may have pondered some kind of apocalyptic vindication of his life and work suggested by the words of the prophet Malachi, "Lo, I will send you the prophet Elijah before the great and terrible day of the Lord comes."

Newman understood that to retain Catholics for the English Church and within the influence of his now prophetic ministry, he must provide them with a place for worship, devotion, and community secure from the ecclesiastical authorities. In terms of the categories of the last days that increasingly dominated his thought, he must provide a refuge for Catholic truth against the advance of evangelical heresy penetrating the Church of England. To that end, in early 1842 he resurrected his project for a monastery, which, as he indicated to Pusey, he had temporarily abandoned the previous summer. He intended to overcome public criticism and possible internal Tractarian hesitancy by portraying his monastery as the solution to the Catholic restlessness about which high churchmen had been complaining. Early in January Newman wrote to Hope, again employing the alarmist rhetoric of the previous November, "I am almost in despair of keeping men together. The only possible way is a monastery. Men want an outlet for their devotional and penitential feelings—and if we do not grant it, to a dead certainty they will go where they can find it. This is the beginning and end of the matter. Yet the clamour is so great, and will be so much greater, that if I persist, I expect (though I am not speaking from anything that has *occurred*) that I shall be stopped. Not that I have any intention of doing more at present than laying the foundation of what may be."[14] In the midst of expanding evangelical heresy by now equated with all Protestant religion, Littlemore in the fashion he had described in *The Church of the Fathers* would function as a monastic haven for Catholic truth. Newman may have feared authorities would seek to stop him, but must have concluded on the ground of his previous experience with Bagot that they would not dare. Newman would function as the Elijah of Littlemore.

THE ASCETIC IMPERATIVE

After the turn of the twentieth century, the eleventh edition of the *Encyclopaedia Britannica* noted, "Few phenomena are more striking than the change that has come over educated Protestant opinion in its estimate of monasticism."[15] In the English-speaking world the short-lived Littlemore monastic community marked a major milestone in that transformation of cultural sensibilities. At Littlemore certain Protestants of the Church of England, calling themselves Catholics and rebelling against modern evangelical religion, reclaimed the benefits of a private monastic devotional setting, such as that from which Luther had himself commenced his own journey. This Tractarian monastic departure almost necessarily assumed the face of a religious schism, as in typical Protestant fashion one small, not firmly constituted congregation split off from a larger body. That schismatic behavior did not necessarily mean, however, that those who wished to pursue a conventual life also wished to pass to the Roman Catholic communion, no matter how much the two were associated in popular opinion.

In founding Littlemore, Newman was doing nothing less than establishing a conventicle of the Church Catholic where men might safely engage in advanced Catholic devotion and communal fellowship. Although as early as September 1841 Newman described himself as "an incipient monk, in my noviciate at the least," he formally established his residence at Littlemore only on April 19, 1842, having his books and other scholarly materials transported there.[16] Newman did not choose a life of isolation. He remained an Oriel fellow, frequenting the college on occasion and maintaining connections with younger fellows. Indeed, Peel withheld patronage from Hawkins for fear that Newman might be elected as his successor. There is no indication that Newman entertained such a possibility, being no doubt convinced that Hawkins's determination to defeat the Tractarians far outweighed any ecclesiastical ambition on his part.

Newman's activities at Littlemore stirred controversy well before he took up residence. In mid-December 1841, Jelf, writing to Pusey, had deplored the well-founded rumors of Newman's building structures for conventual life at Littlemore. Regarding that behavior as schismatic, Jelf thought that the time might have come for Newman and his friends to leave the church or at least to deal with these matters honestly with the Bishop of Oxford. The opportunity for such clarification arose in the spring. On April 12, 1842, responding to press commentary, Bishop Bagot inquired directly whether Newman was attempting to revive monastic orders of a Roman type without episcopal authority. Newman told Bagot that for at least thirteen years he had wished to give himself "to a life of greater religious regularity" than he had previously followed. He felt it "very cruel . . . that very sacred matters between me and my conscience are made a public talk." He claimed that he was no more violating the rule of the church than if he married. Although stating that he undertook his present actions for himself alone, Newman admitted, "It would be a great comfort to me to know that God had put it into the hearts of others to pursue their personal edification in the same way." Furthermore, he suggested the resolution to such a life as "most necessary for keeping a certain class of minds firm in their allegiance to our Church." Then carefully using Bagot's own words, Newman flatly denied "attempting a Revival of the Monastic orders, in any thing approaching to the Romanist sense of the term," and reported instead, "I am attempting nothing ecclesiastical, but something personal and private." To be sure, Newman was not reviving Roman orders, but as his correspondence over the past three years demonstrated, he was attempting to found a monastery. Bagot, as in his previous negotiations with Newman, communicated with Archbishop Howley, who instructed him to accept Newman's explanation.[17] There, so far as the exercise of ecclesiastical authority was concerned, matters at Littlemore rested until its dissolution.

Despite its lack of full candor, Newman's response to Bagot was highly revealing. Littlemore was "something personal and private." Just as evangelicalism represented a religion of the public sphere, the Littlemore monastery constituted an early Victorian experiment in the religion of the private sphere. At Littlemore, in contrast to the bombastic meetings, histrionic preaching, and buzzing committee rooms of Exeter Hall, stood a series of low connected sheds where a few men in pursuit of spiritual edification read, prayed, and lived together largely in silence. The organizational model for Littlemore was not modern business life, as with the Bible and Missionary societies, but rather those medieval monastic associations that such contemporary writers as Walter Scott, A. W. Pugin, Thomas Carlyle, and Benjamin Disraeli used as foils against commercial, urban, and industrial culture.

Almost twenty years later Newman recorded in his journal that he understood his function in the Roman Catholic Church to be that of edifying its members rather than making converts.[18] He had first perfected that role among Catholics in the English Church when at Littlemore he provided his own version of spiritual direction to those who came to him for guidance. This self-defined vocation set him apart within both the English and Roman Churches. At midcentury the most dynamic elements of both institutions eagerly pursued converts for either evangelical crusades or Roman Catholic renewal. Personally, emotionally, and religiously Newman could no more eagerly enter the spectacle of Wiseman's reestablishment of the Roman Catholic hierarchy in England or Manning's vast public ministry than he could join the civic enterprises of Lord Shaftesbury. Newman's pursuit of a religion of the private sphere marked his life and nurtured his frustrations in both communions. He pursued neither Catholicism nor Roman Catholicism for the purpose of making converts but rather sought in each the possibility of a conventual life.

As so often when driven by inner personal needs, Newman described himself in his Littlemore community as functioning as an instrument of Providence. He told Henry Wilberforce shortly after sending his explanation to Bagot, "What will, what can, come of my attempt, I do not see, I do not realize. I should say nothing, yet a good Providence has wonderfully guided me on step by step, without my seeing the path before me, that I cannot but think that something will come of it—yet it may be a failure, and *the experience* may [mainly] be the gain that comes of it. I wish I was a hundredth part as sure that I was in God's favor as I am that He is using me as an instrument; but, alas, it is one of the most common spectacles in the history of the Kingdom that those who are profitable to others, do not save their own souls."[19] On any given occasion, the appeal to Providence was the equivalent of Newman's declaring consequences be damned, as in typical Protestant fashion he carried out the impulses of his private judgment. Long determined to establish a setting for monastic devotion and celibate living, he now set about the task regardless of the obstacles, sustained and justified by his conviction that Catholic truth must be protected against the evangelical heresy arising in what might be the last days.

In January 1843, less than a year after Newman moved to Littlemore, Frederick Oakeley explored some of the difficulties confronting the revival of conventual life in a private letter to Francis Kilvert. There Oakeley pointed to what he regarded as the "insuperable difficulty *as yet* in forming any estabt. which shall be at once *ostensibly* monastic and . . . subject to the jurisdiction of our Bps. or other officers of our Church." Such a "desirable" work of ecclesiastical reform could in all likelihood be brought about "by Clergymen who have the means and the will, forming private estabs. of an *essentially* monastic character (so far as to combine the advantages of strict regulation, intimate social union, charitable works, and joint religious offices) under the *sufferance* rather than the direct authority, which might come as other good things have done, to receive in due time episcopal countenance & encouragement." It appeared to Oakeley perfectly possible to create such a voluntary society, which though lacking official sanction would not otherwise lack "the essential character of a monastery altho without its name." He observed that if reports were correct, "this is just what N. has done at L." and that "whatever he has done, be it less or more, is with the *knowledge,* & I conclude with the concurrence, but incidentally the *permission* of the B. of Oxford." But Oakeley thought "the docility, the unquestioning & uncriticising confidingness, the love of monotonous severity," as well as the "unselfishness" of monastic life, appeared "foreign to our English habits" and would require the English to "get rid of all our national & exclusive & party prejudices." It would demand that the English "try & sympathize with the tone of the middle ages, and with the Catholic Church above the world." He feared that "nationality and the monastic spirit are utterly incompatible." Furthermore, he contended, "Catholicism (as distinct from Anglicanism) and much of what we have been accustomed to call Popery or Romanism must be the basis and bond of such an undertaking."[20] Oakeley did not at that moment see the establishment of conventual life requiring Roman Catholic sponsorship. The location for the experiment, even in a mind so highly sympathetic to Rome as Oakeley's, lay on the margins of the English Church.

The question from the beginning was whether those inhabiting the Littlemore community could remain satisfied in that marginal setting. Many years later William Lockhart, then a Roman Catholic priest, recalled of those living at Littlemore, "We had a sincere desire to remain in the Church of England if we could be satisfied that in doing so we were members of the world-wide visible community of Christianity which was of Apostolic origin." Therein from its inception lay the nub of the inherent instability of Littlemore. Newman had unleashed among his Catholic followers two distinct forces functioning in tension with each other: the pursuit of asceticism and the desire for Catholicity. The former dominated Newman's mind; the latter ultimately, as events unfolded, the minds of his followers. As John Keble observed privately in 1844, "The unhappy circumstance in our present position is that so many of those who are ascetically inclined are also more or less perplexed on that other subject, so that there is danger of their asceticism forcing them out of our Communion, instead of their infecting it with their asceticism."[21] Littlemore became a satisfactory center for the ascetic life, but not, at the end of the day, for the achievement of Catholicity.

Yet for three and a half years Littlemore became the new center for Tractarian Catholicism, capturing the imagination and temporary loyalties of those for whom Newman labored to provide a possible life in the English Church. During late 1841 his friends referred to Littlemore variously as "the embryo monastery," "*the cottages,*" and "the *Union* workhouse." Newman himself by March 1842 described the establishment as "a half College half monastery." At Littlemore, in addition to a Catholic refuge in heretical times, Newman both created a quasi-family setting, in which he was the dominant elder brother, and founded his own college, where he presided over the high table and finally served as the chief tutor. For the satisfaction of those ends, he was willing to undergo the harassment of such people as Benjamin Symons, evangelical Warden of Wadham, who rode out to look at the monastery only to have Newman slam the door in his face, declaring, "We have here no monasteries."[22] Newman did not want to leave the English Church, but he did want to slam the door of his private religious sphere against the intrusions of what he increasingly regarded as heretical ecclesiastical authorities.

The *Morning Chronicle* opined in January 1842, when news of Newman's monastic venture was spreading, "The youth of Oxford will shrink from entering on the cold path of fasting and monastic celibacy, when lit by no hope of preferment at the end."[23] Yet by late spring a few men began to arrive, including John Dobree Dalgairns, William Lockhart, Mark Pattison, James Anthony Froude, F. S. Bowles, Richard Stanton, Albany Christie, Robert Ashton Coffin, and Ambrose St. John. All were younger and standing in various degrees of religious and emotional unsettlement. Some visited, some stayed a few days, others remained for longer periods. As the *Morning Chronicle* had anticipated, none, with the exception of Pattison, Froude, and Dalgairns, proved to be of exceptional ability, and none was at the time recognized as having such ability. Certainly no man of real ambition in the Church of England, nor in all likelihood anyone with immediately good prospects in the university, was about to associate himself with Newman and Littlemore celibacy.

Dalgairns, for whom Littlemore provided a place to think through his decision about taking Holy Orders, described the setting in January 1842, as "nothing but a place where men who have no fellowships may come and read under Newman's inspection, and with his library, which is an excellent one." Because of the excess rooms, "any country parson who likes to retire there for a season will be welcome." Littlemore might serve to receive, he explained, the "individual panting for something higher than he sees about him, who incurs the temptation of playing all sorts of pranks from mere restlessness and craving." Dalgairns insisted that Newman himself was not going over to Rome and that, despite "his deep sense of the wretched state into which the Church has fallen," remained "wonderfully cheerful" in his view "of the designs of Providence in stirring up this Catholic spirit amongst us." Although Newman refused to be treated as a superior, a stance that would seem only to have raised him in the estimation of his community, Oakeley reported a year later that the young men living at Littlemore "look up to him with a veneration which stands in the place of a law of obedience" required in a formal monastic setting. It was about this time that Ward described Newman as his "Pope."[24]

Pattison left a diary account of his two-week sojourn at Littlemore in October 1843, during which he was very clearly confused and depressed. One day he confided to his journal, "How low, mean, selfish, my mind has been to-day; all my good seeds vanished; groveling, sensual, animalish; I am not indeed worthy to come under this roof."[25] Later he complained of the intense fasting and noted that an anonymous benefactor sent the group a goose. He recorded much discussion of patristic theology, miracles, Irish and continental Roman Catholic devotional practices, and university politics. He and others took solitary walks, spent time in prayer, and broke the general silence only for simple daily necessities. Pattison also reported Newman's reminiscing about Hawkins's halting the Oriel tutorial revision and his illness in Sicily in 1833, as well as expressing concern for the Church of England, which Pattison took to indicate Newman's sense of its hopelessness. That observation contrasted with Dalgairns's of more than a year earlier and reflected the genuine shift that had occurred in Newman's mood during 1843.

The buildings of Littlemore were exceedingly modest, with low ceilings and bare rooms. In 1842 there were only a few structures, with rooms for men to live simply, to study alone, to worship, and to undertake communal devotions drawn from Roman Catholic practices. By the summer of 1843, pursuing larger designs for the Littlemore monastery, Newman was "fitting up a room for a *temporary* oratory," with curtains hung round it and with light only from candles. He was concerned about the proper color for the curtains, which were red, and inquired about the appropriateness of "a quasi-altar." When he finally completed the space, it had a South American crucifix on the altar. Certain of the rooms were decorated with Roman

PRIORY

CHURCH

SCHOOL

THROUGH OXFORD TO OSCOTT

9. Newman formally established his residence at Littlemore in the spring of 1842. Hostile evangelicals saw his monastery as a halfway house on the way to Roman Catholicism. This etching of the early 1840s describes Littlemore as "The Newman-ooth College," referring to the Irish Roman Catholic Seminary of Maynooth. The sign at the left reads "Through Oxford to Oscott," Oscott being the Roman Catholic institution over which Bishop Wiseman presided. (Reproduced with the kind permission of Oscott College, Birmingham.)

Catholic devotional prints. He also continued to contemplate more elaborate decoration of the Littlemore village chapel itself—which until the conversions of 1845 the community used for evensong and communion—that would include granite, possibly with alabaster and gilding on the altar. Although any slight devotional decoration of the chapel had long aroused commentary in Oxford, at no point were Newman's plans nearly so elaborate as those of Pusey at Saint Saviour's, Leeds, or of later ritualists. Only by the standards of low Protestantism was the decoration or devotion of Littlemore, whether the monastery or the village chapel, complex or intricate. Father Dominic, who received Newman into the Roman Church, later reported, "A Capuchin monastery would appear a great palace when compared with Littlemore."[26]

Littlemore communal life and devotional activities matched the austerity of the physical surroundings. In December 1841 Dalgairns had noted, "In point of asceticism I take it, that it will be very shady [sic]; each man has to be left to himself." The next month he reported that Newman intended "to establish some sort of rule there in time, whether strict or not he does not himself know, but will be guided by circumstances." On April 25, 1842, Newman confided in Henry Wilberforce, "We are a small household here, small indeed—but we have begun the Breviary Service here this morning. . . . Do not tell, please, *any* one, what we are doing; it would be sure to be misinterpreted." The community arose to recite the Breviary at midnight; matins came at six in the morning. Initially, these services were said not in a chapel but rather in what Dalgairns described as "a most unchapel-like room" because the inhabitants regarded themselves as "only embryo-monks." Most of the day was simply spent in study, with silence observed except during the brief meals. Dalgairns understood the silence as "really the whole mystery of our pseudo-monastery."[27] The members of the community practiced confession and frequent communion. Further services and prayers by those in residence were added during Lent and Advent. No accusations of breach of confidentiality regarding any of these Littlemore confessions is recorded, whereas Pattison claimed that in one instance Pusey had breached confessional confidentiality.

Beginning with Newman's first observation of Lent there in 1839, significant and sometimes severe fasting marked that part of the Littlemore liturgical year. In addition to a restricted diet supplemented with quinine pills, Newman refrained from wearing gloves and for a time attempted to sleep on the floor, a practice that he eventually abandoned. Once a community had been established, fasting appears to have been virtually an obsession among the Littlemore men, for whom "the most austere religious orders of Eastern and Western Christendom" served as the model.[28] The fast was not broken ordinarily until noon and not until five o'clock during Advent and Lent. Dr. John Wooten, the physician who looked after the Littlemore group, was deeply concerned about their health, and for good reason: some people who under Tractarian influence had previously undertaken unregulated fasting had become seriously ill, and one apparently had died. The first meal of the day was dry toast and tea. At dinner there was salt-fish and a pudding. When meat was served, those who partook of it were refused tea morning and evening. Although Pusey had made fasting one of the hallmarks of Tractarian devotion, he appears to have had little relationship to Littlemore and instead pursued his own personal ascetic rigors within his Christ Church residence.

The attraction of the starkly ascetic vision of Tractarian Catholicism has been underestimated as one of the powerful imperatives of the movement. Thomas Arnold had noted this fascination as early as 1836, telling Whately, "The truth is, that a religious Exterior, fasting, etc. has been so long out of fashion, that the Scribe & Pharisee Character now takes people by Surprise, and they are as much deceived by it as they were in the Beginnings of Puritan Times." As if illustrating Arnold's observation, Ward wrote Pusey in July 1841 that Froude's *Remains* had "delighted" him "more than any book of the kind I ever read," not only because of Froude's criticism of the English Reformation and "his sympathy for the rest of Christendom" but also because of "his great strictness." Later the same year, writing in the *British Critic,* Ward criticized Arnold in contrast to Froude, for displaying lax discipline by ignoring fasting and the hidden life of a Christian and for being attracted *"by the vision of good conduct in the many than of eminent holiness in the few."* That Tractarian pursuit of individual personal holiness at Littlemore led Dalgairns in October 1844, with Newman's approval and on behalf of "several persons among us . . . anxious to lead a more mortified life," to ask Father Dominic Barberi to procure for them "shirts or girdles of haircloth," as well as for one person "a discipline, such as ordinary persons use." Dalgairns assured the priest that Newman's presence as a spiritual guide meant that he "need not fear their being indiscreetly used."[29]

Ward and other advanced Tractarians steadfastly distanced themselves from the potential aestheticism of both Catholicism and Roman Catholicism, displaying, for example, no particularly warm feelings toward either the Gothic revival or highly ritualized worship or liturgy. Newman himself had once scribbled in his diary, "The reaction from UltraProtestantism *need* not be to Catholicism, but to ritualism." In a similar vein sharply distinguishing aestheticism from asceticism, Ward in 1843 declared, "Men may join the Catholic side, not from the stirrings of their conscience, but from their aesthetical perceptions; and in so far as they have done so, will be among our most dangerous enemies, while within our very camp and contending externally on our own side. They will seek for converts not where they see strict and wary conscientiousness (which we must never forget is the *real* germ of Catholicism), but where there is a kindred taste for external beauty." To the extent that the beauty of holiness was genuinely allied to personal holiness itself through subservience to the creed and a desire for piety, it was a positive good, but "apart from these it . . . becomes a hollow unsubstantial profane mockery." Also in 1843 Oakeley similarly emphasized the ascetic core of late Tractarian Catholicism, writing, "Greater calamity for the world, we repeat, there could be none, than that Catholic sentiment, or Catholic *effect*, should ever come to be divorced from Catholic strictness."[30] To that end, Oakeley urged a revival of confession, though he also believed that it should be introduced gradually.

From 1842 onward Newman's sermons exhibited an ever-growing ascetic rigorism that spilled over into a critique of the spiritual solace offered by Catholicism itself. In January he denounced those ministers who had recently arisen "speaking heresy, making much of the free grace of the Gospel, but denying that it enjoined a work, as well as conferred a blessing; or, rather, that it gave grace in order that it might enjoin a work." In May, preaching on "Indulgence in Religious Privileges," he criticized the present age for loving "an exclusively cheerful religion" and for determining "to make religion bright and sunny, and joyous, whatever be the form of it which it adopts." The age consequently would not allow itself to drink deeply from the well of Catholic truth—"the deep well, the abyss of God's judgments and God's mercies." Newman, however, deplored not only the ease of evangelical doctrine but also "the luxuries of devotion" associated with the Catholic faith itself, including weekly communions for which "men in general, such as we are, even religious persons" were not fit. Advocating reserve in offering the eucharist that paralleled reserve in preaching the atonement, he argued that worshipers required "a more real understanding of what sin is, and the consequences of sin, a more practical and self-denying rule of conduct, before such a blessed usage will be safely extended among our congregations."[31] Here, as if out of a deep misanthropic anger, Newman preached against the very Catholic religious devotion that had drawn many to the Catholic faith.

In the same sermon, Newman directed toward religious feelings evoked by Catholic devotion the very criticism that for more than a decade he had hurled against evangelical preaching and theology. He told those who had received emotional sustenance from Catholic worship, "Nothing lasts, nothing keeps incorrupt and pure, which comes of mere feeling; feelings die like spring-flowers, and are fit only to be cast into the oven. Persons thus circumstanced will find their religion fail them in time; a revulsion of mind will ensue. They will feel a violent distaste for what pleased them before, a sickness and weariness of mind; or even an enmity towards it; or a great disappointment; or a confusion and perplexity and despondence. They have learned to think religion easier than it is, themselves better than they are; they have drunk their good wine instead of keeping it; and this is the consequence."[32] Newman thus rejected for himself and most certainly for others the comfort afforded by Catholicism if it actually relieved its adherents of a profound sense of personal sin and provided even a modest sense of inner personal assurance. His public and private statements of this moral rigorism indicate less that he thought such forgiveness theologically impossible than that he feared that any substantial subjective sense of personal forgiveness would prove illusory, being vanquished by recurring inner reproaches of sinfulness and unworthiness.

In so powerfully reciting how effervescent religious feelings must necessarily quickly give way to perplexity, confusion, and despondency and eventually to revulsion against the experience itself, Newman was offering an autobiographical confession. By at least 1840 Newman was no longer certain what he really believed, and not only on matters of the Catholicity of the English Church. At the core of Newman's doubt lay not the question of England or Rome but rather that of what faith really could undergird his life. In April 1847, more than a year and a half after having entered the Roman Church and shortly before receiving its ordination, he penned in Latin a personal meditation that provides a glimpse into the interiority of his mind during the Littlemore years and suggests why so many contemporaries thought he was leading men toward skepticism. Although displaying in this meditation a meek, even self-effacing, tone that might be expected on such an occasion, Newman also expressed a sense of profound disillusionment not only with the Church of England but more generally with his experience of evangelical religious faith and with the Catholic faith that had followed.

Writing in Rome itself, Newman recalled that while growing up he had possessed "confidence and hope in God," which allowed him to commit himself "without anxiety to His Providence" and to possess "the greatest faith in the efficacy of prayer."[33] But as over the years he had applied his "intellect to sacred subjects," he recorded having "lost" his "natural and inborn faith" as well as his "simple confidence in the word of God."[34] He complained, "That subtle and delicate vigour of faith has become dulled in me, and remains so to this day." There then followed what Newman regarded as an even more serious experience, as he had "for some years fallen into a kind of despair and a gloomy state of mind" and had then also "fallen away from hope." The faith that had proved insufficient to him was, of course, that of his evangelical youth, based largely on feeling, even if not extravagant emotion, and the authority of Scripture.

Newman continued by recalling the "many detractors," the "mass of calumny," and the misrepresentation he had encountered in the English Church. Within that institution he claimed for a time to have become "an exile in a solitude," not even finding among friends safety from curiosity seekers. Although he had not given way to "anger, indignation, or the like," he had been "oppressed and lost hope." Under those spiritual circumstances he had retreated to Littlemore, where he had pursued new religious beliefs and practices infused with Catholic spiritual rigorism and self-denial. Of the Littlemore community Newman commented, "When I lived in my retreat with certain others, seeking a way of life, we were accustomed to observe many things which are proper to Catholics,—fasts, meditations, retreats, the use of the Breviary, and other practices belonging to the ecclesiastical, or rather to the religious life." Those had, he claimed in 1847, despite other contemporary comments to the contrary, satisfied him while he pursued them as a Protestant, but on the eve of his new ordination Newman recounted, "Now I undergo a reaction, as they say, and have not the courage to continue those things which I did willingly in the Anglican Church." In the midst of that reaction he found himself "always languid in contemplation of divine things, like a man walking with his feet bound together."[35]

This memorandum, along with modulations of despair and apocalypticism in his sermons of the early 1840s, invites the historian to analyze Newman's personal religious development from the mid-1820s through his conversion in terms of the well-known pattern of Victorian loss of evangelical faith. Indeed, his 1847 meditation reads as a quintessential statement of such loss of faith, with the sensitivity of beliefs of childhood and adolescence becoming dulled by the experience, associations, study, and maturity of adulthood. From the late 1820s through the mid-1840s Newman took one step after another not toward the Roman Catholic Church but rather away from the evangelical faith that as an adolescent he had first encountered through Walter Mayers and subsequently nurtured throughout his under-graduate experience. Over the years he lost confidence in and then de-nounced one element after another of that evangelical religion—the theol-ogy of justification by faith alone, the validation of personal faith through internal feeling or conversion experience, the authority of the Bible, the dominance of a preaching ministry, and the concept of the invisible church, as well as the entire apparatus of the evangelical crusade for spreading vital religion through the society. John Newman's path from evangelical religion through varieties of high-church theology to Catholicism to Catholic mo-nasticism to the Roman Catholic communion itself displayed the same in-determinacy that one finds in his brother Francis's passage from estab-lishment evangelicalism through the Plymouth Brethren to Unitarianism recounted in *Phases of Faith* (1850).

Another element in John Newman's loss of evangelical faith also fits the familiar cultural template of a profound moral repugnance with evangelical theology, followed by an emphasis on strict personal morality. Many of the early- and mid-Victorians who left orthodox Protestant Christianity re-belled against what they regarded as the moral inadequacy of the doctrine of the atonement, which with its image of God's sacrifice of his perfect son they saw at odds with progressive contemporary secular morality. But to affirm their own moral commitment, English religious doubters from the 1830s through the agnostics of the late century consistently compensated for their rejection of orthodoxy by leading personal lives of relatively strict morality. Late in the century, Nietzsche acutely quipped, "In England one must rehabilitate oneself after every little emancipation from theology by showing in a veritably awe-inspiring manner what a moral fanatic one is. That is the penance they pay there."[36]

In rejecting evangelicalism, Victorian Protestants had to demonstrate that they had not changed their religion to relieve themselves of the morality that evangelicalism had so firmly embedded in the culture. Newman's quar-rel with evangelical theology followed this pattern, even though unlike the more widely recognized doubters he was moving toward a more highly defined and articulated set of religious beliefs and practices. Because of what he regarded as its promise of easy salvation, Newman found the evangelical doctrine of the atonement morally lax, a failure he also long projected onto elements of unreformed Roman Catholicism. For a time he rejected the spiritual adequacy of both communions. During those months and years of intense ecclesiastical doubt, Newman, no less than an honest doubter moving toward liberal Protestantism or some indeterminate spiritual religion, demonstrated the sincerity of his commitment to a religious outlook at odds with evangelicalism by undertaking an extremely strict moral life involving celibacy, physical self-denial, and a highly regulated daily routine, first on his own and then within the Littlemore community. In that respect, Newman's personal moral rigorism fit, and indeed exceeded, the classic compensatory pattern for the Victorian doubter or unbeliever.

MONASTICISM, HOMOSEXUALITY, AND CELIBACY

One final parallel between Newman and more formally recognized Victorian unbelievers requires comment. Certain of the latter, such as Marian Evans and John Stuart Mill, entered upon irregular domestic relationships, despite which they functioned as widely respected and even revered public moralists. During his religious journey from evangelicalism to Roman Catholicism, Newman embarked on the equally unusual living arrangement of an all-male monastic community. Although realizing a monastic life challenged contemporary norms of family and domesticity, he nonetheless claimed in his April 1842 letter to Bishop Bagot that his personal experiment in conventual living at Littlemore should be no more a matter for public comment than marriage. For a time his detractors thought otherwise, but eventually the asceticism of Littlemore and moral regularity of the Birmingham Oratory earned Newman a grudging respect. Despite his culturally peculiar monasticism, Newman, like Evans and Mill, became one of the late Victorian moral sages, already as an elderly monk long before he was a cardinal, and ironically more often a sage to the Protestant world he had departed than to the Roman Catholic world he inhabited.

Yet ever since the publication of Geoffrey Faber's *Oxford Apostles* (1933), the question of the relationship of Newman's sexuality to the Tractarian Movement has concerned some scholars. The possibility of homosexual or homoerotic affinities between Newman and those living at Littlemore may even have crossed Harriett Mozley's mind when in May 1842, reporting to Jemima after her own visit there, she described Dalgairns, then their brother's only "companion," as "a modest looking blushing youth, all the *men* again talking of his beauty and fine eyes," though she "thought him nothing but a boy, with no harm about him and particularly cleanly looking!"[37] Endless speculation about Newman's sexuality is possible, with the evidence being at best indecisive and the question not firmly resolvable. Commencing in adolescence Newman dwelled in communities of unmarried men that generally excluded women, first as a student, then as a fellow of Oriel, later as proprietor of Littlemore, and finally as head of the Birmingham Oratory, as well as for brief periods in other Roman Catholic settings. His relationships with women occurred within his family, through occasional though often important correspondence, and in conjunction with a few Roman Catholic activities. Generally speaking, however, as much as seeking the company of men, Newman consistently avoided that of women. In the *Apologia* he recounted that he had decided upon a single life at a relatively early age and had confirmed that decision in 1829, but gave no significant reasons.[38] What the decision meant, particularly as he associated it with a virgin life, was that he rejected domesticity, as understood by most of his contemporaries, and thus avoided sexual contact and relations with women. His consequent articulated embrace of celibacy made a virtue of his aversion to women.

Over the years a number of Newman's clerical friends who did not share this aversion encountered his anger and even petulance. From the mid-1820s onward, Newman became troubled, angered, or disappointed over clerical friends' marriages, including those of Hawkins, Pusey, Robert Wilberforce, and George Ryder. Isaac Williams recalled "the great annoyance" Newman "always felt at John Keble's marriage." Each marriage disrupted the sense of personal stability of community and bonds of emotional intimacy and sometimes dependence that he had cultivated in Oriel or among the informal fraternity of Apostolicals. Once the publication of the tracts commenced, an event simultaneous with the appearance of his first "Church of the Fathers" articles championing ancient monasticism, Newman equated marriage by Tractarian colleagues with inadequate commitment to both the larger cause and affectionate deference to himself. At the time Thomas Mozley married Harriett Newman, her brother wrote Christie, "You must not fancy about Mozley—at the same time be sure of this, that every one when he marries is a lost man—a clean good for nothing—I should not be surprised to be told that Mozley would not write another letter all his life." Newman persisted in this outlook telling Dalgairns in 1843 that marriage "reconciles one to any amount of intellectual inconsistency." Indeed the only marriage that Newman while in the English Church seems not to have resented was that of the nonclerical Bowden, his oldest friend from undergraduate days, who after his wedding, Newman remembered, would "call me Elizabeth and her Newman."[39]

Newman encountered enormous difficulty in sharing with a woman the affections of another man, particularly if that man was ordained. In his world, affection was a matter of all or nothing. In early 1834 the news of Henry Wilberforce's engagement occasioned particular pique on Newman's part and the composition of an unsent letter that is the single piece of evidence from his years in the English Church that might point toward latent homoerotic yearnings, but may also have had other origins. Addressing Wilberforce in that unposted letter, Newman wrote,

> You surely are inconsiderate—you ask me to give my heart, when you give yours to another—and because I will not promise to do so, then you augur all sorts of illtreatment towards you from me—Now I do not like to speak of myself, but in selfdefence I must say, it is a little hard for a friend to separate himself from familiarity with me (which he has a perfect right, and perhaps lies under a duty to do,) and then to say, "Love me as closely, give me your familiar heart as you did, though I have parted with mine." Be quite sure that I shall be free to love you, far more than you will me—but I cannot, as a prudent man, forget what is due to my own comfort and independence as not to look to my own resources, make my own mind my wife, and anticipate and provide against that loss of friends which the fashion of the age makes inevitable. This is all I have done and said with respect to you—I have done it towards all my friends, as expecting they will part from me, except the one, who is at Barbados. . . . You knew very little of me, if you think I do not feel at times much the despondence of solitariness. . . . Why must I give my heart to those who will not (naturally, it would be a bad bargain for them,) take charge of it? . . . My dear H.—you have really hurt me—you have *made* a *difficulty* in the very beginning of our separation. You should have reflected that to remove it, you would not only have to justify it to yourself but to explain it to me.

In part, as alluded to in the closing lines of his letter, Newman's anger stemmed from Wilberforce's not having directly informed him of the upcoming marriage. Wilberforce's anxiety over Newman's anticipated response to the news probably accounted for that failure. Beyond indicating a profound inability to understand love between a man and a woman, Newman's condescending portrayal of marriage to his younger friend as a mere fashion of the age suggests a disgust at sexual intimacy between husbands and wives, as did his near contemporaneous offhand reference to the Dissenters' demand for reform of marriage law as a desire for "lawful concubinage."[40] Both comments may point equally well to Newman's aversion to women—especially when as wives they interfered with the affection he had already received from a male friend—as to any homosexual orientation on his part.

It is important to note that Newman's hostility to marriage by clerical friends in the Church of England continued during his later Roman Catholic life when he saw women and family ties preventing those men from becoming Roman Catholics. In 1861 he wrote the Duchess of Norfolk, "I see in the papers that [Mark] Pattison is married! sic transit Gloria. He will never come to us." Newman, however, saved his most astonishingly vitriolic remark against a friend's wife for the late Mrs. John Keble, who in 1866 had survived her husband by just over a month. After her death, Newman told Henry Wilberforce, "She suffered a great deal at last; so, Keble was spared a great deal. When I found she was surviving, it struck me (I trust it is a really charitable thought) that she was to be kept awhile to do penance for having kept Keble from being a Catholic."[41] This last comment more than anything else Newman ever wrote demonstrates the deep and lasting resentment he felt toward his male friends who chose marriage and family over affection for himself and toward the women who had become the new object of their love and affection.

While Newman remained in the English Church, marriage by younger friends, often former students or close religious confidants whose lives Newman for a time dominated, may also have aroused anger for another reason. Those marriages often repeated the pattern first experienced with his younger brothers of Newman's extending love and personal commitment to persons who thus became dependent on him, but who then eventually achieved independence. One of the few marriages to which Newman could reconcile himself was that in 1836 of Thomas Mozley to his sister Harriett. There he thought the marriage would draw Mozley closer, telling Bowden, "I never can approve of a fellow like Mozley marrying—but if it must be, it is a great happiness to find him brought nearer to me by his offence against monastic rule."[42] Thus in his own imagination Newman saw the marriage drawing Mozley as much into greater intimacy with himself as with his bride. And indeed, the new familial relationship allowed Newman to nurture Mozley's emotional dependency and to retain much of the direction of the *British Critic* once Mozley became editor. He had similarly taken advantage of Wilberforce's anxieties in persuading him to write the hostile pamphlet against Hampden during the subscription controversy of 1834.

There is no question that by the mid-1830s Newman looked to his younger male friends, rather than to women, for support and would flatter them with affectionate language. Late in 1839 Frederic Rogers rejected Newman's proffered dedication of *The Church of the Fathers* on the grounds that its language was too intimate and might be misunderstood outside Oxford, commenting, "If I knew the 'dearest, sweetest, etc' was to be contained in those two little volumes I should never be able to see their very backs without colouring up to the eyes."[43] Yet over the years all of Newman's comments about love and affection for men are just that—remarks about love and affection with no hint of sexual relation or contact, which he consistently sought to avoid.

The real issue for Newman was an unfulfilled desire for emotional intimacy. On March 25, 1840, while observing an ascetic Lent at Littlemore, Newman completed an account of his illness in Sicily, in the midst of which he lamented the absence of anyone in his life who might take "an affectionate interest" in him, though he thought Henry Wilberforce might have fulfilled that role. He then concluded, "This is the sort of interest which a wife takes and none but she—it is a woman's interest—and that interest, so be it, shall never be taken in me. Never, so be it, will I be other than God has found me. All my habits for years, my tendencies, are toward celibacy. I could not take that interest in this world which marriage requires. I am too disgusted with this world—And, above all, call it what one will, I have a repugnance to a clergyman's marrying. I do not say it is not lawful—I cannot deny the right—but, whether prejudice or not, it shocks me." A few weeks later Newman suggested to a correspondent that the conclusion of celibacy being "a holier state than matrimony" followed "from the words of the Article 'concupiscence has the nature of sin' " and from the text "In sin hath my mother conceived me."[44] Avoiding "interest in this world" actually allowed Newman to eschew marriage to a woman and its concomitant sexuality. Asserting his particular "repugnance to a clergyman's marrying" gave a higher vocational purpose to his own resolution to celibacy, which, as indicated by the second comment, stood rooted in his disgust at sexual relations and his equation of the conception of human life with sin.

Another factor may also have been at work in Newman's thinking about celibacy and marriage. His avoiding marriage because the institution required an "interest in this world" may have arisen from doubts about his own ability to make his way in the world after having witnessed his father's worldly financial difficulties and the emotional pain, social dislocation, and economic deprivation they had caused his family. His own loss of the income and status accruing from the Oriel tutorship must have impressed on him the fragility of worldly success. In the years immediately after his tutorial work ended and before his mother's death and sisters' marriages, he was extremely short of money. Similarly, Newman's desire for someone to take "an affectionate interest" in him may have reflected an unfulfilled longing for both parental love and the kind of love and aid that he had so steadily provided his brothers, sisters, and aunt without having received what he regarded as sufficient affection and appreciation in return. In both respects, it is by no means clear that Newman ever achieved that level of adult emotional development and personal confidence required for a committed relationship of love or sexuality with either a man or a woman.

Newman's consistent attack on feeling and subjectivity in religion may well have reflected a larger discomfort with his own subjective thoughts, feelings, fantasies, and yearnings sexual and otherwise. The imperative of his sermons pointed toward enormous self-control and asceticism. As he wrote Miss Holmes in 1843, "You are overflowing with feeling and impulse; all these must be restrained, ruled, brought under, converted into principles and habits or elements of character."[45] The very perfectionism of his moral theology and his rejection of preaching what he regarded as a gospel of easy salvation may have been informed by his own subjective fears of how his own unruly inner self might be unleashed without a more demanding gospel message. Newman, as well as other Tractarians, in particular Pusey, feared that a gospel message of ready forgiveness and assurance might open the way for unspoken sins. All of these inner feelings so clearly distrusted by Newman could just as well have been heterosexual as homosexual, or they may have just as much related to fears about his aggressiveness and anger as well as his sexuality.

Pusey had addressed the issue of celibacy in his *Letter to the Bishop of Oxford* of 1839, written during his wife's last illness. There and elsewhere his comments indicate more nearly asceticism toward heterosexual relations rather than any homoerotic tendency. Addressing the bishop, Pusey stated that while the tracts had not taught celibacy, parish work in great industrial cities might require a celibate clergy. While praising marriage, he noted that since the fall in Eden, marriage had produced tainted offspring. Scripture and the primitive church taught a preference for celibacy as a higher state than marriage, and the corruption of Rome lay not in "its *preference* [for priestly celibacy], but its tyrannical and ensnaring and voracious *enforcement*." Yet Pusey at the same time demanded, "Why thus decry and revile as Popish what is Primitive? Why should not celibacy be used by those to whom it is given, to bind men's affections the more firmly to their Lord, instead of to Rome?"[46] Pusey also advocated the creation of orders of celibate sisters, which would become his major personal cause during the next decade. He saw sisterhoods as memorializing his daughter Lucy, who had died in early adolescence and who had indicated to her father, no doubt with his encouragement, her hope for a celibate life. There was, however, an important difference between Newman and Pusey. Although Pusey had become deeply suspicious about sexuality, he displayed no aversion to women. Indeed, through the sisterhoods and women drawn to his mode of spirituality, he found ways to let his religious concerns foster interaction with female company.

Richard Church was a young Oriel fellow and close Newman friend of the early 1840s. In his influential account of the Tractarian Movement, Church described the celibate ideal that seized Newman's coterie as "in the highest degree a religious and romantic one," and recalled a man's shrinking from it as marking, among that group, a "want of strength or intelligence, of an unmanly preference for English home life, of insensibility to the generous devotion and purity of the saints." He also noted, "The hold which it had on the leader of the movement made itself felt, though little was directly said." Church's remarks indicate both the manner in which, as late-twentieth-century scholars have noted, Tractarian celibacy represented one of the transforming modalities of Victorian masculinity and how Newman's own commitment to a celibate life accounted for part of his powerful attraction. Rather than suggesting weakness or effeminacy, clerical celibacy and monasticism appeared to some people as the embodiment of masculine discipline. In this regard, as one scholar has argued, Tractarianism represented "an early and profoundly influential example of the authorization of a dissident masculinity through a conjoint appeal to tradition and to a solidarity manifested through an ostentatious regimen of ascetic discipline."[47]

A complicated, triangular exchange of letters from October 1840 indicates something of what celibacy had come to mean to Newman and advanced Catholics after his decision to undertake his "monastic scheme." Late that month rumors circulated around Oxford that F. W. Faber was to be married. J. B. Morris, Pusey's assistant in teaching Hebrew and one of Newman's more extravagant associates, immediately composed an extraordinary letter to Faber on marriage, family, and celibacy. In reading Morris's letter, it is important to remember that the Prayer Book of the day enjoined persons not to undertake marriage "unadvisedly, lightly, or wantonly, to satisfy men's carnal lusts and appetites, like brute beasts having no understanding," and described marriage as "ordained for a remedy against sin, and to avoid fornication" on the part of "such persons as have not the gift to continency." Morris told Faber, while still believing that he might be about to marry,

High and holy as the joys of Matrimony may be, we surely want in these
days people not entangled in the world as the married are. . . . Those of
certain lustful temperaments have perhaps more excuse, if they find discipline will not crush and break such feelings. Yet short of this, there are
certain softnesses and endearments, which the rude soldier of Him who had
not where to lay His Head were well to try hard too [sic] break of by
abridging his diet, diminishing his sleep, by hard lying, and other stern-
nesses such as are painful, that I say not excruciating postures in prayer. If
Celibacy be an excellent gift, it is one which we *ought* to covet earnestly, and
we do not covet earnestly what we are not bold to toil after in pain and
weariness and fasting and *per*vigilia. And he that endureth in this course to
the end, shall be saved from Matrimony and all its specious holinesses.

Turning to the manner in which his views of celibacy worked themselves
out in his own life, Morris commented,

The sense of past sin, thought [sic] never issued in a day's utter forgetfulness of God, so far as I remember, yet is too great in me to allow me in my
better times ever to entertain long hopes of matrimony, though they have
cost me a violent struggle. . . . What has penance to do with the softnesses of
the marriage bed; or how can Divine wrath be warded off, if we set ourselves in the midst of continual allurements to be easy and comfortable? I
much doubt if there is a woman in England who would not think me stark
mad for taking up the miserable pittance of penance which I do. It is
literally a pittance, no more. I will say nothing of laying up treasures upon
earth which the married are under a strong temptation to do—a sinner
needs all that he can get to buy off God's wrath by alms to His Son's
members, not by household expences.

The phrase "sense of past sin" echoed Pusey's own 1835 letter to his wife
in which he regretted the passion he had felt for her before their marriage
and which he could no longer recall "without the solemn memory of past
sinfulness."[48]

Morris for his part directly advised Faber that if there existed in him
"beginnings of love" or "little sallies of affectionateness," to "break them
off ere too late." Urging him to "consider the miserable and distracted
state of the Church, literally prostrate," Morris stated, "Saint or sinner
ought hardly in such times to marry; when the Bridegroom seems, if ever, to
have left us, what have we to do with Brides?" Then in words that would
have confirmed the worst evangelical suspicions about Pusey's emphasis on
postbaptismal sin, Morris declared, "You may marry as you know without
any dereliction of principles, that is, if since Baptism you have never forsaken God. But if grievous sins, especially if sins issuing in a rebellious *habit*

of mind of long continuance ever possessed you, I for one do not see how consistently with Catholic principles and with the Judgment and its searching fire before you, you can let yourself settle into the comfortableness of married life. Two days without food would often bring us to our senses." Morris himself had found "hard lying and diminishing of drink and sleep" to be "the great preservatives."[49] He thus directly related fasting and asceticism to repression of sexuality, an attitude that he may well have acquired from Pusey, whose own ascetic extravagances had commenced as tragedy struck his life after marriage and family. The same sensibilities would have found confirmation for Morris and others in the pages of Froude's *Remains*, as well as in Newman's ascetic observation of Lent.

Faber, forwarding Morris's letter to Newman and reporting no immediate matrimonial prospects, recounted his own personal loneliness arising from his parents' early deaths, as well as his hope that marriage, in addition to his writing poetry, might eventually provide an outlet for his emotions. Newman replied that there would be nothing wrong in Faber's marrying but advised him to keep Morris's letter and think about it a year later. Describing the letter as "one of overpowering moral force" and making "one feel little," Newman indicated agreement with Morris's "principles heartily in the abstract, especially to his principal view, of celibacy as a penance for past sin." Although considering celibacy "a more holy state," Newman could not urge that view strongly upon others, it "being so much a matter of feeling." Then he added that in regard to celibacy as penance, "I could urge it strongly, did I know on whom to urge it."[50]

A tangle of motives, sensibilities, experiences, and proclivities reinforcing and confusing each other informs these remarks on marriage and celibacy. All of these men had spent much of their lives in exclusively male Oxford settings, where only the heads of the colleges could marry while residing in the university. Tractarian language about marriage in some cases suggests a real, if possibly unconscious, misogyny, which relegated marriage primarily to a sexual union, with little or no part of it embracing love, affection, mutual support, or care through the passages of life. In other cases, their attitudes indicate a genuine desire for all of the emotional comforts of marriage but a deep fear or repugnance about sexuality, which they equate with sinfulness and in so equating explain away. But in all cases, the issue appears more nearly one of aversion to women and sex rather than one of attraction to relationships with other men.

In addition to their comments on celibacy, from the mid-1820s through the mid-1840s another factor that may cast light on Tractarian sexuality appears and reappears. That is the issue of food. Froude wrestled with fasting as a young man, and to a lesser extent so did Newman. In the years before the tracts, Newman organized his university dining club around modest meals. When Newman made his personal retreat to Littlemore in 1839, he observed a strict Lent in regard to his food, as he did in subsequent years. Once he established his community at Littlemore, its members adopted extreme practices of fasting that disturbed their sympathizers. Pusey, for reasons we have explored, became virtually fanatical over the matter of fasting.[51] Morris's letter to Faber indicates a preoccupation with fasting as a means to repress sexuality. In each instance, fasting served as a device to exert self-control over sexual feelings, substituted thoughts about desire for food for those about desire for sex, and simultaneously fulfilled duties of penance.

There have been relatively few studies of male anorexia and other male eating disorders because the problem is so much more prevalent among young women than young men. Furthermore, there exists at this time no strong consensus within the medical community about the causes and character of male anorexia. Nor are the linkages between fasting and anorexia certain; each could lead to the other, or fasting could serve to rationalize anorexia. Nonetheless, the limited body of medical literature suggests that male eating disorders may well be associated with men having no sexual experience, or homosexual men, or men encountering some conflict over sexual orientation.[52] Other characteristics of the men associated with Littlemore, including evidence of depression and perfectionism, are also linked to eating disorders.

The tempered conclusions that may be drawn from such literature in regard to the late Tractarians and Littlemore are modest but suggestive. Several of the persons drawn to Newman, as well as Newman himself, clearly appear at that moment in their lives to have been more comfortable in an exclusively male community, where women touched their lives only on the margins. Moreover, most of them appear to have embraced various kinds of perfectionism, especially moral perfectionism, in their personal behavior. In some cases this characteristic was a permanent feature of their personalities; in others temporary. Although there is no evidence of open homosexual orientation, some of the Newman coterie may well have been latently homosexual. Others may simply not have been able or willing at that point in their lives to engage in either close personal or sexual relationships with women. Still others may have temporarily embraced celibacy and life in an all-male community for reasons of religious conviction or vocation, but then have come to believe those convictions and vocations compatible with marriage. Still others remained celibate for their entire lives.

Whatever the motives, sensibilities, and sexual orientations at work among the late Tractarians in regard to celibacy, their rejection and denigration of marriage and family and their yearning for monasticism both set them apart from the wider English Church and directly challenged evangelical moral theology. Of all the institutions to which evangelicals looked for the nurturing of Christians, none was more important or fundamental than the home. One evangelical crusade after another, such as those against slavery or intemperance, battled forces that disrupted the family and their vision of Christian domesticity. The home, not a monastery, provided the evangelical safe haven within which to communicate the Christian faith so that the next generation might go forth into the world as witnesses and soldiers of Christ. The Tractarians quite simply rejected that outlook.

The issue of sexuality and celibacy in relation to Newman and the late Tractarians requires one additional comment. A number of Newman's most bitter enemies in his later life as a Roman Catholic may well have been reacting in a delayed sense to what they had come to regard as his misguided views on these subjects and his possible earlier manipulation of their own lives and sexuality. It is well known and has been frequently observed that Charles Kingsley loathed Newman and Tractarianism in general because he had for a time been attracted to celibacy and because his wife as a young woman before their sexually joyous marriage had almost entered an Anglican sisterhood. There are other similar cases within Newman's own Littlemore coterie. Among those who remained in the Church of England both Pattison and J. A. Froude had been drawn to asceticism. Both later married and wrote harshly of their experiences with Newman and Tractarianism. As Roman Catholic converts, Ward and Faber came to have long-standing antagonistic relationships to Newman. Ward was Newman's closest young associate during the early 1840s, had deeply imbibed Froudean asceticism, and championed religious rigorism in his Tractarian writings. He married in 1845 and with his wife entered the Roman Catholic Church, having rejected Newman's ideal of penitential celibacy and then embraced genuine religious devotion as compatible with marriage. Faber continued while in the English Church to admire Newman and to be deeply interested in the subject of saintly virginity.[53] But it is by no means certain that Faber's understanding of celibacy was Newman's. Indeed, Faber's own experience of celibacy as a positive element in the vocation of a Roman Catholic priest, rather than as a penance for past sin as expounded by Morris and Newman, may have occasioned as much of his later antagonism toward Newman as did the experience of marriage on the part of other former Tractarians. Indeed, Faber's famous hymn with the lines "There is a wideness in God's mercy, like the wideness of the sea" may indicate just how different was his view of divine love and forgiveness from that of Newman and from the latter's concept of penitential celibacy. What united all these figures was an eventual powerfully emotional rejection of the utter joylessness and relentlessly self-condemnatory character of Newman's religious vision into which they had for a time been drawn. Either within or outside marriage, they had rejected the body-hating, misogynist elements of Tractarian celibacy.

THE BISHOPS AND THE QUESTION OF HONESTY

In the months following Newman's move to Littlemore the bishops of the Church of England issued a second round of critical charges. It is impossible to overemphasize the importance of the episcopal charges of 1842 and 1843 for the rest of Newman's career in the English Church. Theologically these charges, which he did not discuss in the *Apologia*, while often praising early Tractarian motives, firmly reasserted the fundamentally Protestant character of the English Church and sharply criticized the murky quality of the Tractarians' understanding of the Catholic and their disparagement of preaching the atonement and justification by faith alone.[54] Even more important, these charges uncompromisingly and explicitly accused Newman of dishonesty in *Tract 90*.

According to the bishops, Tractarian Catholicism fostered doctrinal vagueness, devotional superstition, and ecclesiastical insubordination. A consensus existed among the bishops that the Tractarians had pursued what Bishop Bagot termed "that shadowy Catholicism, which under the aspect represented by them, has never existed except in their own imaginations." Edward Denison, Bishop of Salisbury, in whose diocese Thomas Mozley resided, denounced the *British Critic* contributors as arrogant men, "fixing their critic's chain in the wide regions of Catholicism, from it boldly and irreverently to examine, to question, and censure, if they do not finally condemn, that Church to which they owe, and in general terms, profess to pay, loving obedience, and filial respect." Denison urged his clergy "to cleave to Catholic truth, without arrogating to yourselves any distinctive title as doing so." Thomas Musgrave of Hereford accused Tractarians of constructing a Catholic tradition through "garbled and disingenuous quotation" from the great Anglican divines. In 1843 Christopher Bethell of Bangor complained of "the phantom of a system" which the Tractarians "call Catholic, and hold up to admiration as something infinitely superior to the imperfect and lifeless Catholicism of our own Church." He could discern no "clear or definite notion of the system which they admire" nor draw "any precise line between Catholic truths and traditions, and Uncatholic errors and corruptions or doctrine and discipline."[55]

The Tractarian pursuit of the Catholic, according to Edward Copleston, Bishop of Llandaff and former Provost of Oriel, fostered a "hankering" after Roman Catholic ritual and formularies that "tend to mislead the ignorant into gross idolatry." He suggested that the Tractarian critique of the supposedly insufficient devotional life of the English Church arose "more from the indulgence of a morbid feeling in religious matters—a feeling which, when supported by ability and learning and a reputation for sanctity, is highly contagious, than from any reasonable cause of dissatisfaction." Although "rash teachers" among the tract party did attempt "here and there to protest against certain Popish corruptions," they nonetheless led their disciples "to the very confines of that treacherous ground," sought "to make its boundaries less distinct and perceptible," and appeared "intent upon smoothing the way and affording facilities for passing on from our own side to the other." Bishop Blomfield similarly condemned sympathy for devotions associated with the Roman Church, which had "forsaken the true faith, and defiled herself with superstition and idolatry." He pointed out that prayers for the dead, triune immersion at baptism, the kiss of peace in the eucharist, and the mixing of water with the wine might be ancient practices, but they were not recognized by the Church of England. He reminded his clergy that their ecclesiastical model was not the early church but rather "the Church of England, as she speaks in plain and obvious cases by her Rubrics and Canons, and doubtful and undecided ones by her Bishops."[56]

James T. O'Brien, the evangelical Bishop of Ossory in Ireland, in a nearly three-hundred-page charge, which Gladstone regarded as the most effective critique ever offered of Tractarianism, criticized the potential for "a good deal of insubordination in a 'witness to Catholic views,' " as set forth in Froude's *Remains*. O'Brien noted, "When once this principle of the paramount duty of obedience to the Catholic Church had released a man from subjection to the authorities which God has set over him, talk of this kind, we know, would never be wanting to justify all that his own notions of Catholic views, or the notions of whatever little party, living or dead, he had chosen as the interpreter of the Catholic Church, might require him to do or say. And so we might be prepared to see as the result of the principle, a great deal of self-will and presumption, under the guise of humility and submission."[57] By claiming primary loyalty to a Church Catholic, the Tractarians could voice the harshest criticism of the inadequacies of an English Church in bondage to the state. At the same time, as Catholics within the national church, they could assume a no less hostile stance toward Dissenters.

The effort to define doctrine from primitive Catholic sources other than revealed Scripture troubled Connop Thirlwall, the great historian of ancient Greece and liberal Bishop of St. David's, who issued a moderate charge, partially sympathetic to the Tractarians and distinctly critical of evangelicals. Thirlwall found little inherent fault with Newman's basic principle of interpreting the Articles in a Catholic sense. He did, however, with Ward and Oakeley in mind, regret restatements of that principle "which the writer's language does not warrant" and which permitted one to reject the "obvious, literal, and grammatical sense" of the Articles and "to substitute another more conformable to his own preconceived notion of Catholic doctrine." Thirlwall also found Newman's application of his own principle "excessively refined and artificial," justifying the sensation of surprise and alarm" that had greeted *Tract 90* even in friendly quarters. Thirlwall specifically denounced "as manifest error" Newman's distinction between Romish practices and the Tridentine decrees. He also directly condemned Newman's effort to expand the area of liberty for private religious belief, explaining, "On subjects, as to which nothing can be known to us but by revelation, it cannot be altogether innocent, or safe, to adopt, even as a matter of private belief, any doctrine which has not been revealed. It is either a presumptuous abuse of our mental faculties, or it is suffering ourselves to be *beguiled* by others, who have rashly and vainly *intruded into those things which they have not seen*. It diverts the mind from the contemplation of certain and useful truths: it tends directly to introduce superstitious practice."[58] In particular, Thirlwall argued that prayers for the dead were not a matter of liberty.

Thirlwall thought the criticism overblown of the Tractarian understanding of reserve, atonement, and justification, stating that the dispute over justification was "one of words, involving no real difference of opinion," and that consequently he looked "upon both parties as in this respect equally orthodox." Other evangelical and nonevangelical bishops, however, thought differently. Urging the forceful preaching of the atonement, Blomfield declared, "I cannot conceive that any teaching, in which it does not occupy a prominent and conspicuous place, can be effectual in *turning the hearts of the disobedient to the wisdom of the just*." Blomfield, of course, received support from such evangelical bishops as Musgrave, who considered the recommendation of reserve as taking "an unwarrantable liberty with the Word and purposes of God," most particularly with Christ's command that the apostles preach the Gospel. If in modern as in apostolic times the atonement proved a stumbling block and foolishness then, Musgrave urged, all the more reason for "pointing at once to the cross of Christ as their only refuge, and stay, and safety." In *The Kingdom of Christ Delineated* of 1842, Whately also sharply condemned the practice of reserve because "by expunging or suppressing at pleasure, that which remains may become totally different from what the religion would have been if exhibited as a whole."[59]

O'Brien also emphasized that the most important role of the clergy was preaching. "It is in the pulpit," he wrote, perhaps drawing upon Sumner's *Apostolic Preaching*, "that a minister appears most distinctly and impressively in his office as *God's ambassador*." Condemning Williams's arguments for reserve as a "mass of sophistry and misrepresentation and confusion," O'Brien accused the Tractarians of having "either passed over in silence, or brought forward to be misrepresented, or disparaged, or explained away, or opposed" in their publications "the great doctrine of justification by Faith only" and consequently having filled members of the Church of England "with an uneasy craving for something more catholic and primitive than they enjoyed in its communion." Similarly, in 1843 Bishop John Kaye of Lincoln, a patristic scholar of high-church outlook, objected that the Tractarian view of justification caused "men to lose sight of Christ, as the Author, the Continuer, the Finisher of their Justification; and to place their reliance on their own works and deservings."[60]

In addition to voicing theological objections to Tractarianism, the episcopal charges of 1842 and 1843 repeatedly and scathingly questioned Newman's personal sincerity and honesty in a fashion that haunted him, as well as other Tractarians, all the rest of their days. Evangelicals had long decried the honesty of the Tractarians, but the guttersniping character of the *Record* had undermined the broader impact of those accusations. Yet there had been similar private criticisms from nonevangelicals. Even before *Tract 90* some persons once close to Newman, such as Benjamin Harrison, thought him disingenuous. Thomas Arnold in 1841, after the publication of *Tract 90*, wrote Archibald Tait that Newman's position conscientiously fostered among the Tractarians a profound confusion "far more objectionable morally than theologically" because of its "utter Perversion of Language . . . according to which a Man may subscribe to an Article when he holds the

very opposite opinions;—believing what it denies, and denying what it affirms." Richard Whately, for whom the Tractarians constituted a "rapidly
spreading pestilence" that was "truly formidable to genuine Christianity,"
decried what he termed "the double doctrine" whereby they expressed one
meaning in public and another in private. Complaining about other Tractarian tactics, he told one correspondent, "Their policy is, to obtain for each
tract whatever influence it may derive, not only from its intrinsic merits, but
from its being part of a series coming out under the sanction of a certain
committee or whatever it may be called (which is quite fair); but then (which
is quite unfair), if the tract be refuted or objected to, to disown it, as 'the
work of a very young man,' for which no one is at all responsible but the
individual author, and our judgment of which is not at all to affect the
general character of the tracts. Now this may be called 'playing fast and
loose.' " In 1843 Whately exclaimed to Hawkins, "It is a thing which makes
me every now & then feel as if I were in a dream, to find people going on
believing men who *proclaim* themselves liars."[61] From the spring of 1842,
however, such denunciations had thundered publicly across the theological
spectrum of the episcopal bench, with Newman being branded as an essentially dishonest person. Thereafter, well before his conversion, he became a
stranger in his own land. It was these accusations of dishonesty in the
argument and intent of *Tract 90* that Newman did not really address in the
Apologia.

In many respects the early-Victorian Church of England still embodied
characteristics of seventeenth-century European culture, within which, according to Steven Shapin, there emerged a particular social construction of
truthfulness and untruthfulness. The mode of subscription advanced in
Tract 90 met all the criteria that Shapin has ascribed to the lie as a social
event in early modern culture.[62] The Tractarian ordinand knew that as a
clergyman of the Church of England as well as of the Church Catholic, he
owed respect and truthfulness to his bishop, yet he intended his subscription
to embrace a meaning different from what his bishop, as well as the wider
church community, thought his words conveyed. In this social context of a
face-to-face ecclesiastical culture, the argument of *Tract 90* that theological beliefs need not be straightforwardly enunciated profoundly offended
and contradicted expectations of truthfulness within the daily social inter-
course of gentlemen as well as within commercial and ecclesiastical relations. Thereafter, the Tractarians, as Pusey had immediately feared upon
first reading the tract, were never able to restore a sense of public or ecclesiastical trust. It is not insignificant that more than a decade after *Tract 90*,

when delineating the character of the gentleman in *The Idea of a University*, Newman did not include truthfulness among genteel qualities.

That omission might not have surprised Henry Phillpotts, the redoubtable high-church Bishop of Exeter, who, directly questioning Newman's historical honesty, described the principles of *Tract 90* "most unsound" and its reasoning "sophistical." The Convocation of 1571, according to Phillpotts, had indeed authorized a Catholic interpretation of the Articles, but Catholic not in Newman's sense, which Phillpotts equated with an exercise of private judgment. Phillpotts argued that "whereas the canon shows the plain, and obvious, and grammatical, is also *the* Catholic sense; and the preacher or minister who shall adopt any other sense, as the Catholic, does, in truth, prefer his own private judgment on the point to the declared judgment of the Church synodically assembled—a procedure as uncatholic and schismatical as can be well imagined."[63] Phillpotts, who had previously written on the subject, fervently denied Newman's contention that for chronological reasons the Articles had not been directed against Trent; he noted that many of the Tridentine decrees had been drawn up before the composition of the Articles. Furthermore, following Trent, the Articles had been adopted by the Convocation of 1571 and had received further commendation in 1603.

For other bishops, however, the incapacity for sincerity and honesty in clerical subscription on the part of Newman and supporters of *Tract 90* was the primary issue, not the historical accuracy of its author. The earliest and perhaps most telling of these indictments, because of its understatement, was that of Bishop Bagot. On the surface, his charge of May 1842, which his chaplain Francis Paget helped compose, was a model of balance, with an understanding of Bagot's precise meaning and intention very much depending upon which paragraph a reader decided to concentrate. Although Bagot acknowledged that the Articles had been drawn up more "with a view of including, than of excluding, men of various shades of opinion" and that Calvinist interpreters had exercised much license in regard to those formularies, he nonetheless declared his inability to persuade himself "that any but the plain obvious meaning is the meaning which as members of the Church we are bound to receive" or to reconcile himself to a system of interpretation "so subtle, that by it the Articles may be made to mean anything or nothing."[64]

Bishop Copleston declared that, regarding subscription, *Tract 90* amounted to a "very loose and dangerous doctrine" that might lead to the most serious kind of moral blindness. Pointing to what many at the time considered the central moral objection to Newman's position, Copleston observed, "To speak of the language of the Articles as being capable of two or more senses, and to teach that the subscriber may therefore take them in his own sense, knowing at the same time that the authority which requires his assent understands them in another, is surely a dishonest course— tending to corrupt the conscience, and to destroy all confidence between man and man." Similarly, Bishop Kaye in 1843 rejected the "subtle and refined interpretations" of *Tract 90*, which appeared "inconsistent with Religious sincerity and calculated to deaden the perception of truth in the mind, both of him who puts forth such interpretations, and of them to whom they are addressed."[65] Within the confines of the guarded language of episcopal charges, neither bishop could have more bluntly denounced what he regarded as the Tractarian incapacity for truthfulness.

Bishop O'Brien related the presumed dishonesty of *Tract 90* directly to the view of the Church Catholic espoused in Froude's *Remains*. The alleged incompatibility of simultaneous loyalty to the Church Catholic and the English Church, as suggested in those volumes, had elicited the "startling solution" of *Tract 90*, with its display of "dishonest casuistry" of a Jesuit variety, as well as "a shifting, evasive, and disingenuous sophistry" that allowed the Anglo-Catholics to remain where they were. Although declining "to speculate upon the effects of such views upon the sacredness of the engagements of private life," O'Brien thought it "very plain that they deprive the most solemn engagements, which those who hold them contract with the Church or with the State—at least with our enthralled Church and tyrannical State—of all force and value." On those grounds, O'Brien concluded, "It would seem . . . that there are no declarations which can be framed of belief in a doctrine—however explicit and unreserved they be, and however voluntarily they be made by one who holds what are called 'Catholic views'—which will give any absolute security that he believes the doctrine. His belief of it will, after all, be contingent upon his being able to make out for himself, or by the aid of some one else, that it was held by the Catholic Church." Through *Tract 90* and its broad defense, according to O'Brien, the Tractarians had indicated a readiness to escape "from the fair force of the most solemn and sacred obligations by such sophistry and evasion, such shifts and contrivances as a man could not apply to the very lightest of the engagements of common life, without forfeiting all reputation for integrity and good faith."[66] O'Brien and other bishops questioning the honesty of *Tract 90* as it might affect daily life may have been particularly sensitive to the element of nonperformance of contract in the tract, as well as to the challenge to clerical subscription, because theirs was an episcopal generation deeply engaged in all manner of commercial dealings arising from church extension, expansion of education, economic reform of the church, and extensive church building.

Shortly before the appearance of *Tract 90*, Newman had told Frederic Rogers, "I declare I think it is as rare a thing, candour in controversy, as to be a Saint." The publication of that tract rendered Tractarian candor and honesty deeply problematical within a cultural climate where, as Lionel Trilling once argued, sincerity had become a daily moral imperative. Newman had sought a way to allow clergy to assume the burden of personal sincerity in subscription, but at the cost of sacrificing mutual trust between themselves and their bishops. He had attempted nothing less than to establish a device whereby sets of persons holding really very different and conflicting beliefs could remain together in the Church of England without sincerely or honestly accepting, acknowledging, or approving what each other thought or believed. He was in effect saying that discourse between priests and their bishops was to be a personally privileged discourse, with the former determining without the concurrence of the latter the meaning of promises and commitments exchanged. Newman was encouraging the absence of mutual sincerity between priests and bishops as well as among priests, and he was understood to be doing so at the time. In 1853, pursuing his unrelenting critique of the Tractarians for having taught "openly, through the *Tracts*, one set of opinions, while, in private, they taught another," Whately demanded, "And what limit is there to such insincerity?" Driving home his point, he denounced "the exhibition of this disingenuousness" for being "likely to endanger the faith both of those who are and those who are not, themselves of an honest and open disposition." As people saw "that the sincerity with which a supposed good object is pursued is allowed to excuse insincerity in the means employed . . . all this cannot but tend to disparage Christianity itself . . . in the eyes of the scrupulously honest and guileless, in proportion to their abhorrence of all double dealing."[67]

Tract 90 defended any Catholic clergyman from accusations of violating the terms of his subscription to the Articles—that is, the implicit contract between himself and his ordaining bishop—on the grounds that the cleric had himself privately drawn up the terms of that contract to suit his own religious conscience without necessarily having shared those private terms with the other contracting party. In other words, what appeared to be a *public* agreement between a clergyman and his bishop was actually a *private* contract of the clergyman with himself or with the Church Catholic. In effect Newman had urged Catholic ordinands to make a contract with their bishop that without mutual transparency would allow those clergy according to their own consciences to retain the benefits of ordination while holding their own concealed Catholic convictions. The ordinand and the bishop attached different meanings, though unacknowledged publicly as such, to the language of their contractual agreement, with no independent authority to adjudicate disputes. In other words, according to the thrust of *Tract 90*, no Catholic clergyman could, like Newman's father, stand accused of theological bankruptcy or failure to meet the terms of his ecclesiastical contract because he had himself constructed the terms and was their sole interpreter.

All but an extremely narrow circle of stalwart late Tractarian supporters regarded the reasoning of *Tract 90* as exemplifying principle sacrificed to at best a scantily disguised expediency. Bonamy Price of Rugby stated in the *Edinburgh Review* of 1841 that the arguments in *Tract 90* violated "the cardinal rule for the observance of engagements, that they are to be kept in the sense with which he who gives the promise believes the other to impose it."[68] To do otherwise was to "vitiate the pledge given, and convert it into an instrument of deceit." Newman's passing off "*his interpretation*" of the Articles to comfort scrupulous consciences "as the *genuine sense*" struck Price "as being destructive of public morality, and one of the worst forms of falsehood." The writer propounding such a position stood as "the open enemy of truth," teaching "men to be reckless of what assertions they make . . . provided only verbal sophistry and special pleading may enable them to retain hold of the letter." The author of *Tract 90* and those agreeing with him clearly were not men to be trusted. In 1843 the Congregationalist Henry Rogers stated the issue more succinctly in the same journal, declaring that *Tract 90* "ought by right to be called the 'Act of Perjury made Easy.' "[69]

Newman's perceived rejection of the trust expectations of early Victorian contractual relationships impinged upon an intersection in English life and culture between secular and evangelical values. Evangelical moral theology had long emphasized the necessity of honesty in the act of promising, whether in one's private or commercial conduct. Newman's renunciation within ecclesiastical relationships of that standard of honesty directly repudiated the moral injunctions of Thomas Scott, who had described "the true believer" as "habitually" aiming "to be just and honest in all his dealings" and as "not grasping at gains which custom may have sanctioned, but which accord not with strict probity" nor "taking advantage of any man's ignorance or necessity, to circumvent or exact from him." To be a good

Christian consciously required for Scott the keeping of commercial contracts and other business agreements. As he had further urged, "The Christian cannot consistently trifle with so sacred a matter as truth, for the sake of a jest, an humorous tale, or a compliment; much less to gratify anger, malice, or avarice, or in flattery, slander, or religious controversy. He will aim to avoid all prevarication and equivocal expressions, and whatever has a tendency to deceive; his 'yea will be yea, and his nay, nay': he will study undisguised sincerity, and not, under professions of friendship, raise expectations which he hath no intention or prospect of answering."[70] The relationship of these moral injunctions to commercial life appears reasonably straightforward, but for Scott they were also to obtain in one's religious life. One could not be commercially honest and religiously dishonest or the reverse. A person who would be dishonest in one sphere would be dishonest in the other.

Beyond the rejection of evangelical moral theology, Newman repudiated open contracts and the straightforward keeping of promises at quite possibly the worst historical moment for a figure in English public and religious life to do so. P. A. Atiyah, the historian of contract law, has pointed to the first half of the nineteenth century as "an age of principles," when in one area of thought and endeavor after another a "stress on rule or principle" became a central ideal and the gentleman defined "above all" as "a man of principles." Expediency contrasted with principle, and acts based on expediency appeared throughout the society as morally wrong. Fundamental to this outlook was "the principle of the due observance of promises" among gentlemen, in commercial relations, in social behavior, and as a principle of justice. More specifically, during this period there emerged a legal formalism, which among other things "combined with a tendency to 'literalism,' that is, a refusal to read into the contract anything which the parties had not expressly provided for, and an insistence that implications could only be made when absolutely necessary to make the contract workable."[71]

Simultaneously, there occurred a decline in "the very concept of equity" as "a form of mercy" to be applied in a discretionary sense by courts. Throughout the early and mid-nineteenth century, Atiyah states, "It was widely believed that the chief functions of the law of contract were to encourage people to keep their promises and pay their debts." Much of the case law on the formulation of contracts with an eye to future performance developed only between 1789 and 1830 (almost exactly the years of John Newman's business career) as a result of the legal and commercial disorderliness of the emerging industrial society and the uncertainty of business relationships. The most fundamental point to emerge from these cases was that "contracts must be two-sided exchanges, and not one-sided promises." Furthermore, courts began to rule that a person "who behaved in such a way as to lead another to suppose that he meant one thing was to be treated as though he did mean that thing." As Atiyah has explained, "Lawyers tended increasingly to ignore the reasons for which promises were given, and to assume that promises were always made with a view to creating a binding future commitment."[72] It was just exactly this presumption that Newman in 1841 and his followers in the years immediately thereafter violated.

REDEFINITIONS

The episcopal charges of 1842 eroded still further what little remained of Newman's fragile deference toward ecclesiastical authority. In late September he told Thomas Mozley that there might be "questions on which the Bps word is not law." In "Feasting in Captivity," delivered the same month, Newman announced that the Kingdom of God had "to all appearance broken into fragments," with "authority in abeyance,—separate portions in insurrections,—brother against brother,—truth, not a matter of faith, but of controversy." In the midst of this turmoil "heresies of the most deadly character" worked around and in the English Church, with "error stalking abroad in the light of day and over the length of the land unrebuked, nay, invading high places," while "the maintainers of Christian truth" found themselves "afraid to speak, lest it should offend those to whom it is a duty to defer." The church had abandoned discipline with "the sacraments and ordinances of grace open to those who cannot come without profaning them and getting harm from them" and virtually no thought given to works of penance. Those who mourned over the situation were "looked upon with aversion, because they will not prophesy smooth things and speak peace where there is no peace."[73] Yet in that situation, comparable to the Jewish Babylonian captivity, Christians must be cheerful as Christ himself had been while keeping festivals and rejoicing in the days and weeks before his Passion.

Calling themselves Catholics, Newman contended, constituted for modern Christians the first step in their becoming Catholics truly. In the language of a potential seceder, he exclaimed, "In a word, if we claim to *be* the Church, let us act *like* the Church, and we shall *become* the Church," adding, "Here, as in other matters, to doubt is to fail, to go forward is to succeed." In so moving, however, Catholics must pursue the entire apostolical faith, including both the severe and the beautiful, and not raise "a high superstructure ere they have laid a deep foundation." Presumably referring to high churchmen who criticized asceticism as Romish, Newman decried those Catholics who, like the backsliders of ancient Israel, "scoff at the ascetic life of the Saints as an extravagance or corruption" or "slur over their austerities, as if they were an accident of their religion peculiar to *their* times" and "would live like the world, yet worship like the Angels." Rejecting the current fascination with church architecture and decoration, he implored Catholics to emulate the example of Christ and the apostles, who had enjoyed "no high cathedrals, no decorated altars, no white-robed priests, no choirs for sacred psalmody,—nothing of the order, majesty, and beauty of devotional services" but rather "trials, afflictions, solitariness, contempt, ill-usage." Newman then asked, "If we have only the enjoyment and none of the pain, and they only the pain and none of the enjoyment, in what does our Christianity resemble theirs?"[74] Thus Newman championed the prophetic asceticism of the penitential fasts at Littlemore as the answer to the dangers the world posed to the Catholic faith.

Newman also continued private resistance to evangelical theology. Writing to an unknown correspondent in March 1843, he repeated his longstanding objection to the open preaching of the atonement "when people are *unfit* to receive it." Such preaching, as he had argued so often in the past, should not serve as "the *means of conversion* . . . of those who are *not* religious." Congregations that had lapsed into sin after baptism required the law rather than grace and needed "to be brought to a sense of sin" that the preaching of the atonement would not achieve. Baptism alone stood as the appointed means "*revealed in Scripture* for regeneration." After baptism, "the promises of forgiveness of sin" were to be "regained gradually, with fear and trembling—by repentance, prayer, deprecation, penance, patience." Turning to the eucharist, Newman portrayed the sacrament as "a proper Sacrifice made by the Priest as Christ's *representative.*" He further asserted, "Justification by Faith without the Sacraments is the essence of sectarian and (modern) heretical doctrine."[75] Each of the positions Newman advocated had been condemned by at least one bishop during the past eighteen months.

Newman also resisted one of the evangelicals' favorite religious practices and their claims to a monopoly on genuine Bible-based religion. In "The Apostolical Christian" of February 1843 Newman radically redefined for Catholic purposes the Bible Christian—"that much abused term" by which so many evangelicals identified themselves. "Christians of Scripture," Newman explained, had lost their "taste for this world," with "sweet and bitter being the same." For those Christians, "no barrier, no cloud, no earthly object, interposed" between their souls and their Saviour and Redeemer, but he warned that while the religion of Christians as described by Scripture might have begun "with the heart" and "with the conversion of the heart from earth to heaven, the stripping off and casting away all worldly aims," it did "not end there." Rather among those "whom our Lord's precepts formed," religion "drew up all the faculties of the soul, all the members of the body, to Him who was in their heart." Newman then admonished his congregation and later readers, "Bear to look at the Christianity of the Bible; bear to contemplate the idea of a Christian, traced by inspiration, without gloss, or comment, or tradition of man. . . . Study what a Bible Christian is; be silent over it; pray for grace to comprehend it, to accept it."[76] Newman thus challenged evangelicals to read Scripture in a Catholic manner.

At that point in his sermon, however, in a declaration not heard from English pulpits for hundreds of years, Newman announced, "If the truth must be spoken, what are the humble monk, and the holy nun, and other regulars, as they are called, but Christians after the very pattern given us in Scripture?" Monks and nuns, indelibly associated in the Victorian public mind with superstition, corruption, personal isolation, and celibate rejection of family, suddenly and jarringly emerged as the very embodiment of the much-vaunted Bible Christian. Thus implicitly suggesting that the only real English Bible Christians resided at Littlemore, Newman asked, "What have they done but this,—continue in the world the Christianity of the Bible? Did our Saviour come on earth suddenly, as He will one day visit, in whom would He see the features of the Christians He and His Apostles left behind them, but in them? Who but these give up home and friends, wealth and ease, good name and liberty of will, for the kingdom of heaven?" Admitting that most of his congregation need not so separate themselves from the world, he nonetheless asked them to consider whether or not they might have a duty to pursue such callings. Then turning the evangelical ideal of private judgment to his own Catholic ends, as he had the term Bible Christian, he stated, "It may be your duty to pursue merit. . . . But you cannot tell till you inquire; enough do we hear of private judgment in matters of doctrine; alas! that we will not exercise it where it is to a certain extent allowable and religious; in points, not public and ecclesiastical, and external and independent of ourselves, but personal,—in choice of life, in matters of duty!"[77] Concluding the sermon with what resembled an evangelical call to repentance and conversion, Newman thus invited his congregation to consider for themselves the cloistered life of monks and nuns.

But Newman did not rest with redefining terms of Scripture for the advancement of the Catholic cause. In "Wisdom and Innocence," preached in February 1843, he undertook a series of redefinitions of moral terms whereby he intended to refute the widespread denunciations of Tractarian honesty. By this date he consistently portrayed English Catholics as a small, beleaguered group of faithful Christians surrounded by powerful, destructive forces of evangelical heresy. Their position as a saving remnant dwelling in what might be the last days justified extraordinary means of self-defense, including the resort to guile and craft as devices providentially provided in the divine economy. Throughout "Wisdom and Innocence," the most controversial sermon Newman delivered in the English Church, he cast his bitterly tendentious quarrel with episcopal authority and evangelical religion into the ancient image of the faithful Christian resisting the carnal unbelieving world.[78] Tractarian Catholics in the English Church stood as the latest embodiment of the true church working its way through history, and everyone else in that institution became simply equated with the world. A struggle among Christians within the Church of England thus assumed the features of a battle between true Christians and non-Christian enemies where no holds were barred and no nonviolent weapon forbidden. Newman claimed that actions and statements that might appear dishonest to observers outside the body of Catholic faithful constituted legitimate weapons in the present struggle. Honesty and dishonesty, right and wrong became for Newman largely a matter of one's perspective. In this respect, "Wisdom and Innocence," which presages Nietzsche's critiques of Christianity, constitutes a brilliant defense of hypocrisy, deception, and duplicity in the cause of a self-perceived and self-defined higher good.

From its inception, the church, according to Newman, had like Christ been a lamb or sheep among wolves. The "purer," the "less worldly," the more cultivating of "its proper gifts," and the more refusing to rely "upon sword and bow, chariots and horse, and arm of man" the church had chosen to be, the more did it stand "defenceless" and "exposed to ill-usage." In addition, "the more it has invited oppression, the more it has irritated the proud and powerful."[79] Thus Newman suggested that persecution and ill usage by those in authority, such as the Tractarians were then experiencing, denoted the presence of the true church fulfilling its peaceful, nonviolent character.

Asking what weapons God did allow to "those who are helpless and persecuted, as the Holy Spouse of Christ," Newman responded, "the arms, that is, the arts, of the defenceless." The Creator had compensated weak animals and nonviolent human beings with qualities that allowed them to protect themselves. Nations "destitute of material force" taking "recourse to the arts of the unwarlike" proved "fraudulent and crafty" and would "dissemble, negotiate, procrastinate, evading what they cannot resist, and wearing out what they cannot crush." Those employing such tactics included "captive effeminate" races living "under the rule of the strong and haughty," "slaves," and "ill-used and oppressed children," all of whom "learn to be cowardly and deceitful towards their tyrants," as also did "subjects of a despot" who resisted his authority "with the secret influence of intrigue and conspiracy, the dagger and the poisoned cup." Those downtrodden groups exercised "the unalienable right of self-defence in such methods as they best may; only, since human nature is unscrupulous, guilt or innocence is all the same to them, if it works to their purpose." Although in the Garden of Eden the serpent had been the instrument of temptation, Christ had nonetheless urged his followers to be wise as serpents. Through that injunction, Newman urged, it was as if Christ had appealed "to the whole world of sin, and to the bad arts by which the feeble gain advantages here over the strong," and as if he had thus "set before us the craft, the treachery, the perfidy of the captive and the slave, and bade us extract a lesson even from so great an evil."[80]

After so dissolving any distinct identity between good and evil, guilt and innocence, and making their definitions and reality, even in Christ's sight, dependent upon the point of view of the various actors, Newman declared that Christ had not forbidden "the exercise of that instinct of self-defence which is born with us" and which might manifest itself in foresight, avoidance, prudence, and skill. He further argued, "It is as if the more we are forbidden violence, the more we are exhorted to prudence; as if it were our bounden duty to rival the wicked in endowments of mind, and to excel them in their exercise." Through the centuries the church had followed Christ's injunction. As a result, Christians from the time of St. Paul had been reproached for using fraud, cunning, and priestcraft "partly, nay, for the most part, not truly, but slanderously, and merely because the world called their wisdom craft, when it was found to be a match for its own numbers and power."[81]

Further pursuing his tactic of definition based on point of vantage, Newman declared, "The words 'craft' and 'hypocrisy,' are but the version of 'wisdom' and 'harmlessness,' in the language of the world." He equated innocence or harmlessness with "simplicity in act, purity in motive, honesty in aim; acting conscientiously and religiously, according to the matter in hand, without caring for consequences or appearances; doing what appears one's duty, and being obedient for obedience-sake, and leaving the event to God." Such conduct, he declared, "accordingly has pre-eminently the appearance of craft."[82]

During periods of oppression and persecution, such as that in which Newman saw himself living, the Christian, in order to avoid both the vehemence and the corruption of the world, must in both speech and action exercise an enormous self restraint, which made "holy persons seem wanting in openness and manliness." To the "gross, carnal, unbelieving world" incapable of understanding them and ascribing to them unreal motives, truly religious people remained "a mystery," being defensively called by that world "mysterious, dark, subtle, designing." As Christians obeyed authorities in all things outward and not sinful, their conformity might cause a confused world to believe they had "renounced their opinions as well as submitted their actions." The world, then surprised to learn "that their opinions remain," interpreted that situation as manifesting "an inconsistency, or a duplicity." Indeed, because they obey outwardly but refuse to assent inwardly, Christians "are called deceitful and double-dealing, because they do as much as they can, and not more than they may." If such Christians resorted to silence and resignation, they again became the objects of suspicion. Newman stated, "The truest wisdom is to stand still and trust in God, and to the world it is also the strongest evidence of craft."[83] It was designs of God that made his servants appear to be designing. Newman had satisfied himself that behavior appearing to both religious and nonreligious observers as dishonest, crafty, and duplicitous actually fulfilled the will of God and quite legitimately embodied weapons provided by God to the weak in the face of the powerful. By this point in his life, he essentially equated heresy and sin with the frustration of his own will and the exercise of his will with the providence of God.

"Wisdom and Innocence" convinced non-Catholics of Newman's persistent recourse to arguments that undermined truthfulness, honesty, and sincerity in daily life, as well as casting doubt on the sanctity of promises and contracts. The positioning of the sermon in *Sermons, Bearing on Subjects of the Day,* published in late autumn 1843, confirmed those suspicions. In that volume "Wisdom and Innocence" directly preceded his four revised late-1841 sermons on the safety of Catholics continuing in the Church of England. This arrangement rendered Newman's intention in those sermons, as published, highly problematical. It appears that, in the face of episcopal criticism and after his own resignation from St. Mary's, he urged those Catholics who could remain in the English Church only on the terms of *Tract 90* (however interpreted) to conform outwardly while retaining their own internal beliefs no matter how duplicitous this behavior may appear to observers outside the Catholic fold. Through "Wisdom and Innocence" he was assuring those Catholics of their real honesty despite the accusations of dishonesty from the surrounding world.

RESIGNATION, FAMILY TURMOIL, AND CATHOLIC CONFUSION

In February 1843 for uncertain reasons Newman published in the *Conservative Journal* a curious anonymous retraction, dated December 12 of the previous year, of certain of his anti-Roman statements published between 1833 and 1837. Yet he saw no reason to depart the English Church, still contending that his understanding of Christian belief and practice might be achieved within it. During the early months of 1843, however, Newman did once more contemplate resigning St. Mary's, formally raising the issue with Keble in early March. Indicating that his own subscription stood on the basis of *Tract 90*, Newman admitted that his particular interpretation of the Articles had actually "never been drawn out, to say the least, before" even by Catholic-minded divines. He further recognized that he led men "to lean towards doctrines and practices which our Church does not sanction." Indeed, he confessed to "not promoting, the Anglican system of doctrine, but one very much more resembling in matter of fact, the doctrine of the Roman Church." At the same time he found at Littlemore a new vocation growing upon him in "directing (as I best may) the consciences of persons."[84] If he surrendered St. Mary's, he hoped to retain the church at Littlemore, but Oriel authorities quickly closed that alternative.

In two separate letters to Keble on May 4, Newman more fully than ever before revealed his thinking. In the first, he spoke of personal consciousness of his capacity for "insincerity and double dealing," voiced anxiety over "culpable inconsistency," and lamented his difficulty in discriminating "between passing thoughts and permanent impressions, particularly when they are unwelcome." He recounted having had thoughts resembling "hideous dreams, and we wake from them, and think they will never return; and though they do return, we cannot be sure still that they are more than vague fancies," and then concluded that until one was sure whether they were real or not, it was "wrong, to mention them to another."[85]

Later in the day, thinking better of the first letter, Newman composed a second, apparently enclosed with the first, in which he finally confessed to Keble, as he had to Henry Wilberforce and Frederic Rogers in 1839 and Robert Wilberforce early in 1842, his difficulties regarding the Catholicity of the English Church when viewed as a modern parallel to the Donatists and the Monophysites. Newman stated that he considered "the Roman Catholic Communion the Church of the Apostles" and any grace present in the English Church as "extraordinary, and from the overflowings of His Dispensation." He indicated that he was "far *more* sure that England is in schism, than that the Roman additions to the Primitive Creed may not be developments, arising out of a keen and vivid realizing of the Divine Depositum of faith." From that standpoint, the bishops' charges appeared as "protests and witnesses" to his conscience against his "secret unfaithfulness to the English Church" and "average samples of her teaching and tokens of how very far she is from even aspiring to Catholicity." Newman nonetheless still mentioned to Keble the imagined possibility of Rome's changing and thus healing the schism rather than men having to go over to Rome from the English Church. Furthermore, despite the momentous contents of the second May 4 letter, Newman wrote Keble six days later making no mention of it.[86]

On May 14, in advice not unlike that he had given more than twenty years earlier to the young doubting Thomas Arnold, Keble urged Newman to move slowly. He feared that Newman's resigning St. Mary's might also lead him to go over to Rome, which would be "a grievous event" because neither of them was responsible for the faults in the English Church into which God's Providence had placed them. He also noted that Newman grounded his general impressions "chiefly on points of *historical* evidence" which even he spoke of as "a 'hideous dream,' from which you would gladly awake," rather than as overpowering him as "a sort of intrinsical lustre, as many divine truths, I suppose, might." One could not expect "more than toleration" from bishops for the Catholic feelings arising in the church. Newman might now be overestimating the claims of Rome "from a kind of feeling that your earlier expressions had done her wrong." Keble advised Newman to follow his own early teaching that "where the Succession and the Creeds, are, there is the Covenant, even without visible intercommunion."[87]

Keble intuitively recognized that Newman often wrote speculative letters that functioned as safety valves for expressing anxieties of the moment, after which he settled back into inactivity. Such an interpretation of his letter writing seems confirmed by the presence among his papers of long, important unsent letters. But Newman's later use of personal correspondence to establish the powerful self-narrative of the *Apologia* set a pattern for succeeding generations of reading those letters as marking milestones in a meditative spiritual journey, a practice that the later scholarly publication of his correspondence has continued to invite. Consequently, the letters have tended to be interpreted in light of his eventual reception into the Roman Catholic Church rather than as products of particular circumstances of a particular moment.

Newman's closest friends seem to have known better and often saw his letters as thought experiments. Many of Newman's correspondents, though of course by no means all, also realized by 1840 that he actually wrote and said quite different things to different people. The letters that aroused the most intense reactions were normally those received by infrequent correspondents, who did not realize that his letters embodied thoughts of the moment rather than indicating either firm adherence to particular outlooks or firm decision for action. Indeed, the longer the letter, the more likely that no immediate action would follow on Newman's part. Failing to recognize the actual function and character of Newman's almost feverish letter writing, historians and biographers have often overinterpreted much of his correspondence. As a consequence, commentators have too often paid more attention to what Newman wrote than to what he actually did. Usually only the potential or actual precipitous actions of others, rather than any systematic or even unsystematic development of his own thought, caused Newman to act. His was a deeply reactive rather than proactive personality.

In that respect, Newman's actual attitude toward the English and Roman Churches at any given moment was generally the product of his reaction to immediate events rather than of long meditation. For example, his January 1842 letter to Robert Wilberforce restating the parallel between ancient and modern heresies followed Pusey's doubt about the wisdom of publishing *Tract 90,* the modest accommodations of several Catholics to the Jerusalem bishopric, Gladstone's effort to conclude the poetry professorship contest, and Peel's appointment of Gilbert, leader of the anti-Tractarian opposition in that contest, to a bishopric. On May 18, 1843, Newman admitted to Keble that his present lack of confidence in the English Church arose in part from his recent breach with Frederic Rogers, who now found him too sympathetic to Rome, and a cut from C. P. Eden, an Oriel fellow who had indicated that he would not even let Newman read prayers at Littlemore should he replace him at St. Mary's. Newman candidly stated, "For surely I should feel no anxiety at all about treachery to the Church, if they, as organs of prevailing opinion as well as Bishops, had one and all *approved* and *recommended* No. 90, instead of censuring it."[88]

It is also worth noting in this same context that in early autumn 1839, when Wiseman's *Dublin Review* article so impressed Newman with its questioning of the Catholicity of the English Church, Newman was still recovering from the high-church critique of Froude's *Remains*, a mild admonishment by Bishop Bagot, and the widespread support, initially including even Pusey, for the erection of the Martyrs' Monument in Oxford.[89] The monument had been the brainchild of Golightly, who saw the subscription for its erection as a test of whether Tractarians and their sympathizers would contribute to a memorial for the English Reformers. In other words, each instance of Newman's encountering and then stating doubt about the Catholicity of the Church of England followed upon instances of confusion or accommodation by Catholics and indications of clear Protestant self-identity on the part of leaders of the establishment and traditional high churchmen. Newman's doubt about the Catholicity of the English Church thus rose and fell with his perception of resistance to the Catholic experiment he was forwarding—resistance and opposition to which he now equated with heresy in the form of either evangelical or moderate Protestantism.

By May 1843 Newman was also concerned about the manner in which his retention of St. Mary's kept him under the authority of a bishop. Perhaps with his trimming letter of the previous April to Bagot in mind, he asked Keble, "With what sort of sincerity can I obey the Bishop?"[90] Furthermore, his position at St. Mary's was "an offence and stumbling block" to those who thought that because he retained the pulpit, they could remain in the church on the grounds enunciated in *Tract 90*. His personal religious goals might best be achieved outside St. Mary's pulpit by fostering the Littlemore community and by publishing a series on the lives of the English saints to further practical devotion. By May 30 Keble, agreeing that he could not press Newman to retain St. Mary's, returned to the position of his own immediate post–*Tract 90* pamphlet and cautioned him against giving too much authority to the opinions of one generation of bishops.

Newman decided to continue at St. Mary's, but while he had been corresponding with Keble, another event turned against the Tractarians. On Sunday, May 14, Pusey preached a sermon which Philip Wynter, the Vice Chancellor, and Edward Hawkins considered somewhat heterodox but warranting no action. By Tuesday, May 16, however, Dr. Faussett, the Lady Margaret Professor of Divinity, who had attacked the Tractarians years before and who had himself been more recently the target of *British Critic* ridicule, requested Wynter according to the university statutes to convene six doctors to determine whether Pusey's sermon conformed to the doctrines of the Church of England. Because of Hampden's censure of 1836, Faussett himself in his capacity as Lady Margaret Professor of Divinity would serve as one of the six. That day Wynter asked Pusey for a copy of the sermon. This request itself posed difficulty because Pusey had preached from notes rather than a full text. He delayed sending the notes on the grounds that he was ill and wanted to indicate his patristic sources. It is fundamental to the whole incident that the text of the sermon as delivered did not exist.

Wynter convened the six doctors, who included Richard Jenkyns of Balliol, Hawkins of Oriel, Symons of Wadham, Jelf of Christ Church, C. A. Ogilvie, the Regius Professor of Pastoral Theology, and Faussett. With the exception of Jelf, none of the doctors, who met four times in secret commencing May 24, was friendly to Pusey. Even Jelf, who saw nothing contrary to the teaching of the Church of England in the sermon, thought its contents nonetheless problematical. Hawkins contended that Pusey had been "led into erroneous views and expressions, partly by a pious desire to magnify the grace of God in the Holy Eucharist, and partly by an indiscreet adoption, in its literal sense, of the highly figurative, mystical, and incautious language of certain of the old Fathers." The Vice Chancellor, on the basis of the judgment of the six doctors, concluded that Pusey had indeed "preached certain things which were either dissonant from or contrary to the doctrine of the Church of England," but neither he nor anyone else ever specified the exact character of those "certain things."[91]

Wynter could either suspend Pusey from preaching or permit him to recant. At that point, the Vice Chancellor sent Jelf on a series of confidential visits to Pusey with proposals for a recantation, the initial text for which Wynter and Hawkins had written. Wynter and the six doctors seem to have undertaken the negotiation as an effort to allow Pusey a graceful exit from the condemnation. Pusey believed that the documents regarding recantation implied that the panel had acted on incorrect theological presumptions about the contents of his sermon. At no point had Pusey been allowed to confront the six doctors directly to make his case. Throughout the entire affair, of course, there was no certainty as to exactly what Pusey had said during the delivery of the sermon.[92] Believing himself under the strictest vow of silence regarding the negotiations, though newspapers had made the fact of the process public, Pusey did not consult any of his friends. The negotiation collapsed, and Pusey was suspended from preaching for two years, becoming the third major religious Oxford figure since 1836 to receive some form of university theological condemnation.

Jelf informed Pusey of the decision and penalty on June 2. Like Hampden and Newman before him, having lost in university forums, Pusey immediately issued a public protest, claiming to have been condemned "either on a mistaken construction of my words, founded upon the doctrinal opinions of my judges, or on grounds distinct from the Formularies of our Church." He also declared the sentence against him to be "unstatutable as well as unjust." Pusey's protest, as well as his eventual publication of a text of the sermon, stirred a public debate that concentrated on the process of adjudication, characterized by the *Morning Post* as "a sentence without a judgment," rather than on the substance of the original sermon, which could never actually be known.[93] By mid-June Pusey's supporters presented a formal address to the Vice Chancellor, and similar addresses arrived over the course of the summer. Pusey also took advice of various lawyers whether to make some form of legal appeal of his case and attempted unsuccessfully to seek redress from the Bishop of Oxford. The bishop turned the matter over to the Archbishop of Canterbury, who also provided none.

It is always difficult to fathom Pusey's actions and motives. On May 18 he had written to Newman, "You will be very sorry that the storm has at last reached me. God guide me through it, for it may be a heavy one, not for myself, but for its effects on others." Pusey may very well have hoped to invite sympathetic attention to himself as well as eventually a self-validating martyrdom or censure akin to Newman's. Initially, however, Newman was only marginally sympathetic, seeing the event as exposing Catholics to the very kind of official condemnation that for the past two years he had hoped to avoid. As with the poetry professorship, Pusey's precipitate action had led to a public defeat for the larger Tractarian cause. Newman actually cautioned Mozley as editor of the *British Critic* against depending on information contained in Pusey's protest for fear of exposing the journal to legal action. Nonetheless by late June, Newman concluded from Pusey's suspension that the Oxford authorities intended to "put down Catholicism at any risk."[94] Pusey's fate, arising from his continuing public Catholic aggressiveness, now fit into Newman's wider vision of Catholicism endangered by heresy, but all of his comments on the matter were private.

What had commenced as a chiefly university high-church disciplining

10. Edward Bouverie Pusey (1800–1882) was an Oriel fellow until appointed Regius Professor of Hebrew in 1828. In the public mind and in the press he was incorrectly regarded as the chief leader of the Tractarians, hence the epithet of Puseyite. This drawing by Francis Kilvert portrays Pusey in the spring of 1843 delivering the sermon for which he was condemned by a university panel of six doctors. (Reproduced from frontispiece, Liddon, *Pusey*, vol. 2.)

of Pusey appeared in the wider press as still another evangelical victory over the Tractarians. High churchmen, by now with little sympathy for the Tractarians, regretted how Pusey's case roused evangelicals and the low church forces in general. Pusey's supporters only made matters worse during the summer of 1843. When by mid-August they had not received satisfaction from their addresses and protests to the Vice Chancellor, they released the correspondence to newspapers.

In a remarkably blunt letter of August 18, following the publication of that correspondence, Jelf told Pusey that he had "put the truth in peril" by his "rambling, incoherent, confused mode of stating it" and that he should not "run away with the idea" that the sermon was "generally approved of by men of good Church principles." Many such people lamented its delivery and "more its publication" and thought that, owing to his state of health, "as a work *of art*, it was a very poor *composition* not worthy" of his reputation as a writer. Deeply regretting factional strife within the church, Jelf pressed his annoyance even further, declaring to Pusey, "You forgot that your first act gave at once a *factious* character to the whole proceeding, followed as it was by the signatures to declarations, *so far as they were genuine*. Your *protest* had not a shadow of ground, & the declarations were mere party movements not of the most creditable kind; & this alone wd have determined me from any overt act of sanctioning whatever I could sanction in the Sermon." About the same time that Pusey received Jelf's sharp private scolding, Newman learned that William Palmer had undertaken a major pamphlet, which would appear in a matter of weeks, attacking the *British Critic* and other examples of Tractarian excess. Jelf's letter and Palmer's anticipated pamphlet simply confirmed the veracity of the *Morning Chronicle* comment of more than a year earlier: "The old High Church party have got to hate the Puseyites even worse than the Liberals."[95]

Then on August 22 William Lockhart, one of the young men who had lived at Littlemore, informed Newman that against long-standing advice he was entering the Roman Church. Edward Churton characterized the event as "the defection of that rogue, Lockhart; who has played the *Monastery* a thorough Jesuitical trick, and left N. to bear the obloquy." Lockhart's conversion and the prospect of others triggered Newman's decision to resign St. Mary's, having become convinced that within the constraints of a traditional English Church ministry he could not restrain men from Rome. His family knew of the decision by August 30; on September 7 Newman informed Bishop Bagot. Alerted of Newman's impending resignation, Archbishop Howley counseled Bagot that he was no longer responsible for

Newman while regretting "the aberration of mind which has rendered his eminence in ability, attainments, and piety, a cause of disturbance instead of peace and strength to the Church."[96] On September 18, 1843, Newman formally resigned his living at St. Mary's before a notary. The resignation of his living was the second major redefinition of Newman's relationship to the Church of England directly provoked by the religious difficulties of his followers, the first having been the publication of *Tract 90*. In that regard, as will again be seen in his passage to Rome, he followed a pattern of displaying enormous hesitation, often involving considerable correspondence filled with self-doubt and introspection, followed by an action precipitated by the behavior of a more radical Catholic associate.

Lockhart's departure for the Roman Catholic Church bespoke Newman's lack of control over the monastic family he had created for himself at Littlemore. Similar trouble soon erupted in the extended Newman family itself. During the late summer Thomas and Harriett Mozley had been on holiday in France, but Thomas returned home to complete editorial work for the next number of the *British Critic*. Early in September, just as Newman was informing Bagot of his resignation, Mozley wrote to Harriett of his intention to convert to the Roman Church. Upon first receiving the unanticipated news, she bitterly responded, "Is it not enough that I should suffer by J.H.N.?" From her lonely holiday isolation, Harriett told Jemima that Mozley's announcement had struck her "like a thunderclap" and that he had not given "the slightest idea of what was passing in his mind" except for his always being "far more favorable and indulgent to the R.C.s than seems to me at all right." For her part, Harriett could not condemn strongly enough what she was witnessing "every where [in France] of the working of this wretched religion" which each hour convinced her "what a showy, fallacious, false and hollow system it is."[97]

Newman bore direct personal responsibility for his brother-in-law's religious turmoil. He had used Mozley as a young surrogate against various enemies, particularly Faussett, as in 1834 he had employed Henry Wilberforce to attack Hampden and in late 1841 had directed Ward against Arnold and Whately. Throughout 1841 and 1842 Newman had pressed Mozley toward a more radical stance in the *British Critic*, gave mixed signals on the most controversial articles, and criticized him for lack of proper sympathy for Ward. All the while Newman assured other Tractarians, such as Keble, that he was trying to restrain Mozley. When the Bishop of Salisbury vehemently attacked the *British Critic* in September 1842, Newman had suggested that his brother-in-law directly confront him as Newman himself would never have confronted Bishop Bagot. Mozley wisely refused, taking a more moderate course.[98] During 1843, reversing himself, Newman began to suggest more restraint in the *British Critic*, advice that Mozley now resisted. By the late summer of 1843, Mozley was thoroughly confused and deeply depressed about the ongoing public attacks on his journal and his relationship to Newman. His marriage was under strain from lack of money and Harriett's illness. The holiday in France, the couple's first experience on the Continent, was planned to improve Harriett's health.

After hearing of Mozley's letter to Harriett, Newman moved rapidly to persuade him to delay any decision which, of course, would have been a personal political disaster for Newman, following immediately upon Lockhart's conversion. Throughout the days of family crisis Newman displayed little sympathy or even understanding for his sister's situation, emphasizing instead his own plight and focusing on the difficulties that advanced Catholic men were then encountering. Writing on September 22, after his resignation but before his last sermon at Littlemore, in an effort to explain Mozley's predicament, he told Jemima, "You cannot estimate what so many (alas!) feel at present, the strange effect produced on the mind when the conviction flashes, or rather pours, in upon it that Rome is the true Church. Of course it is a most revolutionary, and therefore a most exciting, tumultuous conviction. For this reason persons should not act under it, for it is impossible in such a state of emotion that they can tell whether their conviction is well founded or not. They cannot judge calmly."[99] Newman was here consistent with his previous disapproval of other conversions, most particularly that of Sibthorp, which he regarded as equivalent to a Methodist or evangelical religious experience based upon subjective feelings.

A week later, berating Harriett for her impatience with himself and her husband, Newman wrote, "Only see what a position we are in—how difficult to please you. T. you blame for telling you, me for not telling. T. is cruel and I am disingenuous." Newman expressed his despair over the Church of England, his feeling of being cast off by it, and his being so drawn to the Church of Rome that he thought it "*safer*, as a matter of honesty," not to keep his living. Then no doubt to the puzzlement if not astonishment of his sister, he claimed, "This is a very different thing from having any *intention* of joining the Church of Rome. However, to avow generally as much as I have said would be wrong for ten thousand reasons. People cannot understand a man being in a state of *doubt*, of *misgiving*, of being unequal to *responsibilities*, &c.; but they will conclude that he has clear views either one way or the other. All I know is, that I could not without hypocrisy profess myself any longer a *teacher* and a *champion* for our Church."[100] This statement indicates the very real indeterminacy of Newman's thought and action in the coming months. This outlook may also explain why so many of the young men at Littlemore and others under his influence experienced so much personal religious confusion. Mozley himself was to leave the *British Critic* and eventually the active priesthood, becoming a London newspaper writer.

Only after thus defending his own situation did Newman report to Harriett that he had dissuaded her husband from taking any immediate step toward Rome or from surrendering his living and that he had acquiesced in Mozley's resignation of the *British Critic* editorship. He also explained to Harriett, after what must have been one of the worst months of her life, "If you knew what the feeling is for it to break upon a man that he is out of the Church, and that in the Church only is salvation, you would excuse anything in him." He closed the letter, "My dear H., you must learn patience, so must we all, and resignation to the will of God."[101] It is difficult to imagine a letter displaying less understanding about the relationship between a husband and a wife as in early middle age Newman reassumed the role of eldest sibling attempting to impose both order and personal dominance among his now extended family. His behavior puzzled and angered Harriett, who had reconciled herself to her brother's resigning St. Mary's because he had persuaded her that he had "made the act a sacrifice of duty."[102]

In September 1843 Newman appears to have felt that while retaining his Oriel fellowship outside a Church of England living but within the confines of the Littlemore monastery, he could pursue an increasingly experimental, Roman Catholic-like devotional life that would retain men of Catholic beliefs as an almost hidden presence within the English Church. The resignation formally removed him from direct episcopal supervision, but he still remained an ordained fellow of Oriel and must have known that Wesley had used his own ordination at Oxford to justify preaching without episcopal authority. On September 2, 1843, Newman had told Faber, "One thing . . . I feel very strongly—that a very great experiment, if the word may be used, is going on in our Church—going on, not over. Let us see it out." Furthermore, through at least the end of 1843 he discouraged Pusey from encouraging the use of Roman Catholic devotional manuals lest they persuade men to move to Rome. Like Elijah, Newman would remain in the wilderness, apart from all religious institutions, awaiting the day of the Lord or simply living at peace and without external ecclesiastical interference in his community of male friends. This view is supported by his decision, following long consultation with Keble, to publish two months after his resignation *Sermons,*

Bearing on Subjects of the Day, which included those sermons on Elijah from late 1841 urging patience for Catholics in the church. Even before his resignation Newman had been eager to publish the volume for the income it would generate and no doubt felt that need even more after losing the stipend associated with St. Mary's.[103]

Newman preached "The Parting of Friends," his final sermon as a priest in the Church of England, at Littlemore on September 25, 1843, the Sunday commemorating the dedication of the chapel in 1836. In the midst of a private family crisis and on the verge of a public crisis of renewed high-church criticism, he defined the moment as one of impending doom and judgment paralleling the last days of Jesus' life. Again identifying with Christ, as he had in his December 1841 letter to Rickards, Newman pointed to the current autumn harvest season as recalling Jesus' decision to observe Passover with his disciples in Jerusalem before his arrest and crucifixion. Speaking of the final week of Jesus' ministry, Newman exclaimed, "O wonderful pattern, the type of all trial and of all duty under it, while the Church endures!" Then recalling the happy day of the chapel's dedication, he urged the congregation to maintain the anniversary just as the Jews before their flight from Egypt had observed the first Passover before the angel of death visited Egyptian homes, "even though in haste, and with bitter herbes, and with loins girded, and with a staff in our hand, as they who have 'no continuing city, but seek one to come.' "[104]

Newman recalled several biblical scenes of farewell and departure, first of Jacob and Ishmael sent from their homes and then of Naomi returning to hers from the land of the Moabites, with whom she had lived so happily and lovingly. He described Orpah's kissing Naomi while not accompanying her back to Bethlehem as "the pain of a wound, not the yearning regret of love," and "the pain we feel when friends disappoint us, and fall in our esteem." Orpah's kiss was "not a loving token" but "the hollow profession of those who use smooth words, that they may part company with us with least trouble and discomfort to themselves." With tears that were "but dregs of affection," Orpah had "clasped her mother-in-law once for all, that she might not cleave to her."[105] That scene of concealed betrayal contrasted with the parting kiss between David and Jonathan and the emotion of St. Paul departing one of the early Christian congregations.

Then, recalling Jesus' persecution by the rulers of Israel, his desertion by his friends, his crying out in a barren land, and his finding only a stone as a pillow, Newman commented, "Heavily did He leave, tenderly did He mourn over the country and city which rejected Him." Jesus' lamentation over Jerusalem for killing the prophets and leaving its house desolate stood as "a lesson surely, and a warning to us all" of the danger of being cold to God's gifts. Then in an apostrophe to the Church of England, Newman declared, "O my mother, whence is this unto thee, that thou hast good things poured upon thee and canst not keep them, and bearest children, yet darest not own them?"[106] He pondered why the English Church lacked "the skill to use their services" and "the heart to rejoice in their love?" More darkly, he queried, "Who hast put this note upon thee, to have 'a miscarrying womb, and dry breasts,' to be strange to thine own flesh, and thine eye cruel to thy little ones?" He accused the English Church of gazing upon those children who yearned to love and serve it "with fear, as though a portent" or "as an offence," and at best enduring them "as if they had no claim" on its "patience, self-possession, and vigilance," and in expectation of being "rid of them as easily" as it might. The church made them " 'stand all the day idle,' as the very condition of . . . bearing with them," or bid "them be gone, where they will be more welcome" or sold them "for nought to the stranger that passes by."[107] In conclusion, Newman asked the congregation to remember him in times to come, even though they would not hear him, and to pray that he might know God's will and stand ready to fulfill it. With such disillusionment, self-indulgent anger, and the anguished regression of a child who believes his mother wills not to understand him, Newman completed the sermon, stepped from the pulpit, and deliberately laid his hood over the railing. The university-silenced Pusey celebrated the eucharist.

Yet the carefully constructed scene on that September day in the Littlemore chapel filled with Catholic sympathizers was a problematic one, as was also clear in the family correspondence of the same week. In this sermon, Newman sought to delineate an appropriate religious model for himself, but what emerged was the image of a man confused and distraught. The mixture of references to biblical farewells, the first Passover, and Jesus' final days indicated that perplexity. In this farewell sermon, Newman had himself assumed that profoundly Protestant stance of a self-convinced person believing himself providentially called to faith and practice determined by his own private judgment over and against ecclesiastical authority, whether English or Roman. At least one contemporary observer, however, a local workman constructing bookcases for the library at Littlemore, recognized a familiar pattern in Newman's behavior and wondered why he did not construct his own chapel like the Rev. Henry Bulteel before him.[108] Truth to tell in late September 1843, Newman looked very much like one more Oxford seceder from the Church of England. Local people, not caught up in church and university politics, knew a renegade priest when they saw one, and so, for that matter, did John Henry Newman. As he told Charles Cornish in the autumn of 1843, "I inculcate a body of doctrine, which as a body is now universally reprobated and was never avowed at any time."[109] As he departed the living of the Church of St. Mary the Virgin, Newman had attempted to clothe himself in the martyrdom of that reprobation without admitting the heterodoxy that had elicited it.

Although Tractarian hagiography almost immediately imposed an aura of sorrow about Newman's departure, much Oxford opinion was anything but regretful. The powerfully anti-Tractarian *Oxford Chronicle and Reading Gazette* spared no contempt, voicing "an overwhelming sense of the awful amount of evil, to the church, to this realm, to the world which has been connected with the occupancy of the pulpit of St. Mary's by Mr. Newman." The newspaper deplored his having "been permitted to destroy veneration for the authority of Holy Scripture," "to cast the seeds of spiritual pride and fanaticism into the minds of those who are now the teachers of the people," and "to benumb the moral perceptions" of those who could not reconcile Tractarian dogmas with subscription to Protestant Articles. After his last sermon, the Oxford editor reminded readers that in *Tract 90* Newman had demonstrated "how every man may be a law unto himself; and set up a dispensing power in his own mind, by which oaths and subscriptions may be relaxed, and their authority overruled, by the cabalistic letters—CATHO-LIC."[110] For the next two years, Newman did in fact function exactly as such a law unto himself.

THE HIGH-CHURCH ONSLAUGHT

Newman's resignation bought no more patience from once sympathetic high churchmen than from the long hostile *Oxford Chronicle*. The Tractarians had by now become a serious embarrassment to high-church clergy and laity. None of them intended, if they could avoid it, to be permanently blemished by duplicitous Catholic clerical subscription, Romanizing devotional practice, and radical *British Critic* excesses. Political and ecclesiastical careers needed to be salvaged.

Gladstone, weary of facilitating compromises between Tractarian demands and London political and ecclesiastical realities and disillusioned by his sister's conversion to Roman Catholicism, made the initial public move. In the *Foreign and Colonial Quarterly Review* of October 1843, Gladstone published an anonymous article, composed the previous summer, on the "Present Aspect of the Church." Along with many of the bishops, Gladstone wanted to harvest much of the post-1833 Catholic revival while separating himself from "its chequered characteristics" of the past four or five years. For Gladstone, as others, Froude's *Remains* marked the turning point. Since its publication, the Tractarians had demonstrated "an unmeasured and unmitigated aversion to the Reformation and the Reformers" and had displayed "a measured but yet undeniable and substantial estrangement of the heart from the actual Church of England, and a disposition not only to respect Catholicity in the Church of Rome, but to take the actual Church of Rome, in the mass, as being upon the whole the best living model of the Christian Church." Secessions to Rome had occurred only since such departures from "the masculine theology of the seventeenth century" and from a proper understanding of Romish corruptions.[111] Gladstone's imputing of effeminacy to Tractarianism by asserting the masculine character of the theology they had abandoned would not have been lost on contemporaries often pruriently fascinated by the monastic experiment of Littlemore.

Gladstone emphasized that early supporters of the tracts, including Perceval, Hook, and Palmer, had nothing to do with the radical Catholicism of the *British Critic;* nor, he claimed, had Keble, Williams, and Pusey. In contrast to those sound Catholic churchmen, the new school had "too frequently adopted a strain of language which, in plain terms, is not loyal towards the Church of England." Although appealing to Thirlwall's 1842 charge to defend criticism of the Reformation as a matter of freedom within the church, Gladstone protested the refusal of extreme Tractarians to acknowledge the Reformers' achievements in restoring the cup to the laity, stemming the corruption of indulgences, and spurring Roman Catholics to the reforms of Trent. Originally the Tractarians had sought "to catholicise the members of the Church of England, but without 'unprotestantizing' them." Such remained the true and proper goal of Catholics who aimed "at assimilation, not to Rome, but to something quite distinct, something higher and better than Rome; to that original of which Rome is a mutilated copy."[112]

Acknowledging Newman's retraction of his anti-Roman remarks, Gladstone asked what he now proposed "to substitute for the protestations thus withdrawn." Gladstone also wished to see the *British Critic* undertake "some similar retraction of their many hard speeches against men and things which England in her inmost heart reveres" and "against that 'Protestantism,' which, in the language of those by whom they are chiefly read . . . is not a symbol of a bare cold negation, or of a license for infidelity, but is the usual exponent of a substantive, undoubting, Christian, Catholic belief." He trusted that the theology of Newman, Oakeley, and others would "be corrected and counterbalanced by the soundest ethical habits, and by the great Christian specifics of earnestness, humility, and prayer."[113]

The secular press presented Gladstone's anonymous article, immediately recognized as his, either as a fair statement of Tractarianism or as the effort of a clever politician to mute the Tractarian excesses.[114] In either case there was no doubt in the public mind that high churchmen were in the process of mightily casting off the Tractarian albatross, which they had once hoped might be a noble creature exalting church principles. The formal appearance of William Palmer's previously privately circulated pamphlet almost simultaneously with publication of Gladstone's article further confirmed that perception.

In 1841 Palmer had briefly supported Newman over *Tract 90* but had quickly rethought his position after Bishop Blomfield directly rebuked his "declared determination to stand or fall with Mr. Newman, *as the author of the Tract No. 90*," while indicating his pain in thinking "that you will henceforth be identified . . . with the writers of the Tracts for the Times."[115] Thereafter Palmer attempted unsuccessfully to recoup his position by organizing the public declaration clarifying matters on the part of the upholders of church principles, which gained the support of neither the Bishop of Oxford nor Pusey. Palmer then engaged in a long controversy with Bishop Wiseman over *Tract 90*, devoting much of his effort to attacking Roman errors. During early 1842 Sibthorp's conversion to Rome occasioned a Palmer pamphlet suggesting that sympathy for Romish practices made such a conversion plausible. He also made revisions to one of his earlier publications, adding comments hostile to the Catholic interpretation of the Articles in *Tract 90*. These efforts failed to restore ecclesiastical confidence, as witnessed by Palmer's failure to gain either the Oxford chair in modern history upon Thomas Arnold's death in 1842 or a parish under the patronage of the Archbishop of Canterbury.

Palmer's next vehicle for rescuing his career was *A Narrative of Events Connected with the Publication of the Tracts for the Times, with Reflections on Existing Tendencies to Romanism, and on the Present Duties and Prospects of Members of the Church*, a signed pamphlet of October 4, 1843, dedicated to Bishop Bagot. By the end of the year it had gone through three editions. Just before its publication Palmer had told Bagot, as he had Pusey, that "a line of distinction" must be drawn "between *genuine* Church Principles and those who uphold them on the one hand, and Ultra and Romanizing doctrines on the other." If that were not done, "the tendency of things will be, to give Puritanism a complete triumph."[116] Palmer thus hoped to associate himself with the critical charges of the bishops while maintaining his long-standing opposition to evangelicalism.

Palmer's *Narrative* portrayed a movement that had commenced within the boundaries of church principles only to have been later captured by young Froude-inspired Romanizers, associated with the *British Critic*. These younger Tractarians had embraced "a kind of personal enmity, which, with a steady and unremitting scent for destruction, tracked and hunted down every fault, each mistake in doctrine, each folly in practice, every unguarded word, or look, or deed; and found in them all damning proof of dishonesty and of all imaginable crimes against the Church of England." Despite these excesses, men of church principles had continued to support the Tractarians until the events surrounding *Tract 90*. Palmer limply defended his initial commendation of the pamphlet on the grounds that he feared that the personal attack on Newman would be taken "as a blow aimed, not merely against the author of Tract 90 . . . but . . . against all that Churchmen are bound to value and defend." The post–*Tract 90* Romanizing of the *British Critic*, however, now required Palmer to denounce what had become "a spirit of—almost *servility* and *adulation* to Rome, an enthusiastic and exaggerated praise of its merits, an appeal to all deep feelings and sympathies in its favour, a tendency to look to Rome as the model and the standard of all that is beautiful and correct in art, all that is sublime in poetry, all that is elevated in devotion." Palmer feared that these extremists had decided to secede, but remained in the church "to insinuate their own persuasion amongst the duped and blinded members of the English Church," thus gaining adherents who would otherwise not be drawn to Rome. The conduct of the *British Critic* had placed high churchmen in an impossible position by legitimating the evangelical charge that their views led to Romanism. The upholders of church principles must recognize that "the dangers which now threaten us, are not inferior to those which surrounded the Church in 1833; that the tendency to latitudinarianism has been replaced by a different, but not less dangerous tendency; while the spirit of disaffection to the Church has only taken a new form."[117]

In late October 1843, pursuing his own call to action, Palmer, accompanied by other high churchmen, requested Rivingtons to cease publication of the *British Critic*, and the firm agreed. Mozley's previous resignation as editor had made the publisher's decision easier. Palmer shortly thereafter established the *English Review* as a journal of conservative high-church opinion and as a demonstration of his towing the anti-Tractarian line now handed down from the episcopal bench.[118] Yet, as will be seen, by isolating Ward and Oakeley, both Palmer's pamphlet and the closing of the *British Critic* provoked still more excessive actions on their part.

Throughout September, Newman had known that politically opportunistic attacks were in the offing from both lay and clerical high churchmen. His angry resentment, which had informed "The Parting of Friends," exploded when Manning on October 8 asked for a fuller explanation of his departure from St. Mary's. After stating the difficulty of providing an extensive view of his feelings and pointing to the general hostility to *Tract 90*, Newman on October 14 stated, "It is felt, I am far from denying, justly felt, that I am a foreign material—and cannot assimilate with the *Church* of England." Specifically complaining of Bishop Bagot's charge, he confessed that to the extent the Church of England displayed herself "intrinsically and radically alien from Catholic principles," he could not defend its claims to be a branch of the Church Catholic. Indeed, he thought it "a dream to call a communion Catholic, when one can neither appeal to any clear statement of Catholic doctrine in its formularies, nor interpret ambiguous formularies by the received and living sense past or present."[119]

Manning immediately shared Newman's letter with Gladstone, who thought it revealed a "powerful man" who had suffered much "in the healthful tone of his judgment from exclusiveness of mental habit, and from affections partly wounded through cruelty, partly overwrought into morbid action from gloating as it were continually and immediately upon the most absorbing and exciting subjects." With enormous insight into the indeterminacy of Newman's mind, Gladstone observed, "The Newman of 1843 is not the Newman of 1842, nor is he of 1842 the same with him of 1841: and how different, how far drifted down, are any of these from the Newman of the 'Romanism and Popular Protestantism.'" He further thought it "frightful" that Newman wavered in his allegiance to the Church of England on the grounds of "the general repudiation of the view contained in Tract 90" because in reality the uproar and censure were "more ascribable to the manner and language of a publication as contrasted with its substance." Newman simply ignored the vast progress that Catholic principles had achieved until the "rude shocks" occasioned by the publication of Froude's *Remains*. By quitting the Church of England from a sense of general repudiation, Newman could certainly "contribute much to the religious disorganization of the country," but little to its reorganization on a Roman Catholic model.[120]

Both Manning and Gladstone would have been even more deeply

disturbed had they known of Newman's other recent correspondence. On September 1, in a letter that he instructed J. B. Mozley to burn, Newman had stated, "The truth . . . is, I am not a good son enough of the Church of England to feel I can in conscience hold preferment under her. I love the Church of Rome too well."[121] It is actually difficult to know what in this letter or others of the next two years Newman meant by "the Church of Rome," for he had virtually no experience with that institution and only occasional contacts with its representatives. "Rome" was a word that for Newman embodied hopes for ecclesiastical reform, yearnings for Christian unity, and imaginings of personal religious tranquility as much as any concrete, contemporary social and institutional reality. "Rome" in these months and earlier functioned in his thought almost as the evangelical concept of an "invisible church," shorn of the contemporary trappings of popular Protestantism, existing through the ages but never quite achieving adequately pure realization and most particularly not adequately realized within any ecclesiastical institution of his own day.

Rome so imagined also served as a counterpoint to what Newman regarded as the hopelessly Protestant character of the English Church. On October 13 he told Woodgate that he did "not doubt that the articles were drawn up by persons either heretic or heretical" and that he also did "not believe that the compilers acknowledged *any* Catholic sense," which appeared only with those who received them after their promulgation in 1571 and 1662. Newman further observed, "But leave the Articles in their *intended* meaning and they are Protestant." With the bishops having now decided they were to be taken "in their Protestant sense," the question arises whether people "have not as much right to do so, as the Convocations of 1571 and 1662 to take them in their Catholic sense." This situation was why Newman called "our system rotten," because it had no meaning other than that determined by those who administered it. Since *Tract 90* those administering the church had decided that it "is *not* Catholic, i.e. that it does not hold Catholic doctrine."[122] Two weeks later, writing to Bowden, Newman deplored the English episcopal bench as "ultra-protestant" and as having "nothing else in them, i.e., speaking of them as Bps."[123]

Having no inkling that Newman held such opinions, Manning replied to him in the dark, and as Gladstone had suggested, reminded him of the progress of Catholicism during the past decade. On October 25 Newman stated directly to Manning that he had resigned St. Mary's "from no disappointment, irritation, or impatience" but rather "because I think the Church of Rome the Catholic Church, and ours not a part of the Catholic

Church, because not in communion with Rome, and I felt I could not honestly be a teacher in it any longer." He related this conviction as having come upon him in the summer of 1839 as a result of his study of the Donatist and Monophysite controversies and his having then quieted himself for a time on the issue with his *British Critic* article "Catholicity of the Church." Newman wrote that circumstances had later forced him to publish *Tract 90*. He then claimed, "You know how unwillingly I wrote my letter to the Bishop of Oxford, in which (as the safest course under circumstances) I committed myself again." This comment reflected either a complete mis-remembering of his well-documented negotiation with the Bishop of Oxford and subsequent correspondence on that event or an example of monumental disingenuousness on Newman's part. In contradiction to what he had written to Keble in the spring, he insisted that the events of the past two years had not been "the cause of my state of opinion" but had functioned as "keen stimulants and weighty confirmations of a conviction forced on me, while engaged in *the course* of duty, viz. the theological reading which I had given myself." Describing himself as relieved to have disclosed "a heavy secret," Newman told Manning, who not unnaturally assumed the letter signaled an impending passage to Rome, that he might make whatever use of the two letters that he thought right.[124] Once again, it should be noted, Newman appealed to the parallel of ancient and modern heresy after encountering prolonged criticism from both bishops and high churchmen numbered among the Catholics in the English Church. The specter of internal contemporary heresy arose proportionally with his own self-perception of being "a foreign material" in that institution.

Manning again consulted Gladstone. Unable to make the second Newman "letter hang together," Gladstone told Manning, "My first thought is, 'I stagger to and fro, like a drunken man, and am at my wit's end.'" Gladstone found Newman's remarks about his *Letter to the Bishop of Oxford* "frightful" and "more like the expressions of some Faust gambling for his soul, than the records of the inner life of a great Christian teacher." Newman's letter, he told Manning, could not be publicized as it stood because its contents would certainly "damage and disparage his authority and character in the manner which one perhaps should desire as to a confirmed enemy of truth, but which, with respect to him, it would be most wicked to do otherwise than deeply lament." Returning to the subject two days later, Gladstone stated that, upon publication of those letters, Newman would stand "in the general view *a disgraced man*, and all men, all principles, with which he has had to do, disparaged in proportion to the proximity of their connection." Many people would say that Newman's " 'committing himself again' was simply a deliberate protestation of what he knew to be untrue." For Gladstone, the letter bore "the construction of dishonesty, of mental disease, or of great credulity and incompleteness." Its whole aspect was "so *inharmonious* in its tone, so dark in its moral colour upon the surface, and so uncertain" that Manning would require divine guidance in knowing what to do with it.[125]

Moving to cover both his political and ecclesiastical flanks, Gladstone proposed "something in the nature of an united protest on the part of those whom the public voice has associated with Newman, declaring together their adherence to Catholic principles, their loyalty to the actual English Church and their firm resistance to the actual system and claims of Rome."[126] At the same time nothing must be done to precipitate Newman to act. On November 5 Manning, apparently following Gladstone's strategy of disassociating Catholics from Newman, preached a powerful no-popery sermon before the university. Thereafter Newman famously refused to see him when he called at Littlemore.

Manning had by this point also sent Newman's letters to Pusey, who had previously served as a conduit for information about Newman's state of mind. In 1842, attempting to account for Newman's relationship to the radical *British Critic* Catholics, Pusey had explained to Manning that "persons near Newman do him injustice: they fasten their own corollaries upon his principles, and because Newman cannot deny that they may be plausibly drawn, though he does not see them or appropriate them, they assume that he is with them." He had also at that time indicated the pain that Newman felt over the insularity of the English Church, its toleration of heresy, and its approximation to Protestantism, but had assured Manning that these sentiments did not "alter" Newman's "sense of duty." In November 1843 Pusey correctly believed that Newman's recent communications did not indicate an imminent conversion to Rome. Yet he could no longer suggest a plausible explanation for Newman's opinions, reporting to Manning, "I have been gradually recovering since the very painful letters wh. you showed me, & I cannot but strongly hope that in all practical bearings they seemed to us to say more than they do. I have not said any thing of them to the writer; I shd expect only harm wd come of it; it is so sensitive a mind & so shrinks from speaking of itself, that for years I have found that I would be violating a sanctuary by wishing it to do so. Thus in a quick sharp way, as if it was almost avenging itself on itself for doing so. Then also that mind is so refined, that it may be that if we take its language in an ordinary way, we may be mistranslating it." Even Pusey recognized that no one could accept or interpret Newman's language at ordinary face value. Pusey's reference to Newman's refinement of mind was only a more polite version of Gladstone's image of a Faust gambling with his soul. The same month, retreating from such candor, Pusey told Gladstone in regard to Newman, "It is not the natural effects of any principles, but the actual state of things, our disorganization, the tolerance of heresy, the conduct of our Bishops" which so disturbed his and others' minds. "Blow comes, after blow."[127]

Pusey had counseled Manning to discontinue his vehement preaching against Rome. Manning, however, remained true to Gladstone's advice that Catholics must separate themselves from the uncertain Newman. Defending his no-popery rhetoric and renouncing Newman and his other Tractarian acquaintances, Manning told Pusey, "I feel to have been for four years on the brink of I know not what; all the while persuading myself and others that all was well; and more—that none were so true and steadfast to the English Church; none so safe as guides. I feel as if I had been a deceiver speaking lies . . . and this has caused a sort of shock in my mind that makes me tremble. . . . I have been using his books, defending and endeavouring to spread the system which carried this dreadful secret in its heart. There remains for me nothing but to be plain henceforward on points which hitherto I have almost resented, or ridiculed the suspicion. . . . I am reduced to the painful, saddening, sickening necessity of saying what I feel about Rome." Preaching against popery was Manning's compensation for onetime admiration for Newman and his subsequent loss of faith in the man. By the close of the year, however, Manning, feeling the bite of Newman's portrayal of Orpah in the published version of "The Parting of Friends," attempted a modest reconciliation, which resulted in a polite exchange of letters but in no restoration of mutual trust. Late in the century Gladstone recalled that shortly after Newman's conversion, he had asked Manning what united those who in late 1845 had passed to Rome and had received the answer, "Their common bond is their want of truth." Manning and other moderate Catholics had certainly already reached that conclusion in the late autumn of 1843, by which time Newman had become a complete mystery to them. Fully recognizing the situation, Newman himself toward the end of October reported to Miss Giberne, "All the Anglo Catholics are trooping off."[128]

CHAPTER 10

Monks, Miracles, and Popery

NEWMAN PURSUED two distinct goals in the publication of *Tract 90* and his formal establishment of the Littlemore monastery, each of which roused opposition from both evangelicals and high churchmen. The first was a determination to secure toleration for Catholics within the ministry of the Church of England through implicit recognition of Catholic latitude in clerical subscription to the 39 Articles. His second goal was to continue and to expand the Tractarian devotional experiment. The latter effort has received much less scholarly attention than the former. Advanced Tractarian Catholic devotion and theology largely disappeared from the Victorian religious scene when its leading progenitors entered the Roman Catholic Church in 1845. In later life, neither they nor those Tractarians who remained in the English Church found it wise or useful to resurrect the details of their earlier experiment. Indeed, their ecclesiastically schismatic and devotionally eclectic activities of the early 1840s generally embarrassed them. Consequently, one of the boldest efforts at constructive theology and devotion in Victorian religious and intellectual life largely vanished from collective memory and later historical accounts.

The advanced Tractarian Catholicism of the late 1830s and early 1840s combined two features that to most early-twenty-first-century readers appear quite separate. On the one hand, the late Tractarians steadily advanced an agenda of unapologetically supernatural religion involving miracles. On the other hand, many of these same people, including Newman, encountered profound religious skepticism. Indeed, many Victorians eventually associated the Tractarian Movement as much with such skepticism as with Roman Catholic sympathies and saw people who had passed through the movement as having sometimes lost faith in any religion. Whereas later in the century, religious doubt was associated with questions about the validity of the Bible and natural theology, the Tractarians' skepticism involved doubt about their capacity to discern the presence of a true church to which they could extend their faith and devote their lives.

ECCLESIASTICAL MIRACLES

As early as 1839 in *Tradition Unveiled,* Baden Powell had predicted that the Tractarians' view of tradition and the consequent dissolution of the boundaries between an original revelation and later Christian history would necessarily lead them to embrace ecclesiastical as well as biblical miracles. Although Newman briefly did so the next year in *The Church of the Fathers,* it was in *An Essay on the Miracles Recorded in the Ecclesiastical History of the Early Ages,* prefaced by an advertisement dated June 4, 1842, that he most strongly and memorably defended the factual, historical validity of miracles alleged to have occurred in Christian communities after the age of the apostles. This essay, which perplexed admirers and confirmed opponents' hostile suspicions, presented sacred history as being distinguished from profane history "by the nature of the facts which enter into its composition, and which are not always such as occur in the ordinary course of things, but are extraordinary and divine." Miracles, along with monasticism, celibacy, poverty, papal power, and methods of teaching doctrine that startled modern readers, constituted essential and undeniable facts in the postapostolic sacred history of the Christian Church. Despite differences in the character and evidence of miracles in different eras of sacred history, Newman insisted that there had existed "no Age of miracles, after which miracles ceased." To treat the subject otherwise, as had long been the practice of English Protestant commentators, proved "both false and dangerous to revealed religion altogether." If one assumed that "the ordinary Providence of God is conducted upon a *system,*" it became "more probable than not that there is also a law of supernatural manifestations" in the age of the church as well as in the age of the apostles. Acceptance of the validity of the accounts of scriptural miracles coupled with rejection of ecclesiastical ones meant that previous commentators had acted "towards the miracles of the Church as Hume towards the miracles of Scripture."[1]

According to Newman, the Protestant frame of mind itself accounted for the long and dangerous rejection of postapostolic ecclesiastical miracles. Those alleged miracles appeared improbable, if not impossible, to

Protestants because they believed "that Christianity is little more than a creed or doctrine, introduced into the world once for all, and then left to itself, after the manner of human institutions . . . containing certain general promises of aid for this life, but unattended by any special Divine Presence or any immediately supernatural gift." Within this Protestant historical vision, ecclesiastical miracles "must needs be a shock, and almost an outrage" disturbing "feelings" and unsettling the "most elementary notions and thoroughly received opinions."[2]

Catholics, however, who in contrast to Protestants believed the church to be "a supernatural ordinance," had no difficulty in assuming the possibility of such miracles. Furthermore, Newman asserted, "If we disbelieve the divinity of the Church, then we shall do our best to deny that the facts attested are miraculous, even admitting them to be true." Once again, as in his recent sermons, he contended that one's theology determined one's evaluation of evidence, explaining, "As the admission of a Creator is necessary for the argumentative force of the miracles of Moses or St. Paul, so does the doctrine of a Divine Presence in the church clear up what is ambiguous in the miracles of St. Gregory Thaumaturgus or St. Martin." Following Gibbon without adopting his irony, Newman argued that it had been the miracles of the early church that most accounted for the adhesion of new members. It was just such miracles that Protestants now denied. The Church Fathers, who had expressed their faith in and expectation of miracles, had not foreseen a day when "evidence would become a science" or when "doubt would be thought a merit, and disbelief a privilege."[3]

Newman did admit differences in the circumstances of scriptural and ecclesiastical miracles, as well as the frequent triviality of the latter. Scriptural miracles in one way or another contributed directly to the purposes of divine revelation, whereas ecclesiastical miracles had "sometimes no discoverable or direct object, or but a slight object." He also confessed that reports of ecclesiastical miracles, like other aspects of Prophetical Tradition, were at best only "floating rumours, popular traditions, vague, various, inconsistent in detail, tales which only *happen* to have survived, or which in the course of years obtained a permanent place in local usages or in particular rites or in certain spots," often having been recorded long after and far from the place where they were alleged to have occurred. Much falsehood as well as truth appeared in such stories. Moreover, after reciting a long record of ecclesiastical miracles from the first four centuries, Newman confessed that they did actually differ from the Gospel miracles and that, according to some of the Church Fathers, "*Apostolic* miracles, or miracles *like* the Apostles'," had indeed ceased with the apostles.[4]

Drawing upon a framework of successive, developing religious dispensations, Newman distinguished first between Mosaic and prophetic miracles recorded in Hebrew Scripture and then between those and the Gospel miracles, presenting each as representing a different stage of revelation. If one rejected the latest stage, so his argument went, one must also potentially reject earlier ones: "As a gradual revelation of Gospel truth accompanied the miracles of the Prophets, so to those who admit the Catholic doctrines as enunciated in the Creed, and commented on by the Fathers, the subsequent expansion and variation of supernatural agency in the Church, instead of suggesting difficulties, will seem but parallel, as they are contemporaneous, to the developments, additions, and changes in dogmatic statements which have occurred between the Apostolic and the present age, and which are but a result and an evidence of life." Newman reminded his readers that pagan observers had associated Christian scriptural miracles "with the prodigies of Jewish strollers, heathen magicians and astrologers, and idolatrous rites," but the assumption of scriptural inspiration made the divine purpose of such miracles clear. Because inspiration itself had ceased, ecclesiastical miracles must consequently remain "dimly seen in twilight and amid shadows," but remain seen they must.[5]

Whatever arguements worked against the divine power of the church as manifested in ecclesiastical miracles ultimately also worked against Christianity itself as manifested in the miracles of the Bible. In a sentence recalling the skeptical strategy of *Tract 85*, where he had dared readers to diminish ecclesiastical authority at the cost of diminishing scriptural, Newman wrote, "On the whole . . . it will be found that the greater part of the miracles of revelation are as little evidence for revelation at this day, as the miracles of the Church are evidence for the Church." Moving to an even more tendentious conclusion, he declaimed, "Superstition is a corruption of Christianity, not merely of the Church; and if it discredits the Divine origin of the Church, it discredits the Divine origin of Christianity also."[6] Thus to protect the validity of ecclesiastical miracles, Newman threatened to poison the well of all supernatural religious belief.

For some years Newman had argued that for the natural theologian to discern evidence for the presence of God in nature, he must first necessarily assume that presence. Without the latter predisposition, the multitude of plants and animals, as well as the ugliness of many, might well lead one to discern no purpose or evidence of divinity in the natural order. Newman believed that Protestant commentators approached scriptural miracles as natural theologians approached nature and hence found evidence of God's miraculous activity. But when those same Protestant commentators examined ecclesiastical miracles, they did so in the pattern of certain unnamed irreligious men of science who studied nature without presupposing a divine presence. To these scientists, nature did not bespeak the presence of God, just as to the Protestant commentator ecclesiastical miracles had not occurred in sacred history. Pursuing an elaborate metaphor based on this analogy, Newman explained, "Scripture is to us a garden of Eden, and its creations are beautiful as well as 'very good'; but when we pass from the Apostolic to the following ages, it is as if we left the choicest valleys of the earth, the quietest and most harmonious scenery, and the most cultivated soil, for the luxuriant wildernesses of Africa or Asia, the natural home or kingdom of brute nature, uninfluenced by man." Within that wild terrain of ecclesiastical history, miracles functioned as "in some sense an innovation" upon the divine revelation that Scripture had previously afforded human beings.[7]

The miracles of Scripture, Newman urged, actually deviated more from the economy of nature than ecclesiastical miracles did from the economy of Scripture and should thus pose no less a problem to belief. For example, Christ's walking on water or raising the dead directly reversed nature, whereas, Newman wrote, "The narrative of the combats of St. Anthony with evil spirits, is a development rather than a contradiction of revelation, viz. of such texts as speak of Satan being cast out by prayer and fasting." Consequently, he asserted, "To be shocked . . . at the miracles of Ecclesiastical history, or to ridicule them for their strangeness, is no part of a scriptural philosophy." In his view there was no logical stopping point between skepticism toward postapostolic ecclesiastical miracles and skepticism about the most important miracles recorded in the Bible. Newman closed perhaps the most theologically controversial and puzzling essay ever to come from his pen by confessing that his views might be condemned as "subtle" and "sophistical." Such, he observed, was "ever the language" used by men "concerning the arguments of others, when they dissent from their *first principles*,—which take them by surprise, and which they have not mastered."[8]

Much of the skeptical potential of Tractarian thought lay embedded in this essay, which even Keble considered "too clever," fearing "that such a man [as its author] could prove anything." Newman's polemical strategy in support of ecclesiastical miracles led him perilously close to Nietzsche's later assertion, "There are no moral phenomena at all, but only a moral interpretation of phenomena."[9] Newman in effect had said there are no distinctly religious or spiritual phenomena in either nature or history, but only a religious interpretation of such phenomena originating in a particular moral disposition that first assumes Catholic truth. If that disposition were removed, the entire conceptual structure and conclusions flowing therefrom collapsed. The common source of potential skepticism shared by Newman and Nietzsche, who at first appear so disparate, lay in their mutual understanding of truth as rooted in the perspective of the speaker or observer, an outlook Newman had advocated in his sermons of 1839. Furthermore, both Newman and Nietzsche were reacting against Protestantism, which each often saw as deeply intermeshed with the wider Enlightenment hopes for human reason about which they were profoundly skeptical. Neither wished to be encased entirely in a rational Apollonian world. Indeed, Newman's fascination with all of the emotional, experimental expansiveness of Prophetical Tradition bears a certain though to be sure inexact parallel to the young Nietzsche's appeal to the Dionysian.

LIVES OF THE ENGLISH SAINTS

Less than a year later Newman transferred his attention to the miraculous terrain of the Middle Ages. In early April 1843, following the successful publication of *Sermons, Chiefly on the Theory of Religious Belief,* he proposed to Francis Rivington a series on British saints. The publisher liked the idea but substituted "English" for "British." On May 18, 1843, while discussing with Keble his possible resignation from St. Mary's, Newman stated that he had initially thought such biographies useful for "employing the minds of persons who were in danger of running wild, and bringing them from doctrine to history, from speculation to fact," and to keep "them from seeking sympathy in Rome as she is," as well "as tending to promote the spread of right views." More recently, however, he had conceived the series as "a practical carrying out of No. 90, from the character of the usages and opinions of Ante-reformation times."[10] Newman thus envisioned the *Lives of the English Saints* as sustaining *Tract 90* by recording from the pre-Reformation history of the English Church many of those contested elements of religious life that he and his coterie believed a Catholic interpretation of the 39 Articles necessarily embraced.

In his prospectus for the series, dated September 9, 1843, shortly after having informed Bagot of his resignation from St. Mary's and when marital turmoil arising from Thomas Mozley's desire to enter the Roman Church was about to embroil his sister, Newman wrote that just as the earliest Christians had received the blessing of having seen "the fresh traces of their Lord" and having "heard the echoes of Apostolic voices," modern Christians stood blessed by being allowed "to see that same Lord revealed in His Saints." Through reading the lives of those postapostolic saints, modern Christians might experience in a manner not possible to the earliest Christians "the wonders" of God's grace revealed "in the soul of man, its creative power, its inexhaustible resources, its manifold operations."[11] Newman thus transferred to the realm of ecclesiastical history the privileged reading applied by many contemporary English Christians to biblical history alone and urged readers to draw from English ecclesiastical history devotional solace that others thought available only in the Bible itself. Christian history thus served as a supplemental revelation of the spiritual patterns that God intended for human beings in the church.

Newman had understood for some time that the success of his Catholic religious experiment required the nation to embrace an entirely new perspective on its culture, history, and destiny. As early as 1841 he had opined to Bowden that people shrank from Catholicity because they thought "it implies want of affection to our *national* Church." In order "to disarm people of their prejudice against Catholicity as anti-national," he suggested refusing to date the founding of the English Church from the Reformation and then rousing love for both a national church and "a Catholic tone" by appealing to the experience of "our Church in the middle ages." Three years later Newman quite myopically hoped the series of saints' lives would help to replace the English sense of a national Protestant mission with a new appreciation of its Catholic heritage and associations. To that end, he claimed that recurring to the medieval English saints at the present time might "serve to make us love our country better, and on truer grounds than heretofore; to teach us to invest her territory, her cities and villages, her hills and springs with sacred associations; to give us an insight into her present historical position in the course of the Divine Dispensation; to instruct us in the capabilities of the English character; and to open upon us the duties and the hopes to which that Church is heir, which was in former times the Mother of St. Boniface and St. Etheldreda."[12] Such was the vocation that Newman set forth for himself and those around him as he departed St. Mary's pulpit, a vocation directly linked to sympathy for medieval English Roman Catholicism and for mystery in religious life as advanced in the *British Critic*. The early Victorian medieval revival associated with the novels of Scott and with Pugin's ecclesiastical architecture, as well as with the secular gothic design of the new Houses of Parliament, gave plausibility to Newman's new venture achieving resonance in the world of contemporary religious publication.

The authors Newman recruited for *Lives of the English Saints* were generally though not always associated with Littlemore. They included John Barrow, R. W. Church, Robert Aston Coffin, John Dobree Dalgairns, F. W. Faber, James Anthony Froude, William Lockhart, Thomas Meyrick, Thomas Mozley, Frederick Oakeley, Robert Ornsby, Mark Pattison, and John Walker. Except for Oakeley, all were significantly younger than Newman. Several were encountering personal religious turmoil about their relationship to the English Church and their often powerful attraction to Roman Catholicism. Composing lives of English saints was to demonstrate that through their beliefs and devotional practices Newman's coterie constituted a contemporary saving remnant of an earlier English Church that had once borne witness to the Catholic faith. But the publication of these medieval saints' lives also powerfully and controversially expanded the possible prescribed content and character of that Catholic faith to encompass historical credulity, ascetic behavior, Romish ecclesiastical loyalties, and monastic celibacy disruptive of family bonds that even zealous modern English Catholics quickly rejected.

Almost from its inception, the series veered out of Newman's control, once more convincing observers that, in the words of William Palmer, he was "under (in some degree) the influence of very unsound men." In organizing the *Lives of the English Saints* as a series, Newman had badly underestimated the animosity toward Protestantism and the determination to disparage it on the part of his enlisted authors. For example, in May 1843, Faber had written privately, "My whole life, God willing, shall be one crusade against the detestable and *diabolical* heresy of Protestantism, the very name even of which has been publicly and authoritatively abjured by my own Church. Arianism, Pelagianism, and the like are awful enough, and soul-destroying: but Protestantism is the devil's masterpiece. It has broken into the English pastures, and must be hunted down. I will do my best in my little way, because I *doubt* the salvation of Protestants, and my office is to save souls."[13] The same month Oakeley told Newman that potential authors might well wish to treat miracles in a manner that even Newman himself might not approve for inclusion in publications devised for the general public. As the events of the summer and autumn of 1843 unfolded and high churchmen deserted the Tractarians, Newman became increasingly unlikely to caution his authors, particularly if it meant losing their by now even more precious friendships, loyalties, and intimacies.

Newman's determination to pursue the radical Catholicism associated with those friends appears in another complicated triangular exchange that had become a way of life for the Tractarians. On November 2, following the correspondence with Manning over his doubts about the Catholicity of the English Church, Newman wrote to James Robert Hope that he understood Pusey had told Hope that the saints' lives "would cause a sensation" particularly because of a tone of *"liking for Rome"* that would appear in them. Admitting that others would react even more intensely, Newman still thought that despite "great perplexity," the series must move ahead lest cessation "tend to precipitate certain persons . . . toward Rome." Besides those who thought the Church of England external to the Church Catholic, Rome attracted two other groups. There were first people "unconsciously near Rome, and whose *despair* about our Church, if anyhow caused, would at once develop into a state of conscious approximation and *quasi*-resolution to go over." A second group thought it safe to remain in the Church of England only if permitted "to testify in behalf of Catholicism, and to promote its interests."[14] Composing lives of the saints might preserve both for the English Church, presumably by convincing them that genuinely pious, holy Catholics trod the halls of its history and could yet again bear witness to that holy faith. Preserving these authors within the English Church would also, of course, sustain Newman's own life, position, and work at Littlemore, which would collapse if a serious wave of conversions occurred.

Counseling caution so that "the Roman leaning" of the lives of the saints would not give undue offense, Hope asked whether it was possible "to *commence* by lives which will not once bring the whole series into popular disrepute? the less palatable ones being kept for a more advanced stage." Particularly uneasy about the authority that Dalgairns in the draft manuscript of his life of St. Stephen Harding ascribed to the Pope and the Church of Rome, Hope thought he might instead refer "to the asceticism, devotion, and anti-secular spirit of the English saints" as "displayed in necessary relation to Rome, or to Roman institutions," without including the latter among their merits. Hope thought it also feasible "simply to take the Church of their times as *the* Church, without entering into the question whether any of the conditions under which it then existed are necessary for its existence now." In that manner the acts of those saints "done in relation to the Church of their day may be dwelt upon, while the further question whether the Church of our day is capable of eliciting such acts may be left to the judgment of the reader."[15] Hope thus rejected any modern normative role for medieval practices.

On November 6, the day after Manning's antipopery sermon, Newman passionately rejected Hope's plea for prudence, thundering at him, "Now Church History is made up of these three elements—miracles, monkery, Popery. If any sympathetic feeling is expressed on behalf of the persons and events of Church history, it is a feeling in favour of miracles, or monkery, or Popery, one or all." The unethical alternative was to adopt "Milner's or Neander's device of dropping part of the history, praising what one has a fancy for, and thus putting a theory and dream in the place of facts." Newman further declared it impossible "that a leaning to Rome, a strong offensive leaning should be hidden." Contrary to Hope's wish, there really were no easy or inoffensive lives, and those that were published would "make a sensation" because "to do it without offence is impossible." Noting the financial commitments already made to authors, Newman stated that if he did not conduct the series, someone else would. "What right," he asked, "have I to be quiet, having the means of making a protest, when there is so great an effort on the other side to put down the Pope!" Recalling what he regarded as his nearly three years of silence, he demanded, "Am I never to move?" Abandoning the project would inevitably raise the question, " 'What then, cannot the Anglican Church bear the Lives of her Saints!' "[16] Throughout these exchanges Newman repeatedly aligned himself with the more radical of his authors, who, he knew, would not submit to compromise.

Although Hope failed to dissuade Newman, events quickly overtook the series. Rivington, being unable to accept the draft life of St. Stephen Harding, withdrew as publisher in late November, having closed the *British Critic* only days before. Unwilling to demand changes from Dalgairns, Newman thought the publishing situation would improve in a few months. But new warning voices soon appeared on the scene. On December 2 J. B. Mozley told Newman, "One cannot read the prospectus without feeling that such accounts would be pretty sure to contain much to do violence to the feelings of many who yet are very far from thinking themselves as being low Churchmen." A day later Gladstone, who at Hope's request read one of the draft lives, protested that the character assigned to the English Church repelled him, as did "the introduction with apparent approval of particular points & phrases of Roman doctrine, such as the devotion to St. Mary." Following Gladstone's hostile response, Hope, thinking he might halt the series, offered two hundred pounds to defray any expenses Newman had incurred from Rivington. But upon reading Gladstone's critique, Newman replied that it had shown him "the *hopelessness* by delay, or any other means of escaping the disapprobation" of persons he respected. In a later note, in which he used his own possible departure as a prod to frighten critics and give space to his experiment, Newman told Hope, "I assure you, to find that the English Church cannot bear the Lives of her Saints . . . does not tend to increase my faith and confidence in her."[17] Newman had, of course, only a few weeks earlier told Manning of his lack of such confidence.

By December 11 Newman had decided to relinquish the editorship of the series, while still undertaking to publish as separate works the lives already set in type by Rivington. Newman angrily informed Hope, "I do consider, then, I have given up a great deal. But what I have *not* given up is the *wish* that the work should be done; only I have put it under great disadvantages—so great that I think it never will be done—at the utmost fragments will be done—and that without method, precision, unity, and a name."[18] Despite his formal withdrawal as editor, Newman arranged for James Toovey to replace Rivington as publisher, oversaw publication of the life of St. Stephen Harding, wrote two brief lives himself, and continued until at least June 1845 to consult with authors and the publisher.

In the public mind, the series was always connected with Newman, and his thinking determined much of its character. Toward the conclusion of his essay on ecclesiastical miracles, he had announced, "What, indeed, is very obvious, but still may require a distinct acknowledgment, that the view here taken of the primitive miracles is applicable in defence of those of the medieval period also." He further declared that if the occurrence of miracles "depends upon the presence of the Catholic Church, and if that Church is to remain on earth until the end of the world," there was no reason why prejudice should "attend the medieval miracles at first hearing, though no distinct opinion can be formed about them before examination." These presuppositions deeply informed the *Lives of the English Saints*. In his own signed preface of February 21, 1844, to the lives of the family of St. Richard, Newman asserted that to the question of "whether the miracles recorded in these narratives" were to be received as matters of fact, "we can only reply, that there is no reason why they should not be," because they constituted "the kind of facts proper to ecclesiastical history, just as instances of sagacity and daring, personal prowess or crime, are the facts proper to secular history." Somewhat more guardedly, he stated that nothing existed "*primâ facie,* in the miraculous accounts in question to repel a properly taught and religiously disposed mind," which would "accordingly, give them a prompt and hearty acquiescence, or a passive admission, or receive them in part, or hold them in suspense, or absolutely reject them, according as the evidence makes for or against them, or is or is not of a trustworthy character." But in his life of St. Gundleus, without any formal criticism of the documentary evidence, Newman advised, "We can do nothing else but accept what has come down to us as symbolical of the unknown, and use it in a religious way for religious uses." He continued, "At the best it is the true record of a divine life; but at the very worst it is not less than the pious thoughts of religious minds,—thoughts frequent, recurrent, habitual, of minds of many in many generations." In the life of St. Bettelin, departing even further from critical analysis, Newman insisted that in examining contemporary reports and later legends of miraculous occurrences in the lives of medieval saints, "There is no room for the exercise of reason—we are in the region of faith. We must believe and act where we cannot discriminate; we must be content to take the history as sacred on the whole, and leave the verification of particulars as unnecessary for devotion, and for criticism impossible."[19]

Newman's fellow hagiographers followed his lead in regard to the miraculous, with differing degrees of conviction. Thomas Meyrick in his life of St. Richard simply declared, "The lives of Christian saints are a standing miracle." In the life of St. Augustine, Oakeley asked, "If Christianity did not make its way into Saxon England by miracles, how came its progress to be so rapid and so wide?" After writing that Christians looked to the individual saint "as the work of Divine grace" in history, Pattison then recorded miracles in his life of St. Ninian. He and Dalgairns reported the continuation through the late seventeenth century of miracles at the tomb of St. Edmund at Pontigny, the evidence for which "is so full, complete, and satisfactory, that all history might as well be rejected if these are to be."[20]

Other contributors qualified their support of the necessity and validity of medieval miracles. The unsigned preface to the life of St. German, presumably written by John Walker, merely asserted, "Those miracles, which have been given without any stress upon the authority or evidence, are considered true and credible as far as testimony can make anything credible." Thomas Mozley urged in the life of St. Bartholomew, "The visions seen and the voices heard by the Saints are expressed in terms, so to speak, of Time and Space to which we are at present bound, so that it is often hard to distinguish them from the phantoms of imagination." Church, in his life of St. Wulstan, more reservedly noted "But whether he did these miracles, or they were only reported of him, so he lived, and so he died, that men readily believed them of him."[21]

The authors disagreed about whether miracles confirmed the faith of the church or whether the church provided the authority for faith in the miracles. According to Faber in his life of St. Bega, beyond displaying romance and poetry, miracles "attest the power and heavenliness of that system of Catholic morals, so often stigmatised as degrading, servile, and superstitious" and to that end they should be kept in view. But in his lives of St. Waltheof and St. Robert, Dalgairns argued the reverse, contending that men would believe or disbelieve the truth of miracles "in proportion as they are disposed to admit or reject the antecedent probability of the existence of a perpetual church endowed with unfailing divine powers." He further asserted very much in line with the incipient skepticism of Newman's essay, "Ecclesiastical miracles presuppose the Catholic faith just as Scripture miracles, and Scripture itself presuppose the existence of God." Consequently, "the real reason for rejecting the account of the vision which appeared to St. Waltheof in the Holy Eucharist, must be disbelief of the Catholic doctrine." Then explaining why such visions of Christian saints were true and those of false gods and of "beings created by superstition" were untrue, he wrote, "the answer is, that . . . the visions in the lives of Saints presuppose the truth of the Catholic faith, and are real because the faith is true." Dalgairns concluded, "We believe Christian visions to be real because Christianity is real, and the portents of heathen mythology are false because they are part of a false religion."[22]

Accounting for the origins of saintly visions, Dalgairns explained that God imparted supernatural power to his saints to carry out healing and to experience visions. He further contended, "Imagination, translated into the language of the Church, means devotion; and no one can tell how far Almighty God may have made use of the Saint's own devotion in framing the vision before the eyes of his soul." People who excluded such divine explanations of the world simply excluded "whatever does not necessarily come within their system, even though it may not be incompatible with it." God could work his own purposes through natural causes, including the laws and faculties of the human mind. Dalgairns further claimed, "What is meant by a law is only the human way of viewing in succession, what to Almighty God, and it may be even to the angels, is one and undivided." Then, drawing an analogy between natural and spiritual sight, possibly derivative of Newman's university sermons, he urged, "Substance is taken for granted in our bodily vision, as the faith is presupposed in supernatural visions."[23]

The authors of *Lives of the English Saints*, however, did more than record their protagonists' ecstatic visions. Many of the biographies reported miracles of an indefinite character occurring at their saints' burial sites. According to Pattison, the divine judgment that St. Thomas à Becket's "life had been offered to God" as a sacrifice "acceptable in His sight" had received verification "in that way that is least of all liable to mistake, by the visible and tangible evidence of miracles." Pattison explained that "to the humble monk and the helpless poor, the obscure and the oppressed, but, withal, faithful and obedient, God dispenses help and healing by the medium of the remains of the dead." In that fashion, "As a miracle is a co-operation of God's power with man's faith, the more the prayers of the believing are attracted to any particular relic, the more is its hidden virtue developed; so continually fresh prodigies were performed at Canterbury."[24]

Some narratives described with differing degrees of certainty miracles performed by saints during their own lifetimes. In regard to miracles accorded to St. Wulstan, Church observed, "How far they may have been fictions, imagined and circulated under shelter of the general belief in supernatural agency for good and evil, we have now little means of ascertaining." Other authors directly reported supernatural occurrences. After relating the story of heavy rain first being deflected from St. Ninian but then falling upon him as his mind became distracted from religious reading, Pattison commented, "No useless lesson this—that the unseen guardianship which is over us in prayer, which screens us from evil, that the grace which is then around us, is for the time withdrawn, if wilful distractions are admitted." Faber reported apparitions of the dead St. Ebba, as well as visionaries receiving instructions from another departed saint about healing. Froude, who experienced much difficulty evaluating the miraculous elements of the life of St. Neot, nonetheless included the story of that physically short saint having successfully prayed to God to open a high lock on a monastery door in order to admit a person needing aid. Walker recorded accounts of a paralyzed man regaining the use of his limbs after washing in water that had bathed the corpse of St. Amator before burial and of St. German's having restored the sight of a blind man, as well as repelling a nest of large snakes and numerous other miracles. Dalgairns in the life of St. Stephen Harding recorded the reappearance of a dead monk. Despite the inclusion of modest qualifications, the general thrust of the narratives suggested that the miraculous events had occurred even if, as in the case of St. Wilfrid's healing a young boy who had fallen from a building, the story was admitted to have progressed only gradually among the faithful.[25]

Beyond finding their rational and scientific sensibilities affronted by the revelry in the irrational appearing in Newman's essay on ecclesiastical miracles and the *Lives of the English Saints*, learned early Victorian Protestant reviewers discerned either revival of long-discarded superstitions or profound theological and religious skepticism at work in the Tractarian approach to Christian history. Such commentators throughout the transatlantic world, including numerous men of science, accepted in some manner biblical miracles, but they believed that miracles, like divine revelation itself, had ceased after the apostolic age. Protestants saw numerous religious and theological perils associated with breaking the boundaries of that delimited age of miracles.

Discrediting the faith among people of intelligence and good sense was one such danger. An anonymous comment in the high-church *British Magazine* derided the series of saints' lives for palming upon the church with "pernicious zeal and industry" the "old sophistry, lying legends, forged writings, and all the worst things of the worst defenders of the worst times and practices of irreligious popery." If religion appeared equated with superstition, as it did in recent Tractarian writings, thinking persons would reject it. W. F. Hook thought the *Lives of the English Saints* would "have the same effect in England as the fanatical movement in France; they will make men decided infidels." The Congregationalist Henry Rogers wrote in the *Edinburgh Review*, "If Mr. Newman's tests be thought sufficient, we hardly know any legend wild enough to be unworthy of human belief." He further claimed that it was useless to quarrel with the authors of the *Lives of the English Saints*, because "if we speak of the veriest mummeries of that period, it will be said, 'but what a deep feeling of faith' accompanied these seeming follies!"[26]

Even more serious than a revival of superstition, Baden Powell saw in the Tractarian emphasis on the miraculous in ecclesiastical history the possibility of "nothing less than an entire rejection of all distinctive evidences of Scripture revelation, and, under the most flimsy and transparent professions of faith and sanctity, the adoption of a system undistinguishable from that of rationalism or deism." Writing in the *British and Foreign Review*, he asked whether Newman's language and method of argument could prove "*consistent with* ANY real belief in revelation." Having become confused and uncertain about proofs of either natural or revealed religion, the Tractarians had sunk "into a hopeless apathy," merging "all thought in a confused visionary mysticism, which is but the counterpart of universal skepticism." To escape "the strife of conflicting opinions and the gloom of universal doubt," they consequently looked to the church which in the process, rather than "a household of faith," they made "a refuge for those destitute" of faith. Two years later, Powell concluded in the *Westminster Review* that Newman's analysis of ecclesiastical miracles, of which he regarded the *Lives of the English Saints* as an extension, tended to "*invalidate all commonly received ideas of a distinct revelation of Christianity evinced by miracles.*" By refusing to distinguish between an original revelation in Scripture and the later postapostolic history of the church, the Tractarians had broken down "the line of demarcation between the divine and the human, the natural and the supernatural" upon which "all rationalism proceeds."[27] Without infallibility being ascribed to the church, it was unclear how the Tractarians' reasoning differed from that of rationalists. The danger that Newman had raised among believers was the temptation of transferring to the biblical narrative itself the critical skepticism traditionally applied to postapostolic miracles.

Apprehension about religious skepticism flowing from the Tractarian embrace of ecclesiastical and medieval miracles occurred to quite sophisticated theological minds. Other portions of the *Lives of the English Saints*, however, fed the more widespread, commonplace fears that the Tractarians sought to foster Roman Catholicism within the confines of the Church of England. Outlooks, attitudes, and assertions that Protestant contemporaries of all persuasions regarded as distinctly Roman Catholic permeated the *Lives of the English Saints*. Merely writing about the medieval English Church, of course, brought to the fore allegiance to Rome because the authors of the historical sources assumed papal supremacy, about which the various biographies indicated very considerable modern enthusiasm. Dalgairns described Rome as "the bourn to which the hearts of all Englishmen naturally turned at that day across the wide tract of land and sea which separated them," because England never forgot that Rome was "her mother church." He further presented medieval Rome as "the principal treasurehouse of Christ's blessings on earth, the centre of Catholic communion, and the rallying-point of all that was good." Suggesting that admiration for Rome transcended any particular historical epoch, Faber claimed, "To look Romeward is a Catholic instinct, seemingly implanted in us for the safety of the faith." He described St. Wilfrid as seeing Rome "as a legitimate fountain of Catholic teaching, desiring to measure and compare his English faith with it, and prepared to abandon whatever was opposed to the doctrine, spirit, or usage of Rome." Passing beyond any acceptable Protestant boundaries, Faber praised "the happy chains which held England to St. Peter's chair,—chains never snapped, as sad experience tells us, without the loss of many precious Christian things." Pattison in his life of St. Stephen Langton stridently defended the papal interdict over England during the reign of King John as "a measure of mercy, an appeal, on its Divine side, to Providence; on its human side, to all the generous feelings of the heart." Commending King John's excommunication, Pattison declared that one need not entertain "a Catholic bias" but only lack "the anti-Catholic bias" to understand such papal acts as "no far-fetched, high-flown usurpations, but only the natural, inevitable results of a public and established Christianity."[28] The only reason that such papal authority could no longer hold sway was that a united Christendom itself had ceased to be.

As Newman had promised Hope, monkery as well as miracles and the papacy filled the volumes of *Lives of the English Saints*. Monkery as explored by the Tractarian authors doubly offended Protestant readers by simultaneously embracing the Roman Catholic monastic ideal and casting aspersions on the ideal of the Victorian family. In the life of St. Wilfrid, Faber, reasserting a main argument of Newman's *Church of the Fathers*, declared, "Monastic orders are the very life's blood of a Church, monuments of true apostolic Christianity, the refuges of spirituality in the worst times, the nurseries of heroic bishops, the mothers of rough-handed and great-hearted missionaries." Then, implicitly condemning the modern English Church, in which he still held orders, he announced, "A Church without monasteries is a body with its right arm paralyzed." Oakeley for his part thought the history of monasteries read "almost like meditations" which to outsiders would appear "wearisome as the tales of dreamers, their chronicles of events read like fiction, their comments sound like the ravings of fanaticism." For Dalgairns, however, "The very object of Monasticism is to give a proper outlet to devotional feelings, which are stifled in the world, because it would be fanatical to indulge them."[29]

The championing of monasticism in *Lives of the English Saints* struck at the heart of early Victorian cultural expectations of marriage, family, and gender roles.[30] The narratives questioned the autonomy of the individual within families, cast doubt on patriarchal family structure, and suggested the wisdom of abstinence from sexual relationships between husbands and wives, as well as providing unbecoming details about saints' efforts to preserve their own virginity and celibacy.

At least one of the authors the *Lives of the English Saints* genuinely wanted to replace his own Victorian family with a Victorian monastery. An ardent Tractarian supporter from his student days, Dalgairns, after taking his degree in 1839, had received financial support from Newman and was the first inhabitant of Littlemore. That setting provided a refuge from his parents' pressure that he enter the Church of England ministry despite his uncertainty as a Catholic of being able conscientiously to subscribe to the Articles.[31] Like many late adolescents, he genuinely desired to establish his own independent existence separate from his family. Littlemore provided for Dalgairns a family-like setting with a paternal figure extending to him the kind of sympathy and religious understanding then lacking in his own family. Littlemore was also the place where he self-consciously decided to reject his family, choosing in late September 1845 to enter the Roman communion immediately before his parents arrived there for a visit.

Dalgairns's life of St. Aelred reflected those yearnings for separation and independence from family. There he declared the monastic system as "an expansion of the love of the domestic circle upon a large community," "a supernatural home raised by Christianity out of man's Natural affections, an expansion of the narrowed sphere of usefulness allowed to most men in the world," and "a very large family." Indeed at one point Dalgairns exclaimed, "After casting our eyes on the holy rood, does it never occur to us to wonder how it can be possible to be saved in the midst of the endearments of a family, and the joys of domestic life?" He suggested that St. Benedict's rule had actually permitted parents to consign their children to monasteries and to take the vows on their behalf. Dalgairns argued that what appeared to modern people as an arbitrary action had been a kindness to those children. In the Middle Ages, he explained, "Monastic discipline was not then con- sidered so dreadful as it is now thought to have been; nor was this world looked upon as so very sweet that it was an act of madness to quit it for God's service. Rather, they were thought happy to whom God had given the grace of a monastic vocation, and they surely were called by Him to the happy seclusion of the cloister, who were placed there by their parents' will; just as now we find the wish of a father and mother decides on the profession or state of life of their child." Parents thus leaving a child in a monastery were "in one sense" completing their baptismal vows by placing a child "in the way of best fulfilling the vows to which they themselves had bound him in his infancy."[32] To readers unfamiliar with Dalgairns's personal situation or unsympathetic to his Catholic rebellion against his family, his comments suggested that the baptismal vows of parents superseded their responsibili- ties to nurture loving families and might transform parenthood into a mech- anism for supplying monks to monasteries.

The passages in the *Lives of the English Saints* that contemporaries found most remarkable and abhorrent related to virginity and celibacy as prescriptions for holy living. As John Cross Crosthwaite, a high-church critic, without undue exaggeration observed of the biographers, "According to their doctrine, there is something of impurity in the married state, and the state itself is something to be repented of." Near the conclusion of the life of St. Wilfrid, for example, Faber, urging "another more excellent way of advancing the Catholic cause," inquired, "What poetry more sweet, and yet withal more awfully real—indeed, hourly realised by the sensible cuttings of the very Cross—than the pursuit of Holy Virginity? . . . What are the troubles and the pains of life to the struggles of the sealed affections, struggles which come never to the surface, plaints which have no audience, sorrows which cannot ask for sympathy, and haply joys of which it is but a weak thing to say that they are not fathomable? What, O young men and maidens! what is more like an actual, protracted, lifelong Crucifixion, than the preservation of Holy Virginity, while every action of your gentle lives sings, like our sweet Lady, a perpetual Magnificat?" Dalgairns and Lockhart in the life of St. Gilbert urged, "Holy virginity is no less a portion of Christianity than holy penitence, and the denial of the virtue of the one most certainly impairs the full belief in the other . . . and they who deny the merit of virginity leave out a portion of Christian morals."[33]

Pressing the issue of virginity into extreme prominence in his life of St. Bega, Faber reported that even when St. Bega was a child, God had "inspired her with an ardent love of holy virginity." Although while a young woman in Ireland she received many offers of marriage, "Her thoughts were ever running upon the excellences of a monastic life; to be a nun was more after her heart than to be a queen, for that sweet truth was never out of her mind that the angels neither marry nor are given in marriage." Admitting that "this panting after holy virginity" would seem unreal to many, Faber reported that according to the medieval record Bega had received a visitation from either an angel or a departed saint or a holy man who had "admonished her to keep the laudable vow of chastity" and that thereafter she determined to fulfill that vow. Her father nonetheless contracted her marriage to a Norwegian prince, who upon visiting her father's palace ended the night in drunken revelry. During these hours St. Bega, having prayed to find a way to preserve her virginity, heard a voice, which she obeyed, telling her to flee her father's house. Contending "that Bega was justified in this act of flying from her father's house to fulfil her vow of virginity," Faber explained that certain persons having received divine supernatural election for a particular course of life were justified in pursuing the demands of that election rather than obedience to parents. He supposed that Bega, being one "who so loved chaste virginity," must have remembered how Christ, her heavenly spouse, had left his parents at the age of twelve upon their visit to the Temple. Faber concluded, "Great and dazzling was all that she left behind, but greater still and brighter the prize of holy virginity after which she pressed through the dreary prospect before her." She at last landed in England and for a time lived in a cave near the shore which she fled when pirates threatened "her treasure," which was "her chastity."[34] Bega eventually settled in Northumbria, ending her life as the chaste abbess of Hartlepool.

The question of virginity fascinated Faber more than any other of the authors. For example, he wrote of the young St. Ebba's "thirst for holy virginity" and her longing "to draw with her a band of virgins into the same divine espousals." In Faber's accounts men as well as women labored to protect their vows. Drawing here as elsewhere on Bede, he wrote that St. Cuthbert for many years allowed no women into his sanctuary. When St. Cuthbert came at St. Ebba's request to visit her convent, at night he resided outside the gates, "spending the hours of darkness in prayer, either up to his neck in the water, or in the chilly air." Although there was less information about St. Oswin, Faber observed, "We may suppose that one who all his life long so earnestly coveted the best gifts was not likely to be without a holy ambition for the coronal of virgins, and that in virginity, that great fountain of almsgiving, and preceptress of humility, his holy soul would much delight." Faber was no less specific about St. Wilfrid's concern for preserving his chastity, asserting, "He watched over his chastity as his main treasure, and was by an unusual grace preserved from pollution; and to this end he chiefly mortified his thirst, and even in the heats of summer and during his long pedestrian visitations, he drank only a little phial of liquid daily. So through the day he kept down evil thoughts, and when night came on, to tame nature and to intimidate the dark angels, no matter how cold the winter, he washed his body all over with holy water, till Pope John forbade him this great austerity. Thus, year after year, never desisting from his vigilance, did Wilfrid keep his virginity to the Lord."[35] These portions of the lives of the saints appeared to contemporaries as the prurient fantasies of unmarried Catholic men who knew too little of life, love, and family responsibilities. To readers of the early twenty-first century they denote the enormous apprehension and disgust with sexuality in general and women in particular of which we have already seen evidence. At the same time, the writing of these lives allowed their authors to spend a good deal of time and energy thinking about sexuality, all in the cause of advancing Catholicism.

Beyond what Crosthwaite condemned as "fanatical panegyrics of virginity," some biographers commended saints who had decided upon a religious calling only after marriage and who had thereafter rejected sexual relations with their spouses and then completely abandoned their marriages. For example, there was St. Etheldreda, who had wed Prince Egfrid about 660 but shortly thereafter informed him of her desire to live a continent life. The prince, unhappy about this unforeseen development, asked St. Wilfrid to intervene, promising him land and money if the intervention proved successful. St. Wilfrid, however, apparently dissembled. According to Faber, "Wilfrid, at her husband's desire, did lay before St. Etheldreda what Egfrid required; at the same time pointing out to her that obedience in such a matter was a clear duty, which nothing could supersede but a well-ascertained vocation from God. St. Etheldreda, it would appear, satisfied the bishop on this very point; and then his duty was at once shifted. So far from urging her to comply with her husband's desires, he did all he could to strengthen her in her chaste resolve, and to render her obedient to the heavenly calling." Etheldreda sought refuge from her husband in a monastery to which St. Ebba told her to flee and to which she was delivered by a miracle. Thereafter she founded a monastery of her own at Ely. The tale, of course, confirmed all the worst anti-Catholic prejudices about the duplicity of priests and their possible interference in the marital relationships of husbands and wives. Faber attempted to sidestep that problem by acknowledging that objections "would be raised in these days" to Etheldreda's "conduct as a wife, and to her marrying Egfrid at all," but then stated that "her defence belongs to her own life, not to Wilfrid's."[36]

Other examples of what Dalgairns had termed "the romance of monastic life" involved direct hostility toward domestic affection and family. Walker recounted that St. German had been "lulled in the arms of domestic happiness" but had then experienced a conversion, leading him to take on the cause of the church. Thereafter, apparently with little difficulty or turmoil, "His wife Eustachia became his sister."[37] She may have retired to a monastery herself, because after St. German took his vow of poverty, he had no property or worldly goods to share with his wife (or sister). Other authors presented women as potential sexual temptresses to young saints who fled their presence or escaped their designs for marriage in order to lead celibate lives in the priesthood.

Crosthwaite contended that in these discussions of celibacy, virginity, and rejection of sexual relations in marriage and of marriage itself the authors of the saints' lives "cast very grave suspicion on the purity of their own minds" and that "young persons who talk and think in this way, are in extreme danger of falling into sinful habits." Denouncing the praise for St. Cuthbert's nights in cold water, he wrote, "A *saint,* according to Mr. Newman's teaching, is, plainly, a person of no ordinary degree of natural viciousness, and of unusual, and almost preternatural violence of animal passions. His sanctity consists mainly, in the curious and farfetched ingenuity of the torments by which he contrives to keep himself within the bounds of decency." Even while recognizing the anti-Catholic animosity in Crosthwaite's judgment, one must note that the championing of chastity and celibacy in *Lives of the English Saints,* as well as the founding of Littlemore, challenged all the wider contemporary cultural expectations of domesticity against which the Tractarians had largely set themselves. Newman himself recognized the situation. In March 1842 he told Maria Giberne, a woman who over a decade earlier had rebuffed the romantic interests of his brother Francis and who later herself became a Roman Catholic nun, "We are trying to set up a half College half monastery at Littlemore, which does very well as far as it has gone, i.e. without inmates yet. Men enough are *willing*—but parents, friends, etc. are in the way." Eschewing deference toward the influence of parents over young adult children, Newman fully approved Dalgairns's converting in September 1845 before the arrival at Littlemore of his disapproving parents. Accounting for the widespread criticism of the saints' lives, he explained to Faber earlier in 1845, "The dread of a Romeward tendency has been increased by the paternal and maternal dread of children being decoyed away from their homes or being [un]protected on leaving it, or turning hermits, and the like, which the old Lives appear to countenance . . . and many a pater-familias I can conceive saying, 'Such trash shalln't come into my house.' "[38] Beyond embodying a secret Roman Catholicism in the English Church and rejecting the everyday middle-class commercial understandings of truth, Tractarians had now repudiated sexuality in marriage, keeping of marital vows, the attractions of family life, and deference of children to their parents.

The skepticism implicit in the essay on ecclesiastical miracles and the absence of critical historical judgment and the all too abundant prurience and challenge to domesticity present in the *Lives of the English Saints* constituted an intellectual penumbra surrounding all of Newman's activities during his last years in the English Church. By early 1844 evangelicals, high churchmen, liberals, and Catholics took their measure of Newman, his goals, and his character on the basis of the methods, approaches to evidence, and means of persuasion affronting common sense and widely shared social values that appeared with such extravagance in those publications. The mysticism, superstitious credulity, and potential skepticism of those publications, in addition to their flagrant Romish sympathies, raised questions of the most profound kind about not only Newman's reasoning and honesty but also about his good sense and good intentions. The man who in 1845 was to explore the idea of doctrinal development and then enter the Roman Church was the same person whom contemporaries necessarily associated with a tendentious defense of ecclesiastical miracles and with medieval saints' lives that offended one religious, moral, intellectual, and social sensibility after another.

TOWARD DEVELOPMENT

Like the leaders of other new nineteenth-century Protestant religious departures, Newman advocated a concept of ongoing or progressive revelation. His essay on ecclesiastical miracles and the *Lives of the English Saints* sought to demonstrate that God's revelation to Christians and his direct presence in the history of the church had not ceased at the close of the apostolic age. Newman's personal defense of progressive, extrabiblical revelation attained its full flowering, of course, in *An Essay on the Development of Christian Doctrine* of 1845, but his thinking on the matter extended deeply into his earlier preaching and writing. It will be recalled that in the early 1830s he had located the origins of religion, or of what he called natural religion, in the human response to the internal demands of conscience. Thereafter, through first the Jewish and later the Christian dispensations, God had supplemented that natural religion by revealing divine truths to humankind and establishing priesthoods to convey and preserve that truth. In *The Arians of the Fourth Century* Newman had expanded the scope of revelation to include the controversial idea of a dispensation of paganism. Not long thereafter, through the concept of Prophetical Tradition, he embraced an even more expansive vision of advancing religious revelation not wholly defined by ecclesiastical authority or by the high-church understanding of antiquity. Regarding the latter, he had acquiesced in Keble's radical, prescriptive appropriation of "the propriety of any sentiment, allowed to be general in Christian Antiquity, how remote soever from present views and usages."[39] *Tract 90* had defended an interpretation of the Articles that in an indeterminate manner legitimated many of these postbiblical, pre-Reformation religious ideas and practices as fitting for contemporary Catholic faith and devotion.

During the 1830s, however, Newman, while pressing against constraints of religious truth defined in terms of the Bible and antiquity, had given at best modest systematic attention to the manner in which additional religious knowledge might have emerged over the course of Christian history. But eventually a twofold challenge to his call to religious obedience and asceticism led him to speculate about how religious thought and practice developed. First, numerous critics, such as Thomas Arnold, faulted the Tractarian emphasis on law over grace as a modern version of the Judaizing that St. Paul had rejected in the life of early Christian congregations. Second, other critics had accused the Tractarians of Romanizing because of their emphasis on obedience and moral behavior and their favoring devotional practices associated in the popular mind with continental Roman Catholicism. Consequently, Newman found himself required to defend both religious continuity, in response to the accusations of Judaizing, and innovation, in response to accusations of Romanizing. He used the concept of development to address both challenges. By defending the ongoing presence of Jewish elements in Christianity, he laid the groundwork for the continued presence of Roman Catholic practices in post-Reformation Tractarian Catholicism.

In a sermon of May 1840, Newman first worked through the relationship of Judaism to Christianity in order to support the ongoing necessity of Christian obedience to the law. His chief presupposition was that Christianity represented a continuation, not a repudiation, of Judaism. After defining "religion" as "worship," he stated that "whatever changes" were made "in the sense of its letter" could not "be of a nature to reverse that letter," but might only "enlarge the letter" or "introduce a sense parallel to it," with "the substance of the ideas expressed" remaining "the same." Christians, according to Newman, through further knowledge of God's revelation had developed but not entirely rejected Jewish practices, Scripture, and law. Consequently, there was nothing wrong or inherently un-Christian with the Tractarians' advocacy of "reverence for sacred places, observance of holy days, adoption of a minute ceremonial, and the like," which their critics saw as redolent of Jewish religion. If, according to Newman, the Jewish Psalms could admit "of a Christian and spiritual sense, it does not appear why rites and ceremonies [similar to those given to the Jews] may not be practised spiritually also."[40] The Christian revelation had not displaced Judaism altogether but had reshaped it, as was the correct procedure with religious change. Implicit in this argument was a second contention. If the early Christian assimilation of elements of Jewish worship provided a legitimate model for religious development, then modern Christians might reappropriate practices drawn from earlier Christian ages and locales improperly repudiated during the Protestant Reformation. Two years later Newman was to return to the subject of the relationship of Judaism and Christianity.

Meanwhile, Newman and Oakeley defended the extension of the arena of devotional appropriation beyond Keble's radical 1839 expansion of the authority of antiquity to include the life and history of the Roman Catholic Church and beyond. These claims appeared in separate *British Critic* articles, published one month before *Tract 90*. For both writers Catholicism appeared to be a floating body of indeterminate truths ever in process of both recovery and discovery. Once again with the Tractarians, reclamation became a justification for innovation.

In the first essay Oakeley, redefining traditional high-church ecclesiology, warned readers against "identifying the Church with the Establishment" and regarding it "merely, or chiefly, in the light of a National institution." That " 'Rule Britannia' sentiment in matters ecclesiastical" frequently caused people to forget "that the basis of Christian union is not Nationality, but Catholicism." Recognition of that binding power of Catholicism, however, would require high churchmen, who often mindlessly attacked Roman Catholics and Protestant Dissenters alike, to see themselves as "better employed in trying to regain principles, to which, with all her faults, Rome has been, on the whole, a faithful witness." Asserting the great issue of the day as reunifying truths either ignored or broadly dispersed across both communions, Oakeley exclaimed, "O, when shall the Catholic elements, which now lie scattered in different and dissociated regions, but every where in combination with grievous error, be separated from their noxious adjuncts, and brought into effectual coalition! when shall true Catholic hearts, which now mourn (must we say hopelessly?) apart; forced by the pressure of disastrous influences upon the painful alternative of an almost morose reserve, or an almost disingenuous disguise; be unchained, each from his solitary cell, and restored to that energetic life, and active communion, after which they fondly yearn!"[41] Oakeley's vision was that of a union of Catholics now isolated in both the Roman and the English communions, where each, until so unified, possessed shreds of tattered Catholic truth without grasping the whole fabric. The image, however, of Catholics resorting to "morose reserve" and "disingenuous disguise" while protecting their truth was to haunt the Tractarians for years and further cast their everyday honesty into the most severe public doubt.

The same month Newman adopted a similar, remarkably open-ended vision of Catholicism in his important review of Henry Hart Milman's *History of Christianity*. Newman denounced Milman for implicitly holding, in typical Protestant fashion, "that nothing belongs to the Gospel but what originated in it; and that whatever, professing to belong to it, is found in anterior or collateral systems, may be put out of it as a foreign element." Newman's disapproval of that outlook implicitly reasserted his contention of 1840 about elements of proper continuity as one religion develops from another. Newman then criticized Milman's understanding of Christian history, which he associated with Socinianism and heresy despite Milman's serious criticism of Strauss's *Life of Jesus,* for failing to conceive of "the possibility of a visible and an invisible course of things going on at once." Historians who failed to grasp that metaphysical possibility while examining the emergence of the creed would "deny that what is historically human can be doctrinally divine, confuse the outward process with the secret providence, and argue as if instruments in nature preclude the operation of grace." Asserting the existence of particular manifestations of divine Providence coterminous "through, with, and beneath . . . physical, social, and moral laws" as imposed by God and directly experienced by human beings, Newman declared in the fashion of Carlylean natural supernaturalism, "All that is seen—the world, the Bible, the Church, the civil polity, and man, are types, and, in their degree and place, representatives and organs of an unseen world, truer, and higher than themselves. The only difference between them is, that some things bear their supernatural character upon their surface, are historically creations of the supernatural system, or are perceptibly instrumental or obviously symbolical: while others rather seem to be complete in themselves, or run counter to the unseen system which they really subserve, and so make demands upon our faith." Catholics recognized this dual reality in the manifestation of matter and spirit, the natural and the supernatural. Consequently, in contrast to Protestants, who understood revelation as "a single, entire, solitary act, or nearly so, introducing a certain message," Catholics maintained instead "that divine teaching has been in fact, what the analogy of nature would lead us to expect, 'at sundry times and in divers manners,' various, complex, progressive, and supplemental of itself."[42] The key last phrase, "supplemental of itself," opened for Newman the possibility of vast ongoing changes from and within any original deposit of divine truth that had occurred before, during, or after the age of the apostles. Moreover, those providential transformations occurred through what appeared to be natural causes. Consequently, beyond exploding both the evangelical standard of Scripture and the high-church standard of antiquity, Newman implicitly naturalized the course of religious change and progressive divine revelation.

Rather than limiting divine revelation to the single epoch of the life of Christ or the age of the Fathers, one could, Newman asserted, understand that "the Moral Governor of the world" had "scattered the seeds of truth far and wide over its extent," where they had taken root and grown as "wild plants indeed but living." Just as animals inferior to man "have tokens of an immaterial principle in them yet have not souls so the philosophies and religions of men have their life in certain true ideas, though they are not divine." The Church Catholic, as it passed through history, had ever actively functioned as "a treasure house, giving forth things old and new, casting the gold of fresh tributaries into her refiner's fire, or stamping upon her own, as time required it, a deeper impress of her Master's image."[43]

This concept of a divine institution working its way syncretistically through history allowed Catholics to "conceive that the church, like Aaron's rod, devours the serpents of the magicians," while Protestants remained "ever hunting for a fabulous primitive simplicity." Whereas Protestants "are driven to maintain . . . that the church's doctrine was never pure," Catholics "readily grant . . . that it can never be corrupt." Catholics believe "that a divine promise keeps the Church Catholic from doctrinal corruption," but "on what promise, or on what encouragement" Protestants seek "their visionary purity does not appear."[44] Newman thus in the name of latitudinarian, indeed expansionary, Catholicism enthusiastically embraced doctrinal and devotional indeterminacy lacking authoritative guides, boundaries, or definitions. Catholic truth existed in the eye of its beholder, the Church Catholic, for which Newman provided no clear or distinct definition or delineation, except as perceived in the private judgment of the Tractarians themselves. In defending such an expansive vision of religious truth, Newman, somewhat unlike Oakeley, sought not to reconcile himself to the contemporary Roman Catholic Church or the decrees of the Council of Trent but rather to defend the faith and practice that he and his followers wished to pursue in their utopian quest for an idealized Catholicism.

In a sermon of November 1842 Newman returned to the continuities between Judaism and Christianity, this time within the more general framework of human religious development. He portrayed Judaism as a religion closely related historically to the earlier religions of the region where it arose. As such, Judaism represented "the correction, the restoration, of those degenerate and corrupt religions [which preceded and surrounded it], just as Christianity is the development and spiritual perfection of the Jewish." Again countering accusations of Judaizing by then additionally germane because of the devotional rigor emerging at Littlemore, Newman contended, "Now, if it is a good argument against our Christian priesthood, Christian sacrifices, Christian Sabbaths, and Christian sacraments, that they are like ordinances of the Jewish Law, which came from God, much more would it be an argument against that Law in Samuel's time or David's, as infidels have made it since, that in some chief portions of it, it is like the paganism of Egypt or Syria." In effect, Newman contended that all religious truth would simply evaporate into nothingness or skepticism if one disallowed elements of continuity between successive religions. Drawing the issue into the immediate present, he declaimed, "And if it is a good argument against our [Tractarian] Church system, that St. Paul denounces Judaism, surely it is not a worse argument against the Jewish system, that Moses denounces paganism." Further pressing the analogy of Christianity emerging from Judaism, Newman announced in a statement replete with as yet untapped theological complexity, "The Gospel is but a development of the Law; and creeds and systems may at first sight be very far removed from certain known originals, and yet, after all, be but developments of them."[45] This sweeping assertion, unsupported by any substantially articulated argument, provided a theoretical basis for enormous latitude in pursuing novel, modern beliefs or practices in the cause of either religious restoration or progressive religious development.

In February 1843 Newman published *Sermons, Chiefly on the Theory of Religious Belief,* a collection intended among other things to provide a firm theological basis for Tractarian asceticism. Throughout the volume, which included his sermons of the early 1830s on natural religion rooted in human conscience and his later sermons redefining faith and Reason, he defined religion, whether understood in terms of behavior or in terms of faith, primarily as a matter of morality and obedience. He concluded this collection with "The Theory of Developments in Religious Doctrine," a sermon delivered in February 1843, the same month as "The Apostolical Christian," in which he equated the genuine Bible Christian with monks and nuns. In "The Theory of Developments in Religious Doctrine," Newman defended the validity of the strict doctrines and devotional practices that underscored his long-standing call to a religion of obedience and sustained his monastic experiment. In the process, he further explored the mechanisms of ongoing religious revelation.

The words from Luke 2:19, "But Mary kept all these things, and pondered them in her heart," provided Newman's text for this Feast of the Purification sermon. More boldly associating himself with the mother of Jesus than on previous occasions, Newman announced, "St. Mary is our

pattern of Faith, both in the reception and in the study of Divine Truth."
She had embodied the faith that, as championed by the early church, had
sought "the overthrow of the wisdom of the world," that phrase by now
almost always indicating for Newman evangelical religion. The triumph of
the ancient church had required of the heathen world what Newman and his
Catholic followers were now demanding of the English Church: "to confess,
what yet they could not deny, that a Superstition, as they considered it, was
attracting to itself all the energy, the keenness, the originality, and the
eloquence of the age." The early saints who, like the Littlemore coterie,
stood accused of superstition had "given up the comforts of earth and the
charities of home, and surrendered themselves to an austere rule, nay, even
to confessorship and persecution," in order to advance the progress of the
faith. Those saints had succeeded in rearing "a large fabric of divinity" that,
while "irregular in its structure, and diverse in its style," and "anomalous
in its details, from the peculiarities of individuals, or the interference of
strangers," remained "still, on the whole, the development of an idea, and
like itself, and unlike any thing else, its most widely-separated parts having
relations with each other, and betokening a common origin." That body of
postapostolic Catholic divinity stood as "the expansion of a few words,
uttered, as if casually, by the fishermen of Galilee." Over time Reason,
ministering to this faith, had elicited from those words meaning that their
first hearers "little suspected." That very capacity to develop religious truth
progressively constituted one of the notes of Catholic truth, while by contrast heresies remained "in themselves, without development, because they
are words" proving "barren, because they are dead."[46]

Newman directly rebuked Protestants, such as R. D. Hampden (though
without naming him), for teaching "that the development of ideas and
formation of dogmas is a mere abuse of Reason" working "beyond its
powers" and doing nothing more than multiplying "words without meaning, and deductions which come to nothing." In response to Hampden's
contention that discursive reason applied to the great facts of religious
revelation resulted largely, if not exclusively, in a confused narrowing of the
original truth of divine revelation, Newman urged that revelation set before
the mind "certain supernatural facts and actions, beings and principles"
actually intended to invite the mind's reflections and hence development
and change. Impressions made by the original apostolically revealed truth
might long remain an unconscious presence in the collective human mind of
the church, which itself functioned differently according to mood or circumstance. What Newman termed "the reality and permanence of inward

knowledge" of Catholic doctrines, thus unconsciously retained in the minds of the faithful, existed "distinct from explicit confession," which might not emerge until many centuries after the apostles. Newman directly asserted, "Even centuries might pass without the formal expression of a truth, which had been all along the secret life of millions of faithful souls."[47] The church collectively had just as much difficulty in making explicit ideas that had long resided latent within its mind as did individuals who often experienced difficulty in easily or quickly articulating their own inner thoughts.

Establishing genuine, historical connections between those latent, unarticulated ideas and their public development posed a genuine problem for Newman—indeed, one he never really solved. He eschewed discursive historical analysis that would reduce developments in Christian doctrines to moments in a secular narrative. Rather, as in his January 1841 *British Critic* article, he postulated a theological history that, while manifesting itself naturalistically within secular history, was driven through the workings of hidden sacred forces and determinants. According to Newman's theory, one thought about God led expansively to another without the persons so contemplating those divine thoughts necessarily knowing where that contemplation would ultimately lead or whether it was complete. As he explained this unconscious dynamic, "One proposition necessarily leads to another, and a second to a third; then some limitation is required; and the combination of these opposites occasions some fresh evolutions from the original idea, which indeed can never be said to be entirely exhausted. This process is its development, and results in a series, or rather body of dogmatic statements, till what was at first an impression on the Imagination has become a system or creed in the Reason."[48] The divine thought or idea apparently produced on the Imagination an impression which in turn the Reason further explored. The process appears to have been a cumulative one, with the implications of the original ideas receiving further articulation rather than a dialectical one whereby older or previous ideas are overcome, transformed, and discarded. But through this cumulative articulation, actual substantive change did occur.

Newman thus outlined a dynamic concept of Christian truth originating in biblical revelation and in an extrabiblical deposit of apostolic truth but substantially transforming itself over the ages. The reading of the Bible constituted only one of many religious situations from which human beings came to receive divine impressions. Others included keeping company with those possessing sacred ideas, studying dogmatic theology, pursuing the life of devotion, and allowing the operation of faith in oneself. The formulation of creeds was "a chief mode of perpetuating the impression" of the divine gleaned from these sources, with the Scriptures themselves providing the main outlines of the dogmatic system. Admitting that one might wonder why "such inspired statements [of Scripture] are not enough without further developments," Newman replied that once reason "has been put on the investigation, it cannot stop till it has finished it." Consequently, one dogma would create another "by the same right by which it was itself created." The statements of Scripture functioned "as sanctions as well as informants in the inquiry." Those statements "begin and they do not exhaust." Because Scripture so instigates developments in doctrine that it does not contain, "it is a mistake to look for every separate proposition of the Catholic doctrine in Scripture."[49] Rather, the primary role of Scripture is to impress on human beings the Catholic idea, with the peculiar function of the church being that of realizing its developments.

Newman concluded the sermon by wondering whether even under his developmental analysis the explicit statements of Catholic dogma might not still confuse words with things. As in the past, he assumed an empiricist philosophical framework, with the human mind receiving sense impressions. He then introduced into that framework the analogous concept of distinct religious impressions upon which the mind worked as it did upon sense impressions. Pressing that analogy, he argued that neither set of impressions may actually convey knowledge of its own particular reality—that is to say, human beings might experience only a myriad of material and religious impressions, providing no knowledge of any reality or certainty beyond themselves. Consequently, reasoning based on such impressions might not actually lead to any knowledge beyond conclusions about those impressions. On that basis, Newman observed, "Let, then, the Catholic dogmas, as such, be freely admitted to convey no true idea of Almighty God, but only an earthly one, gained from earthly figures, provided it be allowed, on the other hand, that the senses do not convey to us any true idea of matter, but only an idea commensurate with sensible impressions."[50] Here Newman brought his readers to the brink of a radical Humean skepticism, a cauldron of doubt and uncertainty that would produce the agnosticism of the next Victorian generation. For his own purposes, Newman avoided that conclusion by contending that Catholic dogma, though conditioned by our present earthly state, nonetheless corresponded to its heavenly archetype.

Yet, Newman's analysis did result in an immediate skepticism, though he sought to elude it. When he delivered and published this sermon, no authority existed among English Catholics to define the precise meaning of

"Catholic Dogmas." Even if it had existed, such an authority, according to Newman's own analysis, could not have set doctrinal limits. Newman had outlined a process of indeterminate theological development arising from an original revelation inexhaustible in its capacity for future elucidation and interpretation. He claimed that no necessary identity existed between the original idea or impression, presumably rooted in revelation, and its later development, for the development represented carrying out the impression to its consequences. Without falling into heresy, dogmatic statements about God could not "say more than is implied in the original idea," but Newman gave little indication about how to determine the exact content of that original idea. Indeed, he argued that Catholic dogmas constituted "after all, but symbols of a Divine fact, which, far from being compassed by those very propositions, would not be exhausted, nor fathomed, by a thousand."[51] Doctrines just kept developing with no future end point in sight.

Although evangelicals regarded Newman's concept of development as still one more indication of his having rejected biblical theology, high churchmen took offense at his bursting the boundaries of antiquity, which they believed separated the ancient Catholic faith from later Roman Catholic corruptions. In the least analyzed portions of his *Narrative*, published only a few months after Newman's sermon, William Palmer identified the principle of development as the heart of Tractarian errors resulting in Romanizing. He explained that for the Roman Catholic apologists Joseph De-Maistre and J. A. Möhler, development evaded "the objection" to Roman Catholicism "founded on the *silence of primitive tradition*, in regard to the papal supremacy, the worship of Saints and Angels, and other Romish doctrines and practices; or *its actual opposition* to Rome in such points." Using development to replace an unwritten tradition or a *disciplina arcani*, these modern Roman Catholic apologists had contended that "it is the nature of Christianity *to develope itself gradually* in the course of ages, and under change of circumstances." Palmer associated this novel principle with Rationalism on the grounds that Rationalists, who remained unnamed, identified the development of religion with ongoing accomplishments of human reason while the Roman Catholic apologists similarly identified such development with the office of the church. Both the Rationalist and the Roman Catholic concept of development involved a progressive definition of religion that portrayed "the religion of the present day" as "more perfect than that of the early Church" and that consequently taught modern men and women "*to set aside the testimony of Catholic antiquity*, on pretense, that religion was then but imperfectly understood." By contrast, the principle of the Church Catholic, according to Palmer, had always been "*to hand down and bear witness to the Catholic verities which she received from the Apostles, and not to argue, to develop, to invent.*"[52]

While admitting that reason led by faith could "systematize, harmonize, and illustrate" the original truth of the apostles, Palmer saw only confusion and inconsistency in the current rhetoric of development, as most recently illustrated in Newman's sermon. Newman had suggested that development amounted simply to *inferences* from revelation, which unlike *expressions* from revelation itself could not constitute articles of faith. Apparently believing that Newman's explication of development of doctrine actually resulted in creeds that confused the great facts of revelation, the situation about which a decade earlier Hampden had so controversially warned, Palmer urged, "These Catholic doctrines, and others included in the doctrine of the Trinity and the Incarnation, should not be confounded with mere theological dogmas deduced from the truths of Revelation by action of reason; lest in advocating both on the same principles and in the same mode, the Faith should be in danger of being mingled with the doctrines of men." Newman's concept of development was in Palmer's opinion genuinely rationalistic because it imagined doctrines emerging through the exercise of reason on revelation and then upon previous reasonings about revelation. Palmer also argued that development might legitimize and validate all manner of unexpected religious and theological outcomes including the Reformation so hated by the Tractarians. Moreover, through the principle of development, the Gospel itself might be mistaken for "only a philosophy, a science, a creation of the intellect." In the end Palmer believed that those who embraced development might "discover, too late, that a philosophy which has commenced its speculations in the service of Romanism, may have found its legitimate conclusion in Rationalism, or in St. Simonianism."[53]

Deeply troubled by the profound indeterminacy inherent in the metaphor, Palmer rejected the idea that Christian revelation could on developmental premises "be compared to a plant which only gradually attains its perfection." Carried to one possible conclusion, that metaphor might suggest that the Christian faith could enter a period not only of growth but also of "*corruption and death,*" or that anything allowed or tolerated by church authorities "*cannot be a corruption.*" Palmer noted that on the basis of development the Romanizing contributors to the *British Critic* had championed medieval practices "as being in essential respects superior to our own" and had portrayed "the Papal supremacy, the invocation of Saints, &c. as divinely instituted." Indeed, Palmer argued that these *British Critic* authors appeared to have concluded from the theory of development "that Rome *as she is* should be our actual model in religion."[54] All of those tendencies manifested themselves even more fully, of course, during the next two years in the *Lives of the English Saints*.

Newman did not respond to Palmer or to any other theological equal. Indeed, after the 1836 correspondence with Rose, Newman never again while in the Church of England carried out an extended correspondence about theology with another man, including Keble and Pusey, who might check the expansion of his thought. He reported his thoughts to men, though by no means fully, but did not ask for theological advice or criticism. Instead, from late 1843 onward Catherine Holdsworth Froude, Mary Holmes, Maria Giberne, and his sister Jemima were the recipients of Newman's most elaborate musings over his theological opinions and ecclesiastical situation. From these female correspondents, who did not include his sister Harriett, by then estranged from her brother because of her husband's near conversion, Newman sought sympathy, understanding, and deference, which he generally received. Moreover, unlike Newman's immediate male coterie, these women did not run wild with his ideas, but with the exception of Jemima proved benignly receptive to his musings. This pattern largely replicated the situation prevailing in his family from the late 1820s to the early 1840s, when his mother and sisters were always more tolerantly interested in Newman's thought and activity than his disapproving brothers.

Catherine Holdsworth Froude, always addressed as Mrs. Froude, received Newman's most extensive speculations over the idea of development. She was the wife of William Froude, the brother of Hurrell and James Anthony Froude and a scientist then himself undergoing a period of religious doubt. Why Newman wrote so extensively to Mrs. Froude is not certain. He may have felt himself carrying out a vicarious dialogue with the now long dead Hurrell. He may have believed himself more likely to receive an empathetic hearing from the spouse of someone experiencing religious difficulties, an empathy unavailable from his family. He may also have thought that his sharing his inner thoughts with Mrs. Froude would simply fascinate her and her husband. Furthermore, the absence of significant previous correspondence with the Froudes allowed Newman to use these letters to construct a highly selective personal narrative that traced the emergence of his recent religious thought with virtually no references to the turmoil and conflict of the past four years—that is to say, a history of his religious opinions and experience without the presence of *Tract 90*.

Commencing on April 3, 1844, Newman told Mrs. Froude that since at

least 1833 he had "felt both admiration and love of Rome, as far as I dare."
Only "a strong positive difficulty or repulsion" arising from particular Roman doctrines had prevented him from surrendering his heart. That "very
circumstance" had caused him "to be violent against the church of Rome—
because it was the only way of resisting it." Indeed, he reported, "To be
violent against Rome was to be dutiful to England, as well as a measure of
necessity for the English theory." Then in 1839, he reported, "It flashed
upon me in the course of reading the Fathers" that the English theory was
"disproved by Antiquity."[55] In a very real sense, Newman admitted to Mrs.
Froude that by 1839 his mind had eventually devised an argument to sustain
the love for Rome that had arisen six years earlier and that had continued to
stir his inner being.

   Throughout this correspondence Newman urged that the changing of
one's religious affiliation need not necessarily result in a general skepticism
about all religion. He stated on April 4 that his own personal alteration
of opinion should not shake other people's faith in truth as "a real objective thing." Actually, just the opposite was the case because, he explained,
"Surely the *continuance* of a person who wishes to go right in a wrong
system, and not his giving it up, would be that which militated against the
objectiveness of Truth—leading to the suspicion that one thing and another
were equally pleasing to our Maker where men were sincere." One should
not, however, begin with private judgment but rather "throw oneself generously into that form of religion which is providentially put before one." He
did not want his regret over his anti-Roman statements or "all sorts of
faults" in his "*mode* of doing things" to be seen as having caused him to
surrender "feeling an *assurance* that I have been brought on by a divine
guidance to my present point." At the same time he indicated having "so
bad a conscience in details as to have *very little* claim to feel confidence that I
am right."[56] Again, as in his sermons of December 1841, Newman resorted
in an evangelical fashion to personal inner assurance and conviction.

   A day later Newman further rehearsed to Mrs. Froude his loss of confidence in the Catholicity of the English Church originating in 1839. Through
an insight that provided "*a key,* which interpreted large passages of history"
previously "locked up" to him, he had then discovered in the Council of
Chalcedon "a complete and wonderful parallel, as if a prophecy, of the state
of the Reformation controversy, and that we were on the Anti-Catholic
side." Thereafter he repeatedly found "one and the same picture, prophetic
of our present state, the Church in communion with Rome decreeing, and
heretics resisting." Ancient anti-Catholics had charged Catholic opponents

with "introducing novel and unscriptural terms into the Creed of the Church," most particularly when the Nicene Council had adopted a term condemned by the Council of Antioch more than a half-century earlier. On April 9 Newman stated that he had concluded "that separation from the body of Christendom, and again, or especially, from the see of Rome, is (for those who would go by primitive views of Christianity) a *presumption* of error." He could not "recollect by what degrees or at what time it became an unsettling principle in my mind, though I perfectly recollect the lively feelings produced in me by the Monophysite history."[57] He then recounted reading Wiseman's *Dublin Review* article about the Donatists and his effort to refute its argument. What Newman did not say to Mrs. Froude, and what he may genuinely have forgotten, was that he had himself formulated almost exactly the same argument in "Home Thoughts Abroad."

Having traced the impact of these ideas, Newman informed Mrs. Froude of his now "sincere belief and principle that it is right to resist doubts and to put aside objections to the form of doctrine and the religious system in which we find ourselves." He further repeated his conviction that "the system in which we have been placed is God's voice to us till He supersede it, and those means by which He supersedes it must be more distinct than the impression produced on us by that system itself." Three days later, Newman declared to Mrs. Froude, as he had to his sister more than six months earlier, "Be sure that I am in no danger of moving at present. Of course I cannot prophesy what may happen towards me from without; but I can have no intention of doing anything, or I should not just now have put out those Sermons," by which he meant the December 1841 sermons published a few months earlier in *Sermons, Bearing on Subjects of the Day*.[58] There the correspondence rested for over a month.

It is significant that twice in the letter of April 5 and once in that of April 12 Newman referred to the parallel he discerned between ancient and modern times as "prophetic," a point he had also made directly to Robert Wilberforce early in 1842 and implicitly to Manning in late 1843. Although Newman had abandoned most evangelical theology, an evangelical proclivity to interpret the present through categories of sacred prophecy and biblical narrative provided him with insights to reframe his understanding of the contemporary religious world.[59] He tended to do so at times of considerable personal stress. In 1833, following the loss of the Oriel tutorship and difficulties over publishing *The Arians of the Fourth Century*, his sudden understanding of Rome as not being the Antichrist had allowed him to expand the scope of possible Christian unity. His epiphany of 1839, following upon high-church repudiation of Froude's *Remains,* that the English Church might not be part of the Church Catholic, became, as he recalled it later, an explanation for the immediate problems confronting Tractarian Catholics. He wrote of the prophetic character of the ancient example to Wilberforce in the wake of the Jerusalem bishopric and poetry professorship contest and to Mrs. Froude in the face of mounting high-church abandonment of the Tractarians as seen in Gladstone's article of the previous October, Palmer's *Narrative,* and Catholic disapproval of the *Lives of the English Saints.* Viewing the position of the contemporary English Church as prophetically foreshadowed in conflicts from the fourth century allowed Newman to explain the failure of Catholicism to establish itself in that church without having to ascribe any responsibility or blame to his own actions. He and his fellow Tractarian Catholics could not find a place in the Church of England because it was not actually a part of the Church Catholic. He was experiencing the plight of the faithful Catholic dwelling in the midst of heretics. Newman thus understood the increasingly problematic situation of Tractarian Catholics by grasping radically new prophetic insights from ecclesiastical history as the advanced evangelicals of the 1820s had discerned their new religious calling from discovering radically new premillennialist interpretations of biblical prophecy.

On May 28 Newman posted a letter to Mrs. Froude authorizing her and her husband to say publicly that he had been very much unsettled over the question of Rome in 1839 but asking them to indicate nothing of his present frame of mind. He added, "It is very unpleasant to be trusted when I do not deserve it."[60] This is a curious statement to come from a person distrusted not only by the general English public but also for several months even by close Catholic associates. Just over a week later, and then again in July, Newman would also ask Henry Wilberforce to let it be known that since 1839 he had entertained doubts about the Catholicity of the Church of England. The spreading of this self-narrative, which eight months earlier he had posed to Manning, allowed Newman to explain his thoughts and actions on the grounds of a theological conviction predating *Tract 90* and all that followed. He thus located his doubt about the Church of England to its standing in a prophetically foreshadowed schism from the Church Catholic rather than to his personal treatment by that institution. He thereby sought to transform the most vicious and corrosive controversy in the recent history of the English Church into a small bump in his own larger spiritual and ecclesiastical journey. He could not admit that he had been defeated by the evangelicals and abandoned by the high churchmen. Nor could he admit that he no longer was really certain about what he himself believed in regard to either faith or practice. He must provide himself with a history that might either make sense of his next step or defend his taking no step at all. He must create his own historical reality.

Meanwhile, over a ten-day interval in late May, Newman composed an extensive letter to Mrs. Froude on the subject of the claims of the Roman Church. Rejecting the high-church branch theory of the Christian Church as both "absurd" and "hypocritical" for reducing differences over "*doctrine and practice*" to a quarrel about "ecclesiastical arrangement," he explained that the Reformation had really created two churches, each of which "claims its inherent original jurisdiction over the whole Church." Stating that he had begun to find no fundamental problem with papal authority, Newman interpreted history through biblical prophecy, suggesting that papal power, as brought about by "natural and human means," might fulfill "the prophetic promise to St. Peter as recorded in xvi of St Matthew." Because the issues required to be addressed by ecclesiastical law and canons had presented themselves only gradually over time, papal authority would necessarily have grown slowly. Consequently, so far as the legitimate power of the papacy was concerned, "All then that we look for in antiquity, is tendencies and beginnings of its greatness, and these are found abundantly."[61]

Citing from memory occasions when the authority of Rome had received some kind of acknowledgment in the early centuries of the church, Newman asserted that "the doctrine of the Papacy was a primitive one." That St. Cyprian and others had resisted papal authority proved nothing, "for when a doctrine or ordinance has to be developed, collision or disturbances seem previous conditions of its final adjustment." Nor did possible alternative interpretations of the ancient authorities and incidents that he had cited cause difficulty, "for the question is which of the two interpretations is the more likely—and the event seems to suggest the true interpretation, as in the case of a prophecy." Thus supporting his case for papal authority and other Roman Catholic practices not manifestly existing in antiquity, Newman commented, "If we do not allow of developments, especially in a matter which from the nature of the case *requires* time for its due exhibition, hardly any doctrine can be proved by antiquity."[62]

On July 14, 1844, the anniversary of Keble's assize sermon, to which no reference appears in his letter, Newman continued to explain to Mrs. Froude "the mode in which I have got reconciled to the (apparently) modern portions of the Roman system." He stated that since composing his volume on "the Arians, or at least from 1836, I have had in my thought, though I could

not bring it out, that argument or theory" of development that had publicly
appeared in his sermon of February 1843. He believed that that theory as it
stood did not provide "the whole length of theory which is necessary for the
Roman system, and that something is still necessary to the discussion of the
theory, though I have no difficulties about receiving the system in matter of
fact." He had already been led to a series of important conclusions that
allowed him to believe that it was not more certain that the Church of
England lay "in a state of culpable separation *than* that developments do *not*
exist under the gospel, and that the Roman developments are *not* true ones."
Assuming the hypothesis of divine guidance of the church, antiquity furnished sufficient primitive traces of evidence for the special Roman Catholic
doctrines, including the necessity of church unity, the supremacy of the
papacy, and invocation of saints as much as it did for apostolical succession, a
real presence in the eucharist, and the inclusion of certain books in the canon
of Scripture, all of which were accepted by Anglicans. Furthermore, the
analogy of the Old and New Testaments, the gradual revelation of the call of
the Gentiles through St. Peter and St. Paul, the distinct theological pronouncements of the Gospel of John, the emergence of the doctrine of the
Holy Trinity, and the rule for baptizing heretics and infants all suggested
"the acknowledgment of doctrinal developments."[63]

    In acknowledging these developments, Newman rejected both the gen-
eral Protestant view that such changes constituted corruptions of the original apostolic truth and the high-church view that they marked departures
from antiquity. He now believed that both the English Church, whether
defined by evangelicals or by high churchmen, and Roman Catholicism
differed from Scripture and the early church. The choice confronting the
contemporary Christian in either case was that of two institutions, each
different from the early church and each requiring reform. Although indicating to Mrs. Froude considerable sympathy for Rome, Newman nonetheless still believed that the Roman Catholic Church needed to reform
certain practices, which he seems not to have regarded as developments. A
profound theological indeterminacy marked this entire correspondence, as
Palmer would have been quick to observe. Unlike the latter, Newman did
not fully recognize that it was one thing to understand ecclesiastical history
in terms of theological development but quite another to make development
one's own device for understanding or defining Christian faith and practice.
Development, as Newman speculated to Mrs. Froude, appeared to say that
true Christianity was what Christianity had become.

    The letters to Mrs. Froude, and the frequently convoluted character of their prose, indicate the enormous confusion and skepticism present in Newman's thought at this time. Over years of polemical exchanges he had undercut the religious authority of Scripture, internal feeling, episcopal authority, antiquity, natural theology, and discursive reason. Moreover, his disappointment and fundamental distrust of subjectivity rendered him increasingly passive and indecisive. In late January 1844 he had written Keble, "What I wish is, not to go by my own judgment, but by something external, like the pillar of the cloud in the desert." Deeply sensitive to Newman's ecclesiastical skepticism and emotional paralysis, Keble on June 12 asked him, "Do you not think it possible (I dare say I borrow the view from yourself) that the whole Church may be so lowered by sin as to hinder one's finding on earth anything which seems really to answer to the Church of the Saints? and will it not be well to prepare yourself for disappointment, lest you fall into something like scepticism? You know I have always fancied that perhaps you were over-sanguine in making things square, and did not quite allow enough for Bishop Butler's notion of doubt and intellectual difficulty being some men's intended element and appropriate trial."[64] At some intuitive level Keble recognized that Newman was undergoing a loss of religious faith that channeled itself through meditation upon a perfectionist ecclesiology. Keble recognized that his friend sought utopian perfection in the realm of history, where it was not to be found. His subtle advice was that Newman take upon himself something resembling a vocation of doubt and not try to solve problems that perhaps could not be solved. Keble feared, perhaps because he already discerned its presence, that Newman's disappointment stemming from the failure of his utopian search would end in skepticism.

So in a sense it already had. Rehearsing to Keble his doubts about the English Church and his inability to move to Rome that elicited the advice quoted above, Newman asked, "Am I in a delusion, given over to believe a lie?" The indications of doubt that he was sending to others about not only the English Church but his own religious convictions may have culminated on November 18 when he told Gladstone, "After all I do not think I should mind the attack of ever so many, if I had any thing to fall back upon. But for a long time past I have nothing." Reciting absence of support from bishops, rubrics, Articles, Reformers, English theology, its usage and books, he explained, "Thus I must stand by myself or seek external support."[65]

Newman's was among the most profound and painful of the many Victorian experiences of loss of faith. In most other cases, the protagonist retained confidence in human reason or human goodness or a loving God. For his part, Newman was skeptical of reason, possessed of no confidence in human goodness, and remained uncertain about the love and redemption of God. In his skepticism and fear of delusion of 1844, Newman had actually arrived at a psychological position that he had occupied previously. In fact, neither the doctrines of the high church nor those of Tractarian Catholicism had been the religion in which Providence had originally placed him. Newman concealed from his correspondents, and perhaps more important from himself, that he had on another occasion significantly changed his articulated religious beliefs by moving from his original moderate evangelicalism to the high church and then to Catholicism. It was no wonder that he asked if he was in a state of delusion. He had been firmly convinced of his early evangelical faith, then of high-church doctrines, and finally of radical Catholicism, but throughout this process of religious transformation his mind attained no firm ground as the pillar of the cloud kept moving before him, an unsettledness that had not been lost on Isaac Williams, Gladstone, Keble, or Pusey. These changes in faith had paralleled shifting loyalties of friendship from Mayers to Hawkins and Whately to Froude, Keble, and Pusey to Henry Wilberforce and Rogers to Mozley, Ward, Dalgairns, and others associated with Littlemore. His beliefs changed in response to those of newfound friends every bit as much as they informed those relationships. Repeatedly he modified his theology to cultivate new relationships and never the reverse. Changes in affection more often than modification of intellect drove Newman's own theological development. Newman's theological reasoning was and long continued to be the slave of his passions.

Throughout these changes of friendship and faith the evangelical template provided Newman with his pattern for thought and action. His private comments of 1844 in no small degree replicate Thomas Scott's account of his evangelical conversion in *The Force of Truth* (1797). Newman could have described himself, as easily as did Scott, as a person "in an uncommon manner, being led on from one thing to another, to embrace a system of doctrine which he once heartily despised."[66] In his own day Scott had been a Church of England clergyman, originally of near Unitarian opinions, who eventually embraced much that was associated with Methodism. In *The Force of Truth* he recounted how he found himself attracted to Methodist and enthusiastic religion as by something forbidden, but had eventually come to understand it as compatible with the faith of the Reformers. He presented his conversion to evangelical religion not as the result of Methodist enthusiasm but rather largely as the product of reading and the study of history.

At the end of the day, moderate evangelicals such as Scott remained for Newman the cultural models of religious change, with important elements of Scott's transformation replicating themselves in Newman's experience. First, Scott emphasized the need to prove to himself that his slow movement toward evangelical religion had not been a delusion or a dream. Second, Scott felt that he had to demonstrate that the religious practices derisively termed *Methodistical* and *enthusiastic* bore in reality little resemblance to the negative qualities popularly associated with them. For his part Newman repeatedly portrayed his movement toward Rome as the result of reading the Fathers and church history and then coming through the principle of development to a more complete understanding of the history of the Christian faith. He devoted enormous energy to demonstrating to himself and possibly others that Roman Catholicism was not the same as popery or corruptions of the original Christian revelation. Finally, Newman long hoped that he, like Scott's generation of evangelicals, could secure within the English Church a tolerated presence for himself and his followers. That last option vanished forever when in 1844 W. G. Ward published *The Ideal of a Christian Church,* setting off a train of events that wrecked the Tractarian experiment and eventually caused Newman and several of his followers to depart the Church of England.

W. G. WARD'S CALL TO RADICAL CATHOLICISM

By late November 1843, while Newman was quarrelling with Catholic colleagues over the *Lives of the English Saints,* the irrepressible W. G. Ward had decided that Palmer's *Narrative* must not pass unnoticed and that the closing of the *British Critic* should not silence radical Catholics, whom he soon dubbed "the new anti-Protestant school." Early the following June, Ward published *The Ideal of a Christian Church Considered in Comparison with Existing Practice, Containing a Defence of Certain Articles in The British Critic in Reply to Remarks on Them in Mr. Palmer's "Narrative,"* a book that the *Record* described as "an open declaration of war" against high churchmen and moderate Tractarians. While claiming "to lay down a sufficient basis, on which all who profess what are called 'high-church' sentiments might be able to cooperate, without compromise on any side," Ward, as an embodiment of Froude's spirit, insisted in effect that the original differences among the high churchmen of the Hadleigh conference of July 1833 be fought out to a conclusion.[67] His strategy was to denounce the practical results of evangelical theology and then to argue that traditional or moderate high churchmanship was inadequate to repair the damage evangelicals had inflicted on the English Church. He thus linked the Tractarian assault on the Protestant to an equally vigorous critique of the spiritual adequacy of the high church. Determined to establish an *ideal* for a Christian Church that could draw the Church of England out of its spiritual torpor, Ward eagerly and unapologetically looked to Rome—its heritage, its practices, and its devotional literature—for major elements informing that ideal.

Throughout Ward's volume Thomas Keble discerned a strong tincture of "Arnoldianism" that recalled the late Rugby headmaster's "particular delight . . . in speaking *provokingly* . . . of persons and things whom one respected out of mere tame duty."[68] Indeed, Ward did share with his former headmaster, if from a totally different theological vantage point, Arnold's moral disgust with the contemporary Church of England. Whereas Arnold's impatience led him to propose latitudinarian cooperation with Protestant Dissenters, Ward's resulted in admiration for Roman Catholicism. Both men deeply offended high churchmen.

For Ward evangelicalism and high churchmanship alike had failed to produce a church marked by the quality of holiness. Confessing a "ceaseless and ever-increasing inward repugnance, against the habits of thought and action prevalent in our Church," by which he meant evangelicalism, Ward declared the standard of holiness in the English Church to be "miserably low" and even belief in Christ's divinity "very far less firmly rooted than we are apt to think." In particular, a "deplorable inadequacy" marked that institution in regard to the "careful and individual moral discipline" of its members, a discipline that he considered "the only possible basis, on which Christian faith and practice can be reared." But beyond blaming evangelicals for these shortcomings, Ward also rejected the high-church notion that faithfulness to the Prayer Book, Articles, and antiquity could reinvigorate the piety and discipline of the English Church. Instead, in the spirit of the defunct *British Critic,* he demanded a theological transformation that would forge a church possessing "a profound and accurate system of *moral,* of *ascetic,* and of *mystical* theology" and a clergy capable of inculcating "holiness of life and orthodoxy of faith" among their congregations.[69]

Evangelical preaching of justification by faith alone constituted the core of the problem. Ward described "as the master-piece of Satan's craft" a system of theology that counted "sinful impulses" as "Christian graces" and that extended a promise to "self-deceiving men of enjoying at once carnal security and spiritual peace." Drawing upon Newman's thought, Ward declaimed that "many, who professed a full assurance of salvation, have lived lives of open and unblushing profligacy," and declared that it was incumbent

11. William George Ward (1812–1882), here portrayed at the age of twenty, became the most radical of the advanced Tractarians. The publication of his *Ideal of a Christian Church* in 1844 set the stage for the end of the Tractarian Movement. (Reproduced from frontispiece, Wilfrid Ward, *William George Ward and the Oxford Movement* [London: Macmillan, 1889].)

upon " 'evangelicals' " to provide "some test whereby this spurious faith shall be distinguished from the Gospel virtue." Until the latter task was accomplished, "that very feeling of security from fear of punishment, which is their great boast, has no more warrant than a madman's dream." Rather than justification by faith alone, the church must proclaim "the intrinsic hatefulness and peril of sin" and must inculcate "habits of daily observance" that would allow Christians to safeguard themselves from "the snare" and "the triumphs of Satan." Beyond furnishing the sacraments, the church must use its offices to train up saints, who are its "very hidden life" and who "cannot be nurtured on less than the full Catholic doctrine."[70]

Deploring "the Great Sin of the 16th century," Ward announced his own personal "intense abhorrence of the Reformation," which had denied "those great principles" of "obedience and faith." In having made intellect rather than conscience the judge of religious truth, the English Reformers had fostered a Protestant theology that for three centuries had pursued biblical criticism pressed "into the service of rationalism and heresy." Indeed, Ward confessed that the identification of the English Church with the principles of the Reformation made it "literally impossible" for him and unnamed others "to indulge in that affection towards her, which would otherwise be natural." In a footnote, Ward even more hostilely stated, "I know no single movement in the Church, except Arianism in the fourth century, which seems to me so wholly destitute of all claims on our sympathy and regard, as the English Reformation" with its rejection of both supremacy of conscience and reverence for hereditary religion.[71]

Having thoroughly criticized both historic and more recent evangelical Protestantism, Ward turned his sights on the high-church view of the English Reformation. He first denied that the Reformers had actually returned to antiquity and then challenged the idea that antiquity could actually provide the modern English Church with a functional prescriptive ideal. He elucidated numerous problems posed by the effort to use antiquity as a guide for contemporary faith and practice. These included the difficulty of really understanding the historical character of antiquity, the inability of antiquity to meet the moral needs arising from modern subjectivity, the overly harsh asceticism of the primitive church, the discrepancy between ancient church government and that possible in the modern world, and the differences between the eucharist of the early church and that of the English Prayer Book. Drawing upon Froude and Keble, he argued that recognition of the lively presence in antiquity of mystical reading of Scripture, belief in miracles, monasticism, a passion for martyrdom, veneration of relics, honor paid to celibacy, prominence accorded priests, and habitual thought of angels served "to impress upon the most unimaginative and insensible the wide contrariety between the religious spirit which ruled respectively Nicene Christendom and modern 'high church' Anglicanism."[72] Indeed, despite all their references to antiquity, high churchmen did not really follow its examples, precedents, or prescriptions.

After so enumerating the difficulties associated with any modern appropriation of antiquity, Ward turned for an alternative model to the Church of
Rome, an appeal to which "on a great number of points," he claimed,
displayed no disloyalty to the English Church. Indeed, he announced, the
English Church "should be taught from above to discern and appreciate the
plain marks of Divine wisdom and authority in the Roman Church, to
repent in sorrow and bitterness of heart our great sin in deserting her
communion, and to sue humbly at her feet for pardon and restoration."
Urging the importation of post-Tridentine Roman Catholic spiritual exercises and devotional practices, Ward explained, "What *will* be the external
manifestation of Catholicism in England, is a question then which it is idle
to ask; but we may be very certain what it will *not* be; it will not be the same
with its manifestation in Belgium or Normandy, Naples or Palermo." He
understood his idealized "Catholicism" to be "something moral and spiritual, not formal, external, circumstantial; in doctrine, in sentiment, in principle, ever one and the same; but elastic and pliant to adapt itself to all
conceivable circumstances, vigorous and full of life to cope with all conceivable emergencies."[73] In effect, Ward had declared that only Roman Catholic
devotion adjusted to the English setting rather than a spurious high-church
appeal to antiquity could overcome the evil influence of evangelical religion
and inculcate the English Church with genuine holiness.

The enormous controversy that Ward's book rapidly elicited has obscured its power and purpose, which should allow it to be included among
the prophetic jeremiads of the better-known Victorian sages. No less than
Wilberforce's *Practical View* of the late eighteenth century, Ward's *Ideal of a
Christian Church* summoned English Christians to a life of holy living and
personal devotion. Whereas Wilberforce had condemned the nominal Christianity of the respectable eighteenth-century Church of England, Ward denounced the religious smugness of now culturally established evangelicals
and ecclesiastically secure high churchmen, demanding from both lives of
practical self-denial, devotion, and obedience. Just as Wilberforce had appealed to the invisible church transcending the ages and denominational
boundaries of Christian history, Ward presented an idealized Catholicism
not limited by time and existing religious divides. Moreover, just as Wilberforce had sympathized with the devotional life of Methodists and Dissenters
while firmly adhering to the Church of England, Ward as a clergyman of that
church commended Roman Catholics for having "witnessed the pure Gospel to a blind and carnal age" and for providing a useful devotional apparatus

for holy living.[74] All of these remarkable qualities of Ward's volume were immediately lost in the internecine conflict it spawned and its necessary association with the complexities of his personality.

Numerous problems and objections soon confronted Ward, many of his own making. First, in his own mind and that of his readers, the proposed accommodations of the English Church to Roman Catholicism that permeated his *Ideal* were rooted in what he and Oakeley in 1841 had presented as the actual argument of *Tract 90:* that the Articles prohibited no official Roman Catholic teaching. When critics had pointed to the injunction that the Articles be read in their grammatical and natural sense, Ward had privately claimed around Oxford that he subscribed to them in a "non-natural" sense. In the *Ideal of a Christian Church,* he put that claim into print, declaring that in regard to Article 12, "Of course I think its natural meaning may be explained away, for I subscribe it myself in a non-natural sense."[75]

That assertion immediately revived denunciations of Tractarian dishonesty. Nassau Senior in the *Edinburgh Review* contended that the person who subscribed according to Ward's argument "gains this privilege by the sacrifice of all honour, all veracity—all that enables men to confide in one another." The *Christian Observer* declared that according to Ward's view, "A man may . . . promise to pay a thousand pounds, and say that he meant a thousand pounds of clay, or, in a still more unnatural sense, a thousand kicks." Bishop Musgrave denounced the "scandalous and shameful dishonesty" of Ward's mode of subscription, which served "to annihilate all confidence among men, and to equivocate with God."[76]

A second circumstance also poisoned the atmosphere around Ward's book. Although neither Newman nor Pusey approved Ward's view that the Articles prohibited no official Roman Catholic teaching, both were in 1844 associated with books that contemporaries rightly regarded as akin to Roman Catholic devotionals. In the case of Newman, it was the *Lives of the English Saints,* which despite his withdrawal as editor remained indelibly linked to him in the public mind. Pusey, while prohibited from preaching, was translating and editing continental Roman Catholic works intended for the kind of ascetic devotion that Ward advocated as a cure for evangelical spiritual laxity. In his preface to Avillon's *A Guide for Passing Lent Holily,* published shortly before Ward's book, Pusey contrasted evangelical preaching of the atonement with Roman Catholic meditation on Christ's suffering during the crucifixion, observing, "Our very Church has not yet adapted herself to the new wants of her children." Then, later in 1844, Pusey formally endorsed the *Ideal of a Christian Church* in his preface to Surin's

Foundations of the Spiritual Life, where, like Ward, he lamented the impact of evangelical religion on the English Church. Pusey particularly criticized Methodists for emphasizing personal assurance of salvation, a practice that he described as "one of the most dreadful scourges with which the Church was ever afflicted, the great antagonist of penitence, as those who have the charge of souls most sorrowfully find." To assuage the "practical deficiencies" of evangelical religion flowing from the assumptions "that acts have nothing to do with formation of habits or that feelings sustain good habits," Pusey prescribed Roman Catholic practices including recitation of the rosary and contemplation of the passion and wounds of Christ as vehicles aiding the formation of such habits through ascetic discipline. He also commended the lives of saints which were "alas! a new world to us."[77] Consequently, Ward's commendation of Roman Catholic devotion, despite his clear qualifications regarding what that meant, appeared as one more element in a larger Tractarian effort to import continental Roman Catholic spiritual discipline into the English Church.

A third factor that caused Ward difficulty was his locating the origin of religion in the experience of the individual conscience, a faculty he distinguished from feelings, emotions, and reason. Some Tractarians and high churchmen saw little difference in Ward's radical appeal to conscience and the more general evangelical religious subjectivity. As early as 1843, on the basis of having read one of his *British Critic* articles, Keble had opined that Ward exercised "private judgment more boldly and daringly than almost any one else" and applied his own test of holiness "as boldly and unscrupulously as the most ultra-Protestant could his." An Oxford handbill of early October 1844, signed by Hook, described Ward's *Ideal* as a book "which defends Popery on Ultra-Protestant Principles and is therefore subversive both of principle and truth." The same month continuing to distance himself from the radical Tractarians, Gladstone criticized the culturally Protestant quality of Ward's argument, observing,

Even as a murderer for religion . . . is more difficult to bring to repentance than any other murderer, so a heretic who has reached his heresy through Mr. Ward's system will be more hopeless than any other heretic, because he has done evil under the notion of good; and the very faculty which ought to have assisted him to detect his iniquity is become its cloak. Every case under that theory would become that of the Quaker called upon to pay church-rates. He is doing wrong, and he is more obstinate than any other person in doing that wrong; and why?—because he has been told he must make the immediate impression of his own conscience the sole criterion of

duty; and that immediate impression is against his paying the rate. The act
in his mind may be pure or impure, but great is the responsibility of those
who furnish such a plea.[78]

To be sure, Ward had attempted to avoid the extremes of this subjective
theory by presupposing that moral discipline curbed conscience, but he had
nonetheless based his theory on the radical subjectivity that had become the
chief hallmark of late Tractarian thought.

A minor event in October 1844 appears to have prepared the university
for action against Ward as a representative of Tractarianism. In what Pusey
termed "a protest against heresy and heretical decisions," his unpredictable
assistant J. B. Morris staged a vocal protest over the election as Vice Chancellor of the evangelical Benjamin Symons, one of the six doctors who
had suspended Pusey. Again as with his public letter about the poetry
professorship and his protest over his suspension, Pusey had alienated Oxford high churchmen from the Tractarian cause. Hook stood aloof from any
protest. Palmer, Churton, and even the aged, redoubtable, high-church
Martin Routh of Magdalen supported Symons. Newman had opposed the
protest, thinking it might backfire and strengthen the Heads in their determination to move against Catholics. When exactly such events transpired,
Newman in great exasperation exclaimed to Pusey, "It is deplorable to think
what harm J. Morris has done by blowing up the last contest. . . . Why will
he not stick to his Sanskrit? Oh that men did but know their place and their
work."[79] Newman also no doubt suspected that Pusey had done nothing to
discourage Morris.

More directly precipitating action by the Heads was pressure from
Whately, who in late October privately raised the issue of the future confidence of the bishops in Oxford. Copleston also urged Hawkins to take action
against Ward, declaring, "The Church of England will now be the rallying
point. We shall no longer be deluded by sophistical evasions. They will be
put down with a strong hand. The University must set the example—for
there the mischief began & ripened."[80] At the end of November and again in
early December, the Vice Chancellor demanded that Ward retract certain
portions of *The Ideal of a Christian Church*. Ward, after consultation, refused to do so, and the fray erupted once again in Oxford.

The Heads of Houses then decided to submit to Convocation two statutes, the first condemning certain passages in *The Ideal of a Christian Church*
and the second annulling Ward's degrees. These statutes alone would not
have been particularly controversial, even if widely regarded as grossly

unfair. What provoked a serious controversy was a third proposal, already feared by Newman in the late summer, to establish a new test whereby the Vice Chancellor, now the evangelical Symons, could ask any member of the university to resubscribe to the 39 Articles in a clearly Protestant manner. The proposal for a new test, eagerly supported by the evangelical *Record,* proved a blunder of considerable magnitude by transferring, as Whately observed, "the dread and indignation which was felt against the Tractites, to their opponents."[81] The issue of clerical subscription replaced that of Ward's extravagances.

As the university attack proceeded, a fourth factor, hidden for several months from the public and in this case affecting Tractarian attitudes toward Ward, also came into play. At some point during 1844, Ward had fallen in love with Frances Mary Wingfield, a member of Oakeley's Margaret Chapel Congregation, and he became engaged to her during the autumn. Domesticity had triumphed over celibate asceticism. Many of Ward's Tractarian associates, who had been championing medieval monasticism and saintly virginity in the *Lives of the English Saints,* saw him breaking ranks and becoming an embarrassment to the cause. Tractarian leaders were willing to extend only modest support to him in the weeks before the meeting of Convocation They feared being condemned, as in fact they later were, for having defended at considerable political cost an uncertain person who had failed to lived up to the Tractarian ascetic model. For that reason, the fact of Ward's engagement remained carefully concealed from the public as the February 13 meeting of Convocation approached.

Once announced afterward, Ward's engagement and forthcoming marriage occasioned not unsurprisingly much ironic newspaper commentary. Making the situation even worse, shortly before his marriage Ward astonished Tractarians and non-Tractarians alike by stating in *The Times,* "How any one can imagine that I have ever professed any vocation to a high and ascetic life, I am utterly at a loss to conceive."[82] The whole intellectual and religious integrity of *The Ideal of a Christian Church* and its author appeared to friend and foe alike compromised, if not outright sacrificed, on the altar of marital bliss.

Ward's engagement, the first among his post–*Tract 90* followers, no doubt accounted for the steady cooling of Newman's affection for him, as had been the case with so many previous Tractarian colleagues who married.[83] But Ward's choice of marriage represented only one of several displays of independence among those Catholic men for whom Newman had written *Tract 90* and then borne persecution and isolation in the hope of securing them a place in the English Church and in his own personal life. The inherent instability of the Tractarian Catholic social circle had begun to manifest itself.

While nurturing an expansive devotional life at Littlemore and among his Catholic followers, Newman had consistently discouraged some Roman Catholic practices, particularly certain invocations. In late November 1844, Faber asked Newman to revoke his prohibition "of invoking our Blessed Lady, the Saints, and Angels." On December 1 Newman firmly chastised Faber, and by implication Ward, Oakeley, and Pusey, for attempting to draw Roman Catholic devotion into the English Church. Newman stated his "great repugnance at mixing religions or worships together," a practice that amounted to "sowing the field with mingled seed." Having warned Pusey a year earlier that the introduction of the Breviary would tempt men to Rome, Newman now told Faber, "I do not like decanting Rome into England; the bottles may break." He expressed "much anxiety" over religious behavior that embraced "the inculcation of extraordinary degrees of asceticism; extreme strictness about indifferent matters, heights of devotion and meditation, self-forgetfulness and self-abandonment, and the like." He thought that what might be "natural in Saints and in a saintly system, becomes a mere form in others." Newman described the devotional eclecticism that Faber requested as a presumptuous act of private judgment, indicating "an absence of submission to religion as a rule."[84]

Newman's chastisement of Faber echoed the injunction to restraint and avoidance of private judgment in penitential devotion that he had urged two years earlier in his sermon on "Dangers to the Penitent."[85] Yet other factors influenced Newman's late 1844 letter to Faber. Newman's firm prohibition to Faber represented his resistance to a potential burgeoning of radical pluralism in Catholic belief and devotion over which he could no longer exert leadership and personal authority. In 1841 through the device of *Tract 90* Newman had attempted to accommodate Catholics to the English Church. By late 1844 those Catholics were again careening out of his control, with Faber seeking still more advanced devotions, Ward embracing all elements of Roman Catholicism through a "non-natural" subscription to the Articles, and Pusey publishing translations of continental Roman Catholic devotional manuals. All of this behavior could provoke the possibility of formal university condemnation and threaten the perseverance of Newman's monastic experiment. Newman, like Dalgairns, believed that monasteries tamed religious behavior that might otherwise result in fanaticism and those errors of popular Catholicism which he had distinctly *not* defended in

Tract 90. Unrestrained devotion could, as Newman had often predicted, nurture a taste for Roman Catholicism itself, rendering his own life and self-defined Catholic vocation at Littlemore functionless.

Newman believed that he knew how much Catholicism the English Church could and would tolerate. If that boundary was exceeded, as Ward and Pusey had done publicly and Faber wished to do privately, Newman believed formal, authoritative repudiation of *Tract 90* would follow and the entire position of Catholics in the English Church would be lost. As long as *Tract 90* escaped a formal, authoritative condemnation that Newman and other Catholics must acknowledge, it survived. As long as *Tract 90* so passively endured, the Littlemore enclave could function with all that its life and work meant to Newman religiously and personally. For Newman, the devotional venturesomeness of Ward, Faber, and Pusey amounted to an ascetic antinomianism challenging the model he had established. Their behavior threatened an advanced Catholic schism within the Tractarian schism. Once again Newman's family—this time the family he had created for himself—was in turmoil. His response to this situation, seen in the letter to Faber as well as in expressions of doubt about Ward, closely resemble his responses during the late 1820s to both Charles and Francis Newman on their leaving his sphere of elder sibling influence.

While holding off the Romanizers, Newman remained troubled by his own indecision, which had led to unsettlement in other people's minds and families. On November 21 he wrote to Keble of "the deep confidence I have at present that Christianity and the Roman Catholic system are convertible terms" and indicated concern for his own soul while he remained in the Church of England. Yet despite those sentiments, Newman almost desperately looked to the furor that Ward's *Ideal of a Christian Church* had elicited to give him reasons for remaining in the English Church rather than departing. On December 8, after telling the Froudes of his hope that something external might guide him, he speculated that Ward's case might prove such an event, explaining, "The series of measures in prospect is quite independent of any act of mine, and an external coincidence with my own personal convictions." Ward's expulsion from the university "for holding certain things which I hold" might provide that external indication. But Newman then immediately attached the further complicated condition of the bishops "virtually, if not formally" acquiescing in that sentence while the bulk of the clergy and laity remained quiet. During these weeks, Newman remained capable of curious, almost wishful thinking. He wrote to Jemima on December 24 that university rejection of the new test would constitute "a virtual repeal of the censure on No. 90," and he told Keble five days later that a rejection of the new test would be "an indirect assertion of No. 90."[86]

Much of this late 1844 correspondence suggests a person not wishing to change his situation and grasping at one desperate reason after another not to do so or to be compelled to do so. In the December 29 letter to Keble, Newman directly separated himself from Ward and described as shocking to common sense the latter's contention that the Articles are compatible with the whole of Roman Catholic doctrine. He suspected that Ward, unlike himself, held "that we are simply external to the Church." Further hedging his position, Newman wrote, "Now, it is one thing to say (as I have said) that our Church has lost its external notes of Catholicity, another to say that she has no Catholicity at all." He was not sure that Ward was "always consistent" in the view imputed to him, but if he was, Newman could "but think it very dangerous" because "to remain knowingly out of the Church" seemed to him "next door to maintaining some bad heresy." He should "not wonder at a person so acting falling any day into any error." Newman finally asserted with reference to his own situation, "It is quite another thing to be in doubt."[87] On the basis of this analysis of what he supposed Ward to think, he advised Keble to attack the new test rather than to defend Ward, because those who opposed the new test would eventually aid Ward. Newman obviously realized that the new test could be used directly against him while in his eyes condemnation of Ward's position did not condemn his own. Newman also knew that Ward would soon marry and thus effectively abandon the Tractarian cause.

The issue of the new test resolved itself relatively quickly. On January 13 the Heads withdrew the proposal, which was by then opposed by people as different as Pusey, Tait, and Whately.[88] Too many people who disagreed about many other things had concluded that the new test might be turned against groups other than the radical Tractarians. Two principles had stood in conflict—anti-Catholicism and moderate freedom of thought in the church, or more pointedly theological self-protection—with the latter ultimately triumphing. The threat to *Tract 90* had passed, but only for the moment. On February 3 the Heads accepted a petition, sponsored by the ever persistent Golightly, evangelicals, and high churchmen and signed by more than 450 university members, to submit to Convocation on February 13 a condemnation of *Tract 90* itself.

CHAPTER II

Endgame

I N ONE OF THE MOST PERSUASIVE passages of the *Apologia Pro Vita Sua* Newman invoked the memory of "three blows which broke me" between July and November 1841, causing him to lose faith in the Catholicity of the Church of England. These incidents included his coming to perceive even more than previously the analogy between the English Church, presumably including his own sect therein, and the ancient Monophysite communion, his encountering the first of the fierce episcopal charges against *Tract 90,* and the launching of the Jerusalem bishopric project. Thereafter, the English Church in his eyes bore all the signs of heresy, heresy that for him only intensified in coming months. Having portrayed his own spirit as well as his ecclesiastical confidence as shattered by these three events, Newman then wrote of his "death-bed, as regards my membership with the Anglican Church." He invited the reader of the *Apologia* to share the grief and inevitability of a distressingly long process, as he commented, "A death-bed has scarcely a history; it is a tedious decline, with seasons of rallying and seasons of falling back; and since the end is foreseen, or what is called a matter of time, it has little interest for the reader, especially if he has a kind heart. Moreover, it is a season when doors are closed and curtains drawn, and when the sick man neither cares nor is able to record the stages of his malady. I was in these circumstances, except so far as I was not allowed to die in peace,—except so far as friends, who had still a full right to come in upon me, and the public world which had not, have given a sort of history to those last four years."[1] Newman in 1864 thus transferred his restless, painfully disappointing four final years in the Church of England into a deathbed scene, evocative of both St. Augustine's *Confessions* and lives of pious evangelicals.

Resorting to the trope of a final deathwatch allowed Newman quite specifically to deny an articulated historical narrative to his last years in the English Church. In the *Apologia* his personality during that crucial period assumes the guise of a fluctuating, disembodied state of mind wherein the protagonist finds himself hesitantly but insistently drawn forward inwardly by the concept of doctrinal development, while standing much removed from any direct activity of its own or of others. The extended deathbed metaphor allowed the Roman Catholic Newman, surrounded by suspicious critics in his second religious communion, to portray his religious hesitations of two decades earlier as resistances to the inevitable rather than as choices and delays made in hope of alternatives. It concealed the possibility that his death in the English Church and passage to Rome may have been as sudden, rapid, and to some observers as unexpected as the deaths of his sister Mary and his mother. Moreover, by closing his autobiographical, psychological narrative with an historically unexplained event—that is, his change of religious affiliation—Newman avoided discussing in detail the publication and reception of *An Essay on the Development of Christian Doctrine* of 1845. Finally, portraying his departure from one church and his entry into another as a passage from death to an afterlife allowed him to say little about the continuity of monastic living that marked his last years in the English Church and the rest of his life in the Roman communion. In other words, in the *Apologia*, Newman eluded the necessity of relating the endgame to the religious movement that he had initiated with the publication of *Tracts for the Times*. No doubt, in 1864 he would have claimed that he intended only to relate the history of his religious opinions, but during 1845 he acted as a result of events occurring around him as well as of opinions developing within him. Indeed the events generated many of the opinions.

EXTERNAL TRANSFORMATIONS OF 1845

On December 29, 1844, while distinguishing his own thinking from W. G. Ward's, Newman declared to Keble, "No one can have a more unfavorable view than I of the present state of the Roman Catholics—so much so, that any who join them would be like the Cistercians of Fountains, living under trees till their house was built." About a week later Newman told Miss Giberne that he found "the state of the RCs . . . at present so unsatisfactory" that he could easily acquiesce should God "in His inscrutable wisdom *delay* to take the veil from the eyes of Catholic-minded men, or to make them see whither their present faith leads." At that moment Newman could only

imagine his position in either the English or Roman communion as that of a
Catholic awaiting institutional reform. After her brother's conversion Harriet Mozley thought this situation a source of possible future difficulties as
she reminded Jemima of John's "very low and degraded idea of the Church
of Rome" and his long-standing refusal to "retract the smallest particle of
his bad opinion."[2] As Harriett understood, there exists no substantial evidence that between late 1844 and October 1845 Newman's outlook toward
the Roman Church underwent substantial change.

Rather during those months there occurred a series of interrelated,
transforming events that modified his attitude not toward Roman Catholicism but toward his own personal situation in the English Church. These
events rendered virtually impossible the position he had hoped, sometimes
through the most strained and contorted arguments, to maintain for himself
and his followers therein. Keble judged more correctly than he realized
when in 1847 he told Justice Coleridge, "I am more than convinced, between
ourselves, that N. went (unconsciously of course,) rather from impulse than
from reason, & that good treatment & sympathy would probably have kept
him here."[3] Such good treatment and sympathy were, however, completely
lacking for Newman in 1845 as he received a second set of three sharp blows,
even more crushing to his situation in the English Church than the auto-
biographically more famous ones of 1841.

The Aftermath of Ward's Case

The first of these events occurred in early February when the Oxford
Heads, having abandoned the new test, precipitously decided to bring a
formal condemnation of *Tract 90* before the same meeting of Convocation
that would decide Ward's fate.[4]

Convocation would thus address two related, but theologically distinct,
problems on one tumultuous day. Ward was to be condemned on the supposed demerits of his book, and the tract regarded as the source of his "non-
natural" mode of clerical subscription would receive similar censure. On
February 13 Convocation condemned *The Ideal of a Christian Church* by a
vote of 777 to 386, and then passed, 569 to 511, a measure to degrade Ward
of his degrees. The frustrated Heads, angry evangelicals, and disgruntled
high churchmen had won the day, but, as indicated by the substantial minority vote, at enormous cost to their prestige and any sense of fairness
on their part. The proposal to condemn *Tract 90* met a different fate from
those relating to Ward. The proctors, one of whom was R. W. Church, a

contributor to *Lives of the English Saints*, as promised beforehand, vetoed the *Tract 90* censure in the same fashion that nine years earlier proctors had vetoed the first effort to censure Hampden. Consequently, *Tract 90* did not receive official university condemnation.[5]

Tract 90 never again came before Convocation, apparently because the Archbishop of Canterbury signaled that there had been enough divisive controversy.[6] Some critics of the tract may also have feared that should the measure actually come to a future vote, a coalition of Tractarians and liberals might defeat it, thus creating the situation that Newman forecast in December: the appearance of a repeal of the 1841 Heads' censure. In any case, the institutions of the university had finished with the Tractarians.

But Newman could not have known this with any certainty and had reason to fear the contrary. During the spring of 1845 a requisition demanding that Convocation be permitted to vote on the *Tract 90* condemnation was circulated and acquired more than four hundred signatures. In late April the Hebdomadal Board, after receiving the requisition, referred it to committee for an anticipated negative decision regarding further action. On May 1 Newman expressed gratitude for friends who had persuaded university officials to give up "the condemnation of No 90," cautiously adding, "at least for the present." That skeptical caution was well founded. Archbishop Whately had wanted to press the censure, fearing that the Tractarians would interpret its absence as a tacit approval and further believing that henceforth some people would all too cleverly assume "that you may sign the Articles in a sense wh. every man must perceive to be contrary to that of the framers, provided you do not *call* it a non-natural sense."[7] Whately's views were not insignificant, for his pressure a few months earlier had led to the action against Ward. Consequently Newman took little real comfort from the earlier recension of the new test, the survival of *Tract 90* in February, or the decision to carry the matter no further in April.

Newman furthermore could not altogether regard himself as genuinely uncondemned through a proctoral veto, as he had so disparaged the same action in Hampden's case. Newman also believed that if Convocation did ever again consider *Tract 90*, it would be censured as had Hampden's views on a similar second occasion. Though many years later expressing effusive thanks to Church, Newman had not been certain before the fact that he wanted the proctoral veto.[8] From late January 1845 onward, a pervasive ambivalence marked all Newman's thought and emotion. On February 6 he had written to Pusey, as he had to the Froudes several weeks earlier, "I should not be honest, if I did not begin by saying that I shall be glad, selfishly speaking, if this decree passes. Long indeed have I been looking for external circumstances to determine my course—and I do not wish this daylight to be withdrawn." Although "really glad and relieved" to find himself "at last in the scrape," Newman regretted the confusion that Ward's presence brought to the situation, making his own position less dignified than if he could have stood by himself. Ward's ecclesiology was not Newman's, and what Ward believed about the Articles Newman did not. Newman told Hope later in the spring, "You are quite right in saying I do not take Ward and Oakeley's grounds that all Roman doctrine may be held in our Church, and that *as* Roman. I have always and everywhere resisted it."[9]

Newman privately continued to make that distinction between himself and Ward and Oakeley throughout the remainder of his months in the English Church, but it was a distinction that persuaded few people. Most important, he made no bold public statement distinguishing his views from theirs in 1845, as he had not in 1841, when he actually defended the two writers privately in the months after they published radical interpretations of *Tract 90*. The public at large, and even those whom he had earlier termed "Conservative Apostolicals" and "the regular Anglican party," as well as the newspapers, saw *Tract 90* as "that atrocious work, the parent of Mr. Ward's volume" and "the origin of the whole mischief." Nor could anyone deny the assertion of the *Christian Observer* that no one had heard of taking an oath in a nonnatural sense until *Tract 90* had "beamed upon the world." Only in a letter to *The Times* in February 1863 did Newman publicly disassociate himself from Ward's and Oakeley's position.[10] Newman's ambivalence during the 1840s may have been calculated. As long as some people asserted and he did not forthrightly contradict the belief that it was possible to hold all things Roman in the English Church, Newman may have believed the more radical of his coterie would remain with him, providing him with a constituency in the Church of England.

Just before Convocation gathered, Newman had recognized further complexities in the situation. He told Jemima that moderates, speculating that the Hebdomadal Board had actually played into his hands, believed "that if I wished people to be unsettled and inclined towards Rome, I could not have better fortune than a condemnation of No 90." He stated, however, "I *do* wish people to agree with me in turning Romeward; but, as I do not wish them so to feel because *I* am so feeling, so do I deprecate their so feeling from mere disgust with what is happening among ourselves."[11] He may have been expressing concern over his own feelings at the time, as much as that of others. He also mentioned to Jemima apprehension that if the debate over the condemnation of *Tract 90* continued, his conduct since its publication might come under public scrutiny. He understood that his behavior, publications, and correspondence had involved far too many expedient twists and turns for any clear explanation or defense. He may have feared that his highly compromising correspondence with Thomas Mozley over the conduct of the *British Critic*, in which he had expressed his generally strong support for Ward and Oakeley, would somehow become public, possibly at Harriett's angry urging. He may have thought that Manning might publish those highly compromising letters of October 1843 which had so flabbergasted Gladstone. There would also no doubt have been much more extensive publicity about Littlemore devotional life and his private conversations with visitors to the monastery, his exchange with Bishop Bagot over that community, and the extent of his involvement with the *Lives of the English Saints*, as well as the interactions of some of his friends with Roman Catholics. He knew his private actions and private statements stood at odds with his public reticence.

By February 25 Newman wrote Pusey, "I am as much gone over as if I *were already gone.*" On Good Friday, which fell in March that year, Pusey told Woodgate that he expected Newman to pass over to Rome before the next Advent season, "so now my only hope is that he may be an instrument to restore the Roman Church, since our own knows not how to employ him." Jemima Mozley, assuming a more imminent departure, wrote her brother that news of his likely entrance into the Roman Church, though not unexpected, struck her like hearing that a friend must die. Then in a moment of rare criticism she observed, "It is to me the great proof of the badness of this world and the unfortunate times we live in that such a one as you should take the line you have taken."[12]

To these expressions of melancholy disappointment her brother replied on March 15, first with a self-portrayal, quite common among Victorians changing religious faith, wherein he sought to demonstrate his sincerity by citing all the losses he was about to encounter for the sake of following his convictions:

> At my time of life men love ease. I love ease myself. I am giving up a maintenance involving no duties, and adequate to all my wants. What in the world am I doing this for (I ask *myself* this), except that I think I am called to do so? I am making a large income by my sermons. I am, to say the very least, risking this; the chance is that my sermons will have no further sale at all. I have a good name with many; I am deliberately sacrificing it. I have a bad name with more. I am fulfilling all their worst wishes, and giving them

their most coveted triumph. I am distressing all I love, unsettling all I have instructed or aided. I am going to those whom I do not know, and of whom I expect very little. I am making myself an outcast, and that at my age. Oh, what can it be but a stern necessity which causes this?

After expressing perplexity, indeed profound self-puzzlement, over his inner unsettlement, he demanded, "Pity me, my dear Jemima. What have I done thus to be deserted, thus to be left to take a wrong course, if it is wrong?"[13] If he found himself suddenly dying, Newman wrote, he would send for a priest. He also feared traveling lest he should meet a deadly accident in this state. He had hoped to wait until the summer of 1846, but certainly could not wait beyond the next Christmas.

Another element in this letter, however, differed from those typical of Victorian doubters. Newman's characteristic narcissism soon displayed itself, as he remarked to Jemima, "Meanwhile may not I, may not you and all of us, humbly take comfort in the thought that so many persons are considerately praying for me?"[14] He was employing the process of self-doubt and possible, but not yet executed, conversion to intrude himself into the lives of a whole series of people—Jemima, Keble, Pusey, Henry Wilberforce, and the Froudes—who might otherwise not necessarily be thinking very much about him. Wishing for renewed personal engagement, Newman used his letters as vehicles for energizing old relationships and causing disillusioned friends to respond in the possible hope of retaining him for the English Church. He had taken himself to a brink over which he had no real desire to step and from which he repeatedly distanced himself. As he had said to Jemima, he may well not have genuinely known or been able to admit to himself what inner forces then really drew him to Rome.

But while still writing to Jemima, Newman quickly moved from submissive sincerity and self-pity to the aggressiveness of an elder sibling attempting to exert dominance. He reminded her that he was certainly not the first person to give pain to others by leaving one faith for another and then cited St. Paul's conversion. The appeal to St. Paul's example allowed Newman first to draw a parallel between himself as a persecutor of Roman Catholics and Paul as a persecutor of Christians and in so doing possibly to block in his sister's mind, as well as his own, the more relevant parallel between his behavior and that of his two brothers, whose unorthodox religious departures he had so sharply condemned and disowned. In words that Francis Newman or other Oxford seceders might have written fifteen years earlier, John asserted, "Surely all the distress and unsettlement I shall give, however great a warning to me not to act hastily, cannot be *a real reason* against moving, for it is, so it happens, the very condition under which a follower of Christ is drawn in Scripture."[15] Toward the end of the letter he asked Jemima, this time in the spirit more of Charles than of Francis, "What right have you to judge me? Have the multitude, who will judge me any right to judge me? Who of my equals, who of the many who will talk flippantly about me, has a right? Who has a right to judge me but my Judge? Who has taken such pains to know *my* duty (poor as they have been) as myself?" Here was the voice of the radical Protestant following his private judgment into Catholicism and eventually the Roman Church, but it could just as easily have been the voice of his brother Charles departing for Owenite socialism.

In April, as the requisition to resurrect the condemnation of *Tract 90* circulated, the ghostly figure of Blanco White, through the publication of his biography, suddenly haunted Newman, who told Henry Wilberforce that he thought he understood what intellectual faults had touched White and Thomas Arnold, leading both of them to go wrong while "yet sincere." But Newman asked, "How do I know that I too have not my weak points which occasion me to think as I think? how can I be sure I have not committed sins which bring this unsettled state of mind on me as a judgment?" But from this self-doubt Newman moved to a long litany of the wrongs he had suffered within the university, as he recounted, "No one has spoken well of me. My friends who had had means of knowing me have spoken against me. Whately and Hawkins have both used opprobrious language about me, till I began to think myself really deceitful and double dealing. . . . Others have kept silent in my greatest troubles. The mass of men in Oxford who know me a little, have shown a coldness and suspicion which I did not deserve. In the affair of No 90 few indeed showed me any sympathy, or gave me reason to believe that I was at all in their hearts. . . . Heads of houses whom I knew have been unkind to me, and have set the fashion; and now my prime of life is past, and I am nothing." He mentioned others, such as Golightly and Eden, who had harmed him, and then pondered the mystery that while his gifts were that of the "tuition or the oversight of young men," he had "all along been so wonderfully kept out of that occupation." He also wondered what influence he might have exerted had he been assigned some station of responsibility in the university. Having recited the wrongs he had suffered since being excluded from the Oriel tutorship, he concluded, "And now it is all gone & over, and there is no redress, no retrieving." Yet he did not "think anything of ambition or longing is mixed with these feelings, as far as I can tell."[16]

What emerges in this letter is the enormous pent-up anger that had so long driven Newman since his ouster as an Oriel tutor, an anger that often channeled itself into personal self-abasement and self-pity as well as condescension toward others. The letter also displays his enormous incapacity to catch even a glimpse of how his own personality and actions might have appeared to persons who had once cared for and valued him. At that moment the kind of warm appreciation for Hawkins and even Whately that later appeared in the *Apologia* eluded Newman as he saw himself surrounded by enemies, including those two former Oriel mentors now determined to crush all that Tractarianism had spawned.

The final public effort of the spring to have Convocation condemn *Tract 90* had unleashed all of these feelings of resentment and abandonment. The university authorities, the country parsons, the evangelicals, and the onetime sympathetic high churchmen would not leave him alone even when he had, for all intents and purposes, at least in his own view, withdrawn from their lives. His most zealous followers would not defer to him but stood determined to drive his own opinions to conclusions from which he demurred. The lesson of the events around Ward's degradation and the attempted condemnation of *Tract 90* was that even passivity would bring him no peace. Of course, those who viewed him from outside Littlemore and who read *Sermons, Chiefly on the Theory of Religious Belief* and *Sermons Bearing on Subjects of the Day*, as well as the *Lives of the English Saints* and Ward's *Ideal of a Christian Church*, did not regard Newman as passive but saw his ideas and influence as remarkably active, still deeply pernicious, and requiring condemnation.

Oakeley's Case

By June 1 Newman told the Froudes that he had set his reception into the Roman Church for October and did not wish to resign his fellowship until that time.[17] In light of his March comments to Jemima regarding his income, he may well have wanted to ensure that he received his annual Oriel stipend, to be distributed in October. By this point in the early summer, however, a second fundamentally transforming external event had begun to remove doubts and to confirm Newman's convictions of the necessity of his leaving the English Church. Its roots went back to the controversy provoked by Ward's *Ideal of a Christian Church*.

On February 18, five days after Convocation condemned Ward's book and degraded its author, Pusey wrote to Gladstone, "People would be glad of an armistice in statu quo, each working on as they may; they by Select

Preachers, Bampton Lecturers, Professors; we by tutors and books." Such was not to be, as the issues raised by Ward's case erupted outside the boundaries and authorities of Oxford itself. Frederick Oakeley, whom Churton once described as "a man destitute of all self-control," had undertaken a public initiative of his own. As earnestly myopic as Ward was ironic, Oakeley determined to press the cause of the radical interpretation of *Tract 90* to a decisive conclusion, the very conclusion Newman had so assiduously avoided. Oakeley had first entered the Ward controversy during November 1844 by publishing letters to explain why, with his advanced views, he remained in the English Church, which he insisted did possess Catholicity, but only as he understood it. More fully expanding on his *Tract 90* pamphlet of 1841, now republished to aid Ward's cause, Oakeley on December 23 forthrightly claimed the right "of holding (as distinct from teaching) all Roman doctrine, and that notwithstanding my subscription to the Thirty-nine Articles." This assertion went beyond anything that Newman had ever advocated publicly or presumably privately, though it was exactly what most of the public thought he believed. Moreover, Oakeley presented his and Ward's writings as evidence that while the *British Critic* had been closed, "its spirit is not allowed to rest."[18] Oakeley's extravagant public declarations had contributed to the drive for a formal Convocation condemnation of *Tract 90* on February 13. The day after that gathering, throughout which he had literally stood beside Ward at the rostrum, Oakeley, a Balliol fellow, submitted to newspapers a letter to the Vice Chancellor of Oxford reasserting his position of holding but not teaching Roman Catholic doctrines and associating himself with Ward's condemned views. That letter itself was generally understood to relate to the university and its authorities and in the post-Convocation climate might not have received any formal response.

Oakeley, however, rapidly transferred the dispute over clerical subscription from the auspices of Oxford authorities to those of the Bishop of London. On February 18 Bishop Blomfield had conferred privately with Oakeley about his letter to the Vice Chancellor. The next day, responding to that conversation, Oakeley published *A Letter to the Lord Bishop of London, on a Subject Connected with the Recent Proceedings at Oxford*, there declaring his conviction that the Articles were "*subscribable* in what may be called an ultra-Catholic sense." Assuring the bishop that at Margaret Chapel he preached against sin rather than about doctrine, Oakeley wrote that if in addition, "my obligations as an English Clergyman require me to controvert the doctrines of Rome, then I freely admit that I do not fulfill those obligations." He also unnecessarily and belligerently stated his supposition that

"It is nowhere even maintained or imagined that individual bishops of our Church are invested with the power of authoritatively determining the sense of the Articles."[19]

The same day that Oakeley's pamphlet appeared, Bishop Blomfield, who had a few weeks earlier refused Pusey permission to preach in his diocese as long as the university suspension remained in effect, forbade Oakeley from officiating at Margaret Chapel. Shortly thereafter, he relented on the condition that Oakeley promise "not to preach untruth" or "any of those doctrines which are considered to be peculiar to the Church of Rome, as distinguished from the Church of England." After Oakeley awkwardly released confused information to the press, Blomfield decided to take the matter to the Court of Arches under the auspices of the Church Discipline Act. Apparently, like *The Times*, Blomfield had concluded, "There ought to be some means—some power lodged somewhere—of suspending or silencing a clergyman who avowedly professes and proclaims what is fundamentally opposed to our Church." To halt what that newspaper termed Oakeley's "mischievous and disingenuous system of conduct," the bishop opted for the ecclesiastical courts, claiming in his letter of request to the Court of Arches that Oakeley's *Letter to the Lord Bishop of London* contained statements "directly contrary or repugnant to the true, usual, literal meaning of the Articles of Religion."[20]

In late February, in a state of emotional headiness following his appearance at the Oxford Convocation, Oakeley actually believed that he might rescue the entire advanced Catholic cause by achieving episcopal or judicial approval of his provocative position on clerical subscription. Pondering his immediate response to Blomfield's initial letter of suspension, Oakeley had outlined to an unconvinced, disapproving Pusey the victories to be achieved if only he could prevail over the most powerful bishop of the day: "*Only conceive what will be won*, if Margaret C[hapel] is *now* spared! I wish persons cd . . . have felt that I wd not have risked so much but for a great end: that no great good ever comes without risk: that great personal risk is in itself generally some security against great & real harm. I wish it cd have been felt that *if* I shd be unharmed, *immense* points are gained inclusively in mine—No. 90—Ward, etc. etc."[21] Of course, all that was to be won was also to be sacrificed if Oakeley failed in his cause. Most of the Tractarians understood just exactly how high Oakeley's impetuosity had raised the stakes. Newman must have reconsidered the wisdom of his having persuaded Oakeley not to enter the Roman Communion in 1843.

Once his case was at law, Oakeley seems to have persevered for some time in his fantasy of saving the Tractarian cause and seems also to have received less than excellent legal advice. Hope, according to Oakeley, advised him against resigning Margaret Chapel, thinking it possible that the doctrinal questions in the case might "possibly be evaded." Eventually, however, Oakeley, fearing loss of the suit and possibly concerned over legal costs, decided on June 3 to decline his defense at the hearing and to resign his license as minister of Margaret Chapel. The *Morning Herald* observed "that there is nothing of which Mr. Oakeley is less desirous than this, that the question should be decided *at all*." Once indicating his willingness to resign, Oakeley had expected Blomfield to "have given up the Suit."[22] To his surprise, Blomfield persisted, no doubt convinced from prior experience that Oakeley would prove unpredictable in his public presentation of the matter and, more important, desiring a clear legal decision on the matter. Even as Oakeley's case continued without his own participation, some people, presumably including Hope, led him to expect an acquittal. But what transpired during June in the Court of Arches was anything but the routine or benign hearing that the naive Oakeley anticipated.

Sir Herbert Jenner Fust heard the case on June 10, somewhat professionally uncomfortable, with only the complaint being presented. The prosecution set out to demonstrate "that the Articles of the Church of England have been drawn up in direct opposition to the then recent decrees of the Council of Trent."[23] Oakeley had in both 1841 and 1844 presented a historical argument to the contrary that, he believed, buttressed Newman's fundamental position in *Tract 90*. Both Newman and Oakeley had asserted that because the Articles were adopted before the close of the Council of Trent, they could not condemn official Roman Catholic doctrine as opposed to popular piety. Oakeley's stubborn bad judgment had thus transferred the issues of *Tract 90* from the world of unaccountable university pamphlet controversy to a court of ecclesiastical law where litigation, unlike pamphlet warfare, did come to a decisive end, with a judge having the last word.

The Court of Arches handed down its decision on June 30, five days before which Oakeley had issued another public defense of his views. Jenner Fust held that in fact Oakeley did not simply hold the disputed doctrines privately without teaching them publicly, observing, "If he does not teach them in his public ministrations, is not the Pamphlet [*A Letter to the Lord Bishop of London*] which is now under consideration of the Court, sufficient to show that he publicly maintains and affirms them? And *that* is the question which the Court is called up to decide." In an assessment with import for public evaluation of all previous Tractarian rhetoric as well as Oakeley's, the court further concluded that for Oakeley the term "Catholic" was equal to "Roman Catholic." Moving upon that basis to a much more sweeping judgment, Jenner Fust declared that Oakeley's "own statement as to the conduct which he pursues, when he is consulted upon the propriety of a person leaving the Church of England for the Church of Rome, is, in fact, an evasion." Moreover, Jenner Fust asserted that Oakeley's "outwardly professing to be a member of one Church, whilst he is inwardly attached to the doctrine of another; and his declaration, that he signs the Thirty-nine Articles in a sense different from their grammatical construction, in which he knows they ought to be signed, can hardly be reconciled with integrity." Eschewing constructions of the Articles arising "from the different opinions of persons concerning them," Jenner Fust firmly stated, "No minister of the Church of England has a right to put his own private interpretation upon the Articles, which he has sworn to, and which he has subscribed." Most important, Oakeley possessed no right "to put his own construction upon the Articles of the Church, in order to justify the holding and maintaining of doctrines contrary to the views of that Church."[24] In all these respects, Jenner Fust provided the judicial authority of the Court of Arches to the injunctions regarding subscription asserted by several bishops in their charges of 1841 through 1844. His use of the term *evasion* echoed the Hebdomadal Board's censure of *Tract 90* in 1841, and his emphasis on integrity was redolent of the vast public criticism of the dishonesty in the reasoning of that tract. His decision also resembled Blomfield's letter of 1830 to the then young Pusey regarding the purpose and function of articles of faith.

Jenner Fust then proceeded to examine the 39 Articles in regard to the most controverted issues raised in *Tract 90*, as well as to Oakeley's radical interpretation of it. Stating again that the Articles must be interpreted in their plain, grammatical sense and without recourse to other authorities—and thus directly rejecting the authority of either the Church Catholic or nonnatural reasoning in interpreting the Articles—Jenner Fust found that in regard to tradition, purgatory, the invocation and worship of saints, the sacraments, and the doctrine of the sacrifice of the mass, there existed "irreconcilable differences between the two Churches" and that "in all these respects the two Churches differ entirely." He finally commented, "When, therefore, Mr. Oakeley publicly declares his belief in, and publicly maintains, the doctrine of the Church of Rome, not only in these respects, but in all others, there can be no doubt of his affirming and maintaining doctrines directly opposed, and contrary to the plain words of the Articles of the Church of England. And . . . where the Articles are plain, distinct, and definite, affording no room for doubt as to their real meaning, no attempt can be sanctioned which goes to distort their language, and so to extort by unfair means, if fair means will not do, a sense consistent with the ultra-Catholic, or Roman Doctrine, which Mr. Oakeley professes." Jenner Fust thus repudiated not only Oakeley's advanced position that the Articles were compatible with all Roman Catholic doctrine but even Newman's more moderate position in *Tract 90* of their not being incompatible with certain Roman Catholic doctrines. Oakeley's understanding of the Articles was not Newman's, and Oakeley admitted as much. Yet Ward's and Oakeley's radical readings of *Tract 90* had remained in the public domain since 1841, as Oakeley once quietly observed, "without disclaimer, though also without direct sanction, from its author." Jenner Fust's decision had effectively rejected both interpretations despite Newman's private assertion in September 1845 to the contrary. As Oakeley stated years later, "The judge . . . unwilling to lose so good an opportunity of entering the protest of the highest ecclesiastical court against what were called 'Romanizing opinions,' pronounced a condemnation of Catholic doctrines *seriatim*."[25]

The Court of Arches decreed that Oakeley had "advisedly maintained and affirmed Doctrines directly contrary to the Articles of the Church of England, and that, therefore, he is liable to Ecclesiastical censures."[26] Consequently, the Court revoked Oakeley's clerical license and his right to minister throughout the province of Canterbury until he had repented and retracted his errors.

After the Court of Arches decision, *Tract 90* could no longer comfort the consciences of advanced Catholics who wished to remain or become clergy of the English Church. Even the hapless Oakeley, whom the decision "both in substance and in tone" had taken by surprise, entertained no illusions as to its import. Over the summer, as Pusey composed a public letter dismissive of the wider impact of the court's decision, a much chastened Oakeley told Pusey, "When the Judgment is treated as nugatory, it shd. be recollected that in its operation it is very powerful & stringent, as I no doubt should find were I to attempt to act against it. It is not . . . a mere declaration, as for instance—[a] Bp might make in a Charge, or such as the Heads made about N. 90, it includes a palpable effect and a sweeping penalty." Oakeley was personally "disposed to think that a Clergyman . . . after the Sentence agst me, [who] *officiates* in the Ch. of England must be understood to surrender *something* for which I contended" and further thought that advanced Tractarians could not "help the fact of the Sentence telling in the case of sensitive persons."[27] The Oakeley case, despite some

Tractarian efforts to contend otherwise, condemned the principles of *Tract 90* in the very manner that Newman had so steadfastly sought to avoid.

The wider Tractarian camp had contemplated the potential difficulties of such an adverse judgment and had attempted to dissuade Oakeley from the moment he first confronted the Vice Chancellor and subsequently his bishop. E. L. Badeley presciently concluded, "It will be a most serious grievance to us all if Oakeley is censured." The Tractarians might wonder where the true Church Catholic was to be found, but they did understand that within England ecclesiastical courts had the last word regarding the established church itself. Moreover, they did not themselves on principle reject resort to ecclesiastical courts. Newman, for example, in 1841 had expressed the wish that Tractarian views receive the approval of the Court of Arches. During the summer of 1843 he had believed Pusey should judicially appeal his university suspension. But no one seems to have favored Oakeley's actions, partly for Badeley's reasons and partly because it was widely believed that Oakeley had every intention of very soon entering the Roman Church and was thus behaving disingenuously as well as recklessly in attempting to achieve a legal decision for a church he was about to depart. As James Mozley complained, Oakeley "may be ever so ready to take all the *onus* on himself; but he cannot prevent it from falling on others besides himself." Pusey, Keble, and Newman strongly opposed Oakeley's behavior, with Newman telling Edward Bellasis, another London lawyer sympathetic to the Tractarians, just before the hearing that "the risk of failure" on Oakeley's part "is great, from the *extreme* character of those opinions . . . and very serious, considering what interests would suffer if he was unsuccessful."[28]

The Court of Arches decision in Oakeley's case effectively ended the radical Catholic experiment that had commenced with the publication of Froude's *Remains*. Newman could no longer legally play even the role of Elijah in the English Church. Some months earlier in the *Edinburgh Review* the Congregationalist Henry Rogers had delineated the difficulty of the situation that Newman had long been attempting to sustain at Littlemore, observing, "Mr. Newman having retracted almost all his objections to the Church of Rome, from which, however, he is still a separatist, and having *not* retracted any of the several things he has uttered against the Church of England, in which he still remains—having also, in his zeal for the dark ages, undertaken the defence of an indefinite number of primitive and *mediaeval* miracles, and affixed his Editorial *imprimatur* on a series of publications advocating the religious system of the middle ages, and, amongst other things, the supremacy of the Apostolic see, (which, nevertheless, he will not obey,) may be considered to be by this time a Church of himself."[29] Jenner Fust's decision cast Newman into exactly the situation Rogers had so uncharitably, if not incorrectly, described. Before the Oakeley decision Newman and his followers might have remained a conventicle unto themselves, awaiting the day when their views became officially tolerated within the English Church. After the Oakeley decision the position they hoped to realize over time had become legally, if not necessarily theologically, untenable.

The journalistic coverage of both Ward's case and Oakeley's confrontation with Blomfield had also focused public attention once more on the issue of Tractarian honesty. The *Morning Herald* blatantly accused the Tractarians of reducing "falsehood to a system," of "promulgating the duty of being *insincere*," and of infecting their supporters "with a blindness to the dictates of plain duty and moral obligation." The same paper asked whether Oakeley had not moved "away from plain English and common honesty into regions of equivocation, double-dealing, and jesuitry." *The Times* was more moderate but claimed of the likes of Oakeley, "Men holding opinions that they have again and again solemnly abjured, as far as plain words convey plain meaning, expect at once to pass muster with the rest of the Anglican priesthood, and to be acquitted of insincerity and treachery." No longer supporting the Tractarians, *The Times* announced that the day of Ward's and Oakeley's "Jesuitical double-dealing is happily over." The ever sympathetic *Morning Post* wished to keep as an open question "whether the doctrines of the Church of Rome and the doctrines of the Church of England may *both* be honestly and rationally held by one and the same individual at once and the same time," but even that paper admitted that Jenner Fust had decided "the question in the negative, and so will most men." It further commented rather limply, "*That* must be regarded as the law; yet that law may not bind the consciences of all men."[30]

On July 11, just over a week after Jenner Fust rendered his decision, Newman told the sculptor Richard Westmacott "that it is morally certain I shall join the R.C. Church, though I don't wish this *told* from me." Presenting still again his by now well-rehearsed account of acting upon the study of ancient church history and not upon pressures of recent events and also stating views from his work-in-progress on development of Christian doctrine, he explained to Westmacott, "I think the Church of Rome in every respect the continuation of the early Church. I think she is the early Church *in* these times, and the early Church is she *in* these times. They differ in doctrine and discipline as child and grown man differ, not otherwise. I do not see any medium between disowning Christianity, and taking the Church of Rome." Responding to Westmacott's criticism of Ward and Oakeley's interpretation of the Articles, Newman wrote, "You call them disingenuous in trying to *stretch* the articles of our Church. Well then, do you wish them to *leave* our Church? that I suppose would not please you better. You abuse them for staying—you remonstrate with me for going. What middle course is there?" In an important further remark, he stated that middle-aged men might consider entering lay communion, but such a course for persons as young as Ward and Oakeley was "a more fantastic idea than turning Mormonite or Jumper."[31] The last was a curious comment because Newman and Oakeley were not far apart in age.

On September 21, 1845, in a brief reply to a question about his present religious intentions, Newman told an unidentified inquirer "that no reason for leaving our Church for the Roman comes home to me as sufficient, except this,—the conviction that such a step is necessary for our salvation." He further insisted, "As I have never held that 'all Roman doctrine' could be held in our Church, I have not myself been at all affected by recent decisions." He concluded, "The simple question to my mind is whether St. Athanasius or St. Augustine would have acknowledged us as a Church."[32] The three points of the letter do not hold together. He had mentioned the question of salvation for several months but had not acted upon that concern, which he had previously addressed by suggesting that God's grace did extend to members of the English Church. The appeal to St. Athanasius and St. Augustine required a private historical speculation on Newman's part about their view of modern churches and did not indicate his own reservations about the contemporary Roman Catholic Church. Perhaps most important, his comment on the Oakeley case represented still again his determination to allow no existing ecclesiastical authority actually to touch him. His was a very narrow reading of that decision, the content of which certainly might apply to him should he be placed in any kind of ecclesiastically problematical situation. On September 21 Newman was not yet prepared to move. He still had not completed his book on development, the contents of which he wished to keep secret, and the appearance of which he had told Jemima would in all probability indicate his departure.

On October 3, with the book still unfinished, Newman submitted his resignation from the Oriel fellowship, though college records indicate that he received the stipend distributed at the audit later that month. He had not dined at Oriel since March. In late 1844 he had worried that Hawkins might use the then contemplated new test against him. He may now have feared that despite his own contention of its inapplicability, Hawkins might seek to

use the Oakeley judgment against him. On October 6, acknowledging Newman's resignation, Hawkins observed that he knew nothing specific about
Newman's present position or intentions but understood from rumors that
he intended to join the Roman Church. Although feeling unable to dissuade
him, Hawkins continued, "And yet I cannot forbear expressing the most
earnest hope (in all sincerity and with feelings of real kindness), that whatever course you may have resolved upon, you may still at least be saved from
some of the worst errors of the Church of Rome, such as praying to human
Mediators or falling down before images—because in you, with all the great
advantages with which God has blessed and tried you, I must believe such
errors to be most deeply sinful. But may He protect you!" One can only
wonder about Hawkins's feelings on this occasion, knowing as he did that
his sermon of a quarter-century earlier on unauthorized tradition had awakened the undergraduate Newman to the possibility of religious truth beyond the letter of Scripture. Did Hawkins also recall those summer conversations of two decades earlier that began to draw that younger Oriel fellow
out of his Calvinism, or did he understand that by relieving Newman of his
tutorial duties, he had provided the time and necessity for personal redirec-
tion that led him to undertake the tracts and all that followed therefrom?
Although in 1874 Richard Church described Hawkins as "the ablest and
most hurtful opponent" of the Tractarians within Oxford, the Provost of
Oriel had also unwittingly been one of their chief progenitors.[33]

As throughout the late summer Newman had continued to indicate that
he would move to Rome, his sister Harriett, still angry over her husband's
near conversion two years earlier, supplied instructive, if not generous,
comments to Jemima about their brother. Harriett thought no one could
have "any weight" with John, who "had made up his mind to the step some
years," further noting that "in such a case reasons are never wanting." She
found John's situation "like a disgraceful marriage, and he has been breaking it to his friends and to the world, just as a step of that kind is done."
Three months after her brother had converted, Harriett returned to the
same metaphor, this time telling their sister, "The flagrant evil of his present
step, as regards himself, is acting against his reason, and knowing it. If a man
of reason (which J.H.N. especially is) acts against his reason, suffer he must
and ought. If he marries so, he does, and J.H.N. has made a most disgraceful
match—the consequence of which he must bear."[34] Harriett's comments
may probe far more deeply into the sources of her brother's inaction and
passivity than does a more intellectual or theological explanation. Newman's
life in the Roman Church, if not the disgraceful match described by his

sister, was nonetheless at best an imperfect match and no marriage made in heaven. He had told Westmacott, it was the primitive church in modern times, but had not said it was a church without faults.

Newman knew that he was contemplating entering not that idealized Church Catholic he had in 1840 described to Francis Newman as glimpsed at a distance through a mist, but an institution that he firmly believed required reform and whose shortcomings he had repeatedly and recently elucidated. He was moving toward Rome, not as part of a saving remnant of the Church Catholic from the English Church uniting with a saving remnant of the Church Catholic in the Roman Church, but quite simply as an individual uniting himself with the unreformed Roman communion, who must await, like those Cistercians of old under the trees, the construction of a new fabric. After all, the previous autumn the *Tablet* had advised the Tractarians "to remember that *to us they are Protestants;* and that, in fact, the distance between themselves and ourselves is immeasurably greater than between themselves and the class of Protestants whom their writers accuse of blasphemy." In September 1845 the *Tablet* took Ward's conversion earlier that month as "an open confession of failure" on the part of the Tractarian school and hoped that its followers would make "no more attempts to stride over and stand on both sides of the unfathomable abyss."[35]

While Roman Catholic journalists left him under no illusion about his circumstances, Newman may well have been right to hesitate. He had encountered enormous personal abuse and deep psychological pain to avoid exactly this moment. He had eschewed lay communion for Ward and Oakeley in his letter to Westmacott but not for himself. Even *The Times* hoped that Newman would pass a period in contemplation rather than depart the English Church. For his younger Littlemore acolytes, conversion was an act as much of youthful rebellion and personal self-individuation as of faith and conviction. For Newman, who had years before left the evangelical faith, it was still another vast change in religious life and practice. Had it been the conclusion of a deathbed as he portrayed it in the *Apologia*, it would have been easier. Death did not conclude Newman's troubles in 1845, but rather life in a religious subculture where within a few weeks Bishop Wiseman would require him to wait alongside young schoolboys before receiving admission into his office for confession.[36]

Although in the *Apologia* Newman's reception by Father Dominic Barberi serves as a fitting conclusion to the narrative structure of the work, it is not altogether clear why Newman actually entered the Roman Communion *when he did.* His own thinking was not substantially different from what it had been weeks or months before, and, as already noted, his book on development of doctrine was not yet completed. He had also previously indicated that a significant period of time would separate his resigning Oriel and his conversion to Rome. As late as October 4, the day after resigning his Oriel fellowship, knowing that Father Dominic would be arriving at Littlemore later in the week, Newman told Stanton, "It is *likely* that he will admit me. . . . But I *am not* certain; I am so very busy, that is the reason."[37] Such was hardly the statement of a person eager to change churches. On October 9 Newman did find time to allow Father Dominic to receive him into the Roman Catholic Church within the walls of Littlemore. Newman's conversion thus displayed all the haste that he had hoped to avoid, a situation recognized immediately within his new religious communion.

Conversion for Newman was a confession of failure both to secure latitude for Catholics in the English Church and to define a Catholic faith that could hold a congregation. In 1844 Bishop Blomfield privately commented that Newman was hesitating to change communions because he wanted to take "with him to Rome a respectable number of converts."[38] Had there been a large group around Newman, it would not have been necessary for him to go over to Rome. Newman's conventicle of the Church Catholic at Littlemore ultimately collapsed, leading to his conversion not because of external opposition but because, unlike other secessionist Church of England clergy, he failed to establish a stable, faithful congregation supportive of him and his ideas. Rather, in traditional radical Protestant fashion, he had fostered a movement that continued to splinter rapidly from within as enthusiastic Catholic individuals pressed his ideas to what they saw as more extreme logical conclusions and disruptive actions.

During September the advanced Catholic party that had once looked to Newman for leadership had begun rapidly to disintegrate before his eyes. He had long contended, as he had told Keble in 1841, "It is not love of Rome that unsettles people, but *fear of heresy* at home." That opinion had stated his own views, not those of his followers. By the late summer of 1845, within Newman's larger circle, the love of Rome overwhelmed one person after another. The Oakeley decision demonstrated that love of Rome as understood by advanced Catholics was incompatible with priesthood in the English Church. Newman found himself required to react to a situation that he could no longer define or dominate. He had recognized as early as May that conversions might well mean separation for himself and his friends. At that time, he viewed the prospect calmly. But as the reality of conversions commenced, he reacted with a good deal of emotion. On August 22, as their immediate prospect loomed, he later recalled, "I saw my way clear to put a miraculous medal around my neck."[39]

On August 8 Ward had written that whatever Newman's "present feelings" were "about our position," for his own part he could not "but look on the decisions of the Ecclesiastical Courts as final." Even more important, Ward's wife had strong feelings "that she may suffer spiritual detriment by remaining for several months together in a Communion which she cannot now regard with the confidence which it did receive from her, that quite possibly it may be of the greatest importance to her to join the Roman Church sooner." He himself now wanted to begin confession with someone outside the English Church. During the next week Ward allowed a friend to give notice that he would be joining the Roman Church in about a month. He and his wife entered the Roman Catholic Church the first week in September. On September 26, having lost his formerly intimate confidant first to marriage and then under the direct influence of the new spouse to the Roman Church, an angry Newman wrote Ward that he was "pained a good deal" at "the whole series of the acts that extend from the publication of your book" onward. It is not insignificant that Ward's book had appeared about the same time that the romance with his future wife had commenced. Newman continued, "It has been a growing pain. I cannot go into the subject, nor on the other hand can I in one word convey my feeling about it." He advised Ward against continuing a career in theology. This letter proved so disturbing to Frances Wingfield Ward that she herself replied to express her own "grief and pain" at having been "indirectly the cause of Mr. Wards appearing in a disadvantageous light to his friends."[40] Newman had never before confronted a situation in which the new wife answered his anger over a colleague's marriage, however courteously. Mrs. Ward's Roman Catholic zeal, commencing with her conversion a month before his own, would always outdistance Newman's.

Ward's letter of August 8 suggests that Newman at that time still believed that he and his followers might persevere in the English Church. His Littlemore followers, perhaps now looking more to Ward's example than Newman's advice, thought otherwise. Father Dominic received Dalgairns in late September, shortly before his parents came to visit him at Littlemore. St. John, that closest of Newman's Littlemore friends, followed on September 29, and others prepared themselves. Four days later Henry Wilberforce, recognizing the import of what was occurring, wrote, "So St. John has really left you. Well many blessings on you in all times and all places." On October 7, though still wishing to complete his book before his own reception,

Newman told Wilberforce that what he now termed "the accident" of Father Dominic's approaching visit might fulfill his desire for "an external call" indicating he should change communions. He further confessed, "Also, I suppose the departure of others has had something to do with it, for when they went, it was as if I were losing my own bowels."[41] Newman was quite literally losing control of the followers he had attempted to draw around himself for the past five years. These September conversions replicated all of the most painful events of Newman's previous life. People to whom he had been close and whose spiritual edification had provided him a vocation were independently changing their religious views, loyalties, and affiliations. By describing Father Dominic's anticipated arrival to Wilberforce in providential terms, language absent from his October 4 letter to Stanton, Newman imposed a divine pattern upon events that he could no longer influence or determine.

Newman's own passage to Rome—like every other of his major actions since early 1841, including the publication of *Tract 90*, the founding of the Littlemore community, and the resignation of St. Mary's—was still another response to his radical followers with whom he desperately wished to preserve connection and community. His celibate male brotherhood was vanishing before his eyes, and he rushed just to keep up with them, an older man hoping to match the energy of the young whose company he so valued and required. Although the previous June the *Morning Herald* had stated, "Tractarianism, in fact, is at an end when Mr. Newman departs," he actually departed the Church of England only when the advanced Tractarian party deserted him.[42]

A New Bishop for Oxford

There did occur, however, during the same days of late September and early October, 1845, a third transforming external event that *may* (and it must be emphasized only *may*) also have contributed to Newman's deciding to enter the Roman Church when he did. On September 22, 1845, George Henry Law, Bishop of Bath and Wells, died. His succession by Bishop Bagot of Oxford was announced in *The Times* on October 16, but the prospect of Bagot's transfer could very well have been known earlier within Oxford, indeed in time to have influenced Newman. It is difficult to overestimate the impact upon Tractarianism of the removal of Bagot from Oxford to Bath and Wells, where shortly thereafter he suffered a complete mental collapse. The character of Richard Bagot as Bishop of Oxford had been a key factor in the entire history of the Tractarian Movement. A person of low energy, Bagot disliked conflict and publicity, which could rarely redound to his credit. Indeed, A. P. Stanley noted years later that this unexceptional . " 'Dick Bagot' " was the only bishop whom Newman in the *Apologia* singled out for any special commendation. An aristocratic pluralist surviving well into the age of reform, Bagot enjoyed another rich clerical living in addition to the income from the Oxford bishopric, a situation that affronted Sir Robert Peel, the church reformer. Furthermore, as a relatively old-fashioned high churchman, Bagot carried out his London business with the Tory Archbishop Howley, to whom he always deferred in Tractarian matters, and appears to have had no significant interaction with Blomfield, Peel's close conservative ecclesiastical adviser. On Howley's instruction, Bagot had ordered the end of the tracts, subsequently refused to interfere with the Littlemore monastic experiment, and then left Newman alone after his resignation from St. Mary's. No less important, Bagot did not raise difficulties about ordaining men from Oxford. There were no incidents in the Oxford diocese comparable to the refusal of the Bishop of Winchester to ordain Keble's curate Peter Young. J. D. Coleridge noted that Bagot would have willingly ordained certain Oriel men whom, because of their sympathy for *Tract 90*, Hawkins refused testimonials. Bagot's chaplain Francis Paget, denounced by the local Oxford newspaper as a "Romanizing Chaplain," appears to have given ordination candidates neither probing nor extensive examinations.[43] By contrast Bagot vigorously criticized clergy who visited Dissenting congregations. He had also been the bishop who in 1831 suspended Henry Bulteel's clerical license.

Over the years, Newman had played for all it was worth his bishop's fear of a misstep with the Tractarians. Bagot would ask the necessary questions and virtually always accept Newman's answers, no matter how calculating or possibly disingenuous their character. To be sure, Bagot had made mildly critical comments about Tractarianism, including a public warning against the extremes of the followers in 1838 and a private one in late 1840, and had included that single harsh sentence about *Tract 90* in his charge of 1842, issued when he was still angry over Tractarian behavior regarding the poetry professorship. He had also refused, in cooperation with the Archbishop of Canterbury, to intervene in Pusey's suspension. But fundamentally Bagot had provided the Tractarians with consistent protection. Roundell Palmer observed that in the Bishop of Oxford's mildly critical charge of 1842, he "censures in the most uncompromising manner the character of the opposition which [the Tractarians] have encountered. In truth, therefore, he puts himself at their head, and takes the responsibility of publicly approving their acts and avowing their doctrines up to a certain point—and what is more—nothing less than the furthest limits of Anglo-Catholicism."[44] And in 1843 Bagot urged William Palmer to soften some of the anti-Tractarian rhetoric in his *Narrative*.

Whether, as Copleston thought, Bagot's tentative behavior actually emboldened the Tractarians, they did appreciate the importance of his presence. After the first critical episcopal charges appeared during the summer of 1841, Newman reminded Hope that they had "no direct authority except in their own dioceses," and that there was "nothing to hinder any one in the Oxford diocese maintaining just the negative of what those particular Bishops have said." In late December, fearing that the bishops might issue "some stringent declarations of faith," Newman wondered, "Would the Bishop of O. *accept* them?" In January 1842, after expressing his general distrust of the current bench of bishops, Newman told Rickards, "What a blessing it is my own Bishop is the man he is; yet they say he is to go to York on a vacancy." The same day, with more foreboding, he wrote Crawley, "It is a source of great thankfulness, I am sure, that the Bishop of Oxford should be the man he is—but what if he goes to York sometime, and another comes in his place?" In April 1842, after Bagot accepted Newman's reply to his inquiry about Littlemore, Bowden wrote, "What a happiness it is in that most important, now, of sees, to have a right-minded Bishop," and expressed apprehension over likely appointments by Peel to the episcopate. With the rumor of Bagot's possible translation to York still in mind, J. B. Mozley commented later that spring, "It will be a perilous thing his going away—that is, for us."[45]

For a brief time there had even existed a modest personal relationship of sorts between Newman and Bagot. In late February 1841, just before *Tract 90* appeared, the bishop visited Littlemore, as did his family in early March, at the very time the Heads were debating their course of action over the tract. In the late spring of 1842 Newman reported to Jemima that Bagot would call at Littlemore "not as a Bishop but as a friend—out of kindness," an event that took place in November. During this same period, Newman wrote quite confidently of the "good" being done by the Bishop of Oxford's charge, despite certain critical lines, and told Jemima, "It is plain which way he leans." Furthermore, Bagot's daughter became friends with the sister of F. S. Bowles, Newman's curate, with the bishop putting "his daughter into her hands, as to what books she should read, etc." While this friendship continued, Miss Bagot must have visited Littlemore, because she wanted to copy the altar cloth that Jemima Mozley had made for the church. While in Rome for Easter in 1843, however, Miss Bowles herself converted to Roman Catholicism. Whatever personal relationship may have been developing between Newman and Bagot apparently ended at that point. But even in November 1843, after having resigned St. Mary's, Newman told Miss Giberne that he would remain at Littlemore rather than seek a living elsewhere because among other things, "No where can I have a Bp more favorable to me."[46] It is significant that Newman, even when without a living and at a time when he was complaining vituperatively about the lack of Catholicity on the part of the English Church, regarded the presence of a noninterfering bishop as important.

Bagot's personality and caution, unbeknownst to himself, served another function. There existed in Newman's mind an important line of defense against external ecclesiastical criticism and rebuke by which he might have thought himself insulated even from the implications of the Oakeley judgment as long as Bagot remained in place. According to Newman's theory of ecclesiology, the central authority of the English portion of the Church Catholic stood dispersed among its several bishops, who, in his view, functioned as the equivalent of popes in their individual dioceses. Bagot had never taken any significant independent direct action against the Tractarians, as Blomfield had just done against Oakeley. Consequently, even in the wake of the Oakeley decision Newman during the late summer of 1845 might well have felt secure in the diocese of Oxford, having in his own mind never violated any agreement with his bishop or publicly endorsed the views of Ward and Oakeley on subscription. Newman no doubt believed on the basis of past inaction that Bagot would not take steps against him as a result of that judgment.

Sir Robert Peel, of course, knew the Oxford scene well and exercised purposeful ecclesiastical patronage there. Staunchly anti-Tractarian, he retained enormous anger over the "Catholicus Letters" to *The Times* of 1841 and no doubt remembered how university high churchmen had contributed to the loss of his Oxford parliamentary seat in 1829. Religiously Peel's life and convictions displayed "evidence of deep faith and a basically evangelical temper." In 1842, shortly after appointing the anti-Tractarian Gilbert to the episcopal bench, he had written J. W. Croker, "Three *good* appointments in the English Church, indicating the sense of the Government, would do more to allay the fever of Puseyism, than 3000 controversial tracts with a Chillingworth for the author of each of them."[47] This outlook informed Peel's actions when in late September 1845 he contemplated the opportunity for creative exercise of ecclesiastical patronage occasioned by the vacancy of Bath and Wells.

Peel had already once previously attempted to transfer Bagot, a few months after Pusey's suspension and shortly after Newman's leaving St. Mary's. In October 1843, when the see of Lichfield stood vacant, Peel informed Blomfield of his "present *inclination*" to offer it to Bagot. His chief motive "for the offer would be to sever the various Ecclesiastical appointments which the Bishop unites in his own person." With such an appointment to Lichfield opening the see of Oxford, Peel stated, "Particular circumstances will render this vacancy more than ordinarily important." With the Tractarians very much in mind, he told Blomfield, "The existence and influence of that party, and its immediate connections with Oxford make it highly desirable that a man of authority and high character should be selected for the see in the event of a vacancy." Blomfield fully supported the strategy that, if successful, would result in "the extinction of a very objectionable case of accumulated pluralities" and put the residency of the Bishop of Oxford on a more nearly full-time basis than was the case with Bagot. Although he had "steered his course cautiously and upon the whole wisely, in the midst of no ordinary difficulties," Blomfield also asserted, no doubt alluding to Archbishop Howley's influence, that it was widely believed that Bagot "has acted under the guidance and spoken the language of others." Bagot quickly declined the proffered see. Thereafter, the prime minister consulted Archbishop Howley about a list of other candidates, each of whom Peel regarded as "wholly free from any leaning towards Tractarian opinions," adding "This I should consider a sine quâ non."[48]

It is not known whether rumors of Peel's offer of Lichfield to Bagot circulated in Oxford as had rumors of Bagot's possible translation to York the previous year. There were, however, rumors in Oxford and elsewhere that one of the Tractarians' internal university opponents might receive appointment to Lichfield. It was in mid-October 1843 that Newman wrote those extraordinary letters to Manning about his doubting the Catholicity of the English Church on the grounds of the Monophysite parallel and the same time that he complained about the Protestant character of the bench of bishops. Newman could have written the letters and authorized their public release not only because of his anger over leaving St. Mary's but also because he anticipated the appointment of a hostile Oxford bishop and was preparing the groundwork for announcing his principled departure from the English Church. In that respect, the months of August through October 1843, with William Lockhart converting and Thomas Mozley almost converting and the see of Oxford possibly open, resembled late September 1845. More-over, Newman had also extensively explored the parallel of the modern English Church with ancient heresy in his January 1842 letter to Robert Wilberforce, written just after Peel had appointed Gilbert to the episco-pal bench.

After Bagot rejected Lichfield, Peel did not give up his objective of vacating the see of Oxford for a candidate of his own choosing. He could not do so when Ely became vacant in early 1845 because of the expectation of a Cambridge appointment to the see nearest that university. Press specula-tion, however, indicated a general public understanding that Peel would continue to appoint Tractarian opponents to the episcopal bench. For exam-ple, in late June 1845, even before there existed any new vacancy, the *Oxford Chronicle* reported that Hawkins would be Peel's next choice for an open bishopric.[49] Such ongoing public discussion of Peel's ecclesiastical patron-age policy created an atmosphere that would have aroused apprehension among Tractarians about any of his ecclesiastical appointments.

Then on September 22 the death of the Bishop of Bath and Wells actually created a vacancy and simultaneously reopened the question of Oxford. Gossip in and out of the press about the late bishop's replacement commenced immediately, as was usual in such circumstances. Four days later Peel requested advice from Archbishop Howley and a conversation relating to the new episcopal vacancy. By September 29, based on reports certainly circulating the previous day, the *Standard* reported that an Oxford man would be appointed to Bath and Wells, mentioning Samuel Wilberforce and Dr. Jelf as leading candidates. No later than September 30, however, the archbishop wrote to Bagot, sounding him out about moving to the newly vacant diocese. Replying on October 1, Bagot raised concerns about the residence of the Bishop of Bath and Wells. On October 2 the archbishop confirmed to Peel that he could think of no better arrangement than to transfer Bagot. On October 5 and 7, following Howley's advice, Bagot asked permission from Peel to visit the prospective residence. On October 13 Bagot accepted Peel's offer. That same day the prime minister wrote Wil-liam Wilberforce, a great favorite of Victoria and Albert's, offering him the see of Oxford, a decision upon which Peel and Howley must have deter-mined no later than September 30 and possibly before.[50]

Although one cannot be certain, of course, it seems highly unlikely that the possible transfer of Bagot remained an entirely private or confidential matter within the church or Oxford. The rumor of a major change in the political complexion of the English Church could have begun to spread no

later than September 30 and conceivably earlier. It is certainly possible that
Newman at Littlemore *may* have known that the benign, frequently absent
bishop who had protected him largely through inaction, might be departing.
The names then circulating as possible new appointees to the episcopal
bench—Wilberforce, a known Tractarian critic whom Newman had once
called "a humbug," and Jelf, one of the six doctors involved in Pusey's
suspension, as well as that of Hawkins, floated earlier—would have proved
deeply disturbing.[51] But even without knowing exactly whom Peel would
appoint to Oxford, Newman and his friends would certainly have realized
on the basis of Peel's previous episcopal patronage that he would appoint
someone hostile to the Tractarians, thus transforming their immediate ecclesiastical situation. Consequently, simple knowledge that the Oxford diocese was in play would have been enough to have moved Newman to the
action that he had been postponing.

Newman had repeatedly demanded some outer sign, but the two previous signs—the vetoed condemnation of *Tract 90* and the Oakeley decision—left him at least in his own mind with an escape. On October 4 he
wrote that he might be too busy to be received by Father Dominic, but five
days later he was received. It had been between October 5 and 7 that Bagot
had asked to visit Wells and received permission to do so. The possible
imminent departure of Bagot and his presumptive replacement by an unsympathetic bishop would have left Newman no avenue of escape within the
Church of England. Even though Newman no longer held a living under the
authority of the Bishop of Oxford, a new active bishop could have caused
him difficulty and embarrassment, especially if cooperating with the evangelical Symons, the university Vice Chancellor, or with Hawkins in Oriel, or
with both. That new bishop might very well have demanded to know of
Newman just exactly what was going on liturgically at Littlemore or might
have pressed in some manner the precedent of the Oakeley decision or
might have ignored the archbishop's desire for no further university action
regarding *Tract 90*. A new bishop could change the process of ordination so
as to demonstrate quite forcibly to young ordinands that the arguments of
Tract 90 had no validity in his diocese. In short, a new Peelite bishop could
only be trouble to the already beleaguered Tractarians at Littlemore. Suddenly Newman, for whom there was no friendly diocese where he might
seek refuge beyond the borders of Oxford, had no room to maneuver, and
his own theory of episcopal authority now directly worked against his remaining in the English Church. Once he stood in direct opposition to his
bishop, as he had not with Bagot, Newman by his own definitions would

have become schismatic. Under such circumstances he could thus have convinced himself that by entering the Roman Church, he was acting, even if rapidly, upon objective events, as he had long wished, and not on private judgment.

Moreover, had Newman entered the Roman communion *after* direct difficulty with his own bishop, he could not have maintained the stance that he acted upon religious conviction rather than in reaction to formal discipline, conflict, or unpleasantness. After such an occurrence, he would be received into the Roman Church under the most questionable and strained circumstances. He may well have chosen to leave before that situation presented itself, even if it meant the failure to complete, as he wished, his book on development, and the appearance of acting on impulse. From the standpoint of the Roman Church authorities, it was also well to appear to receive a Newman acting upon principle rather than one seeking a final refuge.

It is admittedly not certain that Bagot's transfer to Bath and Wells served as the immediate cause for Newman's conversion. Yet there was, as noted at the time, a precipitous quality about his move. Newman's conversion came upon Keble as a "thunderbolt," and he continued to believe that Newman had acted on impulse rather than long thought. As rumors swirled, the *English Churchman* commented with some plausibility, "In one sense it cannot be said that the event has come upon us by surprise. For the last eight or ten months, it has been generally rumoured that he would resign his Fellowship at the annual meeting of Oriel College, (in the present week); and that this step would be speedily followed by the renunciation of the English Church. *What it was which hastened the movement in the manner above related, is not likely to transpire upon positive authority; and we do not care to repeat the report which has reached us, which the readers of our Journal for the last three or four weeks will have no difficulty in guessing.*"[52] The conversions of Ward, Dalgairns, and St. John were not rumors but actual occurrences. When that edition of the *English Churchman* appeared, it had been more than three weeks since the Bishop of Bath and Wells had died. Rumors regarding the patronage of that diocese and of Oxford had been circulating for the period the journal mentioned.

The vacancy created by Bagot's departure was a passive situation, but the arrival of the new bishop brought a powerful, active force to the scene. Samuel Wilberforce was an outspoken, highly energetic personality who had for some time distanced himself politically and theologically from the Tractarians, and they from him. He intended to employ his episcopal authority to prevent persons of Tractarian persuasion from entering the priesthood. In late 1845, in sharp departure from Bagot's practice, Wilberforce personally examined candidates for ordination, after requiring them to spend as much as three days with him at Cuddesdon. Not all who presented themselves to their new bishop were ordained. Indeed, on December 21, in his first charge to candidates for ordination, Wilberforce announced, "I am sure that a more deadly blow could not be inflicted on our Church than that the people, of whose character, thank God, sterling honesty is the distinctive feature, should have reason to suspect that their clergy believed one thing while they taught another." Because Wilberforce had previously "been much struck by the inferior character of all of Newman's comrades," there seems little question that he would have refused to ordain them or that they would have refused to present themselves for his examination.[53]

One can only speculate about the dialogue that might have ensued between Cuddesdon and Littlemore if Newman had not been received into the Roman Church. Newman had never done direct public battle with an intellectual or theological equal or with a person capable of powerfully expressing convictions at odds with his own. Indeed, in 1841 he had consciously used Ward as a surrogate in the *British Critic* to attack Arnold and Whately, as in 1834 he had used Wilberforce against Hampden and Hawkins over subscription. Newman himself had always chosen opponents, such as Faussett, easily subject to caricature or had constructed his own polemical straw men, as in his *Lectures on the Prophetical Office of the Church*, as well as his two volumes of sermons published in 1843. He had carried unctuous, passive-aggressive obedience to episcopal authority to a fine art. Those strategies would not have succeeded with Wilberforce, who would have liked nothing better than to unveil the self-will encased in Tractarian humility. Moreover, Wilberforce, unlike Bagot, would not have been unhappy to be the bishop under whose auspices Newman, Pusey, or any other advanced Tractarians departed the English Church.

The initial correspondence between Wilberforce and Pusey illustrates what Newman might have confronted under his new bishop. On November 15 Pusey rehearsed to Wilberforce current problems in the English Church, mentioning Newman's conversion and stating that he believed, as most evidence would support, that "despondency about ourselves" rather than attraction to Rome had caused the conversion. Pusey also alluded to his own *Letter to the Bishop of Oxford* (1839) and his subsequent *Letter to the Archbishop of Canterbury* (1842) defending the Tractarian Movement without, however, mentioning his chastisement of bishops contained therein. After delaying a response for over a week, Wilberforce told Pusey that those pamphlets had deeply "pained" him and that he could not feel "that the language therein held as to the errors of the Church of Rome" could "be reconciled with the doctrinal formularies of our own Reformed Church."[54]

Pusey in answer defended both his own mode of subscribing to the Articles as well as *Tract 90*, stated his hope for the eventual reconciliation of the English and Roman Churches, and explained how the practices and authority of the ancient church informed his views. Employing uncompromising language such as Pusey had not encountered since his exchange with Bishop Blomfield a decade and a half earlier, Wilberforce replied that he did not doubt that initially "a longing after greater devotion, after a higher and more self-denying character, and after a greater life of Christian charity, than they met with around them" had stirred the Tractarians. But rather than "seeking for these, where only they could be found, in a fuller and more personal knowledge of God and the eternal relations of the ever-blessed Trinity as revealed in God's Word," they had been "drawn aside by forms and trappings" into a system "which must really obscure the truth to all, and especially to those by whom it was self-chosen." The Tractarians had consequently been led away from rather than toward God, and as a result, Wilberforce declared, "With the appearance to themselves of peculiar self-abasement they lost their humility; and with great outward asceticism they were ruled by an unmortified will; they formed a party; and thus being greatly predisposed to it, the perverted bias of one master-mind has sufficed to draw them close to or absolutely into the Roman Schism, with all its fearful doctrinal errors." Having so attacked the departed Newman, Wilberforce turned his episcopal scorn on Pusey, stating that there appeared in him "too many traces of this evil," including "a subtle and therefore most dangerous form of self-will" as well as "a tendency to view" himself "as one in, if not now the leader of, a party." Those qualities had led Pusey "to judge the Church" which he "ought to obey" and "sometimes to blame, sometimes almost to patronize her; and hence to fall into the further error of undervaluing the One inspired Revelation of God's will given to us in His perfect Word."[55] Clearly a new voice spoke from Cuddesdon, announcing a new day in the diocese of Oxford.

DEVELOPMENT BEFORE AND AFTER

Although Newman had met with Bishop Wiseman as recently as August 9, 1845, and had carried on an important correspondence with Dr. Charles Russell, he did not join the Roman Church under the auspices of either.

Instead Newman entered under the aegis of an Italian priest who had long hoped to draw him into the Roman Catholic fold.[56] The choice of Father Dominic, the priest who had just received Dalgairns, precluded any extensive conversation with Roman Catholic authorities about his conversion. Newman thus guaranteed the fewest possible questions being raised about his timing, his motives, his principles, or his understanding of Roman Catholic beliefs and practices.[57]

Within days, indeed almost hours, of Father Dominic's visit, however, Newman found himself dealing with English Roman Catholic bishops. Harriett's marriage metaphor remained apt because both parties had entered into a union without either quite knowing how the other would behave. The absence of anticipatory groundwork was especially important because Newman was accompanied into the Roman communion not only by his reputation and a number of followers but also by the manuscript of *An Essay on the Development of Christian Doctrine,* then in the course of having proof sheets printed under conditions of secrecy. On October 11, 1845, Roman Catholic Bishop C. M. Baggs, who died a few days later, describing the matter of the uncompleted book as "one of great difficulty and delicacy," recommended that Newman "consult with Dr. Wiseman or some other experienced Catholic Divine, as I should grieve if any one of your expressions were afterward misinterpreted."[58] Consequently, within two days of his reception into the Roman Catholic Church, Newman returned to the familiar situation of negotiating with ecclesiastical superiors over one of his publications.

The encounter between Wiseman and Newman occurred on November 1, 1845, the occasion of Newman's formal confirmation as a Roman Catholic. As during past negotiations, Newman knew exactly what he wanted, while Bishop Wiseman, finding himself in the presence of a religious genius whom he had long desired to adorn his church, hoped primarily, like Bishop Bagot before him, to avoid any untoward incident. Wiseman provided Dr. Russell with an important report of Newman's description of the manuscript:

> The plan is something of this sort. There is a long introductory portion, upon the mode of ascertaining which Church corresponds with the ancient. He shows the *prima facie* evidences or striking features which anyone comparing the primitive Church with modern forms of religion would discover only in that and in the modern Catholic: *e.g.* the importance attached to dogma and accuracy of belief, &c. He then examines different tests, principally Vincent Lirinensis' 'Quod semper &c.,' and shows how in application it would not answer, though true. For this purpose he takes three doctrines admitted by the Anglican Church and shows how difficult it

would be to prove the *semper, ab omnibus* and *ubique* in the first three centuries. . . . He concludes by drawing the consequence that doctrines are developed by time, and do not reach their full manifestation in the Church in the beginning. The main portion of the work is taken up in showing the difference between a development and a corruption, and in giving and applying tests for distinguishing one from the other. . . . He gives, I think, as many as [seven] tests: *e.g.* that the substance of the doctrine must remain unchanged, &c.

Wiseman then further explained, "The work was all written while [Newman was] an Anglican, when he did not contemplate joining us, at least immediately, and gives the history only of the mode in which he was led to his own convictions; but at the end he will state that now he is a Catholic and holds his faith on the authority of the Church, and believes in all things as she teaches, &c." Wiseman reported that Newman believed his work "would be considered decidedly Ultramontane" and would show how the "worship" of the Virgin Mary "as now practised, superseding, overlaying or obscuring the doctrines of the Incarnation, &c . . . seems to bring them out and give them importance." Wiseman emphasized to Russell that Newman's book was "the history of his past mind, the narrative of a fact, not a theoretical or dogmatical work."[59]

Wiseman directly reports that Newman wrote the book before contemplating immediately joining the Roman Catholic Church, which must have been what Newman told him and accords with the evidence in his correspondence of 1845. Furthermore, while indicating that Newman would state that he had become a Roman Catholic and now believed "on the authority of the Church," Wiseman writes that the book itself "gives the history only of the mode in which he was led to his own convictions" and "the history of his past mind," but the bishop does not state with any specificity what was meant on either his or Newman's part by "mode" or "convictions." In actuality, *An Essay on the Development of Christian Doctrine* contained nothing autobiographical and much theoretical, though admittedly not dogmatic. Although Newman, according to Wiseman, had agreed to state that he believed what the Roman Church teaches, the letter indicates nothing about whether he had regarded the defense of the Roman Church as a specific goal in undertaking the book. Wiseman again seems not to have raised that question. From Wiseman's summary, it appears that Newman had described to him a book directed at refuting the high-church standard of antiquity, but not necessarily championing the Roman Catholic Church, except possibly by default.

Newman would have realized that claiming to have reached convictions about joining the Roman Catholic Church on the basis of his own research, reasoning, or feelings would have suggested a Protestant-like conversion based on private judgment about the authority of the Roman Church rather than faithful acceptance of its authority. Wiseman clearly did not want to probe that issue too deeply. Nor did he wish to examine issues surrounding the rapidity of the "how sudden" conversion, which, he reported, Newman had acknowledged as "accidental" in "mode." Wiseman also made no mention of Newman's entering the Roman Church on the basis of his conviction that the English Church stood in schism. Nor did he state anything about Newman's attaching importance to Dr. Russell's correspondence, about which he was to express such gratitude in the *Apologia*. Clearly much was quite consciously left unspoken and unasked during the conversation. As Wiseman told Russell, "I have often said I should be ready to sing my *Nunc dimittis* when Mr. Newman should have joined us; and I must not draw back from my word." For all the docility that Wiseman wished to perceive in Newman, the conversation must have been quite demanding and stressful for the bishop. Two months later, with more prescience than she realized, Harriett Mozley speculated to Jemima regarding their brother, "I should not wonder if the Church of Rome and he cannot come to terms at the onset. J.H.N. has showed less than ever lately, (less even than I expected) that he can bow to any authority, collected or individual."[60] Wiseman might well have appreciated the remark.

During the November 1 conversation, Wiseman agreed to let Newman's book pass into publication without examination. Then, influenced by more skeptical and cautious Roman Catholic colleagues, he decided that he should read it. On November 7, however, Newman told Wiseman that a member of the English Church—it had been James Hope—had informed him that the book would have no impact in that communion if changes were introduced at the behest of a Roman Catholic authority. Wiseman quickly backed down, requesting only comments in the preface indicating Newman's acceptance of the authority of the Roman Church. Once again from long practice, Newman had succeeded in substituting his private judgment for that of his bishop. In late 1841, in the face of the early hostile episcopal charges against *Tract 90*, Newman had asserted his right to exercise "that liberty of prophesying which has ever existed in the reformed Church."[61] He had not yet been prepared to surrender that familiar liberty when he made his first journey to Oscott. Wiseman, like Bagot before him, had been fearful of losing Newman, and Newman knew it. Both let him choose his prose, his arguments, and the grounds of his acceding to their concerns without imposing further examination or criticism. Newman could offer to destroy the manuscript of the widely anticipated book, but Wiseman knew that such an action would confirm every worst English Protestant suspicion of the Roman Church. The rapid publication of the book as a work composed before Newman's conversion provided a relatively straightforward, if expedient, way out of the difficulty.

English Catholics accepted Wiseman's strategy for receiving Newman and his book. Such was not the case in America, where Orestes Brownson, the brilliantly irascible recent lay convert, drawing upon his own considerable editorial experience of reading manuscripts-in-process, shrewdly recognized that Newman's *Essay* had been concluded under a set of circumstances different from those under which it had been commenced. Whereas Stephen Prickett once suggested that the *Essay on Development* was "written in limbo," Brownson understood it had been *published* in limbo. In a review of January 1847 Brownson commented, "It is not likely the work was commenced with the design with which it was completed; and it requires no very profound examination to discover, that, while the main theory is consistently enough set forth, the book is not all of a piece; and the hand of the author, retouching it here and there for the press, and striving to give it a more [Roman] Catholic coloring and expression, is visible enough." By the time Brownson's review appeared, English Roman Catholics appeared to have let Newman's book and its arguments quietly recede from public discussion. Indeed, for well over a century the volume enjoyed at best a mixed career among Roman Catholics commentators, with one noting in 1945, "The reserve with which the *Essay on Development* was originally received seems to have increased rather than diminished with the passing of a century."[62] It enjoyed new prominence during the years leading up to Vatican II and for a time thereafter. Yet overall after 1847, when its sales dropped sharply, *An Essay on the Development of Christian Doctrine* appears more often than not to have been a title cited rather than a volume read, studied, or debated in either of Newman's communions.

But Newman put his own interpretation on the Roman Catholic reaction to his book that followed immediately upon his conversion. Even as a young convert, Newman remained very much himself, having, he believed, drawn his own novel version of development into Roman Catholic circles, just as through his *Letter to the Bishop of Oxford* of 1841, he felt he had injected elements of his own Catholicism into the English Church. In March 1846 Newman interpreted the gift of a silver crucifix with a splinter of the True Cross from Pope Gregory XVI as "an indirect approval of my book—

at least a negative approval—for, if the book had any thing in it very dangerous or unsound, I suppose this honor would not have been paid me."[63] As in the past, Newman chose to regard what had not been forbidden as permitted, expanding the least hint of approval into complete commendation.

Newman also understood that *An Essay on the Development of Christian Doctrine* would make him an object of immediate theological interest in his new communion as well as providing possibly needed income, which may have been the reason that he initially planned not to enter the Roman Church until he had finished the book. In 1843 he had remarked that the obstreperous Ward's "occupation would be almost gone, *did* he join the Church of Rome," because his "powers of argument *tell* now very much, and would not tell then, for he would have no one for them to tell upon." Newman's much anticipated forthcoming discussion of development assured at least for the moment his escaping that fate. J. B. Mozley, his sharpest postconversion English critic, immediately grasped this situation, commenting, "Exerting the privilege of genius, Mr. Newman does not enter the Roman Church as a simple pupil and follower. He enters magisterially. He surveys her with the eye of a teacher. He tells her new truth. He commences a doctrinal rise in her; he takes her by the hand, and lifts her up a whole step, in system and idea, on her very boldest ground of development. . . . He points out, and institutes accordingly, a new doctrinal movement within the Roman pale, before he is himself in it."[64] Although Newman had not originated the concept of development, its presumed role in his conversion infused it at least for the moment with an inherent public theological interest.

Enormous confusion surrounded the composition, content, and authorial intent of Newman's *Essay on Development*, a situation only magnified by his extensive revision of 1878. Nonetheless, during 1845 and immediately thereafter, Newman's conversion itself rather than the events leading up to it became the lens through which the *Essay on Development* would be read. For a cerebral figure known primarily through his publications, the book could explain a change in religious communion. In the minds of contemporary observers, Newman had been headed for the Roman Church all along. They read the *Essay on Development* as confirming what they were predisposed to believe in the first place. Moreover, difficult questions could and would be posed about the complicated book rather than about the complicated details of Newman's final months in the English Church. The text thus quite understandably for contemporaries overpowered the events and for most of them solved the puzzle of Newman's behavior. Consequently, most of them failed to recognize that the actual arguments of Newman's book, taken alone, could have served to justify the ongoing, expansive pursuit within the Church of England of a program of highly controversial, radical Catholic devotion, including veneration of the Virgin Mary within the confines of Littlemore or even, as suggested by Brownson, the organization of Newman's own church independent of the Church of England.[65] As a polemical concept, development could just as easily have provided an apologetic for a radical English Catholicism, independent of either the Roman Catholic or the established church, with its adherents regarding themselves as the Church Catholic in England and embracing devotional practices drawn eclectically from Christian history.

Most important for Newman, development could justify past and present Christian monasticism. He and others sought a personal and communal religious life encompassing elements of pre-Reformation Christian faith and practice, including those of the Middle Ages. Protestant interpretations of the Reformation obviously obstructed such appropriation, as did the high-church boundary of antiquity. According to Newman, development constituted "an expedient" designed to solve "a necessary and an anxious problem" arising from the Protestant critique of pre-Reformation Christianity by transforming the alleged corruptions of that church into valid manifestations of Christianity. At the same time, development allowed a devotional life beyond the high-church boundaries of antiquity because the open-ended character of development also permitted it to constitute "a solution of such a number of the reputed corruptions of Rome, as might form a fair ground for trusting her, where the investigation had not been pursued." Or putting the matter more succinctly, Newman claimed that the fact that the developmental hypothesis accounted "not only for the Athanasian Creed, but for the Creed of Pope Pius, is no fault of those who adopt it."[66] In this manner, Newman broke the prescriptive high-church boundaries of antiquity and the more general Protestant barrier of the Reformation.

Although permanently associated with the event of Newman's conversion and his pursuit of an experimental devotional life, the little-read *Essay on Development* is also as much about the loss of one faith as about the reception of another. In that regard, the book occupies a key place in Victorian discussions of changing religious belief and displays the lack of secure cultural boundaries so characteristic of that considerable literature. In 1841 Newman had described to Richard Church certain people who if the Church of England "committed herself to heresy, sooner than think that there was no Church any where, would believe the Roman to be the

Church—and therefore would on faith accept what they could not otherwise acquiesce in."[67] That was why Newman had to interpret as legitimate developments those changes in Christian faith and practice that Protestants regarded as illicit corruptions. He employed the concept of development to provide a reason for himself to acquiesce in such faith and practice and thus to avoid the ecclesiastically skeptical conclusion "that there was no Church any where." In this respect, the problem for Newman and others of the 1840s was not skepticism about existential religious truth or the historical and scientific accuracy of the Bible associated with late Victorian agnosticism, but rather skepticism about the spiritual and theological adequacy of ecclesiastical institutions. That institutional doubt could prove just as corrosive to a person's religious life and commitment as the doctrinal.

Throughout 1845 Newman endured one event after another indicating that he could not maintain a position, however marginal, in the English Church. At that point, given his previous critiques of both Protestantism and Roman Catholicism, without his resort to development he might very well have had to conclude "that there was no Church any where." On March 14, 1845, a month after the February Convocation and with Oakeley headed toward judicial confrontation with Blomfield, Newman explained to Pusey how development relieved him of that skeptical conclusion, "I thank God that He has shielded me morally from what intellectually might easily come on me—general scepticism. Why should I believe the most sacred and fundamental doctrines of our faith, if you cut off from me the ground of development? But if that ground is given me, I must go further. I cannot hold precisely what the English Church holds and nothing more. I must go forward or backward, *else* I sink into a dead scepticism, a heartless *acedia*, into which too many in Oxford, I fear, are sinking." Newman's solution to such skepticism, for which he was largely responsible, was to believe more rather than less. Later in the summer, discussing the same issues with Richard Westmacott, who was himself encountering religious doubt, Newman stated that it seemed "a most serious thing to tell a person so inclined [to skepticism] that one's conviction was that he must believe everything or nothing." Finding it impossible to believe only what the Reformers had taught, Newman stated, "If Christianity is one and the same at all times, then I must believe not what the Reformers have carved out of it, but what the Catholic Church holds."[68] The embrace of fuller faith, including matters against which he had once polemicized, was the only path Newman believed would allow him to continue the life of Catholic devotion and monastic community he so strongly sought. In that respect, it is important to recognize that Newman's argument for development served as an after-the-fact justification of his previous appropriation of what he understood to be Catholic faith and practice. At the same time, it is not certain, and may not have been clear in his own mind, whether, in the letter to Westmacott, by "Catholic Church" he meant the Roman Catholic Church or his still much sought after Church Catholic independent of England and Rome.

Despite these statements, the principle of development concealed within Newman's mind and spirit religious skepticism as deep and profound as that of any enlightenment *philosophe* or late Victorian agnostic. In 1846 Hawkins wrote Whately, "My own suspicion indeed is that Newman is only seeking to escape Infidelity by a violent plunge into credulity." Toward the close of the century, A. M. Fairbairn, the deeply learned Congregationalist Principal of Mansfield College, Oxford, incisively explicating that powerful strain of skepticism, described Newman's conversion as "the victory of unbelief." He argued that Newman's submission to the Roman Catholic Church exemplified a person accepting authority "because he dare not trust his intellect, lest it lead him into Atheism" and as a consequence actually standing "vanquished by the Atheism he fears." Such a person in effect, Fairbairn urged, "unconsciously" subscribed "to the impious principle, that the God he believes, has given him so godless a reason that were he to follow it, it would lead him to a faith without God." Thus Newman's religious acceding to Roman Catholicism represented "the surrender of nature to unbelief." He had appealed to conscience as the basis of religion without giving reason any significant relationship to conscience and had then called in "an infallible church" in order "to determine the issue, confirm and support the conscience," and rescue religion by restraining thought. From Fairbairn's perspective, Newman personified one "who places the rational nature of man on the side of Atheism, that he may the better defend a church," and thus "saves the church at the expense of religion and God."[69] Newman's faith in ecclesiastical authority, according to Fairbairn, had thus flowed from the skepticism inherent in British empiricism itself.

Newman would have asserted that development allowed him to avoid skepticism that he found inherent in other approaches to Christianity. Long before the rise of the higher criticism of Scripture, Paine's *Age of Reason* had nurtured in Newman profound doubts about the Bible. In his early adulthood, perhaps drawing upon Hume, he also seems to have intuited the inherent fragility of contemporary natural theology that decades later so quickly collapsed under the weight of Darwinian evolution and the subsequent tailspin of rationality into agnosticism. His yearning for ascetic devotion and monastic community led him to reject the narrow high-church appeal to the authority of antiquity. Eventually in his own mind only the totality of Christian history interpreted as progress rather than decline relieved him of the skeptical conclusions he had encountered and largely assimilated throughout his life in the English Church.

Refusing to privilege Scripture, nature, or antiquity as sources of information about Christianity, Newman in 1845 declared instead that "the history of eighteen hundred years" itself constituted "our most natural informant concerning the doctrine and worship of Christianity." Christianity was what Christians, or more precisely, what those Christians calling themselves Catholics, had done in a religiously progressive march through the ages. The process of the development of Christian faith and practice throughout human history displaced an original deposit of faith articulated among the apostles and Fathers as the source of knowledge about the content and character of the Christian religion. There existed no original deposit of faith to be corrupted, but rather a religion originating with the apostles to be fulfilled and realized. Because the human mind could achieve "the full comprehension and perfection of great ideas" only over time and because human beings could not comprehend all at once the "highest and most wonderful truths, though communicated to the world once for all by inspired teachers," those ideas had "required only the longer time and deeper thought for their full elucidation," thus resulting in a progressive development of doctrine over time.[70] Christianity for Newman was an idea, but not an idea of the disembodied Platonic sort to be grasped through refined intellection. Rather, Christianity understood historically resembled more nearly an Aristotelian form that must realize itself only through a material embodiment, in this case in the embodied material life of human beings in human society.

Newman's arguments in the *Essay on Development* presented difficulties that he failed to overcome to almost anyone's genuine satisfaction. His position required him to defend developments associated with Roman Catholicism from being equated with corruptions while, as Palmer had already noted in 1843, simultaneously rejecting Protestantism as a legitimate historical development. As in the past, Newman's tactic was to denigrate Protestantism. After declaring at his outset that Christianity constitutes "a fact in the world's history," Newman formally denounced Protestant private judgment according to which, he urged, Christianity constituted "to each man what each man thinks it to be, and nothing else," thus representing only a collection of individual religions under a single name. He then repudiated the Protestant declinsionist argument that original Christianity had "died out of the world at its birth" only to be succeeded by "a counterfeit or counterfeits" assuming the name but teaching only a portion of the faith. He also spurned the evangelical idea of Christianity existing "as a secret and hidden doctrine, which does but revive here and there under a supernatural influence in the hearts of individuals, and is manifested to the world only by glimpses or in gleams, according to the number or the station of the illuminated, and their connection with the history of their times." Finally, Newman asserted without qualification or equivocation, "Whatever be historical Christianity, it is not Protestantism. If ever there were a safe truth, it is this." Protestants, he claimed, had implicitly admitted this embarrassing truth by "dispensing with historical Christianity altogether" and "forming a Christianity from the Bible alone."[71] As in his previous writings, Newman essentially conflated historical Protestantism with radical evangelicalism, in this case through an extensive analysis of the history of Methodism, to illustrate that Protestantism was not an example of a legitimate development.

The novel feature of the *Essay on Development* was not Newman's attack on evangelicalism or "ultra-Protestantism," which at least as early as the preface to his third volume of sermons he had denied could have been the original Christian faith later "silently corrupted into Popery." Rather, the new element in 1845 was his rejection of the high-church position that the original deposit of faith resided in ante-Nicene patristic writings. In particular, Newman pointed to the absence of "a *consensus* of primitive divines" from the ante-Nicene era in favor of the doctrine of the Trinity. A reading of the ante-Nicene fathers provided, according to Newman, no stronger evidence for the Trinity than did other ante-Nicene evidence "for certain doctrines of the Roman Church" rejected by high churchmen.[72] Again, in order to avoid skeptical conclusions about already prized religious truth, one must accept additional truths as well, even if unpalatable ones.

Pressing further this argumentative strategy against the high church, Newman observed, "In truth, scanty as the Ante-Nicene notices may be of the Papal Supremacy, they are both more numerous and more definite than the adducible testimonies in favour of the Real Presence." More fully explaining his position to Henry Wilberforce in June 1846 and confirming some reviewers' critical reading of his book, Newman wrote, "The fact I believe to be this—the early Fathers made incorrect intellectual developments of portions or aspects of that whole Catholic doctrine which they held, and so far were inconsistent with themselves. Their opinions contradicted their implicit faith—and they said and held things which they would have shrunk from, had they seen, as heretics afterwards exhibited, that they were really destructive of the doctrine of Christ." Newman ominously added, "I really do not think you can deny, that the Fathers, not merely did not contemplate true propositions, (afterwards established) but actually contemplated false."[73] Newman carefully avoided the issue of later Fathers and Christian theologians having made errors that would have required corrections supplied by the Reformation.

High churchmen as well as others in the Church of England immediately grasped the impact of Newman's argument against patristic authority. As a writer in William Palmer's *English Review* boldly announced, "Antiquity is gone." William Archer Butler, an Irish churchman, declared, "The claim of antiquity and the hypothesis of development (in Mr. Newman's application of the term) are absolutely incompatible." In 1848 Bishop Thirwall told his clergy, "The right of innovation cannot be reconciled with the claim of antiquity."[74] Churchmen who had looked to antiquity along with Scripture for the rule of faith found themselves cast adrift if Newman's argument triumphed. The confusion Newman delineated among the pre-Nicene Fathers presented high churchmen with a skeptical challenge parallel to the assertion of incoherence of Scripture that he had launched against evangelical belief. High churchmen, according to Newman, could find the Catholic doctrine of the Trinity in the ante-Nicene fathers only by interpreting them through what came afterward and must thus also logically accept later Roman Catholic beliefs and practices. Here Newman's tactic resembled his essay on ecclesiastical miracles, where he had posed the alternatives of accepting the miracles of the church or surrendering those of Scripture. In the *Essay on Development* he demanded receiving the theological and devotional developments of the medieval church or surrendering the doctrine of the Trinity.

Paradoxically, Newman's analysis of the ante-Nicene fathers drew him near to some old theological enemies. Evangelicals, who believed the original deposit of faith from the apostolic age had suffered corruption over time, would not have contested Newman's assertion of confusion among the fathers. On this matter, they had always differed from high churchmen. Moreover, their confidence in the existence of the original deposit and of human capacity with divine help to reclaim it relieved them of the indeterminacy inherent in Newman's own position. Furthermore, Newman's analysis of the historical formulation of the doctrine of the Trinity distinctly resembled that of Unitarians such as Joseph Priestley, who traced the doctrine of the Trinity to corruptions of the original Christian faith. Indeed the

Unitarian *Christian Reformer* boasted that Newman's pages might be read "as comprising a view, by an orthodox hand, of the progress of Trinitarian theology, replete with every admission which an Unitarian can desire."[75]

Despite his critique of antiquity, Newman's most persistent theme in the *Essay on Development* remained what George Stanley Faber termed his "intense hatred of Scriptural Protestantism," a polemic generally ignored by historians. Whatever Newman's love of Rome, it was always outdistanced by his hatred of evangelical Protestantism and its championing of the Bible. Indeed, Newman regarded the Bible as a far greater obstacle to the concept of development of doctrine than antiquity. Scripture, according to Newman in 1845, did not determine Christian doctrine but rather was intended to create in the reader's mind an idea that "expands in his heart and intellect, and comes to perfection in the course of time." By so lodging the meaning of Scripture in its readers' responses, Newman emphasized that the letter of Scripture could thus comprise "a delineation of all possible forms which a divine message will assume when submitted to a multitude of minds." The reality that the meaning of Scripture, as well as the establishment of its canon and authority, required explanation and explication through subjective reception on the part of its readers suggested to Newman the actual fact of development: "Since then Scripture needs completion, the question is brought to this issue, whether defect or inchoateness in its doctrines be or be not an antecedent probability in favour of a development of them." Scripture itself, Newman contended, drawing upon evangelical exegesis, presented revelation as "a process of development" with the early primitive scriptural types constituting prophecies of larger, more complete truths revealed later "as the course of revelation proceeds." Indeed, he concluded, "the whole Bible, not its prophetical portions only, is written on the principle of development." Christ himself, according to Newman, had suggested as much when he spoke of his kingdom as a mustard seed. Furthermore, with the failure of the immediate return of Christ to the early Christian community, "a different application of the revealed word became necessary, that is, a development."[76]

In both his disparagement of Scripture and his assertion of ongoing revelation, Newman inevitably encountered the problem of how to distinguish a legitimate development from "a false or unfaithful development," which "is called a corruption." Determined to elude the Protestant equation of developments in Roman Catholicism with corruptions, Newman thoroughly confused his argument by proposing a host of different definitions of development itself. After noting that "from defect of our language," *development* could mean either a process or a result and either true or false development, he pointed to a variety of developments, including logical developments, such as are found in mathematical equations, physical developments, such as are found in organic nature, material development of natural resources, political developments, historical developments, moral developments, and metaphysical developments. Attempting to overcome the discrepancies between the relative simplicity of early Christianity and the complexities of its medieval and subsequent manifestations, he quoted one of his own university sermons, "Ideas and their developments are commonly not identical, the development being but the carrying out of the idea into its consequences." But that statement hardly prescribed how to identify a legitimate development or its connection with the original idea. Adding several other supposedly clarifying statements about distinguishing developments from corruptions, Newman claimed that "real perversions and corruptions are often not so unlike externally to the doctrine to which they belong, as are changes which are consistent with it and true developments," and he then stated, "One cause of corruption in religion is the refusal to follow the course of doctrine as it moves on, and an obstinacy in the notions of the past." He further observed, "The Gospel is the development of the Law; yet what difference can seem wider more than that which separates the unbending rule of Moses from the 'grace and truth' which 'came by Jesus Christ'?" Finally, he declared, "Natural then as it is at first sight to suppose that an idea will always be the exact image of itself in all stages of its history, experience does not bear out the anticipation." No additional precision or sustained argument informed Newman's discussion when he announced, "The corruption of an idea is that state of a development which undoes its previous advances." He wrote further, "That development . . . is to be considered a corruption which *obscures or prejudices its essential idea,* or which *disturbs the laws of development* which constitute its organization, or which *reverses its course of development;* that is *not* a corruption which is *both a chronic and an active state,* or which is *capable of holding together* the component parts of a system."[77] The more Newman explained the differences between developments and corruptions, the more the confusion grew.

To clarify these supposed distinctions Newman established seven tests of a true development: preservation of type, continuity of principles, power of assimilation, early anticipation, logical sequence, preservative additions, and chronic continuance. His tests appear to have convinced none of his contemporaries or, for that matter, later commentators. These confusions and obfuscations over the distinction between development and corruptions, as well as the lack of clarity about what actually constituted Christianity as an idea, may account for the failure of his *Essay on Development* to find a sustained readership after an initial burst of sales to curious readers in the English Church who, as will be seen, emerged from its pages relieved to find themselves and their faith exactly where they had been when they entered.[78] As a consequence, Roman Catholics had little reason to champion the book. After all, it had not actually been written for them, but for those in the Church of England who wished to burst the bonds of both the Bible and antiquity.

Yet in the midst of these tendentious, largely unconvincing assertions about developments and corruptions, Newman introduced brilliant comments on what can only be termed a Victorian social history of ideas as he emphasized that the never quite defined or delineated ideas constituting Christianity had manifested themselves and come to be grasped only in a social setting where they had received life. Within that social setting Christianity stood as one of many ideas to achieve vitality, the achievement of which did not in itself guarantee truth content. Such a living idea, "whether true or false," was "not only passively admitted in this or that form into the minds of men, but it becomes a living principle within them, leading them to an ever-new contemplation of itself, an acting upon it and a propagation of it." These ideas for Newman included doctrines as different as freedom and bondage of the human will, the divine right of kings, the tyranny of priesthoods, and the rights of man. The power of those ideas once possessed by the popular mind could not be calculated. Over time such an idea embodied in the minds of individuals and of the community would grow into a code or system that would embody "the adequate representation of the original idea, being nothing else than what the very idea *meant* from the first,—its exact image as seen in a combination of the most diversified aspects, with the suggestions and corrections of many minds, and the illustration of many trials." The purity of the idea consisted "not in isolation, but in its continuity and sovereignty." Directly rejecting the evangelical and high-church concept that ideas, like streams, are purer at their source in either Scripture or antiquity, he argued, "Whatever use may fairly be made of this image, it does not apply to the history of a philosophy or sect, which, on the contrary, is more equable, and purer and stronger, when its bed has become deep, and broad, and full." Indeed, the beginnings of an idea provided "no measure of its capabilities, nor of its scope." The idea must change as it encounters new situations and circumstances "in order to remain the same." Newman then famously commented, "In a higher world it is otherwise; but here below to live is to change, and to be perfect is to have changed often."[79]

Because living ideas, such as Christianity, manifest themselves in a social setting, there existed, according to Newman, an antecedent argument "for its progressive development." He thus found the dynamic element in his understanding of Christianity not by looking to a theology of the Holy Spirit or to a vision of human reason coming to a more complete understanding of an original revelation, but rather simply by equating Christianity with its changing concrete social embodiments. Despite himself, Newman's discussion of developing Christianity was no less naturalistic than eighteenth-century Scottish writers' accounts of the development of commercial society or Gibbon's narrative of the triumph of the early church. But Newman's understanding of the original idea of Christianity that manifested itself in history through true developments and false corruptions remained elusive. His naturalistic bent of mind led him so far as to observe, "As to Christianity, considering the unsystematic character of its inspired documents and the all but silence of contemporary history, if we attempt to determine its one original profession, undertaking, or announcement, we shall be reduced to those eclectic and arbitrary decisions which have in all ages been so common." Then quoting from *Tract 85*, the most profoundly skeptical of all the tracts, he advised against efforts based on private judgment to reduce the Christian faith to " 'the essentials, the peculiar doctrines, the vital doctrines, the great truths, simple views, or leading idea of the Gospel.' " As J. B. Mozley quite correctly noted, "As soon as ever Mr. Newman's theory approaches its elementary region, it disappears, and we are left, without any theory at all, to make out the original idea of Christianity, to as much or as little as we like." More ominously, Baden Powell observed that Newman's backward reading of Christianity reduced "*everything to utter vagueness and confusion, so that we lose all perception of the original nature of Christianity.*"[80]

To overcome this challenge, Newman had pointed to the difficulty of ever actually grasping a great idea in its entirety. He argued that just as the human mind by its very character could not take into cognizance as a whole an object such as the fact of Christianity, neither could two individuals possess an identical view of such a fact. Nor could a single representation present the complete idea of Christianity, "For Christianity has many aspects: it has its imaginative side, its philosophical, its ethical, its political; it is solemn, and it is cheerful; it is indulgent, and it is strict; it is light, and it is dark; it is love, and it is fear." Moreover, he thought, "The holy Apostles would know without words all the truths concerning the high doctrines of theology, which controversialists after them have piously and charitably reduced to formulae, and developed through argument."[81] In other words, only in the centuries after the apostles, if then, could Christians or for that matter non-Christians know the actual truths of the Christian religion. The process whereby they came eventually to know such truths was that of the formation of creeds. Here Newman's *Essay on Development* stood in direct opposition to the argument of Hampden's Bampton Lectures, which had so strenuously argued for decline from original truth into later corruption through the same process.

With the abandonment of a discernible original Christian teaching, institutional descent, in Newman's mind, replaced adherence to primitive doctrine as the chief indication of the presence of a faith rooted in the apostolic age. The longevity and durability of the Roman Catholic Church in and of itself suggested the purity of its developments. In light of all the change, controversy, enthusiasm, and responsibilities that the Roman Catholic Church had encountered over the centuries, "it is quite inconceivable that it should not have been broken up and lost, were it a corruption of Christianity." Buttressing this contention at another point, Newman declared, "A corruption is of brief duration, runs itself out quickly, and ends in death." The Roman Catholic Church had been able to bear "principles or doctrines, which in other systems of religion quickly degenerate into fanaticism or infidelity." The doctrines that he regarded as having so developed were the invocation of the saints, the veneration of Mary, penance, purgatory, and monasticism, each of which manifested "an instance of the mind of the Church working out dogmatic truths from implicit feelings under secret supernatural guidance."[82] Newman did not opine on either the theological or metaphysical character of that "secret supernatural guidance." Finally, unable to provide on the basis of his own analysis a definition or even substantive discussion of the core idea of Christianity that would allow for its contemporary location, Newman fell back in his book, as in contemporary private letters, upon an imagined visit of St. Ambrose and St. Athanasius to modern England, where he assured his readers that those ancient saints would seek out a Roman Catholic Church for purposes of worship. One of Newman's critics responded that he would prefer to know which church Jesus or St. Paul would attend.

Newman had once accused Protestant theologians of creating particular theological problems so they could then supply the answers. Such was his own procedure in the *Essay on Development*. His argument for the antecedent probability of developments beyond Scripture and antiquity required in turn an antecedent probability "in favour of a provision in the Dispensation for putting a seal of authority upon those developments." If, Newman argued, the Creator of the order of nature stands as a permanent guardian of the fact and operation of that creation, the same Creator breaking into the natural order through revelation would presumably wish to oversee and preserve that revelation. The Bible itself could not serve that purpose: "We have tried it, and it disappoints; it disappoints, that most holy and blessed gift, not from fault of its own, but because it is used for a purpose for which it was not given." A divinely supplied infallible authority external to Scripture both permitted developments and served to distinguish true developments from corruptions. Without recourse to an extrabiblical authority, which Newman now saw in Rome, religion declined into the chaos of private judgment or the "hollow uniformity" of the Church of England or the "interminable divisions" of the Protestant sects. On the basis of those assertions, Newman elliptically concluded, "As creation argues continual governance, so are Apostles harbingers of Popes." He further claimed, presumably to the surprise of most of his English readers, that few people would deny "the very strong presumption which exists, that, if there are developments in Christianity, the doctrines propounded by successive Popes and Councils, through so many ages, are they."[83]

Newman's book on development differed markedly from his exploration of the concept in his late 1840 correspondence with his brother Francis. John had concluded that previous discussion by stating, "The argument, as I have above put it, is quite independent of the proper *authority* of the Church." By the second half of 1845 Newman had come to ascribe extensive authority to the Roman Catholic Church in regard to developments, but, as he had quite correctly stated years before, the ascription of such authority was not intrinsic to his argument. The presence of such authority, to which as Mozley noted Newman actually devoted little space, was really the only thing that prevented Newman's argument from presupposing an utter indeterminacy of religious development as well as extensive skepticism about religious truth. The turn to the authority of Rome may, as Brownson deeply suspected, have come very late in the composition of the book to assure that he had somewhere to go. Newman embraced papal authority to halt and channel the ever-expanding vision that he had set forth of Christianity as a creature of social reality rather than a theological understanding of an original divine revelation. Papal authority was the answer to the problem of

Newman's own creation. Even the papacy provided an uncertain vehicle for those purposes because, as Bishop Thirlwall noted, Newman actually portrayed developments as validating Church authorities and not the reverse.[84] His entry into the Roman Catholic Church before completing the book saved him from that skeptical theological and ecclesiastical indeterminacy inherent in his intellectual position and previous religious practice, an indeterminacy inescapable according to his own reasoning outside any Christian institution save the Roman Catholic Church.

Although always portraying himself as a fierce opponent of evangelical heresy in the modern English Church and personally identifying with St. Athanasius, throughout the *Essay on Development* Newman displayed surprising and significant sympathy for ancient heresy. During early Christian history, even heretics, Newman suggested, had advocated some doctrines providing "indices and anticipations of the mind of the Church." He went so far as to state, "As the first step in settling a point of doctrine is to raise and debate it, so heresies in every age may be taken as the measure of the existing state of thought in the Church, and of the movement of her theology; they determine in what way the current is setting, and the rate at which it flows." Newman in particular pointed to the anticipatory character of Montanism, with its fasts, visions, celibacy, martyrdom, penitential discipline, and rejection of worldly goods which stood as "a remarkable anticipation or presage of developments which soon began to show themselves in the Church, though they were not perfected for centuries after," with their true fulfillment occurring in "the doctrinal determinations and the ecclesiastical usages of the middle ages."[85] The Tractarians themselves had embraced each of those practices. Newman himself appears on at least one occasion to have known a mystical experience while celebrating the eucharist. Though none of them suffered physically, the Tractarians certainly had courted varieties of martyrdom in the university and church.

Newman thus implicitly presented an eclectically dynamic ancient church, not the essentially static one so admired by high churchmen, as a model for the modern English Church. The self-transforming ancient institution, unlike the modern from its dealings with the Methodists to the Tractarians, had been able to convert the most unlikely elements to its own uses and had "succeeded in thus rejecting evil without sacrificing the good, and in holding together in one things which in all other schools are incompatible." Perhaps with reference to Tractarian efforts to appropriate Roman Catholic devotion, Newman contended that there existed "a certain virtue

or grace in the Gospel" that could change "the quality of doctrines, opinions, usages, actions, and personal characters which become incorporated
with it," making them "right and acceptable" to God "when before they
were either contrary to truth, or at best but shadows of it." The Fathers
believed that Christianity could resist infection from evil practices that it
embraced and could "transmute the very instruments and appendages of
demon-worship to an evangelical use." In this process the church had simply exercised a discretion arising from its having "been entrusted with the
dispensation of grace." In contrast to other religions and systems, "The
Church can extract good from evil, or at least get no harm from it."[86] Such
was exactly the course that Newman believed he had provided for the
English Church by introducing or reviving Catholic practices that might be
unacceptable in a Roman context but pure and spiritually edifying in an
English Catholic context. Such was the plea that the *Essay on Development*
might have made to the authorities of the Church of England had it been
published without Newman's having converted.

As a writer in the *English Review* observed, while composing the book,
Newman "was living and acting neither under the authority of his own
Church, nor under that of Rome, but under an authority within his own
heart; which after all was a self-indulged bias, working to realize a self-
invented and ideal model."[87] That model differed from both Rome and the
English Church, and Newman's tactic in supporting it differed sharply from
the disruptive behavior of the more radical Catholics, including Ward and
Oakeley, from whom he was distancing himself in 1844 and 1845. He had
originally designed the *Essay on Development* to counter high-church objections to the emergence of advanced Catholic devotion and monasticism in
the English Church without at the same time provoking the powerful anti–
Roman Catholic reaction occasioned by Ward's *Ideal*. Stripped of his mini-
malist advocacy of papal authority, Newman's assertion of development
could have justified the advanced ascetic pursuit of holiness that Ward urged
but without the latter's controversial appeal to the contemporary Roman
Catholic models and gratuitously offensive language about clerical subscription. In that respect, as originally undertaken, the *Essay on Development*
would have continued the argument of *Tract 90* by delineating the prescriptive character of pre-Reformation Catholicism to meet the present and
possible future aspirations of the Littlemore community and other advanced
Catholics. The Oakeley judgment that followed upon radical Catholic challenges to ecclesiastical authority and that resulted in the repudiation of

Tract 90 had made all those goals impossible, as Newman's followers recognized more quickly than he.

THE CRITIQUE OF DEVELOPMENT

All parties in the Church of England felt required to criticize Newman's *Essay on Development* because in his postscript he stated that he had originally hoped to postpone "deciding" on joining the Roman Catholic Church until the book had been published, "But when he had got some way in the printing, he recognized in himself a conviction of the truth of the conclusion to which the discussion leads, so clear as to supersede further deliberation." Furthermore, the *Dublin Review*, in almost exactly the terms Wiseman had used when writing to Russell, described the book as recording "the process of reasoning which brought Mr. Newman to the Catholic faith."[88] Consequently, the link stood established in the public mind, and to that presumed connection commentators from the English Church responded.

First and foremost, moderate Protestant observers in the English Church rejected any claim to progressive revelation, asserting that revelation, like miracles, had ceased with the age of the apostles. As early as 1843, responding to Newman's university sermon on development, Archbishop Whately, pointing to "the line of demarcation between what ordinary Christians call the *Scriptures*, and every thing subsequent," had insisted on the difference "between what *we* call the Christian Revelation, considered as an historical transaction recorded in the New Testament; and any pretended after-revelation, or improvement, or completion or perfect development, of 'the system of true Religion.'" Three years later, after Newman's volume appeared, Hampden declared that the New Testament constituted "not an expansion of doctrine from doctrine, or series of developments, but rather, a combined view of the whole Doctrine and Discipline of Christ, as revived and impressed, through the operation of the Holy Spirit, on the hearts and minds of the Apostles, once for all, and left in writing as the one indelible Divine record for each succeeding age." George Moberly, Headmaster of Winchester College, quite correctly understood Newman's concept of development to suggest "the imperfection of the faith of the Apostles and first Fathers." William Archer Butler stated that Christianity had not been designed to become "known at last, by striking, from age to age, a precarious and difficult average among hesitating teachers" and that it had not been "nursed through an infancy and childhood of centuries into a slow and imperfect adolescence." Rather, he assured his readers, "Christianity was born full-grown." Hawkins contended, "It has never yet been given to uninspired men to improve upon a Divine Revelation, and reproduce it under new forms. The very thought is profane."[89]

Orestes Brownson, differing little from English Protestant commentators in his criticism of development, declared that the Roman Catholic Church "asserts that there has been no progress, no increase, no variation of faith; that what she believes and teaches now is precisely what she has always and everywhere believed and taught from the first." Such was, of course, just exactly what Newman had denied. George Stanley Faber, an evangelical with whom Newman had corresponded, similarly grasping the implication of Newman's position for traditional Roman Catholic apologetics, noted that "our oracle from Littlemore" had relinquished Rome's "old stock . . . claim of an undeviating perpetuity of faith and practice . . . for a fantastic progressive expansion of *Nothing* into *Something,* or a virtual acknowledgment of the indubitable fact of A PERPETUITY OF CHANGE on the part of the Romish Church." For Faber, this outlook confirmed the evangelical understanding of the story of Christianity after the age of the Primitive Church as "little more than the History of the Rise and Completion of that fearful Apostasy which . . . forms the grand subject of Evangelical Prophecy." Consequently, in Faber's view, for Newman to say that historical Christianity was not Protestantism was "only to say that 'Protestantism' is not the predicted Apostasy."[90]

Other reviewers examined the *Essay on Development* more nearly from the standpoint of historical scholarship than of theology, though the two were not rigidly separated. For example, Henry Hart Milman, whose history of Christianity Newman had so harshly criticized in 1841, declared, "The whole history of Christianity is a development—a development of its internal powers, its irresistible influences over the mind of man. Every page of Mr. Newman's book then, so far as regards the fact of development, is true. . . . We are all Developists; every writer of the history of Christianity describes its development." To Newman's contention that an original act of revelation presupposed continuation in revelation, J. B. Mozley, one of the advanced Catholic contributors to the *British Critic* now distancing himself from Newman, simply responded, "Why?" Mozley also believed that Newman's broader argument amounted to little more than claiming that whatever had occurred in Christian history was valid and true and commented, "The fact of certain ideas getting established becomes itself the proof of their truth." Contending that Newman "reposes in fact," Mozley observed,

"The authority of fact becomes itself a fact, and is ever seen in the background as the supreme authority, beyond which no appeal lies." Newman's mode of argument thus lay less "in proving than in simply unfolding his assumption." Other commentators similarly faulted Newman's practice of taking historical existence itself as an indication of legitimate development. Hampden declared, "Nothing is, then, a corruption, but what has not been incorporated into the system of the Church." Butler saw Newman presenting a mode of progressive revelation, which assumed that "the *mere historical eventuation* of dogmas in a certain particular division of the Christian Church, is a sufficient evidence of dogmatic *truth,* and a sufficient ground for the absolute *authority* of these dogmas over the belief and conscience of all mankind." Newman had substituted "high-toned and elaborate descriptions of the course of mere *historical eventuation,* or little more than this, for the legitimate *logical connexion* of the disputed with admitted doctrines." He had thus contended that "the security of development resolves into that which is *itself* a development."[91]

One after another reviewer observed that on Newman's own presuppositions the concept of development might or might not actually lead to modern Roman Catholicism. William Palmer in 1846, rehearsing his previous critique of development, declared that Newman's principles could as easily lead to Anabaptists, the Family of Love, or puritanism as to Roman Catholicism. Faber thought that Newman's position might equally well support Socinian as Roman Catholic conclusions. Butler described development as "the principle of revolution enlisted in behalf of the principle of immutability; perpetual motion demonstrating the absolute duty of perpetual repose" and asserted that the theory might consequently "be made to vindicate every historical variety of religious revolution altogether as well." Milman noted that, according to Newman, "*preservative additions*" displayed "an invariable tendency to usurp more than their proper place: their development knows not where to cease." Mozley declared, "The general state of development may be, for anything he knows, neither wholly true nor wholly false, but a mixture of both." Insisting that corruptions could occur through exaggeration of truth as easily as through departure from original type, Mozley explained, "Mr. Newman limits deterioration to that form in which it does not apply to the Roman system, and then confidently determines that there has been no deterioration."[92]

Because, according to Newman, the Christian revelation was never complete, his critics thought that the theory rendered religious certainty impossible and religious skepticism inevitable. Hampden asked the Christ Church congregation, "Where can be the steadiness of profession in the man who is the disciple of a system of faith, which is continually developing itself; of which he cannot be assured at any given moment, that it is what it shall be; or what he shall believe, or act upon, at some future period of his life?" Behind such a system of doctrinal development Hampden could find nothing except the private subjective judgment of John Henry Newman. While admitting that Newman stopped just short of the infidel conclusion that "the [Christian] Religion itself has no fixed Eternal Reality at all," W. J. Irons nonetheless argued, "This system of development, in attempting to enlarge, really invades and destroys Objective Truth."[93]

In a trenchant *Edinburgh Review* article, significantly entitled "Mysticism and Skepticism," Henry Rogers accused Newman of having transformed Christianity into "a wholly progressive scheme of doctrine, undistinguishable in authority in any of the epochs of its gradual disclosure; undistinguishable in its earliest phase from the merely human aspect of the later," and thereby of rendering "the New Testament not superior in authority, and inferior in value, to the systematized formularies of the church, down to the present times." Newman, consequently, had eradicated "the boundary between inspiration and opinion, between Divine and human doctrine, between the voice of revelation and the conclusions of reason, or the suggestions of mere feeling or imagination; and in thus effacing the landmarks of the Christian's spiritual inheritance, it cannot but hazard the secure enjoyment of it." Using "the mystified language of ultra-orthodoxy," Newman espoused a theory incorporating "the worst tenets of Neology" long denounced by spokesmen for both the English and Roman Churches.[94]

Brownson largely agreed with Rogers and with his linking Newman's thought to that of Ralph Waldo Emerson. In Newman's emphasis on Christianity as an idea, Brownson smelled the same indeterminate theology characterizing the New England Unitarianism he had recently abandoned. Both Newman and Brownson's former Unitarian colleagues, by assuming the idea of Christianity to have been "thrown upon the great concourse of men, to be developed and embodied by the action of their minds, stimulated and directed by it," believed they might use such knowledge abstracted from that history of development to organize "a new institution, a new church, in advance of the old by all the developments which these eighteen hundred years have effected." Brownson pictured Newman as earnestly seeking "to develope Protestantism into Catholicity" by using a theory "not necessary to the defence of the Church" and "utterly repugnant to her claims to be the authoritative and infallible Church of God." Brownson further stated,

"Christian doctrine is the revelation itself, not the view which men take of that revelation. . . . And here is the grand error Mr. Newman commits. He is still, while writing, a decided Protestant, mistaking our notions of Christianity for Christianity itself."[95] In this respect, Brownson took Newman's postscript quite literally at its word and refused to see Newman as a Roman Catholic until he had actually converted. Brownson was determined that Newman's book not be considered a Roman Catholic document, thus firmly drawing a line that Bishop Wiseman had consciously blurred.

To later readers the most surprising response to the *Essay on Development* is the high-church accusation that Newman himself had become a rationalist.[96] This charge was quite complicated, but it was one to which Newman was fully attuned and which he never refuted.

In 1844 Edward H. Dewar, a high churchman who had studied at Exeter College, Oxford, and later served as the chaplain to British residents in Hamburg, published *German Protestantism and the Right of Private Judgment in the Interpretation of Holy Scripture,* a work Newman read and cited in his *Essay*. Well informed about both German philosophy and theology, Dewar distinguished between what he termed a Catholic and a rationalist reading of Scripture, indicating that for all practical purposes he used the term *rationalistic* interchangeably with Protestant. Catholics, Dewar claimed, in traditional high-church fashion, interpreted Scripture according to "that which has been held by the Church in all ages, and especially in her youngest and purest days." Rationalists, by contrast, contended "that Christian doctrine admits of and requires to be constantly acted upon by the human intellect, to be ever searched into, developed, altered, improved." That rationalist or Protestant approach to Scripture constituted the "very principle of development which we have to struggle against." The Roman Church, according to Dewar, had effectively embraced "this principle of development" by transferring to the Pope as an individual "an unlimited, an arbitrary power in determining what shall be her faith," thus rendering "his private judgment the rule according to which the sense of Scripture shall be determined." In this fashion, the Roman Church allowed "human intellect, in the person of her chief Bishop, to alter, modify, develope, in a word, to tamper with, the faith once delivered."[97] Papal supremacy thus constituted a privileged mode of private judgment not altogether different from that of Protestants. Consequently, only the rationalistic principle of development allowed Rome to explain how its teachings and practices could legitimately differ from both Scripture and early patristic writings.

Dewar's understanding of rationalism haunted Newman. He attempted to counter Dewar through the long-established Tractarian tactic of making and remaking definitions to fit their own concerns without coming to grips with their critics' arguments. In the *Essay on Development* Newman defined rationalism as consisting of theological systematization based on personal experience or evidence of the senses. He then claimed, "If this be rationalism, it is totally distinct from development; to develop is to receive conclusions from received truth, to rationalize is to receive *nothing* but conclusions from received truths; to develop is positive, to rationalize is negative; the essence of development is to extend belief, of rationalism to contract it." Undoubtedly with Dewar's argument in mind, Newman claimed there was no difference "between a Pope *ex cathedra* and an individual Protestant, except that their authority is not on a par."[98] But Newman did not account for the relative superiority of papal authority except through the process of development itself.

Despite Newman's assertions to the contrary, high-church commentators did regard him as having fallen into that mode of rationalism which, in accord with Dewar's analysis, equated the private judgment of the Pope or other ecclesiastical authorities with divine truth. Butler wrote, "It is . . . quite vainly that Mr. Newman would vindicate his system from being a defence of Romanism on the principles of Rationalism, by alleging that the tendency of the Development Theory is positive, and to extend belief; of Rationalism negative, and to contract it." Butler saw in Newman's critique of antiquity the hand of a rationalist now ripping apart the Fathers as others had previously torn apart Scripture. For high churchmen, if antiquity failed, then the truth of Christian doctrine was simply that of the rationalists who reasoned or who constructed doctrine on their own or that of the Roman Church, which Butler dubbed "a huge corporate Rationalist."[99]

Other contemporaries saw modern German philosophical and historical rationalism at work in Newman's thought. Archbishop Whately had discerned parallels between German neology and the Tractarians as early as Williams's tracts on reserve, with both theological camps advocating the language of a double truth—one for general circulation, another for the initiated few. Both also appealed to the historical experience of Christianity to inform themselves of religious truth subsequent to the revelation contained in the Bible. A commentator in *Fraser's Magazine,* who portrayed Newman "traveling to Germany by way of Italy," characterized development as "German infidelity communicated in the music and perfume of St. Peter's" and as "Strauss in the garment and rope of the Franciscan." Milman, who was deeply read in German historical criticism, elaborated a detailed analogy between Newman's development and Strauss's evolving the main features of Christianity "from the *subjective Idea* in the mind of man." According to Milman, "Strauss may . . . appear to begin higher up than Mr. Newman. But Mr. Newman, by annulling the authority—as he inevitably does by impugning the early and universal acceptance—of the written word—by resting the divine origin of Christianity on tradition alone, or on something more dubious than tradition—abandons the whole field to the mythic expositor. Still further: admit, with Mr. Newman, so much which is clearly and almost avowedly *mythic* into Christianity—and ingenuity like his own will claim free scope to resolve the whole into a myth." Milman feared that Newman, like Strauss, discerned no historical reality in the early history of Christianity and most particularly in the life of Jesus. Hampden, perhaps drawing upon Milman's review, contended that Newman's theory made "the fundamental historical truths of the Gospel but as germs to vanish in their perfect expansion, whilst it ascribes to the existing Church the realization of what was shadowed out by the life and doctrine of Christ. The existing Church then becomes the true Christ; as in the German theory, his own philosophy becomes to the idealist his phantom-substitute for the real body of the Lord." Both Newman and Strauss substituted "a latent sense of the text for the manifest one" and explained "the primary sense by the secondary, the direct and proper by the mystical." Blomfield in his charge of 1846 portrayed the disciples of Newman and other Roman Catholic advocates of development as "in a state of hopeful training for the school of Strauss."[100]

The profoundly naturalistic vision of both human and ecclesiastical history that characterizes Newman's *Essay on Development* was recognized immediately upon its publication. Brownson claimed Newman had removed the Roman Catholic Church from the order of grace and left it merely part of the order of nature. Had Newman not attempted to relate his theory to the authority of the Roman Catholic Church, Brownson thought that he might have published a fine, unobjectionable book entitled "*An Essay on the Development of Christian Doctrine, when withdrawn from the Authority and Supervision of the Church.*" F. D. Maurice, similarly perceiving this absence of supervisory authority, strikingly compared Newman's volume to Robert Chambers's then anonymous *Vestiges of the Natural History of Creation*, published in 1844. Maurice explained that Newman

> finds an established system, not indeed a dead system, but a living one—
> such a one as the author of the *Vestiges of Creation* recognises the system of
> nature to be—a system of generative powers, vital energies; in unceasing
> movement and operation, with a correcting power, like that which Mr.
> Babbage says resides in his machine, gradually evolving itself in the course

of these workings, and no doubt, contemplated from the first by the great Demiurgus. This is his hypothesis to explain, not the physical world, but the life and history of man; not of man only considered as dwelling in some outward circle, but of man brought into the family of God! This hypothesis is to be the substitute for the unbelief of Protestantism, for the coldness of Anglicanism;—this is to teach us what the Church really means!

Maurice declared, "Once adopt Mr. Newman's hypothesis, and the belief of . . . living Divine Government is at an end." Just as Darwin, privately in the late 1830s and early 1840s and then publicly in *On The Origin of Species* in 1859, appropriated much of the vision and rhetoric of natural theology but excluded from it the presence of the Creator, Newman effectively naturalized the history of the Christian church, interpreting it with all of its usual features except the presence of divine Providence or the guidance of the Holy Spirit. As Fairbairn later commented regarding Newman's position, "A miracle by becoming continuous ceases to be miraculous; a supernatural which has descended into the bosom of the natural becomes part of its order, and must be handled like the other forces and phenomena of history."[101]

From the early 1830s through 1845 Newman had portrayed religion as a concrete manifestation of human social interaction, combining the human and the divine, in an ongoing effort to satisfy the demands of conscience. In the pages of his *Essay on Development* the human clearly predominated over the divine, with one rearrangement simply supplementing and sometimes supplanting another. Hampden, who had read carefully, critically, but not unfairly, Newman's sermons published since 1843, as well as the volume on development, elaborated upon the fundamental, relativistic naturalism inherent in Newman's analysis of the emergence of Christian doctrine:

> Imagine ideas, according to this philosophy [of development], at one time appearing in the form of heathen doctrine and heathen worship, or the speculations of heathen philosophy—and then only imperfectly developed; assuming accordingly wild, grotesque, unreal forms; distorted in shadow, or faintly pictured in legend and fable; then, as the state of the world affords them happier occasions of development, issuing in more and more perfect forms, more according to their own proper nature, as the true and real types of things; first, however, still in shadows and symbols under the Law and the Prophets then in an elementary manner at the outset of the Gospel; afterwards expanding in their native vigour, and reaching their maturity, as the elaboration of the Church's Doctrine and Discipline proceeds;— conceive all this,—and you have then a just view of what is now recommended to us for the Gospel of Christ, under the name of the Development of Christian Doctrine.[102]

Hampden here managed quite succinctly to explain how through the concept of development Newman had transformed the murkiness of both his
dispensation of paganism and his Prophetical Tradition into official doctrines of faith and practice. But in doing so Newman had avoided neither
relativism nor indeterminacy.

Originally intending his book to defend an advanced, expansive devotional life for Catholics whom he hoped to retain in the Church of England,
Newman had actually written the *Essay on Development* to champion just
such indeterminacy in the face of evangelical appeals to the Bible and high-
church appeals to antiquity. Within the Littlemore setting and his wider
circles of influence, Newman believed that he himself could function as a
deterrent against ever-evolving doctrinal venturesomeness. Events intervened; he entered the Roman Catholic Church; and his hastily added paragraphs on the papacy served the purpose of inhibiting the indeterminacy
the rest of the book nurtured. Yet to readers left unconvinced by those
paragraphs or always having rejected papal authority, the *Essay on Development* stood as a monument to religion without certain beginning or certain
end. For those readers, and they were certainly the majority, Newman left
the English Church and entered the Roman Church as a voice of religious
doubt, uncertainty, and skepticism

That situation gratified those whom Newman left behind. Before the
publication of the *Essay on Development* many in the Church of England
feared that Newman might have devised some deeply persuasive argument
in favor of Rome. When such proved not to be the case, English clergy gave a
collective sigh of relief. Samuel Wilberforce from his new episcopal vantage
point found Newman's volume "acute . . . perhaps beyond anything even he
has written," but thought it not "calculated to overthrow the faith of many."
Indeed, the book had "no force whatsoever" with those who believed "that
the first Divine afflatus conveyed to the Church in the persons of the Apostles all truth concerning God which man could know; & that the inspired
Word of God is the written transcript of that entire knowledge, which it was
but given to the Church afterwards to draw out & define with logical accuracy as heresy created the necessity." Though not acquiescing in Wilberforce's view of the relative roles of the church and Scripture, Gladstone
replied that Newman's work had made "upon me no impression adverse" to
the claims of the English Church "on my allegiance." He also thought
Innocent III would not have thanked Newman "for this kind of Popery" and
might have found himself "beyond measure shocked at the Doctrine of the
book concerning the Blessed Virgin." Manning, who shared Gladstone's
shock over Newman's treatment of Mary, told Robert Wilberforce, "After

reading the book I am left where I was found by it." Henry Wilberforce found Newman's *Essay* "very able but very skeptical," "in parts . . . very sophistical," and "more fitted . . . to damage us than to advance Rome." Upon reading only part of the book, Hawkins similarly concluded "that it is far more likely to make Sceptics than Romanists" and could not believe "that the Romanists will like it at all." Keble, who studied Newman's *Essay* only after an anxious two-year delay, happily concluded that "it seemed . . . not so strong in argument, nor yet so scornful & unpleasant in tone, as I expected."[103]

It is significant that the *Essay on Development* produced no more impact on men such as Manning and the Wilberforce brothers who later converted to Rome than it did on those who concluded their lives in the English Church. As Roundell Palmer observed later in the century regarding those who followed Newman to Rome in 1845: "With them, nothing really turned upon the development theory; and, upon those who remained behind, it had no effect."[104] It is equally uncertain whether the concept of the development of Christian doctrine accounted significantly for Newman's own choice of being received into his new communion.

CHAPTER 12

Paths Taken and Not

WHY, after the events of 1845, John Henry Newman departed the Church of England is reasonably clear, but why he entered the Roman Catholic Church is not self-explanatory. That question is not a theoretical issue but one much pondered by observers at the time. The assumption of the inevitability of Newman's reception into the Roman Church precludes the query, "Inevitable in lieu of what?" The answer is in lieu of still other available contemporary religious alternatives. Recognizing the problematic rather than inevitable character of Newman's conversion opens the way for reconsidering both his life goals and the manner in which they shaped the conclusion of the Tractarian Movement itself.

CONTEMPORARY REACTIONS TO NEWMAN'S CONVERSION

Many contemporaries, to be sure, did regard Newman's reception into the Roman Church as inevitable. Evangelicals, who regarded him as a disguised Roman Catholic illicitly dwelling in the Church of England, had long anticipated his conversion. For them Newman was going to the place where he had always belonged. Similar anti-Catholic assumptions made even some moderate figures no more generous in their judgments. The theological liberal Julius Hare, for example, told Manning that he could "only feel thankful" that Newman "is no longer amongst us, occupying what to him was a false position incompatible with the simplicity of truth & deluding our most hopeful youths within our very sanctuary." Hare further stated that though for himself "going over to Rome seems . . . equivalent to giving

12. John Henry Newman (1801–1890), portrayed in 1844. At this time Newman stood aloof from the English Church as well as from the Roman Catholic Church, envisioning what he hoped might be a Catholic reform of each. (Portrait by George Richmond, reproduced with the permission of the National Portrait Gallery.)

oneself up to believe a lie," Newman had "so warpt his mind, he will doubtless feel more at home in the midst of lies, than when engaged in a continual wrestling with inconvenient truths."[1]

The secular press also generally displayed smug satisfaction over Newman's departure, alternatively decried as *secession* or *perversion* as well as conversion. Before the event, but after months of public rumors swirling about the Littlemore coterie, the *Globe* had denounced "Newmanite monkfanciers" as constituting a "priesthood playing the incendiary" that had commenced as an "Anti-Radical, Anti-Papist movement" but ended in "sheer Radicalism and Popery." Newman's secession served to confirm that judgment. The *Standard* regarded the conversion as "Mr. Newman's first *honest* act" and demanded the return with interest of his university income for the past eight or ten years. Similarly raising the question of Newman's financial honesty, the *Morning Herald* asserted, "Most assuredly the Free Presbyterians of Scotland will cut a far more respectable figure in history." The *Morning Post* reminded readers of the days when Newman's "zeal was inflamed against what was then 'popular Protestantism,'" which he thought was "driving men to embrace the errors of Romanism." The newspaper regretted that with the storm of criticism having grown "too strong for him," Newman himself had fallen "into this very pitfall" from which he had sought "to save others" and had "gone to abide in the midst of those errors which he himself exposed."[2]

Newman's entrance into the Roman Church at once saddened and angered high churchmen, who regarded the event as one not to be assumed as having been inevitable but one that demanded explanation and assignment of blame. Although Benjamin Harrison thought that Newman had succumbed to a long-standing attraction to Rome, others did not see his action as quite so uncomplicated. Pusey blamed Newman himself for having lost control of the movement to the Romanizers, commenting, "Ward took the reins out of his hands and has been like Phaeton." Hook, who in 1845 privately thought Newman "yielding to the temptation of Satan" and putting his salvation in peril through an "overt act of apostasy," nonetheless later argued publicly that ultra-Protestant harassment had finally driven him from the church. James Mozley adopted a near-scatological metaphor, describing Newman and the advanced Tractarians as exemplifying "a body of opinion rising in the Church, passing through her, and going out of her, without ever having really belonged to her." These incensed Catholic high churchmen could never overcome their personal disillusionment at having trusted themselves and their apologetic to someone whom they then had watched become an uncertain, independent force in their communion. Nor could they ever really forgive Newman for exposing them through his conversion to evangelical invective such as that of the *Christian Observer,* which, after rejoicing that through Newman's entry into the Roman Church "gross Tractarianism is checked," expressed the hope that his "apostasy" would stop the "cant" among "those do-nothing hirelings who affect what are called high-church notions" and who had been "pleased to esteem" Tractarianism as "'a cure for Methodism.'"[3]

Early Victorian culture generally provided only hostile terms to explain why an English Protestant might choose to become a Roman Catholic. In 1845 Newman's actions, as well as those of the men associated with him, represented a cultural as well as a religious apostasy that contemporaries generally could not interpret as following from honest conviction but could see only as the result of seduction by falsehood, fault of character, or emotive lapse of judgment more often than not associated with women or less than fully masculine men. Nonetheless, before the publication of *Tract 90* and all that flowed therefrom, some commentators though deeply hostile to the Tractarians had still understood them not as disguised Roman Catholics but as one among numerous groups of contemporary religious rebels. For example, as early as 1837 R. D. Hampden, still smarting from his censure the previous year, pointed to parallels between the Tractarians and the Irvingites, most particularly in their common refusal to acknowledge any external religious authorities. Commenting to Whately on their mutual Tractarian enemies, Hampden wrote,

> They exhibit themselves before the public as the living representation of their own extravagant and false theory of tradition. They expect to be listened to accordingly as sacred oracles, as carrying weight in their ministerial capacity. Holding themselves as the proper maintainers of the divine apostolical tradition, the true inheritors of what Keble calls the "episcopal grace," they feel themselves far above the condition of mere teachers and persuaders of men. . . . It is no wonder that persons actuated by such a spirit should be despisers of all authority except that which founds itself on views such as their own, and while they profess the highest reverence for Church authority in the abstract—authority, *i.e.*, grounded on their theory of tradition—treat with disrespect any existing authority, or an actual minister of religion not of their party.[4]

Although on other occasions Hampden cast his critique of the Tractarians in stark terms of Protestantism versus Roman Catholicism, he here clearly grasped the powerfully self-referential sense of religious authority concealed in their rhetoric of deference to tradition. As far as Hampden was concerned, the Tractarians sought to constitute their own church within the larger English Church. Whatever their Roman Catholic sympathies, they were not Roman Catholics but clergy of the English Church rejecting the faith and practice of historic Protestantism for a religion of their own self-willed devising.

Ironically, in 1845 the Roman Catholic *Tablet* approximated Hampden's judgment as it evaluated the behavior within the English Church of the recent Tractarian converts and their former associates still remaining there. In one of the most brilliant of all contemporary assessments of Tractarianism, the *Tablet* characterized "the party which had attached itself" to Newman as appearing publicly "most zealous for Church Authority" and "for the subjugation of the individual judgment and intelligence beneath the yoke of an outward, public, authorized and compulsory rule." On that basis, they had undertaken a "quarrel with all the forms of Ultra-Protestantism," which in the end had left them "to the guidance of their individual fancies, or subjected them to the unauthorized guidance of teachers self-chosen and self-choosing." Despite their vigorous contention "for the necessity of an external Church authority, to repress the excesses of undisciplined zeal and of straggling imaginations," they had transformed themselves into "the followers of a man" and "his followers not in any special discipline or rule of life and manners, but in the choice of a Church!" The *Tablet* continued, "Professing the utmost abhorrence of Protestantism and of all private choice in matters of religion, they were yet by virtue of their position the most Ultra-Protestants in existence; for the complexion of their creed was the result of three acts of individual choosing. They chose in general; they chose in special; they chose in individual. . . . They chose the Anglican Establishment for their Church; they chose a party in the Establishment as the interpreter of its doctrines; they chose a man as the interpreter of that party."[5] Though calling themselves Catholics, the Tractarians in their challenge to evangelical religion had actually behaved as an ultra-Protestant conventicle within a larger Protestant body. Similar Roman Catholic suspicions about inherent Tractarian tendencies to independent religious action, which Bishop Wiseman so quickly smoothed over in England, reappeared several months later in Orestes Brownson's American commentary on Newman's *Essay on Development*. Both the *Tablet* and Brownson recognized that Newman and his followers had resorted to the Roman Catholic Church only after their own ultra-Protestantlike experiment within the Church of England had encountered a series of failures and after Newman himself had rejected various alternatives for sustaining it outside either the English or Roman communions.

In 1853 Richard Whately remarked that the taste for "Romish-like practices and notions," which during the past decade had led many to the Roman Catholic Church, "did not *come to* us from Rome" and was "not *imported* into England at first." Rather, he noted, "First a *taste* was formed, and then a *craving* came on for things of that sort; and when it was found that our Church could not satisfy that craving, the customers were driven to the Roman market." Whately was correct in his appraisal. From Newman's sermons of at least the late 1820s and Pusey's tract on fasting through Ward's *Ideal of a Christian Church*, the Tractarians had sparked and nurtured yearnings for Catholic religious experiences and ascetic devotion unfulfilled and indeed rejected in the English Church. But those impulses had arisen among themselves, not from interaction with Roman Catholics nor

from receiving Roman Catholic instruction. Indeed, many years later Newman wrote, "Catholics did not make us Catholics; Oxford made us Catholics." In the spring of 1841, after concluding his negotiation with Bagot over
Tract 90, Newman told Richard Westmacott that he had "no thought whatever of going over to Rome, or letting others," but at the same time admitted
to pursuing "a great wish to make our Church more Catholic in its tone, and
to introduce into it the good points of Rome—and if the consequence is a
more friendly feeling between the Churches, it may tend to the improvement of Rome herself."[6]

Observers across the spectrum of Victorian religious life, watching what
Henry Christmas soon termed "the great Tractarian epic," were deeply
impressed by the range of disruptive activities, particularly in terms of
publication and university politics, that Newman and his associates generated in their effort to forge a place for their radical Catholicism inside the
English Church.[7] To evangelicals, traditional high churchmen, and eventually moderate Catholics, the Tractarians were genuinely challenging the
understood limits of faith, worship, devotional practice, and asceticism in
the established church as well as declaring their intention to interpret the
39 Articles in their own fashion. Contemporaries did not associate reticence or restraint with Tractarianism. Yet Newman's behavior is much more
fully clarified and opened to a more nearly consistent explanation if the historian recognizes within his personality a fundamental pattern of self-
delimitation. This penchant to self-delimitation is no less important to
understanding Newman's life and thought than is his more familiar polemical ferocity. Newman was willing to envision a Catholic reformation in both
the Church of England and the Church of Rome, but he was not willing to
allow himself or his followers to move aggressively toward that end. In this
respect, his self-identification during the early 1840s with the delimited
prophetic ministry of Elijah is telling. Various examples of conscious self-
delimitation on Newman's part represent a series of paths taken and, more
important, paths not taken. Recognition of the paths not taken serves to
illustrate the kind of religious figure Newman chose not to become and thus
helps to illuminate more clearly what he actually did seek to accomplish.

THE ABSENCE OF A
SEARCH FOR SALVATION

As indicated in his letter to Westmacott, the most conspicuous example of
self-delimiting action on Newman's part was his extreme reluctance to

transfer his religious affiliation itself. Unlike most people in both early- and late-Victorian England, Newman believed that a change in religious affiliation *need not* necessarily follow a change in religious conviction. Indeed, he considered such action, if in any way peremptory, to denote an evangelical frame of mind driven by temporary inner feelings. He told a correspondent in the summer of 1843, "I have a great horror of acting upon private judgment. . . . We are not Protestants, who think religions may be changed about, as coats of different colors."[8]

To one degree or another, Newman had doubted the Catholicity of the English Church since the summer of 1839, but he repeatedly claimed that such doubt did not require him to change churches because from his standpoint his questioning of the English Church only marginally involved the salvation of his own soul. Newman did not doubt the validity of his baptism, nor does he appear ever to have doubted that something lasting had occurred between him and his God at the time of his first conversion. In other words, his assurance of heaven did not have to wait until he had settled on his church membership. This stance puzzled many of his friends in whose experience other Protestants encountering serious religious doubt generally changed religious affiliation or ceased religious observance. Newman's behavior by contrast appeared peculiar, insincere, and hypocritical.

Although in 1860 Newman told a correspondent, "For myself, I came into the [Roman Catholic] Church to save my soul, which I considered I could not save by remaining in the establishment," between 1839 and the middle of 1845 Newman repeatedly said that he did not question the possibility of salvation for himself or others within the English Church. On November 8, 1841, after telling Henry Wilberforce a second time of his doubt about the Catholicity of the Church of England, Newman pointed to the presence of "over-flowings of grace" in that institution and firmly stated, "I have no doubt, nor do I think I am likely to have, of the salvability of persons dying in the English Church." Almost two months later Robert Wilberforce learned the story of 1839 and expected Newman to leave the Church of England, but the latter replied, "You over state what I have said. . . . I have said *not a word* of any thing practical following as regards individuals from even a *conviction* that our Church were without the pale of Catholicity." In late 1843 Manning and Gladstone, who did not press the issue, were mystified that Newman did not enter the Roman Church after so stridently expressing doubt about the English Church. Throughout the same period the question of salvation did not appear in his correspondence with Keble or Pusey. On November 16, 1844, however, he told Edward

Coleridge, "As far as I know myself the one single over-powering feeling is that our Church is in schism—and that there is no salvation in it *for one who is convinced of this.*" In December 1844, he told Jemima, "I believe our Church to be separated from Catholic communion; but still I know very well that all divines, ancient and modern, Roman as well as our own, grant even to a Church in schism, which has the Apostolical Succession, and the right form of consecrating the sacraments, very large privileges." The real problem, he thought, arose in the case of one such as himself who was not in ignorance of the state of schism. There the issue became "whether it is not his duty, if he would be saved, to act upon knowledge vouchsafed to him concerning the state of his Church; which acting is not required for salvation in those who have not that knowledge. Our Church may be a place of grace and security to another, yet not to me?" But still he did not act. Finally, Newman did not raise the issue of salvation in June 1845 when defending to Dalgairns's father his son's imminent conversion to Roman Catholicism. Nor did Newman allude to the issue of salvation in his letter to Westmacott of July 11.[9]

When on rare occasion Newman did raise the matter of salvation, he did so to halt discussion rather than to precipitate action. In the late summer of 1845, he stated quite directly to Francis Newman his belief in the Roman Catholic Church as the only true church in order to forestall the full exploration of his religious behavior that Francis had invited. Similarly, on September 21 Newman asserted that his conviction that the Roman Catholic Church could assure salvation was the only basis for entering that institution in order to diminish the immediate or direct relevance of the Oakeley decision for his own situation.[10] Around the time of his reception into the Roman Church, he wrote far more publicly and privately about the image of St. Augustine and St. Athanasius finding themselves in Oxford and attending the Roman Church as drawing him toward Rome than about concern for his personal salvation.

Nor did Newman raise the issue of salvation when counseling others about their possible conversions. In his long, often moving, exchanges with Miss Mary Holmes, a correspondence that constituted a spiritual direction for himself as much as for her, Newman repeatedly advised against action based on feeling or impulse. For example, in 1843 when Miss Holmes was about to receive a visit from Bishop Wiseman, Newman advised, "Do consider that you are about to be submitted to temptation; that is, the temptation of acting not on *judgment* but on *feeling.* Your feelings are in favor of Rome, so are mine—your judgment is against joining it—so is mine." He told her in August 1843, "I cannot conceive a more painful situation, that [than?] for a person to find himself joined, committed irreversibly, to the Church of Rome—and then to find he wanted something more or else, which he could not get."[11] Newman himself entered the Roman Church only when he was certain that he could no longer find what he wanted in the English Church and could almost certainly find it in the Roman. What he sought there, however, was not new assurance of salvation—or, for that matter, affiliation with an institution that he was certain possessed Catholicity.

Deeply distrustful of his own feelings, Newman publicly and privately warned other Catholics against sudden, emotion-driven conversions. In advising friends and acquaintances who were considering conversion, Newman consistently told them—often in the starkest terms—that they must not act on impulse. He deplored R. W. Sibthorp's movements to and from Rome and had repeatedly urged William Lockhart to delay action. Lockhart's conversion in August 1843 precipitated Newman's resignation from St. Mary's, in part because he believed his preaching there was encouraging Roman sympathies that might result in the young moving unthinkingly to Rome. Less than a month later Newman demanded that his brother-in-law Thomas Mozley not enter the Roman Church. After discussing the upheaval in Mozley's marriage to his sister as well as in their wider family, Newman bluntly, even brutally, declared, "And again how unseemly to seem to be acting under excitement! If you ask me, I must plainly tell you that you *are* under excitement, and in no fit state to act for your self."[12] Newman understood that the overwrought frame of mind under which his brother-in-law labored because of the episcopal onslaught against the *British Critic* could not sustain any lasting loyalty to the Roman Church.

After all, Newman had not raised aspirations for the Catholic in men such as Lockhart and Mozley to foster their passage to Rome. Indeed, such conversions represented the failure of Newman's larger ends. Within the Littlemore coterie, conversions threatened to destroy, and eventually did destroy, the family-like situation he had created for himself. Conversion of anyone in or near his close circle of acquaintances removed them from his direct influence and company and undermined his self-defined religious vocation of edification. Without exception he fought against the impulse and deplored it when it was realized. In this respect, he reacted to people pursuing their emotions toward conversion as he had to earlier companions following their emotions into matrimony. In both situations, he ceased to be the center of their attention and affection.

With people either converting or threatening to convert, as with those

PATHS TAKEN AND NOT

friends who married, Newman used the tactic of withholding not only his approval but also his friendship and ongoing presence in their lives. This pattern was consistent. The most extreme example was that of Mozley, for whom the collapse of his marriage and the loss of Newman's affection loomed as an immediate prospect. A few months later in 1844, Miss Holmes announced to Newman her intention of being received into the Roman Church. He immediately threatened to cease correspondence on the grounds that as a priest of the Church of England he could no longer counsel her: "In its *nature* it would be the same sort of impropriety as saying mass or dressing in Pontifical vestments." In May 1845, when Dalgairns considered entering the Roman Church, he asked whether he and Newman would be able to remain together once they had both taken the step. Newman said that they very well might not, a reply possibly designed to discourage Dalgairns from action at a time when Newman himself still hoped to avoid the step.[13] The conversion of Ward and his wife in late September effectively ended the already tenuous intimacy of their relationship to Newman, which had briefly survived their marriage.

Through conversion to Rome or in Mozley's case near-conversion, people in some manner close to Newman directly rejected the authority of his vocation of edification. This self-defined calling on Newman's part very much replicated the role that at his parents' behest he had once played in the education and moral instruction of his brothers and sisters. When his brothers eventually challenged his influence, John's reaction had been first to argue with them and then to withhold affection. He remained close to his sisters only as long as there were no substantial religious quarrels. For John Newman in his early forties the prospect of the conversion of people who had placed themselves under his religious or spiritual influence evoked the lingering angers and unresolved turmoil from his young adulthood. Then he had assumed numerous family responsibilities, had at much personal financial and emotional sacrifice defined his vocation as the oversight of his brothers and sisters, had failed to recognize that those siblings would eventually become independent adults, and had then felt himself badly used and little appreciated. He had attempted to reconstruct that situation in a more nearly satisfactory fashion in the aborted Oriel tutorial reform. After that failure, he surrounded himself with men and corresponded with women who welcomed his religious counsel and in some cases his financial aid. For them he had written *Tract 90* and borne all the abuse flowing therefrom. Then after those sacrifices there arose the possibility that those same Catholic companions would leave him and the monastic refuge of Littlemore for the Roman Catholic Church. The anger and frustration that he felt over those possible or actual conversions arose in part from the fundamental frustration of an adult who could not imagine a role for himself other than that of an older sibling and who was thus almost bound to see relationships disintegrate because they were never based on a recognition of mutual maturity and independence.

Furthermore, by 1843 the conversion of men to Roman Catholicism threatened both directly and indirectly the Littlemore community. The conversion of someone who had lived at Littlemore directly undermined the life of the community as an end in itself rather than as a halfway house to Rome. Conversions meant the community might erode without prospect of renewal. But conversions also suggested that what Newman had to offer at Littlemore was religiously or spiritually inadequate to the advanced Catholic aspirations he had personally nurtured. He understood Littlemore to be the realization of the Church Catholic in England in the face of advancing heresy in the English Church and popular corruption in the Roman. If the Littlemore enclave lost its members and associates through conversion, that institutionalization of the Church Catholic would fail. Newman thus had to prevent conversions to sustain the prospect of his own institution making its way however modestly in the world. At some level he grasped that his ministry, if it were to be successful, must make people discontented with the English Church but not so discontented as to leave that institution for Rome. In the long run, he found no device to achieve that delicate and perhaps impossible balance.

RETREAT FROM REFORMED CATHOLICISM

As demonstrated in 1841 by Ward and Dalgairns's letter to *L'Univers* and their correspondence with Ambrose Phillipps, Newman had aroused in his followers a strong vision of a utopian Catholicism that would reform two Christian communions. But Newman himself retreated from that vision of reformed Catholicism, a retreat that provides a second example of his proclivity to self-delimitation. This Catholic utopianism, presupposing the necessity of significant reform in both the English and Roman Churches, displayed itself most extensively during the last three years of the *British Critic* and in Ward's *Ideal of a Christian Church*. Although Newman must have for a time encouraged such utopianism in private conversation and had defended its advocates' articles in the *British Critic*, he was rarely comfortable with its public presentation because he anticipated destructive

responses from ecclesiastical and university authorities that would endanger
his monastic religious experiment.

From *Tract 90* through *An Essay on the Development of Christian Doctrine* Newman advocated what contemporaries regarded as enormous innovation in ecclesiology, devotion, and historical theology. Yet in reality his
innovations lacked a powerful, integrative, forward-looking religious vision
such as characterized other new religious movements in the contemporary
transatlantic world, including Wiseman's launching of a Roman Catholic
revival in England. The absence of vision meant that Newman did not
formulate a genuine alternative to the English and Roman Churches, even
when he regarded each as decidedly inadequate. Newman was a religious
leader who led his followers not toward a future reformed Catholicism but
rather toward a Catholic monastic life apart from either communion. Rather
than advancing an agenda of expansive reformed Catholicism that Ward and
others imagined during late 1841 and beyond, Newman offered a ministry
of nonexpansive ascetic edification in which except for the composition of
the *Lives of the English Saints* his followers were actually given very little to
do with their days, a problem that continued into the early years of the
Birmingham Oratory.[14]

This tone of self-delimitation marked the *Essay on Development*. Indeed,
one could express the same disappointment about this book that Newman in
the *Essay* directed toward the Bible, which he believed must disappoint
those who incorrectly looked to it for the teaching of doctrine. Similarly, the
Essay must deeply disappoint the reader, who expects to find in it a sweeping
vision of Christian history or a forcefully persuasive argument favoring
Roman Catholicism. Newman could in principle have assumed an open-
ended agenda of religious change, but he did not, only marginally probing
postmedieval developments. As more than one contemporary observed,
rather than explaining what religious faith and practice ought to be, Newman's argument defended a selective status quo. At its most extensive,
Newman's concept of development instrumentally explained the past while
implicitly defending novel contemporary usages in the English Church, but
it did not point toward any brave religious future. Instead, Newman's vision
of development rather than pointing toward a reformed Catholicism, primarily justified the legitimacy of Littlemore devotional life. That is to say,
he wrote a very long, intricate book to defend the practices of a very small
and never cohesive monastic community.

Two major factors account for the delimited character of Newman's
understanding of development, which cast the Christian past in profoundly

naturalistic terms. The first is the absence of a significantly articulated consideration of the third person of the Trinity. In this respect, Newman stood at one with other early-nineteenth-century theologians of established Protestant denominations who failed to work through a major theology of Holy Spirit. Theirs was, after all, the century of Jesus, with enormous theological attention directed toward the atonement, the incarnation, and historical debates surrounding Jesus' life and times. Although the Tractarians had harshly criticized the open preaching of the atonement, their emphasis on the real presence of Christ in the eucharist represented another facet of Christology rather than a departure from it. Emphasis on either the atonement or the real presence represented elements of what Richard Niebuhr once called "the Unitarianism of the Son," which so deeply informed nineteenth-century theology, devotion, and worship.[15]

Historically, attention to the Holy Spirit had constituted the third rail of Protestant theology. Appeals to the Holy Spirit had long characterized disruptive, radical groups on the margins of established Protestantism, including many associated with advanced nineteenth-century evangelicals. Newman could not easily for his own purposes have moved to an outright antinomian position, though there is evidence of a temptation in his descriptions of himself as an instrument of Providence. Furthermore, the Tractarian determination to transform theology and ecclesiology, while retaining appointments and income within the English Church, functioned as a limitation on anti-institutional or antinomian appeals to the Holy Spirit. Consequently, for Newman the history of Christianity was essentially the history of the Christian Church and not the history of the Holy Spirit working through history.

The second factor limiting the scope of vision that Newman attached to development was the empiricist philosophy that, despite his efforts to resist, nonetheless largely determined his frame of mind. That outlook meant that Newman lacked any metaphysical foundation that might have provided a dynamic element to his thinking about development. The situation might well have been different had he drunk from the philosophical springs of even moderate German idealism or studied idealist theologians, who emphasized a theology of divine immanentism.

That a vision of a reformed Catholicism might flow from a concept of development pursued with different, more dynamic philosophical presuppositions stands importantly demonstrated in the contemporaneous publications of Philip Schaff. Born in 1819, only a year after Dalgairns, in German-speaking Switzerland, Schaff attended the University of Tübingen, which

had both a Protestant and a Roman Catholic theological faculty. J. A. Moehler, the Roman Catholic theologian of development, had taught there before
Schaff's arrival, and Isaac Dorner, a Lutheran, had published his *History of
the Development of the Doctrine of the Person of Christ* while Schaff was in
residence. After two years at Tübingen, Schaff moved to Halle, where he
studied with Pusey's friend F. A. G. Tholuck. Later in Berlin he encountered the religious activists who encouraged Frederick William IV's policy
of unifying the Prussian Lutheran and Reformed Churches.[16] Thus Schaff,
as a student, had encountered German idealism, ecumenical settings for
theological training, the concept of the development of doctrine, and a
strong appreciation for the corporate role of the church—sensibilities that
might be described as German Protestant high churchmanship. In 1843 he
received an appointment at the Mercersberg Theological Seminary of the
German Reformed Synod in Pennsylvania, where he became a major figure
in American religious life.

In 1843, while traveling to America, Schaff called on Pusey in Oxford
and Newman at Littlemore. Once relocated across the Atlantic, Schaff immediately found himself appalled by American Protestant evangelical sectarianism, with its omnipresent itinerant clergy. Reacting to that new environment in *The Principle of Protestantism,* his Mercersburg inaugural lecture
of October 1844, Schaff shrewdly and sympathetically described English
Tractarianism as "*an entirely legitimate and necessary reaction against rationalistic and sectaristic pseudo-protestantism, as well as the religious subjectiv-
ism of the so called Low Church Party.*" Those pseudo-Protestants had "forgotten" or "at least practically undervalued" the importance of the Church
"in favour of personal individual piety, the sacraments in favor of faith,
sanctification in favour of justification, and tradition in its right sense in
favour of the holy scriptures." Institutionally minded Protestants, possessing a firm sense of their faith and tradition, must oppose evangelical sec-
tarians with "the power of history, and the idea of the Church, as the pillar
and ground of the truth, the mother of all believers, with due subordination
always to the written word." In words that might have delighted the late
Tractarians, Schaff announced, "All conventicles and chapels must perish,
that from their ashes may rise the One Church of God, phoenix like and
resplendent with glory, as a bride adorned for her bridegroom."[17] Schaff's
"One Church of God" would have been no less difficult to delineate with
any precision than the Tractarian Church Catholic.

After commending the Tractarians' assault on sectarian Protestant subjectivity and their appreciation for the corporate church, the sacraments,

and religious discipline, Schaff denounced as their "grand defect" the "*utter misapprehension of the divine significance of the Reformation, with its consequent development, that is of the entire Protestant period of the Church.*" The Tractarian emphasis on a static concept of Christianity embodied in antiquity meant that, at least in 1844, they lacked "the true idea of *development* altogether," and for "all their historical feeling" had proved themselves "with regard to the Reformation absolutely unhistorical."[18] But Schaff's conviction of the importance of the various stages of growth allowed him, though a firm Protestant, to appreciate the Middle Ages as well as antiquity. He argued that Protestants should refrain from wholesale condemnation of the medieval church and should appreciate the sanctity and piety of those who had lived and died in its bosom. Nonetheless, enormous corruption in doctrine had characterized that institution, necessarily calling forth the Reformers.

Schaff saw the Tractarians' hostility to the Reformation, their diminishment of the authority of Scripture, and their embrace of religious novelties under the term *Catholicism* as discrediting their important original opposition to evangelicalism. Moreover, in the *Lives of the English Saints* he discerned "the old Jewish work-righteousness" presenting "itself again in its full arrogant parade." Tractarian sanctity embodied "the character of an outward legalism, an unfree, anxious piety, reminding us of monkhood, with undue stress laid upon the observance of particular Church forms, fasts, and self-imposed discipline." All these shortcomings stemmed from the Tractarians' possessing "no proper sense of the world-historical importance of Protestantism in its origin and later development" and their failure to comprehend that "Protestantism is the principle of movement, of progress in the history of the Church." Schaff saw Protestantism in this world-historical role as embodying "*an ever extending knowledge* of the bible itself, and an *ever deepening appropriation* of Christianity as the power of a divine life, which is destined to make *all* things new."[19]

Liberated by German idealism from the stark naturalism of empiricism, Schaff, unlike Newman, discerned in the work of the spirit an internal, divine dynamic to Christian history and the historical development of Christian doctrine. Through that idealist philosophy Schaff championed sympathy for ecumenical Protestant–Roman Catholic relations that very much resembled radical Tractarian comments on the same subject but which did not similarly disparage Protestantism. Looking to a final development and consummation of Christianity in the future, Schaff urged Protestants to extend themselves to Roman Catholics in pursuit of a higher religious synthesis, declaring, "Protestantism cannot be consummated, without [Roman] Catholicism; not in the way of falling back to the past, but as coming into reconciliation with it finally in a higher position, in which all past errors shall be left behind whether protestant or catholic, and the truth of both tendencies be actualized, as the power of one and the same life, in the full revelation of the kingdom of God."[20] German idealism thus furnished Schaff with a metaphysical foundation making the divine immanent in history that might otherwise have been filled by a theology of the Holy Spirit.

This vision of Christian history determined Schaff's negative reaction to Newman's *Essay on Development*, which in 1846 he criticized for "a wretched want of acquaintance with the better productions of modern German historical inquiry." In contrast to Newman's profound silence on the matter, Schaff repeatedly stressed that the life of the developing Church "involves the uninterrupted presence of Christ, the God-man, in and among his people." Positing through Hegelian terminology that objective truth had been present in both Christ and the Scriptures, he explained, "Subjective Christianity . . . or the life of the God-man in his Church, is a process, a development, which begins small, and grows always larger, till it comes at last to full manhood in Christ; that is, till the believing human world may have appropriated to itself, both outwardly and inwardly, the entire fulness of objective Christianity, or the life of Christ." Human growth into fuller spiritual truth, including a better understanding of the Bible, occurred from age to age through "a process of annihilation, preservation, and exaltation." Pointing again to the emergence of a more fully perfected Christian faith in the future, Schaff emphasized that "the grand leading phases of church historical development, [Roman] Catholicism and Protestantism, do not, separately taken, exhibit the *full* compass of Christian truth." Schaff forecast "a higher stadium of development" where the errors of Roman Catholicism and Protestantism would "be effectually surmounted" and "the divine element comprehended in each" would appear "happily preserved and perfected, in a higher form of church life," culminating in a transformed ecumenical Christianity—"evangelical Catholicity or churchly Protestantism"—that transcended present divisions.[21] Newman's concept of development, by contrast, would have led either to his own eclectic Christian communion or to reconciliation with contemporary unreformed Roman Catholicism. In either case Newman did not fundamentally point beyond the present.

One may wonder, as did Victorian observers, where Newman's restless intellect might have arrived in its thinking about history had he possessed a significant, or perhaps even modest, knowledge of German idealist philosophy. It might have allowed him to resist the Tractarian conflation of evangelical religion and historical Protestantism with the consequent attacks on the Reformation that proved so politically devastating to the movement. It might also have permitted him to persist in a vision of a reformed Roman Catholicism such as he had hinted to Westmacott in 1841. Yet the question is itself misplaced. It too readily accepts the invitation of the *Apologia* that to understand Newman is to follow the history of his religious opinions. German philosophy and theology would in all likelihood have made little difference in his actions and behavior because factors other than religious opinion drove Newman from the early 1830s through 1845.

THE SELF-IMPOSED ISOLATION OF THE MONOPHYSITE NIGHTMARE

While Newman steadily retreated from envisioning any kind of expansive reformed Catholicism, he increasingly pressed his perception of a powerful parallel between the contemporary Church of England and the ancient church surrounded by heresies. In January 1842 he explained this idea in some detail to Robert Wilberforce, recalling that "about two years and a half ago I began reading the Monophysite controversy, and with great concern and dismay found how much we were in the position of the Monophysites. . . . After that I turned my mind to the Donatists, and there the same truth, or a parallel one, came out in the strongest colours. In the Monophysite history it is that the Church of Rome, in the Donatist that body which spreads through the world, is always ipso facto right. . . . Since then whatever line of early history I look into, I see as in a glass reflected our own Church in the heretical party, and the Roman Church in the Catholic. This is an appalling fact—which, do what I will, I cannot shake off."[22] Here and elsewhere Newman dated this insight to the summer of 1839, when he had devoted much study to ancient heresy and then subsequently read Bishop Wiseman's *Dublin Review* article comparing the English Church with ancient heresies. Beginning in the autumn of 1839, Newman selectively informed certain of his friends of his understanding of the parallel and the conclusion that he drew from it—that is, that the modern Church of England quite possibly lacked Catholicity. He repeated this argument in the months and years after his conversion, mentioned it in the dedication to his *Discourses Addressed to Mixed Congregations* in 1849, explored it fully in *Lectures on Certain Difficulties Felt by Anglicans* of 1850, and again recounted it in the *Apologia*. What became lost from Newman's later recountings of the Monophysite parallel was its profound interconnection in his mind with a fierce hatred toward evangelical religion. In its retelling in the *Apologia*, the target became the Church of England establishment, but in its origin the target was the established Church of England as overwhelmed by ultra-Protestantism.

From the publication of the *Apologia* onward, commentators have extensively explored the Monophysite parallel. Teachers have attempted to explicate its intricacies to undergraduate, graduate, and divinity students. Neither at the time nor later was the idea easy or simple to explain, as is evident from the labored early-twentieth-century elaboration by the editor of *The Correspondence of John Henry Newman with John Keble and Others*. These later interpretive difficulties are not insignificant to understanding Newman's position in the 1840s and have obscured an important historical fact. The parallel upon which Newman so fervently insisted between heresy in the ancient church and the modern Church of England appears to have convinced no one to whom he privately communicated it between 1839 and 1845. It was his peculiar argument and his alone. His confidants—including Frederic Rogers, Henry and Robert Wilberforce, the Froudes, Manning, Gladstone, Pusey, and J. B. Mozley—were to one degree or another shaken by Newman's personal doubt about the Catholicity of the English Church, but none was drawn to the parallel itself. Immediately after Newman's conversion, E. L. Badeley wrote, "I know not the ground on which you have proceeded & am consequently distracted [?] at present between your teaching & your example." Had he known of the Monophysite parallel, there is no reason to believe that he would have understood Newman's decision any better. None of Newman's close friends pointed to the parallel in explaining his departure. Moreover, across the years Newman gave mixed signals as to its meaning even for himself, telling Pusey early in 1844, "I am too much accustomed to this idea to feel pain at it. I could only feel pain, if I found it led me to action. At present I do not feel any such call."[23]

Both Newman's private emphasis upon the ancient and modern parallel and his ever-growing conviction of the infection of the English Church by modern evangelical heresy represent another highly complicated facet of his tendency toward a narrow self-delimitation. In the letter of January 26, 1842, he explained to Robert Wilberforce, "Nor is it the mere *coincidence* between the state of things now and formerly which harasses me, but it seems something *prophetic*—it scares me." He then wrote of "a growing dread lest in speaking against the Church of Rome I may be speaking against the Holy

Ghost." Newman admitted that he had returned to the parallel only when he found that his "fears," which had "slept for many months," had become "re-animated by our dreadful divisions, the Bishops' charges, and this Prussian affair."[24] The analogy of ancient and modern heresy served to make personal sense of the terrible pressures and rejections that Newman had encountered for the past several months at the hands of evangelicals and departing high churchmen. For their part his Catholic correspondents found the parallel puzzling, troubling, misguided, or simply odd and arcane.

Nonetheless, the perceived analogy of ancient and modern heresy assaulting the Church Catholic remained for Newman intensely real. From at least the autumn of 1841, like a man seized by a nightmare that will not desist, Newman became nothing less than obsessed with his vision of an ever-expanding evangelical heresy, the view that informed what his friends found to be his largely inexplicable fury at the Jerusalem bishopric. For a brief time in 1842, Newman's apprehensions subsided, as he told Simeon Pope, "My great hope and belief is, that the so-called Evangelical party is a failing and declining one; so that we may hope that the clamours will be less and less every year."[25] When the power of evangelical heresy reasserted itself in the bishops' charges of 1842 and 1843, as well as in Pusey's suspension, Newman became even angrier, seeing the influence of what he by then regarded as an ultra-Protestant bench of bishops manifesting itself everywhere. Throughout this period friends, including Hope, Manning, Gladstone, J. B. Mozley, and Edward Badeley, attempted to persuade him that he was wrong and that he should recognize the enormous advance made in the past decade by Catholicism in the English Church. They believed Newman was out of touch with reality.

In June 1844, as any remaining high-church support for the Tractarians waned with the appearance of the *Lives of the English Saints*, Newman told Henry Wilberforce, "I want you, if you do not object, to do this:—to state *historically*, that you know that in 1839 I was very unsettled on the subject of the Catholicity of our Church. You may speak as strongly as your recollections enable you. But I should not like, first, any mention what my *present feelings are*—next, any hint that *I* have put you on doing this." He wanted the story told so that people might be prepared for a future action on his part. He further stated, "I don't care who knows. The only fear is, that, being so long ago, people may think I have got over it." Wilberforce was "puzzled" by this request, most particularly about how he could circulate the information without encountering the charge "that I am betraying the confidence of private friendship publishing what you said in conversation five years ago without either authority from you or even without knowing what your present feelings on the matter are." Newman's concern, he told Wilberforce, was communicating that whatever might result from his present state of mind, his friends should know that "at least it is not an accidental state of mind, but a part of my character or history—that they should not be relying on a person, even if he continued where he is, without knowing what they rely on. And still more if something is to come of it, they ought to be prepared for it." He concluded, "That friends should know a *fact,* and a fact five years old, seems an easy way of leading them to conjecture what my present state of mind is."[26] By 1845 Newman's recounting the parallel of ancient heresy and the modern church and thus the conclusion that the English Church lacked Catholicity had become almost a litany in his correspondence.

Throughout 1844 Pusey's suspension continued to fester in Newman's mind. Although he had only marginal sympathy for Pusey's own somewhat bungled handling of matters, Newman nonetheless had hoped for an appeal to the Court of Arches. Even sympathetic Catholic lawyers, however, argued against that appeal. Though Newman did not challenge their legal judgment, he still regarded the suspension, as he told Badeley in late summer, as having been directed against "a sermon, which is an understatement of a doctrine which must be called Catholic—and now . . . [the suspension stood] accepted by the silence of the Church and her Bishops," who could "charge against other errors, but even when they have that opportunity and call to speak, . . . can be silent here." Coming after the Jerusalem bishopric, the suspension convinced him "that we have long been unchurched." He further complained, "Every form of heresy is tolerated, but there is an instinctive irritation, or shudder, at anything too Catholic." Newman then cited a host of minor local ecclesiastical events that in his mind furnished powerful evidence of the descent into evangelical heresy. He related all of these "very fearful thoughts, which have long, very long, crowded upon my mind, and oppressed it."[27] In each instance Newman was attaching vast meaning to incidents that close Catholic friends outside his Littlemore circle regarded as unimportant or trivial.

On August 28, 1844, Badeley argued, as had other Catholics, that Pusey's suspension could "hardly be deemed an *authoritative* condemnation" and had in fact actually brought discussion of Catholic doctrine before a wider public. Furthermore, the Jerusalem bishopric seemed "already to have well nigh come to naught." He also sought to defuse each and every one of the recent small incidents to which Newman had attached so much importance, and he reminded Newman, "In the state to which we have been reduced, it requires a long time for a healing process to bring the system to its proper state—but when the younger & more healthy blood has been gradually diffused thro its veins, the Body may recover its true character, & bring itself into a right position." Despite "disheartening events" real progress and recovery were under way in the English Church.[28]

For some time other Catholic friends had similarly attempted to help bring what they regarded as a better sense of proportion to Newman's interpretation of contemporary events. J. B. Mozley in 1843, about the time Newman was deciding to resign St. Mary's, had attempted to refute his pessimistic view of the state of the English Church. He urged Newman to understand that he had been "singled out for attack by Bishops" because they knew that he and not Pusey was the leader of the movement and that he was more sympathetic to Rome than Pusey. Mozley had further explained, "What I mean is that they attack your position, & not you personally." Almost exactly a year later, hoping to convince Newman that he had genuinely miscalculated the character of the evangelical presence in the English Church, Mozley strongly assured him that within broad popular public opinion "the Evangelicals are not considered Churchmen, strictly speaking, but thought of and put under the same religious category in peoples' minds, with Dissenters—that is to say popular opinion recognizes a certain existing reality in the Church, of wh the Evangelicals do not partake, & the absence of wh in them makes their position in the Church a questionable one. What I mean is that as long as Evangelicals are looked on as *quasi* dissenters, so long there is a testimony to the existence of a something in the Church, making it a Church in distinction to being the natural and congenial communion to wh an Evangelical would belong spontaneously." Mozley saw the main strength of Catholics as lying "not in striking blows but in existing in it." He concluded, "So long as we *exist* in the Church we must be gaining power."[29]

Yet neither Mozley nor Badeley nor others could turn Newman's mind away from the specter of expanding heresy he saw all about him. He told Badeley that his "convictions about it are of very long standing" and that "for years" he had "been engaged in overcoming them, under the idea that possibly they were unfounded." He reported having acted "like persons who pinch themselves to be sure that they are not asleep and dreaming." But now he told Badeley,

> To show that they may possibly be otherwise explained, as you kindly do, is to *my feelings* like the conduct of a patient in a consumption and of his friends, who satisfactorily show that no one of his symptoms but may be referred to some cause short of the fatal malady, not one which involves the necessity of death. Yet a bystander or physician has a view, though he

cannot out-argue; and the event justifies it. We are naturally friends, for we are children, of this dying or dead system in which we have lived all our days. We cannot, we will not, believe what the real state of the case is. We cannot be persuaded to open our eyes. . . . There is no bier and funeral of a Church. The fact then escapes unwilling minds: yet it may be as certain to others, as the prospective termination of a fatal malady is to the physician.[30]

Newman could not believe, as he now insisted, that he had been living in a delusion for the past five years. In the autumn of 1844 the advancement to the Vice Chancellorship of Symons, the evangelical Warden of Wadham who years before had presided over the Oxford Church Missionary Society meeting that ejected Newman from office in the society, further confirmed his vision of English ecclesiastical institutions overwhelmed by evangelical heresy, as did, of course, the subsequent persecution in Convocation of Ward and *Tract 90*.

There is no question about the sincerity of Newman's vision of an English Church dying in the chains of evangelical heresy—a vision that constituted a major psychic reality for him and a framework for his thought and actions during his last years in that communion. This image permitted Newman, dwelling in ever-narrowing social and theological isolation, to see himself as fulfilling the role of the early desert saints and isolated monastic communities first outlined in the "Letters on the Church of the Fathers." This image further confirmed him in the prophetic role later articulated in those sermons in which he identified with Elijah. From at least late 1841 onward Newman was voicing self-generated fears, apprehensions, and anxieties that could be resolved only in his own prophetic enclave at Littlemore. Ironically, this fearful vision in Newman's mind was the exact counterimage of the contemporary evangelical conviction of Romish intrusions into the English Church carried out by the Tractarians. Both Newman and his evangelical detractors were creating their own sense of contemporary religious reality and acting on it.

Newman's post–*Tract 90* image of an English Church steadily falling to the forces of ultra-Protestantism paralleled the apocalypticism of his earlier vision of an English Church ravaged by the forces of secular reform in league with evangelical Dissent. Each scenario justified for him some kind of radical independent, separatist, or schismatic religious departure from the establishment. The belief in forces of real evil affecting the English Church in each instance justified his pushing beyond its present boundaries; both times sympathetic friends protested the unreality of Newman's fears. Both in 1833 and after late 1841 Newman saw himself as the only person of high-church persuasion adequate to the challenge of evangelical heresy. On both occasions he embraced rhetoric far more extreme than that of other high churchmen and also set himself in opposition to bishops who were willing to accommodate the forces of evangelicalism either among Dissenters or within the establishment.

On both occasions the apocalyptic stance radicalized his actions: in 1833 the extreme rhetoric and ecclesiology of the tracts and in 1842 the departure into a monastic community organized around his own leadership and personality.[31] In 1833, after witnessing in Italy the results of continental anticlericalism and having himself just experienced a loss of substantial tutorial income, Newman had projected a vision of English clergy cast out of their livings by revolutionary forces of Protestant Dissent who had captured the English government. There was no basis in reality for such extreme fears. Launching the tracts and envisioning an Apostolic Brotherhood to resist these alleged dangers to the English Church provided Newman with a new sense of vocation after the loss of the Oriel tutorship, the rejection of his Arians manuscript by two high churchmen, and Froude's report of the tepid actions contemplated at the Hadleigh conference. Newman's extreme rhetoric in 1833 found a wide response among the politically disillusioned establishment clergy and achieved a major, lasting impact on the English Church, as virtually all the bishops later recognized even when criticizing *Tract 90* and the *British Critic*. Newman also forged for himself a position of note in the university, where not unwillingly he became the center of a personality cult. The collective worry over the danger posed by political reform to the church, as well as Newman's sense of personal anger and hurt, had largely diminished by 1836 when he seriously considered halting the publication of the tracts.

In late 1841 the second crisis of the English Church that generated itself in Newman's mind had origins similar to those of the first. In the wake of *Tract 90*, Newman confronted doubts from close but more moderate Catholic supporters, censure from the Hebdomadal Board with Hawkins in the lead, the disapproval of his bishop, extremely critical episcopal charges, and unprecedented criticism in the religious and secular press. In his Catholic battle against evangelical religion, he again suddenly stood thoroughly rejected in the university, in Oriel, and by high churchmen. Early in 1842 it was also clear that Peel would appoint anti-Tractarians to the episcopal bench. Under those circumstances Newman entertained his nightmare image of a university and church overwhelmed by evangelical heresy, an image that in his mind now again reflected a parallel with ancient times. His editing of Athanasius meant that in 1841 and thereafter, as in 1833, he was working through the materials from the ancient Arian controversy that provided interpretive categories for his own immediate personal experience. The life of the English Church in the early 1840s, however, differed quite sharply from that of the early 1830s, and so did the clerical response to Newman's actions on this second occasion. During the 1840s there existed no larger collective ecclesiastical crisis leading people to tie their concerns with Newman's. In fact, just the opposite was the case. Peel's policy toward Irish Roman Catholics provoked the eruption of enormous anti-Catholicism that only further fueled hostility to the Tractarians. Newman consequently roused no friendly response in the larger ecclesiastical world as people inside and outside the Tractarian camp either distanced themselves or abandoned him altogether. Newman found himself left with a smaller and smaller circle who could or would embrace his vision of the supposed contemporary crisis. He turned this growing isolation into the opportunity of formally establishing the Littlemore community after the pattern of ancient monasteries protecting truth in times of crisis. Thereafter, the Monophysite parallel became absolutely essential for the justification of the Littlemore departure.

In this climate Newman's appeal to the Monophysite precedent served two distinct purposes. First, it allowed him to say to high churchmen, both traditional and moderately Catholic, that the establishment, which they were so determined to protect, was ecclesiastically a hollow sham distinct from the Church Catholic, a body incapable of standing against the heretical forces of evangelical religion and one now hopelessly permeated by its influence. Under these conditions what was required was a different church or ecclesiastical institution, the faith and practice of which necessarily went beyond the high-church boundaries of antiquity. The whole thrust of his argument for the development of doctrine contended that the true Christian faith was not to be located in antiquity or in Protestantism but in a faith and practice growing and developing through the ages from which Newman initially believed he might pick and choose and which only in his very final days in the English Church he identified with Roman Catholicism.

Second, the appeal to the Monophysite parallel served at the time and later an important personal function for Newman. It provided a plausible, even if difficult to grasp, explanation of his personal religious behavior that avoided his admitting to his enormous anger over the treatment meted out to him by one group after another in the English Church. Virtually all contemporary observers writing from a religious or secular standpoint saw Newman after 1841 as responding to the array of criticism and hostility to his theology and ecclesiology. He refused, however, except in the rarest moments of sheer exhaustion, to admit to such anger or frustration. In a letter of early 1843 he did confess, "As to Church matters, I have so long been (if it be not wrong or presumptuous to say so) in a certain sense without hope or fear about them, that I am no judge and can give no opinion, like a person whose fingers are numbed. I have such a dreadful impression of our corruption and heresies and unrealities, viewing us as a body, that the holiness of individuals, and the good that it is doing in externals and on its surface, are insufficient to over come this deep despondency." By that point in his life he admitted to Henry Wilberforce, "It is very difficult to steer between being hypocritical, and revolutionary." Still later that year, as he contemplated resigning St. Mary's, he told Mrs. Froude, "As time has gone on, *I* have become more dissatisfied with the established system, and *its conductors* have become more dissatisfied with me; I do not see what good can come of continuing a relation, which each party wishes brought to an end."[32]

Newman had enormous difficulty dealing with his anger toward the English Church. The behavior of evangelicals, high churchmen, and the bishops provided him with every good reason to leave that institution, but he needed to demonstrate that he was acting on the basis of sincere religious conviction rather than from spite, rage, or animosity. He had to demonstrate his sincerity through undergoing a painful religious change rather than one that was ecclesiastically liberating or spiritually joyful. His appeal to the Monophysite parallel provided a private, calm, rational historical explanation for his own emotionally driven actions. Through the Monophysite parallel he cast himself not as an angry righteous rebel against an unrighteous church but rather as a privileged interpreter of sacred history, who had recognized a profound problem with his church but still tried for some time to be its obedient son refusing to respond to his private judgment.

Henry Wilberforce, upon whose almost reflexive sympathy Newman could normally depend, believed that Newman paid too little attention to the role of his feelings and emotions and almost recognized how he employed the Monophysite insight of 1839 to appear calm when he was really deeply perturbed. In early June 1845, replying to Newman's indicating his likely passage to Rome, Wilberforce wrote of "how much mental suffering you have been passing through," and worried about the personal impact of the "agitation of mind like that under which you have been suffering." He then immediately offered himself, as Newman had requested a year earlier, as a witness "that so far from truth is the notion of your having been influenced" against the Church of England "by the unjust treatment you have personally received; or by any disappointment either personal or as to the success of your labours for reviving Catholicism in her that on the other hand when you first entertained the doubts which have since grown upon you (in autumn 1839) you felt & repeatedly said to me that success of so wonderful a nature was attending your labours that there seemed nothing at all to fear as to their triumph among us." Wilberforce also said that the weight Newman gave to the issue of the Catholicity of the English Church, because of its repudiation of his previous declarations against Rome, represented "a deliberate sacrifice to your own conscience such that I do not know where to look for another similar example." Should Newman convert, Wilberforce assured him that some friends would continue to "love & revere you, the more even while we do not see the way to follow you in this respect as a guide as we have been wont to do."[33]

Wilberforce then departed from Newman's proposed conversion scenario to make an observation of his own. He asked Newman "how far the tone of feeling in your letter is one which often assails you" and urged him to "be on your guard" against taking action on that basis. He noted that Newman seemed "to have been haunted by feelings of loneliness & desertion as if no one had sympathy or affection for you." Wilberforce gently reminded him, "But is it not true, my dearest Newman, that to a sensitive mind there is nothing so dangerous as the allowing itself to feel unjustly [or] unkindly treated by all around? It is commonly said to be the first sign of mental disorder. I should think it quite as often one of the first causes." Though asking forgiveness for his boldness, he felt compelled "to say something; for you are going through so much that perhaps even inferiors to you, may see some of your danger more than you do."[34]

Wilberforce had written one of the wisest and most incisive letters Newman would ever receive while still in the Church of England. Wilberforce, like Badeley and Mozley months earlier, recognized the psychological burden that Newman carried and the damage that had been done to his confidence, self-esteem, sense of proportion, and emotional stability. But their voices, like that of Richard Westmacott, who thought Newman had been "too long *cloistered*," were from outside the Littlemore coterie to whom Newman by then so deeply deferred. Those younger, extravagant men played to his deepest fears, which they, like he, now believed realities. For example, in May 1845 Dalgairns was visiting his family in Jersey, where an evangelical clergyman was in charge of the local church. That situation provoked him to write to Newman criticizing Pusey's moderation and patience with the English Church. After confessing that it was "a shame . . . to talk so of so good a man," Dalgairns explained, "However I am savage just now, as you must bear with me. The more I see of Protestantism the more I hate it with a deadly hatred. It is a miracle if Protestants are left [?] out of mortal sin any day of their lives. What a mystery it is that such a wicked, worldly system should have been allowed to overspread the earth! I don't know what you will say to me, but I cannot go to the Communion here. It is a mockery to receive it from such heretics." On June 13 John Walker, one of the contributors to the *Lives of the English Saints,* angered over the Oakeley hearing, wrote "This nation certainly has committed itself to Protestantism in the most positive manner." Both remarks demonstrate the ongoing climate of anti-Protestantism that had surrounded Newman and that he had nurtured and to which he responded ever since he gathered a Catholic community around himself at Littlemore, and more especially since he had set those men to composing lives of English Saints. Newman and his coterie fed on each other's apprehensions about the rising evangelical heresy they saw about to engulf them. That situation would only have intensified Newman's conviction of the validity of his analogy of ancient and modern heresy. To the men of Littlemore it would have made sense as it did not to Catholics dwelling elsewhere. Nor at this point would Newman have encountered any really serious caution from Pusey, who in November 1844 privately told Hook that he no longer thought the Roman Church Antichrist, but now believed that "Anti-Christ will be Infidel and arise out of what calls itself Protestantism and that Rome and England will be united in one to oppose it."[35]

THE REJECTION OF THE
SECTARIAN ALTERNATIVE

In 1845 Newman converted to Roman Catholicism only after consciously rejecting the suggestion that he organize a new church. As contemporary observers recognized and as he himself feared, Newman came very near to making a sectarian or schismatic departure from the Church of England. In late 1840 he had discussed sectarian sentiments in some detail with Francis. At that time, John accepted the concept of the Church of England establishment as itself constituting a sect. Once he had so conceived the English Church, it was not a major conceptual leap to lead his own group, which he equated with the Church Catholic, into schism to protect Catholic truth.

Thereafter, he sought some way of both remaining in the English Church and living apart from it, in a manner that he associated with early Methodists, St. Meletius, and Elijah.

Francis resurrected the sectarian alternative in well-thought-out detail during 1845 in a correspondence with John occasioned by the necessity of dealing with the financial and mental instability of their brother Charles. In May 1845, displaying rare sympathy for his brother's situation, Francis offered financial assistance, which John did not accept.[36] Later that summer Francis directly addressed the issue of John's possible change in religious affiliation, an issue that he himself well understood, having resigned his Balliol fellowship many years before over his own departure from the English Church. In August 1845, while clearly grasping John's concern for Christian unity, Francis nonetheless called his brother's bluff on the matter of conversion, writing, "If you choose the Romish Communion as in *itself good*, you would be in it already, and would long and long since have abandoned your ostensible position." John's hesitancy, Francis correctly perceived, indicated that the Roman Church "must needs have in it points which make you reluctant to enter it." He reminded John of the difficulty that he would confront at his age in making a career for himself in the Roman Church, where his "attainment" and "acquired influence" did not fit him and where he would be at once incapacitated. Francis further correctly warned that John "would at once lose all influence with nine-tenths of those who were used to respect" him and that within the Roman Church he "would be received with condescending pity, as a novice who had yet much to learn and to unlearn."[37]

Francis, who had himself surrendered much for the cause of his own religious convictions, regarded the issue confronting his brother as one not of how to follow conscience but rather of how practically to be useful. Under those circumstances, he wrote, "I say it would be better for obtaining what I believe to be your ends,—*not* to join Rome, *but* to stay unconnected with any thing, until you can form and join some independent Episcopal System, similar to that of Scotland or New York." He thought John might well achieve his goal of Christian unity by taking "even a leading part in organizing the nucleus of an Anglo-Episcopal Free Church with succession of Bishops derived from New York or Scotland." This proposed religious group need profess "no hostility to Rome" but might rather keep that question "carefully open." This departure would link his brother and other like-minded clergy with an episcopacy possessing, according to their lights, apostolical succession and at the same time allow a basis for some future union with Rome but without John and his followers "*surrendering their own liberties,* which liberties, it strikes me, your friends have never liked to surrender to our English Bishops." Francis, like their sister Harriett, thus fully comprehended the difficulty that John might encounter with Roman Catholic episcopal authority, a problem anticipated almost a year earlier when the *Tablet* had commented, "An indocile Puseyite may be many degrees further from the Church than a teachable Atheist."[38]

In 1845 Francis Newman was not alone in speculating that his brother might organize a free episcopal secession. Predicting a large defection of Newman's followers, Bishop Blomfield in March had written the Bishop of Gibraltar, "It is however possible, that they may endeavour to set up an Episcopal church not in connexion with the state, if they can get a Bishop from Scotland, or America, but I hope that neither of the Churches of those countries will abet so schismatical a proceeding." Six months later Francis advised his brother to "boldly face the charge of 'Schism' " and "not enslave yourself to your past words" by undertaking just such a newly organized church as Blomfield privately feared. Francis concluded, "In such a church you would have an immediate sphere of useful actions—and, if you succeeded, you would by it *prepare materials for a future union* [with Rome], such as you desire; and this would be work enough surely for one life."[39]

In response to Francis's elaborately articulated suggestion, John replied, "My reason for going to Rome is this:—I think the English Church is in schism. I think the faith of the Roman Church the only true religion. I do not think there is salvation out of the Church of Rome." No matter how strongly stated, the letter carries little conviction because its author, if so convinced, had nonetheless long remained in the English Church. When, as an elderly man, John recopied Francis's letter, he added the note, "That I could be contemplating questions of Truth & Falsehood never entered into his imagination!"[40] This comment, like those that he appended to the reprinted editions of his Anglican works during his Roman Catholic years, attempted to reduce his life from 1833 to 1845 to the contours of the narrative of the *Apologia.* Francis Newman, however, had understood both his brother and his brother's situation differently. He would have been familiar with the ecclesiastical ideas John shared with Froude. He would have recalled John's sympathetic remarks of 1840 about independent sects. He had observed John living almost four years at Littlemore, where he largely ignored episcopal opinion. On the basis of that knowledge, Francis had advised John to undertake a secession from the Church of England analogous to the contemporary Free Church secession from the Church of Scotland.

Nor was the liberal, freethinking Francis the first person to have raised with his brother such an alternative to Roman Catholicism. In October 1841 J. W. Bowden, then perhaps Newman's closest friend, had written, "And even admitting our *English* Bishops should be able to un-Church—so to say—the Church under their charge—it does not follow,—*necessarily*—that men should go *to Rome*. There is Scotland—there is America." Later that year, on Christmas Day, Newman himself actually speculated to Richard Church about joining another communion, "*What* communion could we join? Could the Scotch or American sanction the presence of its Bishops and congregations in England without incurring the imputation of schism, unless indeed (and is that likely?) they denounced the English as heretical?" A few days later, he told Miss Giberne, "And you think we are going to be non-jurors. I think not. No, depend upon it, this is not a day for non-juring. . . . Certainly most dreadful things are in progress or done by persons in authority—and I shall never be loth, when necessary, to call heresy heresy, and am never going to retreat before heresy, until like mephytic gas it is suffocating outright."[41] Certainly by 1845 the mephitic gas of evangelical heresy and legal rejection of Catholic truth was suffocating Newman. Under those circumstances it is not altogether inconceivable that Newman, who proved himself a skilled ecclesiastical negotiator, might have convinced an American or Scottish bishop for some kind of help. Or he might even have changed his country of residence.

Jemima, in contrast to Francis, actually feared that John would undertake what she thought might amount to a separatist Roman Catholic departure by remaining after his conversion at Littlemore, among the parish where he and his sisters and mother had together ministered a decade earlier. On October 6, 1845, just before his reception into the Roman Church, she wrote,

> One thing has been on my mind since I saw you, and the more I think of it, the more it seems to be the case—it is that you purpose remaining at Littlemore under your altered circumstances. I certainly had not expected it, and shall be very sorry if it should be so. Now I know it would be a great trial to leave, but yet I am sure, you who are sacrificing so much would think it light indeed to the rest, and that therefore you are acting with due thought & deliberation—but yet, dear John, I cannot help wishing to think you as far right as ever I can. I should indeed have been glad if it had been otherwise, for with my views and feelings, it does not seem right. I do not think I should have had courage to mention it to you but that I have heard so many express the same thing, almost without exception—at least I may say with only one.[42]

This painful note provides further evidence that at least within Newman's family circle there existed very real apprehension that John might found his own Roman Catholic congregation in the Littlemore neighborhood, something in the character of a radical evangelical seceder.

To reconceptualize Newman as a potential secessionist clergyman who did not secede emphasizes that his life and career emerged from a series of choices made and not from a web of inevitabilities in which he stood entangled. Enterprising clergy within and without the historic denominations were a significant social fact of nineteenth-century English religious life. Richard Helmstadter once used the terms *religious entrepreneur* and *businessman* to characterize the life of Andrew Reed, an early-nineteenth-century Dissenting clergyman who successfully expanded his chapel membership, paid down its debt, founded a number of charities, and sustained an excellent salary for himself.[43] Numerous contemporary seceders from the English Church, such as Bulteel in Oxford and Darby in Ireland, had similarly established themselves as self-sustaining independent clergy, serving either their own chapels or new denominational networks. The Irvingites, with roots in the Scottish Church, also constituted themselves into the independent Catholic Apostolic Church. Other early-nineteenth-century clergy, most particularly among the Methodists, founded their own freestanding religious bodies through secession from older Dissenting denominational structures. The clergy who seceded from the Church of Scotland established a whole infrastructure for the Free Church, including schools and other voluntary agencies, as well as distinct congregations. Although such groups differed in size and influence, most managed to sustain themselves for several decades.

Newman had actually long pondered this world of voluntary religious entrepreneurship. He had demonstrated such capacities when serving St. Clement's, where he had revived a congregation and raised money for capital repairs. Whately's anonymous *Letters on the Church* of 1826, advocating ecclesiastical independence from the state, had deeply influenced Newman, as it had Froude.[44] Newman had witnessed Bulteel's success, as well as his brother's association with the quickly independent Darbyite Plymouth Brethren. He was familiar, if not deeply so, with the experience of the Episcopal Church in the United States, operating in the arena of evangelical religion. He and Froude had considered how under the possible impact of Dissenting political persecution the Church of England and its clergy might survive and function as an independent denomination competing in the English religious marketplace. When, however, the anticipated anticlerical political disaster and property confiscation requiring their imagined new organization for the English Church failed to occur, Froude and Newman decided to carry out their antievangelical strategy within the established Church of England. Competition for place and recognition inside the establishment replaced the projected competition within a religious marketplace lacking an established religion. This situation eventually drew the Tractarians away from defending episcopal power and toward passive resistance to it and finally to Newman's institutionalization of a quasi-independent Church Catholic at Littlemore.

Between late 1841 and 1845 Newman and his coterie might have attempted to form a distinct, independent religious group, as many observers thought they had in fact done. Yet Newman and the other advanced Tractarians did not form such a distinct separatist group even at Littlemore, which remained to the end a shifting community. Their restraint arose from genuine apprehension over schism, but there existed a deeper cause as well. The advanced Tractarians had rejected not only evangelical theology but also the evangelical commercialization of religion—a mistake that Wiseman's and later Manning's resurgent Roman Catholicism did not make. The Tractarians conflated the message and methods of evangelicalism and consequently rejected the very commercial tactics that might have attracted more people to their cause and made their enterprise institutionally viable either inside or outside the English Church.

First, whereas the Tractarians devoted enormous energy to publishing and polemical controversy, they turned almost none to the kind of institution building that characterized both their establishment and Dissenting evangelical opponents. Their initial goal had been to protect the role of Catholic clerics within the English Church, "fighting the battle of a priesthood," according to the *Edinburgh Review*.[45] They did not attempt to organize the laity, to raise up Catholic congregations, or even to demonstrate particular pastoral and spiritual concern for the needs of the laity. In fact, except for the early tracts themselves, they championed religious products largely inaccessible to the laity or inaccessible except through an apostolic priesthood. The Tractarians urged the wisdom of the Book of Common Prayer, the Homilies, works by earlier divines of the English Church, and the writings of the Church Fathers, none of which was so readily available as the Bible published and distributed by the Bible Society or so accessible as the scores of evangelical biblical commentaries. Even the Book of Common Prayer, as Ward came to recognize, was not oriented to the religious consumer but rather to the priest who conducted the liturgy. The Homilies similarly held few attractions for the lay reader and enjoyed a modest circulation. The problems of language and availability of the texts, as well as the inherent difficulty of the works themselves, rendered access to the Fathers and earlier English divines virtually impossible.

Newman himself was not even sure that works of genuinely Catholic devotion could be supplied to laity in the immediate future. The experiment of ascetic devotion must in his view realize itself before such a devotional literature developed. As he once told Miss Holmes, "Our literature is essentially Protestant—All our great writers are such—all the strength, richness, and elegance of the language is devoted to the maintenance of Protestantism. . . . As to supplying our great deficiency in devotional works, it is a matter of time, it cannot be done by the stroke of a pen. When we have ascetical livers, we shall have devotional writers."[46] In all these respects, while Tractarian leaders insisted on the insufficient breadth of devotional practice in the Church of England, they made few efforts to provide necessary materials. Ironically, Newman's sermons, a typically evangelical vehicle, remained the chief Tractarian publication for wider audiences.

The Tractarians also refused to avail themselves of one of the cleverest devices used by evangelicals in the Church of England—the purchase of livings. The Simeon Trust had acquired livings and then placed evangelical clergy in them. It is not certain why the Tractarians did not follow this course of action. It may simply have been lack of funds or the inability to raise them. Several people, Charles Marriott being the most important, had supplied money to purchase the land at Littlemore. Pusey had significant income, and contributed generously to the building of new churches in London and to the construction of St. Saviour's Church in Leeds. He and others believed that what the English Church most required were new churches in the cities and may thus have refrained from the Simeon Trust example for that reason. The real problem after the bishops' hostility to *Tract 90* may have been assuring any ongoing supply of ordained clergy of strongly Tractarian persuasion. But such would not have been the case earlier. Money did appear in the 1840s for the financing of the small sisterhoods, and ironically the absence of the ordination of women removed Catholic subscription as an issue for recruitment of sisters.

What the Tractarians did supply for the religious marketplace were publications extensively and articulately criticizing evangelical Protestantism. In a remark describing Newman but applicable to the entire Tractarian Movement, Pusey once told Hook, "The battle against rationalism and heresy is his special calling." But beyond that assault on the Protestant the

Tractarians failed to supply a clear, consistent Catholic message in the religious marketplace. Henry Rogers, writing in late 1844 for the *Edinburgh Review*, pointed to the "instable equilibrium" that characterized Tractarian Catholicism. He observed that the pursuit of Catholic unity had in actuality resulted in "the widest diversities of opinion" and "the amplest scope" for "the exercise of private judgment, in determining what is that only system of Catholic truth—which always and for ever excludes it!" While rejecting private judgment, the Oxford writers could inevitably trust nothing else to interpret the vast and varied patristic sources, their appeal to which had "only increased the difficulty which they affirm so insurmountable to the Bible Protestant." Unable even to agree about which centuries constituted antiquity or which elements in antiquity were authoritative for the faith, its Tractarian expositors found that "that limit of Catholicity still lies beyond them." Furthermore, whereas Roman Catholics could point to a visible Church and Protestants to an invisible one, the Catholics in the Church of England could point to no visible or invisible manifestation of the Church Catholic. Rogers asked, "Can we wonder that many of the disciples of this school feel compelled to go a little further in search of that *one invisible church* which they are persuaded exists, and sigh for that unity which they have as yet found only in name?" In 1845 the *Morning Herald* rather more impatiently complained that for the Tractarians "such expressions" as " '*the Church,*' 'Catholic principles,' the 'decrees of the Catholic Church,' " had "no distinct significance, and mean nothing," but appeared instead to be "mere moonshine and vapour when taken in the sense in which these Romanisers use them."[47] In reality, no two Tractarian writers really agreed on what they meant by the Church Catholic or its faith and practice.

Finally, the Tractarians encountered enormous difficulty in advancing their effort because their tactics and rhetoric so deeply offended the values and expectations associated with truthfulness in personal and public social engagements. In the *Apologia* Newman transformed that issue into the question of the truthfulness of Roman Catholic clergy in polemical situations. That, however, was not the real question in the mid-1840s. Within early-Victorian intellectual and religious life there were many examples of both men and women abandoning religious orthodoxy on the grounds of pursuing honest convictions of conscience and often paying a high price for those convictions. The Tractarians, by contrast, appeared to spurn the religious orthodoxy of the establishment while enjoying its clerical livings, college fellowships, university professorships, and other sources of ecclesiastical income.[48] The moral doubt that hovered as a dark cloud over the Tractarians made significant recruitment after 1841 exceedingly difficult.

Each of these elements of the rejection of the commercialization of religion worked against Newman's forming a distinct religious group or congregation separate from the English Church. Nonetheless, he did assume the mantle of the Anglo-Catholic Elijah of Littlemore, where a religion of the private sphere provided a direct, if modest, institutional alternative to the evangelical religion of the public sphere. Newman's ministry and pursuit of monastic devotion at Littlemore certainly lay outside the acknowledged latitude of the English Church. Yet the local bishop, on the instructions of the Archbishop of Canterbury, left him alone; and the university authorities could not really directly touch him. He had realized a situation in no small measure resembling Lady Huntingdon's household and college for Methodist clergy, clergy who it should be noted were as distinct from the mainstream of Methodism as Tractarianism was from that of the traditional high church. In all these respects Newman displayed a talent for modest entrepreneurship and for defining a new monastic religious product that met a small, but real demand in the contemporary religious marketplace.

The difficulties for his experiment came from the growing rhetorical and devotional extravagance of his followers and their determination to take actions independent of his influence. For them the desire for Catholicism and Christian unity proved more urgent than for monasticism. For some time Newman implicitly promised that the foundation of *Tract 90*, his spiritual direction, participation in the *Lives of the English Saints*, and the community of Littlemore could satisfy both. But the Oakeley decision in the Court of Arches precipitated all the confusion and contradiction inherent in this situation. Had *Tract 90* been condemned by Convocation, Newman's position at Littlemore would have become more tenuous but, at least in his own mind, not impossible if that condemnation remained unconfirmed either by his own bishop or by a collective act of all the bishops. The Oakeley judgment, however, effectively put Littlemore out of business as an enclave of the Church Catholic standing on the edges of the established church.

That decision, despite Newman's private and Pusey's public notions to the contrary, undermined the survival in the religious marketplace of Tractarian Catholicism based on *Tract 90*, and every one knew it. For the second time an English court had disrupted Newman's life, this time telling him and his Catholic followers, as a different court had told his father before

him, that public contracts must be observed as courts prescribe.[49] Thereafter, the religious product that Newman offered at Littlemore, though not
exactly that of Oakeley or Ward, was sufficiently similar to be regarded as
having been declared on legal grounds theologically and ecclesiastically
defective. It was no longer really feasible for a clergyman to make his way in
the English Church while publicly declaring, on the basis of an argument
provided by Newman, that he held some or all distinctively Roman Catholic
doctrines and yet still properly conformed to the Articles. Persons who
hoped to have careers in the Church of England would no longer come to
Littlemore.

Of more immediate importance in the late summer and early autumn of
1845, once Newman's religious product had been ruled defective, he began
to lose his existing constituency at Littlemore and in the wider English
Church. Although Newman repeatedly stated that no departures for Rome
occurred until after the Hebdomadal censure of *Tract 90*, the major secessions from Littlemore, except for Lockhart's in 1843, came only after Oakeley's defeat in the Court of Arches.[50] If the Articles did, as the Court of
Arches had decreed, establish distinct boundaries between the English and
Roman communions, Catholic clerics and laity who wished to experience
elements of Roman Catholic faith and practice must either do so within the
confines of that church or, as both Bishop Blomfield and Francis Newman
had understood, formally separate from the English Church.

Although Newman rejected the secessionist course in part because of
genuine abhorrence of schism, his more important reason was his incapacity
by the autumn of 1845 to persuade his closest Littlemore followers to
remain with him outside both the Church of England and the Church of
Rome. By September 1845 Newman's followers understood that they would
have no place in the English Church and wanted Rome, not a separatist
Catholic conventicle. They sought the experience of a universal Catholicism, not Newman's ultimately parochial, self-constructed Catholicism.
Their desire for Christian unity, as well as the beckoning of friendly Roman
Catholic priests and bishops, the recognition of truly saintly figures in the
post-Reformation Roman Church, and in Ward's case the influence of his
wife, overcame whatever qualms they still entertained about unreformed
aspects of the Roman Church. They had been willing to reside at Littlemore
or elsewhere under Newman's spiritual direction as long as they could still
see themselves as a part of the Church Catholic that might eventually
receive recognition in the Church of England. They were not, however,
willing to dwell in a religious and ecclesiastical wilderness. After the Oake-

ley decision, Newman had lost his authority and personal influence. The Wards' early September conversions may well have precipitated the others, a possibility that would account for Newman's exceptionally hostile September 26 note to Ward, written about the time Dalgairns himself left Littlemore to be received. The dam had broken and no one would soon be left to reside with Newman at Littlemore. All his efforts to hold men in the English Church and thus under his edification had failed. Like his siblings and later Oriel colleagues, they were going their separate ways. On this occasion, with a change in the Oxford bishopric looming, Newman quickly *followed* his young friends, so as not to lose them.

Consequently, Newman's conversion in October 1845 represented a confession of abject failure to establish a stable conventicle of the Church Catholic. His conversion followed upon an act of private judgment whereby he recognized the collapse of the small but significant religious enterprise that he had been constructing for the past several years. He later presented these events, of course, as a collapse of conviction in a *via media*. But what actually collapsed under numerous weights in 1845 was his fragile network of personal social relationships sustained by Catholic aspirations. Within the world of contemporary Victorian religion, with its burgeoning new congregations, denominations, and independent ministries, Newman stood at that moment as a failed, discredited, untrustworthy religious businessman, finally putting himself into receivership. Or, as Francis Newman had predicted shortly before, John Henry Newman entered the Roman Church because "nothing *better* can be found."[51]

THE PATH TAKEN

In early October 1845 Newman might have chosen to remain a priest in the English Church. He might even have continued to collect his Oriel stipend. Or he might possibly have received from a sympathetic Catholic layman the kind of living about which he once allowed himself to fantasize to Miss Giberne and then have faded into the countryside, as eventually did his Oxford high-church nemesis William Palmer.[52] Newman might have put together a life of sorts in lay communion, as *The Times* advised upon first learning of his resignation of his fellowship. Newman's personal financial needs were modest; his books would have continued to sell at least for a significant transitional interim.

Even if the opportunity had been offered, however, Newman had no wish to dwell alone in a country parish or in the isolation of a lay vocation.

He was a man who wanted to live in the company of other men. The single most consistent emotional element in Newman's adult life was his sustained determination to dwell among other celibate males and outside the company of women. Newman, unlike the other Tractarian leaders, with the possible exception of the prematurely deceased Froude, had pursued Catholicism so that he might achieve and legitimate a monastic life. Monasticism was his experiment in living, as Catholicism was his experiment in ecclesiology, devotion, and theology, with Catholicism more often than not serving the goal of monasticism. It was the conflation and confusion of these two enterprises that produced his perplexing examples of personal self-delimitation, muddled so much of his experience in the Church of England, prevented him from undertaking a formal secessionist movement, and ultimately led him into the Roman Catholic communion.

Newman's dual personal aspirations, religiously to Catholicism and emotionally to monastic celibacy, had necessarily led him to challenge evangelical religion. The inner tensions leading to Newman's drive against evangelicalism may have originated psychologically in the religious instruction associated with his conversion following his father's first business failure. After urging the individual Christian to achieve a correct relationship with God through justification by faith, many of the evangelical works that Walter Mayers recommended to the young Newman or that informed his own mentoring portrayed the Christian's next duty as fulfilling family responsibilities and commercial honesty. Among these works, however, Newman also read Milner's evangelical history of Christianity, where he encountered in the early monasticism of the desert fathers a Christian alternative to Victorian domesticity. In ancient times pious Christian men dwelled in monastic settings without the pressures and disappointments Newman had just encountered in family and commercial relations.[53] About the same time Newman recalled becoming convinced that he should lead a single life, a conviction that took permanent hold of him in 1829 after several years of study in the ancient Church Fathers. His gradual liberation from evangelical religion was also a liberation from expectations of traditional domesticity that he articulated through the denunciation of feeling and the championing of an ascetic theology of Christian obedience.

Newman had lived primarily among men in his secondary school and at Trinity College, Oxford. From his election to the Oriel fellowship through his time at Littlemore, Newman managed to secure for himself a social setting in which he could dwell outside the company of women with celibate males, who at least for a time recognized in him that measure of leadership that he had failed to sustain in his family. Newman had one set of expectations from these relationships while his friends had another. Each effort saw him forging friendships that later often dissolved into either personal independence or marriage on the part of those men whom he wished to influence or edify. Throughout his years in the English Church, Newman consistently expressed anger or disapproval over friends, especially clerical friends, who married and who like his own brothers established lives independent of his influence and direction, thus breaking the circle of male friendship he had constructed for himself. The most notable exception was J. W. Bowden, who married, whose wife Newman admired, and who was himself not a clergyman.

During his first decade in Oriel, Newman achieved positions of acknowledged respect and leadership within the college community. His opposition of 1829 to Peel's reelection, however, overturned many of those college relationships, as had recent marriages by fellows, such as Hawkins and Pusey, with whom he had been on close terms. This was also the moment when he fully committed himself to a single life. Shortly thereafter, seeking a new circle of male friends, he had organized the dining club of Oxford colleagues, who gathered for simple meals. Then, along with other Oriel tutors, he began the experimental tutorial program that would have brought him into a dominant relationship with a few selected male students. Hawkins closed down the experiment once he discovered it. After undertaking *The Arians of the Fourth Century*, Newman began to imagine forging an apostolic brotherhood to defend the church against evangelical enemies within and without.

At that point in mid-1833 his twin goals of Catholicism and monasticism publicly emerged simultaneously, the former in *Tracts for the Times* and the latter in the "Letters on the Church of the Fathers." In that *British Magazine* series he outlined a role for monasteries in protecting Catholic truth in a climate of ecclesiastical heresy, which in the tracts, his sermons, and his exactly contemporary book on the Arians he directly associated with contemporary evangelical religion. Monasteries provided models for preserving religious truth in difficult times either if the establishment collapsed or if it survived penetrated by heretical religious forces. That vision of monasticism at once provided Newman with a religious vocation while satisfying his deepest personal social yearnings. The necessity of saving the Catholic faith from evangelical heresy justified his determination to live among celibate men. At every major turning point, his desire for life in a monastic setting, wherein interaction with women was strictly excluded and his leadership acknowledged, more than any other single factor explains why he risked and endured all of the personal pain and public abuse that he encountered first in the English Church and then on the occasion of his conversion to Rome.

The publication of the tracts sustained for a time around Newman a group of male supporters who followed him as their leader. But within a couple of years several of these men, including both Henry Wilberforce and John Keble, married and in Newman's mind compromised their devotion to the Catholic cause. As the brotherhood involved in the tracts dissolved, Newman devised new ways to draw other men, generally younger than he, to his side. These included nurturing the Theological Society, conducting the weekly soirées in his Oriel rooms, hearing personal, private confessions, securing the house of study near St. Aldate's, and later establishing the fund to support study among men who had completed their degrees but not gained fellowships. Ironically, as Newmania blossomed in Oxford, he acquired far more influence than the defunct tutorial program would have provided him.

Newman's theology solidified these relationships. Publicly and privately he reduced evangelical religion based on subjective religious experience and biblical authority to a meaningless spiritual chaos. He conflated evangelical religion and historic Protestantism, thus closing off the latter as a path to spiritual solace. In the process he raised Catholic aspirations to a fever pitch among the young and among a few men of his own generation. Simultaneously, with his powerful anti-Roman polemic, especially in *The Prophetical Office of the Church*, he denied those same men access to Roman Catholicism and thus left himself, his theology, and devotional life as the only vehicles that could fulfill Catholic feelings. The more Newman made Rome impermissible, the more important he became as the authority explaining what course their religious lives must take. Monasticism lay at the center of his concern. During the mid-1830s Blanco White observed that Newman's and Keble's thinking could lead to monasticism, and about the same time Faber wrote privately of Newman's followers as Christian Essenes.[54] By 1839 Newman secretly began establishing his monastery at Littlemore and in 1840 published a book-length edition of *The Church of the Fathers*. He saw such a monastery functioning to protect religious truth as had the desert fathers and resembling early Methodist chapels, which in theory and organization supplemented rather than supplanted the activities of the local parish church. He presumably anticipated that men from his personal coterie would eventually join him at Littlemore, again outside the company and influence of women. Much of this thinking was hesitant and even secret through 1840.

But at just that point Newman suddenly confronted a more dynamic and disruptive situation than he had anticipated or previously experienced. Several of his profoundly antievangelical Catholic male friends found themselves deeply attracted to the devotion and liturgy of the Roman Catholic Church, and others believed they could not in good Catholic conscience subscribe to the 39 Articles. Newman had indoctrinated them too well with his antipathy for evangelicalism and his aspiration to the Catholic. If, however, in pursuit of the Catholic they departed the English Church, Newman would again find himself abandoned and his most recent effort at devising the possibility of a life for himself in a celibate male community a failure. To forestall that eventuality, he published *Tract 90*, hoping to persuade those of tender Catholic conscience that they could pursue various controversial elements of Catholicism, including hostility to the English Reformation and affection for Roman Catholic devotion, while at the same time still conscientiously remaining or becoming clergy in the English Church. If through the resolution of his negotiations with Bishop Bagot, he could convince those advanced, restless Catholics that the English Church implicitly tolerated their position, he hoped his followers might find religious stability. Then the storm of the hostile episcopal charges struck, and the power of evangelicalism manifested itself still further in the Jerusalem bishopric, his own reaction to which generated a feverish sense of impending evangelical heretical hegemony. A monastery functioning in the midst of that engulfing heresy led by himself after the model of Elijah became Newman's immediate vehicle to retain men both in the English Church and within his own orbit. After 1841 the protection of Catholic truth and his personal monastic imperative became self-reinforcing. Littlemore furnished an environment in which Newman, replicating the failed Oriel tutorial revision, could have a close, instructional relationship to unmarried men of Catholic outlook. In that respect though unfailingly hostile, the *Christian Observer* had not been incorrect to observe "the monastic system" to be "the key-stone of the Tractarian fabric" as it denounced the Tractarians for advocating "the spiritual meritoriousness of an unmarried life," "the meritorious sanctity of celibacy," and "the iron yoke of monastic ascetics."[55]

Newman's personal softening of mind and spirit in regard to the Roman Catholic Church mirrored and followed that of his coterie. Their attraction to Rome and Roman Catholic devotion persistently outran his, and he repeatedly needed to take steps to prove that he was still with them, the publication of *Tract 90* being the most conspicuous of these. Moreover, he was willing to sacrifice older friendships, such as that of Frederic Rogers, over his accommodating advanced Catholic sentiments in order to secure new friends and admirers whom he hoped would stay with him. This situation explains at least in part his disowning in early 1843 certain of his anti-Roman statements while yet remaining in the Church of England, an act that would have indicated to his followers that his sensibilities were not necessarily incompatible with theirs. At the same time he strongly resisted the introduction of formal Roman Catholic devotionals, the printing of the Breviary, and the invocation of saints and of the Virgin Mary lest those practices lead men further Romeward or toward religious lives and authorities independent of his. Newman clearly understood that once men were received into the Roman Church, they would leave his influence, his monastic community would dissolve, and the vocation he had established for himself would collapse. He did nothing to encourage these dire eventualities. His conversations with them in early 1845 about their all converting together may have been just that, conversations to bond with them, to postpone action, and to send signals to the English Church, which he may have still hoped would respond by accommodating the religious needs of his Catholic community. Certainly as late as the summer of 1845 some admirers, such as Richard Westmacott, believed that Newman remained "one of the Reformers of our Anglican Church—& one of those whose learning, piety, and good intentions must eventually have such influence in restoring a right feeling both on to faith & proper observances."[56] Newman had long used the threat or prospect of conversions to press the establishment toward change and accommodation.

The desire to preserve his life in a community of celibate males that excluded any significant relationships with women also helps to explain Newman's separation from Keble and Pusey. Although in principle both of the latter approved the idea of monasteries for both men and women, neither personally wished to dwell in one. Keble devoted his life to an invalid wife, whom he appears to have deeply loved, while enjoying the comforts of a well-paid living and the pleasures of country life. Though clearly a person of deep spirituality, Keble was no ascetic. Pusey's household after his wife's death may have amounted to an individual monk's cell, but it was not a monastery. He did not seek community, the accolades (as opposed to the deference) of younger men, or the abandonment of his professorship. This difference accounted for the difficulties he and Newman confronted in 1841 and beyond when it became clear that Newman had a closer relationship with the *British Critic* circle than with Pusey and was allowing himself to be influenced by the radical Catholics. Pusey had no intention of placing himself under the real direction of anyone else and most certainly not men younger than himself. Moreover, from the late 1840s onward, Pusey was actively involved with Anglican nuns and became deeply involved, some thought too deeply, as director of their devotional lives.[57]

The primary, though by no means uncomplicated, religious goal of Pusey and Keble was the pursuit of Catholicism, spiritual, ecclesiastical, and possibly ascetic, but not primarily monastic. Newman's goal was that of a Catholic religious life pursued in a setting of celibate Christian males. By the late summer of 1845, as the Littlemore community disintegrated around him, that monastic alternative was no longer possible to Newman under any foreseeable circumstances within the Church of England or for that matter through a separatist congregation, now that his followers were deserting him for Rome. Quite simply put, Newman became a Roman Catholic so that he could continue to remain a monk, and if possible, a monk surrounded by his Littlemore male friends. It was more nearly Newman's personal social salvation than his eternal salvation that lay in the Roman Catholic Church in October 1845. Just a month after entering the Roman Church, he told Dalgairns, "The problem is, how to get education and orders (for those who wish it) yet to keep together." On the same day, he rather more forthrightly told Miss Giberne that despite the Oscott building that Bishop Wiseman offered him being "dismally ugly," it would nonetheless "bring with it this advantage, which is a great temptation—that my friends could get educated for orders, etc. without separating from each other or from me." Newman's resolve in this matter caused Hope, who was advising him on his new position in the Roman Catholic Church, to warn about "the risk of giving a party aspect to your position."[58]

The concept of development of Christian doctrine, which Newman pondered so extensively between 1843 and 1845, was also not wholly unrelated to his monastic aspirations. His earliest exploration of the monastic ideal involved the desert fathers living in isolation, but as he sought to surround himself with sympathetic friends, he embraced the medieval model of collective monastic communities. As long as he could see doctrine and devotion developing, he could justify monasticism itself as a development rather than as a corruption of the early faith or as an institution prone to corruption. No single act of the English Reformation had involved so much violence as the confiscation of the monasteries. Since that time, the

13. During the middle of the twentieth century the buildings of Littlemore were restored to the conditions of Newman's day. The structures now house the International Centre of Newman Friends and the Society of The Work. (Reproduced with the kind permission of The International Centre of Newman Friends, c/o The Society of The Work, Littlemore.)

accusations of corruption and immorality used to justify that destruction had continued to mar popular thinking about monasteries and monastic celibacy. A theology of development sustained Newman's efforts to resurrect monasteries, which as early as 1841 he had described as the "most sacred and heavenly abodes" in the Roman Catholic Church.[59]

Newman recognized that monasticism flew in the face of contemporary assumptions about marriage and the family. In the *Essay on Development* he confessed that monastic ideals "strangely grate upon the feelings of an age, which is formed on principles of which marriage is the centre." In his championing of monastic celibacy, Newman rarely lost the opportunity to criticize traditional domestic settings, which he associated with personal turmoil and disapproval. While surveying the array of fourth-century Christian sects advancing one heresy or another, he commented, "The Church is a kingdom; a heresy is a family rather than a kingdom: and as a family continually divides and sends out branches, founding new houses, and propagating itself in colonies, each of them as independent as its original head, so was it with heresy." Newman might well have been describing his own family, in which each of the brothers departed the original moderate family religion—Charles to Owenism; Francis to evangelicalism, then to Darbyism, and finally Unitarianism; and John to evangelicalism, then to Catholicism, and finally to Roman Catholicism. As events finally determined, the theory of development justified Newman's personal departure from Victorian domesticity and the establishment of a different kind of monastic family at the Birmingham Oratory wherein he could, he hoped, dwell with more nearly orthodox, docile siblings. Newman actually once equated the life of an oratory with that of a family. In 1849, arguing to Faber for the division of the oratorians into distinct London and Birmingham houses, he wrote, "The Oratory is a family—6 children form a fair fire side— I would allow 11 including novices which makes 12 with the Padre."[60] It is not insignificant that there had been six children in Newman's own family. In the oratory, however, unlike in his own family he would preside as the paterfamilias.

There exists another possible relationship between Newman's ongoing issues with his family and his conversion to Roman Catholicism, as well as his embrace of the theory of development. The exploration of this issue, though both speculative and tendentious, is nonetheless invited by the documents. The theory of development permitted Newman to include within his monastic family setting the one sibling with whom he appears to have enjoyed an uncomplicated, unproblematic, loving relationship: his youngest sister Mary, who had died on January 5, 1828, before the age of twenty. As we have seen, there was no one else in his life whom he appears to have loved so deeply or lastingly as this sister. In 1828, a few weeks after her sudden death, he had confided in his journal, "For some time I had a presentiment more or less strong that we should lose dear Mary. I was led to this by her extreme loveliness of character, and by the circumstance of my great affection for her. I thought I loved her too well, and hardly ever dared to take my full swing of enjoyment in her dear society. It must have been in October 1826 that, as I looked at her, beautiful as she was, I seemed to say to myself, not so much 'will you live?' as 'how strange that you are still alive!' " It is almost as if Newman was distancing himself from his intense feelings for his young sister by imagining her death and thus her removal as an object stimulating those feelings. In 1833, as his own near-fatal illness came upon him in Sicily, Newman "fell to tears thinking of dear Mary" as he looked over the movingly beautiful landscape. As years passed, he recalled the anniversary of her death and mentioned his mother's grief when sympathizing with parents who had themselves lost children. In 1860 he wrote Jemima, "Mary would be above 50, had she lived. How wonderful it seems when the only picture the mind can form of her is of a young girl!" The next year, when visiting Brighton, he described it to Miss Holmes as the place where "in 1828, I had one of my greatest losses—my sister, cut off in a few hours, lies in the cemetery attached to the Old Church." Six years later he again wrote Jemima, "To think that Mary would now be in her 59th year, if now alive! But she, taken away young, looks always young to us, and would be so, though her birthday were a hundred years off. And to think that that picture, vivid as it is to us, is now confined to the imaginations of half a dozen persons." A decade later in a private marginal note he commented, "I have as vivid feelings of love, tenderness, and sorrow, when I think of dear Mary, as ever I had since her death." In 1878 he confessed to Pusey, "For myself, I do not exaggerate when I say that I have not even now got over my Sister's death." In his eighties Newman told Miss Giberne, who had been visiting the Newman home at the time of Mary's sudden demise in 1828, "she is as fresh in my memory and as dear to my heart, as if it were yesterday; and often I cannot mention her name without tears coming into my eyes."[61] With the possible exception of events that he associated with the feast of the Virgin Mary's Purification, which included both the founding of Oriel and the establishment of the Oratory in England, there was no anniversary that Newman noted so frequently over the years as that of the death of his sister Mary.

Some of the most eloquent passages of the *Essay on Development* relate to the development of veneration of the Virgin, passages that aroused considerable private and public criticism at the time. Although in both his private correspondence of the 1840s and in the *Apologia* he indicated long-standing dislike of excessive or Italianate Marian devotion, in the *Essay* he treated the more general subject of Mary with enormous warmth. Although these passages signaled to anyone who might have doubted that Newman had fully committed himself to the Roman Church, at the same time his manner of discussing Mary served other ends, which even he did not recognize.[62]

Newman was determined to demonstrate that Marian veneration did not confuse worship of the Creator and the creature. To that end, he explained that the Arians had assigned one high quality after another to Christ without confessing "Him to be the One, Everlasting, Infinite, Supreme Being." The great achievement of the Nicene Council had been to recognize "the eventful principle, that, while we believe and profess any being to be a creature, such a being is really no God to us, though honoured by us with whatever high titles and with whatever homage." Those who venerated Mary at most accorded her no higher position than that which the Arians had accorded Christ. Consequently, according to the principles of Nicea, Roman Catholics who venerated Mary did not deify her or raise her to the level of God or confuse her status with that of her son. Therefore, Newman declared, "The votaries of Mary do not exceed the true faith, unless the blasphemers of her Son came up to it. The Church of Rome is not idolatrous, unless Arianism is orthodoxy." According to Newman, mistaking the veneration of Mary for the worship of God originated in an inadequate or heretical Christology, and not surprisingly, "If those who never rise higher in their notions of our Lord's Divinity than to consider Him a man singularly inhabited by a Divine Presence, that is, a Catholic Saint,—if such men should recognize, in the honour paid by the Church to St Mary, the very honour which, and which alone, they offer to her Eternal Son." Modern writers who decried Marian devotion, he asserted, were unconscious Socinians, Sabellians, and Nestorians, who had never in the first place entertained a proper understanding of Christ's divinity and had thus confused Roman Catholic Marian devotion with their own inadequate views of Christ. In a later passage, Newman caustically observed, "Carnal minds will ever create a carnal worship for themselves; and to forbid them the service of the Saints will have no tendency to teach them the worship of God."[63]

The important discussion of Marian devotion illustrates a pattern running throughout the *Essay on Development*. Repeatedly Newman argued that Roman Catholic doctrines, practices, and devotions, *if properly interpreted,* are not the corruptions that both high churchmen and evangelical Protestants claimed them to be. For example, for Newman Christianity is not purer at its origins but rather in its later developments. Corruptions are not corruptions but rather developments if they persist in particular ways. The church was not harmed by embracing pagan practices or ideas but had transformed them to its own higher purpose. Heresy could foretell later true doctrine. Invocations of saints and the veneration of Mary do not confuse the priority of worship to be accorded Christ.

It seems possible that if Newman could convince himself that Marian devotion did not obscure the distinction between Creator and creature, then his intense affection for his own sister Mary had not challenged the decencies of family relationships. He told St. John in 1864, "It is 36 years yesterday, since I lost my dear Sister, and shortly after, on my return home, I slept in her bed—and I thought what a sweet saint had died there." Whatever the depths of his love for her, Newman had not confused his sister with a wife or with a woman with whom he might have sexual relations. (It is perhaps not insignificant that within the English Church the Virgin Mary was usually referred to as St. Mary.) Indeed, Newman's sustained criticism of what he regarded as excessive Marian devotion or Marian devotion carried out in bad taste may have been another way in which he protested that his love for his own sister Mary had not exceeded the boundaries of good taste and morality. It is also possible that his determination in the early 1840s to forbid his fervent followers, such as Faber, from invoking Mary was the product not only of Newman's determination to prevent men from slipping over to Roman Catholicism but also at a deeper personal level to withhold and protect his sister Mary from becoming an object of their unbridled affections. The same may have been true of the later tentativeness of his Marian devotion as a Roman Catholic tied to his warm welcome of the papal enunciation of the doctrine of the Immaculate Conception.

Throughout writing the *Essay on Development* in 1845, Newman confronted serious family as well as religious problems, and only the now long-dead Mary remained an easy object of his familial affection. Charles suddenly reappeared with his usual financial problems and mental instability. Harriett remained unremittingly hostile. Jemima disapproved his direction, and her husband refused to print the book for Newman. Francis gave him unwanted advice. John's imminent departure for Rome required a rearrangement of family financial support for their Aunt Elizabeth. Writing at that time while not yet instructed in the Roman Catholic faith, Newman may have felt that in his escape from an English Church fallen into evangelical heresy he could also remove the beloved Mary from the turmoil and heresy of the Newman family and carry her to the safety of the monarchy of the Roman Catholic Church. There her virginity, which may have mystified and attracted him during her life, as virginity and celibacy with Newman's full approval contemporaneously so stirred his authors of the *Lives of the English Saints*, stood protected and transformed from an object of temptation into one of safe devotion. Only Mary among his siblings had never caused him trouble, offered criticism, expressed disapproval, or become old enough to achieve personal independence. Isaac Williams many years later regretted that Newman "partly from circumstances and partly under the false guise of mortification" had "stifled . . . his domestic affections," thus increasing his "constitutional restlessness of intellect." By contrast, he observed that Newman "never seemed to me, so saintlike and high in his character as when he was with his mother and sisters," when "the softness and repose of his character . . . came out, and so corrected that restless intellect to which he has been a prey."[64] As he wrote the *Essay on Development* during 1845 while confronting so much hostility and criticism from his surviving siblings, Newman at some level may have yearned for the presence of his sister Mary as possibly leading to such intellectual repose which he claimed to have achieved in the Roman Catholic Church.

As already acknowledged, these comments are obviously speculative and tendentious, but a fascination with the Virgin Mary marked Newman from his early adulthood. Oriel College, where he had found a home after his family's financial collapse, had been dedicated to Mary. As early as the mid-1820s he had a print of a painting of the Madonna by Correggio on the walls of his Oriel rooms. He soon became Vicar of the Church of St. Mary the Virgin. In 1840, regarding a book of prayers he used at Littlemore written by two women, each named Mary, he had written to Wilberforce, "I think all nice persons are called Mary." Two of his closest female correspondents, Miss Giberne and Miss Holmes were named Mary, and both, like his sister of the same name, remained unmarried and generally received his advice and instruction docilely. In 1841 he accepted a gift of an image of the Madonna from the young John Walter, then an ardent advanced Tractarian Catholic. In his first major public statement on development, the sermon of February 1843, Newman portrayed the Virgin as a model of faith. His defense of Marian devotion through the concept of development allowed him to sustain in his own mind a relationship with Mary in the Littlemore setting after he was no longer vicar of a church named for her. The medal he placed around his neck on August 22, 1845, was of a design revealed by the Virgin in 1830 to Sister Catherine Labouré in Paris. Perhaps most telling, when on November 1, 1845, Newman was confirmed as a Roman Catholic, thus invaliding his priestly orders in the English Church that had so deeply defined his being, he took the name of Mary, thus establishing a link between his new life and his beloved deceased sister. When Newman and his Littlemore friends moved to Oscott, they renamed the building they inhabited *Maryvale*. In July 1846 Newman wrote to Dalgairns about having "sketched out the faint outlines of a community under the patronage of St Mary . . . with the object of 1st adoring, 2nd defending the *Mysteries* of Faith." In late 1848 Newman visited Loreto and later reported to Henry Wilberforce, "We went there to get the Blessed Virgin's blessing on us. I have ever been under her shadow, if I may say it. My College was St. Mary's, and my Church; and when I went to Littlemore, there, by my own previous disposition, our Blessed Lady was waiting for me. Nor did she do nothing for me in that low habitation, of which I always think with pleasure."[65] That he did not, as he insisted, while in the Church of England invoke Mary does not detract from his long-standing interest in both the name and person of the mother of Christ.

Moreover, not insignificantly in the *Essay on Development*, following his refutation of the usual Protestant condemnation of Marian veneration for being equivalent to the worship of God, Newman discussed penance, purgatory, and the monastic rule as similar developments. In this sense, Newman moved from the veneration of the Virgin to a consideration of doctrines and practices meant to address sinfulness. He insisted on the necessity for Catholic monastic orders to return to a greater observance of penance. Of purgatory Newman wrote, "For thus the sins of youth are turned to account by the profitable penance of manhood; and terrors which the philosopher scorns in the individual, become the benefactors and earn the gratitude of nations."[66] This statement recalls his remarks of several years earlier that celibacy could serve as a penance for some earlier unspecified sin in a person's life. He had himself permanently determined to lead a celibate life about a year after Mary's death and only a few months after indications of intense grief ceased to appear in his letters. It is possible that in his mind he entertained a sense of sin over some thought or fantasy related to his deceased sister that required the asceticism he had initially espoused at Littlemore and now urged upon the Roman Catholic Church.

Once a part of the English Roman Catholic community, Newman could from the standpoint of the surrounding culture live unproblematically in a community of celibate males who venerated Mary. Most Victorians may have disliked monasticism, but they understood that within the context of Roman Catholicism it occupied a defined place. The Roman Catholic Newman, like the Anglican Newman, wanted such a life defined within an orderly, ascetic community of men, living self-consciously apart from women. While contemplating the possible formation of some kind of teaching or preaching order, he complained that Wiseman's Oscott was insufficiently monastic, describing it as "a place of dissipation" with "tribes of women, and hosts of visitors." Newman appears to have had little but contempt for the religious proclivities of women independent of firm spiritual direction, speculating to J. M. Capes in 1850 that should the Church of England finally collapse, "Infidelity would take possession of the bulk of the men, and the women, so they had something to worship, would not care whether it was an unknown tongue, or a book of Mormon, or a pudding sleeve gown."[67]

By contrast, when Newman found himself in the company of celibate priests, he experienced contentment. After recounting his visiting Roman churches in late 1846 with Ambrose St. John, he told Henry Wilberforce, "I was happy at Oriel, happier at Littlemore, as happy or happier still at Maryvale—and happiest here."[68] In papal Rome and later in the Birmingham Oratory, Newman found settings where without the necessity for sophistic arguments he could live unproblematically with other celibate males. By establishing himself and certain of his friends as oratorians in the Roman Catholic Church, Newman achieved several related goals. The oratorian rules of St. Philip Neri, as Newman understood them from 1847 onward, made him directly answerable to no local ecclesiastical superior, required him to take no monastic vows, including that of poverty, but strictly excluded him from certain pastoral relationships with women.

Newman was prepared to permit no breach of the all-male community that he had thus created for himself. In the autumn of 1855 a quarrel erupted between the Birmingham and London Oratories, ultimately resulting in their separation. Although numerous previous tensions had existed between the two houses, the issue that brought matters to a head was the determination of Frederick Faber, head of the London house, and the other London fathers to hear the confessions of nuns. Dalgairns, then one of the Birmingham fathers, had already independently begun to hear such confessions and urged the Birmingham Oratory to follow the London example. Newman believed that the London house had wrongly represented the situation in Rome and was violating St. Philip's oratorian rule, which as

early as 1847 Newman had told Bishop Wiseman made "impossible" oratorians undertaking "the spiritual care of the Sisters of Mercy." In 1855
Newman wrote to Ambrose St. John, "The absence of the possible care of
Nuns may in particular cases be the turning point of an individual being
drawn to the Oratory." A few months later he told Richard Stanton, "Our
Rule is our vocation, as far as any thing external can be so called. . . . To
touch a Rule, is to unsettle vocations; to create suspicions about its stability,
is to weaken the hope, which those who have embraced it humbly entertain
of their own perseverance." Although Newman contested the dispute in
terms of process and faithfulness to the oratorian rule, what was at issue was
whether the fathers of his oratory would undertake a confessional relationship with religious women. Newman would have none of it, declaring "that
the spirit of Father Faber's house is different from that of our own."[69] With
this dispute Dalgairns, the first of Newman's earlier coterie to reside at
Littlemore, departed Birmingham for London, and another of Newman's
friendships finally shattered over a relationship with women.

That wonderful valedictory in the *Apologia* concealed, however, as much
Furthermore, within the Roman Church Newman could and did ar-
range and rearrange his monastic family until eventually, after no little conflict, he found fellow oratorians with whom he wished to live and who would
accord him the superior position as both a brother and father that he had so
long desired. Near the close of the *Apologia Pro Vita Sua* Newman wrote
movingly, lovingly, if with characteristic self-referentiality, of his brother
priests in the Birmingham Oratory, describing them as those "who have
been so faithful to me; who have been so sensitive to my needs; who have
been so indulgent to my failings; who have carried me through so many
trials; who have grudged no sacrifice, if I asked for it; who have been so
cheerful under discouragements of my causing; who have done so many
good works, and let me have the credit of them;—with whom I have lived so
long, with whom I hope to die."[70] It is significant that Newman closed the
Apologia, which he insisted constituted a history of his religious opinions,
not with a theological discussion but with this meditation on his monastic
family community within which he played the dominant role and received
the kind of support he wished had been his in his own family.

That wonderful valedictory in the *Apologia* concealed, however, as much
as it revealed. Six years earlier, in 1858, Isaac Williams, having heard a report of Newman's life in the oratory, privately commented, "Bishop Forbes
was mentioning that a friend of his had been lately with Newman at the
Oratory at Egbaston, and was giving a curious account of his life; but what
struck me was, how like Newman it all was, though the Bishop did not know

this; I mean Newman's living with persons younger than himself, a party reflecting his opinions, his constraint in public, his entirely throwing it off with friends in private afterwards."[71] As was so often the case, Williams evinced shrewd insight into Newman's personality. In that closing passage of the *Apologia* Newman had listed by name his six "dearest brothers," the priests of the Birmingham Oratory, each of whom was from thirteen to thirty-six years younger than himself. Although three of them could boast modest publications, not one of his brother priests was a person of any outstanding ability or possessed the capacity to challenge Newman as even a near equal. None of them could prove to be another Charles or Francis. And in the midst of that quiescent oratory brotherhood, as Bishop Ullathorne once wrote to assure Newman's Roman Catholic detractors, stood a statue of the Blessed Virgin Mary.

Newman's ambition for a monastic life defined largely on his own terms accounts for both his entrance into the Roman Catholic Church in the autumn of 1845 and for the self-delimitation that marked so much of the rest of his personal and religious behavior. The perplexingly narrow focus of the *Essay on Development*, which defended only a limited Catholic vision rather than one of expansive Catholic reform, arose from his personally self-contained religious goal. He embraced development for the purpose of justifying devotional practices that he either wished to embrace himself or that his coterie wished to undertake. He had not desired a wider religious mission. Newman persisted in the Monophysite explanation of his doubts about the English Church because those fostered the image of a religious world overwhelmed by heresy in which his monastery provided a possible refuge. Newman's monastic yearning explains why he chose Rome rather than founding his own schismatic church. By the time of his conversion those people willing to undertake a monastic life with him would do so only in a Roman Catholic setting, and he could thus remain with them only by entering that communion. Finally, Newman's determination for life in a monastery may explain his reticence as a Roman Catholic to become deeply involved in controversial issues, a stance that disappointed many of his later colleagues. Once he had achieved a male community as his personal household, nothing within English life or within the Roman Catholic Church would lead him to take any action that might require its sacrifice.

Because of the power of the monastic imperative in his life, the aspiration to the Catholic in Newman seems invariably to have served the personal and the parochial. That parochial focus was not the problem of Newman's thought but the very point of it, whether exploring development to defend

Littlemore or propounding an expansive liberal education for the sake of a tiny, yet unfounded, Irish Catholic university, or defending himself against Kingsley. His religious and theological genius realized first in the English Church and later in the Roman was his capacity to address local problems through a universalistic rhetoric that resonated far beyond his immediate and often narrow precincts. His life was filled with institutions, ambitions, philosophy, theology, conflicts, and friendships incommensurable to the enormous power of his mind and spirit. Newman's personal institutional world was always constrained: Ealing School, Trinity College, Oriel College, Littlemore, the Birmingham Oratory, and briefly the small Catholic University in Dublin. His gift was to transform his concerns and passions over the particular into a larger vision to which he virtually always appealed for his own limited polemical purposes, but which as the memories of the polemic faded left the universal categories of his message standing. Consequently, the power and scope of his prose allowed it to outlast the incidents of its origins, and through his gift for the English language he changed the religious and spiritual life of two major communions of the modern Christian world and beyond.

Historians and literary scholars normally think of the late Victorian agnostics, scientists, and critical biblical scholars as having reoriented nineteenth-century English Christianity by removing the older signposts. Yet Newman had actually been the first major Victorian Christian intellectual to do so. Through the publication of *The Arians of the Fourth Century*, *Lectures on the Prophetical Office of the Church*, and *An Essay on the Development of Christian Doctrine*, as well as *Tracts for the Times*, he steadily and uncompromisingly displaced the theological presuppositions and intellectual boundaries whereby clergy and engaged laity of the English Church defined and located themselves in Christendom and English society. In particular, he provided powerful critiques of both the Bible and natural theology as bases for the Christian faith. Moreover, Newman and other Tractarians called into question the cultural self-confidence once afforded all things Protestant. They did so less by appropriating elements of Roman Catholicism than by criticizing the spiritual adequacy and the theological doctrines first of evangelical religion and then of historic Protestantism, as well as the social values contemporaries derived therefrom. In this respect, the Tractarians created new cultural space in English life and society by thrusting back the evangelical hegemony. Their assault on the Protestant proved so effective because it originated within the core of the Church of England itself and not from outside that national institution.

Newman stands among the first cultural apostates, who established new foundations for a late Victorian English culture that would be pluralistic religiously, morally, and intellectually, rather than exclusively Protestant in character.[72] Conservative as he and his fellow Tractarians may have been politically, they nonetheless paradoxically demanded a pluralism in the English Church that mirrored the political pluralism they so disliked external to it. In the process, they helped to break the Protestant religious–cultural mold into which they had been born, and because that mold determined so much of English life and values beyond religion, they prepared the way for wider cultural transformations. In conducting his own experiment in monastic living and religious observance at Littlemore, Newman had challenged the domestic expectations of his society and the devotional expectations of his church. During his ministry in the English Church, though often clothing himself in a rhetoric of unctuous obedience, Newman had actually pursued the practice of "doing as one likes," later so deplored by his admirer Matthew Arnold. The restlessness of Newman's mind, the inability of his spirit to find a steady spiritual refuge, his family conflicts, his resentment of authority, his frustrated personal ambitions, and his determination to dwell with other celibate males had led him to challenge evangelicalism and all its works. Through that cultural as well as religious apostasy, Newman emerged as the first great, and perhaps the most enduring, Victorian skeptic. Nothing so bore witness to the long-term effectiveness of his enterprise as the transatlantic recognition of the elderly John Henry Cardinal Newman, celibate Roman Catholic priest of the Birmingham Oratory, as one of the foremost sage voices of late-Victorian intellectual as well as religious life. The earlier John Henry Newman, fellow of Oriel College and Vicar of the Church of St. Mary the Virgin in Oxford, could hardly have imagined such a development.

Abbreviations

NAMES

EBP—Edward Bouverie Pusey
FWN—Francis William Newman
HNM—Harriett Newman Mozley
JHN—John Henry Newman
JK—John Keble
JNM—Jemima Newman Mozley
RHF—Richard Hurrell Froude

FREQUENTLY CITED WORKS

Apologia—John Henry Newman. *Apologia Pro Vita Sua: Being a History of His Religious Opinions.* Ed. Martin J. Svaglic. Oxford: Clarendon, 1967.

Arians—John Henry Newman, *The Arians of the Fourth Century, Their Doctrine, Temper and Conduct, Chiefly as Exhibited in the Councils of the Church between A.D. 325, and A.D. 381.* London: J. G. and F. Rivington, 1833.

AW—Henry Tristram, ed. *John Henry Newman: Autobiographical Writings.* New York: Sheed and Ward, 1957.

Certain Difficulties—John Henry Newman. *Certain Difficulties Felt by Anglicans in Catholic Teaching Considered: In Twelve Lectures Addressed in 1850 to the Party of the Religious Movement of 1833.* Westminster, Md.: Christian Classics, 1969.

Corrs. with J K—[Joseph Bacchus, ed.] *Correspondence of John Henry Newman with John Keble and Others . . . 1839–1845.* London: Longmans, Green, 1917.

Development—John Henry Newman. *An Essay on the Development of Christian Doctrine.* London: James Toovey, 1845.

Froude, *Remains*—[J. H. Newman and John Keble, eds.] *Remains of the Late Reverend Richard Hurrell Froude, M.A., Fellow of Oriel College, Oxford.* London: J. G. and F. Rivington, 1838, 1839, 4 vols. Published with volumes 1 and 2 (1838) designated part I and volumes 3 and 4 (1839) designated part II. References in the notes are to the individual volumes without notation of the part designation.

Justification—John Henry Newman. *Lectures on Justification.* London: J. G. and F. Rivington, 1838.

L&D—*The Letters and Diaries of John Henry Newman.* Vols. 1–8 ed. Ian Ker, Thomas Gornall, Gerard Tracey. (Oxford: Clarendon, 1978–1999). Vols. 11–31 ed. Charles Stephen Dessain, Edward E. Kelly, Thomas Gornall. (Oxford: Clarendon, 1961–1972).

Liddon, *Pusey*—H. P. Liddon. *Life of Edward Bouverie Pusey, Doctor of Divinity, Canon of Christ Church; Regius Professor of Hebrew in the University of Oxford.* London: Longmans, Green, 1893.

Mozley, *Letters and Correspondence*—A. Mozley, ed. *Letters and Correspondence of John Henry Newman during His Life in the English Church with a Brief Autobiography* (London: Longmans, Green, 1890), 2 vols.

Newman Family Letters—Dorothea Mozley, ed. *Newman Family Letters.* London: S.P.C.K., 1962.

Newman Microfilms—John Henry Newman Papers from the Birmingham Oratory Microfilm. Yale University Library System.

PPS—John Henry Newman. *Parochial and Plain Sermons.* New edition. London: Longmans, Green, 1894, 8 vols.

Prophetical Office—John Henry Newman, *Lectures on the Prophetical Office of the Church, Viewed Relatively to Romanism and Popular Protestantism.* London: J. G. and F. Rivington, 1837.

Tract N—*Tracts for the Times by Members of the University of Oxford.* New edition. London: J. G. F. and J. Rivington, 1840, 5 vols. Unless otherwise noted, all quotations from the tracts are from this 1840 edition. Volume 3 as published in 1840 carries the words New Edition on the title page.

University Sermons—John Henry Newman. *Fifteen Sermons Preached Before the University of Oxford, Between A.D. 1826 and 1843.* New edition. London: Rivingtons, 1880.

Via Media—John Henry Newman. *The Via Media of the Anglican Church, Illustrated in Lectures, Letters, and Tracts Written Between 1830 and 1841.* London: Longmans, Green, 1899.

Notes

INTRODUCTION

1. Pope John Paul II, "Letter on the Occasion of the 2nd Centenary of the Birth of Cardinal John Henry Newman," January 22, 2001, quoted from *L'Osservatore Romano*, Weekly English Edition, as provided by Eternal World Television Network, Irondale, Australia.

2. Matthew Arnold, *Discourses in America* (New York: Macmillan, 1924), p. 139.

3. *Christian Reformer*, n.s. 7 (1840): 382. An effort to downplay this conflict marked the otherwise important work of Owen Chadwick in *The Victorian Church* (New York: Oxford University Press, 1966), 1: 121–126; *From Bossuet to Newman*, 2d ed. (Cambridge: Cambridge University Press, 1987); and *The Spirit of the Oxford Movement: Tractarian Essays* (Cambridge: Cambridge University Press, 1990). W. R. Ward and Peter Nockles fully recognize the presence of Tractarian-initiated conflict. See W. R. Ward, *Victorian Oxford* (Oxford: Clarendon, 1965), and P. B. Nockles, " 'Lost Causes and . . . Impossible Loyalties': The Oxford Movement and the University," in M. G. Brock and M. C. Curthoys, eds., *The History of the University of Oxford*, vol. 6, *Nineteenth-Century Oxford, Part I* (Oxford: Oxford University Press), pp. 196–267.

4. W. G. Ward to JHN, August 8, 1845, Newman Microfilms, reel 74, batch 80.

5. Journal, January 21, 1863, *AW*, p. 254.

6. JHN to A. St. John, July 15, 1857, *L&D*, 18: 94.

7. Richard Holt Hutton, *Criticisms on Contemporary Thought and Thinkers Selected from the Spectator* (London: Macmillan, 1894), 2: 278. Regarding the impact of Newman's thought and writing on late Victorian prose, see David J. DeLaura, *Hebrew and Hellene in Victorian England: Newman, Arnold, and Pater* (Austin: University of Texas Press, 1969).

8. JHN to P. W. Bunting, May 14, 1883, *L&D*, 30: 218. For further comment on this process of the domestication of Victorian polemics, see Frank M. Turner, *Contesting Cultural Authority: Essays in Victorian Intellectual Life* (Cambridge: Cambridge University Press, 1993), pp. 38–43.

9. F. J. A. Hort to Rev. John Ellerton, May 7, 1865; F. J. A. Hort to his wife, August 24, 1890, Arthur Fenton Hort, *Life and Letters of Fenton John Anthony Hort* (London, 1896), 2: 36, 423, 424, 425, 423, 424.

10. James Martineau, *Essays, Reviews, and Addresses* (London: Longmans, Green, and Col, 1890), 1: 223. See also Peter Nockles, *The Oxford Movement in Context: Anglican High Churchmanship 1760–1857* (Cambridge: Cambridge University Press, 1994), p. 171.

11. *Apologia*, 184–185; see also Martin J. Svaglic, "Why Newman Wrote the *Apologia*," and Edward Kelly, "The *Apologia* and the Ultramontanes," in Vincent Ferrer Blehl and Francis X. Connolly, eds., *Newman's Apologia: A Classic Reconsidered* (New York: Harcourt, Brace and World, 1964), pp. 1–46; Nockles, *Oxford Movement in Context*, pp. 136–142, 309; Peter Nockles, "Oxford, Tract 90, and the Bishops," and P. J. FitzPatrick, "Newman and Kingsley," in David Nicholls and Fergus Kerr, eds., *John Henry Newman: Reason, Rhetoric, and Romanticism* (Carbondale: Southern Illinois University Press, 1991), pp. 28–87, 108. FitzPatrick had presented an expanded version of his skepticism about Newman's forthrightness in the *Apologia* in P. J. FitzPatrick, *Apologia pro Charles Kingsley* (London: Sheed and Ward, 1969), published under the pseudonym of G. Egner.

12. *Apologia*, pp. 255–256, 262; see also JHN to R. H. Hutton, June 3, 1865, *L&D*, 21: 482 and 450 n.

13. Peter Nockles, "The Oxford Movement: Historical Background 1780–1833," and Reginald H. Fuller, "The Classical High Church Reaction to the Tractarians," in Geoffrey Rowell, ed., *Tradition Renewed: The Oxford Movement Conference Papers* (London: Darton, Longman and Todd, 1986), pp. 24–63; Peter Nockles, "Church Parties in the Pre-Tractarian Church of England 1750–1833: The 'Orthodox'—Some Problems of Definition and Identity," in John Walsh, Colin Haydon, and Stephen Tayler, eds., *The Church of England, c. 1689–c. 1833: From Toleration to Tractarianism* (Cambridge: Cambridge University Press, 1993), p. 334. See also Nockles, *Oxford Movement in Context*, pp. 25–43. Here and elsewhere throughout this book I very much follow Nockles's useful and sensible definitions.

14. On the difficulties of terminology during these disputes, see J. C. D. Clark, *English Society, 1688–1832* (Cambridge: Cambridge University Press, 1985), pp. 315–348; Richard J. Helmstadter, "Orthodox Nonconformity," and R. K. Webb, "Quakers and Unitarians," in D. G. Paz, ed., *Nineteenth-Century English Religious Traditions: Retrospect and Prospect* (Westport: Greenwood, 1995), pp. 57–116.

15. R. K. Webb, "The Emergence of Rational Dissent," in Knud Haakonssen, ed., *Enlightenment and Religion: Rational Dissent in Eighteenth-Century Britain* (Cambridge: Cambridge University Press, 1996), p. 37; also consult other essays in this volume; B. W. Young, *Religion and Enlightenment in Eighteenth-Century England* (Oxford: Clarendon, 1998); and Clark, *English Society* for discussions of the eighteenth-century political impact of actual and alleged Socinianism; and "The Anatomy of Socinianism," *British Magazine*, 8 (1835): 241–247, 375–380, for an example of a high-church exploration of the subject contemporary with the Tractarian Movement.

16. Turner, *Contesting Cultural Authority*, pp. 3–37.

17. Olive J. Brose, *Church and Parliament: The Reshaping of the Church of England, 1828–1860* (Stanford: Stanford University Press, 1959); Robert Bruce Mullin, *Episcopal Vision/American Reality: High Church Theology and Social Thought in Evangelical America* (New Haven: Yale University Press, 1986); Richard J. Helmstadter, ed., *Freedom and Religion in the Nineteenth Century* (Stanford: Stanford University Press, 1997); Frank J. Coppa, *The Modern Papacy Since 1789* (London: Longman, 1998), pp. 1–100.

18. Much of this scholarly research has flowed from the controversies raised by the publication in 1985 of Clark's previously cited *English Society, 1688–1832*.

19. Michael R. Watts, *The Dissenters*, vol. 2, *The Expansion of Evangelical Nonconformity, 1719–1859* (Oxford: Clarendon, 1995), pp. 417–426.

20. G. I. T. Machin, *The Catholic Question in English Politics, 1820–1830* (Oxford: Oxford University Press, 1964); Clark, *English Society*, 349–420; Robert Hole, *Pulpits, Politics, and Public Order in England, 1760–1832* (Cambridge: Cambridge University Press, 1989), pp. 29–247.

21. Asa Briggs, *The Age of Improvement 1783–1867*, Second Impression with Corrections (New York: David McKay, 1962), p. 230. The newspaper quoted is the *Birmingham Argus*, May 1, 1829.

22. M. B. Brock, "The Oxford of Peel and Gladstone," in Brock and Curthoys, *The History of the University of Oxford*, 6: 7–71.

23. *Certain Difficulties*, p. 102. See John R. Griffin, *A Historical Commentary on the Major Catholic Works of Cardinal Newman*, American University Studies, series 9, History, vol. 125 (New York: Peter Lang, 1993), pp. 35–48, for a brief overview of the literature on these lectures. See also Chadwick, *The Victorian Church*, 1: 250–271.

24. *Certain Difficulties*, pp. 35, 48, 68.

25. *Certain Difficulties*, pp. 15, 20, 145.

CHAPTER 1. THE EVANGELICAL IMPULSE

1. David Hempton, *The Religion of the People: Methodism and Popular Religion, c. 1750–1900* (London: Routledge, 1996), p. 50.

2. Quoted from the preface to *Horae Homileticae* (1820) in William Carus, *Memoirs of the Life of the Rev. Charles Simeon, M.A., Late Senior Fellow of King's College, and Minister of Trinity Church, Cambridge, with a Selection from His Writings and Correspondence*, American ed., ed. the Right Rev. Charles P. McIlvaine (New York: Robert Carter, 1847), p. 311. See also D. W. Bebbington, *Evangelicalism in Modern Britain: A History from the 1730s to the 1980s* (London: Unwin Hyman, 1989), pp. 75–104.

3. W. R. Ward, *The Protestant Evangelical Awakening* (Cambridge: Cambridge University Press, 1992), pp. 54–160; Frank Lambert, *Inventing the "Great Awakening"* (Princeton: Princeton University Press, 1999); John Walsh, " 'Methodism' and the Origins of English-Speaking Evangelicalism," and David Hempton, "Evangelicalism in English and Irish Society, 1780–1840," in Mark A. Noll, David W. Bebbington, George A. Rawlyk, eds., *Evangelicalism: Comparative Studies of Popular Protestantism in North America, the British Isles, and Beyond, 1700–1990* (New York: Oxford University Press, 1994), pp. 19–37, 156–179.

4. Alan D. Gilbert, *Religion and Society in Industrial England: Church, Chapel, and Social Change, 1740–1914* (London: Longman, 1976), p. 51; Mark Smith, *Religion in Industrial Society: Oldham and Saddleworth, 1740–1865* (Oxford: Clarendon, 1994), p. 227; Bebbington, *Evangelicalism in Modern Britain*, pp. 1–17; Elizabeth Jay, *The Religion of the Heart: Anglican Evangelicalism and the Nineteenth-Century Novel* (Oxford: Clarendon, 1979), pp. 51–105.

5. David Newsome, *The Wilberforces and Henry Manning: The Parting of Friends* (Cambridge: Harvard University Press, 1966), pp. 1–15; Sheridan Gilley, "Edward Irving: Prophet of the Millennium," in Jane Garnett and Colin Matthew, eds., *Revival and Religion Since 1700: Essays for John Walsh* (London: Hambledon, 1993), p. 95. See E. M. Howse, *Saints in Politics: The "Clapham Sect" and the Growth of Freedom* (Toronto: University of Toronto Press, 1952); Ford K. Brown, *Fathers of the Victorians: The Age of Wilberforce* (Cambridge: Cambridge University Press, 1961); Michael Hennell, *Sons of the Prophets: Evangelical Leaders of the Victorian Church* (London: S.P.C.K., 1979); E. M. Forster, *Marianne Thornton: A Domestic Biography, 1797–1887* (New York: Harcourt, Brace, 1956), pp. 130–149.

6. Isaac Watts, "An Humble Attempt Towards the Revival of Practical Religion," in *The Works of the Reverend and Learned Isaac Watts, D.D.* (London, 1810–1811), 3: 25, as quoted in Michael J. Crawford, *Seasons of Grace: Colonial New England's Revival Tradition in Its British Context* (New York: Oxford University Press, 1991), p. 84. For discussions of this transformation in preaching, consult Isabel Rivers, *Reason, Grace, and Sentiment: A Study of the Language of Religion and Ethics in England 1660–1780* (Cambridge: Cambridge University Press, 1991), pp. 164–204; W. R. Ward, *Religion and Society in England, 1790–1850* (New York: Schocken, 1973); Michael R. Watts, *The Dissenters*, vol. 1,

From the Reformation to the French Revolution (Oxford: Clarendon, 1978), pp. 394–464; Gordon Rupp, *Religion in England, 1688–1791* (Oxford: Clarendon, 1986), pp. 325–485; Gilbert, *Religion and Society*, pp. 23–50; Deborah M. Valenze, *Prophetic Sons and Daughters: Female Preaching and Popular Religion in Industrial England* (Princeton: Princeton University Press, 1985); Ted A. Campbell, *The Religion of the Heart: A Study of European Religious Life in the Seventeenth and Eighteenth Centuries* (Columbia: University of South Carolina Press, 1991); Hempton, *Religion of the People*, pp. 49–76; Geoffrey Best, "Evangelicalism and the Victorians," in Anthony Symondson, ed., *The Victorian Crisis of Faith* (London: S.P.C.K., 1979), pp. 37–56; and Robert E. Sullivan, "The Birth of Modern Christianity," 1998 (typescript furnished privately to the author). For an overview of the manner in which such evangelical preaching was interpreted and reinterpreted during the first century of evangelicalism, see William G. McLoughlin, introduction to Charles Grandison Finney, *Lectures on Revivals of Religion*, ed. William G. McLoughlin (Cambridge: Harvard University Press, 1960), pp. vii–lii.

7. J. C. Philpot to the Provost of Worcester College, Oxford, March 28, 1835, in J. H. Philpot, ed., *The Seceders (1829–1869): The Story of a Spiritual Awakening as Told in the Letters of Joseph Charles Philpot, M.A., and William Tiptaft, M. A.* (London: C. J. Farncombe, 1930), pp. 284–285. This letter was published and received wide circulation.

8. Boyd Hilton, *The Age of Atonement: The Influence of Evangelicalism on Social and Economic Thought, 1795–1865* (Oxford: Clarendon, 1988), p. 12. See also Alan C. Clifford, *Atonement and Justification: English Evangelical Theology, 1640–1790* (Oxford: Oxford University Press, 1990), pp. 51–69, 125–166, 186–220; D. Bruce Hindmarsh, *John Newton and the English Evangelical Tradition Between the Conversions of Wesley and Wilberforce* (Oxford: Clarendon, 1996), pp. 119–168; Bernard Semmel, *The Methodist Revolution* (New York: Basic, 1973), pp. 106–109; Michael Watts, *The Dissenters*, vol. 2, *The Expansion of Evangelical Nonconformity, 1791–1859* (Oxford: Clarendon, 1995), pp. 1–3; Roger H. Martin, *Evangelicals United: Ecumenical Stirrings in Pre-Victorian Britain, 1794–1840* (Metuchen, N. J.: Scarecrow, 1983); Thomas J. Sheridan, *Newman on Justification* (New York: Alba House, 1967), pp. 15–66; and Bebbington, *Evangelicalism in Modern Britain*, pp. 42–50, 63–65, 92–94. I wish to acknowledge the influence on this paragraph of conversations and correspondence with Professors Mark Noll and Harry Stout.

9. On conversion and accompanying concerns over excess of enthusiasm in revivals, see Watts, *The Dissenters*, 2: 49–81; Rivers, *Reason, Grace, and Sentiment*, 1: 243–253; Bebbington, *Evangelicalism in Modern Britain*, pp. 42–50; F. W. B. Bullock, *Evangelical Conversion in Great Britain, 1696–1845* (St. Leonards-on-Sea: Budd and Gillatt, 1959); Donald M. Lewis, *Lighten Their Darkness: The Evangelical Mission to Working-Class London, 1828–1860* (New York: Greenwood, 1986), pp. 29–34; Semmel, *Methodist Revolution*, pp. 81–109; Hempton, *Religion of the People*, pp. 91–108, 130–144.

10. William Wilberforce, *A Practical View of the Prevailing Religious System of Professed Christians, in the Higher and Middle Classes, Contrasted with Real Christianity*, From a Late London Edition (New York: American Tract Society, n.d.), pp. 69, 71, 114.

11. Frank M. Turner, *Contesting Cultural Authority: Essays in Victorian Intellectual Life* (Cambridge: Cambridge University Press, 1993), pp. 73–100; Jeffrey von Arx, "The Victorian Crisis of Faith as a Crisis of Vocation," in Richard Helmstadter and Bernard Lightman, eds., *Victorian Faith in Crisis: Essays in Continuity and Change in Nineteenth-Century Religious Belief* (Stanford: Stanford University Press, 1990), pp. 262–282; Perry Butler, *Gladstone: Church, State, and Tractarianism: A Study of His Religious Ideas and Attitudes, 1809–1859* (Oxford: Clarendon, 1982); Basil Willey, *Nineteenth Century Studies: Coleridge to Matthew Arnold* (New York: Columbia University Press, 1949); Basil Willey, *More Nineteenth Century Studies: A Group of Honest Doubters* (New York: Columbia University Press, 1956).

12. Christopher Tolley, *Domestic Biography: The Legacy of Evangelicalism in Four Nineteenth-Century Families* (Oxford: Clarendon, 1997), pp. 25–41; Charles Smyth, *Simeon*

and *Church Order: A Study of the Origin of the Evangelical Revival in Cambridge in the Eighteenth Century* (Cambridge: Cambridge University Press, 1940), pp. 1–43; Watts, *The Dissenters*, 2: 54–58; Henry Abelove, *The Evangelist of Desire: John Wesley and the Methodists* (Stanford: Stanford University Press, 1990), pp. 49–73; Steven Ozment, "Marriage and Ministry in the Protestant Churches," in William Bassett and Peter Huizing, eds., *Celibacy in the Church* (New York: Herder and Herder, 1972), pp. 39–56.

13. Henry Venn, *The Complete Duty of Man; or, A System of Doctrinal and Practical Christianity, Designed for the Use of Families*, A New Edition Carefully Revised and Corrected by Rev. H. Venn, B.D. (New York: American Tract Society, n.d.), pp. 282, 283, 285. See also Thomas Scott, *The Theological Works of the Rev. Thomas Scott, Author of a Commentary on the Bible* (Edinburgh: Peter Brown and Thomas Nelson, 1835), pp. 295–305.

14. Thornton as quoted in Standish Meacham, *Henry Thornton of Clapham, 1760–1815* (Cambridge: Harvard University Press, 1964), p. 52.

15. Thomas Walter Laqueur, *Religion and Respectability: Sunday Schools and Working Class Culture* (New Haven: Yale University Press, 1976), pp. 5–9.

16. J. H. Newman, "Notes on Reading of Scripture," Newman Microfilms, reel 7, batch 43.

17. Bebbington, *Evangelicalism in Modern Britain*, pp. 13–14, 86–91; Doreen M. Rosman, *Evangelicals and Culture* (London: Croom Helm, 1984), pp. 28–32

18. *Apologia*, p. 18; Thomas Scott, *The Holy Bible, Containing the Old and New Testaments, with Original Notes, Practical Observations, and Copious Marginal References*, The Fourth American, from the Second London Edition, Improved and Enlarged (New York: Dodge and Sayre, 1814), 1: xvi (hereafter cited as *Scott's Bible*).

19. *Scott's Bible*, 1: vi, vii, x.

20. *Scott's Bible*, 1: v, vi, xvii, xviii. The impact of print culture on the study and appreciation of ancient texts may also be seen in the emergence of the Homeric Question toward the end of the eighteenth century. See Anthony Grafton, introduction to F. A. Wolf, *Prolegomena to Homer* (Princeton: Princeton University Press, 1985), pp. 3–36.

21. *Scott's Bible*, 1: xvii; 4: Practical Observations on Matthew 22: 23–33 (volume unpaginated); Thomas Chalmers, *Sermons and Discourses*, Third Complete American Edition, from the Late Glasgow Stereotype Edition, Revised and Corrected by the Author (New York: Robert Carter, 1848), p. 15.

22. Rosman, *Evangelicals and Culture*, pp. 25–31, 223–233; Ernest R. Sandeen, *The Roots of Fundamentalism: British and American Millenarianism, 1800–1930* (Chicago: University of Chicago Press, 1970), pp. 1–41; W. H. Oliver, *Prophets and Millennialists: The Uses of Biblical Prophecy in England from the 1790s to the 1840s* (Auckland: Auckland University Press and Oxford University Press, 1978), pp. 42–98; J. F. C. Harrison, *The Second Coming: Popular Millenarianism, 1780–1850* (London: Routledge and Kegan Paul, 1979), passim; Jack Fruchtman, Jr., *The Apocalyptic Politics of Richard Prince and Joseph Priestley: A Study in Late Eighteenth Century English Republican Millennialism* (Philadelphia: American Philosophical Society, 1983); Bebbington, *Evangelicalism*, pp. 81–86; Paul Misner, "Newman and the Tradition Concerning the Papal Antichrist," *Church History*, 42 (1973): 377–395; D. N. Hempton, "Evangelicalism and Eschatology," *Journal of Ecclesiastical History*, 31 (1980): 179–194; Sheridan Gilley, "Newman and Prophecy, Evangelical and Catholic," *Journal of the United Reformed Church History Society*, 3 (1985): 160–188; Hilton, *Age of Atonement*, pp. 14–19, 94–97, and passim.

23. Lewis, *Lighten Their Darkness*, pp. 14–17; Joseph L. Altholz, "Alexander Haldane, *The Record*, and Religious Journalism," *Victorian Periodicals Review*, 20 (Spring 1987): 23–31; Joseph L. Altholz, *The Religious Press in Britain, 1760–1900* (New York: Greenwood, 1989), pp. 17–19; J. Wolffe, *The Protestant Crusade in Great Britain, 1829–1860* (Oxford: Clarendon, 1991), pp. 31–33; Ian S. Rennie, "Fundamentalism and the Varieties of North Atlantic Evangelicalism," in Noll, Bebbington, and Rawlyk, *Evangelicalism*, pp. 333–350;

G. R. Balleine, *History of the Evangelical Party in the Church of England* (London, 1909), p. 207.

24. G. F. A. Best, "Popular Protestantism in Victorian England," in R. Robson, ed., *Ideas and Institutions of Victorian Britain* (London: G. Bell, 1967), pp. 115–142; E. R. Norman, *Anti-Catholicism in Mid-Victorian Britain* (London: Allen and Unwin, 1968); Wolffe, *Protestant Crusade;* D. G. Paz, *Popular Anti-Catholicism in Mid-Victorian England* (Stanford: Stanford University Press, 1992).

25. On the issue of the alleged doubtfulness of Roman Catholic loyalty, see Sheridan Gilley, "Nationality and Liberty, Protestant and Catholic: Robert Southey's Book of the Church," in Stuart Mews, ed., *Religion and National Identity* (Oxford: Basil Blackwell, 1982), pp. 409–432.

26. Joseph Milner, *The History of the Church of Christ,* With Additions and Corrections by the Late Rev. Isaac Milner, From the Last London Edition (Philadelphia: Hogan and Thompson, 1835), 1: 3, 5; W. H. Proby, *Annals of the Low Church Party Down to the Death of Archbishop Tait* (1888), 1: 203, quoted in Walsh, "Joseph Milner's Evangelical Church History," *Journal of Ecclesiastical History,* 10 (1959): 185.

27. Benedict Anderson, *Imagined Communities: Reflections on the Origin and Spread of Nationalism,* rev. ed. (London: Verso, 1991), p. 83. Frank Lambert has also independently pointed to this parallel. See Lambert, *Inventing the "Great Awakening,"* p. 270, n. 47. For considerations of the reality that evangelical Christians attached to their imagined community, see Ward, *Protestant Evangelical Awakening,* passim; Susan O'Brien, "A Transatlantic Community of Saints: The Great Awakening and the First Evangelical Network, 1735–1755," *American Historical Review,* 91 (1986): 811–832; Susan O'Brien, "Eighteenth-Century Publishing Networks in the First Years of Transatlantic Evangelicalism," in Noll, Bebbington, and Rawlyk, *Evangelicalism,* pp. 38–57; Michael J. Crawford, *Seasons of Grace,* passim; Patrick Scott, "The Business of Belief: The Emergence of 'Religious' Publishing," in Derek Baker, ed., *Sanctity and Secularity: The Church and the World* (Oxford: Basil Blackwell, 1973), pp. 213–224; Leonore Davidoff and Catherine Hall, *Family Fortunes: Men and Women of the English Middle Class, 1780–1850* (Chicago: University of Chicago Press, 1987), pp. 76–148. Consult Altholz, *The Religious Press in Britain,* for the structure of British evangelical print culture.

28. On the issue of evangelicals and ecclesiastical establishment, see Geoffrey Best, "The Evangelicals and the Established Church in the Early Nineteenth Century," *Journal of Theological Studies,* n.s. 10 (1959): 63–78; Lewis, *Lighten Their Darkness,* pp. 9–49; J. P. Ellens, *Religious Routes to Gladstonian Liberalism: The Church Rate Conflict in England and Wales, 1832–1868* (University Park: Pennsylvania State University Press, 1994), pp. 1–114; G. I. T. Machin, *Politics and the Churches in Great Britain, 1832–1868* (Oxford: Clarendon, 1977), pp. 28–74, 91–112, 148–180; Raymond G. Cowherd, *The Politics of English Dissent* (New York: New York University Press, 1956), pp. 84–96; Paz, *Popular Anti-Catholicism,* pp. 153–196; Martin, *Evangelicals United,* passim.

29. Johnson Grant, *History of the English Church and of the Principal Bodies of Dissenters with Answers to Each from A.D. 1800 to the End of George III* (London: J. Hatchard, 1820), 2: 96.

30. Grant, *History,* 2: 115, 86–87. Furthermore, Grant also pointed out that the evangelicals often placed in their pulpits clergy who had not received university education, thus edging out university-educated clergy whose parents had made considerable investments to assure their sons a respectable clerical career. (Grant, *History,* 2: 86–91.) Writing during his Roman Catholic years, Newman also described "the Evangelicals of the Establishment" as "making a Church within a Church" by talking of " 'vital religion' and 'vital doctrines,' " and not allowing "that their brethren 'know the Gospel' or are 'Gospel preachers' unless they profess the small shibboleths of their own sect." JHN to W. G. Ward, May 9, 1867, *L&D,* 23: 217. See also Wesley Balda, "Simeon's 'Protestant Papists': A Sampling of Moderate Evan-

gelicalism Within the Church of England 1839–1865," *Fides et Historia*, 16 (1983): 55–67; Meacham, *Henry Thornton of Clapham*, pp. 2–6.

31. Watts, *The Dissenters*, 2: 27–29; Robert Hole, *Pulpits, Politics, and Public Order in England, 1760–1832* (Cambridge: Cambridge University Press, 1989), pp. 195–198; Deryck W. Lovegrove, *Established Church, Sectarian People: Itinerancy and the Transformation of English Dissent, 1780–1830* (Cambridge: Cambridge University Press, 1988); Semmel, *Methodist Revolution*, pp. 133–134; Hempton, *Religion of the People*, pp. 110–115; Deborah M. Valenze, *Prophetic Sons and Daughters*, pp. 50–74, 101–108, 205–244; Neil J. Smelzer, *Social Paralysis and Social Change: British Working-Class Education in the Nineteenth Century* (Berkeley: University of California Press, 1991), passim; Theodore Koditschek, *Class Formation and Urban-Industrial Society: Bradford, 1750–1850* (Cambridge: Cambridge University Press, 1990), pp. 252–292; K. D. M. Snell and Paul S. Ell, *Rival Jerusalems: The Geography of Victorian Religion* (Cambridge: Cambridge University Press, 2000), pp. 1–201.

32. Quoted in Lovegrove, *Established Church, Sectarian People*, p. 21.

33. Richard Carwardine, *Transatlantic Revivalism: Popular Evangelicalism in Britain and America, 1790–1865* (Westport, Connecticut: Greenwood, 1978), pp. 59–133.

34. Sheridan Gilley, "Edward Irving: Prophet of the Millennium," in Garnett and Matthew, *Revival and Religion*, pp. 95–110; Columba Graham Flegg, *"Gathered Under Apostles": A Study of the Catholic Apostolic Church* (Oxford: Clarendon, 1992), pp. 46–63; W. H. Oliver, *Prophets and Millennialists*, pp. 99–149; Sandeen, *Roots of Fundamentalism*, pp. 14–30.

35. Stewart J. Brown, *Thomas Chalmers and the Godly Commonwealth in Scotland* (Oxford: Oxford University Press, 1982), pp. 211–220; Flegg, *"Gathered Under Apostles,"* pp. 41–46.

36. Sandeen, *Roots of Fundamentalism*, p. 14.

37. Harold H. Rowdon, *The Origins of the Brethren, 1825–1850* (London: Pickering and Inglis, 1967), pp. 37–111.

38. Francis William Newman, *Phases of Faith; or, Passages from the History of My Creed*, 6th ed., 1860 (rpt. New York: Humanities, 1970), pp. 16–28.

39. Henry Bellenden Bulteel, *A Sermon on I. Corinthians II. 12. Preached before the University of Oxford at St. Mary's on Sunday, Feb. 6, 1831, to which is added, A Sequel, Containing an Account of the Author's Ejectment from His Curacy by the Bishop of Oxford for Indiscriminate Preaching*, 6th ed. (Oxford: W. Baxter, 1831), pp. 23, 45, 46, 47. See also Edward Burton, *Remarks upon a Sermon Preached at St. Mary's on Sunday, February 6, 1831* (Oxford: W. Baxter, 1831); "Henry Bellenden Bulteel," *Dictionary of National Biography;* Philpot, *The Seceders*, pp. 57–60, 163–174, 184; Harold H. Rowdon, *Origins of the Brethren*, pp. 64–73; J. S. Reynolds, *The Evangelicals at Oxford, 1735–1871* (Appleford: Marcham Manor, 1975), p. 162; G. Carter, *Evangelical Seceders from the Church of England, c. 1829–1850* (Oxford diss., 1990).

40. William Tiptaft to his brother, May 2, 1831, quoted in Philpot, *The Seceders*, p. 163; Bulteel, *A Sermon*, pp. 55, 57, 59.

41. Rowdon, *Origins of the Brethren, 1825–1850*, pp. 74–108.

42. J. C. Philpot to the Provost of Worcester College, Oxford, March 28, 1835, in Philpot, *The Seceders*, pp. 284–285.

43. For departures from that midcentury outlook see, for example, Richard B. Sher, *Church and University in the Scottish Enlightenment: The Moderate Literati of Edinburgh* (Princeton: Princeton University Press, 1985); Knud Haakonssen, ed., *Enlightenment and Religion: Rational Dissent in Eighteenth-Century Britain* (Cambridge: Cambridge University Press, 1996); B. W. Young, *Religion and Enlightenment in Eighteenth-Century England: Theological Debate from Locke to Burke* (Oxford: Clarendon, 1998); J. G. A. Pocock, *Barbarism and Religion* (Cambridge: Cambridge University Press, 1999), 2 vols.; Roy Porter, *The Creation of the Modern World: The Untold Story of the British Enlightenment* (New York: Norton, 2000).

44. See Semmel, *Methodist Revolution*, for an extensive argument on the manner in which both Methodist theology and Methodist organization served to prepare adherents to that religion for participation in liberal political and commercial society, and David W. Bebbington, "Revival and Enlightenment in Eighteenth-Century England," in Edith L. Blumhofer and Randall Balmer, eds., *Modern Christian Revivals* (Urbana: University of Illinois Press, 1993), pp. 17–41, for a discussion of the alignment of evangelicalism and the Enlightenment.

45. Jürgen Habermas, *The Structural Transformation of the Public Sphere: An Inquiry into a Category of Bourgeois Society*, trans. Thomas Burger (Cambridge: MIT Press, 1991; 1st pub. 1962), pp. 37, 40, 42–43, 52.

46. J. Wesley, *The Works of John Wesley, Sermons*, ed. A. C. Outler (Nashville, 1984–1987) 1: 103–104, as quoted in Isabel Rivers, *Reason, Grace, and Sentiment*, 1: 215; Simeon quoted in Carus, *Memoirs of the Life of the Rev. Charles Simeon*, p. 309.

47. Donald Winch, *Riches and Poverty: An Intellectual History of Political Economy in Britain, 1750–1834* (Cambridge: Cambridge University Press, 1996), pp. 349–388; A. M. C. Waterman, *Revolution, Economics, and Religion: Christian Political Economy, 1798–1833* (Cambridge: Cambridge University Press, 1991), pp. 150–263; Hilton, *Age of Atonement*, passim. See also Frank Lambert, *"Peddler in Divinity": George Whitfield and the Transatlantic Revivals, 1737–1770* (Princeton: Princeton University Press, 1994); Harry S. Stout, *The Divine Dramatist: George Whitfield and the Rise of Modern Evangelicalism* (Grand Rapids, Mich.: Eerdmans, 1991); R. Laurence Moore, *Selling God: American Religion in the Marketplace of Culture* (Oxford: Oxford University Press, 1994), pp. 2–66; Richard J. Helmstadter, "The Reverend Andrew Reed (1787–1862): Evangelical Pastor as Entrepreneur," in R. W. Davis and R. J. Helmstadter, eds., *Religion and Irreligion in Victorian Society: Essays in Honor of R. K. Webb* (London: Routledge, 1992), pp. 7–28; Gregory H. Singleton, "Protestant Voluntary Organizations and the Shaping of Victorian America," in Daniel Walker Howe, ed., *Victorian America* (Philadelphia: University of Pennsylvania Press, 1976), pp. 47–58.

48. Charles Simeon to unknown correspondent, August 8, 1836, quoted in Carus, *Memoirs of the Life of the Rev. Charles Simeon*, p. 455.

49. Hilton, *The Age of Atonement*, p. 8; Thomas Scott, "On Justification," from *Essays on the Most Important Subjects in Religion*, in *The Theological Works of the Rev. Thomas Scott*, p. 241; *Scott's Bible*, 3: Commentary on Chapter 53 of Isaiah; Thomas Chalmers, *Lectures on the Epistle of Paul the Apostle to the Romans*, in *The Works of Thomas Chalmers* (Glasgow: William Collins, n.d.), 23: 92–93. I owe this Chalmers reference to Hilton, *Age of Atonement*, p. 291. In regard to the debate over Methodist views, see Alan C. Clifford, *Atonement and Justification*, pp. 126–134. For criticisms of the debtor-creditor metaphor first on theological grounds and then on moral grounds see, R. P Buddicom, "The Atonement Indispensable to the Necessities of Guilty Man; and Shown to Stand or Fall with the Deity of Our Lord Jesus Christ," in *Unitarianism Confuted: A Series of Lectures Delivered in Christ Church, Liverpool in MDCCCXXXIX by Thirteen Clergymen of the Church of England* (Liverpool: Henry Perris, 1839), pp. 453–456, and Francis Power Cobbe, *Broken Lights: An Inquiry into the Present Condition and Future Prospect of Religious Faith* (Boston: J. E. Tilton, 1864), p. 53; Hilton, *Age of Atonement*, p. 288–297; Semmel, *Methodist Revolution*, pp. 10–13.

50. W. E. G. Gladstone, *Gleanings of Past Years* (London: John Murray, 1879; rpt. New York: AMS, 1976), 7: 219; Venn, *Complete Duty of Man*, pp. 232–233, 233, 234, 236, 237. See Thomas Gisborne, *An Enquiry into the Duties of Men in the Higher and Middle Classes of Society in Great Britain, Resulting from Their Respective Stations, Professions, and Employments*, Fourth Edition, Corrected (London: B. and J. White and Cadell and Davies, 1797), 2:

NOTES TO PAGES 60–68

199–341, on the various duties of bankers to insure probity in commerce and to make credit available for commercial enterprise.

51. Cobbe, *Broken Lights*, p. 64.

52. Quoted in Leslie Howsam, *Cheap Bibles: Nineteenth-Century Publishing and the British and Foreign Bible Society* (Cambridge: Cambridge University Press, 1991), pp. 6, 7. It is worth noting that the Quakers themselves became an evangelical religious group in the course of the nineteenth century. On the Bible Society and other religious publication, see also Martin, *Evangelicals United*, pp. 80–172; Foster, *An Errand of Mercy*, pp. 70–118; Patricia Anderson, *The Printed Image and the Transformation of Popular Culture, 1790–1860* (Oxford: Clarendon, 1991), pp. 29–35; and Colleen McDannell, *Material Christianity: Religion and Popular Culture in America* (New Haven: Yale University Press, 1995), pp. 67–102; for high-church criticism, see Grant, *History*, 2: 263–307.

53. Quoted in John Hedley Brooke, *Science and Religion: Some Historical Perspectives* (Cambridge: Cambridge University Press, 1991), p. 191. See also John Hedley Brooke, "The History of Science and Religion: Some Evangelical Dimensions"; David D. Bebbington, "Science and Evangelical Theology in Britain from Wesley to Orr"; and Jonathan R. Topham, "Science, Natural Theology, and Evangelicalism in Early Nineteenth-Century Scotland: Thomas Chalmers and the *Evidence* Controversy," in David N. Livingstone, D. G. Hart, and Mark A. Noll, eds., *Evangelicals and Science in Historical Perspective* (New York: Oxford University Press, 1999), pp. 17–42, 120–141, 142–176; Brown, *Thomas Chalmers*, pp. 107–109; Hilton, *Age of Atonement*, pp. 19–25.

54. Theodore Dwight Bozeman, *Protestants in an Age of Science: The Baconian Ideal and Antebellum American Religious Thought* (Chapel Hill: University of North Carolina Press, 1977), pp. 72–116.

55. Arnold Thackray and Jack Morrell, *Gentlemen of Science: Early Years of the British Association for the Advancement of Science* (Oxford: Clarendon Press, 1981), pp. 21–35, 224–245. Thackray and Morrell use the term "Broad churchmen," which is associated with the theological liberals of the third quarter of the century, to describe the founders of the British Association. The activity they subsume under that term actually much more closely parallels the contemporary evangelical ethos than the later ethos of liberal Anglicanism.

56. Brian Stanley, " 'Commerce and Christianity': Providence Theory, the Missionary Movement, and the Imperialism of Free Trade, 1842–1860," *Historical Journal*, 26 (1983): 76. For a criticism of Stanley, see Andrew Porter, " 'Commerce and Christianity': The Rise and Fall of a Nineteenth-Century Missionary Slogan," *Historical Journal*, 28 (1985): 597–621; see also David Brion Davis, *Slavery and Human Progress* (Oxford: Oxford University Press, 1984), pp. 231–258, 279–320.

57. *Apologia*, pp. 216, 217.

CHAPTER 2. MEN IN MOTION

1. Richard Brent, "Note: The Oriel Noetics," in M. G. Brock and M. C. Curthoys, eds., *The History of the University of Oxford*, vol. 6, *Nineteenth-Century Oxford, Part I* (Oxford: Clarendon, 1997), pp. 72–76. Even this cautious note suggests a stronger sense of collegiality to this group than evidence exists to sustain. See also Pietro Corsi, *Science and Religion: Baden Powell and the Anglican Debate, 1800–1860* (Cambridge: Cambridge University Press, 1988), pp. 83–95, and Thomas C. Hummel, "John Henry Newman and the Oriel Noetics," *Anglican Theological Review*, 74 (1992): 203–215.

2. H. C. G. Matthew, "Noetics, Tractarians, and the Reform of the University of Oxford in the Nineteenth Century," *History of Universities*, 9 (1990): 212.

3. JK to R. Wilberforce, December 31, 1827, John Keble Papers, Keble College; J. T.

Coleridge, *A Memoir of the Rev. John Keble, M. A., Late Vicar of Hursley*, Second Edition with Corrections and Additions (London: James Parker, 1869), 1: 175–182; *L&D*, 2: 44–47. Newman in his age saw the election of Hawkins as providentially allowing him to undertake the Tractarian Movement. See JHN to EBP, June 9, 1882; JHN to Lord Blatchford, November 4, 1884, *L&D*, 30: 106–107, 432.

4. Brock and Curthoys, *History of the University of Oxford*, 6: 56–63, 201–206; John Hamilton Thom, ed., *The Life of the Rev. Joseph Blanco White, Written by Himself; with Portions of His Correspondence* (London: John Chapman, 1845), 2: 198–199; 3: 130–132.

5. "Autobiographical Memoir" (1874), *AW*, pp. 86–107; *L&D*, 2: 202–250; A. Dwight Culler, *The Imperial Intellect: A Study of Newman's Educational Ideal* (New Haven: Yale University Press, 1955), pp. 96–122.

6. F. L. Cross, *John Henry Newman* (London: Philip Allan, 1933), pp. 162–163; G. F. A. Best, *Temporal Pillars: Queen Anne's Bounty, the Ecclesiastical Commissioners, and the Church of England* (Cambridge: Cambridge University Press, 1964), pp. 273–275; John R. Griffin, "The Meaning of *National Apostasy:* A Note on Newman's *Apologia,*" *Faith and Reason*, 2 (1972): 19–33; John R. Griffin, *The Oxford Movement: A Revision* (Edinburgh: Pentland, 1984), pp. 5–17; John R. Griffin, "John Keble, Radical," *Anglican Theological Review*, 53 (1971): 167–173; John R. Griffin, "The Radical Phase of the Oxford Movement," *Journal of Ecclesiastical History*, 27 (1976): 47–56; John Henry Lewis Rowlands, *Church, State, and Society: The Attitudes of John Keble, Richard Hurrell Froude, and John Henry Newman, 1827–1845* (Worthing, Sussex: Churchman, 1989), pp. 27–52.

7. John Keble, "National Apostasy," in Eugene R. Fairweather, ed., *The Oxford Movement* (New York: Oxford University Press, 1964), p. 41.

8. Keble, "National Apostasy," in Fairweather, *Oxford Movement*, pp. 40–43. Keble's text, 1 Samuel, 12:23, reads: "As for me, God forbid that I should sin against the Lord in ceasing to pray for you: but I will teach you the good and the right way."

9. Keble, "National Apostasy," in Fairweather, *Oxford Movement*, pp. 44, 45, 47.

10. John Keble, "Advertisement to the First Edition"(July 22, 1833) of "National Apostasy," in Fairweather, *Oxford Movement*, pp. 48–49.

11. Isaac Williams, *The Autobiography of Isaac Williams, B.D.*, ed. George Prevost (London: Longmans, Green, 1892), p. 118. On Keble's life, see Coleridge, *Memoir of Keble;* Walter Lock, *John Keble: A Biography* (Boston: Houghton, Mifflin, 1893); Georgina Battiscombe, *John Keble: A Study in Limitations* (New York: Knopf, 1964); Willem Joseph Antoine Marie Beek, *John Keble's Literary and Religious Contribution to the Oxford Movement* (Nijmegen: Centrale Drukkerij N.V., 1959); Owen Chadwick, *The Spirit of the Oxford Movement: Tractarian Essays* (Cambridge: Cambridge University Press, 1990), pp. 54–62.

12. Coleridge, *Memoir of Keble*, 1: 149–150; Lock, *John Keble*, pp. 204–222.

13. JK to J. T. Coleridge, January 26, 1819, Bodleian Library, Ms. Eng. lett. d. 134, f. 94. See also Arthur Penrhyn Stanley, *The Life and Correspondence of Thomas Arnold, D.D.*, Two Volumes in One (New York: Scriber's, n.d.), 1: 33–35; 2: 127–128.

14. T. Arnold to J. T. Coleridge, February 5, 1819; April 29, 1820, Bodleian Library, Ms. Eng. lett. d. 130, f. 13, 29. See also T. Arnold to J. T. Coleridge, January 31 and March 16, 1819, and June 19, 1820, Bodleian Library, Ms. Eng. lett. d. 130, f. 11, 15, 33.

15. Frank M. Turner, *Contesting Cultural Authority: Essays in Victorian Intellectual Life* (Cambridge: Cambridge University Press, 1993), pp. 73–100.

16. G. B. Tennyson, *Victorian Devotional Poetry: The Tractarian Mode* (Cambridge: Harvard University Press, 1981), pp. 1–113.

17. John Keble, *Sermons, Occasional and Parochial* (Oxford: James Parker, 1869), pp. 119, 184–185, 186, 193, 218, 236, 273–282.

18. JK to C. Dyson, Coleridge, *Memoir of Keble*, 1: 94. On the issue of establishment, see

also JK to J. T. Coleridge, June 22 and March 31, 1831, J. T. Coleridge Correspondence, Bodleian Library, Ms. Eng. lett. d. 134, pp. 196, 230. See also Griffin, *Oxford Movement*, pp. 7–8; John R. Griffin, "John Keble: Radical," *Anglican Theological Review*, 53 (1971): 167–173; Peter B. Nockles, *The Oxford Movement in Context: Anglican High Churchmanship 1760–1857* (Cambridge: Cambridge University Press, 1994), pp. 82–83.

19. JK to J. T. Coleridge, December, 1831; January, 1833, J. T. Coleridge Correspondence, Bodleian Library, Ms. Eng. lett. d. 134. f. 234 238. By 1833, according to Froude, "Keble . . . thinks the union of church and State, as it is now understood, actually sinful." RHF to A. P. Perceval in A. P. Perceval, *A Collection of Papers Connected with the Theological Movement of 1833*, 2d ed. (London: J. G. F. & J. Rivington, 1843), p. 12. See also Battiscombe, *John Keble*, p. 136–137.

20. JK to J. T. Coleridge, May 8, 1832, J. T. Coleridge Correspondence, Bodleian Library, Ms. Eng. lett. d. 134, f. 240.

21. JK to J. T. Coleridge, early 1832, quoted in Battiscombe, *John Keble*, p. 135; JK to C. A. Olgilvie, January, 1835, Bodleian Library, Ms. Eng. lett. d. 124, f. 71; JK to J. T. Coleridge, October 6, 1836, J. T. Coleridge Correspondence, Bodleian Library, Ms. Eng. lett. d. 134, f. 264. For Arnold's offending "Principles of Church Reform; with Postscript" (1833), see A. P. Stanley, ed., *The Miscellaneous Works of Thomas Arnold, D.D.* (London: B. Fellowes, 1845), pp. 257–338. On Keble's attitude toward and relationship with Arnold, see also Coleridge, *Memoir of Keble*, 1: 183; Griffin, "John Keble: Radical," *Anglican Theological Review*, 53 (1971): 167–173; and T. Arnold to J. T. Coleridge, July 1, 1835, and January 2, 1841, J. T. Coleridge Correspondence, Bodleian Library, Ms. Eng. lett. d. 130, f. 129, 191. In the second letter, Arnold wrote that he now understood Keble's estrangement: "It appears that he says that 'I do not believe in the Holy Catholic Church.' Now that I do not believe in it in Keble's Sense is most true. I would just as soon worship Jupiter, and Jupiter's Idolatry is scarcely further from Christianity in my Judgment than the Idolatry of the Priesthood."

22. T. Arnold to J. T. Coleridge, October 23, 1833, Bodleian Library, Ms. Eng. lett. d. 130, f. 121. On the Tractarian resemblance to Irving, see also T. Arnold to R. Whately, November 8, 1833, Stanley, *Life and Correspondence of Arnold*, 1: 328

23. JK to J. T. Coleridge, St. John's Day, 1843, Coleridge, *Memoir of Keble*, 2: 299, 300. For the full text see J. T. Coleridge Correspondence, Bodleian Library, Ms. Eng. lett, d. 135, f. 105. See also JHN to RHF, October 18, 1835, Newman, *L&D*, 5: 154.

24. JK to J. T. Coleridge, Feast of the Purification, 1844, Coleridge, *Memoir of Keble*, 2: 300, 301. For the full text see J. T. Coleridge Correspondence, Bodleian Library, Ms. Eng. lett, d. 135, f. 107.

25. JK to J. T. Coleridge, April 3, 1826, J. T. Coleridge Correspondence, Bodleian Library, Ms. Eng. lett. d. 134, f. 184. See also RHF to R. Froude, August 10, 1823, cited in William J. Baker, "Hurrell Froude and the Reformers," *Journal of Ecclesiastical History*, 21 (1970): 246n.

26. Froude, *Remains*, 1: 1–70; Piers Brenden, *Hurrell Froude and the Oxford Movement* (London: Paul Elek, 1974), pp. 60–74.

27. Froude, *Remains*, 2: 166–172.

28. Froude, *Remains*, 2: 27, 56–57, 103, 146, 158, 253.

29. Culler, *Imperial Intellect*, pp. 96–122. See further discussion of this incident in chapter 3.

30. RHF to Archdeacon Froude, November 28, 1830, as quoted in Brenden, *Froude and the Oxford Movement*, p. 105. See also J. H. Newman to JNM, July 25, 1847, *L&D*, 12: 203–204; Nockles, *Oxford Movement in Context*, pp. 67–85; Rowlands, *Church, State, and Society*, pp. 78–133.

31. Froude, *Remains*, 1: 250; Williams, *Autobiography*, pp. 63–64. On Froude's radical views of establishment, see Nockles, *The Oxford Movement in Context*, pp. 79–83.

32. RHF to JHN, July 30, 1833, *L&D*, 4: 16–17; Hadleigh Conference Sermon, presumably delivered by A. P. Perceval but quoted without attribution of authorship in Perceval, *Collection of Papers*, p. 42. See also Brenden, *Froude and the Oxford Movement*, pp. 128–131.

33. RHF to JHN, February 17, 1832; November 17, 1833, *L&D*, 3: 17–18; 4: 112. In this respect Froude differed from his supposed Nonjuror models. See Robert D. Cornwell, *Visible and Apostolic: The Constitution of the Church in High Church Anglican and Non-Juror Thought* (Newark: University of Delaware Press, 1993), pp. 44–58.

34. Froude, *Remains*, 1: 389, 391; 3: 7–10. See also Baker, "Hurrell Froude and the Reformers."

35. Froude, *Remains*, 1: 336; RHF to JHN, April 8, 1834; RHF to JHN, March 4, 1835, *L&D*, 4: 254; 5: 68. See Nockles, *Oxford Movement in Context*, pp. 122–127.

36. RHF to J. F. Christie, April, 1833, *L&D*, 3: 276n. See also JHN to Editor of the *Spectator*, May 5, 1883, *L&D*, 30: 214–215.

37. Froude, *Remains*, 1: 355, 356; RHF to JHN, April 8, 1834, *L&D*, 4: 254.

38. Froude, *Remains*, 3: 273–274.

39. Froude, *Remains*, 1: 404, 405, 407. He thought that in the end such endowments might not succeed because they might be confiscated by a future government or appropriated by a neighboring bishop.

40. John R. Griffin, "Dr. Pusey and the Oxford Movement," *Historical Magazine of the Protestant Episcopal Church*, (1972): 137–153; Peter Nockles, "Pusey on the Question of Church and State," in Perry Butler, ed., *Pusey Rediscovered* (London: S.P.C.K., 1983), pp. 255–298; A. M. Coleman, "'Puseyite' as General Term of Abuse," *Notes and Queries*, 166 (1934): 241–242, 428–429; Williams, *Autobiography*, pp. 70–72.

41. EBP to W. E. Gladstone, February 15, 1833, Gladstone Papers, British Library, Add. Ms. 44281, f. 4; EBP to H. P. Liddon, March 21, 1868, Liddon, *Pusey*, 4: 200–201.

42. EBP to M. Barker, October, 1827, Pusey-Barker Correspondence (transcripts), Pusey House, reprinted in Liddon, *Pusey*, 1: 4.

43. JHN to H. P. Liddon, March 19, 1884, *L&D*, 30:330; EBP to M. Barker, February 21, 1828, in Pusey-Barker Correspondence (transcripts), Pusey House, as quoted in Liddon, *Pusey*, 1: 132; see also EBP to M. Barker February 12 and 28 and March 5, 1828, in Pusey-Barker Correspondence (transcripts), Pusey House, and David Forrester, *Young Doctor Pusey: A Study in Development* (London: Mowbray, 1989), pp. 18–25. For Newman's recollection of Pusey's passion for Maria Barker, see JHN to H. P. Liddon, February 24, 1884, *L&D*, 30: 314. On Pusey's relationship with Charles Lloyd, who as Bishop of Oxford supported Catholic emancipation, see EBP to C. Lloyd, June 10, September 18, November 13, 18, 23, 1826, and February 26, March 30, April 22, 1827, E. B. Pusey-Charles Lloyd Correspondence (transcripts), Pusey House.

44. Liddon, *Pusey*, 1: 146–177; Albrecht Geck, "The Concept of History in E. B. Pusey's First Enquiry into German Theology and Its German Background," *Journal of Theological Studies*, n.s. 38 (1987): 387–408; Leighton Frappell, "'Science' in the Service of Orthodoxy: The Early Intellectual Development of E. B. Pusey," in Butler, *Pusey Rediscovered*, pp. 1–33; H. C. G. Matthew, "Edward Bouverie Pusey: From Scholar to Tractarian," *Journal of Theological Studies*, n.s. 32 (1981): 101–124; Forrester, *Young Doctor Pusey*, pp. 32–50, 211–231; H. J. Rose, *The State of the Protestant Religion in Germany; In a Series of Discourses Preached Before the University of Cambridge* (Cambridge: J. Deighton, 1825); David A. Valone, "Hugh James Rose's Anglican Critique of Cambridge: Science, Antirationalism, and Coleridgean Idealism in Late Georgian England," *Albion*, 33 (2001): 218–242.

45. E. B. Pusey, *An Historical Enquiry into the Probable Causes of the Rationalist Character Lately Predominant in the Theology of Germany, to which is Prefixed a Letter from Professor Sack, upon Rev. H. J. Rose's Discourses on German Protestantism; Translated from the German* (London: C. and J. Rivington, 1828), pp. 28–32 [see also pp. 39–43], 49, 50, 53.

46. Pusey, *Historical Enquiry*, p. 90. See also Liddon, *Pusey*, 1: 174–175; Forrester, *Young Doctor Pusey*, pp. 109 ff.; W. R. Ward, *The Protestant Evangelical Awakening* (Cambridge: Cambridge University Press, 1992), pp. 54–92.

47. Pusey, *Historical Enquiry*, p. 100, 101, 103, 105, 110.

48. Pusey, *Historical Enquiry*, p. 147.

49. Pusey, *Historical Enquiry*, pp. ix–x, x.

50. David W. F. Forrester, "Dr. Pusey's Marriage," in Butler, *Pusey Rediscovered*, pp. 131–133; Forrester, *Young Dr. Pusey*, pp. 58–63. See Maria Marcia Fanny French, *The Story of Dr. Pusey's Life* (New York: Longman, Green, 1900) for numerous letters relating to Pusey's marriage, generally undated, that were not printed in Liddon's volumes.

51. EBP to M. Barker, October 16, 1827; early 1828 or late 1827; January 8, 1828, Liddon, *Pusey*, 1: 125, 127–128, 132. In the letter of early 1828 or late 1827 he praised recent efforts in Germany to lead Jews to conversion, but clearly was not convinced that the salvability of Jews depended upon such conversion.

52. Pusey, *Historical Enquiry*, p. 105; M. Barker to EBP, October 18, 1827, Pusey-Barker Correspondence (transcripts), Pusey House; EBP to M. Barker, October, November, 1827, EBP–Mrs. Pusey Correspondence, Pusey House as quoted in Liddon, *Pusey*, 1: 124 [see also EBP to Mrs. Pusey, November 4, 1835, for a comment on this letter, EBP–Mrs. Pusey Correspondence, Pusey House]; EBP to M. Barker, March 5, 1828, Pusey-Barker Correspondence (transcripts), Pusey House. EBP to M. Barker, May 16, 1828, Pusey-Barker Correspondence (transcripts), Pusey House, as quoted in Forrester, *Young Doctor Pusey*, p. 62. In 1829 Pusey would again criticize evangelical use of religious feeling to Keble, "On the province of 'feeling' in Religion, I fear that I shall be widely mistaken: it would be almost too much to expect that a distinction should be made between 'feelings' and 'feeling': the one the faculty of the mind, the other the outward manifestations of that faculty—the emotions. It is I think the employment of the latter as a test of religion, which has caused so much mischief and self-deception and misery: while the neglect of the former appeared to me also to have been injurious to Religion by causing the intellect to be alone considered." EBP to JK, April 18, 1829, Pusey-Keble Correspondence (transcripts) Pusey House, as quoted in Forrester, *Young Doctor Pusey*, pp. 131–132.

53. EBP to M. Barker, May 30, 1828, E. B. Pusey-Maria Barker Correspondence (transcripts), Pusey House.

54. EBP to C. Lloyd, October 6, 1828, E. B. Pusey-Charles Lloyd Correspondence (transcripts), Pusey House as quoted in Liddon, *Pusey*, 1: 184, 185. See also EBP to C. Lloyd, October 9, 1828, and another undated letter of October 1828 in EBP-Charles Lloyd Correspondence, Pusey House. The trimming quality of this letter particularly emerges when compared to Pusey's letter to John Keble of May 1829, in which he forthrightly stated, "On 'historical inspiration' I own that, if taken in its most extensive and rigid sense, I have felt myself obliged to abandon it: that is, if applied to all the minute facts, not immediately connected with religious truth." EBP to JK, May, 1829, E. B. Pusey-John Keble Correspondence (transcripts), Pusey House, as quoted in Forrester, *Young Doctor Pusey*, p. 225.

55. E. B. Pusey, *An Historical Enquiry into the Causes of the Rationalist Character Lately Predominant in the Theology of Germany. Part II. Containing an Explanation of the Views Misconceived by Mr. Rose, and Further Illustrations* (London: C. J. G. and F. Rivington, 1830), p. vii. See also Liddon, *Pusey*, 1: 160–172.

56. C. Blomfield to EBP, January 4, 16, 1830, E. B. Pusey-Charles Blomfield Correspondence, Pusey House.

57. Pusey, *Historical Enquiry, Part II*, pp. 11, 14.

58. Pusey, *Historical Enquiry, Part II*, pp. 33–34.

59. Pusey, *Historical Enquiry, Part II*, pp. 370–371.

60. Pusey and Maria were married on June 12, 1828. The wedding had been scheduled

for April, but Pusey's father died just a week before the date originally set, causing its postponement. EBP to M. Barker, April 14, 15, 16, 17, 18, 19, 20, 1828, Pusey-Barker Correspondence (transcripts), Pusey House.

61. See James R. Moore, "Of Life and Death: Why Darwin 'Gave up Christianity,' " in James R. Moore, ed., *History, Humanity, and Evolution: Essays for John C. Greene* (Cambridge: Cambridge University Press, 1989), pp. 195–230; Michael Wheeler, *Death and the Future Life in Victorian Literature and Theology* (Cambridge: Cambridge University Press, 1990).

62. EBP to Mrs. Pusey, November 4, 6, 13, 19, 1835 in EBP–Mrs. Pusey Correspondence (transcripts), Pusey House. See Gabriel O'Donnell, "The Spirituality of E. B. Pusey," in Butler, *Pusey Reconsidered*, pp. 233–234, for more extensive quotation from the November 6, 1835, letter.

63. EBP to Mrs. Pusey, June 2, 1839, in E. B. Pusey–Mrs. Pusey Correspondence (transcripts), Pusey House. In 1837, in response to a friend's belief that his sister's decline in health resulted from her following Pusey's advice in his tract on fasting, Pusey complained that the absence of clerical agreement about the value of fasting meant "that people have no individual advisors, and one has to resort to this quackery of printing, which sends out a medicine into the world without being able to say how, or in what proportions, or by what individuals it is to be used." EBP to Mrs. Pusey, June 4, 1837. See also EBP to Mrs. Pusey, June 4, 1837, and May 1, 5, 9, 20, 1838; and Mrs. Pusey to EBP, June 21 (begun June 19), 1838. All citations in E. B. Pusey–Mrs. Pusey Correspondence (transcripts), Pusey House. On the more general issue of fasting within an evangelical culture, see Julius H. Rubin, *Religious Melancholy and Protestant Experience in America* (New York: Oxford University Press, 1994), pp. 156–196.

64. Mrs. Pusey to EBP, June 14 (letter begun June 12), 1838; EBP to Mrs. Pusey, October 25, 1836. See also Mrs. Pusey to EBP, June 11, 1838. EBP to Mrs. Pusey, April 29, 30 1834, states the earliest instances of the stern corporal punishment of his children recorded in his letters. All citations in E. B. Pusey–Mrs. Pusey Correspondence (transcripts), Pusey House.

65. EBP to B. Harrison, April 16, 1835, Liddon, *Pusey*, 1: 317–318. See also Pusey's statement of 1840 in which he distinguished the differing views of those associated with Puseyism and those he termed Calvinist, but who appear to have been evangelicals in regard to "the means whereby a man, having been justified, remains so." Pusey explained, "The one would say (the Calvinist), by renouncing his own works and trusting to Christ alone; the other, by striving to keep God's commandments through the grace of Christ, trusting to Him for strength to do what is pleasing to God, and for pardon for what is displeasing, and these bestowed especially through the Holy Eucharist as that which chiefly unites them with their Lord." Liddon, *Pusey*, 2: 140.

66. EBP to W. B. Pusey, May 18, 1835, Liddon, *Pusey*, 1: 317; T. L. Claughton to R. Palmer, February 23, 1836, Selborne Papers, Lambeth Palace Library, Ms. 1861, f. 18. See also C. P. Golightly to P. S. Dodd, February 13, 1836, Golightly Papers, Lambeth Palace Library, Ms. 1805, f. 126.

67. Rune Imberg, *In Quest of Authority: The "Tracts for the Times" and the Development of the Tractarian Leaders, 1833–1841* (Lund: Lund University Press, 1987), pp. 166–169, 171–174; Forrester, *Young Doctor Pusey*, pp. 229, 265n60; Liddon, *Pusey*, 2: 89–90; *L&D*, 6: 234n–235n.; JHN to H. P. Liddon, November 20, 1885, *L&D*, 31: 97.

68. Keith Denison, "Dr Pusey as Confessor and Spiritual Director," in Butler, *Pusey Rediscovered*, pp. 210–230; Liddon, *Pusey*, 3: 4, 12.

69. EBP to JK, September 26, 1844, in Liddon, *Pusey*, 3: 96–97

70. JHN to EBP, January 12, 1836, *L&D*, 5: 198, 199; JHN to C. Ward, September 25, 1848, *L&D*, 12: 273–274. See also Gabriel O'Donnell, "The Spirituality of E. B. Pusey," in Butler, *Pusey Rediscovered*, pp. 231–254, and Rubin, *Religious Melancholy*, pp. 125–196.

CHAPTER 3. JOHN HENRY NEWMAN AND THE CALL TO OBEDIENCE

1. The two now-standard biographies of Newman are Ian Ker, *John Henry Newman: A Biography* (Oxford: Oxford University Press, 1988), and Sheridan Gilley, *Newman and His Age* (London: Darton, Longman, and Todd, 1990), to which should also be added Maisie Ward, *Young Mr. Newman* (New York: Sheed and Ward, 1948); Meriol Trevor, *Newman: The Pillar of the Cloud* (Garden City: Doubleday, 1961); Paul Vaiss, *Newman: Sa Vie, Sa Pensée, et Sa Spiritualité* (Paris: L'Harmattan, 1991); and Vincent Ferrer Blehl, *Pilgrim Journey: John Henry Newman, 1801–1845* (New York: Paulist, 2001). For the financial aspects of the Newman family and related matters, see *L&D*, 1: 18–19, 26–28, 60–61; Sean O'Faolain, *Newman's Way: The Odyssey of John Henry Newman* (New York: Devin-Adair, 1952), pp, 1–20, 49–85; Barbara Weiss, *The Hell of the English: Bankruptcy and the Victorian Novel* (Lewisburg: Bucknell University Press, 1986), pp. 13–47; Boyd Hilton, *The Age of Atonement: The Influence of Evangelicalism on Social and Economic Thought 1785–1865* (Oxford: Clarendon, 1988), pp. 117–162, 288–297.

2. Journal, June 25, 1869, AW, p. 268. In his old age, Newman was deeply concerned to assure people that in 1816 his father's bank had paid all its creditors; see JHN to T. Mozley, June 9, 1882, *L&D*, 30: 94; see also John Newman to JHN, April 2, 1816, and JHN Memorandum, March 17, 1874, *L&D*, 1: 18 and 18nn. 2, 3.

3. Stephen Dessain, "Newman's First Conversion," *Newman Studien*, 3 (1957): 37–53. The father of Henry Manning, the other convert-cardinal from the Church of England to Roman Catholicism, experienced bankruptcy just after his son's completing his Oxford degree. In the months thereafter Manning decided to take Holy Orders to improve his chances of a college fellowship. Edmund Sheridan Purcell, *Life of Cardinal Manning, Archbishop of Westminster* (New York: Macmillan, 1896), 1: 70–105.

4. *Apologia*, p. 17. For Romaine's discussion of final perseverance, see William Romaine, "Treatise on the Triumph of Faith," in *The Whole Works of the Late Reverend William Romaine, M.A.*, New Edition, Carefully Revised (Edinburgh: T. Nelson, 1840), pp. 343–346, 359–371.

5. W. Mayers to JHN, April 14, 1817, *L&D*, 1: 32. On Newman's general evangelical background, consult John E. Linnan, *The Evangelical Background of John Henry Newman*, 2 vols. (Louvain thesis, 1965); John E. Linnan, "The Search for Absolute Holiness: A Study of Newman's Evangelical Period," *Ampleforth Journal*, 73 (1968): 161–174. On the social standing of evangelicals at Oxford, see S. Wilberforce to W. Wilberforce, June 21, 1823, quoted in David Newsome, *The Wilberforces and Henry Manning: The Parting of Friends* (Cambridge: Harvard University Press, 1966), p. 73.

6. *Apologia*, pp. 20, 484n. See also Trevor, *Newman*, pp. 19–22, 88–96; F. W. Newman, *Contributions Chiefly to the Early History of the Late Cardinal Newman, with Comments* (London: Kegan, Paul, Trench, Trübner, 1891), pp. 2–3.

7. *L&D*, 1: 86–99; Office of the Commissioners and Successors: Order Books Relating to Petitions against Declarations of Bankruptcy, pp. 263–265, Public Record Office b1 / 160; *London Gazette*, May 21, 1822, p. 856; September 3, 1822, p. 1451; *Law Chronicle, Commercial, and Bankruptcy Register*, no. 552, September 5, 1822, p. 283; no. 537, May 23, 1822, p. 162. I wish to thank Professor David Sacks for his comments on matters relating to the law and process of bankruptcy.

8. JHN to JNM, July 2, 1871; "Memorandum, The Delation to Rome," January 14, 1860; JHN to E. Bellasis, August 20, 1862, *L&D*, 25: 351; 19: 282; 20: 34.

9. Journal, November 15, 1821; January 11, July 12, 1822, *AW*, 177, 180, 186–187.

10. JHN to R. Greaves, February 27, 1828, *L&D*, 2: 58; Journal, January 12, 1822, February 21, 1826, *AW*, pp. 180, 208. On John Newman's apprehensions about his son's intense evangelicalism and Newman's comments on his Oriel colleagues, see Journal, January 6, December 1, 1822; April 4, May 2, 1823; February 21, 1826, *AW*, pp. 179, 188, 190–191, 209.

11. "Autobiographical Memoir" (1874) *AW,* 73, 74.

12. Edward Copleston, *An Enquiry into the Doctrines of Necessity and Predestination in Four Discourses Preached Before the University of Oxford. With Notes and an Appendix on the Seventeenth Article of the Church of England,* 2d ed. (London: John Murray, 1821), pp. 175–176; Journal, May 16, 1824; February 21, 1826, *AW,* pp. 199, 209.

13. Journal, February 21, 1825; August 9, 1823, *AW,* p. 204, 193; JHN to Mr. Newman, August 9, 1824, *L&D,* 1: 184. [Newman may have written parts of this letter to suggest that he was refraining from the excessive zeal against which his father had once warned him.] Richard Whately, *The Use and Abuse of Party-Feeling in Matters of Religion Preached Before the University of Oxford in the Year MDCCCXXII, at the Lecture Founded by the Late Rev. John Bampton, M. A., Canon of Salisbury* (Oxford: [Oxford] University Press, 1822), p. 232; JHN to Mrs. Newman, August 30, 1824; see also JHN to Mrs. Newman, July 28, 1824, and Newman's remarks on his stern preaching, *L&D,* 1: 177–180, 180–181, 189.

14. JHN to JK, December 19, 1827; see also JHN to Mrs. E. Hawkins, November 21, 1882, *L&D,* 2: 44, 30: 153.

15. J. B. Sumner, *Apostolical Preaching Considered, in an Examination of St. Paul's Epistles,* 3d ed. (London: J. Hatchard, 1820), pp. 10, 247. As a Roman Catholic, Newman once recommended Sumner's volume; see JHN to Unknown Correspondent, February 4, 1867, *L&D,* 23: 50.

16. Sumner, *Apostolical Preaching,* pp. 25, 26, 27, 135, 212.

17. Edward Hawkins, *A Dissertation upon the Use and Importance of Unauthoritative Tradition as an Introduction to the Christian Doctrines; Including the Substance of a Sermon Preached Before the University of Oxford, May 31, 1818* (Oxford: W. Baxter, 1819), pp. 1 [see also p. 14], 17, 18, 20.

18. Hawkins, *Dissertation,* pp. 43, 46, 77; see also pp. 52–53, 76–77.

19. See Richard Whately's anonymous *Letters on the Church. By an Episcopalian* (London: Longman, 1826). The estimate of the income from the tutorship is based on the entry into the Oriel College *Fellows and Exhibitions Account Book for the Year Ending March, 1830,* Birmingham Oratory. Reference 10.7.9. That account book records each of the Oriel tutors in that year as having received £308. For the Oriel fellowship income I am indebted to information furnished by the Librarian of Oriel College.

20. Journal, February 21, 1826, *AW,* p. 208; Mr. Newman to JHN, October 27, 1821; Mrs. Newman to JHN, February 21, 1822; see also Mrs. Newman to JHN, November 23, 1821, *L&D,* 1: 114, 117, 122.

21. Journal, February 9, 1824; June 5, 1826; February 21, 1827; see also Journal, February 21 and November 4, 1823; June 9, 1824, *AW,* pp. 189, 194, 196, 199–200, 209, 210. Newman had continued to receive some money from his father even after the bankruptcy, but in 1824 he sent a payment to his father; see Blue Account Book from early 1820s, Birmingham Oratory. For the manner in which Newman's personality in the 1820s conforms to that of persons believing in magic, consult Stuart A. Vyse, *Believing in Magic: The Psychology of Superstition* (New York: Oxford University Press, 1997), pp. 24–58.

22. Journal, August 9, 1823, *AW,* pp. 192, 193; C. R. Newman to JHN, February 23, 1825; JHN to C. R. Newman, March 3 and 24, July 7, August 25, 1825, *L&D,* 1: 212n., 213, 219, 240, 254. See also F. W. Newman, *Contributions,* pp. vii–viii.

23. C. R. Newman quoted in Journal, August 9, 1823, *AW,* p. 193. For the movement of his brothers toward independent thought, consult Mrs. Newman to JHN, February 18, 1828; Aunt Elizabeth Newman to JHN, February 21, 1828; HNM to JHN, February 23, 1828, *L&D,* 2: 56, 56n., 57, and Francis William Newman, *Phases of Faith; or Passages from the History of My Creed,* 6th ed., 1860 (rpt. New York: Humanities, 1970), pp. 16–64; William Robbins, *The Newman Brothers: An Essay in Comparative Intellectual Biography* (Cambridge: Harvard University Press, 1966), pp. 14–39.

24. JHN to Mrs. Newman, October 28, 1827, *L&D,* 2: 33. On the issue of baptism and

justification, see HNM to JHN, April 23, 1828; JNM to JHN, May 17, 1828, *L&D*, 2: 5n., 67, 67n.; F. W. Newman, *Phases of Faith*, pp. 6–11; Thomas J. Sheridan, *Newman on Justification* (New York: Alba House, 1967), pp. 127–134; Robbins, *The Newman Brothers*, pp. 14–30.

25. Journal, October 30, 1825; see also February 21, 1828, *AW*, pp. 207, 213; JHN to E. Hawkins, January 18, 1828, *L&D*, 2: 51. See also M. R. Giberne to JHN, January 8, 1882, *L&D*, 30: 50, for an account of Mary's sudden demise. For an important, sensitive discussion of the significance of his sister's death for Newman, consult Louis Bouyer, *Newman: His Life and Spirituality* (London: Burns and Oates, 1958), pp. 96–115.

26. JHN to JNM, March 9, May 10, 1828; JHN to HNM, June 4, August 20, November 23, 1828; February 17, 1829, *L&D*, 2: 62, 69, 74, 91, 108, 123; see also JHN to R. Wilberforce, July 16, 1828, *L&D*, 2: 82. On sleeping in his deceased sister's bed, see JHN to A. St. John, January 6, 1864, *L&D*, 21: 7.

27. JHN to JNM, May 10, 1828, *L&D*, 2: 68–69 [see also 2: 67, 143]; F. W. Newman, *Contributions*, p. 4; JHN to HNM, November 23, 1828, *L&D*, 2: 108. The members of the dining club included Charles Awdry, John Bramston, Henry Deane, George Anthony Denison, William Falconer, R. H. Froude, James Garbett, William Jacobson, Richard Martin, Frederick Oakeley, Joseph Loscombe Richards, James Thomas Round, Augustus Page Saunders, Robert Walker, Henry Wilberforce, and Henry Arthur Woodgate.

28. JHN to JK, July 31, 1828, *L&D*, 2: 85; Froude, *Remains*, 1: 233.

29. JHN to JNM, March 4, 1829; JHN to Mrs. Newman, March 13, 1829, *L&D*, 2: 128, 130.

30. *PPS*, 7: 53. For a complete listing of subjects and dates of Newman's sermons, see John Henry Newman, *Sermons, 1824–1843*, Placid Murray, ed. (Oxford: Clarendon, 1991), 1: 353–372.

31. JHN to JNM, March 17, 1829; Mrs. Newman to JHN, December 11, 1829; HNM to JHN, July 16, 1830, *L&D*, 2: 133, 177, 254.

32. *PPS*, 3: 190, 192, 200, 201, 202, 204.

33. *Via Media*, 2: 10–11. See also JHN to G. T. Edwards, February 8, 1883, *L&D*, 30: 180–181; Isaac Williams, *The Autobiography of Isaac Williams, B.D.*, ed. George Prevost (London: Longmans, Green, 1892), pp. 43, 47–48; and T. C. F. Stunt, "John Henry Newman and the Evangelicals," *Journal of Ecclesiastical History*, 21 (1970): 65–74.

34. *L&D*, 2: 97, 181–182, 188, 197–199; see *Via Media*, 2: 7–8.

35. JHN to HNM, October 16, 1831, *L&D*, 2: 367. He served one year as Dean of Oriel as a result of the college election of October 17, 1833.

36. JHN to C. R. Newman, May 25, August 19, 1830, and "Memorandum on Revelation," January 2, 1831; see also JHN to JNM, September 2, 1830, *L&D*, 2: 224, 266–283, 285–286.

37. JHN to JNM, May 27, 1830; Mrs. Newman to JHN, May 31, August 9, 1830; JHN to Mrs. Newman, August 27, 1830, *L&D*, 2: 226, 228, 263, 284.

38. JHN to S. L. Pope, August 15, 1830, *L&D*, 2: 264, 265. On Newman's resignation from the Bible Society, see *L&D*, 2: 228. Newman continued, however, to take interest in the internal quarrels of the Bible Society, for reports of which consult *Christian Observer*, 32 (1832): 117–124, 141–190, 206–300, 358–365.

39. JHN to FWN, 1830, *L&D*, 2: 183, 184.

40. JHN to Unknown Correspondent, February 4, 1867; JHN to H. T. Ellacombe, January 21, 1870; JHN to G. T. Edwards, February 24, June 2, 1883, *L&D*, 23: 51; 25: 12; 30: 188–189, 225. See also Vaiss, *Newman*, pp. 293–428, for an exploration of his preaching that emphasizes the presence of both evangelical and high-church sentiments.

41. *PPS*, 3: 80, 81, 87, 88.

42. *University Sermons*, pp. 18, 19, 18, 23, 21, 25, 34, 27. Newman thought that the heathen who in the past and present may not have possessed the special spiritual gifts made possible by revelation "are not in danger of perishing, except so far as all are in such danger,

whether in heathen or Christian countries, who do not follow the secret voice of conscience, leading them on by faith to their true though unseen good." *University Sermons*, p. 33. See also JHN to C. R. Newman, August 19, 1830, and "Memorandum on Revelation," January 2, 1831 in *L&D*, 2: 266–283. See also Francis McGrath, *John Henry Newman: Universal Revelation* (Macon, Georgia: Mercer University Press, 1997).

43. *PPS*, 8: 202–205. See also R. H. Froude, "The Gospel the Completion of Natural Religion," in *Remains*, 2: 58–69.

44. *PPS*, 8: 211, 212, 215; 1: 179, 188. For the expression of similar sentiments, consult Froude, *Remains*, 2: 27, 46, 56, 68, 103, 116–117, 158, 169–170. See Francis Joseph Butler, *John Henry Newman's Parochial and Plain Sermons Viewed as a Critique of Religious Evangelicalism* (Catholic University of America, S.T.D., 1972), pp. 105–158.

45. *PPS*, 1: 115, 118.

46. *PPS*, 1: 119, 119–20, 120.

47. *University Sermons*, p. 137.

48. JHN to W. J. Trower, April 16, 1833; JHN to S. Wilberforce, February 4, 1835; JHN to S. Wilberforce, March 10, 1835, *L&D*, 3: 292; 5: 21–22, 39, 40. See also Newman's critique of Chalmers's theology in this regard, "Critical Remarks on Dr. Chalmers' Theology" (dated 1834), Newman Microfilms, A. 9. 1., reel 7, batch 43, as well as David Newsome, "Justification and Sanctification: Newman and the Evangelicals," *Journal of Theological Studies*, n.s. 15 (1964): 32–53.

49. *University Sermons*, pp. 117, 118. See Richard Whately, *Essays on the Errors of Romanism, Having Their Origins in Human Nature* (London: B. Fellowes, 1830), pp. 26 ff., 45 ff., 123 ff., for an extensive criticism of superstition from which Newman may here be dissenting.

50. *University Sermons*, pp. 104, 111.

51. *PPS*, 1: 309, 311, 315–316.

52. *PPS*, 1: 320, 322, 323.

53. *University Sermons*, p. 69.

54. JHN to S. L. Pope, August 21, 1834; JHN to J. Stephen, February 27, 1835; JHN to S. Wilberforce, March 10, 1835, *L&D*, 4: 324; 5: 32, 40.

55. *Arians*, pp. 89, 41, 55. Regarding the publication background of this volume, see H. J. Rose to JHN, March 9, 1831; JHN to H. J. Rose, March 28, 1831, *L&D*, 2: 321–322. See also *L&D*, 3: 104–105, 112; Rowan Williams, "Newman's *Arians* and the Question of Method in Doctrinal History," in Ian Ker and Alan G. Hill, eds., *Newman After a Hundred Years* (Oxford: Clarendon, 1990), pp. 263–286; Jaroslav Pelikan, "Newman and the Fathers: The Vindication of Tradition," *Studia Patristica*, 18 (1990): 379–390. Consult [G. Vance Smith], "Newman's Arians of the Fourth Century," *Christian Reformer*, n.s. 1 (1834): 226–233, 316–323, 399–406, and [Bonamy Price], "Newman's *History of the Arians*," *Edinburgh Review*, 63 (1836): 44–72, for examples of the relatively few contemporary comments. Also note that both in *The Arians of the Fourth Century* and in his 1830 sermon, the concept of "the Dispensation of Paganism" appears to be equivalent to what in the private memorandum on revelation, originally associated with correspondence to his brother Charles, he termed "an *universal* revelation." "Memorandum on Revelation," January 2, 1831, *L&D*, 2: 281–283.

56. *Arians*, pp. 41–42, 50–51, 166, 167, 171. These phrases are strikingly similar to passages in Hawkins's *Unauthorized Tradition*.

57. *Arians*, pp. 153–156. On evangelical women preaching see Deborah M. Valenze, *Prophetic Sons and Daughters: Female Preaching and Popular Religion in Industrial England* (Princeton: Princeton University Press, 1985).

58. *Arians*, pp. 157, 161, 163, 162, 195.

59. *Arians*, pp. 421, 422.

60. JHN to H. Wilberforce, July 20, 1859, *L&D*, 19: 181. On the circumstances of the rejection of Newman's manuscript, see W. R. Lyall to H. J. Rose, October 19, 1832; H. J. Rose to JHN, October 21, 1832; JHN to H. J. Rose, October 23, 1832; W. R. Lyall to JHN, November 3 and 9, 1832, *L&D*, 3: 103–105, 112–113.

61. JHN to Mrs. Newman, February 28, 1833, *L&D*, 3: 224–225, 227.

62. JHN to H. Wilberforce, March 9, 1833; JHN to G. Ryder, March 14, 1833, JHN to JNM, March 20, 1833, *L&D*, 3: 247, 249, 264. In so mentioning Keble, Newman seems to have been completing or anticipating the thought of the conclusion of *The Arians of the Fourth Century*, taken through the press in the late autumn of 1833.

63. JHN to J. F. Christie, March 7, 1833; JHN to JNM, March 20, 1833; JHN to EBP, March 19, 1833; JHN to John Frederic Christie, April 6, 1833; JHN to JNM, April 11, 1833, *L&D*, 3: 239, 265, 259, 277, 284; see also JHN to S. Rickards, April 14, 1833, *L&D*, 3: 290. It is not altogether clear whether the last clause of Pusey's letter refers to the English and Roman Churches or to the various Christian groups in England.

64. JHN to H. Jenkyns, April 7, 1833; JHN to HNM and JNM, March 25, 1833; JHN to Mrs. Newman, April 5, February 28, 1833, *L&D*, 3: 280, 270, 274, 227.

65. JHN to W. J. Trower, April 16, 1833, *L&D*, 3: 293.

66. JHN to JNM, April 11, 1833, *L&D*, 3: 283.

67. JHN to Mrs. Newman, April 17, 1833, *L&D*, 3: 295, 296.

68. For the correspondence of June, July, and September 1832 between Newman and Jenkyns on the matter of the authority of the Oriel provost vis-à-vis the Oriel dean, see *L&D*, 3: 58–64, 97–98.

69. JHN to H. A. Woodgate, April 17, 1833, *L&D*, 3: 300.

70. For the first major argument in this direction, see F. L. Cross, *John Henry Newman* (London: Philip Allan, 1933), pp. 162–163.

71. JHN to R. H. Froude, August 1, 1833; JK to JHN, August 8, 1833; JHN to C. P. Golightly, August 11, 1833, *L&D*, 4: 17–18, 23, 28; see also A. P. Perceval, *A Collection of Papers Connected with the Theological Movement of 1833*, 2d ed. (London: J. G. F. and J. Rivington, 1843), pp. 12–13. For a discussion of thinking about liturgical matters, see "Liturgical Reform," *Quarterly Review*, 50 (1834): 508–561.

72. JHN to T. Mozley, August 5, 1833, *L&D*, 4: 24.

73. [J. H. Newman], "Letters on the Church of the Fathers," *British Magazine*, 4 (1833), 421, 763, 767; 5 (1834): 256.

74. [Newman], "Letters on the Church of the Fathers," *British Magazine*, 7 (1835): 662, 663. See also [Newman], "Letters on the Church of the Fathers," *British Magazine*, 4 (1833): 764; 6 (1834): 45, 156–158.

75. [Newman], "Letters on the Church of the Fathers," *British Magazine*, 8 (1835): 41. See also JHN to RHF, July 16, 1835, *L&D*, 5: 99–100.

76. [Newman], "Letters on the Church of the Fathers," *British Magazine*, 8 (1835): 42.

77. [Newman], "Letters on the Church of the Fathers," *British Magazine*, 8 (1835): 158, 43, 45, 283.

78. [J.H. Newman], "Home Thoughts Abroad," *British Magazine*, 9 (1836): 365–366.

79. [Newman], "Home Thoughts Abroad," *British Magazine*, 9 (1836): 366, 367, 369.

80. John Hamilton Thom, ed., *The Life of the Rev. Joseph Blanco White, Written by Himself; with Portions of His Correspondence* (London: John Chapman, 1845) 2: 33–36. See also Martin Murphy, *Blanco White: Self-Banished Spaniard* (New Haven: Yale University Press, 1989).

81. [Newman], "Home Thoughts Abroad," *British Magazine*, 9 (1836): 367–368.

82. Charles Smyth, *Simeon and Church Order* (Cambridge: Cambridge University Press, 1940), pp. 250–253. For the self-reference to Elijah, see JHN to Mrs. Henry Wilberforce, December 23, 1836, *L&D*, 5: 397.

CHAPTER 4. WHAT THE EARLY TRACTS SAID

1. Proposed Declaration by William Palmer, March 31, 1841, in Liddon, *Pusey*, 2: 205–206; R. W. Church, *The Oxford Movement: Twelve Years, 1833–1845*, ed. Geoffrey Best (Chicago: University of Chicago Press, 1970), pp. 86, 87.

2. S. Rickards to JHN, November 20, 1833, *L&D*, 4: 115; [J. H. Newman], "Advertisement," *Tracts for the Times*, 3: v, vi. For Newman's powerfully uncompromising response to Rickards and other early friendly criticism, see JHN to S. Rickards, November 22/23, 1833, *L&D*, 4: 116–119. For comments on the early view of the tracts within Oxford, see R. Palmer to C. Wordsworth, December 14, 1833, Correspondence of Christopher Wordsworth, Lambeth Palace Library, Ms. 1824, f. 33.

3. Quoted in A. P. Perceval, *A Collection of Papers Connected with the Theological Movement of 1833*, Second Edition (London: J. G. F. and J. Rivington, 1843), pp. 18, 19. See also JHN to H. J. Rose, January 1, 1834, *L&D*, 4: 155–159, and [William Scott], "State of the Church—Mr. Palmer's Narrative," *Christian Remembrancer*, 6 (1843): 538–568. Consult Marvin O'Connell, *The Oxford Conspirators: A History of the Oxford Movement, 1833–1845* (New York: Macmillan, 1969), pp. 123–173, for the fullest narrative of the events surrounding the launching of the tracts and William Seth Adams, *William Palmer of Worcester, 1803–1885, the Only Really Learned Man Among Them* (Princeton diss., 1973), for the best discussion of the struggle between the Tractarians and high churchmen during the autumn of 1833. For information on the temporary suspension of publication, see JHN to J. W. Bowden, November 13, 1833; JHN to RHF, November 13, 1833; JHN to Unknown Correspondent, January 28, 1882, *L&D*, 4: 98, 99–100; 30: 55.

4. JHN to S. Rickards, November 22/23, 1833, *L&D*, 4: 116–117; see also JHN to J. W. Bowden, November 17, 1833, *L&D*, 4: 108–110.

5. J. W. Bowden to JHN, November 15, 1833, *L&D*, 4: 110.

6. For titles and authors of the tracts, see Liddon, *Pusey*, 3: 473–480.

7. JK to JHN, January 30, 1834, John Keble Papers, Keble College, Oxford; JHN to J. W. Bowden, November 17, 1833, *L&D*, 4: 108–110; *Christian Observer*, 34 (1834): 324. See also Peter Nockles, " 'Lost Causes and . . . impossible loyalties': the Oxford Movement and the University," in M. B. Brock and M. C. Curthoys, eds., *The History of the University of Oxford*, vol. 6, *Nineteenth-Century Oxford, Part I* (Oxford: Clarendon, 1997), pp. 195–267.

8. JHN to J. W. Bowden, November 17, 1833, *L&D*, 4: 109, 110.

9. JHN to S. Rickards, November 22, 1833, *L&D*, 4: 117.

10. *Christian Observer*, 37 (1837): 256n. Rune Imberg has traced the tortured and complex publication history of the tracts and related publications in *Tracts for the Times: A Complete Survey of All the Editions* (Lund: Lund University Press, 1987); see also pp. 143–164 for a long list of revisions. For other important information regarding the publication of the tracts, see Lawrence N. Crumb, "Publishing the Oxford Movement: Francis Rivington's Letters to Newman," *Publishing History*, 28 (1990): 5–53, and Rune Imberg, *In Quest of Authority: The "Tracts for the Times" and the Development of the Tractarian Leaders, 1833–1841* (Lund: Lund University Press, 1987), pp. 215–234.

11. Richard H. Hutton, *Cardinal Newman* (London: Methuen, 1891), p. 47.

12. On the social condition of the clergy see Brian Heeney, *A Different Kind of Gentleman: Parish Clergy as Professional Men in Early and Mid-Victorian England* (Hamden, Conn.: Archon, 1976); Anthony Russell, *The Clerical Profession* (London: S.P.C.K., 1980); and Alan Haig, *The Victorian Clergy* (London: Croom Helm, 1984).

13. *Tract 1:* 1–2. Consult the index for titles and authors of cited tracts.

14. See Michael R. Watts, *The Dissenters*, vol. 2, *The Expansion of Evangelical Nonconformity* (Oxford: Oxford University Press, 1995), pp. 240–264, and [William Pitt Scargill], *The Autobiography of a Dissenting Minister* (London: Smith, Elder, 1834), on the congregational difficulties that Dissenting clergy confronted.

15. *Tract 1:* 2; *Tract 2:* 2.

16. *Tract 1:* 2–4.

17. *Tract 2:* 2–3; *Tract 11:* 5; *Tract 15:* 1; *Tract 16:* 8.

18. *Tract 52:* 3, 8.

19. *Tract 54:* 3, 12. See also Peter B. Nockles, *The Oxford Movement in Context: Anglican High Churchmanship, 1760–1857* (Cambridge: Cambridge University Press, 1994), pp. 146–152, and Robert Bruce Mullin, *Episcopal Vision/American Reality: High Church Theology and Social Thought in Evangelical America* (New Haven: Yale University Press, 1986), pp. 60–98.

20. *Christian Observer,* 34 (1834): iii, 88–89, 186; see also *Christian Observer,* 34 (1834): 324, for another association of the Oxford tracts with both bigotry and Popery, and *Christian Observer,* 34 (1834): 515, on the issue of Christian unity.

21. *Record,* December 5, 1833.

22. *Record,* April 21, August 18, 1836; August 7, December 14, 18, 1837. See also *Record,* December 15, 1834; June 30, 1835, for early comments critical of the Tractarians, and *Record,* September 18, 1837, for a defense of "Puseyite" understood as a term standing in stark contrast to evangelicalism.

23. This clericizing of the sacraments lay at the fountainhead of the Tractarian endeavor as seen in a private statement of principles, which Keble had produced in September 1833. Though later modified even for very limited private circulation, the original draft clearly displayed the manner in which Keble linked the validity of the sacraments to apostolical succession and hence to the social status and utility of the clergy. Keble wrote, "Considering 1. That the only way of salvation is the partaking of the Body and Blood of our sacrificed Redeemer; 2. That the means expressly authorized by Him for that purpose is the holy Sacrament of His Supper; 3. That the security, by Him no less expressly authorized, for the continuance and due application of that Sacrament, is the Apostolical commission of the Bishops, and, under them, the Presbyters of the Church; 4. That, under the present circumstances of the Church of England, there is peculiar danger of these truths being slighted and practically disavowed, and of numbers of Christians being left or tempted to precarious and unauthorized ways of communion, which must terminate often in virtual apostasy . . . " (Printed in *L&D,* 4: 42.) See *L&D,* 4: 129 for the narrowly circulated final draft, which modified Keble's first point to "Considering, that the Lord's Supper is the great means of applying to individuals the benefits of Christ's Sacrifice on the Cross." He then urged that a committee of clergy seek to circulate various publications declaiming the importance of the apostolical succession and the desirability of more frequent communions. See also JHN to J. Stephen, March 16, 1835, *L&D,* 5: 44–48. In 1833 all of this correspondence was private, but in 1843 A. P. Perceval made it public. Read in the climate of late Tractarianism, this correspondence convinced some people that early Tractarian sacramentalism was actually "Romish" in intention. See Perceval, *Collection of Papers,* pp. 10–17.

24. *Evangelical Magazine,* n.s. 12 (April 1834): 154, as quoted in Donald M. Lewis, *Lighten Their Darkness: The Evangelical Mission to Working-Class London, 1838–1860* (New York: Greenwood, 1986), p. 19.

25. "My sermons are a constituent part of the literature of the movement, as much as the Tracts for the Times are. The Tracts are from 1833 to 1841. The Sermons overlapped them, viz they ran from 1825 to 1843." JHN to G. T. Edwards, February 24, 1883, *L&D,* 30: 189.

26. *Tract 2:* 2; *Tract 11:* 1; *Tract 29:* 4; *Tract 52:* 5; *Tract 60:* 3. See JHN to W. G. Todd, August 12, 1850, *L&D,* 14: 37, in which he states that the objects of the attacks of the movement of 1833 were evangelicals. In undated notes for an unwritten narrative of the Tractarian Movement, C. P. Golightly, once Newman's curate and later his implacable enemy, associated the Tractarians with "a violent dislike of that class of serious persons whom they call Evangelicals or Peculiars and a harsh and contemptuous way of speaking of them."

C. P. Golightly Papers, Lambeth Palace Library, Ms. 1811, f. 263. It is again one of the ironies of the Tractarian Movement that when Newman a quarter-century later wrote his *Apologia,* he adopted the evangelical emphasis on sincerity as one of his chief rhetorical devices.

27. *Tract 4:* 5, 7.

28. *Tract 4:* 1, 2; JK to JHN, autumn 1833, John Keble Papers, Keble College.

29. *Tract 10:* 4 (italics added); on the revision of this passage, see also S. Rickards to JHN, November 20, 1833; J. Dean to JHN, December 2, 16, 1833; JHN to H. J. Rose, January 1, 1834, *L&D,* 4: 115, 131, 144, 158.

30. S. Rickards to JHN, November 28, 1833; JHN to H. J. Rose, November 23, December 15, 1833, *L&D,* 4: 119, 120, 143. For Rickards's highly critical comments on the view of the eucharist advanced in the original edition of *Tract 10;* see S. Rickards to JHN, September 20, 1833, *L&D,* 4: 115.

31. Letter of August 22, 1834, Froude, *Remains,* 1: 370–372. Froude continued in the same letter, "If you are determined to have a pulpit in your church, which I would much rather be without, do put it at the west end of the church, or leave it where it is: every one can hear you perfectly; and what can they want more? But whatever you do, pray don't let it stand in the light of the Altar, which, if there is any truth in my notions of Ordination, is more sacred than the Holy of Holies was in the Jewish Temple." Froude, *Remains,* 1: 372. See also Nockles, *Oxford Movement in Context,* pp. 235–248; A. Hardelin, *The Tractarian Understanding of the Eucharist* (Studia Historico-ecclesiastica Upsaliensia, 8, Upsala [Distributors: Almqvist and Wiksell, Stockholm, 1965]).

32. Adam Smith, *An Inquiry into the Nature and Causes of the Wealth of Nations,* R. H. Campbell and A. S. Skinner, eds. (Oxford: Clarendon, 1979), pp. 789, 791, quoting David Hume, *History of England* (1778), 3: 30–31. Hume had thought the government should bribe clergy into indolence rather than face the disruptive social and religious behavior that would arise when clergy shorn of establishment needed to provide for themselves.

33. *Tract 7:* 2, 4; *Tract 15:* 3.

34. *Tract 35:* 3, 4.

35. *Tract 36:* 1–3, 5.

36. *Tract 36:* 7.

37. *Tract 29:* 2, 4, 5; *Tract 30:* 7.

38. *Tract 47:* 3, 3–4; see also [J. H. Newman], "Home Thoughts Abroad," *British Magazine,* 9 (1836): 242–243.

39. *Tract 51:* 2, 4, 11, 14, 2, 5.

40. *Tract 61:* 3

41. *Tract 54:* 1–3.

42. *Tract 57:* 1, 3, 6.

43. *Tract 57:* 8, 11, 9, 9–10, 11, 12. See Timothy C. F. Stunt, "Geneva and British Evangelicals in the Early Nineteenth Century," *Journal of Ecclesiastical History,* 32 (1981): 35–46.

44. *Tract 57:* 13, 14.

45. JK to JHN, March 22 or 27, 1834, John Keble Papers, Keble College.

46. Nockles, *Oxford Movement in Context,* pp. 229–234; John C. S. Nias, *Gorham and the Bishop of Exeter* (London: S.P.C.K., 1951). See also *Tract 76* for a Tractarian survey of various contemporary positions on baptismal regeneration.

47. EBP to H. A. Woodgate, September 14, 1843, H. A. Woodgate Letters, Lambeth Palace Library, Ms. 3535, f. 22.

48. E. B. Pusey, *Scriptural Views of Holy Baptism* (1835), pp. 14–16. This rare first edition of *Tracts 67, 68,* and *69* is to be found in the Beinecke Library of Yale University. The volume contains all three tracts paginated continuously and like the other tracts printed

without publication information. Unless otherwise indicated all quotations from *Tracts 67, 68,* and *69* are cited from this 1835 volume rather than with the individual tract number.

49. Pusey, *Scriptural Views of Holy Baptism,* pp. 1, 9.

50. Pusey, *Scriptural Views of Holy Baptism,* pp. 29, 37.

51. Pusey, *Scriptural Views of Holy Baptism,* pp. 62–63, 65. 81.

52. [J. H. Newman], "Advertisement," October 31, 1835, *Tracts for the Times,* 2: v, vi. See also, "Tracts for the Times," *Christian Remembrancer,* 18 (1836): 645–656.

53. *Record,* August 29, 1836 [see also *Record,* August 25 and September 5, 1836]; October 12, 1837, "High Church Principles, No. VII," September, 1837, January 1, 1838.

54. *Christian Observer,* 36 (1836): 789–791n.

55. JHN to A. Mozley, January 26, 1885, *L&D,* 31: 20; *Christian Observer,* 37 (1837): 119n., 120n., 332n.; see also pp. 122n.–123n., 195n.; consult 114–126, 141–198, 243–263, 317–352 for Newman's original letters to the journal.

56. *Christian Observer,* 37 (1837): 121n., 249n. [see also 37 (1837): 319n.–321n., and 39 (1839): 163n., 654n.], 122n. [see also 336n.], 259n. The *Christian Observer* editor accused Newman of misapplying the meaning of their critique of Pusey and more importantly of misquoting the Homilies by omitting sentences without indication of the omission. *Christian Observer,* 37 (1837): 192n.–193n.

57. *Tract 20:* 3. The most extensive discussion of the Tractarian views of Roman Catholicism remains R. H. Greenfield, *The Attitude of the Tractarians to the Roman Catholic Church, 1833–1850* (Oxford D. Phil. thesis, 1956).

58. JHN to J. W. Bowden, September 11, October 10, 1835, *L & D,* 5: 142, 150.

59. *Tract 71:* 1, 2.

60. *Tract 75:* 23.

61. *Tract 71:* 4.

62. *Tract 71:* 9, 34.

63. *Tract 71:* 27, 31, 32.

64. [J. H. Newman], "Advertisement," November 1, 1834, *Tracts for the Times,* 1: iii–v.

65. JHN to S. Rickards, November 22, 1833, L&D, 4: 118; *Tract 75:* 1.

66. William Palmer, *Origines Liturgicae, or Antiquities of the English Ritual,* 2 vols. (London, 1832).

67. *Tract 57:* 7; *Tract 71:* 30.

68. See *Tract 15:* 11 in its first edition in Beinecke Library, Yale University. Palmer's modification came in a subsequent edition of *Tract 15:* 11. See also Imberg, *In Quest of Authority,* p. 224

69. *Tract 45:* 1–3; *Tract 45:* 6; F. W. Newman, *Contributions to the Early History of the Late Cardinal Newman, with Comments* (London: Kegan Paul, Trench, Trübner, 1891), p. 22.

70. Pusey, *Scriptural Views of Holy Baptism,* pp. 90, 103, 90. 107, 127.

71. E. B. Pusey, *Scriptural Views of Holy Baptism with an Appendix* (London: J. G. and F. Rivington, 1836), pp. x, xi. Pusey wrote the preface and appendix to this second printing of his tract after Newman's *Tract 73* on Rationalism. On the publication history of Pusey's tract, see Liddon, *Pusey,* 1: 352–354. Pusey's attack on Zwingli and the continental Reformers was especially harsh in the first edition of his three tracts and in the prefatory letter to the one-volume reprint of that edition published in 1836, here cited. In the second enlarged edition of the tract, published in 1839, and in the third edition of 1840 the criticisms were still present but much softened and less extensive. He may have quietly made these revisions in light of the hostile reception accorded the remarks on the Reformation in Froude's *Remains.* The first edition became a quite rare publication, and in most collections of the tracts it is the second edition that was included. This was a not unusual Tractarian tactic of pushing their point very far in the first edition and then silently backtracking later.

72. Pusey, *Scriptural Views of Holy Baptism,* pp. 193–194.

73. *Tract 38:* 2, 3, 4, 6, 5. Significantly, in this tract entitled the *Via Media,* Newman devoted only a single page to Roman Catholicism while directing the remaining pages to a polemic explaining how the proliferation of evangelical Protestantism had driven English Protestant religious life far beyond the original boundaries of the Reformation.

74. *Tract 38:* 9–10.

75. *Tract 41:* 6, 12.

CHAPTER 5. THE HAMPDEN CASE

1. Handbill on the 1834 Bill on Subscription, Radnor Papers, Pusey House; *L&D,* 4: 208–212, 245–247, 318–320; V. Thomas to the Duke of Wellington, May 2, 1834; J. Griffiths to the Duke of Wellington, July 31, 1834; Wellington Papers, University of Southampton, 2/245/ff. 6, 105a, 105d. On the more general background to the Subscription controversy, see R. W. Church, *The Oxford Movement: Twelve Years, 1833–1845* (Chicago: University of Chicago Press, 1970), pp. 113–124; W. R. Ward, *Georgian Oxford: University Politics in the Eighteenth Century* (Oxford: Clarendon, 1958), pp. 239–256; W. R. Ward, *Victorian Oxford* (Oxford: Clarendon, 1965), pp. 80–103; Owen Chadwick, *The Victorian Church* (New York: Oxford University Press, 1966), 1: 121–126; Marvin O'Connell, *The Oxford Conspirators: A History of the Oxford Movement, 1833–1845* (New York: Macmillan, 1969), pp. 191–206; P. B. Nockles, "'Lost Causes and . . . Impossible Loyalties': The Oxford Movement and the University," in M. G. Brock and M. C. Curthoys, eds., *The History of the University of Oxford,* vol. 6, *Nineteenth-Century Oxford, Part I* (Oxford: Oxford University Press, 1997), pp. 121–225.

2. E. Cardwell to the Duke of Wellington, April 19, 1834; Duke of Wellington to G. Rowley, August 27, 1834; G. Rowley to the Duke of Wellington, August 29, 1834, Wellington Papers, University of Southampton, 2/244 f. 137; 2/245 ff. 121–122. See also the Wellington–Cardwell Correspondence of October 27, November 3, 10, 17, 24, 1834, Wellington Papers, University of Southampton, 2/245 ff. 128, 131, 134–136, 138, 140.

3. Renn Dickson Hampden, *Observations on Religious Dissent with Particular Reference to the Use of Religious Tests in the University,* 2d ed. rev. (Oxford: S. Collingwood; London: B. Fellowes and J. G. and F. Rivington, 1834), pp. 3, 7, 8, 11. The second edition here cited was the edition consistently cited by the Tractarians.

4. Renn Dickson Hampden, *The Scholastic Philosophy Considered in Its Relation to Christian Theology, in a Course of Lectures Delivered before the University of Oxford, in the Year MDCCCXXXII. at the Lecture Founded by John Bampton, M. A., Canon of Salisbury* (Oxford: J. H. Parker, 1833), pp. 149, 374, 383. See Pietro Corsi, *Science and Religion: Baden Powell and the Anglican Debate, 1800–1860,* (Cambridge University Press, 1988), pp. 67–72, 96–105, for discussions of other Oxford figures, including Baden Powell and Samuel Hinds, who had published arguments similar to Hampden's, but without provoking any significant reaction in the university.

5. Hampden, *Observations on Religious Dissent,* pp. 20–21, 25, 28.

6. Hampden, *Observations on Religious Dissent,* p. 35.

7. P. N. Shuttleworth to Lord Holland, October 2, 1834, Holland House Papers, British Library, Add. Ms. 51597, f. 131. Throughout the controversy Shuttleworth seems to have played a double game. He was a Whig seeking patronage through Holland, but as a member of the Hebdomadal Board, he pursued a moderate, trimming policy and occasionally criticized the Whig ministry.

8. R. D. Hampden to Lord Radnor, June 2, 1835, Radnor Papers, Pusey House. For the impact of Hampden's pamphlet on his opportunity for receiving patronage, see R. Whately to R. D. Hampden, October 16, 1835, Hampden Collection, Oriel College, Oxford; Lloyd C. Sanders, ed., *Lord Melbourne's Papers* (London: Longmans, Green, 1889), pp. 496–497. For

an excellent discussion of Whig religious policy and outlooks, consult Richard Brent, *Liberal Anglican Politics: Whiggery, Religion, and Reform, 1830–1841* (Oxford: Clarendon, 1987).

9. JHN to J. W. Bowden, January 30 and February 9, 1834; JHN to JK, Between March 7 and March 24, 1834, *L&D*, 4: 203; see also 4: 201n.; "Autobiographical Memoir," (1874), *AW*, 98. One can only wonder whether Hawkins had some hand in denying Newman the moral philosophy professorship the election to which would have embarrassed him after his dismissal of Newman from Oriel instructional duties.

10. JHN to H. J. Rose, August 20, 1834, *L&D*, 4: 323.

11. JHN to R. D. Hampden, November 28, 1834; see also JHN to Archdeacon Froude, November 13, 1834, *L&D*, 4: 364, 371.

12. For the unsent drafts of Newman to Hampden, see Newman Microfilms, reel 95, batch 140; R. D. Hampden to JHN, November 28, 1834, *L&D*, 4: 372. It is clear from Hampden's response that the word *Socinian* had not appeared in the letter he received from Newman. When Newman authorized the reprinting of this letter in 1871, *Socinian* did not appear in that reprinting [Henry Wilberforce, "Dr. Hampden and Anglicanism," *Dublin Review*, 69 (1871): 79], as it had not in the *Apologia*, p. 62. In later Victorian reprintings of this letter, however, the word *Socinian* did appear—apparently as editors used the original manuscript rather than looking to what Newman printed in the *Apologia* or what he had authorized Wilberforce to publish. See Mozley, *Letters and Correspondence*, 2: 69, and Liddon, *Pusey*, 1: 302. See also *L&D*, 4: 371n.4.

13. JHN to J. W. Bowden, December 1, 1834, *L&D*, 4: 372. See also JHN to H. Wilberforce, March 23, 1835, *L&D*, 5: 50. See also Meriol Trevor, *Newman: The Pillar of the Cloud* (New York: Doubleday, 1961), pp. 158–165; David Newsome, *The Wilberforces and Henry Manning: The Parting of Friends* (Cambridge: Harvard University Press, 1966), pp. 153–154.

14. JHN to Henry Wilberforce, March 23, 1835; Henry Wilberforce to JHN, March 25, 1835, *L&D*, 5: 51, 52. See also [Edward Hawkins], *A Letter to the Earl of Radnor upon the Oaths, Dispensations, and Subscriptions to the XXXIX Articles at the University of Oxford by a Resident Member of Convocation* (Oxford: J. H. Parker; London: B. Fellowes, 1835); L. G. Mitchell, "Politics and Revolution, 1772–1800," in L. S. Sutherland and L. G. Mitchell, eds., *The History of the University of Oxford, The Eighteenth Century* (Oxford: Clarendon, 1986), vol. 5, pp. 171–174; and B. W. Young, *Religion and Enlightenment in Eighteenth-Century England: Theological Debate from Locke to Burke* (Oxford: Clarendon, 1998), pp. 45–82.

15. [Henry Wilberforce], *The Foundation of the Faith Assailed in Oxford: A Letter to His Grace the Archbishop of Canterbury, &c. &c. &c. Visitor of the University, with Particular Reference to the Changes in Its Constitution, Now Under Consideration* (London: J. G. and F. Rivington, 1835), pp. 6–9.

16. [Wilberforce], *Foundation of the Faith Assailed*, pp. 15, 34.

17. R. D. Hampden, *Parochial Sermons Illustrative of the Importance of the Revelation of God in Jesus Christ*, Second Edition: To Which Are Added, Four Sermons Preached to the Children of the Bath National School (London: B. Fellowes, 1836), pp. 23–35.

18. H. Wilberforce to R. D. Hampden; R. D. Hampden to H. Wilberforce, May 20, 1835, *L&D*, 5: 73, 74.

19. R. D. Hampden to EBP, May 20, 1835 (a) and (b); E. Hawkins to EBP, May 27, 1835. In the same letter Hawkins also stated that other pamphlets against Hampden, in particular Wilberforce's, constituted a "gross libel." Marriott Papers, Pusey House; EBP to E. Hawkins, undated, Oriel College Letterbooks, 8: 765, Oriel College, Oxford. The pamphlet that initiated this exchange was [E. B. Pusey], *Subscription to the Thirty-Nine Articles: Questions Respectfully Addressed to Members of Convocation on the Declaration Proposed as a Substitute for the Subscription to the Thirty-Nine Articles, by a Bachelor of Divinity with Answers by a Resident Member of Convocation, and Brief Notes upon Those Answers by the Bachelor of Divinity* (Oxford: J. H. Parker; London: Rivington and Hatchard, 1835) This

pamphlet had a rather complicated publication history. Pusey published the list of questions, which in turn Edward Hawkins republished with answers. Then Pusey republished the second pamphlet with his comments on Hawkins's answers. The present citation includes the entire exchange.

20. R. D. Hampden to Lord Radnor, May 21, 1835, Radnor Papers, Pusey House.

21. *Pamphlets in Defence of the Oxford Usage of Subscription to the XXXIX Articles at Matriculation* (Oxford: J. H. Parker; London: J. G. and F. Rivington, 1835), 10–11, 13–14. The materials surrounding this pamphlet incident are quite rare. The copy I have used is in the Sterling Memorial Library of Yale University [Zeta Collection, Lmd 57/834/3] and consists of the two prefaces and the two tables of contents. It was originally part of a larger pamphlet collection put together in the 1830s and 1840s by John Griffiths of Wadham College, whose notes on the pamphlet indicate that John Keble was the author of the preface. Griffiths's attributions are normally correct, and there is no real reason to doubt that Keble wrote the preface although other of the Tractarians might just as well have written it. See also *L&D*, 5: 80n., 81n.

22. R. D. Hampden to JHN, June 23, 1835; see also JHN to H. Wilberforce, August 7, 1871, *L&D*, 5: 83; 25: 374–375.

23. J. H. Newman to S. Rickards, June 26, 1835; RHN to JHN, July 2, 1835, *L&D*, 5: 88, 97. See also W. Sewell to J. H. Newman, June 14, 1835, Newman Microfilms, reel 95, batch 140; JHN to S. Rickards, June 26, 1835; JHN to EBP, June 27, 1835, *L&D*, 5: 87–90. The other deleted pamphlet was [Benjamin Harrison], *Latitudinarianism in Oxford in 1690, a Page from the Life of Bishop Bull.* On Newman's recollection of this incident, see JHN to H. Wilberforce, August 4, 1871, *L&D*, 25: 370–371.

24. H. J. Rose to JHN, January 1, 1836; JHN to EBP, January 2, 1836; JHN to H. J. Rose, January 3, 1836, *L&D*, 5: 189, 188, 194.

25. JHN to T. Mozley, January 23, 1836 ("forerunner of Antichrist" appears in Greek in the original letter); JHN to EBP, January 24, 1836, *L&D*, 5: 210, 214.

26. EBP to W. E. Gladstone, February 2, 1836, Gladstone Papers, British Library, Add. Ms. 44281. f. 10. See also Sanders, *Lord Melbourne's Papers* p. 497; JHN to JK, January 30, 1836; JHN to RHF, January 31, 1836; JK to JHN, February 10, 1836, *L&D*, 5: 216–217, 219–220, 228.

27. R. D. Hampden to Lord Melbourne, February 8, 1836, Melbourne Papers, Royal Archives, RA MP (M)79/2.

28. Anne Mozley, ed., *Letters of the Rev. J. B. Mozley, D.D., Edited by His Sister* (London: Rivingtons, 1885), p. 50. See also JHN to EBP, Between 7 and 13 May, 1835, *L&D*, 5: 69–70.

29. William Palmer, *A Narrative of Events Connected with the Publication of the Tracts for the Times, with Reflections on Existing Tendencies to Romanism, and on the Present Duties and Prospects of Members of the Church,* Third Edition, with Postscript (Oxford: John Henry Parker; London: J. Burns and J. G. F. and J. Rivington, 1843), pp. 27–30; Church, *Oxford Movement,* pp. 120–121.

30. Nockles, "'Lost Causes and . . . Impossible Loyalties': The Oxford Movement and the University," in Brock and Curthoys, *The History of the University of Oxford,* 6: 230; *Record,* February 25, 1836. See also *Christian Observer,* 36 (1836): 189. Also consult Henrietta Hampden, ed., *Some Memorials of Renn Dickson Hampden* (London: Longmans, Green and Co., 1871), p. 90n.; William Palmer, *A Letter to the Rev. Dr. Hampden, Regius Professor of Divinity in the University of Oxford* (Oxford: John Henry Parker, 1842), p. 8; H. Wilberforce to JHN, May 10, 1831, *L&D*, 2: 329; Roger H. Martin, *Evangelicals United: Ecumenical Stirrings in Pre-Victorian Britain, 1795–1830* (Metuchen, N. J., 1983: Scarecrow), pp. 131–140.

31. JK to JHN, February 10, 1836; JHN to H. J. Rose, February 11, 1836, *L&D*, 5: 228, 232; *True Tablet,* June 4, 1842, p. 233.

32. R. D. Hampden to Lord Melbourne, February 10, 1836, Melbourne Papers, Royal Archives, RA MP (M)/79/5.

33. E. Bayly to Lord Holland, February 12, 1836, Holland House Papers, British Library, Add. Ms. 51597, f. 201.

34. The petition was signed by M. Routh of Magdalen, W. Landon of Worcester, G. W. Hall of Pembroke, R. Jenkyns of Balliol, G. Rowley of University, A. T. Gilbert of Brasenose, T. Gaisford of Christ Church, A. Gradyson of St. Edmund Hall, and E. Cardwell of St. Alban Hall. Melbourne Papers, Royal Archives, RA MP (M)/79/14. See also Wellington Papers, University of Southampton, 2/247/13. In drawing up the petition there had been debate as to whether to accuse Hampden of being opposed to "the theology of the Christian Church," "the Integrity of the Christian faith," or "the Church of England." See Richard Jenkyns Papers, Balliol College, Oxford, VIA, 14.

35. JHN, Diary, February 10, 1836; JHN to H. J. Rose, February 12, 1836, *L&D*, 5: 229–233; A. T. Gilbert to Lord Melbourne, February 16, 1836, Melbourne Papers, Royal Archives, RA MP (M)/79/24; E. Cardwell to the Duke of Wellington, February 15, 1836, Wellington Papers, University of Southampton, 1/247/22.

36. [J. H. Newman], *Elucidations of Dr. Hampden's Theological Statements* (Oxford: J. H. Parker, 1836), pp. 5–6.

37. [Newman], *Elucidations of Dr. Hampden's Theological Statements*, p. 11.

38. [Newman], *Elucidations of Dr. Hampden's Theological Statements*, pp. 18, 41.

39. JHN to John Frederic Christie, February 14, 1836; JHN to J. W. Bowden, February 17, 1836, *L&D*, 5: 234, 236–237. See also J. H. Newman to H. J. Rose, February 21, 1836, *L&D*, 5: 241. That Hampden's *Observations on Religious Dissent* had not appeared before he achieved the moral philosophy professorship was one reason for the absence of controversy over that appointment, but another was the absence of any significant income being attached to the position.

40. JHN to S. L. Pope, March 3, 1836, *L&D*, 5: 251. See Robert Pattison, *The Great Dissent: John Henry Newman and the Liberal Heresy* (New York: Oxford University Press, 1991), pp. 55–96, for the best discussion of the Newman-Hampden relationship and rivalry. It was noted at the time that two of Hampden's children were mentally handicapped, a situation that in addition to Hampden's ambition may have accounted for his drive for additional income. See C. P. Golightly to P. S. Dodd, February 13, 1836, Golightly Papers, Lambeth Palace Library, 1805, f. 126.

41. William Robbins, *The Newman Brothers: An Essay in Comparative Intellectual Biography* (Cambridge: Harvard University Press, 1966), pp. 57–60.

42. JHN to RHF, November 17, 1835, *L&D*, 5: 164.

43. JHN to FWN, November 23, 1835, *L&D*, 5: 166, 167.

44. JHN to FWN, November 23, 1835; Mrs. Newman to JHN, November 26, 1835, *L&D*, 5: 167.

45. JHN to RHF, October 18, 1835, *L&D*, 5: 154.

46. JHN to JNM, February 21, 1836, *L&D*, 5: 241. In the same letter Newman told Jemima, "As to Hampden's appointment, I think we might have had much greater calamities, unless it affects Pusey's health."

47. Louis Allen, ed., *John Henry Newman and the Abbé Jager: A Controversy on Scripture and Tradition (1834–1836)* (London: Oxford University Press, 1974), pp. 149–171. Froude very nearly agreed with Harrison at least in passing; see RHF to JHN, July 2, 1835, *L&D* 5: 98.

48. Melbourne Papers, Royal Archives, RA MP (M) 79/16–18; *L&D*, 5: 238n.1. Archbishop Howley clearly attempted to resist the exercise of Whig ministry patronage at Oxford, but he seems to have been unwilling to become directly associated with the political extremists at Oxford and with their irregular approach to the king.

49. E. Copleston to Lord Melbourne, February 13 and February 16, 1836; R. Whately

to Lord Melbourne, February 17, 1836, Melbourne Papers, Royal Archives, RA MP (M)/79/20, 23, 27. On Melbourne's more general concerns about theological orthodoxy, see Sanders, *Lord Melbourne's Papers*, p. 497; Lord Melbourne to William IV, Melbourne Papers, Royal Archives, RA MP (M)/79/17.

50. R. Whately to Lord Melbourne, February 21, 1836, Melbourne Papers, Royal Archives, RA MP (M)/76/162.

51. T. L. Claughton to R. Palmer, February 23, 1836, Selborne Papers, Lambeth Palace, Ms. 1861, f. 18.

52. EBP to Lord Melbourne, February 22, 1836, Melbourne Papers, Royal Archives, RA MP (M)/79/28; A. P. Stanley to Unknown Correspondent, February, 1836, Hampden File, f. 327, Oriel College, Oxford; C. P. Golightly to P. S. Dodd, February 9, 1836, C. P. Golightly Papers, Lambeth Palace, Ms. 1805, f. 124; JHN to H. J. Rose, February 12, 1836, *L&D*, 5: 233; T. L. Claughton to R. Palmer, February 23, 1836, Selborne Papers, Lambeth Palace, Ms. 1861, f. 18.

53. EBP to Lord Melbourne, February 22, 1836, Melbourne Papers, Royal Archives, RA MP (M)/79/28.

54. Lord Melbourne to EBP, February 24, 1836, Melbourne Papers, Royal Archives, RA MP (M)/79/29.

55. EBP to Lord Melbourne, February 26, 1836, Melbourne Papers, Royal Archives, RA MP (M)/79/30.

56. EBP to Lord Melbourne, February 26, 1836, Melbourne Papers, Royal Archives, RA MP (M)/79/30. Unable to resist a final thrust, Pusey scrawled in a postscript, "May I venture, without offence, to state to your Lordship that there has never, before this, been any instance, wherein a Minister recommended to His Majesty to appoint as the Professor in this place an individual, unacceptable to the University generally, much less one to whom they, upon principle, objected, & and thus rendered His Majesty's gift of a Professorship for the time an evil instead of what it has been a great benefit." EBP to Lord Melbourne, February 26, 1836, Melbourne Papers, Royal Archives, RA MP (M)/79/30.

57. Broadsides of February 24 and 25 and March 5, 1836, included in the materials under the Hampden Case, Beinecke Library, Mhg 56, vol. 1, Yale University. See also a series of letters from C. P. Golightly to P. S. Dodd written between February 9 and March 24, 1836, which recount the meetings of the Corpus Committee. C. P. Golightly Papers, Lambeth Palace, Ms. 1805, ff. 124-138.

58. "Report and Declaration of the Corpus Common Room Committee," March 10, 1836, *L&D*, 5: 264-265. Pusey sent most of the public attacks on Hampden to William Gladstone along with assurances that Hampden's thought would lead directly to Socinianism. EBP to W. E. Gladstone, March 6, 14, 17, 1836, British Library, Add. Ms. 44281, ff. 12-20. On Semler, see "J. S. Semler," *Encyclopaedia Britannica*, 11th ed. For one of Hampden's own critical comments on "rationalism," consult Hampden, *Scholastic Philosophy*, p. 40. No mention is made of the term *rationalism* in the only extensive review of Hampden's lectures, "Hampden's Bampton Lectures," *British Critic*, 14 (1833): 125-152.

59. [Thomas Moore and R. H. Brabant], "State of Protestantism in Germany," *Edinburgh Review*, 54 (1831): 246-248; E. G. Bayly to Lord Holland, March 13, 1836, Holland House Papers, British Library, Add. Ms. 51597, f. 220.

60. Froude, *Remains*, 3: 7, 14; RHF to JHN, January 30, 1835, *L&D*, 5: 18.

61. JK to R. Wilberforce, April 2, 1835, John Keble Papers, Keble College, Oxford; JK to J. T. Coleridge, October 6, 1836, J. T. Coleridge Correspondence, Bodleian Library, Ms. Eng. lett. d. 134, f. 264.

62. E. B. Pusey, *Tracts for the Times, nos. 67, 68, 69. Scriptural Views of Holy Baptism with an Appendix*, (London: J. G. and F. Rivington, 1836), pp. x-xi.

63. EBP to Augustus Tholuck, 1838, Liddon, *Pusey*, 1: 388.

64. *University Sermons*, p. 69; J. H. Newman, "Holy Baptism," dated 1834, in "Papers on Theological Subjects," A. 9.1, Newman Microfilms, reel 7, batch 43, pp. 3, 25.

65. *Tract 73*: 2. This definition appears to echo passages about rationalism in [Moore and Brabant], "State of Protestantism in Germany," *Edinburgh Review*, 54 (1831): 247–248. See also JHN to HNM, October 10, 1835, *L&D*, 5: 151. A note from Pusey may have instigated Newman's writing of this tract: "Something to stem the tide of American dissenting divinity would be very useful." EBP to JHN, September 4, 1835; Liddon, *Pusey*, 1: 357. See also John B. Logan, "Thomas Erskine of Linlathen, Lay Theologian of the 'Inner Light,' " *Scottish Journal of Theology*, 37 (1984): 23–40.

66. *Tract 73*: 3.

67. *Tract 73*: 4.

68. *Tract 73*: 3–5.

69. *Tract 73*: 13, 53. In a postscript to *Tract 73* Newman criticized Schleiermacher and other German theologians for being united with those who affirmed that the object of Christian Revelation was "to stir the affections, and soothe the heart," that the Christian faith contains "nothing which is unintelligible to the intellect," and that the creeds inhibited the spread of the Gospel, "being stumbling-blocks to the reason and shackles and weights on the affections" (*Tract 73*: 54–55). Newman's knowledge of Schleiermacher came from his reading an article on the German theologian in *The Biblical Repository* (nos. 18 and 19), an American journal.

70. *Tract 73*: 12.

71. JHN to Lord Lifford, September 12, 1837, *L&D*, 6: 133. See also JHN to G. T. Edwards, May 2, 1883, *L&D*, 30: 211–212.

72. "Correspondence—Mr. Perceval and the 'Record,' " *British Magazine*, 12 (1837): 538, 539; *The Record*, December 18, 1837; see also November 20, 1837.

73. *British Magazine*, 14 (1838): 26.

74. [Thomas Mozley], "New Oxford Theological Statute and Revival of the Hampden Question," *British Critic*, 32 (1842): 186–187.

75. For example, in 1836 the term *rationalism* made no appearance in "The Philosophy of Unbelief," *British Critic*, 19 (1836): 395–419.

76. E. Hawkins to R. Whately, March 31, 1836, Letterbooks, 5: 416, Oriel College.

77. Archbishop Howley to Lord John Russell, August 9, 1847, Lord John Russell Papers, Public Record Office, PR 30/22. 6E, f. 61. For Howley's change of mind, consult Howley-Russell correspondence, November 26, 27, and 29, 1847, Russell Papers PR 22/30. 6G, ff. 259, 264, 296. See also Chadwick, *The Victorian Church*, 1: 237–250.

78. S. Wilberforce to Miss L. Noel, December 29, 1847, R. A. Ashwell, *Life of the Right Reverend Samuel Wilberforce, Lord Bishop of Oxford and Afterwards of Winchester with Selections from His Diaries and Correspondence* (London: John Murray, 1880), 1: 498. See also 1: 419–515 for the full account of Wilberforce in 1847 and correspondence between Bishop Wilberforce and Edward Hawkins during late 1847 and early 1848 in Samuel Wilberforce Papers, Bodleian Library, C9, f. 57, ff. 107–135.

79. J. Hare to W. Whewell, December 20, 1847, William Whewell Papers, Trinity College, Cambridge, Add. Ms. a.77. f. 148, as reprinted in N. Merrill Distad, *Guessing at Truth: The Life of Julius Charles Hare, 1795–1855* (Shepherdstown: Patmos, 1979), p. 172. See also Julius Charles Hare, *A Letter to the Very Reverend The Dean of Chichester, on the Agitation Excited by the Appointment of Dr Hampden to the See of Hereford* (London: John William Parker, 1848).

80. W. E. Gladstone to R. D. Hampden, November 9, 1856, as quoted in H. Hampden, *Some Memorials of Renn Dickson Hampden*, p. 200. For Hampden's reply see R. D. Hampden to W. E. Gladstone, November 18, 1856, Gladstone Papers, British Library Add. Ms. 44386, f. 227. Gladstone seems to have forgotten this correspondence as time passed, as indicated in his correspondence with Henrietta Hampden when she was writing her father's biography.

See Henrietta Hampden to W. E. Gladstone, May 8 and 13, 1869, British Library Add. Ms. 44420, ff. 233, 262.

81. W. F. Hook to Bishop Samuel Wilberforce, March 19, 1864, W. R. W. Stephens, *The Life and Letters of Walter Farquhar Hook* (London: Richard Bentley, 1879), 2: 418.

82. Roundell Palmer, *Memorials, Part I, Family and Personal, 1766–1865* (London: Macmillan, 1896), 1: 213.

83. E. Hawkins to R. Whately, March 31, 1836, Letterbooks, 5: 416, Oriel College; E. Cardwell to the Duke of Wellington, March 11, 1836, Wellington Papers, University of Southampton, 2/247/45. Virtually all of the proceedings of the Hebdomadal Board became public or were reported to interested parties. See P. N. Shuttleworth to Lord Holland, March 1, 1836, and E. G. Bayly to Lord Holland, March 2, 3, 4, 5, 7, 9, 11, 13, 17, 20, 21, 1836; Holland House Papers, British Library Add. Ms. 51597, ff. 136, 203–231; E. Cardwell to the Duke of Wellington, February 26, 29, March 4, 7, 9, 11, 22, 1836; R. D. Hampden to the Duke of Wellington, March 9 and 11, 1836; G. Rowley to the Duke of Wellington, March 11, 14, 22, 1836, Wellington Papers, University of Southampton, 2/247/32–47; C. P. Golightly to P. S. Dodd, February 13, March 1, 5, 8, 12, 24, 1836, C. P. Golightly Papers, Lambeth Palace Library, Ms. 1805, ff. 128–138; E. Hawkins to R Whately, March 31, 1836, Letterbooks, 5: 416, Oriel College; JHN to H. J. Rose, February 29, 1836; JHN to R. Wilberforce, March 15, 1836, *L&D*, 5: 245, 260; Liddon, *Pusey*, 1: 373–379. Across the years Hawkins repeatedly and steadily deplored the attack on Hampden's personal religious faith, about which Hawkins entertained no doubts despite misgivings about Hampden's Bampton Lectures and his judgment "that there are many things very rash and incautious in his writings, and, [that] as they stand [they are] unsound." E. Hawkins to R. Whately, February 18, 1836, Letterbooks, 5: 413, Oriel College. Hawkins, ever the steady administrator, attempted to bring the protest into proper channels by insisting that Hampden be tried by the six doctors, an alternative the Hebdomadal Board refused to follow.

84. W. J. Copeland to G. F. Copeland, March 26, 1836, Ollard Papers, Pusey House. The background to the veto can be traced in the contemporary correspondence between Edward Bayly and Lord Holland. Holland House Papers, British Library Add. Ms. 51597, ff. 199–235.

85. H. Hampden, *Some Memorials of Renn Dickson Hampden*, p. 55.

86. R. D. Hampden, *Inaugural Lecture Read Before the University of Oxford in the Divinity School on Thursday, March 17, 1836* (London: B. Fellowes, 1836), pp. 4, 15, 19, 20. See E. Copleston to R. D. Hampden, February 18, 1836, Hampden File, Oriel College.

87. Hampden, *Inaugural Lecture,* pp. 26, 27, 29. See R. Whately to R. D. Hampden, March 6, 1836, Hampden File, Oriel College.

88. Quoted in Chadwick, *Victorian Church,* 1: 119n.; Blanco White to Lord Holland, March 6, 1836, Holland House Papers, British Library, Add. Ms. 51645, f. 230. See also Blanco White to Edward Hawkins, April 11, 1836, Oriel College, Letters, vol. 2, f. 108, in which contrary to Liddon, *Pusey,* 1: 361–364, he states that he had seen drafts of Hampden's Bampton Lectures and had predicted that Hampden would encounter trouble, but had not contributed to their composition.

89. T. Arnold to R. D. Hampden, February 17, 1836, Hampden File, Oriel College. In addition to the hesitant support within Oxford, a few public pamphlets defended Hampden, the most important being the Tory lawyer William Winstanley Hull's systematic analysis of the inaccuracies of Newman's *Elucidations.* Numerous newspaper articles also questioned the fairness of the proceedings. Consult William Winstanley Hull, *Remarks Intended to Shew How Far Dr. Hampden May Have Been Misunderstood and Misrepresented During the Present Controversy at Oxford,* Second Edition, Corrected (London: B. Fellowes, 1836); Anon., *Statements of Christian Doctrine Extracted from the Published Writings of R. D. Hampden, D.D., Regius Professor of Divinity in the University of Oxford* (London: B. Fellowes, 1836); Anon., *A Letter to His Grace the Archbishop of Canterbury, Explanatory of the Proceedings at Oxford, on*

the Appointment of the Present Regius Professor of Divinity by a Member of the University, 3d ed. (London: B. Fellowes, 1836); Anon., *The Oxford Persecution of MDCCCXXXVI: Extracts from the Public Journals; in Defence of the Present Regius Professor of Divinity, and His Appointment to That Chair; and in Condemnation of the Proceedings at Oxford, Subsequent to that Appointment* (London: B. Fellowes, 1836; Oxford: D. A. Talboys, 1836); W. W. Grinfeld, *Reflections after a Visit to the University of Oxford on the Occasion of the Late Proceedings Against the Regius Professor of Divinity in a Letter to the Rector of Lincoln College* (London: B. Fellowes; Oxford: J. H. Parker, 1836); Robert French Laurence, *Remarks on the Hampden Controversy Addressed Principally to Members of Convocation* (Oxford: D. A. Talboys; London: B. Fellowes, 1836).

90. T. Arnold to R. D. Hampden, February 17, 1836, Hampden File, Oriel College; [Thomas Arnold], "The Oxford Malignants and Dr. Hampden," *Edinburgh Review*, 63 (1836): 238–239. On March 28 Arnold had indicated to Hampden that he was writing an article in his support. On April 12, 1836, Arnold, casting Hampden in the role of a firm Protestant reformer, told J. Hearn, "Hampden is doing what real Christian reformers have ever done; what Protestants did with Catholicism, and the Apostles with Judaism. He upholds the Articles as true in substance, he maintains their usefulness, and the truth and importance of their doctrines; but he sees that the time is come when their phraseology requires to be protested against, as having, in fact, obstructed and embarrassed the reception of the very truths which they intend to inculcate." On April 21, 1836, Hampden, thanking Napier for publishing the article, commented, "I have long seen the tendency of all that has been going on here to degrade the University from its proper station & that usefulness as an University, to the rank of a low theological school. The present fury is but a strong manifestation of this." T. Arnold to R. D. Hampden, March 28, 1836, Hampden File, Oriel College; T. Arnold to J. Hearn, April 12, 1836, Arthur Penrhyn Stanley, *The Life and Correspondence of Thomas Arnold, D.D.*, 10th ed. (London: John Murray, 1877), 2: 27; R. D. Hampden to M. Napier, April 21, 1836, M. Napier Papers, British Library, Add. Ms. 34617, f. 407.

91. A. P. Stanley to Unknown Correspondent, April 1836, Rowland E. Prothro, *The Life and Correspondence of Arthur Penrhyn Stanley* (London: John Murray, 1893), 1: 163.

92. "Letter of the Corpus Committee, April 26, 1836," *L&D*, 5: 287–288.

93. EBP to C. A. Olgilvie, June 9, 1836, Bodleian Library, Ms. Eng. lett. d. 124, f. 152.

94. See H. Hampden, *Some Memorials of Renn Dickson Hampden*, p. 93–97, 111, and *Correspondence Between the Rev. Dr. Hampden, Regius Professor of Divinity in the University of Oxford, and the Most Rev. Dr. Howley, Lord Archbishop of Canterbury* (London: B. Fellowes, 1838).

CHAPTER 6. THE ASSAULT ON THE PROTESTANT

1. J. S. Mill to Gustave D'Eichthal, December 27, 1839, in Francis E. Mineke, ed., *The Earlier Letters of John Stuart Mill, 1812–1848* (Toronto: University of Toronto Press, 1963), pp. 415–416. For Matthew Arnold's indebtedness to Newman, see M. Arnold to JHN, November 29, 1871, *L&D*, 25: 440–441. Putting the matter somewhat differently, Lucy Aikin wrote the American William Ellery Channing regarding the Tractarians, "As for the origin of the sect, some say Cambridge having had her Simeon, Oxford must have her Pusey. But the root lies a little deeper than this. Our Church, as you know, is a Janus, having one face towards Geneva, the other towards the city upon the Seven Hills. Of the sour Geneva face, as exhibited by the modern Evangelicals, our gentlemanly clergy began to grow very sick, and to fancy they should prefer the other, which at least becomes a mitre far better." Lucy Aikin to W. E. Channing, March 23, 1839, in Anna Letitia Le Breton, ed., *Correspondence of William Ellery Channing, D.D., and Lucy Aikin, from 1826 to 1842* (Boston: Roberts Brothers, 1874), pp. 331–332. I wish to thank Professor R. K. Webb for furnishing this reference.

2. *Certain Difficulties*, p. 145.

3. John Henry Newman, *The Via Media of the Anglican Church*, ed. H. D. Weidner (Oxford: Clarendon, 1990).

4. JHN to JNM, July 11, 1836. Several years later Newman wrote to Henry Wilberforce, "I will add that my own Mother's death was a most unintentional and startling, but still a fulfillment of a prayer of mine—which wounded me much at the time, for I seemed, as if, to have been praying that God would take her away." JHN to Henry Wilberforce, April 25, 1842, *L&D*, 5: 322; 8: 511–512.

5. JHN to M. R. Giberne, March 20, 1836, *L&D*, 5: 262–263.

6. JHN to JNM, January 5, 1837; JHN to H. Manning, February 24, 1837; JHN to JNM, April 25, 1837, *L&D*, 6: 6, 34, 61. See also JHN to F. Rogers, January 7, 1837, *L&D*, 6: 8.

7. *Prophetical Office*, p. 13.

8. *Prophetical Office*, p. 19. For one of the few recognitions of how much more hostile Newman was to ultra-Protestantism than to Roman Catholicism, see Peter Nockles, *The Oxford Movement in Context: Anglican High Churchmanship, 1760–1857* (Cambridge: Cambridge University Press, 1994), p. 171.

9. *Prophetical Office*, pp. 24, 25. In regard to Germany, Newman was drawing on Pusey's volume of 1829, which had equated rationalistic religion with pietism. This passage also clearly reflects Keble's *Tract 57*. The Socinianism of Geneva referred to the radical evangelicalism associated with the Genevan evangelical ministry of César Malan, who enjoyed numerous contacts with radical British evangelicals. Timothy C. F. Stunt, "Geneva and British Evangelicals in the Early Nineteenth Century," *Journal of Ecclesiastical History*, 32 (1981): 35–46.

10. *Prophetical Office*, pp. v, 2, 3, 5.

11. *Prophetical Office*, pp. 180, 189, 34, 43, 178.

12. *Prophetical Office*, pp. 328, 37, 38, 39, 48, 61. "Scripture is interpreted by Tradition, Tradition verified by Scripture; Tradition gives form to the doctrine, Scripture gives life; Tradition teaches, Scripture proves." *Prophetical Office*, p. 327.

13. *Prophetical Office*, p. 225.

14. *Prophetical Office*, pp. 290, 289, 291.

15. *Prophetical Office*, pp. 315–317.

16. C. Nevile, *A Review of Mr. Newman's Lectures on Romanism with General Observations on the Oxford Tracts, and Dr. Pusey's Letter to the Bishop of Oxford* (London: James Ridgeway, 1839), pp. 147, 82, 82–83.

17. Charles P. M'Ilvaine, *Oxford Divinity Compared with That of the Romish and Anglican Churches: With a Special View of the Doctrine of Justification by Faith, as It Was Made of Primary Importance by the Reformers; and as It Lies at the Foundation of All Scriptural Views of the Gospel Our Lord Jesus Christ* (London: R. B. Seeley and W. Burnside, 1841), p. ii; *Christian Observer*, 37 (1837): 114–126, 141–198, 243–263, 317–352. Newman's two letters are reprinted without the hostile commentary in *Via Media*, 2: 143–194. See also M'Ilvaine, *Oxford Divinity*, pp. 40–53; Thomas L. Sheridan, *Newman on Justification: A Theological Biography* (New York: Alba House, 1967); Peter Toon, *Evangelical Theology, 1833–1856: A Response to Tractarianism* (London: Marshal, Morgan, and Scott, 1979), pp. 141–170; David Newsome, "Justification and Sanctification: Newman and the Evangelicals," *Journal of Theological Studies*, n.s. 15 (1964): 32–53; Peter Toon, "A Critical Review of John Henry Newman's Doctrine of Justification," *Churchman*, 94 (1980): 335–343; Alister E. McGrath, "The Emergence of the Anglican Tradition on Justification, 1600–1700," *Churchman*, 98 (1984): 28–42; Alister E. McGrath, "Justification in Earlier Evangelicalism," *Churchman*, 98 (1984): 217–227; Alister E. McGrath, *Iustitia Dei: A History of the Christian Doctrine of Justification* (Cambridge: Cambridge University Press, 1986), 2: 121–134; Henry Chadwick, "The Lectures on Justification," in Ian Ker and Alan G. Hill, eds., *Newman After a Hundred*

Years (Oxford: Clarendon, 1990), pp. 287–308; Nockles, *Oxford Movement in Context*, pp. 256–269.

18. JHN to Lord Lifford, September 12, 1837, *L&D*, 6: 129.

19. *Record*, April 15, 1839; JHN to Lord Lifford, September 12, 1837, *L&D*, 6: 128–130.

20. *Tract 83:* 12, 13.

21. *Lectures on Justification*, p. v.

22. *Lectures on Justification*, pp. 1, 2.

23. *Lectures on Justification*, pp. 4–5, 12. Henry Chadwick has commented, "His [Newman's] most penetrating critique, however, lies in his pinpointing of a central difficulty of embarrassing proportions for the Protestant Evangelicals, namely that, while asserting faith alone to be the sole instrument of justification, they find it impossible to offer any but the foggiest definition of what they mean by faith: they can say something only of what it is not, namely not a mere assent to belief in God, or to the gospel history, or even submission to due authority." Chadwick, "The *Lectures on Justification*," p. 295.

24. *Lectures on Justification*, pp. 12, 13.

25. *Lectures on Justification*, pp. 25, 18.

26. *Lectures on Justification*, pp. 371, 61, 61–62.

27. *Lectures on Justification*, pp. 362, 372, 372–373, 374.

28. *Lectures on Justification*, p. 389. Although Newman vehemently attacked Luther, he did not read German, nor had he apparently studied extensively the few of Luther's works translated into English. Newman did quote Melanchthon, who published in Latin. See Alister E. McGrath, "John Henry Newman's 'Lectures on Justification': The High Church Misrepresentation of Luther," *Churchman*, 97 (1983): 112–121.

29. *Lectures on Justification*, pp. 389, 127n. Newman defended his attack on the Reformation by stating that if he had "here or elsewhere used 'freedom of speech' concerning Luther and Calvin, I will observe that those who spoke as they did of all who went before them, have no claim on the reverence of those who come after." *Lectures on Justification*, p. 412.

30. *Lectures on Justification*, pp. 33, 67, 38.

31. *Lectures on Justification*, pp. 44, 58, 67. "That the forgiveness of sins is the work of the Holy Ghost was one of *my great points* as a Puseyite. It means that it is conveyed *in* the gift of grace—that justification and sanctification go together—that we are justified, not by external imputation, but by an inward gift." JHN to C. A. Bathurst, October 27, 1856, *L&D*, 17: 421.

32. *Lectures on Justification*, pp. 92, 167; see also p. 85.

33. *Lectures on Justification*, pp. 113, 203, 220. See also the important letter JHN to James Stephen, March 16, 1835, *L&D*, 5: 44–48.

34. *Lectures on Justification*, pp. 291–292, 300–301, 307. See JHN to G. Edwards, April 15, June 2, 1883, *L&D*, 25: 203–204, 224–225, for an extremely clear, succinct statement by Newman late in his life on what he understood to have been his theological differences with evangelicals over the atonement.

35. *Lectures on Justification*, pp. 260, 262.

36. See particularly E. B. Pusey, *A Letter to the Right Rev. Father in God Richard Lord Bishop of Oxford, On the Tendency to Romanism Imputed to Doctrines Held of Old, as Now, in the English Church* (Oxford: J. Parker, 1839), pp. 72, 72n–73n., 82–88, 96. For important evangelical criticism of Tractarian views of justification, see George Stanley Faber, *The Primitive Doctrine of Justification Investigated: Relatively to the Several Definitions of the Church of Rome and the Church of England; and with a Special Reference to the Opinions of the Late Mr. Knox, as Published in his Remains*, Second Edition: With an Appendix, Containing, among Matters, a Notice of Mr. Newman's Lectures on Justification (London: R. B. Seeley and W. Burnside, 1839).

37. On April 8, 1889, Leslie Stephen wrote to T. H. Huxley, "In No. 85 of the Tracts for the Times (in Vol. V 1838–40) J. H. Newman wrote a very well written essay for the confusion of Protestants. Their argument was that the sacraments etc. were not provable by the New Testament. His reply is, no more are the doctrines of the trinity, of Christ's divinity, or in particular, the admissibility of Gentiles to the church. His inference is, as there is no proof of either you may swallow both; but the curious thing is the clearness with which he shows that the gospels do not prove that Christ was more than a Jewish prophet of the usual kind—even taking them to be inspired. If you have to say anything more about it, it would perhaps be worth while to show that you have a cardinal to back you." Huxley took this advice and quoted from Newman in "Agnosticism and Christianity" (1889). Bernard Lightman, *The Origins of Agnosticism: Victorian Unbelief and the Limits of Knowledge* (Baltimore: Johns Hopkins University Press, 1987), pp. 114–115.

38. *Record,* August 22, September 29, August 22, 1836; see also *Record,* September 19, 1836, "High Church Principles VII," for a refutation of baptismal regeneration on the basis of the Fathers set forth only because of the manner in which the Tracts had convinced many people of the supposed stand of the Fathers on this issue. See also *Christian Observer,* 38 (1838): 312–314.

39. *Record,* 29 September 1836; Newman, *Tract 85:* 3, 4. See also *Christian Observer,* 38 (1838): 312–314.

40. *Tract 85:* 102.

41. *Tract 85:* 14, 11.

42. *Tract 85:* 15, 16, 25, 18, 19, 20, 25.

43. *Tract 85:* 22–24.

44. *Tract 85:* 27, 55–56, 35, 27.

45. *Tract 85:* 30, 32–34. It should be noted that Newman believed the same to be the antecedent case with nature, which he thought did not demand the conclusion of the existence of a designer without such a presupposition in the mind of the observer.

46. *Tract 85:* 49.

47. *Tract 85:* 71, 80, 81.

48. *Tract 85:* 87, 88, 90, 100, 115.

49. *Tract 85:* 98, 99. Newman continued to hold this view during his Roman Catholic years, writing in 1863 in the wake of the furor over *Essays and Reviews,* "At this very time we are witnessing the beginning of the end of Protestantism, the breaking of that bubble of 'Bible-Christianity' which has been its life." JHN to Lady Chatterton, June 10, 1863, *L&D,* 20: 465; see also JHN to C. Crawley, March 17, 1861, *L&D,* 19: 482–483.

50. Pusey, *Letter to the Bishop of Oxford,* pp. 23–24. Newman made a similar point while a Roman Catholic; see JHN to W. J. O. Daunt, October 4, 1862, *L&D,* 20: 286–287.

51. Pusey, *Letter to the Bishop of Oxford,* pp. 10, 58, 59, 61.

52. JHN to James Stephen, March 16, 1835, *L&D,* 5: 45. Newman turned this earnest criticism of evangelicals into satire in "Exeter Hall," *British Critic,* 24 (1838): 190–210.

53. *Tract 80:* 61, 62, 69, 72, 63, 79.

54. Isaac Williams, *The Autobiography of Isaac Williams,* ed. George Prevost (London: Longmans, Green, 1892), pp. 91, 92. See also I. Williams to T. Keble, undated (probably 1838), in Thomas Keble–Isaac Williams Box, Pusey House; JK to C. A. Ogilvie, March 17, 1838, calling Williams's tract "as important as anything in a long time," Bodleian Library, Ms. Eng. lett. d. 124, f. 76; and O. W. Jones, *Isaac Williams and His Circle* (London: S.P.C.K., 1971), pp. 28–41.

55. *Tract 80:* 1, 8, 12, 13, 21. Drawing heavily on Newman's *Arians of the Fourth Century,* Williams contended that the early Fathers had so interpreted the parables.

56. *Tract 80:* 45, 49.

57. W. F. Hook to JHN, 1839, *The Life and Letters of Walter Farquhar Hook,* 2d ed. (London: Richard Bentley, 1879), 2: 56–57; *Tract 80:* 55–57.

58. *Tract 80:* 73, 76, 78, 79.

59. *Tract 86:* 63. See John Munsey Turner, *Conflict and Reconciliation: Studies in Methodism and Ecumenism in England, 1740–1982* (London: Epworth, 1985), pp. 44–113, for a number of shrewd comments on the relationship of Methodism and the Tractarians, and W. R. Ward, "The Religion of the People and the Problem of Control, 1790–1830," *Studies in Church History*, 8 (1972): 237–257, on the discipline within Methodism, which the Tractarians ignored.

60. *Tract 87:* 48–49.

61. *Tract 87:* 76, 77, 79, 72, 62, 97.

62. Pusey, *Letter to the Bishop of Oxford*, pp. 10, 22.

63. Pusey, *Letter to the Bishop of Oxford*, pp. 22, 10, 14, 13.

64. Preface (March 7, 1839) to Frederick Oakeley, *Sermons Preached Chiefly in the Chapel Royal at Whitehall* (Oxford: John Henry Parker, 1839), pp. x–xiii, xvii.

65. Preface (March 7, 1839) to Oakeley, *Sermons*, pp. xviii*n.*, xix, xii.

CHAPTER 7. THE PURSUIT OF THE CATHOLIC

1. J. W. Bowden to JHN, October 28, 1833, *L&D*, 4: 67.

2. EBN to JHN, January 8, 1841, *L&D*, 8: 13–14.

3. Frank M. Turner, *Contesting Cultural Authority: Essays in Victorian Intellectual Life* (Cambridge: Cambridge University Press, 1993), pp. 38–72.

4. *Prophetical Office*, p. v.

5. JHN to RHF, December 24, 1835, *L&D*, 5: 185; [J. H. Newman], "Home Thoughts Abroad," *British Magazine*, 5 (1834): 1–11, 121–131; 9 (1836): 237–248, 357–369.

6. [Newman], "Home Thoughts Abroad," *British Magazine*, 5 (1834): 129, 130, 128, 129.

7. [Newman], "Home Thoughts Abroad," *British Magazine*, 5 (1834): 122–126. "It seems as if that spirit had gained subtilty by years; popish Rome has succeeded to Rome pagan; and, would that we had no reason to expect still more crafty development of antichrist amid the wreck of institutions and establishments which will attend the fall of the Papacy!" [Newman], "Home Thoughts Abroad," *British Magazine*, 5 (1834): 125.

8. [Newman], "Home Thoughts Abroad," *British Magazine*, 5 (1834): 130, 127.

9. Louis Allen, ed., *John Henry Newman and the Abbé Jager: A Controversy on Scripture and Tradition, 1834–1836* (London: Oxford University Press, 1975), pp. 35, 117, 37–43, 93. This volume includes a full analysis of this relatively little explored episode in Newman's writings. See pp. 149–172 for correspondence in which Harrison privately objected to such statements as supposedly embodying the very kind of rationalism that he and other Tractarians rejected as opening the door to Unitarianism.

10. Allen, *John Henry Newman and the Abbé Jager*, pp. 94, 95.

11. Allen, *John Henry Newman and the Abbé Jager*, p. 96.

12. RHF to JHN, September 3, 1835; see also RHF to JHN, July 17 and 30, September 3, 1835; JHN to RHF, July 20, August 9 and 23, 1835, *L&D*, 5: 128, 100–102, 116–118, 127–128, 102–104, 118–120, 125–127.

13. F. W. Faber to a Friend, January, 1835, John Edward Bowden, *The Life and Letters of Frederick William Faber, D.D.* (Baltimore: John Murphy, 1869), pp. 42, 43.

14. Sheridan Gilley, *Newman and His Age* (Westminster, Md.: Christian Classics, 1990), p. 140.

15. EBP to JHN, undated, but before November 29, 1835, Liddon, *Pusey*, 2: 6; *Tract 72:* 54.

16. JHN to H. J. Rose, April 10, 1836, *L&D*, 5: 275–276.

17. H. J. Rose to EBP, April 30, 1836, John William Burgon, *Lives of Twelve Good Men* (London: John Murray, 1888), 1: 208; JHN to H. J. Rose, May 1, 1836, *L&D*, 5: 291, 292.

18. H. J. Rose to JHN, May 9, 1836, Burgon, *Lives of Twelve Good Men*, 1: 210–212.

Rose wished that Newman had presented apostolical succession "as a regular, undoubted doctrine, held undoubtingly by all true Churchmen, and only a little neglected,—than as a thing to which they were to recur as a sort of ancient Novelty,—a truth now first recovered." H. H. Rose to JHN, May 9, 1836, Burgon, *Lives of Twelve Good Men,* 1: 211. See also Peter Nockles, *The Oxford Movement in Context: Anglican High Churchmanship, 1760–1857* (Cambridge: Cambridge University Press, 1994), pp. 146–152.

19. JHN to H. J. Rose, May 11, 1836, *L&D,* 5: 295.

20. EBP to H. J. Rose, May 12, 1836, Burgon, *Lives of Twelve Good Men,* 1: 220n.

21. H. J. Rose to JHN, May 13, 1836, Burgon, *Lives of Twelve Good Men,* 1: 217–219.

22. JHN to H. J. Rose, May 23, 1836, *L&D,* 5: 301, 302.

23. JHN to H. J. Rose, May 23, 1836, *L&D,* 5: 302–304. Newman also regretted the character of the dedication of the eucharist, the omission of the Prayer to the Holy Ghost, and omission of the commemoration of the dead in the eucharistic service. He admitted that while celebrating the eucharist, he silently made an offering and prayer for the dead in Christ.

24. Volume 5 of *L&D* included very little of Rose's side of this important correspondence even though it has been available since published by Burgon in 1888. Newman himself was hesitant in 1840 to turn this correspondence over to Rose's proposed biographer. See JHN to EBP, January 9, 19, 21, 1840, *L&D,* 7: 207, 219–221, and EBP to JHN, January 21 and two subsequent undated letters of January 1840 in Newman Microfilms, reel 70, batch 68, ff. 140–142. See JHN to John Murray, November 30, 1887, *L&D,* 31: 237–238, giving permission to J. W. Burgon to reprint the letters.

25. John Keble, *Primitive Tradition Recognized in Holy Scripture: A Sermon Preached in the Cathedral Church of Winchester, at the Visitation of the Worshipful and Reverend William Dealtry, D.D., Chancellor of the Diocese* (London: J. G. and F. Rivington, 1836), pp. 20, 21, 26, 28. Keble's text was similar to 2 Timothy 6:20, which Newman quoted to Jager. See Allen, *John Henry Newman and the Abbé Jager,* p. 95.

26. Keble, *Primitive Tradition,* pp. 48, 46, 53; JHN to M. R. Giberne, November 27, 1836, *L&D,* 5: 385; E. Hawkins to R. Whately, December 5, 1836, Letterbooks, 5: 417, Oriel College.

27. *Prophetical Office,* pp. 296–297. For a discussion of the two traditions see Allen, *John Henry Newman and the Abbé Jager,* pp. 14–20, and Henry Tristram, "In the Lists with Abbé Jager," *John Henry Newman: Centenary Essays* (London: Burns, Oates, and Washbourne, 1945), pp. 201–222. For a careful though severely critical contemporary reading of *The Prophetical Office of the Church,* see "Rev. J. H. Newman on Romanism and Protestantism," *Christian Observer,* 38 (1838): 310–322.

28. *Prophetical Office,* p. 298; Allen, *John Henry Newman and the Abbé Jager,* p. 98; JHN to RHF, July 20, August 9, 1835, *L&D,* 5: 102, 119. For further comments on Prophetical Tradition, see Allen, *John Henry Newman and the Abbé Jager,* pp. 94–95, and RHF to JHN, July 17 and 30, September 3, 1835; JHN to RHF, August 13, 1835, *L&D,* 5: 100–102, 116–118, 127–128, 125–127.

29. *Prophetical Office,* pp. 299, 303.

30. *Christian Observer,* 37 (1837): 119n., 145, 150, 146. See also *Christian Observer,* 37 (1837): 147, 160–162, 319–321, 327–331, for commentary on the Church Fathers, the authority of tradition, and Keble's idea of primitive tradition.

31. *Tract 81:* 1–2.

32. *Tract 81:* 60, 3, 2, 3, 23, 32. Furthermore, according to Pusey, the English Church had not looked to Scripture as the basis of understanding true doctrine. That, he thought, was the path of rationalism, which would unravel the Articles by using the standard of scriptural interpretation through private judgment. Pusey declared, "Such, blessed be God! was not the case with our Anglican Church. For, having seized hold of a fixed standard for scriptural interpretation and for doctrine, in this agreement of Catholic Antiquity, she had no longer need to toss up and down in the fluctuations of human opinion, but was at once arrived in her haven." *Tract 81:* 33.

33. *Tract 81:* 36, 41, 42; furthermore, Pusey stated that "the ambiguity of the language, and the variety of senses in which the terms are used" among Anglican writers cited as upholding the doctrine might perplex superficial readers because the same writer might employ language regarding the eucharist in both a Roman and a Catholic sense (*Tract 81:* 43). See also Liddon, *Pusey*, 2: 33.

34. EBP to JHN, undated, Thursday Night, 1836, Newman Microfilms, reel 70, batch 68. This undated letter must have been written in late 1836 as Newman was completing his tract on purgatory and not in late 1835 as Liddon seems to suggest in *Pusey*, 2: 7. See JHN to M. R. Giberne, November 27, 1836, and Newman's diary entries for November 25, December 2, 1836, *L&D*, 5: 385–386. In his biography of Pusey, Liddon edited this letter to remove the most sharply critical sentences, as was first observed by R. H. Greenfield, *The Attitude of the Tractarians to the Roman Catholic Church, 1833–1850* (Oxford diss., 1956), pp. 189–190.

35. *Tract 79:* 3. Earlier in the tract Newman had asserted, "Romanism in the theory may differ little from our own creed; nay, in the abstract type, it might even be identical, and yet in the actual framework, and still further in the living and breathing form, it might differ essentially"(*Tract 79:* 2).

36. *Tract 79:* 3; *Christian Observer*, 37 (1837): 184, 187, 197.

37. *Prophetical Office*, pp. 61, 71.

38. *Prophetical Office*, pp. 51, 101. "The very force of the word *corruption* implies this to be the peculiarity of Romanism." *Prophetical Office*, p. 51.

39. JHN to J. W. Bowden, March 19, 1838; JHN to H. Wilberforce, March 15, 1838; on *British Critic* circulation, see JHN to H. J. Coleridge, May 2, 1869, *L&D*, 6: 215, 213; 24: 250. See also William J. Baker, "Hurrell Froude and the Reformers," *Journal of Ecclesiastical History*, 21 (1970): 243–259; Piers Brendon, "Newman, Keble, and Froude's *Remains*," *English Historical Review*, 88 (1972): 697–716; Piers Brendon, *Hurrell Froude and the Oxford Movement* (London: Paul Elek, 1974), pp. 180–197.

40. JHN to J. M. Capes, August 23, 1850, *L&D*, 14: 49.

41. JHN to J. W. Bowden, October 6, 1837, *L&D*, 6: 145.

42. JHN to F. Rogers, August 31, 1837; see also JHN to S. F. Wood, June 2, 1837, *L&D*, 6: 120, 77–78, which indicates some initial hesitancy on Newman's part about publishing the earlier Froude manuscripts.

43. JK to JHN, September 12, 1837; JHN to JK, September 17, 1837, *L&D*, 6: 134, 136.

44. [J. Keble], Preface, Froude, *Remains*, 1: xxi. Before publication of Froude's diary, Frederic Rogers had commented, "I cannot doubt at all that they will very materially lessen the influence of the Apostolicals over the Clergy—and perplex many friends." F. Rogers to JHN, July 17, 1837, *L&D*, 6: 100n.

45. [J. H. Newman], Preface, Froude, *Remains*, 1: xiv-xv. Keble wrote virtually all of the preface, as Newman remembered late in life, except for pages ix–xv; authorship in these notes has been assigned accordingly. See *L&D*, 31: 87, and Wilfrid Ward, *William George Ward and the Oxford Movement* (London: Macmillan: 1889), pp. 81–85.

46. [Newman], Preface, Froude, *Remains*, 1: x.

47. JHN to JK, July 16, 1837, *L&D*, 6: 97; [Keble], Preface, Froude, *Remains*, 1: vi.

48. Froude, *Remains*, 1: 433; *Record*, April 19, November 12, 1838; see also May 4, 1840.

49. H. J. Rose to J. Watson, January, 1838, in Edward Churton, *Memoir of Joshua Watson* (Oxford: J. H. and Jas. Parker, 1861), p. 63.

50. Godfrey Faussett, *The Revival of Popery: A Sermon Preached Before the University of Oxford, at St. Mary's, on Sunday, May 20, 1838*, 3d ed. (Oxford: At the University Press, 1838), pp. 13, 15–17, 22, 24. Faussett's reference to priests transforming the elements of the eucharist recalled the wording of the first edition of *Tract 10*, which was changed in later editions. See *Record*, July 2, 1838, for commendation of Faussett's sermon.

51. Faussett, *Revival of Popery*, pp. 31, 36–37.

52. J. H. Newman, *A Letter Addressed to the Rev. the Margaret Professor of Divinity, on*

Mr. R. Hurrell Froude's Statements Concerning the Holy Eucharist, and Other Matters Theological and Ecclesiastical (1838), as reprinted in *Via Media*, 2: 201, 256. Newman did not reply to Faussett's further criticisms attached to later reprintings of his sermon. See Faussett, *Revival of Popery*, p. xiii.

53. [J. H. Newman], "Geraldine—a Tale of Conscience," *British Critic*, 24 (1838): 69–71.

54. Bagot quoted in *L&D*, 6: 286. See also EBP to JK, August 22, 23, 1838, Pusey-Keble Correspondence, f. 74, Pusey House.

55. E. Hawkins to R. Whately, December 5, 1836, Letterbooks, 5: 417, Oriel College; Appendix to E. B. Pusey, *A Letter to the Right Rev. Father in God Richard Lord Bishop of Oxford, On the Tendency to Romanism Imputed to Doctrines Held of Old, as Now, in the English Church* (Oxford: J. Parker, 1839), following main body of the pamphlet.

56. Pusey, *Letter to the Bishop of Oxford*, pp. 182, 237.

57. [Frederic Rogers], "Froude's *Remains*," *British Critic*, 23 (1838): 218–220.

58. [J. W. Bowden], "The British Association for the Advancement of Science," *British Critic*, 25 (1839): 19, 46. See p. 18 of this article for Bowden's direct comparison of the vision of the early Victorian scientific community and the evangelical vision of an invisible church. On the relation of early-Victorian science and religion, consult Jack Morrell and Arnold Thackray, *Gentlemen of Science: Early Years of the British Association for the Advancement of Science* (Oxford: Clarendon, 1981), passim; Robert Young, *Darwin's Metaphor: Nature's Place in Victorian Culture* (Cambridge: Cambridge University Press, 1985), pp. 126–163; Turner, *Contesting Cultural Authority*, pp. 101–130.

59. [J. B. Mozley], "Palgrave—Truths and Fictions of the Middle Ages," *British Critic*, 24 (1838): 376, 380, 383. H. J. Rose deeply disapproved of this outlook, suggesting that Mozley set no limits on mystery nor established any authority for its use. See H. J. Rose to JHN, October 11, 1838, Newman Microfilms, reel 72, batch 71.

60. [Mozley], "Palgrave," 394–397.

61. [William Sewell], "Animal Magnetism," *British Critic*, 24 (1838): 306, 346. See also JHN to Arthur Perceval, January, 1836, *L&D*, 5: 196–197, for a similar criticism of the study of evidences. Mesmerism could prove itself quite compatible with evangelical theology and other nondogmatic religion. See Alison Winter, *Mesmerized: Powers of Mind in Victorian Britain* (Chicago: University of Chicago Press, 1998), pp. 246–275.

62. [T. Mozley], "Study of the Evidences," *British Critic*, 26 (1839): 3, 10, 4, 17, 26, 36, 64.

63. [J. H. Newman], "Palmer's *Treatise on the Church of Christ*," *British Critic*, 24 (1838): 368; Baden Powell, *Tradition Unveiled: or, An Exposition of the Pretensions and Tendency of Authoritative Teaching in the Church* (London: John W. Parker, 1839), pp. 29, 37, 38; Baden Powell, *A Supplement to Tradition Unveiled* (London: John W. Parker, 1840), p. 8. See also Pietro Corsi, *Science and Religion: Baden Powell and the Anglican Debate, 1800–1860* (Cambridge: Cambridge University Press, 1988).

64. Powell, *Tradition Unveiled*, pp. 44, 43, 45, 47.

65. Powell, *Tradition Unveiled*, pp. 61, 62, 63, 64, 67, 70, 67, 68.

66. John Hamilton Thom, ed., *The Life of the Rev. Joseph Blanco White, Written by Himself; with Portions of His Correspondence* (London: John Chapman, 1845), 3: 145, 146.

67. J. B. White to W. E. Channing, October 9, 1839, Thom, *Life of White* 3: 105, 106.

68. [J. H. Newman], "State of Religious Parties," *British Critic*, 25 (1839): 402, 405, 406, 410, 412.

69. [Newman], "State of Religious Parties," 399, 415, 416, 399, 416.

70. [Newman], "State of Religious Parties," 417, 419–420, 425, 423, 425, 426.

71. *Arians*, p. 195.

72. *University Sermons*, pp. 182, 203, 208, 231, 249, 239, 184, 187, 191. The original title for this collection was *Sermons, Chiefly on the Theory of Religious Belief Preached Before the*

University of Oxford (London: J. G. F. and J. Rivington, 1843). This volume, reprinted in 1872 under the more familiar title *Fifteen Sermons Preached Before the University of Oxford between A.D. 1826 and 1843*, provided much of the basis for *A Grammar of Assent* (1870). Newman's change in the title of the book was an example of his attempting to obscure the contexts of his earlier writings when he published them many years later. On Newman and Coleridge, see John Coulson, *Newman and the Common Tradition: A Study in the Language of Church and Society* (Oxford: Clarendon, 1970). Newman insisted that he had never read Coleridge or Kant and that such was also the case with Keble, Froude, and Pusey. See JHN to W. S. Lilly, August 17, 1884; January 7, 1885. *L&D*, 30: 391; 31: 7.

73. *University Sermons*, pp. 194–195.

74. *L&D*, 8: 559–560.

75. *University Sermons*, p. 200. See also Frank M. Turner, "John Henry Newman and the Challenge of a Culture of Science," *European Legacy*, 1 (1996): 1694–1704.

76. *University Sermons*, pp. 232, 233, 234, 233–234, 238, 244, 250, 249.

77. [Newman], "State of Religious Parties," 426.

78. JHN to EBP, January 24, 1836, *L&D*, 5: 215. See also Liddon, *Pusey*, 1: 331–342; Maisie Ward, *Young Mr. Newman* (New York: Sheed and Ward, 1948), pp. 298–321; Meriol Trevor, *Newman: The Pillar of the Cloud* (New York: Doubleday, 1962), pp. 199–225. Mr. Gerard Tracey provided the author with information about the fund that Newman administered.

79. W. Dodsworth to JHN, November 18, 1839; JHN to H. A. Woodgate, October 20, 1839, *L&D*, 7: 184, 169.

80. Nicholas Cardinal Wiseman, *Essays on Various Subjects* (New York: P. O'Shea, 1873), 3: 234, 270.

81. *Apologia*, p. 108; see also pp. 540–542, for Svaglic's very accessible explanations of the complexities of the ancient heresies that Newman discusses, and Stephen Thomas, *Newman and Heresy: The Anglican Years* (Cambridge: Cambridge University Press, 1991), pp. 203–227. Consult also [Newman], "Home Thoughts Abroad—No. II," *British Magazine*, 9 (1836): 240–242. Consult JHN to Mrs. Helbert, October 20, 1869, for a late clarification of Newman's point in which he states that what struck him was not the parallel with the ancient heresies but the quotation from St. Augustine. *L&D*, 24: 354–356. But this clarification may more nearly reflect a point he wished to make among English Roman Catholics in 1869 than his views in 1839.

82. JHN to J. W. Bowden, October 20, 1839; *L&D*, 7: 166, 176–178; JHN to Frederic Rogers, September 22, 1839; JHN to JNM, November 17, 29, 17, 1839, *L&D*, 7: 166, 154, 183. See also JHN to J. W. Bowden, November 4, 1839, and JHN to JNM, November 29, 1839, *L&D*, 7: 176–178, 187–188; Henry Wilberforce, "F[ather] Newman's Oxford *Parochial Sermons*," *Dublin Review*, n.s. 12 (1869): 327–328.

83. Thomas, *Newman and Heresy*, pp 220–222. Also consult Newman's first volume of Roman Catholic sermons, which in the dedication of 1849 to Bishop Wiseman he pointed to the 1839 article as marking when "a doubt first crossed my mind of the tenableness of the theological theory on which Anglicanism is based." John Henry Newman, *Discourses Addressed to Mixed Congregations*, 2d ed. (London: Longman, Brown, Green, and Longmans, 1850), p. 6, as well as *Certain Difficulties*, pp. 370–387. See also chapter 12 of this study.

84. JHN to R. Williams, November 10, 1839; JHN to J. W. Bowden, November 4, 1839; W. Dodsworth to JHN, November 18, 1839; JHN to W. Dodsworth, November 19, 1839; JHN to J. W. Bowden, January 5, 1840; R. Bagot to JHN, November 25 and December 26, 1839, *L&D*, 7: 181, 176, 184, 185–186, 201–204, 184–185, 189, 185, 190.

85. JHN to H. Manning, September 1, 1839, *L&D*, 7: 133; see also JHN to H. A. Woodgate, October 20, 1839, *L&D*, 7: 169. The possibly erotically charged metaphor of a blanket too small for the bed is taken from chapter 28 of the book of the prophet Isaiah.

86. [John Keble], Preface, Froude, *Remains*, 3: xiii, xv, xvii, xviii. As noted Keble was

the author of virtually all of the preface to the second set of Froude's *Remains.* See JK to J. T. Coleridge, May 1, 1839, Bodleian Library, Ms. Eng. lett. d. 134., f. 282, and *L&D,* 31: 87. Neither Keble nor Newman consulted Pusey regarding either the preface or the contents of the volumes. On the importance of this preface to Tractarian history, see Greenfield, *Attitude of the Tractarians,* pp. 160–177, and for its echoes with the Nonjurors, Nockles, *Oxford Movement in Context,* pp. 121–122. As early as 1835 Keble had written to Newman of "the Ultra Protestantism of . . . Cranmer and his school." JK to JHN, Keble-Newman Correspondence (transcripts), Pusey House. I owe this reference to Peter Nockles.

87. [Keble], Preface, Froude, *Remains,* 3: xix, xxviii–xxix.

88. JHN to R. F. Wilson, May 13, 1835, *L&D,* 5: 70; [Keble], Preface, Froude, *Remains,* 3: xxxv. In *Tract 86* Isaac Williams was to claim that the Catholicity of the English Church resided in the Prayer Book.

89. JHN to JNM, January 18, 1840, *L&D,* 7: 218.

90. [J. H. Newman], "Catholicity of the Church," *British Critic,* 27 (1840): 55, 57, 64, 68, 74. Newman also contended that there was less ecclesiastical difference between Rome and England in his time and in the age of St. Cyprian than between the papal monarchy of the age of Hildebrand and that of St. Augustine.

91. [Newman], "Catholicity of the Church," 77–79.

92. [Newman], "Catholicity of the Church," 87, 88.

93. [Newman], "Catholicity of the Church," 84. In the *Apologia* Newman stated that it was during 1841 that he came to recognize the Anglicans as playing a role in modern Christianity equivalent to the semi-Arians of antiquity. What he did not say in the *Apologia* is that in 1841 he had pointed to the semi-Arians as a prescriptive model for a group of Christians embodying vitality and sanctity. *Apologia,* p. 130.

94. JHN to JNM, Nov. 17, 1839; JHN to T. Mozley, Dec. 12, 1839; JHN to J. W. Bowden, Jan. 17, 1840, *L&D,* 7: 183, 192, 217; JHN to EBP, March 14, 1845, Pusey House.

95. JHN to H. A. Woodgate, January 17, 1840, *L&D,* 7: 218; John Henry Newman, *The Church of the Fathers* (London: J. G. F. and J. Rivington, 1840), pp. 250, 251, 252, 253, 283, 331, 251; see also John Henry Newman, "Advertisement to the Third Edition, 1857," *The Church of the Fathers,* 4th ed. (London: Burns, Oates 1868), p. x. For a contemporary, moderate evaluation of ancient monasticism, see H. H. Milman, *The History of Christianity from the Birth of Christ to the Abolition of Paganism in the Roman Empire* (London: John Murray, 1840), 3: 289–340.

96. *AW,* pp. 217–218; *L&D,* 5: 167; 6: 106, 299; 7: 94, 127, 138–139, 158, 299, 312.

97. "Memorandum. Reasons for Living at Littlemore," March 17, 1840; JHN to H. Wilberforce, August 30, 1839; JHN to F. Rogers, September 15, 1839; JHN to T. Mozley, December 12, 1839, *L&D,* 7: 263, 129, 151, 192. Note that Newman's comment to Wilberforce came just one day before he wrote Manning that Catholics in the English Church must demand monasteries. JHN to H. Manning, September 1, 1839, *L&D,* 7: 133.

98. JHN to S. F. Wood, March 17, 1840; JHN to J. R. Bloxam, March 29, 1840; Diary, May 20, 1840; JHN to JNM, May 28, 1840; JHN to Woodgate, June 11, 1840; JHN to M. R. Giberne, July 15, 1840, *L&D,* 7: 267, 282, 327, 334, 343–344, 358.

99. [Newman], "Catholicity of the Church," 78; Newman, *Church of the Fathers* (1840), p. 252. Newman contended that within the Church of England there existed "no *praemunire* attached to the formation of a subsidiary system [of monasticism] as I am speaking of." Newman, *Church of the Fathers* (1840), p. 252.

100. [J. H. Newman], "Memoir of the Countess Huntingdon," *British Critic,* 28 (1840): 263, 264. It seems likely that the first clause of the first cited quotation as drafted, but not printed, must have included the word "more" or "so" between "heresy" and "mixed."

101. [Newman], "Memoir of the Countess Huntingdon," 272, 275–276.

102. [Newman], "Memoir of the Countess Huntingdon," 282. The quotations cited in the article are taken from *Life and Times of Selina Countess Huntingdon. By a Member of the Houses of Shirley and Hastings* (London: William Edward Painter, 1839), 1: 163.

103. [Newman], "Memoir of the Countess Huntingdon," 280, 281.

104. FWN to JHN, April 15, 1840, *L&D*, 7: 308. For the family background of this exchange, see JHN to JNM, November 17, 1839; JHN to Elizabeth Newman, April 1, 1840; JHN to JNM, April 10, 1840; JHN to FWN, April 11, 1840, *L&D*, 7: 182, 286, 300.

105. JHN to FWN, April 16, 1840, *L&D*, 7: 310.

106. FWN to JHN, April 29, 1840, *L&D*, 7: 319.

107. JHN to FWN, May 5, 1840, *L&D*, 7: 320.

108. JHN to W. C. A. Maclaurin, July 26, 1840, *L&D*, 7: 368–70.

109. JHN to FWN, October 22, 1840, *L&D*, 7: 412, 413. Earlier in the year John had told Jemima that he thought perhaps only Roman Catholicism could provide a bulwark against the attack on the Bible. JHN to JNM, February 25, 1840, *L&D*, 7: 244–246.

110. JHN to JK, October 26, 1840, *L&D*, 7: 417, 418.

111. JHN to JK, November 6, 1840, *L&D*, 7: 433–434; ("ethos" appears in Greek in the original). See also JHN to F. Rogers, November 25, 1840, *L&D*, 7: 450–451, where he repeats the same sentiments.

112. JHN to FWN, November 10, 1840, *L&D*, 7: 437. Newman also compared the situation to that of the Jews in the time of Jesus, attempting to keep the law but hoping for its abolition. Compare Newman's view of his acting as an officer separated from his commander with Sewell's 1838 comment (n. 61) that use of the evidences fostered use of private judgment similar to a man of war crew devising their reasons for obeying their commander.

113. JHN to FWN, November 10, 1840, *L&D*, 7: 440–442.

CHAPTER 8. PROVING CANNON

1. JHN to A. P. Perceval, January 11, 1836, *L&D*, 5: 197; *Prophetical Office*, pp. 282, 344. "In the preface to the Articles it is said that we are to understand them in their grammatical sense; which I interpret into a permission to think nothing of the opinion of their framers." Letter of April 8, 1834, Froude, *Remains*, 1: 363.

2. *Tract 81:* 54, 56, 57. In this tract, Pusey largely, if more extensively, repeated Newman's view that the Reformers were not "the founders of our Church" but rather "one link in a chain." (*Tract 78:* 2) Pusey also agreed with Newman's statement, "No greater injury can be done them [the Reformers] than to make it appear, (as is too often done at this day,) that they occupied or professed a position which belongs only to heretics, that of originating the faith they maintained" (*Tract 78:* 2).

3. E. B. Pusey, *A Letter to the Right Rev. Father in God Richard Lord Bishop of Oxford, On the Tendency to Romanism Imputed to Doctrines Held of Old, as Now, in the English Church* (Oxford: J. Parker, 1839), pp. 146–147, 180, 181; [J. Keble], Preface, Froude, *Remains*, 3: xxi.

4. *Christian Observer*, 37 (1837): 170; *Record*, July 11, 1839; January 9, 1840.

5. Edward Hawkins, *Inquiry into the Connected Uses of the Principal Means of Attaining Christian Truth in Eight Sermons Preached Before the University of Oxford at the Bampton Lectures for the Year MDCCCXL*, 2d ed. (Oxford: John Henry Parker, 1841), pp. 108, 63, 207, 249, 257; see also pp. 192–193 for his comments on Roman Catholic authority The first edition of this work appeared in 1840.

6. Hawkins, *Inquiry*, pp. 192, 193.

7. JHN to M. R. Giberne, December 22, 1840, *L&D*, 7: 465–466; see also *L&D* 7: 465n2 and 466n2.

8. EBP to JHN, January 8, 1841; JHN to EBP, January 12, 1841, *L&D*, 8: 13–15. See also Peter Nockles, *The Oxford Movement in Context: Anglican High Churchmanship, 1760–1857* (Cambridge: Cambridge University Press, 1994), pp. 127–129.

9. *Tract 90:* 1. All citations to the very rare first edition are taken from John Henry Newman, *Tract Ninety, or Remarks on Certain Passages in the Thirty-Nine Articles*, ed. A. W. Evans (London: Constable, 1933). All the Tractarians believed that the Articles were

incompatible with various elements of evangelical theology and that evangelical clergy for their part actually and privately relaxed the terms of subscription.

10. *Tract 90:* 5–6; Pusey's comment to Newman in March, 1841, cited in *L&D*, 8: 129n.

11. James Anthony Froude, "The Oxford Counter-Reformation" (1881), in *Short Studies on Great Subjects* (Longmans, Green, 1898), p. 308.

12. *Tract 90:* 10, 20. For an early nineteenth-century Protestant reading of the Articles, see George Tomline, *Elements of Christian Theology,* 14th ed. (London: T. Cadell, 1843), 2: 28–487.

13. *Tract 90:* 26–27.

14. *Tract 90:* 29–30; J. Bowden to JHN, February, 1841, *L&D*, 8: 32n.

15. *Tract 90:* 73, 78.

16. *Tract 90:* 85, 92–93.

17. *Tract 90:* 94–95.

18. *Tract 90:* 98, 100–102; R. F. Wilson to JK, March 15, 1841, *L&D*, 8: 91.

19. HNM to JNM, March 15, 1841, *Newman Family Letters,* p. 103; J. W. Bowden to JHN, March 15, 1841; EBP to J. R. Hope, April 18, 1841, *L&D*, 8: 71, 178; Yngve Brilioth, *The Anglican Revival: Studies in the Oxford Movement* (London: Longmans, Green, 1925), p. 155.

20. JHN to T. Mozley, March 7, 1841; JHN to A. P. Perceval, March 12, 1841, *L&D*, 8: 58, 68; J. H. Newman, "Postscript," *A Letter Addressed to the Rev. R. W. Jelf, D.D. Canon of Christ Church, In Explanation of the Ninetieth Tract in the Series Called the Tracts for the Times,* rpt. in *Via Media,* 2: 390. See also S. F. Wood to JHN, July 13 and 20, 1840, *L&D*, 7: 355, 364.

21. JHN to H. Moore, May 21, 1840, *L&D*, 7: 330–331.

22. "Letter of Four College Tutors," *Via Media,* 2: 359, 360. The signers of the letter were T. T. Churton of Brasenose College, H. B. Wilson of St. John's College, John Griffiths of Wadham, and A. C. Tait of Balliol. Wilson was to become a contributor to *Essays and Reviews,* and Tait was later appointed Bishop of London and then Archbishop of Canterbury. Except for holding strong Protestant convictions and generally disliking the Tractarians, their motives are not altogether clear. See also Tait Papers, vol. 77, ff. 1, 7, 9, 21, 29–30, 33–34, Lambeth Palace Library; Edwin A. Abbott, *The Anglican Career of Cardinal Newman* (London: Macmillan, 1892), 2: 235–293; E. A. Knox, *The Tractarian Movement, 1833–1845: A Study of the Oxford Movement as a Phase of the Religious Revival in Western Europe in the Second Quarter of the Nineteenth Century* (London: Putnam, 1933), pp. 237–264; Ian Ker, *John Henry Newman: A Biography* (Oxford: Oxford University Press, 1990), pp. 213–231; Peter Nockles, "Oxford, Tract 90, and the Bishops," in David Nicholls and Fergus Kerr, eds., *John Henry Newman: Reason, Rhetoric, and Romanticism* (Carbondale: Southern Illinois University Press, 1991), pp. 28–87; and Nockles, *The Oxford Movement in Context,* pp. 136–142.

23. R. W. Greaves, "Golightly and Newman, 1824–1845," *Journal of Ecclesiastical History,* 9 (1958): 209–228; see also C. P. Golightly to C. Blomfield, March 9, 11, 1841, Charles P. Golightly Papers, Lambeth Palace Library, 1804, ff. 49, 51.

24. Edward Cardwell to Duke of Wellington, March 10, 1841; Wellington Papers, 2/251/21, University of Southampton; JHN to HNM, March 12, 1841; EBP to P. Wynter, March 12, 1841, *L&D*, 8: 67, 74. See also transcripts of EBP to B. Harrison, March 11, 14, 15, 20, 1841, Harrison-Pusey Correspondence, Pusey House, and R. W. Church to JHN, March 10, 11, 1841, *Corrs. with JK,* pp. 78–80.

25. P. Wynter to EBP, March 13, 1841, *L&D*, 8: 74, 75. Wynter did, however, present Pusey's letter to the meeting of the Hebdomadal Board. [I read this sentence in the manuscript letter in the Birmingham Oratory *Tract 90* File differently from the editor of New-

man's letters. Where I read "humble declaration," the editor reads "hundred declarations," and where I read "inculcation," the editor reads "circulation."]

26. JHN to E. Hawkins, October 14, 1841, *L&D*, 8: 72; Statement by the Heads of Houses quoted in *Via Media*, 2: 362. See also JHN to W. F. Hook, October 19, 1841, *L&D*, 8: 99.

27. P. Wynter to Duke of Wellington, March 15, 1841, Wellington Papers, 2/251/27, University of Southampton. [See also P. Wynter to Unknown Correspondent, April 23, 1841, Philip Wynter Papers, dep. d. 3, f. 7, Bodleian Library.] JK to EBP, March 18, 1841; JK to JHN, March 18, 1841, Liddon, *Pusey*, 2: 179, 180. On the views of the Archbishop of Canterbury see B. Harrison to Dean Gaisford, March 15 and 17, 1841, University Archives, NW 21.5, ff. 54, 56, Bodleian Library.

28. Joshua Watson as quoted in R. W. Jelf to JHN, March 18, 1841, *L&D*, 8: 90; A. P. Stanley to A. C. Tait, March 30, 1841, Tait Papers, vol. 77, f. 29, Lambeth Palace Library. The *Record*, which in 1837 had demanded episcopal action against the Tractarians, called for an Oxford Convocation condemnation of *Tract 90*. See *Record*, October 12, 1837; March 22, April 12, 1841.

29. *Letter to Dr. Jelf, Via Media*, 2: 368, 371–372, 378; JHN to J. W. Bowden, February 12, 1841, *L&D*, 8: 32. On composition of the *Letter to Dr. Jelf*, see Diary, March 12, 1841, and EBP to JHN, March 9, 13 or 14, 1841: *L&D*, 8: 67, 62–63, 75; W. G. Ward to EBP, July 23, 1841, Wilfrid Ward, *William George Ward and the Oxford Movement* (London: Macmillan, 1889), p. 181.

30. *Letter to Dr. Jelf, Via Media:* 2:378.

31. *Letter to Dr. Jelf, Via Media:* 2:385–387.

32. R. Bagot to EBP, March 17, 1841; R. Bagot to JHN March 17, 1841, *L&D*, 8: 92, 94, 95. See F. Oakeley to EBP, March 15, 1841, and R. W. Jelf to JHN, March 18, 1841, *L&D*, 8: 95–96, 89–90.

33. JHN to R. Bagot, March 18, 1841, *L&D*, 8: 95; R. Bagot to EBP, March [18?], 1841, Liddon, *Pusey*, 2: 188; JHN to R. Bagot, March 20, 1841, *L&D*, 8: 100–101. During the negotiation Pusey also wrote Bagot attempting to explain the background of *Tract 90*. EBP to R. Bagot, March 18, 1841, Liddon, *Pusey*, 2: 186–187.

34. "Postscript *Letter to Dr. Jelf, Via Media*, 2: 389, 390. See also JHN to W. F. Hook, March 19, 1841, *L&D*, 8: 99, and *L&D*, 8: 93, on the timing of the publication of the postscript. See also note 46 in this chapter.

35. In 1865 Newman presented a highly revised account of the writing of the second edition of *Tract 90*, telling Pusey, "As to Number 90, as far as I recollect the 1st Edition is better and truer than the second. The second Edition was altered to meet the views of liberals who objected that I *was not definite*, and therefore shuffling—whereas I did not *mean* nor *could* be definite—for I was introducing a mode of interpretation, not settling its application, or its limits." JHN to EBP, January 31, 1865, *L&D*, 21: 399. The people whom Newman terms liberals in this letter were either high churchmen or Tractarian sympathizers.

36. Archbishop Howley to R. Bagot, March 22, 1841, Liddon, *Pusey*, 2: 190. Howley's reaction to both the *Letter to Dr. Jelf* and the postscript directly contradicts the long-standing Tractarian contention that had the Hebdomadal Board awaited publication of that pamphlet, they would not have voted their censure. For the extensive exchange of letters during the next several days, see Liddon, *Pusey*, 2: 190–204; *Corrs. with JK*, pp. 98–103, Anne Mozley, ed., *Letters of the Rev. J. B. Mozley, D.D., Edited by His Sister* (London: Rivingtons, 1885), pp. 111–12, as well as all of the correspondence in *L&D*, 8, for March, 1841. For the claim that delay would have changed matters, see [E. B. Pusey, ed.], *Tract XC on Certain Passages in the XXXIX Articles by the Rev. J. H. Newman, B.D., 1841, with A Historical Preface by the Rev. E. B. Pusey, D.D., and Catholic Subscription to the XXXIX Articles Considered in Reference to Tract XC by the Rev. John Keble, M. A., 1841* (Oxford:

John Henry and James Parker, 1865), pp. xii–xiii. See also James Garrard, "Archbishop Howley and the Oxford Movement," in Paul Vaiss, ed., *From Oxford to the People: Reconsidering Newman & the Oxford Movement* (Leominster: Gracewing, 1996), pp. 255–268. On Blomfield's important intervention, see C. Blomfield to W. Palmer, March 22, 1841, Blomfield Papers, vol. 28, f. 30, Lambeth Palace Library; C. Blomfield to W. F. Hook, [March] 1841, W. R. W. Stephens, *The Life and Letters of Walter Farquhar Hook*, 2d ed. (London: Richard Bentley, 1880), 2: 64.

    37. JHN to EBP, March 24, 1841, *L&D*, 8: 115, 116. See W. F. Hook to JHN, March 17, 20, 27, 1841; JHN to W. F. Hook, March 25, 1841; JK to JHN, March 25, 1841; JHN to JK, March 26, 1841, *L&D*, 8: 98, 99, 118–121. For the case of a high churchman who had contributed to the tracts but was also repulsed by Newman's *Letter to Dr. Jelf*, see A. P. Perceval, *A Vindication of the Principles of the Authors of "The Tracts for the Times"* (J. G. F. and J. Rivington, 1841).

    38. JHN to EBP, March 24, 1841; JK to JHN, March 26, 1841, *L&D*, 8: 116, 121. See EBP to R. Bagot, March 25, 1841, *L&D*, 8: 123n., for Pusey's communication to Bagot on the contents of Newman's letter of March 24 and its addendum of March 25.

    39. R. Whately to E. Hawkins, March or April 1841, Letterbooks, 3: 232, Oriel College.

    40. J. H. Newman, *A Letter Addressed to the Right Reverend Father in God, Richard, Lord Bishop of Oxford, On Occasion of the Ninetieth Tract in the Series Called The Tracts for the Times*, rpt. in *Via Media*, 2: 400, 417, 421.

    41. JHN to JNM, March 31, 1841; JHN to T. Mozley, March 31, 1841; JHN to JK, April 1, 1841(I), (II); JHN to H. A. Woodgate, April 1, 1841, *L&D*, 8: 145, 148–149, 152. Bishop Blomfield wrote, "I am extremely desirous that no further controversy should be raised at the present moment. . . . Enough has been done to direct the attention of the Church to what is dangerous or questionable in the Tracts. . . . These errors, whether of doctrine or discipline, which are imputed to Mr. Newman and his friends, may now, I think, be left to the vigilance & discretion of the Bishops." C. Blomfield to C. P. Golightly, April 14, 1841, Charles P. Golightly Papers, 1804, f. 54, Lambeth Palace Library.

    42. JHN to T. Mozley, June 18, 1841, *L&D*, 8: 207. The question of the existence or nonexistence of assurances having been given regarding the absence of general episcopal condemnations of *Tract 90* became a vexed question in Newman's history. Pusey claimed to have received Bagot's assurance on this point not only on the basis of Bagot's word but also of other authority. See *L&D*, 8: 106n., 119n., and 123n. for extensive references on the question. Furthermore, on March 22, 1841, Bishop Blomfield sent the following comments to R. W. Jelf: "With regard to the Bishops, it is most probable that some of them will notice the Tract [No. 90] in their charges, as they have already noticed others of the series: but I have no reason to apprehend that there will be any formal censure of it by the Bishops collectively. Indeed neither the Archbishop, nor myself, would consent to such a measure in the present posture of the question." [C. Blomfield to Dr. Jelf, March 22, 1841, Blomfield Papers, vol. 28, f. 33, Lambeth Palace Library.] Blomfield then advised the discontinuation of the tracts. If Jelf either showed Pusey, Bagot, or much less likely Newman, this letter or simply conveyed by paraphrase this passage, Newman might well have concluded that a firm assurance on the basis of authority had been given that he would not be censured by the bishops. See Thomas Gornall, "Newman's Lapses into Subjectivity," *Heythrop Journal*, 23 (1982): 46–50.

    43. *Christian Observer*, 41 (1841): 307, 304; *Record*, June 5, March 29, 1841. For claims of Newman's inconsistency, consult *Christian Observer*, 41 (1841): 295–296; *Record*, March 29, 1841. It is significant that Newman admitted as much himself in 1877; see *Via Media*, 2: 145–154.

    44. EBP to JHN, March 8, 1841, *L&D*, 8: 62. Newman refused to send all of the Pusey correspondence regarding *Tract 90* to Liddon. See notation to this effect in the Newman-Pusey correspondence volumes, Pusey House.

    45. JHN to EBP, March 10, 1841, *L&D*, 8: 64. John Keble also suggested changes in the

original wording of the Tract; JK to JHN, February 19, 1841, *L&D*, 8: 38, and Liddon, *Pusey*, 2: 180–181. On March 17 W. F. Hook, while writing in support of *Tract 90*, demurred from Newman's "*seeming* to assert that High Churchmen generally have found a difficulty in holding Catholic Principles consistently with a subscription to the Articles." He disliked Newman's asserting "that our Reformers were uncatholic" and also his "insinuating that while repudiating the *Romish* Doctrine with reference to Images Relics etc we wish to maintain *some* doctrine on these points on which I presume no *Catholic* Doctrine exists." W. F. Hook to JHN March 17, 1841, *L&D*, 8: 98. Newman took into account several of Hook's criticisms as well as those of Pusey and Keble when he responded to the larger storm of criticism. Virtually all the letters Newman received in support of *Tract 90* voiced one degree or another of hesitation. See W. Palmer to JHN, March 9, 1841; A. Perceval to JHN, March 10, 1841; G. Moberly to R. W. Church, March 18, 1841, *L&D*, 8: 63, 68, 97–98.

46. EBP to J. R. Hope, April 18, 1841, *L&D*, 8: 178. On tension between Newman and Pusey, see R. W. Church to F. Rogers, March 14 (continued on March 21), 1841, and on the discontinuance of the Theological Society, JHN to H. P. Liddon, May 27, 1887, *L&D*, 8: 108–111; 31: 212. On confusion about what Newman meant, consult J. W. Bowden to JHN, March 15, 1841, *L&D*, 8: 63, 71.

47. JHN to JK, April 1, 1841 (II), *L&D*, 8: 149.

48. John Keble, *The Case of Catholic Subscription to the Thirty-Nine Articles Considered: With Especial Reference to the Duties and Difficulties of English Catholics in the Present Crisis: In a Letter to the Hon. Mr. Justice Coleridge*, Not Published (London, 1841), pp. 6, 7, 12, 13, 25, 16, 17. Keble had 250 copies of this pamphlet printed to be sent to the bishops and others, but did not formally publish it.

49. Keble, *The Case of Catholic Subscription*, pp. 19–21, 32. Later in 1841 C. R. Sumner, the evangelical Bishop of Winchester, refused to ordain Peter Young, Keble's curate. Keble appealed without result to the Archbishop of Canterbury, but then as later remained in the church because there was no authority that could reach him personally.

50. [William George Ward], *A Few Words in Support of No. 90 of the Tracts for the Times, Partly with Reference to Mr. Wilson's Letter* (Oxford: John Henry Parker, 1841), pp. 4, 7. See also Ward, *William George Ward and the Oxford Movement*, pp. 156–175.

51. [Ward], *A Few Words*, pp. 28, 30–31, 43.

52. William George Ward, *A Few More Words in Support of No. 90 of the Tracts for the Times* (Oxford: John Henry Parker, 1841), pp. 29, 30, 33, 35.

53. Ward, *A Few More Words*, pp. 32, 35, 32, 79, 80, 91.

54. *Apologia*, pp. 150–151; JHN to T. Mozley, August 23, 1841, *L&D*, 8: 252. Over the years Newman quarreled with Ward and regretted and then in his own mind suppressed his former admiration for the younger man. In 1885 Newman quite remarkably wrote to Ward's son and their mutual biographer Wilfrid Ward, "Your Father was never a High-churchman, never a Tractarian, never a Puseyite, never a Newmanite." JHN to Wilfrid Ward, March 16, 1885, *L&D*, 31: 45.

55. Frederick Oakeley, *The Subject of Tract XC. Examined, in Connection with the History of the Thirty-Nine Articles, and the Statements of Certain English Divines to Which Is Added, The Case of Bishop Mountague, in the Reign of King James I* (London: J. G. F. and J. Rivington, 1841), pp. l, 11, 12, 15, 17, 26, 51. Oakeley had let it be known before publishing this pamphlet that he had supported Ward's recent publications. F. Oakeley to A. C. Tait, May 28, 1841. A. C. Tait Papers, vol. 77, f. 45, Lambeth Palace Library.

56. [F. Oakeley], "Bishop Jewel," *British Critic*, 30 (1841): 2, 3. See also JHN to T. Mozley, April 1, 1841. *L&D*, 8: 150–151. See also W. Palmer to JHN, July 25, 1841, for a sharply critical assessment of Oakeley's article from someone who had initially been enthusiastic about *Tract 90*. Newman Microfilms, reel 102, batch 162. This article generated criticism from Keble and Pusey as well. Newman wrote to them of his hope to moderate Mozley, but he did very little in that direction. Instead he continued to urge Mozley to accept Ward's

articles. JHN to T. Mozley, July 15, August 16, September 1, 1841, *L&D*, 8: 221–222, 249, 257.

57. [Oakeley], "Bishop Jewel," 27–28. Oakeley claimed to have written this passage before the appearance of *Tract 90*.

58. [Oakeley], "Bishop Jewel," 29, 45–46.

59. [J. H. Newman], "Private Judgment," *British Critic*, 30 (1841): 120, 121, 133, 134, 133.

60. J. B. Mozley to T. Mozley, May 19, 1841, Mozley, *Letters of the Rev. J. B. Mozley*, pp. 118–119; E. B. Pusey, *The Articles Treated on in Tract 90 Reconsidered and Their Interpretation Vindicated in a Letter to the Rev. R. W. Jelf.D. D., Canon of Christ Church* (Oxford: John Henry Parker, 1841), pp. 151, 71, 72, 148–149, 11. See also JHN to JK, April 1, 1841 (II); JHN to H. J. Coleridge, October 20, 1865, *L&D*, 8: 149; 22: 78–79.

61. F. Oakeley to EBP, June 22 and 29, 1841, Oakeley-Pusey Correspondence, Pusey House.

62. EBP to JHN, July 15, 1841, Liddon, *Pusey*, 2: 245.

63. EBP to JHN, July 20, 1841, Liddon, *Pusey*, 2: 218, 219; JHN to EBP, July 23 and 30, 1841, *L&D*, 8: 228, 234. See also JHN to JK, July 7 and 20, 1841; and JHN to T. Mozley, *L&D*, 8: 218, 225–226. See also JHN to T. Mozley, July 15, 1841, and T. Mozley to JHN, July 17, 1841, *L&D*, 8: 221–222. Although the editor of the Newman *Letters and Diaries* has included a generous selection of the correspondence coming to Newman from Mozley, the entire file deserves consultation. See Newman Microfilms, reel 102, batch 162.

64. W. G. Ward to EBP, July 23, 1841, CUP 5/91, Pusey House. Ward, *William George Ward and the Oxford Movement*, pp. 177–184, reprinted only portions of this very long document. See also JHN to EBP, August 24, 1841, *L&D*, 8: 253. Ward's statement about Newman's approval also receives confirmation in two letters from F. Oakeley to T. Mozley, May 18 and 27, 1841, Newman Microfilms, reel 104, batch 167. Consult [Newman], "Private Judgment," *British Critic*, 30 (1841): 101, 125, for favorable comments about Ward.

65. W. G. Ward to EBP, July 23, 1841, CUP 5/91, Pusey House.

66. JHN to EBP, August 3, 1841, *L&D*, 8: 237, 238.

67. EBP to JHN, August 9, 1841, *L&D*, 8: 240, 241. [The word *ethos* appears in Greek in the original.] This situation again raises questions about the nature and content of Pusey's conversations with Bishop Bagot over *Tract 90* the previous March. See also JHN to G. Ryder, April 15, 1841, *L&D*, 8: 176.

68. JHN to EBP, August 13, 1841, *L&D*, 8: 242, 243. Newman had viewed the *Remains* as allowing him to present himself more honestly, having told Edward Churton in 1838 that the volumes allowed the world to know his real sentiments toward the Reformation, "While the world thought, I liked Jewell etc. or rather while any of my friends thought it, I was uncomfortable. I am glad an opportunity has been given me to show them what I am." JHN to E. Churton, October 3, 1838, *L&D*, 6: 325. Throughout the autumn of 1841 Newman encouraged Thomas Mozley to look favorably on actions and articles of Oakeley and Ward. See JHN to T. Mozley, August 23, September 1, October 1, 1841, *L&D*, 8: 252–253, 257, 280–281.

69. Quoted in Ward, *William George Ward and the Oxford Movement*, pp. 187, 189. Published in *L'Univers* on April 15, 1841, and later translated and republished in the English Roman Catholic *Orthodox Journal*. See *L&D*, 8: 563–567, for the French text.

70. W. G. Ward to A. L. Phillipps, October 28, 1841, Ward, *William George Ward and the Oxford Movement*, pp. 195, 196.

71. W. G. Ward to A. L. Phillipps, continuation of October 28, 1841, Ward, *William George Ward and the Oxford Movement*, pp. 197–199.

72. JHN to J. R. Bloxam March 2, 1841; JHN to Dr. Russell, May 5, 1841; JHN to A. L. Phillipps, April 8, 1841, *L&D*, 8: 48, 49, 188, 166, 165, . See also JHN to Nicholas Wiseman, April 3, April 6, October 4 (unsent) and 14, 1841, *L&D*, 8: 153, 160–161, 282–285, 297–298.

73. JHN to J. R. Bloxam, March 2, 1841; JHN to JK, *L&D*, December 26, 1841, 8: 48, 389.

74. The bishops in England and Wales, numbering twenty-five, issued charges to their clergy usually at three-year intervals, meaning that between 1841 and 1843 there existed the possibility of twenty-five episcopal charges. Because of deaths and new appointments a total of twenty-eight persons served as bishops during that span. Of that group seventeen issued charges in one degree or another critical of *Tract 90* and other Tractarian writings. Had Bishop Phillip Shuttleworth of Chichester not died in 1842, another highly critical charge would certainly have been issued. No bishop and neither archbishop wrote in approval or sympathy of *Tract 90*.

Of the group of twenty-eight bishops, seventeen had been appointed by Tory or Conservative ministries and eleven by Whig ministries. Tory premiers had appointed both archbishops, not included in the twenty-eight. Of the seventeen charges against the Tractarians, ten emanated from Tory prelates and seven from Whig prelates. In 1841 and 1842 an equal number of Whig and Tory appointees charged the tracts. In 1843 all of the English bishops doing so were Tory appointments. Similarly both Whig and Tory bishops in the Irish Church criticized the Tractarians.

75. John Bird Sumner, *A Charge Delivered to the Clergy of the Dioceses of Chester at the Visitation in June and September, MDCCCXLI* (London: J. Hatchard, 1842), p. 22. See also A. P. Perceval, *A Letter to the Right Rev. John Bird, Lord Bishop of Chester: With Remarks on His Late Charge, More Especially as Relates to the Doctrine of Justification; with a Reference to the State of Things in the University of Oxford* (London: J. G. F. and J. Rivington, 1841), in which Perceval wrote, "I will only add my impression, that the whole confusion at Oxford arises from a dispute about the disposal of *second* votes. All are agreed to give their first votes to the Church of England; but as to their second votes, some would give to Rome, others to Geneva. For myself, I should greatly prefer, in this matter, the system of single voting; but if second votes are to be required or allowed, and some may give theirs to Geneva, it seems only reasonable to allow others to give theirs, if they prefer to, to Rome" (p. 6).

76. Sumner, *Charge to the Clergy*, pp. 28–29, 40, 42, 18. This charge, and particularly Sumner's criticism of Williams on reserve, long vexed Newman, who as late as 1883 recalled, "Bishop Sumner, in a charge, denounced" Williams's tract "as if speaking against the 'distribution of the Scriptures,' whereas Mr. Williams's words were 'the *indiscriminate* distribution of the Scriptures.' " [emphasis Newman's], JHN to G. T. Edwards, June 2, 1883, *L&D*, 30: 225.

77. Sumner, *Charge to the Clergy*, p. 78. Sumner rejected statements to the contrary set forth in *Tract 90, Tract 63*, the *British Critic*, and Newman's *Letter to Dr. Jelf.* For the manner in which this initial charge influenced others, see Charles Richard Sumner, *A Charge Delivered to the Clergy of the Diocese of Winchester at His Fourth Visitation in September, 1841* (London: J. Hatchard, 1841).

78. Charles Thomas Longley, *A Charge Delivered to the Clergy of the Diocese of Ripon at His Triennial Visitation, in July and August, 1841* (London: J. G. F. and J. Rivington, 1841), pp. 19, 20, 24, 25.

79. Edward Maltby, *Salutary Cautions Against the Errors Contained in the Oxford Tracts: A Charge to His Clergy Delivered at St. Nicholas's Church, Newcastle-Upon-Tyne, on Monday, August 9, 1841*, Taken in Short Hand, and Reprinted from the *Newcastle Courant* of August 13, 1841 (Newcastle: J. Blackwell, 1841), pp. 9, 7, 8, 7. Among former Tractarian acquaintances Archbishop Whately was also critical in his charge of 1841, but his remarks were not published that year. See Richard Whately, *The Kingdom of Christ Delineated, in Two Essays on Our Lord's Own Account of His Person and of the Nature of His Kingdom, and as the Constitution, Power, and Ministry of a Christian Church, as Appointed by Himself*, From the Second London Edition with Additions (New York: Wiley and Putnam, 1843).

80. James Henry Monk, *A Charge Delivered to the Clergy of the Diocese of Gloucester and*

Bristol at His Visitation in August and September, MDCCCXLI (London: J. G. F. and J. Rivington, 1841), pp. 35, 36, 30, 35.

81. Monk, *Charge to the Clergy*, p. 35.

82. Monk, *Charge to the Clergy*, pp. 34, 38.

83. Moreover, Catholic-minded Church of England parochial clergy found themselves sincerely confused as they confronted evangelical challenges on the one side and, on the other, the Tractarians, whom they had long admired, moving into Romanish directions, which neither they nor their bishops could approve. See for example, E. B. Cooper to the Bishop of Oxford, January 11, 1842 in Pusey-Bagot Correspondence Transcripts, f. 60, Pusey House. Cooper wrote, "In what a purgatory have these infatuated Tractarians placed all the Parochial Clergy who are anxious to uphold and disseminate those sound Catholic views, which they at first so nobly supported. I heartily trust the dreaded reaction may yet in some degree be averted."

84. JHN to JK, October, 24, 1841; JHN to T. Mozley, October 29, 1841; JHN to H. Wilberforce, November 8, 1841, *L&D*, 8: 305–306, 311, 322. For an earlier complaint to Keble, see also JHN to JK, October 5, 1841, *L&D*, 8: 286. For copies of passages of the bishops' charges in Newman's hand, see Newman Microfilms, reel 98, batch 154.

85. For Arnold's comments on Tractarianism, see T. Arnold to R. Whately, May 16, 1836, Whately Papers, Lambeth Palace, Ms. 2164, f. 30; T. Arnold to E. Hawkins, December 4, 1840, Arnold Papers, Rugby School; Arthur Penrhyn Stanley, *The Life and Correspondence of Thomas Arnold, D. D.*, 10th ed. (London: John Murray, 1877), 1: 227, 324; 2: 35, 46, 53–54, 124–126, 243; Thomas Arnold, *Christian Life, Its Courses, Its Hindrances, and Its Helps* (London: B. Fellowes, 1841), pp. xviii–lvi.

86. Robert Ornsby, *Memoirs of James Robert Hope-Scott of Abbotsford* (London: John Murray, 1884), 1: 283–331; David E. Barclay, *Frederick William IV and the Prussian Monarchy, 1840–1841* (Oxford: Oxford University Press, 1995), pp. 33–34, 74–84; R. W. Greaves, "The Jerusalem Bishopric, 1841," *English Historical Review*, 64 (1949): 328–352; Liddon, *Pusey*, 2: 248–60; Leopold Von Ranke, ed., *Aus dem Briefwechsel Friedrich Wilhelms IV. mit Bunsen* (Leipzig: Dunder and Humbolt, 1873), pp. 85–105; Nockles, *Oxford Movement in Context*, pp. 156–160.

87. JHN to HNM and JNM, October 12, 1841; JHN to the Editor of *The Times*, November 1, 1841 (not published), JHN to JNM, November 21, 1841, *L&D*, 8: 297, 316, 340. See also JHN to T. D. Acland, November 25, 1841, *L&D*, 8: 349 as well as all the Newman-Hope Correspondence throughout October-December, 1841, *L&D*, 8. Gladstone told Manning on November 30, "If Newman lighted the flame of discord by Tract 90 on one side it is a strange way of extinguishing to rival it by a yet wilder glare in another quarter of our close beleaguered camp." W. E. Gladstone to H. Manning, November 30, 1841, Gladstone Papers, British Library, Add. Ms. 44247, f. 106 (reverse side).

88. *Apologia*, p. 135. Newman saw both Lutheranism and Calvinism involved because under Frederick IV of Prussia the Lutheran and Reformed churches in Prussia had been merged.

89. JHN to J. R. Hope, November 24, 1841, *L&D*, 8: 345, 346. See also EBP to B. Harrison, April 13, 1846, in Pusey-Harrison Transcripts, Pusey House.

90. JHN to J. R. Hope, December 8, 1841, *L&D*, 8: 370.

91. W. F. Hook to JHN, March 27, 1841, *L&D*, 8: 119.

92. JHN comment written in 1850 on JHN to W. Dodsworth, January 2, 1842; JHN to JK, November 25, 1841, *L&D*, 8: 351, 405n.

93. *Record*, December 8, 1841; JHN to JNM, November 21, 1841, *L&D*, 8: 338–340. For background to the poetry professorship contest, see Liddon, *Pusey*, 2: 260–271. For Gladstone's exasperated reaction to Pusey's public letter, see W. E. Gladstone to J. R. Hope, November 25, 1841, Hope-Scott Papers, National Library of Scotland, Edinburgh, Ms.

3672, ff. 155–156. It is interesting to note that James Garbett had been a member of Newman's dining group that gathered from 1828 to 1833.

94. *Tablet*, January 2, 1842, p. 50; R. Bagot to EBP, January 26, 1842, Bagot-Pusey Transcripts, ff. 82–84, Pusey House. See also J. Copeland to Mr. Bowdler, December 31, 1841, Pusey House; JK to EBP, St. Andrew's Day, 1841, Keble-Pusey Transcripts, p. 190, Pusey House; Gladstone to Hope, November 25 and 27, 1841, Hope-Scott Papers, National Library of Scotland, Ms. 3672, ff. 155–157. On Gladstone's efforts around the poetry professorship contest, consult W. E. Gladstone to H. Manning, December 3, 14, 16, 18, 20, and 22, 1841, January 1, 1842, British Library, Add. Ms. 44247, ff. 109, 111, 113, 115, 121, 125, 131; see also f. 130 for the circular asking the two candidates for the poetry professorship to withdraw; H. Wilberforce to W. E. Gladstone, December 24, 1841, Gladstone Papers, British Library, Add. Ms. 44358; Correspondence between W. E. Gladstone and R. Bagot of January, 1842, Gladstone Papers, British Library, Add. Ms, 44359, ff. 1, 9, 31, 32, 46, 49, 51, 55.

95. E. Churton to EBP, December 9, 1841, Edward Churton Papers, Pusey House, partially rpt. in Liddon, *Pusey*, 2: 268–270; EBP to E. Churton, December 11, 1841, Liddon, *Pusey*, 2: 270–271; JHN to H. Wilberforce, February 19, 1842, *L&D*, 8: 469. Exacerbating concerns of such high churchmen as Churton, Ward on December 6 wrote a public letter to Pusey, allegedly clarifying Newman's stance toward Rome as well as the more advanced Tractarians and their actions, but in fact only serving to stir more controversy. W. G. Ward, *To the Rev. Dr. Pusey, Canon of Christ Church*, December 6, 1841, published as a privately circulated broadsheet. See E. Churton to EBP, December 13, 1841, Edward Churton Papers, Pusey House, where Churton says, "What I really am afraid of now, is, lest the excesses of the young men, who are supposed to be guided by you shd induce the bishops to put themselves at the head of some movement against you. If they do, what will become of us?"

96. *Christian Observer*, 42 (1842): 127; *Morning Chronicle*, January 29, 1842. See also R. Peel to the Duke of Wellington, January 19, 1842, British Library, Add. Ms. 40459. See also JNM to JHN, January 27, 1842, and H. A. Woodgate to JHN, May 30, 1842, *L&D*, 8: 437 and note. In January 1842, Archdeacon W. R. Lyall wrote to Bagot reporting the Archbishop's personal request to Pusey for a period of silence. Lyall further stated that the Archbishop wanted Pusey and Newman to reply to certain questions in regard to the Fathers that William Goode had posed in *Divine Rule of Faith and Practice*. The Archbishop's hope was that Newman and Pusey might produce a statement of their opinions "such as one may tie them down to *certain distinct propositions and enable those who differ from them in their views of Catholic doctrines to grapple with them in argument.*" W. R. Lyall to R. Bagot, January 14, 1842, in Francis Paget, "A Collection of Letters Bearing on the Oxford Movement, and Especially on Bishop Bagot's Connexion with It," Pusey House. See also Dean of Canterbury to EBP, January 14, 1842, Liddon, *Pusey*, 2: 274–275.

97. JHN to R. Wilberforce, January 26, 1842, *L&D*, 8: 441, 442, [This letter was part of a larger exchange with Wilberforce on these questions; see R. Wilberforce to JHN, December 9, 1841, January 21 and 29, 1842, Newman Microfilms, reel 75, batch 86]; JHN to T. Mozley, January 29, 1842; see also JHN to T. Mozley, August 23, September 1, October 1, 1841, January 26, 1842, *L&D*, 8: 444, 252, 257, 280, 438, 443. For Ward's position, consult T. Mozley to W. G. Ward, Conversion of St. Paul, 1842, Newman Microfilms, reel 103, batch 162.

98. J. R. Hope to EBP, January 31, 1842, Liddon, *Pusey*, 2: 278.

99. E. B. Pusey, *A Letter to His Grace the Archbishop of Canterbury, on Some Circumstances Connected with the Present Crisis in the English Church*, 2d ed. (Oxford: John Henry Parker, 1842), pp. 39, 40.

100. Pusey, *Letter to the Archbishop of Canterbury*, pp. 47, 48, 83, 77, 79. It was no wonder that the Bishop of London was reported to have said that the bishops had been treated worse by the Tractarians than by the evangelicals. T. Henderson to EBP, Ash Wednesday,

1842, *Pusey*, 2: 275. Churton was not pleased with Pusey's *Letter*, which he indicated voiced views different from those Pusey had privately written to him and which years later he described "as written in the style of a leader of mutineers." E. Churton to J. C. Crosthwaite, April 21, 1842; E. Churton to W. Gresley, May 21, 1846 in Edward Churton Papers, Pusey House. See also Nockles, *Oxford Movement in Context*, pp. 309–311.

    101. Pusey, *Letter to the Archbishop of Canterbury*, pp. 51, 60.

    102. Pusey, *Letter to the Archbishop of Canterbury*, pp. 61, 67–68, 71–73.

    103. Pusey, *Letter to the Archbishop of Canterbury*, pp. 98, 140, 156, 149.

CHAPTER 9. IN SCHISM WITH ALL CHRISTENDOM

    1. *Morning Herald*, March 26, 1841, p. 4.

    2. *Morning Chronicle*, March 26, 1841, lead page; R. Whately to E. Hawkins, March or April, 1841, Letterbooks, 3: 232, Oriel College; *Christian Observer*, 42 (1842): 35; *Standard*, January 13, 1842; June 9, 1843; [Baden Powell], "Anglo-Catholicism," *British and Foreign Review*, 16 (1844): 24, 26, 28, 29; [Anon.], "Ancient and Modern Catholicity," *Dublin Review*, December, 1843, p. 510.

    3. For example, on September 23, 1843, the *Morning Herald* wrote, "Tractarianism is an effort to denationalize the Church of England, just as the Free Church is an effort to denationalize the Church of Scotland. The former would Romanize our church; the latter would Americanize that of Scotland." *Morning Herald*, September 22, 1843, p. 4.

    4. JHN to S. Rickards, December 1, 1841, *L&D*, 8: 359, 360. See also JHN to T. Mozley, October 29–31, 1841, *L&D*, 8: 311–312, for an earlier discussion of how heresy might allow rejection of constituted authority, in this case that of a bishop.

    5. JHN to M. R. Giberne, December 27, 1841, *L&D*, 8: 392.

    6. JHN to W. Dodsworth, January 2, 1842, *L&D*, 8: 405. For advice to postpone conversion, see F. Oakeley to JHN and reply, undated, 1843, Newman Microfilms, reel 67, batch 59.

    7. HNM to JNM, November 30, 1841, *Newman Family Letters*, pp. 113; J. D. Dalgairns to Unknown Correspondent, December 1, 1841, *L&D*, 8: 421n.

    8. John Henry Newman, *Sermons, Bearing on Subjects of the Day*, (London: J. G. F. and J. Rivington, 1843) p. 391, 393. The subjectivity of the published sermons appears to have been a toned-down version of the delivered sermons following prepublication suggestions by Keble. JK to JHN, September 4, 5, and 18, 1843, and JHN to JK, September 5 and 6, In fest. S. Mich., 1843, *Corrs. with JK*, pp. 255–260, 263–267. See JHN to J. Hope, November 22, 1841, *L&D*, 8: 345–347. When Newman's sermons of December 1841 were published in 1843 in *Sermons, Bearing on Subjects of the Day*, the Roman Catholic *Dublin Review* criticized him for encouraging men to stay in the Church of England and for his emphasis on inwardness. "Newman's Sermons," *Dublin Review*, 15 (1843): 557.

    9. *Sermons, Bearing on Subjects of the Day*, pp. 359, 365, 371, 376, 379, 383.

    10. *Sermons, Bearing on Subjects of the Day*, p. 408.

    11. *Sermons, Bearing on Subjects of the Day*, pp. 415, 419, 421, 422.

    12. *Sermons, Bearing on Subjects of the Day*, pp. 423, 428.

    13. *Sermons, Bearing on Subjects of the Day*, pp. 136, 355, 366, 417, 422; JHN to S. F. Wood, December 13, 1841, *L&D*, 8: 375. Newman's self-identification with Elijah was noted at the time; see "Newman's Sermons on Subjects of the Day," *English Review*, 1 (1844): 328–330. Newman had made a personal reference to Elijah almost exactly six years earlier. In late 1836 Mrs. Henry Wilberforce presented him a new surplice, for which he thanked her, commenting, "May it be Elijah's mantle—an omen of better things coming!" JHN to Mrs. Henry Wilberforce, December 23, 1836, *L&D*, 5: 397.

14. JHN to J. Hope, January 3, 1842, *L&D*, 8: 410.
15. "Monasticism," *Encyclopaedia Britannica*, 11th ed. (1910–1911).
16. JHN to H. A. Woodgate, September 22, 1841, *L&D*, 8: 277. On Peel's patronage concerns, see Duke of Wellington to R. Peel, April 14 or 19, 1842, Sir Robert Peel Papers, British Library, Add. Ms. 40459, f. 224. Concerns on the part of both Peel and members of the university affected other patronage. See correspondence between Edward Cardwell and R. Peel, November 22, 23, and 28, 1844, and between Thomas Gaisford and R. Peel, November 27 and 28, 1844, May 1845, Sir Robert Peel Papers, British Library, Add. Ms. 40554, ff. 284, 286, 288, 382, 384; Add. Ms., 40568, ff. 49–58; Add. Ms. 40567, ff. 409–412.
17. R. W. Jelf to EBP, December 10 and 12, 1841, Jelf-Pusey Correspondence (transcripts), Pusey House; R. Bagot to JHN, April 12, 1842; JHN to R. Bagot, April 14, 1842, *L&D*, 8: 504, 505, 507; Archbishop Howley to R. Bagot, April 16, 1842, in Francis Paget, "A Collection of Letters Bearing on the Oxford Movement, and Especially Bishop Bagot's Connexion with It," Pusey House.
18. Journal, January 21, 1863, *AW*, p. 258
19. JHN to H. Wilberforce, April 25, 1842, *L&D*, 8: 512.
20. F. Oakeley to F. Kilvert, January 19, 1843, Bodleian Library, Ms. Don. d. 120, f. 132. I owe the reference to this letter to Dr. Richard Lofthouse. See also Peter Nockles, *The Oxford Movement in Context: Anglican High Churchmanship, 1760–1857* (Cambridge: Cambridge University Press, 1994), pp. 184–190, for earlier high-church attitudes toward asceticism.
21. William Lockhart, *Cardinal Newman: Reminiscences of Fifty Years* (London: Burns and Oates, 1891), p. 10; JK to F. Kilvert, March 28, 1844, Bodleian Library, Ms. Don. d. 120, f. 114. See also JK to F. Kilvert, December 2/3, 1842; EBP to F. Kilvert, November 3, no year, Bodleian Library, Ms. Don. d. 120, ff. 112, 138. See also Peter F. Anson, *The Call of the Cloister: Religious Communities and Kindred Bodies in the Anglican Communion* (London: S.P.C.K., 1956), pp. 29–46; A. M. Allchin, *The Silent Rebellion: Anglican Religious Communities, 1845–1900* (London: SCM, 1958), pp. 52–68.
22. J. D. Dalgairns to Unknown Correspondent, December 1, 1841, "Letters from Oxford and Littlemore," E. Hermitage Day, *Treasury*, 1911, p. 25, as quoted in R. D. Middleton, *Newman and Bloxam: An Oxford Friendship* (London: Oxford University Press, 1947), p. 86; JHN to M. R. Giberne, March 30, 1842, *L&D*, 8: 497; Newman quoted in Mark Pattison, *Memoirs* (London: Macmillan, 1885), p. 190.
23. *Morning Chronicle*, January 29, 1842. See John Oldcastle [pseudonym for Wilfrid Meynell], *Cardinal Newman: A Monograph* (London: John Sinkins, 1890), pp. 18–31.
24. J. D. Dalgairns to Unknown Correspondent, January, 1842, "Letters from Oxford and Littlemore," E. Hermitage Day, *Treasury*, 1911, p. 25, as quoted in Middleton, *Newman and Bloxam*, pp. 86–87; F. Oakeley to F. Kilvert, January 19, 1843, Bodleian Library, Ms. Don. d. 120, f. 132; Wilfrid Ward, *William George Ward and the Oxford Movement* (London: Macmillan, 1889), p. 240.
25. Pattison, *Memoirs*, p. 190. See also F. Nolan, *A Study of Mark Pattison's Religious Experience, 1813–1850* (Oxford diss., 1977).
26. JHN to J. R. Bloxam, June 12, 1843, in Middleton, *Newman and Bloxam*, p. 92; Urban Young, *Life and Letters of the Venerable Father Dominic* (London: Burns, Oates, and Washbourne, 1926), p. 265. See G. P. Grantham, *A History of Saint Saviour's Leeds with Full Description of the Church* (London: Joseph Masters, 1872).
27. J. D. Dalgairns to Unknown Correspondent, December 1, 1841, January, May, September, 1842, "Letters from Oxford and Littlemore," E. Hermitage Day, *Treasury*, 1911, pp. 25, 26, as quoted in Middleton, *Newman and Bloxam*, pp. 86–89; JHN to H. Wilberforce, April 25, 1842, *L&D*, 8: 511–512. Note that Newman records the beginning of the Breviary service as dating after his letter to the Bishop of Oxford. Robert Williams had undertaken a

translation of the Breviary, which Newman first supported and then ceased to support when he found that Keble had translated parts of it. Middleton, *Newman and Bloxam*, 93–95. See also Pattison, *Memoirs*, p. 189.

28. Lockhart, *Cardinal Newman*, p. 10. See also Journals for 1839–1844, *AW*, pp. 216–236; Oldcastle, *Cardinal Newman*, p. 25; EBP to Mrs. Pusey, June 4, 1837. E. B. Pusey–Mrs. Pusey Correspondence (transcripts), Pusey House.

29. T. Arnold to R. Whately, undated, but forwarded by Whately to Lord Melbourne, April 13, 1836, with internal comments indicating it had been written in late March or early April 1836, Melbourne Papers, Royal Archives, RA MP (M) 76/171; W. G. Ward to EBP, July 23, 1841 CUP 5/91, Pusey House; [W. G. Ward], "Arnold's Sermons," *British Critic*, 30 (1841): 318; Dalgairns to Father Dominic, October 1844, as quoted in Meriol Trevor, *Newman: The Pillar of the Cloud* (New York: Doubleday, 1962), p. 332. Ward further criticized the inadequacy of Arnold's views on the sacraments, the indwelling of the Holy Ghost, the priesthood, and the authority of Scripture over Catholic truth. It should be noted that in 1838 the hostile *Edinburgh Review* article on Froude's *Remains* had simultaneously reviewed and criticized a biography illustrating evangelical asceticism. See [James Stephen], "The Lives of Whitfield and Froude—Oxford Catholicism," *Edinburgh Review*, 67 (1838): 500–535. Only the case of Gladstone's personal asceticism has received serious attention; see H. C. G. Matthew, *Gladstone: 1809–1874* (Oxford: Clarendon, 1986), pp. 87–102.

30. Newman's Diary Notes, 1839–1840, *L&D*, 7: 487; [W. G. Ward], "St. Athanasius Against the Arians," *British Critic*, 32 (1842): 392, 393; [Frederick Oakeley], "Sacramental Confession," *British Critic*, 33 (1843): 299. See also [W. G. Ward], "The Synagogue and the Church," *British Critic*, 34 (1843): 7, 17–18. In late 1842 Newman himself wrote, "I think we are in great danger of becoming, if I may use a harsh word, *theatrical* in our Religion. All true attention to rites must be founded on deep inward convictions, and this makes me dread the fine arts when disjoined from what is practical and personal." JHN to [?] Russell, December 29, 1842, Birmingham Oratory Typescript.

31. *Sermons, Bearing on Subjects of the Day*, pp. 4, 132, 133. See also p. 132, where Newman gives a reference to *PPS*, 1: 309–324, as an indication that he had said this before.

32. *Sermons, Bearing on Subjects of the Day*, p. 135.

33. "Notes of the Retreat Before Ordination," April 8–17, 1847, *AW*, p. 247. For the Latin text, see pp. 239–242.

34. "Notes of the Retreat Before Ordination," p. 247.

35. "Notes of the Retreat Before Ordination," pp. 247–248. In a journal entry of 1863 Newman traced the change in his inner feelings and outward physical appearance to the events around *Tract 90*, but such was not the picture he drew in 1847. Journal, January 21, 1863, *AW*, pp. 254–255.

36. Friedrich Nietzsche, *Twilight of the Idols* (1888), in Walter Kaufman, ed., *The Portable Nietzsche* (New York: Viking, 1954), p. 515.

37. HNM to JNM, May 13, 1842, *Newman Family Letters*, p. 122. Ten years earlier Harriett had indicated difficulty with her brother's friends; see Harriett Newman to JHN, October 20 and 26, 1832, *L&D*, 3: 107–108.

38. For a general discussion with a different argument from mine, see Trevor, *Newman*, pp. 19–20, 88–96, 235–236. See also Oliver S. Buckton, *Secret Selves: Confession and Same-Sex Desire in Victorian Autobiography* (Chapel Hill: University of North Carolina Press, 1998), pp. 21–59, for a consideration of the manner in which suspicion of homosexuality on Newman's part may have informed Charles Kingsley's attack in 1864, and James Eli Adams, *Dandies and Desert Saints: Styles of Victorian Masculinity* (Ithaca: Cornell University Press, 1995), pp. 61–106, for a nuanced exploration of the attractions that Newman's personality and message held for young men. Also important for this topic, consult Herbert Sussman, *Victorian Masculinities: Manhood and Masculine Poetics in Early Victorian Literature and Art* (Cambridge: Cambridge University Press, 1995); Linda Dowling, *Hellenism and Homosex-*

uality in Victorian Oxford (Ithaca: Cornell University Press, 1994), pp. 36–44; Eve Kosofsky Sedgwick, *Epistemology of the Closet* (Berkeley: University of California Press, 1990), pp. 1–90; and Susan Chitty, *The Beast and the Monk: A Life of Charles Kingsley* (New York: Maston/Charter, 1975), pp. 229–237.

39. Isaac Williams, *The Autobiography of Isaac Williams, B.D.*, ed. George Prevost (London: Longmans, Green, 1892), p. 107; JHN to J. F. Christie, January 29, 1837, *L&D*, 6: 18; JHN to J. D. Dalgairns, April 26, 1843, *Corrs. with JK*, p. 215; JHN to JK, September 14, 1844, Mozley, *Letters and Correspondence*, 2: 392. See also David Newsome, *The Wilberforces and Henry Manning: The Parting of Friends* (Cambridge: Harvard University Press, 1966), pp. 146–156.

40. JHN to H. Wilberforce, January 8, 1834 (not sent), *L&D*, 4: 169–170; JHN to H. J. Rose, March 17, 1834 (I), *L&D*, 4: 206.

41. JHN to the Duchess of Norfolk, September 19, 1862; JHN to H. Wilberforce, May 15, 1866, *L&D*, 20: 45; 22: 234.

42. JHN to J. W. Bowden, August 28, 1836, *L&D*, 5: 345.

43. As quoted in Trevor, *Newman*, p. 234. For the original, see Frederic Rogers to JHN, December 31, 1839, Newman Microfilms, reel 33, batch 6.

44. "My Illness in Sicily," March 25, 1840, *AW*, 137; JHN to Henry Moore, May 21, 1840, *L&D*, 7: 330–331.

45. JHN to M. Holmes, March 8, 1843, Anne Mozley, ed., *Letters of the Rev. J. B. Mozley, D.D., Edited by His Sister* (London: Rivingtons, 1885), 2: 366.

46. E. B. Pusey, *A Letter to the Right Rev. Father in God, Richard, Lord Bishop of Oxford, in the Tendency to Romanism Imputed to Doctrines Held of Old, as Now, in the English Church* (Oxford: J. H. Parker, 1839), pp. 212, 213.

47. R. W. Church, *The Oxford Movement: Twelve Years, 1833–1845*, ed. Geoffrey Best (Chicago: University of Chicago Press, 1970), p. 248; Adams, *Dandies and Desert Saints*, p. 60.

48. JHN to EBP, March 17, 1840, *L&D*, 7: 264; "The Form of Solemnization of Matrimony," *Book of Common Prayer;* J. B. Morris to F. W. Faber, October 20, 1840, *L&D*, 7: 420; EBP to Mrs. Pusey, November 6, 1835, in E. B. Pusey–Mrs. Pusey Correspondence (transcripts), Pusey House.

49. J. B. Morris to F. W. Faber, October 20, 1840, *L&D*, 7: 420–421. I have substituted "yourself" in the next-to-last sentence of this quotation for the apparently mistranscribed "ourself" in the cited printed version.

50. JHN to F. W. Faber, October 27, 1840, *L&D*, 7: 422.

51. See also F. Oakeley to EBP, December 3, 1838, Oakeley-Pusey Correspondence, Pusey House.

52. D. B. Herzog, D. K. Norman, C. Gordon, M. Pepose, "Sexual Conflict and Eating Disorders in 27 Males," *American Journal of Psychiatry*, 141: 8 (1984): 989–990; J. W. Sterling and J. D. Segal, "Anorexia Nervosa in Males: A Critical Review," *International Journal of Eating Disorders*, 4 (1985): 559–572; N. Joughin, A. H. Crisp, C. Halek, H. Humphrey, "Religious Belief and Anorexia Nervosa," *International Journal of Eating Disorders*, 12 (1992): 397–406; S. A. French, M. Story, G. Remafedi, M. D. Resnick, R. W. Blum, "Sexual Orientation and Prevalence of Body Dissatisfaction and Eating Disordered Behaviors: A Population-Based Study of Adolescents," *International Journal of Eating Disorders*, 19 (1996): 119–126; P. M. Keel, K. L. Klump, G. R. Leon, J. A. Fulkerson, "Disordered Eating in Adolescent Males from a School-Based Sample," *International Journal of Eating Disorders*, 23 (1998): 125–132; Walter Vandereycken and Ron Van Deth, *From Fasting Saints to Anorexic Girls: The History of Self-Starvation* (London: Athlone, 1994), pp. 181–217.

53. As we have seen, Faber had described Newman's coterie in the mid-1830s as Essenes. At that time the Essenes were understood to be a Jewish order whose celibacy was grounded in a low view of women. F. W. Faber to a Friend, January 1835, John Edward

Bowden, *The Life and Letters of Frederick William Faber, D.D.* (Baltimore: John Murphy, 1869), p. 43.

54. Peter Nockles, "Oxford, Tract 90, and the Bishops," in David Nicholls and Fergus Kerr, eds., *John Henry Newman: Reason, Rhetoric, and Romanticism* (Carbondale: Southern Illinois University Press, 1991), pp. 28–87.

55. Richard Bagot, *A Charge Delivered to the Clergy of the Diocese of Oxford, May, 1842* (Oxford: John Henry Parker, 1842), p. 23; Edward Denison, *A Charge Delivered to the Clergy of the Diocese of Salisbury by Edward Denison, D.D. Bishop of Salisbury at His Second Visitation, September, 1842,* 2d ed. (London: J. G. F. and J. Rivington, 1842), pp. 17, 20; Musgrave quoted in W. Simon Bricknell, ed., *The Judgment of the Bishops upon Tractarian Theology: A Complete Analytical Arrangement of the Charges Delivered by the Prelates of the Anglican Church, from 1837 to 1842 Inclusive; So Far as They Relate to the Tractarian Movement,* (Oxford: J. Vincent, 1845), p. 73 [although this volume is the most easily accessible source for the bishops' charges, they are only excerpted therein, with numerous comments favorable to the early tracts omitted]; Christopher Bethell, *Charge to the Clergy of the Diocese of Bangor, Delivered in the Month of September, 1843* (London: J. G. F. and J. Rivington, 1843), pp. 18–19; see also pp. 33–52 in the appendix to this charge, in which Bethell systematically criticizes Tractarian clericalism.

56. Edward Copleston, *A Charge Delivered to the Clergy of the Diocese of Llandaff at the Triennial Visitation in October, 1842* (London: J. G. F. and J. Rivington, 1842), pp. 15, 25–26, 28; Charles James Blomfield, *A Charge Delivered to the Clergy of the Diocese of London at the Visitation in October MDCCCXLII,* 2d ed. (London: B. Fellowes, 1842), pp. 59, 51–52.

57. James Thomas O'Brien, *A Charge Delivered to the Clergy of the United Dioceses of Ossory, Ferns, and Leighlin, at His Primary Visitation in September, 1842* (London: Seeley, Burnside, and Seeley, 1843), pp. 150, 152.

58. Connop Thirlwall, *Remains Literary and Theological of Connop Thirlwall,* ed. J. J. Stewart Perowne (London: Daldy, Isbister, 1877–1878), pp. 29–30, 42–45.

59. Thirlwall, *Remains,* p. 33; Blomfield, *Charge Delivered to the Clergy,* p. 28; Musgrave quoted in Bricknell, *Judgment of the Bishops,* p. 435; Richard Whately, *The Kingdom of Christ Delineated, in Two Essays on Our Lord's Own Account of His Person and of the Nature of His Kingdom, and as the Constitution, Power, and Ministry of a Christian Church, as Appointed by Himself,* 3d ed. (London: B. Fellowes, 1842), p. 208.

60. O'Brien, *Charge Delivered to the Clergy,* pp. 26, 46, 121–122 [see also p. 10 for O'Brien's rejection of Pusey's view of postbaptismal sin]; John Kaye, *A Charge to the Clergy of the Diocese of Lincoln* (London: J. G. F. and J. Rivington, 1843), p. 52.

61. T. Arnold to A. C. Tait, March 11, 1841, A. C. Tait Papers, vol. 77, f. 11, Lambeth Palace Library; E. Jane Whately, *Life and Correspondence of Richard Whately, D.D,* New Edition, in One Volume, with Additional Correspondence (London: Longmans, Green, 1875), pp. 192–193, 170, 204; R. Whately to E. Hawkins, March 20, 1843, Letterbooks, 3: 251, Oriel College. See also B. Harrison to EBP, March 14, 1841, Pusey-Harrison Correspondence (transcripts), p. 12, Pusey House.

62. Steven Shapin, *A Social History of Truth: Civility and Science in Seventeenth-Century England* (Chicago: University of Chicago Press, 1994), pp. 106–107.

63. Henry Phillpotts, *A Charge Delivered to the Clergy of the Diocese of Exeter at the Triennial Visitation in June, July, August, and September, 1842* (London: John Murray, 1842), pp. 31, 34–35.

64. Bagot, *Charge Delivered to the Clergy,* pp. 17–18. Francis Paget wrote the final quoted phrase; see F. Paget to Bishop Eden, January 24, 1879, in "Collection of Letters," Pusey House. See also *Christian Observer,* 42 (1842): 504–511, for a reading of Bagot's charge that saw it as an apology for the tracts.

65. Copleston, *Charge Delivered to the Clergy,* p. 32; Kaye, *Charge Delivered to the Clergy,* p. 12.

66. O'Brien, *Charge Delivered to the Clergy*, pp. 165, 172, 174, 158, 183.

67. JHN to F. Rogers, January 10, 1841, *L&D*, 8: 10–11; Richard Whately, *Cautions for the Times Addressed to the Parishioners of a Parish in England, by Their Former Rector* (London: John W. Parker, 1853), pp. 236, 237. See also Lionel Trilling, *Sincerity and Authenticity* (Cambridge: Harvard University Press, 1972).

68. [Bonamy Price], "Tracts for the Times—Number Ninety," *Edinburgh Review*, 73 (1841): 286. See also [Baden Powell], "Anglo-Catholicism," *British and Foreign Review*, 16 (1844): 532, 559.

69. [Price], "Tracts for the Times—Number Ninety," 286, 288, 289, 297; [Henry Rogers], "Puseyism, or The Oxford Tractarian School," *Edinburgh Review*, 77 (1843): 505. In 1845 the *Christian Observer* noted that Tractarian interpretations of subscription would end all human compacts and most particularly contracts to repay debts. *Christian Observer*, 45 (1845): 15. See also [Powell], "Anglo-Catholicism," 532, 559.

70. Thomas Scott, "On the Dispositions and Character Peculiar to the True Believer," in *Essays on the Most Important Subjects in Religion* in Thomas Scott, *The Theological Works of the Rev. Thomas Scott* (Edinburgh: Peter Brown and Thomas Nelson, 1835), p. 291.

71. P. S. Atiyah, *The Rise and Fall of Freedom of Contract* (Oxford: Clarendon, 1979), pp. 345, 347, 348, 353, 389.

72. Atiyah, *Freedom of Contract*, pp. 393, 395–396, 447, 459; P. S. Atiyah, *Promises, Morals, and Law* (Oxford: Clarendon, 1981), p. 4.

73. JHN to T. Mozley, September 26, 1842, Newman Microfilms, reel 103, batch 162; *Sermons, Bearing on Subjects of the Day*, p. 432.

74. *Sermons, Bearing on Subjects of the Day*, pp. 442–445.

75. JHN to Unknown Correspondent, March 4, 1843, *Corrs. with JK*, pp. 205–207.

76. *Sermons, Bearing on Subjects of the Day*, pp. 244, 313, 317, 327. Here Newman faults the circulation of the Bible in editions that included marginal notes; in the mid-1830s he had similarly rejected the Bible Society practice of circulating the Bible without any notes or commentary.

77. *Sermons, Bearing on Subjects of the Day*, pp. 328, 330.

78. For the specific exclusion of evangelicals from Newman's definition of the church, see his note of many years later on "Wisdom and Innocence." *Apologia*, p. 274.

79. *Sermons, Bearing on Subjects of the Day*, p. 332.

80. *Sermons, Bearing on Subjects of the Day*, pp. 332–335.

81. *Sermons, Bearing on Subjects of the Day*, pp. 334, 335, 337.

82. *Sermons, Bearing on Subjects of the Day*, pp. 337, 338.

83. *Sermons, Bearing on Subjects of the Day*, pp. 339–342.

84. JHN to JK, March 14, 1843, *Corrs. with JK*, pp. 210–212. On Newman's retraction of previous opinions and views of the Roman Church, see *Via Media*, 2: 425–433; *Corrs. with JK*, 202–204. See also Mozley, *Letters and Correspondence*, 2: 364. The contents of this letter should be contrasted with the claims Newman made in a letter of 1845. See JHN to S. Wilks, November 8, 1845, *L&D*, 11: 27–28. See also JHN to M. Holmes, March 8, 1843, Mozley, *Letters and Correspondence*, 2: 366–367

85. JHN to JK, May 4, 1843 (a), *Corrs. with JK*, p. 218.

86. JHN to JK, May 4 (b), 10, 1843, *Corrs. with JK*, pp. 219, 220, 222.

87. JK to JHN, May 14, 1843; JHN to JK, May 4, 1843, *Corrs. with JK*, pp. 223–225.

88. JHN to JK, May 18, 1843, *Corrs. with JK*, p. 227.

89. On Pusey's ambivalence about the Martyrs Monument, see Liddon, *Pusey*, 2: 65–76.

90. JHN to JK, May 18, 1843; see also JK to JHN, May 30, 1843, *Corrs. with JK*, pp. 227, 231–232.

91. E. Hawkins and P. Wynter as quoted in Liddon, *Pusey*, 2: 317. For materials surrounding Pusey's sermon, see H. P. Liddon, *Pusey*, 2: 306–369; Wynter Papers, dep. c. 3,

Bodleian Library; E. Cardwell to Duke of Wellington, May 25 and 30, June 1 and 2, 1843; P. Wynter to Duke of Wellington, July 10, 1843, Wellington Papers, 2/253/24–27, 43, 49–53, Southampton University; R. Jenkyns Papers, Balliol College, VI A, 21; *Oxford Chronicle and Reading Gazette*, May 20 and 27, June 3 and 10, 1843; *Morning Chronicle*, May 24 and 27, June 2, 7, and 9, 1843; *Standard*, June 3, 6, 7, 8, 9, 10, 1843.

92. Contemporaries were well aware that the sermon Pusey printed was not the sermon he had actually delivered. *Christian Observer*, 43 (1843): 511; *Standard*, July 17, 18, 1843; and *Oxford Chronicle and Reading Gazette*, July 8, 1843.

93. Liddon, *Pusey*, 2: 329; *Morning Post*, June 12, 1843, p. 4. See also EBP to I. Williams, Ascension Day, 1843, Isaac Williams Papers, 3/102, Lambeth Palace Library; *Morning Chronicle*, August 19, 1843; [Thomas Mozley], "The Six Doctors," *British Critic*, 34 (1843): 195–271; [Anon.], "The Vice-Chancellorship of Dr. Wynter," *Christian Remembrancer*, 9 (1845): 133–187. Also consult the extensive correspondence between Pusey and Bagot and between Bagot and Archbishop Howley between October 22 and December 19, 1844, in Paget, "Collection of Letters," Pusey House.

94. EBP to JHN, May 18, 1843, Liddon, *Pusey*, 2: 312; JHN to A. St. John, June 20, 1843, *Corrs. with JK*, p. 237. There appears to have been some concern on Newman's part about the clarity and consistency of Pusey's statements. See JHN to E. L. Badeley, June 18, 1843, *Corres. with JK*, p. 235–236, and JHN to T. Mozley, June 19, 1843, Newman Microfilms, reel 103, batch 162. For Keble's opinion, see JK to EBP, July 1, 1843; see also JK to EBP of May 30, June 4, 10, and 21, 1843. Keble-Pusey Correspondence (transcripts), Pusey House.

95. R. Jelf to EBP, August 18, 1843, Jelf-Pusey Correspondence (transcripts), Pusey House; *Morning Chronicle*, May 30, 1842, p. 2. See also R. Jelf to EBP, July 12 and August 19, 1843, Jelf-Pusey Correspondence (transcripts), Pusey House. On Palmer's forthcoming pamphlet, consult JK to JHN, August 30, 1843; JHN to JK, August 31, 1843, *Corrs. with JK*, pp. 249–250. By early September, Palmer had shown the narrative to W. F. Hook, W. Gresley, E. Churton, and Bishop Bagot; see W. Palmer to R. Bagot, September 4, 1843, Pusey-Bagot Correspondence, Pusey House.

96. E. Churton to J. Watson, September 18, 1843, Edward Churton Papers, CHUR 2/3/8, Pusey House; Archbishop Howley to R. Bagot, September 11, 1843, in Paget, "Collection of Letters," Pusey House. J. D. Coleridge wrote a friend about the same time, "I grieve to see an Exeter man of the name of Lockhardt [*sic*] and one of the 'mynckerie' at Littlemore has seceded. It is not a thing to be surprised at nor, I think, very much vexed at, except as far as it concerns Newman himself. There is a man who has lived a great deal with him gone—which would seem to show, either that he is a more dangerous man than most people (I, for one,) believed, or that he can't keep these 'myncks' of his in proper order. I should be sorry to adopt either alternative." J. D. Coleridge to J. B. Seymour, September 16, 1843, Ernest Hartley Coleridge, *Life and Correspondence of John Duke Lord Coleridge Lord Chief Justice of England* (London: Heinemann, 1904), 1: 138–139. See W. Lockhart to JHN, August 22 and 30, 1843, Newman Microfilms, reel 44, batch 44. JNM to JHN, August 30, 1843; HNM to JNM, September 9, 1843, *Newman Family Letters*, pp. 138–139.

97. HNM to T. Mozley, September 12, 1843; HNM to JNM, September 16, 1843, *Newman Family Letters*, pp. 141, 142.

98. JHN to T. Mozley, June 7, 12, 18, 1841, January 26, 29, 1842; T. Mozley to JHN, January 28, 1842; JK to JHN, July 4, 1841; JHN to JK, July 20, 1841, *L&D*, 8: 202, 204, 207, 438, 443, 439n., 217, 225; T. Mozley to JHN, September 9 and 16, November 1, St. Martins, December 24, 1842; JHN to T. Mozley, September 14 and 26, October 18 and 30, December 11, 1842, Newman Microfilms, reel 103, batch 162.

99. JHN to JNM, September 22, 1843, Mozley, *Letters and Correspondence*, 2: 379–380. As Newman's comments are published in this edition, there is no indication that they were directed specifically toward the situation in his own family.

100. JHN to HNM, September 29, 1843, Louis Bouyer, *Newman: His Life and Spirituality* (London: Burns and Oates, 1958), p. 232. Heavily edited versions of this letter appear in *Newman Family Letters*, p. 143, and Mozley, *Letters and Correspondence*, 2: 380–381.

101. JHN to HNM, September 29, 1843, Bouyer, *Newman*, p. 232. For Mozley's defense of his actions to his wife, see T. Mozley to JNM, October 3, 1843, *Newman Family Letters*, p. 144.

102. HNM to JNM, September 9, 1843, Mozley, *Newman Family Letters*, p. 139.

103. JHN to F. W. Faber, September 2, 1843, *Corrs. with JK*, p. 253; JHN to EBP, December 16, 1843, Liddon, *Pusey*, 2: 391. See also JHN to JK, August 20, 1843, *Corrs. with JK*, p. 247. Newman had good reason to expect such income because his *Sermons Chiefly on the Theory of Religious Belief* had gone into a second edition very quickly after initial publication. The forfeited income associated with St. Mary's and Littlemore was approximately £90 per annum. (Figure furnished by the Librarian of Oriel College.)

104. *Sermons, Bearing on Subjects of the Day*, pp. 448, 452. For a previous comparison of himself to Christ, see JHN to Samuel Rickards, December 1, 1841, *L&D*, 8: 359.

105. *Sermons, Bearing on Subjects of the Day*, pp. 455–456.

106. *Sermons, Bearing on Subjects of the Day*, p. 461.

107. *Sermons, Bearing on Subjects of the Day*, pp. 460–462.

108. F. S. Bowles to J. R. Bloxam, December 16, 1885, Middleton, *Newman and Bloxam*, p. 90

109. JHN to C. Cornish, In fest. S. Mich, 1843, Birmingham Oratory Typescript.

110. *Oxford Chronicle and Reading Gazette*, September 23, October 7, 1843.

111. [W. E. Gladstone], "Present Aspect of the Church," *Foreign and Colonial Review*, 2 (1843): 554, 575. See also Perry Butler, *Gladstone: Church, State, and Tractarianism: A Study of His Religious Ideas and Attitudes, 1809–1859* (Oxford: Clarendon, 1982), pp. 175–186.

112. [Gladstone], "Present Aspect of the Church," 576, 592, 594. Gladstone apparently did not know that Keble had written most of both prefaces to Froude's *Remains*.

113. [Gladstone], "Present Aspect of the Church," 595, 596.

114. *Morning Chronicle*, October 14, 1843, lead page; *Morning Post*, October 28, 1843, p. 2. See also, F. Oakeley to W. E. Gladstone, November 16, 1843, Gladstone Papers, British Library, Add. Ms. 44360, f. 307.

115. C. Blomfield to W. Palmer, March 22, 1841, Blomfield Papers, vol. 28, f. 30, Lambeth Palace Library. William Seth Adams, *William Palmer of Worcester, 1803–1885, The Only Really Learned Man Among Them* (Princeton Diss., 1973), pp. 147–249. For a statement by Palmer on his relationship with the Tractarians, see W. Palmer to A. P. Perceval, n.d., *L&D*, 8: 5n. See also William Palmer, *Letters to N. Wiseman, D.D., on the Errors of Romanism, in Respect to the Worship of Saints, Satisfactions, Purgatory, Indulgences, and the Worship of Images and Relics* (Oxford: John Henry Parker, 1841); *An Examination of the Rev. R. W. Sibthorp's Reasons for His Secession from the Church* (Oxford: John Henry Parker, 1842); Nockles, *The Oxford Movement in Context* (Cambridge: Cambridge University Press, 1994), pp. 140–141.

116. W. Palmer to R. Bagot, September 4, 1843, in Pusey-Bagot Correspondence, 2: 163–164, Pusey House. See also W. Palmer to EBP, August 2, September 12, 1843, CUP/83, Pusey House; and W. Palmer to W. E. Gladstone, November 9, 1843, Gladstone Papers, British Library, Add. Ms. 44360, f. 299.

117. William Palmer, *A Narrative of Events Connected with the Publication of the Tracts for the Times, with Reflections on Existing Tendencies to Romanism, and on the Present Duties and Prospects of Members of the Church*, Third Edition, with Postscript (Oxford: John Henry Parker, 1843), pp. 30, 32, 44, 68, 70. The essay had circulated in a printed but unpublished format for two months before its actual publication. See *Christian Remembrancer*, n.s. 6 (1843): 550–553, for a disclaimer of the identity of interests in 1833 between the traditional high churchmen and the Tractarians. A. P. Perceval's *A Collection of Papers Connected with the*

Theological Movement of 1833 (London: Rivington, 1842; 2d ed. 1843), which made claims not unlike those of Gladstone and Palmer, produced very little impact among either Tractarians or their critics. Archbishop Whately believed that the two publications necessarily complemented each other for a correct understanding of the origins of the movement; see R. Whately to H. More, September 11, 1844, E. Jane Whately, *Life and Correspondence of Richard Whately, D.D., Late Archbishop of Dublin* (London: Longmans, Green, 1866), 2: 59. See also William Seth Adams, "William Palmer's *Narrative of Events:* The First History of the 'Tracts for the Times,' " in John E. Booty, ed., *The Divine Drama in History and Liturgy: Essays Presented to Horton Davies on his Retirement from Princeton University* (Allison Park, Pa.: Pickwick, 1984), pp. 81–106.

118. Lawrence N. Crumb, "Publishing the Oxford Movement: Francis Rivington's Letters to Newman," *Publishing History,* 28 (1990): 38–40; Septimus Rivington, *The Publishing Family of Rivington* (London: Rivingtons, 1919), pp. 112–147. On Palmer's founding of the *English Review,* see W. Palmer to W. E. Gladstone, November 9, 13, 19, and 21, December 14 and 15, 1843, April 31, May 21 and 22, 1844; W. E. Gladstone to W. Palmer, May 21, 1844; W. E. Gladstone to F. Rogers, December 14, 1843, Gladstone Papers, British Library, Add. Mss. 44360, ff. 299, 303, 315, 346, 384, 388; 44361, ff. 111, 123, 126, 133; 44107, f. 223.

119. JHN to H. Manning, October 14, 1843, *Corrs. with JK,* pp. 272, 273.

120. W. E. Gladstone to H. Manning, October 24, 1843, D. C. Lathbury, ed., *Correspondence on Church and Religion of William Ewart Gladstone* (New York: Macmillan, 1910), 1: 281, 282.

121. JHN to J. B. Mozley, September 1, 1843, Mozley, *Letters and Correspondence,* 2: 379.

122. JHN to H. A. Woodgate, October 13, 1843, Birmingham Oratory typescript.

123. JHN to H. A. Woodgate, October 13, 1843, Birmingham Oratory typescript; JHN to J. Bowden, October 31, 1843, Newman Microfilms, reel 36, batch 11.

124. JHN to H. Manning, October 25, 1843, *Corrs. with JK,* pp. 276–278. Newman's accounts of why he wrote his *Letter to the Bishop of Oxford* varied over the years; see JHN to T. Flanagan, July 28, 1857, *L&D,* 18: 101–102, where he stated, "I wrote with great violence against the doctrines received at Rome and in her communion; with violence, but if I may so say, not violently—I mean, I spoke what I internally felt, and what I was called by my Bishop to say, but what (from my love of the Roman Church) I would not have said *then,* (though I had said worse things in years past,) unless it had been extorted from me by what I held to be then competent authority."

125. W. E. Gladstone to H. Manning, October 28, 30, 1843, Lathbury, *Correspondence of Gladstone,* 1: 283–286.

126. W. E. Gladstone to H. Manning, October 30, 1843, Lathbury, *Correspondence of Gladstone,* 1: 286. See also Edmund Sheridan Purcell, *Life of Cardinal Manning, Archbishop of Westminster* (New York: Macmillan, 1896), 1: 243–260. The failure of Manning to gain admission to Littlemore in early November 1843 resounded across the years. See "Memorandum. Manning's Call at Littlemore," November 18, 1884, JHN to R. W. Church, December 23, 1884, January 4, 1885, *L&D,* 30: 437–438, 448–449; 31: 4–5.

127. EBP to H. Manning, Eve of St. Luke's, 1842, Pusey-Manning Correspondence (transcripts), Pusey House; EBP to H. Manning, November 17, 1843, Bodleian Library, Ms. Eng lett. c. 654, f. 206; EBP to W. E. Gladstone, November 1843, Gladstone Papers, British Library, Add. Ms. 44247, f. 192. See also EBP to H. Manning, August 22, 1842, Pusey-Manning Correspondence (transcripts), Pusey House; and JHN to EBP, October 16, 1842, *Corrs. with JK,* pp. 198–199.

128. H. Manning to EBP, November 19, 1843; Gladstone quoting Manning as recounted in Purcell, *Life of Cardinal Manning,* 1: 251–252, 318; JHN to M. R. Giberne, October 27, 1843, Birmingham Oratory. For Manning's attempted reconciliation, see also

H. Manning to JHN, December 21, 1843; JHN to H. Manning, December 24, 1843, *Corrs. with JK*, pp. 290–293.

CHAPTER 10. MONKS, MIRACLES, AND POPERY

1. John Henry Newman, *An Essay on the Miracles Recorded in the Ecclesiastical History of the Early Ages* (London: J. G. and F. Rivington, 1843), pp. xi, xiii, xxii, xx. The essay first appeared in 1842 as a supplement to *The Ecclesiastical History of M. L'Abbé Fleury, from the Second Ecumenical Council to the End of the Fourth Century;* it was separately reprinted in 1843. See also Newman, *The Church of the Fathers* (London: J. G. F. and J. Rivington, 1840), p. 42.

2. *Essay on the Miracles*, p. lxxii

3. *Essay on the Miracles*, pp. lxxiii, lxxvi, ciii.

4. *Essay on the Miracles*, pp. xxiv, xxv, xxxviii.

5. *Essay on the Miracles*, pp. lxii–lxiii, lxv.

6. *Essay on the Miracles*, pp. cix, cxiii.

7. *Essay on the Miracles*, pp. xlix, li. Historians of science have for some time noted that it was exactly the removal of the divinity from natural theology without removing its other presuppositions about nature that accounted for much of Darwin's view of nature.

8. *Essay on the Miracles*, pp. liii–liv, ccxv. Newman had defended in detail the historical validity of accounts of Christians in the Roman army receiving through the power of prayer much needed rain when perishing from thirst, St. Narcissus of Jerusalem changing water into oil, St. Gregory of Thaumaturgus altering the course of the River Lycus, the appearance of the cross in the sky to Constantine, his mother St. Helena's discovery of the True Cross, the death of Arius, the fiery eruption occurring when Julian attempted to rebuild the Jewish Temple, the recovery of the blind man through the relics of St. Gervasius and St. Protasius, and the miracles of the African confessors mutilated by Hunneric during the Arian persecution.

9. Keble conversation reported, Journal of J. D. Coleridge, January 16, 1843; Ernest Hartley Coleridge, *Life and Correspondence of John Duke Lord Coleridge Lord Chief Justice of England* (London: Heinemann, 1904), 1: 116; Friedrich Nietzsche, *Beyond Good and Evil* in Walter Kaufman, ed. and trans., *The Basic Writings of Nietzsche* (New York: Modern Library, 1968), p. 275.

10. F. Rivington to JHN, April 1, 1843, and May 3, 1843, Newman Microfilms, reel 96, batch 150; JHN to JK, May 18, 1843, *Corrs. with JK*, p. 228. See also A. W. Hutton, Introduction, *The Lives of the English Saints* (London: St. T. Freemantle, 1901), 1: vii–xxx; J. Derek Holmes, "Newman's Reputation and *The Lives of the English Saints*," *Catholic Historical Review*, 51 (1965–1966): 528–538; J. A. Froude, "The Oxford Counter-Reformation," *Short Studies on Great Subjects* (Longmans, Green, 1898), 4: 315–339.

11. "Note D, Series of Saints' Lives of 1843–1844," *Apologia*, p. 280.

12. JHN to J. W. Bowden, April 4, 1841, *L&D*, 8: 155; "Note D, Series of Saints' Lives of 1843–1844," pp. 280–281.

13. W. Palmer to W. E. Gladstone, November 9, 1843, Gladstone Papers, British Library, Add. Ms. 44360, f. 299; F. W. Faber to F. A. Faber, May 27, 1843, John Edward Bowden, *The Life and Letters of Frederick William Faber, D.D.* (Baltimore: John Murphy, 1869), pp. 192–193; F. Oakeley to JHN, May 4, 1843, Newman Microfilms, reel 96, batch 150.

14. JHN to J. R. Hope, November 2, 1843, *Corrs. with JK*, pp. 280–281. See also JHN to J. W. Bowden, January 22, 1844, in which Newman criticizes Pusey's stance. Newman Microfilms, reel 36, batch 11.

15. J. R. Hope to JHN, November 4, 1843, Robert Ornsby, *Memoirs of James Robert Hope-Scott of Abbotsford with Selections from His Correspondence* (London: John Murray, 1884), 2: 25–26. For the originals of this correspondence see Newman Microfilms, reel 42, batch 35.

16. JHN to J. R. Hope, November 6, 1843, *Corrs. with JK*, pp. 282–284. Although he claimed to have remained silent for three years, Newman had preached during those years and by November 1843 had published at least three additional volumes of sermons since *Tract 90*. He continued to reprint his earlier volumes of sermons, and the tracts also continued to circulate.

17. J. B. Mozley to JHN, December 2, 1843; W. E. Gladstone to J. R. Hope, December 3, 1843, forwarded by Hope to Newman; J. R. Hope to JHN December 5, 1843, Newman Microfilms, reel 96, batch 150; reel 42, batch 35; J. R. Hope to JHN, December 5, 1843, Ornsby, *Memoirs of James Robert Hope-Scott*, 2: 33; JHN to J. R. Hope, December 5, 11, 1843, *Corrs. with JK*, pp. 286, 287. For Hope's initial effort to dissuade Newman from undertaking the series, see J. R. Hope to J. H. Newman, November 8, 1843, Ornsby, *Memoirs of James Robert Hope-Scott*, 2: 28–30; J. H. Newman to J. R. Hope, November 26, 1843, *Corrs. with JK*, pp. 285–286; F. Rivington to J. H. Newman, November 22, 1843, Newman Microfilms, reel 96, batch 150.

18. J. H. Newman to J. R. Hope, December 16, 1843; for other aspects of publication of the series, see JHN to J. R. Hope, March 14, May 14, 1844; JHN to E. Bellasis, June 8, 1844, *Corrs. with JK*, pp. 289, 310–313. Pusey had enthusiastically reconciled himself to more advanced devotional literature. On the second Sunday of Advent, 1844, he wrote to Francis Kilvert, "Lives . . . of eminent saints wd. be very useful," and noted that most people had "no idea of the high spiritual character & devotedness" among those in monastic orders. He also stated that he understood that a London publisher would be publishing a series of lives of saints. EBP to F. Kilvert, Second Sunday in Advent, 1844, Bodleian Library, Ms. Don. d. 120, f. 140, 142. See also J. Toovey to JHN, January 2 and 11, April 3, May 7, 8, 15, and 21, June 3, 5, and 25, August 2 and 30, December 9, 1844; June 26, 1845, Newman Microfilms, reel 137, batch 276.

19. *Essay on the Miracles*, pp. ccxiv, ccxv; *Lives of the English Saints*, 2: 3, 4; 3: 10, 66.

20. *Lives of the English Saints*, 2: 19; 3: 388; 5: 222; 6: 97.

21. *Lives of the English Saints*, 2: 135; 3: 142; 5: 50.

22. *Lives of the English Saints*, 4: 326; 5: 382, 390.

23. *Lives of the English Saints*, 5: 389, 386–387, 387, 390.

24. *Lives of the English Saints*, 6: 374, 375.

25. *Lives of the English Saints*, 5: 48, 337; 4: 262–265; 3: 104; 2: 181–182, 225–228; 1: 114, 296–297.

26. *British Magazine*, 28 (1845): 364n.; W. F. Hook to EBP, February 6, 1845, Liddon, *Pusey*, 2: 431; [Henry Rogers], "Recent Developments in Puseyism," *Edinburgh Review*, 80 (1844): 346, 365. See H. Rogers to M. Napier, January 12, April 15, July 18, 1844, Napier Papers, British Library, Add. Ms. 34624, ff. 307, 414, 535. On the general subject of miracles, consult Robert Bruce Mullin, *Miracles and the Modern Religious Imagination* (New Haven: Yale University Press, 1996), pp. 9–30.

27. [Baden Powell], "Anglo-Catholicism," *British and Foreign Review*, 16 (1844): 556, 557; [Baden Powell], "Tendency of Puseyism," *Westminster Review*, 14 (1846): 339, 317. See also [Anon.], "Ecclesiastical Miracles," *North British Review*, 4 (1846): 451–486.

28. *Lives of the English Saints*, 1: 10, 11, 220, 228–229, 310; 6: 277, 315–316. The comments on Rome in the *Lives of the English English Saints* would appear to reflect long-standing attitudes among Newman's coterie. See R. Williams to W. E. Gladstone, July 11, 25, 1842; November 23, 1843, Gladstone Papers, British Library, Add. Mss. 44359, ff. 41, 77, 143; 44360, f. 332.

29. *Lives of the English Saints*, 1: 286; 3: 385; 5: 129–130.

30. See Walter L. Arnstein, *Protestant versus Catholic in Mid-Victorian England: Mr. Newdegate and the Nuns* (Columbia: University of Missouri Press, 1982).

31. J. D. Dalgairns to JHN, November 1841; January 1, March 11, April 18, 1842; May 23, June 24, July 6, 1845, Newman Microfilms, reel 103, batch 164; JHN to EBP, September 28, 1845, Pusey House.

32. *Lives of the English Saints*, 5: 131, 132; 1: 129, 7.

33. John Cross Crosthwaite, *Modern Hagiology: An Examination of the Nature and Tendency of Some Legendary and Devotional Works Lately Published Under the Sanction of the Rev. J. H. Newman, the Rev. Dr. Pusey, and the Rev. F. Oakeley* (London: John W. Parker, 1846), 1: 97; *Lives of the English Saints*, 1: 447–448; 4: 61–62. Crosthwaite's critique originally appeared in *The British Magazine*, 27 (1844–1845): 1–17, 105–120, 225–240, 345–360, 465–480, 585–600; 28 (1845): 1–16, 99–114, 219–234, 339–362, 459–470, 595–606. For similar evangelical criticism, see *Christian Observer*, 44 (1844): 559–575, 730–768.

34. *Lives of the English Saints*, 4: 305, 307, 309, 316, 322, 327.

35. *Lives of the English Saints*, 4: 275, 277, 281, 256; 1: 288.

36. Crosthwaite, *Modern Hagiology*, 1: 26; *Lives of the English Saints*, 1: 298.

37. *Lives of the English Saints*, 1: 19; 2: 193; 4: 31–32, 5: 10.

38. Crosthwaite, *Modern Hagiology*, 1: 26, 99–100; JHN to M. R. Giberne, March 30, 1842, *L&D*, 8: 497; JHN to F. Faber, January 31, 1845, Birmingham Oratory typescript. [Original letter in London Oratory.] At the time of Dalgairns's conversion, Newman wrote, "Dalgairns left us yesterday. His Father and Mother come into Oxford in a few days, and he thought it best that it should be over before he saw them. He does not wish it known at present. Indeed, though his Father and Mother have long known it was to be, yet the very time was not mentioned; and if you happened to see them, you had better not speak about it. Of course what he has wished, has been to do what was lightest for them." JHN to EBP, September 28, 1845, Newman-Pusey Correspondence, Pusey House. See also JHN to Dalgairns Senior, February 18, 1845, Birmingham Oratory typescript, in which Newman defends Dalgairns's possible reception into the Roman Church to his father.

39. [J. Keble], Preface, Froude, *Remains*, 3: xiii.

40. John Henry Newman *Sermons, Bearing on Subjects of the Day* (London: J. G. F. and J. Rivington, 1843), p. 292. Thomas Arnold particularly leveled such charges. See T. Arnold to R. Whately, 16 May, 1836, Whately Papers, Lambeth Palace, Ms. 2164, f. 30; T. Arnold to E. Hawkins, 4 December, 1840, Arnold Papers, Rugby School. In rejecting such charges of judaizing, Newman may, however, have had another figure in mind. In relation to the error of justification by works, Bishop Sumner in *Apostolical Preaching*, which Newman had studied in the 1820s, had specifically listed the doctrine of purgatory and the practices of pardons, masses, auricular confessions, fasts, celibacy, and penances as having arisen from Judaizing practices and embodying "curious refinements and proud pretensions to sanctity, joined to unprofitable ceremonies and bodily austerities," eventually culminating in the "apostasy of Papal Rome" and superseding "the righteousness which is by faith" and destroying "the spirit of the Gospel." J. B. Sumner, *Apostolical Preaching Considered, in an Examination of St. Paul's Epistles*, 3d ed. (London: J. Hatchard, 1820), pp. 207–208.

41. [Frederick Oakeley], "Ancient and Modern Ways of Charity," *British Critic*, 29 (1841): 68, 69, 68, 69.

42. [J. H. Newman], "Milman's History of Christianity," *British Critic*, 29 (1841): 76, 100–102. For Milman's critique of Strauss, see H. H. Milman, *The History of Christianity from the Birth of Christ to the Abolition of Paganism in the Roman Empire* (London: John Murray, 1840), 1: 115–124. See also Francis McGrath, *John Henry Newman: Universal Revelation* (Macon, Ga.: Mercer University Press, 1997), pp. 25–85.

43. [Newman], "Milman's History of Christianity," 101, 102.

44. [Newman], "Milman's History of Christianity," 103.

45. *Sermons, Bearing on Subjects of the Day,* pp. 241, 243.

46. *University Sermons,* pp. 313–318.

47. *University Sermons,* pp. 319, 320, 323.

48. *University Sermons,* p. 329.

49. *University Sermons,* pp. 333, 335.

50. *University Sermons,* p. 340.

51. *University Sermons,* pp. 331, 332.

52. William Palmer, *Narrative of Events Connected with the Publication of the Tracts for the Times, with Reflections on Existing Tendencies to Romanism, and on the Present Duties and Prospects of Members of the Church,* Third Edition, with Postscript (Oxford: John Henry Parker, 1843), pp. 57, 58. Palmer also privately complained about the concept of development. See W. Palmer to EBP, August 2, 1843, Pusey House.

53. Palmer, *Narrative,* pp. 59, 60, 62. See also William Brudenell Barter, *A Postscript to the English Church Not in Schism: Containing a Few Words on Mr. Newman's Essay on Development* (London: Francis and John Rivington, 1846), pp. 15–16, which quotes a letter of October 1, 1844, to *The Times* in which he contended that evangelical Protestantism was a development as illegitimate as Roman Catholic developments.

54. Palmer, *Narrative,* pp. 61, 62, 64, 65.

55. JHN to C. H. Froude, April 3, 1844, Gordon Huntington Harper, ed. *Cardinal Newman and William Froude, F.R.S.: A Correspondence* (Baltimore: Johns Hopkins University Press, 1933), pp. 39, 40. It is significant that in this first mention of 1839 to Mrs. Froude, Newman pointed to his reading of the Fathers rather than of Wiseman's *Dublin Review* article as the key factor redirecting his thought. Harper's editorial commentary interspersed with the letters includes important and incisive remarks on the manner in which Newman's comments to the Froudes contrast with the narrative of the *Apologia.*

56. JHN to C. H. Froude, April 4, 1844, Harper, *Cardinal Newman and William Froude,* pp. 40–41, 43.

57. JHN to C. H. Froude, April 5, 9, 1844, Harper, *Cardinal Newman and William Froude,* pp. 45, 46.

58. JHN to C. H. Froude, April 9, 12, 1844, Harper, *Cardinal Newman and William Froude,* pp. 48, 51.

59. Sheridan Gilley, "Newman and Prophecy, Evangelical and Catholic," *Journal of the United Reformed Church History Society,* 3 (1985): 160–188.

60. JHN to C. H. Froude, May 28, 1844, Harper, *Cardinal Newman and William Froude,* p. 58; JHN to H. Wilberforce, June 8, July 4 and 17, 1844, Ushaw College, OS/N24, N25, N26.

61. JHN to C. H. Froude, May 19, 1844, Harper, *Cardinal Newman and William Froude,* pp. 52, 54, 55.

62. JHN to C. H. Froude, May 19, 1844, Harper, *Cardinal Newman and William Froude,* pp. 56–57.

63. JHN to C. H. Froude, July 14, 1844, Harper, *Cardinal Newman and William Froude,* pp. 58, 59.

64. JHN to JK, January 23, 1844; JK to JHN, June 12, 1844, *Corrs. with JK,* pp. 300, 320. See also JHN to EBP, December 2, 1843; February 14, 1844, Liddon, *Pusey,* 2: 290. It was perhaps his keen sense of possibly committing error that allowed Newman to separate himself from other contemporary religious seekers, most particularly Blanco White. See JHN to H. Wilberforce, April 27, 1845, Ushaw College, OD/N34; JHN to W. E. Gladstone, undated and June 17, 1845, Gladstone Papers, British Library, Add. Ms. 44362, ff. 233, 246.

65. JHN to JK, June 8, 1844, *Corrs. with JK,* p. 318; JHN to W. E. Gladstone, November 18, 1844, Gladstone Papers, British Library, Add. Ms. 44361, f. 290. See also JHN to EBP, August 28, 1844, Pusey House; JHN to C. H. Froude, November 12, 1844, Harper, *Cardinal Newman and William Froude,* pp. 62–63.

66. Thomas Scott, *The Theological Works of the Rev. Thomas Scott* (Edinburgh: Peter Brown and Thomas Nelson, 1835), pp. 38–39. See also Thomas L. Sheridan, *Newman on Justification* (New York: Alba House, 1967), pp. 15–134.

67. William George Ward, *The Ideal of a Christian Church Considered in Comparison with Existing Practice, Containing a Defence of Certain Articles in The British Critic in Reply to Remarks on Them in Mr. Palmer's "Narrative,"* 2d ed. (London: James Toovey, 1844), p. 568; viii; *Record*, August 8, 1844.

68. T. Keble to JK, February, 1845, Keble College. The *Morning Post* stated on February 20, 1845, p. 5, "Mr. Ward's entire publications are, in effect, neither more nor less than a series of *High Church* (or, if you will, Romanizing) *Arnoldianisms*." As an example of Thomas Arnold's critique of the English Church, in October 1833 he had written privately, "Historically, the Church of England is surely of a motley complexion, with much good about it, and much evil, no more fit subject for enthusiastic admiration than for violent obloquy." T. Arnold to S. Coleridge, October 23, 1833, A. P. Stanley, *Life and Correspondence of Thomas Arnold, D.D.* (New York, Scribners, n.d.), 1: 323.

69. Ward, *Ideal*, pp. 56, vii, 17, 25.

70. Ward, *Ideal*, pp. 221–222, 200, 11, 12, 13, 20; see pp. 237–238 for a summary of the faults of evangelicalism.

71. Ward, *Ideal*, pp. 292, 587, 588, 37, 96, 45n. Ward's anti-Protestantism once led him to write Gladstone of the "unmixed wickedness" of the Reformation and to express his inability to consider that "in our present state of discipline, & of faith, or in any state which has existed since the Reformation, the free circulation of Scripture is other than a real serious evil." W. G. Ward to W. E. Gladstone, November 22, 26, 1843. Gladstone had pointed to the free circulation of Scripture as one of the benefits of the reformation, thus eliciting Ward's second comment. W. E. Gladstone to W. G. Ward, November 23, 1843, Gladstone Papers, British Library, Add. Ms. 44360, ff. 328, 330, 342.

72. Ward, *Ideal*, p. 141; see also pp. 61, 69.

73. Ward, *Ideal*, pp. 54, 473, 84. Moreover, Ward believed that the high-church defense of the English Church against Rome had no basis in the ideal of antiquity but simply derived its "whole force from a denial of the doctrine of 'development.'" Ward, *Ideal*, p. 126. Once that denial stood abandoned, the Roman communion appeared the source of many truths and devices for holy living. Very much in line with Newman's original advertisement for the *Lives of the English Saints*, Ward envisioned a distinctly English version of Catholic piety.

74. Ward, *Ideal*, p. 260. See also George P. Landow, *Elegant Jeremiahs: The Sage from Carlyle to Mailer* (Ithaca: Cornell University Press, 1986), pp. 17–72.

75. Wilfrid Ward, *William George Ward and the Oxford Movement* (London: Macmillan, 1889), p. 173; Ward, *Ideal* p. 479; see also pp. 474–481, 567–568.

76. [Nassau Senior], "Oxford and Mr. Ward," *Edinburgh Review*, 81 (1845): 390; *Christian Observer*, 45 (1845): 115; Thomas Musgrave, *A Charge Delivered to the Clergy of the Diocese of Hereford, June, 1845, at His Third Triennial Visitation* (London: John W. Parker, 1845), p. 34.

77. E. B. Pusey, Preface, Seragesimis, J. B. E. Avrillon, *A Guide for Passing Lent Holily*, E. B. Pusey, trans. and ed. (London: James Burns, 1844), p. vii; E. B. Pusey, Preface, Vigil of St. James, 1844, F. Surin, *The Foundations of the Spiritual Life: Drawn from the Book of the Imitation of Jesus Christ*, E. B. Pusey, trans. (London: James Burns, 1844), pp. lvn, vna, xv, xxiii. Pusey's reported objections to the early draft of one of the lives in Newman's series had been its praise for the papacy, not the implicit recommendation of the sanctity of the saint's life. Pusey also privately urged the adoption of continental Roman Catholic devotional practice; see EBP to W. K. Hamilton, St. Thomas' Day, 1844, Liddon, *Pusey*, 2: 394–395, as well as Liddon, *Pusey*, 2: 415, and Surin, *Foundations of the Spiritual Life*, 1st ed., preface, p. 55na. Oakeley had previously published a volume of similar Roman Catholic devotional literature dedicated to Pusey; see Frederick Oakeley, ed., *Homilies for Holy Days and Seasons*

Commemorative of Our Lord and Saviour Jesus Christ, from Advent to Whitsuntide Inclusive, Translated from the Writings of the Saints with Biographical Notices of the Writers (London: James Burns, 1842). Also consult Peter Nockles, *The Oxford Movement in Context: Anglican High Churchmanship, 1760–1857* (Cambridge: Cambridge University Press, 1994), pp. 223–227.

78. Keble conversation reported in J. D. Coleridge Journal, January 14, 1843, Coleridge, *Life and Correspondence*, 1: 115; handbill by W. F. Hook, October 4, 1844, Warden Symons Miscellaneous Papers, Wadham College Archives, 210/5; [W. E. Gladstone], "Ward's *Ideal of a Christian Church*," *Quarterly Review*, 75 (1844): 185–186. On the issue of the Tractarian appeal to conscience, see also William Palmer, *The Doctrine of Development and Conscience Considered in Relation to the Evidence of Christianity and of the Catholic System* (London: Francis and John Rivington, 1846), pp. 53, 46, 73, 83.

79. EBP to W. B. Pusey, October 1844, Liddon, *Pusey*, 2: 412; JHN to EBP, In fest. S. Joan, 1844, Pusey-Newman Correspondence, Pusey House; see also JHN to J. B. Mozley, August 25, 1844, for Newman's initial opposition to the protest against Symons election. Birmingham Oratory Typescript. Also consult W. G. Ward to JHN, October 4, 1844, Newman Microfilms, reel 74, batch 80. For the exasperation and disapproval of high churchmen, see E. Churton to J. Griffiths, October 1, 1844; W. Palmer to J. Griffiths, October 2, 1844; M. J. Routh to Principal of St. Alban Hall, October 4, 1844; handbill by W. F. Hook, October 4, 1844, in Warden Symons Miscellaneous Papers, 210/5, Wadham College Archives. It is not at all clear that before the protest the Oxford authorities intended to act, because Ward's most vocal critics had been evangelicals, and the Hebdomadal Board generally did not wish to strengthen their hand. See *Record*, August 8 and 22, September 5, 16, 26, and 30, and October 3, 1844. Morris had long been a provocative thorn in Newman's side and continued to be so when both were in the Roman Catholic Church; see JHN to J. B. Morris, May 8, 1846, *L&D*, 11: 156–159.

80. E. Copleston to E. Hawkins, November 13, 1844, Letterbooks 1, f. 57, Oriel College. For Whately's intervention, see R. Whately to the Vice Chancellor of Oxford, October 26, 1844, E. Jane Whately, *Life and Correspondence of Richard Whately, D.D., Late Archbishop of Dublin* (London: Longmans, Green, 1866), 2: 60–63; W. R. Ward, *Victorian Oxford* (London: Frank Cass, 1965), pp. 120–121. See also Notebooks with Materials on Ward Case Kept by B. P. Symons, Wadham College Archives, A12.6. and Wellington Papers, 2/254/103–108, 112, 114, 117, 118, 132, University of Southampton. Whately's prediction of further episcopal criticism following the publication of Ward's volume was confirmed in James Henry Monk, *A Charge Delivered to the Clergy of the Diocese of Gloucester and Bristol, at His Visitation in August and September, MDCCCXLIV* (London: Francis and John Rivington, 1844), p. 35, and Musgrave, *Charge Delivered to the Clergy*, pp. 33–37.

81. R. Whately to N. Senior, January 10, 1845, Whately, *Life and Correspondence*, 2: 78.

82. W. G. Ward to the Editor of *The Times*, March 1, 1845, *The Times*, March 3, 1845, p. 5. On the circumstances surrounding the engagement, see Ward, *William George Ward and the Oxford Movement*, pp. 348–352.

83. See Newman's hostile criticism of Ward in JHN to JK, December 16, 27, 29, 1844, *Corrs. with JK*, 360–364. Shortly after publication of Ward's book, Newman had told Bowden, "There is a great deal of good in it—and a great deal which reads to me like a theory." JHN to Bowden, June 17, 1844, Newman Microfilms, reel 36, batch 11.

84. F. W. Faber, to JHN, November 28, 1844, Bowden, *The Life and Letters of Frederick William Faber*, p. 219. [The year of this letter is printed incorrectly.] JHN to F. W. Faber, December 1, 1844, *Corrs. with JK*, pp. 356–357. The same argument could be advanced against vows of celibacy in the English Church and was so used by Ward in the public defense of his marriage in *The Times*. See also JHN to EBP, December 2, 1843, Liddon, *Pusey*, 2: 390.

85. *Sermons Bearing on Subjects of the Day*, pp. 47–59. Joseph Bacchus, the anonymous

editor of *Corrs. with JK*, made this important point on p. 358 of that volume. He did not note, however, that much of the sermon may be read as an autobiographical meditation as well as prescriptive advice.

86. JHN to JK, November 21, 1844, *Corrs. with JK*, p. 350; JHN to C. H. Froude, November 12, December 8, 1844, Harper, *Cardinal Newman and William Froude*, pp. 62–64; Newman to JNM, *In vig. Nativit*, 1844, Mozley, *Letters and Correspondence*, 2: 405; JHN to JK, December 29, 1844, *Corrs. with JK*, p. 363.

87. JHN to JK, December 29, 1844, *Corrs. with JK*, p. 363. In January, when the rejection of the new test appeared assured, Newman turned some real sympathy to Ward. JHN to J. B. Mozley, January 5, 1845, Mozley, *Letters and Correspondence*, 2: 405

88. Liddon, *Pusey*, 2: 417–419; A. C. Tait, *A Letter to the Rev. The Vice-Chancellor of the University of Oxford*, pp. 13–15; E. Hawkins to A. C. Tait, January 15, 1845, A. C. Tait Papers, Lambeth Palace Library, vol. 77, f. 282; [A. P. Stanley], "The Oxford School," *Edinburgh Review*, 153 (1881): 305–335. For evangelical support of the new test, consult *Record*, December 23, 26, 1844; January 9, 13, 16, 20, 23, 1845.

CHAPTER 11. ENDGAME

1. *Apologia*, pp. 130, 137. On the relationship of Newman's image to St. Augustine, see Linda H. Peterson, *Victorian Autobiography: The Tradition of Self-Interpretation* (New Haven: Yale University Press, 1986), pp. 111–116.

2. JHN to JK, December 29, 1844, *Corrs. with JK*, p. 364; JHN to M. R. Giberne, January 8, 1845, Birmingham Oratory; HNM to JNH, January, 1846, *Newman Family Letters*, p. 166.

3. JK to J. T. Coleridge, October 25, 1847, Bodleian Library, Ms. Eng. lett. d. 135, f. 354.

4. W. Wimcox Bricknell, *Oxford; Tract 90; And Ward's Ideal of a Christian Church. A Practical Suggestion Respectively Submitted to Members of Convocation* (Oxford: J. Vincent, 1844); Lydia Symons to W. Bricknell, January 24, 1845, Bricknell Papers, Pusey House.

5. For reports of the meeting of Convocation, see *The Times*, February 13, 1845, p. 5, and February 14, 1845, p. 6; "Notebook with Materials on Ward Case Kept by B. P. Symons," Archives, A12.6, Wadham College; W. G. Ward, *An Address to Members of Convocation in Protest Against the Proposed Statute* (London: James Toovey, 1845). During the previous February the *Record* had already noted the Tractarian sympathies of the newly elected proctors. *Record*, February 22, 1844. For hostility of various persons toward Ward, consult JHN to E. Bowden, December 7, 17, 1844; JHN to JNM, January 5, 1845, Birmingham Oratory; S. Wilberforce to W. E. Gladstone, January 14, 1845, Gladstone Papers, British Library, Add. Ms. 44343, f. 68; JHN to W. E. Gladstone, January 22, 1845, Gladstone Papers, British Library, Add. Ms. 44362, f. 32; H. Manning to EBP, March 5, 1845, Ms. Eng. lett. d. 654, f. 257, Bodleian Library. Ward himself did not disagree with the harsh judgments of friends, telling Gladstone that he did not feel personally "aggrieved at severe comments on my writing," understanding that "in the present case it wd. be most preposterous, considering that, as you observe, the very extreme measure [?] in wh I have myself indulged." W. G. Ward to W. E. Gladstone, January, 1845, Gladstone Papers, British Library, Add Ms. 44362, f. 2.

6. Archbishop of Canterbury to W. E. Gladstone, February 21, 1845, Gladstone Papers, British Library, Add. Ms. 44362, f. 97; W. E. Gladstone to EBP, February 22, 1845, Liddon, *Pusey*, 2: 438.

7. JHN to W. E. Gladstone, May 1, 1845, Gladstone Papers, British Library, Add. Ms. 44362, f. 180; R. Whately to E. Hawkins, March 9, 1845, Letterbooks, 1: 38, Oriel College.

Consult *Morning Chronicle*, April 29, 1845, p. 11; JHN to R. W. Church, April 3, 1845, Mozley, *Letters and Correspondence*, 2: 416–417; and R. Whately to E. Hawkins, April 29, 1845; Letterbooks, 3: 258, Oriel College.

8. Newman had indicated his hesitancy regarding a proctoral veto of the new test when he told Elizabeth Bowden, "If the Test *is* thrown out, this remarkable consequence will follow, that the Hebdomadal Censure on No 90 will virtually be reversed. But at the same time this effect would *not* follow, if the Test were merely vetoed by the Proctors." JHN to E. Bowden, December 27, 1844, Birmingham Oratory Typescript. See also Dedication to R. C. Church, dated Advent, 1871, in John Henry Newman, *Fifteen Sermons Preached Before The University of Oxford*, New Edition (London: Rivingtons, 1880).

9. JHN to EBP, February 6, 1845, Liddon, *Pusey*, 2: 428; JHN to J. R. Hope, May 14, 1845, *Corrs. with JK*, p. 380.

10. JHN to T. Mozley, September 26, 1842, Newman Microfilms, reel 103, batch 162; JHN to E. Bowden, December 7, 1844, Birmingham Oratory; *Morning Herald*, February 5, 1845, p. 7; February 13, 1845, p. 4; *Christian Observer*, 45 (1845), p. 119; JHN to the Editor of *The Times*, February 24, 1863, *L&D*, 20: 413–415. Newman's statements regarding Ward and Oakeley's opinions were consistent only when he addressed the issue of his not accepting their view that a Church of England clergyman could hold all Roman doctrine. Newman reserved his clearest statement on this matter for Mary Holmes, to whom he wrote in 1843, "It is a great mistake, if people think that the object of Tract No 90 was to *reconcile* the Articles and the Tridentine Decrees—if they say so, they do not believe my own assertions, but impute to me meaning which I do not avow. I was not unwilling in writing the Tract to bring them as near as I could, and most glad should I be, (ought not every one to be so?) *could* they be proved to agree; but I have no wish at all to wrest any one phrase, and I trust, I should be given grace to resign my living rather than do so." [JHN to M. Holmes, March 8, 1843, Birmingham Oratory; see also JHN to John Kaye, Bishop of Lincoln, March 2, 7, 1843, Birmingham Oratory Typescript.] Yet on September 26, 1842, Newman had told Thomas Mozley that he in the main agreed with Ward and Oakeley and regarded them as "reformers." JHN to T. Mozley, September 26, 1842. Newman Microfilms, reel 103, batch 162.

11. JHN to JNM, February 11, 1845, Birmingham Oratory.

12. JHN to EBP, February 25, 1845, Liddon, *Pusey*, 2: 448; EBP to H. A. Woodgate, Good Friday, 1845, H. A. Woodgate Letters, Lambeth Palace Library, Ms. 3535, f. 47; JNM to JHN, March 13, 1845, Mozley, *Letters and Correspondence*, 2: 410. See also JHN to C. H. Froude, April 20, 1845, Gordon Huntington Harper, ed. *Cardinal Newman and William Froude, F.R.S.: A Correspondence* (Baltimore: Johns Hopkins University Press, 1933), p. 65.

13. JHN to JNM, March 15, 1845, Birmingham Oratory. This letter appears with the omission of important passages in Mozley, *Letters and Correspondence*, 2: 410–413. On Newman's fear of dying outside the Roman Communion while traveling, see also EBP to JK, July 8, 1845, Keble-Pusey Correspondence (transcripts), Pusey House. Newman's income for his published sermons during 1844 had been approximately £400. See J. H. Newman Account Book, A7.5, Birmingham Oratory.

14. JHN to JNM, March 15, 1845, Birmingham Oratory. On March 14 Newman told Pusey that despite his wish that people not turn to Rome because he was doing so, "It cannot pain me that they should take my change as a sort of warning, or call to consider where the Truth lies." JHN to EBP, March 14, 1845, Liddon, *Pusey*, 2: 450.

15. JHN to JNM, March 15, 1845, Birmingham Oratory.

16. JHN to H. Wilberforce, April 27, 1845, Ushaw College, OS/N34. On drawing a possible parallel between himself and Blanco White, see also JHN to W. E. Gladstone, June 12, 1845, Gladstone Papers, British Library, Add. Ms. 44362, f. 233.

17. JHN to C. H. Froude, June 1, 1845, Harper, *Cardinal Newman and William Froude*, p. 66.

18. EBP to W. E. Gladstone [transcript], February 18, 1845, Pusey-Gladstone Corre-

spondence (transcripts); E. Churton to EBP, December 9, 1841, Edward Churton Papers, Pusey House; Frederick Oakeley, *The Subject of Tract XC. Examined, in Connection with the History of the Thirty-Nine Articles, and the Statements of Certain English Divines to Which is added, The Case of Bishop Mountague, in the Reign of King James I*, Second Edition Revised (London: James Toovey, 1845), pp. xiii, xiv. For the documentation of the dispute commencing in November 1844, consult Frederick Oakeley, "To a Roman Catholic Friend," subsequent comments, and a reply, November 18 and 21, December 26, 1844, *English Churchman*, pp. 742–743, 761–762, 821–823; "Romish Subscription to the Articles," *English Review*, 3 (1845): 157–178; and "Mr. Oakeley's Puseyism," *Tablet*, December 7, 1844, pp. 769–770. Consult William Goode, *Tract XC. Historically Refuted; or, a Reply to a Work by the Rev. F. Oakeley, Entitled, 'The Subject of Tract XC. Historically Examined* (London: J. Hatchard, 1845), and *Christian Observer*, 45 (1845): 511–12, 557–571, which contended that both Oakeley and Newman had argued from an incorrect historical understanding of the composition of the 39 Articles. On a previous related dispute, see C. J. Blomfield to F. Oakeley, November 26, 1842, Blomfield Papers, vol. 34, f. 94, Lambeth Palace Library. I wish to thank Dr. Richard Lofthouse for pointing me to the last reference.

19. Frederick Oakeley, *A Letter to the Lord Bishop of London, on a Subject Connected with the Recent Proceedings at Oxford* (London: James Toovey, 1845), pp. 11, 14, 26. That pamphlet had been preceded by Frederick Oakeley to the Vice Chancellor of Oxford, February 14, 1845, *The Times*, February 15, 1845. See correspondence between F. Oakeley and W. E. Gladstone, January 8, 10, 15, 1845, Gladstone Papers, British Library, Add. Ms. 44362, ff. 5, 11, 21.

20. C. Blomfield to F. Oakeley, February 19, 20, 26, 1845, Blomfield Papers, vol. 42: 115, 117–118, 121, 133, Lambeth Palace Library; *The Times*, March 4, 1845, p. 4; "Letter of Request," April 3, 1845, Court of Arches, H/672, item 1, Lambeth Palace Library. For Blomfield's specific concerns about Oakeley, see C. Blomfield to George Chandler, Dean of Chichester, February 24, 1845, Blomfield Papers, 42: 124. (I owe these references with gratitude to Dr. Richard Lofthouse.) Oakeley asked Gladstone for help in his negotiation with Blomfield; see F. Oakeley to W. E. Gladstone, February 20, 21, 27, 1845, and a draft of a letter from W. E. Gladstone to C. Blomfield, February 24, 1845, which may have briefly moderated the latter. Gladstone Papers, British Library, Add. Ms. 44362, ff. 95, 99, 102, 104. Oakeley could not see how his own actions caused Blomfield to act but blamed the influence of others on the Bishop of London. See F. Oakeley to EBP, February 21, 22, 24, 1845, Pusey House. For Blomfield and Pusey, see also C. Blomfield to EBP, December 30, 1844; May 20, 1845, Blomfield Papers, vols. 41, f. 389; 42, f. 284, Lambeth Palace Library. See also *Morning Chronicle*, March 1, 3, 4, 1845; *Standard*, March 1, 1845, p. 2; *Morning Post*, March 3, 1845, p. 5, and March 4, 1845, p. 4; and *The Times*, March 4, 1845, pp. 4, 5.

21. F. Oakeley to EBP, February 24, 1845, Pusey-Oakeley Correspondence, f. 36, Pusey House. On Oakeley's possible conversion in 1843, see F. Oakeley to JHN, undated, 1843, Newman Microfilms, reel 67, batch 59.

22. F. Oakeley to EBP, May 20, 1845, Pusey-Oakeley Correspondence, f. 38, Pusey House; *Morning Herald*, June 7, 1845, p. 10; F. Oakeley to EBP, undated, 1845, Pusey-Oakeley Correspondence, f. 37, Pusey House. Blomfield had already experienced Oakeley's going to the newspapers to put his own explanation on events and probably wished to preclude its happening again in this instance. The Court of Arches had indicated its lack of sympathy with Tractarian theology in the recent Stone Altar case, which rejected certain high interpretations of the eucharist. See C. Blomfield to F. Oakeley, March 10, 1845, Blomfield Papers, vol. 42. f. 157, Lambeth Palace Library. See also JHN to E. Bellasis, May 30, 1845, Newman Microfilms, reel 32, batch 5; F. Oakeley to C. Blomfield, June 3, 1845, and F. H. Dyke, Bishop of London's Proctor, to F. Oakeley, June 4, 1845, *British Magazine*, 28 (1845): 65; and *The Times*, June 6, 1845, p. 4; *English Churchman*, June 26, 1845, p. 404.

23. A. F. Bayford, ed., *A Full Report of the Proceedings in the Office of the Judge Promoted*

by Hodgson v. Rev. F. Oakeley, before the Rt. Hon. Sir Herbert Jenner Fust, KT., Dean of the Arches (London: William Benning, 1845), p. 11. The standpoint of the prosecution had actually been stated the previous October in the Roman Catholic *Tablet,* which decried the efforts of the advanced Tractarians to claim that in some manner those English clergy who subscribed to the 39 Articles taught the doctrine of the Council of Trent. *Tablet,* October 26, November 16, 1844, pp. 673–674, 721–722; February 22, 1845, 113–114. For the documentation of the case in the Court of Arches, most of which was also reprinted in the major London newspapers, see Court of Arches, H/672, Lambeth Palace Library. See also *Index of Cases in the Records of the Court of Arches at Lambeth Palace Library, 1660–1913* (London: Phillimore, 1972), pp. 196–197.

24. Bayford, *Full Report of the Proceedings,* pp. 128–129, 134–135, 144, 151. See also Frederick Oakeley, *The Claim to "Hold, as Distinct from Teaching," Explained in A Letter to a Friend,* dated June 25, 1845 (London: James Toovey, 1845).

25. Bayford, *Full Report of the Proceedings,* pp. 165, 166; F. Oakeley to EBP, undated, 1845, *English Churchman,* October 9, 1845, p. 645; Frederick Oakeley, *Historical Notes of the Tractarian Movement, A.D. 1833–1845* (London: Longman, Green, Longman, Roberts, and Green, 1865), p. 96; JHN to Unknown Correspondent, September 21, 1845, Birmingham Oratory. An editorial in the *English Churchman* and an extensive letter from Pusey published in the same journal attempted with no particular success to deflect the obvious impact of the Oakeley decision. See *English Churchman,* July 10 and October 2, 9, 1845, pp. 435–436, 626–628, 642–645. See also Liddon, *Pusey,* 2: 439–440. In private Oakeley had been quite forthright about the differences among the Tractarians regarding subscription to the 39 Articles, telling Pusey in late 1844, "You sign upon a different view; you, (like J.H.N.) *do* think that the Articles preclude *some* Roman doctrine. I wish to believe that they do not, because I think they were drawn up on a principle of latitude in respect of R. Catholicism." F. Oakeley to EBP, December 21, 1844; see also F. Oakeley to EBP, December 24, 1844, Pusey-Oakeley Correspondence, ff. 32, 33, Pusey House.

26. Bayford, *Full Report of the Proceedings,* p. 166.

27. F. Oakeley to EBP, September 18, 1845, and undated summer 1845, Pusey-Oakeley Correspondence, ff. 40, 44, Pusey House. See also F. Oakeley to EBP, September 20, 23, 25, Pusey-Oakeley Correspondence, ff. 41–43, Pusey House; W. G. Ward to Undesignated Recipient, August 13, 1845, Wilfrid Ward, *William George Ward and the Oxford Movement* (London: Macmillan, 1889), p. 361, *The Times,* September 1, 1845, p. 5.

28. E. Badeley to JHN, February 21, 1845, Birmingham Oratory; [James Mozley], "Recent Proceeding at Oxford," *Christian Remembrancer,* n.s. 9 (1845): 53; JHN to E. Bellasis, May 30, 1845, Birmingham Oratory. Badeley also disapproved Oakeley's legal course because at that time it appeared that Ward might also take legal action against the decision of Convocation in his own case. On the more general subject of Tractarian appeals to ecclesiastical courts, see JHN to T. Mozley, October 29, 1841; JHN to JK, December 26, 1841; JHN to H. Wilberforce, December 27, 1841, *L&D,* 8: 311–312, 389, 393–394; JHN to EBP, July 11, 31, 1843, Pusey House, and JHN to W. H. Anderson, August 24, 1843, Birmingham Oratory Typescript, as well as the entire Newman-Bellasis Correspondence for 1843 to 1845, Birmingham Oratory. For further references to Pusey's possible case, see correspondence between JK and J. T. Coleridge, Oct. 3 and 30, November 10, 11 and 26, 1844, Bodleian Library, Ms. Eng. Lett, d. 135, ff. 133, 135, 137, 141, 145; E. Badeley to JHN, August 22 and 28, November 7 and 15, 1844; JHN to E. Badeley, November 16, 1844; JHN to E. Bellasis, May 30, 1845, Birmingham Oratory, and Newman Microfilms, reel 32, batch 5. For the extensive correspondence surrounding Oakeley's case, which indicates the importance that the Tractarians attached to it, see JHN to J. R. Hope, May 14, 1845, *Corrs. with JK,* p. 380; JHN to E. Bellasis, May 30, 1845; see also JHN to E. Bellasis, June 3, 4, 1845, Birmingham Oratory, and JHN to F. W. Faber, December 1, 1844, *Corrs. with JK,* p. 357. For Pusey's disapproval of Oakeley's action, which for a time led him to cease correspondence with

Oakeley, see F. Oakeley to EBP, February 27, undated, May 20, 1845, Pusey-Oakeley Correspondence (transcripts), Pusey House; W. G. Ward to EBP, March 1845, Ward, *William George Ward and the Oxford Movement,* pp. 353–356; F. Oakeley to EBP, undated, 1845, *English Churchman,* October 9, 1845, p. 645. For Keble's views, see JK to EBP, February 26, March 1, 1845, Pusey-Keble Correspondence, Pusey House.

29. [Henry Rogers], "Recent Developments in Puseyism," *Edinburgh Review,* 80 (1844): 314.

30. *Morning Herald,* December 28, 1844, p. 4; February 5, 1845, p. 6; March 13, 1845, p. 10; *The Times,* July 1, 1845, p. 4; *Morning Post,* July 2, 1845, p. 4.

31. JHN to R. Westmacott, July 11, 1845, Birmingham Oratory Transcript. On the identity of the modern Roman Catholic and the primitive church, see JHN to Unknown Correspondent, June 19, 1870, *L&D,* 25: 147.

32. JHN to Unknown Correspondent, September 21, 1845, Birmingham Oratory; see also JHN to JNM, August 17, 1845, Birmingham Oratory; J. Toovey to JHN, September 2, 1845, Newman Microfilms, reel 137, batch 276.

33. Edward Hawkins to JHN, October 6, 1845, *Corrs. with JK,* p. 388; R. W. Church, *Occasional Papers* (London: Macmillan, 1897), 2: 346. Hawkins could confirm Newman's conversion only by rumor more than a week after the fact. See E. Hawkins to S. Wilberforce, October 18–19, 1845, Wilberforce Papers, c. 8, ff. 37–38, Bodleian Library. I owe this reference to Ms. Elisa Milkes. On Newman's appearances in Oriel, see Cecil S. Emden, *Oriel Papers* (Oxford: Clarendon, 1948), pp. 168–175. I am grateful to Mr. Gerard Tracey for this reference. Concerning the Oriel stipend, I acknowledge with thanks information supplied by the Librarian of Oriel College. See also JHN to H. E. Manning, November 24, 1844, Birmingham Oratory Typescript; JHN to Father Dominic Barberi, December 17, 1845, *L&D,* 11: 67.

34. HNM to JNM, July 6, 1845; January, 1846, *Newman Family Letters,* pp. 163, 166.

35. *Tablet,* November 16, 1844, p. 722; September 6, 1845, p. 561.

36. *The Times,* October 11, 1845; Journal, January 21, 1863, *AW,* p. 255. *The Times* editorial leader was written to comment upon Newman's resignation of his fellowship; the writer was unaware that Newman had already been received into the Roman Catholic Church.

37. JHN to R. Stanton, October 4, 1845, Oratory Letters I, f. 57a, Birmingham Oratory.

38. C. Blomfield to Unknown Correspondent, April 25, 1844, Blomfield Papers, vol. 40, f. 40b, Lambeth Palace Library

39. JHN to JK, December 26, 1841; JHN to EBP, August 22, 1867, *L&D,* 8: 389; 23: 318. It was a medal associated with the appearance of the Virgin to St. Catherine Labouré in Paris during 1830. See also JHN to J. D. Dalgairns, May 28, 1845, Birmingham Oratory Typescript.

40. W. G. Ward to JHN, August 8, 1845, Newman Microfilms, reel 74, batch 80; JHN to W. G. Ward, September 26, 1845, Birmingham Oratory typescript; F. W. Ward to JHN, undated September, 1845, Birmingham Oratory; consult Anne Mozley, ed., *Letters of the Rev. J. B. Mozley, D.D., Edited by His Sister* (London: Rivingtons, 1885), p. 166. See also JHN to W. G. Ward, February 15, 1845, Birmingham Oratory typescript, for an earlier sympathetic note regarding Ward's degradation by Convocation. Mrs. Ward seems never to have believed that Newman after his conversion was a wholehearted Roman Catholic. See JHN to Emily Bowles, December 9, 1871, and note to this letter, *L&D,* 25: 445. Ward's wife was the third woman whose conversion had a negative impact on Newman's goals. There can be little question that Helen Gladstone's conversion in the summer of 1842 had impressed her brother with the dangers of Romanizing, which he attacked in late 1843. As will be seen later in this chapter, the conversion also in 1843 of F. S. Bowles's sister, who had become a close friend of Bishop Bagot's daughter, could only have upset the warm relationship that seemed to have been developing between Bagot and Newman.

41. H. Wilberforce to JHN, October 3, 1845, Newman Microfilms, reel 74, batch 85; JHN to H. Wilberforce, October 7, 1845, *L&D*, 11: 3.

42. *Morning Herald,* June 20, 1845, p. 10.

43. [A. P. Stanley], "The Oxford School," *Edinburgh Review,* 153 (1881): 319; *Oxford Chronicle and Reading Gazette,* August 9, 16, 23, 1845. On Bagot's tolerant views toward ordination of Tractarian sympathizers, see J. D. Coleridge to his Father, October 31, 1843, Ernest Hartley Coleridge, *Life and Correspondence of John Duke Lord Coleridge Lord Chief Justice of England* (London: Heinemann, 1904), 1: 140-141. When Newman wrote the *Apologia,* he met private opposition to his warm remarks about Bagot; see *L&D,* 21: 108n.

44. R. Palmer to J. R. Godley, January 27, 1842, Selborne Papers, 2498, f. 28, Lambeth Palace Library, as quoted in Peter Nockles, *The Oxford Movement in Context: Anglican High Churchmanship, 1760-1857* (Cambridge: Cambridge University Press, 1994), p. 298n., and p. 301 for Bagot's urging Palmer to moderation.

45. JHN to J. R. Hope, October 17, 1841; JHN to R. W. Church, December 24, 1841; JHN to S. Rickards, January 2, 1842; JHN to Charles Crawley, January 2, 1841; J. W. Bowden to JHN, undated, 1841, *L&D,* 8: 300, 384, 404, 408, 508n.; J. B. Mozley to A. Mozley, May 22, 1842, Mozley, *Letters of the Rev. J. B. Mozley,* p. 130. See also E. Copleston to E. Hawkins, November 6, 1843, Letterbooks, 5: 405, Oriel College.

46. HN to JNM, June 12, 1842; JHN to Miss Holmes, July 3, 1842; JHN to JNM, May 24, 1843; JHN to M. R. Giberne, November 13, 1843, Birmingham Oratory. See also JHN, Diary, February 25, March 11, 1841, *L&D,* 8: 44, 64; Diary, November 17, 1842, Newman Microfilms, reel 2, batch 17; JHN to JNM, August 5, 1842, Birmingham Oratory Typescript, original, Bodleian Library, Ms. Eng. lett. d. 102. f. 22.

47. Boyd Hilton, *The Age of Atonement: The Influence of Evangelicalism on Social and Economic Thought, 1785-1865* (Oxford: Clarendon, 1988), p. 229; R. Peel to J. W. Croker, February 21, 1842, Louis J. Jennings, *The Correspondence and Diaries of the Late Right Honourable John Wilson Croker, LL.D., F.R.S., Secretary to the Admiralty from 1809 to 1830,* 2d ed., rev. (London: John Murray, 1885), 2: 379. J. B. Mozley had reported in early 1842, "Peel told Lord Ashley the other day that he need not be afraid of the Oxford party, for he should take care they got into no preferment while he was in office." J. B Mozley to A. Mozley, January 27, 1842, Mozley, *Letters of the Rev. J. B. Mozley,* p. 127. Regarding an appointment to the Deanery of Carlisle, Peel wrote in 1844, "I should certainly wish that such Divine should not hold Tractarian opinions or have any marked learning towards them." R. Peel to Dean of Christ Church, November 27, 1844, Peel Papers, British Library, Add. Ms. 40554, f. 382. See also Boyd Hilton, "Peel: A Reappraisal," *Historical Journal,* 22 (1979): 585-614.

48. R. Peel to C. Blomfield, October 13, 1843; C. Blomfield to R. Peel, October 15, 1843; R. Peel to Archbishop Howley, October 20, 1843, Peel Papers, British Library, Add Mss. 40533, f. 403; 40534, ff. 168, 239. The candidates Peel mentioned to Blomfield for Oxford were the Dean of Christ Church, the Dean of Salisbury, the Provost of Oriel, and Dr. Cardwell. In 1843 Peel thought Wilberforce's appointment not yet advisable. Blomfield favored Cardwell, thinking that Wilberforce's appointment at that time "would be a hazardous measure & he is young enough to wait." He reported Hawkins was known to be "crotchety." On rumors in Oxford around the time of the Lichfield appointment, see "University & Clerical Intelligence," *Oxford Chronicle and Reading Gazette,* October 21, 1843.

49. *Oxford Chronicle and Reading Gazette,* June 28, 1845.

50. R. Peel to Archbishop Howley, September 26, 1845; R. Bagot to Archbishop Howley, October 1, 1845; Archbishop Howley to R. Peel, October 2, 4, 1845; R. Bagot to R. Peel, October 5, 7, 1845; R. Bagot to R. Peel, and R. Peel to W. Wilberforce, October 13, 1845; R. Peel to Archbishop Howley, October 13, 1845, Peel Papers, British Library, Add. Mss. 40574, f. 261; 40575, ff. 97-103; 40574, ff. 163-165; 40575, ff. 103, 167, 373. See also the *Standard,* September 29, 1845, p. 6, under "Oxford Intelligence" from September 27, 1845. Newman

was in the city of Oxford on September 29, 1845; see Diary, September 29, 1845, Newman Microfilms, reel 2, batch 20.

51. JHN to H. A. Woodgate, September 22, 1841, *L&D*, 8: 277.

52. JK to J. T. Coleridge, October 16, 1845; italics added. See also JK to J. T. Coleridge, October 25, 1847, Bodleian Library, Ms. Eng. lett. d. 135, ff. 209, 354; *English Churchman*, October 16, 1845, p. 661.

53. Quoted in [R. A. Willmott (probable author)], "Mr. Newman; His Theories and Character," *Fraser's Magazine*, 33 (1846): 268; S. Wilberforce to E. Hawkins, October 25, 1845, Letterbooks, 11: 1097, Oriel College. See *Oxford Chronicle and Berks and Bucks Gazette*, December 27, 1845, under "University Chronicle," for Wilberforce's ordination process; S. Wilberforce to W. F. Hook, January 29, 1839, Ms. Wilberforce, d. 38, f. 129, Bodleian Library. For Wilberforce's earlier view of the Tractarians see S. Wilberforce to J. W. Croker, January 31, 1842, *Correspondence and Diaries of Croker*, 2: 409. On Newman's encouraging younger associates to write against Tractarian opponents, consult JHN to T. Mozley, July 15, August 23, October 24, 1841, *L&D*, 8: 222, 252, 307. See also W. G. Ward, "Arnold's Sermons," and "Whately's *Essays*," *British Critic* 30 (1841): 298–364; 31 (1842): 255–302. For an indication that both Henry Wilberforce and Newman may have had some regret over the anti-Hampden pamphlet of 1834 as far as their own relationship was concerned, see JHN to H. Wilberforce, June 13, 1854, *L&D*, 16: 160.

54. EBP to S. Wilberforce, November 15, 1845; S. Wilberforce to EBP, November 24, 1845, R. A. Ashwell, *Life of the Right Reverend Samuel Wilberforce, D.D.* (London: John Murray, 1880), 1: 301, 303. It appears that some of the Tractarians, including Henry Wilberforce, feared that Samuel Wilberforce as Bishop of Oxford would attempt to force Pusey from the church. See H. Wilberforce to W. E. Gladstone, November 19, 1845, in which the former pleads with the latter to intervene with Samuel Wilberforce on Pusey's behalf. Gladstone Papers, British Library, Add. Ms. 44362, f. 373.

55. S. Wilberforce to EBP, December 5, 1845, Ashwell, *Life of Wilberforce*, 1: 307–308; see 1: 302–307 for EBP to S. Wilberforce, November 27, 1845, the letter that elicited the quoted reply.

56. JHN, Diary, August 9, 1845, Newman Microfilms, reel 2, batch 20.

57. See JK to EBP, July 20, 1845; EBP to JK, July 8, 1845, Keble-Pusey Correspondence (Transcripts), Pusey House, for Keble's hope that Newman would convert in some geographically distant part of the Continent.

58. Bishop C. M. Baggs to JHN, October 11, 1845, Newman Microfilms, reel 95, batch 142. Newman had arranged strict confidentiality for the printing of the early proofs of *An Essay on the Development of Christian Doctrine*. In early September his publisher James Toovey assured Newman, "In reply to yours received this morning, I would engage that no intimation should escape me that any such work was in progress, and sending the proofs, etc. to me the printer would know nothing." J. Toovey to JHN, September 2, 1845, Newman Microfilms, reel 137, batch 276. Newman's brother-in-law John Mozley, a printer, had firmly refused to produce the book; see JHN to JNM, August 16, 1846, *L&D*, 31: supplement, p. 9.

59. N. Wiseman to C. Russell, early November 1845, Wilfrid Ward, *The Life and Times of Cardinal Wiseman*, 2d ed. (London: Longmans, Green, 1897), 1: 434, 435. The letter continues to say that Wiseman has not yet seen the book and hesitates in having it revised because it has been long expected and relates to Newman's past mind.

60. HNM to JNM, January 1846, *Newman Family Letters*, p. 165; N. Wiseman to C. Russell, early November 1845, Ward, *Life of Cardinal Wiseman*, 1: 433, 436.

61. JHN to T. Henderson, November 8, 1841, *L&D*, 8: 319. See JHN to J. R. Hope, November 2, 1845; JHN to N. Wiseman, November 7, 1845, *L&D*, 11: 23, 25–26; Owen Chadwick, *From Bossuet to Newman*, 2d ed. (Cambridge: Cambridge University Press, 1987), pp. 160–163. At least one contemporary Unitarian commentator saw "cunning policy" in

Newman's negotiation and the achievement of the exercise of private judgment in determining what he would and would not permit the Roman Catholic Church to sanction and not sanction. See "Doctrine of Development," *Christian Reformer*, n.s. 2 (1846): 464. In regard to Newman's negotiating with an episcopal superior, there exists another more somber parallel between *Tract 90* and *An Essay on the Development of Christian Doctrine*. Generally speaking, with the exception of Richard Church, public adherence to the principles of *Tract 90* resulted in either lack of clerical promotion in the English Church or conversion to Roman Catholicism. To the extent that around the turn of the twentieth century the *Essay on Development*, as the book became almost invariably called, informed Roman Catholic modernism, Newman's theology similarly led certain Roman Catholic clergy toward condemnation by the highest authorities of their church. The history of both the English and Roman Churches would have been far different had either Bishop Bagot or Bishop Wiseman negotiated more firmly with Newman; see Marvin R. O'Connell, *Critics on Trial: An Introduction to the Catholic Modernist Crisis* (Washington, D.C.: Catholic University of America Press, 1994), pp. 177–197.

62. Stephen Prickett, *Romanticism and Religion: The Tradition of Coleridge and Wordsworth in the Victorian Church* (Cambridge: Cambridge University Press, 1976), p. 153; [Orestes Brownson], "Newman's Theory of Christian Doctrine," *Brownson's Quarterly Review*, n.s. 1 (1847): 45; William J. Philbin, "The *Essay on Development*," in Michael Tierney, ed., *A Tribute to Newman* (Dublin: Browne and Nolan, 1945), p. 116. There is only modest evidence for Bishop Connop Thirlwall's statement that the theory had been made "a legitimate and efficacious instrument of proselytism." Connop Thirlwall, *Remains Literary and Theological of Connop Thirlwall*, ed. J. J. Stewart Perowne (London: Daldy, Isbister, 1877–1878), p. 102. For Newman's ongoing anger toward Brownson, see JHN to W. G. Ward, August 14, 1850; JHN to J. M. Capes, September 6, 1850; JHN to Editor of the *Tablet*, September 14, 1852, *L&D*, 14: 41–42, 60; 15: 164–165.

63. JHN to M. R. Giberne, March 20, 1846, *L&D*, 11: 140.

64. JHN to C. H. Froude, July 28, 1843, Newman Microfilms, reel 39, batch 29; [J. B. Mozley], "Newman on Development," *Christian Remembrancer*, 13 (1847): 153. See also "The Development Controversy in the Church of Rome and the Position of the Recent Converts," *English Review*, 9 (1848): 96–127. Newman had negotiated royalties for the volume in September 1845. In March 1846 he inquired of Toovey what payments would be due him. The publisher replied that he owed Newman approximately £279 in the forthcoming September, but that he could receive immediate payment at a 5 percent discount; see J. Toovey to JHN, September 5, 10, 1845; March 6, 1846, Newman Microfilms, reel 137, batch 276.

65. [Brownson], "Newman's Theory of Christian Doctrine," *Brownson's Quarterly Review*, 3 (1846): 355–356. See particularly Chadwick, *From Bossuet to Newman*, and Nicholas Lash, *Newman on Development: The Search for an Explanation in History* (Shepherdstown, W.Va., 1975). In reference to Newman's edition of his volume on development as published in 1878, Charles Frederick Harrold wrote, "No other work of Newman's underwent so much revision as did the *Essay on Development*." Charles Frederick Harrold, Preface, John Henry Newman, *An Essay on the Development of Christian Doctrine*, ed. Charles Frederick Harrold (New York: Longmans, Green, 1949), p. vii. In the same edition consult O. I. Schreiber, "Newman's Revisions in the *Essay on the Development of Christian Doctrine*," pp. 417–435.

66. *Development*, pp. 28, 29. Other Victorians suggested different solutions. For example, in *Stones of Venice* (1851–1853) John Ruskin located the date of the corruption of Christianity in the Renaissance, thus saving the art and social values of the Middle Ages.

67. JHN to R. W. Church, December 24, 1841, *L&D*, 8: 383.

68. JHN to EBP, March 14, 1845, Liddon, *Pusey*, 2: 450; JHN to R. Westmacott, July 11, 1845, Birmingham Oratory Typescript.

69. E. Hawkins to R. Whately, January 19, 1846, Letterbooks, 3: 260, Oriel College;

A. M. Fairbairn, *Catholicism: Roman and Anglican*, 3d ed. (London: Hodder and Stroughton, 1899), pp. 137, 140; see also pp. 298–305. For an earlier critique of the Tractarian view of reason and faith, consult T. Arnold to A. P. Stanley, October 21, 1836, Arthur Penrhyn Stanley, *The Life and Correspondence of Thomas Arnold, D.D.*, 10th ed. (London: John Murray, 1877), 2: 46.

70. *Development*, p. 27.

71. *Development*, pp. 1, 2, 5. For a contemporary comment on the hostility displayed toward Protestantism in Newman's *Essay*, as opposed to his attraction to Roman Catholicism, see [Willmott (probable author)], "Mr. Newman," 253–268

72. John Henry Newman, Advertisement to the Second Edition, *Parochial Sermons*, 2d ed. (London: J. G. and F. Rivington, 1837), p. viii; *Development*, p. 11.

73. *Development*, p. 20; JHN to H. Wilberforce, June 25, 1846; see also JHN to Lord Adare, August 31, 1846, *L&D*, 11: 183, 239.

74. "Newman's Essay on Development," *English Review*, 4 (1845): 399; William Archer Butler, *Letters on the Development of Christian Doctrine, In Reply to Mr. Newman's Essay*, ed. Thomas Woodward (Dublin: Hodges and Smith, 1850), p. 16; Thirlwall, *Remains*, p. 104. See also "Dr. Wordsworth on Romanism," *English Review*, 7 (1847): 143.

75. *Christian Reformer*, n.s. 2 (1846): 359. On the resemblances with Joseph Priestley, *The History of the Corruptions of Christianity* (2 vols., 1782) and *General History of the Christian Church to the Fall of the Western Empire* (2 vols., 1790), see "Doctrine of Development," *Christian Reformer*, n.s. 2 (1846): 465.

76. George Stanley Faber, *Letter on the Tractarian Secession to Popery: With Remarks on Mr. Newman's Principle of Development, Dr. Moehler's Symbolism, and the Adduced Evidence in Favour of the Romish Practice of Mariolatry* (London: Protestant Association, by W. H. Dalton, 1846), p. 84; *Development*, pp. 95, 100–103.

77. *Development*, pp. 44, 55, 61–64.

78. James Toovey published 1,500 copies of the first edition and 1,250 of the second edition of *An Essay on the Development of Christian Doctrine*. By the summer of 1846 sales had fallen, with Toovey telling Newman, "I need scarcely mention to you that within the last few months there has been a considerable reaction in the mind of the public & that it is nearly impossible to excite the least attention by any work if the subject is religious." By mid-1848 Toovey reported that the sale of the volume "ceased very suddenly and I do not think any expense in the way of advertising would assist it." In January 1870 Toovey stated that 430 copies of the second edition remained on hand. Newman note on J. Toovey to JHN, March 14, 1846; J. Toovey to JHN, June 30, 1846; August 25, 1848; January 8, 1870, Newman Microfilms, reel 137, batch 276.

79. *Development*, pp. 35–39.

80. *Development*, pp. 95, 66; [Mozley], "Newman on Development," 262; [Baden Powell], "Tendency of Puseyism," *Westminster Review*, 45 (1846): 325.

81. *Development*, pp. 35, 83.

82. *Development*, pp. 446, 451, 417; see also Butler, *Letters on the Development of Christian Doctrine*, pp. 296–298.

83. *Development*, pp. 118, 126, 128, 124, 136. See also JHN to Unknown Correspondents, September 14, 19, 1875, *L&D*, 27: 354–355, 357–358.

84. JHN to FWN, November 10, 1840, *L&D*, 7: 442; [Mozley], "Newman on Development," 172; Thirlwall, *Remains*, pp. 102–105. As Mozley particularly observed, Newman devoted relatively little space to his defense of papal infallibility, though most reviewers thought that point absolutely essential to his argument. It may actually not have been. Newman and other high Anglicans had long seen the clergy or certainly some kind of properly constituted synod of clergy as constituting a voice for the church. Newman in the early 1840s had envisioned some kind of mutually agreed upon merger between the Church of Rome and the Church of England. It may well have been possible for him to have

conceived of a papacy much more benign than that imagined by most English Protestants. The sparse discussion of the papacy and its authority may also simply have reflected Newman's own lack of clarity on where a verifying authority for development resided.

85. Newman, *Development*, pp. 349–351; on Newman's own possibly mystical experience, see JHN to M. Holmes, December 6, 1841, *L&D*, 8: 367.

86. Newman, *Development*, pp. 352, 354–355, 358, 365, 449.

87. "Newman's Essay on Development," *English Review*, 4 (1845): 391.

88. Newman, *Development*, p. x; JHN to R. Stanton, October 4, 1845, Oratory Letters I, f. 57a, Birmingham Oratory; "The Religious Movement," *Dublin Review*, 19 (1845): 532; see also 527–528.

89. Richard Whately, *The Kingdom of Christ Delineated, in Two Essays on Our Lord's Own Account of His Person and of the Nature of His Kingdom, and on the Constitution, Powers, and Ministry of a Christian Church Appointed by Himself,* From the Second London Edition, with Additions (New York: Wiley and Putnam, 1843), p. 297; R. D. Hampden, *Sermons Preached Before the University of Oxford in the Cathedral of Christ Church from 1836 to 1847* (London: B. Fellowes, 1848), p. 461; George Moberly, *The Sayings of the Great Forty Days, Between the Resurrection and Ascension, Regarded as the Outlines of the Kingdom of God: In Five Discourses, with an Examination of Mr. Newman's Theory of Development*, 3d ed. (London: Francis and John Rivington, 1846), p. L; Butler, *Letters on the Development of Christian Doctrine*, p. 391; Edward Hawkins, *Sermons on the Church Preached before the University of Oxford* (London: B. Fellowes, 1847), p. 116. For the most extensive discussion of the reception of Newman's work, see Henry Lawrence Joseph, *Newman and Development: The Genesis of John Henry Newman's Theory of Development and the Reception of His Essay on the Development of Christian Doctrine* (Texas [Austin] diss., 1973); see also David Nicholls, "Newman's Anglican Critics, "*Anglican Theological Review*, 47 (1965): 379–385.

90. [Orestes Brownson], "Newman's Development of Christian Doctrine," *Brownson's Quarterly Review*, 3 (1846): 352; Faber, *Letter on Tractarian Secession to Popery*, p. 119.

91. [H. H. Milman], "Newman on the Development of Christian Doctrine," *Quarterly Review*, 77 (1846): 421; [Mozley], "Newman on Development," 178, 195; Hampden, *Sermons*, p. 506; Butler, *Letters on the Development of Christian Doctrine*, pp. 81, 85, 275. Similarly, for William J. Irons, development was "an attempt to make a statement of fact stand for its theory" and represented in "itself a retrospective development of his mind from existing facts." William J. Irons, *The Theory of Development Examined, with Reference Specially to Mr. Newman's Essay, and to the Rule of St. Vincent of Lerins* (London: Francis and John Rivington, 1846), p. 49.

92. William Palmer, *The Doctrine of Development and Conscience Considered in Relation to the Evidences of Christianity and of the Catholic System* (London: Francis and John Rivington, 1846), p. 84; Faber, *Letter on the Tractarian Secession to Popery*, pp. 76–80; Butler, *Letters on the Development of Christian Doctrine*, pp. 147–148; 168–169; [Milman], "Newman on the Development of Christian Doctrine," 454; [Mozley], "Newman on Development," 142, 178.

93. Hampden, *Sermons*, p. 479; Irons, *Theory of Development Examined*, pp. 58–59.

94. [Henry Rogers], "Mysticism and Scepticism," *Edinburgh Review*, 84 (1846): 219, 221. See also [Powell], "Tendency of Puseyism," 314.

95. [Brownson], "Newman's Development of Christian Doctrine," 355–356, 345, 346, 357n.

96. See also the same charge from outside the high-church circle in [Powell], "Tendency of Puseyism," 335.

97. Edward H. Dewar, *German Protestantism and the Right of Private Judgment in the Interpretation of Holy Scripture: A Brief History of German Theology from the Reformation to the Present Time in a Series of Letters to a Layman* (London: J. G. F. and J. Rivington, 1844), pp. 15, 2, 6, 8, 8–9, 16. Dewar explained that by rationalism he meant "the principle of

submitting the Holy Scripture to the investigation of man's understanding, in order that he may thence frame the articles of his faith; hence you will see, a man, according to my meaning of the word, may be a Rationalist in principle, and yet possibly orthodox in all the principal articles of faith." Dewar, *German Protestantism*, p. 17.

98. *Development*, pp. 82–83, 97.

99. Butler, *Letters on the Development of Christian Doctrine*, pp. 88, 351. Newman himself may well have come to a similar conclusion many years later, when in 1871 he told Richard Holt Hutton, "A Catholic believes that the Church is, so to call it, a standing Apostolic committee—to answer questions, which the Apostles are not here to answer, concerning what they received and preached. As the Church does not know more than the Apostles knew, there are many questions which the Church cannot answer—but it can put before us clearly, what the Apostles (being in heaven) cannot, what their doctrine is, what is to be believed, and what is not such." See JHN to R. H. Hutton, October 20, 1871, *L&D*, 25: 418, and also Palmer, *Doctrine of Development and Conscience*, pp. 88–113.

100. Whately, *Kingdom of Christ*, pp. 296–297; [Willmott (probable author)], "Mr. Newman," 265, 256; [Milman], "Newman on the Development of Christian Doctrine," 437–438; Hampden, *Sermons*, pp. 495, 496; Charles James Blomfield, *A Charge Delivered to the Clergy of the Diocese of London at the Visitation in October, MDCCCXLVI*, 2d ed. (London: B. Fellowes, 1846), p. 27. For Milman's own previous, critical discussion of Strauss, consult, H. H. Milman, *The History of Christianity, from the Birth of Christ to the Abolition of Paganism in the Roman Empire* (London: John Murray, 1840), 1: vi–viii, 115–132.

101. [Brownson], "Newman's Development of Christian Doctrine," 366; Frederick Denison Maurice, *The Epistle to the Hebrews; Being the Substance of Three Lectures Delivered in the Chapel of the Honourable Society of Lincoln's Inn, on the Foundation of Bishop Warburton. With a Preface Containing a Review of Mr. Newman's Theory of Development* (London: John W. Parker, 1846), p. xliii; Fairbairn, *Catholicism: Roman and Anglican*, p. 141. See also [Powell], "Tendency of Puseyism," 317, and Hampden, *Sermons*, p. 431 ff.

102. Hampden, *Sermons*, pp. 440–441.

103. S. Wilberforce to W. E. Gladstone, December 6, 1845; W. E. Gladstone to S. Wilberforce, December 10, 1845, Gladstone Papers, British Library, Add. Ms., 44343, ff. 81, 83; H. Manning to W. E. Gladstone, December 28, 1845; H. Manning to R. Wilberforce, December 30, 1845, Edmund Sheridan Purcell, *Life of Cardinal Manning, Archbishop of Westminster* (New York: Macmillan, 1896), pp. 315, 311; H. Wilberforce to W. E. Gladstone, December 27, 1845, Gladstone Papers, British Library, Add. Ms. 44363, f. 64 [Wilberforce also criticized the omission of consideration of the Greek Church]; E. Hawkins to R. Whately, January 19, 1846, Letterbooks, 3: 260, Oriel College; JK to J. T. Coleridge, October 25, 1847, Bodleian Library, Ms. Eng. lett., d. 135, f. 354. See also W. E. Gladstone to R. Wilberforce, December 30, 1845, Ms. Wilberforce, c. 67, f. 14, Bodleian Library.

104. Roundell Palmer, *Memorials. Part I, Family and Personal, 1766–1865* (London: Macmillan, 1896), 1: 397.

CHAPTER 12. PATHS TAKEN AND NOT

1. J. Hare to H. Manning, November 5, 1845, Bodleian Library, Ms. Eng. lett. c.653, f. 318.

2. *Globe*, October 4, 1845, p. 4; *Standard*, October 10, 1845; *Morning Herald*, October 22, 1845 (Supplement), p. 14; *Morning Post*, October 18, 1845, p. 5.

3. B. Harrison to EBP, April 16, 1846, Harrison-Pusey Correspondence; EBP to W. F. Hook, undated, autumn 1845; W. F. Hook to EBP, October 6, 15, 1845, Hook-Pusey

Correspondence (Transcripts), ff. 278, 286, 293, Pusey House; [James Mozley], "The Recent Schism," *Christian Remembrance*, 11 (1846): 209; *Christian Observer*, 45 (1845): 704. See also W. F. Hook, *"She Leaveth Much: And the Hem of His Garment." Two Sermons, with a Preface Containing Some Remarks on the Late Schism* (London: F. and J. Rivington, 1846); *British Magazine*, 29 (1846): 234–236.

4. R. D. Hampden to R. Whately, undated, 1836, Henrietta Hampden, *Some Memorials of Renn Dickson Hampden, Bishop of Hereford* (London: Longmans, Green, 1871), pp. 90–97; see also R. D. Hampden to R. Whately, undated, 1836, p. 88. Ironically, thirty years later Newman directed exactly the same kind of charge against the ultramontane behavior of W. G. Ward in the Roman Catholic Church; see JHN to W. G. Ward, May 9, 1867, *L&D*, 23: 217.

5. *Tablet*, October 25, 1845, p. 673, and rpt. in *English Churchman*, October 30, 1845, p. 694. See also *Tablet*, September 20, 1845, p. 593, on the Tractarian exercise of private judgment.

6. Richard Whately, *Cautions for the Times: Addressed to the Parishioners of a Parish in England by Their Former Rector*, 2d ed. (London: John W. Parker, 1854), p. 194; JHN to E. E. Estcourt, June 2, 1860, *L&D*, 19: 352; JHN to Richard Westmacott, April 8, 1841, *L&D*, 8: 166. See also Connop Thirlwall, *Remains Literary and Theological of Connop Thirlwall*, ed. J. J. Stewart Perowne (London: Daldy, Isbister, 1877–1878), pp. 106–107.

7. Henry Christmas, *A Concise History of the Hampden Controversy, from the Period of Its Commencement in 1832 to the Present Time* (London: Smith, Elder, 1848), p. 2.

8. JHN to Unknown Correspondent, June 23, 1844, Birmingham Oratory typescript. Newman was not the first clergyman of the English Church to find a parallel between Methodism and Roman Catholicism as both being based on emotion. See George Lavington, *The Enthusiasm of Methodists and Papists Compared* (London: J. and P. Knapton, 1749), 2 vols.

9. JHN to E. Walford, May 13, 1860, *L&D*, 19: 336; JHN to H. Wilberforce, November 8, 1841; JHN to R. Wilberforce, February 1, 1842, *L&D*, 8: 321, 451–452; JHN to E. Coleridge, November 16, 1844, *Corrs. with JK*, p. 345; JHN to JNM, December 22, 1844, Mozley, *Letters and Correspondence*, 2: 404; JHN to Dalgairns Senior, February 18, 1845; JHN to R. Westmacott, July 11, 1845, Birmingham Oratory Transcript.

10. JHN to FWN, August 1845, "Copies of Letters Personal and Family, 1817–1845," N. IV, book 2, letter 183," Newman Microfilms, reel 81, batch 107; JHN to Unknown Correspondent, September 21, 1845, Birmingham Oratory.

11. JHN to M. Holmes, February 8, August 16, 1843, Newman Microfilms, reel 43, batch 36. See also JHN to M. Holmes, March 8, 1843, Newman Microfilms, reel 43, batch 36, and partially reprinted in Mozley, *Letters and Correspondence*, 2: 366–367.

12. JHN to T. Mozley, September 21, 1843, Newman Microfilms, reel 103, batch 162. It should be noted that the handwriting in this letter is exceptionally difficult to read. Almost a half-century later Newman wrote Mozley, "I ought to have reminded myself that before I became a Catholic I hindered you from becoming one. This leads me to say that I think my second judgment in all respects a better than the first." JHN to T. Mozley [End of 1882?], *L&D*, 30: 167.

13. JHN to M. Holmes, April 22, 1844, Newman Microfilms, reel 43, batch 36; JHN to J. D. Dalgairns, May 28, 1845, Birmingham Oratory Typescript (original in London Oratory).

14. In early September 1855 J. D. Dalgairns wrote to Newman, who was then in Dublin, "We in Birmingham have nothing to do in comparison with our numbers and strength. I am going to write a book because I have not enough to do; and other minds in the congregation are stagnating for want of objects to fix themselves upon. There is just as much danger of health going and brains over-working from the painful consciousness of doing nothing for God as from having too much to do. We have no right to be living as comfortably as we do

unless we are wearing ourselves out with work for Christ; and if you could see into the interiors of some of those about you you would know how painful is the sense that after all that God has done for them they are doing nothing for Him. I cannot see what is ever to bring a novice to the Birmingham Oratory in its present state of unattractive inaction." J. D. Dalgairns to JHN, September 1855, *L&D*, 17: 33–34n3.

15. H. Richard Niebuhr, *Theology, History, and Culture: Major Unpublished Writings*, ed. William Stacy Johnson (New Haven: Yale University Press, 1996), p. 52; see also pp. 53–55. See also A. M. Fairbairn, *The Place of Christ in Modern Theology*, 5th ed. (London: Hodder and Stoughton, 1894); Daniel L. Pals, *The Victorian "Lives" of Jesus* (San Antonio: Trinity University Press, 1982); Charlotte Allen, *The Human Christ: The Search for the Historical Jesus* (New York: Free Press, 1998).

16. James Hastings Nichols, *Romanticism in American Theology: Nevin and Schaff at Mercersburg* (Chicago: University of Chicago Press, 1961), pp. 64–83; Stephen R. Graham, *Cosmos in the Chaos: Philip Schaff's Interpretation of Nineteenth-Century American Religion* (Grand Rapids, Michigan: Eerdmans, 1995), pp. 1–72; David E. Barclay, *Frederick William IV and the Prussian Monarchy, 1840–1861* (Oxford: Clarendon, 1995), pp. 75–98.

17. Philip Schaff, *The Principle of Protestantism as Related to the Present State of the Church* (Chambersburg, Pa.: Publication Office of the German Reformed Church, 1845), pp. 120–123.

18. Schaff, *Principle of Protestantism*, p. 124.

19. Schaff, *Principle of Protestantism*, pp. 127, 169, 160, 160–161.

20. Schaff, *Principle of Protestantism*, pp. 173–174.

21. Philip Schaff, *What is Church History? Vindication of the Idea of Historical Development* (Philadelphia: J. B. Lippincott, 1846), pp. 6, 36, 81, 85, 98; see also pp. 46–48 with notes for a discussion of the manner in which Schaff briefly explained how his view of development differed from Newman's and where he cites W. A. Butler's criticism of Newman.

22. JHN to R. Wilberforce, January 26, 1842, *L&D*, 8: 440.

23. E. L. Badeley to JHN, October 13, 1845, Newman Microfilms, reel 32, batch 4; JHN to EBP, February 19, 1844, Liddon, *Pusey*, 2: 381.

24. JHN to R. Wilberforce, January 26, 1842, *L&D*, 8: 441; see also R. Wilberforce to JHN, January 21, 29, 1842, Newman Microfilms, reel 75, batch 86.

25. JHN to S. L. Pope, September 4, 1842, Birmingham Oratory Typescript.

26. JHN to H. Wilberforce, June 8, 1844, Ushaw College, OS/N 24; H. Wilberforce to JHN, Eve of St. Peter and St. Paul, 1844, Newman Microfilms, reel 74, batch 85; JHN to H. Wilberforce, July 4, 17, 1844, Ushaw College, OS/N 25, N26.

27. JHN to E. L. Badeley, August 23, 1844, *Corrs. with JK*, pp. 327, 328.

28. E. L. Badeley to JHN, August 28, 1844; see also E. L. Badeley to JHN, November 15, 1844, in which he states that Gladstone and others saw the judgment on Pusey as lacking constitutional and thus authoritative standing. Newman Microfilms, reel 32, batch 4.

29. J. B. Mozley to JHN, August 31, 1843; August 24, 1844; see also J. B. Mozley to JHN, September 4 or 9, 1843, Newman Microfilms, reel 67, batch 56.

30. JHN to E. L. Badeley, September 9, 1844, *Corrs. with JK*, pp. 329–330.

31. For incisive comments on the eschatological outlook that so marked Newman's thinking in the 1830s, see Stephen Thomas, *Newman and Heresy: The Anglican Years* (Cambridge: Cambridge University Press, 1991), pp. 55–58

32. JHN to [?] Anderson, January 21, 1843, Birmingham Oratory Typescript; JHN to H. Wilberforce, February 3, 1843, Ushaw College, OS/N 16; JHN to Mrs. Froude, July 28, 1843, Birmingham Oratory.

33. H. Wilberforce to JHN, June 5, 1845, Newman Microfilms, reel 74, batch 85.

34. H. Wilberforce to JHN, June 5, 1845, Newman Microfilms, reel 74, batch 85.

35. R. Westmacott to JHN, July 8, 1845, Birmingham Oratory; J. D. Dalgairns to JHN,

May 23, 1845; J. Walker to JHN, June 13, 1845, Newman Microfilms, reel 104, batch 164; EBP to W. F. Hook, November 24, 1844, Hook-Pusey Correspondence (Transcripts), Pusey House.

36. FWN to JHN, May 1, 1845, "Copies of Letters," N. IV, book 2, letter 181, Newman Microfilms, reel 81, batch 107.

37. FWN to JHN, August, 1845, "Copies of Letters," N. IV, book 2, letter 182, Newman Microfilms, reel 81, batch 107. Francis's comments in this letter suggest that Jemima may have been sharing with him her correspondence with John.

38. FWN to JHN, August, 1845, "Copies of Letters," N. IV, book 2, letter 182, Newman Microfilms, reel 81, batch 107; *Tablet*, October 26, 1844, p. 674. For Harriett Newman's views of John's independent spirit discussed in chapter 11, see HNM to JNM, January 1846, *Newman Family Letters*, p. 165.

39. C. Blomfield to the Lord Bishop of Gibraltar, March 3, 1845, Blomfield Papers, 42: 145, Lambeth Palace Library; FWN to JHN, August, 1845, "Copies of Letters," N. IV, book 2, letter 182, Newman Microfilms, reel 81, batch 107. What Blomfield feared and Francis Newman urged was an ecclesiastical departure on John Henry Newman's part that would have resembled the actions undertaken in 2001 by the Anglican Mission in America, a group ordaining Episcopalian priests through the Bishops of the Anglican Church in Rwanda and Singapore for ministry in the United States outside the authority of the presiding bishop of the American Episcopal Church. *New York Times*, March 6, 2001.

40. JHN notation at conclusion of FWN to JHN, August, 1845, "Copies of Letters," N. IV, book 2, letters 182, 183, bottom p. 153, Newman Microfilms, reel 81, batch 107. See also J. H. Newman, "Two Papers from 1879," Newman Microfilms, reel 14, batch 80, ref. A. 26. 13. Newman again negatively recalled his brother's advice in 1883, JHN to the Editor of the *Fortnightly Review*, June 14, 1883, *L&D*, 30: 233. It is unclear whether this letter was sent.

41. J. W. Bowden to JHN, October 11, 1841; JHN to R. W. Church, December 25, 1841; JHN to M. R. Giberne, December 27, 1841, *L&D*, 8: 294, 387, 392.

42. JNM to JHN, October 6, 1845; see also JHN to JNM, October 9, 14, 1845, *L&D*, 11: 13n., 13-14, 16-17.

43. Richard J. Helmstadter, "The Reverend Andrew Reed, 1787-1862: Evangelical Pastor as Entrepreneur," in R. W. Davis and R. J. Helmstadter, eds., *Religion and Irreligion in Victorian Society: Essays in Honor of R. K. Webb* (London: Routledge, 1992), pp. 7-28; Harold H. Rowdon, "Secession from the Established Church in the Early Nineteenth Century," *Vox Evangelica*, 3 (1964): 76-88.

44. [Richard Whately], *Letters on the Church by an Episcopalian* (London: Longman, Ress, Orme, Brown, and Green, 1826).

45. [Bonamy Price]., "Newman's *History of the Arians*," *Edinburgh Review*, 63 (1836): 65.

46. JHN to M. Holmes, March 8, 1843, Newman Microfilms, reel 43, batch 36.

47. EBP to W. F. Hook, undated, autumn 1845, Pusey-Hook Correspondence (Transcripts), Pusey House; [Henry Rogers], "Recent Developments in Puseyism," *Edinburgh Review*, 80 (1844): 310, 311, 318, 322, 326; *Morning Herald*, May 21, 1845, p. 10.

48. *Morning Herald*, February 24, 1845, p. 4. This point had been made even before the appearance of *Tract 90*.

49. There was to be a third instance of judicial condemnation in Newman's life in 1853 in the Achilli Case; see Sheridan Gilley, *Newman and His Age* (London: Darton, Longman and Todd, 1990), pp. 269-274.

50. JHN to M. R. Giberne, November 13, 1843, Newman Microfilms, reel 43, batch 36.

51. FWN to JHN, August, 1845; see also JHN to FWN, August, 1845, "Copies of Letters," N. IV, book 2, letters 182, 183, Newman Microfilms, reel 81, batch 107.

52. JHN to M. R. Giberne, November 13, 1843, Newman Microfilms, reel 43, batch 36.

53. Less than a year after entering the Roman Catholic Church, Newman recalled his

first conversion and subsequent reading of Joseph Milner's history. JHN to H. Wilberforce, September 24, 1846, *L&D*, 11: 252.

54. John Hamilton Thom, ed., *The Life of the Rev. Joseph Blanco White, Written by Himself; with Portions of His Correspondence* (London: John Chapman, 1845), 2: 34–35; F. W. Faber to a Friend, January 1835, John Edward Bowden, *The Life and Letters of Frederick William Faber, D.D.* (Baltimore: John Murphy, 1869), p. 43.

55. *Christian Observer*, 44 (1844): 731, 732, 742.

56. Richard Westmacott to JHN, July 8, 1845, Birmingham Oratory.

57. See Liddon, *Pusey*, 3: 1–32, 191–200.

58. JHN to J. D. Dalgairns, November 9, 1845, *L&D*, 11: 29; J. R. Hope to JHN, November 1, 1845, Birmingham Oratory. See also JHN to J. R. Hope, November 28, 1845, (*L&D*, 11: 46–48), in which he clearly backs off from the idea of maintaining any group that might appear as a party. On future plans, see JHN to J. D. Dalgairns, November 9, 1845, and JHN to T. F. Knox, August 20, 1846, *L&D* 11: 30, 226–228.

59. JHN to M. Holmes, August 15, 1841, *L&D*, 8: 247.

60. *Development*, pp. 382, 246; JHN to F. W. Faber, February 17, 1849, *L&D*, 13: 56.

61. Journal, February, 1828; "My Illness in Sicily," *AW*, pp. 123, 213; JHN to JNM, Epiphany Eve, 1860, *L&D*, 19: 272; JHN to M. Holmes, August 5, 1861, *L&D*, 20, 23; JHN to JNM, May 19, 1867; Note dated October 23, 1877; JHN to EBP, October 7, 1878; JHN to M. R. Giberne, January, 1882, *L&D*, 23: 234; 28: 256n., 406; 30: 48. See also JHN to M. R. Giberne, January 4, 1864; JHN to A. St. John, Epiphany, 1864; JHN to Louisa Elizabeth Deane, January 7, 1874; JHN to Robert Monteith, July 9, 1877; JHN to R. W. Church, January 5, 1878; JHN to EBP, October 7, 1878, *L&D*, 21: 6, 7; 27: 6; 28: 220, 295, 406.

62. In regard to Newman's comments on Mary in the *Essay on Development*, Gladstone took special offence. See W. E. Gladstone to S. Wilberforce, December 10, 1845, and W. Gladstone to H. Manning, Dec. 23, 1845, William Gladstone Papers, British Library, Add. Mss. 44343, f. 83; 44247, f. 249. See also [J. B. Mozley], "Newman on Development," *Christian Remembrancer*, 13 (1847): 151–162, and [H. H. Milman], "Newman on the Development of Christian Doctrine," *Quarterly Review*, 77 (1846): 448–451. The issue of Newman and Marian devotion in the Roman Catholic Church goes well beyond the boundaries of the present study, but for confirmation of Newman's devotion to Mary, see W. B. Ullathorne to the Editor of the *Tablet*, April 4, 1866, *L&D*, 24: 341–344; on Newman's concern about Marian devotion and good taste, see JHN to M. Holmes, September 6, 1841; JHN to Ambrose L. Phillipps, September 12, 1841; JHN to Mrs. William Froude, January 2, 1855, *L&D*, 8: 261–265, 268–271; 16: 341; John Henry Newman, *Discourses Addressed to Mixed Congregations*, 2d ed. (London: Longman, Brown, Green, and Longmans, 1850), pp. 362–402. An image of the Virgin Mary is on the title page of the last cited work.

63. *Development*, pp. 405, 406, 438.

64. Isaac Williams, *The Autobiography of Isaac Williams, B.D.*, ed. George Prevost (London: Longmans, Green, 1892), p. 61. I wish to thank Professor Linda Peterson for reminding me of this passage.

65. JHN to H. Wilberforce, January 1841, *L&D*, 8: 3; JHN to A. Hutchison, December 2, 1850; JHN to J. Walter, December 6, 1850, *L&D*, 14: 152–153, 161–162, and 153n., 159n.; JHN to J. D. Dalgairns, July 6, 1846, *L&D*, 11: 196; JHN to H. Wilberforce, January 12, 1848, *L&D*, 12: 153–154. John Newman apparently offered this print to Francis during his student years, but Francis regarded it as Romish. Consult J. H. Newman, "Two Papers from 1879," Newman Microfilms, reel 14, batch 80, ref. A. 26. 13; F. W. Newman, *Contributions to the Early History of the Late Cardinal Newman, with Comments* (London: Kegan Paul, Trench, Trübner, 1891), pp. 18–23. See also *L&D*, 23: 318n., and N. Wiseman to Dr. Murray, undated, 1845, Wilfrid Ward, *Life and Times of Cardinal Wiseman*, 2d ed. (London: Longmans, Green, 1897), 1: 433. See also P. Paul Schneider, "Das Marienbild des Anglikanischen Newman," *Newman Studien*, 2 (1954): 103–119.

66. *Development*, p. 423.

67. JHN to J. D. Dalgairns, June 6, 1846, *L&D* 11: 195; JHN to J. M. Capes, In Vigil N. Dñe, 1850, *L&D*, 14: 173

68. JHN to H. Wilberforce, December 13, 1846, *L&D* 11: 294;

69. JHN to N. Wiseman, February 23, 1847; JHN to A. St. John, November 9, 1855; JHN to R. Stanton, May 27, 1856; JHN to R. B. Tillotson, October 31, 1856, *L&D*, 12: 52; 17: 45, 248, 431. See also JHN to Cardinal Fransoni, October 18, 1855; JHN to J. R. Hope-Scott, December 20, 1860, *L&D*, 17: 8–11; 19: 443–446, as well as letters and annotation on the split between the London and Birmingham houses throughout *L&D*, vol. 17.

70. *Apologia*, p. 252.

71. Williams, *Autobiography*, pp. 61n.–62n.; *Apologia*, p. 252. In 1864 the Birmingham Fathers were Ambrose St. John (1815–1875), Henry Austin Mills (1823–1903), Henry Bittleston (1818–1886), Edward Caswall (1814–1878), William Paine Neville (1824–1905), and Henry Dudley Ryder (1837–1907). Except for St. John, none of them had been among the 1845 converts. Once those converts associated with the Littlemore years had entered the Roman Catholic Church, Newman reexperienced the very kind of rejection of deference that he had first encountered with his brothers during the 1820s. In 1863 he recalled the scene at Maryvale during 1846, "J. B. Morris undertook to lecture me. This has been the way with those who had been Protestants, & who felt themselves (seemingly) on a level with me now. Morris lectured me as the organ of Dr. Wiseman, Dalgairns lectured me still more from France, as the organ of M. Laurent, John Walker lectured me, from the inspiration of Dr. Acqueroni, Capes had lectured us from Prior Park, as put up to it by Dr. Baggs. A smaller fry afterwards presumed to cut at me, and at a later date others, whom just now I cannot call to mind." Journal, January 21, 1863, *AW*, p. 255. See also JHN to D. Moriarty, May 8, 1870, *L&D*, 25: 122.

72. Frank M. Turner, *Contesting Cultural Authority: Essays in Victorian Intellectual Life* (Cambridge: Cambridge University Press, 1993), pp. 38–72.

Index

Aaron, 500

Abbott, Jacob, 239, 329

Abiram, 182

Achilli, Giovanni, 4

Aikin, Lucy, 675n1

Albert, Prince, 553

Albury Conferences, 39–40

Anderson, Benedict, 42–43

Andrewes, Lancelot, 107, 165, 304

Anglican Mission in America, 722n30

Anglo-Catholicism, 333, 256, 349, 442, 473

Anorexia, 434–435. *See also* Asceticism; Fasting; Homosexuality

Anticatholicism, 40–41, 311, 313. *See also* Anti-Romanism

Antichrist, 264, 267, 290, 295–296, 362, 509

Antioch, Council of, 509

Antiquity, 23, 35, 283, 305, 312, 335, 338–340, 373, 383, 392–393, 496, 508, 516, 518, 566, 568–569, 571, 574, 585, 610

Anti-Romanism, 9, 311–313, 341–342, 528–529, 702n124

Apocrypha dispute, 39

Apostasy, cultural. *See* Cultural apostasy

Apostles Creed, 356, 298

Apostolicals (and related terms), 84, 127, 164, 293, 342, 426

Apostolical succession, 154, 168–174, 177, 185, 200, 277, 594

Arianism, 218, 263, 518, 633. *See also* Newman, John Henry—Published works, *The Arians of the Fourth Century*

Arius, 144, 186

Arminians, 371

Arnold, Matthew, 1, 77, 256, 641

Arnold, Thomas, 215–216, 223, 231, 420, 439–440, 453, 460, 467, 497, 516, 534, 556, 655n21, 675n90, 707n68; relationship with J. Keble, 72–73, 77–78, 81; defends Hampden, 250–251; portrait, 251; appointed Regius Professor of Modern History, 395

Articles of religion, use of, 99–102. *See also* Blomfield, Charles J.; Clerical subscription; Hampden, Renn Dickson; Newman, John Henry; Oakeley case; Pusey, Edward Bouverie; Subscription, university; 39 Articles; Ward, William George

Asceticism, 79, 97, 103–109, 158–159, 415–425. *See also* Celibacy; Fasting; Monasticism

Ashley, Lord. *See* Cooper, Anthony Ashley

Athanasian Creed, 298, 563

Atiyah, P. A., 445–446

Atonement, 28–30, 42–43, 57–58, 106, 135, 218, 271, 286, 288, 392, 394, 438, 447. *See also* Justification by faith; Reserve; Williams, Isaac

Avillon, J. B. E., 520

Badeley, Edward Lowth, 541, 604–607, 612

Baggs, Charles Michael, 558

Bagot, Richard, 100, 321, 376, 390, 394, 396, 398–399, 406, 412, 414, 425, 436, 455, 457, 459–461, 467, 469, 471, 479, 532, 556, 560, 592, 627; revokes Bulteel's license, 50; permits Maria Barker Pusey's conditional baptism, 106; *1838* charge, 320; cautions Newman on activities of his followers, 337; *1841* negotiation with Newman, 370–375; inquiry about Littlemore, 413; on *Tract 90*, 441; importance of presence to Tractarian Movement, 548–553; removal from diocese of Oxford, 551–553

Balaam, 281

Baptism, 14, 30, 91, 16–107, 112, 187–193, 197, 202, 267–270, 273–275, 277, 373, 392, 402, 447. *See also* Pusey, Edward Bouverie; *Tracts* 67, 68, 69

Baptist Midland Association, 45

Baptists, 182

Barberi, Dominic, 419–420, 545–547, 554, 558

Barker, Maria. *See* Pusey, Maria Barker

Barrow, John, 481

Bayly, Edmund Goodenough, 224, 236

Bebbington, David, 27

Bede, 493

Bellasis, Edward, 541

Bethell, Christopher, 437

Beveridge, William, 165

Bible, 67, 96–97, 120–121, 564–569, 571, 574, 585, 640. *See also* Newman, John Henry; Scripture; *Tract 85*

Bible Christians, 264–265, 447–448

Bible Society. *See* British and Foreign Bible Society

Biblical Figures. *See specific names*

Birmingham Oratory. *See* Oratory of St. Philip Neri

Blomfield, Charles J., 209, 101–102, 145, 236, 356, 372, 398, 437–439, 546, 549, 551, 564, 583, 615, 622, 688n41; on Pusey's *Historical Inquiry*, 99–101; advice to Palmer, 372; clash with Oakeley, 536–538; comment on Newman's potential secession, 546, 615; on Bagot, 552

Bloxam, John Rouse, 334, 337, 344, 387, 389, 406

Bowden, John William, 165, 176, 182–183, 193–194, 227, 293, 322, 336, 364, 426, 470, 480, 550, 616, 625

Bowles, Frederick S., 416, 550

Breviary, 90, 166, 290, 293, 300, 305, 373, 423

Bridgewater Treatises, 324

Briggs, Asa, 17

British and Foreign Bible Society, 15, 39, 60–62, 120–121, 124, 133–134, 142, 144, 223, 322, 413, 618

British and Foreign Review, 405, 488

British Association for the Advancement of Science, 62, 142, 322–323

British Critic, 2, 198, 313–314, 317, 319, 321, 334, 345, 340, 375, 380, 382, 384, 395, 420, 428, 436, 456–457, 459–462, 465–466, 468–469, 471, 480, 483, 498, 503, 506, 516, 521, 524, 532, 536, 556, 578–579, 595, 597, 609, 629

British Magazine, 84, 157, 207, 225, 242, 295, 301, 488

British Society For Promoting the Religious Principles of the Reformation, 40

"Broad churchmen," 653n55

Brooke, John, 61

Brownson, Orestes, 561, 580–581, 591

Bucer, Martin, 204

Buchman, Frank, 2

Bull, William, 165

Buller, Anthony, 165, 184–185

Bulteel, Henry B., 49–51, 100, 130, 132, 318, 342, 405, 464, 549, 617

Bunsen, Christian Charles Josias, Baron von, 395

Bunting, Jabez, 56

Bunyan, John, 33

Burnet, Gilbert, 329

Burton, Edward, 50, 220–221, 318

Butler, Joseph, 513

Butler, William Archer, 568, 577, 579, 582

Calvin, John, 41, 346

Calvinism (and cognates), 45, 30, 50, 57–58, 67, 112, 116, 118, 120, 186, 188, 201, 203–204, 288, 290–291, 304, 318, 320, 371, 385, 396, 441, 658n65

Cambridge University, 212

Canterbury, Archbishop of. *See* Howley, William

Capes, John Moore, 637

Cardale, John Bate, 47–48

Cardwell, Edward, 225, 247, 366

Carlyle, Thomas, 328, 413, 499

Cartwright, Thomas, 204

Catholic, problematic character of term, 293

Catholic Apostolic Church, 48, 89, 293, 617

Catholic emancipation, 16–17, 67–68, 71, 99

Catholicism, 158, 161, 304, 313, 329, 333–341, 352, 358, 436, 519, 534, 605, 621–622, 624

Caughey, James, 46

Celibacy, 127, 130, 149, 155, 294, 319, 339, 425, 429, 434–435, 475, 523, 624, 626–627, 631, 635–636, 641, 708n84; Froude's, 81, 83, 90; Newman's, 113, 428–431; Pusey on, 430–431; Morris, Faber, Newman correspondence on, 431–433; late resentment of those drawn to ideal of, 435–436. See also *Lives of the English Saints*

Chadwick, Henry, 677n23

Chalmers, Thomas, 38, 46, 58, 61, 324

Channing, William Ellery, 327

Chester, Bishop of. *See* Sumner, John Bird

Chillingworth, William, 551

Christ, 28–30, 37, 58, 67, 136–138, 141, 156, 172, 176–178, 183–184, 208–209, 226, 269–271, 273, 285–288, 296, 307, 315, 338, 391,

393–394, 439, 446–450, 463–464, 489, 521, 573, 583, 599, 602, 633

Christian Herald, 39

Christian Observer, 40, 168, 173, 191–192, 223, 253, 266, 276, 308–309, 312, 355, 400, 404, 520, 531, 589, 627

Christian Reformer, 569

Christian Witness, 51

Christie, Albany, 416

Christie, John Frederick, 150

Christmas, Henry, 592

Church, Richard W., 162, 334, 343, 481, 529, 544, 563, 616; on celibacy, 431

Church Catholic, 89–90, 160, 163, 265, 273, 278, 282, 315–316, 340, 401, 412, 438, 442, 500, 510, 545–546, 551, 597, 605, 618, 622

Church Missionary Society, 43, 121, 130–132, 134, 136, 413

Church of Scotland, 615, 617. *See also* Chalmers, Thomas; Irving, Edward

Churton, Edward, 399, 459, 693n95

Clapham Sect, 25, 27, 31, 94

Clarendon Code, 45

Clarke, Adam, 237

Claughton, Thomas Legh, 106, 232

Clericalism, sacramental, 174–180, 188–189, 267–268, 665n23

Clerical itinerancy, 45, 600

Clerical subscription, 356, 365, 391, 441–443, 474, 520, 530

Close, Francis, 96–97

Cobbe, Frances Power, 32, 60

Coffin, Robert Ashton, 416, 481

Coleridge, Edward, 594

Coleridge, J. D., 594

Coleridge, J. T., 73, 76–80, 237, 529

Coleridge, Samuel Taylor, 56, 328, 330

Confession, 79, 107–108, 333, 419

Congregationalists, 20

Conservative Journal, 452

Contracts, observance of, 443–446

Conventicle Act, repeal of, 45

Convocation, Oxford University, 166, 207, 216, 226, 234, 246, 367, 376, 523, 526, 535, 537, 564, 608, 621; Peel re-election, 18, 127; Hampden censure, 247, 253; Newman's apprehension of, 398–399, 530–532; Ward condemnation, 529; *Tract 90* escapes condemnation, 529–530

Convocation of *1662,* 383

Cooper, Anthony Ashley (Lord Ashley; later seventh Earl of Shaftesbury), 396, 398

Copeland, W. J., 247, 334, 343

Copleston, Edward, 66, 68, 70, 116, 231, 248, 437, 441–442, 550; portrait, 117

Copleston, William James, 150

Cornish, Charles, 343

Corporation Act of *1661,* repeal of, 16

Corpus Christi Common Room Committee, 222, 234–236, 244, 252–253

Cosin, John, 165, 237

Court of Arches, 538–542, 621–623

Cranmer, Thomas, 148, 310, 378

Creed of Pope Pius IV, 563

Crellius, 216, 218

Croker, John Wilson, 551

Crosthewaite, John Cross, 491–495

Cullen, Paul, 3

Cultural apostasy, 294, 641

Dalgairns, John Dobree, 334, 387, 397, 407, 416–420, 425–426, 481–483, 486–487, 489–492, 494–495, 514, 524, 547, 555, 558, 565, 594, 596–597, 599, 612–613, 623, 629, 631, 636–638, 705n38, 720n14

Darby, John Nelson, 32, 48–51, 89–90, 124, 617

Darbyites, 161

Darwin, Charles, 332, 584

Dathan, 182

David, 463, 501

Davison, John, 66

Deists, 192

DeMaistre, Joseph, 505

Denison, George A., 150

Dennison, Edward, 436

Dewar, Edward H., 581–582

Disciplina arcani, 143, 145, 294, 309, 341

Dispensation of Paganism, 136, 143, 145, 496

Disraeli, Benjamin, 413

Dissent, Dissenters, 12–16, 18–20, 25–31, 43–45, 51–52, 60–61, 71–72, 157, 255, 292, 334, 353, 427, 608–609; Keble view of, 76–78; lack of apostolical succession, 170–171; Tractarian denigration of, 180–187; admission to Oxford, 207–211. *See also* Methodism, Methodists

Doddridge, Philip, 35, 242, 406, 600

Dodsworth, William, 334

Donatists (and cognates), 335, 341, 453, 471, 603

Dornford, Joseph, 69, 149

Dow, Lorenzo, 46

Drummond, Henry, 39

Dublin Review, 336, 405, 455, 509, 577, 603

Ealing School, 111, 640

Eden, Charles Page, 165, 454, 534

Edinburgh Review, 251, 444, 488, 520, 541, 580, 618, 620

Edwards, Jonathan, 28, 31
Egfrid, Prince, 494
Elgar, Edward, 1
Elijah, 406, 409–411, 462–463, 541, 613, 621, 627
Elisha, 239, 409–410
Emerson, Ralph Waldo, 580
English Review, 468, 555, 568, 576
Episcopal authority. *See* Apostolical succession
Episcopal Tradition, 307–308
Equity, changing concept of, 445–446
Erastianism, 22
Erskine, Thomas, 239
Essays and Reviews, 9–11, 101, 246, 280, 299, 325
Essenes, 626, 697n53
Eucharist, 106, 178, 197, 202, 318, 309–310, 373, 394
Eustachia, 494
Eutychians, 335
Evangelical religion: generational change, 24–27, 39–41; conversion and affectionate religion, 26, 28–33; chief doctrines of, 27; home and family, 33–34, 113; biblical emphasis, 34–38; radicalization of, 39–41; clerical itinerancy, 40, 600; invisible church, concept of, 41–46; church establishment, 43–45, 176, 187, 650n30; seceders from, 46–52; as religion of the public sphere, 52–56; commercial life, 56–63, 142, 444–445; natural theology, 61–62, 142; early response to *Tracts for the Times*, 173-174. *See also* Atonement; Baptism; *Christian Observer;* Clapham Sect; Dissent, Dissenters; Justification by faith; Methodism; *Record;* Scripture; Ultra-Protestantism; Wesleyans
Evans, Marian, 32, 425
Evidences, study of, 324–325
Exeter Hall, 52, 413, 678n52

Faber, Frederick William, 298–299, 334, 431–436, 462, 481, 486–487, 489–490, 492–495, 524–525, 626, 631, 634, 637–638
Faber, Geoffrey, 425
Faber, George Stanley, 569, 578–579
Fairbairn, Andrew Martin, 565, 584
Fasting, 81–82, 104–107, 339, 419–420, 423, 433–435, 591, 658n63. *See also* Asceticism; Littlemore
Faussett, Godfrey, 220, 318–319, 320, 357, 456, 460, 556
Finney, Charles Grandison, 46
Five Mile Act, repeal of, 45
Food. *See* Fasting
Foreign and Colonial Quarterly Review, 465
Foundations, 101
Fraser's Magazine, 582

Frederick William IV of Prussia, 395, 600
Free Church of Scotland, 47, 405, 615, 617
Froude, Catherine Holdsworth, 507–512, 611. *See also* Froude, Mr. and Mrs. William
Froude, James Anthony, 32, 359, 481, 487, 507
Froude, Mr. and Mrs. William, 507, 525, 530, 533, 535, 604
Froude, Mrs. William. *See* Froude, Catherine Holdsworth
Froude, Richard Hurrell, 2, 65–66, 68–69, 79, 91, 93, 110, 115, 126–127, 135, 146, 150, 153, 158–159, 164–165, 179–180, 220, 228–229, 261, 294, 308, 468, 507, 514–515, 518, 609, 617–618, 624, 656n39; *Remains*, 2, 80, 82, 86, 90, 198, 313–321, 332, 338–339, 355, 363, 379, 380–381, 384, 386–387, 420, 433, 437, 442, 466, 469, 510, 541; opposes Peel's re-election, 18; fasting and asceticism, 80–82; Mediterranean trip, 83; on ecclesiastical establishments, 83–84, 87–88; dislike of traditional high churchmen, 84; criticism of Reformation, 85–86, 90, 317, 339; on 39 Articles, 85, 87, 685n1; conversations with Wiseman, 86–87; on Nonjurors, 87; on church discipline, 87–88; refounding the national church, 88–89; influence on Newman, 89–90; on frequent communion, 179; death of, 230, 258; on Prophetical Tradition, 298; late Tractarians drawn to, 317; on Keble, 655n19; on position of pulpit and altar, 666n231
Froude, Robert, 83, 169, 314

Gaisford, Thomas, 227
Garbett, James, 398
Geneva, 186, 261, 283, 401
George IV, 17
Gibbon, Edward, 476, 572
Giberne, Maria, 258, 345, 357, 473, 507, 528, 551, 616, 623, 629, 632, 635
Gilbert, Alan, 26
Gilbert, Ashurst Turner, 225, 400, 454, 553
Gilley, Sheridan, 27, 299
Gisborne, Thomas, 59
Gladstone, William Ewart, 32, 58, 108, 221, 454, 472–473, 510, 514, 532, 535, 585, 593, 604–605, 673n80, 692n87; regret over Hampden censure, 245; role in poetry professorship contest, 399; criticism of radical Catholicism, 465–467; on Newman-Manning correspondence of October *1843*, 469–472; on *Lives of the English Saints*, 483–484; on Ward, 521–522
Globe, 588
Golightly, Charles Pourtales, 154, 365–366, 526, 534–535, 665n26

Gordon, Charles George, 1
Gorham Judgment, 21–22, 188
Grant, Johnson, 44, 650n30
Great Disruption, 89, 694n3
Gregory XVI, 561
Greswell, Edward, 222

Habermas, Jürgen, 53–55
Hadleigh Conference, 84, 153, 300, 515, 609
Haldane, Alexander, 40
Hammond, Henry, 304
Hampden, Renn Dickson, 66, 101, 167, 194, 201, 206, 208, 216, 259, 265, 300, 357, 366, 395, 401, 456–457, 460, 502, 530, 573, 577, 669n12, 674n83, 675n90; brought back to Oriel as tutor, 69; signs Oxford petition against subscription reform, 208, 210; *Observations on Religious Dissent*, 208–212, 219–220, 226, 245, 247; Bampton Lectures, 209, 218; rivalry with Newman, 212–214; portrait, 213; clash with Pusey over subscription, 217; Newman effort to publish pamphlet collection against, 218–220; controversy over his appointment as Regius Professor of Divinity, 221–234; accused of rationalism, 235–236; censured, 247, 253; defense of himself, 274–249; on development of doctrine, 579–580, 583–585; characterization of Tractarians, 590
Hare, Julius, 245, 587–588
Harrison, Benjamin, 165, 171, 230, 297, 309, 589
Hawkins, Edward, 66, 82, 115, 124–127, 132, 149, 150–152, 212, 244–246, 307, 320, 367, 395, 412, 417, 426, 440, 514, 553–534, 556, 565, 578, 586, 609, 625, 669n9, 674n83; elected Oriel Provost, 68; blocks Oriel tutorial reform, 68–69, 128–129; early friendship with Newman, 118–121; portrait, 129; on Oxford subscription reform, 214–217; on clerical subscription to 39 Articles, 355–356; Pusey's suspension, 455–456; on Newman's resignation of Oriel fellowship, 543–544
Heads of Houses. *See* Hebdomadal Board
Heathcote, William, 78
Hebdomadal Board, 208, 212–213, 243, 247, 367, 405, 530–531, 539, 609, 622
Hegel, G. F. W., 602
Helmstadter, Richard, 617
Hempton, David, 24
Henry VIII, 304
High Church, defined, 12–13; criticism of evangelicals, 45; split with Tractarians over Reformation, 300–301; general attack on radical Tractarians, 465–473. *See also* Churton, Edward; Faussett, Godfrey; Gladstone, William

Ewart; Hook, Walter Farquar; Palmer, William; Rose, Hugh James
Hildebrand, 329
Hill, John, 222–223
Hilton, Boyd, 29, 57
Hinds, Samuel, 67
Hoadley, Benjamin, 237
Holland, third Lord, 224, 237, 249
Holmes, Maria, 430, 507, 594–596, 619, 632, 635
Holy Spirit, Theology of, 599
Homilies, Book of, 275, 392, 361–362, 371, 378, 402, 618
Homosexuality, 425–436
Honesty, 439–446, 520
Hook, Walter Farquar, 242, 245, 286, 371, 373, 396, 398, 466, 488, 589, 613, 619, 688–689n45
Hope, James Robert, 376, 397–398, 400–401, 411, 482–484, 538, 550, 560, 605
Hort, Fenton John Anthony, 7–8
Howard, Luke, 61
Howley, William, 165, 221, 224, 227, 231, 233, 244–245, 247, 413, 367, 372, 390, 396, 413, 457, 459–460, 530, 549, 552–553, 671n48. *See also* Bagot, Richard
Hume, David, 180, 263, 330, 475, 504, 565, 666n32
Huntingdon, Selina Countess, 345–346, 621
Hutton, R. H., 168
Huxley, Thomas Henry, 111, 275, 678n37

Idealism, German, 599–603
Incarnation, 172
Independents, 182, 263
Inglis, Robert, 18, 68
Innocent III, Pope, 585
Investigator, 39
Invisible Church, 41–44, 264, 620
Ireland, 16–17, 194, 223
Irish Temporalities Act, 18–19, 69–71, 146–147, 153
Irons, William J., 580
Irving, Edward, 32, 47–48, 293
Irvingites, 182, 405, 617
Ishmael, 463

Jacob, 463
Jager, Jean Nicolas, 297–298, 307–308
Jay, Elizabeth, 27
Jehu, 410
Jelf, Richard W., 370, 383, 412, 456–457, 459, 553–554
Jenkyns, Henry, 148–149
Jenkyns, Richard, 456
Jenner Fust, Herbert, 538–540, 542

Jerusalem Bishopric, 395–397, 399, 405, 454, 510, 527, 605–606, 627

Jesus. *See* Christ

Jewel, John, 329, 378, 380

Jews, 96, 182. *See also* Newman, John Henry— Theological and ecclesiastical themes, Development

John I, Pope, 490

John Paul II, Pope, 1

Jonathan, 463

Jowett, Benjamin, 280

Judas, 280

Justification by faith, 120, 266–275, 359, 391, 438, 447, 516–518. *See also* Atonement; Evangelical religion; Newman, John Henry— Theological and ecclesiastical themes, Justification; Reserve; William, Isaac

Kant, Immanuel, 54

Kaye, John, 439, 442

Keble, John, 2, 65, 80, 82–84, 91–92, 107, 110, 127, 147, 154, 158–159, 163–165, 169, 175–177, 180, 185–186, 218–219, 221, 223, 284, 292, 328, 334, 343, 350–351, 355, 367, 368, 371, 373, 374, 387, 390, 396, 398–399, 401, 428, 460, 462, 466, 471, 478–479, 496, 507, 511, 513, 514, 518, 521, 525–526, 528–529, 535, 546, 555, 586, 593, 628–629, 655nn19,21; opposes Peel's re-election, 18; sermon on national apostasy, 19, 69–71, 153, 168; Oriel election, 68; years in Oriel, 72–73; advice to Thomas Arnold, 72–73; years in father's parish, 73–74; Christian *Year*, 74; poetry professorship, 74, 127; portrait, 74; critique of religious feelings, 74–75; on ecclesiastical establishment, 76; hostility to evangelicalism, 76–77, 79; break with Thomas Arnold, 77–78; hostility to Dissent, 76, 78; marriage, 78, 89, 230, 426; achieves his own parish, 78–79; confession, 79; relationship to youthful R. H. Froude, 80–81; Pusey's confessor, 107; on apostolical succession, 171–172; survey of contemporary Christendom, 186–187; on Reformation, 199; on rationalism, 237; on primitive tradition, 306–307; edits Froude's *Remains*, 314–316; Preface to second installment of Froude's *Remains*, 338–340; defends *Tract 90*, 376–377; on tension between asceticism and Catholicism, 415–416; on Oakeley's case, 541; counseling Newman, 452–455; on sacraments, 665n23; on problem with his curate's ordination, 689n49

Keble, Mrs. John, 428

Keble, Thomas, 165, 284, 516

Ken, Thomas, 304

Kilvert, Francis, 414

Kingsley, Charles, 4–7, 435, 646

Korah, 181, 184

Labouré, Catherine, 636

Latitudinarian (and cognates), 13, 278–279, 289, 322, 329, 349–350

Laud, William, 12, 303

Law, George Henry, 548

Lazarus, 280

Leo XIII, Pope, 5

Liberals and Liberalism, 9–11, 23, 133–134, 142, 223, 277, 289

Library of Anglo-Catholic Theology, 166, 294, 358

Library of the Fathers, 166, 294

Liddon, Henry Parry, 92, 375

Lifford, James Hewitt Lord, 266

Littlemore, 3, 55, 82, 109, 197, 284, 334, 365, 386, 389–390, 395, 410, 447–448, 462, 474, 482, 490, 495, 500–502, 514, 525, 532, 535, 545, 549–550, 554, 556, 563, 576, 596–598, 600, 606, 608, 610, 612–613, 615–616, 618–619, 621, 623–624, 626–627, 629–630, 635, 637, 640, 641; Newman's plans for, 343–345; life there, 412–417; worship space, 417–419; fasting, 419–420, 433–435; dissolution of the community, 546–548

Lives of the English Saints, 334, 507, 510, 515, 520, 523, 530, 532, 535, 598, 601, 605, 613, 621, 635; origin of series, 479; Newman's prospectus, 479–480; authors, 481; editorial difficulties, 481–484; Catholic hostility to, 482–484, 496; credibility of miracles therein, 484–487; attraction to papal Rome discussed therein, 488–490; monasticism, 490–491; celibacy, 490–496; attention to virginity, 490–495; challenge to domesticity, 495

—References to specific saints: St. Aelred, 491; St. Amator, 487; St. Augustine (English), 485; St. Bartholomew, 485; St. Bega, 486, 492–493; St. Benedict, 491; St. Bettelin, 485; St. Boniface, 480; St. Cuthbert, 493, 495; St. Ebba, 487, 493–494; St. Edmund, 485; St. Ethelreda, 480; St. German, 485, 487, 494; St. Gilbert, 492; St. Gundleus, 485; St. Martin, 476; St. Neot, 487; St. Ninian, 485, 487; St. Oswin, 493; St. Richard, 484–486; St. Stephen Harding, 482–484, 487; St. Stephen Langton, 489–490; St. Thomas à Becket, 487; St. Waltheof, 486; St. Wilfrid, 487, 489–490, 492–494; St. Wulstan, 485, 487

Lloyd, Charles, 80, 93, 98–99, 102, 116, 118

Locke, John, 211

Lockhart, William, 334, 406, 415–416, 459–461, 481, 492, 552, 595, 622, 700n96

Longley, Charles Thomas, 391–392

Low church party or views, 237, 284

Loyola, Ignatius, 329

Lucifer, Bishop of Cagliari, 342

Luther, Martin, 41, 93–94, 102, 200–201, 204, 268–269, 271, 329, 346, 412

Lutheranism, 93–96, 102–103, 268–269, 329, 388, 396

Lux Mundi, 101

Lyall, William Rowe, 145–146

Maclaurin, William C. A, 349–350

Malachi, Book of, 411

Maltby, Edward, 92, 392–393

Manning, Henry, 165, 197, 259, 337, 414, 473–474, 482–483, 500–510, 532, 552, 585–587, 593, 604–605, 618, 659n3; October *1843* exchange with Newman, 469–472

Marriage. *See* Celibacy

Marriott, Charles, 165, 334, 344, 619

Martineau, James, 9

Martyrs' Monument, 455

Marx, Karl, 53

Mary, Blessed Virgin, 265, 287, 305, 319, 345, 501–502, 559, 563, 573, 585, 628, 632–634, 637, 639

Matthew, Colin, 67

Matthias, 172

Maurice, Frederick Denison, 245, 583–584

Mayers, Walter, 111–113, 115–116, 118, 126–127, 135, 424, 514, 624

Maynooth, 191, 376, 389, 636

McNeile, Hugh, 175–176

Melbourne, Lord, 207, 211, 220–221, 224–225, 230–232, 253, 395, 401; exchange with Pusey, 232–234, 667n56

Meletius. *See* St. Meletius

Menzies, Alfred, 165

Methodism, Methodists, 20, 30–31, 45–46, 88–89, 106, 144, 182, 197, 405–406, 514, 521, 567, 589, 614, 617, 621, 626, 652n44. *See also* Evangelical religion; Wesley, John; Wesleyans; Whitfield, George

Meyrick, Thomas, 481, 485

Mill, John Stuart, 53, 81, 255–256, 344, 425

Milman, Henry Hart, 498–499, 578, 582–583

Milner, Joseph, 41–42, 266, 483, 624

M'Ilvaine, Charles, 266

Miracles, 319, 475–479, 484–487. See also *Lives of the English Saints* and individual saints

Moberly, George, 577

Möhler, J. A., 505, 600

Monachism. *See* Monasticism

Monasticism, 90, 108, 155–159, 197, 294, 305, 319, 342–354, 369, 386, 390, 410–412, 426, 448, 475, 491, 524, 566, 598, 624–627. *See also* Celibacy; Littlemore

Monk, James, 393–394

Monophysites, Newman's perception of modern parallel with ancient Monophysites, 335–337, 400, 453, 471, 509, 527, 552, 603–613

Montanism, 575

More, Hannah, 25–26, 32–33

Mormon, Book of, 637

Morning Chronicle, 400, 404, 416, 459

Morning Herald, 404, 538, 542, 548, 589, 620

Morning Post, 457, 542, 589

Morning Watch, 39

Morrell, J. D., 62

Morris, John Brande, 337, 434–435, 522, 708n79, 724n71; on celibacy and asceticism, 431–433

Moses, 37, 285, 476, 501

Mozley, Harriett Newman, 110, 125, 363, 407, 425, 426, 428, 507, 529, 532, 558; marriage to Thomas Mozley, 258; near conversion of her husband, 460–462; on her brother's conversion, 544, 560, 615

Mozley, James B., 222, 258, 323–324, 326, 343, 383, 470, 483, 541, 550, 562, 572, 574, 578, 589, 604–605, 607, 612

Mozley, Jemima Newman, 111, 114, 125–126, 230, 259, 336, 344, 363, 407, 425, 461, 507, 525–526, 529, 531–535, 544, 550–551, 594, 616–617, 632, 634; marriage to John Mozley, 258

Mozley, Thomas, 154 324–325, 334, 344, 364, 474–375, 380, 394, 400, 406, 426, 436, 446, 457, 480–481, 485, 532, 552, 595–596; on rationalism, 243; marriage, 258, 428; near conversion, 460–462, 720n12

Musgrave, Thomas, 436–437, 439, 520

Mystery, Tractarian appeal to, 321–333

Naaman, 239

Naomi, 463

Napier, McNavy, 250

Natural religion, Newman's explication of, 136–137

Natural theology, 142, 323–325, 406, 565, 640

Neander, August, 483

Nestorians, 633

Nevile, Christopher, 265–266

Newman, Charles, 110–111, 117, 123–124, 128, 132–133, 136, 139, 151, 176, 262–263, 525, 534, 614, 631, 634, 639

Newman, Elizabeth, 123, 634

Newman, Francis, 11, 32, 49, 89–90, 110–113, 128, 130, 132, 134–135, 138, 139, 143, 149, 151, 200, 205, 228–230, 262–263, 392, 424, 525, 533–534, 545, 574, 594, 622, 623, 631, 634, 639; at Oxford, 122–123; associates with radical evangelicals, 124; resigns Balliol Fellowship, 133; breach between himself and John and resulting family tensions, 228–230; exchange of religious views with his brother John, 347–352; portrait, 458; advises John to start his own denomination, 613–615

Newman, Harriett. See Mozley, Harriett Newman

Newman, Jemima. See Mozley, Jemima Newman

Newman, Jemima Fourdrinier (Mrs. John Newman), 122, 130, 133, 146, 229–230, 258, 343

Newman, John, 112–114, 120, 170

Newman, John Henry

—Biographical matters: overview of his reputation and the writing of the *Apologia*, 1–11; portrays his life as a battle against liberalism, 9–12; conversion as fitting pattern of Victorian loss of faith, 11, 532–533; his career in opposition to evangelicalism, 21–23; Oriel tutorial reform collapse, 68–69, 128–129, 429, 509, 534–535, 596, 627; developing friendship with Froude, 82, 126–127; Mediterranean trip with Froudes, 83, 146–153, 261–262; influence of Froude upon, 89–90; early Oriel years and friendships, 92, 114–122; conditional baptism of Mrs. Pusey, 106–107; early childhood, 110–111; impact of father's business failures, 111, 113–114, 659n2; influence of Walter Mayers, 111–112; enters Trinity College, 112; first conversion, 112; decision for celibacy, 112–113, 426, 429–430; poor examination performance, 113; death of his father, 116, 124; St. Clement's ministry, 116–118, 122, 617; concerns about income, 122–123, 429, 660n21, 676n4, 716n64, 717n78, 701n103; religious debates with Charles Newman, 123, 132–133; conflict with Francis over latter's radical evangelicalism, 124, 132–133; death of Mary Newman, 124–126; becomes Vicar of St. Mary the Virgin, 126; organizes intercollegiate dining group, 126, 661n27; *1829* Oxford election, 127–128; sermons against evangelical theology and organizations and championing of a religion of conscience, 130–131, 133–142; Oxford Church Missionary Society dispute, 130–132; criticizes and resigns from Bible Society, 133–134, 661n38; draws parallels between ancient and modern heresy in *The Arians of the Fourth Century*, 142–146; reaction to Roman Catholicism in Italy, 146–148; dream in Naples, 149–152; desires apostolic brotherhood, 152–153, 609, 626; illness in Sicily, 153, 417; return from Italy, 153–154; articles on ancient monasticism, 154–159; apocalyptic sensibilities, 160–161, 163, 178, 292, 698–609; personal identification with the prophet Elijah, 161, 409–412, 592, 608, 627; launching of *Tracts for the Times*, 163–165, 167; failure to achieve moral philosophy professorship, 212, 227; rivalry with R. D. Hampden, 212–214, 228; effort to publish anti-Hampden pamphlet collection, 218–220; publishes *Elucidations of Dr. Hampden's Theological Statements*, 225–227; further break with Francis Newman, 228–230; death of Froude, 230; B. Harrison accuses him of rationalism, 230, 679n9; publishes tract against rationalism in religion, 239–242; further comment on Hampden, 258; death of his mother and marriages of his sisters, 258, 676n4; attack on appeal to private judgment in popular Protestantism, 258–263; shifts attacks to establishment evangelicals, 259–260; defends Pusey's tract on baptism, 266; discussion of justification by faith, 267–275; attack on Protestant understanding of Bible, 275–283; elaborates concept of Prophetical Tradition, 294–299, 307–309; Jager exchange, 297–298; *1836* exchange with Rose, 300–305; his anti-Romanism, 311–313; edits Froude's *Remains* with Keble not consulting Keble, 314–316, 683n86; attacked by Godfrey Faussett, 318–319; expands scope of Prophetical Tradition, 319–320; chastened by Bagot's *1838* charge, 320; exploration of faith and reason, 328–333; attacks Peel in "Catholicus Letters," 331; development of personal coterie, 333–334; impact of Wiseman's *Dublin Review* article, 335–337, 455; perception of modern parallel with Monophysites, 335–337, 639, 400, 453, 471, 509, 527, 552, 603–613, 684n93; followers drawn to Rome, 337–338; demand for Catholic latitude, 337–338; envisions Littlemore monastery, 343–345; publishes article sympathetic to early Methodism, 345–347; exchanges views of sectarianism with Francis Newman, 347–352; contemplates resigning St. Mary's, 350–351, 452–453, 455; faulty analysis of Oxford scene, 357; publishes *Tract 90*, 358, 364, 687n35; Hebdomadal Board condemns *Tract 90*, 365–367; Bagot negotiation, 370–375; disagreements with Pusey, 376, 382–383; sees evangelical heresy growing throughout the English Church, 389–403, 604–610; criticizes Jerusalem Bishopric, 395–397; poetry professorship contest, 398–399; sermons on reasons to remain in English Church, 406–410; asceticism of himself and his Littlemore coterie, 412–425; letter to Bagot on Littlemore, 413; vocation of edification, 413–414; desire for a monastic life, 414, 631, 624, 229, 639; sermons on asceticism, 421–422; skepticism of, 422–425; *1847* memorandum before Roman Catholic ordination, 422–424; aversion to women and difficulty with marriages of clerical friends, 425–429, 624–625, 637–638; accused of dishonesty by bishops and press, 439–446; retracts anti-Roman comments, 452; character of correspondence, 454; reaction to Pusey's suspension, 457; resignation from St. Mary's, 459–460; response to Thomas Mozley's near conversion, 460–465; attacked by Gladstone and Palmer, 465–469; October *1843* exchange with Manning; 469–472; discussion of ecclesiastical miracles, 475–479; difficulties associated with *Lives of the English Saints*, 481–484; thinking moves toward concept of doctrinal development, 496–505; discusses development in correspondence with Catherine Holdsworth Froude, 507–512; change in affections leading to change in opinions, 514; Scott's *Force of Truth* as model for religious change, 515; opposed to advanced Catholic devotions, 524–525; indecision, 525–526; three blows of *1841*; 527; proctorial veto saves *Tract 90* from condemnation, 530–531; disagreement with Ward and Oakely over 39 Articles, 531; comments on imminent departure to Rome, 532–533; recollections of personal slights against him, 534; resigns Oriel fellowship, 543, 546; conversion as a failure to establish independent congregation, 546, 623; conversions among his coterie, 547–548; reception by Father Dominic, 548; importance of Bagot to his career, 549–553; possible impact of change in bishop of Oxford, 553–556; postconversion conversation with Wiseman, 557–561; character and arguments of *Essay on Development*, 559–577; critique of *Essay on Development*, 577–586; Dewar and rationalism, 581–582; contemporary reaction to conversion, 587–592; portrait, 588; penchant for self-delimitation, 592, 639–640; anxiety over rapid religious change, 593–597; retreat from vision of reformed Catholicism, 597–603; concept of development compared with Philip Schaff's, 599–603; rejects becoming an independent sectarian, 613–617; seen as a po-

tential religious seceder, 617–618; distinction in life goals from Keble and Pusey, 628–629; possible association in his mind of the Virgin Mary and his sister Mary, 631–637; life associations with Virgin Mary, 635–636; as surrounded by celibate fathers in Birmingham Oratory, 639–641; importance of his sermons to the movement, 665n25; sense of assurances given regarding *Tract 90*, 688n42; sense of isolation among new converts, 724n71

—Comments on: Bagot, Richard, 548–553; Hampden, R. D., 241–242; Luther, Martin, 271; Milman, Henry Hart, 498–499; Mozley, Thomas, 258, 720n12; Oakeley, Frederick, 543; Presbyterians, 181; Pusey, Edward Bouverie, 92, 399, 541; Schleiermacher, Friedrich, 673n69; Sumner, John Bird, 394–395, 691n76; Ward, William George, 379–380, 400, 543, 547, 689nn54,56, 708n83

—Published works:

Apologia Pro Vita Sua, 16–11, 19, 21, 23, 110, 123, 162, 171, 248, 257, 260, 314, 329, 335, 336, 357, 396, 426, 436, 454, 527–528, 545, 549, 560, 603–604, 615, 620, 633, 638–639

Arians of the Fourth Century, The, 142–145, 154–155, 168, 176, 179, 209, 211, 295, 329, 406, 509, 625, 640

"Catholicity of the English Church, The" 340–342, 345, 471, 603–606

"Catholicus Letters," 331, 551

Certain Difficulties Felt by Anglicans in Catholic Teaching, 21–23, 335–336, 603

Church of the Fathers, 342–345, 411, 428, 475, 626

Discourses Addressed to Mixed Congregations, 603

Elucidations of Dr. Hampden's Theological Statements, 225–227, 247, 250

Essay on the Development of Christian Doctrine, An, 347, 496, 528, 558–559, 561–563, 566–577, 591, 598, 602, 629–636, 639–640, 715n58; contemporary criticism of, 577–586

Grammar of Assent, A, 1

"Home Thoughts Abroad," 157–158, 160, 184, 295–296, 301, 305, 335, 509

Idea of a University, 1, 3–4, 441

Lectures on Justification, 2, 192, 266–267, 275, 359

Lectures on the Prophetical Office of the Church, 2, 257–259, 261–262, 268, 307, 312, 345, 556, 626, 640

"Letters on the Church of the Fathers," 154–157, 160, 426, 608, 625

Letter to Dr. Faussett, 319

Newman, John Henry—Published works (continued)

Letter to Dr. Jelf, 368–370, 373

Letter to the Bishop of Oxford, 373–374, 389, 471, 561

"On Consulting the Faithful in Matters of Doctrine," 4

Postscript to the Letter to Dr. Jelf, 371–372

Sermons: "Apostolical Christian, The," 447–449, 501; "Danger to the Penitent," 524; "Feasting in Captivity," 446–447; "Influence of Natural and Revealed Religion Respectively, The," 136–137; "Obedience to God the Way to Faith in Christ," 137–238; "Parting of Friends, The," 463–464, 469, 473; "Religion of the Day, The," 141; "Religious Emotion," 138; "Religious Use of Excited Feelings, The," 138–139; "Theory of Developments in Religious Doctrines, The," 501–505; "Wisdom and Innocence," 449–452

Sermons, Bearing on Subjects of the Day, 451, 463, 509, 535

Sermons, Chiefly on the Theory of Religious Belief, 475–479, 501, 535

"State of Religious Parties, The," 328–329

Suggestions in Behalf of the Church Missionary Society, 131–132

"Tamworth Reading Room, The," 331

Tracts for the Times. See individual tracts by author

—Theological and ecclesiastical themes:

Antichrist, 295–296, 679n9. *See also* Roman Catholic Church, Roman Catholicism

Ante-Nicene fathers, 567–568

Anti-Romanism, 9, 295–296, 311–313, 341–342, 528–529, 702n124

Apostolical succession, 170–171

Baptism, 190, 238–239, 268–269, 274–275, 447

Bible Christianity, 678n49

Christian history, 566

Commercialized religion, rejection of, 617–623

Development, 496–505, 500, 503–504, 507, 569–571. *See also* Froude, Catherine Holdsworth; under Published works, *Essay on the Development of Christian Doctrine*

Dispensation of paganism, 662n55

Dissenting clergy, plight of, 170

Ecclesiastical skepticism, 11

English bishops as heretics, 470

English Church, Catholicity of, 593–594, 612

Eucharist, 680n23

Evangelical preaching, 135, 137–140, 269, 447

Evangelical Protestantism, criticisms of, 9, 21–23, 135, 237–140, 201, 256, 261, 269, 294, 345–347, 389–390, 396, 405–406, 430, 447, 627, 650n30, 665n26, 650n30. *See also* Ultra-Protestantism

Evangelical Protestantism as heresy in Church of England, 264, 389–390, 396, 405–406, 446, 604–610, 627

Faith and reason, 328–333

Heresy, ancient, sympathy for, 575–576

Judaism, Christianity a development of, 497–498, 500

Justification, 268, 447, 677n31. *See also* under Published works, *Lectures on Justification*

Marian devotion, 633–635

Monasticism. *See general index entry*

Monophysites, perception of modern parallel with, 335–337, 639, 400, 453, 471, 509, 527, 552, 603–613, 684n93

Natural theology, 330–332, 478

Obedience, 137–140

Prayers for the dead, 195, 300, 302, 321, 438

Private judgment, 256–266

Prophetical Tradition, 205, 240, 297–299, 307–308, 585. *See also* Froude, Richard Hurrell; Jager, Jean Nicolas; under Published works, *Lectures on the Prophetical Office of the Church*

Purgatory, 195, 263, 265, 295, 302, 311–312, 360, 636

Rationalism, associated with rejection of baptismal regeneration, 238–239

Reason and faith, 328–333

Reformation, 148, 200–201, 203–205, 270–271, 300, 304–305, 384, 387, 564, 677n29, 685n2, 690n68, 696n30

Roman Catholic Church, 9, 193–198, 265, 295–296, 311–313, 341–342, 528–529, 542, 574–575, 592–597, 627–628, 681nn35,38, 702n124. *See also* under Published works, "Home Thoughts Abroad," *Lectures on the Prophetical Office of the Church*

Salvability of heathen, 661n42

Scripture, 144, 264–265, 297, 503–504, 569, 574, 676n12, 699n76. *See also Tract 85;* under Published works, *Essay on the Development of Christian Doctrine;* under Theological and ecclesiastical themes, Private judgment

Sectarianism, sources of, 156–157, 196–197

Superstition, 140, 477

Theatrical religion, 696n30

39 Articles, 354, 368–370, 479, 710n10. See also *Tract 90*

Tradition, 263–264, 676n12. See also under Published works, *Lectures on Prophetical Office of the Church*

Via media, 260–261, 668n73

Newman, Mary, 111, 125, 127, 345, 631–632, 634–637

"Newmania," 333, 626

Newsome, David, 27

Newspapers. *See specific titles*

Newton, B. F., 49, 51

Nicene Council, 509, 633

Nicene Creed, 264, 298

Nicholl, Alexander, 98

Nicodemus, 239

Niebuhr, Richard, 599

Nietzsche, Friedrich, 424, 449, 478–479

Nockles, Peter, 12, 223

Noetics, 66–67, 121, 146. *See also* Oriel College

Nominal Christianity, 26, 42, 59

Nonjurors, 13, 74, 87, 147, 156, 310, 397; Froude on, 87; Newman rejects example of, 616

Norfolk, Duchess of, 428

Oakeley, Frederick, 100, 317, 334, 377, 383–385, 387, 400, 406, 417, 419, 421, 467, 481, 485, 490, 498, 500, 520, 523–524, 532, 542–543, 545, 551, 564, 576–577, 622; on Catholicism as a negative force, 290–292; Catholicism distinguished from Popery, 291; defense of *Tract 90*, 380; on clerical subscription, 381–382; on the Reformation, 381–382; Pusey's criticism of, 383–384; on revival of monasticism, 414–415; disagreement with Newman on 39 Articles, 531; case in Court of Arches, 536–544, 546, 551, 554, 576–577, 621–623

Oakeley case, 536–544, 546, 551, 554, 576–577, 621–623

O'Brien, James T., 437–439, 442

O'Connell, Daniel, 16, 194, 223

Olgilvie, Charles Atmore, 253, 456

Oratory of St. Philip Neri, 3, 598, 631, 638–640

Oriel College, 226, 555, 635, 640–641; position in early nineteenth-century Oxford life, 65–69; Noetics, 66–67; provostial election, 68; tutorial dispute, 68–69, 128–129; willingness to welcome evangelicals, 115–116; Oxford election of *1829*, 127. *See also* Copleston, Edward; Hawkins, Edward; Keble, John; Newman, John Henry; Whately, Richard

Origen, 299

Ornsby, Robert, 481

Orpah, 463, 473

Owen, Robert, 123

Owenites, 132, 134, 161, 534, 631

Oxford Chronicle and Reading Gazette, 465, 553

Oxford election of *1829*, 17–18, 68, 82–84, 166, 211, 252, 625. *See also* Froude, Richard Hurrell; Keble, John; Newman, John Henry; Oriel College; Peel, Robert

Oxford Movement, as term, 2. *See also* Buchman, Frank

Paget, Francis, 441, 549

Paine, Thomas, 565

Paley, William, 140, 324, 329

Palmer, Roundell, 232, 246, 549

Palmer, William, 84, 153, 181, 199, 200, 222, 372, 396, 459, 466, 481, 510, 512, 550, 566, 568, 579, 623; effort to begin a clerical association and involvement with early *Tracts*, 164–165; Blomfield criticizes, 372; publishes *A Narrative of Events*, 467–468, 505; advises closing of the *British Critic*, 468; begins *English Review*, 468–469; critique of concept of development, 505–507; Ward's *Ideal of a Christian Church* a response to, 515–516

Papal infallibility, 717n84

Papal supremacy, 263, 265, 506, 567, 581, 605

Parker Society, 357

Pattison, Mark, 334, 416, 428, 435, 481, 485, 487, 489, 490; on life at Littlemore, 417; Newman's comment on his marriage, 428. See also *Lives of the English Saints*

Peel, Robert, 72, 126–127, 208, 331, 400, 549, 609–610, 625; moves Catholic Emancipation, 16; *1829* Oxford election, 17–18, 68, 166, 211, 252, 625; Oxford-related ecclesiastical patronage, 412, 551–553, 714n47

Pennefather, Sergeant, 49

Perceval, Arthur P., 54, 165, 364, 396, 466; on apostolical succession, 181–182; on rationalism, 242

Phillips, Ambrose, 387, 395, 597

Phillpotts, Henry, 441

Philpot, J. C., 29, 51–52

Pietism, German, Pusey on, 94–96

Pius IV, Pope, Creed of, 563

Pius IX, Pope, 3

Plato, 291

Plymouth Brethren, 48–49, 51, 89, 124, 405, 424, 617. *See also* Darby, John Nelson; Newman, Francis

Poetry professorship contest, 398–399, 454, 510. *See also* Bagot, Richard; Gladstone, William Ewart; Newman, John Henry; Pusey, Edward Bouverie; Williams, Isaac

Pole, Reginald, 85

Pope, Simeon Lloyd, 133, 142

Popery, 158, 193, 197, 291, 312, 316–318, 320, 329, 333, 567, 586, 588; proposed series of tracts against, 194–194

Popular Protestantism, 9, 268, 326; defined, 262–263. *See also* Evangelical religion; Ultra-Protestantism

Powell, Baden, 66–67, 325–330, 332, 405, 475, 488–489, 572

Prayers for the dead, 195, 300, 302, 321, 438

Premillenialism, 39–40

Presbyterians, 181–182, 186, 201

Prevost, George, 165

Price, Bonamy, 444

Priestly, Joseph, 300, 568

Private judgment, 10, 229, 322, 351, 389, 392, 534

Prophetical Tradition, 205, 240, 297–299, 307–308, 585. *See also* Froude, Richard Hurrell; Jager, Jean Nicolas; Newman, John Henry

Protestantism: significance of Tractarian critique of, 256–257; as rationalism, 261–262. *See also* Atonement; Justification by faith; Luther, Martin; Popular Protestantism; Rationalism; Ultra-Protestantism; Zwingli, Ulrich

Prussian Lutheran Church, 600

Prussian Reformed Church, 600

Public sphere, 52–56, 258, 289, 413

Pugin, Augustus Welby, 413

Purgatory, 195, 263, 265, 295, 302, 311–312, 360, 636. *See also* Newman, John Henry; Pusey, Edward Bouverie

Puritanism (and cognates), 257, 290, 304, 385, 402, 468, 579

Pusey, Edward Bouverie, 2, 65, 68–69, 72, 110, 115, 126–127, 132, 145, 147, 158–159, 163–164, 166, 168, 175, 182, 209, 218, 219, 221–223, 225, 227, 235–236, 240, 245, 249, 252–253, 291–292, 299, 300–301, 303–304, 307, 311, 318, 333–334, 358, 364, 368, 370–371, 373, 386–387, 390, 392, 396, 411–412, 420, 426, 430, 432, 440, 454–455, 464, 466, 507, 514, 520, 522, 524–526, 530, 532–533, 535, 537, 589, 591, 593, 600, 604–605, 607, 613, 619, 621, 625, 628–629, 632; importance to Tractarian Movement, 90–91; on ecclesiastical establishments, 91–92; courtship with Maria Barker, 92, 96–98; early political liberalism, 92; and Germany, 92–93; *Historical Inquiry,* 93–96, 102–103, 145–146; articles of faith and

subscription to the 39 Articles, 95–96, 101–102, 217, 354–355; Regius Professorship of Hebrew, 98–99; privately criticized by Bishop Blomfield, 99–100; sadness of family life, 103–104; household asceticism, 103–109; on repentance and Mrs. Pusey, 104; corporal punishment of children, 105; *Scriptural Views of Holy Baptism,* 106, 167, 188–190, 202–203, 203, 255, 260, 266, 300, 667n71; on evangelical view of the atonement, 106; and confession, 107–108; favors sisterhoods, 107, 430, 629; on Reformation, 201–203, 310, 354–355, 685n2; clash with Hampden over subscription, 217; exchange with Lord Melbourne on Hampden nomination, 232–234, 667n56; on rationalism, 237–238; *Letter to the Bishop of Oxford,* 283, 289–290, 320–321, 337, 430, 355, 556; on *via media,* 289–290; on the Eucharist, 309–310; criticism of Newman's anti-Romanism, 311; on *Tract 90,* 375–376, 383; disagreement with Newman, 376, 382–383; criticism of Ward and Oakeley, 383–385, 387; on Irish Roman Catholicism, 384; poetry professorship contest, 398–399; *Letter to the Archbishop of Canterbury,* 399–403, 556; on celibacy, 430; on fasting, 434, 658n63; suspended from preaching, 455–459; portrait, 458; comment on Newman's state of mind in late *1843,* 472–473; reaction to *Lives of the English Saints,* 482; edits Roman Catholic devotional manuals, 520–521; on Oakeley case, 540–541; exchange with Samuel Wilberforce, 556–557; on Jews, 657n51; on religion of feeling, 657n52; on biblical inspiration, 657n54, 680n32; on Calvinists, 658n65; on saints' lives, 704n18

Pusey, Lucy, 107

Pusey, Maria Barker, 92, 92–98, 103–106, 126; conditional baptism of, 106–107

"Puseyite," origin of term, 91, 188, 665n22. *See also* Baptism; Pusey, Edward Bouverie; *Record*

Quakers, 182, 653n52

Radnor, seventh Earl of, 215, 217

Rambler, 4

Rational Dissent, 14, 243. *See also* Dissent, Dissenters; Unitarians

Rationalism, 104, 186, 192, 195, 200–201, 253, 261–262, 277, 283, 289–290, 352, 505–506, 581–583, 672n58; Froude introduces term, 85; Newman accused of, 230, 581–583, 679n9; meaning during Hampden dispute, 234–244; accusation against Hampden, 235–236; in *Edinburgh Review,* 236; debated by Hebdomadal Board, 236–237; Froude on, 237; Keble on, 237; Pusey on, 237–238; Newman on, 238–241; A. P. Perceval on, 242; *Record* on, 242; Thomas Mozley on, 243

Ray, John, 62

Record, 40, 188, 253, 276, 308, 317–318, 355, 367, 439, 523; "Puseyite," origin of term, 91, 188, 665n22; on early *Tracts*, 173–174; on Pusey and baptism, 190–191; opposes Hampden, 223; on rationalism, 242; on Newman and justification, 266

Records of the Church, 166

Reed, Andrew, 617

Reform Act (1832), 15–18, 25, 169

Reformation, 188, 196, 271, 393, 466, 498, 568, 627, 629; Froude on, 85–86, 317; Newman on, 148, 200–201, 203–205, 270–271, 300, 304–305, 384, 387, 564, 677n29, 685n2, 690n68, 696n3; in the *Tracts*, 198–206; Pusey on, 202–203; Ward on; 378, 518, 707n71

Religious Movement of *1833*, 2, 21

Religious Tract Society, 60

Reserve, 391, 394, 438, 582. See also *Tracts 80, 86, 87;* Williams, Isaac

Revelation, as progressive, 496

Revivalism, American, 45–46

Revolution of *1688*, 13, 87, 303, 310, 320

Rickards, Samuel, 165, 167, 178, 405, 493, 550

Rivington, Francis, 479, 483

Rivingtons, 225, 468, 484

Rogers, Frederic, 149–152, 321, 334, 336, 344, 428, 443, 453–454, 514, 604, 626, 681n44

Rogers, Henry, 444, 488, 541, 580, 620

Romaine, William, 112

Roman Catholic Church, Roman Catholicism, 157, 182, 261, 278, 283, 290–292, 294–296, 305, 329, 350, 470–471; Newman on, 9, 193–198, 265, 295–296, 311–313, 341–342, 528–529, 542, 574–575, 592–597, 627–628, 681nn35,38, 702n124; and the Noetics, 67; Froude on, 86–87; Pusey on, 96; in Italy, 146–147; in the *Tracts*, 193–198; union with, 193; specific alleged errors, 196; neglect of antiquity, 263–264; doctrine of justification, 271–272; as needing reform, 388–389; Ward on, 519

Rose, Hugh James, 84, 93, 95, 98–99, 101–102, 145–146, 153, 179, 185, 212, 225, 236, 295, 306–307, 311, 333, 356, 382, 507, 799n18; on Hampden, 220; *1836* exchange with Newman, 300–305; on antiquity, 302; on Froude's *Remains*, 318

Routh, Martin, 522

Russell, Charles, 389, 557–560, 577

Russell, Lord John, 244

Ryder, George, 147, 426

Sabellians, 263, 633

St. Ambrose, 147, 155, 230, 573

St. Anthony, 108, 156–157, 478

St. Athanasius, 108, 145, 335, 341, 354, 406, 543, 573, 575, 594, 610

St. Augustine, 354, 378, 382, 527, 543, 594

St. Basil, 145, 155, 354, 382

St. Chrysostom, 354, 382

St. Cyprian, 511

St. Francis, 346

St. Gregory, 155, 378

St. Gregory Thaumaturgus, 476

St. James, 277, 281

St. John, Ambrose, 334, 416, 547, 555, 634, 638

St. John, Gospel of, 281

St. Jude, 281

St. Luke, Gospel of, 280

St. Matthew, Gospel of, 280, 511

St. Meletius, 342, 382, 400, 406, 614

St. Paul, 42, 121, 123, 272, 277, 295, 306, 382, 450, 463, 476, 497, 501, 512, 533, 573

St. Peter, 281, 295, 382, 489, 511–512

St. Philip Neri, 346, 637

St. Simonianism, 506

Saints treated in *Lives of the English Saints.* See *Lives of the English Saints*—References to specific saints

St. Thomas, 239

Samuel, 501

Satan, 145–146, 182, 321, 391, 516, 518

Schaff, Philip, 599–602

Schleiermacher, Friedrich, 673n69

Scotland, Church of, 46–47, 186

Scott, J. R., 334

Scott, Thomas, 32, 35, 39, 58–59, 112, 212, 266, 444–445, 514–515; biblical commentary, 35–38; portrait, 36

Scott, Walter, 328, 413

Scripture: Tractarian critique of, 275–283; and private judgment, 22–263. *See also* Bible; Newman, John Henry

Seceders, evangelical, 46–52

Second Reformation, 2, 149, 205, 260

Semler, J. J., 235

Senior, Nassau, 520

Sewell, William, 219, 222, 324

Sexuality, and asceticism, 80–82, 103–105, 107–109, 113. *See also* Celibacy; Fasting; Homosexuality

Shaftesbury, Earl. *See* Cooper, Anthony Ashely

Shapin, Steven, 440

Shrewsbury, Lord, 337
Shuttleworth, Philip Nicholas, 211, 668n7
Sibthorp, R. W, 406, 461, 467, 595
Sidmouth, first Vicount, 45
Simeon, Charles, 25, 31–33, 55–57, 237, 266
Simeon Trust, 56–57, 619
Sincerity, 59, 176–177, 443–446
Sisterhoods, 207, 430–431, 629
Skepticism, 350, 474–475, 489, 495, 504–505, 513–514, 564, 580, 585, 641
Smith, Adam, 180
Smith, Mark, 26
Smith, Sidney, 249
Society for Investigating Prophecy, 39
Socinian (and cognates), 14–15, 140, 142, 154, 182, 185–187, 192–193, 200–203, 214–216, 218, 226, 228–229, 241–244, 253, 255, 261–262, 283, 287, 289–290, 304, 499, 579, 633, 669n12, 676n9
Southcottians, 182
Sozzini, Lelio, 14
Spener, Jacob, 94–95, 99
Spranger, Robert, 334, 343
Standard, 207, 404–405, 553, 588
Stanley, Arthur Penrhyn, 251–252, 367, 549
Stanton, Richard, 334, 416, 546, 548, 638
Stephen, James Fitzjames, 25, 142, 284
Stephen, Leslie, 275
Strachey, Lytton, 6
Strauss, David Friedrich, 499, 582–583
Subscription, clerical. See Clerical subscription
Subscription, university, 21, 140, 166, 207–221, 226, 332, 477. See also Hampden, Renn Dickson; Hawkins, Edward; Newman, John Henry; Pusey, Edward Bouverie; Wilberforce, Henry
Sumner, Charles, 391, 402
Sumner, John Bird, 61, 121, 127, 324, 394–395, 402, 405, 439, 705n40; influence on Newman's early theological development, 118–119; hostile 1841 charge, 390–391
Superstition, 140, 332, 477
Surin, F., 520–521
Swedenborgians, 182
Syllabus of Errors, 10
Symons, Benjamin P., 132, 416, 456, 522–523, 608

Tablet, 224, 399, 545, 590–591, 615
Tait, Archibald, 365, 367, 439, 526
Tertullian, 144
Test Act of 1673, 16
Test Act of 1678, 16
Thackray, Arnold, 62

Theological Society, 333, 376, 626
Thirlwall, Connop, 438–439, 466, 568, 575
39 Articles, 22, 100, 109, 133, 196, 198, 204, 217, 273, 275, 305, 310, 339–340, 354–355, 357–363, 367–371, 374, 377–381, 392–393, 441–443, 467, 470, 474, 479, 491, 516, 520, 523–524, 526, 530–531, 536, 538–540, 557, 622, 627, 685n1, 711n23, 711–712n25; Froude on, 85–87; as a problem for the Tractarians, 353–356. See also Articles of religion; Blomfield, Charles J.; Clerical subscription; Newman, John Henry; Oakeley, Frederick; Oakeley case; Pusey, Edward Bouverie; Subscription, university; Tract 90; Ward, William George
—Individual articles: Article 6, 393; Article 11, 359, 274; Article 12, 359; Article 13, 359; Article 21, 360; Article 22, 360; Article 31, 311, 361; Article 35, 361; Article 37, 362
Tholuck, Augustus, 238, 240, 600
Thomas, Stephen, 335
Thomas, Vaughan, 207, 222
Thornton, 25, 33
Times, The, 247, 331, 365–366, 396, 523, 531, 542, 545, 548, 551, 623
Timothy, 306–307
Tiptaft, William, 50
Tocqueville, Alexis de, 53
Toleration Act of 1812, 71
Toovey, James, 484
Tractarian Movement: use of term, 2–3; conflict with Dissent, 13; conflict with establishment evangelicals over baptism, 13–14; as Catholic Dissenters, 20–21; as schismatics, 21, 404–405; not necessarily Roman Catholic in tendency, 197–198; rejection of commercial religious tactics, 617–623
Tract 1, Thoughts on the Ministerial Commission (J. H. Newman), 169–170, 177
Tract 2, The Catholic Church (J. H. Newman), 170–171, 176
Tract 7, The Episcopal Church Apostolical (J. H. Newman), 181
Tract 10, Heads of a Week-day Lecture, delivered to a Country Congregation (J. H. Newman), 178, 197
Tract 11, The Visible Church, Letters I and II (J. H. Newman), 176
Tract 15, On the Apostolical Succession in the English Church (W. Palmer; revised and completed by J. H. Newman), 171, 181, 200
Tract 16, Advent (B. Harrison), 171
Tract 20, The Visible Church, Letter III (J. H. Newman), 193

Tract 29, Christian Liberty, or, Why Should We Belong to the Church of England (J. W. Bowden), 176, 182

Tract 30, Christian Liberty, or, Why Should We Belong to the Church of England (J. W. Bowden), continued, 182

Tract 35, The People's Interest in Their Minister's Commission (A. P. Perceval), 181

Tract 36, Account of Religious Sects at Present Existing in England (A. P. Perceval), 182

Tract 38, Via Media, No. I (J. H. Newman), 353

Tract 45, The Grounds of Our Faith (J. H. Newman), 200

Tract 47, The Visible Church, Letter IV (J. H. Newman), 183–184

Tract 51, On Dissent without Reason in Conscience (R. F. Wilson), 184

Tract 52, Sermons for Saints' Days and Holidays. No. I, St. Matthias (J. Keble), 172, 176

Tract 54, Sermons for Saints' Days and Holidays. No. II, The Annunciation of the Blessed Virgin Mary (J. Keble), 185

Tract 57, Sermons for Saints' Days and Holidays. No. III, St. Mark's Day (J. Keble), 185–186, 199

Tract 60, Sermons for Saints' Days and Holidays. No. IV, St. Philip and St. James (J. Keble), 176–177

Tract 61, The Catholic Church a Witness against Illiberality (A. Buller), 184

Tracts 67, 68, 69, Scriptural Views of Holy Baptism (E. B. Pusey). *See* Baptism; Pusey, Edward Bouverie

Tract 71, On the Controversy with the Romanists (No. I, Against Romanism) (J. H. Newman), 199, 194, 265

Tract 72, Archbishop Ussher on Prayers for the Dead (No. II, Against Romanism) (preface, J. H. Newman), 195, 300

Tract 73, On the Introduction of Rationalistic Principles into Religion (J. H. Newman), 239–240. *See also* Rationalism

Tract 77, An Earnest Remonstrance to the Author of "The Pope's Letter" (E. B. Pusey), 300

Tract 79, On Purgatory (No. III, Against Romanism) (J. H. Newman), 195, 312

Tract 80, On Reserve in Communicating Religious Knowledge (Isaac Williams), 283; directed against Low Church party, 284; divine revelation gradual, 285; necessity of obedience, 285–286; critique of religious enthusiasm, 286; critique of frequent preaching of the atonement,

286–287. *See also* Atonement; Reserve; Williams, Isaac

Tract 83, Advent Sermons on Antichrist (J. H. Newman), 267

Tract 85, Lectures on Scripture Proof of the Doctrines of the Church. Part I (J. H. Newman), 275–276, 282–283, 331, 477, 572

Tract 86, Indications of a Superintending Providence in the Preservation of the Prayerbook and in the Changes Which It Has Undergone (Isaac Williams), 287

Tract 87, On Reserve in Communicating Religious Knowledge (conclusion) (Isaac Williams): critique of religion of feeling, 288; evangelicalism as "new scheme of religion," 288; necessity of obedience, 288–289

Tract 90, Remarks on Certain Passages in the Thirty-Nine Articles (J. H. Newman), 3, 9, 86, 101, 162, 167, 198, 283, 336, 340, 352–353, 357, 390–391, 393–395, 399, 404, 407, 436, 438, 452, 454–455, 460, 465, 467–468, 470–471, 474, 479, 496, 498, 507, 510, 520, 523–527, 529–532, 534–536, 538–541, 548–550, 554, 557, 560, 576, 590, 592, 596, 598, 608–609, 619, 621–622, 627–628, 710n10; analysis of, 358–364; condemned by Hebdomadal Board, 365–367; and Bishop Bagot, 370–375; Pusey's defense of, 375–376, 383; Keble's defense of, 376–377; Ward's defense of, 376–377; Oakeley's defense of, 380; and honesty, 439–446. *See also* Oakeley case

Tracts against Popery, proposed series, 194–195

Tracts for the Times, 1–2, 18, 84–85, 255, 404, 528, 625, 640; launching, 154; ignored historically, 162–164; publication details, 164–168; authors, 165–168; Archbishop Howley demands conclusion to, 372. *See also individual tracts*

Trent, Council of, 85–86, 173, 195, 200, 202–204, 297–298, 317, 318–319, 360–361, 368, 378, 383, 393, 441, 500, 538, 710n10, 711n23

Trilling, Lionel, 443

Trinity College, 624, 640

Trower, Walker Johnson, 148

Ullathorne, W. B., 639

Ultra-Protestantism, 9, 25, 201, 229, 255, 258, 268, 283–284, 289–291, 299, 310, 327, 343, 420, 470, 521, 567, 591. *See also* Dissent, Dissenters; Evangelical religion; Methodism, Methodists; Wesleyans

Unitarians, 14–15, 58, 186, 210, 214, 227, 244,

Unitarians (continued)
    263, 300, 320, 328, 349, 424, 514, 568–569,
    580, 631, 679n9
Ussher, James, 165, 195, 300

Venn, Henry, 25, 33, 59
Vestiges of the Natural History of Creation, 583–
    584
Via media, 163, 203, 265, 289, 335, 623
Victoria, 553
Vital religion, 25–26, 59
Voltaire, 191

Walker, John, 481, 485, 487, 494, 613
Walter, John, 635
Ward, Frances Mary Wingfield, 523, 547–548,
    596, 622, 713n40
Ward, William George, 249, 290, 317, 334, 343,
    368, 387–389, 395, 397, 400, 420–421, 435,
    460, 514, 524–526, 528, 532, 535, 542–543,
    545, 551, 555–556, 562, 576, 596, 598, 608,
    618, 622–623, 707n68; quoted, 3; defense of
    Tract 90, 377–379; on Reformers and Refor-
    mation, 378, 518, 707n71; Newman defends,
    380; Pusey criticizes, 383–385; correspon-
    dence with Pusey, 385–386; letter to *L'Uni-
    vers*, 387, 597; need for reform in Roman
    Catholic and English Churches, 388–389;
    Ideal of a Christian Church, 515–521, 523, 525,
    535, 576, 591, 597; standard of holiness, 516;
    on justification by faith, 516–518; portrait,
    517; criticism of high churchmen, 518; on Ro-
    man Catholicism, 519; "non-natural" sub-
    scription, 520, 524; university action against,
    522–523, 529; engagement and marriage, 523–
    524; degrees revoked, 529; disagreement with
    Newman on 39 Articles, 531; on Oakeley deci-
    sion, 536–537, 547; conversion to Roman
    Catholic Church, 545, 547
Watson, Joshua, 399, 367
Watts, Isaac, 28, 242
Watts, Michael R., 45
Webb, Robert K., 15
Wellington, Duke of, Arthur Wellesley, 16, 207,
    225, 247, 366–367
Wesley, John, 25, 30, 33, 50, 55, 61, 144, 287, 397,
    408, 462
Wesleyans, 204, 287, 301, 303. *See also* Dissent,
    Dissenters; Methodism, Methodists

Westmacott, Richard, 343, 542–543, 545, 564–
    565, 592, 594, 603, 628
Westminster Review, 489
Whately, Richard, 66, 70, 115, 118, 122, 132, 211,
    215, 231, 231–232, 244, 248, 307, 373, 395,
    404, 420, 439–440, 443, 460, 514, 522, 526,
    530, 534–535, 556, 565, 577, 582, 590–591,
    617; portrait, 119
Whewell, William, 245
White, Joseph Blanco, 67–68, 127, 159, 214–216,
    226, 229, 243–244, 249, 327–328, 534, 626
Whitfield, George, 25, 346, 408
Wilberforce, Henry, 69, 147, 218, 225, 336, 344,
    395, 399, 414, 427, 428–429, 453, 460, 510,
    514, 533–534, 547–548, 567, 586, 593, 604–
    606, 611–612, 626, 636; pamphlet against
    Hampden and subscription reform, 214–216,
    219–220, 223, 252
Wilberforce, Robert, 135, 237, 337, 400, 426,
    453–454, 509–510, 553, 585, 593, 603, 612
Wilberforce, Samuel, 112, 139–140, 142, 245,
    553–554, 585; exchange with Pusey, 555–557
Wilberforce, William, 25, 59, 116, 519; on re-
    ligious emotion, 31–32
William III, 304
William IV, 230–231
Williams, Isaac, 72, 84, 165, 290, 333, 391, 399,
    401, 426, 466, 514, 582; on reserve in commu-
    nicating religious knowledge, 283–289; poetry
    professorship contest, 398–399; on Newman
    and his family, 635; on Newman living in the
    Birmingham Oratory, 638–639
Williams, Robert, 334
Wilson, Robert Francis, 165, 184
Wilson, Thomas, 165
Winchester, Bishop of. *See* Sumner, Charles
Wiseman, Nicholas, 86–87, 148, 194, 298, 339–
    340, 414, 455, 467, 509, 545, 557–561, 577,
    581, 591, 594, 598, 603, 618, 629, 637, 638;
    Dublin Review article, 335–337; postconver-
    sion conversations with Newman, 557–561
Wood, S. F., 411
Woodgate, H. A., 152–153, 334, 344, 374, 470
Wooten, John, 420
Wynter, Philip, 366–367, 455–457

Young, Peter, 549, 689n49

Zwingli, Ulrich, 201, 203, 320, 387